SOUTHEAST
ASIA
HANDBOOK

SOUTHEAST ASIA HANDBOOK

THIRD EDITION

CARL PARKES

MOON
TRAVEL
HANDBOOKS

SOUTHEAST ASIA HANDBOOK
THIRD EDITION

Published by
Moon Publications, Inc.
P.O. Box 3040
Chico, California 95927-3040, USA

Printed by
Colorcraft Ltd.

© Text and photographs copyright Carl Parkes, 1998.
All rights reserved.

© Illustrations and maps copyright Moon Publications, Inc., 1998.
All rights reserved.

Some photos and illustrations are used by permission
and are the property of the original copyright owners.

ISBN: 1-56691-127-3
ISSN: 1099-1867

Map Editor: Gina Wilson Birtcil
Copy Editor: Asha Johnson
Production & Design: Carey Wilson
Cartography: Brian Bardwell, Chris Folks and Mike Morgenfeld
Index: Valerie Sellers Blanton

Front cover photo: Phi Phi Don Island, Thailand. Credit: © 1998, Raga/Picture Cube

All photos by Carl Parkes unless otherwise noted.

Distributed in the United States and Canada by Publishers Group West

Printed in China

Please send all comments,
corrections, additions,
amendments, and critiques to:

**SOUTHEAST ASIA HANDBOOK
MOON TRAVEL HANDBOOKS
P.O. BOX 3040
CHICO, CA 95927-3040, USA
e-mail: travel@moon.com
www.moon.com**

Printing History
1st edition—August 1990
3rd edition—August 1998

All rights reserved. No part of this book may be translated or reproduced in any form, except brief extracts by a reviewer for the purpose of a review, without written permission of the copyright owner.

Although the author and publisher have made every effort to ensure that the information was correct at the time of going to press, the author and publisher do not assume and hereby disclaim any liability to any party for any loss or damage caused by errors, omissions, or any potential travel disruption due to labor or financial difficulty, whether such errors or omissions result from negligence, accident, or any other cause.

CONTENTS

INTRODUCTION 1-42
Introduction 3
Southeast Asia Highlights 6
Travel with a Theme 11
On the Road 19
Health 23
  Information; Principal Problems; Warnings
Visas and Officialdom 28
  Passports; Visas; Other Documents
Money 30
  Traveler's Checks; Money Transfers; Credit Cards; ATM Withdrawals
Communications 33
  Mail; Telephone; Travel Resources
Getting There 36
  Ticket Tips; Sources of Tickets; By Air from North America

SPECIAL TOPICS

Historical and Architectural
  Highlights of Southeast Asia 7
Performing Arts Venues
  in Southeast Asia 12
Major Festivals of Southeast Asia . . . 13
Art and Handicraft
  Centers in Southeast Asia 14
Beach Resorts of Southeast Asia . . . 15

Diving Destinations
  in Southeast Asia 16
Southeast Asia Highlights 17-19
Suggested Packing List 22
Responsible Tourism 26
Save the Wildlife 35
Selecting a
  Responsible Tour Operator 40

BRUNEI 43-54
Introduction 45
  History; Government; Economy
On the Road 48
  Getting There; Travel Practicalities
Bandar Seri Begawan 49
  Attractions; Accommodations
Exploring Brunei 52
  Western Brunei; Eastern Brunei

CAMBODIA 55-90
Introduction 57
  The Land; History; The People
On the Road 65
  Getting There; Getting Around; Travel Practicalities
Phnom Penh 68
  Attractions; Accommodations; Restaurants; Nightlife; Services;
  Transportation
Excursions from Phnom Penh 79
  Choeung Ek; Tonle Bati; Phnom Chisor; Udong

Coastal Towns 81
   Kampot; Kep; Sihanoukville
Angkor 82
   Siem Reap; The Monuments

SPECIAL TOPICS

Sightseeing Highlights 60   *Cinema Cambodia* 76
Kampucambodian Conundrum 62   *Temple Symbolism* 85

HONG KONG **91-146**

Introduction 93
   The Land; History; Government; Economy; The People
On the Road 104
   Getting There; Getting Around; Travel Practicalities
Kowloon 108
   Attractions; Accommodations; Restaurants; Nightlife
Central and Western 119
   Central Attractions; Western District Walking Tour; Accommodations;
   Restaurants; Nightlife
Wanchai 127
   Accommodations; Restaurants; Nightlife; Attractions; Accommodations;
   Restaurants
Hong Kong Island—South Side 134
   Attractions
New Territories 136
   Attractions
Outlying Islands 139
   Cheung Chau; Lamma Island; Lantau Island

SPECIAL TOPICS

Sightseeing Highlights 98-99   *Floating Sleeves*
What's Changed, What Hasn't 100   *and Painted Faces* 118
Hong Kong's   *Movies about Hong Kong* 130
   Vanishing Peoples 101   *New Territories Hiking* 138
Festivals 102-103   *Hiking on the Outlying Islands* . . 139
Taoist Geomancy 113   *Funerals on Cheung Chau* 142

INDONESIA **147-374**

Introduction 149
   The Land; History; The People; Language
On the Road 157
   Getting There; Getting Around; Travel Practicalities

JAVA **166**

Jakarta 168
   Attractions; Accommodations; Restaurants; Entertainment; Shopping;
   Services; Transportation
West Java 177
   Merak; Carita Beach; Krakatau Volcano; Ujung Kulon Reserve; Bogor;
   Puncak Pass; Bandung; Pangandaran

Yogyakarta 188
Attractions; Attractions near Yogya; Accommodations; Restaurants;
Performing Arts; Shopping; Services; Transportation
Central Java 201
Prambanan; Borobudur; Kaliurang and Mt. Merapi; Dieng Plateau; Solo
(Surakarta)
The North Coast 211
Cirebon; Pekalongan; Semarang; Vicinity of Semarang
East Java 216
Surabaya; Attractions near Surabaya; Madura Island; Malang; Temples
near Malang; Mount Bromo; Gunung Semeru; East Java Parks;
Banyuwangi

BALI **231**
Introduction; Practical Information
South Bali—Kuta, Sanur, and Nusa Dua 240
Kuta Beach; Sanur Beach; Nusa Dua
Central Bali 252
Denpasar; Northwest of Denpasar; Denpasar to Ubud; Ubud; Ubud
Vicinity; Bangli
East Bali 266
Klungkung; Besakih; Nusa Penida and Lembongan; Padangbai;
Candidasa; Tenganan; Amlapura; Tirtagangga; Amed and Tulamben
Central Mountains 274
Penelokan; Gunung Batur; Batur and Kintamani; Bedugul and Lake
Bratan
North Bali 278
Singaraja; Lovina Beach; Northwest Bali

SUMATRA **284**
Getting There
North Sumatra 286
Medan; Bukit Lawang; Banda Aceh; Banda Aceh to Lake Toba; Brastagi
(Berastagi)
Lake Toba 291
Prapat; Tomok; Tuk Tuk; Ambarita; Simanindo
West Sumatra 298
Sibolga; Nias Island; Bukittinggi; Vicinity of Bukittinggi; Padang; Mentawi
Islands
South Sumatra 307
Pekanbaru; Bengkulu
Riau Islands 310
Batam Island; Bintan Island

NUSA TENGGARA **314**
Transportation
Lombok 315
Ampenan, Mataram, and Cakranegara; Senggigi Beach; Gili Islands;
Southwest Peninsula; Praya and Vicinity; Sade (Rambitan); Kuta Beach;
Gunung Rinjani; Tetebatu; Labuhan Lombok

Sumbawa 330
   Sumbawa Besar; Gunung Tambora; Huu; Bima-Raba; Sape
Komodo 333
Flores 335
   Labuhanbajo; Ruteng; Bajawa; Riung; Ende; Keli Mutu; Moni (Mone);
   Maumere; Waiara Beach; Larantuka; Solor and Alor
Sumba 346
   Waingapu; Villages near Waingapu; Waikabubak; East of Waikabubak;
   South of Waikabubak; West of Waikabubak
Timor 350
   Kupang; Roti; Soe; Atambua; Dili

SULAWESI **355**
   Transportation
Southern Sulawesi 357
   Ujung Pandang; Other Southern Destinations
Tana Toraja 361
   Makale; Rantepao; Rantepao Vicinity
Central Sulawesi 367
   Mangkutana; Pendolo and Lake Poso; Tentena; Poso; Palu; Donggala;
   Lore Lindu and Bada Valley
North Sulawesi 371
   Manado; Gorontalo

SPECIAL TOPICS
....
Sightseeing Highlights 152-153   *Running of the Bulls* 223
Railyard Dinosaurs 162   *Balinese Performing Arts* 236-237
Javanese Culture 195-197

LAOS
    . . . . **375-406**
Introduction 377
   The Land; History; Government; Economy; The People
On the Road 383
   Getting There; Getting Around; Visas; Travel Practicalities
Vientiane 386
   Attractions; Accommodations; Restaurants; Services; Transportation
Luang Prabang 393
   Attractions; Accommodations; Services
Plain of Jars 397
   Phonsavan; Phonsavan Vicinity
Southern Laos 399
   Savannakhet; Pakse (Pakxe); Champasak and Wat Phu; Bolovens
   Plateau; Mekong Islands

SPECIAL TOPICS
....
Sightseeing Highlights 379   *The Final King—*
Lao Food 391   *Savang Vatthana* 394

MACAU 407-430
Introduction 409
The Land; History; Government and Economy; The People
On the Road 412
Getting There; Getting Around; Travel Practicalities
Attractions 415
South Macau; Central Macau; North Macau; Taipa Island; Coloane
Island
Practicalities 423
Accommodations; Restaurants; Nightlife

SPECIAL TOPICS
....

Festivals 413   A Portuguese Menu 426

MALAYSIA 431-542
Introduction 433
The Land; History; The People; Arts and Crafts
On the Road 446
Getting There; Getting Around; Travel Practicalities

PENINSULAR MALAYSIA—WEST COAST 450
Johor to Kuala Lumpur 450
Johor Bharu; Malacca; Seremban
Kuala Lumpur 460
Attractions; Accommodations; Restaurants; Travel Practicalities;
Transportation
Kuala Lumpur to Penang 470
Taman Negara; Fraser's Hill; Cameron Highlands; Ipoh; Pangkor Island;
Kuala Kangsar; Taiping; Maxwell Hill
Penang 479
Attractions; Accommodations; Food; Travel Practicalities
Langkawi Island 493
Alor Setar; Langkawi Island

PENINSULAR MALAYSIA—EAST COAST 497
Mersing
Tioman Island and Vicinity 499
Attractions; Accommodations; Getting There; Other Islands near Tioman
Central Coast—Kuantan to Kota Bharu 502
Kuantan; Teluk Chempedak; Cherating; Rantau Abang; Marang; Kuala
Trengganu; Merang and Redang Island; Perhentian Island
Kota Bharu and Vicinity 512
Attractions; Attractions near Kota Bharu; Accommodations;
Transportation

EAST MALAYSIA 517
Sarawak 517
Transportation; Travel Practicalities; Kuching; Kuching Vicinity; Skrang
River; Sri Aman; Sibu; Rejang River; Kapit; Belaga; Bintulu; Niah Caves;
Miri; Baram River and The Interior; Gunung Mulu National Park

Sabah 532
  Transportation; Kota Kinabalu; Penampang and Papar; Beaufort;
  Labuan Island; Tenom; Tuaran and Kota Belud; Kinabalu National Park;
  Sandakan; Lahad Datu; Tawau

SPECIAL TOPICS

Sightseeing Highlights	436	Culture Clash in Kuala Lumpur	468
Affirmative Action— Malay Style	441	A Hawker Menu	490
Festivals	442-444	East Coast Highlights	498
Movies Filmed in Malaysia	445	The Brink of Extinction	505
West Coast Highlights	452	Sarawak Highlights	519
Futuristic Architecture	462	End of the Rainforests	521
Petronas Towers	465	Sabah Highlights	533

MYANMAR (BURMA) 543-598

Introduction 545
  The Land; History; Government; Economy; The People
On the Road 556
  Getting There; Getting Around; Visas and Travel Permits; Money; Travel
  Practicalities
Yangon (Rangoon) 560
  Attractions; Accommodations; Restaurants; Shopping; Practicalities;
  Getting Around; Leaving Yangon
Vicinity of Yangon 569
  Thanlyin (Syriam) and Kyauktan; Bago (Pegu)
Southeast of Yangon 570
  Kyaiktiyo; Mawlamyin (Moulmein)
Mandalay 572
  Attractions; Accommodations; Restaurants; Transportation
Vicinity of Mandalay 578
  Amarapura; Ava; Sagaing; Mingun; Pyin U Lwin (Maymyo)
Bagan 582
  Old Bagan Monuments; Monuments toward Nyaung U; Monuments
  toward Minnanthu; Monuments South; Accommodations; Shopping;
  Transportation; Mount Popa
Inle Lake and Vicinity 594
  Transportation; Kalaw; Pindaya Caves; Taunggyi; Nyaungshwe
  (Yaunghwe); Inle Lake

SPECIAL TOPICS

Destination Names	548	Burmese Language	559
Sightseeing Highlights	549	The Arts of Myanmar	571
Opium King Khun Sa	553	Bagan Marionettes	591
Festivals	555	Buddha and the Nats	593

PHILIPPINES 599-698

Introduction 601
  The Land; History; Government; Economy; The People

On the Road **615**
  Getting There; Getting Around; Travel Practicalities; Food and Drink;
  Cautions

LUZON **626**

Manila 626
  Attractions; Accommodations; Restaurants; Entertainment; Shopping;
  Services; Transportation

Around Manila 636
  Corregidor Island; Las Pinas Organ; Sarao Jeepney Factory; Tagaytay;
  Talisay and Lake Taal; San Pablo; Pagsanjan

Mountain Provinces 641
  Angeles City; Olongapo and Subic; Banaue; Bontoc; Sagada; Bontoc to
  Baguio; Baguio

Northwest Coast 652
  Hundred Islands; Bauang (La Union) Beaches; Vigan

Southern Luzon 654
  Daet and San Miguel Bay; Naga; Legaspi; Sorsogon and Rizal Beach;
  Matnog

ISLANDS TO THE SOUTH **660**

  Routes around the Visayas

Bohol 661
  Transportation; Tagbilaran; Panglao Island; Chocolate Hills; Jao Island

Boracay 665

Camiguin Island 667
  Mambajao; Around the Island

Cebu 669
  Transportation; Cebu City; Bantayan Island; Santandar; Moalboal; South
  of Moalboal

Leyte 675
  Transportation; Tacloban; Biliran Island; Ormoc

Mindanao 677
  Surigao and Siargao Island; Butuan; Balingoan; Cagayan de Oro;
  Dipolog and Dapitan; Davao City; Lake Sebu; Zamboanga

Mindoro 683
  Puerto Galera; Roxas City

Negros 685
  Bacolod; Dumaguete City; Siquijor Island

Palawan 689
  Puerto Princesa; Southern Palawan; Sabang; Port Barton; Roxas;
  Taytay; El Nido

Panay 694
  Iloilo; Kalibo

Samar 697
  Catbalogan

SPECIAL TOPICS

Sightseeing Highlights	604-605	Festivals	616-618
Filipino Customs	610-611	Movies Filmed in the Philippines	625
Speaking the Language	613	Island-by-Island Highlights	662-663

SINGAPORE **699-770**
Introduction 701
   The Land; History; The People
On the Road 711
   Getting There; Points of Arrival; Getting Around; Travel Practicalities
Attractions 715
   Colonial Singapore; Chinatown; Little India; Arab Street; West Singapore
   Attractions
Accommodations 731
   Budget; Moderate
Restaurants 741
   Orchard Road; Central Singapore; Boat Quay; Clarke Quay; Chinatown;
   Tanjong Pagar; Little India
Entertainment 763
   Classical; Nightlife
Shopping 767
   Orchard Road; Central Singapore; Speciality Shops

SPECIAL TOPICS

Restoration of the Past 706   *Taste of Singapore* 742-743
Festivals 707-709

THAILAND **771-938**
Introduction 773
   History; Government; The People; Festivals
On the Road 785
   Getting There; Getting Around; Visas; Tourist Information; Travel
   Practicalities; Etiquette and Customs; Cautions

BANGKOK AND VICINITY **794**
   Attractions; Accommodations; Restaurants; Cultural Entertainment;
   Nightlife; Nightclubs and Discos; Shopping; Services; Transportation
East Coast 833
   Pattaya; Ko Samet; Trat; Ko Chang
West of Bangkok 839
   Nakhon Pathom; Kanchanaburi; Kanchanaburi Region; Sangklaburi
North of Bangkok 845
   Bang Pa In; Ayuthaya; Lopburi

CENTRAL THAILAND **852**
   Phitsanulok; Sukothai; Si Satchanalai; Kamphang Phet; Tak; Mae Sot;
   Mae Sot to Mae Sariang

NORTHERN THAILAND **861**
   Chiang Mai; Hilltribe Trekking; Lamphun; Lampang; Mae Sariang; Mae
   Hong Son; Pai
Chiang Rai and the Golden Triangle 880
   Thaton and Kok River; Chiang Rai; Mae Salong (Santikhiri); Mae Sai;
   Chiang Saen; Sop Ruak; Chiang Khong; Phayao; Phrae; Nan

NORTHEASTERN THAILAND **888**

Khao Yai National Park; Korat (Nakhon Ratchasima); Khon Kaen; Udon
Thani; Nong Khai; Si Chiang Mai; Sang Khom; Pak Chong; Chiang
Khan; Loei; Beung Khan; Sakhon Nakhon; Nakhon Phanom; That
Phanom; Yasothon; Ubon Ratchathani; Surin; Buriram

SOUTHERN THAILAND **901**

Phetburi; Hua Hin; Prachuap Khiri Khan; Chumphon; Surat Thani; Ko
Samui; Ko Phangan; Ko Tao; Phuket; Phangnga; Ko Phi Phi; Krabi; Ao
Nang (Beach); Pranang; Ko Lanta; Trang; Ko Tarutao National Park;
Satun; Hat Yai; Songkhla; Narathiwat; Sungai Golok

SPECIAL TOPICS

Sightseeing Highlights 776-777	Food and Drink 818-819
Contemporary Buddhism	Performing Arts 823-824
in Thailand 780-781	Live Thai Rock 'N' Roll 826
Movies Filmed in Thailand 793	The Arts of Sukothai 855
Temple Architecture 799-801	Peoples of the Hills 872-875
Iconography of	The Opium Trail 883
the Buddha Image 802-803	Festivals of the Northeast 889
Magical Medallions 804	Khmer Monuments 892-893
Thailand's Futuristic Architecture . . . 808	

VIETNAM **939-1016**

Introduction 941
The Land; History; The People

On the Road 949
Getting There; Getting Around; Travel Practicalities; Money; Other
Practicalities

SOUTH VIETNAM **955**

Ho Chi Minh City (Saigon) 955
Attractions in Central Saigon; Attractions in Cholon; Attractions near
Saigon; Accommodations; Restaurants; Practicalities; Transportation

Vicinity of Ho Chi Minh City 968
Cu Chi Tunnels; Cao Dai Cathedral; Vung Tau

The Mekong Delta 971
Mytho; Vinh Long; Cantho

Dalat to Nha Trang 972
Dalat; Phan Rang; Nha Trang

CENTRAL VIETNAM **981**

Qui Nhon to Hue 981
Qui Nhon; Quang Ngai and My Lai; Hoi An; Danang; Attractions near
Danang; Hue

Vicinity of Hue 994
Quang Tri; Dong Ha; Khe Sanh; DMZ Sites

NORTH VIETNAM **997**
Dong Hoi; Vinh; Thanh Hoa; Ninh Binh

Hanoi **1000**
 Central Hanoi Attractions; Northwestern Hanoi Attractions;
 Accommodations; Restaurants; Entertainment; Other Practicalities;
 Transportation
The Northeast Coast **1008**
 Haiphong; Halong Bay; Cat Ba National Park
Northwest Vietnam **1012**
 Hoa Binh; Mai Chau; Son La; Dien Bien Phu; Sapa; Lao Cai; Bac Ha
SPECIAL TOPIC
....
Sightseeing Highlights *944-945*

SUGGESTED READING **1017**

INDEX **1027**

MAPS

INTRODUCTION

Southeast Asia 4-5
Historical and Cultural
   Attractions of Southeast Asia 8-9

BRUNEI

Brunei 46
Bandar Seri Begawan. 50

CAMBODIA

Cambodia 58-59
Phnom Penh 70-71
Central Phnom Penh 72-73
Siem Reap. 83
Angkor Wat and Angkok Thom. 86
Monuments of Angkor. 87

HONG KONG

Hong Kong, China. 94-95
Kowloon. 110-111
Yaumatei and Mongkok 112
Central. 120-121
Sheung Wan (Western District). 124
Wanchai 128
Causeway Bay 132
Hong Kong Island 135
Cheung Chau 140

INDONESIA

Indonesia 150-151
Pelni Shipping Routes 160-161

JAVA

Java 166-167
Jakarta 169
Central Jakarta 170
Jalan Jaksa Area 172
Bogor 179
Bandung. 182
Pagandaran. 186
Yogyakarta 189
Central Yogyakarta 191
Vicinity of Yogyakarta 193
Prambanan Plain, The 201
Dieng Plateau. 205
Solo 207
Solo, Central 209
Cirebon 212
Semarang 215
Surabaya 218
Central Surabaya. 219

Trowulan 222
Malang 224
Bromo-Tengger-Semeru
   National Park. 227

BALI

Bali 232-233
South Bali 241
Kuta Beach 242
Sanur 249
Nusa Dua and Tanjung Benoa. 251
Denpasar 253
Ubud 258-259
Goa Gajah 264
Gunung Kawi 265
Bangli 265
Klungkung (Semarapura) 267
Padangbai 269
Candidasa. 270
Tenganan 271
Amlapura 272
Tirtagangga 273
Gunung Batur and Vicinity 275
Bedugul Area 277
Singaraja 279
Lovina Beach Area 280-281

SUMATRA

Sumatra 285
Medan. 287
Brastagi 290
Lake Toba 292-293
Prapat. 294
Samosir Island 296
Nias Island 299
Bukittinggi 302
Padang 305
Pekanbaru 308
Batam and Bintan Islands 311

NUSA TENGGARA

Nusa Tenggara 316-317
Lombok. 318-319
Ampenan-Mataram-Cakranegara 320
Gunung Rinjani Approaches. 327
Sumbawa 330
Komodo Island 334
Flores. 336-337
Sumba. 347
Kupang 352

SULAWESI

Sulawesi. 356
Ujung Pandang 358

MAPS
(continued)

SULAWESI *(continued)*

Tana Toraja 362
Rantepao 364
Manado 372

LAOS

Laos 378
Vientiane 387
Central Vientiane 388-389
Luang Prabang 395

MACAU

Macau 411
Central Macau 417
Taipa and Coloane Islands 421

MALAYSIA

Malaysia 434-435
Peninsular Malaysia 451

PENINSULAR MALAYSIA ~ WEST COAST

Malacca (Melaka) 453
Kuala Lumpur 461
Central Kuala Lumpur 463
Cameron Highlands 473
Ipoh 475
Pangkor Island 476
Kuala Kangsar 478
Penang Island 480
Georgetown 482
Batu Ferringhi 487
Central Georgetown 488
Langkawi Island 494

PENINSULAR MALAYSIA ~ EAST COAST

Tioman Island 499
Kuantan 502
Teluk Chempedak 503
Cherating 504
Marang 506
Kuala Trengganu 508
Kota Bharu 513

EAST MALAYSIA

Sarawak, Brunei, and Sabah 518
Kuching 522
Kota Kinabalu 535

MYANMAR (BURMA)

Myanmar (Burma) 546-547
Yangon (Rangoon) 561
Shwedagon Pagoda 563
Central Yangon 564
Mandalay 573
Vicinity of Mandalay 579
Bagan (Pagan) 583
Old Bagan 586
Inle Lake and Vicinity 594

THE PHILIPPINES

The Philippines 602-603

LUZON

Central Manila 628-629
Ermita and Malate 627
Banaue and Vicinity 642
Bontoc 644
Sagada-Bontoc Region 646
Sagada 648
Central Baguio 650
Legaspi 657

ISLANDS TO THE SOUTH

Boracay 666
Cebu City 671
Puerto Galera 684
Bacolod 687
Iloilo 696

SINGAPORE

Singapore Island 702-703
Singapore City 716
Colonial Singapore 718-719
Chinatown 724-725
Little India 726-727
Colonial Singapore Accommodations 732
Chinatown Accommodations 734
Little India Accommodations 736
Orchard Road 737
Colonial Singapore Restaurants 748
Boat Quay Restaurants and Nightclubs . . . 752
Chinatown Restaurants 757
Little India Restaurants 762

THAILAND

Thailand 774

BANGKOK AND VICINITY

Central Bangkok 795
Bangkok 796-797
Wat Pra Keo and The Royal Palace . . 798
Banglampoo 809
Malaysia Hotel Area 811
Silom Surawong 813
Siam Square 814
Sukumvit 816
Pattaya 834
Ko Samet 837
Kanchanaburi 841
Kanchanaburi Region 843
Ayuthaya 846
Lopburi 850

CENTRAL THAILAND

New Sukothai 854
Old Sukothai 853

NORTHERN THAILAND

Chiang Mai 862
Central Chiang Mai 866
Chiang Rai 881

NORTHEASTERN THAILAND

Korat 890-891

SOUTHERN THAILAND

Phetburi 902
Hua Hin 904
Ko Samui 907

Chaweng Beach 909
Phuket Island 917
Phuket Town 918
Patong Beach 920
Karon and Kata Beach 922
Krabi 928
Hat Yai 932

VIETNAM

Vietnam 942-943

SOUTH VIETNAM

Ho Chi Minh City (Saigon) 956-957
Central Saigon 958-959
Cholon 962
Vung Tao 969
Dalat 973
Downtown Dalat 975
Nha Trang Area 977
Nha Trang 978

CENTRAL VIETNAM

Qui Nhon 981
Hoi An 984
Danang 986
Hue 990-991
Hue Vicinity 995

NORTH VIETNAM

Vinh 998
Central Hanoi 1002-1003
Northwest Hanoi 1004
Haiphong 1009

MAP SYMBOLS

	PARKWAY (EXPRESSWAY)	★	POINT OF INTEREST SIGHTSEEING ATTRACTION		....	TRAM / CABLE CAR
	MAIN ROAD	■	POINT OF INTEREST / RESTAURANT			RAIL ROAD
	MINOR ROAD	●	HOTEL / ACCOMMODATION		-----	FERRY
	UNPAVED RD.	▲	MOUNTAIN		I.	ISLAND
	FOOT PATH	♣	SACRED TREE		RD.	ROAD
	INTERNATIONAL BORDER		WATERFALL		N.P.	NATIONAL PARK
	STATE BORDER	O	CITY		GH	GUESTHOUSE
	BRIDGE	o	TOWN			WATER
	TUNNEL	o	BOAT STOP			
	PARK, OPEN SPACE, OTHER				♣	TEMPLE

ABBREVIATIONS

A$—Australian dollars
APEX—advance-purchase excursion fare
B—Thai *baht* (currency)
B$—Brunei dollars
d—double
GH—guesthouse
GPO—General Post Office
HK$—Hong Kong dollars

HKTA—Hong Kong Tourist Association
Jl—Jalan (street)
K—Burmese *kyat* (currency)
KK—Kota Kinabalu
KL—Kuala Lumpur
km—kilometers
km/h—kilometers per hour
M$—Malaysian dollars

MTPB—Malaysian Tourism Promotion Board
MTR—Hong Kong public transit
PAL—Philippines Airlines
RTW—round-the-world fare
s—single
S$—Singapore dollars

IS THIS BOOK OUT OF DATE?

Travel books are a collaboration between author and reader. Every effort has been made to keep this book accurate and timely, but conditions change quickly in a region as dynamic as Southeast Asia. Please let us know about price hikes, new guesthouses, closed restaurants, transportation tips, map errors, and anything else that may prove useful to the next traveler. A questionnaire in the back of this book will help us find out who you are and what improvements might help the next edition of this book. Send your comments to:

Southeast Asia Handbook
Moon Publications
P.O. Box 3040
Chico, CA 95927-3040, USA
e-mail: travel@moon.com

ACKNOWLEDGMENTS

Writers write alone, but survive only with generous doses of help and encouragement. Top marks at Moon Publications go to copy editor and computer whiz Asha Johnson, and art director Dave Hurst, all of whom labored well beyond the call of duty. The superb maps are credited to Bob Race, Brian Bardwell, Chris Folks, and Mike Morgenfeld. Gratitude is also given to founder Bill Dalton, publisher Bill Newlin, and other Moonbeams who helped realize the book.

Contributions from Readers

I would also like to thank the many readers who wrote to me about their travel adventures:

America: Susan Brown (New York), Burt Blackburn (Austin), Thomas Burns (Ocean Park), Alan Cartledge (AZ), Robert Chiang (San Antonio), Frank Cotter (Mounds View), Pat Crowley (San Diego), Stephen Downes (Marion), Rhys Evans (Grover City), Kathleen Flynn (Los Angeles), Leigh Fox (Guam), Steve Gilman (Norcross), Leslie Hamersly (Index), Stefan Hammond (San Francisco), Dr. Martin Hane (Chicago), Celeste Holmes (Oakland), Harry Hunter (Olympia), Dana Kizlaitis (Oak Lawn), Kate Klein, Irene Malone (San Pablo) Angelo Mercure (San Diego), Dan Moody (Studio City), Jan Morris (Louisville), Michael Newman (Los Angeles), Martin Offenberger (La Habre), James Patterson (Santa Cruz), Mark Peters (Muscatine), John Pierkarski (Huntington Beach), John Pike (Redondo Beach), Rachel Rinaldo (Wilton), William Ring (San Diego), Yancey Rousek (Los Angeles), Priscilla Rowe (San Francisco), Claudia Siegel (Hackensack), Howard Spector (Dallas), Jefferson Swycaffer (San Diego), Michael Triff (Atlanta), Bruce Willis (Glendale), Ray Varn Buhler (Wilseyville), Chantal Yang (Cambridge).

Asia: Philip Drury (China), Chieko Ishikawa (Japan), Bruce Swenson (Japan).

Australia: Gary Deering (True East), Greg Duffy (Burleigh Waters), Martin Ellison (Darlinghurst), Cas Liber (Elizabeth Bay), Kevin Mulrain (Sydney), Morgana Oliver (Wodonga), Catherine Spence (Mona Vale), Keith Stephans (Noose).

Austria: Herber Walland (Graz).

Belgium: Guy Crouna (Tieuen).

Canada: Bob Cadloff (Montreal), Bruce Fraser (Calgary), Melvin Green (Toronto), Pat and Tom Jorgrinson (Webb), Bruce Moore (Ganges), Lenny Morgan (Richmond), Scott Pegg (Vancouver), Laura White (Toronto), Tanya Whiteside (Ottawa).

England: Alan Cummings, Jon Bonnin (Sanderfest), Tim Eyre (Nottingham), Linda Grace (Oxford), Mark Gregory (Leeds), David Host (Bulkington), John Maidment (Southbourne), Anthony Maude (Canterbury), C. Miller (London), Peter Moorhouse (Seathwaite), Tina Ottman (Cambridge), Tim Prentice (Kent), Nick Slade (Flackwell Health), Lois Tadd (Chesham), David Veale (Fishbourne).

Germany: Christiane Moll (Berlin), Marcus Muller (Tubingen), Ralf Neugebauer (Lubeck), Wolfgang and Mosgit (Brey), Hans Zagorski (Gunterleben).

Netherlands: Vander Bel-Kampschuur (Eindhoven), Maarten Camps (Ryswyh), Claantie van der Grinten (Ryswyh), E. Cornelissen (Castricum), Rick Dubbeldam (Sas Van Gert), Jan Valkenbury (Heerlen), Michel van Dam (Den Haag), Erik van Velzen (Zoetermeer), Helle Nielson (Silkeborg), Herbert Walland.

New Zealand: Barry Wells (Wellington).

Spain: Sevvy (Madrid).

Sweden: Stefan Sandelsson (Lomma)

Switzerland: Nicolas Chiriotti (Grand Lancy), Rolf Huber (Uitikon-Waldegg), Katharina Hug (Enalinpes).

A Personal Note

Finally, I would like to extend my deepest gratitude and sincerest love to all my friends in San Francisco and throughout the world:

Terra and radio king Nick Marnell, Norton, Dean (Wolfman) Bowden, Dave "Art Seen" Howard, Hai Sun, Suzi C., Roy T. Maloney, jetsetter Michael McKenna & Laurie, John Kaeuper, Jimbo & Kelly, amazing Amos, Wayne, Jim & Amy, Eric Dibbern & Sue, Linda & Geek, Ellen & Dave, Vince "Dude," Lee & Pam, Ab-Fab Bruce, Kim Kacere, beam-me-up Scotty & Juiceteen, lovely Rita & Eric, Dara & Rog, zenbullet Stefan, Bali Joel, Cuba Chris, Vera, Peachy, Genievieve, Deke, Tatoo Jerome, Ed Samarin, Karen (we'll always have Tahoe), Larsen (you still owe me $40), Zimmie da giant, Stephanie, Hugh, Guru Das, Donna, Hazel & Rick, Richard (North Beach '75), Dianne (Aspen '76), Nam Chu (R.I.P.), Doctor Bob & German Ralph, Joe & divine Dyan, Homeless Jim, sweet June, Sheila, Marty, Ray Jason, Bodewes (Amsterdam), Flynn (Down Under), Jennifer (Manila), David Stanley (who knows), Joe Biz (R.I.P.), Bob Nilsen (Chico), Marael, Rachel (Singapore), Nicole (Paris), Escola Nova de Samba, Lulu and the Atomics, sister Claud, fab Stan, cool Kev and Heather, Mom & Dad.

INTRODUCTION

INTRODUCTION

I would rather be ashes than dust—
I would rather my spark should
burn out in a brilliant blaze
Than it should be stifled in dry rot.
I would rather be a superb meteor,
Every atom of me in magnificent glow,
Than a sleepy and permanent planet.
Man's chief purpose is to live, not to exist:
I shall not waste my days trying to prolong them.
I shall use my time.

—JACK LONDON

The use of traveling is to regulate imagination by reality,
and instead of thinking how things may be,
to see them as they are.

—SAMUEL JOHNSON

If the doors of perception were cleansed
every thing would appear to man as it is, infinite.

—WILLIAM BLAKE

INTRODUCTION

Borneo and Bali, Mandalay and Macau, Sulawesi and Zamboanga—names that fire the imagination. In a world gone increasingly dull, Southeast Asia remains a land of magic and mystery, adventure and romance, far-flung destinations still strange and exciting in a Westernized world.

Travel with an open mind and you'll find many magical moments: sunrise on a volcano above a sea of swirling clouds, saffron-robed monks slowly encircling a gold-encrusted pagoda, old women burning incense and finding their fortunes in a smoky temple, sinewy fishermen setting sail from blazing white beaches, tribal villagers who don't believe that man has walked on the moon, river journeys through the heart of darkness. This is a land blessed with an incredibly rich tapestry of races, languages, natural wonders, histories, cultures, and peoples, ranging from the rulers of international banking empires to isolated tribes just emerging from Stone Age lifestyles.

Much of Asia's strong imagery derives from writers and adventurers who recorded their own journeys of discovery and inner exploration. Marco Polo's early records were followed by the verses of Conrad, Verne, Hesse, Maugham, Gurdjieff, Malraux, Fleming, Ginsberg, and Watts. Today a new generation of writers, Theroux, Iyer, Hansen, Krich, and the Blairs, continues to explore and examine the Brave New World of modern Asia.

And what a strange, surprising place it is. Both exotic and contemporary, Southeast Asia is no place for sentimental colonialism or quaint desires that unspoiled paradises will remain forever lost. The lament, "You should have been here last year," becomes a traveler's fraud when you consider that Southeast Asian cities are some of the most highly developed and technologically advanced in the world and that most Asians prefer Hollywood and holograms to meditation and mantras. The collision of East and West is modern reality but also, at times, just as fascinating and revealing as the relics of empire and history.

To see the real Asia—the Asia that lies just underneath the Western veneer—you must travel with wide eyes and an open mind. Avoid spending money just to isolate yourself against what appears to be an alien culture. Treat the residents and other travelers as you would have them treat

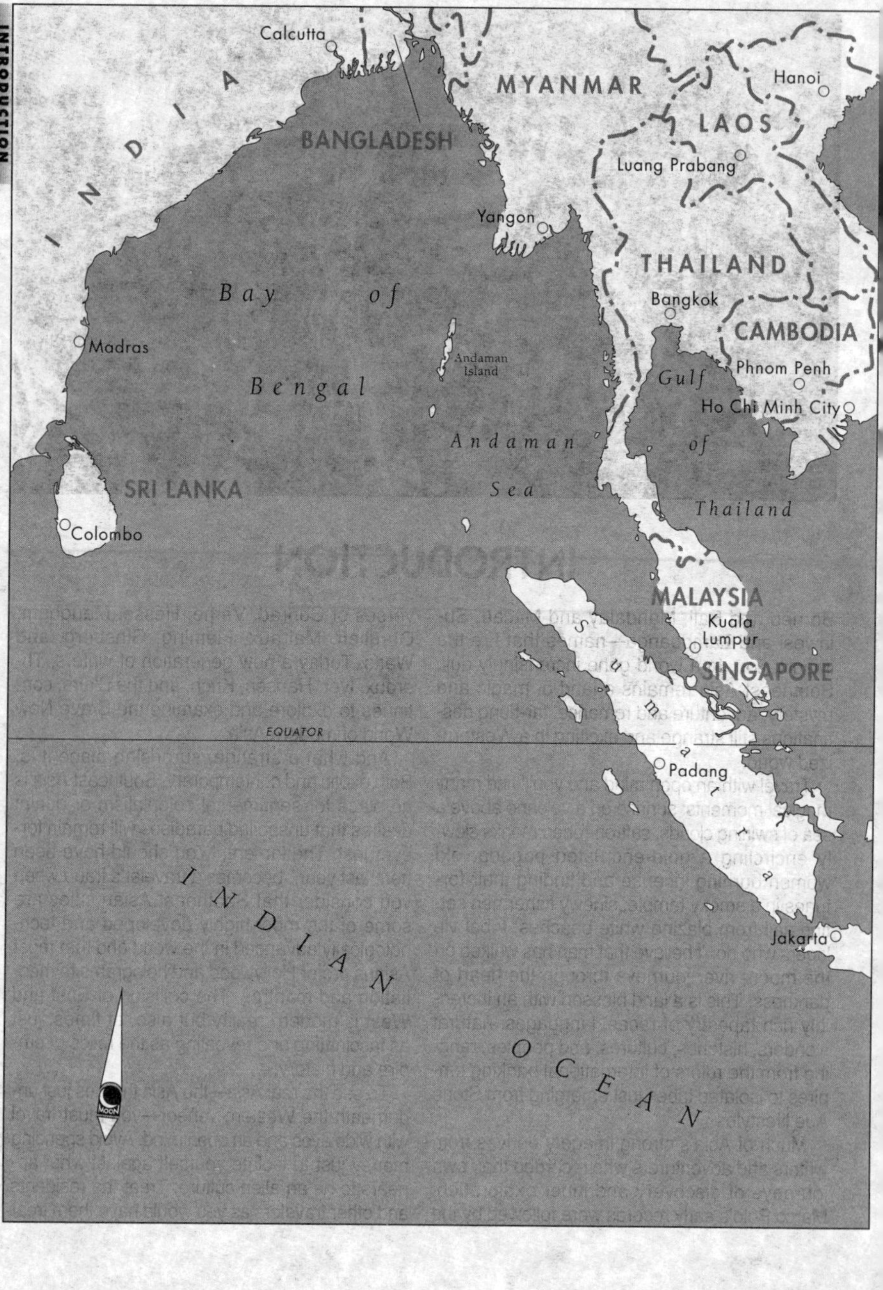

Calcutta
INDIA
MYANMAR
Hanoi
LAOS
BANGLADESH
Luang Prabang
Yangon
THAILAND
Bay of Bengal
Bangkok
CAMBODIA
Madras
Andaman Island
Gulf of Thailand
Phnom Penh
Ho Chi Minh City
Andaman Sea
SRI LANKA
Colombo
MALAYSIA
Kuala Lumpur
SINGAPORE
Sumatra
EQUATOR
Padang
Jakarta
INDIAN OCEAN
MOON

SOUTHEAST ASIA

CHINA
Guangzhou

TAIWAN

HONG
KONG

Hainan
Dao

VIETNAM

Luzon

Manila

Mindoro

Philippines

Sea

PHILIPPINES

South China Sea

Samar

Panay

Palawan

Negros

Mindanao

Davao

Kota Kinabalu

BRUNEI

MALAYSIA

Kalimantan

Celebes
Sea

Halmahera

EQUATOR

Banjarmasin

Sulawesi

Buru

Ceram

New
Guinea

Ujung
Pandang

INDONESIA

Java

Bali

Sumbawa

Flores

Arafura

Lombok

Sumba

Timor

Sea

Melville
Island

Timor
Sea

Darwin

AUSTRALIA

0   1,000 mi
0   1,000 km

© MOON PUBLICATIONS, INC.

you. Don't measure people by Western standards or your own cultural values. Keep a cool heart but an optimistic attitude. Remain open to chance en-counters with travelers, shopkeepers, students, and monks. The success of your journey ultimately lies in your hands. Have a great adventure.

SOUTHEAST ASIA HIGHLIGHTS

Where to go and what to see is often a difficult decision since few Westerners are familiar with the history, geography, or tourist attractions of Southeast Asia. Sadly, few people contemplating a vacation in the region could even name or find a country on a globe in this unknown corner of the world. Southeast Asia is located east of India, south of China, north of Australia, and west of the South Pacific. The region is as wide as the United States and stretches across the equator from the latitude of New Orleans as far south as that of Bahia, Brazil. It's formed by almost a dozen countries, each with distinctive histories, archaeologies, topographies, flora, fauna, peoples, cultures, traditions, handicrafts, cuisines, political landscapes, and economic promises.

Despite the amazing number of possibilities, travel destinations familiar to the general public are largely limited to Hong Kong (because of its reputation as a shopping mecca), the tropical paradise of Bali (an island in Indonesia, *not* an independent country or a movie soundtrack), Singapore (credit goes to historical novels), and Thailand (promotional campaigns and word of mouth). A fine beginning, but there's more—far, far, more—to Southeast Asia than just this short list.

The following thumbnail sketches will provide quick glimpses of the major attractions found in this book. Further descriptions are provided at the beginning of each chapter under "Sightseeing Highlights." But to really make an intelligent decision on where to go and what to see, you'll need to diligently study maps to become familiar with the geography and conduct an organized reading campaign of travel guidebooks, background histories, and armchair travelogues to fire up your imagination.

Far too many travelers begin a long and expensive journey without even spending a single evening at the local library or bookstore. Often the only advance reading consists of a few destination pieces in the Sunday travel sections or a travel agent's promo brochures. Without some advance research, the trip quickly be-comes a confusing trail of shrines, ruins, lectured commentaries, and strange customs, without any real understanding of it all. It is absolutely essential that you prepare yourself with a thorough examination of these pages, plus some of the general background reading suggested below and specific books listed under each country. A well-rounded reading program, together with the following thumbnail sketches and suggestions for travel themes, will point the way to a successful vacation.

Brunei

The small but immensely rich oil sultanate on the northern coast of Borneo is primarily a stopover between the Malaysian states of Sabah and Sarawak. Ruled by Sultan Hassanal Bolkia—the world's richest man according to *Forbes* magazine and the *Guinness Book of World Records*—Brunei is one of Southeast Asia's more intriguing destinations because of its curious marriage of oil, Islam, and Western materialism.

Myanmar (Burma)

Myanmar, formerly called Burma, is a country forever frozen, where timelessness and the search for Buddhist nirvana fly in the face of Western efficiency and capitalistic wealth. One of the world's most isolated and exotic countries, Myanmar is well worth a visit despite recent political turmoil, primitive internal transportation, decrepit hotels, and an official policy that limits visitors to four-week visits. Both independent travelers and group tours are welcome.

Tourists can visit Yangon (formerly Rangoon), a crumbling city with a faded colonial atmosphere chiefly known for the world-famous Shwedagon Pagoda. The dusty and somewhat undistinguished town of Mandalay offers a handful of magnificent temples and monasteries. Travelers jaded by archaeology and old temples will enjoy the splendid natural environment and ethnic minorities of Inle Lake. The highlight

HISTORICAL AND ARCHITECTURAL HIGHLIGHTS OF SOUTHEAST ASIA

CAMBODIA

Angkor Wat: Southeast Asia's finest architectural site

HONG KONG

Hong Kong Island: amazing modern architecture

INDONESIA

Borobudur: world's largest Buddhist stupa;
Yogyakarta: Prambanan, Hindu counterpart to Borobudur;
Bali: Gunung Kawi, Goa Gajah, Kerta Gosa, Tanah Lot
Surabaya: Dutch colonial architecture, the last of its kind
Nias: megalithic architecture, powerful villages

LAOS

Luang Prabang: timeless atmosphere on the Mekong

MALAYSIA

Penang: Peranakan architecture, old-world atmosphere
Kuala Lumpur: Blue Mosque, colonial relics, Petronas Towers
Kuala Kangsar: the classic mosque of Southeast Asia

MYANMAR

Yangon: Shwedagon Pagoda—Southeast Asia's most impressive monument
Bagan: 12th-century lost city, mysterious and expansive
Bago: massive pagoda to rival Shwedagon

SINGAPORE

Chinatown: Chinese temples, Peranakan neighborhoods
Little India: Hindu temples and seedy alleys
Central: British colonial churches, museums, homes

THAILAND

Bangkok: Wat Pra Keo, Grand Palace, Wat Po, Marble Temple
Sukothai: Thailand's original 15th-century capital
Ayuthaya: Thailand's second capital, well restored
Northeast: Khmer temples on the Cambodian border
Chiang Mai: temples and pagodas of the Lanna Kingdom
Lampang: Wat Prathat Lampang Luang

VIETNAM

Hue: ancient capital with elaborate temples
Hanoi: Old Quarter filled with unrestored French-style homes
Ho Chi Minh City: American symbols of the Vietnam war

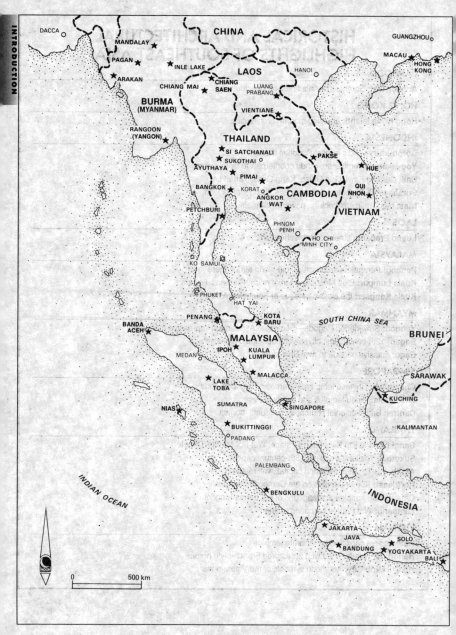

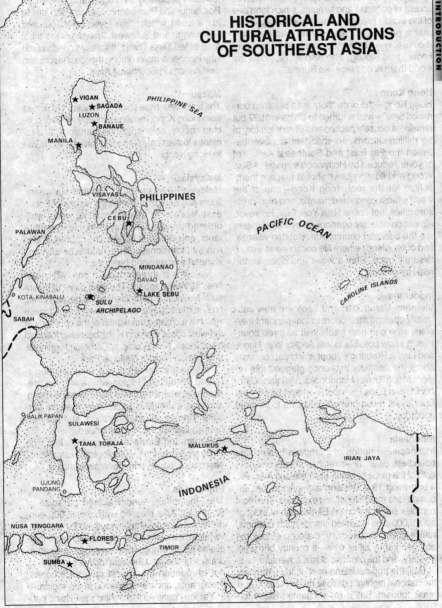

HISTORICAL AND
CULTURAL ATTRACTIONS
OF SOUTHEAST ASIA

PHILIPPINE SEA

★ VIGAN
★ SAGADA
LUZON
BANAUE ★
MANILA ★

PACIFIC OCEAN

VISAYAS
PHILIPPINES
★ CEBU

PALAWAN

MINDANAO
DAVAO
★ LAKE SEBU

KOTA KINABALU
SULU
ARCHIPELAGO

SABAH

CAROLINE ISLANDS

BALIK PAPAN
SULAWESI
★ TANA TORAJA

MALUKUS ★

IRIAN JAYA

UJUNG
PANDANG

INDONESIA

NUSA TENGGARA
★ FLORES

TIMOR

SUMBA ★

© MOON PUBLICATIONS, INC.

is Pagan (now called Bagan), an awesome sprawl of pagodas and temples, which form one of the world's premier archaeological sites. Myanmar is primitive, untamed, and extraordinarily memorable—"Quite unlike any land you will ever know," said Kipling, who also wrote, "In all the world there is no place like Burma."

Hong Kong

Hong Kong—the once "borrowed place on borrowed time"—was returned to China in 1997 but remains a densely packed and vibrant territory of six million citizens, an important stopover between the Far East and Southeast Asia. Yet anyone seduced by Hollywood's image of Suzi Wong and floating junks should prepare themselves for the real Hong Kong—one of the world's most congested, frantic, and high-pressure cities, not unlike New York City. However, almost completely overlooked by most visitors are the peaceful countryside, isolated villages, and outer islands where life continues at a more leisurely pace. Stay a week and discover the real Hong Kong.

Indochina

Vietnam, Cambodia, and Laos are now cautiously opening their doors to independent travelers, who can now freely visit all three countries. It's now possible to visit Angkor Wat, Hanoi, and Luang Prabang without any great concerns about the conflicts that once plagued this region. Moon Travel Handbooks' *Vietnam, Cambodia, and Laos Handbook*, written by Michael Buckley, is a comprehensive guide to all three countries.

Indonesia

Indonesia—a nation of incredible beauty and boundless diversity—stretches across one-seventh of the globe between Malaysia and Australia, a sprawling 13,000-island archipelago that encompasses mind-stupefying extremes. The most complex single nation on Earth, each of Indonesia's 6,000-plus inhabited islands holds customs, native dress, architecture, dialects, ethnology, and geography all its own—a country of magic, mystery, and the promise of real adventure.

Bali, the tropical island east of Java, remains the national highlight despite modernization and mass tourism. Bali is an enchanted island followed in popularity by Yogyakarta, known for Borobudur and Prambanan; Sumatra, fifth largest in the world, which offers idyllic Lake Toba and Bukittinggi; and Sulawesi, known for the tribal area called Tana Toraja. It's easy to understand why Indonesia ranks among the most fascinating destinations in Southeast Asia.

Macau

The tiny Portuguese colony of Macau, just across from Hong Kong, remains a sleepy world of cobbled streets, color-splashed mansions, and romantic Iberian cafes—a real highlight to any visit to Hong Kong.

Malaysia

Malaysia—the land of Kipling and Maugham, tigers and *stengahs*—holds title as one of Southeast Asia's most affluent nations, with a well-ordered transportation system, clean restaurants, and excellent hotels. The country is also rich with traditional culture, natural beauty, and wonderful white-sand beaches.

Malaysia is three worlds in one, which defines its tourist appeal. The west coast of peninsular Malaysia is characterized by modern cities, busy expressways, and hard-working Chinese who have created the wealth of the country. On the west coast, Penang is the best stop followed by Malacca, Kuala Lumpur, Cameron Highlands, and Taman Negara National Park.

The east coast remains a relatively undisturbed, traditional region where Malays predominate, where the call of Islam remains strong, and where leisure is prized over material pursuits. Tioman Island, Cherating, and the Perhentian Islands are recommended.

Sabah and Sarawak are for travelers who enjoy long river trips, ethnological explorations, vast caves, parks, and mountain climbing.

Philippines

The Philippines—undiscovered paradise of Southeast Asia blessed with over 7,000 sun-drenched islands—has everything for a superb vacation: exquisite white-sand beaches, unparalleled scuba diving, volcanoes, baroque cathedrals, nightlife, and the best festivals in Asia . . . not to mention the lowest prices for hotels, restaurants, and transportation in the region.

Yet the country's highlight is the Filipino people, whose warmth, love, and enthusiasm are legendary throughout Asia. The Thais may be nicely detached and the Indonesians politely curious but seldom will you meet such hospitable souls, so ready to smile, joke, laugh, and make friends with perfect strangers. If you believe travel is relationships, then the Philippines is your country—the best rest-and-relaxation destination in Southeast Asia.

Singapore
Singapore may surprise you with its soaring architecture, luxurious hotels, air-conditioned shopping centers, and city center, which remains among the cleanest and safest places in the world. It's an ideal place to shop, recover from the hardships of overland travel, and enjoy the best food in Southeast Asia. Check out the Singapore Zoo, Jurong Bird Park, and what remains of the old colonial architecture.

Thailand
Thailand offers the best mix of history, beaches, and culture of all the countries in Southeast Asia. In addition you'll find superb archaeological sites, expansive national parks, glittering temples, and a society not completely dominated by Western influence.

Bangkok ranks as among the most fascinating cities in Asia, a place where the temples, museums, and shopping centers would require months if not years to explore. Near Bangkok are beach resorts, the world's tallest Buddhist monument, the Bridge on the River Kwai, and the ruins of Ayuthaya and Sukothai. Chiang Mai is a convenient base for trekking into the "golden triangle," while northeast Thailand offers outstanding Khmer monuments and an opportunity to get somewhat off the beaten track. Southern Thailand boasts beaches and resort islands—some of the best in Asia.

TRAVEL WITH A THEME

Another approach to travel is to specifically seek out those destinations or activities that carry the strongest appeal. Far too many visitors find themselves wandering from country to country, unsure of where to go or what to see. Remember that travel can be a craft done well or badly, conscientiously or with a general disregard for detail, but like most things, it is much more satisfying if you do it properly. Imagine Southeast Asia as a colossal gallery that can only be sensibly explored selectively. Mash too many experiences together and you end up with an unsatisfying mess. Find a few themes and follow them. It doesn't really matter what they are—just don't spread yourself too thin.

A well-thought-out itinerary begins with a logical travel plan followed with flexibility and a sense of spontaneity. What kind of a traveler are you and what are your interests—history, art, culture, dance, people, beaches, sports, nightlife? If you enjoy history and museums, you should focus on those countries, such as Thailand, Myanmar, and Indonesia, where museums and archaeology are the major attractions. Most importantly, do your background reading *before* you go. Music, dance, and performing-arts aficionados should concentrate on places where

traditional theater and festivals still survive. Top choices are Yogyakarta, Bali, and Chiang Mai. Shopping—always one of the top attractions—is best conducted in the handful of towns which specialize in local crafts. Or would you prefer a total escape at a beach resort? The list is almost endless—educational tours, study programs, cultural minorities, adventure travel, restaurants, nightlife—but research and planning are essential for a successful and rewarding journey.

History and Architecture
While an endless procession of decaying old temples or ruined cities may not appeal to everyone, most visitors enjoy visiting a limited cross section of the more impressive monuments and historical sites. Each country offers a selection of architectural gems, but Thailand, Myanmar, and Indonesia offer the richest range when measured by antiquity and artistic merit. Singapore, Malaysia, and Macau are best for colonial architecture and 1930s domestic architecture. Though largely Westernized, Hong Kong has a handful of colorful Chinese temples and some outstanding modern architecture. Filipino churches are more intriguing than might be expected,

since they often combine both Spanish and Asian architectural themes. Quick walking tours are given for most historical neighborhoods, but visitors with limited time should concentrate on the following sites.

Performing Arts

Travelers who enjoy dance and drama will be thrilled with Southeast Asia's extraordinarily rich bounty of performing arts: Hindu ballets on Java, Buddhist/animist dance troupes in Bangkok, shadow plays on Bali, Christian passion dramas in the Philippines, Islamic martial arts in Malaysia, Chinese street opera in Singapore, puppet theater in Myanmar. Local theater and dance-dramas are recommended both as great entertainment and windows into the histories, cultures, and value systems of the people.

Performances can be either tourist-oriented or authentic spectacles intended for the local population. Though tourist performances are sometimes dismissed as mere contrived ripoffs, they're well advertised, reasonably priced, and often employ the finest dancers, musicians, and actors from the local community. However, anyone who would like to really understand Southeast Asian theater must also search out local performances. Here you'll experience the real Asia, complete with sweating crowds, old women cracking peanuts, kids running up and down the

center aisle, and a dozen other distractions that make the performance so memorable.

The major drawback to authentic theater is that performances are often difficult to find. Outside a handful of towns which have developed strong theatrical traditions (see the "Performing Arts Venues in Southeast Asia" chart), you'll need to conduct an organized search by scanning English-language newspapers and magazines, inquiring at local tourist offices, and asking everyone from taxi drivers to waitresses. Your best chances are on temple grounds during religious festivals. Even in such sacred settings, high-brow classical theater is often wedged between blasting rock 'n' roll bands, reruns of old Hollywood films, and slapstick comedies heavy with sexual innuendo. Venues are subject to changes and last-minute cancellations.

Festivals

A highly recommended travel theme is the religious, ethnic, and national celebrations of Southeast Asia. No matter their size or importance, festivals generally guarantee a colorful parade filled with floats, exotically costumed participants, the exhibition of valuable religious icons, traditional dance and drama, foodstalls, charlatans, hucksters, and rare opportunities to photograph without the risk of offending somebody's sense of privacy.

PERFORMING ARTS VENUES IN SOUTHEAST ASIA

COUNTRY	LOCATION	THEATER	PERFORMANCES
Indonesia	Jakarta	Taman Ismail Marzuki	dance, drama, comedy
	Yogyakarta	Dalem Pujokusuman	Ramayana theater
	Solo	Royal Palace	Central Javanese dance-drama
	Bali	Ubud	Balinese dance and drama
Malaysia	Kuala Lumpur	Central Market	Malay and Chinese theater
	Kota Bharu	Gelanggang Seni	traditional Malay arts
Myanmar	Yangon	Karaweik	dance, music, puppets
	Bagan		famous puppet performances
Philippines	Manila	Cultural Center	drama, dance, music
Singapore	Orchard Road	Luxury Hotels	cultural dance shows
Thailand	Bangkok	National Theater	classical theater, Thai drama
	Chiang Mai	Cultural Center	Lanna-era dance and drama

MAJOR FESTIVALS OF SOUTHEAST ASIA

MONTH	FESTIVAL	LOCATION	PERFORMANCE
January	Thaipusam	Hindu communities	Hindu parade of penance
	Independence Day	Myanmar, Yangon	Parades on 4 January
	Sinulog, Ati Atihan	Philippines	Carnival in the tropics
February	Chinese New Year	Chinese communities	dragons and firecrackers
	Union Day	Myanmar, Yangon	ethnic celebration
March	Moriones	Philippines	Easter Passion plays
April	Buddhist New Year	Thailand and Myanmar	water-throwing festival
	Ching Ming	Chinese communities	All Souls Day
	Tin Hau Birthday	Hong Kong	decorated fishing boats
May	Buddha's Enlightenment	Thailand and Myanmar	temple processions, fairs
	Bun Festival	Hong Kong	Floating children parade
June	Independence Day	Manila	parades on 12 June
	Kandazan Harvest	Malaysia, Sabah	tribal festival
	Dayak Festival	Malaysia, Sarawak	Dayak music and dance
July	Buddhist Lent	Thailand and Myanmar	Monks' ordination
	Candle Festival	Thailand, Ubon	parade of giant candles
August	Independence Day	Singapore	parades on 9 August
	Independence Day	Indonesia	parades on 17 August
	Independence Day	Malaysia	parades on 31 August
	Hungry Ghosts	Chinese communities	Chinese opera
September	Mooncake Festival	Chinese communities	lanterns and foods
	Boat Festival	Myanmar, Inle Lake	elaborate boats
October	Cheung Yeung	Chinese communities	Moon Watching Festival
	Asian Arts Festival	Hong Kong	Asian performing arts
	MassKara	Philippines, Negros	masked celebration
	Thimithi	Hindu communities	firewalking
	Deepavali	Hindu communities	festival of lights
November	Loy Kratong	Thailand, Sukothai	festival of lights
	Golden Mt. Festival	Thailand, Bangkok	Temple fair
	Elephant Round Up	Thailand, Surin	pachyderm polo
December	Christmas	Philippines	Passion plays

Religious celebrations predominate. Those listed in the "Major Festivals of Southeast Asia" chart are worth planning into your itinerary even if it involves additional time and expenses. Festivals are described in greater detail in each chapter. Chinese and Hindu festivals are detailed in the Singapore chapter.

Approximate dates are indicated despite festival dating being an inexact science in South-east Asia. National celebrations, such as independence days, are dated by Western calendars and fall on the same date annually. However, religious and agricultural festivals are dated by lunar calendars and change year to year, consequently floating around the calendar from month to month. Exact dates of religious and agricultural festivals should be confirmed with national tourist offices.

Shopping

While shopping might seem to be somewhat of an artificial theme for travel, visitors who understand the markets and enjoy bargaining will find Southeast Asia one of the world's great emporiums. Each country produces a unique range of goods: jewelry and masks in Bali, shellwork and baskets in the Philippines, batik and leatherwork in Java, pewter in Malaysia, puppets in Myanmar, silks and silverware in Thailand. The trick is to know what to buy and where to buy it. Unlike in Western countries where distribution networks efficiently spread products across dozens of markets, handicrafts in Southeast Asia tend to be sold only near the points of origin. Of course, many Thai products are available in Bangkok and Filipino handicrafts are sold in Manila, but villages where the handicrafts are originally produced generally offer the highest-quality product at the lowest prices.

The "Art and Handicraft Centers in Southeast Asia" chart will help point you toward the best places to shop. Shopping directly from the producer has several advantages. You'll be able to watch the craftsman in action and gain a greater appreciation for the work. You can also request custom jobs and negotiate prices. Perhaps most important is that money spent goes directly into the artist's pocket rather than to the middlemen.

Beaches

History, culture, and the performing arts may be rewarding themes for travel, but relaxing on an Asian beach is unquestionably a far more popular pastime. And what a great place for escape . . . stunning sands, crystal-clear waters, water sports, and glorious sunsets. Beach resorts are plentiful in all price ranges, from luxurious developments with first-class facilities to isolated beaches where the cost of lodging and food hardly breaks US$10 per day. Twenty dollars a day almost guarantees a clean and comfortable bungalow with a private verandah, barbecued fish dinners, and a bottle of rum. Even short-term visitors who generally limit their vacations to Hawaii or Mexico should consider a holiday in Southeast Asia since higher airfares are largely balanced by the lower costs of food and accommodations.

Selecting a beach without some background research can be a difficult task since Southeast Asia offers scores of resorts in varying states of development. One key to finding the perfect hideaway with the proper mix of primitivism and comfort is to consider the evolutionary cycle of Southeast Asian beach resorts. Virtually all of today's leading resorts—Phuket, Kuta, Ko Samui, Boracay, Puerto Galera, Batu Ferringhi—began as deserted beaches favored by independent travelers who lived in simple grass shacks and survived on fish and rice. Discovering the financial incentives of tourism, local villagers soon constructed guesthouses and cafes. Increasing numbers of travelers quietly tiptoed down, hoping that nobody else would discover their secret paradises. But word leaked out and soon the trickle became a rush as planeloads of land speculators and hotel operators joined the deluge. Within a decade what was once

---

ART AND HANDICRAFT CENTERS IN SOUTHEAST ASIA

INDONESIA

Jakarta: antiques, modern batiks
Bali: silverwork, painting, stonework, wood
Yogyakarta: batiks, leatherwork, clothing, puppets
Sulawesi: tribal carvings, textiles

MALAYSIA

Kota Bharu: batik, embroidered fabrics, kites

MYANMAR

Yangon: handmade umbrellas, wooden puppets
Bagan: lacquerware, ceramics

PHILIPPINES

Sagada: woodcarvings, tribal weavings
Banaue and Bontoc: woodcarvings, tribal weavings
Cebu City: shellwork, guitars

THAILAND

Bangkok: silks, brassware, clothing, antiques, gems
Chiang Mai: silverwork, jewelry, instant antiques

BEACH RESORTS OF SOUTHEAST ASIA

THAILAND

Ko Samui: Peaceful paradise yet well developed

Phuket: The Waikiki of Southeast Asia—noisy but fun

Ko Samet: Exceptional sand, primitive facilities

Pattaya: Heady yet family-friendly resort near Bangkok

Ko Chang: Emerging backpacker's destination near Cambodia

Krabi: Seaside town near spectacular Ao Pranang

Ko Phi Phi: Surrealistic landscape threatened by unchecked tourism

Ko Phangan: Backpackers' hedonistic escape near Ko Samui

Tarutao: Unspoiled islands near Malaysian border

MALAYSIA

Tioman Island: Spectacular natural setting; mediocre beaches

Cherating: Romantic and rural; simple bungalows

Pulau Pangkor: A quick escape on the west coast

Penang: Disappointing beach but superb town

Perhentian: Most spectacular islands in West Malaysia

Langkawi: Commercialized but with excellent beaches

PHILIPPINES

Puerto Galera: Beautiful topography but poorly developed

Boracay: Stunning island threatened by pollution, greedy developers

El Nido: The best in the Philippines—perhaps Southeast Asia

Panglao: Superb diving for mid-level travelers

Siargao: Remote Mindanao location; famous surf

INDONESIA

Kuta, Bali: Noisy, raucous, commercialized, fun

Pangandaran, Java: Mediocre beach but worthwhile national park

Gilis, Lombok: Small, remote, beautiful islands near Bali

Nusa Lembongan, Bali: Famous surfing spot near Sanur

Nias, Sumatra: Another world-class surfing destination

---

an idyllic stretch of sand had become an international clone of Waikiki or Mazatlán.

Although this sounds discouraging—and it is hard to deny that the hippie trails of the '60s have surrendered to mass tourism of the '90s—all is not lost. Even today, all over Southeast Asia, a small number of adventurous backpackers are sitting on deserted tropical beaches, being welcomed into the homes of villagers, and exchanging smiles with friendly children.

What's the perfect resort? Opinions differ, but for this author it begins with a long and wide

stretch of thick, clean, powder-white sand. Water should be warm, clear, and aquamarine blue. The ocean floor should be flat and sandy. The wind should blow with enough velocity for windsurfing and sailing but not so hard as to ruin sunbathing. Behind the beach should stand a forest of palm trees interspersed with hiking trails and isolated villages. Beaches fitting this description are relatively plentiful in Southeast Asia. However, facilities that harmonize with the environment are often lacking. Imagine a major resort being developed without any sort of

DIVING DESTINATIONS IN SOUTHEAST ASIA

COUNTRY	LOCATION	COMMENTS
Indonesia	Jakarta	Thousand Islands—decent diving, comfortable resorts
	Bali	Outstanding coral reefs and sunken wrecks
	Flores	Remote, untouched, Indonesia's best?
	Sulawesi	Coral gardens near Manado, popular with Japanese.
Malaysia	Tioman Island	Spectacular landscape with limited diving
	Sabah	Best dive sites in Malaysia
Philippines	El Nido	Superb diving, remote location
	Puerto Galera	Best diving near Manila
	Mactan Island	Convenient dive sites near Cebu City
	Bohol	Good beaches but limited dive facilities
Thailand	Similan Islands	Best diving in Thailand, accessible from Phuket
	Surin Islands	More great diving north of Phuket
	Phuket	Decent beaches but mediocre diving

zoning, government controls, or centralized planning.

Tragically, many of Southeast Asia's most promising beach resorts have transformed themselves into not tropical paradises but travelers' ghettos of dilapidated guesthouses or touristy nightmares of faceless high-rises and noisy bars. Perfect resorts are neither backpackers' slums nor Asian Waikikis. They are locally developed, owned, and operated so that profits return to the people rather than the New York Stock Exchange. Guesthouses are clean, spacious, and constructed from natural materials such as bamboo and palm fronds. Restaurants serve local fare, such as fish and vegetables, rather than pseudo-French or American fast food. Nightlife should include traditional entertainment and folk music along with the inevitable discos and video bars. Traffic and noise is minimized by limiting local traffic to service vehicles only. Cars and motorcycles are kept well away from the beach and residential areas. I've saved the best for last: Lanterns and candles are used rather than electricity . . . a radical idea now proving successful at several resorts.

The "Beach Resorts of Southeast Asia" chart includes both highly developed destinations and upcoming beaches popular with world travelers. None are secret destinations since it is not the intention of this author to accelerate commercial development or ruin tropical hideaways. The more remote beaches are hinted at in this book but you'll need to read between the lines.

Scuba Diving

The world's fastest-growing sport is quickly gaining popularity in Southeast Asia, where tropical waters host outstanding coral reefs, colorful marinelife, and sunken ships. Dives can be arranged with shops located in large Asian hotels or in advance from international tour operators such as See and Sea Travel Service. More dive operators are listed below and in *Skin Diver* magazine.

Philippines: Southeast Asia's top dive destination remains the Philippines, despite unscrupulous fishing practices and devastating typhoons, which have damaged some of the more accessible coral gardens. Diving is most spectacular off the north coast of Palawan and at the widely proclaimed Tubbataha Reef in the Sulu Sea. Organized dive expeditions are necessary to reach these destinations, though independent divers can find good offshore corals near Cebu and Bohol. The Department of Tourism in Manila distributes a useful brochure entitled *Philippines, A Diver's Paradise*, which lists dive resorts, shops, operators, and packagers.

Thailand: Diving in Thailand revolves around the Similan and Surin Islands, a few hours north of Phuket. Dives can be easily organized with dive shops in Bangkok and Phuket.

SOUTHEAST ASIA HIGHLIGHTS

TOP HOTELS

HOTEL	LOCATION	FEATURES
Oriental	Bangkok	19th-century ambiance with 20th-century comforts
Regent Hong Kong	Hong Kong	Darth Vader-style with incredible lobby views
Peninsula	Hong Kong	Oriental classic with impeccable service
Shangri-La	Bangkok	Stunning modern architecture
Regent Bangkok	Bangkok	Understated elegance in the heart of the beast
Mandarin Hong Kong	Hong Kong	Perfect service plus outstanding restaurants
Manila	Manila	MacArthur's favorite and national centerpiece
Raffles	Singapore	The classic yet over-restored colonial legend
Bela Vista	Macau	Once seedy, now lavishly restored
E & O	Penang	The final, unrestored classic from the Sarkie brothers
Four Seasons Bali	Bali	The world's top-rated tropical resort
Amankila	Bali	Surrealistic, zen-like atmosphere for sophisticates
Strand	Yangon	Once funky, now extremely posh and fabulous

FOOD CENTERS

COUNTRY	LOCATION	VENUE	COMMENTS
Hong Kong	Kowloon	Temple Street	Clams in black-bean sauce, beer
	Causeway Bay	Lockhart Road	Chinese, Thai, and vegetarian cafes
Indonesia	Bali	Kuta Beach	Fresh seafood, thick coffee
	Solo	street stalls	Unique Javanese specialties
	Yogyakarta	street stalls	Best vegetarian food in Southeast Asia
Malaysia	Penang	street stalls	Chinese and Nonya specialties
	Kuala Lumpur	Chinatown	Alfresco dining, Malay dishes
	Kota Baru	night market	Wonderful sweets
Macau	Macau	cafes	Portuguese dishes and cheap wine
Philippines	Sagada	guesthouses	Vegetarian dishes, great coffee
Singapore	Singapore	hawker centers	Best food in Southeast Asia
Thailand	Chiang Mai	night market	Oyster omelets, soups, seafood

NIGHTLIFE

COUNTRY	CITY	LOCATIONS	ENTERTAINMENT
Thailand	Bangkok	Patpong, Soi Cowboy	Famous bars and live revues
	Pattaya	Beach Road	Transvestite shows
	Phuket	Patong Beach	Discos, nightclubs, "beer bars"
Philippines	Manila	Makati	Upscale nightclubs, bars
	Manila	Ermita	Live bands and folk music nightclubs
	Angeles	Fields Avenue	Bachelor bars, live shows
Hong Kong	Hong Kong	Kowloon	British pubs, live bands

SOUTHEAST ASIA HIGHLIGHTS
(continued)

NIGHTLIFE *(continued)*

COUNTRY	CITY	LOCATIONS	ENTERTAINMENT
	Hong Kong	Wanchai	Yuppie watering holes;
	Hong Kong	Lan Kwai Fong	Expatriate clubs, delis, flashy discos
Singapore	Singapore	Orchard Road	Jazz bars, trendy discos, cozy pubs;
	Singapore	Singapore River	Folk clubs and jazz on the river
Indonesia	Bali	Kuta	Aussie bars and discos
	Bali	Seminyak	Sophisticated nightclubs, full-moon parties

MOUNTAIN CLIMBS

COUNTRY	MOUNTAIN	LOCATION	METERS	COMMENTS
Indonesia	Gunung Merapi	Central Java	2,911	Difficult 1-day trek
	Bromo	East Java	2,300	Easy early morning trek
	Gunung Ijen	East Java	2,800	Moderate 2-day trek
	Gunung Agung	Bali	3,142	Difficult 1-day trek
	Gunung Rinjani	Lombok	3,726	Moderate 2-3 day trek
	Gunung Tambora	Sumbawa	2,821	Difficult 3-day trek
	Keli Mutu	Flores	1,731	Easy 2-3 hours trek
Malaysia	Mount Kinabalu	Sabah	4,110	Highest peak in Southeast Asia
Myanmar	Kyaiktiyo	East of Yangon	1,102	Religious site, easy 2-day trek
Philippines	Mount Mayon	Southern Luzon	2,422	Difficult 2-day trek
	Mount Apo	Mindanao	3,143	Moderate 3-4 day trek

TREKKING

COUNTRY	LOCATION	COMMENTS
Hong Kong	Lantau	Lantau Trail, 70 km in 12 sections, camping
	Victoria Peak	Easy walks, spectacular views over Hong Kong harbor
Indonesia	Java	Ujong Kulon National Park, wildlife reserve
	Java	Kaliurang, trails at base of Mt. Merapi
	Java	Baluran National Park, wildlife reserve
	Bali	Ubud, hiking through rice fields, art villages
	Sumatra	Lake Toba, pleasant, easy, one-day hikes
	Sumatra	Bukittingi, canyons, lakes, nature reserves
	Sulawesi	Tana Toraja, rich ethnological region
	Kalimantan	Kapuas to Mahakam rivers, 1-2 months
Malaysia	Taman Negara	National park, original rainforest, wildlife
	Sarawak	Belaga to Bintulu, Ibans and logging
	Sarawak	Gunung Mulu National Park, tremendous caves
Philippines	Sagada	Limestone canyons, caves, superb villages
	Bontoc	Amazing rice terraces, great hikes, friendly people

COUNTRY	LOCATION	COMMENTS
	Lake Sebu	Mindanao, remote tribal homeland, beautiful topography
Thailand	Chiang Mai	Hilltribe villages, memorable yet controversial
	Khao Yai	National park, dozens of trails, campsites, limited wildlife
	Phu Kradung	National park, remote, profuse vegetation, chilly nights

RIVER JOURNEYS

COUNTRY	RIVER	COMMENTS
Indonesia	Siak	Sumatra—slow, cheap boat to/from Singapore
	Alas	Sumatra—whitewater rafting near orangutan reserve
	Kapuas	Kalimantan—longest river in Indonesia
	Makaham	Kalimantan—2 months, Samarinda to Apo Kayan
Malaysia	Skrang	Sarawak—Iban tribal area, commercialized
	Rejang	Sarawak—Iban tribal area, changing quickly
Myanmar	Ayeyarwady	Mandalay to Bagan—1 day, timeless journey
Philippines	Pagsanhan Falls	Luzon—whitewater and falls, touristy but fun
Thailand	Kok	Golden Triangle—5 noisy hours to Chiang Rai;
	Chao Praya	Bangkok canals—fast and exciting longboats

Malaysia: Dives off the east coast of peninsular Malaysia include the offshore islands of Tioman and Kapas. Arrangements can be made through the Tanjung Jara Hotel near Kuala Dungun and Tioman Island Resort. Malaysia's most spectacular diving, however, is found in Sabah near Kota Kinabalu and at Sipadan Island in the southeast. Contact Borneo Divers at the Tanjung Aru Beach Hotel or Hyatt in Kota Kinabalu.

Indonesia: The vast archipelago of Indonesia offers endless dive possibilities, although the diving industry remains quite undeveloped. Thousand Islands near Jakarta boasts professional facilities but diving is mediocre because of dynamiting and silting. Bali, the tropical island famed mostly for its arts and crafts, offers surprisingly good diving off the north coast around Menjangan and at the submerged maritime wreck east of Karangasem. Dives can be easily arranged through most large hotels or directly at several private dive operators. Indonesia's two most promising dive locations are the 62,000-hectare marine reserve at Flores and the gigantic coral gardens off Manado in North Sulawesi. Contact Dive Indonesia, Borobudur Intercontinental Hotel, Shop 34, Jakarta, or Jakarta Dive School, Jakarta Hilton, Jalan Subroto, Jakarta.

ON THE ROAD

Time

Allow as much time as possible. The two most common mistakes for first-time travelers to Asia are overpacking their bags and trying to cram too many destinations into their schedule. With only two or three weeks, it's much better to visit a single place such as Thailand or Bali than to attempt the if-it's-Tuesday-it-must-be-Singapore tour.

Travelers with an open schedule will find that Southeast Asia divides itself into convenient boxes which correspond to the length of visa. For example, the Philippines and Indonesia grant most nationalities a two-month stay, about an ideal amount of time to spend in each country. Thailand and Myanmar grant one month while most visitors spend about a week in Singapore and Hong Kong. Figured together, allow about

SAMPLE TIMETABLES FOR SOUTHEAST ASIA

COUNTRY	2 MONTHS	3 MONTHS	4 MONTHS	6 MONTHS	8 MONTHS
Hong Kong	1 week	1 week	1 week	1 week	1 week
Indonesia			1 month	2 months	2 months
Malaysia	2 weeks	2 weeks	2 weeks	2 weeks	1 month
Myanmar		1 week	1 week	2 weeks	2 weeks
Philippines		3 weeks	3 weeks	1 month	2 months
Singapore	1 week	1 week	1 week	1 week	1 week
Thailand	1 month	1 month	1 month	6 weeks	2 months

six months to properly explore Southeast Asia. Shorter options are listed in the "Sample Timetables for Southeast Asia" chart.

Costs

The basic rule for estimating costs is that time and money are inversely related. Short-term travelers must spend substantially more for guaranteed hotel reservations and air connections. Long-term travelers willing to use local transportation, budget hotels, and streets stalls can travel more cheaply in Southeast Asia than almost anywhere else in the world. Expenses vary widely, but many budget travelers report that land costs average about US$20-25 per day or US$500-800 per month. Total costs can be divided into four main categories: airfare, local transportation, accommodations, and food.

Airfare: Airfare takes a big chunk of everybody's budget, but you'll be surprised at how many kilometers can be covered per dollar with some planning and careful shopping. Roundtrip airfare from the United States or Europe should average under US$1,000. Figure on US$500-800 for additional flights around the region.

The best strategy for independent travelers on an extended vacation is to buy a one-way ticket to Southeast Asia and onward tickets from travel agencies along the way. Located in nearly every large town and city in Southeast Asia, these discount agencies offer some of the world's lowest prices because of fierce competition and the unwillingness of local agents to follow fares suggested by international consortiums. Unless you're on a tight schedule, roundtrip tickets and fixed-stop tickets are not advised since your travel plans will change en route and changing tickets is also a hassle. Note, however, that some countries will refuse entrance to anyone entering by air without an onward ticket. Details below.

Local Transportation: Trains, buses, taxis, and other forms of internal transportation are ridiculously cheap by Western standards. For example, a two-day train ride from Singapore to Bangkok costs under US$40; a bus from Bali to Jakarta costs US$25; a taxi from the airport to most hotels in Manila costs US$5.

Accommodations: While air tickets and ground transportation costs are rather fixed, eating and sleeping expenses can be carefully controlled. Hotels are available in all price ranges, depending on the country, size of city, and level of comfort. Industrialized countries such as Thailand and Malaysia are, quite naturally, more expensive than less-developed countries such as Indonesia and Myanmar. On the other hand, it's also possible to spend over US$200 for a luxury hotel in Indonesia or less than US$5 for a backpackers' dorm in Singapore.

Secondly, hotels in large cities are generally more expensive than those in smaller towns. Probably the most important pricing factor is comfort. Shoestring travelers who don't mind simple rooms with common bath and minimal furniture can sleep for under US$5 in most towns. Some of these places are desultory and noisy Chinese hotels located near the train or bus terminals, but others are clean and friendly guesthouses filled with Western backpackers. This informal network of guesthouses is the ideal solution for long-term travelers since they're great spots in which to relax, meet other people, and exchange travel information. Many have dormitories under US$2.

Guesthouses come under different names, depending on the country, and offer varying degrees of cleanliness, but most are a vast improvement over the sterility of large international hotels. Travelers who want better rooms with decent furnishings and private baths should figure on US$6-10 per day. Prices jump to US$10-20 with air-conditioning. While not a necessity at breezy beach resorts or in the hills, a/c becomes almost a necessity in hot and smoggy cities such as Bangkok. Moderately priced hotels in the US$25-50 range usually include hotel restaurants, lounges, TV, room service, and other standard amenities. Southeast Asia's top-end hotels are considered some of the finest in the world. Although recommended for an occasional splurge, it must be said that generally the cheaper the hotel, the more intriguing the people you'll meet and the more memorable the travel experience.

Food: Another old axiom encourages one to sleep rough but eat well. A great deal of money can sensibly be saved by staying in guesthouses rather than flashy hotels. The tragedy is that many travelers extend this bare-bones philosophy to dining, refusing to spend an extra 50 cents to enjoy a far superior meal. This is hardly recommended since surviving on a steady diet of fried rice and noodle dishes is not only monotonous and detrimental to your mental health, it deprives you of one of life's great travel experiences . . . food! Finding good food at bargain prices is the same anywhere in the world. Avoid those places signposted "We Speak English" or displaying credit card stickers. Instead, search out cafes filled with local customers, not groups of tourists. Don't be shy about road stalls and simple cafes; as mentioned above, these often provide the tastiest food at rock-bottom prices. By carefully patronizing a selection of local cafes

CLIMATES AROUND SOUTHEAST ASIA

	JAN.	FEB.	MAR.	APR.	MAY	JUNE	JULY	AUG.	SEPT.	OCT.	NOV.	DEC.
BURMA												
Rangoon	hot . . . . . . extremely hot . . . monsoon . . . . hot . . . . .
HONG KONG												
Hong Kong	cool . . . . warm . hot . . monsoon . . . . warm . . . .
INDONESIA												
Jakarta	rainy . . . . hot . . . . rainy . . . . .
Bali	rainy . . . . hot . . . . rainy . . . . .
Sumatra	rainy . . . . hot . . . . rainy . . . . .
Maluku	hot . . . . rainy . . . . hot . . . .
MALAYSIA												
K. Lumpur	warm . . . . hot . . . . monsoon . . . .
Kota Bharu	warm . . . . . hot . . . . monsoon . . . .
Kuching	monsoon. . . . . hot . . . . monsoon . . . . .
PHILIPPINES												
Manila	hot . . . . . . extremely hot . . . . monsoon . . . . hot . . . . .
SINGAPORE												
Singapore	warm . . . . rainy . . . . .
THAILAND												
Bangkok	hot . . . . . . extremely hot . . . . monsoon . . . . hot . . . . . .

and quality street stalls, it's surprisingly easy to enjoy three outstanding meals for less than US$10 a day.

Weather

Heat and rain can raise hell with your vacation plans. Southeast Asia is an equatorial land with a tropical climate. Temperatures perpetually hover between hot and excruciatingly hot, depending on whether it's the so-called "cool" winter season from November to March or the hot summer months from March to June. High temperatures and a humidity factor of almost 100% can be quite a shock for Westerners accustomed to more moderate climes, but there's little you can really do about it except stay out of the midday sun and escape into an air-conditioned hotel or restaurant. On the other hand, if you have control over your travel schedule, the best time to visit Southeast Asia—especially Thailand and Myanmar—is during the cooler winter months.

Monsoons, not temperature, are the most important weather factor in Southeast Asia. Derived from the Arabic word *mansim* (seasonal winds), monsoons are created by the differences in annual temperature trends over land and water. From May through September, winds from the southwest bring heavy rains to most of Asia lying north of the equator. In winter they reverse, bringing cool, dry air across mainland Southeast Asia and carrying rains to Indonesia and the northeast coastlines of mainland countries. The dividing line is formed by the equator. Best time to visit countries north of the equator (Myanmar, Thailand, Philippines, Hong Kong) is from November to March when the dry monsoons sweep down from China. Countries south of the equator are driest March to November. Monsoons flood streets and ruin holidays on the beach, but they're no cause for real alarm. For many seasoned travelers, the violent but brief rains of summer bring the real drama of Asia, providing an opportunity to witness nature in all her uncontrolled fury.

Luggage

Overpacking is perhaps the most serious mistake made by first-time travelers. Experienced vagabonders know that heavy and bulky absolutely guarantees a hellish vacation. Travel light and you'll be *free* to choose your style of travel. With a single carry-on pack weighing less than 10 kilos you can board the plane assured that your bags won't be pilfered, damaged, or lost by baggage handlers. You're first off the plane and you can cheerfully skip the long wait at the baggage carousel. You grab the first bus and get the best room at the hotel. Porters with their smiling faces and greased palms become somebody else's problem.

First consideration should be given to your bag. The modern solution for world travel is a convertible backpack/shoulder bag with zip-away shoulder straps. Huge suitcases that withstand gorilla attacks and truck collisions are best left to group tours and immigrant families moving to a new country. Serious trekking packs with outside frames are only suitable for the genuine backpackers they were designed for. Your bag should have an internal frame, a single-cell, lockable compartment without outside pockets to tempt Asian thieves. A light, soft, and functional bag should fit under an airplane

---

SUGGESTED PACKING LIST

- ☐ two pairs of pants, one casual, one formal
- ☐ one stylish pair of shorts
- ☐ two short-sleeved shirts with pockets
- ☐ five pairs of underwear and socks
- ☐ modest bathing suit
- ☐ one pair of comfortable walking shoes
- ☐ sandals or rubber thongs
- ☐ mini towel
- ☐ mini umbrella, or poncho
- ☐ medical kit
- ☐ sewing kit
- ☐ insect repellent
- ☐ two small padlocks
- ☐ Swiss Army knife
- ☐ photocopies of essential documents
- ☐ spare passport photos
- ☐ plastic Ziploc freezer bags
- ☐ alarm clock
- ☐ sunglasses
- ☐ International Drivers License
- ☐ *Southeast Asia Handbook*

seat and measure no more than 18 x 21 x 13 inches. Impossible, you say? It's done every day by thousands of smart and experienced travelers who know they are the most liberated people on the road.

Second consideration is what to pack. The rule of thumb is that total weight should never exceed 10 kg (22 pounds). Avoid vagabondage by laying out everything you *think* you'll need and then cutting the pile in half. (To truly appreciate the importance of traveling light, pack up and take a practice stroll around your neighborhood on the hottest day of the year.) Take the absolute minimum and do your shopping on the road. The reasons are obvious: Asia is a giant shopping bazaar filled with everything from toothpaste to light cotton clothing, prices are much lower than back home, and local products are perfectly suited for the weather.

Half of your pack will be filled with clothing. Minimize your needs by bringing only two sets of garments: wash one, wear one. A spartan wardrobe means freedom, flexibility, and variety, plus it's great fun to purchase a new wardrobe when the old clothing no longer comes clean. Give some serious thought to what you *don't* need. Sleeping bags, parkas, bedding, and foul-weather gear are completely unnecessary in Southeast Asia. Experienced travelers buy their umbrellas when it rains and sweaters when it gets chilly.

Then pack everything into individual plastic bags. Plastic compartmentalization keeps your bag neat and organized, and possibly even dry when the *banca* capsizes in the Philippines!

HEALTH

Southeast Asia is a surprisingly healthy place and it's very unlikely that you will lose even a single day to sickness. The secret to healthy travel is adequate preparation, watching your health during your vacation, and understanding how to find adequate medical attention in the event of an emergency.

INFORMATION

Background Reading

Detailed information on overseas medical problems is given in the following books.

Staying Healthy in Asia, Africa, and Latin America. Dr. Dirk Schroeder, Moon Publications, 1996. A handy and compact guide which updates the original publication from Volunteers in Asia. The book includes three chapters discussing the prevention of illness and general health maintenance on the road, while the remainder describes the diagnosis and treatment of illnesses common to foreign countries. It's written for the average traveler in a lively and direct tone.

Travellers Health, How to Stay Healthy Abroad. Dr. Richard Dawood, Oxford University Press, 1994. This newly revised guide to healthy travel is very comprehensive and medically authoritative though perhaps too technical for the average traveler.

Where There Is No Doctor. David Werner, Hesperian Foundation, 1992. A health-care handbook written in non-technical language with information on children's diseases, pregnancy, use of drugs with dosages, and first aid in third-world countries. Designed for both certified professionals and Peace Corp volunteers who intend to work abroad in remote villages.

The Tropical Traveller. John Hatt, Hippocrene, 1984. A readable book that served as the Bible for healthy travel for many years and can still be recommended for its clear descriptions of health and travel issues such as theft, communication, and culture shock.

IAMAT Directory. The International Association for Medical Assistance to Travelers in Lewiston, New York, publishes a worldwide directory of English-speaking physicians whose qualifications meet IAMAT standards and who have agreed to treat members for a set fee. Membership is free.

The Travel Clinic Directory. This free list of U.S. physicians specializing in travel medicine is available from Connaught Laboratories, Swiftwater, Pennsylvania, tel. (717) 839-7187.

U.S. Government Health Advice

Current health recommendations of the United States government can be checked by calling the Centers for Disease Control and Prevention (CDC) in Atlanta at (404) 332-4559 (general information), (404) 639-1610 (malaria tips). The annual CDC publication, *Health Information for International Travel*, is available from the U.S. Government Printing Office, tel. (202) 783-3238.

A handy new service is the **CDC Fax Information Service,** which sends country specific information to your fax machine in a few minutes. Call (404) 332-4565 and follow the voice prompts for instant advice on medical risk and prevention by region, diarrhea and disease outbreak bulletins, prescription drugs recommended for malaria, AIDS updates, and notes from their biweekly *Blue Sheets.*

Medical Kit
Most of the following supplies are available in cities and larger towns, though a small medical kit may be useful in remote villages. Recommended supplies depend on the length of your vacation, time of year, and remoteness of your travels. Most travelers need only the following:

- bandages, Band-Aids, scissors, tweezers
- insect repellent, sunscreen, Chap Stick, foot powder
- Pepto-Bismol tablets for mild diarrhea
- antiseptic for cuts and grazes
- antihistamine for allergies and colds
- antibiotics as prescribed by your doctor
- malaria pills (if necessary)
- contraception

Vaccinations
Contact a doctor who specializes in travel medicine for a general checkup, necessary shots, and perhaps an International Certificate of Vaccination, a small yellow booklet that records your immunizations. However, it is rarely demanded by immigration officials. The CDC *does not recommend* a yellow fever vaccination unless you intend to travel to or from an infected country in Africa or South America.

Cholera and smallpox vaccination requirements for Southeast Asia have been dropped, though the normal "childhood" vaccinations—tetanus; diphtheria; typhoid; measles, mumps, rubella (MMR vaccine); pertussis (DTP vaccine); and polio—should be up-to-date. All should be boosted, if necessary, by your doctor.

Insurance
Insurance is one item many travelers overlook until they face hospitalization abroad or emergency evacuation to medical facilities back home. Finding the right policy at the right price can be tricky. First, review your personal insurance policy to find out whether you are covered for medical treatments and emergency evacuations while traveling overseas; no need to pay twice for the same services. Don't rely on either homeowner's insurance, which generally only covers theft to US$500, or credit card insurance, which is often limited to flight insurance.

PRINCIPAL PROBLEMS

Diarrhea
The Centers for Disease Control and Prevention (CDC) in the U.S. reports that the most frequent problem is common traveler's diarrhea, transmitted by bacteria and parasites found in contaminated food or water. Common sense will minimize the risks: eat only thoroughly cooked food, drink safe water, wear shoes, resist swimming in fresh waters possibly contaminated with schistosomiasis flatworms, and take precautions against contact with insects, particularly mosquitoes.

Two drugs recommended by the National Institutes of Health for mild diarrhea can be purchased over the counter: Pepto-Bismol Diarrhea Control and Imodium A-D. Both contain loperamide, an antidiarrheal not found in regular Pepto-Bismol.

An alternative to loperamide is three days of a single 500 mm dose of the antibiotic ciprofloxacin, approved by the U.S. Food and Drug Administration for traveler's diarrhea.

Hepatitis A
The two main hepatitis varieties, A and B, are highly contagious liver diseases marked by debilitating, long-term symptoms such as jaundice and a feeling of malaise.

Hepatitis A ("infectious hepatitis") is a liver disease spread by contaminated water and food—conditions common in countries with poor standards of hygiene and sanitation. The disease is associated with feces and often spread by infected food handlers who don't wash their hands. Hepatitis A is a problem in Burma, India,

Nepal, and Indochina, but rarely contracted elsewhere in Southeast Asia by travelers who exercise a degree of caution with their drink and food. On the other hand, hepatitis A is figured to cost each infected adult in the United States about US$2,600 in lost wages, US$700 in medical costs, with an additional US$2,800 for hospitalized patients. About 20% of those infected experience a relapse and an estimated three percent of adults over 49 years old will die from hepatitis A.

Until a few years ago, hepatitis A was regarded as an incurable condition without any effective form of prevention or treatment. A dose of gamma globulin (immune serum globulin) was the only known antibody which reduced the likelihood of contracting the disease. Gamma globulin was effective for only one month, declining to near zero after three months, while appearing to reduce the body's natural immune system. Antibiotics administered after infection were useless and other drugs only increased liver damage. The only treatment was rest and liquids; travelers were told to "go home and rest."

In early 1995 the U.S. Food and Drug Administration approved a new vaccine called Havrix, the first vaccine proven effective in the prevention of hepatitis A. Developed by SmithKline Beecham, Havrix requires two injections one month apart with a booster after six months, and should be taken at least three weeks prior to departure. The newly approved drug is somewhat expensive—US$50-60 for each of the two recommended doses—but it's extremely beneficial since it offers long-term immunity, estimated to be up to 10 or 15 years. For more information, contact SmithKline Beecham at (800) 437-2829.

Hepatitis B

Hepatitis B—formerly called serum hepatitis—is another liver disease passed through sexual intercourse and the exchange of body fluids such as blood or semen. Hepatitis B may cause irreparable liver damage, liver cancer, and cirrhosis of the liver.

Hepatitis B is considered 100 times more infectious than HIV and is a particular risk to homosexuals, intravenous drug users, and health workers who handle body fluids. Approximately 1.2 million Americans carry the highly contagious virus and spread the disease to more than 300,000 new people each year. According to the National Foundation for Infectious Diseases (NFID), three-quarters of all cases strike sexually active young adults between the ages of 15 and 39.

Early symptoms include loss of appetite, nausea, vomiting, fatigue, and joint and muscle pain, though the CDC reports that 50% of the people exposed to the virus show no symptoms and may not even realize they are infected. While almost 90% will recover within months, 6-10% will retain the virus and become lifelong carriers.

Hepatitis B can be prevented with three shots of Hepvac B vaccine over a five-month period, with a booster shot every four or five years. Private physicians charge US$75-150 for the three-shot sequence, while public clinics offer it on a sliding scale. For more information about hepatitis B, contact the National Foundation for Infectious Diseases at (800) 437-2873.

Malaria

After a general checkup, discuss the possibility of malaria with your doctor. The nine-page CDC regional profile on Southeast Asia recently stated that the risk of malaria throughout the year is low in all parts of the region, except for remote and undeveloped countries such as Cambodia, Burma, and Laos. Visitors who stick to the standard routes have little risk of exposure and should perhaps avoid powerful anti-malarial drugs.

Travelers who plan to get well off the beaten track—explore remote jungles during the rainy season, camp around equatorial lakes—should take malaria pills, remain well covered, wear dark clothing, use mosquito nets, purchase insect repellents which contain deet (diethylmetatoluamide), and faithfully follow the recommended regimen of antimalarial pills.

Malaria Pills

Prescription drugs recommended by the CDC include chloroquine, mefloquine, doxcycline, proguanil, and primaquine. These drugs resist various strains of malaria with different side effects. About 50% of malaria cases in Southeast Asia are due to *Plasmodium falciparum,* a strain of malaria that gives flu-like malaise and high fever with shakes, and if not treated can lead to organ disease, anemia, and even death.

As a general rule, visitors should consider any fever as a sign of malaria and seek early

RESPONSIBLE TOURISM

Tourism, some say, broadens the mind, enriches our lives, spreads prosperity, dissolves political barriers, and promotes international peace. While concurring with most of these sentiments, others feel that mass tourism often destroys what it seeks to discover; it disrupts the economy by funneling dollars into international travel consortiums rather than local enterprise, exploits the people who find themselves ever more dependent on the tourist dollar, and reinforces cultural stereotypes rather than encouraging authentic dialogue between peoples. Responsible tourism is a movement that attempts to address both the virtues and vices of mass tourism by making each traveler more sensitive to these issues. The fundamental tenet is that travel should benefit *both* the traveler and the host country, and that travelers should travel softly and thoughtfully, with great awareness of their impact on the people and the environment.

Spearheading this movement is the Center for Responsible Tourism (2 Kensington Road, San Anselmo, CA 94960), a Christian group that holds annual conferences on the impact of mass tourism, publishes a thought-provoking newsletter, and offers workshops on how to lead a responsible tour. Visitors are encouraged to seek out low-impact and lo-cally based travel experiences by patronizing cafes, guesthouses, and pensions owned by indigenous people. Their guidelines:

1. Travel in a spirit of humility, with a genuine desire to meet and talk with the local people.

2. Sensitize yourself to the feelings of your hosts.

3. Cultivate the habit of listening and observing, rather than merely hearing and seeing.

4. Realize that other people's concepts of time and thought patterns may be dramatically different—not inferior—to your own.

5. Seek out the richness of foreign cultures, not just the escapist lures of tourist posters.

6. Respect and understand local customs.

7. Ask questions and keep a sense of humor.

8. Understand your role as a guest in the country; do not expect special privileges.

9. Spend wisely and bargain with compassion.

10. Fulfill any obligations or promises you make to local people.

11. Reflect on your daily experiences; seek to deepen your understanding of the people, the culture, and the environment.

---

diagnosis and treatment for an uncomplicated and complete cure.

Doxycycline: The CDC currently recommends the use of doxycycline for travelers intending to spend significant time in dangerous areas. Doxycycline is a more effective drug than mefloquine due to mefloquine-resistant malarial mosquitoes found in infected regions. Common trade names for doxycycline include Vibramycine, Banndoclin, Doxin, Dumoxin, Interdoxin, and Siclidon. The chief disadvantages to doxycycline are that the drug must be taken every day at an adult dose of 100 milligrams beginning the day before entering the malarious area and four weeks after departure, and the possible side effects such as skin photosensitivity, which may result in sunburn.

Mefloquine: Travelers should also ask their doctor about the suitability of mefloquine, marketed in the U.S. under the trade name of Lariam and dosed out at 250 milligrams once a week.

Mefloquine been proven effective against chloroquine- and Fansidar-resistant *P. falciparum*, but is no longer recommended as a prophylactic due to mefloquine-resistant parasites found in certain regions of Southeast Asia. Mefloquine also carries the risk of side effects such as gastrointestinal disturbances and dizziness.

Chloroquine: Chloroquine is a possible choice for travelers who cannot take mefloquine or doxycycline. The adult dosage is 500 milligrams once a week, starting one week before entering a malarious area, then weekly for four weeks after leaving the area. Chloroquine is marketed in the U.S. under the brand name Aralen and elsewhere as Resochin, Avoclor, Nivaguine, and Kalguin. Chloroquine is **no longer recommended** for visitors to Southeast Asia but remains effective in the Caribbean, South America, and the Middle East.

Proguanil: The CDC recommends that travelers taking chloroquine should also simultaneously take proguanil. Though not available in the United States, proguanil can be purchased overseas under the brand name Paludrine. The dosage is 200 milligrams daily in combination with a weekly dose of chloroquine.

Fansidar: Fansidar, the trade name for sulfadoxine and pyrimethamine, is a powerful and potentially dangerous drug taken only as temporary self-treatment. Fansidar is also sold as Maloprim, the trade name on dapsone and pyrimethamine. The CDC advises that Fansidar should be taken to treat a fever only if professional medical assistance is not available within 24 hours.

WARNINGS

Theft

Theft can be a problem in Southeast Asia. Losing your passport, air ticket, traveler's checks, and cash can be a devastating experience. Each country and each city seems to have its own peculiar type of thief—razor-blade artists on Bangkok buses; the hooked-pole trick in Kuta, trapdoor thieves in Manila—but with a certain amount of caution you can hold the damage down to a minimum. First, bring as few valuables as possible. Leave the jewelry, flashy camera bags, and other signs of wealth at home. To speed up the replacement of valuable documents, keep a duplicate copy of all valuable papers separate from the papers themselves. Immediately report any theft to the local police and obtain a written report. Check the security of your hotel room and ask for a room with barred windows and a private lock. Valuables should be checked in the hotel safe and an accurate receipt obtained.

Be cautious about fellow travelers, especially in dormitories. Keep your pack in full sight whenever possible. Be cautious about pickpockets in crowds, on buses, during festivals, and at boat harbors. Finally, try to maintain a balance between suspicion and trust. Most Asians are honest, so don't get paranoid about everybody who wants to show you around or practice their English. Meeting the people will almost certainly provide your most cherished moments while on the road.

Drugs

Unless you care to spend the next 20 years of your life in an Asian prison, don't mess with drugs in Southeast Asia. All countries in Southeast Asia execute convicted drug smugglers. There are plenty of drugs floating around—from marijuana to mushrooms and smack—but hundreds of foreigners are arrested and thrown into prison each year. Beware of scams. Organized drug raids of budget travelers' hotels are conducted by local police who haul suspects down to jail and demand stiff fines. Taxi drivers often sell drugs to travelers and turn them in for the reward the and return of the drug! Drugs are not worth the risk.

Just say no to drugs while traveling in Southeast Asia.

AIDS

Love and lust in Southeast Asia have taken an ugly turn since authorities first detected AIDS in 1984. According to a government survey released in 1992, Thailand alone has over 300,000 HIV-positive cases, while several thousand people had developed AIDS-related complex. The World Health Organization (WHO) reckons that AIDS could infect over five million Southeast Asians by the year 2000.

Heterosexual sex—not homosexual sex or intravenous drug use—is the most common source of AIDS in Southeast Asia. The scourge has moved from the prostitution industries of Thailand and the Philippines to all other countries. Former Thai Population and Community Development Association (PDA) head Mechai Viravaidhya estimates that 50% of the prostitutes in Thailand now carry the virus, and that up to 10% of the male population are infected. The WHO recently reported over 200 HIV-positive cases in Singapore, 200-300 new cases each month in Malaysia, a rapid rise in the once-untouched countries of Vietnam and Cambodia, and a frightening increase in Indonesia, Myanmar, and Laos.

The eerie quality of the raging epidemic is its invisibility. Most of those infected with HIV have not yet developed symptoms of AIDS and continue to engage in prostitution, unwittingly infecting their customers. Southeast Asia's sex-for-money trade will continue growing into the next century. And so will AIDS cases. Sexually active Westerners and Thais alike would do well to practice the only proven form of safe sex: complete abstinence.

VISAS AND OFFICIALDOM

PASSPORTS

American Passports

Essential travel documents include a valid passport and necessary visas. Passports should be valid for at least six months after the day of entry.

Passports are available from U.S. government agencies listed below and from many post offices and courthouses. American passports are valid for 10 years and cost US$65; renewals are US$50. Allow six weeks for processing during the busy spring and summer months. You can obtain an emergency passport in 24 hours with an additional US$35 fee.

The U.S. Passport Information office (tel. 202-647-0518) provides a 24-hour recording about fees and documentation. *Passports: Applying The Easy Way* and *Foreign Entry Requirements* are two useful brochures, available from Consumer Information Center, Pueblo, CO 81009.

Safeguard Your Documents

Losing passports can be an unpleasant experience. Overseas embassies and consulates can replace passports in two days to two weeks depending on the office. Visitors missing passports and faced with a dire emergency such as family death or legal problems can request temporary traveling permits and proceed to airports for immediate flights back home.

To speed replacement of important documents, make two photocopies of the stamped pages in your passport, airline tickets, identification cards, insurance policies, and credit cards. One copy should be left with friends back home who can be contacted in emergencies. Keep your photocopies in a separate place from the actual documents.

VISAS

Visas are stamps placed in your passport by foreign governments that permit you to visit that country for a limited time and for a specified purpose, such as tourism or business. Visas are issued by embassies and consulates located both at home and in most large Asian cities.

The good news is that visa requirements are being eased throughout Southeast Asia. Most countries now permit visa-free entry for a limited time. For instance, Indonesian immigration officials stamp a two-month permit into your passport upon arrival. Visas are also unnecessary for short visits to Singapore, Hong Kong, Macau, Brunei, Malaysia, and Thailand, which now grants 30 days on arrival. The Philippines only

U.S. PASSPORT AGENCIES

Boston	(617) 565-6990
Chicago	(312) 353-7155
Dallas	(214) 653-7691
Honolulu	(808) 522-8283
Los Angeles	(310) 235-7070
Miami	(305) 536-4681
New Orleans	(504) 589-6161
New York	(212) 399-5290
Philadelphia	(215) 597-7480
San Francisco	(415) 744-4010
Seattle	(206) 220-7777
Washington	(202) 647-0518

grants 21 days on arrival but extensions are fairly easy in Manila and Cebu.

Whether to get your visas prior to departure or on the road depends on what countries you intend to visit, how long you wish to stay, and your approximate dates of arrival. Travelers on short vacations can obtain the necessary visas in advance from consulates, travel agents, or visa agencies. On an extended trip, it's much better to pick up your visas as you travel. For example, most travelers get their Thai visa in a neighboring country shortly before crossing the border. This also circumvents the problem of visas with limited validities (unused visas often expire in six to 12 months; see below). Visas can be obtained in person from embassies located in most Asian capitals, but it's much faster to let a travel agent or

visa service do the necessary paperwork. Wasting half a day wrestling with disgruntled consulate officials just isn't worth the modest service charge.

OTHER DOCUMENTS

International Health Certificate

Under the International Health Regulations adopted by the World Health Organization (WHO), a country may, under certain conditions, require from travelers an International Certificate of Vaccination against yellow fever. The WHO has recently eliminated the special page for cholera vaccinations and an international health certificate is no longer required for entry into Singapore or Malaysia. Find more detailed information under "Health," above.

International Student Identity Card (ISIC)

The green-and-white ISIC card offers airline, hotel, and museum discounts in Europe and the United States, but provides few benefits for travelers in Southeast Asia. Qualified students may want to obtain the card if only for its insurance policies, which cover up to US$3,000 in total medical expenses as well as US$100 per day in a hospital. The annual fee is US$16. To purchase a card contact ISIC Headquarters, P.O. Box 9045, 1000 Copenhagen, Denmark, tel. (45) 33-93-9393.

Students 12-25 years of age can obtain an ISIC card at any of the following offices: Council Travel Services, tel. (212) 661-1450; STA Travel, tel. (800) 777-0112; Let's Go Travel, tel.

ENTRY REQUIREMENTS FOR SOUTHEAST ASIA

COUNTRY	VISAS	LENGTH	EXTENSIONS	OPTIONAL
Brunei	None	1 week	1 week	
Myanmar	Required	1 month	None	
Hong Kong	None	1 month	1 month	
Indonesia	None	2 months	None	
Macau	None	20 days	None	
Malaysia	None	30 days	30 days	
Philippines	None	21 days	38 days	60-day visa
Singapore	None	2 weeks	None	
Thailand	None	30 days	None	60-day visa

INTRODUCTION

(800) 553-8746; and Travel CUTS, tel. (416) 798-CUTS

International Youth Hostel Card

As with the ISIC card, membership in the International Youth Hostel Federation offers only minimal benefits since Southeast Asia has very few youth hostels, except in Japan. IYH offices throughout the world sell membership cards and background material such as their *International Youth Hostel Handbook to Africa, America, Asia, and Australasia.*

International Driving Permit

Officially, an International Driving Permit (IDP) may be required to rent cars and motorcycles in many countries in Southeast Asia; despite this fact, most rental agencies have dropped this requirement and simply ask to see your home country driver's license. The IDP is only recommended for really inexperienced and very nervous travelers.

The card costs US$10 per year and is sold by the Canadian Automobile Association and American Automobile Association (AAA).

MONEY

Smart travelers bring a combination of cash, traveler's checks, credit cards, and a bank ATM card. Each has its own advantages and drawbacks depending on the circumstances.

Cash is useful in emergencies, so stash a few U.S. twenties in your pack, well removed from your main money supply. Traveler's checks remain the favorite form of money despite the growing popularity of bank cards and ATMs. Credit and debit cards used for withdrawals from ATMs are slowly becoming a feasible alternative to traveler's checks, though a few kinks need to be worked out before traveler's checks can be considered obsolete. Finally, visitors on longer vacations should consider opening a bank account in Southeast Asia to earn interest on their deposited traveler's checks and provide easy access to instant cash.

The secret to successful money management is to keep your money working in interest-bearing accounts, minimize fees for transfers of funds, demand commission-free traveler's checks, bring along a credit or debit card, and perhaps open a bank account in the region.

TRAVELER'S CHECKS

Most of your currency will probably be in traveler's checks, the familiar standby that provides a degree of safety and fairly quick refunds when lost or stolen. The most widely recognized brands are American Express, Bank of America, Citicorp, Thomas Cook, Visa, and MasterCard.

Most checks should be in larger denominations such as US$50 and US$100 to minimize paperwork and garner slightly better rates. Bring a few smaller checks to cash when exchange rates are dismal, and for the end of your trip to minimize the aggravation of excess currency.

Keep a list of serial numbers and an accurate record of each exchange. This provides a running balance of your finances and helps speed up the refund process in the event of loss.

Fees

Traveler's checks are safe and convenient but they certainly aren't free. Most banks and commercial issuers charge 1-3% for purchase and then keep all accrued interest until the checks are cashed. Banks actually make far more profit using your float than whatever sales fees they might collect. These fees can be minimized by purchasing only commission-free checks and keeping your funds in interest-bearing accounts until the moment of transfer.

MONEY TRANSFERS

Money can be transferred from banks, private companies, and stock brokerage firms at home to financial institutions in Southeast Asia. Be sure to open an account prior to departure and request a list of their international affiliates, plus ask about all transfer fees and for suggestions on more economical methods of receiving money abroad.

Bank Transfers

Bank transfers by telex are safe and fast but quite expensive due to mandatory service charges (US$20 per transaction), telex fees (US$20 each way), commissions on traveler's checks (1-3%), and currency spreads between the buy and sell rates. Bank fees for wire transfers average 6-10% or US$60-100 per US$1,000.

Transfers by mail take two or three weeks but eliminate the need for expensive telexes.

American Express

AMEX MoneyGrams can be sent and received from any participating AMEX Travel Office and you don't need to be a cardholder. The first US$1,000 may be paid by credit card but additional amounts must be paid in cash. Money-Grams take about 30 minutes and funds can be picked up in either local currency or U.S. dollar-denominated traveler's checks.

MoneyGram service fees of 4-10% are based on the amount of funds transferred, the final destination, and method of payment. This means you'll pay US$40-100 per US$1,000, or about the same rate as bank transfers by telex.

AMEX cardholders can withdraw funds directly from their home account up to a limit of US$1,000 per week. This can be an economical alternative to MoneyGrams or wire transfers through banks. For more information and overseas AMEX locations, call (800) 926-9400 in the U.S. and (800) 933-3278 in Canada.

Western Union

Money can also be wired in about 30 minutes from Western Union to representative offices in Southeast Asia. To wire money, take cash or a cashier's check to the nearest office of Western Union. You can also use your Visa or MasterCard by calling (800) 325-6000 in the U.S. or (800) 321-2923 in Canada. Service fees range 4-10% depending on the amount transferred and method of payment.

U.S. Embassies

Emergency funds *only* can be sent abroad through U.S. embassies or consulates at fees of US$15-40 per US$1,000. Details are provided in the U.S. government brochure, *Sending Money to Overseas Citizens Abroad.* Call (202) 647-5225 or fax (202) 647-3000.

CREDIT CARDS

Advantages

Smart travelers bring credit cards for several reasons.

Purchases: First, credit cards are invaluable for major purchases such as airline tickets and electronic equipment since you don't need to haul around buckets of cash or a suitcase packed with traveler's checks. Credit cards are also somewhat economical since they provide interest-free loans until the bill arrives back home. Just be sure to make arrangements to have a friend or family member pay the bill.

Cash Advances: Credit cards are also useful for instant cash advances from banks in Southeast Asia. For example, you can walk into any major bank, present your credit card to the clerk, fill out a short form, and quickly pocket up to US$500 in local currency. Another advantage is that funds are normally converted into local currencies at favorable "interbank foreign exchange rates," the wholesale benchmark used by international banks.

Cash advances carry some financial drawbacks. Advances are loans—not lines of credit—and interest charges accrue from the moment of transaction, plus cash advances completed overseas generally carry higher transaction fees than similar services in the West.

Credit Card Guarantees

Credit card protection is often less than assumed by most travelers, perhaps due to the aggressive marketing campaigns of most card companies. Anyone contemplating large overseas purchases by credit card should read the fine print *very* carefully. United States law states that credit cards must provide a degree of protection against defective, switched, inauthentic, and inferior goods, but *only* on items purchased in your home state or within 100 miles of your home address.

On overseas purchases, credit card companies only help with items that never arrive; they provide no legal protection against defective, switched, and inauthentic merchandise purchased abroad. In most cases, the customer pays by credit card and agrees to let the merchant ship the items back home. Upon arrival (if it arrives at all), the customer discovers the item to be defective, broken, or switched with an inferior replacement. The cardholder then turns to their credit card company for help. The card company attempts to resolve the issue by contacting the merchant by mail or phone, but companies are helpless if the merchant quibbles or fails to respond to their inquiries. The cardholder is not only stuck with the merchandise, but also legally obligated to pay the bill.

The straightforward solution is to hand carry all purchases back home. Otherwise, ask for an itemized invoice that details exactly what you bought, the date of purchase, and all shipping and insurance costs. Take several photographs of the store owner and yourself standing next to the item. Write down the merchant's name, address, and phone number, and all other verbal guarantees and legal documentation. Detailed paperwork often helps to settle problems with recalcitrant merchants.

Credit Card Fraud

Southeast Asia is a relatively honest region, though American Express reports that a few countries here carry some of the highest ratios of fraudulent-to-legitimate transactions in the worldwide market.

Hotel Scams: Far too many visitors return home to discover that large bills have been run up by dishonest hotel employees who remove cards from stored luggage or hotel safes and then go on shopping sprees with the cooperation of unscrupulous merchants. You return home to find that you somehow purchased 20 color TVs and 16 stereo systems during your brief vacation.

Credit cards should be carefully guarded and carried on your person at all times. Cards checked with baggage handlers or deposited in hotel safes should be tightly sealed in theft-proof compartments and a complete receipt should be listed of all valuables including credit cards and serial numbers of traveler's checks. Carefully inspect the contents of your package when you reclaim your valuables from the front desk or baggage storage room.

Duplicate Receipts: Fraud is also practiced by dishonest merchants who surreptitiously run cards through machines several times to produce multiple copies and then fill out the extra copies before submitting the receipts to local

banks for collection. The best prevention is to keep an eye on your credit card during purchases and never allow merchants to disappear into a back room with your card.

Illegal Surcharges: Merchants sometimes add illegal surcharges to credit card purchases, such as value-added taxes (VAT) and merchant fees of 3-5% collected by the credit card company. Both practices are against international law and violate the legal agreements signed between the merchant and credit card companies. Customers charged such fees should immediately object and demand that all surcharges be eliminated from the bill. If the merchant refuses but you still want the item, ask for an itemized receipt that clearly states the cost of the product and the amount of surcharge. After your return home, submit photocopies of these receipts to your credit card company for a refund and to aid them with legal action against the merchant.

ATM WITHDRAWALS

A sensible alternative to carrying excessive cash is to withdraw funds from ATMs with a credit or debit card issued by a domestic or foreign bank. ATMs dispense cash 24 hours a day, seven days a week, and then charge your credit card or debit your bank account. Debit and credit cards are now honored at most ATMs in Southeast Asia.

Debit cards are issued by banks in conjunction with either the Cirrus system owned by Visa or the PLUS system owned by MasterCard. The MasterCard/Cirrus card works at ATM machines located in airports, major hotels, and at banks throughout the region. To obtain an international ATM directory, call MasterCard/Cirrus at (800) 424-7787 or Visa/PLUS at (800) 843-7587.

Visitors spending a month or so in Southeast Asia should seriously consider opening a local bank account and obtaining a debit card.

Using Your Card

The logos of the types of cards accepted at a given ATM are posted on the machine. Some ATMs take both debit and credit cards while others are limited to one particular card.

Daily withdrawal limits are predetermined by your bank and usually range from US$100-200 per day. Insert your card, enter your personal identification number (PIN), and follow the instructions shown in English on the screen or posted nearby. Local currency is given but your account is debited in your national currency at favorable exchange rates.

Ghosts in the Machine
There are a few problems with using ATM cards, which appear to be the inevitable replacement for traveler's checks. Some ATMs do not have the ability to ask whether you want the money withdrawn from your checking or savings account but automatically try the primary (usually checking) account. Contact your institution prior to departure to insure that sufficient funds are in your primary account and that your card withdraws from the correct account. It can be an unpleasant surprise to discover that your card is programmed to withdraw funds from your checking account, but all your money has been left in your savings account.

Another glitch is that some Asian ATMs often do not accept PIN numbers longer that four digits. Travelers with six-digit PINs should ask their bank to reprogram their card with a four-digit number.

Finally, consider the fees. ATM withdrawals carry either flat fees demanded by the institution that issued the card or transaction fees based on the amount of withdrawal. Visa and MasterCard fees are determined by the issuing bank, American Express charges a minimum of two percent or US$2 per transaction, Diners Club charges 3-4%.

COMMUNICATIONS

MAIL

The most dependable way to receive mail is at large post offices via poste restante, a French term which means general delivery. Instruct your friends to capitalize and underline your last name to prevent your mail being misfiled under your first name. You will need to show your passport and pay a small fee when you pick up your mail. Letters are held for several months before being returned to sender.

Mail should not be sent to embassies since they deal only with official correspondence. Neither is American Express recommended since the company's mail services are being cut back. Mailing packages home is best done from major cities, where post offices sometimes provide packing services. Packages are limited to 10 kilos; above that you'll need to use private shipping firms. Use registered mail for important documents and keep all receipts to help trace missing parcels.

TELEPHONE

International Calls to Southeast Asia
International calls can be made from the United States by dialing the international access code (011), the country code, and then the local number. To make an operator-assisted call (person-to-person, collect, calling card), dial the international access code for operator-assisted calls (01) and give the country code plus the local telephone number.

Consider the time differential before calling and waking your friends at some hellish hour. Southeast Asia is 8-10 hours ahead of GMT, 14-16 hours ahead of San Francisco and Los Angeles, 12-14 hours ahead of Chicago, and 11-13 hours ahead of New York. Daylight saving time adds one hour to these figures.

International Calls from Southeast Asia
Overseas calls can be made from hotels, telecommunication centers, selected post offices, and public phones labeled World Phone. Some phones only accept payment by phone cards, which can be purchased from pharmacies, bookstores, post offices, 7-Elevens, and supermarkets. Instructions are clearly labeled in English and special buttons for Home Direct Service are common in many locations.

International calls are made by dialing the international access code for each particular country followed by the country code, the area code minus the initial zero, and finally the local number. The least expensive calls are those made through discount calling plans offered by AT&T, MCI, and Sprint, followed by government telecommunication offices and finally hotels,

INTERNATIONAL TELEPHONE CODES

To make an international call from Southeast Asia, dial the outside access number, the appropriate country code (given below), the area code (minus the initial zero), and finally the local number.

INTERNATIONAL ACCESS CODE— WESTERN NATIONS

Australia	61
Canada	1
France	33
Germany	49
Ireland	353
Netherlands	31
New Zealand	64
United Kingdom	44
U.S.A.	011

SOUTHEAST ASIA COUNTRY CODES

Brunei	673
Cambodia	855
Hong Kong	852
Indonesia	62
Laos	856
Macau	853
Malaysia	60
Myanmar	95
Philippines	63
Singapore	65
Thailand	66
Vietnam	84

which often add surcharges or connection fees. Discount calling plans allow travelers to dial a toll-free access number from their hotel room and most public phones and speak directly with an operator in their home country—a convenient service which eliminates language problems, minimizes hotel surcharges, and allows phone bills to be charged to either your telephone calling card or major credit card.

AT&T estimates that their program cuts 20-60% off the direct dial rates imposed by hotels. As you might expect, some hotels block access to these discount programs or impose stiff surcharges on permitted calls. Be sure to inquire about all charges prior to making lengthy phone calls from your hotel room.

Calling Card Access: Customers with telephone calling cards issued by AT&T, MCI, or Sprint can simply dial the access number, punch in their PIN number, and then follow the English-language voice prompts to make direct connections. To obtain a calling card in the United States contact AT&T USA Direct, tel. (800) 331-1140; MCI Call USA, tel. (800) 444-3333; or Sprint Express, tel. (800) 767-4625.

TRAVEL RESOURCES

The following section will help you uncover reliable travel information before you leave home.

First visit your public library for books on history, culture, people, politics, and the arts. The "Recommended Readings" section in the back of this guidebook summarizes many of the author's personal favorites and provides recommendations for travelers with limited reading time.

Travel agents experienced with Southeast Asia are a godsend, but as rare as whale's teeth. Student travel agencies often provide more reliable travel advice than the average agency. Finally, talk with other travelers who have recently returned from Southeast Asia for the latest details.

Internet

Surfing the Internet is a great way to find travel tips on every nook and cranny of the planet including an amazing amount of information about every country in Southeast Asia. With a bit of time, you can download:

• A country report from the U.S. government

• CIA assessments including concise and detailed advice for the traveler

• Current travel advisories issued by the U.S. State Department

• Thousands of visitor comments from usenet groups

• Satellite photos of current weather patterns

- Political and economic news from wire services
- Currency exchange rates
- Tips from travel writers
- Advice from local residents
- Hotel prices from regional hotel associations
- The latest issue of the Southeast Asian newspapers

You can then print the whole thing out and return your copy of *Southeast Asia Handbook* for a refund. Suggested Internet sites are listed in the back of this book under Recommended Reading.

Magazines

The following magazines publish a limited number of stories on Southeast Asia.

Escape: The best periodical for adventurous travelers with stories on Zanskar ice capades, Northern Ireland without a flack jacket, the Golden Triangle ruby business, cosmic surfing, and the Tibetan Wheel of Life. US$18/6 issues. P.O. Box 5159, Santa Monica, CA 90409.

International Travel News: Big, opinionated, and highly informative monthly magazine with dozens of down-to-earth travel articles, plus columns on cruising and helpful tips from readers. Geared to the older traveler but still an ex-

cellent deal. US$14/12 issues. 2120 28th St., Sacramento, CA 95818, tel. (916) 457-3643.

EcoTraveler: Publisher Lisa Tabb covers the world of ecotourism and responsible travel with an eye on more accessible destinations than the ones covered in the magazines mentioned above. US$12/6 issues. 2535 N.W. Upshur St., Portland, OR 97210, tel. (503) 224-9080, ecotrav@aol.com.

Condé Nast Traveler: Superb writing, photography, and graphics on Europe and the Americas, though few stories on anything exotic such as Southeast Asia. US$15/12 issues. P.O. Box 52469, Boulder, CO 80321, tel. (800) 777-0700, http:\\www.cntraveler.com.

Consumer Reports Travel Letter: A professional 12-page monthly newsletter with honest advice on airline and hotel discounts, auto rentals, coupon books, and rail travel but little information on specific destinations. It's expensive at US$37/12 issues. P.O. Box 51366, Boulder, CO 80321.

Globetrotters Club: Membership in England's leading club for budget travelers includes a handbook, six annual newsletters, and a list of over 1,200 members who accept homestays. Monthly travel club meetings are held in New York, Southern California, and in London at 52 St. Martins Lane. US$14/year, US$5 initiation fee. BCM/Roving, London WC1N 3XX, England.

SAVE THE WILDLIFE

As Asian rainforests are destroyed by man, the first casualties are wildlife. Rainforests are home to 90% of the world's primates, such as monkeys and orangutans; 80% of the world's insects; and half of the world's plants. According to the U.S. Academy of Sciences, a four-square-mile patch of forest will hold 125 different mammals, 400 species of birds, and hundreds of reptiles and amphibians. The region's endangered species include famous animals such as the orangutan, the Asian elephant, the Sumatran rhino, and the Philippines eagle, plus less-well-known animals such as Ridley's leaf-nosed bat, the flat-headed cat, and the violin beetle; an international study lists 166 endangered species in Southeast Asia. The end of the rainforests will bring destruction to wildlife comparable only to the mass extinction that wiped out the dinosaurs 65 million years ago.

Spreading the message has largely been the work of rainforest groups, plus the efforts of the

World Wildlife Fund and Friends of the Earth. But you, as a traveler, can also help by refusing to purchase animal goods made from protected or endangered species. The United States is the world's largest consumer of wildlife! Travelers often don't realize that seemingly innocuous products made from hides, shells, and feathers—and on sale in public markets in Asia—are often illegal and life-threatening souvenirs. Regulations are complex, but prohibited products include *all* sea-turtle items, Philippine crocodile hides, pangolin (anteater) leather from Thailand and Indonesia, most wild bird feathers, and all ivory products. Just as destructive is the purchase of coral items, since coral collection is directly responsible for the near-complete destruction of sea beds in many Southeast Asian countries. Prohibited items will be seized by customs officials, and you will risk a substantial fine: when in doubt, don't buy!

GETTING THERE

TICKET TIPS

Southeast Asia can be reached from North America, Australia, and Europe on dozens of airlines at all possible prices. Airline tariffs vary widely and substantial savings can be made by using legal loopholes and the services of a well-trained travel agent. To both novice travelers and professionals in the field, airfares and routings seem a disorganized mess. Much of the confusion and controversy revolve around the International Air Transport Association (IATA), a trade association of over 100 of the world's scheduled airlines, which attempts to enforce airfares agreed to bilaterally by national airlines and their respective governments. Fortunately, their efforts are frustrated by the realities of modern ticketing, which say that empty seats should be filled no matter the demands of a price-fixing cartel.

Do-it-yourself travelers can benefit by learning some of the tools of the travel trade. First, read the local newspapers and then call airline, cruise, student, and discount-travel agencies for ticket and tour information. Contact all the national tourist offices for more information. Serious travelers can plan their itinerary and discover obscure air routes by studying the *Official Airline Guide* at the library and checking out Web sites on the Internet. Then call an experienced travel agent. Even the most independent of travelers can save money and countless hours by letting a travel agent do the actual booking.

Types of Tickets

Ticket prices vary enormously depending on dozens of factors, including type of ticket, season, choice of airline, flexibility, and experience of the travel agent. It's confusing, but since airfare comprises a major portion of total travel expenses, no amount of time getting it right is wasted. The rule of thumb is that price and restrictions are inversely related; the cheaper the ticket, the more hassles such as penalties, odd departure hours, layovers, and risk of last-minute cancellations.

First Class and Business Tickets: First class (coded F) and business class (coded J) are designed for travelers who need maximum flexibility and comfort, and are willing to pay the price.

Economy Tickets: Economy tickets (coded Y) are cheaper than first and business classes, plus they often lack advance-purchase requirements and cancellation charges.

APEX Tickets: Advance-purchase excursion (APEX) tickets—the airlines' main method for deep discounts—are about 25% less than economy but often come loaded with restrictions which require advance payment, dictate your length of stay, and carry heavy penalties for cancellations or amendments. Read the fine print *very* carefully.

CIRCLE-PACIFIC AND ROUND-THE-WORLD FARES

CIRCLE-PACIFIC FARES

U.S.A. (West Coast)-Hong Kong-Bangkok-Bali-Hawaii-U.S.A.: US$999

U.S.A.-Tahiti-Cook Islands-Fiji-New Zealand-Australia-Bali-Bangkok-Hong Kong-U.S.A.: US$1,699

ROUND-THE-WORLD FARES

U.S.A.-London-Bangkok-Hong Kong-U.S.A.: US$1,399

U.S.A.-Hawaii-Bali-Bangkok-Kathmandu-Delhi-Amsterdam-U.S.A.: US$1,599

U.S.A.-Tahiti-New Zealand-Noumea-Sydney-Jakarta-Singapore-Amman-Vienna-U.S.A.: US$1,799

U.S.A.-Tahiti-Cooks Islands-Fiji-New Zealand-Australia-Bali-Bangkok-Kathmandu-Delhi-Vienna-U.S.A.: US$2,199

U.S.A.-Dublin-Amsterdam-Athens-Cairo-Nairobi-Bombay-Delhi-Kathmandu-Bangkok-Singapore-Jakarta-Bali-Hawaii-U.S.A.: US$2,299

Super-APEX Tickets: Super-APEX tickets, somewhat cheaper than regular APEX, are limited in quantity and often sell out quickly. APEX and super-APEX tickets are recommended for visitors with limited time who need guaranteed air reservations.

Mileage Tickets: Mileage tickets permit the traveler to pay the fare from A to B and make unlimited stops en route. For example, the ticket from San Francisco to Bangkok costs US$1,361 and permits 9,559 miles on a route that might include San Francisco-Tokyo-Seoul-Taipei-Hong Kong-Manila-Bangkok. Mileage tickets are generally good for one year and mileage surcharges are tacked on for travel beyond the allotted distance. Many airlines have phased out this type of ticket.

Circle-Pacific: Scheduled on major international airlines, Circle-Pacific tickets allow you to circle the North Pacific, Southeast Asia, and South Pacific for about US$2,400 in economy class. Restrictions are a problem, however, since they're limited to four stopovers, cost US$50 per extra stop, demand 14 days advance purchase, carry cancellation penalties, have a six-month expiration, and charge US$50 for each reissuance. Worse yet, only those cities served by the principal carrier and partner are possible stopovers—a restriction that eliminates many of the smaller but vitally important connections. Budget and student travel agencies put together the least expensive Circle-Pacific tickets.

Round-the-World: Another variation of APEX are RTW tickets sold by several international carriers in conjunction with foreign airlines. RTW tickets cost US$2,700 in economy class on the North Pacific route and US$3,400 economy on the South Pacific route through Australia and New Zealand. Tickets are good for one year and stops are limited to cities served by the airlines.

One-way or Roundtrip?

Travelers on short holidays—under three weeks—should purchase roundtrip tickets to ensure reserved seats or consider package tours, which include discounted hotels and internal flights within Southeast Asia.

Travelers with flexible schedules should skip roundtrip tickets and purchase a one-way ticket to Southeast Asia and then make all future travel arrangements after arrival—an option that adds

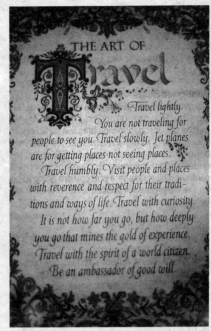

THE ART OF Travel

Travel lightly. You are not traveling for people to see you. Travel slowly. Jet planes are for getting places not seeing places. Travel humbly. Visit people and places with reverence and respect for their traditions and ways of life. Travel with curiosity. It is not how far you go, but how deeply you go that mines the gold of experience. Travel with the spirit of a world citizen. Be an ambassador of good will.

adaptability and can save money. Tickets sold in Southeast Asia are lower than abroad since local agents do not follow IATA price recommendations and are free to sell tickets at minimal markup.

The Intra-Orient Marketing Program (IMP), an airline cartel set up to regulate minimum ticket prices, was dissolved in 1995 after complaints about its unfavorable image as a "price fixer" and the wholesale disregard of its price recommendations. The collapse of IMP has brought prices down and made return tickets an even better proposition, generally 10-25% cheaper than one-way tickets purchased in North America.

Proof of Onward Passage

Some countries in Asia require incoming travelers to show proof of onward passage. Proof of onward passage can be a plane ticket to some foreign destination or a miscellaneous charge order (MCO). Fortunately, immigration officials rarely check for onward tickets.

Passengers concerned about not having proof of onward passage can purchase the cheapest outbound ticket and request a refund after arrival in Southeast Asia. Tickets should be purchased with cash or traveler's checks from a major airline carrier since trying to obtain refunds for unused tickets on an obscure airline can be a Kafkaesque experience.

Confirmed Seats

Tickets issued by travel agents will be marked either OK, RQ, or "on request." The OK stamp next to the destination indicates the travel agent has checked with the airline and the seat has been reserved in your name. An RQ or "on request" stamp means your seat has not been confirmed by your agent and you are going to be on standby. Be sure your ticket is marked "OK" before payment.

Low and High Seasons

All airlines and discount agencies price their tickets according to the season.

Airlines in North America and Europe consider the low season the winter months Oct.-April and the high season the summer months May-September. The holiday period Dec.-Jan. is also considered a high season. An intermediate or "shoulder season" is often wedged between the high and low seasons.

The high season for airlines in Australia and New Zealand runs Dec.-15 Jan., school holiday periods are shoulder seasons, and the low season is the rest of the year.

Reconfirmations

Passengers are required to reconfirm all flights at least 72 hours prior to departure. Reconfirmations aren't necessary on the first flight or on flights with layovers less than 72 hours, but passengers who otherwise fail to reconfirm their flights may have their seats automatically canceled and reassigned to other passengers. Some travelers even reconfirm their reconfirmations!

More Tips

For passengers, air travel is getting worse. The number of passengers angry enough to complain to the Department of Transportation has risen to record levels in recent years. A few tips may help reduce the aggravation.

Try to avoid flying on weekends or holidays when airport congestion is bad and flight cancellations and delays are most common. Avoid rush hours in the early mornings and evenings. Request your boarding pass when you make your reservation or take advantage of the new "ticketless" travel options offered by many airlines.

Don't check additional baggage; carry everything possible onto the plane. Ask your travel agent about legal limits and pack accordingly. Remove old airport destination tags and write your permanent business address and phone number at your destination on your luggage tag. File claims for lost baggage before you leave the airport.

Know your legal rights. Contact the U.S. Department of Transportation's Office of Consumer Affairs (tel. 202-366-2220) for a copy of *Fly Rights: A Guide to Air Travel in the U.S.*

SOURCES OF TICKETS

Consolidators

The cheapest tickets to Asia are sold by wholesalers who purchase large blocks of unsold seats from major airlines. Once an airline concludes it can't sell all of its seats, consolidators are offered a whopping 20-40% commission to do the job. They then hand most of the commission back to the clients in the form of reduced ticket prices. Consolidators are the industry's equivalent of a factory outlet and the last resort for airlines with too many empty seats.

Consolidator tickets are legal and generally trustworthy. The advantages are obvious: tickets are 25-40% less than standard economy fares and consolidators offer a range of departures and guaranteed reservations on first-class airlines.

DISCOUNT AND LAST-MINUTE TRAVEL CLUBS

Cruise Line	(800) 327-3021
Cruises Inc	(800) 854-0500
Entertainment Travel	(800) 445-4137
Great American Traveler	(800) 548-2812
Moment's Notice	(212) 486-0503
Privilege Card	(800) 236-9732
Traveler's Advantage	(800) 548-1116
Vacations To Go	(800) 338-4962
Worldwide Discount	(305) 534-2082

CONSOLIDATOR PHONE NUMBERS

Airbrokers	(800) 883-3273
AirHitch	(212) 864-2000
AirTech	(800) 575-TECH
Cheap Tickets	(800) 377-1000
Euram	(800) 848-6789
Global	(800) 283-5333
Overseas	(800) 878-8718
Skylink	800-247-6659
TFI	(800) 745-8000
Time Travel	(800) 847-7026
Travac	(800) 872-8800
UniTravel	(800) 325-2222

The drawbacks are that consolidator tickets may carry stiff penalties for changes or cancellation and routings can be slow and byzantine. Many tickets may be nonendorsable and may not earn frequent flyer miles or allow you to use miles to upgrade to business or first class. Travelers should attempt to find the cheapest ticket on the best airline with the fewest restrictions and unnecessary stops.

Where do you purchase these cheap tickets? Consolidators rarely deal directly with the public, but rather sell their tickets through student agencies, travel clubs, and independent travel franchises. In fact, you can buy consolidator tickets from almost everyone except the consolidators themselves. The safest way to negotiate this mystifying maze of rules and conditions is to ask your travel agent to buy your consolidator ticket. A good agent knows the restrictions and vagaries better than anyone else.

Roundtrip prices currently average US$500-600 from the West Coast of North America to Tokyo, US$550/650 low season/high season to Hong Kong, and US$750/950 to Bangkok, Singapore, and Manila. Roundtrip surcharges for East Coast departures are US$150-200. Current fares are advertised in the Sunday travel sections of major newspapers such as the *New York Times, Los Angeles Times,* and *San Francisco Examiner.* Advance planning is essential since the best deals often sell out months in advance.

COURIER COMPANIES

SAN FRANCISCO DEPARTURES

Jupiter Air: tel. (415) 872-0845
UTL Travel: tel. (415) 583-5074
I.B.C.: tel. (310) 607-0125

LOS ANGELES DEPARTURES

Jupiter Air: tel. (310) 670-5123
I.B.C.: tel. (310) 607-0125
Midnight: tel. (310) 330-7096

NEW YORK DEPARTURES

Air Facility: tel. (718) 712-1769
Now Voyager: tel. (212) 431-1616
Halbart: tel. (718) 656-5000
Jupiter Air: tel. (718) 656-6050
Discount Travel: tel. (212) 362-3636
Bridges: tel. (718) 244-7244
World Courier: tel. (718) 978-9408
East West: tel. (718) 656-6246

MIAMI DEPARTURES

I.B.C.: tel. (305) 591-8080
TransAir: tel. (305) 592-1771

LineHaul: tel. (305) 477-0651
Now Voyager: tel. (212) 431-1616
Going Places: tel. (305) 373-5813

CHICAGO DEPARTURES

I.B.C.: tel. (708) 699-3324
Courier Travel: tel. (708) 620-8080
Discount Travel: tel. (212) 362-3636
UTL Travel: tel. (415) 583-5074

CANADA DEPARTURES

FB Couriers: tel. (514) 633-0740
Jet Services: tel. (514) 331-7470

LONDON DEPARTURES

Courier Travel: tel. (171) 351-0300
Bridges: tel. (181) 759-5040
BA Travel: tel. (181) 564-7009
Norwood Travel: tel. (181) 674-8214

SYDNEY DEPARTURES

Polo Express: tel. (2) 693-5866
Jupiter: tel. (2) 369-2704

SELECTING A RESPONSIBLE TOUR OPERATOR

Before selecting an adventure travel or tour company, you might want to consider the following guidelines suggested by the Center for Responsible Tourism. If your prospective tour group or travel agent fails the test, investigate the alternative travel options listed in the text or go as an independent traveler.

1. Does the tour organizer demonstrate a cultural and environmental sensitivity? How are local people and culture portrayed in advertising brochures?

2. Who benefits financially from your trip? What percentage of your dollar stays in the country you visit rather than ends up with an international hotel chain, airline, or travel agency?

3. Is a realistic picture of your host country presented, or a sanitized version packaged for tourists?

4. Will you use local accommodations and transportation or be assigned to tourist facilities that prevent a real understanding of the environment?

5. Does your travel itinerary allow adequate time for meeting with local people? If it doesn't, don't go!

6. Has the tour operator or travel agent mentioned anything beyond what's listed in the glossy advertisements? Ask about the social, economic, and political realities of Southeast Asia.

Note the following penalties and restrictions: Peak fares are in effect from June to August (add US$50-100). Tickets purchased less than 90 days in advance are subject to an additional US$50-150 surcharge. Flight cancellations or changes before the ticket is issued usually cost US$50. Cancel your flight within 30 days of departure or any time after the ticket has been issued and you'll forfeit up to 25% of the fare.

Couriers

Aside from working as a travel agent or hijacking a plane, the cheapest way to reach Southeast Asia is by carrying urgent mail for one of the following courier companies. Roundtrip tickets from the West Coast of North America average US$350-400 to Taipei, US$400-450 to Tokyo and Hong Kong, US$365-450 to Bangkok, and US$400-450 to Singapore and Sydney. Courier service is also available to Malaysia (Kuala Lumpur), Indonesia (Jakarta), and Indochina.

Anyone can do this, and it's perfectly legal—no drugs or guns are carried, just stock certificates and registered mail. Restrictions mean you're generally limited to carry-on luggage and the length of stay averages just 2-4 weeks.

Frequent Flyer Miles: Some airlines used by couriers allow the couriers to collect frequent flyer miles. One traveler makes courier trips to Southeast Asia and collects frequent flyer miles, which he then resells for a hefty profit.

Current Information: The best source of accurate information on courier flights is an extremely helpful monthly newsletter from Travel Unlimited, P.O. Box 1058, Allston, MA 02134. Editor Steve Lantos (Steve_Lantos@brookline.mec.edu) charges US$25 for 12 monthly issues—a great deal since you'll save hundreds on your first flight whether heading to Asia, Europe, or South America.

Standby Couriers: Absolutely the cheapest way to reach Southeast Asia is as standby courier. Courier companies welcome standby volunteers since important documents need to be delivered to important people and courier companies face little financial risk since they retain the nonrefundable deposits paid by the original client. The courier companies listed in the accompanying chart maintain a list of potential clients who can fill last minute cancellations.

Standby prices decline as the departure approaches. For example, a flight leaving in five days may only be discounted US$100-150 since the courier company has plenty of time to find a replacement. Flights departing in under two days force the company to offer terrific discounts such as US$100 roundtrip to Asia or even absolutely free tickets.

I recently took a roundtrip courier flight to Singapore for just US$25—the cost of the departure taxes. I was allowed full baggage allowance and was greeted by a courier representative at both the San Francisco and Singapore airports who handles all my papers and took me to the front of the line.

BY AIR FROM NORTH AMERICA

Routes

By studying the introduction and "Sightseeing Highlights" sections of each country, you should be able to plan an itinerary composed of the best mixture of history and recreation. A well-planned route that addresses the issues of sights, time, and budget can easily save hundreds of dollars and avoid the hassles of backtracking, wasted opportunities, and unnecessary expenses. A map will help to orient yourself. The basic overland route runs between Bangkok and Bali, through Malaysia and Singapore. Tramped since the hippie days of the '60s, today it's a busy path firmly networked with hotels, restaurants, and other facilities for value-minded overlanders.

To add those remote and exotic destinations located off the familiar trail, you'll need to include side trips to Myanmar (Burma), the Philippines, and the outer islands of Indonesia. Myanmar can be reached on an inexpensive roundtrip ticket from Bangkok or visited as a stop en route to India. The Philippines can be easily reached on roundtrip tickets from Bangkok or Hong Kong, although more adventurous travelers might consider entering or exiting Manila from Kota Kinabalu. Because Indonesia's outer islands such as Kalimantan and Sulawesi are so time-consuming to properly explore, these are often considered separate journeys starting from Singapore.

After touring Southeast Asia, you'll want to continue your Asian odyssey through the Indian subcontinent, north to Japan, or eastward through the South Pacific. Two popular options from Bangkok include a flight to India or Nepal via Myanmar, or a flight to Japan via Hong Kong. Options from Bali include a direct flight to Australia, an overland journey across Nusa Tenggara followed by the short flight from Timor to Darwin, or a return flight to Singapore with stops in Sulawesi or Kalimantan. No matter what route, it's a grand adventure through one of the world's great regions.

North Pacific Route: Americans have two fascinating choices. The North Pacific loop includes stops in Japan, Korea, Taiwan, and Hong Kong before continuing into China or down to Bangkok. This one-way ticket—often on an airline such as Korean or China Air—costs under US$900 from budget travel agencies in San Francisco and Los Angeles.

South Pacific Loop: The southern loop includes stops in the South Pacific, New Zealand, and Australia before arriving in Bali and continuing up to Thailand. This ticket—often standby on various carriers—costs around US$1,200-1,400 to Bali from student agencies.

Roundtrip: Another popular and relatively inexpensive itinerary begins with the northern Pacific loop, travels through Thailand and Southeast Asia, routes across the South Pacific, then returns to the United States for about US$2,000 in total airfare—a once-in-a-lifetime travel experience.

Budget Travel Agencies

Some of the best advice on ticketing can be found at agencies that specialize in the youth and student markets.

Student Travel Australia: STA Travel serves not only students and youths, but also nonstudents and tour groups. 48 East 11th St., New York, NY 10003. In the United States call (800) 777-0112 for the nearest office.

Hostelling International (HI): The former International Youth Hostel Federation (IYH) and their associated American Youth Hostels (AYH)

TOLL-FREE TELEPHONE NUMBERS FOR MAJOR AIRLINES

British Airlines	(800) 247-9297
Cathay Pacific	(800) 233-2742
China Airlines	(800) 227-5118
Delta	(800) 241-4141
Finnair	(800) 950-5000
Garuda	(800) 342-7832
Japan	(800) 525-3663
KLM	(800) 347-7747
Lufthansa	(800) 645-3880
Malaysia	(800) 421-8641
Northwest	(800) 447-4747
Philippines	(800) 435-9725
Silk Air	(800) 745-5247
Singapore	(800) 742-3333
Swiss Air	(800) 221-4750
Thai Airways	(800) 426-5204
United Airlines	(800) 538-2929

provide budget travel information and confirmed reservations at any of almost 200 HI hostels in the U.S. and abroad. HI-AYH, 733 15th St. NW, Suite 840, Washington D.C. 20005, tel. (202) 783-6161.

Travel CUTS: The largest student travel agency in Canada with branches in most major cities. 187 College St., Toronto, Ontario M5T 1P7, tel. (416) 979-2406.

Air Brokers International: A dependable discount agency with many years of experience in the Asian market. Sells discount tickets and can help with Circle-Pacific and Round-the-World airfares. 323 Geary St., Suite 411, San Francisco, CA 94102, tel. (800) 883-3273, fax (415) 397-4767.

Council Travel: This excellent travel organization, a division of the Council on International Educational Exchange, has 37 offices in the U.S. and representatives in Europe and

Australia. Prices are low and service reliable since they deal only with reputable airlines to minimize travel problems. Best of all, Council Travel sales agents are experienced travelers who often have firsthand knowledge of Southeast Asia. Council Travel also sells the Youth Hostel Association Card, International Student Identity Card (ISIC), the Youth International Educational Exchange Card (for nonstudents under 26), plus travel and health insurance. 205 East 42nd St., New York, NY 10017, tel. (800) 743-1823.

Contact numbers at their larger offices are as follows:

- San Francisco . . . . (415) 421-3473
- Los Angeles . . . . (213) 208-3551
- Seattle . . . . (206) 632-2448
- Chicago . . . . (312) 951-0585
- Boston . . . . (617) 266-1926
- New York . . . . (212) 661-1450

Either I am a traveller in ancient times, and faced with a prodigious spectacle which would be almost entirely unintelligible to me and might, indeed, provoke me to mockery or disgust; or I am a traveller of our own day, hastening in search of a vanished reality. In either case I am the loser.

—CLAUDE LEVI-STRAUSS,
TRISTES TROPIQUES

"Are you a god?" they asked. "No."
"An Angel?" "No."
"A saint?" "No."
"Then, what are you?"
Buddha answered, "I am awake."

—BUDDHA

Between the Idea and the Reality . . . Falls the Shadow.

—T.S. ELIOT

BRUNEI

*If you go only once around the room, you are wiser
than he who stands still.*

—ESTONIAN PROVERB

*I travel light; as light,
That is, as a man can travel who will
Still carry his body around because
Of its sentimental value.*

—CHRISTOPHER FRY,
THE LADY'S NOT FOR BURNING

*Follow the first rules of a frequent traveler: Don't
overpack; leave all that excess emotional baggage
at home.*

—LETTER IN *CONDÉ NAST TRAVELER*

INTRODUCTION

The tiny but wealthy country of Brunei, a 500-year-old sultanate situated on the north coast of Borneo between the Malaysian states of Sabah and Sarawak, offers an impressive mosque, river journeys, and untouched rainforests outside the capital city of Bandar Seri Begawan. Since Brunei hardly needs tourist income, the country has remained one of the least touristy in Southeast Asia. Residents are warm and friendly and quick to display traditional Malay hospitality.

Best of all, Brunei has remained a physically beautiful country since oil wealth has helped preserve the rainforests and traditional ways of life. Hospitable people, unspoiled jungle, and the curious marriage of oil, Islam, and Western materialism make Brunei one of the more unique destinations in Southeast Asia.

HISTORY

Brunei has a strange, almost tragic history. When Magellan's ships landed at Brunei in 1521, Spanish conquistadors reported finding a rich and powerful Islamic sultanate which controlled most of Borneo and the trading routes from Indonesia to Manila. Brunei's golden age centered on two rulers, Sultan Bolkiah and Sultan Hassan, who mastered empires whose splendor rivaled that of any power in Southeast Asia.

But the following centuries saw its influence diffused among hereditary chieftains—the Pengirans—who resorted to piracy and the sales of large tracts of Borneo to foreign nationals. By the early 19th century Brunei had been reduced to an emasculated shell, ruled by corrupt sultans who lived off taxes and slave auctions and plagued by roving bands of pirates who preyed on shipping merchants and upriver villages.

Into this desperate situation sailed an English adventurer named James Brooke, the first of Sarawak's White Rajahs. Brooke forced the weakened sultanate to disgorge vast areas of Borneo as reward for his suppression of piracy and headhunting. His brilliant campaigns brought peace to North Borneo but also bankrupted the sultan, who could no longer rely on taxes, piracy, and revenue from slave auctions. By the time the sultanate appealed to Britain for protection in 1888, the once-powerful empire was little more than a small and powerless trading post situated on equatorial swampland.

BRUNEI

SOUTH CHINA SEA

MUARA

JERUDONG

BANDAR SERI BEGAWAN

PUNANG

LAWAS

TUTONG

BUNUT

KLUDANG

LIMBANG

TRUSAN

LAYONG

LABU

LUMUT

SINOKOH MERIMBUN

BANGAR

KUALA BARAM

KUALA BELAIT

SERIA BADAS

BUKIT SAWAT

APAK APAK

KUALA BALAI

LABI

SUKANG

MIRI

BELAIT RIVER

BARAM RIVER

LIMBANG RIVER

MALAYSIA (SARAWAK)

TO KUCHING

MARUDI

TUTOH RIVER

BAKONG RIVER

MOUNT MULU (2,371 m)

GUNUNG MULU NATIONAL PARK

0   20 km

MOON

© MOON PUBLICATIONS, INC.

Political change followed the discovery of oil at the first Seria oilfield in 1929. During the postwar decolonization period, in 1963 the British urged Sultan Omar Ali Saifuddin to try democracy and join the new nation of Malaysia. Although Omar was intrigued with the concept of a united Malaysia, he declined the invitation because of his brief experiment with parliamentary elections in 1962. Omar had allowed free and open elections based on a 1959 constitution, but after 54 of 55 seats were won by the opposition Brunei People's Party (reputedly an antimonarchist and pro-Indonesia coalition) Omar suspended the constitution and refused to seat the winners.

The subsequent civil rebellion was crushed by British Gurkha troops from Singapore who imprisoned or deported about 300 political dissidents. Although the monarchy was saved, this traumatic experiment sealed the political forum and ended the sultan's venture into democracy. Ironically enough, the following year saw the Brunei Legislative Assembly approve the country's

entry into Malaysia. This bold move was reversed after objections from British Petroleum and Shell Oil, two international consortiums who apparently didn't want to see the country's enormous oil profits being funneled to Kuala Lumpur.

In 1967 Sultan Omar voluntarily abdicated the throne to his son, Hassanal Bolkiah. Politely enduring a 15-year power struggle with his father, Hassanal finally asserted his rights by marrying his second wife, Mariam (a former hostess with Royal Brunei Airlines), and granting her status equal to that of his first wife, Raja Isteri Saleha. Although furious about the marriage, Sultan Omar lost the ensuing political maneuvering and eventually resigned himself to a largely ceremonial role. Brunei became a sovereign and independent country in 1984. Omar died in September 1987.

The tiny country received some unwanted publicity in 1987 when it was revealed during the Iran-Contra hearings that Hassanal had contributed US$10 million to the Contras and, in a somewhat comical footnote, it was revealed that the money was returned to the sultan after Oliver North and Elliott Abrams mixed up the digits and deposited the funds in the wrong Swiss bank account.

The sultan received some better publicity in 1994 when it was revealed that he gave the world's largest tip to the 320 workers at the Four Seasons Hotel on Cyprus—US$531.25 per employee. Hassanal Bolkian also made news that same year when he invited football stars Joe Montana and Herschel Walker to Brunei to teach the secrets of the sport to his four children. The following year, the sultan purchased the Beverly Hills Hotel for US$187 million and promptly invested another US$100 million in a much-needed face-lift.

GOVERNMENT

Brunei is an autocratic monarchy ruled by Sultan Hassanal Bolkiah, the 29th ruler of the dynasty. Plucked at age 21 from Britain's Sandhurst Royal Military Academy, Hassanal in his younger days enjoyed a playboy lifestyle filled with racehorses, polo, and excursions to London while his father continued to rule the tiny country. After taking control of Brunei in the early 1980s, Hassanal gave up his racy image and settled down to the business of running the country. Brunei today is a hereditary autocracy ruled by Hassanal, who serves as head of state, head of the Islamic religion, prime minister, and minister of defense.

Though the absolute statesman of Brunei, Hassanal has proven himself to be a surprisingly progressive ruler who has made some remarkable changes in his government, such as splitting up ministerial positions and forming a cabinet no longer dominated by the royal family. As a result, Brunei now more closely resembles a modern parliamentary state than an autocratic monarchy, though it's unclear how much real power is shared between the sultan and his cabinet.

Hassanal has also allowed the formation of political parties, including the National Democratic Party (PNDB), which supports the nationalization of Brunei Shell and gently encourages the sultan to step down from his position as prime minister. Blatant criticism isn't tolerated, however, and the government is quick to shut down political parties who criticize the sultan's absolutism or demand open elections.

Another taboo subject is the personal wealth of Sultan Hassanal, the world's richest man according to *Forbes* and the *Guinness Book of World Records*. The exact extent of his personal fortune is unknown since the division between the Bolkiah family's private assets and the public purse is one of Brunei's most closely guarded mysteries. Yet it hardly strained his pocketbook when he spent over US$600 million in 1984 to construct and furnish his 1,788-room riverside palace, which now serves as residence to his extended family of about 30 people, including his two wives, six daughters, three sons, three brothers, and their families.

ECONOMY

The postage-stamp-sized country of Brunei—more properly called Negara Brunei Darussalam—is a paradox unlike any other country in Southeast Asia. With a population of just over 280,000, Brunei boasts a staggering per-capita national income of US$18,000, one of the highest in the world and surpassed in Asia only by Japan, Korea, and Singapore. This figure is misleading, however, since most of the income goes to the government and the sultan, who distributes a portion of the income to the general population.

Most citizens—aside from ethnic Chinese who have little hope of gaining citizenship—are provided with free education, health care, and interest-free loans for buying homes, cars, and making a pilgrimage to Mecca. As a result, cars are almost as plentiful as people, making for surprising rush-hour traffic jams in one of the world's smallest capitals.

Brunei has no national debt, no trade deficit, and levies no income tax except on 30% of corporate profits. Unemployment is rare because of the manpower shortage. Symbols of success and conspicuous consumption are everywhere—fleets of Mercedeses, air-conditioned shopping centers, color televisions and microwave telephones in remote longhouses, and an international airport larger than the older Kai Tak airport in Hong Kong.

This tremendous wealth comes from oil and gas reserves discovered near Seria by the Royal

BRUNEI

Dutch Shell Group in 1929. While relatively small in total world production, Brunei produces a great deal of oil on a per-capita basis, with hydrocarbons accounting for 96% of all exports plus additional income from rubber, timber, and jelutong, an ingredient for making chewing gum. So complete is oil domination that local wags have dubbed Brunei the "Shellfare State."

Gross domestic product from oil alone is breathtaking—US$15,000 yearly per person and foreign reserves of US$20 billion, a bank account that generates about US$7,000 yearly per person in interest. Brunei, dubbed the "Kuwait of Southeast Asia," has few financial worries about the future—even if the wells ran dry tomorrow, its gigantic foreign-exchange reserves would generate enough investment income to support the entire population of 250,000 people for almost two decades.

Still, the oil *is* dwindling at a steady rate. It's estimated that Brunei will run dry in 20-30 years and the government is now making large overseas investments to diversify the economy. Today almost 50% of the national income comes from foreign investments rather than domestic oil reserves. Government tax structures have been changed to encourage local business formation, though this strategy appears less than successful: few citizens appear motivated to create new enterprises due to the small domestic economic base and the high cost of labor. Brunei after the oil windfall is an open question.

ON THE ROAD

GETTING THERE

From Sarawak
Both Malaysia Airlines and Royal Brunei fly daily from Kuching to Bandar Seri Begawan. The overland journey from Miri can be made by public bus, minibus, or share taxi in a single day with an early start.

Six buses leave Miri daily for Kuala Belait, the first town in Brunei. The bus crosses the wide Baram River and the narrow but congested Belait River. Brunei customs and immigration are located just before Kuala Belait. Delays at river crossings, especially the time-consuming ordeal at the Belait River, can be avoided by taking your gear off the bus and walking to the front of the line. Take the motorized boat or ask a car driver for a lift and then hitchhike from the opposite side.

Buses from Miri to Kuala Belait take about 2.5 hours. Buses from Kuala Belait to Bandar Seri Begawan leave several times daily, take 2.5 hours, and sometimes race along the beach past monkeys and oil platforms to avoid the rough road. Hitching is fairly easy and a good way to meet Bruneians. Traveler's checks can be changed in Kuala Belait.

From Sabah
Both Malaysia Airlines and Royal Brunei fly daily from Kota Kinabalu to Bandar Seri Begawan.

Since there are no roads from KK and BSB (two popular abbreviations for the capitals of Sabah and Brunei, respectively), overland travelers must use a combination of bus and water transport. There are two time-consuming routes from KK to BSB.

Labuan Island Route: Buses and taxis directly to Labuan leave from the bus stand on Jalan Balai Polis in Kota Kinabalu. Otherwise, take the bus to Beaufort and then continue up to Mempakol and Menumbok by taxi. Boats make the 45-minute crossing from Menumbok to Labuan daily at 1030 and 1600. Ferries in the opposite direction from Labuan to Menumbok leave at 0800 and 1300.

Taxi drivers in Beaufort usually know the latest schedules and will deliver you in time for the boat. Launches from Labuan to Bandar Seri Begawan leave twice daily and take about two hours. You will most likely find yourself stranded for a night in the expensive and charmless town of Labuan.

Sipitang-Lawas Route: The road west from Beaufort passes through Sipitang and Merapok before grinding to a halt in the one-horse town of Lawas. Ferries from Lawas to Bandar Seri Begawan leave twice daily and take two hours. Accommodations in Sipitang and Lawas include a government resthouse and several grubby hotels. Boat schedules can be checked with taxi drivers in Beaufort.

TRAVEL PRACTICALITIES

Visas

Visas for 14-day visits are not required for citizens of Belgium, Britain, Canada, France, Germany, Japan, Netherlands, Sweden, Switzerland, and most ASEAN countries. Visa-exemption status is granted with a valid passport, confirmed onward ticket, and sufficient funds.

Travelers of other nationalities can obtain visas from Brunei diplomatic missions in Washington, D.C., New York, London, Singapore, Tokyo, Kuala Lumpur, Bangkok, Manila, and Jakarta, or from British High Commissions and embassies where there are no Brunei diplomatic missions.

Visitors arriving from Sabah and Sarawak are given one-week visas; two-week visas are granted upon request.

Tourist Information

Brunei has a small information booth at the airport and an official tourist office at the Economic Development Board in the State Secretariat Building.

Money

The Brunei dollar is convertible at par with the Singapore dollar, but Malaysian currency is about 40% cheaper. Merchants prefer Singapore currency and traveler's checks which can be exchanged in larger towns at a 10% discount from cash. The current exchange rate is about US$1=B$1.40.

Communications

The dialing code for Brunei is International Direct Dial access code followed by 673 then the appropriate area code—2 for Bandar Seri Begawan, 3 for Seria and Kuala Belait, 4 for Tutong, and 5 for Temburong. International phone calls can be made 24 hours a day from hotels and the telecommunications counter at the General Post Office.

Background Reading

The government publishes the Malay *Pelita Brunei.* English periodicals include the weekly *Borneo Bulletin* from Kuala Belait and newspapers from Singapore and Malaysia. The *Borneo Bulletin* has a Web site with useful news and travel stories.

Books include *By God's Will: A Portrait of the Sultan of Brunei,* by Lord Chalfont, and *The Richest Man in the World: The Sultan of Brunei,* by James Bartholomew, an inside look at the inner workings of the monarchy. The Brunei Shell publication, *Brunei Darussalam, A Guide,* explores the more remote corners of the country.

Festivals

Brunei celebrates several Muslim holidays including Hari Raya Haji, to commemorate the sacrifice of Abraham, the first day of the Ramadan (March), the Koran Revelation (April), the end of Ramadan (April), and the Prophets Birthday (August).

Chinese, Hindu, and Christian holidays include Chinese New Year (February or March), National Day (23 February), Armed Forces Day (31 May), Sultan's Birthday (15 July), and Christmas (25 December).

BANDAR SERI BEGAWAN

Brunei's capital city, often called simply Bandar or BSB, is a low-rise and surprisingly clean town that makes for a pleasant change from the urban messes that dominate most of Borneo. The national wealth of Brunei is reflected in the modern government buildings, manicured lawns, fountains, and lines of air-conditioned cars that briefly clog the streets at rush hour. Bandar is compact enough that most attractions can be reached on foot.

Buses around BSB and to outlying destinations leave infrequently from the terminal behind the Brunei Hotel. Metered taxis are available but very expensive.

ATTRACTIONS

Omar Ali Saifuddin Mosque

The highlight of any visit to BSB is a tour of this magnificent mosque, which ranks as one of the most impressive pieces of modern architecture in Southeast Asia. Set in the middle of a reflecting lagoon, this Saracenic wonder is capped by a

BANDAR SERI BEGAWAN

TO AIRPORT, GADONG, RIVERVIEW HOTEL, AND CENTREPOINT HOTEL

JL. HAJI BASIR

JL. KUMBANG PASANG

TERRACE HOTEL

IMMIGRATION

SHERATON HOTEL

JL. TUTONG

JL. BERANGAN

TO ROYAL PALACE AND PRINCESS INN

CAPITAL HOSTEL

YOUTH CENTER (PUSAT BELIA)

ROYAL REGALIA MUSEUM ★

JL. SUNGAI KIANGGEH

JL. KIANGGEH

JUBILEE HOTEL

BRUNEI HISTORICAL CENTRE

CEREMONIAL HALL ★

■ INFORMATION

JL. STONEY

LEGISLATIVE ASSEMBLY

JL. SULTAN

JL. ELIZABETH DUA

GPO

KEDAYAN RIVER

OMAR ALI SAIFUDDIEN MOSQUE ★

CENTRAL PARK ★

BRUNEI AIR ■

BRITISH CONSULATE

■ FOODSTALLS

JL. PEMANCHA

■ BRUNEI HOTEL

■ MALAYSIA AIR

SINGAPORE AIR

JL. CATOR

JL. PRETTY

BUS TERMINAL

US EMBASSY

JL. McARTHUR

HARRISON'S

■ INFORMATION

TO MUSEUM, SULTAN'S TOMB

KAMPONG AYER ★

BOATS TO LIMBANG AND LAWAS

BOATS TO BANGAR

BRUNEI RIVER

0   250 m

© MOON PUBLICATIONS, INC.

vast golden dome speckled by millions of gleaming fragments of Venetian gold-leaf mosaic.

No expense was spared during its construction in 1958. The exterior walls are cut from Hong Kong granite, interior walls and floors are inlaid with the finest Italian marble, the stained-glass windows and chandeliers were imported from England, and luxurious Persian prayer carpets are stacked up like sacks of potatoes waiting for the next call to prayer. Outstanding views of the city can be enjoyed from the 44-meter minaret served by an elevator.

The mosque is open to non-Muslims Saturday to Wednesday 0800-1200 and 1300-1600, closed Thursday and Friday. Entry rules and dress regulations are strictly described at the front gate.

Kampong Ayer

Brunei's 400-year-old Malay water village, the world's largest community built on stilts, is actually a series of 28 separate *kampongs* connected by concrete footbridges and piping systems for sewage, running water, and electricity. Most of the houses are equipped with TVs and VCRs which blast out reruns of "Dynasty" and kung-fu tapes brought in from Hong Kong.

The nearby village can be toured on foot while the villages across the river can be toured inexpensively on public water buses, which leave from the main wharf and then circumnavigate the village. Private boats charge B$20-30 per hour.

Royal Regalia Museum and History Museum

The former Churchill Memorial Museum has been converted to the Royal Regalia Museum, which extols the virtues of the sultan. The nearby Brunei History Centre is similar. Both are open daily 0900-1700 except Friday when both are closed 1130-1430.

Brunei Museum and Malay Technology Museum

Brunei's national museum is in Kota Batu, six km from town on the banks of the Brunei River. Among the exhibits are Chinese ceramics, oil-industry paraphernalia, and displays of Kenyah, Murut, Dusun, and Kadayan ethnic art. Although the Kenyah reside in the Baram River region in Sarawak and not in Brunei, the museum's collection of Kenyah artwork is considered the finest in Borneo, especially the pieces by Trusau, who also created much of the work displayed in Kuching's Sarawak Museum. The national museum is open daily except Monday 0900-1700. Closed Friday 1130-1430.

A short walk from the Brunei Museum is the Malay Technology Museum, providing excellent displays of the handicrafts and architecture of the Malay and Dayak peoples. Open daily except Tuesday 0930-1700. Closed Friday 1130-1430.

Sultan's Palace

Sultan Hassanal Bolkiah may rule one of the smallest countries in the world, but his 1,788-room palace on the banks of the Brunei River is believed to be the largest royal residence in the world, having displaced the 1,400-room Vatican in the *Guinness Book of World Records*. The Moorish-Islamic-styled palace is studded with golden domes, cavernous banquet halls, a throne room, private mosque, heliport, an immense underground parking lot, and a polo field surrounded by landscaped gardens. Formally opened in 1984 as the private residence for the sultan and his extended family, Istana Nurul Iman was designed by "Lucky" Leandro Locsin—the Filipino architect who also designed the Philippine Cultural Center in Manila. A Japanese group did the landscaping, American Dale Keller did the interiors, and Bechtel built the roads. Total cost has been estimated at over US$600 million.

Istana Nurul Iman, four km from town, is closed to the public but can be easily seen from the opposite bank of the river.

Jame Asr Hassanil Bolkiah Mosque

Brunei's newest, largest, and most impressive mosque is in Gadong, three km north of town, in the Kampong Kiarong district.

ACCOMMODATIONS

Bandar has one inexpensive place and almost a dozen mid-to-top level hotels for the visiting businessperson.

Budget

Pusat Belia (Youth Hostel): A government-operated youth hostel with dorms for men and women, swimming pool, gym, library, and budget cafeteria. Open only to students and those holding youth hostel cards. Others are admitted on a space-available basis at the discretion of the manager. Jalan Sungai Kianggeh, tel. (02) 229423, B$10.

Moderate

Moderate is a relative term in Brunei where rooms priced under B$200 aren't considered luxurious—just moderate.

Capital Hostel: BSB's least expensive hotel is on a small street just behind the Pusat Belia. 7 Simpang 2, tel. (02) 223561, fax 228789, B$75-140.

Terrace Hotel: Simple but comfortable a/c hotel with pool, restaurant, and lounge. Jalan Tasek Lama, tel. (02) 243553, fax 227302, B$80-140.

Princess Inn: Another mid-level hotel inconveniently located in the Seri Commercial Complex across the river about two km from town. Jalan Tutong, tel. (02) 241128, B$80-150.

Jubilee Hotel: New hotel in a good location

with a supermarket and restaurant. Jalan Kampong Kianggeh, tel. (02) 228070, fax 228080, B$120-180.

Brunei Hotel: An older four-story hotel with 73 renovated rooms with a/c, private bath, and TV. 95 Jalan Pemancha, tel. (02) 242372, fax 226196, B$140-200.

Luxury

The Sheraton has been joined by two new hotels in the high-end price category.

Riverview Hotel: Luxurious digs north of town near the airport with pool, health club, business center, and 126 a/c rooms. Jalan Gadong, tel. (02) 238238, fax 237999, B$150-240.

Centrepoint Hotel: Bandar's newest hotel is also located north of town near the airport in the Abdul Razak Complex above the Yaohan Megamart. Jalan Gadong, tel. (02) 430430, B$190-280.

Sheraton Utama: Brunei's most luxurious hotel with 154 a/c rooms, pool, and other facilities for the business traveler. Jalan Tasek Lama, tel. (02) 244272, fax 221579, B$240-360.

EXPLORING BRUNEI

WESTERN BRUNEI

Brunei has beaches, waterfalls, and untouched jungle within a few hours' journey of the capital. Buses reach most locations though service is unpredictable. Hitching is fairly easy, and cars can be rented from Avis, Budget, or National for about B$100 per day.

Murara

Brunei's most popular beach, 28 km northeast of Bandar, draws oil workers and their families on weekends for sunbathing and socializing. It's a mediocre beach, but pleasant walks can be made around the tip of the peninsula.

Jerudong

Jerudong serves as a recreation center for the sultan, who maintains a polo stadium and golf course at the seaside town, and for the general population who can enjoy the huge amusement park which opened a few years ago.

Lake Merimbun

Tasik Merimbun, a remote and beautiful lake, is a birdwatcher's paradise and popular weekend retreat for Bruneians. Facilities include an island campsite and boat rentals for fishermen and birdwatchers. Merimbun can be reached by taking a bus to Tutong, then hitching a ride to the lake.

Labi Falls

En route to Kampong Labi in Belait district is Luagan Lalak, an elevated lake a few kilometers beyond Bukit Puan. The road continues past Labi and ends at a Chinese store, where a narrow path continues up to Labi Falls.

Because of the oil wealth, Brunei hasn't logged its rainforests into oblivion. Jungle paths from Labi lead to Murut villages where both traditional and modern longhouses can be found.

Buses run to Labi from Tutong or Lumut.

Kuala Belait

The last town at the western edge of Brunei serves as the access point for Malaysia. Visitors can stroll the beach or hire a boat for the one-hour upriver journey to Kuala Balai, a pleasant passage through jungle and sago palms.

Kuala Belait has an inexpensive government resthouse on the beach, the Sentosa Hotel near the bus terminal with rooms from B$100, and the Sea View Hotel two km east of town where immaculate a/c rooms start at B$130.

EASTERN BRUNEI

Limbang

Limbang, a Malaysian town in the slice of land between the two sections of Brunei, has little of interest except for upriver trips to Iban longhouses and seedy brothels which have earned it a racy reputation. A curious mix of Christian tribalists and Muslim hedonists, Limbang prostitutes often live in hotels nicknamed "embassies," such as the Thai or Filipino embassy.

Few Western travelers visit the town, which can be reached in about 30 minutes by speedboat. Boats from Limbang to Punang in Sarawak depart daily except Sunday several times before noon. Taxis shuttle boat passengers to Lawas, where public transportation continues east toward Kota Kinabalu.

The Borneo Hotel has rooms from M$25. Upriver boat trips can be arranged at Limbang Trading, next door to the Borneo Hotel. Malaysian Air flies daily from Limbang to Lawas in Sabah and Miri in Sarawak.

Bangar

Bangar, a small town on the banks of the Temburong River, features a handful of traditional longhouses inhabited by Muruts. Accommodation is limited to a government resthouse which costs B$10 per night but requires advance reservations.

Boats to Bangar leave every morning from the BSB wharf and take about an hour. Bangar is also served by bus from Limbang.

*I never travel without my diary. One should always
have something sensational to read in the train.*

—OSCAR WILDE,
THE IMPORTANCE OF BEING EARNEST

*A traveler has a right to relate and embellish his
adventures as he pleases, and it is very impolite to
refuse that deference and applause they deserve.*

—RUDOLF ERICH RASPE,
TRAVELS OF BARON MUNCHAUSEN

*Order some golf shoes. Otherwise, we'll never get out
of this place alive. You notice these lizards don't have
any trouble moving around in this muck—that's
because they have claws on their feet.*

—HUNTER S. THOMPSON,
FEAR AND LOATHING IN LAS VEGAS

CAMBODIA

Before the fall of Sihanouk, Cambodia was the last paradise, the last paradise.

—HELICOPTER PILOT,
VICTORY IN VIETNAM

Angkor is not orchestral; it is monumental. It is an epic poem which makes its effect, like the Odyssey *and* Paradise Lost, *by the grandeur of its structure as well as by the beauty of the details. Angkor is an epic in rectangular forms imposed upon the Cambodian jungle.*

—ARNOLD TOYNBEE,
EAST TO WEST

I have lived seventy-eight years without hearing of bloody places like Cambodia.

—SIR WINSTON CHURCHILL,
THE STRUGGLE FOR SURVIVAL

INTRODUCTION

Life has returned to Cambodia. The Vietnamese occupation army which drove the Khmer Rouge from their "Killing Fields" has packed up and gone home. Kampuchea has been renamed Cambodia in a literary effort to eradicate the painful images created by the Khmer Rouge during their five-year reign of terror. And, after a long gestation period criticized by almost everyone connected with Asian politics, United Nations-supervised elections in May 1993 finally settled the question of who will run the country and be formally recognized by the international community.

Today, thousands of tourists cautiously venture back each year to visit Phnom Penh and the famed ruins at Angkor, considered among the world's greatest archaeological achievements.

And yet some people still say "don't go," including the American State Department, which offers stern warnings about political dangers, and travelers who complain that Cambodia is unbearably hot, accommodations are dismal and overpriced, and you can't escape the rat-tat-tat of machine-gun fire late at night. Others warn you about depressing economic condi-

tions, the sorry state of the capital city, and a life-threatening malaria epidemic, which strikes a third of the population.

Should you go?

By anyone's standards, Cambodia is hardly a typical tourist destination. For one thing, a civil war still rages between Cambodian troops and the outlaw Khmer Rouge on the borders of Thailand and Laos. Diplomatic protection—for what it's worth—is minimal since the present government is helpless to protect tourists who stray off the approved path and venture into unsecured territories: everywhere but Phnom Penh and (perhaps) Angkor. And most of Cambodia remains economically and psychologically devastated by the terror of the Khmer Rouge, who refuse to surrender and lay down their arms.

But, encouraged by improved travel connections and the lure of an untouched land, visitors now arrive in the greatest numbers since the mid-1960s, when over 30,000 tourists ignored the impending dangers and made the journey to Cambodia. According to recent statistics, over 280,000 travelers—70% Asian and 30% Western—now manage to visit Cambodia each year and few problems are reported by those who

CAMBODIA

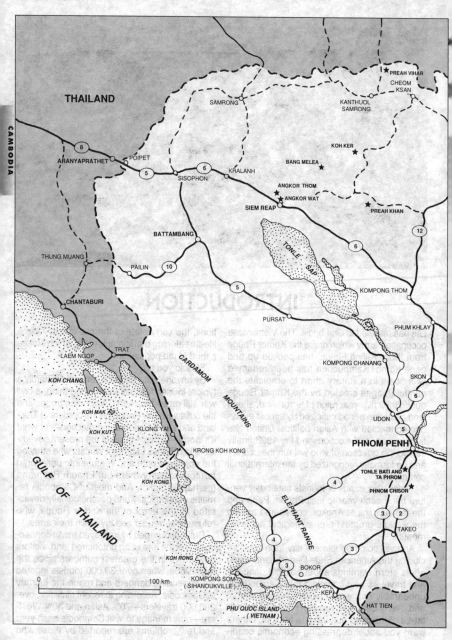

© MOON PUBLICATIONS, INC.

stick to the primary destinations of Phnom Penh and Angkor.

Cambodia is adventure travel at its most adventurous.

THE LAND

Wedged between Thailand, Vietnam, and Laos, Cambodia is a sparsely populated country of 181,035 square kilometers—about the size of Great Britain or half the land area of Vietnam. Most Cambodians live in the central low-lying alluvial plain along the Mekong River and around the Tonle Sap ("Great Lake"). North of the central plains are the Dangrek Mountains, which form a natural barrier with Thailand, while the southern perimeter is delineated by the romantically named Cardamom and Elephant mountains. Cambodia is separated from Vietnam and southern Laos by the densely forested mountains and high plateaus of the Eastern Highlands.

Cambodia's two dominant geographical features are the Mekong River, which rises in Tibet and traverses over 500 km of Cambodian territory, and the Tonle Sap, an immense but very shallow lake which ranks among the richest sources of freshwater fish in the world. The Mekong is navigable all the way to Laos, while the Tonle Sap is served by ferries which connect Angkor Wat with Phnom Penh via the Tonle Sap River.

Climate

Cambodia is a monsoonal country characterized by two major seasons. Strong prevailing winds from the southwest bring heavy rains and high humidity during the rainy season from June to November. Travel is possible though you should expect daily afternoon rains. Summer months from March to June can be overwhelming to Westerners unaccustomed to the searing temperatures, which often soar above 40° C. The dry and somewhat cooler season from December to March is the best time to visit Cambodia.

HISTORY

Cambodia's importance in the evolution of Southeast Asian culture and history is far greater than its limited size and political power would suggest. Lying on the trade routes between China and India, Cambodia has been the center of several powerful empires—Angkor being the most famous—and later the centerpiece of struggle between European and nationalist movements. The tragic history of Cambodia continues today with the ongoing struggle between democratic forces of a U.N.-supported government, the Vietnamese desire to control events in their troublesome neighbor, and the communist war of insurgency waged by the Khmer Rouge.

SIGHTSEEING HIGHLIGHTS

ANGKOR WAT

Cambodia's chief attraction is the dazzling 1,000-year-old ruins of Angkor, hidden away in tropical jungles some 300 km northwest of Phnom Penh. Constructed by the Khmers before the 12th century, Angkor is widely considered the premier architectural attraction in Southeast Asia and among the wonders of the Eastern world.

PHNOM PENH

Phnom Penh may be a city with a tragic recent history—and it's certainly a city in decline—but it has an excellent museum that presents an overview of Khmer history and arts, memorials to the horrific days of the Khmer Rouge, and an atmosphere quite refreshing after the cacophony of Bangkok.

SIHANOUKVILLE

Cambodia's best beach resort is a place on the move, with new shipping harbors, plenty of hotels and guesthouses, and some surprisingly fine beaches with dazzling sand and clear, cool water.

NORTHEAST CAMBODIA

Still completely off the tourist trail, northeastern Cambodia will appeal to adventurous types with its authentic, local markets, plentiful rivers, and tribal minorities. Ban Luang (Ratanakiri)—the main town with several adequate guesthouses—can be reached quickly by air from Phnom Penh.

The Funan Empire

Knowledge of Cambodian history prior to the Funan era is limited to Neolithic artifacts uncovered near Tonle Sap and Bronze Age implements excavated near Phnom Penh and the seaport of Oc Eo. Historical records begin with the rise of the Funan Empire in the 1st century A.D. until its incorporation into the Chenla state in the 6th century. Centered along the lower reaches of the Mekong and Tonle Sap rivers, and prosperous owing to its location on the east-west trade route between China and India, Funan eventually extended its political power south to the Malay Peninsula and east across most of present-day Vietnam.

Funan was among the earliest Asian kingdoms to embrace the Hindu culture which still profoundly shapes the history, art, and political landscapes of not only Cambodia but all of Southeast Asia. Although populated by indigenous peoples and by immigrants from Indonesia and southern China, Funan accepted much of its knowledge of religion and political organization from Indian merchants and theologians who arrived about 2,000 years ago. By the 5th century, Funan civilization used an Indian-based script, worshipped a pantheon of Hindu gods along with Mahayana deities, and created art inspired by the Gupta movement of India.

Eventually, these Hindu elements merged with original designs to create the first true Cambodian empire and the cultural godfather to Angkor.

The Chenla Empire

The empire of Funan was slowly displaced by the rising powers of Chenla, a Hindu-based dynasty originally located near Stung Treng and in southern Laos near Wat Phu. Diplomatic marriages subsequently gave rise to Chenla strongholds at Kampong Thom, in the center of Cambodia, and Angkor Borei in Takeo. Although rarely visited by Westerners, architectural prototypes discovered north of Kampong Thom inspired many of the innovative forms embraced by Khmer builders.

Chenla survived as a united dynasty until the 7th century, when disputes between feuding families led to the creation of "Land Chenla" near the Tonle Sap and "Water Chenla" on the lower Mekong. The Water Chenla empire is famed for its use of hydraulic techniques for cultivation, a sophisticated system later exploited in the complex and highly successful systems of Angkor.

The rise of Srivijaya in southern Sumatra, and new trade routes which favored Indonesian over Cambodian entrepôts, eventually made Chenla a vassal state of the Sailendra dynasty on the island of Java. Several of Chenla's rulers spent time at the Sailendra court, including Jayavarman II, who returned to Cambodia around 800 to establish the civilization of Angkor. The political connections between Java and Cambodia explain many of the architectural and sculptural similarities between the two civilizations.

The Khmer Empire

Cambodia's most famed empire was that of the Khmers, founded in 802 by King Jayavarman II at his capital of Angkor just north of the Tonle Sap. Renowned for its brilliant achievements in art and architecture, Angkor was also an immensely powerful nation which, between the 9th and 13th centuries, controlled most of Southeast Asia from Burma to Indochina, from China to Malaysia.

The introduction of Mahayana Buddhism, which undermined the prestige of the king, combined with the extravagance of the throne, which bankrupted the nation's elaborate irrigation system, finally led to the decline and fall of the Angkor civilization in the 13th century. Angkor fell to the Siamese in 1431. More details under "Angkor," below.

French Rule

The next 500 years—from the fall of Angkor to the arrival of the French in 1863—was an undistinguished period marked by Siamese control and the flight of Cambodian power to various capitals. In 1863, after a series of devastating battles between Siamese and Vietnamese forces, the French seized Cambodia to counter British and Thai expansion up the Mekong River. Their rule was benign. Although the French did little to develop the country, private-sector investors developed vast rubber estates while the government ensured the survival of the Cambodian state by supporting the king in a splendor unequaled since Angkorian times. It was this support of the Cambodian throne which stifled any nationalist activity comparable to that of Vietnam.

The Japanese seizure of Indochina in WW II left the French in nominal control; in 1941 they crowned the 18-year-old schoolboy Prince Norodom Sihanouk the final king of Cambodia. In March 1944, Japanese forces ousted the French and persuaded Sihanouk to declare independence. The French returned after the war and in 1946 abolished the absolute monarchy, though Sihanouk remained titular head of state. Dien Bien Phu was the site of the 1954 defeat of French forces in Vietnam. The withdrawal of French colonial forces from Cambodia led to the complete independence of Cambodia on 9 November 1953 and the triumphant return of Sihanouk to Phnom Penh. Sihanouk abdicated in 1955—absolute monarchies being no longer popular in Asia—but he has remained the principal political leader to the present day.

The Khmer Rouge

Sihanouk may have enjoyed an almost semidivine status with the Cambodian peasantry, but his intractable problems with both right- and left-wing political forces led to his downfall in March 1970 and the seizure of the government by Army Commander Lon Nol. Lon Nol immediately abolished the monarchy, proclaimed a republic, and started his war against the communist rebels—nicknamed the Khmer Rouge or "Red Khmers" by the deposed Sihanouk.

The Khmer Rouge seized Phnom Penh on 17 April 1975 and soon began one of the world's most horrific reigns of terror. To finalize their goal of a Maoist-style agrarian society, the late Pol Pot and his Khmer Rouge evacuated the cities and forced entire populations into slave labor. Currency was abolished, newspapers outlawed, postal services halted, and the Cambodian calendar was reset to "Year Zero." During their 44-month rule, the Khmer Rouge murdered over a million people in an orgy of death unmatched since the days of Adolf Hitler. But statistics are misleading: the percentage of population slaughtered by the Khmer Rouge is an unchallenged world's record.

The Present Scene

To stop the reign of terror largely ignored by the outside world, Vietnamese forces invaded and took Phnom Penh on 7 January 1979. Vietnam's occupation of Cambodia was condemned by the United Nations and unpopular with many Cambodians, who have traditionally disliked the Vietnamese, but nobody else seemed willing to put an end to the holocaust of the Khmer Rouge. Resistance to Vietnamese rule was organized by the Khmer Rouge from their bases on the Thai border and several other groups such as the Sihanuouk National Army (ANS), headed by Sihanouk, and

---

KAMPUCAMBODIAN CONUNDRUM

Perhaps only the former Yugoslavia could compete with Cambodia as the world's leading nightmare for cartographers.

The word Cambodia is the English version of Kambuja, an ancient term which means "Sons of Kambu." According to Khmer traditions, Kambu was an Indian ascetic who married a goddess and founded the kingdom of Chenla, the precursor empire to that of the Khmers.

Cambodians themselves transliterate Kambuja to Kampuchea, while the English-speaking world says Cambodia and the French call it Cambodge. The Cambodians prefer to call their country Kampuchea, but negative perceptions created by the Khmer Rouge—who insisted on calling the country Kampuchea—have brought the term Cambodia back into official favor.

The four decades since independence in 1953 have witnessed many different terms for the "Sons of Kambu":

1953—Kingdom of Cambodia: The official title adopted after independence from France. Cambodia at the time was a monarchy under the rule of Norodom Sihanouk.

1970—Khmer Republic: Cambodia was renamed by the government of army marshall Lon Nol after the overthrow of Sihanouk and the abolition of the monarchy.

1975—Democratic Kampuchea: The term used by the Khmer Rouge after their victory over Lon Nol in April 1975.

1979—People's Republic of Kampuchea: Vietnamese occupation forces renamed the country with suitably socialist overtones.

1989—State of Cambodia: The present name, although given the ongoing political conditions this could change at any moment.

the anticommunist Khmer People's National Liberation Front (KPNLF), headed by Son Sann, a former prime minister under Sihanouk.

After 11 years of occupation and under considerable pressure from the Soviet Union, the Vietnamese withdrew from Cambodia in September 1989, leaving behind a Vietnamese-installed caretaker government under the control of President Heng Samrin and Prime Minister Hun Sen. Although an imposed government will never be popular, most outside observers and many Cambodians appreciate the efforts of the Vietnamese to stop the Khmer Rouge and feel that Hun Sen has been a fair and essentially effective leader.

In October 1991 a peace agreement signed in Paris established a framework for peace and brought in the United Nations Transitional Authority in Cambodia (UNTAC), which has since proved to be the largest and most costly peacekeeping operation in U.N. history. Elections were held in May 1993. In September 1993, Norodom Sihanouk, one of this century's most resilient political survivors, became king of Cambodia for the second time. Sihanouk named his son, Prince Norodom Ranariddh, as prime minister and Hun Sen, who had led the Vietnam-installed government, was named second in command. The U.S. reestablished formal diplomatic relations in October 1993.

But the war against the Khmer rebels continued to rage on the borderlands. The first sign of hope was the March 1994 capture of the Khmer outpost at Pailin, a gem-rich region which had served as the principal source of funds after China ended economic aid in 1991. The following year, several thousand Khmer soldiers on the western border laid down their arms and further decimated the ranks of the once-powerful rebel faction.

And to help bring a final solution to the problem, King Norodom Sihanouk granted amnesty in late 1996 to Ieng Sary, the Khmer Rouge rebel leader widely blamed for the death of two million Cambodians during his four-year reign of terror.

Pol Pot was arrested and tried by his army in 1997. On 15 April 1998, Pol Pot died in his sleep following months of poor health. His death marks the end of one of the world's most despised rulers.

However, more serious than the scattered remains of the Khmer Rouge are the coups and power struggles of 1997 and 1998. The Cambodian government was reorganized by the United Nations with two heads of state—Second Prime Minister Hun Sen and First Prime Minister Prince Norodom Ranariddh. At first, the two men seemed to get along with the odd sharing of power but by the spring of 1997 it was apparent that Hun Sen had become the most powerful political figure in the country, chiefly through his control of most of the military, police, and local militia.

The political rivalry suddenly ended in July 1997 when Ranariddh was told of an impending coup and took the advice of his generals to flee to Paris. Hun Sen's troops met little resistance as they fanned out through Phnom Penh, then arrested and executed two of Ranariddh's top aides. Ranariddh went on to the U.N. headquarters in New York and the State Department in Washington, where he implored the international community to restore him to power. In the meantime, power struggles, gunfire, and acts of sabotage continued to plague the capital city of Phnom Penh.

The disintegration of Cambodia proved a major disappointment for the United Nations, which has spent over US$2 billion to establish peace in that haunted country. Determined to attempt save Cambodia once again, Japan, the United States, the European Union, and Cambodia's neighbors helped draft another peace plan which was set into motion on 27 February 1998. The plan halted the fighting in the capital and forced Ranariddh to break links with the Khmer Rouge. The former prince agreed to face charges related to the July 1997 fighting in Phnom Penh. Ranariddh moved to Thailand where he was tried in absentia on an arms smuggling charge and convicted of colluding with the outlawed Khmer Rouge group. After receiving the pardon he was gauranteed from his father, King Norodom Sihanouk, Ranariddh is expected to return to Phnom Penh and participate in the national elections scheduled for 26 July 1998.

THE PEOPLE

Prior to Pol Pot's time and the holocaust of the Khmer Rouge, Cambodia had an estimated population of over eight million. This number dropped to around five million by the late 1970s but has since rebounded to about seven million due to a high birth rate and the return of refugees from Thailand. Exact numbers of killed or refugees are impossible to know, but it is believed about two million refugees fled the country and have been held in refugee camps unless repatriated or accepted by foreign countries. Overall population density is low except in the south-central region near Phnom Penh, where it's actually quite high.

Khmers

Cambodian (Khmer) stock accounts for over 90% of the total population—a strikingly high homogeneity unique in Southeast Asia and the source of Cambodia's strong sense of national identity. The Khmers belong to the Mon-Khmer ethnolinguistic group, which migrated into the fertile Mekong delta from southern China, the Korat Plateau in northeastern Thailand, and perhaps even from Indonesia prior to the Angkorian period. Influenced over the centuries by Indian and Javanese kingdoms, the Khmers have intermarried with successive waves of immigrants from Thailand during the 10th to 15th centuries, Vietnamese from the 17th century, and Chinese in the 18th and 19th centuries. Despite this racial admixture, Khmer stock remains the dominant feature of Cambodian society.

Chinese

Prior to 1975, Cambodia's most important racial minority were the Chinese, who controlled the national economy and maintained their high degree of ethnic distinctiveness despite widespread intermarriage with local Cambodians. As in Thailand, the Chinese were able to integrate into Cambodian life without the racial tensions and government discrimination promoted in other Southeast Asian nations. In fact, many of the leading political figures in Cambodian society are of partial Chinese extraction.

All this changed in 1975 when the Khmer Rouge initiated a ruthless campaign to rid Cambodia of all foreign influence, including the Vietnamese, the West, and the Chinese, who abandoned the economic engines of the country. The result is a society without the entrepreneurial talents of the Chinese, who now comprise less than 3% of the population.

Vietnamese

Cambodia's most controversial minority is the Vietnamese, who have traditionally lived in the lower Mekong River delta and make up less than five percent of the population. Mistrust and animosity between the Cambodians and the Vietnamese have now reached a point where many diplomats fear race riots and "Vietnamese bodies floating down the Mekong," according to an American envoy. It has happened before: in 1970, an anti-Vietnamese pogrom supported by the Lon Nol regime saw thousands of Vietnamese murdered by Cambodian soldiers and dumped in the Tonle Sap River.

Ethnic hatred of the Vietnamese, combined with familiar anti-Western diatribes, have been skillfully exploited by the Khmer Rouge in recent years. Ousted from power by the Vietnamese army, they have driven home the centuries-old fear of political and cultural domination by the Vietnamese and widespread concerns about the influx of Vietnamese immigrants drawn by Cambodia's economic boom. While it appears that all Vietnamese occupation soldiers have returned home, the Khmer Rouge continue their relentless attack against "the despicable *Yuon*" (a pejorative Khmer term for the Vietnamese) and often raid remote villages in search of Vietnamese victims. Racial tension between the Cambodians and the Vietnamese —not the Khmer Rouge—is considered by many experts to be the primary threat to peace inside Cambodia.

Cham Muslims

Cambodia also has about 100,000 Cham Muslims, also known as Cham Malays or Khmer Islam, living north of Phnom Penh along the Mekong River. Many are descended from the people of the royal kingdom of Champa in Vietnam, who were driven into Cambodia by the Vietnamese in the 15th century. Others arrived by invitation of the Muslim-Khmer king Chan, who ruled central Cambodia in the mid-17th century.

Cham Muslims were horribly persecuted during the Pol Pot regime, when, according to some experts, half of their population was exterminated and over 80% of their mosques destroyed. The survivors regard Chur Changvra near Phnom Penh as their spiritual center and follow their traditional roles as cattle traders, silk weavers, and butchers (Theravada Buddhism prohibits most Khmers from slaughtering, though not consuming, animals).

Ethnic Minorities

Cambodia's Khmer Loeu, or Upland Khmers, traditionally lived in the forested hills of the northeast until the Vietnam War forced many down to the plains and into more sedentary lives. Today, the surviving groups not assimilated into modern Cambodian society include the Saoch in the Elephant Mountains, the Pear in the Cardamom Mountains, the Brao along the Lao border, and the Kuy in the far northwest. Like other tribes in Southeast Asia, these peoples are animist, semi-nomadic farmers who practice slash-and-burn agriculture.

ON THE ROAD

GETTING THERE

By Air

Land access to Cambodia is possible from Vietnam and occasionally Thailand, but most visitors arrive by air at Pochentong Airport, 12 km outside Phnom Penh.

From Bangkok: There are now over 30 weekly flights to Phnom Penh from Bangkok provided by Thai International and Royal Air Cambodge (RAC) for US$140 one-way or US$220 roundtrip. Direct service to Siem Reap has been proposed by both airlines.

From Vietnam: Vietnam Airlines and RAC fly daily from Saigon to Phnom Penh for US$60 one-way and twice weekly from Hanoi for US$160 one-way.

From Other Cities: Phnom Penh is also served from Kuala Lumpur by Malaysia Airlines, Hong Kong (DragonAir), Singapore (SilkAir), Vientiane (Lao Aviation), and Taipei (Transasia Airways).

International **departure tax** from Pochentong Airport is US$15.

By Land

Land access is legal from Vietnam but before considering an overland journey, read the "Warning" below under "Independent Travel."

From Thailand: The border crossing at Aranyaprathet opened in early 1993 but closed the following year after attacks from the Khmer Rouge. If peace suddenly breaks out in western Cambodia, travelers may once again be able to take a bus or train from Bangkok to Aranyaprathet, cross the border, and continue to Siem Reap or Phnom Penh.

From Vietnam by Bus: Travelers can safely make the 245-km journey from Saigon to Phnom Penh on Route 1, via the border crossings at Moc Bai (Vietnam) and Bavet (Cambodia). The bus ride takes 12-15 grueling hours depending on border hassles, ferry delays, and the condition of the road. Share taxis are much faster and safer since they avoid Vietnamese police and soldiers along the way.

All travelers must have a Cambodian visa and a proper exit endorsement from Vietnamese officials. Travelers whose Vietnamese visa lists "Saigon" or "Hanoi" as their departure point *must* obtain a stamp which states "Moc Bai" as the permitted exit port. These stamps can be picked up in Saigon at the Foreign Ministry office and take three days to process.

Buses leave Saigon early each morning from the stop adjacent to the Rex Hotel. The bus heads across Vietnam to Moc Bai, where immigration officials collect passports and check for the proper exit endorsement. After passing through Cambodian immigration, the bus continues west to Phnom Penh.

Buses from Phnom Penh to Saigon depart daily at 0530 from a ticket office near the intersection of Street 182 and Street 211, close to Nehru Boulevard. Buy tickets one day in advance.

From Vietnam by Share Taxi: A much faster, comfortable, and safer journey can be made with share taxis, which run as far as the border from each side. Share taxis leave Saigon and cost US$10 per person or US$30 for the whole taxi to the Cambodian border. Saigon taxis can be picked up at the Try Mien Tay bus station on the western outskirts of town or find a few fellow travelers and negotiate with a downtown taxi driver. Figure on two hours to Moc Bai, half an

CAMBODIA

hour for paperwork, and another three hours by share taxi to Phnom Penh. Share taxis from Bavet to Phnom Penh cost US$5-10 per person.

Coming from Phnom Penh, share taxis can be picked up at the depot east of Monivong Bridge at Street 369 in the Chbampao Market area from 0600-1300. The trip takes three hours to the Cambodian border town of Bavet, where you take care of immigration formalities and catch a motorcycle taxi into Vietnam for another round of immigration proceedings.

From Laos: Route 13, which heads north from Stung Treng to Khong and Pakse in southern Laos, is currently closed to Western visitors though Laotian officials are now pressing to open this border.

By Sea
Cambodia's main maritime port is at Sihanoukville (formerly Kompong Som), at the terminus of Route 4, some 180 km southwest of Phnom Penh. Western visitors are not allowed to enter Cambodia via Sihanoukville, but this may change within a few years.

Cambodia can be entered by sea at the fishing port of Krong Koah Kong, just opposite Ban Hat Lek in Thailand. This quasi-legal entry point lacks a Thai immigration office, so travelers will not receive a Thai exit stamp in their passport—a big consideration if you plan to return to Thailand. Take a bus from Bangkok to Trat and continue by minitruck to the border town of Ban Hat Lek. Longtail boats take an hour through mangrove swamps to Krong Koah Kong, where Cambodian immigration officials place entry stamps in passports. From Krong Koah Kong, you can either fly direct to Phnom Penh (service is sporadic) or take a large fishing boat on the 12-hour passage to Sihanoukville.

GETTING AROUND

By Air
Royal Air Cambodge flies from Phnom Penh daily to Siem Reap (Angkor) for US$70 one-way and US$130 roundtrip. Service is also provided at sporadic schedules to Sihanoukville, Kratie, Stung Treng, Kampot, and Battambang on Boeing 737s and a few old Russian Tupolevs (TU-134) and Antonovs (AN-24).

Reservations should be made well in advance. Travelers without reservations can arrive early at the airport, sign the waiting list, and hope for no-shows or cancellations. Extra "service fees" may be collected for passengers without reservations.

By Land
Despite roads ranking among the worst in Asia, buses and trucks continue to slowly haul passengers around Cambodia while side-stepping the Khmer Rouge. Yet few Western travelers use the vintage Dodge buses—painfully slow nightmares that bounce relentlessly over the bone-jarring roads and serve as an easy target for terrorist groups.

A better alternative is a share taxi. Most leave from several markets in Phnom Penh and take off for Siem Reap, the Vietnamese border, Sihanoukville to the south, and sometime in the future, Battambang near Thailand and Stung Treng in the northeast.

Get an early start and never travel in the late afternoon, when checkpoint soldiers are drunker and more aggressive about collecting "taxes" and "tips" for onward passage.

By Boat
With such dismal and dangerous roads, most travelers prefer fast boats to Siem Reap. Express boat service is also available to Kompong Cham and Kratie on the Mekong River and to Stung Treng when the waters run high from September to January.

Three types of boats go from Phnom Penh to Siem Reap. The speed boat departs daily at 0700, takes five hours, and costs US$30. Slower and less expensive alternatives include the "fast" boat and the aptly named "slow" boat to Angkor. Fares to other destinations are US$25 (Kratie) and US$35-40 (Stung Treng).

TRAVEL PRACTICALITIES

Visas
Visas, required of all visitors, can be obtained from Cambodian diplomatic offices in Bangkok, Saigon, Hanoi, Vientiane, Paris, Berlin, Prague, and Washington D.C. Cambodian diplomatic offices have also opened in Australia, New Zealand,

and several European countries that recognized Cambodia after the 1993 peace accord.

The Cambodian Embassy in the United States can be contacted at 4500 16th St., NW, Washington D.C., tel. (202) 726-8268, fax 726-8381, e-mail: Cambodia&embassy.org, and at www.embassy.org/cambodia/visa.htm. Visas require three application forms, three photos, a US$20 consular fee, and the passport of the applicant. Visa applications can be downloaded from the embassy's Web site. Tourist visas are normally issued for a single entry of 30 days.

Arrival by Air: Visas are granted on arrival at Pochentong Airport in Phnom Penh. Visitors must fill in the arrival declaration, supply three passport photos, and pay US$20. Visas are valid for one month; current visa limitations should be checked before you arrive at Pochentong Airport.

Travelers should also inquire with several travel agents before booking tours or paying for visas since many agencies—especially on Khao San Road in Bangkok—charge exorbitant fees which can triple or quadruple the price.

Extensions: Visas can be extended at the Ministry of Foreign Affairs in Phnom Penh at the intersection of 240 Street and Quai Karl Marx in Phnom Penh.

Travel Permits: Travel permits are no longer required for travel outside Phnom Penh.

Money

The unit of currency in Cambodia is the *riel,* which is issued in denominations from 1,000 to 100,000. The *riel* is very unstable and has gone from 150 *riels* per dollar in 1990 to over 3,000 riels in 1997.

The American dollar serves as alternative currency, accepted by most hotels and restaurants in the country. Travelers should bring along plenty of small-denomination American bills, which can be easily exchanged and used as payment throughout the country.

Prices in this chapter are quoted in U.S. dollars, rather than unstable *riels.*

Tours

Cambodia is open to both tour groups and independent travelers who can make their own arrangements in Bangkok. Most packages sold by Western travel agents include Vietnam or Laos, and tours over seven days generally visit Phnom Penh, Angkor Wat, Tonle Sap, and several places near Phnom Penh such as Udong, Khaki, and Tonle Bati.

The most critical detail is the number of days at Angkor Wat. Almost unbelievably, several highly advertised tour wholesalers sell packages which include just a single day at the ruins—an immense place worth a minimum of three days and two nights.

Tours from Bangkok include roundtrip airfare to Phnom Penh and Siem Reap, all hotels and meals, internal transport, and guide services for about US$200-250 per day. One of the largest tour operators is Diethelm Travel, www.diethelm-travel.com, in Bangkok with offices in Phnom Penh and Siem Reap.

Warnings

Most of Cambodia remains in a state of turmoil and is extremely dangerous thanks to the terrorist activities of the Khmer Rouge, who have murdered hundreds of Cambodians and over a dozen Western travelers, who were caught in the crossfire. The following words are taken from the U.S. Consular Information Sheet at http://travel.state.gov/cambodia.html. The U.S. Embassy in Phnom Penh may be able to provide Americans traveling outside the capital with more detailed information on areas of conflict, and encourages persons wishing to travel to the western districts near Battambang to check with the embassy first. The embassy is located at 27, Street Angphanouvong Street 240, tel. (855) (23) 426436.

Train travel is dangerous and embassy personnel in Phnom Penh are advised to avoid trains at all costs. Travel by water can be unsafe since boats are overcrowded, lack safety equipment, and owners accept no liability for accidents. It is dangerous to travel to Battambang Province during periods of increased military conflict, and to travel to rural areas of Siem Reap Province beyond the main complexes. The safety of road travel outside of urban areas varies greatly from region to region but potential risks can be reduced by traveling in vehicle convoy dur-

ing daylight hours. There has been an increase in armed robberies of foreigners in Phnom Penh, especially on persons who take motorcycle taxis at night. Travelers should carry photocopies, not originals, of *their passport, driver's license, and other important documents while sightseeing. The loss or theft of a U.S. passport should be reported immediately to the U.S. Embassy in Phnom Penh.*

PHNOM PENH

Prior to the arrival of the Khmer Rouge in 1970, Phnom Penh was called the "Paris of the East" for its wide, tree-lined boulevards, croissants, sidewalk cafes, and elegant villas constructed by French colonialists. Four years of terror under the Khmer Rouge left behind a hollow shell ripped with potholed streets, not a single telephone, and piles of rubble which marked the former locations of the National Bank and Catholic cathedral.

The situation has improved somewhat in recent years. Yes, sanitation is still poor, most colonial architecture remains in disrepair, and serious problems still exist with basic utilities and garbage collection. Yet an effort is being made to sweep the boulevards, and people remain genuinely hospitable to the foreign visitor. Visitors who tour both Saigon and Phnom Penh generally prefer the slower pace and friendlier atmosphere of the Cambodian capital—a city strangely suspended between the horrors of the past and the promise of the future.

Getting Your Bearings

Finding your way around Phnom Penh is somewhat tricky. Hotel addresses can be rendered in variety of ways depending on whether it is based on the old French system, the Khmer nomenclature used in the 1970s, or the Sihanouk royalist preferences imposed after the return of Sihanouk in 1993. The most dependable way to describe locations is by landmarks, such as Wat Phnom, Chruoy Changvar Bridge, the Central Market, the Royal Palace, the National Museum, the Hotel Sofitel Cambodiana, and the Independence Monument.

ATTRACTIONS

Although sometimes considered simply a connection to Angkor, Phnom Penh offers several worthwhile sights that deserve a good look.

As mentioned above, finding your way around the sprawling city can be confusing due to the odd street nomenclature imposed over the years. A simple system might divide the city into the former European quarter around Wat Phnom, Chinatown near the Central Market, the Khmer section near the Royal Palace, and the new neighborhood west of Boulevard Achar Mean.

Remote places can be reached by *samlor* or cyclo which cost about US$1 per hour. Tours generally start with a ride along the riverfront esplanade, continue past the bronze dogs staring out over the Mekong River, and end at the Royal Palace.

Wat Phnom

According to legend, Phnom Penh takes its name from a wealthy Khmer widow named Madame Penh who erected this hilltop monastery in 1372 after her miraculous discovery of four Buddhas hidden inside a floating tree. The present stupa dates from 1894 and has been reconstructed several times to hold a small shrine with an image of Madame Penh and a much larger stupa said to contain the ashes of a post-Angkorian king.

Royal Palace

Cambodia's Royal Palace and auxiliary buildings, erected in the late 19th century after French designs, form the finest collection of traditional architecture left in Phnom Penh. The palace has been closed to the public since 1991 but the Silver Pagoda in the southern courtyard remains open to the public. Noteworthy buildings inside the grounds of the Royal Palace include the Throne Hall, inaugurated in 1919 by King Sisowath as the replacement for a wooden hall constructed in 1869, and the Napoleon III Villa, presented to the king of Cambodia in 1867.

Silver Pagoda

Wat Pra Keo or "Temple of the Emerald Buddha" takes it name from some 5,000 silver blocks—six tons of pure silver—which comprise the magnificent floor and lead the way to a 17th-century "emerald" Buddha carved from jade and a 90-kg solid-gold Buddha studded with over 10,000 diamonds. Also note the Ramayana murals and the smaller structures such as the royal *mondop*, Buddha footprints, and stupas dedicated to King Ang Duong (reigned 1845-59), King Norodom (1859-1904), King Suramarit (1955-60), and one of Prince Sihanouk's daughters.

The Silver Pagoda is open daily, except Monday, 0700-1100 and 1400-1700.

National Museum

The blood-red Khmer-style building, home to the Musée des Beaux Arts, was designed by a French architect and constructed 1917-1920 as the centerpiece of Khmer art in Cambodia.

Masterpiece displays include the pre-Angkor periods of Funan and Chenla (5th-9th centuries), Indravarman works (9th-10th centuries), classical Angkor (10th-14th centuries), and post-Angkor periods (15th-20th centuries). Among the highlights are Hindu images from Bangkor Borei, a pre-Angkorian Harihara statue from Kompong Thom, and bronze Vishnus from the West Baray at Angkor Wat.

The museum is open Tues.-Sun. 0800-1100 and 1400-1700.

Wat Ounalom

Cambodia's most important temple dates from 1443 when the original monastery served as the center of the national Buddhist order. Many of the 500 monks who once lived at the temple were slain by the Khmer Rouge, who also executed the supreme patriarch Somdech Huot Tat and destroyed the library—repository of the complete works of the Cambodian Buddhist Institute.

Wat Ounalom has been partially restored and once again serves as the national headquarters for the Cambodian Buddhist *sangha*.

Tuol Sleng Holocaust Museum

Tuol Sleng—a former high school—was seized in 1975 by the Khmer Rouge and converted into the largest detention and torture center in the country during the years of the "killing fields." An estimated 20,000 Cambodians passed through the school to be eventually murdered by the Khmer Rouge; fewer than 10 prisoners survived. Those who died during torture were tossed into mass graves on the school grounds, while those who survived were shipped outside town to the extermination camp at Choeung Ek.

The horrors of Tuol Sleng are matters of public record since the Khmer Rouge, like the Nazis, kept meticulous records and photographs of their victims. Photos mounted on the walls record countless Cambodians and several Westerners, such as Michael Scott Deeds, an American who fell into Khmer Rouge hands in 1978 while sailing the Gulf of Thailand. Deeds was executed two days before Vietnamese forces liberated the country.

One remembrance book entry provides a chilling summary: *"Auschwitz sur le Mekong."*

Tuol Sleng, at the intersection of 113 and 350 Streets, is open daily 0800-1130 and 1400-1700. A subsequent visit to the Killing Fields at Choeung Ek, 15 km southwest of Phnom Penh, will be the most emotional experience of your visit to Southeast Asia.

ACCOMMODATIONS

Phnom Penh currently has over 100 hotels (3,500 rooms) and 25 guesthouses (275 rooms) while Siem Reap has 14 hotels (450 rooms) and 21 guesthouses (169 rooms). Cambodia has another 16 hotels under construction including six expected to open by 1998—Le Royal in Phnom Penh, the Independence Hotel in Sihanoukville, and the Grand, Royal Angkor, Chedi, and Auberge du Temple in Siem Reap.

Two of the more ambitious projects are the US$1.3 billion tourist casino and resort to be constructed by a Malaysia firm on an island near Sihanoukville and a 400-room Club Med to be opened at Sokha Beach, Sihanoukville.

Budget—South

Almost a dozen guesthouses are tucked away in the streets and alleys just south of the bus terminal on Street 182.

Capitol Hotel: The original backpackers' digs has cheap rooms and managers who can help

(continues on page 74)

CAMBODIA

MEKONG RIVER

CHRUOY CHANGVAR PENINSULA

TONLE SAP

SEE "CENTRAL PHNOM PENH MAP"

SISOWATH QUAY

SAMDECH SOTHEAROS BLVD.

★ NATIONAL MUSEUM

★ ROYAL PALACE

POST OFFICE/TELECOM

■ BOAT TERMINAL

NORODOM BLVD.

CHRUOY CHANGVAR (JAPANESE) BRIDGE

TONLE SAP BOAT DOCKS

A CHA XAO ST.

47

WAT PHNOM

51

63

BUS STATION

★ CENTRAL MARKET

RAILWAY STATION

DOCKS FOR FASTBOATS TO SIEM REAP

■ BAYON HOTEL
■ THAI EMBASSY

HOLIDAY INTERNATIONAL HOTEL

CHEZ LIPP RESTAURANT

MONIVONG BLVD.

TO UDONG, SIEM REAP, BATTAMBANG (ROUTES 5, 6, 7)

■ FRENCH EMBASSY

■ LE SOLEIL
VERT GH
■ CALMETTE HOSPITAL
■ BRITISH EMBASSY

■ CONCOI
■ GUESTHOUSE #9

■ BOENG
K KAK GH

■ CLOUD
9 GH

CHARLES DE GAULLE BLVD.

161

ORIENTAL HOTEL

JULIANA HOTEL

192

ORASEY MARKET

TO BATTAMBANG

■ FINE ARTS SCHOOL

70

BOENG KAK LAKE

171

169

182

SANGKAR

211

NEHRU BLVD.

SAIGON BUS

SHARE-TAXIS TO SHANOUKVILLE

PHNOM PENH

■ TUOL KORK

273

POCHENTONG BLVD.

KAMPUCHEA KROM BLVD.

355

337

315

■ MILLIONAIRE CLUB

TO POCHENTONG AIRPORT, SIHANOUKVILLE (ROUTES 3, 4)

■ PHNOM PENH UNIVERSITY

MAO TSE TUNG BLVD.

CAMBODIA

TONLE BASSAC

169

TO SAIGON (ROUTE 1)

● HOTEL SOFITEL CAMBODIANA

★ CHBAMPAO MARKET BUS STATION

■ SHARE-TAXI RANK/ BUS STATION

MONIVONG BRIDGE

■ RUSSIAN EMBASSY

● ROYAL PHNOM PENH HOTEL

★ PRATVONG BUDDHA FACTORY

308

NORODOM BLVD.

● EUROPEAN DENTAL CLINIC

★ WAT THAN

● ROYAL AIR CAMBODGE

★ INDEPENDENCE MONUMENT

★ BAN THAI RESTAURANT

51

57

302

● ACCESS MEDICAL SERVICES

● CCC

63

● PHNOM PENH GARDEN HOTEL

● LAOTIAN EMBASSY

MAO TSE TUNG BLVD.

● HUA NAM RESTAURANT

436

★ VIETNAMESE EMBASSY

★ CHAM KAR MON PALACE

● INDIAN EMBASSY

466

MONIVONG BLVD.

306

310

TRA BEK LAKE

● BASSAC RESTAURANT

TO TONLE BATI AND TAKEO (ROUTE 2)

271

MONIVONG BLVD.

95

320

● VIETNAM TOURISM

● SYDNEY INTERNATIONAL HOTEL

105

● IMC CLINIC

288

143

★ TUOL SLENG HOLOCAUST MUSEUM

432

● CHINESE EMBASSY

★ RUSSIAN MARKET

155

163

163

PREAH SIHANOUK BLVD.

MONIVONG BLVD.

● OLYMPIC STADIUM

MARKETS

■ BUS STATION

298

338

346

★ OLYMPIC MARKET

MARKETS

286

● PARIS HOTEL

191

MAO TSE TUNG BLVD.

BOREI THMEI

VIMEAN SUOR

MARKET 19

236

205

502

■ INTERCONTINENTAL HOTEL

■ MARTINI BAR

404

414

271

TOMPUN LAKE

1 Km

★ DANG KOR MARKET

■ SHARE-TAXI RANK/BUS STATION

● THE OASIS RESTAURANT

MONIRETH BLVD

TO CHOEUNG EK

0

© MOON PUBLICATIONS, INC.

CAMBODIA

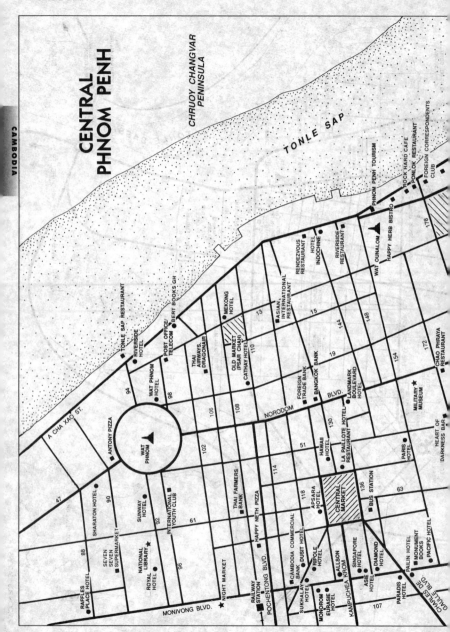

CENTRAL PHNOM PENH

CHRUOY CHANGVAR PENINSULA

TONLE SAP

ROCK HARD CAFE
PONLOK RESTAURANT
FOREIGN CORRESPONDENTS CLUB

178

PHNOM PENH TOURISM

RENDEZVOUS RESTAURANT

HOTEL INDOCHINE

RIVERSIDE RESTAURANT

WAT OUNALOM

HAPPY HERB BISTRO

148

154

172

CHAO PHRAYA RESTAURANT

TONLE SAP RESTAURANT

RIVERSIDE HOTEL

POST OFFICE/TELECOM

BERT BOOKS GH

MEKONG HOTEL

13

ASIAN INTERNATIONAL RESTAURANT

15

144

19

THAI AIRWAYS/DRAGONAIR

OLD MARKET (PSAR CHAH)

CATHAY HOTEL

110

FOREIGN TRADE BANK

BANGKOK BANK

LANDMARK BOULEVARD HOTEL

NORODOM BLVD.

A CHA XAO ST.

WAT PHNOM HOTEL

94

98

106

108

102

MILITARY MUSEUM

HEART OF DARKNESS BAR

ANTONY PIZZA

WAT PHNOM

114

130

51

HAWAI HOTEL

LA PALLOTE RESTAURANT

PARIS HOTEL

47

SHARATON HOTEL

90

SUNWAY HOTEL

92

INTERNATIONAL YOUTH CLUB

61

THAI FARMERS BANK

HAPPY NETH PIZZA

APSARA HOTEL

118

CENTRAL MARKET

136

BUS STATION

63

MONUMENT BOOKS

PACIFIC HOTEL

88

SEVEN SEVEN SUPERMARKET

NATIONAL LIBRARY

ROYAL HOTEL

96

CAMBODIA COMMERCIAL BANK

DUST HOTEL

INDPOLE HOTEL

ALLSON HOTEL

SINGAPORE HOTEL

DIAMOND HOTEL

PALIN HOTEL

MONUMENT

RAFFLES PLACE HOTEL

NIGHT MARKET

POCHENTONG BLVD.

RAILWAY STATION

SUKHALAY HOTEL

MONOROM EURASIE HOTEL

KAMPUCHEA KROM

ASIE HOTEL

PARADIS HOTEL

CHARLES DE GAULLE BLVD.

107

MONIVONG BLVD.

CAMBODIA

CHAKTOMUK THEATER

HOTEL SOFITEL CAMBODIANA

CAMBODIANA INN

REGENT PARK HOTEL

SISOWATH QUAY

RENAKSE HOTEL

UNESCO

SAMDECH SOTHEAROS

EXPOSITION HALL

BASSAC THEATER

PARK

ROYAL PALACE

SILVER PAGODA

NATIONAL MUSEUM

13

184

HONG KONG CENTER

CHIANG MAI RESTAURANT

SAIGON HOUSE RESTAURANT

EID RESTAURANT

7

LANOR THAI RESTAURANT

ART GALLERY

ROYAL PHNOM PENH HOTEL

LA BOUTIQUE

9

NAGA FOUNTAIN

RED HOUSE RESTAURANT

GREEN HOUSE RESTAURANT

21

29

TAJ MAHAL HOTEL

19

MINISTRY OF THE INTERIOR

WAT SENOROM

NORODOM BLVD.

AUSTRALIAN EMBASSY

INDEPENDENCE MONUMENT

LAO AVIATION

GREEN HOUSE 2

GREEN HOTEL

242

PREAH SIHANOUK BLVD.

CACTUS RESTAURANT

294

JAPANESE EMBASSY

BANQUE INDOSUEZ

CHINATOWN HOTEL

MALAYSIAN EMBASSY

51

254

CALIFORNIA RESTAURANT

BEAUTY INN

PHNOM KHIEU RESTAURANT

282

174

HOTEL PASTEUR

INTERNATIONAL HOUSE/MINIMART

178

200

214

US EMBASSY

222

240

63

252

STANDARD CHARTERED BANK

LUCKY MINIMART

CACTUS PUB

LE TROCADERO

TOKYO HOTEL

KIM LY RESTAURANT

AMARA HOTEL

CITY LOTUS GH

REGENT HOTEL

MITTAPHEAP HOTEL

WAT KOH

CAPITOL HOTEL/ RESTAURANT

20 GH

ASIA SOUP

PRINCESS HOTEL

ORIENTAL INN

228

LONG BEACH FAMILY RESTAURANT

MONIVONG BLVD.

MINISTRY OF CULTURE

208

HONG KONG HOTEL

BEEF SOUP

GERMAN EMBASSY

182

198

214

105

107

111

115

GENERAL DIRECTORATE OF TOURISM

FRENCH BAKERY

NEAKPEAN HOTEL

BUS TERMINAL

NAGA GH

232

242

0   250 m

© MOON PUBLICATIONS, INC.

with travel tips. Warnings and updates are posted on the bulletin board. 24 Street 182, tel. (23) 364104, US$4-10.

Happy Guesthouse: Just adjacent to the Capitol Hotel is another budget spot with smaller but somewhat quieter rooms. Street 182, tel. (23) 64104, US$4-10.

Naga Guesthouse: Somewhat better facilities a few blocks south of the Capitol Hotel. 48 Street 111 at Street 232, US$15-40.

Narin Guesthouse: A few blocks west of Naga Guesthouse is a delightful homestay run by the friendly Mr. Narin and his family. Clean, safe, plus great meals served every evening. 50 Street 125 at Street 232, US$3-6.

City Lotus Guesthouse: A few blocks south of the Central Market near Monivong Hospital is a good-value hotel with clean a/c rooms with private bath. 76 Street 172 between Streets 51 and 63, tel. (23) 362409, US$10-15.

Amara Hotel: At the south end of central Phnom Penh is a small concentration of restaurants, pubs, and budget hotels including this colonial-era relic with spacious a/c rooms with private bath and other amenities. The business center provides fax and IDD telephone service. Good value. 126 Street 63 at Street 282, tel. (23) 27260, US$10-15.

Beauty Inn: Hidden away in the south end of town is a reasonably priced minihotel with 17 clean rooms fixed with a/c, refrigerator, and CNN TV. More expensive and somewhat isolated but very good value. 537 Monivong Blvd., tel. (23) 27426, US$12-20.

Budget—River
Among the expensive hotels hugging the banks of the Tonle Sap are a few moderately priced guesthouses and hotels.

Lotus Guesthouse: Near the Tonle Sap River and a few blocks southeast of Wat Phnom is a decent place featuring 10 rooms with private bath. 121 Samdech Sothearos Blvd. at Street 104, US$4-8.

Bert Books & Guesthouse: An American and his Cambodian wife run this funky used bookstore and cafe which has several clean rooms upstairs with private baths and great views over the river. Bert's is a favorite of foreigners teaching English in Phnom Penh. 79 Samdech Sothearos Blvd., US$5-7.

Hotel Indochine: A somewhat sleazy Chinese-run hotel with short-time traffic but decent rooms nicely located near the river. Street 144, tel. (23) 27292, US$20-30.

Budget—North
Some of the quietest and most relaxing guesthouses are north of Wat Phnom near Boeng Kak Lake.

Sok Sin Guesthouse: A quiet place in an alley near the French Embassy with a dozen inexpensive rooms. Street 78, US$5-8.

Number 9 Guesthouse: One of the best places to relax and escape the sleaze of Phnom Penh is this simple place on the banks of Boeng Kak Lake, a few blocks northwest of Wat Phnom. Once known as Cloud 9 for obvious reasons, prior to the crackdown on illegal drugs in Cambodia. 9 Street 93, US$3-6.

Moderate—North
French colonial hotels are plentiful in Phnom Penh near the Central Market and Wat Phnom.

Royal Hotel: A colonial-era hotel constructed in 1910 and the favorite of foreign correspondents during the war. Formerly called the Phnom and Samaki, the Royal has recently been renovated but still exudes old-world charm. Many events depicted in the film *The Killing Fields* took place here, though the Railway Hotel in Hua Hin (Thailand) was used for the film. Monivong Blvd., tel. (23) 24151, US$35-60.

Holiday International: Tucked away in the far northern section near Calmette Hospital is a surprisingly upscale 60-room hotel with business center and small pool. Street 84, tel. (23) 427502, fax 427401, US$70-90.

Moderate—Central
Several great little colonial relics are either in original condition or undergoing renovation for the anticipated tourism boom.

La Paillote Hotel: Opposite the Central Market is a spacious, colonial classic known for its excellent French restaurant and 24 rooms with views over the central district of Phnom Penh. 234 Street 53, tel. (23) 426513, fax 426513, US$25-65.

Hotel Sukhalay: A small and unassuming hotel with temperamental air-conditioning, water-soaked walls, rock-hard pillows, and a pleasant cafe—once a favorite of pre-1975 journalists. Monivong Blvd., tel. (23) 26140, US$18-45.

Hotel Asie: Another mid-priced hotel which, like many other hotels operated by government agencies, is undergoing renovation and will certainly raise room rates. 73 Street 126, tel. (23) 427826, fax 427826, US$25-60.

Hotel Monorom: An older 63-room hotel conveniently located near the post office, banks, and Central Market. Superb city views from the sixth-floor terrace cafe. 89 Monivong Blvd., tel. (23) 26149, fax 26073, US$40-65.

Moderate—River

The following are removed from the action but much quieter than hotels near the Central Market.

Renakse Hotel: Just opposite the Royal Palace is a lovely French colonial building with a good restaurant, travel services, and clean a/c rooms with private bath. Recommended. 40 Samdech Sothearos Blvd., tel. (23) 722457, fax 722457, US$25-35.

Riverside Hotel: East of Wat Phnom is an almost luxurious hotel overlooking the Tonle Sap. Samdech Sothearos Blvd., tel. (23) 27565, US$70-90.

Luxury—Central

Phnom Penh's best hotels are located on Monivong Boulevard east of the Central Market and to the southeast on the banks of the Tonle Sap.

Allson Star Hotel: A Singapore-managed hotel in an ideal location with 68 rooms fixed with satellite TV, IDD telephone, safe, and minibar. 128 Monivong Blvd., tel. (23) 362008, fax 362018, US$85-140.

Landmark Boulevard Hotel: Among the newest hotels in town with all possible facilities two blocks east of the Central Market. 63 Preah Norodom Blvd., tel. (23) 428462, fax 428506, US$90-160.

Luxury—River

Several luxurious hotels have opened southeast of the Royal Palace near the Tonle Sap.

Royal Phnom Phen Hotel: A small, 40-room Thai-managed hotel with plans to add another 300-room wing and swimming pool to compete with the Sofitel property. 26 Samdech Sothearos Blvd., tel. (23) 360026, fax 360026, US$150-240.

Sofitel Cambodiana: Phnom Penh's leading hotel has 280 rooms, three restaurants, several bars, swimming pool, tennis courts, CNN news, and a health center—an amazing touch of luxury on the banks of the Tonle Sap. Originally designed for guests of Prince Sihanouk, construction was halted after Lon Nol's 1970 coup and the shortsighted Khmer Rouge failed to appreciate its money-making potential. Currently managed by the French Sofitel group. 313 Sisowath Quay, tel. (23) 426288, (800) 221-4542 in the U.S., fax (23) 426392, US$160-340.

RESTAURANTS

Phnom Penh hotels and local cafes serve local and Western dishes at reasonable prices and the selection continues to improve with time.

Budget

Some of the most authentic Khmer cooking is found at the night markets, while inexpensive cafes often attached to guesthouses serve Western dishes and a small selection of local dishes.

Night Markets: Join the locals for Khmer specialties at food markets which open at sunset along Monivong Boulevard near Wat Koh and just south of Sihanouk, and along Sihanouk near Victory Monument. Avoid water, ice, and uncooked vegetables.

Phnom Khiev: Perhaps the best inexpensive Khmer cafe in Phnom Penh owned and operated by Cambodians who formerly ran a popular restaurant in France. 138 Sihanouk Boulevard. Open daily 0600-2200.

Kim Ly: Cozy cafe with a fabulous selection of over 100 Chinese, Khmer, and Western dishes with a few French desserts thrown in for the coup de grâce. 336 Monivong Boulevard. Open daily 1000-2300.

Asian International: International fare with an emphasis on Malaysian specialties served in a cool and quiet escape one block south of Pasar Chan. 96 118 Street. Open daily 0700-2200.

Lotus Cafe: Indian curries and Muslim halal vegetarian plus great cheese pizzas and non-vegetarian dishes in a great setting overlooking the Tonle Sap just east of Wat Phnom. 121 Samdech Sothearos Boulevard.

CAMBODIA

Apsara Restaurant: Tasty Khmer dishes prepared by Ms. Malee Um, a Cambodian-American who returned home a few years ago and set up shop just under the Foreign Correspondence Club. 361 Sisowath Quay, tel. (23) 360274.

Cafe No Problem: A colonial mansion with a bar, billiard tables, and a pricey French restaurant upstairs called La Maison. 55 178 Street, tel. (23) 27250. Open daily 0800-0200.

Moderate

Phnom Penh has dozens of cafes and restaurants generally serving Western fare at Western prices.

Raksmey Boeng Kak: Several good cafes are perched around the amusement park at the eastern edge of Boeng Kai Lak and just west of the reconstructed Chruoy Changvar Bridge. Specialties include Khmer-style frogs' legs, spicy crabs, steamed lobster, buffalo steaks, fried baby eels, crispy rice birds, and crunchy crickets served in breezy open-sided huts erected on rickety jetties. Open daily 1000-2300.

Green Room: Well-prepared Western dishes and a reasonably priced luncheon buffet on the ground floor of the Pailin Hotel. 219 Monivong Boulevard. Open daily 0700-2200.

Happy Herb's Bistro: American-style bistro with steaks, chops, burgers, and 17 varieties of pizza including a "double happy Happy Herb pizza." Good atmosphere and convenient riverside location near Phnom Penh Tourism. 345 Sisowath Quay, tel. (23) 62349.

Ponlok: Next to the Rock Café is a large three-story restaurant popular with expatriates and known for its Chinese and Khmer fare served on balconies overlooking the Tonle Sap. 319 Sisowath Quay, tel. (23) 260501. Open daily 1100-2300.

NIGHTLIFE

Nightlife in Phnom Penh is rather tame and tempts few Westerners, who sensibly avoid needless travel in the evenings. If you decide to explore the city after dark, leave all valuables in your hotel and take a small amount of cash. Avoid hailing cyclos or motos at random but rather take the vehicles waiting directly at the hotel or nightclub.

CINEMA CAMBODIA

Several films and documentaries available on videotape will help you understand the tragedies of modern Cambodia.

The Killing Fields: Directed by Roland Joffe and based on Sydney Schanberg's *The Life and Death of Dith Pran,* this powerful film won an Academy Award for its depiction of the Cambodian holocaust. Schanberg returned and screened the film in Phnom Penh in 1989 during the ill-fated Cambodian Conference in Paris.

Swimming to Cambodia: Spalding Gray, America's famed monologist, used his experiences from the filming of *The Killing Fields* to explore the social and political undercurrents of contemporary Southeast Asia.

Year Zero and *Year Ten:* Two superb documentaries that retell Khmer Rouge horrors in 1979 and a follow-up program released in 1989. Directed by David Muroe and distributed by Central Independent Television.

Khmer Dance: Khmer dance performances are occasionally given at the Chaktomuk Conference Hall near the Cambodiana Hotel and at the Ecole des Beaux Arts campus on 70 Street. Schedules can be checked at the Ministry of Tourism and Phnom Penh Tourism.

Heart of Darkness: This seedy yet lively hangout with creepy decor and demonic atmosphere is favored by backpackers and English teachers. 26 Street 51. Open daily 1800-0200.

Rock Hard Cafe: Good place to relax on the patio overlooking the Tonle Sap or watch CNN news on the satellite TV at the bar. Inexpensive drinks and Western food. Open daily 1000-0200.

Cactus Pub: French-owned pub and restaurant with happy hour specials and a popular salad bar. 94 Sihanouk Boulevard. Open daily 1000-0200.

Irish Rover: Irish pub with imported ales and finger food; look for the shamrock sign. 78 Sihanouk Boulevard. Open daily 1000-0200.

Ettamogah Pub: Not to be outdone by the French and Irish, three Australians run a lively Aussie-themed bar with all the down under touches. 154 Sihanouk Blvd., tel. (23) 362461. Open daily 1000-0200.

Foreign Correspondent's Club: A terrific spot to dine and enjoy outstanding views of the river, read daily English-language newspapers, meet other travelers and expats, and catch one of the weekly movies. Unlike other FCCs in Southeast Asia, this outpost is open to the public. 363 Sisowath Quay, tel. (23) 427757, fax 427758. Open daily 0700-midnight.

Martini Bar: An infamous hostess bar-cum-disco in the southwest part of town with blasting tunes and an inordinate number of single females. 205 Street at 404 Street. Open 0800-0200.

Hostess Clubs: Travelers who want to explore the underbelly of Phnom Penh can visit the "dancing restaurants" (karaoke plus companionship) such as Thai San, B.B. Boss, Toeuk Roam Phakar Roam, and the basement nightclub in the former Ambassador Hotel.

Tuol Kork: The seedy entertainment district north of Boeng Kak Lake is the closest alternative to Svay Pak, 12 km north of Phnom Penh. Even closer are the cafes on 154th Street between Norodom and 51st, and those at 184th and 63rd Streets.

SERVICES

Tourist Information

Your best source of travel information is the cafe under the Capitol Hotel and the staff of the hotel, who can arrange visa extensions as well as taxis for trips to Choeung Ek, Tonle Bati, and Udong.

General Directorate of Tourism: Provides lists of hotels and travel agencies but has very little in the way of useful travel information or brochures. Also known as Cambodia Tourism or the Ministry of Tourism. 3 Monivong Blvd., tel. (23) 426107, fax 426364. Open weekdays 0800-1100 and 1400-1700; Saturday 0800-1200.

Phnom Penh Tourism: Fairly useless outfit set up to help group tours rather than individual travelers. No literature or maps but they might be able to advise on safety conditions and cultural performances. 313 Sisowath Quay, tel. (23) 25349, fax 26043. Open weekdays 0800-1130 and 1400-1700; Saturday 0800-1200.

Money

Currency and traveler's checks can be exchanged at the Foreign Trade Bank and Bangkok Bank near the Central Market, Cambodia Commercial Bank on Monivong Boulevard, and Thai Farmers Bank north of Central Market at various or no service charges. Money changers around the Central Market offer better rates but be wary of dishonest dealers who sometimes attempt to pass counterfeit dollars.

The Cambodia Commercial Bank imposes no transaction fee for credit card advances. American Express is at Diethelm Travel, 8 Samdech Sothearos Blvd., tel. (23) 426648, fax 426676.

Communications

Mail: The GPO near Wat Phnom is open daily 0700-1800 while their international phone and fax center is open 24 hours. Courier services include DHL at 28 Monivong, UPS at 8 Street 184, and TNT at 139 Monireth Boulevard.

International Telephone: International calls can be made from Telstra phone booths at the GPO, Ministry of Tourism, and most upscale hotels. Calls cost US$4-6 per minute from the GPO. Phones use phone cards sold at most hotels. Phnom Penh phone numbers recently added either a 3, 4, or 7 to the beginning of the old number.

Internet: Internet e-mail facilities are available at the CCC on 178th Street a few blocks east of Monivong. Messages cost US50 cents per kilobyte each direction.

Newspapers: Recent news about security conditions is reported in the *Phnom Penh Post, Cambodia Times,* and *Cambodia Daily,* while English-language newspapers and magazines can be purchased in supermarkets and gift stores.

Bookstores: Books on Cambodia and Southeast Asia are sold at Bookazine, Cambodia's largest bookstore, at 228 Monivong Boulevard. Useful details are included in the *Guide to Phnom Penh* by the Women's International Group and sold at the 77 Supermarket on 90th near Monivong. Used books can be picked up at Bert Books & Guesthouse, 79 Samdech Sothearos Boulevard.

Diplomatic Offices

Phnom Penh has over 20 embassies and consulates. Visas for Vietnam, Laos, and Thailand are best picked up with the aid of your guest-

CAMBODIA

house or hotel. Western embassies request notification if you intend to travel to remote or dangerous areas.

- **Australia,** 11 Street 254, tel. (23) 26254
- **China,** Issarak at Street 163, tel. (23) 26271
- **France,** Monivong at Street 76, tel. (23) 26278
- **Germany,** 76 Street 214, tel. (23) 26381
- **India,** 777 Monivong Blvd., tel. (23) 25981
- **Japan,** 75 Norodom Blvd., tel. (23) 27161
- **Laos,** 15 Issarak Blvd., tel. (23) 26441
- **Malaysia,** 161 Street 51, tel. (23) 26167
- **Thailand,** 4 Monivong Blvd., tel. (23) 26182
- **United Kingdom,** 29 Street 75, tel. (23) 27124
- **United States,** 27 Street 240, tel. (23) 26804
- **Vietnam,** 436 Monivong Blvd., tel. (23) 25481

Immigration

Cambodian visas are best extended with the help of your guesthouse or hotel but can be done in person at their office at Street 200 near Norodom Boulevard. Visa extensions range from one week (US$20) to six months (US$100) and take three days to process.

Medical Services

Health care in Cambodia remains poor and serious emergencies generally require evacuation to Bangkok or Singapore. Western-style clinics which can help with minor problems include IMC Clinic at 83 Issarak Blvd., mobile tel. 015-912765, associated with SOS International, and Access Medical Services at 203 Street 63.

TRANSPORTATION

Air

Phnom Penh is served by over a dozen international airlines including the national carriers of Cambodia, Vietnam, Laos, Thailand, Malaysia, Singapore, and Hong Kong.

Tickets are best purchased from guesthouses, hotels, or travel agencies but you can also visit the airlines and make your own reservation. Regional airlines include Royal Air Cambodge at 206 Norodom near Wat Tham, Thai International at 19 Street 106 near Wat Phnom, Dragon Air at

19 Street 106, Vietnam Airlines at 35 Sihanouk Blvd., and Lao Aviation at 58 Sihanouk near Victory Monument. Airline offices in hotels include Malaysia Airlines in the Diamond Hotel, Air France in Sofitel Cambodiana, Silk Air in Pailin Hotel, and Aeroflot in Allson Hotel.

Flights leave daily to Siem Reap, Ko Kong, and Sihanoukville, and three times weekly to Kratie, Stung Treng, Kampot, and Battambang. Domestic departure tax is US$5.

Bus

Buses to Ho Chi Minh City (Saigon) leave daily at 0530 from the ticket office near the intersection of Street 182 and Street 211, east of Orasey Market and shown on the map of Phnom Penh. Buses to Battambang, Sihanoukville, and Takeo depart daily from the Central Market.

Train

Trains to Battambang depart alternative days at 0600 and take 12-15 hours with stops in Romeas, Pursat, and Moung. Trains for Sihanoukville also leave alternative days and stop at Takeo and Kampot.

Trains are somewhat risky since diesels double as mine sweepers and most passengers ride on top of coaches or on flatbeds in *front* of the engine. Unless you intend to help clear mine fields in Cambodia, find another form of transportation.

River

Boats operated by Golden Sea Shipping of Malaysia race daily to Siem Reap (six hours), Kompong Cham (two hours), and Kratie (four hours). Service is provided to Stung Treng when waters are high. Water transport is generally safe but expect delays during the dry season from March to July when captains must slowly navigate around sandbars and exposed rocks.

Tickets can be purchased from most guesthouses and travel agencies.

Taxi

Share taxis are the most popular way to reach coastal destinations such as Kep, Kampot, and Sihanoukville, and the Vietnamese border at Bavet. Share taxis to Bavet depart from the Central Market, the stop east of Monivong Bridge, and cost US$5-10 per person depending on the number of passengers crammed into the car. Allow three hours to the border, 30 minutes for paperwork, and another two hours by taxi to Ho Chi Minh City.

Taxis can also be hired to tour Cambodia for US$20-35 per day from the Capitol Hotel and at more exorbitant rates from the Sofitel Cambodiana.

Around Phnom Penh

Cyclos and motos (motorcycles) to most destinations cost US$1 or US$1-2 per hour. Cyclos are slow while most moto drivers have a poor sense of direction and can't speak English. It's best to hire a moto driver near a popular guesthouse or hotel who can speak English and provide a sensible tour around the city without getting lost.

Bicycles and motorcycles can be rented from guesthouses and several shops on Monivong Boulevard. Bikes are a breezy way to tour the city but motorcycles are risky since passports are required as deposit and theft is commonplace; to replace a stolen Honda 100cc Dream runs US$1,200 while replacing a Honda 250cc will set you back US$2,500.

Night travel should be limited to taxis or motos which operate from the front doors of guesthouses and hotels. Armed robberies of Western visitors are on the rise in Phnom Penh.

EXCURSIONS FROM PHNOM PENH

The following sights are single-day journeys from Phnom Penh by motorcycle, bus, or share taxi from the Central or Olympic markets. An experienced motorcycle guide is your best bet to quickly reach the attractions and return to Phnom Penh before nightfall.

CHOEUNG EK

From 1975 to 1979, the murderous Khmer Rouge slaughtered almost 20,000 Cambodians at the Choeung Ek extermination camp, most clubbed to death to save ammunition. A memorial stupa exhibits thousands of Cambodian skulls exhumed from mass graves located in nearby orchards and ricefields, plus the remains of six Americans, three French, two Australians, and one Brit, who were caught up in the national nightmare.

Choeung Ek, 17 km south of Phnom Penh, costs US$5 roundtrip by motorcycle taxi or US$10 roundtrip by taxi, which can be split between several passengers.

TONLE BATI

Tonle Bati

Tonle Bati, a large recreational waterpark 35 km south of Phnom Penh, is deserted during the week but packed on weekends when Khmer families from Phnom Penh arrive to rent bamboo shacks elevated over the lake and spend the day consuming fried chicken, roasted fish, and beer.

Ta Phrom/Yeah Peau

Khmer temples situated at Tonle Bati include Ta Phrom, constructed by King Jayavarman VII (1181-1201) over the site of a 6th-century Khmer shrine. Not up to Angkor Wat standards but still worthwhile, Ta Phrom was originally consecrated by Jayavarman as a Buddha temple but later dedicated to Brahma after Hinduism was embraced by the noble elite.

Ta Phrom, a complex structure with multiple buildings enclosed within two concentric galleries, includes a central sanctuary of five chambers encasing statuary and Hindu lingams, and the Hindu images of Preah Noreay and bas-reliefs of parables from the life of Jayavarman and his consorts.

Yeah Peau, the lesser temple at Bati Lake, is dedicated to the fishermen's daughter, a beautiful woman who bore the son of Jayavarman and the subsequent governor of Takeo province.

Ta Phrom and Yeah Peau, 35 km south of Phnom Penh and three km west of Highway 2, can be reached by bus, motorcycle, or taxi from the Central Market. Transport should cost US$15 by share taxi, not including tips demanded by soldiers and amputee beggars.

CAMBODIA

PHNOM CHISOR

Phnom Chisor, south of Phnom Penh and east of Highway 2, is an 11th-century temple constructed by King Suryagiri and dedicated to Brahma. Phnom Chisor and two lower temples—Sen Thomol and Sen Ravang—were transformed to serve Buddhism, as shown by the interior reclining image inappropriately hidden behind modern, poorly crafted Buddhas.

Buses and share taxis head 55 km south to Prasat Neang Khamu and the wonderfully named Temple of the Black Virgin, where motos continue six km east to Phnom Chisor.

UDONG

Udong (also spelled Oudong) served as the capital of Cambodia from 1618 to 1866 under a series of rulers including King Ang Douong (reigned 1845-55) and his son, King Norodom.

Over the centuries, each dynasty erected temples and continued the construction of a royal palace. Prior to the Cambodian conflict of the 1970s, structures included Viharn Preah Chaual Nipean with its immense reclining Buddha, Tan San Mosque maintained by Cham Muslims, and Phanom Chet Ath Roeus, dedicated by King Sisowath and known for its nine-meter Buddha. Most of these monuments were severely damaged or completely destroyed when Lon Nol launched air strikes against Khmer Rouge hideouts.

Today, Udong offers the ruins of Phanom Chet Ath Roeus (sans the nine-meter Buddha) and a memorial to some 1,000 Cambodians murdered here by the Khmer Rouge and dumped into mass graves.

Udong, 40 km northwest of Phnom Penh along Route 5, can be reached by taxi for US$20.

COASTAL TOWNS

KAMPOT

Kampot, five km from the ocean on the banks of the Tuk Chhou River, is a transit town which largely escaped the mass destruction of the Khmer Rouge. Although it has rebounded with a growing population of fishermen and farmers, Kampot has little of interest aside from a handful of crumbling French-era blue-shuttered shops and villas.

Hotels around the dusty traffic circle in the center of town include the Phnom Kamchay, Phnom Khieu, and Tuk Chhou, which has a restaurant and a seedy nightclub. Kampot, 150 km south of Phnom Penh, can be reached in five hours by share taxi and seven hours by train.

Kampot and Kep are still considered dangerous areas and Western visitors should inquire with authorities before making the journey. Since there is a measure of safety in numbers, both places are best visited on weekends when residents of Phnom Penh deluge the area.

KEP

Once Cambodia's premier beach resort, Kep was, prior to its destruction by the Khmer Rouge, the favorite escape of French colonialists and wealthy Cambodians who came to gamble, yacht, water-ski, and dive in the warm waters. Prince Sihanouk maintained a residence on the hill, still visible but in ruins.

Kep today is a largely deserted and eerie place—weeds poke through the old casino, the Kep Hotel stands empty, and Cambodian fishermen cook meals over open fires in the shells of palatial French villas. Investors are talking about fixing the place up, but at present there's little here but a rather mediocre beach, a few simple guesthouses and restaurants, and proof of a world gone mad.

Kep, 155 km south of Phnom Penh and 25 km southeast of Kampot, can be reached by moto from Kampot.

SIHANOUKVILLE

Sihanoukville, a rapidly expanding commercial center and beach resort, was founded in 1964—helped along by the road built from Phnom Penh to the coast with the American aid. Today the expansive town is undergoing massive changes as money pours in to expand the shipping port and overseas investors arrive to build hotels, a Club Med, and a US$400 million casino on nearby Naga Island.

Sihanoukville offers the best beaches in the country—long stretches of pure white sand backed by swaying palm trees. Boats can be rented to reach nearby islands, which offer excellent snorkeling and diving; check at Sam's Guesthouse just south of the port.

Accommodations
Over 20 guesthouses and hotels are now in operation, chiefly along the southern coastline—the area with the finest sand and water. Accommodations from west to east include the hillside Sam's Guesthouse (US$4-6), Kamsab Hotel (US$30-40), Koh Pos Hotel (US$25-35), the recently renovated Independence Hotel on the main beach (US$40-50), Seaview Hotel (US$10-15), Sokha Bungalows (US$20-40), Hong Kong Hotel (US$20-40), Seaside Hotel (US$25-40), and Eagle's Nest with a/c rooms and satellite TV (US$25-35).

Transportation
Sihanoukville is 230 km from Phnom Penh on Route 4.

Royal Air Cambodge flies several times weekly for US$40 one-way. Air-conditioned buses leave Phnom Penh daily at 0630 and 1300, and take 3-4 hours depending on the number of checkpoints. Taxis from Phnom Penh's Dang Kor Market take three hours and cost US$20. Buses terminate at the bus terminal in the commercial center known weirdly as "Sihanoukville Town," from where motos can be hired to any of the guesthouses and hotels.

CAMBODIA

ANGKOR

Angkor—the colossal and powerful center of the ancient Khmer empire—is the cultural and spiritual heart of the Cambodian people and one of the world's great architectural achievements.

Situated seven km north of Siem Reap, the widely scattered monuments have tantalized Western travelers since 1858 when Henri Mouhot, a French naturalist, stumbled across the ruins and then wrote an account of his voyage and discovery. Today, monuments of the Khmer civilization continue to amaze thousands of visitors who manage to break through the bureaucratic webs and political turmoils which still ensnare the Khmer nation.

SIEM REAP

The town of Siem Reap ("Siamese Defeated") serves as the base for visits to the 100-plus monuments which constitute the empire of Angkor. Siem Reap was badly damaged and largely abandoned during the Khmer Rouge era but has since rebounded and now receives over 50,000 annual visitors.

Angkor Conservancy

The only notable attraction near Siem Reap is the government agency responsible for the restoration and protection of the monuments, located 1.5 km north of Siem Reap. The conservancy trains guides and stores thousands of statues in its guarded compound, which can be visited but only with written permission from the Ministry of Culture in Phnom Penh.

Budget Accommodations

Many of the old French-constructed hotels, including the venerable Auberge Royale and the Hotel Air France, were destroyed by the Khmer Rouge in the late 1970s, but Thai and Cambodian entrepreneurs are now renovating the surviving structures and constructing new facilities for the anticipated upturn in tourism. Siem Reap now has over 20 budget guesthouses and a score of hotels which cater to group tours. Guesthouses are located on Vithei Wat Bo (also

called Achar Hem Chiev) two blocks east of the river, along Vithei Sivutha between the old French quarter and Route 6, and along Route 6 west of Vithei Sivutha. All of the following guesthouses charge US$4-6 for small but adequate rooms and US$10-20 for rooms with a/c and hot showers.

Mahogany Guesthouse: A half-dozen guesthouses are lined up on the road east of the river, yet Mahogany remains the favorite for its expansive verandah, mahogany walls, and small but perfectly clean rooms. 593 Vithei Wat Bo, US$4-8.

Sunrise Guesthouse: High ceilings, Western bathrooms, and friendly managers make this a popular choice east of the river. 592 Vithei Wat Bo, US$4-6.

Mom's Guesthouse: Motherly care and highly polished mahogany floors plus laundry service and complimentary drinking water. 99 Vithei Wat Bo, US$4-6.

Garden House: Khmer homestyle setting and lush tropical gardens attract the more contemplative crowd. 129 Vithei Wat Bo, US$4-6.

Apsaras Angkor Guesthouse: An excellent find about 50 meters west of the bridge near a string of guesthouses superior to those on Vithei Wat Bo. Apsaras has over 20 rooms in the old and new wings with clean bathrooms and ceiling fans to move the heat. 279 Route 6, US$4-8.

Chenla Guesthouse: As tourism moves upscale, Chenla adds new rooms fitted with a/c and private bathrooms to complement their less expensive cubicles in the front building. 260 Route 6, US$4-15.

Villa Royal: Superior to most guesthouses, Villa Royal has a/c rooms furnished with writing tables, hot showers, and mini-refrigerators. 13 Vithei Sivutha, US$13-18.

Moderate Accommodations

Rooms for most of the following hotels can be booked through agents in Phnom Penh and Bangkok.

Koulen Hotel: Popular spot with nightclub, lounge, and 12 a/c rooms with mini-refrigerators and private baths. Route 6, US$30-40.

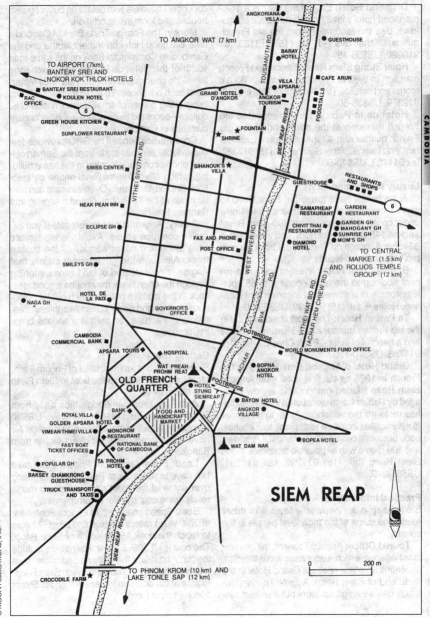

TO ANGKOR WAT (7 km)

ANGKORIANA VILLA

TOUSAMUTH RD.

BARAY HOTEL

GUESTHOUSE

Cambodian Commercial

TO AIRPORT (7km), BANTEAY SREI AND NOKOR KOK THLOK HOTELS

CAFE ARUN

RAC OFFICE

KOULEN HOTEL

BANTEAY SREI RESTAURANT

VILLA APSARA

FOODSTALLS

GRAND HOTEL D'ANGKOR

ANGKOR TOURISM

GREEN HOUSE KITCHEN

SUNFLOWER RESTAURANT

FOUNTAIN

SHRINE

SIEM REAP RIVER

VITHEI SIVUTHA RD.

SIHANOUK'S VILLA

GUESTHOUSE

RESTAURANTS AND SHOPS

6

SWISS CENTER

NEAK PEAN INN

SAMAPHEAP RESTAURANT

GARDEN RESTAURANT

ECLIPSE GH

CHIVIT THAI RESTAURANT

GARDEN GH

MAHOGANY GH

SUNRISE GH

MOM'S GH

FAX AND PHONE

WEST RIVER RD.

DIAMOND HOTEL

TO CENTRAL MARKET (1.5 km) AND ROLUOS TEMPLE GROUP (12 km)

POST OFFICE

SMILEYS GH

HOTEL DE LA PAIX

NAGA GH

GOVERNOR'S OFFICE

SIVA RD.

VITHEI WAT BO RD. (ACHAR HEM CHIEV RD.)

FOOTBRIDGE

CAMBODIA COMMERCIAL BANK

APSARA TOURS

HOSPITAL

WAT PREAH PROHM REAT

WORLD MONUMENTS FUND OFFICE

ACHAR

BOPHA ANGKOR HOTEL

OLD FRENCH QUARTER

HOTEL STUNG SIEMREAP

FOOTBRIDGE

ROYAL VILLA

BANK

BAYON HOTEL

GOLDEN APSARA HOTEL

VIMEAN THMEI VILLA

FOOD AND HANDICRAFT MARKET

MONOROM RESTAURANT

ANGKON VILLAGE

FAST BOAT TICKET OFFICES

NATIONAL BANK OF CAMBODIA

BOPEA HOTEL

POPULAR GH

TA PROHM HOTEL

WAT DAM NAK

BAKSEY CHAMKRONG GUESTHOUSE

TRUCK TRANSPORT AND TAXIS

SIEM REAP RIVER

SIEM REAP

0   200 m

TO PHNOM KROM (10 km) AND LAKE TONLE SAP (12 km)

CROCODILE FARM

© MOON PUBLICATIONS, INC.

CAMBODIA

CAMBODIA

Diamond Hotel: East of the river is a Thai-managed hotel with 27 comfortable a/c bungalows. Use the footbridge from the old French quarter. Achar Sva Rd., tel. (15) 913130, fax 910020, US$35-45.

Hotel Stung Siem Reap: Renovated French mansion in the old French quarter with 33 a/c rooms and satellite TV. Wat Prohm Rd., tel. (15) 912379, US$35-50.

Hotel de la Paix: A lovely renovated old French mansion at the north end of the old French quarter with 40 spacious rooms, restaurant, and lounge. Vithei Sivutha, tel. (15) 912322, fax 911783, US$40-50.

Luxury Accommodations

Upscale hotels have arrived in Siem Reap to serve individuals and group tours. Hotels now under construction include the 300-room Royal Angkor, 145-room Chedi Hotel, and the exclusive 32-room Auberge du Temple; the latter two are projects of AmanResorts.

Banteay Srei Hotel: West of town is a recent addition to the hotel scene with 55 spotless rooms in a somewhat inconvenient location. Route 6, tel. (15) 913839, US$55-80.

Ta Prohm Hotel: The most upscale hotel in the old French quarter has 58 luxurious rooms and a handful of suites. Psah Chas St., tel. (15) 911783, US$70-120.

Grand Hotel d'Angkor: Constructed by the French in 1928 as the first hotel near Angkor, Siem Reap's faded grand dame is now managed by Raffles International of Singapore, which has restored the venerable hotel to its former glory. Facilities include a restaurant, tour agency, pool, business center with fax and IDD phones, and 300 rooms with all possible amenities. North Siem Reap, tel. (15) 911292, fax 911291, US$65-240.

Practical Information

Siem Reap is a sleepy little town with dusty roads and some of the friendliest people in the country.

Tourist Office: Angkor Tourism, the government agency which supervises local tourism, maintains an office near the Grand Hotel in the north end of Siem Reap. Angkor Tourism primarily deals with group tours but also helps independent travelers with details on budget guesthouses and local transportation.

Money: The Foreign Trade Bank of Cambodia near Bakheng Hotel on Vithei Sivutha and the Cambodian Commercial Bank on the same road south of the Hotel de la Paix both exchange traveler's checks and provide Visa and MasterCard cash advances. To avoid transaction fees, bring along plenty of small denomination U.S. dollars—accepted everywhere is the secondary currency of Cambodia.

Communications: The GPO provides few dependable services aside from the Samart cellular phone company located in the same building, which offers international phone connections at exorbitant rates. Overseas calls can also be made at the Ta Prohm, Grand d'Angkor, and Banteay Srei Hotels.

Safety: Angkor is reasonably safe if you exercise common sense. Avoid visiting remote sites alone and never wander off the beaten track. Although the government claims that Angkor is now cleared of land mines, running through the open fields may not be a good idea; stick to the trodden paths. Watch out for poisonous snakes and never collect "worthless" fragments of the ruins; art theft is a serious crime in Cambodia.

Getting There

Siem Reap is 311 km northwest of Phnom Penh. Most travelers take a speed boat to Siem Reap and return by air.

Air: Royal Air Cambodge flies daily from Phnom Penh for US$50 one-way, US$90 roundtrip. Thai International and Bangkok Air have announced plans for direct flights from Bangkok.

Land: Share taxis from Phnom Penh take two days to reach Siem Reap via Battambang over some of the most dangerous and rough roads in the country. Not recommended.

Boat: Speed boats depart Phnom Penh daily at 0700 when waters run high and take 5-7 hours to reach the dock 15 km south of Siem Reap. The cost is US$30. Slower alternatives include the "fast" boat and the aptly named "slow" boat which can take 18-36 hours to reach Siem Reap. Inquire at the docks at the eastern end of Street 108 in Phnom Penh.

THE MONUMENTS

Angkor has an estimated 300 monuments widely scattered throughout the jungle in all directions from Siem Reap. Three days are necessary to visit the three most important sites: the Bayon and Baphuon, which essentially comprise the ancient city of Angkor Thom, Ta Prohm and Preah Khan just outside the city walls, and Angkor Wat to the south of the former capital.

Many visitors first visit the Bayon and Baphuon, two immense temple complexes which face east and are best toured in the fine light of the early morning hours.

Ta Prohm and Preah Khan, outside the perimeter of Angkor Thom, can be visited as side trips between Angkor Thom and Angkor Wat.

Angkor Wat, which faces west, is best visited and photographed in the late afternoon, though several visits are necessary to really appreciate the amazing spectacle.

Admission Fees
Admission fees are US$20 for one day, US$40 for three days, and US$60 for one week. Tickets can be purchased at one of three entry checkpoints, Siem Reap airport, or from Angkor Tourism in Siem Reap.

Transportation
Angkor can be toured with a variety of hired transportation.

Motorcycle: Experienced motorcyclists can rent Honda 70cc and 90cc models for US$5 a day through most guesthouses. Those without motorcycle experience should bring along a driver/guide for an additional US$2 per day.

Bicycle: Bicycles cost US$2 per day from guesthouses, a great way to see the ruins if your bicycle is in dependable condition and you get a very early start.

Car: Cars with driver cost US$25-45 per day, plus an extra US$15-20 for a guide. Travel agents, Angkor Tourism, and many hotels and guesthouses can arrange cars in Siem Reap.

History
Between the 9th and 13th centuries, Southeast Asia from Burma to Indochina and from China to

---

TEMPLE SYMBOLISM

A ngkor was not only a city but, more importantly, an immense representation in stone of Hindu cosmology whose mythological symbolism was intended to preserve spiritual harmony between the gods and mankind.

All major monuments at Angkor can be visualized as magical mandalas that represent the Hindu-Buddhist universe: the central shrines symbolize Mt. Meru, the celestial paradise of both Hindu and Buddhist deities; the gates and cloisters depict the successive outer envelopes of cosmic reality; moats represent the seven oceans which form concentric rings around the holy mountain.

And, similar to Borobudur in Java, causeways and staircases carry the pilgrim on a journey through the mythological worlds of mankind toward the realm of the supreme god.

Malaysia was controlled by a powerful Khmer empire centered just north of the Tonle Sap River.

Angkor's original capital was established in 802 by a Khmer king named Jayavarman II, who made Hinduism the state religion and crowned himself the reincarnation of Shiva. Jayavarman's concept of a god-king—perhaps a combination of Saivite concepts of divinity and older megalithic beliefs—set the style for succeeding rulers who, at times, considered themselves the earthly representatives of Shiva, Vishnu, and ultimately, the Buddha.

Although chiefly noted for its wondrous architecture and sculpture, Angkor was also an immense technological achievement from which central Cambodia derived its agricultural prosperity. By creating an elaborate and highly sophisticated system of lakes, channels, and irrigation canals which radiated from Tonle Sap, the Khmer empire grew into one of the wealthiest and most powerful empires on the face of the earth. Utilizing its vast resources and tens of thousands of slaves, Khmer kings initiated a 400-year building spree which left the world with splendid baroque palaces, towering monuments, royal mausoleums, vast lakes, magnificent highways, and hundreds of immense temples bursting with diamonds, rubies, and gold.

Bantai Srei and the Bakheng—mystical mountains along the lines of Borobudur—were constructed in the 10th century. King Suryavarman II constructed his masterpiece, Angkor Wat, in the early 12th century, though the immense effort and cost almost bankrupted his nation.

It was left to Angkor's final great king, Jayavarman VII, to revitalize the empire and construct his magnificent royal city of Angkor Thom. Breaking all previous Khmer traditions, Jayavarman placed himself under the patronage of Mahayana Buddhism and adopted as his patron deity one of the Buddhist bodhisattvas.

Angkor declined after the reign of Jayavarman, but today the enigmatic faces of Lokesvara, Buddhist Lord of the World, still smile and gaze wondrously over the four directions of the world.

Angkor Wat

The most spectacular and best preserved of Angkor's temples is the self-contained universe of Angkor Wat, erected by Suryavarman II (reigned 1112-52) to honor himself and the Hindu god Vishnu. Angkor Wat is approached from the west along a magnificent road lined with colossal balustrades carved like cosmic serpents.

Recently restored by the Archaeological Survey of India, the complex rises in three concentric enclosures behind the western gate, which is almost as large as the central shrines. An entire day can be spent wandering around the terraces and pinnacles studying the Hindu deities, bullet scars, and row of Buddhas ungraciously decapitated by the Khmer Rouge.

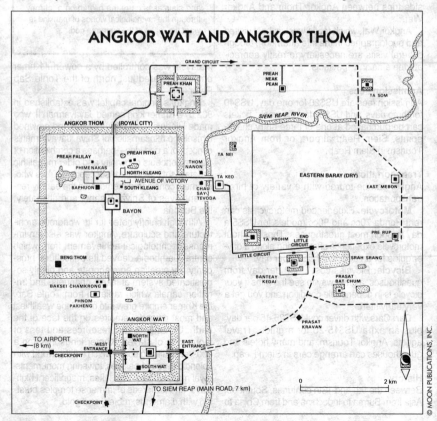

ANGKOR WAT AND ANGKOR THOM

© MOON PUBLICATIONS, INC.

MONUMENTS
OF
ANGKOR

PHNOM BOK

ROLUOS RIVER

ROLUOS
VILLAGE

TO PHNOM KULEN
35 km

BANTEAY
SAMRE

TO KOMPONG THOM
146 km

LOLEI

PREAH KO

BAKONG

CAMBODIA

TO BANTEAY SREI
20 km

TA SOM

EAST BARAY (DRY)

EAST MEBON

TA PROHM

GRAND CIRCUIT

PREAH
NEAK PEAN

LITTLE

CIRCUIT

PREAH KHAN

BAYON

ANGKOR THOM

ANGKOR WAT

BENG
THOM

SIEM REAP

RIVER

CHECKPOINT

CHECKPOINT

PROPOSED TOURISM
DEVELOPMENT ZONE

SIEM REAP

CENTRAL
MARKET

TO PHNOM KROM AND
LAKE TONLE SAP 12 km

PHNOM BAKHENG

CHECKPOINT

CHECKPOINT

WAT THMEY/
KILLING FIELDS
MEMORIAL

ANGKOR CONSERVANCY
(STORAGE BUILDING)

GRAND HOTEL

WALL

WEST MEBON

WEST BARAY

BOAT RENTAL

WALL

WALL

WALL

AIRPORT

TO SISOPHON
103 km

6

0   3 km

= ROAD IN FAIR CONDITION

= DIRT ROAD / ROAD IN BAD CONDITION

= MAJOR ARCHAEOLOGICAL SITES

© MOON PUBLICATIONS, INC.

Perhaps the most spectacular creation is the kilometer-long relief sculpture in the open colonnaded gallery which tells of Hindu epics, Suryavarman's earthly glory, celestial dancing maidens called *apsaras,* fish and flowers, ghastly *makara* demons, arabesque plants, and Vishnu presiding over a tug-of-war between the armies of Khmer good and evil—an appropriate symbol of contemporary Cambodian life.

Phnom Pakheng

Those walking from Angkor Wat to Angkor Thom may want to climb this 65-meter hill for excellent views over the Angkor plains. Highly recommended at sunset.

Angkor Thom (Royal City)

The final and most baroque creation of the Khmers was the Royal City of Angkor Thom, which consists of the central temple, the Bayon, a secondary and older temple called the Baphuon, and several elaborate terraces and victory towers enclosed within ancient city walls.

Though several of the structures are older, the building frenzy of Angkor Thom reached its pinnacle during the reign of King Jayavarman VII (1181-1200), greatest of all Khmer constructionists and the final ruler before the Khmer empire collapsed into economic and spiritual ruin.

Although much of the city has disappeared into the jungle, Angkor Thom once ranked among the most colossal cities anywhere on earth: a million people spread across an area of 10 square km, 12 km of massive walls and wide moats which protected the population against foreign marauders, and two immense artificial lakes (the Western and Eastern Barays) far vaster and more sophisticated than anything seen before in Asia. Angkor Thom was a planned city of greater complexity and spaciousness than any in medieval Europe—larger and perhaps more populous than the whole of ancient Rome.

The Bayon

Focal point and mystic center of the royal city is the temple-mountain of the Bayon, chiefly noted for its 54 powerful four-sided Towers of Faces. Each of the 216 countenances bears the same blank image: Jayavarman as the reincarnation of the Buddha, eyes closed and with an enigmatic and disturbing smile.

The Bayon also features over 1,200 meters of stupendous bas-reliefs carved on the outer walls of the central sanctuary and inner walls of the laterite enclosure. Symbolic differences between the two series of reliefs are noted by the first terrace carvings, which depict realistic tableaux of common life and historical events, and the inner walls, which relate the epic worlds of gods and legends.

And yet, the Bayon's great achievement appears not in its sheer size or hastily carved murals, but in the stupendous architectural arrangement that represented the universe and kingdom—religion and state combined in a single symbol.

The Baphuon

The temple-mountain of King Udayadityavarman II (reigned 1050-66) predates Angkor Wat and the Bayon and, as such, once represented one of the most colossal works of man in the world.

Today, however, it is difficult to appreciate the past splendor since most of the complex has collapsed into a vast accumulation of stone and chaotic ruin. The blame lies with the inadequate technical skills of Khmer architects who erected the monument on an unsteady artificial hill and employed primitive support structures rather than the corbeled arches then known to the Western world.

Royal Enclosure and Phimenakas

From the Baphuon, walk past the moats and through the southeastern gate of the Royal Enclosure into the immense rectangular yard which once formed the heart of the ancient Angkor empire.

Centerpiece of this forbidden city is the now-dilapidated Phimenakas, the pyramidal "Palace of the Winds" constructed by Rajendravarman (reigned 944-968) but later used and embellished by all subsequent kings.

Terrace of the Elephants

Dominating the eastern wall of the Royal Enclosure, some 200 meters north of the Baphuon, is a 350-meter-long terrace once used as a royal audience hall and review stand for public ceremonies. Constructed by Suryavarman I, the terrace derives its name from the bas-reliefs of elephants and rows of life-sized lions and winged garudas which once supported the royal pavilion.

Terrace of the Leper King

Anchoring the northeastern corner of the Royal Enclosure is a seven-meter platform richly carved with dancing *apsaras* and bands of mythological animals which frequented the subterranean slopes and upper elevations of Mt. Meru, Hindu center of the universe.

Perhaps constructed as a cremation tower for Angkorian aristocracy, the platform is surmounted by a mysterious and completely sexless image believed to represent either Shiva, the Hindu god of death, or Yasovarman, founder of Angkor. The original now resides in the courtyard of the National Museum in Phnom Penh.

In any event, the naked and lichen-embalmed image conveys a surrealistic impression of advanced leprosy.

Ta Prohm

The remainder of the widely scattered monuments at Angkor are a long hike from Angkor Thom, but visitors with enough time might follow the Avenue of Victory to the following temple just south of the Eastern Baray.

All of the mystery and romance associated with Angkor is epitomized by this 12th-century temple, which has graciously been allowed to disappear into the jungle. Consumed by gigantic trees and split by destructive vines, Ta Prohm is one of the last great unrestored sanctuaries in the East, an amazing journey back to a lost world.

Ta Prohm was constructed by King Jayavarman VII (ruled 1181-1200) to honor his mother, represented here as Prajnaparamita, the reincarnation of perfect wisdom. A stele discovered at the site indicates the former glory and sheer immensity of the project: 566 stone dwellings, 39 major sanctuaries, 18 chief abbots, 2,740 priests, 2,202 assistants, and 615 dancing girls engaged in service to the priests.

The highly complex plan involves a great variety of buildings enclosed within a series of concentric galleries. The chief structures include several libraries and a central sanctuary of five chambers encasing statuary or Hindu lingams.

All these monuments have collapsed into magnificent ruins; one of the real highlights of Angkor.

CAMBODIA

Some men go skimming over the years of existence to sink gently into a placid grave, ignorant of life to the last, without ever having been made to see all it may contain of perfidy, of violence, and of terror.

—JOSEPH CONRAD,
HEART OF DARKNESS

To many people holidays are not voyages of discovery, but a ritual of reassurance.

—PHILIP ADAMS,
AUSTRALIAN AGE

Countries, like people, are loved for their failings.

—YEATS,
BENGAL LANCER

HONG KONG

He who travels far will often see things far removed from what he believed was Truth. When he talks about it in the fields at home, he is often accused of lying, for the obdurate people will not believe what they do not see and distinctly feel.

—HERMAN HESSE,
JOURNEY TO THE EAST

We are all guilty of crime, the great crime of not living life to the full. But we are all potentially free. We can stop thinking of what we have failed to do and do whatever lies within our power.

—HENRY MILLER

Why do people travel? To escape their creditors. To find a warmer or cooler clime. To sell Coca-Cola to the Chinese. To find out what is over the seas, over the hills and far away, round the corner, over the garden wall.

—ERIC NEWBY,
A TRAVELLER'S LIFE

INTRODUCTION

Once described by the queen's foreign secretary as a "barren rock with hardly a dwelling upon it," Hong Kong today is a land of startling juxtapositions: old and traditional lifestyles set slap-dash against the dynamic world of modern commerce; an exotic backdrop for Hollywood movies; a highly urbanized environment of Eastern lifestyles and Western conveniences; a Chinese city of soaring skyscrapers constructed over the ruins of a colonial outpost; one of the world's most intense, high-strung, frustrating, and fascinating destinations.

At midnight on 30 June 1997, the British Crown Colony of Hong Kong became the Hong Kong Special Administrative Region of China (SAR). Despite the change of leadership, Hong Kong remains an essential Asian destination and one of the world's most popular vacation spots.

Hong Kong is a shoppers' paradise of Chinese craft stores, quality boutiques, and factory outlets overflowing with the trendiest jeans and the latest high-tech wonders. For roaming gourmets with a sense of adventure, Hong Kong offers a wide range of Oriental and Occidental restaurants which serve everything from snake soup to chauteaubriand. There are temples and *tao* and *tai chi* for those interested in Chinese culture, while the enormous range of nightlife options make Hong Kong one of Asia's most exciting cities after dark. Sightseeing beyond the urban core ranges from rural villages and hiking trails to pristine sand beaches and giant water slides. Finally, Hong Kong is a surprisingly easy place to explore, since many of its citizens speak English and public transportation is well organized.

But visitors lured by Hollywood's image of Suzi Wong or the standard tourist hype will be in for a shock. In today's Hong Kong, Chinese junks are powered by noisy diesel engines, the rickshaw pullers only serve as photographers' models, and Suzi plays the stock market while waiting for her exit visa. Nothing stays the same. Locked in a perpetual state of demolition and massive reconstruction, Hong Kong is a place where the national bird is the construction crane and the national anthem the clatter of the jack-hammer. "It'll be a great city when they finish building it."

Situated on little more than 1,000 square km, Hong Kong is both highly urbanized and extra-ordinarily *crowded;* several of its neighborhoods

HONG KONG

HONG KONG, CHINA

GUANGDONG PROVINCE
(SHENZHEN SPECIAL ECONOMIC ZONE)

TO GUANGZHOU

SHENZHEN

LO WU

KCR RAILWAY

LOK MA CHAU

DEEP BAY

SHEKOU

TAI PO MARSHES

LAUFAUSHAN

YUEN LONG

PING SHAN

KAM TIN

SHEK KONG

TO GUANGZHOU

NIM WAN

NEW TERRITORIES

CHING CHUNG KOON TEMPLE

★ MUI FAT MONASTERY

▲ *TAI MO SHAN*
(957 m)

TUEN MUN

▲ *CASTLE PEAK*

TSUEN WAN

TO MACAU

TSING YI ISLAND

CHEK LAP KOK AIRPORT

AIRPORT RAILWAY

EXPRESSWAY

DISCOVERY BAY

PENG CHAU

TUNG CHUNG

ISLAND

MUI WO

SILVERMINE BAY

TAI O

PO LIN MONASTERY

LANTAU

CHEUNG CHAU

YUNG SHUE WAN

LANTAU CHANNEL

SOKO ISLANDS

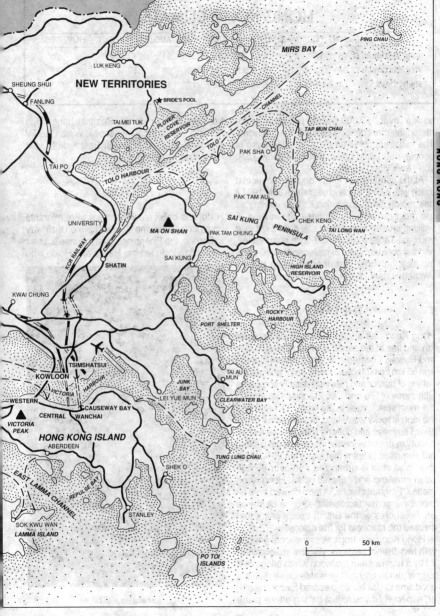

MIRS BAY

PING CHAU

LUK KENG

SHEUNG SHUI

FANLING

NEW TERRITORIES

★ BRIDE'S POOL

TAI MEI TUK

PLOVER COVE RESERVOIR

TAP MUN CHAU

TAI PO

TOLO CHANNEL

TOLO

PAK SHA O

TOLO HARBOUR

PAK TAM AU

CHEK KENG

UNIVERSITY

MA ON SHAN

SAI KUNG

PENINSULA

TAI LONG WAN

PAK TAM CHUNG

KCR RAILWAY

SHATIN

SAI KUNG

HIGH ISLAND RESERVOIR

KWAI CHUNG

ROCKY HARBOUR

PORT SHELTER

TSIMSHATSUI

KOWLOON

HARBOUR

VICTORIA

JUNK BAY

TAI AU MUN

WESTERN

LEI YUE MUN

CLEARWATER BAY

CENTRAL

WANCHAI

CAUSEWAY BAY

VICTORIA PEAK

HONG KONG ISLAND

ABERDEEN

TUNG LUNG CHAU

SHEK O

EAST LAMMA CHANNEL

REPULSE BAY

STANLEY

0   50 km

SOK KWU WAN

LAMMA ISLAND

PO TOI ISLANDS

© MOON PUBLICATIONS, INC.

HONG KONG CLIMATE

	JAN.	FEB.	MAR.	APR.	MAY	JUNE	JULY	AUG.	SEPT.	OCT.	NOV.	DEC.
Avg. Maximum C	18°	17°	19°	24°	28°	29°	31°	31°	29°	27°	23°	20°
Avg. Maximum F	64°	62°	66°	75°	83°	84°	88°	88°	84°	81°	73°	68°
Rainy Days	4	5	7	8	13	18	17	15	12	6	2	3

pack in over 150,000 people per square kilometer, the most densely populated in the world. The initial impact is an overwhelming dose of people, neon, and noise. If you like New York, you'll love Hong Kong.

At the same time, Hong Kong has never lost touch with its origins, and ever since July 1997 it has rapidly been assuming its true identity as the most distinctively Chinese city in Asia. A walking tour through almost any district will lead you past Taoist temples, old-style pharmacies, and the constant rattle of mahjong tiles, all serving as a reminder that beneath Hong Kong's Western exterior beats a Chinese heart.

THE LAND

Hong Kong has a land mass of 1,062 square km and lies at the same latitude as Mexico City and Hawaii. Located only 145 km from Canton and 65 km from Macau, Hong Kong's geographic setting of harbor and hills indisputably compares with those of Rio and San Francisco as among the most spectacular in the world. Over 80% of the land is rocky wasteland, though some of the New Territories and outlying islands have a stark beauty in the brisk winter months. Most visitors are surprised to learn that less than 20% of the total land area is urbanized and over 80% is open farmland and national parks. Hong Kong means "Fragrant Harbor," a term derived from either the incense factories that once clustered on the shores or the British opium ships that created the rationale for the colony.

Hong Kong is a tropical, monsoonal country with two distinct seasons. Winters are dominated by a northeastern monsoon which brings cool temperatures and an agreeable dryness. It's a good time to visit but be prepared for cold weather, especially if you're just getting off the plane

from Bangkok or Manila. Summer brings high humidity and tropical monsoons. Watch the TV and take cover at signal 8. Best time to visit Hong Kong is spring or fall.

HISTORY

Historians believe early settlers were migrants from north China who stopped here on their way to Borneo, the Philippines, and Indonesia. Later migrations included the Hakka and Hoklo who

lips sealed with tar

MAN MO TEMPLE, HOLLYWOOD ROAD

Man Mo Temple

established their farms in the New Territories, followed by the Cantonese who set up their fishing villages at Aberdeen. During the early 16th century, the great commercial potential of the harbor attracted both the Portuguese and the English. In 1557 the Chinese rulers in Peking awarded the trading post of Macau to the Portuguese and a century later allowed the Europeans to establish a mercantile settlement near Canton. It was a profitable but problematical arrangement. The soaring popularity of tea forced the English to import a great deal of Chinese leaf and the Chinese government, being wary of the intentions of foreign devils, began demanding silver as payment. Faced with a deepening trade imbalance, the British proposed an immensely dirty but incredibly profitable solution: sell opium to China's two million drug addicts. Although an unsavory occupation, a certain degree of respectability was maintained by holding opium auctions in Calcutta and letting private British traders export the drugs to China. The history of Hong Kong shows that Noriega and the Colombian drug barons weren't the first to appreciate the advantages of a syndicated drug cartel.

Two of the most successful opium runners were William Jardine and James Matheson, Scottish merchants who were religious in a strict Calvinist way but completely indifferent to moralistic reflections. With the efforts of the Scots and other British merchants, opium exports to the Chinese soon soared to over 50,000 chests per year. Alarmed at the reversal of their economic fortunes, the government in Peking sent an aggressive anti-opium general to clean up the situation in Canton. He promptly dumped thousands of opium chests into the ocean, an act of economic outrage which touched off a series of Opium Wars and treaties which gave the British their foothold in Hong Kong. Looking for a trading post outside Chinese or Macanese control, a young British captain named Charles Elliot annexed the rocky and unwanted island of Hong Kong. In an ironic twist of fate, Elliot discovered his policies so accommodative and his barren rock so worthless that he was ultimately banished to a desolate Texas outpost!

The British proceeded to take Hong Kong in slow but steady bites. In 1842 the Chinese were forced to sign the Treaty of Nanking, which awarded Hong Kong Island to the British in perpetuity. The Convention of Peking in 1850 ceded the Kowloon Peninsula and a final treaty in 1898 gave Britain a 99-year lease on the New Territories. A government opium monopoly was established in 1913 and the trade remained legal in Hong Kong until 1946.

While enjoying a measure of prosperity during the 1920s, Hong Kong was actually the poor stepsister to Shanghai, that glittering yet doomed metropolis strategically located on the Yangtze River. Hong Kong's fortunes changed dramatically with the arrival of WW II. After a short struggle at the now-demolished Repulse Bay Hotel in 1941, the Japanese invaded and with little re-

SIGHTSEEING HIGHLIGHTS

The average visitor stays only 3-4 days in Hong Kong and spends over 60% of the time on Hong Kong's number-one attraction—shopping. Much better: stay a week and discover what makes Hong Kong the most visited city in Southeast Asia. It's not surprising that with so little time most first-time visitors are confused by local geography and place-names. A quick look at the four general areas (Kowloon, Hong Kong Island, New Territories, Outlying Islands) and townships in each area will help you get a handle on the place.

KOWLOON

This densely packed neighborhood of high-rise buildings and rushing crowds is the territories' leading hotel and restaurant area.

Tsimshatsui: This is where you'll find most of Kowloon's hotels, nightlife, and restaurants. Gourmets will love the culinary treats, whether dining at roadside stalls or in five-star restaurants. Tsimshatsui (pronounced Chim-Sa-Choy) also has a new history museum, an impressive cultural center, and, of course, shopping. A good place to start is on Nathan Road, a tree-lined neon strip so packed with shops that it's been nicknamed the Golden Mile; it's a shopping zone where even the deepest of credit cards can run aground in a single afternoon. Bargainers will find lower prices in the night markets of Mongkok and the small factory shops hidden inside Kaiser Estates.

New Tsimshatsui: Directly east is New Tsimshatsui, a landfill project now blanketed with expensive hotels and vast shopping centers. A memorable experience is walking the waterfront promenade as lights blink on at sunset.

Yaumatei and Mongkok: Fifteen minutes north of Tsimshatsui is Yaumatei, a less touristy neighborhood of working-class shops, historic temples, and the famous jade market. Of special note is a walking tour through side streets that still exude some of the flavor of old China. Mongkok, a densely packed neighborhood north of Yaumatei, offers craft stores, brothels, and less expensive hotels. Top pick up here is the Temple Street night market, a nightly happening that typifies what is most exotic and exciting about the territory.

Beyond Kowloon: More sights are located north of Boundary Road, the geographic boundary that separates Kowloon from the New Territories. Temple aficionados will enjoy the architecture of Wong Tai Sin, considered by many Hong Kong's most impressive temple. Also of interest are the Sung Dynasty Village in Lai Chi Kok and seafood restaurants in Lei Yue Mun.

HONG KONG ISLAND

Hong Kong is a geographic term that confuses both locals (who can't decide whether to spell it "Hong Kong" or "Hongkong") and visitors who mix up Hong Kong (the entire territory) with Hong Kong (the island). The mountainous and highly urbanized *island* of Hong Kong is divided into several townships with distinct histories and personalities.

Central: The economic and political capital of

---

sistance conquered Hong Kong. Treatment by the Japanese was so harsh that over one million Chinese fled back into the rural safety of China and Hong Kong's population fell to less than 500,000.

Mao's triumph in 1947 sent waves of refugees back to Hong Kong, including the wealthy industrialists of Shanghai with their financial expertise and vast sums of capital. Hong Kong exploded during the '50s, growing to over five million residents by the end of the decade. Tremendous strains were placed on social services, sanitation, and housing as thousands were forced to live as squatters on barren hillsides and in decaying tenements more suited to cattle than human beings. The British government eventually began an ambitious housing program and, within a single generation, the poor and desperate refugees had achieved an economic miracle few people thought possible.

GOVERNMENT

Prior to the takeover by China, Hong Kong was a British territory headed by a governor appointed by the Queen who was assisted by the Executive and Legislative Councils. There were few politi-

Hong Kong offers a botanical garden, trendy nightlife in the area called Lan Kwai Fong, and some of the world's most striking modern architecture. Looming over the glass-and-steel statuary is Victoria Peak, perhaps the island's best place to escape the crowds and survey the dazzling panorama.

Western: Situated just 15 minutes west is the Western district, a traditional neighborhood of Chinese drugstores, old teahouses, snake restaurants, ginseng emporiums, elderly gentlemen dressed in silk pajamas, and other reminders of old Hong Kong. A highly recommended walking tour is fully described in the text.

Causeway Bay: Causeway is the main hotel, dining, and shopping area for visitors who want to stay on Hong Kong Island rather than in Kowloon. Hugging the landfilled harbor are chic department stores, luxury hotels, and literally hundreds of restaurants with cuisine from Thai to Tunisian. Causeway Bay's other attractions include the weird and wonderful sculptures at Aw Boon Haw and the racetrack in Happy Valley.

Wanchai: The boozy nightlife-and-restaurant area first made famous by Suzi Wong and the movie of the same title is now much less sinful and exotic; most of the girlie joints have been replaced with yuppie bars and Filipino discos. The Wanch has several excellent middle-priced hotels and is conveniently located between Causeway Bay and Central and within easy walking distance of the new convention center.

South Side: Mere minutes from the hustle and bustle of Central you'll find the famous floating community of Aberdeen and expatriate towns of Stanley and Deepwater Bay. Hong Kong's most popular and crowded beaches are located over here. The south side also offers Southeast Asia's largest leisure complex and several country parks with spectacular sea views from wooded hiking trails.

NEW TERRITORIES

North of Kowloon are the New Territories, a hard and rocky land of planned cities firmly rooted in the 21st century and small villages clinging to lifestyles little changed from past centuries. You can explore a temple with more than 10,000 Buddha images or visit protected marshlands filled with various species of migratory birds. A circular day-trip by public bus gives a quick glimpse into this land between.

OUTLYING ISLANDS

Almost completely unknown to the average visitor are the 236 outer islands. All are unhurried places of peaceful walks, Buddhist temples, and wide-open spaces . . . near nirvana after the noise and confusion of Hong Kong. The major islands are linked to Hong Kong and Kowloon by ferries of all types and sizes. Best of the lot is Cheung Chau, a delightful Mediterranean island with great charm and character. Lantau, the largest island in the territory, offers superb hiking opportunities and several relatively untouched villages. A third stop could be made at Lamma just south of Hong Kong Island. All have hotels for overnighters or could be quickly visited on day excursions.

cal parties or special-interest groups until a few years before the transfer of power. Many said that the real power in Hong Kong resided with the Jockey Club, Jardine and Matheson, the Hong Kong and Shanghai Bank, and the governor—*in that order*. Hong Kong lacked political motivation and nationalist fervor; there was no national anthem, pledge of allegiance, or large standing army. Elections attracted so little interest that less than 20% of the population registered to vote and less than a quarter of those turned out on election day. No wonder there was so little concern among most citizens when Hong Kong reverted back to mainland Chinese rule.

Under the terms of the Joint Agreement signed a few years ago by Britain and China, Hong Kong became a Chinese possession at exactly midnight on June 30, 1997. The Joint Agreement, together with the Basic Law, supposedly allows Hong Kong to keep its capitalist system for 50 years with a promise of local autonomy as a Special Administrative Region within the People's Republic of China. Under this "one-country, two-system" arrangement, China has promised that private property, ownership of enterprise, rights of inheritance, and foreign investment will be protected by law and that Hong Kong will remain a free port and international financial center with unrestricted foreign exchange and securities markets. Legal and governmental sys-

WHAT'S CHANGED, WHAT HASN'T

From the visitor's point of view, the Hong Kong Special Administrative Region is no more difficult, nor less fascinating, than the British Crown Colony of Hong Kong. Visa regulations have remained unchanged (except of course that Chinese rather than British consulates will accept applications), and Hong Kong retains the use of its own currency linked to the US dollar. English is still an official language and English signage will be maintained aside from some organizations, which will drop the "Royal" title. And of course the stunning array of sights, including the spectacular skyline, haven't disappeared and aren't likely to no matter what. Hong Kong is too big and powerful and energetic a place to vanish overnight—and vanishing seems to be the last thing it has on its mind.

Post-handover changes focus on the political system. Instead of a governor appointed by London, the SAR is run by a chief executive appointed by Beijing. The old Legislative Council has been replaced by a Provisional Legislature, which shares more than half of the original Legco's members.

According to the Basic Law, Hong Kong retains full autonomy except in matters of foreign affairs and defense. While People's Liberation Army Soldiers have replaced British troops at 14 locations throughout the SAR, they keep a low profile. Domestic security is still maintained by the Hong Kong Police. Hong Kong will keep its separate membership in organizations like the World Trade Organization, and is negotiating for the right to send a "Hong Kong, China" Olympic team.

The legal and judicial system remains the same, based on common law, although the Chinese language has finally been introduced to the courtroom. China is retaining strict border controls to avoid a deluge of immigrants, or even visitors—Chinese still need a special permit to visit the Motherland's latest acquisition, much to their disappointment. According to the terms of a 1995 agreement, 55,000 mainland Chinese will be allowed to settle in Hong Kong each year—a number large enough to strain Hong Kong's overburdened housing resources, yet hardly significant in the big picture.

---

tems are comprised of local people, ruled by a Hong Kong chief executive appointed by Beijing. The Basic Law serves as a sort of mini-constitution, as interpreted by the National People's Congress in Beijing.

Chief Executive
Tung Chee Hwa, a shipping tycoon who was a favorite of Beijing, serves as Hong Kong's first post-1997 leader. Shanghai-born and a refugee from Communist China in 1949, Tung is considered a skilled and honest executive but also critical of democracy and human rights campaigners.

Legislature
The Legislative Council, often called Legco, is the only institution in Hong Kong ever to have enjoyed even a modicum of democracy. For a long time all of its members were either civil servants or appointees, but in 1991, in response to demands provoked by the Tiananmen Square massacre, 18 of its 60 seats were directly elected, a first for Hong Kong.

The 1995 Legco was originally supposed to sit its full four-year term, but the Chinese gov-

ernment, irritated at a unilateral British decision to implement democratic reforms, dissolved Legco on 1 July 1997, replacing it with a hand-picked Provisional Legislature.

Judiciary
The judicial branch remains the least changed by the handover. Chinese has been introduced into court proceedings, but English common law will theoretically remain the basis of practice for the next 50 years. The traditional court attire has also been retained—Chinese tourists reportedly adore the justices' horsehair wigs. A local Court of Final Appeals has replaced Britain's Privy Council as the ultimate arbiter, although China's National People's Congress has the power to overrule its decisions in "acts of state"—a vague clause which could be interpreted a number of ways.

ECONOMY

As the second leading economic power in Asia after Japan, Hong Kong is a testament to what purely unregulated, unbridled, and untamed capitalism can do. The complete lack of natural resources—except for its excellent harbor and energetic work force—makes the economic miracle of Hong Kong all the more remarkable. The economy continues to grow at 6-10% yearly or 3-4 times the rate of most Western countries. Hong Kong's per capita GDP was over US$24,000 a year in 1996, considerably higher than its former colonizer, Britain.

Hong Kong is a textbook value-added economy that imports raw goods and exports finished products to every place on the globe. It's also a more impressive industrial miracle than postwar Japan, since it lacks both a hinterland from which raw materials could come and a large population to absorb its products. Business is religion and Mammon its only god. Marx would have called the citizens of Hong Kong unrepentant petit bourgeois, but unlike Christians, Muslims, or Marxists, the Chinese of Hong Kong have never suffered shame in the pursuit of wealth.

Despite the new bosses in Beijing, Hong Kong's economy is almost completely free of government supervision—there are few import or export duties, incorporation is so easy that one could register a business in the morning and be making profits by lunchtime, and consumer goods remain largely untaxed aside from a handful of luxury items. Beijing seems content, at least for the present, to continue the laissez-faire economics of the previous captains—even during the economic meltdown of October 1997.

Hong Kong's economy, like her skyline, has changed radically in recent years. Many of the British-controlled *hongs* that once sold opium to the Chinese are now controlled by Chinese millionaires who sell their high-quality products back to the British. The Hong Kong and Shanghai Banking Corporation still represents British economic power in the Orient, but its dominance has been surrendered to Chinese and American banking firms.

HONG KONG'S VANISHING PEOPLES

Hong Kong's minority groups include the fishermen and farmers who wandered down from southern China in the 14th century. First on the scene were the Puntis who claimed the most fertile farming lands in the New Territories. Soon afterwards the Hakka (a term that means "Guest People") arrived to become the largest group in the region. The Hakka's matriarchal society permitted women to engage in construction and other work traditionally reserved for Chinese males. Most Hakkas have now integrated into mainstream society, though some elderly Hakka women still dress in their traditional black pajamalike suits *(samfoo)* and wear distinctive hats framed by black curtains. Another group still to be seen in Hong Kong is the Tanka (called the egg people since they once paid their taxes in eggs), who live in junks moored in typhoon shelters at Aberdeen, Causeway Bay, and Yaumatei. Long discriminated against in precommunist China and refused permission to live on land or intermarry with the local population, these hardy seafolk are now moving into housing projects and abandoning their lives on the sea. The Hoklo are another group of fishermen from southern China.

Hakka collecting alms

FESTIVALS

Hong Kong has over 20 annual religious and state festivals that range from subdued family affairs to riotous street celebrations. Chinese festivals common to both Hong Kong and Singapore are fully described in the Singapore chapter. Note that religious festivals that follow the lunar calendar are very difficult to date on the Western calendar. Exact dates can be confirmed with the Hong Kong Tourist Association.

January

Hong Kong Arts Festival: One of Southeast Asia's largest and most important cultural events. Two weeks of concerts by orchestras, dance companies, and internationally known drama groups. Entertainment is Western rather than Oriental; you might be more interested in the October Asian Arts Festival.

February

Chinese New Year: Moon 1, Day 1. Celebrated at nearly all temples. See the Singapore chapter for more details and information on the meaning of "Moon 1, Day 1."

Birthday of the God of Wealth: Moon 1, Day 2. Nearly all Chinese keep the images of the Kitchen God and the God of Wealth in their homes. People celebrate their birthdays by replacing the images and visiting temples to check on their financial luck for the coming year. The Wong Tai Sin Temple in Kowloon is packed with people shaking fortune-telling sticks and tossing fortune-telling blocks.

Lantern Festival: Moon 1, Day 15. Chinese New Year is traditionally ended with children's lantern contests and illuminated processions throughout Hong Kong. The Society for the Advancement of Chinese Folklore hosts cultural shows at Sung Dynasty Village, Tiger Balm Gardens, Edinburgh Place, the Landmark, and many public parks. Ancestral halls in the New Territories are hung with lanterns by villagers to whom a son was born during the previous year.

March

Birthday of Hung Shing Kung: Moon 2, Day 13. Known as the deity who rules the Southern Seas, the Dragon King is honored with celebrations at several Hung Shing Kung temples such as Ap

HONG KONG TOURIST ASSOCIATION

floating child at Cheung Chau Bun Festival

Lei Chau in Aberdeen, Tai O on Lantau, and Kau Sai in the New Territories.

Birthday of Kuan Yin: Moon 2, Day 19. Celebrated at the Buddhist Ku Tung Temple in Fanling. See the Singapore chapter.

April

Ching Ming Festival: Spring Solstice, often 2 or 3 April. An Ancestor Remembrance Day held twice yearly at Hong Kong cemeteries. Best seen (not photographed) at cemeteries in Aberdeen and Wo Hop Shek near Fanling.

Birthday of Pak Tai: Moon 3, Day 3. Pak Tai is the long-haired Ruler of the North who defeated the Demon King in Chinese mythology. Offerings are made at Stanley, Cheung Chau, and Mong Tseng Wai in the New Territories.

May

Birthday of Tin Hau: Moon 3, Day 23. With over 40 temples dedicated to the Queen of Heaven and

Protector of Seamen, Tin Hau is unquestionably the most popular deity in Hong Kong. Celebrations in her honor include Chinese opera, rocket competitions, giant parades of floral shrines called *fa paau,* and huge fleets of gaily decorated boats. Temple celebrations are staggered over a two-week period. The HKTA has the schedule.

Vesak: Moon 4, Day 8. Buddha's birthday is celebrated with great reverence at the Po Lin Monastery on Lantau Island.

Birthday of Tam Kung: Moon 4, Day 8. Tam Kung, God of Weather and second patron saint of the boat people, is honored at the Shaukeiwan Tam Kung Temple on Hong Kong Island. One of Hong Kong's larger celebrations.

Cheung Chau Bun Festival: Date selected by divination. Held on Cheung Chau Island, this great Buddhist-Taoist festival honors Pak Tai, the ferocious warrior god, with Chinese opera, vegetarian feasts, and a parade of "floating children" surrealistically supported by concealed steel frames. The six-day festival is climaxed with the distribution of thousands of pink and white sweet buns mounted on 30-meter-high bamboo and paper towers that serve as talismans against sickness and bad luck. A decade ago the towers were climbed by young men who picked the buns, but the tradition was abandoned after one of the towers collapsed.

June

Dragon Boat Festival: Moon 5, Day 5. Exciting and highly popular boat races are held off Hong Kong's East Tsimshatsui Waterfront in the first week of June. Entries come from over 100 local teams and two-dozen overseas groups from Rome, Nagasaki, and Chicago.

July

Enlightenment of Kuan Yin: Moon 6, Day 19. Celebrated at Pak Sha Wan in Hebe Haven.

August

Festival of the Hungry Ghosts: Moon 7, Day 15. Hong Kong's largest festival is celebrated with free opera in *matshed* (bamboo) theaters. An outstanding opportunity to watch Chinese opera. See Singapore for background notes.

Food Festival: This month-long culinary extravaganza is another highly successful creation of the Hong Kong Tourist Association. Food bazaars and dining tours are held throughout the territory for both locals and visitors alike. Lan Kwai Fong in Central sponsors a two-day street carnival.

September

Mid-autumn or Moon Festival: Moon 8, Day 15. The HKTA has the locations of officially sponsored carnivals held in public parks.

Birthday of the Monkey God: Moon 8, Day 16. The Monkey God shows himself to believers twice monthly on the first and the 15th, but the day after the Mid-autumn Festival is considered especially propitious. Trance mediums under the influence of the monkey demonstrate their invulnerability by cutting tongues, piercing cheeks, drinking boiling oil, and walking across fire. Held at the Sau Mau Ping Temple near Kwun Tong in Kowloon.

October

Birthday of Confucius: Moon 8, Day 27. Celebrated at the Confucius Hall Middle School on Caroline Hill Road in Causeway Bay.

Cheung Yeung Festival: Moon 9, Day 9. The second annual Ancestor Remembrance Day is held in all cemeteries. Also the a day for climbing hills, a tradition taken from a Han dynasty fable.

Asian Arts Festival: Two weeks of Asian dance, music, and theater. A rare opportunity to see some of the best performing-arts companies in Southeast Asia.

THE PEOPLE

Hong Kong's 6.2 million residents include 1.5 million on Hong Kong Island, 3.1 million on the Kowloon Peninsula, and the remainder in the New Territories and outlying islands. Average population density is a modest 5,170 people per square kilometer, but soars to 30 times that figure in certain neighborhoods in Kowloon. (Shamshuipo is currently the most densely populated, with over 165,000 people per square km—a world record according to Guinness.) Chinese comprise 98% of the present population, the majority of whom are descended from refugees.

Most Hong Kong residents are Cantonese from the southern province of Guangdong. A tough and hardworking people with a lively sense of humor and a healthy zest for life, the Cantonese are considered the culinary geniuses of the Chinese world. The Cantonese dialect—arguably the most difficult to learn, with eight tones instead of the usual four—is the most common, although Mandarin is becoming more commonplace ever since the reversion to Chinese rule.

The next largest group are the Shanghainese, who emigrated to Hong Kong in large numbers after the fall of Shanghai, bringing along their factories (literally) and financial expertise—wealthy industrialists who quickly rose to the top of the economic ladder in their new homeland.

Another large group are the Chiu Chow (Teochew in Singapore), who emigrated from the mainland coastal cities of Shantou and Xiamen on China's southern coast.

Perhaps the greatest demographic changes have occurred in Hong Kong's international community: in 1997, the colony counted some 18,000 American expatriates compared to just under 12,000 Britons.

ON THE ROAD

GETTING THERE

Hong Kong is an important gateway to Asia whether coming from America, Europe, or Australia. Exactly where your plane lands will depend on the date of your arrival and how rapidly the new airport at Chek Lap Kok is able to reach full capacity.

Arrival at Kai Tak Airport
Kai Tak, also called Hong Kong International Airport, will be missed by many travelers who enjoyed the amazing and dramatic descent which almost scraped the rooftops of nearby apartment buildings. If you arrive while Kai Tak is still in operation (late 1998), you will need to go through immigration and customs formalities, and can then stop at the Hong Kong Tourist Association (HKTA) counter for maps, brochures, and their weekly magazine.

Hotel vacancies can be checked at the Hong Kong Hotel Association counter, though this doesn't include budget dorms or hostels; their cheapest rooms start at around HK$500. Budget travelers can use the free public phones to check on cheaper facilities, a wise idea if you arrive late at night when vacancies may be scarce.

Departure tax is HK$100 for adults.

Getting Into Town: Kai Tak is 20-30 minutes from Kowloon and 40-50 minutes from Hong Kong Island.

Inexpensive and comfortable KMB Airbuses to most hotels leave every 15 minutes 0700-2300.

There are nine different buses as described on the HKTA brochure, *From Airport to Hotel.* No tickets are issued and passengers must have exact change for the fare-collection box (HK$7-19). Change and route details can also be picked up from the Airbus service center, just outside the terminal exit.

Airbus A1 goes to hotels in Tsimshatsui (Ambassador, Peninsula, Regent, YMCA Salisbury, and Chungking Mansions); Airbus A2 reaches Central and Wanchai hotels (Mandarin, Marriott, Furama, Harbour View International House); Airbus A3 covers Causeway Bay hotels (Excelsior, Lee Gardens, Ramada, Park Lane Radisson). A computerized tape message announces the stops in various languages—a nicely surrealistic introduction to Hong Kong.

Taxis cost HK$45-55 to Kowloon hotels, HK$80 to Central Hong Kong, and HK$100 to Wanchai. Extra surcharges are collected for baggage and tunnel fees.

Arrival at Chek Lap Kok Airport
Flying into the new airport on the north side of Lantau Island may not be as dramatic as flying into Kai Tak, but visitors will unquestionably be amazed by the new airport—a US$30 billion infrastructure project considered one of the world's greatest engineering feats.

Passengers are greeted by a spacious, winged passenger terminal situated on 1,248 hectares of reclaimed land jutting out into the South China Sea. They then proceed quickly along the concourse by travelators to the immigration and baggage claim areas. After customs, visitors enter the arrival hall where they can change currency, make accommodation bookings at the Hong Kong Hotel Association counter, arrange car rentals, and gather information from the Hong Kong Tourist Association.

Airport accommodations are provided at the new HK$2 billion Regal Hotel, with over 1,200 rooms. Nine additional hotels with a total of 5,000 rooms are planned for development along the new expressway which leads to Kowloon and Hong Kong Island.

Getting Into Town: From the arrival hall, passengers move directly into the transportation center, the focal point for all surface transport and the location of the Airport Express Line (AEL) station. Bus tickets can be purchased at the bus counter, though most visitors prefer to take the AEL, which provides speedy transport to Kowloon and Hong Kong's Central business district. No ordinary journey, the route passes over the new Tsing Ma Bridge—the world's longest (1,377 meters) road-and-rail suspension bridge— and alongside the 4.2 km West Kowloon Expressway, offering a whole new perspective of the spectacular Victoria Harbour. The entire 34-km journey to either Kowloon or Hong Kong Island takes just 23 minutes.

GETTING AROUND

Hong Kong's unusual geography and dense population have brought about one of the world's

most efficient and colorful transportation systems. In fact, some of the ferries, streetcars, and funiculars have become tourist attractions in themselves. Because of low fares and the government's policy of discouraging private car ownership almost everybody uses public transport, something you'll notice at rush hour when all systems are standing room only.

Water Transport

Star Ferry: Some of Hong Kong's leading tourist attractions are the green-and-white ferries which began linking the island with Kowloon in 1898. Since then they've starred in almost every movie made about the former colony. All of these historic workhorses, including *Twinkling, Celestial,* and *Golden Star* operate daily 0630-2330. First-class upstairs costs HK$1.40 and is preferred by photographers, but the downstairs section at HK$1.20 allows a look into the chugging engine room. Tsimshatsui to Central takes eight minutes, while the service to Wanchai provides a convenient link to the Hong Kong Convention Center.

Walla Wallas: After the Star Ferry stop, late-night options for shuttling between Central and Kowloon include the MTR (service ends at 0100), public buses (all night), or water taxis called walla wallas (all night). Named for either their coughing engine or the Washington town where the original craft was built, walla wallas leave from the Queen's Pier east of Star Ferry in Central and cost around HK$10 per head.

Outlying Islands Ferries: Over 100 double-decker ferries link Hong Kong with the outer is-

porters with Tai Pan

HONG KONG TOURIST ASSOCIATION

HONG KONG

lands of Cheung Chau, Lamma, and Lantau. Most departures are from the Outlying Districts Ferry Pier on Hong Kong Island, a 10-minute walk west of the Star Ferry.

Ferries to Macau depart from the Macau Ferry Terminal in Central. Jetcats and overnight ferries to Guangzhou depart from the China Ferry Terminal at China Hongkong City in Kowloon.

Mass Transit Railway (MTR)

The 60-km underground MTR provides the quickest way to cross the harbor and reach distant shopping districts. The MTR operates daily 0600-0100; tickets cost HK$3-15. Stored-value tickets, sold in various denominations, can also be used on the Canton-Kowloon Railway. The HKTA publication, *MTR Tourist Guide,* describes how to reach over 40 tourist attractions using buses, trams, and the MTR.

Buses and Trams

Buses: Hong Kong's lumbering British-built, double-decker buses run everywhere 0600-midnight. Destinations are painted on the front. Drop the exact fare in the metal box next to the driver and head upstairs for the best views.

Hong Kong Island Tram: This 86-year-old institution, which chugs along the north side of the island, is one of the best trips in town, especially up front on the top deck. Enjoy this ride while you can—these time machines won't last much longer.

Victoria Peak Tram: Another fascinating experience is the century-old funicular railway, which leaves every 10 minutes 0700-midnight from the terminus on Garden Road near Hong Kong Park. Tickets cost HK$10 one-way and HK$16 roundtrip. Avoid weekends and holidays when lines are long.

Taxis and Trains

Taxis: Hong Kong's 15,000 red-and-silver taxis are convenient and reasonably priced for shorter journeys but can quickly drain the wallet on cross-island jaunts. Taxis can be hailed on the street and at orderly queues near bus stops and ferry terminals. Available taxis are noted by a red For Hire flag on the meter or an illuminated Taxi sign on the roof; wadded rags over meters indicate an "extra charge" during rainstorms and rush hours. Surcharges include HK$5 for luggage, HK$20 for Cross Harbour Tunnel, and HK$1 per minute of waiting.

Kowloon-Canton Railway (KCR): The KCR departs every 10 minutes 0600-midnight from the recently upgraded Hung Hom Terminal in Kowloon. An excellent way to explore the New Territories, popular stops include Shatin (10,000-Buddha Monastery, Shatin Racetrack), University Station (Tolo Harbor Cruise, University Museum), Tai Po (carpet factory), and Fanling. Five daily expresses go to Guangzhou.

Rickshaws: A small cluster of old men and their colorful contraptions still gather at the ferry concourse on Hong Kong Island, and although few visitors are willing to pay HK$50 for a ride around the block, you might want to pay their HK$10 modeling fee. Be prepared to bargain and don't attempt candid photos unless you're using a very long lens—these guys are *quick*. Rickshaw licenses have not been issued since 1975.

TRAVEL PRACTICALITIES

Visas

Visas are unnecessary for most Westerners who are automatically granted one-month visas on arrival, British citizens who receive six-month permits, and Commonwealth subjects who receive three months.

Travelers wishing to stay beyond their visa-free period should apply for a visa at their nearest Chinese embassy or consulate before traveling to Hong Kong. This includes anyone intending to enter employment, establish a business, or enter school as a student.

Tourist Information

The Hong Kong Tourist Association (HKTA) has offices at the new airport, Star Ferry Terminal in Kowloon, and at Jardine House in Central. Its headquarters is in Citicorp Centre, North Point, 18 Whitfield Road, tel. (852) 2807-6543, fax 2806-0303. HKTA offers a deluge of maps, magazines, and brochures including *Places of Interest by Public Transport, Central and Western District Walking Tour, Yaumatei Walking Tour,* and *Visitors Guide to Chinese Food in Hong Kong.* Upcoming cultural shows are listed in their magazine, *Hong Kong.*

A superb resource for current travel information is the HKTA Web site at http://www.hkta.org. You can access the latest information on upcoming festivals, visa requirements, and rates from all the hotels which belong to the Hong Kong Hotel Association (HKHA). Also check the Web site of the HKHA at http://www.hkta.org/hkha.

Other useful publications include the gossipy rag, *Hong Kong Tatler,* and *TV and Entertainment Times,* which includes listings of upcoming arts events. Better libraries include the Urban Council Public Library at City Hall and the British Council Library in Wanchai.

Maps
The best map to the region is Periplus's *Hong Kong plus Kowloon* followed by *Hong Kong Official Guide Map* from the Survey Office of the Buildings and Lands Department. Highly recommended for hikers and backpackers are the *Countryside Series* of topographic maps published by the same group. These show hiking trails, campsites, and youth hostels throughout the territories.

The *Hong Kong Guidebook* by Universal Press is comprehensive, as is the *Map of Hong Kong Territory and Kowloon* from the same group. Universal's *Hong Kong Arrival Survival Map* provides quirky advice similar to the Nancy Chandler maps of Thailand. Good stuff, if they survive.

Money
The Hong Kong dollar (HK$) has been set against the U.S. dollar since 1983, at a rate that fluctuates within a penny of HK$7.80 per U.S. dollar.

INTERNATIONAL CLOCK

Hawaii	-17
California	-15
New York	-12
Europe	-8
Israel	-6
Thailand	-1
Japan	+1

Service charges and exchange commissions vary anywhere from 1-8% at banks, licensed money changers, airport stall, and hotels. Sidewalk vendors charge the highest rates to compensate for high rents, counterfeit notes, holdups, and losses from currency fluctuations. Exchange rates at the airport are also lousy; change only US$20. Banks generally offer the best rates.

Beware of money changers who offer exceptionally good exchange rates. Signs posted with misleading rates and deceptive sales gimmicks are commonplace. "No charge on buy orders" and "no buying commission" doesn't mean commission-free exchanges but rather hefty "buying commissions." The situation is tricky. Unless you have money to burn, *always* check exactly how many Hong Kong dollars you will get before handing over your money.

Mail
Hong Kong has an extremely honest and efficient postal system. The Kowloon post office is at

---

HONG KONG TOURIST OFFICES

Australia: 80 Druitt St., Sydney, N.S.W. 2000, tel. (02) 9251-2855

Canada: 9 Temperance St., Toronto, Ontario, M5H 1Y6, tel. (416) 366-2389

France: 55 rue François, 75008 Paris, tel. (01) 4720-3954

Germany: Humbolt Strasse 94, D-60318, Frankfurt/Main, tel. (069) 959-1290

Italy: Via Monte dei Cenci 20, 00186 Roma, tel. (06) 688-013-36

Japan: Toho Twin Tower, 152 Yurakucho, Chiyoda-ku, tel. (03) 3503-0731

New Zealand: P.O.B. 2120, Auckland, tel. (09) 575-2707

United Kingdom: 125 Pall Mall, London SW1Y 5EA, tel. (0171) 930-4775

U.S.A.: 610 Enterprise Dr., Oak Brook, IL 60521, tel. (630) 575-2828
    590 Fifth Ave., New York, NY 10036, tel. (212) 869-5008
    10940 Wilshire Blvd., Suite 1220, Los Angeles, CA 90024, tel. (310) 208-4582

405 Nathan Road, though the most convenient office is at 10 Middle Road behind the Ambassador Hotel.

The General Post Office (GPO) is in Central next to the Star Ferry at 2 Connaught Place. Post restante letters go here unless another address is specified on the envelope. Postal offices are open Monday-Friday 0800-1800 and Saturday 0800-1400.

Telephone

Local calls are free from private phones and cost HK$1 from public phones. Phone numbers change often in Hong Kong but directory assistance can be contacted for the latest information. International phone calls can be made from hotels, private phones, and 24-hour Hong Kong Telecom offices located in Kowloon on Middle Road and in Central at One Exchange Plaza.

To call overseas from Hong Kong, dial 001 (international access code), country code (1 for the U.S. and Canada), area code, and the local number. To call Hong Kong from abroad, dial 001, 852 (Hong Kong country code), then the local number.

IMPORTANT TELPHONE NUMBERS

Directory Assistance	1081
Emergency	999
Police	999
Ambulance	999
Collect Calls	010
Calling Card	011
IDD Service	013
HKTA	2801-7171
HK Ferry	2542-3081
MTR	2750-0170
KCR	2602-7799
Star Ferry	2366-2576

KOWLOON

Legend relates that after Emperor Ping of the Sung Dynasty counted eight dragons on the hills of Hong Kong and then added one more for his Imperial Self, Kowloon became known as Gau Lung ("Nine Dragons"). Situated at the southernmost tip of the Kowloon Peninsula and seven minutes by ferry from Hong Kong Island, this is where most of the territory's hotels, shopping centers, and restaurants are found.

Kowloon is also one of the world's most crowded cities, with over two million people packed into just 12 square km, a population density almost 20 times greater than that of most Western cities. No matter what hour of the day or night you leave your hotel, it will seem that a large percentage of Kowloon's population is also out there, mixing, moving, and shoving in unison, making it almost impossible to go in any direction other than that of the majority. Westerners accustomed to giving way to the other person should quickly abandon that courtesy and learn to walk Hong Kong-style: charge straight toward oncoming pedestrians and avoid direct eye contact. Just before collision, rotate your shoulder *away* from the other person and make a modest brushing contact. After some practice you should be handling the crowds with ease.

ATTRACTIONS

Kowloon's best diversion is people-watching: bargaining with vegetable vendors, washing clothes in aluminum pots, eating noodles, burning hell notes at the temple, pulling tourists into dimly lit bars, tearing down buildings less than 10 years old. Kowloon is several distinct neighborhoods. Tsimshatsui West has tourist hotels and restaurants; Tsimshatsui East offers super-luxury hotels and expensive nightclubs; Yaumatei is the place for temples and walking tours, Mongkok for nightlife, brothels, and street markets.

Tsimshatsui

The Hong Kong Tourist Association (HKTA) at Star Ferry has maps, brochures, magazines, schedules for upcoming festivals and free cultural performances. International newspapers are sold out front.

Railway Clock Tower: Aside from this nostalgic reminder, the Kowloon-Canton Train Station was torn down decades ago for a quartet of modernistic buildings that form the cultural heartland of Hong Kong.

Hong Kong Cultural Centre: A ski-sloped and highly controversial 100-seat concert hall, 1,750-seat theater, arts library, and cinema with windowless details that guarantee bad *feng shui*.

Hong Kong Museum of Art: Hong Kong's cultural center features six exhibition galleries with old photos, modern art, and the Xubaizhai Collection donated by a local art collector. Highly recommended.

Hong Kong Space Museum: A silly golfball-shaped hall with interactive exhibits and planetarium. Across Salisbury Rd. you might find Mr. Chan Chong-chi, the Taoist from Yunnan who has been weaving grass crickets in the same location since 1946. Has anybody sighted this guy?

Shopping: You could spend weeks exploring Ocean Terminal, Ocean Center, and Harbour City; après shopping, you can enjoy views from the YMCA or sip afternoon tea in the Peninsula Hotel.

Tsimshatsui East: The Regent Hotel, with the best *feng shui* in town, is perfectly complemented by the Darth Vaderesque New World Centre, which marked the arrival of Tsimshatsui East—the gigantic landfill project blanketed with some of Hong Kong's most luxurious hotels, restaurants, and nightclubs.

Hong Kong Science Museum: The HK$350-million museum features 500 hands-on exhibits.

History Museum: The history museum previously located in Kowloon Park has moved to larger facilities near the Science Museum.

Kowloon Park: The HK$30-million Jamai Masjid Mosque, which serves Hong Kong's 50,000 Muslims, is closed to the public but tours can be arranged by calling 2724-0095. Also located in the park are several gardens, an indoor swimming pool, sculpture, and an aviary—a welcome escape from the maddening crowds of Nathan Road.

Yaumatei

Walking remains the single best way to make contact with any city, especially in a neighborhood as colorful as Yaumatei. It's impossible to get lost but useful maps and descriptions are provided in the HKTA *Yaumatei Walking Tour.* From Nathan Road, walk down Jordan and up Ferry Street to the 330-hectare West Kowloon Reclamation Project. No more "one-girl sampans" here, rather plenty of much needed land for residential and commercial development, plus the high-speed train, which carries passengers to the airport on Lantau.

Walking the Streets: Yaumatei's cross web of side streets offers a quick look at traditional Chinese enterprise such as the mahjong and ivory shops on Canton, the Chung Kee Marble Factory and art-deco youth club at No. 601, which once served as a POW holding station during WW II. Battery Street establishments include metal shops, woodcarvers, and print shops featuring old-style wedding invitations, while Reclamation Street remains home to Chinese herbalists, traditional wine shops, and incense makers. Shanghai Street shops sell traditional bridal gowns and Saigon Street has a few street barbers and fortune-tellers. Funerary stores filled with paper models of cars and boats are found on Ning Po Street.

Yaumatei Jade Market: This famous outdoor market is located at the north end of Battery at Kansu Street. Years ago the dealers would spread their wares on the sidewalk and negotiate prices with hand signals hidden under the protective cover of newspapers. Today the jade dealers have moved into organized cubicles and much of the romance has been lost. It's still worth a quick stop between 1000 and 1300 but be forewarned: much of the jade is fake.

Tin Hau Temple

Originally built on the waterfront over 100 years ago, this complex actually comprises four separate temples dedicated to various gods. The temple on the far left honors a half-dozen deities plus Kuan Yin, the Buddhist Goddess of Mercy and one of the most popular deities in the pantheon.

Second from the left is Shing Wong Temple, dedicated to the god who guides the dead through the underground and pleads for mercy on their behalf. The third temple from the left is dedicated to Tin Hau, the Taoist Queen of Heaven and Protector of Fishermen. The scarlet interior is filled with one of the most comprehensive collections of gods in Hong Kong—Tin Hau, General Favorable Wind Ear, General Thou-

KOWLOON

CHINA AND MACAU FERRY TERMINAL

CANTON RD.

★ ST. ANDREW'S CHURCH

★ CHINESE GARDENS

★ OLD KOWLOON BRITISH SCHOOL

WINDSOR HOTEL

KIMBERLEY RD.

● ROYAL PACIFIC HOTEL

KOWLOON   PARK

● MIRAMAR HOTEL

● CHAMPAGNE COURT
■ KIMBERLEY HOTEL

GRANVILLE RD.

NATHAN RD.

CARNARVON RD.

● OMNI PRINCE HOTEL

● AMERICAN EXPRESS

CAMERON RD.

■ BEEFY'S TAVERN

■ STAG PUB

MOSQUE ★

● GRAND HOTEL

HARBOUR
CITY

● LUCKY GH

HUMPHREY'S AVE.

● GOLDEN
CROWN 2 GH

● OMNI MARCO POLO HOTEL

HAIPHONG RD.

● LONDON GH

● VICTORIA HOSTEL

● GOLDEN
CROWN GH

LOCK RD.

■ NEW ASTOR HOTEL

■ BIERGARTEN

CAVERN CLUB

■ NED KELLY'S PUB

■ JUKE BOX

● MIRADOR MANSIONS

● VICTORIA HOSTEL

■ IYAC

MODY RD.

OCEAN CENTER

■ BOTTOM'S UP

● HOLIDAY INN

● VICTORIA GH
■ BLACKSMITH ARMS

MINDEN AVE.

■ RED
LIPS

■ HYATT

● CHUNGKING MANSIONS

● RAMADA RENAISSANCE HOTEL

PEKING RD.

PARK

● IMPERIAL HOTEL

ASHLEY RD.

● AMBASSADOR HOTEL

OCEAN TERMINAL

● POLICE

MIDDLE RD.

HANKOW RD.

● TELEPHONE ■ GPO

● OMNI HONG KONG HOTEL

● KOWLOON HOTEL

● SHERATON HOTEL

★ WATERTOURS

■ STAR HOUSE

● PENINSULA HOTEL

● YMCA

SPACE MUSEUM

■ BUSES

CULTURAL CENTER

★ HK TOURIST ASSOCIATION

★ OLD CLOCK TOWER

STAR FERRY

● REGENT HOTEL

FERRY TO WANCHAI

HONG KONG POLYTECHNIC

SCIENCE MUSEUM

HISTORY MUSEUM

UNITED HOSTEL

JOUSTER BAR

TRAIN STATION

HILLVIEW HOTEL

CHONG WAN RD.

COLISEUM

CHATHAM RD.

KIMBERLEY ST.

RAMADA INN

GRANVILLE RD.

SCIENCE MUSEUM RD.

PARK HOTEL

TSIMSHATSUI EAST

INTERNATIONAL HOTEL

STAR GH

LEE GARDEN GH

NIKKO HOTEL

GRAND STANFORD HARBOUR VIEW HOTEL

GUANGDONG HOTEL

PRAT AVE.

REGAL KOWLOON HOTEL

EMPIRE CENTRE

HART AVE.

NEW HARBOUR HOTEL

ROYAL GARDEN HOTEL

MODY RD.

TSIMSHATSUI CENTRE

BACCARAT/ GINZA HOTEL

RICK'S CAFE

MIRROR TOWER

SHANGRI LA HOTEL

EMPRESS HOTEL

SALISBURY RD.

SIGNAL HILL GARDEN

HONG KONG

HOVER FERRY TO CENTRAL

VICTORIA HARBOR

NEW WORLD CENTRE

NEW WORLD HOTEL

WATERFRONT PROMENADE

MOON

0   200 m

© MOON PUBLICATIONS, INC.

HONG KONG

YAUMATEI
AND MONGKOK

MONGKOK

STB HOSTEL

DUNDAS ST.

WATERLOO RD.

WEST

PITT ST.

YMCA INTERNATIONAL

NATHAN RD.

WATERLOO RD.

YAUMATEI MTR

KOWLOON

FRUIT MARKET

RECLAMATION RD.

FERRY ST.

NIGHT MARKET ENDS

HOT POTS

RECLAMATION

KING'S HOTEL

BOOTH LODGE HOTEL

CARITAS BIANCHI LODGE

AREA

PUBLIC SQUARE ST.

TIN HAU TEMPLE

0   200 m

JADE MARKET

CAR PARK

PALM READERS/OPERA

FOOD MARKET

KANSU ST.

PAK HOI ST.

EATON HOTEL

YAUMATEI

GALAXIE HOTEL

NATHAN HOTEL

SAN DIEGO HOTEL

CANTON ST.

BATTERY ST.

NINGPO ST.

SAIGON ST.

FORTUNA HOTEL

NIGHT MARKET BEGINS

MAJESTIC HOTEL

NANKING ST.

CHUNG HING HOTEL

GASCOIGNE RD

JORDAN ROAD FERRY TERMINAL

JORDAN RD.

JORDAN RD.

JORDAN MTR

PARK

SHANGHAI ST.

TEMPLE ST.

BOWRING ST.

WUSUNG ST.

PARKES ST.

PRUDENTIAL HOTEL

SHAMROCK HOTEL

BANGKOK ROYAL HOTEL

AUSTIN RD.

RITZ HOTEL

FUJI HOTEL

CANTON RD.

NATHAN RD.

CAFE ADRIATICO

JUNGLE PUB

TIBET PUB

KOWLOON PARK

© MOON PUBLICATIONS, INC.

sand Li Eye, the God of Wealth, the black Taoist God of Justice, and 60 identical Tan Sui gods.

The temple on the far right is dedicated to a dozen gods and is a favorite gathering spot for fortune-tellers, palmists, and face readers.

Temple Street Night Market

Kowloon's greatest attraction is the place to buy inexpensive clothing, copy watches, sidewalk charlatans, snake carvers, free opera, acrobatics, and great food at low prices. The market starts on Temple Street two blocks off Jordan and continues north almost to Waterloo. At Kansu Street it seems to dead-end at a large concrete car park . . . but keep walking! Around the corner are palmists, amateur Chinese opera, and a fortune-telling trained bird. Nearby an old man sells false teeth with a sign warning, Not Photo—Each $20.

The market continues up Temple past denim merchants, noodle stalls, and sidewalk chefs who serve incredibly tasty Mongolian hot pots, fried clams, and oysters in black bean sauce. Hong Kong at its very best.

More Sights

Bird Lane: In a city where tiny apartments preclude most pets, people lavish affection on miniature songbirds in delicate cages. Hong Lok Street, a narrow alley two blocks west of Nathan Road best visited in the early morning, is *the* place to hear the birds.

Sung Dynasty Village: A reproduction of a 12th-century Sung Dynasty village with performances of a Chinese wedding, kung-fu, and a fairly clever monkey act. Bored craftsmen demonstrate calligraphy, read palms, and carve ivory. Open daily 1000-2030; admission HK$120. Take bus 6A from the Kowloon Star Ferry terminal to the terminus at Lai Chi Kok Amusement Park. Chinese Opera at Lai Chi Kok has been replaced with third-rate cabaret singers.

TAOIST GEOMANCY

Chinese mythology teaches that one's fortunes and futures can be determined by natural and artificial landscapes, which range from the design of their homes to the placement of their tombs. Since some Chinese believe that mysterious energies race over the face of the Earth and malevolent dragons dwell below the ground, they feel that disturbing the Earth runs the risk of upsetting these spirits. It sounds far-fetched to most Westerners, but prior to high-rise construction or excavations for funeral plots, highly skilled *feng shui* (wind and water) geomancers are called in to determine the proper alignment which will successfully balance the ancient principals of yin and yang. Using both intuition and a compass engraved with ancient trigrams derived from the *I Ching*, Hong Kong geomancers attempt to balance the relationship between landscapes and their resemblance to both mythical and actual animals.

Many Chinese scoff at this emotional concept of the universe and mock the geomancers as charlatans, but almost without fail their services are employed on major construction projects. Consider this: the Regent Hotel was designed with an enormous glass atrium after an influential geomancer announced that the local sea dragon would be displeased if he was walled in. The famous bronze lions in front of the Hong Kong and Shanghai Bank were placed in that exact spot by a geomancer. Modern office buildings often have their main entrances in the *rear* on the advice of geomancers. Fish tanks in corporate offices are thought to ensure good *feng shui*. Many people believe that the new headquarters for the China Bank in Central was designed with sharp angles to cast bad *feng shui* on nearby competitors. Among the more obvious displays of *feng shui* are the eight-sided mirrors placed outside of windows to deflect evil spirits. Called *pat kwa*, you'll see them on shop fronts, hanging from balconies, or stuck on spirit trees. The power of these mirrors is considered so great that some believe that Bruce Lee died because his *pat kwa* was destroyed in a typhoon.

Wong Tai Sin Temple: A large and elaborate temple constructed in 1973 as the most impressive religious monument in Hong Kong. Wong Tai Sin, Taoist God of Healing and God of Good Fortune, discovered the secret of changing cinnabar into the drug of immortality. The temple is jammed with Chinese who seek their fortune by shaking the *chim* until a single bamboo stick falls out. Stick numbers are interpreted by soothsayers. It's all done in a relaxed and fun-loving manner; only young girls appear serious about it. The adjoining buildings and Chinese gardens on the left are remarkable examples of traditional Chinese architecture. To get there, take the MTR to the Wong Tai Sin Station.

ACCOMMODATIONS

Accommodations in Kowloon range from the budget dormitories of Chungking Mansions to the eye-popping spectacles in Tsimshatsui East.

Budget—The Mansions
Hong Kong is a tough place for budget travelers since over 85% of all rooms are in the high-price bracket, 10% in the medium range, and less than 5% are considered budget. Dormitory beds cost HK$80-100 depending on the number of beds per room; you pay more to avoid that sardine feeling. Tiny, tiny, airless rooms slightly larger than shoeboxes cost HK$150-180 with common bath and HK$200-250 with private bath.

Most guesthouses are located in high-rise blocks in Tsimshatsui. Chungking Mansions is the most well known, though less grotty alternatives are within a few blocks. All are cramped, claustrophobic, dirty, and overpriced.

Chungking Mansions: For several decades this dilapidated complex has served as the home base for budget travelers who find dormitory rooms among the floors of doll factories, rug weavers, and Indian cafes. Five separate blocks—A, B, C, D, and E—are served by ridiculously small and slow elevators festooned with plastic signs advertising what's upstairs.

Listings change frequently but Traveller's Hostel on the 16th floor of A block remains a useful if frightfully sleazy starting point. Avoid the room next to the obnoxious television and be prepared for all-night parties. A walk down the stairwell

will teach you more about Hong Kong than any possible guided tour! 36-44 Nathan Road.

Mirador Mansions: Another rambling, collapsing high-rise with several dozen guesthouses and dormitories. Best choices include the relatively clean Garden Hostel, Kowloon Hotel, First Class, and Man Hing Lung Guesthouse. Enter on Mody Street and wander around until you spot the elevator; or walk the stairs for a slice of life. 56-58 Nathan Road.

Golden Crown Court: A small block with a handful of guesthouses including the London Guesthouse, Golden Crown, Silver Crown, Copper Crown, and Wah Tat. 66-70 Nathan Road.

Budget—Beyond the Mansions
The following are relatively independent spots in smaller buildings.

Victoria Hostel: Hot showers, color TV, cooking facilities, visa services, and friendly managers make this a good choice. 33 Hankow Rd., tel. 2376-1182, HK$100-150.

Lee Garden Guesthouse: Clean, newly remodeled rooms with a/c, TV, and private bath. 34 Cameron Rd., 8th floor, tel. 2367-5972, HK$320-440.

Star Guesthouse: Another clean and friendly guesthouse managed by the inimitable Charlie Chan. All rooms are a/c with private bath and TV. 21 Cameron Rd., 6th floor, tel. 2723-8951, HK$300-400.

STB Hostel: Large, very clean, and fully air-conditioned dorm rooms plus hot showers, lockers, and travel services make this a popular if somewhat inconveniently located choice. Great Eastern Mansion, 255-261 Reclamation St., tel. 2710-9199, HK$100 dorm, HK$400-450 rooms.

More Guesthouses: The following guesthouses are all quite adequate and have been shown on the Kowloon map in the event you need some directions or a guesthouse has been recommended by a friend. On the Kowloon map you'll find the **IYAC, Victoria, London, Golden Crown 2, Lucky, Lee Garden, Star,** and **United** guesthouses.

YMCA and YWCA
Kowloon's two YMCAs are hardly budget but rather mid-level hotels with a/c rooms furnished with private bath, phone, and color TV. Reservations should be made several months in advance.

Salisbury YMCA: Great location adjacent to the Peninsula Hotel on one of the most expensive pieces of real estate in the world with swimming pool, sauna, tennis courts, library, and roofgarden. 41 Salisbury Road, tel. 2369-2211, fax 2739-9315, HK$600-950.

YMCA International House: A modern, clean hotel with more vacancies than the Salisbury branch. Facilities include a cafeteria, inexpensive restaurant, gym, and sauna. Well worth the transportation hassle. 23 Waterloo Road, tel. 2771-9111, fax 2388-5926, HK$550-650.

Moderate Accommodations
Many moderate hotels in the HK$500-800 price range are in Yaumatei and Mongkok, both a 20-30 minute walk from Tsimshatsui but conveniently located near the Temple Street Night Market, the Jade Market, Chinese emporiums, department stores, and countless restaurants. Plus it's less touristy than Tsimshatsui—much more of the real Hong Kong. All rooms are a/c with phones and color TV—far more spacious than the claustrophobic guesthouses of Tsimshatsui.

Caritas Bianchi Lodge: Not much atmosphere and rooms are heavy with vinyl, but it's clean, cheap, and reasonably priced. 4 Cliff Road, tel. 2388-1111, fax 2770-6669, HK$540-780.

Salvation Army Booth Lodge: Cheerful and clean with a completely Christian atmosphere. 11 Wing Sing Lane, tel. 2771-9266, fax 2385-1140, HK$550-750.

Bangkok Royal: Gloomy lobby but decent rooms and a great Thai restaurant on the ground floor. 12 Pilkem St., tel. 2735-9181, fax 2730-2209, HK$520-700.

More Moderate Hotels: Decent mid-level hotels shown on the Kowloon map include the **Empress, Ginza, New Astor, Guangdong, International, Park, Ramada, Kimberley, Miramar, Windsor,** and **Hillview** hotels. Moderate hotels shown on the Yaumatei and Mongkok map include the **Fuji, Ritz, Shamrock, Prudential, Chung Hing, Majestic, Fortuna, Nathan, San Diego, Galaxie, Eaton,** and **King's** hotels. These hotels may provide a room if the lodgings listed above are filled to capacity—an important consideration in a city where occupancy rates typically hover in the 80-90% range.

RESTAURANTS

Hong Kong has an estimated 6,000 licensed restaurants and possibly another 10,000 noodle shops, teahouses, and *dai pai dong* (roadside hawkers) that altogether serve some of the best Chinese food in the world. The selection is dazzling, though finding a good restaurant is somewhat different than back home. Rather than the simple and unpretentious places with cheap but great food, in Hong Kong it's often the glitzy neon palaces with elaborate menus that excel.

Dining is casual to the extreme. Even in the better places you might see diners spit out bits of bone, spill sauces on the tablecloth, and slurp soups with abandon, since many feel the more succulent the food the richer the sounds of eating should be. Afterward, diners don't linger but quickly abandon a scene of almost unbelievable gastronomic carnage.

Although Western fast food is very popular (McDonald's is just the sanitized version of a *dai pai dong*), the culinary glory of Hong Kong is the vast array of Chinese cuisines. The Singapore chapter has descriptions of suggested dishes.

Most restaurants in Hong Kong serve Cantonese food, the style most familiar to Westerners, with English-language menus often highly abbreviated and limited to tourist dishes such as sweet-and-sours. The ideal solution is to have a Chinese friend interpret the menus, as the freshest dishes and daily specials are often marked only in Chinese script. The HKTA brochure, *Visitor's Guide to Chinese Food in Hong Kong,* suggests restaurants and specific dishes as well as providing some useful photographs.

Temple Street Night Market
Kowloon's most adventurous eating is at the Temple Street Night Market. Start on Temple Street (clothes, cassette tapes, fake watches), walk around the car park (fortune-tellers, opera singers, acrobats), past the Tin Hau Temple (old men playing checkers and practicing *tai chi*), and keep walking north.

Toward the end of the road (almost to Waterloo Road) you'll find dozens of food vendors serving oysters or snails in black bean sauce, Indonesian *satay*, bubbling hot pot, and dozens of other marvelous creations—all served at rock-bottom prices. This is one of the dining high-lights of Hong Kong.

Cantonese

Dozens of inexpensive cafes and restaurants are tucked away on Mody, Hart, Prat, Cameron, and Granville Roads. Trust your instincts and patronize those restaurants packed with locals.

Cheap Eats: Check the buffets listed in the local newspapers, businessmen's lunch specials, and "happy hours" with complimentary snacks at luxury hotels.

Dim Sum: One of Hong Kong's most popular dining experiences is dim sum, served in nearly all Cantonese restaurants from early morning until late afternoon. Interior decorations are often a chaotic frieze of frenzied dragons and monumental phoenixes emblazoned in garish reds and golds. Ignore the outrageous decor and deafening pandemonium to enjoy these Asian petits fours.

Minden Row Restaurants: Great spots for cheap, fast, and delicious Chinese food. Try a take-away order of oysters in black bean sauce and an ice-cold Tsingtao beer—best in Hong Kong! In the alley just behind Holiday Inn. Inexpensive.

Kau Kee: A brightly lit and primarily pastel cafe known for its seafood hot pots, sautéed prawns in cognac sauce, and steamed chicken with ground ginger. 67 Chatham Rd., tel. 2366-8825. Inexpensive.

Orchard Court: Elegant, cream-colored salon serving seasonal dishes, baked stuffed welk, drunken shrimp flambé, and sautéed minced pigeon. 37 Hankow Rd., tel. 2317-5111. Moderate.

Super Star: Their menu, with helpful photos, provides snapshots of dim sum, deep-fried stuffed crab claws, sliced filet of sole, and baked lobster with minced spinach. 83 Nathan Rd., tel. 2366-0878. Moderate.

Beijing

Northern China's colder climate has influenced its cuisine in the classic dishes of Peking duck, clay-baked beggar's chicken, Mongolian hot pot, handmade noodles in rich gravies, spicy prawns, yellowtail steamed in wine.

North China: Decorated in pink and gray, North China serves traditional northern fare such as freshly carved duck-skin slivers, homemade

noodles, onion cakes, and Peking duck. 21 Prat Ave., tel. 2311-6689. Moderate.

Cheung Kee: One of the less expensive Peking-style restaurants in Kowloon. 75 Lockhart Rd., tel. 2529-0707. Inexpensive.

Peking Garden: Huge menu with all the favorites plus demonstrations of noodle-making in the evenings. Star House, 3 Salisbury Rd., tel. 2735-8211. Moderate.

Spring Deer: An old favorite known for clay-baked beggar's chicken, rice-flour pancakes, and Peking duck. 42 Mody Rd., tel. 2723-3673. Moderate.

Peking: A cheerful, old-style cafe with wooden walls and tasseled lanterns. Yaumatei, 227 Nathan Rd., tel. 2735-1316. Inexpensive.

Chiu Chow

Southern style cooking known for its shark's fin soup, goose simmered in wine, and boiled crab with red rice vinegar. Meals often start and end with a tiny cup of Iron Maiden, a muddy, bitter, and highly charged tea which aids digestion.

Golden Red Chiu Chow: Simple place with excellent braised goose in dipping sauce, suck-ling pig, fried carp in black bean sauce, and steamed pigeon with ham. 13 Prat Ave., tel. 2366-6822. Moderate.

Golden Island: A popular restaurant which serves low cholesterol Chiu Chow specialties. Try the soyed goose then a cup of Iron Maiden. 25 Carnarvon Rd., tel. 2369-5211. Moderate.

Eastern Palace: Homey atmosphere accented by well-stocked fish tanks, glass-enclosed cooking area, and an imposing cabinet holding customers' private brandy bottles. Canton Rd., tel. 2730-6011. Moderate.

Shanghai

Best bets are drunken chicken stewed in rice wine, braised eel, eight treasure duck, and hairy crabs, flown into Hong Kong every fall.

Great Shanghai: Great place to try over 400 time-proven dishes as carefully described by the helpful staff. 26 Prat Ave., tel. 2366-8158. Moderate.

Yap Pan Hong: Clean and spacious cafe with over 350 dishes listed on their trilingual menu. Open daily 1100-0400; good place for a late-night feast. 35 Kimberley Rd., tel. 2311-5078. Moderate.

Wu Kong Shanghai: An Art Deco cafe decorated in cream and peach with Shanghai dishes and other regional specialties such as braised eggplant in hot garlic sauce. Alpha House, 27 Nathan Rd., tel. 2366-7244. Moderate.

Tien Heung Lau: Small, old-fashioned restaurant with top-quality cuisine from the lakeside city of Hangzhou. 18 Austin Ave., tel. 2368-9660. Expensive.

Sichuan

China's spiciest cuisine derives its firepower from chili, bean paste, peppercorns, and heaps of garlic in dishes such as smoked duck, perfumed chicken, and crispy rice covered with spicy seafood sauces.

Crystal Palace: Charming old favorite known for its sizzling prawns in garlic, orange peel beef, braised longbeans, fresh sea cucumber, and crispy rice creations. 16 Cameron Rd., tel. 2366-1754. Moderate.

Fung Lum: Small but consistently popular cafe with fiery dishes carefully noted with asterisks on the menu. 21 Prat Ave., tel. 2367-8686. Moderate.

House of Tang: A stylish wood-paneled restaurant serving Sichuan and Cantonese dishes as prepared by a host of chefs. Metropole Hotel, 75 Waterloo Rd., tel. 2761-1711. Moderate.

Indian

With one of the largest Indian communities outside the subcontinent, it's little wonder that Hong Kong can boast some of the best Indian restaurants this side of Bombay.

Chungking Mansions: A great selection of inexpensive Indian cafes on the ground floor and upstairs such as Umar E Khyam in A Block, Taj Mahal Club Mess in C Block, and Sheri Punjab in C Block. 36-44 Nathan Road. Inexpensive.

Woodlands: South Indian vegetarian dishes served with piping hot breads and fragrant rice in an unpretentious alcohol-free cafe. 61 Mody Rd, tel. 2369-3718. Inexpensive.

New Delhi: Extensive menu with reasonably priced set meals and à la carte specialties such as chicken tikka and alob gobi. 52 Cameron Road. Inexpensive.

Mayur: North and South Indian specialties such as tandoori breads, mutton curries, and salted lassis are served along with Sichuan dishes. BBC Building, 25-31 Carnarvon Road. Moderate.

Other Asian Fare

Sawadee: Reasonable prices, friendly service, and outstanding dishes such as Tom Yam Kung (coconut soup with prawns) and Pla Pae (steamed freshwater fish) make Sawadee a local favorite. Hillwood Road. Moderate.

Java Rijsttafel: Popular, small cafe for fast, informal meals of *nasi goreng, gado gado,* or spicy *satay.* 38 Hankow Rd., tel. 2367-1230. Moderate.

Manila Restaurant: Of all of Asia's diverse cuisines, Filipino food is probably the least known and appreciated. Although Filipinos make up the largest number of expatriates living in Hong Kong—some 40,000 at last count—there are precious few Filipino restaurants here. Visitors curious about Filipino dishes such as pork *adobo,* crispy *pata,* and spicy *sinigang* soup can try the Mabuhay or Manila on Minden. However, no *lugaw.* 9 Minden Avenue. Moderate.

NIGHTLIFE

Kowloon nightlife includes hotel discos, cabaret nightclubs, jazz venues, seedy Suzi Wong bars, and British-style pubs geared toward both locals and visitors.

Pubs and Nightclubs

The least expensive way to pass the evening is in one of the many pubs and small nightclubs on both sides of Nathan Road.

Blacksmith Arms: A cozy place with friendly management; perhaps the best pub in the neighborhood. 16 Minden Avenue.

Rick's Cafe: Casablanca-motif nightclub with terrific local bands. 4 Hart Ave., tel. 2367-2939.

In Place: Lively and very popular place with low cover charges. Midweek specials sometimes include unlimited beer. 42 Hankow Road.

Juke Box: Dance nightclub where the action starts late but doesn't let up till sunrise. Open daily until 0400 or 0600. 42 Hankow Rd., tel. 2739-6331.

Ned Kelly's Last Stand: An Australian pub with live Dixieland entertainment favored by the middle-aged sing-along crowd. No cover charge. 11 Ashley Rd., tel. 2376-0562.

HONG KONG

FLOATING SLEEVES AND PAINTED FACES

Chinese opera, a sometimes bewildering combination of high-pitched singing, clashing music, and stunning costumes, is an artistic form of expression with no real counterpart in the West. That alone makes it worth watching at least once.

To compensate for the stark simplicity of the staging, costumes are brilliant and unbelievably elaborate—heavy embroidered gowns, superb makeup, and amazing water sleeves that float expressively without support. Although the dissonant music irritates most Westerners, it can at times be ravishingly melodic and completely haunting.

Stories taken from ancient Chinese folklore are told with symbolic gestures but few props. Role identification is linked to makeup, which ranges from the heavy paint worn in Peking-style opera (derived from older masked drama) to the lighter shades favored by the Cantonese. The more complicated a character, the more complex the makeup: a red face indicates courageous character, black a warrior's face, blue is cruelty, white face indicates an evil personality, purple is used for barbarian warlords, yellow for emperors. Costumes and movement are also highly stylized. The more important characters wear larger headdresses and express themselves with over 50 different formalized hand and facial movements.

Cantonese opera is the most common genre, followed by the highly refined Peking opera, which is considered the classic version. Soochow opera with its lovely and soft melodies is rarely performed. Hong Kong's 10 Cantonese opera troupes occasionally perform in the streets during temple fairs and religious festivals. Regularly scheduled performances are also given around town—check with the HKTA.

Waltzing Matilda's: Good name but tacky imitation of an Aussie drinking hole. 12 Hart Avenue.

Jouster: An "old medieval pub" with timber beams, mock stone walls, and knights' armor over two floors of bar counters and dining nooks. 19 Hart Ave., tel. 2723-0022.

Hard Rock Cafe: American cuisine, rock memorabilia, and live bands or a disc jockey at night. 100 Canton Rd., tel. 2377-8818.

The Wild Side

The first two places have transcended sleaze to become classics of camp.

Bottom's Up: A topless club featured in the James Bond film *Man with the Golden Gun* still pulls in the curious male and cautious couple. Seems entirely safe . . . maybe *too* safe. 14 Hankow Road.

Red Lips: Another '50s relic with aging hustler-waitresses who remember the days of Suzi Wong, if not Suzi herself. Their sidewalk nags won't take no for an answer. Peking Road.

Ocean City Nightclub: One of Hong Kong's largest Las Vegas-style nightclubs features Cantonese set menus and internationally known cabaret artists. New World Centre, 18 Salisbury Rd., tel. 2369-9688.

CENTRAL AND WESTERN

At first glance Hong Kong's central business districts more closely resembles New York than anything vaguely Oriental. From almost every vantage point overlooking the harbor, you see only the Occidental—shorelines blanketed with tall buildings, office blocks forming windswept canyons, smokestacks in Kowloon, hundreds of ships moored in the harbor, high-rise housing estates, and winding city streets that follow early contours now erased by successive land reclamations. Don't be misled. Hong Kong is a Chinese city populated by Chinese people who have only taken on the more obvious and convenient Western traits.

What you see and remember largely depends on where you stay and what neighborhoods you explore. Central, Hong Kong's financial district, offers some historic government buildings, striking modern architecture, and great panoramas from Victoria Peak. The Western District, on the other hand, is a neighborhood filled with strange sights and medieval insanitariness—one of the last places to see what's left of old Hong Kong. A highly recommended three-hour walking tour is described below.

Wanchai has sailor bars, singles nightclubs, yuppie watering holes, and a handful of moderately priced hotels located near the new convention center. Causeway Bay is where most of the luxurious hotels, chic shopping centers, and restaurants are found. On the south side of the island you'll find the floating village of Aberdeen and wealthy residential neighborhoods such as Stanley and Repulse Bay.

CENTRAL ATTRACTIONS

Downtown

Step off the Star Ferry and you have arrived in Central (formerly called Victoria), Hong Kong's center of finance and government—a curious mix of a few remaining colonial structures and space-age skyscrapers thoughtfully connected with elevated walkways.

Waiting at the ferry halt are some of Hong Kong's last rickshaw "boys." Nineteenth-century Hong Kong had over 7,000 rickshaws but today fewer than 20 old men hang on to licenses that expire forever on their deaths. Short rides around the block cost about HK$50; photos of you lounging in a rickshaw cost HK$20.

The HKTA in the basement of Jardine House (formerly Connaught Centre) distributes free information. The Jardine House's distinctive porthole windows have earned it the nickname "House of 1,000 Assholes." Central's largest bus terminal is hidden underneath the adjacent Exchange Building.

Statue Square: Across the street and wedged between the Italianate Legislative Council (one of the few buildings spared by the wrecker's ball) and the Mandarin Hotel is Statue Square, packed with thousands of Filipino housekeepers on Sundays. The statue of the Queen has been replaced by the first manager of the Hong Kong and Shanghai Bank, an ironic but completely appropriate symbol of modern Hong Kong.

Hong Kong Stock Exchange: West of the ferry pier soars a brooding, almost iridescent monolith designed by architect Remo Riva to house Hong Kong's merged stock exchanges. Tours can be arranged by calling 2522-1122.

Hong Kong and Shanghai Bank: Designed by British architect Norman Foster, this US$1-billion Darth Vader monolith is based on the principles of bridge technology with suspended internal floors and odd touches such as totally visible elevator guts.

Old Bank of China: A classic contrast is provided by the former headquarters of the mainland government. The Tsui Museum of Art on the 11th floor is a privately owned collection of paintings, carvings, and ceramics open weekdays 1000-1800; admission HK$20.

Bank of China: The new financial headquarters for the new ruling body resembles a soaring glass-sheathed rocket ship of blue-glass pyramids twisting into the sky. Designed by Chinese-American architect I.M. Pei with countless threatening and sharp-angled triangles, *feng shui* geomancers note that the building casts ill will toward all nearby institutions.

HONG KONG

FERRIES
TO TUEN MUN AND TAI O
TO LAMMA AND TSUEN WAN
TO CHEUNG CHAU AND MUI WO

TO
TSIMSHATSUI

TO HUNG HOM
TO DISCOVERY BAY
TO TSIMSHATSUI EAST
AND GOLD COAST

STAR FERRY PIER

QUEEN'S PIER

AIRPORT RAILWAY
CENTRAL STATION

BLAKE PIER

GENERAL
POST OFFICE

EDINBURGH PLACE

CITY HALL

TO WESTERN AND MACAU
FERRY TERMINAL

HARBOUR VIEW ST.

MID-LEVELS ESCALATOR

CONNAUGHT RD. CENTRAL

EXCHANGE
SQUARE

CENTRAL
BUS TERMINAL

JARDINE
HOUSE

RITZ-CARLTON

JUBILEE ST.

DES VOEUX
RD. CENTRAL

WORLD
WIDE PLAZA

PEDDER ST.

ICE HOUSE ST.

SWIRE HOUSE

CHATER RD.

MANDARIN
ORIENTAL

LEGISLATIVE
COUNCIL
BUILDING

CENTRAL MARKET

QUEEN VICTORIA ST.

POTTINGER ST.

LI YUEN ST. WEST

LI YUEN ST. EAST

THEATRE LANE

CENTRAL
MTR

ALEXANDRA HOUSE

PRINCE'S
BUILDING

STATUE
SQUARE

BANK OF
CHINA

THE LANDMARK

HONG KONG AND
SHANGHAI BANK

PACIFIC
BUILDING

CENTRAL

QUEEN'S RD. CENTRAL

STANDARD
CHARTERED BANK

STANLEY ST.

WELLINGTON ST.

ICE HOUSE ST.

BATTERY PATH

HOLLYWOOD RD.

WO ON LANE

DUDDELL ST.

LOWER ALBERT RD.

TO MAN MO
TEMPLE AND CAT STREET

LAN KWAI FONG
NIGHTCLUB

D'AGUILAR ST.

LAN KWAI FONG

WYNDHAM ST.

FCC AND
FRINGE CLUB

GOVERNMENT HOUSE

CAINE RD.

UPPER ALBERT RD.

ROBINSON RD.

ZOOLOGICAL AND BOTANICAL GARDENS

0   100 m

MID-LEVELS ESCALATOR

BISHOP LEI
INTERNATIONAL HOUSE

YWCA
GARDEN VIEW

TWO
MACDONNEL RD.

PRINCE OF WALES
BUILDING

CONNAUGHT RD. CENTRAL

HARCOURT RD.

GLOUCESTER RD

HARCOURT
GARDEN

TO WANCHAI

RODNEY ST

FURAMA HOTEL

BANK OF
AMERICA TOWER

FAR EAST
FINANCE
CENTRE

ADMIRALTY CENTRE

QUEENSWAY

MURRAY RD.

LIPPO CENTRE

TAMAR ST.

ADMIRALTY MTR

BUS STOP

UNITED CENTRE

ADMIRALTY

MARRIOTT
HOTEL

JUSTICE DR.

CHATER GARDEN

ONE PACIFIC PLACE

THE FORUM

SUPREME
COURT

ISLAND
SHANGRI-LA

CONRAD HOTEL

TWO PACIFIC PLACE

BANK OF
CHINA TOWER

MUSEUM OF
TEAWARE

COTTON TREE DRIVE

ST. JOHN'S
CATHEDRAL

HONG KONG PARK

U.S.
CONSULATE

GARDEN RD.

LOWER PEAK
TRAM TERMINUS

KENNEDY RD.

CENTRAL

TO VICTORIA PEAK

······· = TRAMLINE

|||||||| = MTR

✳ = MTR STATION ACCESS

© MOON PUBLICATIONS, INC.

The cubist Bond Centre, now called **Lippo Centre,** is another intriguing piece of architecture.

Double-decker Tram: These lumbering 95-year-old trams slowly travel from the western town of Kennedy to the eastern town of Shau Kei Wan, although the 30-minute journey from Western to Causeway Bay will probably suffice for most visitors. Best seats for views and photos are upstairs, front row, center. Pay the driver the posted fare on the way *out*.

Hong Kong Park: Across the street from the Bank of China is a modernistic urban park boasting the largest greenhouse in Southeast Asia and a HK$21-million aviary housing over 100 feathered species gathered from Asian rainforests. The 10-hectare park was opened in 1991 on the site of the venerable Victoria Barracks (now destroyed—a major defeat for preservationists).

Flagstaff House: Hong Kong's oldest surviving colonial-style building now serves as a museum of Chinese teaware. Open daily except Wednesday 1000-1700; free.

Zoological And Botanical Gardens: Stroll up Garden Road past Government House (former residence of the British governors) to the 16-hectare park where people practice *tai chi* in the early morning hours. Associated with the metaphysical principals of Taoism, this sport of shadow boxing is popular with Chinese grandmothers keeping arthritis at bay, business executives loosening up before hitting the market, and young men impressed with the defensive possibilities. Legend has it that this ancient toning technique developed from combat between a bird and a snake, both of which used 108 synchronous movements to get to the same place.

You might also see somebody playing mahjong, a game which uses slamming ceramic tiles in something akin to open warfare. Almost identical to gin rummy, the object of the game is to match the tiles in straights or sets of three.

Victoria Peak

Views from the summit of this 1,305-foot peak are some of the world's most spectacular—like the Holy Grail, if you miss Victoria Peak, then you've missed Hong Kong.

The perfect time to arrive is late afternoon for the captivating sunset. Like New York, Hong Kong takes on a mysterious beauty when viewed from a distance, a galaxy of lights that hide all the blemishes.

The Peak Tram: Victoria Peak can be reached by taxi, bus 15 from Exchange Square, or minibus 1 from Edinburgh Place, but nothing compares with a ride in the renovated Peak Tram. Built in 1888, this 72-passenger relic (perfectly safe) is actually a funicular railway pulled by 1,500-meter steel cables; it leaves every 10 minutes from the terminal 10 minutes from Star Ferry. The historic tram lurches up the hillside at impossible angles and stops nonchalantly at several points before reaching the site of the new Peak Galleria, a three-tiered complex with an uninteresting assortment of souvenir shops

the view from Victoria Peak

HONG KONG TOURIST ASSOCIATION

and restaurants. Best bet is the amusing water fountain which spouts at ridiculous intervals.

Avoid the crowds and urban setting by circumnavigating the peak in an hour along the 3.5-km route comprised of Harlech and Lugard Roads. From the tram terminus, you can also walk up Austin Road and reach Victoria Peak Gardens in about 20 minutes.

More ambitious hikers can walk south all the way down to Aberdeen via Pokfulam Reservoir or to Aberdeen via shady Peel Rise. Both are terrific hikes but bring along the *Hong Kong Island Map—Countryside Series No. 1*.

WESTERN DISTRICT WALKING TOUR

This is old Hong Kong, an undeveloped neighborhood of winding alleyways, street merchants, herbal shops, snake restaurants, and aging temples. The HKTA sells a useful guide called *Central and Western Walking Tour* but the following three or four-hour tour covers much the same ground with a few variations.

Central Market and Alleys

Beginning from the Star Ferry, walk down Des Voeux Road past the cheap clothing stalls on both Li Yuen East and Li Yuen West Streets. Central Market isn't recommended for those with weak stomachs.

Other small alleys quickly follow: Wing On ("Cloth Alley"), once filled with fabric stalls; Wing Wo for jewelry stores; Wing Sing ("Egg St.") for salted and preserved chicken and duck eggs; Wing Lok for herbal medicine stores; Man Wa Lane for chop carvers; and Mercer Street for the Gold and Silver Exchange.

Snake restaurants on Bonham Strand, especially the snake shop at 127 Bonham, are active only during the winter months. Jervois Street is another center of snake dining, most commonly in the old-style snake shop at nearby 13 Hiller Street. Photograph the magnificent tea shop urns at the corner of Possession and Queen's roads.

Western Market and Bonham Strand

Western Market, a late-Victorian/Edwardian red-brick building constructed in 1906, was declared a historical monument in 1990 and completely renovated in 1992. Today it's filled with pricey boutiques, antique shops, and clothing vendors relocated from Wing On Street.

Return to Bonham Strand West and walk past deteriorating buildings filled with wholesale ginseng dealers; visitors are graciously ignored but welcome to browse and smell. Turn left on Des Voeux West and glance inside incense stores and preserved-food shops where old ladies glare at curious Westerners. A sidewalk barber still operates at the corner of Li Sing Street.

Continue walking several blocks farther and turn left on Western Street. Two blocks straight up is a lively fruit-and-vegetable market—good photographic possibilities. Continue back to Central via the upper roads.

Hollywood Road

Ambitious hikers may enjoy a side trip up to the University of Hong Kong for fine views, prewar architecture, and a small museum with pottery and porcelain. The new Hong Kong Museum of Medical Sciences in an Edwardian-style building that dates from 1906 charts the historical development of medical sciences.

Less-determined visitors can return toward Central on Queen's Road West (slightly tricky to find; just keep walking) past stores selling Chinese wedding dresses and paper funeral effigies. Turn right on Hollywood Road and walk past coffin carvers and shops selling Korean chests, Thai brass noodlecarts, Japanese hibachis, Chinese porcelains, and lacquered rosewood furniture.

Man Mo Temple

Eventually you'll find Man Mo Temple, the oldest and most famous religious site on Hong Kong Island. The interior, often cloaked in a smoky haze of burning joss coils, holds mysterious figures of deities and Taoist gods, gigantic hanging incense coils, and a pair of sedan chairs used to carry Emperor Kwan and Emperor Man in annual ceremonies—an exotic and strange world far removed from the hustle and hype of modern Hong Kong. Photography is permitted but small donations to benefit the local hospital are appreciated.

This neighborhood may look vaguely familiar—it served as the backdrop for the film *The World of Suzi Wong*. Suzi's hotel is to the right

HONG KONG

SHEUNG WAN
(WESTERN DISTRICT)

© MOON PUBLICATIONS, INC.

TO KENNEDY TOWN

TO CENTRAL

MACAU FERRY TERMINAL

BUS TERMINAL

SHUN TAK CENTRE

SHEUNG WAN

WESTERN MARKET

SHEUNG WAN MARKET

CONNAUGHT RD. WEST

CONNAUGHT RD. CENTRAL

DES VOEUX RD. CENTRAL

WING ON CENTER

VICWOOD PLAZA

QUEEN'S RD. CENTRAL

GILMAN'S BAZAAR

WING WO ST.

WING KUT ST.

WING SING ST.

HING LUNG ST.

JUBILEE ST.

QUEEN VICTORIA ST.

CENTRAL MARKET

STANLEY ST.

WELLINGTON ST.

COCHRANE ST.

GRAHAM ST.

PEEL ST.

ABERDEEN ST.

GOUGH ST.

STAUNTON ST.

LYNDHURST TERRACE

HILLSIDE ESCALATOR

MAN WAH LANE

MERCER ST.

HILLIER ST.

BONHAM STRAND

JERVOIS ST.

CLEVERLEY ST.

MORRISON ST.

QUEEN'S RD. CENTRAL

LOK KU RD.

UPPER LASCAR ROW (CAT ST.)

HOLLYWOOD RD.

MAN MO

BRIDGES ST.

YMCA

LADDER ST. (STONE STEPS)

SQUARE ST.

TAI PING SHAN ST.

BLAKE GARDEN

TAI PING SHAN

WING LOK ST.

BONHAM STRAND WEST

POSSESSION ST.

QUEEN'S RD. WEST

DES VOEUX RD. WEST

KO SHING ST.

HOLLYWOOD PARK

PO YAN LANE

POUND LANE

PAK SING

SUI CHING PAK

KWUN YAM

0   100 m

and slightly up nearby Ladder Street, though the book was based on imaginary events in Wanchai's old Luk Kwok Hotel—torn down in 1991 and replaced by a businessman's hotel. Is nothing sacred?

A few steps down from Man Mo is Upper Lascar Row (Cat Street), once possibly a brothel area but now filled with expensive antique stores and funky junk stores.

Lan Kwai Fong

Conclude your walking tour in Lan Kwai Fong, a trendy neighborhood thick with chic cafes, Thai bistros, American discos, Scottish bars, and flashy nightclubs frequented by expat yuppies and tony locals. The California is a popular but pricey place to dust off and enjoy a tall cool drink.

One block east is the 1913 Dairy Farm Building, a candy-striped former icehouse which now houses the Foreign Correspondents Club and the artsy Fringe Club, an avant-garde theater company.

ACCOMMODATIONS

Ma Wui Youth Hostel

This inexpensive dormitory at the top of Mt. Davis in the far northwestern corner of Hong Kong Island is peaceful and has great views but, like all official hostels, it's closed daily 1000-1600 and IYHF membership is required for all guests. Another drawback is the isolated location. Take bus 5B from the Hong Kong and Shanghai Bank to Felix Villas terminus then walk back and follow the hostel signs. Mt. Davis Path, tel. 2817-5715, HK$40.

Moderate Accommodations
Garden View International House: A YWCA with swimming pool, business center, conference facilities, cafe, and 130 rooms in a great location across from the Botanical Gardens—a 10-minute walk from Star Ferry. 1 MacDonnell Rd., tel. 2877-3737, fax 2845-6263, HK$850-1,000.

Two MacDonnell Road: A new hotel with 215 rooms, coffee shop, business center, health club, but no swimming pool. 2 MacDonnell Rd., tel. 2132-2132, fax 2131-1000, HK$950-1,200.

Bishop Lei International House: Another new hotel just west of the Botanical Gardens, Bishop Lei features a swimming pool, business

center, gym, smoke-free restaurant, and 205 rooms perched in the Mid-levels district. 4 Robinson Rd., tel. 2868-0828, fax 2868-1551, HK$1,050-1,400.

Emerald Hotel: Western District hotels cater to business travelers on budgets, but they are clean and comfortable alternatives to the much more expensive hotels in Central and Causeway Bay. 152 Connaught Road West, tel. 2546-8111, fax 2559-0255, HK$850-950.

China Merchants Hotel: Another modern hotel priced far below its nearby competitors. 160 Connaught Road West, tel. 2559-6888, HK$750-950.

RESTAURANTS

Lan Kwai Fong
Hong Kong's most fashionable dining and entertainment area sits in a little square block which once served as the 19th-century starting point for sedan-chair carriers. Lan Kwai Fong—a trendy world of fern bars, Western restaurants, and chichi watering holes—provides a refreshing change from endless Chinese cafes, but reservations are advised during main dining hours.

Al's Diner: A 1950's throwback with a Wurlitzer that spits out vintage tunes and period dishes such as tuna melts, potato skins, and root beer floats. 27 D'Aguilar St., tel. 2869-1869.

American Pie: A 4th floor joint known for its homemade lasagna, pork chops, chicken pot pie, salads, Sunday brunch, and rich desserts enjoyed on an outdoor balcony overlooking Lan Kwai Fong. 34 D'Aguilar St., tel. 2877-9779.

California: Cal-Mex food, hamburgers, huge orders of fries, and other variations of California cuisine. There's also a salad bar which is pushed aside on weekends for late-night dancing. 24 Lan Kwai Fong Rd., tel. 2521-1345.

Dillingers Steak House: Steaks and other American dishes served until the disco breaks out around 2300. 17 Lan Kwai Fong Rd., tel. 2521-2202.

Graffiti: The place across the road provides baskets of crayons and paper tablecloths for frustrated artists. 38 D'Aguilar St., tel. 2521-2222.

La Dolce Vita: An Italian style bar and cafe in a trendy nightlife center. 9 Lan Kwai Fong Rd., tel. 2810-9333.

New York Deli: Popular spot and Hong Kong's first Jewish deli serving kosher gefilte fish, cheese blintzes, matzo-ball soup, Texas chili, and American cheesecake. Kosher Texas chili? 17 Lan Kwai Fong Rd., tel. 2882-8600.

Ristorante Il Mercato: Italian cafe with antipastos, pasta and pizza, and homemade Italian ice cream and pastries. 34 D'Aguilar St., tel. 2868-3068.

Tony Roma's: Barbecued ribs, cheese-filled jalapeno peppers, huge salads, succulent prime rib, and pecan pie for dessert. 32 D'Aguilar St., tel. 2521-0292.

Tutto Meglio: Tuscan cafe serving black linguini with baby calamari, imported Italian trout, and buffalo mozzarella with fresh asparagus in balsamic vinaigrette. 33 D'Aguilar St., tel. 2869-7833.

Va Bene: Expensive Venetian cafe famed for its salmon pastas in cream sauce and sinfully rich tiramisu. 58 D'Aguilar St., tel. 2845-5577.

Zona Rosa: Spanish tapas and other regional specialties at moderate prices. 1 Lan Kwai Fong Rd., tel. 2801-5885.

Something Unusual

Bored with yuppie cafes and bankers' restaurants? Try the following for a change of pace.

Poor Man's Nightclub: One of Hong Kong's most memorable experiences is dining al fresco in the parking lot near the Macau Ferry surrounded by denim and handicraft merchants. A dozen-plus foodstalls cook up quick-and-cheap Mongolian hot pots, escargot in black bean sauce, and seafood specialties. Somewhat touristy, but the carnival-like atmosphere and great food make this a real Hong Kong highlight.

Luk Yu Teahouse: An unofficial historical monument, this six-decade-old cafe is a living museum complete with ornate black fans, brass spittoons, marble-backed chairs, and decently prepared Cantonese cuisine. 26 Stanley Street. Inexpensive.

Snake Restaurants: During the cooler winter months, you might want to visit the snake restaurants on Jervois and Hillier Streets where a live snake is brought to your table, split open with a sharp knife and drained of its blood, which is mixed with wine to make an aphrodisiac bile. The snake meat is boiled into soup.

NIGHTLIFE

Lan Kwai Fong

Hong Kong's hottest nightlife scenes are Wanchai and Lan Kwai Fong at the top of D'Aguilar Street. The dozen-plus nightclubs, discos, and delis are filled with Chinese trendsetters and expatriates who stumble down from their midlevel homes.

1997: The well-named 1997 charges HK$85-140 admission but this includes two drinks and three clubs, the Post 97 cafe/bar, Middle Eastern Mecca 97 restaurant, and disco Club 97. Deserted before midnight but then packed until sunrise.

California: Weekend cover includes dancing, two drinks, and all the black-clad intellectuals you can handle.

Jazz Club: The club right above California features superb jazz performances from local and international musicians.

DD II: A reincarnation of the original Disco Disco and cavernous videotheque Underground, DD II attracts the all-night dance-party crowd.

Mad Dogs: For something more sedate, try Mad Dogs at the top of the street—a traditional Scottish-style pub with upstairs drinking and downstairs dancing. Schnurrbart serves German beer, sausages, and Schnurrbart spatzen. The nearby Cellar Bar is also a less yuppie/chuppie alternative to glorious LKF.

Fringe Club: The most alternative venue to alternative LKF is the nearby Fringe Club on Lower Albert Road which serves as one of Hong Kong's few alternative arts centers. Inexpensive drinks, artsy crowd, and live weekend performances from eclectic jazz to ethnic ensembles.

Bankers' Bars

Central is a beehive of traditional English-style pubs that cater to expatriate bankers and the young *hongsters* working the financial district. The cozy and friendly Bull and Bear on Lambeth Walk has all the necessities: darts, dark ale, oak beams, and suitably warm barmaids. The Godown Pub serves as an English restaurant until 2000 when the chairs are pushed aside to make room for dancing. One spot to avoid is the sterile and uninviting Jockey Pub in the Swire House—it's crammed with cell phones and overly tight suits.

WANCHAI

Once filled with the *godowns* of British opium merchants, Wanchai is now primarily a land of department stores, restaurants, nightclubs, businessman hotels, and the Hong Kong Convention Center, which extends out into the bay on a recently completed landfill project. Wanchai is divided by the tram line on Hennessy Road into two distinctive worlds. North of Hennessy is modern Wanchai, with its towering high-rises and immense public facilities constructed on landfill projects that reach out into the harbor. South of Hennessy is old Wanchai—still a world of narrow alleys, strange shops, and vibrant markets—one of the best wandering venues on the island.

South Wanchai

South Wanchai is far more rewarding than the modern sights to the north.

Temples, Alleys, and Views: The alleys connecting Queen's Road East and Johnston Road are crammed with rattan and wooden furniture shops, provision emporiums overflowing with enormous bags of rice, dried fish, lanterns, calligraphy brushes, temple furnishings, incense sticks, bird shops, and snake vendors. Hung Shing Temple dates from the 1860s when, almost unbelievably, it stood on the original waterfront of Wanchai. From there ride the elevator to the 62nd floor lounge of Hopewell Centre, which ranked as Hong Kong's tallest building until the completion of the Bank of China in 1989. Central Plaza, a 78-story wonder erected in 1995, now holds the title of Hong Kong's tallest building.

History, Markets, and Temples: After Hopewell Centre, visit Wanchai Post Office, one of Hong Kong's last remaining protected buildings and now the home of the Environment Resource Centre. Wanchai Market is worth a wander as is Pak Tai Temple, dedicated to the "Supreme Emperor of the Dark Heaven" and located a few blocks south down Stone Nullah Lane.

North Wanchai

The old world of Suzi Wong has transformed itself into a hive of yuppie bars, upscale hotels, artistic performance halls, convention centers, and soaring buildings quite unlike the seedy neighborhood of the 1950s.

Performing Arts: The Hong Kong Academy for Performing Arts and adjacent Hong Kong Arts Centre are home to the 1,188-seat Lyric Theatre, Drama Theatre, and Studio Theatre.

Convention Center: Among the more dazzling pieces of architecture in Hong Kong is the new extension of the Hong Kong Convention and Exhibition Centre which extends over the bay on yet another landfill project. Featuring a unique "bird's wing" design, the innovative, airy, and glass-dominated extension has been kept low to avoid interfering with the spectacular harbor views already enjoyed by both the original convention center and the two adjacent hotels.

Central Plaza: No visit to Wanchai would be complete without a stop at the 78-story Central Plaza, the tallest building in Hong Kong and among the 10 tallest structures in the world. Visitors can ride the high-speed elevators to the observation gallery, where views are nothing short of breathtaking.

Searching for Suzi: Wanchai served as the setting for the novel *The World of Suzi Wong,* and the sleazy old Luk Kwok Hotel on Gloucester Road doubled as Suzi's fictional Nam Kwok brothel. A sign of the times took place in the early 1980s when the original fleabag hotel was pulled down and replaced by the modern, no-frills businessman's hotel of the same name. A few racy bars still exist in Wanchai but most of the action has moved to other sections of Hong Kong.

ACCOMMODATIONS

Moderate

Almost a dozen mid-range hotels are located on the western edge of Wanchai or a few blocks south of Hennessy Road.

Charterhouse: Two blocks south of Hennessy Road with coffee shop, Cantonese restaurant, nightclub, and banquet facilities. 209 Wanchai Rd., tel. 2833-5566, fax 2833-5888, www.charterhouse.com, HK$1,400-2,300.

HONG KONG

WANCHAI

HAPPY VALLEY RACECOURSE

TO ABERDEEN TUNNEL

TO PAK TAI TEMPLE

GLOUCESTER RD.
JAFFE RD.
LOCKHART RD.
TO CAUSEWAY BAY
HENNESSY RD.
MORRISON HILL RD.
TIN LOK LANE
WONG NAI CHUNG RD.

CHINA HARBOUR VIEW HOTEL
SOUTH PACIFIC HOTEL
MORRISON HILL
QUEEN ELIZABETH STADIUM
CHARTERHOUSE HOTEL
KWAN O RD.
OI RD.
QUEEN'S RD. EAST

MARSH RD.
HUNG HING RD.
WANCHAI SPORTS GROUND
NEW TONNACHY NIGHTCLUB
TONNOCHY RD.
STEWART RD.
WANCHAI RD.
WANCHAI PARK

TO HUNG HOM

HARBOUR CENTRE
GREAT EAGLE CENTRE
HARBOUR RD.
CHINA RESOURCES BUILDING
HARBOUR HOTEL
CENTURY HOTEL
FLEMING RD.
RUTTONJEE SANITORIUM
WANCHAI MARKET
STONE NULLAH LANE

TO TSIMSHATSUI
WANCHAI FERRY PIER

NEW WORLD HARBOUR VIEW
CENTRAL PLAZA
JOHNSTON RD.
TAI WO ST.
CROSS ST.
STONE NULLAH ST.

EXPO DRIVE EAST
EXPO DRIVE CENTRAL
EXPO DR.

HONG KONG CONVENTION AND EXHIBITION CENTRE
CONVENTION AVE.
GRAND HYATT
HONG KONG CONVENTION AND EXHIBITION CENTRE
HARBOUR RD.
IMMIGRATION TOWER
O'BRIEN RD.
WANCHAI MTR
TAI YUEN ST.
OLD WANCHAI POST OFFICE
TO BOWEN RD.

YMCA
HK ARTS CENTRE
LUK KWOK HOTEL
MAKATI INN
STRIP JOINTS
SOUTHORN PLAYGROUND
SPRING GARDEN LANE
HOPEWELL CENTRE

GLOUCESTER RD.
LUARD RD.
JOE BANANA'S
JAFFE RD.
NEW HARBOUR HOTEL
HENNESSY RD.
SWATOW ST.
TAI WONG ST. W.
TAI WONG ST. E.

HK ACADEMY FOR PERFORMING ARTS
FENWICK ST.
EMPIRE HOTEL
LOCKHART RD.
FENWICK ST.
JOHNSTON RD.
GRESSON ST.
HUNG SHING

WESLEY HOTEL
QUEENS RD. EAST
KENNEDY RD.

TO CENTRAL

= MTR
= TRAMLINE
✷ = MTR STATION ACCESS

0   200 m

© MOON PUBLICATIONS, INC.

Century Hong Kong: A towering 516-room high-rise with pool, health club, 24-hour coffee shop, golf driving bay, and several bars and lounges. 238 Jaffe Rd., tel. 2598-8888, fax 2598-8866, HK$1,800-2,600.

China Harbour View: Good location midway between Wanchai and Causeway Bay. 189 Gloucester Rd., tel. 2838-2222, HK$950-1,400.

Empire Hotel: Well-priced hotel near Wanchai nightlife and transportation with rooftop swimming pool and sundeck, business center, health club, and several restaurants including the Four Seasons (Continental cuisine), Southern Song (Cantonese), Fenton's wine bar, and the lobby lounge. 33 Hennessy Rd., tel. 2866-9111, fax 2861-3121, www.empire-hotel.com, HK$1,400-2,200.

Harbour Hotel: Excellent location and reasonable prices make this older hotel a good choice for mid-level travelers. 116 Gloucester Rd., tel. 2574-8211, fax 2572-2185, HK$950-1,350.

Harbour View International House (YMCA): Despite the name, this is actually a cleverly disguised but well-priced and wonderfully sited 320-room hotel operated by the YMCA just opposite the Hong Kong Convention Centre. Reservations should be made by fax several months in advance. 4 Harbour Road, tel. 2802-0111, fax 2802-9063, HK$1,100-1,600.

Luk Kwok: Suzi's old hotel, now filled with families and businessmen. 72 Gloucester Rd., tel. 2866-2166, fax 2866-2622, HK$1,200-1,700.

New Harbour: A budget-luxury 173-room hotel near Wanchai nightlife. 41 Hennessy Rd., tel. 2861-1166, fax 2865-6111, HK$1,100-1,800.

South Pacific: Somewhat isolated but new and featuring spotless rooms. 23 Morrison Hill Rd., tel. 2572-3838, HK$950-1,600.

Wesley: A 22-story, 251-room property on the western edge of Wanchai operated in part by the Methodist Church. It has a Western cafe, Chinese restaurant, and business center. 22 Hennessy Rd., tel. 2866-6688, fax 2866-6633, HK$1,200-1,800.

RESTAURANTS

Lockhart Road Restaurants

Lockhart Road from Wanchai to Causeway Bay is an excellent place to find good, cheap, and informal cafes with everything imaginable from Sichuan to Shanghai and Cantonese to Thai. The following cafes don't require reservations and are listed starting from Wanchai.

New American: Strange name for a Beijing restaurant but a good place for northern dishes such as Peking duck, dumplings, sizzling prawns, thick soups, and hot pots. 23 Lockhart Road. Moderate.

Saigon Beach: Vietnamese specialties prepared by Chinese chefs; try Saigon hot pots, spring rolls with fish sauce, glass noodle salads, rich noodle dishes. Good value. 66 Lockhart Road. Inexpensive.

The Curry Pot: Indian specialties from the north and south. 68 Lockhart Road. Inexpensive.

Brett's Seafood: Basic cafe with fried fish, chips, and rice. 86 Lockhart Road. Inexpensive.

Thai Chili Club: A great little Thai cafes known for its spicy *tom yam kai* (coconut soup) and beef in peanut sauce. 88 Lockhart Road. Inexpensive.

SMI Curry Centre: Almost 100 different versions of curry dishes from India, Malaysia, Indonesia, and Burma. 81 Lockhart Road. Inexpensive.

Dai Pai Dong: The street stalls at Lockhart and Luard Road are great for cheap eats but since nobody speaks English, point at your neighbor's dish or at items lying on the chopping block. Inexpensive.

Old China Hand: Menu boards explain their fare: English fish and chips, shepherd's pie, steaks, steak-and-kidney pie, sausages, Scottish nightly specials. 104 Lockhart Road. Moderate.

Yin King Lau: Beijing and Sichuan dishes served by friendly staff. 113 Lockhart Road. Inexpensive.

Wishful Cottage: Outstanding vegetarian dishes carefully prepared by the Hong Kong Buddhist Association in one of the oldest cafes in Causeway Bay. 336 Lockhart Road. Moderate.

Bodhi Vegetarian Restaurant: Bean-curd specialties tasting exactly like chicken and meat abound in this terrific restaurant with a creative, highly descriptive menu. 384 Lockhart Road. Inexpensive.

Yaik Sang: A longtime favorite known for lemon chicken, roast goose, double-boiled soups, and salted beggar's chicken. 454 Lockhart Road. Cantonese. Moderate.

Szechuan Lau: Fiery treats like hot-and-sour soups, smoked duck, prawns sautéed in chili sauce, eggplant with garlic. 446 Lockhart Road. Moderate.

The Jump: American food and a popular singles bar in the Causeway Bay Plaza. 463 Lockhart Road. Moderate.

Chiu Chow: Try the bean-curd dishes, shark's-fin soup, and desserts of sweetened bird's-nest soup. 485 Lockhart Road. Moderate.

Ah Yee Leng Tong: Old-fashioned cafe with soups based on yin-yang principles. 503 Lockhart Road. Moderate.

NIGHTLIFE

Nightclubs and Bars

The discos, English-style pubs, and singles bars in Wanchai are a sensible, less expensive alternative to the trendy clubs in Central's Lan Kwai Fong.

Joe Banana's: A friendly and inexpensive nightclub popular with expatriates who seek singles conversation rather than loud music. Good vibes, great selection of beers, highly recommended. Open daily until 0500 or 0600. 23 Luard Rd., tel. 2529-1811.

The Wanch: First-class club with live rock bands, reggae, samba, and cutting-edge rock groups. Weekend cover HK$45-120. 54 Jaffe Road.

Makati Inn: Homey upstairs club, somewhat run-down, but a popular rendezvous for expatriates socializing with their Filipino girlfriends, who pack the place on Sunday evenings. Hong Kong has over 20,000 Filipino housemaids *(amahs)* who pack Makati Inn and nearby Crossroads, Neptune, and One for Two on Sunday, their only day of freedom from employment. Luard Road.

Girlie Bars

The Wanch achieved lasting fame from Richard Mason's *The World of Suzi Wong* and the memorable movie adaptation starring William Holden and the lovely Nancy Kwan. Once a hotbed of wicked nightclubs packed with sailors in need of drink, drugs, and girls, by the end of the Vietnam War the Wanch had flickered, faded, and died. Today, even Suzi's old hotel, the Luk Kwok, has

MOVIES ABOUT HONG KONG

The World of Suzi Wong: Based on Richard Mason's best-selling novel published in 1957, Ray Stark's story of the love affair between Wanchai prostitute Nancy Kwan and American William Holden is the best Hong Kong flick to date. Although the novel takes place in the Wanchai District, much of the movie was filmed near the Man Mo Temple on Hollywood Road.

PARAMOUNT PICTURES CORPORATION

scene from The World of Suzi Wong

Love is a Many Splendored Thing: The only film worse than the 1986 dud *Tai Pan* is this 1955 melodrama starring William Holden and Jennifer Jones. Portraying a Eurasian doctor torn between family duty and modern love, Miss Jones managed to come up with the single worst Chinese accent ever attempted. Other problems included the lovely theme song, which was played ad nauseam, and the sappy dialogue, which must have mortified Han Su-Yin.

Enter the Dragon: Bruce Lee's masterpiece starts with a few good shots of junks in the harbor. Any suggestions on more films to be included in the next edition?

been torn down and replaced with a conventioneer's hotel. The few strip joints that hang on are best visited during happy hour, when drinks are relatively cheap.

An upscale alternative is the Tonnochy Night-club, though it's geared toward affluent tourists and businessmen with expense accounts.

CAUSEWAY BAY

Causeway Bay—one of Hong Kong's most popular shopping and dining venues—began life as an opium entrepôt for Jardine Matheson when they shifted their headquarters from Macau in 1841. Today, Japanese-owned Daimaru stands on the site of Jardine's old opium godowns and only the street names reflect an earlier era.

Today the district divides itself into two distinct sections. North of the tram line on Hennessy Road are the massive department stores and elegant boutiques which insure more reasonable prices than their competitors in Tsimshatsui. South of Hennessy you'll find more upscale shopping venues but also a diminishing selection of older Chinese markets and cozy traditional cafes.

ATTRACTIONS

North Causeway Bay

Beyond the soaring Japanese department stores are a few relics of the post-consumer era.

Noon Day Gun: This famous recoiling three-pound Hotchkiss was immortalized by Noel Coward who penned, "In Hong Kong they strike a gong and fire off a noon day gun." The traditional salute begun by Jardine and Matheson to announce the arrival of important *taipans* fired its final salvo at midnight 30 June 1997, as control of Hong Kong passed from Britain to mainland China.

Victoria Park: Causeway Bay's enormous green lung is the site of early morning *tai chi*, old men strolling with bird cages, and more mundane facilities such as tennis courts, lawn bowling, an Olympic-size swimming pool, exercise par courses, and a roller skating rink.

South Causeway Bay

South of Hennessy Road you'll find a few old reminders of early Hong Kong and a growing number of monuments to the God of Mammon.

Jardine's Bazaar: Named after the old Chinese enclave once located behind Jardine's headquarters, Jardine's Bazaar today is a somewhat non-descript alley lined with shops and inexpensive cafes. Nearby Jardine's Crescent is better .

Times Square: The nightmarket foodstalls along Russell Street have given way to the district's newest and trendiest shopping center, complete with curving escalators, multiplex cinemas, and dozens of inexpensive cafes and restaurants on the 10-13th floors.

Tin Hau Temple: One of Hong Kong's oldest shrines, constructed in 1747, has been rebuilt several times to honor patron saint Tin Hau, Goddess of the Sea.

Aw Boon Haw Gardens: Chinese-Disneyland kitsch amusement park packed with atrocious Chinese pagodas, bizarre cement figures depicting Chinese mythology, and morality lessons for the young. The park was built in 1935 by inventors of the Asian version of Ben Gay. Tacky Tiger Balm Gardens (the park's old name) is worth visiting if only to gain insight into early moral standards. Open daily 0900-1600. Free. A 20-minute hike from Causeway Bay or take bus 11.

modern architecture in Hong Kong

HONG KONG TOURIST ASSOCIATION

HONG KONG

HONG KONG

TO TIN HAU TEMPLE, (TAI KOO, AND SHAUKEIWAN)

SPORTS GROUND

TUNG LO WAN RD.

TAI HANG RD.

TO AW BOON HAW GARDENS (TIGER BALM GARDENS)

= TRAMLINE
= MTR
= MTR STATION ACCESS

VICTORIA PARK

MORETON TERRACE

NEW CATHAY HOTEL

CAUSEWAY BAY

YEE WO ST. / CAUSEWAY RD.

LEIGHTON RD.

REGAL HOTEL

SUGAR ST.

IRVING ST.

PENNINGTON ST.

TO SOUTH CHINA ATHLETIC ASSOCIATION

GLOUCESTER RD.

GREAT GEORGE ST.

MATSUZAKAYA

PARK LANE HOTEL

CLEVELAND ST.

KINGSTON ST.

FOOD ST.

EXCELSIOR HOTEL

PATTERSON ST.

DAIMARU

NOBEL HOSTEL

SOGO

JARDINE'S BAZAAR

JARDINE'S CRESCENT

SUNING RD.

HOI PING RD.

LEIGHTON HILL

TO NORTH POINT

WORLD TRADE CENTER

MITSUKOSHI

KAI CHIU RD.

LEE GARDEN RD.

YUN PING RD.

LAN FONG RD.

HYSAN AVE.

LEIGHTON RD.

VICTORIA PARK RD.

CAUSEWAY BAY TYPHOON SHELTER

NOONDAY GUN

PERCIVAL ST.

MATHESON ST.

SHARP ST. EAST

LEE THEATRE PLAZA

TO HAPPY VALLEY

TO CROSS-ISLAND TUNNEL

HONG KONG YACHT CLUB

JAFFE RD.

LOCKHART RD.

TANLING ST.

RUSSELL ST.

TIMES SQUARE

CANAL RD.

LEIGHTON RD.

WONG NAI CHUNG RD.

CARGO HANDLING BASIN

TO WANCHAI

HENNESSY RD.

0   200 m

© MOON PUBLICATIONS, INC.

Happy Valley Horse Racing: Horse-racing season (Oct.-May) draws hordes of Chinese who place bets and test their luck on the tracks a few blocks back from Causeway Bay. Each race day an estimated two million residents bet over HK$100 million—six times the average at New York's Belmont Park Racetrack. Almost 20 Hong Kong newspapers are devoted solely to racing news. The century-old Jockey Club, an exclusive organization which controls the racing and lottery market in Hong Kong, is reputedly the world's richest gambling cartel, bringing in over HK$35 billion a year. Western visitors can gain immediate access to the inner circle by presenting their passport at the main entrance and paying a modest fee of HK$50.

A Horse Racing Museum which explains the history of the Jockey Club was opened a few years ago.

ACCOMMODATIONS

Moderate

Nobel Hostel: Three locations with 50 a/c rooms equipped with TVs, towels, and Chinese tea—right in the heart of Causeway Bay. The central office on Paterson Street above Daimaru can advise on nearby vacancies. Paterson Building, 37 Paterson St., Flat C1, 7th floor, tel. 2576-6148, HK$280-450.

New Cathay Hotel: An older 223-room hotel at the eastern edge of Causeway Bay near Vic-toria Park with simple but clean rooms, Cantonese coffee shop, laundry, and tour desk. 17 Tung Lo Wan Rd., tel. 2577-8211 or 2576-9365, HK$950-1,400.

Leishun Court: An apartment and commercial building with guesthouses such as Fuji, Villa Lisboa, and Cannes House. 116 Leighton Road, HK$350-560.

Phoenix Apartments: Near Lee Gardens Hotel. 70 Lee Garden Hill Road, HK$460-620.

RESTAURANTS

Something Different

Along with the listings under Lockhart Road in Wanchai, the following venues feature concentrations of cafes for quick dining choices.

Food Street: A short alley with a dozen restaurants serving Chinese, Taiwanese, Japanese, and dim-sum take-away with lunches costing HK$25-50. Although somewhat artificial and crowded during peak dining hours, Food Street serves as an easy introduction to regional cuisines. Cleveland Street one block east has more quickie cafes.

Causeway Bay Floating Restaurants: The floating sampans in Causeway Bay provide an unusual if touristy dining experience for large groups. Insistent sampan ladies demand HK$150-200 for ride and dinner but beware of those awful floating orchestras. This is a dying institution and may be history by the time of your arrival.

HONG KONG ISLAND ~ SOUTH SIDE

South Hong Kong Island has been called Hong Kong's Riviera—an exaggeration perhaps but there's enough interest to make for an enjoyable day-trip.

Self-guided tours start at the Exchange Square Bus Terminal with bus 6 or 260, which both reach Stanley via the shortcut. Another route is bus 2 to Shaukeiwan then bus 14 to Stanley. Visit the market, beach, and temple, and then take bus 6 or 73 to Repulse Bay or Aberdeen. Visitors short on time can reach Central in 20 minutes with bus 6 or 61 or the slower, more scenic bus 7 along the western coastline.

ATTRACTIONS

Stanley Village: This residential enclave of Stanley is best known for its weekend market where locals and visitors seek out designer-name clothing, fashion over-runs, and rejected seconds sold at reasonable but not bargain prices.

The nearby Tin Hau Temple, constructed 1938, is dedicated to the Goddess of the Sea. Stanley also has a small beach popular with windsurfers, a prison once used as an internment camp by the Japanese, and historic Murray House, which was moved here from Central in 1997 upon being dismantled to make way for the Bank of China. Murray House now features Chinese emporium stores, exhibition areas, pubs, cafes, and specialty restaurants.

Repulse Bay: Repulse Bay, an exclusive neighborhood named after the famous battleship and the place where Hong Kong fell to the Japanese, boasts one of Hong Kong's better beaches—though avoid weekends when it's fully packed and possibly trashed. The Repulse Bay Hotel, once the most popular attraction, was destroyed in 1982 despite impassioned pleas of preservationists. Today, the reconstructed Verandah Restaurant, Bamboo Bar,

and Spices restaurant attract a few visitors in search of nostalgia.

Ocean Park: Hong Kong's largest entertainment complex has dolphin shows, a 3,000-bird aviary, cable cars, an oceanarium, roller-coaster rides, a Shark Tunnel with 40 species of sharks, a butterfly house, a greenhouse, and the world's longest outdoor escalator (no kidding), which climbs the hill from Middle Kingdom—a craft village presenting 13 dynasties in life-size settings. Newer attractions include Toto the Loco leisure ride, the Mine Train in Adventure Land, and the interactive Simulation Theatre. Admission is a stiff HK$140 for adults and HK$70 for children but this includes all rides, shows, Ocean Park, and the Middle Kingdom. Avoid weekends.

Deep Water Bay: Deep Water Bay is an exclusive residential area with a half-kilometer beach where Jennifer Jones swam in a chilly scene from *Love is a Many Splendored Thing;* one assumes that the beach and waters were cleaner back then.

Aberdeen: Several decades ago, some 40,000 boat people lived aboard their junks and sampans moored near the fishing village of Aberdeen—refugees from China's Fukien Province and untouchables of Chinese society routinely denied the right to live on land or marry mainlanders. Today, most of these people have left their boats and moved into the modern housing estates that rise behind Aberdeen like gigantic concrete mushrooms.

Sampan tours are offered (even insisted on) at HK$50 per person, but time seems to be running out for this "tourist attraction."

Floating restaurants across the way have architecture as gaudy as the food is awful, but the setting is unbeatable and the gilded wonders are particularly glorious lit up at night. Back in town there's a Chinese wedding-gown shop filled with *red* dresses, a shrine dedicated to Hung Shing, *mah jong* stores, and the ubiquitous McDonald's.

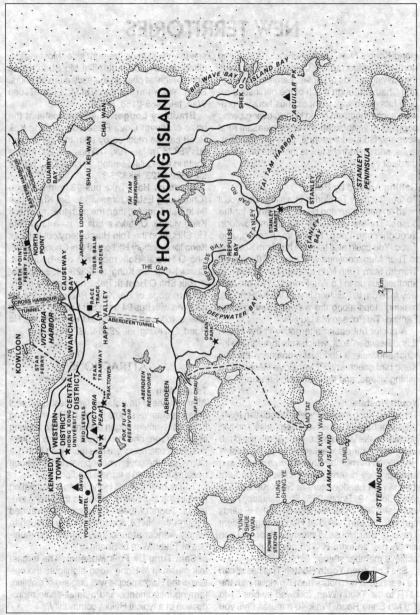

© MOON PUBLICATIONS, INC.

HONG KONG

NEW TERRITORIES

HONG KONG ISLAND

NEW TERRITORIES

Hong Kong's New Territories include the land north of Kowloon to the Chinese border, plus the outlying islands of Lantau, Lamma, and Cheung Chau. Although much of the peninsular region has given way to monstrous housing projects accommodating Hong Kong's ever-growing population, visitors can still enjoy pleasant rural scenery, isolated beaches, simple fishing villages, and old fortress towns that date back hundreds of years.

Getting Around by Bus

To tour the New Territories in a single day you'll need an early start and plenty of change for the buses. Try the clockwise loop from Kowloon through Yuen Long, Kam Tim, Fanling, and Taipo. You could also take the bus from Kowloon to Tuen Mun, continue with the LRT (Light Rail Transit) from Tuen Mun to Yuen Long, and hop another bus up to Lo Wu. From Lo Wu, the best way to return to Kowloon is with the KCR (train), making stops along the way at Sheung Shui, Fanling, Tai Po, and Ma Liu Shui.

A pricier but easier alternative is the HKTA "Land Between" tour, which cuts through the interior and visits a Buddhist monastery, the Luk Keng bird sanctuary, Plover Cove Reservoir, a fishing village, and the market in Fanling.

Youth Hostels

The Hong Kong Youth Hostels Association maintains four hostels in the New Territories and two hostels on the island of Lantau. Some are open year-round, others weekends only; the cost is HK$25. YHA membership cards are required and advance reservations should be made at the HKYHA headquarters at Shek Kip Mei Estate, Block 19, Room 225, Shamshuipo, Kowloon, tel. 2788-1638, fax 2788-3105. IYHF cards can also be purchased at Hong Kong Student Travel in Star House, Tsimshatsui, or you can simply pay an extra HK$25 per night until you achieve member status.

Sze Lok Yuen Youth Hostel: This hostel can be reached in two hours from Kowloon with the MTR to the Tseun Wan, followed by bus 51 to Tai Mo Shan Road. Walk 40 minutes until you see the YH sign on the right side. Most visitors climb nearby 957-meter Tai Mo Shan, Hong Kong's highest peak, in the early morning hours. Bring very warm clothing. Tai Mo Shan, Tsuen Wan, tel. 2488-8188, HK$25.

Bradbury Lodge: This YHA hostel at the base of Plover Cove Reservoir on Ting Kok Road can be reached by train to Tai Po, then bus 75K to Tai Mei Tuk. The hostel is 200 meters south in a beautiful setting. Tai Mei Tuk, Tai Po, tel. 2622-5123, HK$25-32.

Bradbury Hall: Take bus 92 from Kowloon (Choi Hung Estate terminal) to Sai Kung, bus 94 to Pak Tam Au, then the path toward Check Keng village. Or take a bus or train to the Ma Liu Shui, then the Tolo Harbor ferry out to Chek Keng for Bradbury Hall or Lai Chi Chong for Pak Sha O Hostel. Both require a one-hour hike. Check Keng, Sai Kung, tel. 2328-2458, HK$25.

Pak Sha O Hostel: Pak Sha O on the northeastern edge of Sai Kung Peninsula can be reached with bus 94 from Sai Kung to Ko Tong village, followed by a hike to the hostel. Hoi Ha Road, Sai Kung, tel. 2328-2327, HK$25.

ATTRACTIONS

Tsuen Wan

After a series of devastating fires destroyed vast areas of squatters' huts in the 1950s, the Hong Kong government began building public housing in the city core and throughout the New Territories. Early attempts were little more than high-rise slums, but the government persisted and soon became the world's largest landlord.

Today over 50% of Hong Kong's population lives in the eight New Towns in the New Territories. Tours of these cities can be arranged through the HKTA, though it's easy enough to simply wander around the planned communities of Tsuen Wan or Shatin.

Sam Tung Uk Folk Museum: The largest folk museum in Hong Kong highlights the culture of the Hakka people with displays of clothing, farming instruments, and a small-scale reproduction of a typical Hakka community.

Tuen Mun

Tuen Mun, a historic trading post dating from 750 A.D., has two good temples at the north end of town.

Ching Chung Kong Temple: This impressive temple an hour's drive from Kowloon is known for its ancestral halls filled with precious relics, Taoist gods, and countless photographs of departed ancestors—one of the few temples where pure Taoism is still practiced. The modern yet strikingly beautiful structure is to Lui Tung Bun, one of the eight Taoist Immortals who spread the mystical doctrine throughout China. You'll find his gold-leaf, bearded image in the rear of the temple, among images of other Taoist immortals.

Mui Fat Monastery: This HK$60-million three-story temple is considered one of the great temples in Hong Kong. Decorations include more than 10,000 sculptures of Buddha as well as Chinese and Thai paintings.

Both temples are about two km north of Tuen Mun; Mui Fat is to the east on Castle Peak Road while Ching Chung Kong is to the west near the sports grounds. To reach the latter, take the MTR to Tsuen Wan, bus 66M to Tuen Mun, the LRT up to Affluence station, and then walk through the housing estate to the temple. Mui Fat can be reached with bus 68M or LRT to Lam Tei station.

Yuen Long

This gigantic New Town holds little of interest but is a necessary transit point for travelers touring the New Territories by bus. It's also the jumping off point for the Ping Shan Heritage Trail, the oyster village of Laufaushan, and the walled town of Kam Tin.

Most buses terminate in Yuen Long at the western bus terminal at On Tat Square. Buses departing this terminal include 54 to Kam Tin, 76K to Sheung Shui, 68M to Tsuen Wan MTR, and 64K to Tai Po Market KCR.

A smaller bus station on the east side of town near the LRT Terminus provides different services: 53 to Tsuen Wan Ferry, 68 to Jordan Road, 68X to Jordan Road Ferry, and Minibus 655 to Laufaushan. Minibuses shuttle between the two bus terminals.

Ping Shan Heritage Trail

Ping Shan, an old Chinese village a few kilometers northwest of Yuen Long, has been or-ganized into an outstanding heritage trail dotted with exceptionally fine examples of ancestral and study halls.

Take the LRT to Ping Shan station and look for the wooden signposts which point the way to Hung Shing Temple (built 1767), Kun Ting Study Hall (1870), Tang Ancestral Hall (14th century), Yu Kiu Ancestral Hall (16th century), Hau Wong, and finally Tsui Shing Lau (14th century).

Laufaushan

Hong Kong's former oyster capital in the northwest corner of the New Territories is scruffy to the extreme but an excellent place to enjoy seafood in an authentic, reasonably priced locale. A narrow alley heads through the tiny village and terminates at the bay where generations of oyster farmers have deposited mountains of oyster shells. Unfortunately, the local oyster industry has faded away due to unchecked pollution, including cadmium, mercury, and waste from nearby pig farms.

However, simple cafes in town continue to import fresh seafood and oysters, which are prepared in a variety of ways. Well-cooked shellfish is safe but raw oysters should be avoided.

Take minibus 655 from the Yuen Long LRT terminus or minibus 34 or 35 from the eastern minibus terminal on Tai Fung Street.

Kam Tin

A few kilometers east of Yuen Long are several walled villages settled by the Tang family during the 17th century. Surrounded by brick walls and entered through narrow passages, these walled fortresses also feature watchtowers, parapets, and gun slots to complete the scene. Streets are laid out in geometric fashion with narrow lanes separating communal households.

Kat Hing Wai, the largest village, is also highly commercialized. Costumed ladies at the entrance demand payment for both admission and photographs; refuse and they spit at you. Beyond the gates are modern buildings and souvenir stalls selling tourist junk.

Adjacent villages are less touristy but outsiders are unwelcome except in Shui Tau, north along the road from Kat Hing Wai. Other New Territory walled cities include Tsang Tai Uk (see "Shatin," below), Sam Tin near Lok Ma Chau, and Sam Tung Uk located in Tsuen Wan.

Sheung Shui

New Town Sheung Shui has a lively market five minutes north of the KCR station and Man Shek Tong ancestral hall, constructed two centuries ago by the Liu clan. Much of the original architecture was lost in the 1930s when it served as a public school.

Walled city fans might also visit Hakka Wai, a traditional settlement southwest of town that dates from 1905.

Fanling and the Egrets

Fanling is a completely nondescript town promoted for unknown reasons by the HKTA in their *Luen Wo Market* brochure. Skip the boring market and instead walk west from the train station to the Fung Ying Sing Koon Temple where, on Sundays, dozens of people come to shake the *chims,* have their fortunes told by soothsayers, and burn paper money for departed ancestors.

Thousands of white egrets, Chinese pond herons, and *swinhoes* nest in the trees of the protected Luk Keng Egretry during the winter. Take bus 69K from Fanling.

Tai Po

Tours to this New Town visit the dismal Tin Hau Temple and then drop by the Tai Ping Carpet Factory to learn about modern carpet production. The factory is located beyond the temple where the road curves to the right.

Behind the New Market is the Hong Kong Railway Museum, housed in the original 1913 Tai Po Market Railway station. Six old coaches dating from 1911-45 can be seen daily except Tuesday 0900-1600.

University and Tolo Harbor

The Chinese University Museum features an art gallery with calligraphy, Han bronze seals, and jade flower carvings.

Cruises of Tolo Harbor leave twice daily from the harbor at Ma Liu Shui, about 15 minutes by foot from University Station. The four-hour morning ferry does not stop for sightseeing, but the af-

---

NEW TERRITORIES HIKING

Hiking the country parks of the New Territories is a delightful way to escape the noise and congestion of urban Hong Kong. Routes that avoid the urbanized sections can be planned with the *Countryside Maps* published by the Survey Office. These highly recommended maps show hiking trails, youth hostels, campsites, old forts, bus terminals, and all ferry routes. Sold at the Government Publications Centre in the Central GPO and in Kowloon at 382 Nathan Road near Kansu Street, Sheet 4 (the most useful map) covers the youth hostels and hiking trails around the Sai Kung Peninsula. Local authorities advise that you select a route to match your ability, don't hike alone, listen to weather forecasts, and bring water bottles, a good map, flashlights, and some first-aid supplies.

Trail choices are almost limitless, but the MacLehose Trail is considered the most ambitious hike. Named after a former governor of Hong Kong, the trail runs laterally across eight country parks and stretches more than 100 km from Sai King to Tuen Mun. It's been divided into 10 stages, the first two being scenic hikes from High Island Reservoir to remote Tai Long village. The ridgewalker is rewarded with panoramic views form Neele Hill to Tai Mo Shan, Hong Kong's highest mountain.

---

ternoon ferry at 1500 makes six brief stops and a 45-minute layover in Tap Mun. Both youth hostels on the Sai Kung Peninsula can be reached with this ferry.

Shatin

This mind-boggling New Town of a half million people is chiefly known as the home to the Shatin Racecourse, one of the world's most luxurious racetracks with a/c horse stables. Tours organized by the HKTA include transportation, meals, racing guides, and entry to the members' enclosure. Races are held from May to September.

Tsang Tai Uk, a walled village at the northern end of Lion Rock Tunnel Road, was built in 1840 by a wealthy quarryman of Hakka origins. Walk south across the bridge, continue past the intersection, and look left.

Temple of 10,000 Buddhas

Shatin's top attraction is the temple complex north of the Shatin KCR station. From the railway station, walk through the underpass and follow the small signs to the right; don't take the obvious concrete steps that only lead to somebody's house! Exactly 506 steps later (go ahead, count 'em) you'll reach the main temple crammed with 13,000 miniature clay Buddhas. Statues on the lower levels are now covered with thick wire mesh to prevent theft. An escalator has been installed for those who can't take the steps.

The temple was founded shortly after WW II by Yuet Kai, a Shanghai philosophy professor who penned almost 100 books on Buddhism before his death in 1965. A Christ-like image of

Yuet is displayed between a pair of gilded Buddha statues. For something really bizarre, continue up to the upper temple to see his gilded corpse preserved under glass.

The whole place is something of a low-end Aw Boon Haw Gardens with its pagodas, garish statues of Buddha disciples, and assorted gods riding blue lions and white elephants. Views from the hill encompass the housing projects and Amah Rock, which, some say, resembles a woman with child on back.

OUTLYING ISLANDS

Beyond the heat and crowds of Kowloon are 236 rocky islands that form the remainder of the New Territories. Lantau, Lamma, and Cheung Chau are the most popular and Cheung Chau is the best. In any event, the outlying islands are much more peaceful and interesting than the peninsular New Territories.

All can be reached by big ferries departing from the Outlying Districts Ferry Pier in Central, a short walk west of the Star Ferry terminal. Departures are hourly 0600-2000. Call the Hong Kong and Yaumatei Ferry Company at 2542-3081 for more information.

Whatever you do, don't go on weekends, when it seems like half of Hong Kong's population is trying to escape the city.

CHEUNG CHAU

Shaped like a dumbbell with hills on the bells and a town in the waist, this attractive little island is the best choice for visitors with limited time. The somewhat Mediterranean atmosphere (use your imagination) has also made this island popular with locals and expatriates who value the lower rents and unhurried pace of life.

Motorized vehicles are banned except for a few service vehicles that race around with trolleys of Cokes or squealing pigs. Development is on the rise with new resort projects and condo complexes, yet Cheung Chau retains some traditions such as the clan associations and trade guilds.

The central waist is a densely populated village with winding alleys and a handful of good restaurants that face the crowded harbor. The

northern bell is being developed with condominiums and has little of interest, while the scenic southern bell can be walked in three or four hours along a well-marked path.

Cheung Chau is 12 km west of Hong Kong and can be reached in one hour by ordinary or a/c ferry.

The Town

The *praya* (waterfront) is a constant hive of activity where you might discover a junk unloading bas-

---

HIKING ON THE OUTLYING ISLANDS

Few people realize that Hong Kong is more than 70% countryside and boasts over 20 country parks. All offer the visitor uncrowded beaches, fishing villages, farming communities, and rustic monasteries that still reflect traditional architecture and age-old lifestyles. Hiking trails on the islands vary in difficulty from family-style walks through grasslands to arduous treks cutting through forest plantations. Botanists will be surprised at the wide variety of plant life that thrives in Hong Kong's unique climate. Single-day hikes are rewarding, but multiday treks with overnighting at youth hostels and monasteries are also possible. Pick up the *Countryside Series Sheet No. 3—Lantau and Islands* map from the Central GPO or at 382 Nathan Road near Kansu Street in Kowloon. All hiking trails, youth hostels, campsites, old forts, and bus terminals are accurately shown.

HONG KONG

kets of fish or a Chinese funeral in full progress. Waterfront cafes and inexpensive foodstalls south of the pier provide a grandstand view of everything likely to happen. The Cheung Chau Fire Station across from the air-conditioned Amigo Cafe (try their excellent coffee or beef in spicy pepper sauce) has one of the few motorized vehicles allowed on the island, a two-stroke miniature fire truck only two meters long. But it's slow—in a

real emergency the firemen get up and run! Nearby you'll find a small bookstore and Citicorp Bank, which cashes traveler's checks.

Wander through the alleys of Cheung Chau for more discoveries: bakery shops selling miniature egg tarts called *dun tat*, stonemasons fashioning Chinese gravestones for the island's thriving funeral business, fish-processing factories with their distinctive smells, dim-sum restaurants packed in

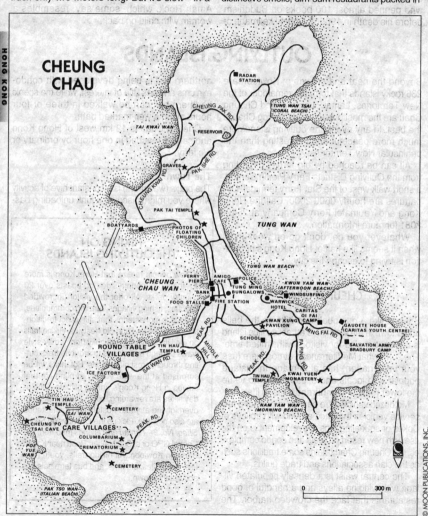

CHEUNG CHAU

RADAR STATION

CHEUNG PAK RD.

TUNG WAN TSAI (CORAL BEACH)

TAI KWAI WAN

RESERVOIR

GRAVES

PAK SHE RD.

CHEUNG KWAI RD.

PAK TAI TEMPLE

BOATYARDS

TUNG WAN

PHOTOS OF FLOATING CHILDREN

'CHEUNG CHAU WAN'

FERRY PIER

AMIGO CAFE

POLICE

TUNG MING BUNGALOWS

BANK

FOOD STALLS

FIRE STATION

TUNG WAN BEACH

KWUN YAM WAN (AFTERNOON BEACH)

WINDSURFING

WARWICK HOTEL

CARITAS OI FAI CAMP

KWAN KUNG PAVILION

GAUDETE HOUSE (CARITAS YOUTH CENTRE)

SALVATION ARMY BRADBURY CAMP

SCHOOL

MING FAI RD.

ROUND TABLE VILLAGES

TIN HAU TEMPLE

MIDDLE HILL

SAI WAN RD.

PEAK RD.

FA PING RD.

ICE FACTORY

KWAI YUEN MONASTERY

TIN HAU TEMPLE

TIN HAU TEMPLE

SAI WAN

CEMETERY

PEAK RD.

NAM TAM WAN (MORNING BEACH)

CHEUNG PO TSAI CAVE

CARE VILLAGES

COLUMBARIUM

CREMATORIUM

PAK YUE WAN

CEMETERY

PAK TSO WAN (ITALIAN BEACH)

0   300 m

© MOON PUBLICATIONS, INC.

HONG KONG TOURIST ASSOCIATION

Cheung Chau

HONG KONG

the early mornings but deserted in the afternoons. The Village Tree Inn next to the post office is a popular social center in the evening. Cheung Chau even has its own floating restaurant; from the pier take the sampan with the yellow flag.

The North

The Pak Tai Temple constructed in 1783 honors the Master of Weather and Emperor of the Dark Heaven. Sometime in the late spring, Pak Tai is paraded around town during the famous Bun Festival before being returned to his corner sedan chair for another 12 months.

The temple is decrepit, but the female temple attendant is enthusiastic about all the garish oddities. Note the well-carved solid granite pillars of dragons clutching pearls in their mouths. Photographs of floating children from the spectacular Bun Festival can be seen in the Temple Association Headquarters down the street on the left.

Southern Walking Tour

Walk south past the sterile concrete shopping centers and take the path up the first hill past a series of planned villages built by the Round Table Association and then an ice factory stuck in a weedy inlet. The nondescript village of Sai Wan and an unimpressive Tin Hau Temple overlook a bay of junks.

The Cave of Cheung Po Tsai at the southern tip is not worth the effort to locate. Return instead to the American-built CARE Village and hike along Peak Road to secluded Italian Beach.

Although considered the best beach on the island, you might feel strange with the hundreds of Chinese gravesites looking down on you. Farther on is a crematorium, a columbarium, and expensive condominium complexes built in a pseudo-Spanish style.

Peak Road eventually passes several Christian churches and youth centers before reaching Tung Wan Beach. Windsurfers are available at the Cheung Chau Activities Center on Afternoon Beach. Both of these crowded and dirty beaches have lost their intimacy to condos and oversized hotels. Like they say in Hong Kong: If you've got the money and want to do it, you can probably get away with it.

Accommodations

Cheung Chau is usually seen on a day visit, although there's a fairly good selection of places to stay. Check the hotel displays near the ferry pier.

Warwick Hotel: A modern hotel on Tung Wan Beach with big rooms, a swimming pool, and a terrace overlooking the beach. Tung Wan Beach, tel. 2981-0081, fax 2981-9174, Hong Kong office tel. 2541-7031, HK$800-1,200.

Tung Ming Bungalows: This small, clean, but overpriced guesthouse is tucked away in a small alley between the ferry terminal and the Warwick. HK$280-380.

Caritas Youth Camp: Cheung Chau also has a pair of youth centers that accept foreign visitors with advance reservations, and this Catholic-run camp is the better of the two.

FUNERALS ON CHEUNG CHAU

Although Chinese religion seems to be a mix of Buddhism and the nonstop pursuit of money, ancestor worship and spirit propitiation actually form the bedrock of their beliefs.

Cheung Chau is a likely place to see a traditional Chinese funeral because of the island's large number of cemeteries. Whether relatives of the departed or professional mourners, everyone will be immaculately dressed in white robes. The procession and a small orchestra of Chinese oboes and crashing cymbals follow the immense clover-shaped coffin through the streets to the distant graveyard. Sites are selected by *feng shui*

geomancers. Paper objects such as hell notes and car replicas are burned in the temple to symbolically ensure the dead receive some material comforts in the hereafter.

Thus laid properly to rest, the dead become focal points for the living. Twice annually, thousands of Chinese return to the gravesites to consecrate offerings and socialize with friends. The rituals continue after the body has decomposed; the bones are exhumed and cleaned with soap and sandpaper. The skeleton is reconstructed by the eldest son, who places the remains into a ceramic urn. The bones are carefully arranged with the foot bones on bottom and skull on top. The urn is reburied in a less costly spot or taken to the family shrine. Few seem concerned that these "grandfather urns" are often purchased by visitors and converted into lamps or flower pots! Traditional practices are changing almost as rapidly as the skyline of Central. Permanent plots in private cemeteries have become so expensive (HK$150,000 and up) that over 65% of the dead are now cremated in the territory's 22 crematoriums.

Salvation Army Youth Camp: Great views but surly management.

LAMMA ISLAND

Hong Kong's third-largest island after Lantau (142 square km) and Hong Kong (77 square km), mountainous Lamma has several mediocre beaches and small fishing towns famous for their seafood restaurants. Also good hiking and views from the hills. The island is blessedly free from motor traffic except for a few vehicles which serve the immense power station.

Although physically attractive, much of the island's idyllic atmosphere was sacrificed to the Po Lo Tsui Power Station—an environmental horror show of the first order.

Hiking around Lamma

Ferries from Central reach both Yung Shue Wan on the northwest corner and Sok Kwu Wan on the east-central side of the island. Most visitors head first to Yung Shue Wan, then hike along concrete paths past Hung Shing beach to the cafes of Sok Kwu Wan. A dozen seafood restaurants line the waterfront but the views have been ruined by the island's other environmental horror show—the noisy cement factory and quarry mines across the narrow bay.

A better idea is to continue hiking 30 minutes over to Mo Tat where the food is equally tasty and the views are far superior. From Mo Tat, you can catch a *kaido* (motorized sampan) over to Aberdeen or return to Sok Kwu Wan for a ferry to Central.

Hikers may want to scale the 353-meter summit of Yin Shan (Shan Tei Tong), known to colonialists as Mount Stenhouse. Fine views on clear days but the path is difficult to find. Time permitting, you might continue to Tung or Mo Tat past red-and-purple bougainvilleas, green bamboo, tattered banana trees, dragonflies, villages of gray-streaked stucco houses, laundry poles heavy with sets of black pajamas, old men doing their wash at communal spigots, fields of vegetables, and a sign reading, Helicopter Landing Site Keep Clear.

Accommodations

Although Lamma is a day-trip for most visitors, accommodations are available in Yung Shue Wan and at Hung Shing Ye Beach.

Man Lai Wah Hotel: Just below the ferry pier is a small, decent hotel with a/c rooms and private baths. Main St., Yung Shue Wan, tel. 2982-0220, HK$450-600.

Lamma Vacation House: Another good spot south of the pier and across from the cafes. 29 Main St., Yung Shue Wan, tel. 2982-0427, HK$300-450.

Concerto Inn: Lamma's most expensive getaway is elegant and romantic. Hung Shing Ye Beach, tel. 2836-3388, HK$700-900.

Han Lok Yuen Hotel: On the steep hill overlooking the beach with rooms and flats. Hung Shing Ye Beach, tel. 2982-0608, HK$300-520.

Transportation

Ferries to Yung Shue Wan and Sok Kwu Wan leave hourly from the Central Outlying Districts Pier. *Kaidos* leave every two hours from Aberdeen to Mot Tat and Sok Kwu Wan, and there is a more irregular *kaido* service between Yung Shue Wan and Kennedy Town.

LANTAU ISLAND

Lantau is twice the size of Hong Kong Island but has only 16,000 inhabitants, the territory's largest and least-densely populated island. Blessed with a rugged landscape of stark beauty and wide-open spaces, Lantau serves as a kind of safety valve for Hong Kong's overcrowded citizens.

Getting Around

Despite the new Chek Lap Kok Airport, most of Lantau remains rugged and wild—an amazing change from the neon jungles of Kowloon and Hong Kong. Although Lantau deserves a few days of leisurely exploration, day-trippers can get a quick impression by taking an early morning ferry from the Outlying Districts Pier in Central to Silvermine Bay (Mui Wo) and heading directly to the big Buddha at Po Lin Monastery, the number one sight on the island.

The ferry makes a brief stop at Peng Chau Island. Those with more time might hop off the ferry and continue by small boat across the narrow straits to the Trappist Monastery on Lantau Island. From here it's a 90-minute hour walk to Silvermine Bay from where buses head out to Po Lin Monastery. This is cutting it close and almost certainly requires an overnight on the island.

Hiking

More than 50% of Lantau is a country park of scraggly mountains, lonely valleys, and remote beaches reached by dozens of trails laid out for the weekend explorer. Hardy hikers might try the 70-km Lantau Trail which starts in Mui Wo and follows a circular path to Po Lin and Tai O before looping back across the southern coast.

Lantau Trail is divided into 12 sections of varying difficulties. The first six sections follow a skyline ridge trail over rugged mountains before finishing at the fishing village of Tai O. The next six stages circle the island counterclockwise, hugging the coastline back to Silvermine Bay. Lantau Trail from start to finish requires about three full days or 24 hours of solid hiking. Most hikers do selected segments as day hikes from Po Lin Monastery—especially the scenic ridge section which heads east to Sunset Peak.

All of the trails, campsites, and youth hostels are shown on the *Countryside Series Map—Lantau and Islands,* available from the Government Publications Office. Hiking trails have also been graded in difficulty.

Accommodations

Visitors can stay in Silvermine Bay, at the Trappist Monastery, Po Lin Monastery, two youth hostels, or one of a dozen campsites.

Campsites: Almost a dozen campsites are located across Lantau with exact locations shown on the *Countryside Series Map—Lantau and Islands.*

Po Lin Monastery: Dormitory accommodations and three vegetarian meals cost HK$175. More information below.

Lantau Tea Gardens: A pleasant alternative to the dormitories at Po Lin. Ngong Ping, tel. 2985-5161, HK$180-300.

Davis Youth Hostel: The morally less fit might stay at the youth hostel near Po Lin Monastery. IYH membership is required and facilities are open weekends only. HK$25.

Trappist Haven Monastery: Visitors willing to abide by the rules (early rising, periods of silence, courteous behavior) may contact the Trappist monastery just across from Peng Chau Island. More information below.

Silvermine Bay: Two modestly priced hotels are located in Lantau's main town to the right of the ferry pier—perhaps necessary if you miss the last ferry back to Hong Kong.

Peng Chau Island

The Lantau ferry pauses at Peng Chau, a tiny C-shaped island across a narrow channel from Lantau. Peng Chau retains some of its pre-industrial charm, although modern houses and occupations have largely replaced traditional structures and cottage industries.

Places of minor interest include a Chinese cemetery and temple and a porcelain factory that supplies ornamental goods for Hong Kong shops. Motorized sampans called *kaidos* leave from the pier for the Trappist Monastery.

Trappist Monastery

An isolated monastery operated by the Trappist Cistercian Order, one of the strictest in all Catholicdom. The order was established in 1644 by a French cleric living in Peking and moved to Hong Kong in the 1950s. Monks maintain complete silence while working the vegetable farms and dairy operations that supply some of the finest restaurants around. Visitors seriously interested in overnights should write to Trappist Haven, Lantau Island, P.O. Box 5, Peng Chau, Hong Kong.

The one-hour hike to Silvermine Bay can be made on the ridgetop or a longer, lower route skirting the coastline.

Silvermine Bay

Lantau's main commercial center and transportation hub takes its name from old silver mines once located in the northern part of the valley. Silvermine Bay (Mui Wo) has a few cafes, small supply shops, and a post office across from the ferry exit and foodstalls to the

right that sell cheap, good meals until late at night.

Farther right lies Silvermine Bay Beach with two hotels and bicycle rental stands. Silvermine Beach Hotel is first on the left followed by Mui Wo Inn across the bridge. Buses leave from the terminal near the pier.

Po Lin Monastery

Southeast Asia's largest outdoor bronze Buddha looms over this ornate temple and monastery complex high atop Ngong Ping Plateau. Visible from Macau almost 70 km away, the 16-meter 250-ton statue was constructed in Nanjing and transported to Hong Kong in 219 numbered segments which were reassembled in record time. The US$6 million project took six years to complete.

Po Lin Monastery itself was modeled after the Temple of Heaven in Beijing, with brilliantly colored shrines and an active community of over 100 monks and nuns. The main temple enshrines the historical Buddha, Sakyamuni, flanked by the Healing Buddha on the right and Amitabha on the left. Across the courtyard is a secondary temple dedicated to Wo Tei, guardian of Buddhist temples. To the rear of the central temple are four buildings—the VIP Room, library, Diamond Grotto, and Hall of Full Enlightenment, where prayers are chanted daily at 0500 and 1600.

Overnight dormitory accommodations in sex-separated quarters plus three meals costs HK$175 per day—recommended as the only way to really experience the tranquillity of the monastery after the crowds have departed. A vegetarian lunch is also served to visitors for HK$45.

There's plenty to do: watch the sun rise from Lantau Peak, rent a pony for the day, learn about tea production at nearby Lantau Tea Gardens, hike the Lantau Trail. A rougher trail leads down to Tung Chung, an ancient farming community near Buddhist temples and an old fort constructed by Chinese troops at war with the Europeans.

Po Lin, or "Precious Lotus" Monastery, is reached with bus 2 from Silvermine Bay. Buses leave hourly and take about 40 minutes to get to the monastery.

Tai O Village

Tai O is home to a large colony of Tanka boat people whose converted junks form three-story apartment complexes permanently anchored in the muddy bay. The Kwan Ti Temple is dedicated to the God of War and Righteousness, who protects the poor from the rich.

Take bus 1 from Silvermine Bay.

The sole cause of man's unhappiness is that he does not know how to stay quietly in his own room.
　　　　　　　　　　　　—BLAISE PASCAL, *PENSÉES*

The world will be meaningless to you.
　　　　　　　　　　　　—KABIR

Peculiar travel suggestions are dancing lessons from God.
　　　　　　　　　　　　—KURT VONNEGUT

INDONESIA

Unexpected encounters far from home can evoke an essential humanity that goes beyond fear and fatigue—and so shows us how, in some deep and important sense, we are never really far from home. Unforgettable connections are the threads that survive long after the museums and monuments have faded and are such the greatest gifts of the world.

—DONALD GEORGE,
SAN FRANCISCO EXAMINER

Travel magnifies and intensifies life. It allows you the opportunity to recapture a feeling of wonder, innocence, and youth; and depending on how vulnerable you are willing to become, it can also deliver a profound experience of unreality that can rattle your most basic beliefs.

—ERIC HANSEN,
THE TRAVELER

Travel can be one of the most rewarding forms of introspection.

—LAWRENCE DURELL,
BITTER LEMONS

INTRODUCTION

Indonesia is a land of superlatives. Arching gracefully between Asia and Australia, this vast archipelago—some 13,000 islands inhabited by over 170 million people—offers overwhelming diversity, from magnificent volcanoes plunging into icy blue lakes to pristine beaches and sparkling coral gardens. Indonesia is a primeval world of astonishing beauty and complexity, kaleidoscopic in culture, perhaps the richest historical and ethnographic destination in the world.

This is a land as varied, complex, and colorful as any place on earth, a "Destination of Endless Diversity" with the power to overwhelm and delight everyone from the one-week visitor to Bali to the multi-entrance traveler en route to Irian Jaya.

THE LAND

The outer limits of this 6,400-km stretch of islands (*Dari Sabang ke Merauke,* or "From Sabang to Merauke") are as far from each other as California is from Bermuda or Perth is from Wellington. Indonesia has a total area of five million square km (about one million more than the United States) of which more than two million are land.

Of the 10 largest islands in the world, Indonesia claims the better part of three (New Guinea, Borneo, and Sumatra); in addition there are about 30 small archipelagoes, each containing literally thousands of islands. Of the 13,677 islands that make up its territory, some 6,000 are named and only 992 are permanently settled. A country of incredible and diverse beauty, there are mind-stupefying extremes: 5,000-meter-high snowcapped mountains of Irian Jaya, sweltering lowland swamps of eastern Sumatra, open eucalyptus savannahs of Timor, lush rainforests of West Java, with lava-spewing volcanoes the whole length.

Climate

Indonesia straddles the equator, so the days are all the same length. This country has a typical equatorial climate with only two seasons: wet and hot. The wet lasts from November to March, and the hot from May to October. Rainfall fluctuates wildly depending on the season. Winter monsoons from the north bring short but drenching cloudbursts. Sometimes it rains so hard it's like falling into a swimming pool; with a roar the skies upend, spilling a solid wall of water on the earth below.

Summer monsoons from the south bring hot winds and little rain.

Rainfall also varies dramatically depending on the island. Locales east of Java have sharply defined dry seasons, the duration increasing the closer the area is to Australia. Sumatra and Kalimantan, lying closer to the equator and farther from Australia, have *no* dry seasons.

Fauna and Flora

Forty different species of mammals are scattered throughout the archipelago and there are 150 state-supervised game parks and nature reserves. Among its mammals are great apes such as the orangutan with its shaggy blazing-orange coat, deep-black wild cattle, 35-centimeter-high miniature deer, clouded leopards, mountain goats *(serow)*, wild warthogs, the sun bear with a large white circle on its chest, and long-snouted tapirs that gallop like stallions tossing their heads and whinnying.

The fauna of Irian Jaya (western New Guinea) resembles that of Australia: vividly colored birds of paradise, spiny anteaters, flying possums, bandicoots. Reptiles include giant monitor lizards, the reticulated python (the world's longest snake, up to nine meters long), and croaking geckos.

Due to its extreme geographic fragmentation, Indonesia is richer in plant species than either the American or the African tropics. Its total number of flowering plant species is more than 35,000. To cite only a sample of Indonesia's floral wealth, there are 250 species of bamboo, 150 species of palm, and in the more fertile

areas flowers are rampant—hibiscus, jasmine, allamanda, frangipani, bougainvillea, lotus lilies a half meter wide.

Java alone has 5,000 plant species, and there are twice as many species of plants on Borneo as in all of Africa. The tall hardwood rainforest trees of Irian Jaya rival the giant sequoias of California; banyan trees planted outside the royal cities of Central Java are connected with authority and are populated by hordes of spirits; the corpse plant of Sumatra smells like putrefying animal flesh; the largest bloom in the world, the rafflesia (one meter wide), inhabits Sumatra; the luxurious vegetation of Borneo hosts the seductive colors of orchids, which glow in the perpetual twilight of the jungle.

HISTORY

When you read Indonesian history, you read world history. Indonesia is a subtle blending of every culture that ever invaded it—Chinese, Indian, Melanesian, Portuguese, Polynesian, Arabian, English, Dutch, and American. Indonesia's history is a story of wave after wave of migrations of peoples who either absorbed earlier arrivals, killed them off, or pushed them into less favorable regions such as deep forests, high mountains, or remote islands. This ongoing and unending process explains Indonesia's ethnic diversity.

Indonesia's prehistory begins on Java, one of the earliest places in the world where man lived.

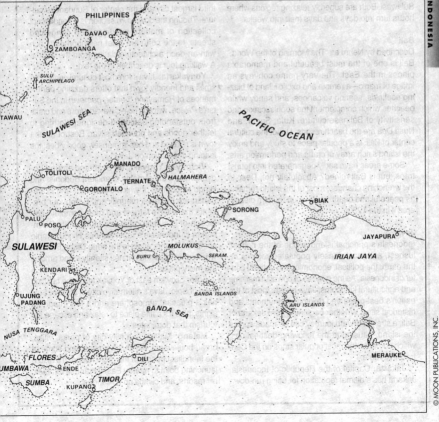

INDONESIA

© MOON PUBLICATIONS, INC.

INDONESIA

SIGHTSEEING HIGHLIGHTS

As the world's largest archipelago, Indonesia boasts an extraordinary number of attractions. Visitors, however, must carefully plan their itineraries since internal transport is rugged and visits are limited to two months per entry.

Bali is deservedly the most popular destination, for despite the impact of tourism, few places in the world are so rich in culture, traditions, and natural beauty. Just across the straits is the island of Java, the second most visited destination in Indonesia. Allow enough time to visit the high points of Yogyakarta, Solo, Mt. Bromo, and Bandung. Third most popular destination is the idyllic Lake Toba region of northern Sumatra, followed closely by the ethnologically rich Tana Toraja region of central Sulawesi. Both are superbly relaxing regions where hours turn into days and days melt into weeks.

Bali

Described by Nehru as "The Morning of the World," Bali is one of the most beautiful and memorable places in the East. The very name conveys an image of magic—a remote and exotic island of blazing ricefields, soaring volcanoes, and sandy white beaches which complement the sophistication and sensitivity of Balinese culture. Kuta, Sanur, and Nusa Dua are the beach resorts. Ubud, the cultural center of Bali, is a popular place to study and enjoy the island's rich array of crafts and performing arts.

Some areas have sadly degenerated into tourist traps, but is Bali ruined? Absolutely not. Despite the wrenching changes, most of the island remains as peaceful and beautiful as when tourism discovered it in the 1930s.

Java

Indonesia's principal island is one of the richest, lushest, and most densely populated regions on the earth: the political, economic, and cultural center of Indonesia. As the genesis of powerful maritime and agricultural kingdoms, Java boasts most of the nation's best-preserved religious monuments and historical sites. Whether beginning from Jakarta or Bali, a straightforward journey can be made across the island, pausing at the following destinations, which comprise the most popular stops on the Central Java route.

Jakarta: Capital of the Republic of Indonesia, Jakarta has a dismal reputation for being run-down and hectic—Asia's most overcrowded, under-planned, and chaotic capital. And yet, beneath the surface is an energetic city full of interest and surprise, including the superb collection of Orientalia inside the National Museum and the wharfside Makassar schooners, which together form the greatest assemblage of traditional sailing crafts in the East. Jakarta deserves a chance.

Bogor: This modest town 60 km south of Jakarta is internationally known for its huge and verdant Botanical Gardens, one of the most magnificent collections of flora in the world.

Bandung: Once referred to as the "Paris of the East" by the Dutch, who valued its tree-lined streets and cool climate, Bandung today is Indonesia's third largest city and the center of Sundanese culture. Though the downtown section is a nondescript collection of modern buildings and congested streets, to the north are quiet neighborhoods rich with art-deco architecture dating from the 1930s. A walking tour is described in the text.

Yogyakarta: Java's foremost cultural center is a small and friendly town that offers dazzling performances of Ramayana theater, *gamelan* in the Sultan's Palace, *wayang golek, wayang kulit,* and crafts from outstanding batik and designer clothing to leather goods and pounded silver. Best of all, the town is relaxed and has immensely good vibes; the leading destination on Java.

Vicinity of Yogyakarta: Scattered around Yogyakarta are the remains of ancient Buddhist and Hindu kingdoms, of which Borobudur and Prambanan are the most magnificent. Borobudur presents the world's largest and most complete collection of Buddhist relief sculpture while Prambanan is Indonesia's most famous Hindu temple complex. Farther afield is the eerie Dieng Plateau, where ancient Hindu shrines silently stand among the misty plains.

Solo: Sixty km east of Yogyakarta is the bustling town of Solo, Java's alternative city of culture. Solo has a pleasant atmosphere and a few important sights, plus it's a fine place to relax and escape the tourism that dominates

Malang: Malang is a hilly city of parks, villas, broad boulevards, old Dutch homes, and some of the friendliest people in the archipelago. It's also a launching point to nearby East Javanese temples, hill resorts, and climbs up volcanoes.

Mt. Bromo: East Java's most spectacular sight is watching the sun rise from the volcanic rim of Gunung Bromo. Just as memorable, and certainly less crowded, is a hike across the sea of sand on the evening of a full moon.

Surabaya: Surabaya, like Jakarta, also deserves a second chance since it offers the determined visitor magnificent Dutch architecture, a wharf with dozens of impressive Makassar schooners, and beautiful little neighborhoods where people smile in amazement at the Western tourist. Beneath the heat, dirt, and noise is a city with more history and atmosphere than most places in Southeast Asia.

Sumatra

This gigantic island—fifth largest in the world—is mainly visited for Lake Toba in the north and Bukittinggi in the west.

Lake Toba: One of the world's largest crater lakes is also home to the Bataks; this remote and relaxing place demands you to do nothing but read a good book and stare out at the glassy waters.

Bukittinggi: West Sumatra boasts some of the most exciting scenery you'll ever see: peaks looming over deep canyons, splendid sheltered valleys, great high plateaus, terraced ricefields, volcanic lakes. Most of the people are Minangkabau, a tribal group remarkable for its unique matrilineal society and magnificent style of domestic architecture. Bukittinggi serves as a good base for exploring the Minangkabau countryside, while nearby Nias Island and its megalithic ruins are also worth visiting.

Nusa Tenggara

The six major islands east of Bali that comprise Nusa Tenggara are home to dozens of ethnic groups, astounding natural wonders, smoking volcanoes, superlative snorkeling, virgin game reserves, megalithic cultures, and the largest reptiles in the world.

Lombok: Though it doesn't compare with its more famous neighbor (just 20 minutes by air from Bali), Lombok compensates with three beautiful islands off the northern coastline and the spectacular peak of Mt. Rinjani.

Komodo: Nusa Tenggara's chief attractions are the giant monitor lizards which live undisturbed on the island of Komodo. The sole survivors of carnivorous dinosaurs, *Varanus komodoensis* now draw thousands of travelers who fly or overland from Bali.

Flores: Considered by many perhaps the most beautiful of all Indonesian islands, Flores has grandiose volcanoes, multicolored lakes, stretches of savannah, and tropical deciduous forests. Roads are rough, but flights go direct from Bali.

Sumba: Sumba is the source of the most handsome and highly prized *ikat* fabrics in Indonesia.

Sulawesi

The world's most peculiarly shaped island is home to an amazing diversity of societies including the fiercely Islamic Bugis, the prosperous Christian Minahasans of the north, and the animist-Christian Torajans in the south-central region. This variety, along with some spectacular scuba diving and natural landscapes, has made Sulawesi the fourth most visited island in Indonesia, after Bali, Java, and Sumatra.

Tana Toraja: Aside from the Balinese, the richest cultural group in Indonesia is the Torajans of Sulawesi. Both Christian and animist, Torajan funerals are amazing ceremonies. The people are also known for their textiles, burial caves, and remarkable domestic architecture with structures that resemble wooden ships riding an ocean of tropical foliage.

North Sulawesi: The northeastern arm of Sulawesi features prosperous towns, refreshing hot springs, friendly people, and some of the best coral in the country.

INDONESIA

In 1891 the fossil skull of an ape man *(Homo erectus)* was discovered at Trinil in Central Java. This erect near-man lived at a time when Europe was under ice, most of Indonesia was a part of Asia, and the Sunda Shelf was above water. He walked to Java, which was then a high mountainous island covered in wild jungle.

Anthropologists say the present-day Malay peoples of Indonesia came in two great waves, spreading through Sumatra, Borneo, Sulawesi, and Java. First came the so-called Proto-Malayans (Caucasoid Malays), who possessed a neolithic-level culture, now represented by the Batak of Sumatra, Toraja of Sulawesi, and Dayak of Borneo. Next came the Deutero-Malays, who carried a more developed Bronze Age civilization from Indochina.

Indian chroniclers wrote of Java as early as 600 B.C., and the ancient Hindu epic, the Ramayana, also gives mention of Indonesia. By the 2nd century A.D. Indian traders had arrived in Sulawesi, Sumatra, and Java. The stage was set for Hinduism. India, at the time of its colonializing efforts, was considered the pinnacle of civilization and at the apex of its cultural vigor. Local Indonesian rulers most likely invited the high-caste Brahmans to immigrate and work as a literate bureaucracy.

Early Kingdoms

The Indonesian-Indian era reached its apogee in the 14th-century Javanese Majapahit Empire. Though the Golden Age of Indonesia thrived just over 100 years (1292-1398), Majapahit is remembered as Indonesia's greatest state because it established Indonesian unification and an Indonesian identity. The Majapahit Empire made a powerful and lasting impact on modern Indonesian culture as new and exciting native styles were fused with the traditions of India.

The results can be seen everywhere. The *kraton* courts of Solo and Yogya remain strong enclaves of Hindu-Javanese Majapahit culture. The religion and culture of Bali, including the *gamelan* orchestra and the five-note scale, were inherited from India. Motifs and styles of old Hindu-Javanese culture permeate modern Indonesian art: all over Java you can see monumental gates constructed in Hindu style; Indian epic poems have been adapted into living Indonesian theater; Indian mythic heroes dominate the plots; Indonesia's present state motto is a Sanskrit phrase; even the national emblem of Indonesia (the largest and most populous Muslim state in the world) is the mythical bird Garuda . . . the mount of the Hindu God Vishnu!

When Islamic traders arrived in the 15th and 16th centuries, they found all the great islands of Indonesia to be a complex of well-established Indianized kingdoms. The expansion of Muslim trade marked the beginning of the Islamic period in the archipelago.

Islam caught fire first in far northern Sumatra and then spread to Java, taking hold most solidly in those areas of Indonesia which had been least affected by the Hindu civilizations of the past. Hindu princes converted to Islam for reasons of trade, wealth, and power. In 1487, a coalition of Muslim princes attacked what was left of the Hindu Majapahit Empire. By the end of the 15th century 20 Muslim kingdoms ruled over the entire archipelago. Indonesia had become, and still remains, the largest Islamic nation in the world.

European Arrivals

The Portuguese were the first bearers of European civilization to Indonesia. Carrying *their* God with them to be embraced by the heathens, these vigorous and bold southern Europeans arrived in Indonesia a full 100 years before the Dutch but lasted only 150 years, until 1512. Keeping the upper hand by virtue of their superior striking power, weaponry, and navigation techniques, the Portuguese were little more than pirates who acquired tribute and booty while exploiting whatever commodities they came upon: slaves, gold, textiles, spices. Portuguese influence ended in 1570 when they foolishly murdered the sultan of Ternate and the inhabitants threw them off the island.

Next in line were the British and the Dutch, who arrived for spices in the early 17th century. Though treaties dictated a degree of cooperation, the underlying rivalry and enmity erupted at last on the island of Ambon in 1623 when the Dutch tortured and executed all the personnel of the English factory. The Ambon Massacre essentially ended English influence in Indonesia, aside from a brief reoccupation in 1811-1816 during the Napoleonic Wars.

By the time Dutch traders reached the East Indies, they discovered they had a government, cities, monumental temples, irrigation systems, handicrafts, orchestras, shipping, art, literature, cannon fire, harems, and astrological systems. The Dutch began with a small trading company at Banten in 1596 and soon entered into the spice trade. Over 65 ships sailed to the East Indies from 1598 to 1605. To prevent rival Dutch companies from competing amongst themselves, a private stock company called the Vereenigde Oost-Indische (VOC) was chartered in 1602 to trade, make treaties, build forts, maintain troops, and operate courts of law in all the East Indies lands.

The Dutch did everything they could to isolate this closed insular world from all outside contact. Using a combination of arms, treaties, treachery, and puppets, they increasingly took control of the internal affairs of Indonesian states and later turned virtually all of Java into a vast state-owned labor camp run somewhat like an American slave plantation. Profits enabled the Dutch masters to build railways, pay off the national debt, and even start a war with Belgium. Indonesians were treated as third-class citizens, always a sure sign that revolution is on the way.

The Rise of Nationalism

Intellectuals and aristocrats were the earliest revolutionaries against Dutch colonial rule. Diponegoro, the eldest son of a Javanese sultan, was the country's first nationalist leader, as well as being a masterful guerrilla tactician. In 1825, Diponegoro embarked on his holy war, a costly struggle of attrition and scorched-earth policy in which 15,000 Dutchmen and 250,000 Indonesians died. At one point the Dutch even considered pulling out of Java. Diponegoro was eventually lured into false negotiations, arrested, and sentenced to death.

Nationalist organizations continued to protest the extreme dissatisfaction and impatience the Javanese masses had for the colonial regime. The final push began in 1926 when an ex-engineer named Sukarno established the PNI (Indonesian National Party). With his oratorical power and domineering, charismatic style, Sukarno soon emerged as Indonesia's most forceful political personality. The PNI demanded complete independence but sought this goal through Gandhi-style non-cooperation. The Dutch responded with further ruthless exploitation of Indonesia's natural resources. A police state was imposed and political opportunists were thrown into jail.

The fall of Indonesia to the Japanese in 1940 showed that the Dutch weren't so powerful. But the Japanese soon showed themselves to be even more ruthless, fascist, and murderous than the Dutch had ever been. Once the Japanese surrendered, bands of politically aligned young people *(laskar)* sprang up to fight the returning Dutch who embarked on ruthless "pacification" exercises, attacking cities and butchering hundreds. The high drama ended on 27 December 1949 when the Dutch reluctantly transferred sovereignty to a free and independent Indonesia.

Modern Challenges

Sukarno was elected president of the new federal state and Indonesia was recognized by the United Nations. But it was a deeply troubled time for the new country. Politicians scrambled after power, cabinets fell every six months, and dissension erupted between the military, religious, left-wing, and conservative factions of the embryonic government.

To end the national nightmare, Sukarno announced his policy of "Guided Democracy," which gave final authority to Jakarta and the ruling military clique. By the late '50s Sukarno had seized total power, press censorship was enforced, and politicians and intellectuals were jailed. Sukarno's mood darkened as his government left the U.N. and grew violently anti-Western and pro-communist. His once-brilliant leadership had broken into disparate political ideologies that borrowed from Marxism, nationalism, and Islam. Indonesia had reached the breaking point.

On the night of 30 September 1965, six top generals and their aides were abducted and brutally murdered, allegedly by communists attempting a coup. What followed was one of the most massive retaliatory bloodbaths in modern world history. An unknown general named Suharto mobilized the army against the communist conspirators while Muslim youths burned the PKI (communist party) headquarters to the ground.

Over the following months all of Java ran amok as an estimated 250,000 to 500,0000 people, including a disproportionate number of Chinese, were murdered by rampaging mobs. Although his implication in the plot was never made clear, Sukarno's power was systematically undermined by the new regime until his death in June 1970.

Suharto and the Economic Meltdown

General Suharto ruled Indonesia from 1967 until his resignation in May 1998, just months after his election to a seventh five-year term. Not everyone was pleased with Suharto's re-election—especially in light of the financial collapse of the country, which had roiled the economy since the summer of 1997.

Protesters in Jakarta and three other cities, angered by a plunging currency, rampant inflation, and soaring unemployment, called on Suharto to quit. Anticipating problems, the 1,000 members of the People's Consultative Assembly (MPR) had earlier extended Suharto's already ample authority by granting him wide emergency powers—measures that could enable him to dissolve Parliament and ban political parties. But a more serious rift had developed with the International Monetary Fund, as assembly delegates accused the Washington-based agency of trampling on Indonesia's sovereignty. Under the US$43-billion bailout plan, Suharto was required to dismantle subsidies and monopolies that had made his family and associates rich over the last three decades.

The crisis started in May 1997 after Thailand's *baht* currency came under attack by speculators, who decided Thailand's slowing economy and political instability meant it was time to sell. Two months later, the Bank of Thailand announced a managed float of the *baht* just as the Indonesian *rupiah* also started to crumble. By mid-July, the Asian currency meltdown was in full swing as the *rupiah, baht,* Malaysian *ringgit,* and Filipino peso all slumped to record lows versus the U.S. dollar. On 14 August 1997, Indonesia abolished its system of a managed exchange rate and the *rupiah* fell down to a low of 3,845 by early October. On 8 October, Indonesia asked the IMF for financial assistance and by the end of the month had received approval for the US$43-billion bailout.

In January 1998, Indonesia unveiled its 1998/99 budget which projected a 32% increase in revenues and expenditures over the current budget and a four percent economic rate. The perception that the budget was not tough enough to meet IMF-mandated austerity measures set off another currency crisis as the *rupiah* broke 10,000 to the dollar over the next five days.

But Suharto continued to hedge his bets on implementing the IMF conditions for the bailout—especially those that hit the pocketbook of the president and his six children. The IMF had stated that Suharto's monopolistic grip on the economy was one of the biggest obstacles to the country's recovery and had demanded an end to some of the pet projects of Suharto's children. Among the IMF prescriptions were that the president end fuel subsidies and price controls on staple goods, which benefited several of his offspring; the end of his son's controversial national car program; the

cancellation of power plants being bankrolled by two of his daughters; the shelving of a quixotically expensive airplane project run by a close friend, the technology minister.

In early 1998, Suharto was forced to survey the wreckage of his economy: annual per-capita income down from US$1,200 to US$300; stock market capitalization down from US$118 billion to US$17 billion; only 22 of Indonesia's 286 publicly listed companies considered solvent; and only four out of 49 firms remaining with market capitalization of US$500 million or more before the crisis.

Suharto received yet another bad piece of news in March when the IMF announced that it would suspend further installments of the US$43 billion bailout package because of worries that Suharto would back off his pledges to dismantle monopolies and tariffs that benefited his family and friends.

Deadly rioting and mass student demonstrations led to the historical 22 May 1998 resignation of General Suharto. His term will be completed by vice president and old friend B.J. Habibie. A measure of stability seems to have returned to Indonesia. The IMF is reassessing the country's economic situation.

THE PEOPLE

Such an influx of peoples has flowed into Indonesia from China, Arabia, Polynesia, Southeast Asia, Indochina, and later from Portugal and Holland, that you can't say that Indonesians are one people. The country is in fact an ethnological gold mine, the variety of its human geography (336 ethnic groups) without parallel on earth. Welded together by a unifying lingua franca and intermarrying freely, Indonesia has all the Asian cultures, races, and religions; they worship Allah, Buddha, Shiva, and the Christian God—and in some places an amalgam of all four.

Shades of skin color vary from yellow to coal black. Each group strives to discover how all these differences can unite all Indonesians in beautiful harmony. The motto clasped in the talons of Garuda, the menacing eagle that is the state crest, is *Bhinneka Tunggal Ika* ("Unity in Diversity").

Indonesia has the fifth largest population in the world (about 200 million), which equals the combined population of all other Southeast Asian countries. The population of Java (the size of California) alone has quadrupled this century to 100 million, well over a third of the population of the United States.

LANGUAGE

Such is the diversity of tongues in Indonesia (250 speech forms, each with its own regional dialects) that often the inhabitants of the same island don't all speak the same native language. Fortunately, one language, Bahasa Indonesia, is taught in all schools from the elementary grades.

If you're traveling in a foreign land it's impossible to understand the culture unless you have some knowledge of the language. Learning the language is the miracle drug that minimizes culture shock. Here are some tips. First learn the numbers, the time, and the calendar systems, the mastering of which will spare you much frustration and money. Avoid Indonesians who try to speak to you in English; they're your most formidable obstacle to learning their language. The only way to learn another language is to never speak your own.

You'll be flabbergasted what you can say with a vocabulary of 500 or so words. In one month of diligent work you'll be speaking the "market talk" or Pasar Melayu. This is all you'll need for bargaining, getting around, and relating to people.

ON THE ROAD

GETTING THERE

Indonesia can be entered by air through seven major gateways. Most travelers, though, still land at Jakarta, Bali, or Medan. Prices of flights into Indonesia change constantly. As soon as the "Official Airlines Guide" is published each month, it's already out of date. Check the latest and cheapest tickets in the Sunday travel section of major metropolitan newspapers. Then call STA, Council Travel, and other budget agencies for ballpark figures.

From America
Current fares from discount agencies and consolidators on the West Coast of North America average US$850-950 roundtrip and US$1,000 roundtrip from New York. STA and Council Travel can advise on Pacific routings. See the main Introduction for addresses and phone numbers. Airlines serving Indonesia from the U.S. include United, TWA, Northwest, Quantas, JAL, and China Air. Most airlines have toll-free numbers for current fares, timetables, connections, etc. Call (800) 555-1212 for airline 800 numbers. Tickets purchased from airlines are generally full fare, although discounts are occasionally given.

Garuda flights from L.A. stop at the remote town of Biak, where the local natives patiently wait at the runway for the twice-weekly arrival. Consider flying one-way to Biak and continuing with local aircraft across the archipelago—the backdoor approach is an excellent alternative since you enter through the most spectacular parts of Indonesia—the outer islands. Other great ways to reach Indonesia include the South Pacific routing through Tahiti and Australia and the North Pacific routing through Japan, Hong Kong, and Southeast Asia. Details in the main Introduction.

From Europe
Most travelers make a stop in Bangkok or Singapore, although several airlines now offer direct flights to Jakarta or Bali. Trailfinders and STA sell budget tickets. Fares average £300-400 one-way to Jakarta or £600-750 roundtrip. Bali costs slightly less one-way but slightly more roundtrip. The weekly *Time Out* contains ads for many bargain airfares and discount travel agencies. Intriguing alternatives to a direct flight are inexpensive round-the-world tickets and one-way tickets to Australia or New Zealand with stops in India, Bangkok, or Hong Kong.

From Australia
Both Qantas and Garuda fly to Bali and Jakarta from Australia's main cities: Sydney, Melbourne,

INDONESIA

Darwin, Perth, and Port Hedland. Tickets are expensive and deep discounts such as those available in London and America are nonexistent. The best deals are APEX tickets, which must be reserved and paid for at least three weeks in advance, and seven- to 28-day excursion fares from travel agencies. Avoid high season from November to February.

Another cheap way to reach Indonesia is to join a group tour, which can cost even less than APEX fares. The cheapest and certainly the most intriguing approach is the twice-weekly Merpati flight from Darwin to Kupang (Timor) for A$225 one-way. The more expensive Darwin to Bali flight is also recommended since stops are permitted in Maumere, Ruteng, Labuhanbajo, Bima, and Ampenan—a sensible way to avoid the nightmare of land travel across Nusa Tenggara.

From Singapore

The most popular approach to Indonesia is the daily flight from Singapore to Jakarta or Bali. One-way fares currently stand at US$100-150 to Jakarta and US$180-250 to Bali. Budget agencies advertise in the *Straits Times,* though the very cheapest deals are passed from traveler to traveler. Ask about the special UTA Singapore-U.S.A. ticket for US$800 with stops in Jakarta, Bali, Australia, New Zealand, and Tahiti; an incredible deal.

Direct sea connections from Singapore to Indonesia do not exist, but indirect passage is possible via Batam and the Indonesian island of Tanjung Pinang. You'll save some money but it can be a slow and frustrating experience filled with delays and cancellations. Step one is a ferry from Finger Pier to the Singaporean island of Batam. A second ferry continues to the Indonesian island of Tanjung Pinang, where passengers proceed through customs and immigration and usually spend a night. The MV *Lawit* leaves Tanjung Pinang twice monthly for either Jakarta *or* Belawan (near Medan in north Sumatra). This luxurious German-built ship has seven first-class cabins, 10 second-class cabins, and covered deck-class accommodations for 866 passengers. Total fare is S$120-240 depending on class. Allow three full days from Singapore. *Arrive in Tanjung Pinang on the correct day unless you don't mind waiting up to two weeks for the next boat!*

APPROVED GATEWAY CITIES

JAVA

Jakarta Airport
Jakarta Seaport
Surabaya Airport
Surabaya Seaport
Semarang Seaport

BALI

Ngurah Rai Airport
Padangbai Seaport
Benoa Seaport

SUMATRA

Medan Airport
Belawan Seaport
Pekanbaru Airport
Padang Airport

RIAU

Tanjung Pinang Seaport
Batam Airport
Batam Seaport

SULAWESI

Manado Airport
Manado Seaport

KALIMANTAN

Pontianak Airport
Balikpapan Airport

MALUKU

Ambon Airport
Ambon Seaport

TIMOR

Kupang Airport

IRIAN JAYA

Biak Airport

You can also fly from Batam to Jakarta if you miss your connection. For reservations and further information in Singapore, contact STA (tel. 734-5681) in the Ming Court Hotel on Tanglin Road, German Asian Travels (tel. 533-5466) in the Straits Trading Building on Battery Road, Yang

Shipping (tel. 223-9902), Dino Shipping (tel. 221-4916), or Inasco Shipping (tel. 224-0698).

An erratic and rugged cargo boat sails weekly from Tanjung Pinang to Pekanbaru in south Sumatra. The Conradesque journey sails up the Siak River for 36 hours to Pekanbaru for 30,000Rp deck class or 45,000Rp in the cabin. The experience has been both highly praised and strongly damned by travelers.

From Malaysia

The second most popular way to reach Indonesia from Southeast Asia is the US$80 daily flight from Penang to Medan in northern Sumatra. Garuda also flies from Kuala Lumpur to several towns in Sumatra, including Medan, Padang, and Pekanbaru. A regular ferry sails from Penang twice weekly to Medan's port of Belawan. Tickets cost US$50 second class. Garuda and Merpati also fly between Kalimantan and the Malaysian states of Sabah and Sarawak.

GETTING AROUND

By Air

Surface transportation, as usual, is cheaper but means a lengthy land or sea passage. Given the limited two months you have in Indonesia, if you want to see the islands beyond Java, Sumatra, and Bali, flying is almost unavoidable. Prices are reasonable, flights are safe, and service is adequate. Always try to get a seat in front of the wings so you can enjoy some of Indonesia's spectacular volcanic and marine scenery during your flight.

State-run **Garuda Indonesia,** tel. (800) 342-7832, the largest Indonesian airline, serves a limited number of domestic routes for international clients who need direct connections. They have essentially withdrawn from the domestic market. All other routes, as well as some border-crossing flights to Australia and eastern Malaysia, are now flown by Merpati using DC-9s, F-28s, Airbuses, and Fokkers. Other airlines such as Bouraq offer additional flights on a zany collection of aircraft including DC-3s, Vanguards, 707s, Viscounts, Skyvans, and Twin Otters. These alternative airlines concentrate in the low-traffic fringe areas not served by Garuda or Merpati. No matter the airline, always confirm flight availability and book a seat well in advance—especially important in the eastern islands where flights are less frequent and seats tend to fill up quickly. Airport departure tax is 2,000-6,000Rp for internal flights and 15,000Rp for external flights. Baggage allowances are from 10 kg on smaller planes such as the 16-passenger Fokker Friendship up to 20 kg on larger aircraft; excess baggage charge is about 5,000Rp per kg (if they even bother to charge you). Airport luggage-storage facilities charge 2,000-3,000Rp per day.

By Sea

Sea transportation—in one form or another—is available to and from all the inhabited islands of Indonesia. The range of sailing craft is nothing short of fantastic: *prahu* which can sail virtually anywhere, Makassarese and Bugis schooners *(kapal layar)* hauling timber from Borneo to Jakarta, speedboats *(spetbot)* and bulky river ferries, outrigger canoes, luxury cruise ships hauling wealthy tourists and veteran travel writers. Frozen as they are in a 19th-century time warp, it's an unforgettable experience riding on Indonesian vessels. Watch the PBS special "Ring of Fire" for inspiration! Check with a *syahbandar* (harbormaster) in any of the thousands of ports of Indonesia about the comings and goings of boats and their prices. Or ask around the harbor first to find a ship sailing where you want to head, then go to the shipping company office. This is when knowing Indonesian really pays off.

The most reliable oceangoing shipping company is state-owned Pelni, which has seven new German ships sailing from one end of the archipelago to the other (Banda Aceh to Sorong) on fixed schedules. Pelni ships are fast, sleek, modern, safe, and comfortable. All are completely air-conditioned (even deck class!) and designed to carry 1,000-1,500 passengers in four classes and *ekonomi*. Pelni gets to just about everywhere at two-week intervals. Fares are standardized and very reasonable; in fourth class you sleep in an eight-berth cabin with your own locker; in third class, there are six beds; in second class, four beds; and in first class, two beds. First-class fare includes TV, day and night videos, bathrooms with hot showers, comfortable beds, palatable meals. Economy-class bunks fit 50-60 people;

INDONESIA

INDONESIA

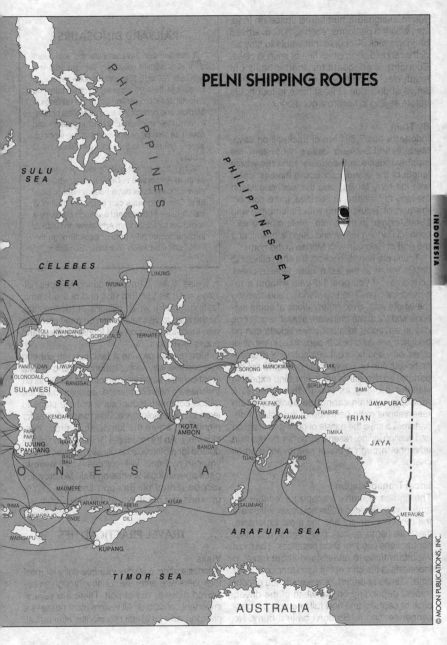

PELNI SHIPPING ROUTES

PHILIPPINES

PHILIPPINE SEA

SULU SEA

CELEBES SEA

LINUNG

TATUNA

TITUNG

TERNATE

TOLI TOLI   KWANDANG   GORONTALO

PANTOLAN   LIWUK

KOLONODALE   BANGGAI

SULAWESI

KENDARI

PARE PARE

UJUNG PANDANG

BAU BAU

SORONG   MANOKWARI   BIAK

SERUI   SAMI

FAK FAK   KAIMANA   NABIRE   JAYAPURA

IRIAN JAYA

TIMIKA

KOTA AMBON

BANDA

TUAL   DOBO

MERAUKE

O N E S I A

MAUMERE

BIMA   LARANTUKA   KALABAHI   KISAR

LABUANBAJO   ENDE   DILI

WAINGAPU

KUPANG

SAUMLAKI

ARAFURA SEA

TIMOR SEA

AUSTRALIA

© MOON PUBLICATIONS, INC.

INDONESIA

you're assigned a numbered space on long, low, wooden platforms, each with its overhead baggage rack. A couple that wants to stay together should book either first or second class. Economy is adequate for shorter hauls but fourth class is preferable for longer journeys. Arrive at dockside at least three to four hours before sailing to secure a good bunk.

By Train

Indonesia has 7,891 km of track, all on Java, Madura, and Sumatra. Java's rail system, the most extensive in Indonesia, runs the whole length of the island, connecting the east coast with the ferry for Bali and the west coast with the ferry for Sumatra. In Sumatra, trains connect the port of Telukbetung with Palembang and Lubuklinggau in the south, while other tracks connect Padang with inland Lake Singkarak and the port of Belawan with Medan in the north.

Trains are heavily booked. It's often difficult to obtain tickets at the last minute. Double-check schedules. If you board a train without a reserved seat, you'll end up standing and swaying the whole way. Seat reservations at some stations and for some trains are available only one day in advance; in other cities tickets can be bought three days before departure; in yet other cities, only one hour before departure! In Jakarta, tickets can be bought only on the day of departure, so rise early, get in line, and expect to wait for as long as two to three hours. A roundtrip by train cannot be booked; return reservations must be made at the point of departure. To save the hassle of getting to a station and waiting in line, reservations may be made in advance through a travel agency for a small charge.

Local Transportation

The choice of native transport available will amaze you. Besides trains and taxis, which are the most convenient and the most expensive, there are *bemo, helicak, bajaj, becak,* and other contraptions used for short distances. The most important thing to understand about travel in Indonesia is the concept of *jam karet,* or "rubber time." Times of departure are stretched or contracted depending on the whim of the driver, pilot, or captain, and how full or empty the passenger seating is. So don't be in a hurry. No

---

RAILYARD DINOSAURS

A decade ago Java was still the equivalent of a wildlife sanctuary for rare engines, with over 700 active steam locomotives made up of no less than 69 classes. Occasionally you can still see locos puffing out of the railyards in Madiun, and behemoths such as Mallets or Hartmanns, their smokestacks belching steam and soot, can also be seen hauling rolling stock up severe gradients in the vicinity of Bandung at Cibatu.

A big draw for rail buffs is the open-air museum at Ambarawa in Central Java, where 22 steam locomotives have been let out to pasture. Charter groups can enjoy the thrill of a steam-hauled ride aboard a vintage Swiss-built cogwheel tank loco from Ambarawa to Bedono through scenic hilly terrain; book through the PJKA office on Jalan Thamrin in Semarang.

---

one else is! Avoid traveling during religious holidays such as Idul Fitri (the end of the Islamic fasting month), when millions of Indonesians hit the road to visit relatives. You must compete with them for transport and tourist facilities, and prices skyrocket.

Motorcycles provide a fast, convenient and inexpensive way to get around. Ride one with great caution, as serious motorcycle accidents on Indonesia's often congested, madcap roads are all too common. Indonesia is not the place to learn to ride a motorcycle. Bring warm clothes for highlands, where the temperature drops considerably. An International Driver's License endorsed for motorcycles is usually required before you can rent one. Without one, you'll need to get a special local license on Bali. Motorcycles can be rented on Bali and Lombok, in Yogyakarta and Surabaya, and at Lake Toba.

TRAVEL PRACTICALITIES

Visas

Indonesia offers a 60-day visa-free entry for most foreigners who enter the country through an approved gateway city or port. There are several important conditions. All visitors must possess a passport valid for at least six months after arrival.

Two-month tourist passes cannot be extended. If you want to stay longer, the only option is to leave the country and return for another stamp. Thirdly, all visitors must possess a ticket out on arrival. This requirement can be satisfied by purchasing the least expensive ticket and then requesting a refund if unused. The two cheapest and most convenient exit points are Medan-Penang (one-way ticket out is US$80) and Jakarta-Singapore (student fare is US$120-150).

Another important restriction is that only those visitors who enter and exit through *approved* gateway cities will be granted the two-month tourist pass. This includes all popular gateway cities, so very few travelers need to worry about this. Those travelers who intend to enter or exit through nonapproved gateway cities must obtain a one-month visa in advance from an Indonesian consulate. These can be extended 30 days by paying a landing tax of 50,000Rp. Nonapproved cities to beware of include Jayapura (Irian Jaya) and Tarakan (Kalimantan). Approved gateway cities are listed below.

Other possible visas include a Business Visa and a Visitor's Visa for students or those with Indonesian sponsors. Special certificates from the police called *surat jalans* are sometimes necessary to explore the more remote areas of Indonesia, such as interior Irian Jaya. This letter must be presented on demand to army, police, immigration, or customs officials: a reassuring sign that you are being a fine, cooperative tourist.

Tourist Information
Indonesian tourist offices, both overseas and domestic, are very poorly stocked aside from a few colorful and relatively generic brochures. Letters and personal visits even to the national headquarters in Jakarta are almost completely useless. Garuda and Natrabu Travel offices in Western countries are often much more helpful than tourist offices. Visiting the regional offices in places like Yogyakarta and Bandung is worthwhile, however, since you may come across an exceptionally knowledgeable employee who sincerely wants to help you discover what is most beautiful about his or her country.

The really valuable and up-to-date travel information you'll get from other travelers along the way—cheapest and friendliest *losmen,* where to eat and drink, best beaches, most beautiful walks, spectacular ruins, mystics, where to learn *kris* making. The many Indonesians you inevitably meet can tell you where *wayang,* dance, or folk dramas are happening, where to find the best crafts. This book will fill in the basics and give you enough maps to find your way around, but the sheer complexity of Indonesia prevents *Southeast Asia Handbook* from going into great detail. To really understand the mind-blowing diversity, rumors, dirt, and glory of Indonesia, buy Moon Travel Handbooks' *Indonesia Handbook* by Bill Dalton.

Maps
The best folded maps of Indonesia available are the APA Roadmaps: *Bali* (scale 1:180,000), *Suma-*

getting around,
Yogya style

tra (1:1,500,000), *Java and West Nusa Tenggara* (1:1,500,000), *Kalimantan* (1:1,500,000), etc. Costing US$6.95 each, these beautiful maps feature vivid eight-color printing, topographic features in realistic relief, and major city plans in close-up margin inserts. These maps can be found at better hotels in Indonesia, but it's best to bring them with you. Another high-quality folded map is *Hildebrand's Travel Map of Western Indonesia*. At US$5.95, this up-to-date map clearly presents the country's topography, roads, towns, and cities. Beware of local maps; village locations seem determined by throwing darts at the map.

Money

The Indonesian monetary unit is called the *rupiah* (Rp). Study Indonesian currency and coins until you're familiar with all the denominations. Bills are all the same size but different colors. When changing large amounts, banks usually give you 10,000Rp notes, which could make it difficult to get your wallet or moneybelt shut! But changing even a 10,000Rp bill in the outlying provinces of Indonesia could prove troublesome. If heading for the outer islands, it's best to accept only 1,000Rp and 5,000Rp notes. In mid 1994 one U.S. dollar was worth 2,150 *rupiah*.

U.S.-dollar traveler's checks are most widely accepted, though it's also easy to cash other well-known currencies such as Australian dollars, Deutschmarks, Netherlands florin, French and Swiss francs. Bank Expor Impor Indonesia, Bank Negara Indonesia, and Bank Rakyat Indonesia have branches virtually the length and breadth of the country, from Aceh to Kupang. When exchanging large amounts, it's worth shopping around to get the best rate. Surprisingly, the highest rates are found in tourist towns such as Kuta, Yogya, and Rantepao. Avoid exchanging money at airports, train stations, and leading hotels. Indonesia has no black market.

Take enough money with you in the first place so you won't have to go through the hassle of having money wired, a service which costs up to US$15. Travelers who've been caught short have found that it may take several weeks to get money remitted by wire from Australia, North America, or Europe. Then there's the horror story of the Indonesian bank that kept the money wired to them for a month and invested it! If you're really stuck, a telex is a much faster way to transfer money than ordinary telegrams or moneygrams. Before you go, get your bank's telex number. A slower way is to wire home and ask for an international money order.

Indonesia's cheapest destinations are right along the travelers' trail, but watch out; you'll spend more here on fruit smoothies and batik underwear than you ever will in Irian Jaya. Ask for receipts for entrance fees to temples but don't raise a fuss since the "guards" are only trying to feed their families. Bribes are often necessary to expedite legal paperwork, get the last seat on the train, obtain a permit to visit a remote tribe, get out of jail. You know when it's coming: "The matter must be referred to another department. Come back next week."

Bargaining

Bargaining will teach you much about the real Indonesia. Always try to get the lowest price the seller will accept. The more Indonesians overcharge, the less interaction there is, the less respect there is, and the more impoverished the communication becomes. Bargain for everything: medicine in drugstores, hospitalization, immigration fees, entrance charges to museums or temple sites, no matter what type of establishment it is, even "fixed-price" shops. Bargaining should be good-humored, not infuriating, a game won by technique and strategy, not by anger or threats. This isn't a one-way process at all—Indonesians enjoy it. It's how most Indonesians relate with you. Before you go shopping, ask your hotel proprietor, houseboy, driver, or anyone who is uninvolved with the shop what the *correct* price for the item or service is.

OVERSEAS TOURIST OFFICES

Australia: 5 Elizabeth St., Sydney, NSW 2000, tel. (02) 9233-3630

Germany: Wiesenhuettenstrasse 17, D-6000 Frankfurt am Main, tel. (069) 233677

Singapore: 10 Collyer Quay, Ocean Building, tel. (01) 534-2837

United Kingdom: 3-4 Hanover St., London WIR 9HH, tel. (0171) 493-0030

U.S.A.: 3457 Wilshire Blvd., Los Angeles, CA 90010, tel. (213) 387-2078

INDONESIAN EMBASSIES

Australia: 8 Darwin Ave., Canberra ACT 2600, tel. (06) 273-3222

Canada: 287 Maclaren St., Ottawa, Ontario K2P 0L9, tel. (613) 236-7403

France: 49 Rue Cartambert, Paris 75116, tel. (01) 4503-0760

Germany: 2 Bernkasteler Strasse 2, Bonn 53175, tel. (0228) 382990

Japan: 9 Higashi Gotanda, 5-Chome, Shingawa, Tokyo, tel. (03) 3441-4201

Netherlands: 8 Tobias Asserlaan, 2517 KC, Den Haag, tel. (070) 310-8100

New Zealand: 70 Glen Rd., Kelburn, Wellington, tel. (04) 475-8697

Papua New Guinea: P.O. Box 7165, Baroko, Port Moresby, tel. (01) 251-3116

United Kingdom: 38 Grosvenor Square, London WIX 9AD, tel. (0171) 499-7661

U.S.A.: 2020 Massachusetts Ave., Washington, D.C. 20036, tel. (202) 775-5200

5 East 68th St., New York, NY 10021, tel. (212) 879-0600

3457 Wilshire Blvd., Los Angeles, CA 90010, tel. (213) 383-5126

1111 Columbus Ave., San Francisco, CA 94133, tel. (415) 474-9571

233 North Michigan Ave., Chicago, IL 60601, tel. (312) 938-0101

Indonesians themselves are always swapping price information as a way of keeping their costs down. Compare prices, learn about the quality, and then ask for the beginning price. Never make the first offer! Offer a quarter to half of the asking price. When you reach your highest price, don't budge. Instead, try "The Walk Away," as feigned disinterest makes for good deals. The real secret to successful bargaining is *never to appear to care.* This is absolutely necessary with *becak* drivers; just smile, shrug your shoulders, and walk slowly away with cocked ears. Often the driver will call you back, agreeing to your last bid. Never hover around, fondle, or show enthusiasm for your *true* interest. Instead, include the item with other articles you want, as if it's a second thought, "Oh, how much for this too?" Finally, remember that it's bad manners to continue to bargain after a deal has been struck, a service has been rendered, or an item has been bought.

JAVA

When fossil remains of the erect ape *Pithecan-thropus erectus* were found on Java in 1891, scientists surmised that Java was the original location of the Garden of Eden.

The most famed of all of Indonesia's islands, Java is also one of the richest, lushest, most densely populated on earth and ranks among the loveliest regions anywhere. Deep purple and fiery volcanoes tower majestically over a land of intense green plains, twisting mountain passes, cool hillside resorts, remote crater lakes, extraordinary Hindu temples, wild game parks, botanical gardens, serene beaches, dense rainforests, vast savannah, thick bamboo groves, stands of teak, and squalling, teeming cities.

Java was the genesis of Indonesia's powerful maritime and agricultural kingdoms and contains the best-preserved and highest number of monuments, many completed centuries before Columbus discovered America. Java is both young and old, rich and poor. Many areas resemble India because of the congestion, the rice paddies, the explosive colors: "I see India everywhere, but I do not recognize it," said the great Bengali poet Tagore when he visited Java in 1927.

The People

Though Java is the smallest of the Greater Sunda islands, it is inhabited by the bulk of Indonesia's population, over 120 million residents packed into only 7% of the country's land mass. With their light brown skin, straight black hair, high cheekbones, and slender builds, the Javanese originally belonged to the Oceanic branch of the Mongoloid race. But the Javanese "race" is actually a blending of every race that ever established itself on the island. Java's people belong to primarily four major cultural-lingual ethnic groups: the Sundanese of West Java (about 30 million), the Javanese of Central

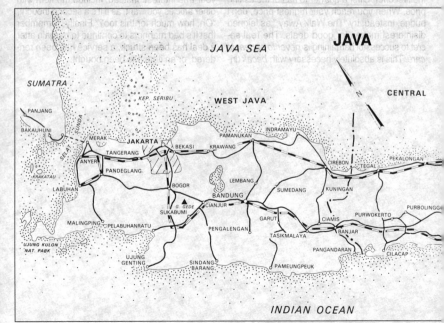

and East Java (about 80 million), the Tenggerese from the area in East Java around Mt. Bromo (300,000), and the Madurese inhabiting the long island of Madura near Surabaya in East Java. The largest group, the Javanese, are also, in terms of cultural and political influence, the most important.

Sightseeing Highlights

Java is officially divided into the provinces of West, Central, and East Java, plus the special territories of Jakarta and Yogyakarta.

Travelers generally follow a route from Jakarta through Bogor, Bandung, Yogyakarta, Solo, Mt. Bromo, and Surabaya to Bali. Central Java offers the greatest number of historical and cultural attractions. Visitors short on time often use Yogyakarta, the cradle of Javanese culture, as a base for exploring the temples and natural sights.

West Java offers beach resorts for wealthy Jakartians and several cities worth brief explorations. Bandung's art-deco architecture and Bogor's famous Botanical Gardens are the top draws but the gateway city of Jakarta also warrants some time.

East Java's top attraction is sunrise at Mt. Bromo, along with visits to Malang, the zoo in Surabaya, and nature reserves in the extreme east.

Transportation

Train: Two parallel train lines run the island's whole length: a northern coastal line (Jakarta-Cirebon-Semarang-Surabaya-Banyuwangi) and a central line (Jakarta-Cirebon-Yogyakarta-Solo-Surabaya-Banyuwangi). Trains are a good way to tour Java since they are far more comfortable than buses and stations are located in the center of town, unlike bus terminals, which are often several kilometers away.

All classes and comfort zones are represented. Java's luxury-class trains such as the Bima and the Mutiara Utara have air-conditioned sleepers and dining cars. Seats can be reserved through travel agencies in most larger towns including those on Jalan Jaksa in Jakarta. The small service charge is well worth avoiding the long ticket lines at most train stations. Westerners can also avoid lines by appealing directly to the stationmaster.

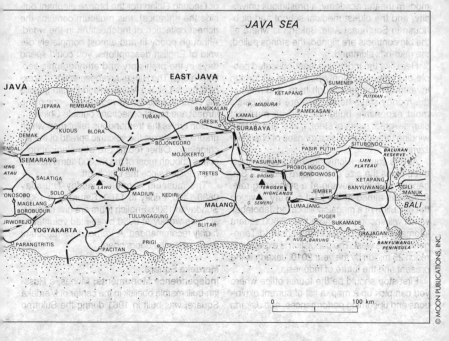

© MOON PUBLICATIONS, INC.

Express and ordinary trains come in three classes. Prices double from third to second class and again from second-class ordinary to second-class express. Second-class express is therefore four times the cost of third-class ordinary. While this may cost more, unreserved train and third-class trains should be avoided since most are badly overcrowded and unbearable in the hot weather. Student discounts are available on most trains.

Bus: Buses on Java are frequent and comprehensive but slow, painful, nerve-wracking, and dangerous. The rule of thumb: trains are best for longer journeys, buses are OK for shorter hauls. Buses, like trains, also come in different types and classes. Ordinary buses are plentiful but less comfortable than *ekspres* or *bis malam* buses, which travel nonstop on all the major roads. *Bis malam* (night buses) depart in the late afternoon or early evening, traveling faster and cooler on less congested roads, but you sacrifice sightseeing for speed. Unless you're in a big rush, it's preferable to take day buses and get a good night's sleep.

Ticket collectors are honest but you should try to present correct fare rather than wait for change.

JAKARTA

Also known as Ibu Kota, the "Mother City," this teeming metropolis of 12 million is Indonesia's capital—the brain, treasury vault, and nerve center of the country. The world's ideas, technology, and fashions first touch Indonesia here. It's the literary center and headquarters for the mass media: a quarter of all of Indonesia's newspapers are printed here. The city has a film industry, a modern theater academy, a prestigious university, and the oldest medical school and clubhouse in Southeast Asia. Jakarta is where all the big contracts are signed, the strings pulled, the rake-offs skimmed.

Here live the most- and least-educated people of Indonesia. Eighty percent of all foreign investment comes through here, and most of the money stays here. Here are Indonesia's most expensive buildings and its murkiest slums—great rivers of steel, glass, and granite winding through endless expanses of one-story *kampongs*.

At 650 square kilometers, Jakarta is almost three times the size of the entire island of Singapore, plus it's growing at a staggering rate. Programs aimed at the 21st century envision the evolution of a megalopolis called Jabotabek which will encompass more than 7,500 square kilometers, from Bogor in the south to Tanggerang in the west. The population is expected to reach 25 million by the year 2010. Jakarta is the present and the future of Indonesia.

First stop should be the tourist office where you can pick up a map, a list of current exhibitions and upcoming performances, and *Jakarta See for Yourself,* which describes buses to the main sights.

ATTRACTIONS

National Museum
Also called the Museum Pusat (Central Museum) or Gedung Gajah (for the bronze elephant outside the entrance), this museum contains the richest collection of Indonesiana in the world. Although poorly lit and almost completely devoid of English descriptions, you could spend days in the prehistory and ethnographic sections alone. The Hindu-Javanese antiquities exhibit rivals Leyden Museum's in Holland, while the ceramic collection is regarded as one of the largest and rarest collections outside China.

Don't miss the tremendous relief map which graphically shows the volcanic spread of the archipelago. Other rooms are ethnological gold mines, though most of the 85,000 items haven't been dusted since the Dutch left.

The museum is open Tuesday-Thursday 0830-1400, Friday to 1100, Saturday to 1300, Sunday to 1500. English tours are given several times weekly at 0930 by spirited volunteers; *highly* recommended. A tremendous museum; arrive when the doors open!

Merdeka Square
Independence Monuments: Monas, a Russian-built marble obelisk in the center of Merdeka Square, was built in 1961 during the Sukarno

JAKARTA BAY

JAKARTA

INDONESIA

OLD SHIPS

PASAR IKAN
MARITIME MUSEUM

MARINA
(BOATS TO PULAU SERIBU)

HORIZON HOTEL

ANCOL AMUSEMENT PARK

JL. PULIT SELATAN

TO AIRPORT (8 km)

JL. MARTINADATA

TO TANJUNG PRIOK HARBOR AREA
(1 km)

MUSEUM OF

DRAWBRIDGE

MUSEUM WAYANG
FINE ARTS

JL. KOPI

JAKARTA CITY MUSEUM

OLD BATAVIA (KOTA)

KOTA TRAIN STATION

PORTUGUESE CHURCH

JAKARTA TOWER HOTEL

JL. GAJAH MADA

CHINATOWN (GLODOK)

CHINESE TEMPLE

NIGHT WARUNGS

PELNI

NATIONAL ARCHIVES BLDG.

NIGHT WARUNGS

TO KALIDERES BUS TERMINAL

JL. HASYIM ASHARI

JL. JUANDA

JL. MERDEKA UTARA

GPO

BHARATA THEATER

JL. PARMAN

JL. CARINGIN

INSCRIPTION PARK

ISTIQLAL MOSQUE

LAPANGAN MERDEKA (FREEDOM SQUARE)

GAMBIR TRAIN STATION

PASAR SENEN TRAIN STATION

JL. SUPRAPTO

ORCHID PALACE HOTEL

NATIONAL MUSEUM

SENEN BUS TERMINAL

TO PULO GADUNG BUS TERMINAL

JL. MERDEKA SELATAN

JL. KEBON SIRIH

HYATT ARYUDATA

JL. KRAMAT RAYA

TOURIST INFORMATION

BUDGET HOTELS

INDONESIA TOURIST OFFICE

TANAH ABANG TRAIN STATION

JL. HASYIM

JL. JAKSA

JL. SUMATRA

JL. MENTENG RAYA

SARINAH DEPT. STORE

TEXTILE MUSEUM

TANAH ABANG BUS TERMINAL

TAMAN ISMAIL MARZUKI (T I M)

TO MERAK

GRAND HYATT

MANDARIN ORIENTAL HOTEL

HOTEL INDONESIA

JL. BONJOL

PASAR SURABAYA ANTIQUES

PHPA

PASAR BLORA

KARTIKA PLAZA HOTEL

JL. DIPONEGORO

PARLIAMENT

JL. SUBROTO

PROCLAMATION MEMORIAL

REGENT HOTEL

TO TAMAN MINI INDONESIA PARK (8 km)

SAHID JAYA HOTEL

TAMAN RIA REMAJA

MERIDIEN HOTEL

TO KEBAYORAN BARU AND BLOK M

JL. RASUNA SAID

STADIUM

JAKARTA HILTON

JL. THAMRIN

TO RAMBUTAN BUS TERMINAL AND ZOO (8 km)

0   1 km

© MOON PUBLICATIONS, INC.

INDONESIA

Map labels:

TO OLD BATAVIA (KOTA)

JL. THAMRIN

JL. PECENONGAN

NIGHT FOODSTALLS

JL. JUANDA

★ JL. PASAR BARU

GEDUNG KESENIAN THEATER
★ GPO

★ CHURCH

PRESIDENTIAL PALACE

ARMY HEADQUARTERS

★ ISTIQLAL MOSQUE

★ IRIAN JAYA MONUMENT

JL. PERWIRA

HOTEL BOROBUDUR INTERCONTINENTAL

★ CEMETERY OF INSCRIPTIONS

JL. TANAH ABANG

DIPONEGORO STATUE ★

MONAS

PEJAMBON

JL. SALAHI

BHARATA THEATER

SENEN TRAIN STATION

★ NATIONAL MUSEUM

● GEDUNG PANCASILA

JL. SENEN RAYA

● DAI ICHI HOTEL

PASAR SENEN

GAMBIR TRAIN STATION

★ EMMANUEL CHURCH

DEPARTMENT OF DEFENSE

LAPANGAN MERDEKA (FREEDOM SQUARE)

■ TANAMUR DISCO

ARJUNA STATUE ★

JL. KWITANG

YOUTH PLEDGE MUSEUM ★

JL. KRAMAT RAYA

■ GARUDA

★ USA EMBASSY

ARYUDATA HOTEL ●

SABANG HOTEL

JL. KEBON SIRIH

JL. JAKSA BUDGET ACCOMODATIONS

★ ANTIQUES

CENTRAL JAKARTA

SARI PACIFIC HOTEL

JL. SALIM

JL. MENTENG RAYA

● WISMA ISE

TOURIST INFORMATION ★

■ RESTAURANTS

JL. HASYIM

● GONDIA GH

JL. R. SALEH

SARINAH DEPT. STORE, HARD ROCK CAFE

■ IMMIGRATION

HOTEL MENTENG 1 ●

■ FRENCH EMBASSY

JL. RATULANGI

TAMAN ISMAIL MARZUKI CULTURAL CENTER

● CIKINI HOTEL

JL. THAMRIN

● PRESIDENT HOTEL

HOTEL MENTENG 2 ●

GRAND HYATT KLM

WELCOME STATUE ★

◆ OASIS RESTAURANT

HOTEL INDONESIA GARUDA AIRLINES

● MANDARIN ORIENTAL HOTEL

JL. SYAHIR

● MARCOPOLO HOTEL

0   500m

JL. BONJOL

JL. SAID

KARTIKA PLAZA HOTEL

★ PASAR CIKINI

■ THAI EMBASSY

PHILIPPINE EMBASSY

★ ANTIQUES

JL. DIPONEGORO

JL. SURABAYA

■ PASAR BLORA NIGHTCLUBS

TO EMBASSIES AND RAGUNAN ZOO

★ PROCLAMATION MONUMENT

© MOON PUBLICATIONS, INC.

Jakarta skyline

era to commemorate the struggle for independence from the Dutch. The gigantic phallic needle rises 137 meters and is topped with 35 kg of pure gold leaf to symbolize the flame of freedom. Wryly called "Sukarno's last erection," it provides an excellent orientation point and a knockout view from the observation room. Beneath the monument is a museum with dioramas relating Indonesia's history from prehistoric Java Man to the struggle for independence.

Merdeka Palace: Surrounding the one-square-kilometer Merdeka Square are several important buildings dating from the early 19th century. The presidential palace, though closed to the public, is lavishly appointed with Dutch colonial furniture, a neoclassic dining hall, and ceiling decorations resembling Ambonese lace. To the rear along Jalan Veteran stands Istana Negara, a palace originally constructed by wealthy Dutch traders.

National Mosque: Designed by a Christian Batak architect and commissioned by Sukarno (this city still very much wears his mark), the massive six-level Istiqlal Mosque, with its minarets and grandiose lines, is reputed to be the largest mosque in Southeast Asia and second largest in the world. Check your shoes and follow the guard past the giant drum to the central prayer hall supported by 12 columns representing the Javanese zodiac and five prayer levels representing the principles of *Pancasila* (the state philosophy). On Fridays, noontime services can be discreetly observed from the upper tiers.

Emmanuel Church: This unique classicist Dutch Protestant church was erected between 1834 and 1839 by architect J.H. Horst, who incorporated elements from Greek temples, Renaissance theaters, and the Roman arena in its circular construction. The whole interior is nicely bathed with an even, well-diffused light.

Old Batavia

Jakarta's best two attractions are the National Museum and the collection of Makassar schooners in Old Batavia. Also called Kota, this relatively small northern area was the waterfront swamp where the Dutch first settled and then remained for 330 years. The ships and all museums can be visited in one morning, but an early start is essential to avoid the afternoon heat. Take buses P1 or 70 from Jalan Thamrin to the Jakarta City Museum.

Dutch Bridge: Begin your walking tour at the sole remaining 17th-century drawbridge, which once marked the southwest corner of the old Dutch fort. Through the 18th century ships could sail under the drawbridge, and continue up the Ciliwung River past the Chartered Bank and Toko Merah building. Jakarta's best old architecture is on this street—so walk slowly!

Watch Tower: Gedung Syahbandar, the towerlike harbormaster's building, once served as a lighthouse and meteorological station equipped with all the high-tech instruments of the day. Chinese inscriptions on the floor are weight standards. Now closed to the public. Have lunch at the nearby cafe or go hungry until you reach Chinatown.

Maritime Museum: Museum Bahari consists of two recently restored Dutch East India Company warehouses (1652) which formerly guarded mountains of coffee, tea, pepper, cloth, tin, and copper. Spice-trade memorabilia and maritime models fill the interior.

Pasar Ikan: Once a fascinating neighborhood of fish markets and old stores selling embalmed turtles, Jakarta's old seafaring center is now a rather ordinary commercial center of clothing and hardware stores.

Harbor: This 500-year-old harbor area remains one of the most important calls for sailing vessels from all over the archipelago. Row upon row of handmade shallow-draft oceangoing Makassar schooners form the world's greatest collection of traditional sailing craft. A scene straight from Conrad; don't miss it! Boatmen can be hired to tour the waterfront.

Wayang Museum: This two-story building has nine rooms containing priceless collections of puppets from all over the world, including fam-ily-planning puppets, Sumatran dolls used during the Indonesian resistance movement, Punch and Judy from England, and French marionettes donated by Fran—ois Mitterand. *Wayang kulit* and *wayang golek* performances accompanied by *gamelan* Sunday mornings at 1000. Jakarta's second-best museum.

Jakarta City Museum: Once the City Hall of Batavia, this magnificent two-story building constructed in 1710 is one of the nation's finest examples of Dutch colonial architecture. Holds an amazingly rich collection of massive antique furniture and VOC memorabilia.

Museum of Fine Arts: Balai Seni Rupa houses a permanent exhibition of Indonesian paintings, from the Raden Saleh era up to contemporary times. The art is poorly lit and mediocre except for a self-portrait of a young painter in front of slums. Museum Keramik, a highly overrated and disappointing ceramics museum, shares the same building.

Portuguese Church: Gereja Sion, Jakarta's oldest standing house of worship, features a magnificent organ, a pulpit, and Dutch tomb-

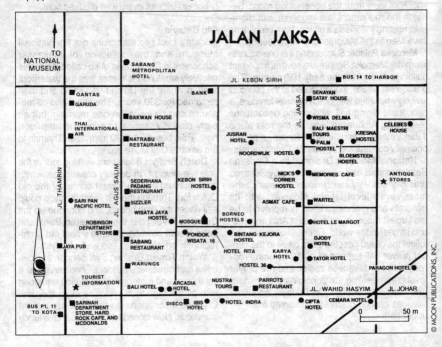

JALAN JAKSA

© MOON PUBLICATIONS, INC.

stones embedded in the northern wall. The most beautiful tomb is of Governor-General Zwaarde-croon, who asked to be buried here so that he might "sleep amongst the common folk."

Glodok: Jakarta's Chinatown has quickly changed from a struggling *kampong* into a thriving commercial center blanketed with air-conditioned shopping centers and luxury hotels—a jarring intersection of old poverty and new wealth. Walk east, sticking to the canals and under bridges: here you'll see poverty as grinding as anywhere in Asia.

Other Attractions

Textile Museum: A permanent exhibition of cloths and weavings from all over Indonesia. Located in Tanah Abang 15 minutes on foot west of Sarinah Department Store.

Taman Mini Indonesia: A 120-hectare open-air cultural/amusement park, 12 km south of the city. Touristy, difficult to reach, exhausting to explore, but a window into the cultural and environmental complexity of Indonesia. Pavilions built in traditional style exhibit artifacts, customs, and lifestyles of the peoples of each of Indonesia's 27 provinces. Indonesians will proudly tell you that there will be no need to see the rest of Indonesia if you visit this park. Free traditional dance performances on Sunday mornings.

Take buses P11, P16, 406, or 408 from Sarinah to the chaotic Cilitan terminal and continue with double-decker bus 408.

ACCOMMODATIONS

Budget

Jakarta's inexpensive guesthouses and hostels are located around Jalan Jaksa, within easy walking distance of the tourist office, sightseeing attractions, and the Gambir train station. All fill up fast, so arrive early for the best rooms.

Noordwijk Hostel: Top choice is the secure and friendly Hostel Noordwijk (or Norbek), where you can practice your Dutch with the amiable owner. Norbek is small, cozy, and filled by noon-time. Jalan Jaksa 14, tel. (021) 330392, US$6-10 fan, US$15-25 a/c.

Wisma Delima: Once the most famous hostel in Jakarta, the Delima has been sabotaged by its own success. Hasn't changed a bit in 10 years—bad lighting, stuffy, noisy, cramped. Jalan Jaksa 5, US$6-10.

Nick's Corner Hostel: Nick's has a pretentious facade, surly management, and grossly overpriced rooms. Jalan Jaksa 16, tel. (021) 314-1988, US$4 dorm, US$30-45 private rooms.

Tator Hotel: Renovated place with superior rooms. Jalan Jaksa 37, tel. (021) 323940, US$7-30.

Jalan Kebon Sirih Barat Dalam: Plenty of inexpensive places are found in the alleys off Jalan Jaksa. Borneo Hostel 1 has rooms for US$7-12 but adjacent Borneo Hostel 2 is cleaner and more spacious. Hostel Bintang Kejora is similarly priced and blessed with surprisingly friendly managers. Also try Pondok Wisata 16 with an inexpensive dorm and rooms from US$6, Pondok Wisata Jaya with rooms for US$6-10, and Kebon Sirih Hostel in the same price range.

Jalan Kebon Sirih Timur: Bloemsteen ("Flower Stone"), Palm Hostel, and Kresna are all rather cramped but reasonably priced at just US$5-10.

Moderate

Jalan Jaksa also has several good middle-priced hotels for those who want air-conditioning and cleaner rooms.

Hotel Karya: An old but renovated hotel with decent rooms. Jalan Jaksa 32, tel. (021) 314-0484, US$30-75.

Djody Hotel: Large and clean if somewhat dark rooms with private bath, either with fan or a/c. Jalan Jaksa 35, tel. (021) 315-1404, US$10-45.

Cipta Hotel: Best bet for mid-level travelers in the Jalan Jaksa neighborhood is this clean and modern hotel, which offers 30% discounts at the front desk. Jl. Wahid Hasyim 53, tel. (021) 390-4701, US$70-80.

Sabang Metropolitan Hotel: Well located on Jalan Agus Alim, the Sabang gives more bang for your buck than most other international-style hotels. Jalan Agus Salim, tel. (021) 373933, US$55-95.

RESTAURANTS

Western food in Jakarta is poorly prepared and overpriced but *warungs* and *warung* complexes *(puja seras)* serve tasty authentic fare at rock-bottom prices. No matter where your hotel is, you're never more than a few hundred meters from a delicious taste experience. Foodstalls are clustered in several neighborhoods:

Jalan Agus Salim (Jalan Sabang): Jakarta's restaurant row is conveniently located just one block from Jalan Jaksa. A nonstop lineup of Indonesian, Chinese, and Western restaurants, from Colonel Sanders and a Japanese bakery to the clean White House Restaurant. The Natrabu Restaurant is one of the most famous Padang restaurants in all of Indonesia. Streetside *sate* vendors set up their carts at the south end of the street.

Other Choices: The Sarinah car park turns into a food market in the early evening hours. Another popular place to *warung* wander is Jalan Pecononan, north of Merdeka Square, where some 50 informal foodstalls operate from twilight to midnight. Chinese foodstalls and flash discos can be found farther north on Jalan Manga Besar. Not a tourist in sight.

ENTERTAINMENT

Performing Arts

The tourist office brochure titled *Jakarta Permanent Exhibitions and Regular Performances* includes a useful guide to theater and dance venues. Current listings are given in their monthly *Guide to Jakarta*.

Taman Ismail Marzuki: Jakarta's cultural center sponsors weekly performances of traditional theater, Islamic poetry readings, comedy competitions, photographic exhibitions, jazz dance, film festivals, and indigenous dramas. A bilingual calendar is available (sometimes) from the tourist office.

Bharata Theater: Authentic *wayang orang* and *ketoprak* performances are given nightly at 2000 except Mondays and Thursdays in the hall on Jalan Kalilio. This is one of Indonesia's few remaining theaters that sponsor classical drama. Packed with Javanese—abundant local color.

National Museum: *Wayang golek, wayang kulit* and *gamelan* performances are given Sunday mornings at 0930, a must-see for anyone passing through Jakarta on a Sunday.

Wayang Museum: Wonderful shadow puppet and wooden marionette theater Sundays at 1000.

Taman Mini Indonesia: Sunday morning performances are given 1000-1200 in the pavilions for West Java, Yogyakarta *(wayang kulit),* East Java, and West Sumatra. The park is incredibly crowded but worth visiting for the shows.

Nightlife

Opinions about nightlife in Jakarta are divided between those who think it's a dull place and others who, perhaps expecting no-alcohol signs and veiled women, are surprised by the number of bars, nightclubs, discos, and massage parlors. Most of the city's nightlife revolves around the luxury hotels, but a fairly active scene has grown up in Chinatown and on Jalan Wahid Hasyim near Jalan Jaksa.

Jalan Jaksa: Admission fees at the clubs near Jalan Jaksa—and elsewhere in the city—are somewhat high but early-bird discounts are common before 2200. For example, discos around Jalan Jaksa are free before 2230 and often run specials to attract visiting Westerners.

The venerable Jaya Pub, behind the Jaya Building across from Sarinah, is a pleasant piano bar where artists, writers, musicians, filmmakers, and expats hang out.

Tanamur: Other nightlife is somewhat distant from the hostels on Jalan Jaksa. Certainly the most famous nightclub in town is the venerable Tanamur at Jalan Tanah Abang Timur 14, where many of the ladies charge for their services. Tanamur has rightly been called the most densely populated disco on the world's most densely populated island.

If Tanamur is packed out, try adjacent J.J. Duit where you can escape the terrors of technopop.

Chinatown: Glodok, Jakarta's Chinatown, is another hot spot for discos such as Stardust on Jalan Hayam Wuruk and Terminal 1, Kanto Pub, Zodiac (Indonesia's largest disco), and Sydney 2000—all located in Glodok Plaza on Jalan Pintu Besar Selatan. These sophisticated clubs are patronized by trendy, young Chinese males and hordes of single, prowling females.

Red Lights: Jakarta's transsexuals and female impersonators *(banci)* hang out in the Pasar Blora area past the sleazy nightclubs on Jalan Tanah Abung Timor. Jakarta's largest red-light district is in north Jakarta near Kramat Tunggak.

SHOPPING

Shopping in Jakarta is something of an ordeal because of the heat and traffic hassles, but a few shops and neighborhoods are worth exploring.

Sarinah Department Store: First stop should be the department store on Jalan Thamrin which, like an Indonesian Macy's, has everything from Borneo *perang* and coral jewelry to batik slippers and Batak woodcarvings. Batiks are on the third floor, reasonably priced handicrafts on the fourth, and a well-stocked bookstore is on the fifth. Sarinah is a good place for newcomers to become acquainted with what's available around the country although at rather high, fixed prices.

Antiques: Antique hunters usually head directly for Jalan Surabaya, where dozens of merchants sell a mixed bag of antiques, fakes, and hopeless discards. The small alley one block east of Jalan Jaksa (Jalan Kebon Sirih Timur Dalam) has several excellent antique shops, plus, of all things, an antique motorcycle dealer who specializes in Harleys.

Shoppers should also check the 40-odd handicraft shops in the Hilton's Indonesian Bazaar.

SERVICES

Tourist Information

The Jakarta Visitor's Information Center in the Jakarta Theatre on Jalan Wahid Hasyim has an excellent supply of maps and other information on Jakarta. This will be your best chance to find out about upcoming festivals in Indonesia.

The free city map provided by the tourist office is comprehensive, but for extended sojourns you'll need either maps from Periplus or Catra Buana.

The Directorate General of Tourism (Indonesia's national tourist organization) on Jalan Kramat Raya offers very little practical information.

Communications

International phone calls can be made around the clock in the Jakarta Theater Building opposite the Sarinah Department Store.

Jakarta's GPO and poste restante on Jalan Pasar Baru northeast of Merdeka Square is open 0800-1600 Mon.-Fri. and 0800-1300 Saturdays. From Sarinah take buses 10, 11, or 12.

Government Office Hours

All Indonesian immigration offices, tourist information centers, and museums are open 0800-1500 Mon.-Thur., 0800-1130 on Fridays, and 0800-1300 Saturdays. Rule of thumb: do all official business and sightseeing *early* in the day!

TRANSPORTATION

Airport Arrival

All international and most domestic flights arrive at the Soekarno-Hatta International Airport, 36 km west of city center in Cengkareng. You can get into town by taxi (35,000Rp plus 7,000Rp toll), private hotel shuttles (20,000Rp), or blue-and-white Damri minibuses (5,000Rp) which leave every 30 minutes 0300-2000 and take about 45 minutes to reach Gambir train station, a 15-minute walk from Jalan Jaksa.

If you want to avoid Jakarta altogether, take a bus or taxi down to the Kampung Rambutan bus terminal, 18 km south of city center, from where you can make onward connections to Bogor, Bandung, or Yogyakarta. An easier idea is to hop on the first train departing from Gambir train station. Train departures are listed below under "Leaving Jakarta by Train."

Getting around Jakarta

Indonesia's premier city—sprawling, bustling, congested—is a bitch to get around in: it's 25 km north to south, hot and muggy; the traffic is horrendous; streets maddeningly change names every two or three blocks; major thoroughfares are freeways without pedestrian overpasses.

The best way to tour Jakarta is by metered, a/c taxi. Drivers are honest and rates are incredibly low. Blue Bird taxis are considered the best in town.

Public buses are slow and crowded but adequate except during rush hour. Most city destinations can be reached with buses from Jalan Thamrin near Sarinah Department Store. Others leave from Gambir train station and from Jalan Kebon Sirih near Bank Duta.

Airlines and Travel Agencies

Air tickets are sold by a variety of airlines and travel agencies. Garuda has offices in the BDN building on Jalan Thamrin and in Hotel Borobudur. Merpati and Bouraq are on Jalan Angkasa in Kemayoram.

Several decent travel agencies are on Jalan Jaksa. Discounts are also available from Carnation Travel on Jalan Menteng Raya and Indo Shangrila Travel on Jalan Gajah Mada in Glodok.

The three largest tour operators in Indonesia are Natrubu on Jalan Agus Salim (near Jalan Jaksa), Pacto in the Borobudur Hotel, and Vayatours on Jalan Batu Tulis. These companies offer some very interesting tours at surprisingly reasonable prices.

Leaving Jakarta by Air

Minibuses leave Gambir train station for the airport every 30 minutes. Airport departure tax is 25,000Rp on international and 12,000Rp on domestic flights. Duty-free cartons of Gudang Garam are sold at the airport!

Flights to Singapore cost US$65-80 on secondary airlines such as Pakistan International and Gulf Air. Sample discounted airfares to other countries (one-way and roundtrip): Bangkok US$200/380, Penang US$180/360, Hong Kong US$320/540, London US$520/840, Los Angeles US$580/1,120, Perth US$300/480, and Sydney US$450/720.

Leaving Jakarta by Train

Jakarta's trains serve most destinations on Java. Tickets can be purchased in advance at the train station or for a small service fee from travel agencies on Jalan Jaksa. The modest service charge is worth avoiding the lines at the train station.

Most trains depart from Gambir station, within walking distance of Jalan Jaksa. Trains head east toward Sumatra from Tanah Abang station but most travelers prefer the faster buses from Kalideres bus station.

Bogor: Trains from Gambir to Bogor take 1.5 hours and depart every 20 minutes 0700-2000.

Bandung: Trains to Bandung take three hours and depart Gambir hourly 0500-2140.

Yogyakarta and Solo: Trains to Yogykarta take 10-11 hours and depart Gambir at 0610, 0720, and 2040. The evening departure puts you in Yogyakarta just as the sun rises—the

perfect time to start searching for your hotel. These trains continue east to Solo.

North Coast: Trains to Cirebon take 3.5 hours and depart Gambir at 0700, 0945, and 1630. Most trains going to Yogyakarta also pass through Cirebon.

Surabaya: Express trains to Surabaya take the shorter northern route through Cirebon and Semerang while other services use the longer southern route through Yogyakarta and Solo.

Leaving Jakarta by Bus

Jakarta has four bus terminals which serve different regions on Java and Sumatra. All are inconveniently located on the outskirts of Jakarta, a hassle which makes trains your best bet.

Kampung Rambutan terminal, 18 km south of city center, has buses to Bogor, Bandung, and Tasikmalaya. Take Patas bus P16 from Jalan Thamrin.

Kalideres terminal, 15 km west of city center, has buses to destinations within west Java such as Merak and Labuan. Take bus 913 or bus 26 from Gambir train station.

Pulo Gadung terminal, 12 km east of city center, has buses to Yogyakarta, Solo, Semerang, Surabaya, and Bali. Pulo Gadung is also the main bus terminal for Sumatra. Deluxe buses to Yogyakarta and East Java leave daily 1500-1800, while deluxe buses to Sumatra generally leave 1000-1500.

Lebak Bulus, 16 km south of city center, also has deluxe buses to central and east Java leaving daily 1500-1800.

Leaving Jakarta by Ship

Pelni ships depart from Tanjung Priok harbor in northeast Jakarta, 14 km from city center. Take a taxi to the harbor for about 10,000Rp or bus 81 from Jalan Thamrin, opposite Sarinah department store.

Pelni schedules change frequently but can be checked at the tourist office or the Pelni office on Jalan Angkasa, northeast of city center near the National Mosque. Tickets are most conveniently purchased from Pelni representatives such as Menara Buana Surya on Jalan Menteng, a short walk east of Jalan Jaksa.

INDONESIA

WEST JAVA

Extending from Krakatau volcano in the west to Cirebon in the east, the province of West Java is a diverse and culturally rich region of beautiful mountains, deep-green tea plantations, rugged wildlife reserves, lush botanical gardens, fertile rice paddies, and beaches with magnificent coral formations.

Transportation is well developed. From Jakarta's Kalideres station, buses leave regularly for the historic town of Banten, the port connection at Merak (to Sumatra), the beautiful beaches at Carita, and Labuan, access point for Ujung Kulon National Reserve.

Buses east to Bogor and Bandung leave from Kampung Rambutan terminal in south Jakarta, though most travelers prefer the convenience of trains from Gambir station.

MERAK

Buses to Merak depart hourly from the Kalideres bus terminal in Jakarta. Trains leave the Tanah Abang train station in Jakarta daily at 0700 and 1400 and take four hours to Merak.

Inexpensive *losmen* are near the train station.

Banten

En route to Merak and the west coast beaches, you may want to make a brief stop at Banten, a small but historic town 18 km east of Merak.

Banten today is known for its historical remains of the once great Bantenese Islamic kingdom such as a partially restored palace, small museum which houses 200-year-old archaeological objects, and an Islamic school where you could run into hundreds of veiled schoolgirls all in white.

Don't miss the impressive mosque outside town on the road to Serang. Banten is also the departure point for boat rides to Nusa Dua, an island bird sanctuary populated by herons, cormorants, and storks.

From Jakarta's Kalideres station, board a bus to Merak, but get off in Serang, from where minibuses continue up to Banten.

Ferries to Sumatra

Ferries depart Merak hourly around the clock and take 1.5 hours to reach Bakauhen in southern Sumatra. There's also a superjet service that leaves hourly 0800-1600 and does the crossing in just 30 minutes. Buses waiting in Bakauhen depart for all destinations in Sumatra, from Palembang to Aceh.

CARITA BEACH

Just a few hours by bus from Jakarta lie some of the more attractive beaches in Java. From Anyer in the north to Labuhan in the south—a stretch of almost 60 km—the Dutch-built road winds past sandy beaches and warm seas just perfect for swimming, snorkeling, fishing, and sailing.

Carita, a beach town midway between Anyer and Labuhan, serves as a convenient base for visits to Krakatau and Ujung Kulong National Park.

Accommodations

Over 20 beach resorts and hotels are located south of the Anyer lighthouse in the direction of Carita Beach, a beautiful stretch of sand situated within the protective enclosure of a U-shaped bay. Most places are overpriced since Carita serves as the vacation escape for wealthy Jakartians.

Rakata Hostel: One of the few inexpensive options in Carita also puts together reasonably priced tours to Krakatau and Ujung Kulon. Jl. Carita, tel. (021) 81171, US$8-25.

Hotel Wira Carita: Clean and friendly resort with swimming pool, tennis court, and gardens. Jl. Raya Anyer, tel. (021) 81116, US$12-40.

Sunset View: Cheapest place in Carita. Jl. Raya Anyer, tel. (021) 81075, US$7-20.

KRAKATAU VOLCANO

Over a century ago, in the early misty hours of 27 August 1883, the island of Rakata Besar disintegrated in the most violent explosion in recorded history. When the central mountain erupted, an enormous amount of rock was heaved out, and the island collapsed, allowing sea water to rush into the fiery crater. The resulting explosion was catastrophic. The volcano unleashed a series of titanic detonations with a force of 100,000 hydrogen bombs. Countless tons of rocks, dust, and pumice were hurled 27 km into the sky. Volcanic clouds circling the earth turned the sun blue and green, causing sensational sunsets for years. Volcanic debris landed on Madagascar on the other side of the Indian Ocean. The boom was heard in Brisbane, over 4,000 km away. Almost 40,000 people died. Afterwards, all remained calm until 1927 when a thick plume of steam roared from the sea bed, giving birth to Anak Krakatau ("Son of Krakatau"), which has since risen 150 meters above the sea.

Excursions

Day-trips to Krakatau can be arranged in Labuhan, Carita, or Pasauran. Though Pasauran is geographically the closest to Krakatau, it's easier to arrange boat transport from Carita. Krakatau is in most cases a one-day roundtrip.

Tours can be arranged with Black Rhino opposite Hotel Desiana and Krakatau Ujung Kulon Tour & Travel at the Rakata Hostel. Day excursions cost US$30-50 per person depending on the number of people in the boat. Visits can also be arranged to nearby Badui villages and Ujung Kulon Wildlife Reserve.

The ideal season is April to September. But no matter what time you go, the volcano is always in a different mood. Surrounding waters could be 60 degrees centigrade, hot ash blackens your face, the roar is deafening, charcoal smoke clouds the sky. If you're there during an active phase, see flaming boulders the size of basketballs tossed out like pebbles.

UJUNG KULON RESERVE

This completely untamed wilderness lies on the far west tip of Java, connected to the rest of the island by a narrow boggy isthmus. Two separate national parks here total more than 420 square km, one located on the Ujung Kulon Peninsula and the other on the island of Panaitan across a narrow strait.

Opened by the Dutch in 1921 as a refuge for the threatened Javan rhinoceros, the establishment of this last large area of lowland forest on Java has since been credited with saving a number of rare life forms from extinction. Observation towers have been erected, and unspoiled beaches with beautiful coral formations lie off the south and west sides.

Excursions

Permits are available from the friendly PPA forestry officers in Labuhan, while accommodations are handled by Wanawisata Alamhayati on the same road. Lodges cost US$10-20 in Tamanjaya and US$20-30 on Handeuleum and Peucang islands.

Most visitors join an organized tour in Carita. Black Rhino and Krakatau Ujung Kulon Tour & Travel put together four-day/three-night tours at US$150 per person with a four person minimum.

BOGOR

Founded over 500 years ago, Bogor is built around a huge, verdant botanical garden, one of the most magnificent in the world and one of Indonesia's major tourist attractions. It's a pleasant but somewhat busy town of pretty Dutch villas, tropical foliage, and the sweetest *murtabaks* in Indonesia.

Attractions

Botanical Gardens (Kebun Raya): This incredible 87-hectare estate is one of the leading botanical institutions in the world, as well as an important scientific research center. The gardens have been here for over 170 years; Bogor has risen up around them. Behind the towering walls you'll discover hundreds of species of trees, an herbarium with 5,620 plant species, a cultivated park of paths, pools, glades, shrubs, lawns, open-air cactus gardens, great twisting foot-thick overhead vines, enormous waterlilies, with a river bubbling through it all. About 13,000 specimens of native plants have been collected not only from all over the Malay Archipelago but from many other tropical regions as well.

The gardens are open daily 0800-1600.

Presidential Palace: Formerly the Dutch governor's mansion, today this is a ceremonial

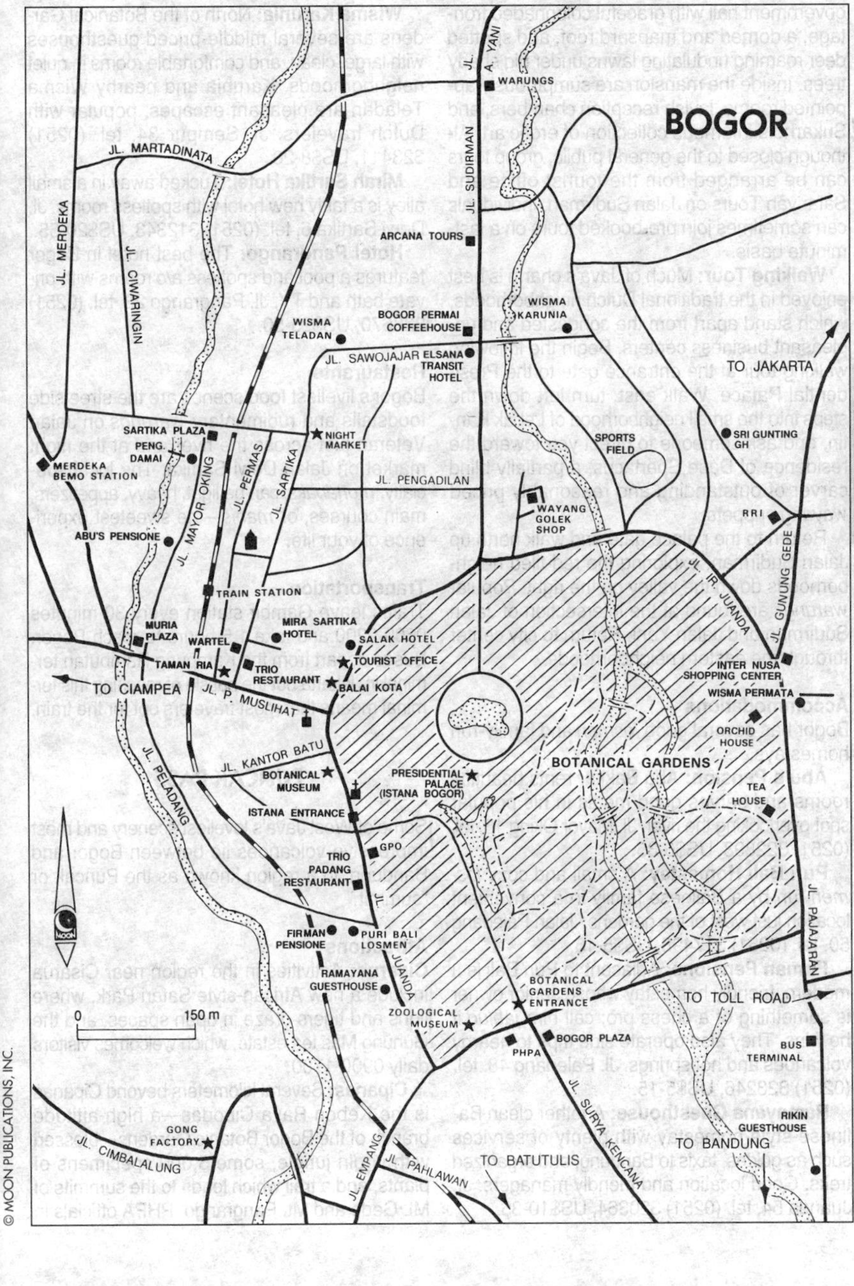

BOGOR

INDONESIA

(map of Bogor showing streets, landmarks, and the Botanical Gardens)

Labels on map (clockwise/by area):

JL. A. YANI — WARUNGS
JL. SUDIRMAN
ARCANA TOURS
WISMA KARUNIA
TO JAKARTA
SRI GUNTING GH
SPORTS FIELD
JL. MARTADINATA
JL. MERDEKA
JL. CIWARINGIN
WISMA TELADAN
BOGOR PERMAI COFFEEHOUSE
JL. SAWOJAJAR — ELSANA TRANSIT HOTEL
SARTIKA PLAZA
PENG. DAMAI
NIGHT MARKET
JL. PERMAS
JL. SARTIKA
JL. PENGADILAN
WAYANG GOLEK SHOP
RRI
JL. IR. JUANDA
JL. GUNUNG GEDE
MERDEKA BEMO STATION
ABU'S PENSIONE
JL. MAYOR OKING
TRAIN STATION
MURIA PLAZA
WARTEL
TAMAN RIA
MIRA SARTIKA HOTEL
SALAK HOTEL
TOURIST OFFICE
TRIO RESTAURANT
BALAI KOTA
INTER NUSA SHOPPING CENTER
WISMA PERMATA
ORCHID HOUSE
TO CIAMPEA
JL. P. MUSLIHAT
JL. KANTOR BATU
BOTANICAL MUSEUM
PRESIDENTIAL PALACE (ISTANA BOGOR)
BOTANICAL GARDENS
TEA HOUSE
JL. PELADANG
ISTANA ENTRANCE
TRIO PADANG RESTAURANT
GPO
JL. PAJAJARAN
FIRMAN PENSIONE
PURI BALI LOSMEN
RAMAYANA GUESTHOUSE
ZOOLOGICAL MUSEUM
JL. JUANDA
BOTANICAL GARDENS ENTRANCE
TO TOLL ROAD
BUS TERMINAL
PHPA
BOGOR PLAZA
JL. SURYA KENCANA
RIKIN GUESTHOUSE
TO BANDUNG
GONG FACTORY
JL. CIMBALALUNG
JL. EMPANG
JL. PAHLAWAN
TO BATUTULIS

0 — 150 m

© MOON PUBLICATIONS, INC.

INDONESIA

government hall with graceful colonnaded frontage, a domed and mansard roof, and spotted deer roaming undulating lawns under big shady trees. Inside the mansion are sumptuously appointed rooms, lavish reception chambers, and Sukarno's infamous collection of erotic art. Although closed to the general public, group tours can be arranged from the tourist office and Safariyah Tours on Jalan Sudirman. Individuals can sometimes join pre-booked tours on a last-minute basis.

Walking Tour: Much of Java's charm is best enjoyed in the traditional Dutch neighborhoods, which stand apart from the congested and unpleasant business centers. Begin the following walking tour at the entrance gate to the Presidential Palace. Walk east, turn left down the steps into the small neighborhood of Lebak Kantin, and ask someone to direct you toward the residence of Dase Spartacus, a partially blind carver of outstanding and reasonably priced *wayang* puppets.

Return to the palace gate and walk north up Jalan Sudirman, exploring the red-tiled neighborhoods down the valley on the right. Popular *warungs* are found at the intersection of Jalan Sudirman and Jalan Yani. Return to city center through the eastern neighborhoods.

Accommodations

Bogor has several good *losmen* and family-run homestays.

Abu's Pension: Abu Bakkar rents beautiful rooms and serves good meals in his popular spot overlooking the river. Jl. Mayor Oking 15, tel. (0251) 322893, US$6-35.

Puri Bali Homestay: A small and cozy *losmen* run by a Balinese family in a convenient location just west of the gardens. Jalan Paledang 50, tel. (0251) 317498, US$5-15.

Firman Pensione: Adjacent to Puri Bali is a modern, friendly homestay whose senior owner is something of a chess pro; call him *jablud* if he wins. They also operate side trips to nearby volcanoes and hot springs. Jl. Paledang 48, tel. (0251) 323246, US$5-15.

Ramayana Guesthouse: Another clean Balinese-style homestay with plenty of services such as guides, taxis to Bandung, and organized treks. Good location and friendly managers. Jl. Juanda 54, tel. (0251) 320364, US$10-35.

Wisma Karunia: North of the Botanical Gardens are several middle-priced guesthouses with large, clean, and comfortable rooms in quiet neighborhoods. Karunia and nearby Wisma Teladan are pleasant escapes, popular with Dutch travelers. Jl. Sempur 34, tel. (0251) 323411, US$8-20.

Mirah Sartika Hotel: Tucked away in a small alley is a fairly new hotel with spotless rooms. Jl. Dewi Sartika 6, tel. (0251) 312343, US$20-55.

Hotel Pangrango: The best hotel in Bogor features a pool and spotless a/c rooms with private bath and TV. Jl. Pangrango 23, tel. (0251) 328670, US$25-50.

Restaurants

Bogor's liveliest food scenes are the streetside foodstalls and rudimentary *warungs* on Jalan Veteran just across the river and at the night market on Jalan Dewi Sartika. The local specialty, *murtabaks,* can be light, heavy, appetizers, main courses, or *manis*—the sweetest experience of your life.

Transportation

Trains leave Gambir station every 30 minutes 0600-2200 and take 1.5 hours to reach Bogor. Buses depart from the Kampung Rambutan terminal in Jakarta but the hassle of reaching this terminal means that most travelers opt for the train.

PUNCAK PASS

Some of West Java's loveliest scenery and most impressive volcanoes lie between Bogor and Bandung, in a region known as the Puncak or "summit."

Attractions

Cisarua: Activities in the region near Cisarua include a new African-style Safari Park, where lions and tigers graze in open spaces, and the Gunung Mas tea estate, which welcomes visitors daily 0900-1700.

Cipanas: Several kilometers beyond Cipanas is the Kebon Raya Cibodas—a high-altitude branch of the Bogor Botanic Gardens—blessed with virgin jungle, some 5,000 specimens of plants, and a trail which leads to the summits of Mt. Gede and Mt. Pangrango. PHPA officials in the parking lot provide permits and route maps to hikers, who should dress warmly and allow six to eight hours to complete the exhilarating climb.

Accommodations

Simple hotels and luxury resorts are in Cisarua and Cipanas and directly at the summit of Puncak Pass. Avoid weekends, when escapees from the city flood the region.

By far, the finest place to stay in the region is in the town of Cibodas, just below the entrance to the botanical gardens—superb views over tea plantations, countless hikes, and day-long treks to Genung Gede and Pangrango. Take a bus from Bogor to the town of Cimacan, then another bus up the hill to Cibodas. Best accommodations include Freddy's Homestay, Wisma Jamur, Pondok Pemuda Cibodas, and Cibodas Guesthouse.

Freddy's Homestay: The small but clean favorite of backpackers on the right side of the road down a narrow alley. Cibodas, tel. (0251) 515473, US$4-10.

Wisma Jamur: The "Mushroom House" run by Miss Nina is another good choice for budget travelers. Guides will find you on arrival. Cibodas, tel. (0251) 515575, US$6-15.

Kopo Youth Hostel: Clean rooms, friendly management, and hearty breakfasts but quite distant from the botanical gardens. Ask the bus driver to drop you at the Cisarua gas station. Cisarua, Jl. Raya Puncak 557, tel. (0251) 254296, US$4-10.

Cibodas Botanical Gardens Guesthouse: A lovely lodge directly inside the gardens. Reservations can be made at the Bogor Botanical Gardens. Cibodas, tel. (0251) 512233, US$10-25.

Pondok Pemuda Cibodas: Excellent location near the PHPA office and very convenient for volcano trekking and visiting nearby tea plantations. Cibodas, tel. (0251) 512807, US$3-15.

Puncak Pass Hotel: A colonial-era hotel with modern additions just below the pass. Jl. Raya Puncak, tel. (0255) 512503, US$45-75.

BANDUNG

Once known as the Paris of Java, Indonesia's third largest city provides a convenient break on the journey from Jakarta and Yogyakarta.

Bandung is a bustling center of Sundanese cultural life, the site of at least 50 universities and colleges, and one of the world's largest concentrations of Dutch art-deco architecture. The Dutch loved it here and constructed most of their colonial government offices not in the sweltering plains of Jakarta but in the cooler elevations of Bandung.

Bandung's great attraction isn't ancient Indonesian ruins or religious monuments, but the phenomenal collection of Dutch architecture constructed between the turn of the century and WW II. The Dutch hired some of their best and brightest architects to build what was intended to be their new capital of Indonesia. Schooled in the art-nouveau and art-deco movements then sweeping Europe, these young and innovative architects successfully adapted contemporary Western styles with Indonesian motifs to create in Bandung a unique tropical Indo-European style. The result is a remarkably rich collection of modern early-20th-century Dutch architecture.

Best of all, Bandung's colonial architecture hasn't been destroyed, as in Jakarta which has torn down most of its most important and beautiful buildings. The city's architectural heritage is guarded and promoted by a coalition of local preservationists, architects, and academics who comprise the Society for Heritage Conservation.

Downtown Bandung

Downtown Bandung is the standard mess of desultory modern buildings and traffic jams. Ignore all this and explore the upper neighborhoods, which have largely retained their colonial charm, broad tree-lined streets, and idyllic pace of life. The following walking tour begins at the tourist office and moves north to the old capitol and Bandung Zoo.

Merdeka Building: An architectural tour of Bandung landmarks should begin with the Gedung Merdeka (Asia-Afrika Building), where two of Bandung's most famous Dutch architects, Wolf Schoemaker and A.F. Albers, combined their talents in the '30s to build what was originally a Dutch clubhouse. The building achieved fame in 1955 when Sukarno invited leaders of 29 developing nonaligned nations to an international solidarity conference. Interior displays and photographs relate the momentous occasion.

INDONESIA

BANDUNG

TO TANGKUBAN PRAHU

JL. CEMARA

LINGGA PUB

TIZI'S RESTAURANT

JL. SILIWANGI

TO DAGO (3 km)

TAMAN SARI

ZOO

TAMAN OKEWAH

JL. CIPAGANTI

ADVENT HOSPITAL

STUDIO EAST DISCO

JL. SUKAJADI

BANDUNG INSTITUTE OF TECHNOLOGY

GANECA

SHERATON INN

JL. I.R.H. JUANDA

PATRA JASA HOTEL

JL. DIPATIUKUR

JL. HASBANUDIN

JL. PROF. EYCKMAN

PONYO RESTAURANT

JL. CIPAGANTI

TAMAN GANECA

JL. TAMANSARI

JL. PASTEUR

JL. CIPAGANTI

JL. CIHAMPELAS

JEANS PARADISE

S. CIKAPUNDUNG

PURI GARDENIA HOTEL

JL. SULJANA

TO PAK UJO'S ANGKLUNG STUDIO

JL. SURAPATI

LAGA PUB

JL. PASIRKALIKI

JL. H. JUANDA

LAPANGAN GASHIBU

GEOLOGICAL MUSEUM

JL. DIPONEGORO

GEDUNG SATE BUILDING

FLOWER MARKET

JL. WASTUKANCANA

JL. SAGUNG

TO AIRPORT

BANDUNG CEPAT BUSES

JL. DR. CIPTO

JL. PAJAJARAN

JL. PASIRKALIKI

YOUTH CENTER

BOURAQ

ANGGREK HOTEL

JL. LAKSMANA

HOTEL SANTIKA

OLD DUTCH HOMES

JL. SUMBAWA

TAMAN MALUKU

JL. ACEH

BIP PLAZA

JL. ACEH

SILIWANGI STADIUM

JL. MERDEKA

CITY HALL

TAMAN LALU LINTAS

GOVERNOR'S HOUSE

JL. KEBON KAWUNG

JL. WASTUKANCANA

JL. SUMATRA

TRAIN STATION

HOTEL GUNTUR

HOTEL SAHARA

JL. GAREJA

BANK OF INDONESIA

JL. JAWA

SAKADARNA LOSMEN

MINIBUS STATION

JL. KEBON JATI

HOTEL SURABAYA

HOTEL MELATI

PASAR BARU

JL. BRAGA

PANGHEGAR HOTEL

JL. LEMBONG BUNGSU

JL. GUDANG SELATAN

JL. SUNDA

TO JAKARTA

JL. NARIPAN

WAYANG THEATER (YPK)

ISTANA HOTEL

LOSMEN INTERNATIONAL

RUMENTANG SIANG CULTURAL HALL

JL. JEN. SUDIRMAN

POST OFFICE

MERDEKA BLDG.

GRAND PREANGER HOTEL

JL. NARIPAN

TO CICAHEUM BUS TERMINAL

JL. CIBADAK

TOURIST OFFICE

JL. ASIA-AFRIKA

TO CICAHEUM BUS TERMINAL

SAVOY HOMANN HOTEL

JL. LENGKONG KECIL

JL. JEN. GATOT SUBROTO

JL. JEN. A. YANI

JL. PAJAGAN

JL. ASTANA ANYAR

JL. ISKANDARDINATA

JL. DEWI SARTIKA

LOSMEN MAWAR

JL. TAMBOLONG

JL. PANGARANG

HOTEL PAPANDAYAN

JL. PASIRKOJA

PACIFIC HOTEL

WAYANG MAKER

PA AMING PUPPETS

JL. KARAPITAN

0   200 m

HOTEL BRAJAWIJAYA

KEBUN KELAPA BUS TERMINAL

JL. PUNGKUR

© MOON PUBLICATIONS, INC.

Savoy Homann Hotel: Bandung's art-deco classic was designed by Albers in 1938 to emulate a luxury steamship complete with portholes and massive lobbies and restaurants that resemble vast open decks. The Savoy was recently purchased and restored by the chairman of the Society for Heritage Conservation.

Grand Preanger Hotel: Designed by C.P. Wolf Schoemaker in 1928, the old sections of this famous lady have been nicely restored by Javanese architects who retained the sleek parallel lines, wide verandahs, and intricate leaded-glass windows. Palm trees and a deco atmosphere now compete with a modern nine-story tower.

Braga Street: A popular place for coffee, pastries, and relaxation in outdoor cafes.

Bank of Indonesia: This pre-art-deco masterpiece was constructed in 1920 by architect Ed Cuypers, who returned to the Netherlands to found the Amsterdam School of Architecture. The nearby park has some unusual statues of white rhinos.

Upper Bandung

The old Dutch neighborhood northwest of Jalan Braga is a delightful escape from the heat, smog, and congestion of downtown Bandung. Continue your walking tour by going east from Jalan Merdeka, slowly wandering around the smaller side streets such as *jalans* Sumatra, Sumbawa, and Aceh, where you'll find the Gedung Kologdam, the residence of the army commander. Nearby Maluku Park is the cruising domain of Bandung's transvestites and *bancis*.

Gedung Sate Building: Bandung's most impressive architectural statement was built in the 1920s by a Dutch architect named James Gerber. Now the administrative center of West Java, the building is nicknamed "Sate" for the metal roof rods which somewhat resemble art-deco satay sticks. Across the street are two more government offices which closely follow the spirit and style of the original.

Geological Museum: An ordinary building but with an impressive collection of fossils, minerals, models of volcanoes, photos of eruptions, and relief maps. Like all other government buildings in Indonesia, it's open Monday-Thursday 0900-1400, Friday 0900-1100, and Saturday 0900-1300.

Bandung Institute of Technology (ITB): Premier among Bandung's myriad colleges and universities, the ITB was designed in 1918 by Dutch architect Maclaine Pont, who used West Javanese styles and spectacular ship-prowed Minangkabau architecture.

Bandung Zoo: Final stop on your walking tour is the large and well-planned zoo in upper Bandung, filled with tropical birds and Sumatran orangutans. Martial and performing arts on Sunday afternoons. Return to Bandung on public minibuses or continue up to Dago Tea House for sunset and dinner.

Jeans Paradise: Kitsch runs amok among the dozens of clothing shops which compete by erecting the most outrageous and extravagant facades: taxis crashing through roofs, alien invaders, sexual goddesses, black caricatures which would make the NAACP howl, and other oddities that perhaps provide insight into the Indonesian mind. Worth a visit.

Vicinity of Bandung

The real joy of Bandung is the surrounding countryside where you can really get away from the congestion of urban Java. The whole regency is situated in the beautiful Parahiangan Highlands, which soar up to 2,000 meters, boasting spectacular and unbelievably varied landscapes.

North: Thirty km north of Bandung is the famous but highly commercialized Tangkuban Crater, complete with car parks, restaurants, and an entrance fee. Buses go there from the train station although it's more dramatic to hike eight km from the Jayagiri dropoff.

Return to Lembang (probably on foot unless a minibus happens by) and continue by minibus either to Ciater hot springs or south to the hot springs at Maribaya. Both are crowded but refreshing on a cold day.

From Maribaya, continue hiking down the river gorge toward Bandung, pausing at the Japanese Cave, a waterfall, and the popular Dago Tea House for a cool drink and sunsets.

South: Two day-trips are possible south of Bandung. The southwest route stops at the market town of Soreang and Ciwidey before reaching Rancabali, where visitors can tour the local tea plantation. From Rancabali you can walk to Pantenggang Lake or the nearby hot springs. The

INDONESIA

tropical treasure

southeast route involves public transport to Cileuleng, from where Mt. Papandayan can be hiked in a full day. Guides and jeeps might be necessary.

Accommodations

The cheap hotel district is around the train station.

Yossie Homestay: Bandung's newest, cleanest, and most popular spot for backpackers is operated by friendly Yosep and his American wife. Rooms are immaculate, plus impromptu folk concerts happen nightly in the dining area. Ask about tours to nearby volcanoes, hot springs, silk weaving villages, and direct minibuses to Pangandaran. Jl. Kebon Jati 53, tel. (022) 420-5453, US$2 dorm, US$5-8 rooms.

Sakadarna International Travellers Homestay: Bandung's super-budget scene also includes this flagged, two-story *losmen* and the older, less spacious but identically named *losmen* on the same street. The owners run a restaurant with Sundanese specialities, sell puppets, and organize sightseeing trips and buses to other points in Java. Two minutes from the train station, eight minutes from downtown, a 20-minute walk from the central bus terminal. Jalan Kebonjati 34, tel. 420-2811, US$5-8.

Sakadarna Losmen: Great information source but perpetually noisy with kids and TV. A real homestay experience. Jalan Kebonjati 50, tel. (022) 439897, US$3-8.

Surabaya Hotel: Recently restored colonial hotel with huge rooms, comfortable (collapsing) furniture, dozing attendants, a seediness both re-

pulsive and memorable. Jalan Kebonjati 71, tel. 436791, US$6-25.

Hotel Sahara: Somewhat dark but quieter and more private than the *losmen* on Jalan Kebonjati. Jalan Otto Iskandar 3, tel. (022) 51684, US$5-15.

Melati II Hotel: A new middle-priced hotel just opposite the Sakadarnas. Comfortable and clean; good enough for an overnight. Jalan Kebonjati 24, tel. (022) 50080, US$8-15.

Panghegar: Bandung's three finest hotels are the Savoy Homann and the Grand Preanger (two art-deco classics described above) and the Panghegar Hotel a few blocks north. While not a relic from the '30s, the Panghegar is modern and clean and features the city's best views from its skyview lounge. Jalan Merdeka 2, tel. (022) 57584, US$75-120.

Grand Hotel Preanger: Bandung's only five-star hotel features a renovated art deco wing and 150 rooms in the new tower, plus pool and nightclub with rockin' Filipino bands. Jl. Asia Afrika 81, tel. (022) 431631, fax (022) 430034, US$140-220.

Restaurants

Start with the foodstalls which set up nightly opposite the tourist office, and try *ikan mas, sayur asam, soto mas, papas* (chicken or fish wrapped in banana leaf), *karadok* and *lontak* (similar to *gado gado*), and other Sundanese and Madurese specialties. Two popular and inexpensive restaurants worth investigating are the Minang Jaya overlooking the central plaza and the self-service Galaya across from the Kumala Preanger Hotel. Babakan Siliwangi in the extreme north is Bandung's most famous Sundanese restaurant.

Performing Arts

Although Bandung is often touted as the center of Sundanese culture, locating a dance or music performance is difficult to impossible; this isn't Yogyakarta, where a strong tourist industry helps keep traditional arts alive. Tourist-office recommendations and schedules for upcoming performances should be taken with a large grain of salt.

Sundanese Dance: Bandung's cultural heart beats around the Music Conservatory (Konservatori Karawitan) on Jalan Buah Batu. Both resident schools—the ASTI (academic, professional level) and the SMKI (high-school students)—occasionally stage performances of Sundanese dance and drama. Traditional Sundanese dance is also performed Wednesday evenings 2000-2200 in the restaurant of the Hotel Panghegar on Jalan Merdeka. One-drink minimum. Jaipongan dance is performed nightly in the Sanggar Langen Setra nightclub on Jalan Tegal Lega south of the Kebu Kelapa bus terminal. Don't waste your time on this sleazy, hokey, and sad spectacle.

Wayang Golek: Traditional wooden puppet plays are given Saturday nights at 2100 at the Yayasan Pusat Kebudayaan (YPK) Cultural Institute on Jalan Naripan. Funky but authentic. Also Fridays and Saturdays at 2000 at the Rumentang Siang Cultural Hall on Jalan Ahmad Yani in the Kusambi shopping district.

Angklung: Tour groups can arrange performances of Sundanese bamboo xylophone orchestras and *wayang golek* by calling Pak Ujo Studios at tel. 71714. Individuals can join the Wednesday afternoon shows on a space-available basis. *Angklung* rehearsals are held Sunday mornings in the Rumentang Siang Cultural hall.

Pencak Silat: Indonesian martial arts can be seen at the student academy on Gang Haji Yakub Mondays and Thursdays 1900-2100. *Pencak silat* is often staged at the zoo on Sunday mornings.

Ram Fights: Exciting contests in which champion rams ferociously butt heads can be seen Sunday mornings 0800-1200 in north Bandung near the town of Lendeng. Matches are local, low-level competitions tied in with breeders' efforts to upgrade the quality of their rams. As orthodox Muslims, the Sundanese are forbidden to gamble. Thus, almost unbelievably, no money changes hands at these contests; they are staged purely for the pleasure of the handlers and breeders! Locations change weekly; the tourist office can help.

Shopping

Bandung's two most acclaimed *wayang golek* carvers are Pa Aming on Jalan Karapitan near the river and Pa Roechiyat at 22 Jalan Pangarang south of the tourist office. Everybody knows what you want; somebody will point the way. Many of Bandung's best antique shops are located on Jalan Barga. Sin Sin Antiques at Jalan Barga 56 offers a wide selection of batik and Sundanese masks. Don't miss the discount-clothing emporiums in Jeans Paradise!

Transportation

Bandung's train station is centrally located near inexpensive *losmen* and within quick trishaw distance of the better hotels on Jalan Asia Afrika.

Bus passengers will be dropped at outlying terminals. Travelers coming from the west (Bogor or Jakarta) will arrive at the Kebu Kelapa bus terminal in south Bandung, about 20 minutes on foot from the train station. Trishaws can also be hired. Bus passengers coming from the east (Pangandaran or Yogyakarta) will be dropped at the *extremely* distant Cicaheum bus terminal on the eastern edge of Bandung. *Bemos* and buses heading west toward the center of town wind through darkened neighborhoods before finally arriving 45 minutes later at the Kebu Kelapa terminal. Don't panic, just stay on the bus.

Choices leaving Bandung include trains, buses from the two public bus terminals described above, or the private buses which leave from Jalan Kebonjai near the train station.

PANGANDARAN

This small fishing village midway between Bandung and Yogyakarta is one of the few beach resorts on the south coast of Java. There's a certain primitive beauty and sense of remoteness to the region. Hikes can be organized through the peninsular national park just south of the town. All

TO KALIPUCANG

TO CIJULANG

◆ HILMAN'S FISHFARM RESTAURANT

JL. MERDEKA

POLICE ■   BANK ■   MAIN BUS   ◆ ROCKET FISH MONUMENT
TERMINAL

GATE ⌐L

GATE L

PAGANDARAN

● BOURGAINVILLE HOTEL

◆ HOSPITAL

● CITRA HOTEL
SURYA BEACH
HOTEL ●
BAMBOO
GUESTHOUSE ●

SURYA PARK   HIDEAWAY ●
ADAMS ●
HOMESTAY ●

● TELEPHONE

● DUTA BEACH
HOTEL
● SANDAAN

JL. BARU

● DAHLIA INDAH
HOTEL
● BULAK LAUT
BUNGALOWS

RELAX RESTAURANT ■

JL. BULAK LAUT

JL. KIDANG PANANJUNG

● LOSMEN
PUSAKA

■ CINEMA

JL. PANUSAPARAN

SARI HARUM TRAVEL ■

■ AGUNG TRAVEL
■ LUTA TRAVEL
■ POST OFFICE   FISH MARKET ■

CAMPING

JL. PRAMUKA

HOTEL BUMI PANANJUNG ●

W E S T   B E A C H

JL. KALEN BUHAYA

JL. TALANCA

MERIDIEN
DISCO ■

SOUTH COAST
HUTS ■

● DAMAR INDAH

■ BUMI DEWI
LAUT
HOTEL
NUSANTARA HOTEL ●

JL. KALEN BUHAYA

● PADANG
JAYA

PANTAI INDAH
BARAT HOTEL ●

SUNRISE
BEACH
HOTEL ●

PANORAMA HOTEL ●

ADEM AYEN
HOTEL ●

E A S T   B E A C H

SUSAN'S
GH ●
MINI
■ LOSMEN
SARI
■ LOSMEN

JL. PASANGGRAHAN

■ NANJUNG
RESTAURANT

CILACAP
RESTAURANT ■

BANK ■
CAFE
SYMPATHY ■

TOHA WARUNG AND
GUIDE ASSOCIATION ■

INTI LAUT
RESTAURANT ■
■ LONELY
PLANET CAFE   GEMINI CAFE ■

JL. JAGALAUTAN

● MANGKUBUMI HOTEL

● NYLUR INDAH HOTEL

FISH MARKET ■

● SAPUTRA HOTEL

● PANGANDARAN BEACH HOTEL

WISMA WAN HOTEL ●

TO PANGANDARAN
NATURE RESERVE

● PHPA OFFICE

0   100 m

© MOON PUBLICATIONS, INC.

INDONESIA

of the original growth was destroyed by fire several decades ago, but guides such as Toha (with his ponytail and antique hiking boots) can point out the black and gray monkeys, *banteng* pasture, flying foxes, Japanese bunkers, caves, and an outstanding waterfall which plunges dramatically into the ocean. White Beach on the western coast offers fine sand and a small bathing pool with a degree of privacy.

Accommodations

Standards of cleanliness of the 50 or so *losmen*, hotels, and bungalows are rising all the time. Pangandaran is now firmly on the tourist trail and five-star hotels will soon be appearing on the once pristine beachfront.

Prices are also rising as organized groups of Europeans and Australians arrive to fill the hotels and resorts. Bare bones *losmens* under US$5 are still available, but most places now charge US$6-10 for fan-cooled rooms and US$12-20 for a/c rooms.

Budget *Losmen*: Much better than the decrepit and overpriced places listed below under Losmen Mini Dua are the small *losmen* in the small alleys in the center of town, away from the beach. Jaya, Budi, Damar Indah, Surya Indah, and the clean South Coast Huts all have decent rooms for US$5-10 and give hefty discounts for longer stays.

Bamboo Guesthouse: A great choice in a very quiet location just one block from the beach behind the Surya Beach Hotel. Jl. Baru, tel. (0265) 379419, US$4-6.

Delta Gecko Village Homestay: Special note must be made of this idyllic escape five km west of Pangandaran in a coconut grove, near the village of Cikembulan. Vegetarian restaurant, lamps at dinnertime, psychedelic bicycles, and small library all run by resident artist "Delta Agus" and his German-Australian wife Kristina. A remote place for contemplation and arts, not party animals or beach hounds. Cikembulan, no phone, US$5-15.

Adam's Homestay: Attractive rooms, small pub, and authentic cappuccino in a fine place run by a German lady and her colorful Indonesian husband and former world traveler. Jl. Pamugaran Bulak Laut, tel. (0265) 379164, US$12-25.

Sandaan Hotel: Good value choice with spotless rooms facing a small but attractive pool.

Recommended. Jl. Pamugaran Bulak Laut, tel. (0265) 379165, US$12-15 fan, US$20- 30 a/c.

Bulak Laut Bungalows: Pseudo-Bukkitingii cottages provide some atmosphere and welcome relief from the uncreative architecture that plagues most of Pangandaran. Jl. Pamugaran Bulak Laut, tel. (0265) 39171, US$10-15 fan.

Pantai Indah Barat Resort Hotel: Upscale hotel with swimming pool, tennis courts at their adjacent sister hotel on the east beach, and a/c rooms with TV and refrigerator. Good central location. Jl. Kidang Pananjung, tel. (0265) 379004, fax (0265) 379327, US$40-65.

Surya Beach Hotel: Best in town is this comfortable hotel with lovely pool, two restaurants, a/c rooms with TV and refrigerator, plus friendly staff. Jl. Pamugaran Bulak Laut, tel. (0265) 379428, fax (0265) 379289, US$40-55.

Pangandaran's dozen-plus *losmen* are clustered near the southern end of the road leading down from the bus terminal. Rates are higher on weekends and doubled during major holidays.

Losmen Mini Dua: Low-end choices include Mini I, Mini II, Laut Biru, the Ramamangun, and Losmen Mini Dua. All are simple homestays where you'll meet the entire family and the teenagers who hang out in town. Jl. Kalenbuhaya, US$2-5.

Panorama Hotel: Hotels facing the beach are more expensive but in better condition than the *losmen* in the center of town. The Panorama offers rather bizarre Tyrolian-style accommodation at bargain rates. 187 Jl. Kidang Pananjung, US$6-15.

Bumi Nusantara Hotel: The best middle-quality hotel on the west coast is a worthy attempt at traditional architecture. Jl. Pantai Barat, US$8-14 fan, US$25-40 a/c.

Getting to Pangandaran

Direct minibuses are available from travelers' *losmen* in Bandung and Yogyakarta. Alternatively, take an ordinary bus to Banjar, 63 km north, and continue to Pangandaran by local bus or minibus. Arrivals at the Pangandaran bus terminal are greeted by a wild collection of aggressive *becak* drivers who grab luggage, yell, beg, plead, and generally scare the hell out of everyone. Stay calm. *Becaks* are necessary since the *losmen* are several kilometers south and too far to walk. The correct fare from the bus terminal to a *losmen*

INDONESIA

is 1,000Rp; the *becak* driver receives a hefty commission from the *losmen* operator.

Pangandaran can be reached in another more intriguing way. Each day around noon a slow boat sails the backwaters from Cilicap to Kalipucang, a small fishing port near Pangandaran. Travel agents in Yogyakarta sell minibus tickets which make the connection. The five- to six-hour journey passes endless mudflats, twisted mangroves, simple villages, and a modern prison which holds detainees from the 1965 revolution. The scenery improves at the western end. On arrival at the Kalipucang Pier, walk 200 meters across the bridge to the main road, from where buses continue into Pangandaran. Boats depart Kalipucang for Cilicap daily at 0700, 0900, and 1300. Only the 0700 departure will get you to Yogyakarta in one day.

YOGYAKARTA

One of the largest villages in the world, Yogyakarta (usually shortened to "Yogya"—pronounced "JOAG-jah") is Java's cultural and educational capital—Indonesia's Kyoto. For centuries a royal city and major trade center, Yogya today has the highest-ranking court in the country; it's a city of monuments, palaces, highly respected music and dance schools, brilliant choreographers, drama and poetry workshops, folk theater, *wayang* troupes . . . a superb destination for world travelers. It's also one of the best places to shop in Southeast Asia, boasting talented batik specialists, leather craftsmen, and some of the country's most successful modern artists. Within easy striking distance are some of Indonesia's finest monuments, including the world-famous ruins of Borobudur and Prambanan. Yogyakarta is also well served by an outstanding selection of budget *losmen,* comfortable hotels, and restaurants serving the regional specialties of Central Java. Small wonder that Yogya, with the possible exception of Bali, has become the leading attraction in all of Indonesia.

History

Yogya lies in the center of Java's "Realm of the Dead," a city surrounded by ancient ruins. A relatively new city, Yogya was founded in the middle of the 18th century after Dutch pressure split the Mataram Empire of Central Java into the twin kingdoms of Solo and Yogya. For the Javanese, Yogya has always been a symbol of nationalistic passion and resistance to alien rule. It was the stubborn center of guerrilla struggle against the Dutch and the first capital of the infant republic during the War of Independence. During the Dutch occupation, the sultan locked himself in his *kraton* and only negotiated with the Europeans from the top of his palace, looking down on them with all his people watching. Finally, in 1948 the Dutch launched an all-out attack on the city, dropping 900 paratroopers, heavy bombs, and rocket fire. Sultan Hamengkubuwono IX, one of Indonesia's most beloved and respected leaders, immediately declared his support for the rebels. When the Dutch finally abandoned their dreams of colonial reconquest, Yogya was designated a Special Territory, responsible to the central government in Jakarta and not the provincial head in Central Java.

Yogya today is ruled by Sultan Hamengkubuwono X (formerly Prince Mangkubumi), a 45-year-old businessman, lawyer, and head of the local chapter of the ruling Golkar Party. Contrary to popular opinion (which assumed the Mataram Dynasty's significance would fade with the death of Hamengkubuwono IX), the 1989 coronation of Prince Mangkubumi was according to tradition and surprisingly lavish. Offerings were presented to the Goddess of the Southern Seas, respects were paid at the royal tombs at Imogiri, and trips were made to the two volcanoes, Merapi and Lawu. The current sultan enjoys the immense goodwill generated by his famous father, but much of his claims to divine rule will depend on whether he can marshal those still-powerful supernatural forces of Central Java.

ATTRACTIONS

Yogya is a compact town and almost everything can be reached on foot, although bicycling is a great alternative. An early start is imperative since all museums and palaces close by 1300. The following sights are described in a walking

INDONESIA

TO BOROBUDUR
AND DIENG PLATEAU

TO KALIURANG

ASTI ★
JL. COLOMBO

CRAZY HORSE DISCO

MINIBUSES TO
KALIURANG, SOLO,
AND PRAMBANAN

INDRALOKA HOMESTAY SERVICE

MERPATI
OFFICE

ARMY
MUSEUM

JL. KYAI MOJO

BUSES TO
BOROBUDUR

SANTIKA
HOTEL

GUNUNG
AGUNG
BOOKSTORE

JL. AM SANGAJI

JL. MAGELANG

JL. RAKYAT MATARAM

JL. SIMANJUNTAK

JL. CIT DITIRO

TO AFFANDI MUSEUM,
AIRPORT, PRAMBANAN,
AND SOLO

JL. P. DIPONEGORO

JL. JEN SUDIRMAN

GARUDA
AIRLINES

ARJUNA PLAZA HOTEL

NEW BATIK PALACE HOTEL

JL. MANGKUBUMI

JL. SUROTO

JL. DR. WAHIDIN

TELEPHONE

SEE "CENTRAL YOGYAKARTA" MAP

TRAIN STATION

PASAR KEMBANG

JL. SOSROWIJAYAN

JL. DAGEN

JL. PAJEKSAN

JL. MALIOBORO

BOURAQ
OFFICE

JL. MAS SUHARTO

JL. COKROAMINOTO

JL. SUPRAPTO

TOURIST
OFFICE ★

MELIA
PUROSANI
HOTEL ●

JL. BAUSASRAN

JL. DR. SUTOMO

JL. SURYOPRANOTO

JL. SARKOTO

AMRI
YAHYA
BATIK ■

ASRI ■

JL. TUBUN

PASAR BERINGHARJO ★

JL. A. YANI

VREDBURG
MUSEUM

PAPILLON
DISCO ■

PAKUALAMAN
KRATON ★

JL. SULTAN AGUNG

TO WATES

JL. DAHLAN

GEDUNG NEGARA ★

POST OFFICE ■

MINIBUSES ■

TAXI STAND ■

JL.
SENOPATI

TO ZOO, WONOSARI, AND
BATIK RESEARCH CENTER

NITOUR ★
PUPPET
SHOW

SONOBUDOYO
MUSEUM ★

KRATON
MUSEUM ★

ALUN-ALUN UTARA

YOGYAKARTA

JL. WAHID HASYIM

PALACE
ENTRANCE

KRATON
YOGYAKARTA ★

PURAWISATA
RAMAYANA ★

JL. TAMAN SISWA

JL. S.
PARMAN

BIRD MARKET ★

SASONO
HINGGIL ★

JL. KATAMSO

MOEJOSOEHARDJO ■

TAMAN SARI
(WATER PALACE) ★

ALUN-ALUN LOR

DALEM
PUJOKUSUMAN
THEATER ★

JL. SUGENG JERONI

JL. HARYONO

JL. SUTOYO

JL. SUGIYONO

BUS TO IMOGIRI ■

TO BUS TERMINAL
AND KOTA GEDE

0   200 m

SWASTHIGITA
WAYANG
KULIT SHOP ■

MODERATE HOMESTAYS

JL. SISINGAMANGARAJA

AGASTYA
ART
INSTITUTE ★

JL. SURYODININGRATAN

TO PARANGTRITIS

BATIK ★
GALLERIES
TO IMOGIRI

JL. PRAWIROTAMAN

© MOON PUBLICATIONS, INC.

tour beginning from the tourist office on Jalan Malioboro.

Central Market
Perhaps the most colorful market in Indonesia. Sprawling out from under an immense shed are hundreds of stalls selling everything from macrame to mutton and mangoes. The narrow access road, clogged with overloaded *becaks* and tremendous piles of vegetables, is a photographer's dream, but you must be quick since Indonesians don't like being treated as foreigner's models. Best experienced at the crack of dawn.

Vredburg (Perjuangan) Museum
This beautiful Dutch fort was constructed directly across from the palace square to consolidate Dutch military advances in the archipelago. With its gun emplacements overlooking the main north gate, it stands today as a reminder of the uneasy relations between the Dutch occupiers and the Javanese sultanate. Now carefully restored, the interior relates recent Yogya history through a series of illuminated dioramas. Best of all, it's air-conditioned! Open Saturday and Sunday 0900-1400.

Sono Budoyo Museum
Yogyakarta's finest museum contains a first-rate collection of Javanese, Madurese, and Balinese arts and crafts; comprehensive exhibits of batik, Dongson drums from Timor, rare *wayang* puppets of long-nosed Dutch soldiers, a special room devoted to Bali, and complete *gamelans* from both Yogya and Cirebon. The building was designed by a Dutch architect who followed the traditional *kraton* (palace) arrangement of a *pendopo* (open Javanese pavilion) with narrow *pringgitan* (passageways) leading to the *dalem* (inner royal courtyards).

The Palace
Founded in 1757 by the first sultan of Yogyakarta, this open-air *kraton* features classical Javanese palace-court architecture at its finest. Facing the immense *alun alun* (open square) are several open pavilions used only for special ceremonies. An educational display of wall reliefs which depict Indonesian history (look for *kraton* construction, Diponegoro, and Sukarno) can be found by walking clockwise around the first

palace, but the main palace entrance is located on the opposite, *western* side. The exterior Museum Kareta Kraton is filled only with an unimpressive collection of royal coaches. The main palace is open Sunday-Thursday 0900-1230, Friday and Saturday to 1100. Everyone must be well dressed; men should wear long pants, women must be very modest.

First Courtyard: Palace tours are conducted by gracious guides dressed in traditional court attire who have often spent their lives in the service of the sultan. First stop is the five *gamelan* orchestras, including the Nagawilaga, tuned to the *slendro* scale (five equal notes per octave), and Gunturmadau, tuned to *pelog* (seven unequal distances per octave). The tour continues past wedding *gamelans* and gilded palanquins through the central entrance into the main pavilion.

Central Courtyard: Buildings inside the main courtyard include the residence of the sultan's family (noted by the three yellow doors), breezy pavilions used for *gamelan* performances and tea ceremonies, and special areas where infidels once drank liquor. The Golden Pavilion, with its well-carved pillars and strong elements of color symbolism, is considered the most distinguished architectural feature of the *kraton.*

Third Courtyard: The Kesatrian Courtyard is dominated by the lovely pavilion in which *gamelan* and dance rehearsals are held Sunday mornings at 1030. Pavilions around the plaza display European-style art, royal regalia, interesting old photographs, and family-tree charts which show that sultans never worried about Indonesia's family-planning slogan, *dua anak cukup* ("two is enough").

Water Palace
Taman Sari is an old pleasure park built in feudal splendor between 1758 and 1765 for the sultan and his family. Like the Hanging Gardens of Babylon, Taman Sari once had lighted underwater corridors, cool subterranean mosques, meditation platforms in the middle of lily ponds, *gamelan* towers, and galleries for dancing, all in mock-Spanish architecture. Princesses bathed in flower-strewn pools, streams flowed above covered passageways, and boats drifted in man-made lakes. Today, most of the "Fragrant Gardens" are in ruins but enough remains to make a visit worthwhile. The accompanying map shows

CENTRAL YOGYAKARTA

BANK JAKARTA

JL. TAMAN GARUDA

TRAIN STATION

URANTS
MOTORCYCLE
RENTALS

WARUNG

TRIMA GH

HOTEL
PARIWISATA

PADANG
RESTAURANT

HOTEL KENCANA

TOKO ASIA ART SHOP

HOTEL
KOTA

BERLIAN
PALACE
HOTEL

WARTEL

BATIK
PALACE
HOTEL

ASIA-AFRICA
HOTEL

RATNA
HOTEL

NATOUR GARUDA
HOTEL

MENDUT
HOTEL

JL. PASAR
KEMBANG

BETA LOSMEN

OLD SUPERMAN'S
RESTAURANT

CITY HALL

SETIA LOSMEN

BAGUS HOTEL

105 HOMESTAY

ANNA'S RESTAURANT

SETIA
KAWAN
LOSMEN

EKO RESTAURANT

LUCY LOSMEN

HOTEL
SELEKTA

DEWI 2
HOTEL
MONICA
HOTEL

GANDHI
LOSMEN

NEW SUPERMAN
RESTAURANT

LIMA LOSMEN

HOTEL
KARINIA

BLADOK
LOSMEN

HOTEL JOGYA

HOTEL
AZIATIC

JL. SOSROWIJAYAN

HOTEL
SALA BARU

HOTEL
RAMA

INDONESIA
HOTEL

MARINA PALACE
HOTEL

POST OFFICE

ORYZA
HOTEL

BAKTI KASIH HOTEL

LEGIAN GARDEN
RESTAURANT

JL. PERWAKILAN

ELLA
HOMESTAY

BATIK PALACE
COTTAGE

MALIOBORO
PLAZA

JL. SOSROKUSUMAN

TENNIS COURTS

INTAN HOTEL

GUESTHOUSES

JL. DAGEN

PUNTO DEWO GH

WISMA
NENDRA

BLUE
SAFIR
HOTEL

LILIK
GH

WISMA
PERSADA

KOMBOKARNO HOTEL

PETIT MAS GH

SRI WIBOWO
HOTEL

MUTIARA HOTEL

MAGA ART SHOP

SHINTA RESTAURANT

OSHIN RESTAURANT

WARGA MULYA ART SHOP

COLUMBO CAFE

TOURIST INFORMATION

JL. PAJEKSAN

WARTEL

TIONG SAN RESTAURANT

JL. SURYATMAJAN

ISTANA BATIK

JL. MANGKUBUMI

JL. MALIOBORO

ONE WAY

ONE WAY

INDONESIA

JL. JOGONEGARAN

0   100 m

© MOON PUBLICATIONS, INC.

the highlights. An excellent bird market is located at the northern end but it's impossible to reach directly from Taman Sari.

ATTRACTIONS NEAR YOGYA

Affandi Art Museum
Indonesia's most famous modern artist's small art museum is in a modern building on Jalan Adisucipto some eight km east of town. Although considered an expressionist with a style somewhat similar to Van Gogh's, his early works in the second gallery display his great talents for naturalism. Affandi died in May 1990 at the age of 83 after a long illness. The batik gallery of Sapto Hudoyo is nearby.

Kota Gede
Once the capital of the old Mataram Kingdom and older than Yogya itself, Kota Gede is now the center of Central Java's thriving silver industry. Visitors are welcome to wander around big workshops full of men and boys hammering on anvils, filing, polishing, heating, and soldering on strips of bright silver, using the simplest of hand-tools. Display rooms sell everything from steelworker's hard hats embossed with your name to silver replicas of Borobudur and Prambanan. Tom's Silver is the largest and the favorite of all tour groups. Kota Gede is six km southeast of Yogya. Take city bus 4 from Jalan Malioboro.

Imogiri
A cemetery for the royal houses of Yogya and Solo since the early kings of Mataram. Climb barefoot up the 346 warm stone steps, a great sun-dappled stairway like a ladder leaning up against the sky to the burial grounds on top. The mighty Sultan Agung was the first Javanese king to be interred here, in the mid-17th century. Since then, nearly every king—including the last sultan, who died in October 1988—has found his final resting place on this highly venerated hill. Imogiri lies 20 km southeast of Yogya, a 30-minute minibus ride from the main terminal. Interior tombs are usually closed, but guides will walk you around the exterior. Take a minibus from Jalan Menteri Superno at Taman Siswo.

Parangtritis Beach
The coast south of Yogya is a windy, wild, and barren region known for its haunted seas, crashing surf, and dangerous riptides. It is also said to be the home of Ratu Loro Kidul, the Sea Goddess who lives beneath the waves and is married not only to the founder of the Mataram Empire but also to the current sultan of Yogya. Like Neptune, her hair is green and full of shells and seaweed; she holds court over sea nymphs and creatures of the deep. Venerated and feared by the Javanese, Loro Kidul is summoned by a gong on the evening of the Muslim day of rest, when a bamboo tray of rice, bananas, jasmine flowers, cosmetics, and coconuts is offered to the eternally youthful goddess. Don't wear green; that's *her* color, and she has been known to yank people into the sea for the transgression. Parangtritis, obviously, isn't a beautiful beach resort with swaying palms, but some people enjoy the primitivism, wild flavor, and end-of-the-world atmosphere. Cheap *losmen* are plentiful. Take an hourly Jatayu bus from the main bus terminal.

ACCOMMODATIONS

Budget
Yogyakarta is Java's *losmen* mecca, with dozens of small but clean and comfortable spots. Almost all are sandwiched in the streets and alleys *(gangs)* immediately south of the train station. Only those which appeared to be clean and friendly, with a degree of atmosphere, are mentioned below. Conditions change frequently; updates are appreciated!

The cheapest places under US$3 are located in the two alleys which run between Jalan Kembang and Jalan Sosrowijayan. First stop might be at a small cafe like Superman's or Bu Sir Gardens for a quick drink and a little networking. Super-budget *losmen* on Gang 1 include Lucy Losmen, Beta Losmen, and Hotel Joyga, but all are rather dark and cramped. Possibilities along Gang 2 include Bagus Hotel and Heru Jaya Losmen, plus the better-than-average Gandhi Losmen. Inspect a few, looking for security and ventilation—Yogya is a hot and muggy city.

Moving up a notch to around US$5-8, you'll find a much better selection of *losmen* and budget hotels. The best are located on Jalan Kembang across from the train station and on Jalan Sosrowijayan just a few steps down from Jalan Malioboro. Both the Indonesia Hotel and Hotel Aziatic on Jalan Sosrowijayan are good places for couples on tight budgets. Ask for a room on the top floor of the Indonesia. Clean and comfortable hotels on Jalan Kembang include the security-conscious Hotel Kota, the Ratna Hotel where rooms cost US$6-12, and the Asia-Afrika Guesthouse where fan-cooled rooms cost US$6-10. All are reasonably well kept and very good value.

Moderate—Central Yogya
Yogya's accommodations really begin to excel in the US$20-35 price range. All of the following are located within easy walking distance of the train station.

Batik Palace Hotels: Directly opposite the station you'll find the luxurious Batik Palace Hotel, where fan-cooled rooms start at US$5 and a/c rooms go from US$26. Another branch of the Batik Palace is located a few blocks north of the train station on Jalan Mangkubumi. Rooms up here cost US$28 single a/c and US$35 double a/c. This one has a swimming pool.

Peti Mas Guesthouse: The neighborhood's other good property in the same price range is the Peti Mas Guesthouse on Jalan Dagen, a couple of blocks south of the train station. Peti Mas consistently receives good reports from

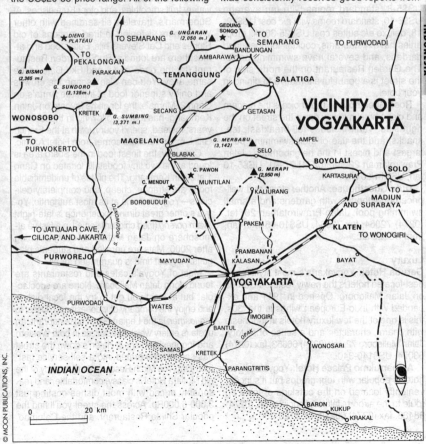

VICINITY OF YOGYAKARTA

travelers who enjoy the small garden and pool. Jalan Dagen 39, tel. (0274) 61938, fax 71175, US$12-15 fan with common bath, US$20-25 a/c with private bath.

Moderate—Jalan Prawirotaman

Yogya's best-value lodgings in the middle price range are located in a residential neighborhood about three km south of the train station. It's a beautiful and relaxing area far removed from the overwhelming urban noise and grit of central Yogyakarta. *Becaks* from the train station to Jalan Prawirotaman cost about 2,000Rp. At last count, the neighborhood harbored 15 guesthouses. Serviceable economy rooms cost just US$5-8, standard rooms with fan average US$6-10, standard rooms with a/c cost US$12-18, deluxe a/c suites cost US$25-30. All properties have restaurants, cocktail lounges, and gardens, and several have swimming pools. The Garden Restaurant on the north side of the street is a beautiful alternative to dining in your hotel.

Rose Guesthouse: Top choice is the modern and clean hotel midway down the street on the right side. Tariff includes full breakfast, tea, snacks, and the use of their swimming pool, largest and nicest in the neighborhood. Jalan Prawirotaman 22, tel. (0274) 77991, US$5-10 fan, US$14-20 a/c.

Duta Guesthouse: Another clean and well-priced guesthouse with gardens and a small swimming pool. Jalan Prawirotaman 20, tel. (0274) 72064, fax 72064, US$10-15 with fan, from US$20 a/c.

Luxury

Garuda Hotel: Yogyakarta's most stylish and best-located hotel is the newly restored Garuda on Jalan Malioboro. Opened in 1911 and expanded with Indo-European wings in the '30s, this is one of the few luxury hotels in Indonesia with charm, character, and a sense of history. Jalan Malioboro 72, tel. (0274) 66353, fax (0274) 63074, US$140-340.

Ambarrukmo Palace Hotel: Yogya's largest hotel is popular with tour groups but it's inconveniently located on the outskirts of town en route to the airport. Jalan Adisucipto, tel. (0274) 88488, fax (0274) 63283, US$120-280.

RESTAURANTS

Yogya is a godsend for vegetarians: bean cakes, *rempeyek* (peanut cookies), vegetable soups, and the *makan asli* speciality called *gudeg,* a delicious mixture of jackfruit cooked in coconut milk with eggs, tofu, and beansprouts covered with a rich and spicy sauce. Also try *opor ayam,* slices of chicken simmered in coconut milk; and sumptuous *mbok berek* or *ayam goreng*—fried chicken that Colonel Sanders can't hold a candle to.

Travelers' cafes near the train station serve the standard road fare of guacamole pancakes, watery fruit smoothies, and other Kuta dishes. At Superman's, travelers sit sardined with other Westerners, listening to tired versions of old Stones and Cat Stevens hits. Better food and atmosphere are found at Bu Sir Garden Restaurant (try the *gado gado*) and Eko Cafe in the same alley. You can also escape the crowds and enjoy superior food at intimate Anna's on Gang 2. Mama's, the longtime favorite on Jalan Kembang, has lost its following in the last few years. Instead, spend your *rupiah* at the French Grill Lima around the corner from Hotel Aziatic.

Curiously, the finest food in the Sosro area is found at the two tiny foodstalls located on Gang 1 at Jalan Kembang. The plates of unidentifiable foods are strange, cheap, and completely delicious—Yogya cuisine at its most authentic. Yogya's other great dining experience is late-night *ayam goreng* (fried chicken) served in a festive atmosphere on Jalan Malioboro every evening after 2000. Mats are unrolled and students play guitar: a great time is guaranteed for all.

Most of Yogya's cafes and restaurants are found along Jalan Malioboro. None are spectacular but at least you get to try the local dishes and enjoy the company of Indonesians. Closest to the *losmen* is the Legian Garden Restaurant, an upstairs eatery which specializes in both Western and Indonesian dishes. Helen's down the street has sadly degenerated into a self-service fast-food joint. The Mirah Restaurant in the lobby of the old Mutiara Hotel is classy, comfortable, and reasonably priced with most dishes costing just 3,000-6,000Rp. Across the street you'll find the popular Shinta Restaurant, and the Columbo,

JAVANESE CULTURE

The *Kraton*

When the temple-city concept arrived from India, the *kraton* developed as the Indonesian counterpart. These walled fortified palaces of Javanese rulers became the centers of political power and culture. Containing several thousand people, each of these self-contained regent mini-cities was tied to a dynasty, and each new dynasty founded a new *kraton*.

The most famous *kraton* of Java are in Yogyakarta and Solo, Central Java. As in India, these fortresses incorporated all that the surrounding region would need in the way of commerce, art, and religion. They contained banks, baths, shops, temples, massage and meditation chambers, schools, workshops, scribes, concubine quarters—everything needed for both body and soul.

Religion

Agama Jawa (The Religion of Java) has evolved into an incredible blending of doctrines and practices. An estimated 148 religious sects exist on Java, mainly in East and Central Java. From its early years, Javanese Islam has been a merger of Sufism (Islamic mysticism), Hinduism, and native superstition. Today Islam is the professed religion of 90% of its inhabitants.

But the Javanese differ widely in the intensity of their beliefs. Only five to 10 percent adhere to a relatively purist form of Islam *(santri)*, some 30% to a syncretic and Javanized version of Islam, while most of the remaining consider themselves only nominal Muslims. The latter group is known as *abangan*, professed adherents of Islam, but whose practices and thinking are closest to the old Javanese mysticism, animism, and Indo-Javanese traditions.

There are vast parts of Java, especially Central Java, that are still Hindu-Buddhist. The *wayang* theater is almost completely non-Islamic, its roots reaching deep into myths and sagas of ancient Javanese heroes. Javanese *pamong* (tutors), black magicians, mystic teachers, and *dukun* (healers), famous for their oracular powers, have often influenced powerful politicians.

Batik

Java produces the world's finest batik, an art of great antiquity. The word is derived from a Javanese word meaning fine point, though in everyday usage it means wax printing or wax-resist painting. Batik is traditionally used for clothing; even on formal occasions one may wear open-necked batik shirts, blouses *(kebaya)*, skirts *(saura)*, or dresses.

Formerly, batik fabrics were used mainly to make *sarong,* women's skirts, scarves, and men's headgear; cloth even had a strong cultic function. Nowadays batik is used in housecoats, long dresses, blouses, ties, belts, slippers, hats, umbrellas, sportjackets, as well as in interior decorating and fashion: wall and carpet designs, lampshades, tablecloths, napkins, bedspreads, shopping bags, briefcases, fans. Even school uniforms in Indonesia have subdued batik patterns in them.

Several sizes are available: *Kain panjang* length is three times its width; a *dodot* used for high court ceremonies is four times its width; the *sarong* is two times its width. Other forms include the *slendang*, a breast and shoulder cloth worn by women, and *kain kepala,* a head cloth worn by men.

Batik tulis is the most prized and expensive batik. Designs of *batik tulis* are usually drawn on fine cotton, linen, or, for those who can afford it, silk. Finely detailed designs are first drawn freehand with a pencil on the textile, then hot liquid wax, impervious to dye, is applied with a penlike instrument called a *canting.* The areas *not* to be colored are filled in with wax. The cloth is then passed through vats of dyes before the unwanted wax is removed, a process repeated four or more times until the overall pattern and effect are created.

Batik cap (pronounced "chop") uses copper stamps to impress the wax patterns onto the fabric—a faster and cheaper method. Made from strips of metal and wire meticulously soldered together, *caps* are themselves collectors' items and objects of great art. In use since 1840, this process is making batik more and more a mass-produced craft, though some *cap batik* is superior to *batik tulis* work.

Gamelan

Gamelan is the broad name for many varieties of xylophonic orchestras with bronze, wooden, or bamboo keys on wooden or bamboo bases or resting on tubular resonators. *Gamelan* is the most widespread type of orchestra in the archipelago, especially on Java and Bali.

The most sophisticated of these orchestras is the Central Javanese *gamelan,* usually composed of

(continues on next page)

JAVANESE CULTURE
(continued)

about a dozen musicians and used as accompaniment in *wayang* and dance performances. In its complete modern form, a *gamelan* orchestra could comprise 70-80 instruments including solo vocalists *(pasinden)* and up to 15 choir *(gerongan)* members. An ethereal sound, from thin tinkles to deep booming reverberations, is created when rows of small bronze kettle-shaped discs of varying sizes, with raised nipples, are hit with cudgel-like sticks.

Gamelan music can't be compared with Western polyphonic music, but it's much looser, freer, more flighty and unpredictable—curiously melancholy, even disturbing.

Dance

Since the split of the Mataram Kingdom into the vassal states of Yogyakarta and Solo in 1775, the art of court dancing has evolved differently in each of these central Javanese *kraton.* These cultural capitals have always been artistic rivals: Solo considers Yogyanese dancers too stiff and Yogyakarta thinks Solonese dancers are too slack and casual. The differences between the two schools are still recognizable today, though unimportant.

The tradition of classical dancing was once looked upon as a sacred legacy by the courts. Dancers selected from the upper-class families of the *kraton* population could take part only in supporting roles in the royal plays. It wasn't until 1918 when the Krida Beksa Wirama Dance School was founded outside the walls of the Yogyakarta *kraton* that Javanese dance was taught to the common Indonesian: the royal monopoly on dancing was at last broken.

In court dancing, the emphasis is on angular graceful poses and smooth subtle gestures. This type of dancing is far removed from Western theories of art and reflects the ultra-refinement of Javanese courts. Having evolved at a time of warring states, classical dancing is executed with all the deliberation of a slow march and the precision of a drill maneuver. Sometimes years of arduous muscular training is required to execute certain gestures such as arching the hand until the fingers touch the forearm (to imitate the opening of flower petals). Dancers are incredibly detached, yet their inaction and long periods of immobility are just as

important as the action. All these pauses, silences, and motions arrested in space, with lowered eyes and meditative poses, make Javanese dance absolutely hypnotic to watch.

The Ramayana is the most widely seen performance, but also watch for the *serimpi,* the slow, graceful, and highly disciplined classical dance of Central Java—one of the oldest and most sacred Javanese court dances. Originating over 400 years ago, this dance is dedicated to the dreaded South Sea Goddess Nyai Loro Kidul, who was said to have appeared to the first ruler of the dynasty, Sultan Agung (1613-45), expressing her love for him by dancing and singing before him.

Other dance forms include the **reyong,** a masked dance in which a great leering tiger's head is worn, and **kuda kepong,** East Java's famous horse-trance dance, in which entranced men ride bamboo-weave hobbyhorses to the mad rhythms of drums, gongs, and flutes.

Wayang

Named for a Javanese word meaning literally "shadow" or "ghost," *wayang* is a theatrical performance of living actors, three-dimensional puppets, or shadow images held before a screen lit from behind. The word can also refer to the puppets themselves. Most often the chants are in Kawi (Old Javanese), as archaic a language today as Shakespearean English.

Wayang performances are staged when some transitional event occurs in a family's life: birthdays, weddings, important religious occasions, or as ritual entertainment during family feasts or *selamatan.* Coming of age (puberty), a circumcision, promotions in rank, even the building of a new swimming pool—all could be excuses for a show.

While providing entertainment, the *wayang* media also teach the meaning and purpose as well as the contradictions and anomalies of modern life. The policies of the government are even explained in terms of *wayang* theater, not only by the puppetmasters but also in newspaper editorials and even in government statements.

Wayangs are led by the *dalang,* an immensely talented playwright, producer, principal narrator, conductor, and director of this shadow world. He's an

INDONESIA

expert in languages and highly skilled in the techniques of ventriloquism. Some *dalang* (or their wives) even carve their own puppets, maintaining a cast of up to 200 which are kept in a big wooden box *(katok)*. He must be familiar with all levels of speech according to the *dramatis personae,* modulating his voice and employing up to nine tonal and pitch variations to suit each of the puppets' temperaments.

The *dalang* has a highly developed dramatic sense, and if he has a good voice, his chants are beautiful and captivating to hear. He must also be intimately versed in history, including complex royal genealogies; music (melodies, modes, phrases, songs); recitation (both *gamelan* and spoken); and eloquence (an extempore poet creating a warm or terrifying atmosphere); and he must possess a familiarity with metaphysics, spiritual knowledge, and perfection of the soul. Traveling from village to village and city to city, he has as many fans as a film star.

Wayang Kulit

A "shadow play" using two-dimensional puppets chiseled by hand out of buffalo or goat parchment, with the appearance of paper dolls but with arms that swivel. Shadow plays are surrealistic collisions of Hindu epic, Muslim folklore, slapstick humor, sexual innuendo, political guidance, and village gossip—Krishna meets Punch and Judy. Since a *wayang kulit* puppet is a stylized exaggeration of a human shape, it's really a shadow of a shadow.

Many different styles exist. Palembang performs its own version, using its own dialect (a sort of Melayu slang), while in South Kalimantan another style called *wayang banjar* is in vogue. In Jakarta, *wayang kulit* is performed in the local Batawi dialects. But by far the most popular is the *wayang kulit* form practiced in Central and East Java and on Bali, where it has been developed as a spellbinding medium for storytelling.

Wayang Golek

Puppets in the round. Since *wayang golek* is the imitation by human actors of the movements of the shadow puppets, the three-dimensional *wayang golek* puppets imitate human beings imitating the shadow puppets. These puppets are much more like our Western ones, except that rods are used to manipulate them, not strings.

No shadow or screen is used. The audience faces the *dalang* and watches realistic people in miniature. Different *gamelan* musical pitches set the mood. Generally performed in the daytime, *wayang golek* is less ceremonial, less magical, and more worldly than shadow puppetry.

Wayang Topeng

Masked theater that mimes the stories of the *wayang golek* in which men act like puppets. Sometimes the dancers themselves speak their roles, other times the *dalang* speaks for them with the actors just marching on and off stage. Although classical Javanese language (Kawi) is most often used, it's spoken in a less stylized form than in *wayang orang.*

Troupes on Java consist of male dancers; female roles are taken by young boys before their voices change. Masks are often similar to the heads of *golek* puppets. Each region of Java and Bali features a different style of *topeng* masks, costuming, and dancing. The most active *topeng* centers are in East Java and on Bali. On stage the shiny beautiful masks with big mysterious eyes seem suspended in the air. An entire *wayang topeng* troupe consists of perhaps 20-25 people, and a set of *topeng* traditionally contains 40-80 pieces.

Wayang Orang

Called *wayang wong* in Javanese, these are abstract, symbolic dance plays, with or without masks, employing actor-dancers who dress up like *golek* puppets. Masks are usually only worn by actors playing animals: monkeys, birds, or monster roles (for example, the King of Demons in the Ramayana). A *dalang* may recite and chant, but the dialogue is most often spoken by live actors and actresses wearing shiny costumes of gold and black, and rich deep-colored batik silks.

Because of its hilarious antics, *wayang orang* is more intelligible and more of a spectacle to Westerners than other *wayang* forms. But *wayang orang* is also by far the most expensive to stage. A boxful of leather or wooden puppets is much cheaper to maintain than a whole troupe of live actors who have to be fed, clothed, transported, and paid. Consequently, *wayang orang* is the rarest *wayang* form—a real privilege to see if you ever get the chance.

which specializes in unusual fruit drinks made from durian, sirzat, and *apel.*

PERFORMING ARTS

Yogyakarta is the performing-arts capital of Java and one of the two finest places in Indonesia to experience the cultural riches of the archipelago. Most of the shows are geared toward the tourist, although this in no way detracts from their excitement or authenticity. Tourist venues are often better funded and have more lavish props and costuming than authentic productions. You will not understand the words but the magical scenes will fascinate and hold your attention for several hours. The tourist office has a list of the latest venues and schedules.

Ramayana
Dalem Pujokuseman: Yogya's most extraordinary performances are held three times weekly in the open-air pavilion a block off Jalan Katamso. Arrive early for the best seats. Photographers can claim the mats at stageside. The Ramayana is performed in four segments over consecutive evenings. Shows begin with a short description by the *dalang,* followed by three introductory dances, usually a *topeng* or *golek* taken from the Mahabharta or Panji cycles. Before the main event, the dancers mentally prepare themselves with a few moments of quiet contemplation. Unlike the frantic movements of the Balinese, Javanese dance is a highly refined and hypnotic choreography which resembles a ballet in slow motion. Battle scenes are reserved for the climactic finish. Do not confuse this performance with the vastly inferior Sasanasuka Ramayana given at the THR.

Prambanan Ramayana: These de Mille-like spectacles take place in the newly constructed 1,011-seat amphitheater which overlooks the Loro Jonggrang temple complex at Prambanan. Performances are held on four successive full-moon nights each month from June to October. This six-episode contemporary *sendratari*-style ballet is based on traditional *wayang orang* dancing of classical Javanese theater. The plot is a modernized, dramatized version of the Indian epic poem, the Ramayana. The Prambanan temple panels are, in effect, re-enacted live. Taking

part are an entire *gamelan* orchestra, scores of beautifully and grotesquely costumed dancers, singers, and musicians, with monkey armies, strutting menacing *rawana,* acrobatic miracles, giant kings on stilts, clashing battles, *real* fire. Tickets for admission and transportation can be purchased in advance from the tourist office, travel agencies, or any large hotel. One of the most spectacular theater productions in Indonesia.

Kraton: Court rehearsals of Javanese dance and *gamelan* can be observed in the royal palace on Sundays at 1030. *Gamelan* only on Mondays and Wednesdays at 1030.

Arjuna Plaza Hotel: Abbreviated versions of the Ramayana are performed in the French Grill Thursdays at 1900.

Sasanasuka: Amateurish and poorly attended shows performed by struggling students, transvestites, and last-minute fill-ins. Forget it.

Wayang
Nitour Show: Wooden puppet shows daily except Sunday at 1100 inside the studio at Jalan Dalhlan 71. Touristy but one of the few guaranteed spots to watch some *wayang golek.*

Agastya Art Institute: A training school for *dalangs* (puppetmasters). Visitors can watch lessons daily from 1500 to 1700. It's on Jalan Gedongkiwo over the RR tracks, about three km from the city in a small *kampong.*

RRI: Radio Republic Indonesia sponsors all-night shadow-puppet plays on the second Saturday of the month in the Sasono Hinggil just south of the *kraton.* A completely authentic experience.

Arjuna Plaza Hotel: Shadow plays for tourists every Tuesday at 1900.

SHOPPING

Yogyakarta is rivaled only by Bali for variety of arts and crafts. Top buys are batiks, leatherwork, and performing-arts tools such as *wayang kulit* and *wayang golek* puppets. Many of the fashion designers have married traditional materials with the latest designs to produce beautiful clothing at outstanding prices.

To get acquainted with the full range of crafts offered, visit first the government-sponsored Yogyakarta Crafts Center across from the Ambarrukmo Hotel and the chaotic Central Market on Jalan Malioboro. Then slowly walk up and down Jalan Malioboro, pausing at the half-dozen shops which specialize in Indonesian crafts. Best bets include the outstanding array of batiks in Terang Bulan (near the market), a handful of small antique stores opposite the Garuda Hotel near the RR tracks, musical instruments and Ramayana costumes in Toko Jawa (opposite the Mutiara Hotel), and Toko Setia for *wayang* puppets.

Batik

Yogya's most famous craft is batik. Outlets can be found throughout the city but a large concentration of shops is located south of the *kraton* near the water palace and on Jalan Prawirotaman near the middle-priced hotels. Some young entrepreneur will almost certainly want to show you around and receive a commission for his services. Although there is absolutely no need to use sales touts, they're worth employing if you enjoy their company and don't mind paying the fee.

Take your time; there's a great deal of mass-produced junk in Yogya. Batik produced with silkscreen printing methods or copper printing stamps called *cap tulis* should be very inexpensive. Hand-painted batik *(batik tulis)* will cost more, but even then, quality varies enormously. Some artists just draw the outline and have teams of girls fill in the intricate details . . . assembly-line fashion. Results are often the worst kinds of clichés: blazing Indonesian sunsets, doe-eyed Balinese dancers, psychedelic crashing beach scenes. Before spending any sizable amount of money, investigate the market and educate yourself. Terang Bulan, Yogya's batik supermarket on Jalan Malioboro, has a good selection in all price ranges. Then visit several private galleries such as Amri Batik west of the river and Kuswadji's near the *kraton.* Batik shops often come down 30% on the original asking price.

Yogyakarta is an excellent place to learn something about the complex art of batik. Dozens of schools here charge 5,000-20,000 *rupiah* weekly, including materials, to teach the history of batik; traditional designs; formulas for waxes; how to prepare and use both chemical and natural dyes; how to hold, use, and clean the *canting* (wax pen) and *jegul* (brush); how to apply wax in fine and thick lines, how to remove wax from cloth. Recommendations from other stu-

dents are best, but the tourist office has an approved list. Before handing over your money, talk to the instructor and look at his work.

SERVICES

Tourist Information

The tourist office (tel. 3543) on Jalan Malioboro is one of the best in Indonesia. They can help with maps, calendars of upcoming festivals, schedules of performing arts, Prambanan shows, and recommendations on where to shop. Train and bus schedules are posted on bulletin boards. Open daily except Sundays 0800-2030.

Yogya's largest bookstore is Gunung Agung, at the corner of Jalan Mangkubumi and Jalan Diponegoro. Look for Michael Smithies's *Yogyakarta, Cultural Heart of Indonesia* or Jacques Dumarcay's *The Temples of Java,* two outstanding guidebooks published by Oxford in Asia.

Mail and Telephone

The post office is located inside the historic building on the corner of Jalan Senopati and Jalan Yani. All packages must be inspected by customs before mailing. The Pos Paket is in a side room; poste restante is just to the left of the main entrance. Telephone calls can be made around the clock from the phone center on Yos Sudarso, about 15 minutes by *becak* from city center.

Travel Agencies

Travel agents around town can help with organized tours to Dieng Plateau, minibuses to Cilicap, and Ramayana plays at Prambanan. Several honest and dependable agents keep shop on Jalan Sosrowijayan near the Indonesia Hotel. Pacto Travel (tel. 2740) on Jalan Mangkubumi sells tours and traveler's checks and functions as the representative of American Express.

TRANSPORTATION

Arrival

Air: Yogya's airport is 10 km from town on the road to Solo. Taxis from the airport to city center cost about US$4. Buses and minibuses leave about 200 meters from the terminal entrance.

Train: Yogya's train station is nicely located right in the middle of town, within easy walking distance of the budget *losmen* and the Garuda Hotel on Jalan Malioboro. Train schedules are posted in the lobby.

Bus: Yogya's main bus terminal is inconveniently located about four km southeast of city center. It's not on the map but about three inches right! Most public buses going west on Jalan Veteran will reach Jalan Malioboro and the budget *losmen* near the train station. *Becaks* cost 2,000Rp to city center. Private bus companies often drop you near the train station; eat at the Padang restaurant just opposite if you arrive before dawn.

Getting Around

Yogyakarta is a compact town and almost everything of interest is within walking distance. A great way to save time and get some exercise is on a bicycle rented from the restaurants and *losmen* near Jalan Sosrowijayan. Streets here are filled with friendly "hellos" and the jangle of bicycle bells. Motorcycles can be rented from several shops on Jalan Kembang. Traffic is light, roads are in good condition, and service stations are plentiful—there is absolutely no finer way to explore the countryside and monuments at Prambanan than on a motorcycle! Minibuses are no longer allowed within the city limits.

Becaks: Prices are extremely reasonable, costing around 600Rp per km or 1,500Rp by the hour. There's no shortage of them, so if you don't get this rate or near it, just walk away and give your business to the competition. Many drivers approach you proposing 300-500Rp per hour, but their intention is to take you on a shopping tour. If you're interested, this is an excellent

way to shop around, though you pay higher prices to cover their commissions.

Leaving Yogyakarta

Air: Tickets can be purchased from Garuda (tel. 4400) on Jalan Mangkubumi, Merpati (tel. 4272) on Jalan Sudirman, and local travel agents. Flights to Jakarta and Bali should be booked several days in advance. To reach the airport from city center, take any minibus going to Solo and get off in front of the terminal.

Train: Train travel is one of the small pleasures of any journey across Java. They're safe, quiet, restful, and allow you the time to meet Indonesians, always the highlight of any visit. A wide variety of trains leaves Yogyakarta every day, but it's best to avoid the slow and crowded third-class coaches. Departure timetables are posted in the train station. Purchase your ticket in advance or expect to stand.

Bus: Buses leave Yogyakarta from several different areas. The main public terminal is about four km southeast of town on the road to Kota Gede. Buses leave 0330-1900 every 10-15 minutes for all the towns on Java. Every public bus that runs down Jalan Malioboro goes to the main bus terminal. Buses also leave from private company headquarters located on Jalan Mangkubumi and Jalan Diponegoro, north of the train station. These long-distance buses usually leave 500-1930 and travel straight through the cool night. Sleep is difficult if not impossible; expect to spend the next day recovering in bed. Minibuses also leave from the travel agencies on Jalan Sosrowijayan in the heart of the tourist quarter. These are fast, convenient, and surprisingly comfortable ways to reach almost all tourist destinations in Central Java.

CENTRAL JAVA

PRAMBANAN

It took a staggering agricultural productivity to enable pompous feudal monarchs to erect temples to their own glorification. Thus the rich Prambanan Plain, 17 km northeast of Yogya on the road to Solo, has the most extensive Hindu temple ruins in all of Indonesia. Between the 8th and 10th centuries, Central Java was the island's wealthiest and most powerful region. South-central Java was controlled by the Hindu-influenced Mataram Kingdom, while the Buddhist Saliendra Dynasty controlled the north. Both kingdoms and religions apparently lived in peace. Lying today among villages and green ricefields with the sharp peak of Mt. Merapi in the background, most of these temple complexes were abandoned in the 13th century when the Hindu-Javanese kings moved from Central to East Java. Around 1600, all extant temples were toppled by an earthquake, then slowly buried by the eruptions of Mt. Merapi. In the 19th cen-

tury their blocks were carried off to pave roads and build sugar mills, bridges, and railroads. The Dutch started restoration work in the late 1930s. The following temples or *candi* (pronounced CHON-di) were used mainly for royal ceremonies rather than religious rites.

To get there, take any minibus on Jalan Mataram going toward Solo. Prambanan is also within reasonable biking distance on a special biking lane. Motorcycles are terrific. Or round up a group and charter a taxi for the day; the ruins are widely scattered. Keep a sharp lookout for small signs posted by the archaeological service.

Prambanan Temple Complex
The largest temple complex on Java, Prambanan's central courtyard contains three large structures: a main temple dedicated to Shiva, flanked by those of Brahma (to the south) and Vishnu (to the north). Besides these, the complex originally contained 244 minor temples *(candi perwara)*, all arranged in four rows. Only two of these have been restored. The two small

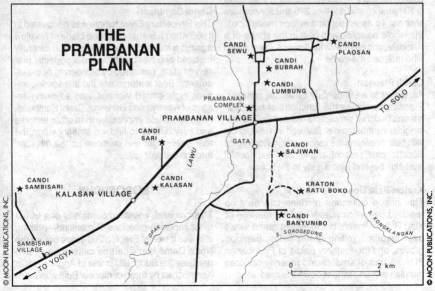

candi at the side of the main terrace were probably the treasuries where the jewels and gold were kept. The tall, elegant central temple is both a wonder of restoration and a synthesis of northern and southern Indian architectural styles. But it is the lavish decorations, panels, motifs, and reliefs that tell the Ramayana stories that remain Prambanan's chief wonder—some of the most famous Hindu sculpture in the world. To follow the story, hire a guide and begin at the east stairway, slowly wandering past trees of heaven surrounded by animals, pots of money, half-women and half-bird creatures, armies of monkeys, noble heroes, beautiful heroines. The four-armed statue of Shiva in the center might remind you of the Jaggernat temple in Bubaneshwar, south of Calcutta.

Candi Sewu

Walk or ride your bicycle to the following temples, which are less crowded, less commercialized, and just as fascinating as the main temple complex. The "1,000 Temples" one km north of Prambanan is now largely in ruins but slowly being reconstructed from the ground up. It consists of a large but disassembled central temple (Candi Induk) surrounded by 28 smaller temples all carved with identical standing Vishnus (à la Kahjuraho) and another 240 smaller *perwara* shrines. To assist pilgrims in their meditations, the whole complex was built in the shape of a mandala, complete with fat demons *(dwarapala)* who guarded the gates.

Candi Plaosan

Attributed to a 9th-century Saliendra princess, Plaosan combines the functions of both Mahayana Buddhist temple and monastery. The rectangular central temple, restored in 1960, is cut with cells displaying the various incarnations of the Buddha: past, present, and future. The peaceful ricefields beyond lend dignity to the scene.

Kraton Ratu Boko

This hilltop collection of ruins can only be reached by motorcycle. Very little remains of King Boko's *kraton,* but there are grand views over luxuriant rolling green fields, bamboo groves, and the feathery palms of Prambanan Plain. A pair of smaller and recently restored temples is found farther down the road.

Candi Kalasan

Kalasan is the oldest Mahayana Buddhist temple in Indonesia to which a date can be set: A.D. 778. Set in a small park just off the Yogya-Solo highway, Kalasan was once a royal mausoleum completely covered in multicolored shining stucco, unique niche decorations, and probably the most beautiful *kala* heads in Central Java. All of the Dhani Buddhas which once stood inside the exterior niches have been plundered, aside from a single figure on the south side. But note the outstanding *kalas* with their crowns of plants and companions of bodhisattvas. The exquisite but empty interior is bathed in light, flooding down from the sky.

Candi Sari

Situated in the middle of coconut and banana groves, the design of Candi Sari is woven together superbly, like a basket. The second floor once served as the priests' dormitory. The entire structure is a sculptor's feast of mythological *kinnaris,* blooming lotus buds, old men with finely carved waterspouts between their legs, and, most importantly, the 36 bodhisattvas dancing and playing instruments. A peaceful, wonderful place.

Candi Sambisari

This 9th-century Shiva temple was discovered in 1966 when a farmer broke the blade of his plow against a stone. Sambasari has been carefully restored and can be studied in a perfectly preserved state, unmarred by plunderers or the elements. Best features are the interior *lingam-yoni,* eight-armed Vishnus, and adjoining images of Agastya and Ganesha. Candi Sambisari, however, is less impressive than other temples and very difficult to find; go straight when the road veers right and continue up the dirt road through the split gate.

BOROBUDUR

This colossal, cosmic mountain is one of the most imposing creations of mankind—nothing else like it exists! Erected 200 years before the Notre Dame and Chartres cathedrals, it also predates the Buddhist temple of Angkor Wat in Kampuchea by three centuries. Built with more

INDONESIA

than two million cubic feet of stone, it's the world's largest stupa, and the largest ancient monument in the Southern Hemisphere. Borobudur is related to both the Indian monuments of northwest India and the terraced sanctuaries of prehistoric Indonesian architecture. Although the structure has many characteristics of the Central Javanese style (A.D. 700-950), it has little else in common with other Buddhist temples in Southeast Asia. Persian, Babylonian, and Greek influences have also been incorporated into Borobudur's art and architecture. Planned by men with a profound knowledge of Buddhist philosophy, on it Buddha and Shiva are spiritually the same being.

Used for veneration, worship, and meditation, this giant monument was an achievement of the Vajrayana sect of the Tantric School of Buddhism, which found acceptance in Indonesia around A.D. 700. The feudal Saliendra princes—not elite savages but highly advanced technicians—erected it with peasant labor between 778 and 850. No one knows how this great structure was built at a time when modern engineering techniques were yet to be developed. No nation or group of men could possibly build it today. Thousands of laborers, slaves, carvers, sculptors, carriers, and expert supervisors worked for decades rolling logs, working ropes, levers, hammers, mallets, and chisels, using only their hands and arms. The monument took perhaps 10,000 men a century to build. Records indicate that the population of the countryside of Central Java was drastically reduced after the completion of Borobudur in the 9th century; it exhausted five generations. The Saliendras were finally overthrown by Hindus on Java in 856, and Borobudur was abandoned soon after completion. It might have started to collapse just when the sculptors were putting on the finishing touches; there's evidence of work initiated to reinforce the base, and some panels were found to have trace marks begun on them.

The monument was buried under a thousand years of volcanic eruptions and tropical growth until discovered by an English colonel during the British occupation of Indonesia in 1814. In 1855 Borobudur was cleared, and the long process of restoration began. The work was at last completed in 1983 at a cost of over US$25 million. Former President Suharto himself presided over the formal opening ceremony in March 1983.

Approached from the main entrance, Borobudur seems to be an unspectacular, almost impassive shape, like something carved out of solid rock. The structure was constructed to look like the holy Mt. Meru of India, the mythological model of the Buddhist universe. This unique building combines symbols of the circle (heaven), of the square (earth), and of the stupa into one coherent whole. The 10 terraces from the base to the main topmost stupa represent the individual stages toward perfection in a man's life. The pilgrim's walk (ignore the Indonesian tourists more interested in you than the carvings) takes you around the temple nine times before reaching the top. Visitors are symbolically swallowed by the *kala* monster upon entering, thus giving new spiritual life. The five-storied pyramid is subdivided vertically into three spheres of Buddhism, symbolizing religious microcosms: the base is the "world of passion" with reliefs illustrating worldly life and toil; the next four terraces depict Buddhas's life and the "world of formlessness." As you climb higher, the reliefs become more heavenly until man has eliminated desire, though still tied to the world of the senses.

Borobudur's crowning glory isn't the complex cosmology or its massive size; it's the phenomenal quality of the sculpture. There are 1,500 pictorial relief panels of Buddha's teachings, plus 1,212 purely ornamental panels—one of the largest and most complete ensembles of Buddhist reliefs in existence, amounting to a virtual textbook of Mahayana Buddhist doctrine in stone. Once glistening with bright purple, crimson, green, blue, and yellow paint, over 8,235 square meters of stone surface are carved in high relief, telling scholars much about the material culture of 8th- and 9th-century Central Java. There are lessons on history, religion, art, morality, literature, clothing styles, family life, architecture, agriculture, shipping, fighting arts, dancing—the whole Buddhist cosmos. Sculptors trained in the best tradition of Indian classical temple building poured their abundant talents into the most delicate, intricate details. The distance through all the galleries to the summit is a walk of over five km, a labyrinth of narrow corridors. To read all the reliefs from the beginning of the story, go through the door on the east side. Take the time to think, dream, sit, and stare.

Also of interest are the nearby temples of Candi Pawon and Mendut, three km east of Borobudur. Mendut is a genuine 9th-century temple of worship, not a *candi* to the dead. Contemporary with Borobudur, the temple has extensive galleries and terraces, and a stupa on its pyramid-shaped roof. A very sophisticated knowledge of Buddhist and Shivaistic texts, Indian iconography, symbolism, and monumental architecture was crucial to build it.

Transportation

The single biggest problem with Borobudur is the gigantic crowds who flood the monument each morning by 0900. Borobudur is open daily 0700-1730. To enjoy it without the crowds you must arrive at the crack of dawn. Buses north to Muntilan, the jumping-off point for Borobudur, depart from Jalan Magelang in north Yogyakarta. You must change buses in Muntilan. Allow two hours by public bus. It's better to find an inexpensive tour that leaves Yogya by 0600 and allows you a minimum of four hours at the site. Tours which also include Dieng Plateau are rushed but acceptable when time is short.

Accommodations

The best way to beat the crowds is to overnight in a *losmen* on the road which approaches the monument. Losmen Citra Rasas, Losmen Saraswati, and Villa Rosita, to the west of the complex, offer decent rooms for US$3-6. Best spot is the spotless and friendly Lotus Guesthouse about 500 meters up the road on the east side of the monument. Perfectly quiet, plus oil lamps—not electricity!

KALIURANG AND MT. MERAPI

Kaliurang is an old Dutch hill resort 26 km north of Yogya nestled on the southern slopes of Mt. Merapi. There's a strong European flavor to the township. It's also a superb place for outdoor activities, hiking, and swimming under icy waterfalls. Almost everybody comes up here to climb Mt. Merapi, but if the weather and horror stories about the climb change your mind, there's plenty of hiking to do for a few days: to the observatory on Mt. Plawangan, east to the dam, west to Tritis for the best volcano views, or the

three-hour trek to Mt. Turgo, a recommended warm-up before the assault on Merapi.

Mt. Merapi is a seriously difficult hike. Its name means "Fire Mountain" for good reasons. Considered one of the most dangerous volcanoes in the world, Merapi has repeatedly exploded, spewing forth lava and ash which devastate the land with disturbing regularity. Vulcanologists see frightening similarities to Mt. St. Helens and fear that the growing pressure dome on the Yogya side will soon explode, unleashing a pyroclastic flow which would consume everything in its path and kill thousands.

With that cheerful thought in mind, Merapi can be climbed either from Kaliurang or from Selo on the north side. From Kaliurang, you must depart at midnight to make sunrise on top. Most hikers are satisfied to fork left above the treeline to see the crater rather than continuing two more hours up to the summit. It's vital to return to the treeline by 0900 or risk getting lost in the thick clouds. From Selo, it's four hours to the summit. Usually less cloudy but still a formidable climb with major risks.

Transportation and Accommodations

Minibuses leave Yogyakarta from Jalan Mataram and from the intersection of Jalan Sudirman and Sangaji (Terminal Terban).

Perhaps the best thing about Kaliurang is a homestay called Vogels, one of the most comfortable and hospitable lodges in Indonesia. Vogel is an effusive Christian who generously dispenses advice and cautions about climbing the mountain, besides running a wonderful guesthouse. A great place to relax, read a book, do some hiking, and socialize with other travelers.

DIENG PLATEAU

The oldest temples of Java lie at 2,093 meters on this pear-shaped plateau, 130 km northwest of Yogyakarta. A religious center possibly since megalithic times and certainly from the beginning of the Java-Hindu era, this enchanting highland offers lovely mountain scenery, a bracing climate, fascinating volcanic fissures, endless hiking possibilities, and ancient Hindu temples named after the heroes of the *wayang*. Dieng was once a huge volcano which erupted. The remaining caldera, after thousands of years of weathering, has become a soggy plateau with dozens of geothermal spots where one can walk right up to the rims of boiling, smoking, odorous cauldrons. In June 1979, poisonous gases rose from underground passages and from several lakes, killing 150 villagers. Dieng is also extremely wet and cold; bring sweaters, jackets, and gloves.

Only eight of perhaps 200 original temples have been restored in the central valley. All were built by the Saliendras sometime in the 8th century and dedicated to Shiva as places of worship, not to glorify kings, as were the later Hindu-Buddhist monuments of Central Java. Candi

Bima, 1.5 km south of Dieng Village, is unique in Indonesia: faces in its roof seem like spectators looking out of windows, reminiscent of its more sophisticated ancestors at Prambanan and Mendut. Named after members of the Pandava clan from the Mahabharta epic, none of the Dieng monuments are very large or particularly impressive, although the location is superb.

Best of all are the hikes though the valley. Maps are available from the tourist office in Dieng and from the Dieng Restaurant in Wonosobo. The energetic can walk to Sembungan, the highest village on Java, or explore the volcanic lakes of Sikidang and Sikumbang. Gua Semar (Semar Cave) is believed to be the exact center of Java

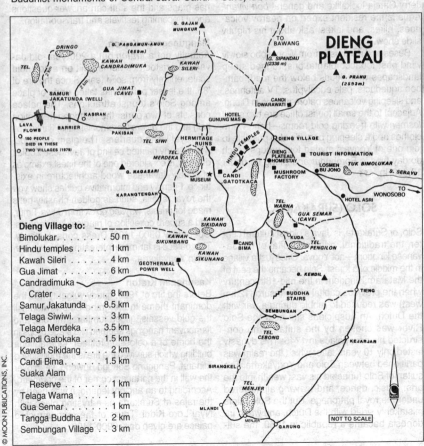

Dieng Village to:

Bimolukar	50 m
Hindu temples	1 km
Kawah Sileri	4 km
Gua Jimat	6 km
Candradimuka Crater	8 km
Samur Jakatunda	8.5 km
Telaga Siwiwi	3 km
Telaga Merdeka	3.5 km
Candi Gatokaka	1.5 km
Kawah Sikidang	2 km
Candi Bima	1.5 km
Suaka Alam Reserve	1 km
Telaga Warna	1 km
Gua Semar	1 km
Tangga Buddha	2 km
Sembungan Village	3 km

NOT TO SCALE

© MOON PUBLICATIONS, INC.

INDONESIA

and the dwelling place of the clown god Semar. Other possibilities include Gua Jimat ("Death Cave") from which so much carbon dioxide pours out that animals can't survive, and the 13-km hike down to Bawang.

Transportation and Accommodations

From Yogya, take a minibus to Muntilan, visit Borobudur, return to Muntilan, change to Magelang, and continue up to Wonosobo. Late-afternoon minibuses climb up to Dieng, but it's better to spend the night with Agus and his wife (ex-lawyer turned "Master of *Nasi Goreng*") at his outstanding Dieng Restaurant and Losmen one block east of the main road. Somewhat of a Jerry Garcia lookalike and general *bon vivant*, Agus is the resident expert on nearby volcanoes, hikes, and lakes; ask about his nightly slide show.

Buses and minibuses from Wonosobo slowly wind past tobacco plantations, rugged steep landscapes with clouds below the road, bamboo aqueducts, pale eucalyptus, TV antennas, and sleeping volcanoes before arriving in Dieng. Adjacent to the small tourist office are two small *losmen* with freezing cold rooms—bring warm clothes and a sleeping bag. It's also possible to join one of Yogya's myriad tour groups which do day-trips to Borobudur and Dieng for under 10,000Rp. 🖢🖢

SOLO (SURAKARTA)

Solo, or Surakarta, is Java's oldest cultural center, the traditional, original capital of the Javanese kingdom—not Yogya. Once just a village in the middle of a forest, Solo became the seat of the Mataram Kingdom in the mid-18th century when the previous capital of Kartosuro (12 km west) was reduced to rubble during a war with the Dutch. An auspicious site near the Solo River was chosen by the sultan, who constructed his new palace in 1745. This dynasty lasted only 10 years, after which the realm was partitioned between Solo and Yogyakarta. The sultan of Solo funneled his vast wealth into the arts: music, dance, and *wayang* all flowered under the royal patronage. But the Solo rulers mistakenly sided with the Dutch, and when Indonesia became a republic in 1950, the sul-

tanate lost all recognized authority. Bad luck continued in 1985 when the palace of Pakubuwono, the youngest of the royal houses, tragically burned down during restoration—a sign that the sultan had lost his *wahyu*, the mystic authority that all Javanese leaders are supposed to possess. In 1988, the 37-year-old Prince Jiwokusomo was proclaimed the 9th sultan of Mankunegara.

Although the city is often compared to Yogya because of its royal palaces and batik industry, cultural offerings and shopping opportunities are far more limited. And yet the town has enough of interest to keep most visitors occupied for a few days. The tourist office on Jalan Slamet Riyadi has maps and the staff can answer questions about upcoming festivals and transportation.

Mangunegaran Kraton

Actually not a *kraton* but a 200-year-old Javanese aristocrat's home built on a splendid scale, entirely from solid teak. Since the fire of '85, the lesser palace has taken pride of place among Solo's tourist attractions. The palace consists of two parts: the *pendopo* (reception hall) and the *dalem* (ceremonial halls) flanked by the royal living quarters. The giant *pendopo*, with its zany painted ceiling of Javanese Zodiac designs, is considered one of the finest examples of stately Javanese wood architecture in existence. Friendly and informative guides show you the royal regalia, such as golden chastity belts made for priests, *wayang golek* from Jawa Timur, and a superb collection of magical *kris* daggers. Open daily 0900-1400. Dress conservatively. This palace is far more interesting than the *kraton* in Yogyakarta.

Kasunanan Kraton

Before the fire of 1985, gaudy vulgarity was the dominant theme in the grand Solo Kraton. All the gold vessels, gilded furniture, mirrors, and flamboyant hangings seemed like stage props in the home of a colossal profiteer. One antique building which survived the fire is the multistoried minaret, Panggung Songgo Buwono, seen over the wall in the northeast corner of the courtyard. According to an ancient legend, it was used by the rajas of Surakarta as a trysting place with Nyai Loro Kidul. Tours of the reconstructed palace are given daily 0900-1400.

INDONESIA

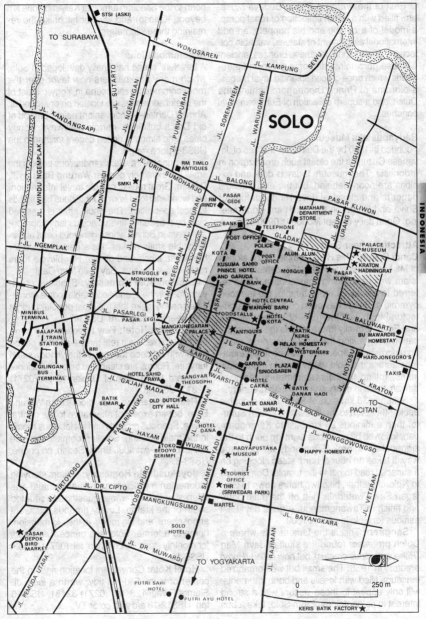

TO SURABAYA

STSI (ASKI)

JL. WONOSAREN

JL. SUTARTO

JL. KAMPUNG SEWU

JL. NGEMINGAN

JL. PURWOPURAN

JL. SORENGENEN

JL. WARUNGMIRI

SOLO

JL. KANDANGSAPI

RM TIMLO ANTIQUES

JL. URIP SUMOHARJO

JL. BALONG

PASAR KLIWON

SMKI

JL. WINDU NGEMPLAK

JL. MONGINSIDI

RM RINDY

PASAR GEDE

MATAHARI DEPARTMENT STORE

JL. SUPIT URANG

JL. PALUGUNAN

JL. NGEMPLAK

JL. KEPUN TON

BANK

JL. WIDURAN

TELEPHONE

GLADAK

PALACE MUSEUM

POST OFFICE

POLICE

ALUN ALUN

KRATON HADININGRAT

KOTA

POST OFFICE

PASAR KLEWER

STRUGGLE 45 MONUMENT

JL. KEBALEN

KUSUMA SAHID PRINCE HOTEL AND GARUDA

MOSQUE

JL. SECOYUDAN

JL. HASANUDIN

JL. TAMBAKSEGARAN

BANK

JL. BALUWARTI

MINIBUS TERMINAL

JL. PASARLEGI

Pasar Legi

HOTEL CENTRAL

WARUNG BARU

FOODSTALLS

HOTEL KOTA

BU MAWARDIS HOMESTAY

BALAPAN TRAIN STATION

JL. BALAPAN

MANGKUNEGARAN PALACE

ASRAMA

ANTIQUES

BATIK KERIS

JL. NOTOSUMAN

RRI

JL. TOTOGAN

RELAX HOMESTAY

WESTERNERS

HARDJONEGORO'S

GILINGAN BUS TERMINAL

JL. KARTINI

JL. SUBROTO

TAXIS

HOTEL SAHID RAYA

SANGYAR THEOSOPHI

JL. WARSITO

GARUDA

PLAZA SINGOSAREN

JL. KRATON

JL. GAJAH MADA

HOTEL CAKRA

BATIK DANAR HADI

TO PACITAN

BATIK SEMAR

OLD DUTCH CITY HALL

JL. SUDIRMAN

BATIK DANAR HARU

SEE "CENTRAL SOLO MAP"

JL. TAGORE

JL. PASARNONGKO

JL. HAYAM WURUK

HOTEL DANA

JL. HONGGOWONGSO

TOKO BEDOYO SERIMPI

RADYAPUSTAKA MUSEUM

HAPPY HOMESTAY

JL. TIRTOYOSO

JL. YOSODIPURO

JL. SLAMET RIYADI

TOURIST OFFICE

THR (SRIWEDARI PARK)

JL. VETERAN

JL. DR. CIPTO

MANGKUNGSUMO

WARTEL

JL. BAYANGKARA

PASAR DEPOK BIRD MARKET

SOLO HOTEL

JL. DR. MUWARDI

JL. RAJIMAN

JL. PEMUDA UTARA

TO YOGYAKARTA

PUTRI SARI HOTEL

PUTRI AYU HOTEL

0   250 m

KERIS BATIK FACTORY

INDONESIA

East of the *kraton* is Suaba Budaya Museum, filled with a lavish collection of regal pomp: a model of a *dalang* and his puppets, an odd international assortment of statues, valuable collections of old Hindu-Javanese bronzes, ancient Chinese porcelains, demonic gargoyle figureheads which once graced splendid royal barges, a diorama of Prince Diponegoro fighting the Dutch, and a superb collection of European royal coaches.

Radyapustaka Museum

Founded in 1890 by the Dutch, the Institute of Javanese Culture is the oldest such organization in Indonesia. The museum today is dark and exhibits are poorly labeled, but the exquisite *kris* daggers and classical Java-Hindu statues of Shiva and Durga on the porch are worth seeing. Open daily except Mondays 0900-1230.

Attractions near Solo

Candi Sukuh: This Hindu temple on the slopes of Mt. Lawu was built in the 15th century just as Islam was penetrating coastal Java. Often referred to as Java's erotic temple, the terraced pyramid at Sukuh has been compared in architectural form with the ruins of ancient Mexico and Egypt. Equally impressive is the superb location overlooking the whole Javanese plain, an unforgettable spectacle of sweeping panoramas across the Solo valley, purple mountains, lakes, rolling foothills, shimmering terraced *sawah,* trees in every shade of lush greenery.

Sukuh is 36 km east of Solo. Take a double decker three km to the terminal on Jalan Sutarto, then a minibus 25 km east to Karangpandan, followed by a minibus eight km north to the signpost at Nglorok. Everybody will point the way. It takes an hour of hard, steep slogging on a surfaced road to get to the temple. Don't return to Nglorok; rather, hike two hours down to Grojagan Sewu waterfalls (left off the main path) and finish in Tawangmangu. A great day! Last minibus for Solo leaves at 1600.

Sangiran: This is the famous site where a Dutch professor found the skull of Java Man *(Pithecanthropus erectus),* but now called *(Homo erectus)* in 1936. The small but well-organized museum, filled with fossils and bone fragments, will only appeal to those visitors with a strong interest in paleontology. From Solo, take a bus north to the Sangiran turnoff at Kalijambi (one km beyond Kalioso) and walk or hitchhike the remaining three kilometers.

Accommodations

A travelers' scene has finally developed in Solo, which many backpackers now favor over the more commercialized scene in Yogya. Most of the useful addresses are located on or around Jl. Ahmad Dahlan—a convenient neighborhood of old Dutch buildings, narrow alleyways, trendy cafes, and almost a dozen decent *losmen* in the US$3-8 price range.

The principal travelers' rendezvous point is the small but extremely popular **Warung Baru** on Jl. Dahlan. Great music, reliable travel information, and wonderful food from mountainous fruit salads to local specialties. The whole affair is presided over by a beautiful and vivacious lady appropriately named Sunny, whose generous heart and irresistible smile makes this a perfect place for breakfast, lunch, and dinner. Her bicycle tours receive rave reviews. Say hello from Carl!

Losmen Solo Homestay: Spacious courtyard, friendly help, and acceptable rooms (sometimes noisy) make this the most popular budget spot near Warung Baru. US$3-5.

Keprabon Hotel: Few travelers stay here, but this old place is a real rarity—a Dutch period hotel with art deco touches in the windows and furniture. Rooms are clean and face a quiet inner courtyard. Good value. Jl. Dahlan 12, tel. (0271) 32811, US$4-8.

Relax Homestay: A few blocks from Warung Baru, but an excellent alternative to the central scene. Spacious grounds and six fabulous rooms in the main building. Smaller rooms to the side are just that—*small.* Jl. Empu Sedah, no phone, US$3-8.

Joyokusuman Homestay: Visitors studying Indonesian mysticism and other spiritual arts often stay in this remote guesthouse situated south of the *kraton.* Lovely grounds, pleasant atmosphere, and big rooms in the old mansion, home to a former Solonese prince. Discounts for monthly stays. Jl. Gajahan, tel. (0271) 32833, US$5-12.

Hotel Kota: Convenient location right in the center of town. Old but tidy; worth a look. Jl. Slamet Riyadi 123, tel. (0271) 32481, US$4-6 fan, US$12-18 a/c with color TV.

CENTRAL SOLO

MANGKUNEGARAN PALACE

KUSUMA SAHID
PRINCE HOTEL

JL. A. DAHLAN

JL. RONGGOWARSITO

FORTUNA
LOSMEN

RAMAYANA
RESTAURANT

TELEKOM
OFFICE

MALIOBORO
RESTAURANT

LOSMEN NIRWANA

JL. TEUKU UMAR

JL. IMAM BONJOL

JL. SUDIRMAN

LOSMEN
SOLO
HOMESTAY

JL. DIPONEGORO

CAFE
GAMELAN

PASAR
TRIWINDU

BU WONGSO LEMU

JL. A. DAHLAN

WARUNGS

BU NAHYO

WARUNG
BARU

GPO

CINEMA

KEPRABON
HOTEL

HOTEL
WIGATI

TO SURABAYA

JL. SLAMET RIYADI

AMERICAN
DONUT

NEW
HOLLAND
BAKERY

WARTEL

KOTA
HOTEL

KASUMA
SARI
RESTAURANT

ADPURA
KENCANA
MONUMENT

BALAI
AGUNG

TO
YOGYAKARTA

JL. EMPU BARDAH

JL. YOS SUDARSO

MAMA
HOMESTAY

OLD DUTCH
HOMES

ALUN-ALUN

RELAX HOMESTAY

JL. EMPU SEDAH

CENDANA
HOMESTAY

BATIK KERIS

PARADISE GH

AGUNG MOSQUE

JL. KEMLAYAN KIDUL

WESTERNERS

SINGOSAREN PLAZA

OLD HERB SHOP

GOLD SHOPS

JL. SECOYUDAN

PASAR KLEWER

JL. SUBROTO

JL. YOS SUDARSO

JL. GAJAHAN

JL. KUSUMA

JL. HASYIM

KRATON

0   50 m

MOON

INDONESIA

© MOON PUBLICATIONS, INC.

Westerners Losmen: Pak and Ibu Mawardi's Homestay is a friendly and clean spot where almost all travelers spend their time in Solo. Singing birds and bicycle rentals—an island of peace in the center of the city. Difficult to find and poorly marked; in the narrow alley down from the modern Singosaran market. Kemlayan Kidul II, tel. (0271) 33106, US$3-6.

Putri Sari Hotel: Simple, modern, and clean hotel on the western edge of town. Jalan Riyadi 382, tel. (0271) 46995, US$4-8.

Dana Hotel: A sprawling, somewhat decrepit hotel with an old-world atmosphere. Great lobby. Jalan Riyadi 286, tel. (0271) 33891, US$8-18.

Kusuma Sahid Prince Hotel: Solo's finest hotel is situated on five acres of landscaped gardens near the Mangunegaran Palace. Beautiful pool and live *gamelan* in the lobby nightly from 1700. Jalan Sugiyopranoto 22, tel. (0271) 46356, fax 44788, US$95-235.

Restaurants

Jalan Teuku Umar foodstalls: Solo is a city with a distinctive local cuisine. Try *nasi liwet* (rice in a delicious coconut sauce), *nasi gudeg* (rice with jackfruit), *susu sugar* (fresh milk), *wedhang ronde* (ginger tea with peanut), and *serabi* (miniature pancakes). All can be inexpensively sampled in the terrific night foodstalls just off Jalan Riyadi. Here, tents emblazoned with their specialties serve some of the best food in Indonesia to *becak* drivers, students, businessmen, Chinese laborers, and travelers.

Jalan Diponegoro: Solo's restaurant row has a half-dozen cafes which serve local dishes at fair prices. Malioboro looks the best.

Centrum Restaurant: This popular Chinese restaurant near Westerners Losmen serves tasty but somewhat expensive dishes. Try giant spring rolls and frog's legs fried in butter and garlic.

Performing Arts

Kraton Mangunegaran: Javanese dance rehearsals accompanied by *gamelan* are given on Wednesday mornings at 1000; *gamelan* only on Saturday mornings. The Javanese orchestra, originally from Demak and dating to 1778, has been given the honorific name Kyai Kanyut Mesem ("Drifting in Smiles"). Swallows dip and dive amongst the rafters as the *gamelan* plays, as if enraptured by the music.

Kasunan Kraton: Javanese dance rehearsals are given on Sundays at 1000 in the reconstructed Morokoto Hall.

Sriwidari Amusement Park: *Wayang orang* shows are given nightly, 2000-2300 except Fridays and Sundays, in the theater next to the tourist office. Simple to the extreme, but one of Indonesia's last venues for traditional Javanese drama.

ASKI: Solo's leading fine-arts conservatory occasionally sponsors student recitals. Check with the tourist office.

RRI: Solo's best *wayang kulit* and *wayang orang* can be experienced on irregular Saturday evenings at 2000 in the Radio Republic Indonesia building on Jalan Marconi near the train station.

Instruction

Solo is an important center for Javanese mysticism and white-magic meditation techniques called *sumarah*. Classes are given in the home of Ananda Suyono on Jalan Ronggowarsito 60, half a block east of Kraton Mangkunegaran. Also by Pak Swondo on Gang 1 Jalan Kratonan. Puppet instruction and monthly all-night performances can be seen in the home of Dalang Anom Suroto on Jalan Notodiningrotan behind the Hotel Cakra. Classes in Javanese performing arts are given at the SMKI (high-school level) and the STSI (university level) located north of Jalan Sahrir. The tourist office can help with referrals and exact locations.

Shopping

Batik: Solo is a batik-producing center of long standing; it's an artform that remains an important source of local revenue and pride. Solo-style batik designs with their somber classical colors of indigo, brown, and cream are noticeably more traditional than Yogya's. Many claim that Solo is a better place to buy than Yogya. Shops are located all over town; the tourist office has a list. Batik Semar, Dinar Hadi, and Batik Keris—three major producers of Solo-style batik—are all safe, reliable, and reasonable. You should compare quality and prices inside Pasar Klewer, Indonesia's largest emporium of fabrics and batiks.

Handicrafts: Antique buffs should wander the confusing maze of stalls inside Pasar Triwindu, just east of Jalan Diponegoro. Hardjonegoro on Jalan Kratonan offers one of the largest *kris* collections in Java, but expect to pay anywhere from 100,000 to five million *rupiah! Gamelans* are tailor-made at the Bale Agung shop just north of the Kraton Kasusunan. A meager and disappointing collection of theatrical supplies and dancers' costumes is sold at Toko Bedoyo Serimpi.

Transportation

Solo's principal bus terminal is located three km north of downtown, about 1,200Rp by *becak* to Westerners. Minibuses from the adjacent terminal are faster and less crowded than public buses. To reach Yogya, hail a westbound bus from the main bus terminal. Trains to Surabaya leave five times daily from the Balapan station.

THE NORTH COAST

CIREBON

Cirebon (pronounced chirry-BON), along with the other cities along the north coast, remains well off the tourist routes of Java. It boasts no golden sandy beaches or trendy travelers' hotels or restaurants, but it's a clean, well-run town, and it's worth a diversion—especially for its rich variety of arts and crafts and historical attractions.

An ancient pre-colonial port town on the border of West and Central Java, Cirebon is the meeting point of the Sundanese and Javanese cultures; its local dialect is a blending of the two (the city's name derives from the Javanese *caruban*, or "mixture"). The sultanate here was split into two main houses, Kanoman and Kesepuhan, both of whose palaces are open to visitors, occasionally hosting court dances and *gamelan* recitals.

Kraton Kasepuhan

In 1478, Kraton Pakungwati surrendered to Sunan Gunung Jati. In that same year, the city of Cirebon proclaimed itself an Islamic principality and work began immediately on Kraton Kasepuhan. Over the centuries, the palace grew decrepit, but it was partially restored in 1928 by a Dutch archaeologist.

Cirebon's most famous reliefs—cloud patterns *(mega mendung)* and rocks *(wadas)*—are seen on the whitewashed entrance. A comatose place very much smelling its age, the sultanate has long since been deposed and the sultan is now a banker.

Kraton Kanoman

Walk straight through the market, Pasar Kanoman, to this palace built by Pangeran Cakrabua-

na in the 17th century. Woodcarvings on the main door of the hall symbolize the opening date (the Javanese date of 1510 translates to A.D. 1670). Kraton Kanoman has a restful courtyard of shady banyan trees and kids flying kites.

Find the man with the key to the Gedung Pusaka ("Heirloom Building") inside the *kraton* compound to see the incredible coach, prize attraction of Kanoman. The three creatures depicted on this royal carriage are symbols of earthly and metaphysical powers: the *paksi* or great mythical *garuda* bird represents the realm of the air; the *naga* (snake bird) represents sea; and the *liman* or *gajah* represents land. All of them are combined in one Pegasus-like creation, the *paksi naga liman,* considered by Javanese to be the strongest creatures of their elements.

Cirebon Batik

Stylistic nuances and the bright accents of Cirebon batik—an art which is a composite of so many incoming cultures and religions—are found nowhere else on Java.

Traditionally, the motifs most associated with Cirebon batik are Chinese in origin. Glorious mythological animals such as dragons, tigers, lions, and elephants, and of course "rocks and clouds" (likened to weather patterns), are executed in light to dark coloring. Sealife, so vital to the economic well-being of the city, is also frequently portrayed.

Since the artists' guilds decreed that only men may work in batik, Cirebon became one of the few locales on Java where females did not draw and paint the cloth. This has infused the area's batik with bold, masculine designs, a minimum of busy detail, and large, dramatic portions of free space, quite distinct from the batik of other north-coastal or Central Java areas.

INDONESIA

CIREBON

TO JAKARTA, GUNUNG JATI, AND INDRAMAYU

TO BANDUNG AND BATIK TRUSMI

TO TOURIST OFFICE AND AIRPORT

TO SEMARANG

TO SEMARANG

TO YOGYAKARTA

PENYU BAY

★ DUTCH CEMETERY

J.L. DIPONEGORO

J.L. PENAMPARAN

HOTEL PURI SANTIKA

BENTANI HOTEL
CORDOVA HOTEL
SLAMET HOTEL
TRAIN STATION

J.L. SILIWANGI

J.L. MOH. TOHA

J.L. KAPTEN SAMADIKUN

J.L. KUSNAN

HOTEL PRIMA

★ BALAIKOTA (TOWN HALL)

GRAND HOTEL

LANGENSARI HOTEL

J.L. VETERAN

WARTEL

YOGYA DEPARTMENT STORE

DUMAI HOTEL

PASAR PAGI

HOTEL ASIA

HOTEL NIAGA

J.L. SUKALILA

KALI SUKALILA

OLD SHIPS

J.L. SISINGAMANGA RAJA

J.L. BANAGIA

PELNI

CHINESE TEMPLE

J.L. PAGONGAN

SEMERANG LOSMEN

TELEPHONE OFFICE

YOGYA DEPARTMENT STORE

POST OFFICE

J.L. KENDURUAN

J.L. PANJUNAN

CIREBON MALL PASUKETAN

DUTCH WAREHOUSE

KEBON CAI

J.L. KANOMAN

MAIN POST OFFICE

PASAR

MARKET

KRATON KANOMAN

ST. JOSEPH'S CATHOLIC CHURCH

J.L. MERDEKA

J.L. ASTANA GARIB

HOSPITAL

PASAR

J.L. LAWANGGADA

KRATON KACIREBONAN

J.L. PULASAREN

GRAND MOSQUE

ALUN-ALUN

KRATON KASEPUHAN

J.L. MAYOR SASTRAATMAJA

KALI KASUNEAN

★ TAMAN SUNYARAGI

J.L. SUNYARAGI

BUS STATION

KALIJAGA CEMETERY

J.L. BYPASS

J.L. PRONGGOL

0   250 m

© MOON PUBLICATIONS, INC.

INDONESIA

Accommodations

Asia Hotel: Most travelers stay here at the Hotel Asia, about 15 minutes from the train station and down near the waterfront, in this old Dutch home—something of a Cirebon antique all fixed up with old wooden furniture and whitewashed walls. Jl. Kalibaru 15, tel. (0231) 202183, US$6-15.

Grand Hotel: A colonial relic with a multitude of large rooms in every price range, restaurant with extensive menu, and splendid verandah. Jl. Siliwangi 18, tel. (0231) 208867, US$15-35.

Cirebon Plaza Hotel: A clean, modern hotel five minutes from the train station and intercity bus terminal. Jl. Kartini 54, tel. (0231) 202062, US$35-70.

Transportation

Cirebon is 256 km east of Jakarta and 245 km west of Semarang.

Train: Almost a dozen trains pass through Cirebon daily since it's located on both the northern Jakarta-Semarang-Surabaya train route and the southern Jakarta-Yogyakarta-Surabaya line. Trains take 3.5 hours to Jakarta, 4.5 hours to Semarang, five hours to Yogyakarta, and six hours to Surabaya.

Trains are the most convenient way to reach Cirebon since the train station is right in the center of town.

Bus: The Cirebon bus terminal is inconveniently located four km southeast of city center. Taxis from the terminal to downtown cost about 4,000Rp.

Several express minibus companies have offices on Jalan Karanggetas in the center of town.

PEKALONGAN

Pronounced "Pek-KAL-long-ahn," Pekalongan lies on the north coast 101 km west of Semarang on the road to Jakarta.

Pekalongan has always been a fortress and trade city; visible to this day are the remains of a VOC fort built in 1753, later turned into a prison by the Dutch. On 7 October 1945, the Pekalongan residency became the first in Indonesia to free itself of Japanese rule.

Attractions

Pekalongan is worth a single day of exploration.

Batik: Pekalongan is chiefly famed for its distinctive batiks sold in a half dozen shops scattered around town. Most of the fabric appears mundane so expect a hard search for better quality product.

Old Dutch Quarter: Try the following half-day walking tour of the old Dutch and Chinese sections, a few blocks north of the main street. First, wander around the old Dutch quarter just across the Loji Bridge and enjoy the former Resident's Mansion, imposing Post Office, Dutch Reformed Church (1852), Kota Madya (former Dutch City Hall), Societeit Corcle (Dutch Clubhouse), and remains of the VOC Fort, now a prison.

Chinatown: Cross the bridge, turn right, and stop in the active Po An Thian Chinese Temple for a few moments, then continue south past a street lined with impressive old homes inhabited by Chinese merchants.

Pasar Banjarsari: A fascinating market filled with all the standard food products, plus batik merchants selling the less expensive stamped fabric. Then walk east to the small Arab Quarter and batik shops such as Jacky's, Toko Yen, and Tobal Batik Factory.

Accommodations

Few travelers pause here, but several acceptable *losmen* are near the train station.

Hotel Gaja Mada: The most cheery and personable option of the budget spots opposite the train station, Jl. Gajah Mada 11, tel. (0285) 41185, US$5-8.

Hayam Wuruk Hotel: Pekalongan's best mid-level hotel is in the middle of town, a 10-minute walk east from the train station. Jl. Hayan Wuruk 152, tel. (0285) 22832, US$10-18

Hotel Istana: The top-end choice is also in the city center, 300 meters west of the train station. Jl. Gajah Mada 23, tel. (0285) 61581, US$15-30.

Transportation

As with Cirebon, Pekalongan is best reached by train since the train station is conveniently located a few hundred yards west of city center and within spitting distance of several decent hotels. Train schedules are almost identical to those of Cirebon since both towns share the same northern and southern train routes.

The bus terminal is four km southeast of town. Colts and *becaks* shuttle between the two points.

INDONESIA

SEMARANG

Central Java's administrative center is unlike the gentle, age-mellowed *kraton* cities of Yogyakarta and Solo, since it has long been a major trading hub populated both by Javanese and Chinese, who now make up over 40% of the population. The city is large but has a spacious, open feel, plus there's a great deal of old Dutch architecture to inspect while wandering around town.

Another good thing about Semarang is that you almost certainly will be the only Westerner in town.

Attractions

The Semarang tourist office in Plaza Simpang Lima, on "five-road square" (Simpang Lima), has maps and brochures.

Dutch Architecture: A quick walk around city center will uncover some grand old buildings, including Lawang Sewu ("1,000 Doors"), which formerly served as the headquarters of the Netherlands Indies Railway company, and the 18th-century Blenduk Church, a domed Protestant church once used as the Dutch state church.

Despite the almost complete modernization of southern Semarang, peeling VOC warehouses still overlook the old harbor and a great deal of traditional architecture survives in the small alleys near Pasar Johar and everywhere in Chinatown. Be sure to walk along the banks of the smelly river which winds from Chinatown to the old warehouse district.

Sam Poo Kong: Semarang's most famous sight is Gedung Batu ("Stone Building") and Sam Poo Kong Temple, a great cave-temple complex about 30 minutes southwest of downtown. One of the largest and most honored Chinese temples in Indonesia, Gedung Batu houses the spirit of a Ming Dynasty Chinese admiral who landed on Java in 1406 with a fleet of 62 vessels and 27,000 sailors.

Accommodations

Most of the inexpensive *losmen* are in the center of town, near the traffic circle and Johar Shopping Center.

Singapore Hotel: Right in the center of town and only a 10-minute walk from the Tawang train station is a fairly clean and quiet place with

surprisingly friendly managers. Jl. Imam Bonjol 12, tel. (024) 543757, US$5-10.

Hotel Rahayu: Popular mid-priced choice with decent rooms and good vibes. Jl. Imam Bonjol 35, tel. (024) 542532, US$8-20.

Oewa-Asia Hotel: An old Dutch colonial hotel with small but quieter rooms in the rear and more expensive a/c rooms up front. Jl. Imam Bonjol 12, tel. (024) 542547, US$10-25.

Losmen Jaya: A big, breezy place with somewhat overpriced rooms, but breakfast is included and the managers are friendly. Jl. Haryono 87, tel. (024) 543604, US$6-10.

Graha Santika Hotel: Luxury hotel five blocks south of the train station near the tourist office and Matahari Shopping Center. Jl. Pandanaran 116, tel. (0231) 318850, US$110-150.

Patra Jasa Hotel: Four-star hotel with swimming pool, bowling alley, and tennis courts in a quiet location in the hills above Semerang. Jl. Sisingamangaraja, tel. (024) 314441, US$110-180.

Transportation

Air: Ahmad Yani airport, six km west of town, can be reached by taxi for about 6,000Rp or with Damri bus No 2. Merpati, Sempati, Bouraq, and Mandala Air all provide flights to and from Semerang.

Train: Semarang is on the main Jakarta-Cirebon-Surabaya line and almost a dozen trains pass through town each day heading east or west. Trains take 8-10 hours to Jakarta.

Tawang train station is conveniently located three blocks north of the hotels on Jalan Pemuda and Bonjol.

Bus: The Terboyo bus terminal is six km east of city center. From the bus terminal, flag down a local bus heading west on the nearby highway.

Around town the main conveyances are Damri buses and bright orange Daihatsus, which run like ants all over town.

VICINITY OF SEMARANG

Ambarawa

The train museum in this small mountain town some 40 km south of Semarang boasts about 25 steam engines constructed from 1891 to 1927 in Germany, Holland, and England.

The only operating cog railway on Java runs from from Ambarawa to the villages of Jambu and Bedono, 15 km uphill. Organized groups can charter the antique coaches, remodeled according to the original designs and hauled by a 1903 steam locomotive. The cogwheel is still running, its beautiful engine in prime shape.

The engineer starts burning fuel wood and coal in the locomotive around 0400 and by 0900 the engine is ready for the climb. In the middle of the climb the cogwheel stops and the passengers hop down, take pictures, rest, and have a picnic.

Train excursions can be booked at Central Java Exploitation Office on Jalan Thamrin in Semarang.

Gedung Songo

At a delightful elevation of around 900 meters, this archaeological park is probably the most beautiful temple location on Java.

Constructed sometime in the 8th century, the modern name means "Nine Temples"—even though only seven are still standing. Though most of the shrines are dedicated to Shiva, one

is set aside for Vishnu, a Hindu god rarely worshipped on Java. See Temple II with its well-preserved *kala-makara* relief on the portal; this site was chosen with great care for magnificent views that take in Ungaran (2,050 meters), Danau Rawapening, Merbabu (3,142 meters), and even hazy Merapi (2,914 meters).

Gedung Songo is 15 km from Ambarawa and seven km from Bandungan on the southern slopes of Gunung Ungaran. Take a minibus from Bandungan or, better yet, walk from Bandungan through a region of vegetable patches, roses, and pine trees.

Bandungan has several inexpensive *losmen.*

Kudus

The name Kudus has its origins in the founding of a mosque here in 1546 by Sunan Kudus, one of Java's *wali* (holy men). Though a staunch Islamic town (censuring looks if you wear shorts), some old Hindu customs prevail: cows may not be slaughtered within the city limits and schoolboys still spend a night at the shrine of Sunan Muria to improve their chances in exams.

Sights include the ancient Al Manar Mosque which, by combining both Hindu and Islamic architecture, actually looks like a Javanese Hindu temple. To the rear is the elaborately carved and inlaid mausoleum of Sunan Kudus.

Cloves: Kudus is the Indonesian clove center. Clove cigarettes were invented in the 1920s by an entrepreneur who claimed the smoke ameliorated his asthma. Indonesians now smoke over 36,000 tons of cloves a year, outstripping domestic supplies, as well as importing cloves from Madagascar and Zanzibar.

Free tours are given at the factories of Noryorono, Seokun, Jambu Boh, and Chinese-owned Djarum, now the biggest clove factory in Indonesia, having made spectacular ground on Gudang Garam in recent years. Djarum's 17 factory buildings each produce a million hand-rolled *kretek* cigarettes per day. Five hundred people work in gigantic rolling sheds; some roll up to 5,000 a day. It's a scene from early-18th-century England, on the eve of the Industrial Revolution.

Jepara

Once the main port of the mighty 8th-century Hindu Mataram Empire, Jepara today is a scruffy country town noted only for its wood-carving industry. Except for the hinges, no nails, screws, or metal joinery are used. The wood comes from Blora and Cepu in East Java—teakwood mostly, but also mahogany, *kayu meranti,* and *sono* wood.

Coming into town you start to see shops with bedstands, tables, chairs, couches, and cabinets piled high inside and out. Paid by the meter, men come in from the surrounding villages to carve in the shops. To see them in action, visit the nearby villages of Tahunan, Mantingan, and Blakanggunung.

EAST JAVA

A heavily populated but undertouristed area of 30 million, East Java abounds with bursting cities, towns, and *kampongs* along roads which run through ceaselessly nurtured ricefields and mountain slopes patched with fruit, coffee, and tea plantations. East Java is to Central Java as Mississippi is to Virginia: deep, deep Java, considerably more rural and less touched by the West.

Regional history began in the 10th century with the rise of King Airlangga, who forged a unified nation before his death and the subsequent division of his fragile empire. The Kediri Dynasty (1049-1222) was followed by the murderous but artistically inclined Singosari Kingdom (1222-1292), which constructed dozens of beautiful and highly original temples near Malang. Kartanagara, last of the Singosari rulers, was succeeded by King Wijaya, who founded the Majapahit Empire (1294-1478), which ruled most of Java from its headquarters at Trowulan. The most powerful and famous of all early East Javanese kingdoms, Majapahit mastery declined after the death of Hayam Wuruk in 1349 and the arrival of Islamic power in the 15th century. East Java fell to the Mataram Empire of Central Java in the 17th century; most of the Hindu-Buddhist artisans, philosophers, and politicians fled to Bali.

Except for a brief stay in Surabaya and the sunrise hike on Mt. Bromo, travelers usually pass straight through on the Yogya-Bali stretch. Although the province is well off the beaten tourist path, the area's far-flung attractions can provide some unusual side trips through magnificent countryside. East Java has seven towering volcanoes and seven wilderness reserves, including Meru Betiri, probably the last habitat of the Java tiger. For batik lovers, virtually every textile center in East Java—Sidoharjo, Madura, Tulungagung, Trenggalak, and Tuban—uses its own motifs and styles.

SURABAYA

Its melodious name belies the true nature of this city—a hot and dirty industrial hub with broad, busy streets, red-tiled houses with neat little gardens, a six-lane boulevard, horrendous traffic jams, quiet cul-de-sacs, technical universities and religious schools, thriving nightclubs, 40 cinemas, bowling and billiards centers, four railway stations, at least 30,000 *becaks,* a splendid zoo, and multistory shopping complexes with speed lifts and freezing air-conditioning. But with a reputation hardly better than Jakarta's, few travelers spend more than a single night in the city.

Surabaya, however, is the last traditional Indonesian city in the archipelago, the final place to see old Dutch architecture on a large scale, timeless neighborhoods little changed from the '30s, and Islamic enclaves where men in fezlike hats gather around minaret-topped mosques. This city exudes an extraordinarily strong atmosphere. The following one-day tour will give you a quick glimpse at Indonesia's second most important city.

Surabaya Harbor

The accompanying map is adequate for most visitors, but to really find the back streets you'll need the large-scale Sena map of Surabaya, available from the bookstores on Jalan Tunjungan. To begin your tour of old Surabaya, take bus 1 from Tunjungan Shopping Center to Surabaya Harbor, where you can check shipping schedules on the second floor and grab a dish of *gado gado* from the nearby *warungs. Becaks* cost 300Rp down Jalan Kalimas Baru to Position IV Gate, the entrance to the old Kalimas Harbor where some 50 tall-masted Bugis

schooners continually load and unload timber from Kalimantan. Before approaching the guardhouse, hide your camera and promise "no photo"—the Indonesian Naval Yard is just opposite and paranoia runs high.

Ampel Mosque

Exit the harbor area and hire another *becak* for 300Rp to Mesjid Ampel, the large but unassuming mosque hidden up an alley filled with heady perfume shops, veiled women hawking dates, and emporiums of religious goods. Ampel Mosque was constructed by Sunan Ampel, one of the nine saints credited with bringing Islam to Indonesia; his tomb in the rear is generally closed to infidels. Visitors must be well dressed to walk through Surabaya's Arab Quarter.

Dutch Architecture

Unlike Jakarta, which has largely destroyed most of its old Dutch warehouses and government centers, Surabaya has retained a great deal of its old colonial atmosphere. From Ampel Mosque, walk south through the old casbah area to Jembatan Merah (Red Bridge), once the throbbing center of the Dutch commercial district, today a haunted ghostland of impressive Dutch warehouses and business emporiums. The interior of the GPO is most impressive.

Recross the bridge and continue on foot through Chinatown to the Old Dutch Cemetery. It's best to walk along the canal and avoid the major thoroughfares. This deserted and weedy cemetery is incredibly rich with memories; crumbling and rusting headstones tell history better than any guidebook. The adjacent neighborhood is a delightful cross-hatching of narrow alleys with original Dutch street signs and lovely Dutch homes displaying graceful art-deco glasswork. Many of Surabaya's wealthiest citizens live on the nearby streets of Ambengan, Kamboja, and Kemuning.

City Center

Grahadi: The former residence of the Dutch governor but now the official residence of East Java's governor. In front is another of Surabaya's atrocious heroic monuments that commemorate Indonesia's 1945 war for independence.

Joko Dolog Statue: The Singosari Dynasty "Fat Boy," a Buddhist stone statue 100 meters back from Jalan Pemuda (look for the green

INDONESIA

SURABAYA

TO HARBOR

POS III

TANJUNG PERAK BARAT/TIMUR

NYAMPLUNGAN

PEGIRIAN

Ampel Mosque

TO GRESIK

GRESIK

Jembatan Merah Station

Pasar Pabean

RAJAWALI

INDRAPURA

KAPASAN

KAPASARI

KENJERAN

Old Dutch Architecture

Central Post Office

Kota Train Station

TOL DUPAK

Pasar Turi Shopping Center

Heroes' Monument

Pelni Office

TO GRESIK

DUPAK

Pasar Turi Train Station

P. BESAR W.

KALI NGAGLIK

KAPAS KRAMPUNG

SEE "CENTRAL SURABAYA" MAP

Dutch Cemetery

Surabaya Mall

WIJAYA SHOPPING CENTER

KRANGGAN

Garuda

Taman Budaya (Performing Arts Center)

AMBENGAN

RAYA ARJUNA

PASANG KEMBANG KUNING BLAURAN

EMBONG MALANG

Genteng Walikota

Bamboo Denn

Ketabang Kali

Gubeng Train Station

DHARMA HUSADA

TOL BANYUURIP

Tunjungan Shopping Center

Tunjungan Plaza

J. PEMUDA

Joko Dolog Statue

Surabaya Plaza

TO TANDES

BANYUURIP

Elmi Hotel

PL. SUDIRMAN

Tourist Offices

Hyatt Regency

Flower Market

AIRLANGGA UNIVERSITY

PANDEGILING

Antique Shops

Y. KAYOON

Y. SUMATRA

Dutch Consulate

DHARMA WANGSA

JALAN TOL SURABAYA- MALANG

U. SUMOHARJO

JARAK S. "DOLLY'S" DISTRICTS

DIPONEGORO

POST OFFICE

JL. KERTAJAYA INDAH

PUTAT BANYUURIP WETAN

JL. DR. SOETOMO

United States Consulate

JL. GIRILAYO

RAYA DARMO

French Consulate

TOL KOTA SATELIT

Taman Tirta Swimming Pool

Museum Ankatan '45

JL. MAY. JEN. SUNGKONO

Empu Tantular Museum

TO PURABAYA (BUNGURASIH) BUS TERMINAL (4 km)

ZOO

0   500 m

GEDE BARATA JAYA

TO MOJOKERTO

TO MALANG, AIRPORT, AND PURABAYA BUS TERMINAL

© MOON PUBLICATIONS, INC.

Garuda gate), depicts the great King Kartana-gara seated on a pedestal inscribed 1289. The statue was transferred to this spot from its site near Malang by the Dutch about 300 years ago.

Majapahit Hotel: Known as the "Oranji Hotel" during Dutch times and the "Yamato Hotel" during the Japanese occupation, the Majapahit is where East Javanese independence from the Dutch was declared shortly after WW II. The ensuing Battle of Surabaya was a turning point in their five-year struggle.

Surabaya Zoo

One of the most complete, largest, and oldest zoos in all of Indonesia and probably the num-ber-one attraction in Surabaya. The zoo boasts over 500 species of animals, including three large adult and six infant Komodo dragons which sleep peacefully in a large sandy pit. Open daily 0730-1700.

North of the zoo on Jalan Taman Mayangkera is a small historical and archaeological museum which houses Mesolithic farming tools, stone statuary from the Majapahit period, Koranic manuscripts, ceremonial beds, *wayang,* photos of old Surabaya, a very good paper-money collection, and early 20th-century technology including a Daimler steam-driven motorcycle. English texts. Take Bemo V opposite the Garden Palace Hotel.

CENTRAL SURABAYA

© MOON PUBLICATIONS, INC.

INDONESIA

Accommodations

Surabaya would be much more tolerable if it had just a single good travelers' hostel. Unfortunately, it doesn't have anything to compare with the *losmen* in Bali or Yogyakarta.

Bamboo Denn: Top choice in the cheap segment is this dank *losmen* in the center of town, 20 minutes from the Gubeng Train Station. Claustrophobic but about the only game in town. 6 Jalan Ketabang Kali, tel. (031) 40333, US$3-8.

Wisma Maharani: Best value in central Surabaya is this large, rambling guesthouse located on a quiet side street back from the tourist office. Good vibes; room prices are negotiable. Jalan Embong Kenongo 73, tel. (031) 44839, fax (031) 45435, US$30-40.

Remaja Hotel: Clean, modern, and air-conditioned businessman's hotel in the center of town. Excellent value for mid-level travelers. Jalan Embong Kenongo 12, tel. (031) 41359, fax (031) 510009, US$30-40.

Garden Hotel: Centrally located hotel with a/c rooms, a swimming pool, and a Chinese restaurant with a popular Friday-evening buffet. Jalan Pemuda 21, tel. (031) 470001, US$100-180.

Hyatt Regency: Surabaya's first luxury hotel is 30 minutes by taxi from the airport, 15 minutes from the harbor, and five minutes from the train station. The air-conditioned three-story open atrium is a welcome relief from the heat and congestion of downtown Surabaya. Jalan Basuki Rakhmat 124, tel. (031) 511234, fax (031) 521508, US$180-360.

Restaurants

For a city of its size, the food scene in Surabaya is disappointing: expensive and poorly prepared dishes served in noisy, desultory cafes. Perhaps the best venue for good value and pleasant surroundings is the Pasar Kayoon night market a few blocks from the Bamboo Denn. *Warungs* opposite the train station are hot and crowded and serve little worth recommending. To eat well in Surabaya, you'll need to spend some extra *rupiah*. The Friday-evening *ristafel* buffet in the Garden Hotel is a worthy splurge. Other places to escape the searing heat and eat in comfort include the Chez Rose for familiar Western dishes and Max's Restaurant a few blocks south. Both Tunjungan and Surabaya Delta shopping centers have countless fast-food joints like Colonel Sanders and Swensen's. Remember the travelers' axiom: sleep hard but eat well.

Entertainment

Sriwandowo Theater: Adjacent to the massive new shopping complex and down the alley from the THR (pronounced TAY-HAH-AIR) Amusement Park, you'll find a miserable tin shed where some of Indonesia's last *ketoprak* and *wayang orang* take place. Completely authentic performances of lowbrow Javanese comedy rich in sexual innuendo, heroic tales taken from the Ramayana, and live *gamelan*. Great entertainment.

Taman Budaya: Students at Surabaya's Performing Arts Center can be seen in the mornings rehearsing *negremo* and *gandrung* dances and practicing bamboo *kalintang* music, *ketoprak, janur* (young coconut-leaves arrangement), Chinese historical dramas, and old Javanese legends like *Aryopenangsang* and *Angreni Larung*. Student recitals are given weekly.

Siswo Bodoyo: The rather deserted theater just outside the zoo sponsors entertaining *keto-*

legong *dancer*

INDONESIA

prak, gaudy Javanese soap operas overacted by flaming transsexuals, fat spinsters, and comely young maidens in full Majapahit costumes.

Red Lights: The Jarak and Bangunrejo districts are world-renowned brothels, superb sociological studies in the dynamics of poverty-sharing. Take a W *bemo* from downtown Surabaya to Jarak, a huge honky-tonk Mexican border town in the Orient. In row upon row of gaudy little dollhouse shanties, 15,000 girls and women of all sizes, shapes, ages, races, and humors work and live. Tandes is another entertainment district. Take a *becak* through market and canal areas that never sleep.

Shopping

Good hunting along Jalan Tunungun. The second-floor batik showroom in the Sarinah department store sells "hand-drawn high and medium quality" *sarongs* from 25,000Rp and machine-stamped wraparounds for 8,000-12,000Rp. Surabaya is also known for its Chinese and Javanese tailors on Jalan Embong Malang ("Street of 1,000 Tailors"), who can cut you a pair of made-to-measure trousers in an hour or so for only 9,000Rp! A whole row of small antique and curio shops lies near the Bumi Hyatt on Jalan Basuki Rakhmat and along Jalan Urip Sumohardjo. On Jalan Raya Darmo are the Rokhim (no. 27) and the Whisnu (nos. 68-74). If you know what you're looking for and know how to bargain, you can still find some good buys. Both the Tunjungan and Surabaya Delta shopping centers have dozens of shops worth exploring.

Services

The Surabaya tourist office on Jalan Pemuda has basic literature and can answer questions about upcoming festivals, the bull races on Madura Island, dance performances at Padaan, and transportation to outlying attractions. There's a convenient post office near the Joko Dolog statue. The telephone office (Kantor Telepon) is on Jalan Diponegoro at the corner of Jalan Kapuas.

Transportation

Air: Surabaya's airport is 15 km south of the city, 8,000Rp by taxi—or walk one km from the terminal for public buses. Taxis to the airport wait at the Gubeng Train Station.

Trains: Trains from Jakarta and Semarang arrive at the Pasar Turi Station. Trains from Yogyakarta, Solo, and Bali arrive at the Gubeng Station, within walking distance of most *losmen* and hotels. Trains leave from Gubeng Station two times daily to Bali, three times daily to Yogyakarta, and seven times daily to Malang. Remember: train travel is safer and less grueling than bus journeys.

Buses: Buses arrive at the Bungurasih (Purabaya) Terminal, some 10 km southwest of city center. Walk over to the main street and take a public *bemo* or bus 2 north to Jalan Pemuda. Get off when you see the big, modern Tunjungan shopping center on your left. Buses to towns on the north coast of Java depart from the Jembatan Merah Terminal. Several private bus companies with direct services and reserved seats are located on Jalan Rakhmat just opposite the Ramayana Hotel.

Ship: Surabaya is an important departure point for Pelni ships to Sulawesi and Kalimantan. Schedules are posted on the second floor at the harbor and at the Pelni ticketing office (tel. 21694) on Jalan Pahlawan. Pelni is open daily except Sundays 0900-1600, Saturdays until 1300. Appeal directly to the ticketmaster, book your passage, and escape to Malang.

ATTRACTIONS NEAR SURABAYA

Mojokerto

Forty-two km southwest of Surabaya, the small town of Mojokerto is a convenient base for exploring the Majapahit ruins around Trowulan. Visit the local museum to see the magnificent sculptural group of Vishnu being carried on the back of Garuda, the centerpiece of a fascinating series of reliefs around the main room. Taken from the Belahan baths near Trawas and known as the Airlangga Statue, one theory holds that the 11th-century Vishnu figure is that of King Airlangga himself. Many other lifelike statues, relics, carved stoned reliefs showing daily scenes—and umpteen plaques with ancient writing on them—fill this museum. Afterwards, wander through the original quarter of town with its finely made old Dutch houses. Inexpensive *losmen* are situated near the bus terminal and in the center of town, three km distant.

INDONESIA

Trowulan
This small agricultural community 12 km south-west of Mojokerto was once the capital of the mighty Majapahit Empire (1292-1389), which, under the ruthless and efficient Gajah Mada, controlled most of the islands of the archipelago in the 14th century. The arrival of Islam forced the Majapahits, the final Hindu kingdom in Indonesia, to flee east to Bali, taking with them their religion, culture, and artistic traditions.

Constructed entirely from brick with no stonework, granite, or sandstone, the temple remains of Trowulan lie scattered over a 15-square-km area. First visit the small but informative Museum Purbakala, renowned for its remarkable collection of terra-cotta figurines and small heads, toys, clay masks, bronze statues, and much more. It's a museum of fragments, so you really have to use your imagination. A large tabletop map shows the locations of the nearby temples and tombs. Day visitors can leave their packs at the museum and either hire a *becak* (four hours for about 7,000Rp) or hike along the winding lanes. A sensible route is up to Candi Siti Inggil, back to Candi Berahu, then northeast down the highway to Waringan Lawang. From here walk on to Bajang Ratu; it's less than one km between Bajang Ratu and Candi Tikus. You might have to cut (carefully) across ricefields in your meanderings. To spend 15-20 minutes at each site will take six hours walking. The walk down lanes of laughing children and people working *padi* is at least as satisfying as the temples themselves.

Buses from Surabaya's Bungurasih Station toward Jombang fly past the turnoff to Museum Purbakala; ask to get off at the main intersection and hire a *becak*. If coming from Jombang, go to Mojoagung first, then take a minibus to Trowulan.

TROWULAN

NOT TO SCALE

CANDI BHRE KAHURIPAN

TO MOJOKERTO (15 km)

WARINGAN LAWANG (200 m FROM ROAD)

CANDI BERAHU

MAKAM PUTERI CEMPA

CANDI SITI INGGIL

KOLAM SEGARAN

MAKAM PANJANG

TO JOMBANG (15 km)

MUSEUM PURBAKALA

SANGGAR PEMELENGAN

CANDI BAJANG RATU

PENDOPO AGUNG

VILLAGE

SUMUR UPAS

TO MAKAM TROLOYO

CANDI TIKUS

From museum to:	
C. Berahu	1 km
C. Siti Inggil	½ km
C. Tikus	4 km
C. Bajang Ratu	4 km
Sanggar Pemelengan	2 km
Kolam Segaran	1 km
Makam Pankamg	2 km
Waringan Lawang	1½ km
C. Bhre Kahuripan	6 km
Pendopo Agung	1½ km
Sumur Upas	1 km
Makam Troloyo	2 km

Pandaan
Spectacular performances of the Ramayana are given twice monthly from May to October in the open-air Candra Wilwatikta amphitheater 45 km south of Surabaya. Held against the flawless cone of Mt. Penanggungan, this is Indonesia's most famous Ramayana production after the spectacle at Prambanan. Exact dates can be confirmed with the Surabaya tourist office.

MADURA ISLAND

One of Indonesia's undiscovered gems, this large, rugged island is blessed with numerous fine white-sand beaches, unpeopled countryside, inexpensive and uncrowded *losmen,* and unique cuisine. Here you can glimpse a bygone rural life, extinct in many other parts of Java. Although only 30 minutes from Surabaya by ferry, Madura is almost totally free of tourists; you could spend a week here and not see another Westerner.

RUNNING OF THE BULLS

Madura is chiefly famous for its bull races, which attract visitors from around the world, but it's also known for its small and dark women who walk with a sensual grace and are renowned all over Indonesia for a special style of movement during lovemaking called *goyang madura.*

As intriguing as that may sound, the island is mainly visited for its *kerapan sapi* bull races held from late July to early October near Pamekasan. Like a scene out of *Ben Hur,* these thrilling, high-speed spectacles of sleek racing bulls also take place around the year with the arrival of large tour groups and cruise ships.

Prior to the grand finale, traditional games, ceremonies, parades of decorated bulls, *gamelan* orchestras, and night bazaars fill the towns. The bulls are decorated with gilt and tinsel, leather bibs, flower-tasseled horn sheaths, silver-studded head harnesses, and bells that jangle from the high, enameled yokes that couple the two bulls of each team. The teams are paraded through the town under ceremonial parasols to the ac-companiment of drums, gongs, flutes, and bells before the rostrums fill with wild spectators.

The race is held on a grassy straightaway 120 meters long: 24 pairs of racing bulls are matched up, their ornaments stripped off, and the beasts lined up with their brightly dressed jockeys. Each is given a generous tote of *arak* from a bamboo tube, then *gamelan* music is played to excite the bulls. The three-man judging panel takes its place. Dead silence before the race begins.

The bulls look heavy and awkward, but watch: the starter drops his flag and the teams lunge forward, the riders straddling skids slung between the yoked bulls, the rear of the skids dragging along the ground. Jockeys prod and flog the animals mercilessly with thorns and spiked rods. With snorting nostrils and mud flying, the bulls look determined to trample the crowd.

They can cover 100 meters in nine seconds flat, faster than the world's human track record. Race dates can be checked at the Surabaya tourist office.

Attractions

Sights on Madura include Air Mata, the island's oldest and most beautiful cemetery. Located on a hill in the northwest near Arasbaya, 11 km northeast of Bangkalan, Air Mata ("Water of the Eye") is a vast complex of very old graves, including that of Ratu Ibu (1546-1569), a descendant of Sunan Giri, the great East Javanese saint.

Accommodations

Inexpensive *losmen* are found in all the principal towns, though the best base for island explorations is Sumenep, an urbanized town with far more atmosphere than Pamekasan.

Losmen Wijaya I: Sumenep's budget spot, near the bus terminal and town square, is clean, friendly, and helpful. 1 Jl. Wahid Hasyim, tel. (0351) 21532, US$3-12.

Hotel Safari Jaya: Another inexpensive option in Sumenep, just five minutes from the town square by *becak*. 90 Jl. Trunojoyo, tel. (0351) 21989, US$3-12.

Hotel Garuda: A fairly clean old house with high ceilings and spacious rooms. The best bud-get option in Pamekasan, though you might also consider the Trunojoyo Hotel around the corner. 1 Jl. Masigit, tel. (0351) 81589, US$3-6.

Transportation

Ferries leave hourly from Tanjung Perak, Surabaya's port, across the narrow strait to the harbor town of Kamal. An alternative approach is from Panarukan, west of Situbondo; ferries leave daily at 1300 for Kalianget in eastern Madura, returning to Panarukan at 0700 the next day. Madura's transportation system is outstanding; minibuses travel to practically everywhere worth going to on the island.

MALANG

One of Java's most pleasant and attractive provincial towns is located in the mountains 90 km south of Surabaya. Established by the Dutch in the late 18th century as a coffee-growing center, Malang today is a bustling city of well-planned parks, sprawling markets, big villas, wide clean streets, one-hour photo shops, abun-

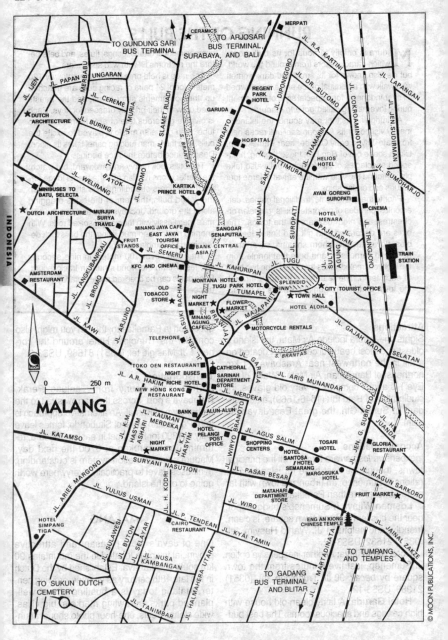

MALANG

TO GUNDUNG SARI BUS TERMINAL

CERAMICS

TO ARJOSARI BUS TERMINAL, SURABAYA, AND BALI

MERPATI

JL. R.A. KARTINI

JL. LAPANGAN

JL. UEN

JL. PAPAN

JL. MERBABU

UNGARAN

JL. CEREME

JL. MURIA

JL. BURING

JL. SLAMET RIJADI

S. BRANTAS

JL. SUPRAPTO

JL. SUPRAPTO

GARUDA

REGENT PARK HOTEL

JL. DIPONEGORO

JL. DR. SUTOMO

JL. COKROAMINOTO

JL. JEN. SUDIRMAN

JL. SUMOHARJO

DUTCH ARCHITECTURE

JL. BATOK

JL. BROMO

HOSPITAL

JL. PATTIMURA

JL. THAMARIN

HELIOS HOTEL

JL. WELIRANG

KARTIKA PRINCE HOTEL

JL. RUMAH SAKIT

JL. SUROPATI

AYAM GORENG SUROPATI

CINEMA

MINIBUSES TO BATU, SELECTA

DUTCH ARCHITECTURE

MURJUR SURYA TRAVEL

MINANG JAYA CAFE

EAST JAVA TOURISM OFFICE

SANGGAR SENAPUTRA

HOTEL MENARA

PAJAJARAN

FRUIT STANDS

JL. SEMERU

BANK CENTRAL ASIA

JL. SULTAN AGUNG

JL. TRUNOJOYO

TRAIN STATION

JL. TANGKUBANPRAU

KFC AND CINEMA

JL. KAHURIPAN

JL. TUGU

SPLENDID INN

CITY TOURIST OFFICE

AMSTERDAM RESTAURANT

JL. BROMO

OLD TOBACCO STORE

MONTANA HOTEL

TUGU PARK HOTEL

TUMAPEL

TOWN HALL

JL. KAWI

JL. ARJUNO

JEN. BASUKI RACHMAT

NIGHT MARKET

FLOWER MARKET

MINANG AGUNG CAFE

JL. MAJAPAHIT

HOTEL ALOHA

JL. GAJAH MADA

TELEPHONE

MOTORCYCLE RENTALS

JL. BRAWIJAYA

S. BRANTAS

SELATAN

JL. GARELA

TOKO OEN RESTAURANT

NIGHT BUSES

CATHEDRAL

JL. A.R. HAKIM

RICHE HOTEL

SARINAH DEPARTMENT STORE

JL. ARIS MUNANDAR

NEW HONG KONG RESTAURANT

JL. MERDEKA

JL. JEN. G. SUBROTO

JL. JUANDA

BANK

ALUN-ALUN

JL. KATAMSO

JL. K.M. HASYIM ASHARI

KAUMAN MERDEKA

HOTEL PELANGI POST OFFICE

JL. WIRYO BRANOTO

JL. AGUS SALIM

JL. KAUMAN

NIGHT MARKET

JL. K.H. HASYIM

SHOPPING CENTERS

HOTEL SANTOSA

HOTEL SEMARANG

TOSARI HOTEL

GLORIA RESTAURANT

JL. SURYANI NASUTION

JL. PASAR BESAR

MARGOSUKA HOTEL

JL. MAGUN SARKORO

JL. ARIEF MARGONO

JL. YULIUS USMAN

JL. H. KODRI

JL. P. TENDEAN

JL. WIRO

MATAHARI DEPARTMENT STORE

FRUIT MARKET

HOTEL SIMPANG TIGA

JL. SULAWESI

JL. BUTON

JL. SELAYAR

CAIRO RESTAURANT

JL. KYAI TAMIN

ENG AN KIONG CHINESE TEMPLE

JL. JAINAL ZAKZE

JL. NUSA KAMBANGAN

TO TUMPANG AND TEMPLES

TO SUKUN DUTCH CEMETERY

TO GADANG BUS TERMINAL AND BLITAR

JL. L. MARTADINATA

JL. TANIMBAR

JL. HALMAHERA UTARA

0   250 m

MOON

INDONESIA

© MOON PUBLICATIONS, INC.

dant trees, air-conditioned shopping centers, and old Dutch architecture—a resort city for overheated lowlanders and dynamic proof of Indonesia's amazing economic gains in the last decade. Although Malang can't compare culturally with a city like Yogya, its surrounding countryside boasts a half-dozen small but precise temples constructed by ancient East Javanese Hindu kingdoms and an easygoing atmosphere that provides a welcome relief from the exhausting journey across Java.

Attractions

Malang itself has little of importance aside from a few markets and people-watching. At Pasar Besar, in the old section below the town park, tobacco traders haggle and *becak* drivers doze in the morning sunshine. The night market on Jalan Brawijaya is mostly just a lineup of simple *warungs*. Best bet is to wander the town square at sunset, cracking hot peanuts and picking out handmade toys (*wayang kulit,* flutes, robot heads, wooden dragons) from the itinerant merchants. The calls of "Hallo!" and "Where are you going?" will drive you nuts, but as Bill Dalton points out in his *Indonesia Handbook,* "You can't get angry at 160 million Indonesians." Nearby Batu, Selecta, and Tretes are expensive and highly commercialized hill resorts.

Accommodations

Malang offers a good selection of inexpensive *losmen* and several fancy new hotels for upscale visitors.

Bamboo Denn: Malang probably gets only a few hundred Westerners per year, and most budget travelers head directly for the Bamboo Denn, a 15-minute walk from the bus terminal. Run by Mr. Achmad, this one-room eight-bed dormitory is friendly and very, very quiet. Jl. Hakim, tel. (0341) 66256, US$2.

Helios Hotel: Another good choice for budget travelers is the Helios just down from the bus terminal. Clean, comfortable, and breakfast is included. Recommended. Jl. Pattimura, tel. (0341) 62741, US$5-15.

Margosuka Hotel: Downtown Malang has over a dozen mid-priced hotels, but the Margosuka is clean, modern, and good value. 15 Jl. Dahlan, tel. (0341) 24841, US$8-15.

Richie Hotel: Decent middle-class accommodations are also found in this centrally located hotel, just across from the town park. Jl. Basuki Rachmat, tel. (0341) 24877, US$10-18.

Splendid Inn: Malang's most worthwhile splurge feels like a European guesthouse with its cozy vibes, flowering plants, library, and formal breakfasts. The bar is a favorite watering hole of the MHHH (Malang Hash House Harriers). 4 Jl. Majapahit, tel. (0341) 66860, fax (0341) 63618, US$14-28

Regent Park Hotel: A three-star hotel with a Chinese restaurant, a nightclub, and business services. 12 Jl. Jaksa Agung Suprapto, tel. (0341) 63388, fax (0341) 61408, US$75-90.

Tugu Park Hotel: Fabulous boutique hotel filled with antiques and the priceless art collection of a local attorney. Cozy and elegantly understated, Tugu Park is considered one of the finest hotels in Indonesia. A real gem. Jl. Tugu 3, tel. (0341) 63891, fax (0341) 62747, US$80-110.

Restaurants

As mentioned above, the night market is where most of Malang's *warung* vendors set up their tents in the early evening. Both the Minang Agung Padang and the Rumah Makan Minang Jaya Restaurant bring dozens of individual dishes to your table (and charge you for everything you touch!) unless you point out your favorite entree before you sit down. For something more formal, try the pricey but excellent Chinese dishes at the New Hong Kong or the Golden Phoenix. Nostalgia buffs will enjoy the colonial atmosphere and anachronistic standbys such as *uitsmijter* (Dutch sandwiches) and *haagsehopjes* (mocha candies) in the Toko Oen ("Castrated Donkey") just off the square near the Richie Hotel.

Transportation

Buses and trains from Surabaya and Yogyakarta are plentiful, but for an unusual approach try taking buses through the mountain passes around Batu or hike down from Mt. Bromo. Leaving Malang, take the day train (best), a public bus from the main terminal, or a private night coach from the Permudi office adjacent to the Richie Hotel. Malang has three bus terminals: Arjosari for Bromo, Surabaya, and Bali; Gadang (five km south of town) for Blitar; Landung Sari for Batu, Selecta, Mojokerto, and Kediri.

INDONESIA

TEMPLES NEAR MALANG

Malang is an excellent base for visiting the astonishingly rich Hindu ruins of East Java. A popular day-trip is from the Blimbing *bemo* station in north Malang to Candi Singosari, backtrack to Blimbing, another *bemo* east to Candi Jago at Tumpang, and another to Candi Kidal in Kidal. Finally, return to Malang via Tajinan.

East Javanese temples and bas-reliefs are distinct from those in Central Java. In Central Javanese art, mastery is shown in the handling and modifying of Hindu styles, but characteristic Indonesian elements are much more dominant in East Javanese ruins. The nationalistic Majapahit Kingdom, which lasted only the lifetime of Gajah Mada, introduced a Javanization of styles, a return to a flatter and highly stylized method of carving in which the figures resemble shadow puppets used in *wayang*. Bodies are sculpted delicately and seen from the front, while the head and feet are turned sideways; a sculptural technique perhaps borrowed from the ancient Egyptians. The temples themselves are more slender, with narrow bases, and on a less grandiose scale than those of Central Java. Many of the following have been completely disassembled and reconstructed by the Indonesian government.

Candi Singosari

Dating from the 13th century, this Shiva shrine is the most imposing monument left of the murderous Singosari Dynasty. It was built to honor King Kartanagara, the mad despot who mortified Kublai Khan's emissaries by cutting off their noses and tattooing "NO!" across their foreheads, an act which precipitated the launching of 1,000 Mongol troop ships against Java in 1293. Candi Singosari's unique feature is its base and central *cella* (inner sanctum), but overall this temple is rather ordinary for its lack of ornamentation. Most of the original statues now form the backbone of the world-famous Hindu-Javanese collection at the Leiden Museum in Holland, including the renowned Prajnaparamita image. Take a *bemo* to Blimbing or direct to the town of Singosari, 10 km north of Malang, and walk left 500 meters down Jalan Kartanagara. Twin Singosari demons glare at passersby an-

other 200 meters up the country road. Time permitting, turn right and head northwest for six km until you reach Sumberawan village, where one of Indonesia's two sole surviving stupas is located (the other is Borobudur).

Candi Jago

Candi Jago, a memorial to Singosari King Vishnuvardhana, dates from 1268 and yet has distinct connections with the prehistoric monuments and terraced sanctuaries found in Java's mountains. Take a *bemo* to Tumpang, walk 100 meters up Jalan Wardhana, and look just beyond the mosque. To the right of the entrance are a pair of finely carved *kala* heads flanking an impressive six-armed image of Durga. The monument incorporates Buddhist sculptures, Krishna reliefs, Arjuna's fretful night in his hermitage, earthy scenes from everyday life, superb *wayang*-style reliefs of bulbous-nosed Semeru and Chinese pagodas, and some of the earliest and most grotesque *panakawan* carvings.

Candi Kidal

This small but lovely sanctuary is an architectural jewel, one of the most perfect examples of Singosari temple art. Hidden inside a papaya grove, the richly carved 13th-century *candi* has elaborate reliefs of medallions and *kala*-heads on the main body, while statues of Garuda guard its base. The entire temple was recently disassembled, each brick labeled, and then laboriously reconstructed from the ground up. Kidal is eight km southwest of Tumpang. *Bemos* out here are absolutely the most crowded vehicles I've ever ridden (except for rush-hour buses in Rangoon).

Panataran

Ten km north of Blitar and 80 km southwest of Malang, this is the largest and most imposing complex of ruins in East Java, and one of the largest temple sanctuaries in all of Indonesia. The Panataran temple group took 250 years to build, starting in about 1197, during the Singosari Dynasty. Three gradually rising walled courtyards are laid out on a long field; see dance-play platforms, terraces, shrines, and the same *gapura* gateways found in almost every village in East Java today. Temple reliefs show the transition from three-dimensional to two-dimensional representations: figures tend to take second place to the decorations. One of the most striking structures is the Naga Temple on the second terrace and the surrounding colossal carvings of protective coiled serpents carried by priests—a sight that would make any medieval thief shudder. The whole complex has been completely restored and is very well maintained. To get there, take a bus to Blitar and continue by *bemo* or minibus to Nglegok village, from where *dokars* go to Desa Panataran, two km farther northeast along the main road.

Hotel Sri Lestari: Most visitors to Blitar overnight in this clean and centrally located hotel, which also arranges quick transportation up to Panataran and the imposing tomb of President Sukarno. Great restaurant. Jl. Merdeka 173, tel. (0342) 81766, US$4-6 fan, US$20-32 a/c.

MOUNT BROMO

A convenient stop for travelers between Bali and Surabaya and the most popular of all of East Java's travel destinations, this active 2,392-meter-high volcano is enclosed by perpendicular walls and an awesome sea of sand. The tremendous caldera has three mountains within it—craters within one huge crater—the Bromo-Semeru Massif. From Bromo's peak are stunning views of active Gunung Semeru, Java's highest mountain. Although Bromo can still vent steam and ash, smoke profusely, and occasionally boom from the central crater, lava has not been ejected in historical times.

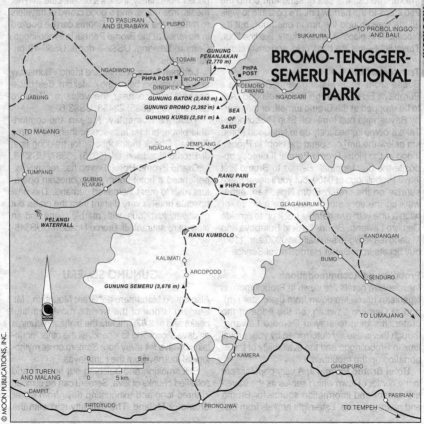

The Trek

No matter how much you've heard about it, you won't be prepared for this ethereal, unforgettable spectacle. Dry-season visitors (April-November) stand the best chance of seeing a bloodred sunrise; in the wet season, you might as well sleep late and stroll across the sand sea during the warmer part of the day. Dress warmly and be prepared for *hundreds* of tourists: Bromo is to Java as Yosemite is to California. The entire hike takes about five hours. The ascent to the Bromo crater from Cemoro Lawang takes about two hours by foot on a well-marked trail; just follow the yellow brick road. Guides and horses are unnecessary. Under clear skies sparkling with stars, with the wind whistling, follow the long line of trekkers across the sea of sand and climb the 250 steps to the narrow rim. It's possible to walk all the way around the rim in one hour, but it's precarious in places and very dusty, like fine flour. Travel light—this is a hard, cold, and dusty climb.

Transportation

Buses from Bali, Malang, and Surabaya's Purabaya Bus Station go to Probolinggo. Ask to be dropped at the Bromo turnoff, or the nearby Bayuangga bus terminal. Skip Probolinggo! Take a *bemo* immediately up to Ngadisari (three km below the rim) or spend the night in Probolinggo at the Hotel Bromo Permai II directly opposite the bus terminal. *Bemos* to Bromo first leave Probolinggo at 0400, but you'll never make sunrise on the crater. From Ngadisari, either walk up the very steep road, hire a horse, or hitch a ride with a vegetable truck up to rimside Cemoro Lawang. *Bemos* back to Surabaya and Malang leave Ngadisari daily at 0900 and 1100; buy tickets from Daftar Harga Travel Service.

Probolinggo Accommodations

Inexpensive hotels are down in Probolinggo, in Ngadisari (three km down from the crater rim), and at Cemoro Lawang, on the edge of the crater. It's best to stay in Cemoro Lawang, though this is usually determined by your arrival time in Probolinggo and the availability of transportation up the mountain.

Hotel Bromo Permai II: A very popular spot in the center of town which serves as the travelers' center and information source for Bromo and nearby regions. Late-night arrivals from Bali can crash in the lobby or drink thick, rich coffee in the Depot Siola beyond the mosque. 237 Jl. Sudirman, tel. (0335) 41256, US$3-8.

Ratna Hotel: Better-quality a/c rooms at very reasonable prices. 16 Jl. Sudirman, tel. (0335) 21597, US$10-15.

Mt. Bromo Accommodations

Ngadisari is the small town at the end of the line for all minibuses from Probolinggo. You can spend the night here, hike up to the rim in about an hour, or catch a ride on a jeep for about 1,000Rp. Ngadisari is rough, but homestays are plentiful and the local people are quite friendly.

Hotel Bromo Permai: Right on the rim with wonderful views, but rooms are small and overpriced. Fortunately, there's a decent cafe with hot meals, free maps, and a good crowd of travelers to meet in the evenings. Rooms can be booked in advance at the Bromo Permai in Probolinggo. Cemoro Lawang, US$2-3 dorm, US$6-12 private rooms.

Losmen Lava: A small and friendly homestay about 50 meters below the crater rim. Best backpackers choice near the volcano. Cemoro Lawang, tel. (0335) 23458, US$3-6.

Yoschi's Homestay: A clean and comfortable place, but far less scenic than the Bromo Permai. Check their logbook for trekking tips. Jl. Bromo-Ngadisari, tel. (0335) 23387, US$3-8.

Grand Bromo Hotel: Bromo has recently experienced a hotel boom as Indonesian operators rush to meet increased demand. This new upscale hotel is very distant from the crater but positively luxurious, with marble baths and an elegant restaurant. Jl. Bromo Ngadisari, US$45-80.

GUNUNG SEMERU

Also called Mahameru or "Great Mountain," Mt. Semeru is one of the world's most beautiful peaks and at 3,676 meters the highest mountain on Java. According to legend, all the other mountains of Java fell away from Semeru on its mythological journey from the Himalayas.

Still smoking and belching out hot ash and solidified chunks of lava, Semeru can be climbed in three long and exhausting days from either Bromo or Malang. The difficulty isn't with the climb but rather with the extreme cold and long walks from your last possible *bemo* stop. Bring food, companionship, a flashlight, and *very* warm clothing.

From Bromo, hike five hours across the sea of sand to Ranopani and register with the PPM. From Malang, take a *bemo* to Tumpang, Gubugklakah, Ngadas, and finally Ranopani. It's then a four-hour walk along a soil path through bamboo and tall grasses to Ranu Kumbolo, where a deserted lakeside hut serves for overnighters. Time permitting, it's better to continue hiking four hours to a shelter marked Arcopodo. Depart the next morning at 0330 for the 0530 sunrise. From the summit, it's five hours to Ranu Kumbolo, four more to Ranopani, and eight more to Tumpang. Recovery takes several days.

EAST JAVA PARKS

Baluran National Park

A reserve since Dutch times, created as a national park only in 1980, Baluran is one of Indonesia's most accessible yet little-known game reserves. Baluran is unusual for Java in that it encompasses a mountainous area that gives way to open forests, scrubland, and white-sand beaches washed by the Bali Straits. Baluran has coastal marshes, open rolling savannah, swampy groves, crab-eating monkeys, and grasslands with huge wild oxen. For Java, the game-watching conditions are unique. This is Java's one bit of Africa.

The entrance to this 250-square-km reserve is at Batangan, just three km north of Wonorejo and 37 km from Banyuwangi. Report to the PPA guardpost and head 12 km down the all-weather road to park headquarters at Bekol. Accommodations are available at the Bekol Guesthouse and the Bama Guesthouse three km east on the beach. Wildlife is most abundant around the watering holes and salt licks in the early morning or sunset hours.

Ijen Plateau

This remote region offers savannah landscapes, ruggedly beautiful panoramas, cool weather, grand hiking, dormant volcanoes, and a placid, bright crater lake. Tourists haven't made it up

here yet and it's still quite primitive, but that's part of the appeal. Bring food, warm clothing, and rain-gear.

The Ijen crater, with its haunting turquoise-blue lake streaked with yellow sulfurous patterns, is a one-hour hike from the vulcanologist station at Ungkup Ungkup. Buses from Banyuwangi reach Licin, a six-hour hike from Ungkup Ungkup. *Bemos* from Bondowoso or Wonosari in the west terminate at Jampit, five hours from Ungkup Ungkup.

Meru Betiri Reserve

From a conservation point of view, this is one of the most important reserves on Java. Established in 1972, the 50,000-hectare Meru Betiri game park lies on Java's rugged southeast coast where thickly wooded hills rise steeply to an elevation of over 1,000 meters. Though best known as the last refuge of the Javan tiger, Meru Betiri is also of considerable botanical importance as one of the few remaining areas of relatively undisturbed primal montane forest on Java. It is the only known habitat of two of the island's endemic plant species, the *Rafflesia zollingeriana* and *Balanphora fungosa*. The reserve's two highest peaks, Mt. Betiri and Mt. Tajem, catch the rain and create a sort of rain pocket; this makes the reserve often wetter than surrounding areas and accounts for the unbelievably thick jungles. The reserve's steep, densely wooded hills also provide a final stronghold for the indigenous Javan tiger *(harimau macan jawa)*, which inhabits the estate's hilly eastern boundary.

The fastest access to the reserve is from Glenmore, which is reachable by bus or *bemo* from Banyuwangi. A comfortable PPA resthouse provides food and lodging within the reserve.

Another resthouse, closer to the turtle nesting beach, is Wisma Sukamade, an elegant old Dutch plantation surrounded by dense jungles and a breathless expanse of coastline. Highly recommended.

Banyuwangi Reserve and Granjagan Surfing

Java's finest surf crashes down at Plengkung, 15 km east of Grajagan. Surfers claim that picture-perfect waves roll in every five minutes, average three to four meters, and can break for miles.

Organized surfing ventures can be arranged through travel agents in Bali. Otherwise, take a bus from Banyuwangi to Granjagan and continue by fishing boat to Plengkung, where bamboo bungalows and simple *warungs* have been constructed on the beach. Bring food and drink from Bali.

BANYUWANGI

This is the jumping-off point for Bali. The ferry terminal is at Ketapang, eight km north. *Bemos* shuttle between the Banyuwangi public bus station and the ferry terminal. Being an important travel junction, Banyuwangi also has several private bus companies with terminals scattered around the city. Travelers who purchase direct bus or train tickets between Bali and Java will simply bypass Banyuwangi. Independent travelers who need detailed advice on regional attractions can visit the tourist office on Jalan

Diponegoro for maps, information about the parks described above, or surfing conditions in Granjangan.

Accommodations

Over 30 *losmen* and hotels are found in this messy, noisy town. Pass straight through unless you want to visit one of the East Java national parks or simply enjoy Javanese cacophony at its finest.

Hotel Baru: The best spot for budget travelers has 42 spacious, airy rooms adjacent to their popular cafe. The owners also help with tips on nearby surfing beaches. 82 Jl. Pattimura, tel. (0333) 21369, US$3-8

Wisma Blambangan: Situated right on the town square with cleanish rooms in all price ranges. 4 Jl. Wahidin, tel. (0333) 21598, US$5-12.

Manyar Hotel: The best hotel in town is overpriced but conveniently located just one km south of the ferry terminal for Bali. Jl. Situbondo, tel. US$12-35.

BALI

When the first Dutch war yacht pulled into Bali in the late 16th century, the whole crew immediately jumped ship—it was heaven on earth and it took the captain two years to round up his men before he could set sail back to Holland. Bali was really put on the map back in the 1930s when several popular documentaries were made about this paradise-like island. Then the world knew, and Bali has remained a tourist colony for well-nigh 50 years now—an Isle of Capri of the Western Pacific.

This tiny tropical island just off the eastern coast of Java is both Indonesia's masterpiece and one of the world's greatest cultural jewels, a 5,500-square-km vision of towering volcanoes, beautiful beaches, and magnificent layers of sculpted ricefields.

But it's not volcanoes, beaches, or ricefields that has entranced the world for centuries but rather Balinese culture, where life and art are completely interwoven to an extent unheard of in the West. Every Balinese citizen, from the simplest peasant to the highest-caste noble, considers himself an artist whose birthright demands the continual creation of music, dance, and crafts to honor the gods, generate karma, and maintain the island's natural balance.

Ruined?

The island's physical beauty and artistic heritage attracts enormous numbers of tourists from all over the world who flood the temples, beaches, resorts, mountains, nightclubs, and remote extensions of the island. Although this sounds negative, commercialization has also brought higher standards of living and served to revitalize and preserve traditional Balinese culture, since the Balinese have somehow grown stronger in their basic faiths fueled with the financial support of the mighty tourist dollar.

Kuta Beach and other commercialized tourist centers have little to do with the "real" Bali, but authentic lifestyles remain alive and well in hundreds of villages which haven't changed in 50 years. Bali is a place to get lost—you don't need directions, just head for the hills. Best of all, the best of Bali is still free: orange and gold tropical sunsets, an astoundingly rich culture, the dynamite smiles of the children, sounds of rustling palms, hidden coves of talcum-powder beaches, and pristine corals.

INTRODUCTION

History

Historically speaking, Bali is a fossilized Java.

After the Balinese escaped the control of the Sumatran Srivijaya Empire (7th-13th centuries), the island came under the control of various East Javanese kingdoms who introduced the same Hindu theologies and artistic models that dominated the Javanese courts. Balinese culture came of age in the 16th century when Islam began to move across the island of Java.

To escape Islamic domination, most of the Hindu Majapahit aristocracy, court philosophers, priests, architects, artisans, painters, and craftsmen took refuge on Bali. The tiny island became the last remaining Hindu outpost in Southeast Asia, an important repository of traditional Majapahit religion and culture, and the final resting place for the old Indo-Javanese civilization.

Except for occasional incursions by the Dutch and English, Bali remained almost completely isolated until the tragic events of 1894. To avenge a massacre of Dutch soldiers by the Balinese, the Dutch government ordered an attack on the royal court of Mataram. Rather than surrender, the king and his entourage committed *puputan,* a form of ritualistic suicide in which the unarmed Balinese hurled themselves against the heavily fortified Dutch.

The gruesome spectacle was repeated in Denpasar in 1906, and later at the royal courts at Gelgel and Klungkung. Bali was incorporated into the Dutch Empire, but only after all remaining lineal descendants of the Majapahit Empire had committed suicide or been killed by the Dutch.

Tourism began in the 1930s after several famous artists, photographers, and writers took residence in Bali. Walter Spies (formerly the

BALI SEA

P. MENJANGAN

TELUK
TERIMA

BANYUWEDANG

TERIMA

BANYUPOH

PEMARON
TUKADMUNGGA
ANTURAN
KALIBUBUK
TEMUKUS KALIASEM

GILIMANUK

SUMBERLAMPOK

PEMUTERAN

GONDOL

GEROKGAK

SERIRIT DENCARIK

SELAT
TIGAWASA

BANJAR

CEKIK

BALI BARAT

BLIMBINGSARI

NATIONAL PARK

G. MERBUK
(1,385 m)

G. MESEHE
(1,344 m)

BULELENG

SIDETAPA

CEMPAGA
PEDAWA
JEMBONG
BEJI

PALAREJO

MAYONG

BUSUNGBIU

GESING

MELAYA

CANDIKUSAMA

JEMBRANA

PUPUAN

RENING

BATUNGSEL

CUPEL

NEGARA

MENDOYO

ASAHDUREN

BLIMBING

PERANCAK

PEKUTATAN

INDIAN

ANTOSARI

LALANG
LINGGAH

BAJERA

SOKA

BERABAN

OCEAN

INDONESIA

0   20 km

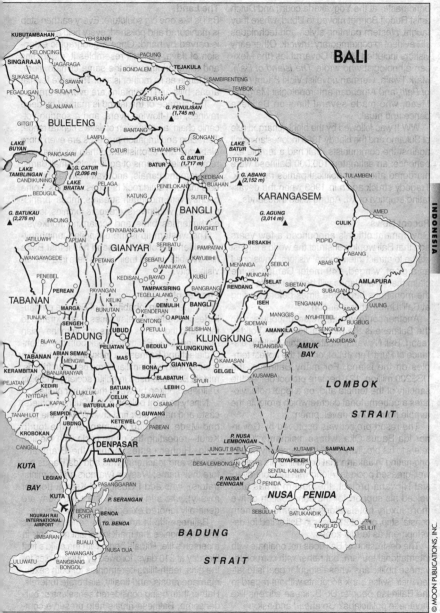

BALI

INDONESIA

KUBUTAMBAHAN
KELONCING
SINGARAJA
SUKASADA
PEGADUGAN
SILANJANA
GITGIT
BULELENG
YEH SANIH
JAGARAGA
SAWAN
SUDAJI
PACUNG
BONDALEM
TEJAKULA
SAMBIRENTENG
TEMBOK
LES
KEDURAN
G. PENULISAN
(1,745 m)
SONGAN
LAMPU
BANTANG
CATUR
YEHMAMPEH
BATUR
LAKE
BUYAN
PANCASARI
LAKE
TAMBLINGAN
CANDIKUNING
LAKE
BRATAN
G. CATUR
(2,096 m)
BEDUGUL
PELAGA
KATUNG
PENELOKAN
G. BATUR
(1,717 m)
KEDISAN
BUAHAN
SUTER
OTERUNYAN
LAKE
BATUR
G. ABANG
(2,152 m)
KARANGASEM
TULAMBEN
AMED
G. BATUKAU
(2,276 m)
PACUNG
JATILUWIH
WANGAYAGEDE
APUAN
PENYABANGAN
PETANG
GIANYAR
SEBATU
MANUKAYA
KEDISAN
BAYAD
KUBU
SERIBATU
PAMPATAN
KAYUBIHI
BANGKET
BESAKIH
MENANGA
SEBUDI
G. AGUNG
(3,014 m)
PIDPID
ABANG
ABABI
CULIK
PENEBEL
PEREAN
PAYANGAN
KELIKI
TAMPAKSIRING
TEGELLALANG
BANGBANG
RENDANG
MUNCAN
SELAT
SIBETAN
SUBAGAN
AMLAPURA
TABANAN
MARGA
SENGEH
BADUNG
UBUD
BUNUTAN
GENTONG
OKENDERAN
DEMULIH
APUAN
PETULU
SELISIHAN
BANGLI
ISEH
TENGANAN
MANGGIS
SIDEMAN
NYUHTEBEL
ASAK
BUGBUG
UJUNG
TUNJUK
BLAYA
PELIATAN
MAS
BEDULU
KLUNGKUNG
KLUNGKUNG
AMANKILA
SENGKIDU
CANDIDASA
TABANAN
ABIAN SEMAL
MENGWI
BANJARANYAR
BONA
BLABATUH
GIANYAR
KAMASAN
GELGEL
PADANGBAI
AMUK
BAY
KERAMBITAN
PEJATAN
KEDIRI
NYITDAH
KAPAL
BATUAN
CELUK
SABA
SUKAWATI
LEBIH
SIYUT
KUSAMBA
LOMBOK
STRAIT
TANAH LOT
SEMPIDI
UBUNG
BATUBULAN
GUWANG
KETEWEL
PABEAN
P. NUSA
LEMBONGAN
JUNGUT BATU
KUTAMPI
SAMPALAN
KROBOKAN
CANGGU
DENPASAR
SANUR
DESA LEMBONGAN
TOYAPEKEH
SENTAL KANJIN
KUTA
BAY
LEGIAN
KUTA
PASANGGARAN
P. SERANGAN
P. NUSA
CENINGAN
PENIDA
NUSA PENIDA
SEBULUH
BATUKANDIK
PELILIT
NGURAH RAI
INTERNATIONAL
AIRPORT
BENOA
PORT
BENOA
TG. BENOA
BADUNG
TANGLAD
JIMBARAN
BUALU
NUSA DUA
ULUWATU
BANGBANG
BONGOL
SAWANGAN
STRAIT

© MOON PUBLICATIONS, INC.

bandmaster at the Yogyakarta court) and Dutch artist Rudolf Bonnet moved to Ubud, where they taught Western painting styles and techniques still evident in contemporary artwork. Other early visitors included Miguel Covarrubias (the Mexican ethnologist who wrote *The Island of Bali*), Mark Twain, German novelist Vicki Baum *(Tale of Bali),* and American anthropologist Margaret Mead, who made several films on Balinese dance and ritual.

WW II was followed by the highly charged rule of Sukarno and the bloody 1965 Indonesian revolt against the communists. Bali had a terrible experience: an estimated 100,000 Balinese were murdered after rival political parties ran amok. Tragedy struck again in 1963 when the devastating eruption of Mt. Agung killed thousands.

Recent News

Government officials announced a few years ago that Bali would construct the world's largest statue to attract international visitors. Envisioned as a giant, winged, 149-meter Garuda, some claim that all airplanes will be required to circle the monstrous bird three times before landing at Bali's international airport.

Another controversial project unpopular with the Balinese is the multi-million dollar holiday resort, Bali Nirwana, located within walking distance of Pura Tanah Lot, one of the holiest temples on the island. For many Balinese, the US$200 million, 121-hectare project defiles the sanctity of the temple and, on a legal note, violates a gubernatorial decree which protects the temple from tourist development.

The resort project was approved by Governor Ida Bagus Oka, whose nickname "O.K." refers to his proclivity to rubber stamp any project originating in Jakarta that could line his already well-greased pockets. Along with the controversial Nirwana project, the governor has also voiced his support for the construction of five more luxury hotels along the same southern coastal strip, one of 21 areas in Bali slated for development as tourist zones.

The destruction of Bali does not originate with international tourism, but rather with corrupt Javanese politicians whose singular goal is to fatten their Swiss bank accounts without regard to the Balinese people. Do Balinese citizens like Javanese politicians? Go ahead and ask.

The Land

Bali is like one big sculpture. Every earthen step is manicured and polished, every field and niche is carved by hand. Once a geographic extension of Java, Bali still resembles it, mountains and all, sharing much the same climate, flora, and fauna as its mother island. There are few flat areas; hills and mountains are everywhere.

The surface of the island is marked by deep ravines, fast-flowing rivers, and a soaring volcanic chain, an extension of Java's central range. Terracing and irrigation practices are even more elaborate and sophisticated than on Java, with remarkable systems of aqueducts, small dams, underground canals, and water carried by tunnels through solid rock hillsides. There's alpine country with mountain streams, moss, prehistoric ferns, wildflowers, creepers, orchids, leeches, butterflies, birds, and screaming monkeys.

The western tip is the unspoiled, uninhabited wilderness of Bali. Legend has it that Bali's first inhabitants had their origins here in a lost, invisible city.

The People

The three million inhabitants of Bali are primarily descendants of Malay races that migrated to the island thousands of years ago from the Asian mainland. Most Balinese speak both the national dialect and Balinese, a tricky language which is subdivided into familiar forms between friends, middle Balinese used in polite society, and high Balinese spoken between the higher castes.

Ninety percent belong to the Sudra (workers) caste and name their first child Wayan, the second Made, the third Nyoman, and the fourth Ketut—repeating the name cycle with the fifth child. Higher castes include the Brahmans (priests and teachers), who add Ida Bagus before their name; Wesyas (warriors and administrators), who add I Gusti; and Ksatria (former royalty), who add Dewa. Caste rules today are generally ignored except at formal occasions.

Balinese life is an endless series of rituals and ceremonies that mark important moments in a person's life. Rituals begin with the child's first birthday at 210 days, followed by puberty rites for the girls, teeth-filing ceremonies for both sexes, marriage rituals, and finally, elaborate funerals. Rather than being considered senseless or burdensome, Balinese rituals help preserve community values, encourage artistic pageantry, and give the people a firm sense of self-worth and emotional security.

Village life also involves community service. Most of the important decisions are made according to the customary laws of *adat* by the *desa* (village) council of married adults. Meetings are often held in the *bale agung*, open-air pavilions located inside temple courtyards. Large *desas* are subdivided into cooperative groups called *banjars*, which help each other with home building, festivals, and cremations.

Balinese farmers are also expected to join the village *subak*, a farmers' federation which distributes the water from the higher ricefields down to the lower levels. Balinese society derives much of its economic and spiritual success from these powerful social organizations.

Religion

Bali is the largest Hindu outpost in the world outside of India. Although Hinduism originated in India, on Bali it has developed along lines all its own. Indeed, the forms of Hinduism practiced in the two lands are as different as the forms of Christianity practiced by the Ethiopians and the Episcopalians. And the way the Balinese practice their island form of frontier Hinduism is still their greatest art.

Balinese practice Agama Tirtal ("Religion of the Holy Water"), an unusual combination of indigenous animism, ancestor worship, Hinduism, and Javanese mysticism. Agama Tirtal is essentially a monotheistic faith with one supreme deity (Sanghyang Widi) who rules over Brahma,

Vishnu, Shiva, and dozens of lesser gods such as Dewi Sri (Rice Goddess), Surya (Sun God), Candra (Moon God), Sakenon (Sea God), and Hyang Gunung (Mountain God) . . . not to mention hundreds of minor spirits who can destroy crops, cause insanity, or bring sickness and death.

Whether benevolent or evil, all spirits must be appeased with daily offerings to maintain balance between the forces of good and evil.

Temples

Bali has an estimated 20,000 temples found in villages, seashores, on mountaintops, and in the ricefields. All *pura* (temples) are oriented from *kaja* (mountain) direction to *kelod* (sea) direction, with secondary shrines located in the *kangin* (sunrise) direction.

Each Balinese village has three primary temples. The Pura Puseh (Temple of Origin) is dedicated to Vishnu and used to worship the village founders; always found in the *kaja* end of the village. The Pura Desa (Town Temple) is dedicated to Brahma and used for ceremonies involving the living; found in the middle of town. The Pura Dalem (Temple of the Dead) is dedicated to Shiva and used to worship the deities of death; located in the *kelod* end. Temple courtyards have several individual shrines *(merus)* dedicated to family clans, village social organizations, and nature spirits.

In addition, each family has a Home Temple, former rajadoms keep Royal Temples to honor their deified ancestors, and the entire population shares a number of National Temples located at the sea (Ulu Watu), in the mountains (Besakih),

SHANTI DIGENOVA

INDONESIA

BALINESE PERFORMING ARTS

The world marvels at the complexity, refinement, and grace of Balinese art. Life and artistic creation are completely intertwined to the point where there are no words for "art" or "artist"—everyone is expected to be an artist.

Dance and drama come in three general forms: *wali* (sacred performances) that serve as rites of exorcism, *bebali* (ceremonial performances), and *bali balihan* (simple amusement) sponsored in staging areas and accompanied by *gamelan* orchestras. Balinese dance—from the squatting "Indian" stances to the darting eyes and elaborate costuming—are derived from Indian origins, though modified by centuries of Javanese and Balinese refinements. Like everything else on the island, dance and drama fashions change as new fads are absorbed by dance troupes and *gamelans*.

Ramayana Ballet

Together with the epic war story of the Mahabharta, the romantic adventure of the Ramayana forms the basis for most local dance and drama. Complete Ramayanas were rarely performed until just a few years ago, when the Denpasar Conservatory of Art and Dance began popularizing full performances with elaborately costumed performers and *gamelan gong* orchestras. Today, abbreviated spectacles are given in the tourist venues; excellent introductions to the lovely and enchanting story.

Barong (Kris Dance)

The *barong* dance serves to exorcise evil spirits and ensure the triumph of the *barong* white magic over the witch Rangda's black magic—a powerful and sacred struggle between the powers of good and evil. Magical masks must be treated with great respect: carved by village masters, purified with prayer, stored in a special pavilion, covered with sacred cloth to contain the magic, and meditated upon by the actors who believe that the spirits of the gods inhabit the masks when worn.

Extensive offerings are first made to protect the performers against evil spirits. Then the *barong*—a furry female lion-like creature manipulated by two men—enters the stage. Slowly, the fingernails of Rangda slide around the corner. Evil and horrible, she is the stuff of nightmares. The fight seems lost until a group of *kris*-armed men attempt to kill Rangda. The evil witch uses her hypnotic magic to force the men into a suicidal stabbing spectacle, but this is soon countered by the superior power of the *barong*. The men are later revived from their trances by holy water sprinkled by the village priests.

Kechak (Monkey Dance)

Picture this: A moonlit night in front of the temple, burning torches encircle the 100 dark-skinned men who sit on the ground in concentric circles, arms waving and continuously chanting "chak-a-chak chak" in perfect synchronization while the Ramayana is performed by costumed actors in the center. This is the *kechak*—Bali's most famous dance.

A powerful and mesmerizing male chorus represents Hanuman's monkey army, which aids Rama in his quest for Sita, his captured queen. The hypnotic chanting serves to drive off black spirits and ensure the triumph of good over evil.

There is good reason why the *kechak* seems so Hollywood. In 1928, German artist Walter Spies and Baron Von Messon (a film director) collaborated with Kathryn Myerson (a Martha Graham choreographer) to create the *kechak*, an event filmed by Von Messon!

Legong Dance

Balinese dance connoisseurs consider this highly stylized dance between two divine maidens the epitome of Balinese femininity, coquettishness, and supreme dance technique. Reciting a 13th-century East Javanese fable, three women enter the stage: a female attendant *(condong)* and two beautiful young girls tightly wrapped in gold brocade with headdresses of frangipani flowers.

After a short introductory dance by the *condong*, the young girls (chosen for their beauty, suppleness, and pre-menstrual purity) perform a tightly-choreographed duet of dramatic gestures, angular body movements, and dozens of special hand movements that help tell the story. The nose-to-nose love scene is especially moving! The *legong* is worth seeing a dozen times.

Sanghyang (Trance Dances)

Balinese dances are often performed by auto-hypnotized trance dancers who have allowed the spirits of gods *(sanghyang)* to descend from heaven and take control of their actions. Rather than a sign of insanity or senility, trance is regarded as a higher, but completely natural, state of consciousness, a conduit between the gods and mortals.

Closely related to the more familiar *legong* is *sanghyang dedari*, a shamanistic trance dance performed by two young girls. Both stand on the shoulders of male dancers and exactly mimic the movements of their partners. After collapsing on the ground, the girls are revived by priests. *Sanghyang jaran*, the hobbyhorse trance dance called the "fire dance" in the tourist brochures, features an auto-hypnotized man possessed by horse spirits who runs through bonfires of coconut husks, kicking up a real firestorm. It's good fun when he punts burning coconuts into the tourist seats!

Topeng (Masked Drama)

Topeng relates the deeds and adventures of local Balinese kings and warriors; a symbolic meeting ground for spiritual and worldly concerns. The finely carved masks link the wearer to a spiritual realm charged with magic potency. Talented performers make their masks breathe, sweat, and cry, but amateurs are disparagingly referred to as carpenters who do nothing but push around wood.

The special bond *(taksu)* that develops between the actor and his mask can only be discovered with meditation, prayers, dreams, and deep trance. Full-masked kings and gods are unable to talk—it is the half-masked clowns who provide the ribald and hilarious dialogue. Acting as interpreters for their dignified masters, clowns satirize the self-importance of their masters, teach lessons to the children, and make fun of the tourists. Recent additions include a long-nosed, camera-laden, and bad-mannered tourist; he draws the biggest laughs.

Other Dances

Kebyar: A dramatic and strenuous male solo dance that portrays the stylized movements of the Balinese warrior. *Kebyar* can be performed in either a standing or sitting position, as popularized by Mario, the legendary dance musician.

Baris: A male warrior dance performed by soldiers brandishing spears, lances, *kris* daggers, swords, and shields.

Janger: A group of a dozen seated men and women who juxtapose the graceful femininity of the girls against the dramatic gestures of the aggressive male warriors.

Oleg Tambulilingan: A tender love duet between a lovely maiden and her handsome suitor that depicts the courting ritual of two bumblebees.

Barong Landung: Usually performed on Serangan Island, this giant puppet dance is sung in Balinese with plenty of bawdy humor.

Arja and **Drama Gong:** Balinese soap operas filled with love, humor, misery, and slapstick melodrama.

Performance Venues

Balinese dance is presented in highly abbreviated versions at tourist venues, though the best performances take place during temple anniversaries *(odalan)* held every 210 days; tourist offices have weekly schedules.

Don't dismiss the tourist shows as worthless or inauthentic—they feature some of the best dancers and musicians, besides providing their communities with an important source of income. It's best to see both: tourist performances are good introductions, and temple festivals uncover the emotional realism often missing from tourist performances.

and in the lowlands (Mengwi). Now you see why the tiny island of Bali has perhaps the highest temple-per-capita ratio of any place on the planet.

Temples are entered through an imposing *candi bentar* (monumental split gate) on the *kelod* side, designed to confuse evil spirits, who have difficulty with sharp corners. The large outer courtyard features pavilions where the village *gamelan* is stored, assembly halls for community meetings, and frequently a pit for cockfighting. Through the second gateway you'll find sacred relics, temple heirlooms, and multiroofed *merus* modeled after Mahameru, the Hindu holy mountain.

Festivals aside, Balinese temples are rather quiet, deserted, and peaceful.

Festivals

Besides serving as points for contact with the gods, Balinese temples serve as centers for art and culture during the yearly *odalan*—temple birthdays celebrated every 210 days on the anniversary of the temple's consecration. Since each Balinese village has three temples with annual *odalan* celebrations, it is highly likely you will discover a few while on the island; the tourist offices in Kuta and Denpasar have a complete list.

Festivals are designed to invite the gods down for food and entertainment before requesting favors such as a bountiful rice crop or help in battling evil spirits. Rather than solemn occasions, festivals are lively social events with smiling kids, dancing grandmothers, gambling, myriad foodstalls, chanting priests, *gamelan* music, and performances of *wayang.*

Women bring enormous pyramids of rice cakes and flowers; offerings for evil spirits are placed on the ground, those for good spirits are stacked around the main altars. *Pemangku* (temple priests) chant in Sanskrit before the rice-cake towers and sacred images are carried to the ocean for a ceremonial bath and purification rites.

At night, old women slowly dance the *pendet,* puppeteers perform *wayang,* and *pemangkus* enter into trances. *Odalans* end with the rising sun and final prayer as the villagers return to their homes—an excellent way to appreciate the religious devotion and zest for life that characterize the Balinese.

Funerals

Another event worth attending is a Balinese funeral—among the most spectacular sights on the island. Rather than sad and solemn affairs, Balinese funerals are joyous celebrations that liberate the soul from the body for the journey back to heaven. First, the corpse is cleaned and displayed in the house for friends and neighbors. Most are temporarily buried until an auspicious date arises and enough money has been raised for the ceremony.

On the appointed day, the entire village constructs a gigantic tower, carves the coffin, and creates art for burning. En route to the Temple of the Dead, the procession spins the coffin to confuse the soul (so it won't return to the village and raise hell!) and then transfers the corpse to a funeral sarcophagus. The magnificent tower is set on fire before the ashes are carried to the sea.

Tourists are welcome to watch and even photograph the event, but it's best to be well dressed (no shorts or halter tops) and remain unobtrusive and respectful of local traditions.

Proper Attire

Great importance is laid on proper dress when visiting temples and attending local festivals.

The recommended attire for males includes *sarong, saput* (second smaller *sarong*), *slendang* (sash around waist), sleeved shirt, and *udung* (headdress).

Ladies should be fitted in *sarong, kebaya* or sleeved shirt, and *selendang.* On no account should you *ever* visit a temple in shorts, halter tops, or anything that appears immodest—this is scandalous behavior that only serves to insult the Balinese.

PRACTICAL INFORMATION

Getting There

Air: Bali's Ngurah Rai International Airport is three km south of Kuta and 12 km south of Denpasar. Airport transport goes to Kuta (10 minutes), Legian (15 minutes), Seminyak (20 minutes), Sanur (30 minutes), Nusa Dua (35 minutes), and Ubud (one hour).

Garuda operates flights to Bali from most major Indonesian cities, plus flights from Singapore, Bangkok, Manila, Hong Kong, Tokyo, Europe, and Los Angeles. Qantas serves Bali direct from Sydney, Melbourne, Perth, and Darwin. Other international airlines generally stop in Jakarta, where you must transfer to a connecting Garuda flight.

The arrival lounge has a hotel booking counter (more expensive hotels only), poorly stocked tourist-information counter, money changers, and transportation touts. Fixed-rate taxi coupons are sold at the taxi counter, or walk out 200 meters to the *bemo* stand for a cheap ride to Kuta. Hooking up with a hotel tout isn't a bad idea.

Bus: Direct a/c buses leave mornings and evenings to most destinations in Java, including Surabaya (10-12 hours), Yogyakarta (15-16 hours), and Jakarta (26-30 hours). Buses to all destinations within Bali depart from the Ubung bus terminal in Denpasar. Tickets can be purchased from agents in Kuta and less expensively directly from bus companies offices at Ubung.

Boat: Ferries connect Ketapang in East Java with Gilimanuk in west Bali every 30 minutes around the clock, and Padangbai in east Bali with Lembar harbor in Lombok several times daily.

The quickest sea route to Lombok is with Mabua Ekspres which operates express boats twice daily from Benoa to Lembar.

Four Pelni ships stop at Benoa on their scheduled routes through Nusa Tenggara and other points in the Indonesian archipelago. Schedules can be picked up at the Pelni office in Benoa port and from travel agencies in Kuta, Legian, Sanur, Nusa Dua, and Ubud.

Getting Around

Bemos **(Minibuses):** Minibuses (formerly covered trucks) serve every possible place on Bali and provide the cheapest but most time-consuming way to get around. From Kuta, Sanur, and Nusa Dua, *bemos* reach Denpasar, from where other *bemos* leave for all destinations.

Prices are negotiable and unsuspecting tourists are always overcharged. You should check the correct fare with your *losmen* manager or tourist office before setting off. Many *bemos* stop running at sunset and some are infested with thieves—be cautious about leaving your bags unattended.

Cars and Motorcycles: Despite safety concerns, cars, jeeps, and motorcycles are certainly the best way to find festivals and explore the back roads of Bali. Motorcycles cost US$5-8 per day, while cars and jeeps run US$15-45 depending on the model, agency, and your bargaining abilities.

Be sure to purchase insurance, inspect the vehicle before leaving the rental agency, and exercise caution on Bali's crowded and dangerous roads—this is *not* the place to learn how to ride a motorcycle or test your rusty skills with a clutch in a rented jeep.

International driver's licenses are still required on Bali although this rule is rarely enforced expect by local police looking for a little grease money from nabbed tourists. If you get pinched without the license, the policeman will show a book listing the suggested penalty fee for your transgression (US$25-40), but will be happy to accept an offer of US$5-8.

International driver's licenses can be obtain in Denpasar for visitors who intend to stay in Bali a great deal of time and want to protect themselves against rapacious policemen.

Tourist Information

Government tourist offices in Kuta and Denpasar can help to a limited degree with maps and schedules of upcoming festivals, but the lack of printed,

accurate, useful material is a measurement of the success of tourism minister Joop Ave. Ubud's privately operated tourist office is just as hopeless as government tourist offices.

Tourist offices are open daily 0900-1600 except Fridays, when they close around noon.

Diplomatic Offices

Denpasar consulates include Australia, France, Japan, Norway, and Denmark, while Sanur consulates include Germany, Italy, Sweden, and the United States. Consulates elsewhere include the Netherlands in Kuta and Switzerland in Legian. Addresses and phone numbers—which change annually—are listed in the phone book.

Immigration

Indonesian immigration on Jalan Puputan Raya, near the main post office in Denpasar, is open Monday-Thursday 0900-1400 and Friday and Saturday 0900-1100. Another office is near the airport.

Mail

Mail should be directed to the small post offices in Kuta or Ubud, rather than the inconvenient postal center in Denpasar.

Telephone

International phone calls from hotels are more expensive than calls from wartels and other public telecommunications offices. Area codes are southern Bali (0361), northern Bali (0362), and eastern Bali (0366).

To dial Bali from the United States or Europe, dial the international access code (011), the country code for Indonesia (62), the area code for Bali *minus the zero* (361 in most cases), and finally the local number.

Weather and Hotel Reservations

Bali is best visited during the dry season from April to October, although the monsoons from November to March are relatively light and usually only disrupt the afternoons. Bali is packed out with Australians during Christmas holidays and Europeans in July/August, when advance hotel reservations are strongly recommended.

Health

Minor medical problems can be handled at the General Hospital in Denpasar and at private clinics in Sanur and Nusa Dua. Serious medical problems and emergency evacuations may require the assistance of your consulate.

Suggested Readings

Bali guidebooks with far more detail than this overall survey include those published by Moon Publications, Lonely Planet, APA Insight, and Cadogan. Hugh Mabbett's *The Balinese* is an outstanding survey of modern Balinese lifestyles, plus it's available on the island.

Background reading includes *Island of Bali* by Miguel Covarrubias, *Dance and Drama In Bali* by Walter Spies, and *Trance in Bali* by Jane Belo—three classics which offer tremendous insight into Balinese culture but should be read *before* you arrive.

Shopping

Shopping runs the gamut from quality paintings and woodcarvings to mass-produced junk churned out for indiscriminate tourists. Check Kuta shops and villages that concentrate on one particular craft, then seek out artisans' homes for top quality at lowest prices.

Many handicraft villages described below are on the road between Denpasar and Ubud.

Paintings: Bali's art center is in Ubud, where dozens of artists maintain home studios, and museums serve as excellent introductions to contemporary styles. Traditional *wayang* paintings and astrological calendars are produced in Klungkung and near Kamasan, two km south of Klungkung. Excellent *wayang* paintings are

displayed on the ceiling of the Kerta Gosa (Hall of Justice) in Klungkung.

Woodcarving: Mas, a small town just south of Ubud, serves as Bali's woodcarving center although lower prices are found in nearby Batuan and Pujung.

Stone, Weaving, and Silver: Stonecarving, one of the few Balinese arts that still serves religion rather than tourism, is best found in Batubulan, Bali's stonecarving center. Batik is plentiful around the island but you might find superior work in Gianyar and Pujung, two important weaving villages. Tenganan produces some double *ikat,* though this labor-intensive craft appears to be a dying art form. Celuk is known for silver and gold filigree work.

Sports

Surfing: Surfers may start at Kuta where decent-sized tubes are common on the reef one km offshore, but most move south to Uluwatu, Padang Padang north of Uluwatu, Sanur Beach during the windy winter months, Nusa Dua (surprise), and Nusa Lembongan across from Sanur. Surfing shops help with details and arrange package surf trips to G-Spot in East Java.

Scuba: Bali has outstanding diving at Pulau Menjangan in northwest Bali, Tulamben in the northeast where a well-preserved wreck of an American steamship lies in shallow waters, and in the coral reefs and submerged cliffs off the south coast near Candidasa.

Dive shops are everywhere: Kuta, Legian, Sanur, and Nusa Dua.

SOUTH BALI ~ KUTA, SANUR, AND NUSA DUA

Each of the three beach resorts of southern Bali—Kuta, Sanur, and Nusa Dua—offer distinct personalities that attract their own breed of traveler.

Kuta—subdivided into the beaches of Kuta, Legian, and Seminyak—is mainly for budget and moderate-rate visitors who want a beach plus plenty of nightlife, from raunchy rock n' roll to sophisticated nightclubs. Tuban is a somewhat upscale neighborhood just south of Kuta with luxury hotels facing the beach and a handful of cheaper places on the east side of the main road.

Sanur is the original luxury area set with older but luxurious hotels on a quiet beach which remains quite true to its original character despite four decades of tourism.

Nusa Dua is Bali's most expensive and luxurious spot—a bold attempt by the Indonesian government to limit tourism to one region and protect the environment from destruction.

None of these beach resorts have much to do with the "real" Bali, but their superb sand, shopping, restaurants, and nightlife make them

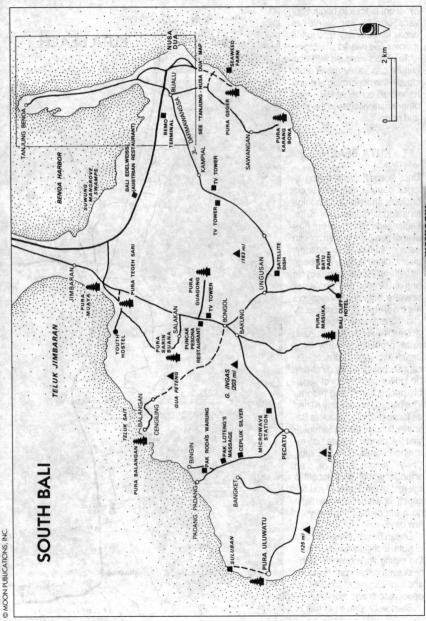

SOUTH BALI

© MOON PUBLICATIONS, INC.

INDONESIA

2 km

NUSA DUA

TANJUNG BENOA

BENOA HARBOR

SUWUNG MANGROVE SWAMPS

TELUK JIMBARAN

BEMO TERMINAL

BUALU

JL. DARMAWANGSA

SEE "TANJUNG - NUSA DUA" MAP

SEAWEED FARM

PURA GEGER

PURA KARANG BONA

BALI EDELWEISS (AUSTRIAN RESTAURANT)

KAMPIAL

TV TOWER

SAWANGAN

JIMBARAN

PURA MUAYA

PURA TEGEH SARI

PURA SARIN BUANA

SALAKAN

PURA GUAGONG

TV TOWER

BONGOL

UNGUSAN

SATELLITE DISH

PURA BATU PAGEH

YOUTH HOSTEL

PUNCAK PESONA RESTAURANT

BAKUNG

PURA MASUKA

BALI CLIFF HOTEL

GUA PETENG

BALANGAN

CENGILING

G. INGAS (203 m)

(163 m)

TELUK SAIT

PURA BALANGAN

BINGIN

PAK RODA'S WARUNG

PAK LOTENG'S MASSAGE

CEPLUK SILVER

MICROWAVE STATION

PECATU

(184 m)

PADANG PADANG

BANGKET

SULUBAN

(125 m)

PURA ULUWATU

excellent places to begin your vacation. All can serve as bases for easy day-trips to the temples and handicraft villages, while visitors intrigued with local culture can easily move on to Ubud—the performing arts and handicraft center of Bali—and other small villages in the east and north.

KUTA BEACH

Once sleepy Balinese fishing villages popular only with backpackers, the rollicking honky-tonk tourist villages of Kuta, Legian, and Seminyak are now almost completely overrun with Aussie students on holiday, bleach-blond surfers, European jetsetters, local motorcycle punks, pimps, and armies of hawkers. Kuta and its neighbors are mad, crazy, and completely chaotic, but *never* boring.

Despite the negative press, Kuta provides a fairly nice beach, wonderful sunsets, decent shopping, nonstop cut-rate hedonism, and plenty of sensibly priced hotels and resorts. The place is completely ruined as far as providing a look at Balinese culture, but it's fortunate that the cancer of Kuta has remained confined to this relatively small enclave, an arrangement of great benefit to the rest of the island. If you accept it for what it is, Kuta might be a fun place to spend your few days.

Legian Beach, three km north of Kuta, is slightly removed from the raging vortex, while Seminyak even farther north is a quiet and sophisticated scene with superior resorts and restaurants.

Start your visit in either of

© MOON PUBLICATIONS, INC.

these three places, but don't let local pleasures seduce you from discovering the rest of the island.

Name Changes
Many of the old, familiar street and place names are in the process of changing to conform with local nomenclature regulations. These new names are generally those of national heroes, ancient kingdoms, religious figures, or famous Balinese landmarks.

The old names are listed here with their new counterparts following in parentheses: Jalan Double Six (Jalan Arjuna), Jalan Dyhana Pura (Jalan Abimanyu), Jalan Tanjung Mekar (Jalan Majapahit), Jalan Kayu Aya (Jalan Laksamana), Jalan Tegal Wangi (Jalan Ciungwanara), Jalan Bakungsari (Jalan Singosari), Jalan Tanjungsari (Jalan Blambangan), Jalan Tamansari (Jalan Tukad Biluk Poh), Jalan Kartika Plaza (Jalan Dewi Sartika), Jalan Padma (Jalan Yudistira), and Jalan Imam Bonjol (Jalan Nakula).

The changes will take place over several years and, until complete, the original names will be used in this guidebook.

Accommodations
Kuta, Legian, Tuban, and Seminyak now offer over 6,000 hotel rooms, ranging from luxurious US$1,500-per-night presidential suites with private swimming pools to simple *losmen* which cost US$5-15 depending on facilities.

Rooms under US$15 are simple affairs with bare walls, double beds, and shared bathrooms, but often include a free breakfast of tea and bananas. Rooms for US$15-25 should be comfortably furnished, include a private bath, and be very clean. Most places are now in the US$25-50 price range and will include an a/c room with TV, cafe, room service, swimming pool, and other standard hotel amenities. The backpackers of yesterday are now comfortably lazing around the pool with cocktail in hand; times have changed remarkably since the author's first visit in 1979.

Hotels and resorts near the beach are more expensive, while the least expensive and quietest places are in the back alleys, not on the main roads. Prices are negotiable during the slower spring and fall months but rise sharply in August for the French invasion and around Christmas and Easter for the Aussie wave.

Categorizing any *losmen* or hotel as "budget" or "moderately priced" is difficult, since most offer older rooms under US$10, more luxurious cottages in the US$15-30 range, and a/c chalets for US$35-60.

Budget Accommodations
The nicest places are the smaller, family-run homestays located down the smaller lanes, rather than the impersonal large hotels that make up most of the current hotel stock.

Hotel touts at the airport south of Kuta Beach and the Denpasar bus station often provide free transportation to their hotel, an easy way to get settled for the first night. The following morning you can hunt for a *losmen* which better fits your needs and budget. A few samples in alphabetical order:

Tuban
Anom Dewi Hostel	US$5-10
Bamboo Inn	US$10-15
Bunti Gardens	US$10-15
Jesen's Inn II	US$8-20
Pendawa Bungalows	US$15-45

Kuta
Arena Bungalows	US$10-25
Bali Duta Wisata	US$6-10
Bali Dwipa	US$6-10
Bali Indah	US$6-10
Bali Sandy Cottages	US$10-20
Bamboo Inn	US$8-15
Bendesa; US$6-10	
Beneyasa Beach Inn	US$6-10
Berlian Inn	US$8-15
Budi Beach Inn	US$8-25
Fat Yogi	US$8-25
Jus Edith	US$6-10
Kedin's Inn	US$8-18
Kodja Beach Inn	US$10-25
Komala Indah I	US$5-10
Kuta Puri Bungalows	US$15-25
Kuta Suci Bungalows	US$8-15
Losmen Cempaka	US$6-10
Meka Jaya	US$6-10
Nagasari Beach Inn	US$10-20
Palm Gardens Homestay	US$8-15
Puri Ayodia Inn	US$6-12
Rita's House	US$8-15
Rempan House	US$8-15
Ronta Bungalows	US$6-15

Sari Bali Bungalows	US$12-35
Sorga Cottages	US$10-25
Suci Bungalows	US$10-15
Suji Bungalows	US$15-30
Suka Beach Inn	US$6-10
Yulia Beach Inn	US$8-30
Zet Inn	US$8-20

Legian

Ady's Inn	US$7-15
Legian Beach Bungalows	US$8-15
Legian Mas Beach Inn	US$8-12
LG Beach Club	US$15-25
Puri Damai Cottages I	US$6-12
Puri Tanah Lot Cottages	US$8-20
Rum Jungle Road Hotel	US$10-35
Sayang Beach Inn	US$8-30
Sinar Beach Cottages	US$10-15
Sinar Indah Beach Cottages	US$10-20
Three Brothers Inn	US$12-30

Seminyak

Mesari Beach Inn	US$8-20
Puri Cendana	US$15-25

Moderate Accommodations

Kuta, Legian, and Seminyak really excel when it comes to hotels in the US$25-75 price range. Most represent great value, since you'll get an a/c room with private bath and a swimming pool at prices well below the luxury hotels of Sanur or Nusa Dua.

Prices listed below are the "rack rates" published in their hotel brochures, though independent travelers should be able to negotiate discounts of 30-50% at the front desk. The rack rates are established for group tours but most owners are flexible about granting hefty discounts to walk-ins.

Tuban

Adhi Jaya Cottages	US$20-45
Karthi Inn	US$35-50
Melasti Beach Bungalows	US$40-80
Palm Beach Cottages	US$50-80
Palm Beach Inn	US$50-75
Sandi Phala Beach Resort	US$30-55

Kuta

Agung Beach Bungalows	US$25-45
Aneka Beach Bungalows	US$55-80
Asana Santhi Homestay	US$30-45
Bali Summer Hote	US$35-55
Bakungsari Cottages Kuta	US$25-45
Flora Beach Hotel	US$40-80
Ida Beach Inn	US$25-45
Kuta Beach Club	US$45-70
Kuta Seaview Cottages	US$55-80
Kuta Village Inn	US$25-45
La Walon Bungalows	US$20-55
Mimpi Bungalows	US$30-45
Poppies Cottages II	US$25-35
Ramayana Seaside Cottages	US$45-65
Sari Yasa Samudra Bungalows	US$30-65

Legian

Adika Sari Bungalows	US$35-65
Bali Niksoma Beach Cottages	US$25-60
Bali Coconut Hotel	US$25-60
Bruna Beach Hotel	US$20-40
Garden View Cottages	US$40-55
Hotel Baleka	US$20-40
Hotel Camplung Mas	US$45-80
Kuta Bungalows	US$30-45
Legian Beach Hotel	US$85-160
Legian Village Hotel	US$35-50
Maharta Beach Inn	US$45-60
Orchid Garden Cottages	US$15-35
Puspasari Beach Cottages	US$25-50
Puri Tantra Beach Bungalows	US$45-60

Seminyak

Baleka Beach Hotel	US$20-45
Bali Holiday Resort	US$55-75
Bali Village Hotel	US$45-80
Dhyana Pura Hotel	US$50-70
Legian Garden Cottages	US$40-55
Nusa di Nusa Hotel	US$35-45
Puri Bunga Cottages	US$55-75
Puri Naga Hotel	US$55-70
Ramah Village	US$45-60
Sari Uma Cottages	US$45-85
Sarinande Beach Inn	US$45-55
Sing Ken Ken	US$30-55
Surya Dharma Cottages	US$30-45
Topi Koki Hotel	US$45-60

Luxury Accommodations

Kuta is home to upscale hotels with every possible convenience, such as lobbies so large you get lost, open-air dining rooms, luxurious gardens, and evening *gamelan* performances around the swimming pool. Rates quoted below include the 17.5% government tax and service charges.

Tuban

Bali Dynasty Resort	US$110-250
Bali Garden Hotel	US$110-180
Bali Rani Hotel	US$60-90
Bintang Bali Hotel	US$140-220
Holiday Inn Bali Hai	US$140-200
Hotel Patra Jasa Bali	US$130-160
Kartika Plaza Hotel	US$140-380
Rama Beach Cottages	US$75-120
Risata Bali Resort	US$75-150
Santika Beach Hotel	US$110-180

Kuta

Maharani Hotel	US$75-100
Natour Kuta Beach Hotel	US$120-300
Poppies Cottages I	US$80-120
Rama Palace Hotel	US$85-200
Sahid Bali Seaside Hotel	US$90-240
The Bounty Hotel	US$75-150

Legian

Bali Anggrek Inn	US$55-165
Bali Intan Cottages	US$95-180
Bali Mandira Cottages	US$85-180
Bali Padma Hotel	US$120-360
Balisani Hotel	US$75-110
Kuta Jaya Cottages	US$90-140
Kul Kul Resort	US$90-140
Legian Beach Hotel	US$80-140
Mabisa Beach Side Hotel	US$65-130

Seminyak

Bali Agung Village	US$75-180
Bali Imperial Hotel	US$160-480
Bali Oberoi Hotel	US$220-480
Balisani Suites	US$120-250
Intan Bali Village	US$160-320
Persona Bali Hotel	US$100-180
The Legian Bali	US$180-450
Tjendana Paradise Resort	US$95-200

Kuta Restaurants

Kuta, Legian, Tuban, and Seminyak are packed with cafes and restaurants serving everything from Chinese seafood and Mexican tacos to Balinese steaks and fiery Padang dishes. Whether you choose a simple *warung* or a first-class retreat, the choices are excellent and reasonably priced.

Made's Warung: Recommended for people-watching, music, vibes, cappuccino, and tasty Indonesian specialties served in a very eclectic atmosphere that attracts bohemian drifters, local expats, Japanese tourists, and Aussie surfers. The multitiered, open-air cafe has great music and tasty dishes served by Balinese employees decked out in ridiculous T-shirts. Be sure to try the "half-half," a wonderful combination of gado gado and nasi campur. Jalan Pantai Kuta. Moderate.

Maharani Hotel Cafe: Enjoying a beachside meal during sunset hours can be a difficult assignment in Kuta since the beachside area is devoid of cafes, and luxury hotels to the south generally place their restaurants far back from the sand. One exception is the small cafe in front of the Maharani Hotel, which offers decent views and happy hour deals on both domestic and foreign beers. Go early for the best seats. Jalan Pantai Kuta. Moderate.

Mini Restaurant: There are dozens of seafood restaurants in Kuta where you select your fish from display cases and then select your sauce and preparation method—boiled, baked, fried, sautéed, etc. What puts the Mini—a surprisingly large operation despite the name—above the rest is the freshness of the fish and the enormous selection, not to mention the sheer size of the prawns. Jalan Legian. Moderate to Expensive.

Indah Sari Restaurant: A seafood-and-barbecue restaurant which serves well-prepared dishes, from prawns to grouper, that you can order either spicy or bland. Jalan Legian. Moderate.

Poppies Restaurant: Tucked away in a narrow alley and removed from the beer-chugging revelries of Kuta, Poppies guarantees upscale dining in a wonderfully romantic atmosphere. Set with candle-lit tables in a tropical garden environment, Kuta's original yuppie hangout features avocado seafood salads, sashimi, grilled lobster, and other Western dishes at reasonable prices. However, skip the Indonesian dishes (especially the gado gado), which are prepared blandly for timid Western palates. Make reservations or go early to secure a table. Poppies Gang I. Moderate.

Western Fast Food: Travelers adverse to Indonesian fare or tired of exotic seafood will be happy to note that Kuta now has many familiar fast-food joints. Prices aren't any lower than in Los Angeles, but it's amazing how identical the flavors are at Burger King, Pizza Hut, KFC, and McDonalds. Afterwards, head over to Hard Rock Café—it's like you never left home. Jalan Legian. Inexpensive.

TJ's Restaurant: Kuta's loveliest and most relaxing Mexican restaurant is a goldmine for delicious south-of-the-border specialties such as savory enchiladas, imaginative salads, and the tastiest margaritas west of Ensenada. Best of all is the idyllic atmosphere that combines tropical vegetation with ponds and swaying palm trees. Say hello to Jean Murniati, the gregarious owner who has lived on Bali for almost 30 years. Poppies Gang I. Moderate.

Legian Restaurants

Legian restaurants are unpretentious spots that serve great food at reasonable prices, but at times it can be difficult if not impossible to find anything resembling Balinese or Indonesian cuisine.

Joni's Bar and Restaurant: For something unique, enjoy a cocktail, Western meal, or gado gado salad while relaxing in the small pool at Joni's. Here, in a setting somewhat like a Star Wars scene, patrons dine in watery splendor while sitting on semi-submerged bar stools. The chief advantage is that inebriated customers won't knock their heads when they collapse from too many Mai Tais, though watery entrées may be a problem. Jalan Padma. Moderate.

Warung Kopi: Warung Kopi, universally recommended by expatriates, has five marble-topped tables facing the street and another ten in the rear garden, which provides an oasis from the surrounding honky-tonk atmosphere. The menu is eclectic: Indonesian fish, vegetable and rice dishes, Indian curries, Western beef and lamb. Jalan Legian. Moderate.

Yanies Restaurant: An old favorite serving Australian-style food since 1985 in a traditional thatched roof garden setting. The owner and his wife are infamous characters, to say the least. Jalan Tanjung Mekar. Moderate.

Rum Jungle Cafe: The original restaurant and accommodation center in the neighborhood still sets the standard for good vibes, reasonable prices, eclectic atmosphere, and friendly service, not to mention specialties such as pumpkin soup, fried "schnapper," malakoff (deep-fried

cheese on toast), and shepherd's pie. To the rear is a cozy pool room and mini-sushi bar. Jalan Rum Jungle (Jalan Pura Bagus Taruna). Moderate.

Glory Bar and Restaurant: Legian expatriates often recommend this large and rather cacophonous restaurant at the north end of Legian where you select your fish, sauce, and the method of preparation. Seafood choices include a variety of fish in Technicolor hues, giant prawns, strange-looking mollusks, mud crabs, and monstrous lobsters. Jalan Legian. Moderate to Expensive.

Warung Alle Zoo: Simple cafe with well-prepared meals and an upstairs buffet room. Jalan Double Six. Inexpensive.

Topi Koki: French restaurant and wine bar in a cozy hotel decorated with Francophile memorabilia. Jalan Pura Bagus Taruna. Moderate.

Poco Loco: Tucked away in a quiet side-street, spacious open-air Poco Loco serves Mexican specialties, Indonesian favorites, and margaritas that compete with those of TJ's. The restaurant also offers live music on weekends, from light jazz to Batak singers who crank out Mexican ballads. Jalan Padma Utara. Moderate.

Swiss Restaurant: Twenty years of operation makes this among the most venerable and famous restaurants on Bali, largely due to Jon Zurcher, the Swiss Consul General who represents his country from a small office in the rear. Entertainment ranges from Batak singers to Jon and his expatriate buddies attempting Dixieland classics for the amusement of their friends. Jalan Rum Jungle (Jalan Pura Bagus Taruna). Moderate.

Seminyak Restaurants

Restaurants in Seminyak tend to be somewhat expensive but certainly have far more atmosphere and style than those in Kuta and Legian.

Bali Agung Village: One of the prettiest places to stay and eat in Seminyak is the superbly located villa at the extreme north end of town, facing spectacular ricefields and the mountains to the north. European, Chinese, and Indonesian dishes are served in the poolside verandah—an oasis of calm and the perfect escape from the conundrum of hectic Kuta. Jalan Dhyana Pura. Moderate to Expensive.

Café Luna: The premier place to see-and-be-seen by cool Europeans who comprise much of the expatriate community. Here they sit—slowly smoking imported cigarettes and checking out the Gucci loafers on the adjacent diners. Pity the poor slob who arrives in anything less than a white Italian suit or avant-garde creation from a local designer. Jalan Seminyak. Moderate to Expensive.

La Lucciola: The final word in elegance, style, and location is this wonderful Italian restaurant about 10 minutes north of the Oberoi Hotel and facing deserted Kayu Aya Beach. La Lucciola is unquestionably the finest place to enjoy a cocktail at sunset and perhaps watch the local kung fu school go through their paces on the broad beach. The gay Australian-owned restaurant features seafood risotto, tuna with salsa verde, a wonderful antipasto platter, and tiramisu for dessert. Also, check out the tastefully designed bathrooms and muse upon the steel lines that support the open-air restaurant during heavy storms. Jalan Oberoi. Moderate to Expensive.

Café Krakatoa: Simple but popular cafe serving Western dishes, homebaked breads, and what they claim are the "best eggs Benedict in Southeast Asia." Laser disc movies are shown nightly at 2030. Jalan Seminyak. Inexpensive.

Pica Pica Tapa Bar: The only Spanish bar on the island serves *tapas* as well as paella, imported steaks, seafood, and the ever popular sangria. Jalan Dhyana Pura. Moderate.

Teras: A rooftop restaurant with open-air dining on a spacious courtyard and meals from bountiful salad buffets to all manner of seafoods. Another place favored by the local expatriate community. Jalan Legian. Moderate.

Goa 2001: Goa 2001 is generally regarded as a nightclub, though locals also claim it serves some of the best food in town at reasonable prices. To accompany your tasty meal, try the local "arak attack," a potent jolt of Balinese firewater, then retire to the cozy sushi room in the rear for a game of pool. Jalan Seminyak. Moderate.

Warisan Restaurant: A sophisticated Italian restaurant north of Seminyak surrounded by ricefields; Warisan sponsors special events and theme parties twice a month—look for posters in Seminyak. Annual events include Brazilian Carnaval with samba entertainment, Bastille Day attended by belly dancers and snake charmers, and AIDS benefits supported by local jazz musicians. Well worth attending if only to appreciate the eccentricities of the local expatriate commu-

nity. Jalan Kerobokan. Moderate to Expensive.

Double Six Restaurant: One of the more popular seaside restaurants with mostly Italian dishes and a limited seafood grill. Double Six is the place to dine in peace before night owls arrive around midnight and continue to party until the sun comes up. Jalan Double Six. Moderate to Expensive.

Gado Gado: A well-located restaurant facing the beach in the outer reaches of Seminyak, where many expatriates enjoy sunset cocktails and dinner before heading home for a quick nap—the so-called "disco nap." They rise around 2300 and head out for an all-night marathon at Goa 2001, Double Six, Gado Gado, or, heaven forbid, the Hard Rock Café down in touristy Kuta Beach. Jalan Dhyana Pura. Moderate to Expensive.

Riyoshi: Small and narrow, Riyoshi's wins the local award for the best sushi on the island, plus it's air-conditioned (important during the hotter months) and provides take-out service for homebodies. Diners can sit at the sushi counter for tempura, robata, or soba, or relax on tatami mats in typical Japanese fashion. Jalan Seminyak. Moderate.

Taj Mahal: Bali's finest Indian restaurant compensates for its remote location near the Oberoi Hotel with memorable dishes such as curries, dahl, and tandoor specialties, all created by a renowned Indian chef. No parking problems out here. Jalan Oberoi. Expensive.

Practicalities

Kuta and Legian are self-contained communities with money changers, postal services, travel agents, motorcycle shops, one-hour photo labs, and whatever else you could possibly need.

Tourist Information: The tourist offices in Kuta and Legian distribute a surprisingly good collection of brochures and schedules. Kuta and Legian used and new bookstores sell guides to Bali and Indonesia, but at fairly steep prices.

Money: Several banks around Kuta will exchange traveler's checks and provide cash advances on Visa and MasterCard. Money changers are quicker than banks and offer the same exchange rates on cash and traveler's checks.

Mail: Mail can be directed to the Kuta post office or, better yet, to any of the private postal agents in Tuban, Kuta, Legian, and Seminyak. The private postal agents are shown on the maps in this chapter.

INDONESIA

Telephone: International phone calls can be made from most hotels and the half-dozen wartel offices in Tuban, Kuta, Legian, and Seminyak. The least expensive calls are from government-operated Telekom Wartel offices rather than the privately operated wartel outlets.

The area code for most of Bali is 0361; other codes include Tabanan and Klungkung (0366), Amlapura (0363), and Singaraja (0362).

Transportation

Transport around and from Bali includes every possible option from public minibuses to private helicopters.

Air: Be sure to reconfirm your outbound ticket as most flights from Bali are fully booked. Those who fail to reconfirm departures may find themselves stranded on Bali—not a bad option if you're wealthy and self-employed.

Airlines with offices in the Grand Bali Beach Hotel in Sanur include Air France, Ansett Australia, British Airways, Cathay Pacific, Continental, Kayanmas Bali, Lufthansa, Malaysia Airlines, Qantas, Scandinavian Airlines, Singapore Airlines, and Thai Airways International.

Airline offices at the airport include Air New Zealand, Cathay Pacific, China Airlines, Garuda Indonesia, KLM Royal Dutch Airlines, Lufthansa, Merpati, Pelita Air Service, Qantas, Singapore Airlines, and Thai Airways International.

Bourag, Merpati, and Sempati have offices in Denpasar.

Bus: Buses to Java leave every morning 0600-0900 and evening 1700-2000 from the Ubung bus terminal in Denpasar. Destinations include Probolinggo (eight hours), Surabaya (10-12 hours), Yogyakarta (15-18 hours), and Jakarta (26-32 hours). Most buses are a/c and the crossing from Bali to Java is included in the fare.

The least expensive tickets are purchased directly from the bus company offices at Ubung terminal, while agents in Kuta and Legian add varying service charges from reasonable to ridiculous.

Minibus *(Bemo):* Minibuses (formerly called *bemos*) to the Tegal terminal in Denpasar depart from "*bemo* corner" in the middle of Kuta, while blue buses can be hailed on the main Kuta-Denpasar road.

From Tegal, you must take a three-wheeler across town to the appropriate terminal. Kereneng Terminal is for minibuses and *bemos* to

Ubud, Kintamani, Gianyar, Padangbai, Amlapura, and Tampaksiring. Ubung Terminal is for Singaraja, Gilimanuk, Bedugul.

Fares for public minibuses are set by the government and can be checked at the tourist offices in Kuta and Legian. To avoid problems, it's best to know the correct fare before taking any form of public transportation on the island.

Taxi: Metered taxis can be called in Kuta, Sanur, and Denpasar, but won't pick up passengers on streets controlled by the minibus cartels. Bali taxis and Praja taxis cost 1,000Rp for the first kilometer plus 500Rp for each additional kilometer.

SANUR BEACH

Bali's Waikiki is the quiet, safe, and more expensive alternative to Kuta and Legian. European and American tour groups come here to luxuriate in fine hotels, attend poolside performances of *legong* and *wayang,* and feast on Balinese seafood—everything except walk on the beach.

Sanur is a sleepy place where all the restaurants are hidden in hotel lobbies and nightlife fades away before midnight. On the other hand, the beach is broad and clean, swimming is safe, and sunrises over Nusa Penida are unforgettable.

Attractions

Sanur in the 1920s and '30s was the favored spot of Western artists such as Walter Spies and American anthropologist Margaret Mead. Most of the original residences have disappeared, except for the former home of Jean Le Mayeur, the Belgian impressionist painter who moved to Sanur in 1932 and stayed for 26 years. The house-turned-museum is shabby, smothered by the Bali Beach Hotel, and often closed; knock loudly, somebody will open the door.

Sanur water sports are superior to those in Kuta or Legian. Visitors can rent brightly painted outriggers to visit offshore islands, water-ski, tour the lagoon in glass-bottomed boats, snorkel over coral gardens, dive, spearfish, and windsurf.

Culture, of the organized type, is equally plentiful. Public performances of Balinese dance are given nightly in all major hotels. Dinner plus show costs about US$20, but remember that many of Bali's finest dancers work the hotels in Sanur and Nusa Dua.

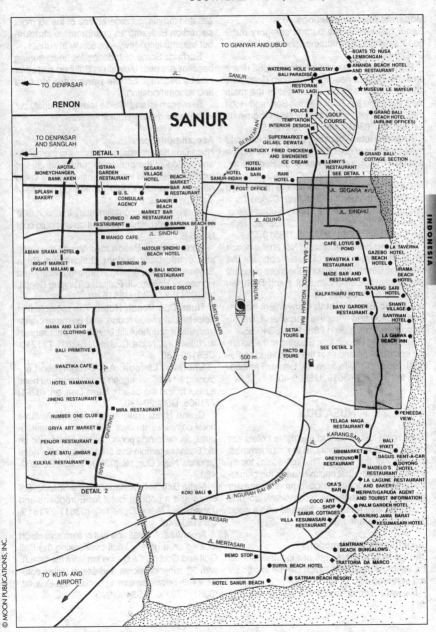

TO GIANYAR AND UBUD

TO DENPASAR

RENON

TO DENPASAR
AND SANGLAH

JL. SANUR

SANUR

BOATS TO NUSA
LEMBONGAN

WATERING HOLE HOMESTAY
BALI PARADISE

ANANDA BEACH HOTEL
AND RESTAURANT

RESTORAN
SATU LAGI

MUSEUM LE MAYEUR

POLICE

TEMPTATION
INTERIOR DESIGN

GRAND BALI
BEACH HOTEL
(AIRLINE OFFICES)

GOLF
COURSE

SUPERMARKET
GELAEL DEWATA

DETAIL 1

KENTUCKY FRIED CHICKEN
AND SWENSENS
ICE CREAM

GRAND BALI
COTTAGE SECTION

LENNY'S
RESTAURANT
SEE DETAIL 1

APOTIK,
MONEYCHANGER,
BANK AKEN

ISTANA
GARDEN
RESTAURANT

SEGARA
VILLAGE
HOTEL

HOTEL
TAMAN
SARI

HOTEL
SANUR-INDAH

RANI
HOTEL

SPLASH
BAKERY

U.S.
CONSULAR
AGENCY

BEACH
MARKET
BAR AND
RESTAURANT

POST OFFICE

JL. SEGARA AYU

JL. SINDHU

SANUR
BEACH
MARKET BAR
AND RESTAURANT

JL. AGUNG

BORNEO
RESTAURANT

BARUNA BEACH INN

JL. SINDHU

MANGO CAFE

ABIAN SRAMA HOTEL

NATOUR SINDHU
BEACH HOTEL

CAFE LOTUS
POND

LA TAVERNA

GAZEBO HOTEL

BEACH HOTEL

NIGHT MARKET
(PASAR MALAM)

BERINGIN 59

BALI MOON
RESTAURANT

SWASTIKA I
RESTAURANT

IRAMA
BEACH
HOTEL

MADE BAR AND
RESTAURANT

SUBEC DISCO

TANJUNG SARI
HOTEL

SHANTI
VILLAGE

KALPATHARU HOTEL

MAMA AND LEON
CLOTHING

BAYU GARDEN
RESTAURANT

SANTRIAN
HOTEL

BALI PRIMITIVE

LA GHAWA
BEACH INN

SWAZTIKA CAFE

SETIA
TOURS

SEE DETAIL 2

HOTEL RAMAYANA

JINENG RESTAURANT

PACTO
TOURS

PENEEDA
VIEW.

MIRA RESTAURANT

NUMBER ONE CLUB

TELAGA NAGA
RESTAURANT

GRIYA ART MARKET

JL. KARANGSARI

BALI
HYATT

PENJOR RESTAURANT

MINIMARKET

BAGUS RENT-A-CAR

CAFE BATU JIMBAR

GREYHOUND
RESTAURANT

DUYONG
HOTEL

KULKUL RESTAURANT

MADELO'S
RESTAURANT

DETAIL 2

OKA'S
BAR

LA LAGUNE RESTAURANT
AND BAKERY

KOKI BALI

MERPATI/GARUDA AGENT
AND TOURIST INFORMATION

COCO ART
SHOP

PALM GARDEN HOTEL

SANUR
COTTAGES

WARUNG JAWA BARAT

VILLA KESUMASARI
RESTAURANT

KESUMASARI HOTEL

JL. NGURAH RAI (BYPASS)

JL. SRI KESARI

SANTRIAN
BEACH BUNGALOWS

BEMO STOP

JL. MERTASARI

TO KUTA AND
AIRPORT

SURYA BEACH HOTEL

TRATTORIA DA MARCO

HOTEL SANUR BEACH

SATRIAN BEACH RESORT

0   500 m

JL. BATUR SARI

JL. SEKUTA

JL. BAJA LETKOL NGURAH RAI

JL. TANJUNG SARI

JL. BERATARAN

INDONESIA

© MOON PUBLICATIONS, INC.

Moderate Accommodations

Sanur has little in the budget category but a good selection of middle-priced hotels in the US$25-50 range.

Rani Hotel: Cheap *losmen* under US$10 are on Jalan Segara near the American Consulate and the police station, plus west of the main road you'll find the Rani, Taman Sari, and Hotel Sanur Indah with old but fairly clean rooms. Jl. Segara, tel. (0361) 288578, US$10-15.

Ananda Hotel: An older place with clean and quiet rooms very near the beach and behind the restaurant of the same name. Jl. Segara, tel. (0361) 288327, US$12-20.

Yulia Homestay: Three simple homestays are found at the north end of Jalan Danau Tamblingan, just opposite the sleazy Subec Disco. Check with the shop owners. Jl. Danau Tamblingan 38, tel. (0361) 288236, US$10-15.

Watering Hole Homestay: Not on the beach but at the northern end of Sanur opposite the Hotel Bali Beach, and among the more pleasant inexpensive places in Sanur. Jl. Hang Tuah, tel. (0361) 288289, US$12-18.

Gazebo Beach Hotel: Convenient beachfront location and attractive gardens. Jl. Danau Tamblingan, tel. (0361) 288212, US$40-65.

Semawang Beach Inn: Situated at the southern end of Sanur and near the beach and somewhat seedy nightlife area. Jl. Danau Tamblingan, tel. (0361) 288619, US$25-40.

NUSA DUA

Bali's most luxurious and exclusive hotels are located on Bukit Peninsula, at the southernmost extremity of the island. This full-scale, totally self-contained tourist enclave forms the centerpiece of the Indonesian government's master plan for regional tourism—a completely isolated tourist enclave fortunately blessed with a good beach and decent diving.

Bukit Peninsula Attractions

Several worthwhile sights are located around the desolate peninsula which can be toured by taxi or rented car.

Uluwatu: Top draw is this small but superbly

situated temple, considered one of the six most sacred on Bali, with an unimpressive structure but breathtaking views, especially at sunset.

Surfing: Some of Indonesia's finest surfing beaches are near Uluwatu at Sulubun and other nearby beaches. Simple *warung* provide food and accommodation.

Serangan Island: Turtle Island is touristy but worth visiting during major festivals.

Accommodations

Nusa Dua has international chains in the southern portion of the peninsula, and a handful of locally owned and less expensive hotels in the northern stretches near the fishing village of Tanjung Benoa.

Most hotels offer complimentary transportation from the airport, while metered taxis should cost US$6-8.

Rasa Sayang Beach Inn: Among the clean and comfortable budget choices are Rasa Sayang, Pondok Agung, Tanjung Mekar, and Homestay Hasam. Jl. Pratama, Tanjung Benoa, tel. (0361) 771643, US$15-40.

Nusa Dua Beach Hotel: The region's first hotel has over 400 rooms and Balinese craftsmanship throughout its bewildering acreage of architecture. Nusa Dua, tel. (0361) 771210, US$180-480.

Sheraton Lagoon: A 276-room resort enclosing an artificial lagoon so massive you need a map to find the beach. Nusa Dua, tel. (0361) 771906, US$220-480.

Grand Hyatt Bali: An almost unbelievable hotel complex with over 700 rooms, 10 restaurants, six swimming pools, squash courts, and an old Balinese temple that still stands on the hotel grounds. Nusa Dua, tel. (0361) 771234, US$200-480.

Melia Bali Sol: Managed by the Spanish Sol chain and a popular hotel for Europeans and Japanese. Nusa Dua, tel. (0361) 771510, US$180-240.

Amanusa: A small and highly exclusive resort located on a grassy knoll overlooking the Bali Golf and Country Club, one km from the beach, with 32 superior rooms and seven suites complete with private swimming pools. Nusa Dua, tel. (0361) 772333, US$460-940.

Map: NUSA DUA AND TANJUNG BENOA

SRIWIJAYA RESORT RESTAURANT
CHINESE TEMPLE
BELUGA WATER SPORTS
TANJUNG BENOA
POLICE
MEKAR SARI SEASPORTS
ELMI BEACH RESORT
BMR (WATER SPORTS)
SORGA NUSA DUA HOTEL
BENOA BEHARI SEASPORTS
TONNY MARINDO SEASPORTS
RASA SAYANG INN
WATER SPORTS CENTER
HASAN BUNGALOWS
BALI RESORT
BALI PALACE HOTEL
MATAHARI TERBIT BUNGALOWS
THALASSO BALI HOTEL
MIRAGE HOTEL
NYOMAN BALI
NUSA DUA MEDICAL SERVICE
BALI ROYAL HOTEL
PURI TANJUNG HOTEL
HEMINGWAY BAR
TAMAN SARI HOTEL
PURI JOMA HOTEL
BALI TROPIC PALACE
BADUNG STRAIT
CLUB MED
NUSA DUA BEACH HOTEL
SHERATON NUSA INDAH HOTEL
TO AIRPORT AND KUTA
JL. NGURAH RAI BYPASS
BEMO TERMINAL
WARTEL
PUBLIC TELEPHONE
NUSA DUA
BANK
POST OFFICE
CAR RENTAL
SHERATON LAGOON
MELIA BALI SOL
BUALU VILLAGE
GOLF COURSE
GARUDA
GALLERIA SHOPS
GRAND HYATT
TO UNGUSAN AND ULUWATU
JL. PANTAI MENGIAT
PUTRI BALI HOTEL
HOTEL BUALU
HILTON HOTEL
GOLF COURSE
AMANUSA
SURFING CAMP AND OUTRIGGER RENTALS
NIKKO NUSA DUA HOTEL
TEMPLE
JL. PEMINGE
0 1 km
© MOON PUBLICATIONS, INC.
INDONESIA

CENTRAL BALI

Bali's scenic wonders, architectural heritage, and artistic achievements are best experienced in the land located between Denpasar and the mountains. Central Bali is a region blessed with terraced ricefields carved exquisitely out of hills and valleys, densely settled villages surrounded by groves of coconut palms, and long stretches of sandy beaches almost completely unvisited by foreign travelers.

Highlights can easily be seen on day-trips from the southern beach resorts, but those who wish to enjoy a more traditional side of Bali can easily steer clear of the tourist stomping grounds and spend a few days unwinding in a remote Balinese village.

Sightseeing Problems

The major attractions are described below, but be forewarned that all are badly overrun with super-aggressive salesmen who rank among the most obnoxious in Asia. Quite honestly, it's unnecessary to visit any of the following temples if you intensely dislike touts and beggars.

To minimize the ordeal, never join a group tour (unless you want to serve as a moving target) but rather hire a motorcycle or jeep, get an early start, and bring along patience and humor.

Most temples now collect fees for parking, entrance, and sash rental, a minor irritation that can be avoided by bringing along your own sash and sarong. Visitors wearing shorts or immodest halter tops may be denied entrance; arrive well dressed or expect to be turned away.

DENPASAR

Bali's largest city is a disaster: roaring motorcycles, smelly buses, unending congestion, and drab modern architecture. Denpasar is also the island's transportation center through which all *bemos* circulate, and the government hub for postal services, immigration, hospitals, and telecommunications. Conduct sightseeing and official business early; government offices and museums close in the early afternoon.

Services

Consulates: Denpasar has consulates for or honorary consuls for Australia, France, Germany, Netherlands, Norway, Denmark, Sweden, Finland, Switzerland, and the United States.

Mail: The main Denpasar post office with the poste restante for the island is southeast of city center in the Renon District.

Immigration: The immigration office for Bali is also in the Renon District just around the corner from the GPO.

Attractions

Denpasar (Badung is the local name) has few charms aside from an excellent museum and some antique shops on the main road. First visit the Badung Tourist Office for maps and information on transportation and upcoming festivals.

Bali Museum: The Bali Museum off Puputan Square houses an outstanding collection of masks, puppets, and archaeological treasures from Neolithic implements to recent discoveries. Museum architecture incorporates three distinct styles of Balinese palaces: the main building resembles the Karangasem palaces of eastern Bali, the left structure is modeled after the northern Singaraja style, and on the right is a Tabanan prototype from western Bali. Adjacent Pura Jaganatha is a state

legong dancers

BOB RACE

INDONESIA

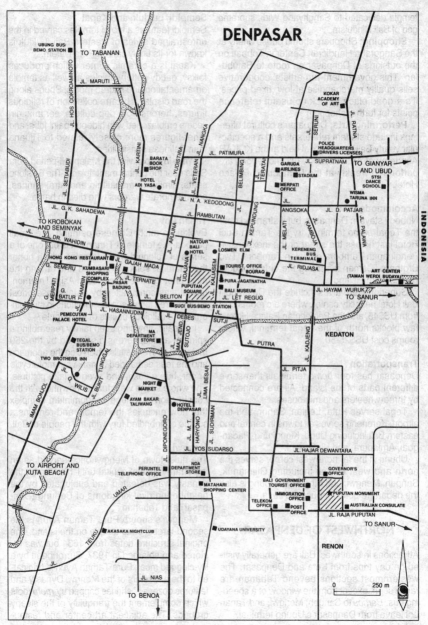

DENPASAR

TO TABANAN

UBUNG BUS/
BEMO STATION

JL. MARUTI

JL. HOS COKROAMINOTO

JL. KARTINI

JL. SETIABUDI

BARATA
BOOK
SHOP

HOTEL
ADI YASA

JL. YUDISTIRA

JL. VETERAN

JL. NANGKA

JL. PATIMURA

BELIMBING

JL. TERATAI

JL. N. A. KEDODONG

JL. RAMBUTAN

JL. G. K. SAHADEWA

TO KROBOKAN
AND SEMINYAK

JL. DR. WAHIDIN

G. SEMERU

HONG KONG RESTAURANT

KUMBASARI
SHOPPING
COMPLEX

G. MERPATI

G. BATUR

G. THAMRIN

KMK

JL. ARJUNA

NATOUR
BALI
HOTEL

JL. GAJAH MADA

JL. UDAYANA

JL. TERNATE

PASAR
BADUNG

JL. BELITON

LOSMEN ELIM

JL. KALIASEM

PUPUTAN
SQUARE

PURA JAGATNATHA

BALI MUSEUM

JL. LET REGUG

KOKAR
ACADEMY
OF ART

JL. RATNA

JL. SERUNI

POLICE
HEADQUARTERS
(DRIVERS LICENSES)

JL. SUPRATNAM

GARUDA
AIRLINES

STADIUM

MERPATI
OFFICE

JL.
ANGSOKA

JL. MELATI

JL. KAMBOJA

KERENENG
BUS
TERMINAL

JL. RIDJASA

TOURIST OFFICE
BOURAQ

TO GIANYAR
AND UBUD

STSI
DANCE
SCHOOL

WISMA
TARUNA INN

JL. D. PATJAR

JL. PALAWA

ART CENTER
(TAMAN WERDI BUDAYA)

JL. HAYAM WURUK
TO SANUR

INDONESIA

PEMECUTAN
PALACE HOTEL

JL. HASANNUDIN

SUCI BUS/BEMO STATION

JL. DEBES

SUTJI

JL. KADJENG

KEDATON

TEGAL BUS/BEMO
STATION

TWO BROTHERS INN

G. WILIS

JL. G. BUKIT TUNGGAL

MA
DEPARTMENT
STORE

JL. MAJ JENG.

SUTOJO

JL. LIMA BESAR

JL. PUTRA

JL. PITJA

NIGHT
MARKET

JL. IMAM BONJOL

AYAM BAKAR
TALIWANG

HOTEL
DENPASAR

JL. M. T.
HARYONO

JL. SUDIRMAN

JL. DIPONEGORO

JL. YOS SUDARSO

JL. HAJAR DEWANTARA

TO AIRPORT AND
KUTA BEACH

PERUNTEL
TELEPHONE OFFICE

NDA
DEPARTMENT
STORE

MATAHARI
SHOPPING CENTER

UMAR

TEUKU

AKASAKA NIGHTCLUB

UDAYANA UNIVERSITY

JL. NIAS

TO BENOA

BALI GOVERNMENT
TOURIST OFFICE

IMMIGRATION
OFFICE

TELEKOM
OFFICE

POST
OFFICE

JL. RAJA PUPUTAN

GOVERNOR'S
OFFICE

PUPUTAN MONUMENT

AUSTRALIAN CONSULATE

TO SANUR

RENON

0   250 m

© MOON PUBLICATIONS, INC.

temple dedicated to Sanghyang Widi, supreme god of Bali Hinduism.

Shopping: Shoppers should pause briefly at the Sanggraha Handicraft Center in Tohpati on the outskirts of Denpasar en route to Batubulan. This government-run artists' cooperative sells quality merchandise at low, fixed prices; it's a good place to pick up useful reference points for further shopping.

Performing Arts: Denpasar's cultural offerings include student rehearsals and a spectacular yearly Bali Arts Festival held at the KOKAR Academy of Art. *Wayang kulit* and *legong* are performed weekly at the Pemecutan Palace Hotel.

Accommodations

Nobody stays in Denpasar, but if stranded near the Tegal *bemo* terminal, try the Taman Suci Hotel just across the street or the inexpensive Penginapan Tambora on Jalan Tambora. Two Brothers Losmen is among the oldest budget places on the island.

Superior alternatives include the Dutch-built Bali Hotel near city center, where a/c rooms cost from US$45, and the Pemecutan Palace Hotel a few blocks north of the Tegal terminal, where rooms cost US$25-50.

Transportation

Denpasar has four *bemo* terminals that serve different parts of the island. All are connected by three-wheelers and minibuses.

Tegal serves Kuta, Legian, Sanur, and the airport. Kereneng serves all towns in central and eastern Bali including Ubud, Klungkung, Padangbai, Amlapura, and Kintamani.

Ubung in the far northwest corner serves the north and west of Bali including Gilimanuk, Sangeh, Mengwi, and Singaraja. Ubung is also the departure point for buses to Java.

NORTHWEST OF DENPASAR

Attractions in southwest Bali are generally visited on day-trips from Kuta and Denpasar. The westernmost sections beyond Tabanan are rarely seen, except from the window of a speeding bus. *Bemos* to Sangeh, Mengwi, and Tanah Lot leave from Denpasar's Ubung terminal.

Sempidi, Lukluk, and Kapal

Sempidi features a trio of temples carved in the unrestrained styles of western Bali. Lukluk is known for its finely carved Pura Dalem.

Kapal is a ceramic center which produces folksy, gaudy pottery articles as well as temple ornamentation and sacred motifs. Shops along the road display a bizarre collection of religious figures, heroes from pop culture, ceramic girl scouts emblazoned with hideous paint jobs, and other figures more closely related to Tijuana than Balinese sensibilities.

While in Kapal, visit the Majapahit-period Pura Sada near the central marketplace. The 64 stone seats, similar to megalithic ancestral shrines, commemorate warriors who died in battle.

Tanah Lot

Evoking a misty Chinese painting, the small pagoda-like temple at Tanah Lot is but one of a series of splendid water temples which honor the guardian spirits of the sea and among the most photographed temples in Asia. The monument was constructed by a Javanese priest remembered for his successful efforts in strengthening the religious beliefs of the people.

Ironically, anything even faintly resembling a spiritual atmosphere is dissipated by the 250 meters of souvenir stalls which clog the approach and the fees demanded to park your motorcycle or car, hire a sash, and even to take pictures. The whole scene went further downhill with the construction of a huge condominium complex that now encircles the temple and remains a source of unbridled fury with the people of Bali.

Mengwi

The quiet town of Mengwi once served as an important regional capital until 1891 when the dynasty was defeated and subjugated by the neighboring rival kingdoms of Badung (Denpasar) and Tabanan.

Mengwi's superb Pura Taman Ayun is the second-largest state temple on the island. The original structure dates from 1634 but was restored and enlarged in 1937. Surrounded by a lily-clogged moat, Pura Taman Ayun is dedicated to the ancestors of the Mengwi Dynasty and features dozens of shrines capped by *meru* roofs which complement the tranquility of the sleepy grounds. The adjacent art center and restaurant are equally deserted except when tour buses arrive.

Sangeh

Built by the royal family of Mengwi in the 17th century, the holy monkey forest of Sangeh is dedicated to Vishnu as a place of quiet meditation. Today it functions as a *subak* temple where hundreds of wild and aggressive monkeys earn their keep by stealing glasses, cameras, and hats from tourists. Before entering the darkened walkway, secure all valuables and carry a stick to fend off the beasts. Booty can sometimes be repurchased from Balinese touts who control the mischievous animals.

Visitors foolish enough to arrive with a tour group will find Sangeh a rude place of pestering peddlers and begging children; otherwise, it's a quiet and serene nature reserve in the middle of an enchanted forest.

DENPASAR TO UBUD

The road from Denpasar to Ubud has evolved into a nonstop lineup of villages that specialize in particular crafts, including junk churned out for indiscriminate tourists and high-quality art priced accordingly. From Denpasar, first visit the Sanggraha Craft Center for a general overview of crafts at fixed prices. Visitors staying in Kuta, Sanur, or Nusa Dua should leave early enough to catch the outstanding *barong* performance at 0900 in Batubulan.

Batubulan

Renowned for its decorative stonecarving, Batubulan offers a handful of shops where child artisans chip away to liberate the heroes, gods, and demons from the silent blocks. Stone sculpture is seldom bought by tourists and therefore remains a nearly intact artform.

The talent of its artisans can be seen on the gate of Batubulan's Pura Puseh, only 150 meters east of the main road. The outstanding gateway is mindful of South Indian gateways, though the sculptures aren't old but modern copies taken from library books borrowed from the archaeological service.

Batubulan's great attraction is the daily 0900 performance of the *barong*. Shows are given

at several locations marked by parked tourist buses. While strictly geared to the tourist, all are professional and provide great photographic opportunities.

Celuk

Bali's silver- and goldsmithing centers are located at Kuta, Kamasan near Klungkung, and in Celuk, where generations of craftsmen have maintained their hereditary trade. Silver filigree work here is amazingly detailed with designs of vivid imagination. Prices soar when the tourist buses pull up between 1000 and 1130 but return to more sensible levels in the early afternoon.

Sukawati and Batuan

These large crafts villages 15 km from Denpasar specialize in both wind chimes and *wayang kulit* production, while puppet masters still practice their craft in Puri Sukawati. Shopping is best in the two-story Pasar Seni just opposite the marketplace.

Batuan is a painting and weaving village where young painters continue to paint in traditional styles and performances of *baris* and *topeng* are given in the evenings.

Mas

Mas is the woodcarving center of Bali where some shops churn out mass-produced knockoffs for the international market, while others stock exquisite and pricey pieces produced by the hands of Balinese masters.

Ida Bagu Gelodog, Ida Bagus Ambara, Ida Bagus Anom, and I Wayan Muka carve phantasmagoric masks used in traditional dramas. You can continue up to Bali or head east to Blahbatuh.

Blahbatuh

The remarkable Pura Gaduh features a massive head of the fearsome mythological giant, Kebo Iwo, a legendary strongman who served as the final minister of Bedulu prior to its conquest by the Majapahit Kingdom in 1343. It's said he carved with his fingernails many of the ancient stone monuments on Bali.

The nearby village of Bona is known for its basketry and nightly performances of *kechak*. Unfortunately, many of the companies have lost their touch and now hack through overpriced and disappointing shows.

Bukit Dharma

North of Blahbatuh near Kutri is the hill of Bukit Dharma, from where a steep path leads to the worn but arresting statue of King Airlangga's mother. Surrounded by flames, she is in the shape of the six-armed goddess of death Durga delivering the death blow atop a bull possessed by a demon; considered one of the most finely wrought sculptures left from the early Pejeng Kingdom. Views of Sanur and eastern Bali can be enjoyed through the fields of coconut palms.

Gianyar

The small, bustling administrative center of Gianyar is known for its hand-woven and hand-dyed textiles produced by textile shops and factories scattered along the main road. The old Gianyar Palace in the center of town is one of the few royal palaces that survived the Dutch invasion in the early 20th century. It's closed to the public but visitors can peer in through the gates.

Sidan Pura Dalem

Gianyar is disappointing, but Pura Dalem near Sidan is perhaps Bali's finest Temple of the Dead. To the right of the extraordinary split-gate entrance stands a *kulkul* drum tower covered with reliefs of tormented sinners being punished by hungry dogs and devil giants. To the left is Pura Rajapati, capped by three electric lights! Beyond the gate in the right corner is the throne of witch-queen Rangda. Don't miss this temple.

UBUD

Ubud—the art and culture center of Bali—is the place to get closer to the *real* Bali. Culturally speaking, Ubud is to Bali as Yogyakarta is to Java and Kyoto to Japan.

Ubud has grown dramatically in recent years yet still lacks a tourist infrastructure; big hotels with nightclubs and golf courses are not here, though luxurious bungalows with comfortable amenities are springing up by the week.

Your first impression on arrival will be negative. Central Ubud is a messy place plagued with belching *bemos,* an uninspiring modern market, and tacky souvenir shops. Don't be discouraged. Within five minutes of *bemo* corner you'll discover idyllic *losmen* perched precariously in the middle of verdant ricefields, splashing rivers filled with smiling children, and small villages where many of Bali's finest artists can teach you the secrets of batik, *gamelan, barong,* mask carving, painting, and the art of the *dalang.*

The Art

Ubud was popularized in the 1930s by Walter Spies and Rudolf Bonnet, two Western artists who moved here to study and then revolutionized contemporary Balinese art. At the time, traditional religious art had degenerated into highly formalized and rigid forms no longer in demand by the Balinese themselves.

German artist Spies and Dutchman Bonnet demonstrated to the Balinese artists that painting could be free of set formulas, using real people in a natural environment rather than courtly models. They introduced the concept of the three dimensions, the imaginative use of strong colors, modern graphic elements, a wider range of subject matter, and provided the materials for the work. A new realism was born which soon developed into a sophisticated, naturalistic style.

Ubud and neighboring communities today support hundreds of artisans who are constantly creating new styles of painting and sculpture.

Attractions

Ubud Museum: Puri Lukisan ("Palace of Paintings") includes a range of art spanning the years from the 1930s to the present, arranged in chronological order to demonstrate the evolution of contemporary styles. Set around beautiful gardens of fountains, statues, and pools, Puri Lukisan features exclusively Balinese art created by Kembang, Lempad, Medja, Gerudug, and a small room with examples of the gaudy Young Artists School. Unfortunately, the non-air-conditioned museum is poorly lit and neglected to the point of scandal.

Antonio Blanco House: Erotic sketches and the illustrated poetry of Ubud's mad Filipino-Catalan artist can be viewed inside his private residence in Campuan. Better than the gallery is the airy workspace where Antonio watches American soap operas on his satellite TV.

Museum Neka: Ubud's finest museum exhibits painters from all over Indonesia as well as foreign artists who have worked on Bali.

The complex is divided into seven buildings

arranged around distinct styles and artistic movements: Room 1 offers Kamasan and Pengosekan artwork; Room 2 features 16 outstanding pieces by I Gusti Nyoman Lempad; Room 3 is devoted to Affandi portraits, three dancers by Anton, and works by Azia; Room 4 specializes in foreign artists such as Spies, Bonnet, and Arie Smit; Room 5 boasts more work by Meier, Snel, Blanco, Friend, Covarrubias, and 15 outstanding works by W.G. Hofker, a Dutch artist who lived on Bali from 1938 to 1944; Room 6 serves as a pavilion-library. Neka is a superb art trip.

Artist Villages: Penestanan, a small village one km through the ricefields beyond Campuan, is where the Young Artists School developed in the mid-1950s under the influence of Arie Smit. Here, strong colors and bold modern designs are favored over the soft pastels of their predecessors; it's a style not beloved by everyone.

Pengosekan, five km south of Ubud, is another famous artist village known for its classical traditions and production of more lucrative decorative arts. Homestays and study groups are found in both villages.

Monkey Forest: Monkey Forest Road curves around the perimeter of Ubud's leading tourist temple; wear a sash and feed the baby monkeys (hold onto your camera).

Walks around Ubud

Ubud's finest experience isn't touring museums or temples, but rather a long day of meandering through the stunning ricefields, deep gorges, and swift flowing rivers which surround Ubud. Suddenly, Bali becomes a magical place, far removed from the hype and hustle of the tourist traps.

Most of the following routes are too far for hikers but with a bicycle, motorcycle, or even a car you can follow the paths and stop whenever the mood strikes. There's also plenty of tourists driving around these roads, so if you hike and get tired, you should be able to hitch a ride back to Ubud.

Northern Ricefields: Ubud's best scenery is north through the fields to Petulu. Motorbikes can maneuver along the narrow paths, but most are now wide enough to handle cars and jeeps.

From *bemo* corner near the cinema, head north through Sambahan, Sakti, and Bentuyung to the right fork toward Jun Jun Gan. Turn left at the intersection in Jun Jun Gan, pass the temple, and take the right fork to Petulu and the heron

sanctuary. Rather than continuing down the busy main road, return to Jun Jun Gan and head south past the small temple to Kutuh and the Neka Art Gallery in Ubud.

Monkey Forest Walk: Walk south down Monkey Forest Road, pause for coffee and music at Kubu Ku Windchimes, and continue south to Pengosekan and then west to Sing Kerta. Then it's north to Penestanan and back to Ubud; a wonderful tour of monkeys, windchimes, and artist villages.

Northwest to Sayan: Take the trail north under the viaduct (*before* the river) to Keliki and Yeh Tengah, then west to Kelusa and the main road at Payangan. Pause at Sayan Terrace Cottages for coffee and explore the scenic Ayung River valley before returning to Ubud.

East to Pejeng: Hike east or drive from the Apotik to the Petanu River, Titiapi, and Pejeng to tour the temples, the museum, Yeh Pulu, and Goa Gajah; an outstanding combination of scenery and history.

Budget Accommodations

Ubud has over 100 *losmen* that offer simple but clean rooms for US$5-25, constructed to resemble traditional Balinese family compounds rather than the commercialized resorts of Kuta and Sanur. Some are residences of painters and dancers who offer personal instruction on the performing arts.

The Bina Wisata Tourist Office near the main crossroads can tell you about budget homestays operated by performing artists, upcoming festivals, dance performances, shuttles down to Kuta and Candidasa, and proper dress for temple touring.

The sheer range is almost staggering, though homestays are most plentiful down Monkey Forest Road and tucked away on the small lanes in all directions. Others, less touristy and much quieter, are found in the neighboring villages of Campuan, Penestanan, Peliatan, and Pengosekan.

After arriving in Ubud, it's best to inspect a few for the perfect combination of atmosphere and amenities. Travelers who wish to escape the schlock shops of Ubud should go directly to one of the smaller villages mentioned above or check those homestays well off Monkey Forest Road.

INDONESIA

To Penelokan

To Pejeng

JL. PETULU

JL. RAYA UBUD

Andong

■ POLICE

To Junjungan

JL. TIRTA TAWAR

Kutuh

JEDBOGADUNG

■ TELEKOM WARTEL

■ MUNUT ART GALLERY

★ PELIATAN DANCE

To Tegal Lantang

JL. SRIWEDARI

Taman

■ NEKA ART GALLERY

★ SENIWATI ART GALLERY

★ LEMPAD HOUSE

OKA KARTINI'S ■

JL. SUGRIWA

JL. JEMBAWAN

■ POST OFFICE

■ WENA

To Sakti and Junjungan

JL. SUWETA

UBUD

JL. KAJENG

★ SANTI

HANS SNEL GARDEN RESTAURANT ■

SITI (HANS SNEL) BUNGALOW ■

■ SUCI INN

HOTEL PURI ★ SAREN AGUNG

MARKET

■ BCA BANK

★ NIRVANA'S

■ MERTA

SUARTHA PENSION ■

■ YOGYA CAFE

MUMBUL CAFE ■

CAFE LOTUS ■

POSTAL AGENT ■

UBUD MUSEUM (PURI LUKISAN) ★

JL. RAYA UBUD

CASA LUNA ■

ARY'S TELEKOM ■

TOURIST OFFICE ■

■ KERTA

To Sayan and Penelokan

JL. RAYA UBUD

★ MUSEUM NEKA

● YASA BUNGALOWS

● PITA MAHA

● WISATA COTTAGES

● HOTEL CAMPUHAN (TJAMPUHAN)

PURA DALEM ★ UBUD

GRIYA BARBEQUE ■

MENARA RESTAURANT ■

MURNI CAFE ■

OKA WATT'S SUNSET BUNGALOWS ●

■ SHANTI

HAPPY INN ●

● PONDOK UBUD

Campuhan

● ANANDA COTTAGES

BEGGAR'S BUSH ●

★ ANTONIO BLANCO HOUSE

● BALI UBUD

● SARI BAMBOO

JAGI ●

Penestanan

To Gianyar

Peliatan

Teges

★ AGUNG RAI ART GALLERY

To Mas and Denpasar

PELIATAN

● RONI
● BADRI
● PURI AYA
● PURI ASRI

● SITI BUNGALOWS

● MATAHARI

TEBESAYA

★ PENGOSEKAN ARTIST COMMUNITY

Pengosekan

Padang Tegal

Tebesaya

★ PADANG TEGAL DANCE

● ARTINI

HANOMAN

★ AGUNG RAI ART MUSEUM

■ DIRTY DUCK DINER
■ PERAMA TRANSPORT

● JAYA 2 BUNGALOWS

● KEBUN INDAH

To Batuan and Celuk

■ Café WAYAN
● MANDIA
● PURI GARDEN
● SRI BUNGALOW
● KARSI
● IBUNDA INN
● FIBRA INN
● UBUD TERRACE
● PERTIWI BUNGALOWS
● VILLA RASA SAYANG
● JAYA BUNGALOW
● DEWI AYU
● UBUD INN
MONKEY FOREST RD

★ CHAMPLUNG SARI
★ KUBU KU WINDCHIMES

● AGUNG RAKA

● PONDOK UBUD

LEMPUNG ACCOMMODATIONS ●
PANDE PERMAI ●
MONKEY FOREST HIDEAWAY ★
MONKEY FOREST
★ PURA DALEM

Nyuh Kuning

● ALAM INDAH

● BALI SPIRIT HOTEL

Ubud

River

Katiklantang

To Sayan and Denpasar

To Sayan and Denpasar

INDONESIA

100 yds
100 m

© MOON PUBLICATIONS, INC.

Some places continue to quote prices in *rupiah,* but after the currency crisis of 1997-98, many now quote room rates in U.S. dollars. All give discounts for longer stays, so be sure to ask if you intend to stay for more than a few days in a single spot.

The following suggestions give only a small sampling of the possibilities.

Monkey Forest Road

Dewi Ayu	US$6-24
Fibra Inn.	US$7-28
Frog Pond Inn.	US$6-15
Ibunda Inn.	US$6-15
Jaya Bungalows	US$6-15
Karsi.	US$6-22
Kerta.	US$6-25
Lempung.	US$10-25
Mandia.	US$10-15
Monkey Forest Hideaway	US$6-28
Pande Permai	US$12-35
Puri Garden.	US$8-30
Sri Bungalows	US$6-15
Ubud Inn.	US$10-30
Ubud Terrace	US$12-30

North Ubud

Ananda Cottages	US$10-28
Santi.	US$5-14
Suci Inn	US$6-15
Wisata Cottages.	US$15-45
Yasa Bungalows	US$10-35

Southeast Ubud

Agung Raka	US$15-45
Artini.	US$5-18
Badri.	US$5-15
Bali Spirit.	US$25-65
Jaya Bungalows.	US$45-10
Jaya 2	US$10-25
Kebun Indah.	US$15-45
Matahari.	US$5-15
Merta	US$6-12
Nirvana's	US$6-15
Pondok Ubud	US$15-35
Puri Asri.	US$5-12
Puri Ayu	US$5-15
Roni	US$8-15
Siti.	US$5-10
Suartha Pension	US$5-12
Weda	US$5-12

West Ubud

Bali Ubud	US$5-15
Happy Inn.	US$5-15
Jagi	US$5-10
Pondok Ubud	US$5-10
Sari Bamboo.	US$10-15
Shanti	US$5-12

Moderate Accommodations

Ubud also has dozens of semiluxurious bungalows for US$30-85, often constructed in traditional styles converted to Western tastes with large rooms set with native furniture, modern bathrooms, and verandahs with views of inner courtyards or across ricefields and rivers. As more of the inexpensive spots disappear each year, this class of hotel seems to be the wave of the future for Ubud.

Hotel Puri Saren Agung: Cokorda Agung, descendant of Ubud's noble family, operates bungalows within his royal compound, decorated with handcarved furniture and Balinese antiques. Traditional dance performances are given weekly within the courtyard. Puri Saren is the oldest hotel in Ubud and dates from the Dutch era. All rooms with fan. Ubud, tel. (0361) 975057, US$45-60.

Oka Kartini's: Oka's homestay features lovely bungalows surrounded by gardens and elaborately carved statuary, plus puppet shows given weekly. Oka's is opposite the big Neka art gallery in Padangtegal, tel. (0361) 975193, US$35-50.

Cendana Cottages: Decent, centrally located spot with swimming pool, popular restaurant, and ricefield views from many of the fan-cooled rooms. Monkey Forest Rd., tel. (0361) 796243, US$25-45.

Puri Saraswati Cottages: Central location, good reputation, pool, and extensive gardens have long made this one of Ubud's classic Balinese homestays. All rooms with fan. On the main road adjacent to the Saraswati temple, tel. (0361) 975164, US$35-55.

Oka Wati's Sunset Bungalows: One of the oldest, and therefore most legendary, homestays in Ubud provides quiet rooms overlooking verdant sawah, plus a small swimming pool and restaurant supervised by Oka herself. Monkey Forest Rd., tel. (0361) 975063, US$35-60.

Siti (Hans Snel) Bungalows: Now managed by his wife, Hans Snel's seven bungalows, orchid gardens, and tiny pool are a favorite with return visitors. All rooms with fan. Jalan Kajeng 3, tel. (0361) 975699, US$55-70.

Champlung Sari Hotel: Modern hotel constructed in traditional Balinese style with L-shaped pool and limited views of nearby rice-fields. All rooms are a/c with private bath and hot showers. Monkey Forest Rd., tel. (0361) 975418, US$55-95.

Pertiwi Bungalows: Spacious grounds, large pool, and both fan-cooled and a/c rooms overlooking a very large pool. Monkey Forest Rd., tel. (0361) 975236, US$40-80.

Ubud Village Hotel: Large complex of bungalows with individual garden entrances plus pool and complimentary breakfast. Monkey Forest Rd., tel. (0361) 975571, US$45-75.

Villa Sanggingan: A few km northwest of town but with a superb garden and pleasant views from its hillside location. Jalan Ubud, tel. (0361) 975389, US$50-75.

Hotel Campuhan (Tjampuhan): Older but well-maintained bungalows in a spectacular location overlooking the Ubud River. Walter Spies stayed here in the 1930s. Jalan Raya Campuhan, tel. (0361) 975368, US$55-85.

Pita Maha: Perhaps the most luxurious place in central Ubud with fashionable chalets overlooking the river. Jalan Raya Campuhan, tel. (0361) 975225, US$120-180.

Alam Indah: Situated a few km south of Ubud proper in the village of Nyuhkuning and one of the loveliest spots in all of Bali. Alam Indah also serves some of the best food on the island since the owner is responsible for the famous Wayan Café on Monkey Forest Road. P.O. Box 165, Ubud, tel. (0361) 974629, US$75-120.

Waka di Ume Resort: Another classy yet traditional resort a few minutes north of town with pool, Balinese massage, and meditation chapel on the top floor. Very Zen, very hip. Jalan Suweta, tel. (0361) 976436, US$80-125.

Restaurants

Ubud has an astounding range of cafes and restaurants that serve every possible cuisine.

Griya Barbecue: Owner Ida Bagus Dalem operates a small cafe that serves the best barbecue in Ubud: succulent chicken, beef, or pork cooked on a charcoal grill. The building itself wraps around a small Balinese temple, which keeps the staff busy with offerings of flowers and incense. Jalan Raya Ubud. Inexpensive.

Ketut's Place: Authentic Balinese food is rarely served anywhere on the island except in private homes or during temple festivals. Most restaurants serve Indonesian food from Java and Sumatra rather than Balinese fare such as duck sate, duck livers wrapped in banana leaves, boiled ferns, and steamed fruits like jackfruit and papaya. Ketut's home, up the street from *bemo* corner, provides a unique insight into regional dishes at reasonable prices. Jalan Suweta. Inexpensive.

Menara Restaurant: Directly opposite Museum Puri Lukisan is one of the larger and more popular traditional restaurants in Ubud. Menara serves both Balinese dishes and continental specialties such as steak Diana and chicken cordon bleu, plus a large variety of Chinese dishes in their spacious setting. Jalan Raya Ubud. Moderate.

Lotus Cafe: Owned and managed by a Balinese couple after the departure of the Australian founder, this peaceful and charming restaurant has blue-and-white tiled tables in a small garden with a Hindu temple and lotus-filled pond at the back. The menu is creative and refreshing. A lovely place to start your restaurant tour of Ubud. Jalan Raya Ubud. Moderate.

Mumbul's Cafe: A small but popular cafe superbly located under a big tree and perched on a terrace overlooking a gurgling stream. The ambience is set by jazz tunes wafting from the stereo. Jalan Raya Ubud. Moderate.

Murni's Warung: On the side of a small ravine in Campuan (say CHAM-puan), this simple terraced restaurant with bamboo furniture offers both Indonesian and Western dishes, plus homemade yogurt and other desserts. Murni's has two dining rooms: one is at the street level and bustles with activity; the other, a steep flight down, is often empty and has the best views of the waterfall 50 feet away. Jalan Raya Ubud. Moderate.

Ary's Warung: Rather than the upscale decor currently in favor, Ary's resembles an old Javanese cafe decorated with furniture, artifacts, and photography from past Balinese days. No MSG or coconut oil used in the preparation of the Indonesian, Western, and Thai dishes; try the delicious dessert, *biu lablab*. Jalan Raya Ubud. Moderate.

Han Snel's Garden Restaurant: One of Ubud's more intimate dining experiences is the historic cafe just north of Café Lotus up the narrow street paved with embellished plaques. Here, painter Han Snel and his wife Sita are your gracious hosts, serving tasty Balinese specialties while frogs croak in the adjacent pond. Prices are somewhat high, but the atmosphere, large portions, and smooth service make this a worthwhile splurge. Jalan Kajeng. Expensive.

Dirty Duck: Many of Ubud's cafes with better atmosphere are located on the edge of town, removed from the traffic and congestion that now disrupts central Ubud. Dirty Duck, in Padang Tegal, offers ricefield ambience (for the next few years) and views toward Gunung Agung in the mornings before the clouds roll in. The menu lists Western, Indonesian, and "nouvelle Bali" desserts. Jalan Hanoman. Inexpensive.

Café Wayan: Run by Wayan Kelepon and her gregarious family, Café Wayan is one of the oldest and most popular cafes on the island. Wayan herself is known for her sparkling sense of humor, infectious laugh, and expertise in cooking. Be sure to try her desserts such as coconut pie and death by chocolate. Prices are extremely reasonable considering the high quality of the food. Finally, be sure to say hello from Carl. Monkey Forest Road. Moderate.

Casa Luna: Casa Luna has become the most popular place to hang out and network with the local expatriates in Ubud. The well designed cafe/bar/bakery and gallery serves fresh home-baked breads in the morning, light lunches such as Vietnamese salads and foccacia New York, and hearty dinners of jungle chicken, calzones, and pumpkin ravioli. Best of all, Casa Luna conducts a wide variety of classes in their downstairs room: art, holistic dance, and Balinese cooking. Jalan Raya Ubud. Moderate.

Yogyakarta Cafe: Midway down Monkey Forest Road it's an old favorite of backpackers and world travelers, who pack the tiny hole-in-the-wall for its central Javanese specialties: *soto ayam* (chicken soup), *ayam panggang* (grilled chicken in spicy sauce), and steamed whole fish. Yogyakarta is reminiscent of the simple style favored in Bali before the arrival of tourism and trendy marketing concepts—a nice change from the current move toward aquamarine walls and designer bathrooms. Monkey Forest Road. Inexpensive.

Begger's Bush: One of the few nightlife spots in town with Western dishes. Fabulous location near the river in Campuan. The owner, well, he's a trip. Jalan Raya Ubud. Moderate.

Performing Arts

Ubud and its neighboring villages are major dance centers where a performance is held nearly every night of the week. Schedules are available from the Ubud tourist office and from touts selling tickets around the town's main crossroads. Seats are unreserved, so it's best to arrive at least 45 minutes early for front-row views.

Performances vary according to the quality of the *gamelan* and skill of the individual dancers who rotate throughout the week: see the *legong* a dozen times and you'll experience both ineptitude and brilliance. For example, the *legong* at Balai Banjar (Sekehe Gong Sadha Budaya Ubud) is breathtaking, while the Peliatan Dance (Tirtasari) troupe in Peliatan does a poor *legong* but compensates with Bali's finest *gamelan*. See the stunning Mahabharta at Banjar Teges, but avoid the disastrous *kechak* in Bona. Padang Tegal Dance is know for its performances by young Balinese children.

Traditional Art

Ubud is chiefly famed as a performing arts center rather than for handicrafts, though its location near the surrounding art villages of Penestanan, Padang Tegal, and Peliatan make it a convenient shopping venue. Many of the shops in the center of town display junk but enough quality flows through to guarantee a full day of good hunting.

Ubud and neighboring villages produce the most famous and technically advanced painting on the island. First, visit Puri Lukisan and Neka Museums for historical and aesthetic background before visiting any shops or the painting villages. Private studios around town (ask the tourist office for directions) include the workshops of Sobart (the first modern Balinese artist), Gusti Ketut Kobot (former student of Rudolf Bonnet), I Made Poleng, Mujawan, Sudiarto, and I Bagus Nadra.

Among the most honored painters was I Gusti Nyoman Lempad (1862-1978), who established the famous Pita Maha art group in 1936 with Walter Spies and Rudolf Bonnet. His modest home on Jalan Raya Ubud is an intriguing building to briefly wander around; though his descendants don't sell his work, it's all in the nearby museums.

Penestanan, one km from Ubud through the ricefields, is where the "Young Artists School" developed in the 1950s under the tutelage of Arie Smit; ask for the studios of Sadia, Ridi, Jaga, Arsana, Regig, and Garda. Finally, there's the village of Pengosekan, whose "Community of Artists" produces both classical paintings and more lucrative decorative items such as big parasols and children's furniture. Best bets include the Agung Rai Art Museum and Pengosekan Artist Community center near Teges.

Contemporary Art Galleries

Some of Bali's finest modern work is displayed and sold in the following galleries. Neka Art Gallery and Munut Gallery, both on Jalan Raya Ubud, represent contemporary Indonesian and Balinese artists. Agung Rai Art Gallery in Peliatan contains one of the best collections of paintings on Bali. Continue 500 meters east to Teges and you'll find Sumertha Art Gallery, a spacious place with all styles: traditional pre-western Kamasan, moody Batuan works, colorful art from Penestanan, and modern works from the adjacent art school. Rudana Gallery in Teges is also recommended.

For something unique, visit Seniwati Gallery on Jalan Sriwedari in Banjar Taman. Founded by Mary Northmore, a British-born Indonesian citizen married to a famous Central Javanese artist, Seniwati is Indonesia's first and only gallery devoted solely to the works of women artists: ask Mary about an upcoming opening and say hello from the author!

Practicalities

Tourist Information: A unique nongovernmental tourist information center is on the main road just west of bemo corner and diagonally across from Puri Lukisan. It's staffed by volunteers who answer questions, post dance schedules, and work to preserve the fragile environment and culture of Ubud.

The best map available is *Ubud Surroundings* published by Travel Treasure under the watchful eye of Max Knaus. Along with the standard map information, Max provides personal recommendations on hotels, restaurants, and nightlife and sporting activities.

Money: Cash and traveler's checks can be exchanged at several banks on Jalan Raya Ubud and money changers scattered all over town.

Mail: The post office on Jalan Raya Ubud is well organized and can help with mailing packages home up to 20 kilograms. Beyond that you must use a freight forwarder such as Bali Surya Agung.

Telephone: International phone calls and faxes can be made at Telekom Wartel, Nomad Telecom, and Ary's Business Center a few steps west of the tourist office. Ubud also has several Internet cafes where you can quickly check your e-mail on your Hotmail account or other free e-mail services.

Bookstores: The Ubud Bookshop and Ganesha Bookshop on Jalan Raya Ubud opposite the post office sell travel guides, Indonesian novels, and newspapers and magazines from Europe and America.

Transportation

Ubud is a major transportation center with countless *bemos,* minibuses, and shuttle service buses fanning out to all corners of the island.

Bemo: Bemos and minibuses arrive and depart from the market in the center of town. Rates are fixed but should be checked with your hotel owner before jumping on any vehicle.

Shuttle Bus: The quickest and most convenient way to reach most destinations is on a private shuttle bus operated by either Nomads at the Nomad Restaurant or Perama south of Ubud in Padang Tegal. The price is about double that of a *bemo* but you arrive in one-third the time and departures are often scheduled based on connecting flights, bus departures, and boat services.

The Mabua Express boat service from Benoa harbor to Lombok provides complimentary pick-up and drop-off service from Ubud.

Cars and Motorcycles: Rental cars cost about 40,000Rp per day including insurance, while motorcycles cost around 15,000Rp per day.

Charters: Chartered transport to Sanur or Denpasar costs about 20,000Rp and about 30,000Rp to Kuta or the airport. Allow at least one hour to any of these destinations.

INDONESIA

UBUD VICINITY

Bedulu

With over 40 old temples in the region near Bedulu and Pejeng, this area contains Bali's richest collection of antiquities, from the earliest known kettledrums and clay stupas to relatively modern Shivaite sculptures and cut-rock Buddhist sanctuaries.

Bedulu was once the seat of the old Balinese kingdom of Pejeng and the last indigenous dynasty to hold out against the mighty Majapahit Empire, which invaded Bali in 1343 and introduced Majapahit culture and institutions. After the fall of the Pejeng Dynasty, the Hinduization of Bali accelerated, culminating in the massive cultural migration to Bali of the Majapahit court around 1515.

Archaeological Museum: Two km north of Bedulu is Gedong Arca, a small museum with such pre-Hindu artifacts as megaliths, bone ornaments, and copperplate inscriptions.

Pura Kobo Edan: Across the road and up a dirt alley is the "Mad Buffalo Temple," home to a four-meter image of a dancing figure endowed with a remarkably realistic penis. Perhaps a Balinese version of the East Javanese Singosari magic temples, the conquering Bima figure seems inspired by both Shivaite and Tantric Buddhist cults, two religions which merged on Bali by the 14th century.

Pura Penataran Sasih: Chief shrine of the old Pejeng Kingdom, this temple boasts one of the most famous examples of Bronze Age art in Indonesia. The so-called "Moon of Pejeng" is considered a masterpiece of bronzesmithing, though its origins might be Indonesian, Kublai Khan, Chinese Ming, or the Dongson culture of North Vietnam. The treasure is poorly located at the top of a towerlike shrine; bring binoculars.

Yeh Pulu

Lying between the Petanu and Pakerisan rivers, the ruins of this 14th-century rock relief form perhaps the most important and mysterious sculpture of the Middle Balinese Period. The carvings are enigmatic and stylistically unique, a 25-meter-long frieze of lifelike vignettes chiseled with an earthy, insightful touch. Yeh Pulu

represents stories from the life of of Lord Krishna, one of Vishnu's reincarnations, though the only deity directly portrayed is Ganesh, the elephant-headed son of Shiva.

Hike or ride your motorcycle to the extreme southeast corner of town, then walk 30 minutes through the ricefields; a good place to escape the tour buses.

Goa Gajah

A large car park packed with souvenir stalls and *warungs* marks the entrance to Bali's famous Elephant Cave. Formerly a monastery for both Hindu and Buddhists pilgrims, Goa Gajah centers around an enormous bulging-eyed demon

GOA GAJAH

TO UBUD

TO TAMPAKSIRING

SOUVENIR STALLS & PARKING

HARITI & OTHER STATUES

ELEPHANT CAVE

BALE

BATHING PLACE

PURA TAMAN

MEDITATION NICHE

MOON

PETANU RIVER

BUDDHIST ANTIQUITIES

BUDDHA STATUES

NOT TO SCALE

© MOON PUBLICATIONS, INC.

INDONESIA

© MOON PUBLICATIONS, INC.

who appears to be splitting and pushing the rock apart with his bare hands—Disney meets Balinese mythology. Below the baroque facade are bathing pools fed by well-endowed nymphs and a path which leads down to a small *candi* and Buddha statues sitting in the attitude of mediation.

Visitors must be well dressed, pay an admission fee, and hire a scarf.

Gunung Kawi

Two km south of Tampaksiring, on the banks of the sacred Pakerisan River, is one of the more impressive historical sites of Bali: a blinding green watery canyon where two rows of ancient blackened tombs have been hewn out of a natural rock hillside as royal memorials. Equated with the Ellora Caves of India and the rock temples of Mamallapuram (near Madras), these temples preserve in stone the architectural styles otherwise destroyed by nature. Although built in the 10th century, the facade temples remain remarkably well preserved.

Tampaksiring

The sacred springs of Tirta Empul, situated in a valley beyond the last houses of Tampaksiring, provide the essential holy waters needed for religion and ritual. The complex features two rectangular bathing pools with 15 spouts that purify, cure illness, and bring immortality. Sadly, the entire place has degenerated into a messy collection of souvenir stalls filled with super-aggressive touts who plead, beg, and voraciously molest Western visitors: Bali gone bad.

BANGLI

Nestled on the slopes of Mt. Batur, Bangli is a friendly little town which served as Bali's most powerful upland court in the late 19th century, largely as a reaction to the Dutch presence in Buleleng. Today it slumbers along, largely ignored except for an occasional tour bus that deposits visitors at Pura Kehen.

Bangli lacks the artistic temperament of Ubud, but it offers a rare chance to get off the beaten track and escape the tourist mentality that permeates much of modern Bali.

Attractions
Pura Kehen: Top draw is Pura Kehen, second largest and among the most impressive temples on Bali. Magnificently situated Pura Kehen

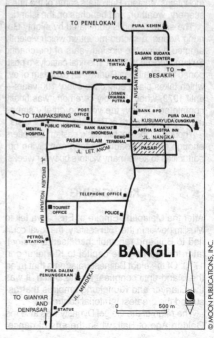

© MOON PUBLICATIONS, INC.

INDONESIA

was founded in the 11th century and consists of three levels connected by soaring flights of stairs. Gateways feature the splayed hands and hideous faces of *kala makara* demons whose function is to prevent malevolent spirits from entering the sacred grounds. Ornamentation on the highest temple is so overdone and uncontrolled that it's even rare for Bali—a stirring testament to the virtuosity of Bangli's stonecarvers.

Bangli Art Center: The art center, around the corner from Pura Kehen, occasionally sponsors art exhibits and performances of *kechak* and *wayang*.

Pura Dalem Penunggekan: South of Bangli is a grotesque temple of the dead carved with hellish scenes straight from Dante.

Hiking: Bangli also offers great hiking: three km west to Demulih Hill for views of Sanur, and a

range of nine mountains named after the nipple-like *trompang* percussion plates in the *gamelan;* it's five km farther to Apuan, where the house of the *kepala desa* is as beautiful as a king's palace.

Accommodations

Artha Sastra Inn: Bangli's rising popularity will bring more hotels, but for the present the best choice is the clean and comfortable former palace residence across from the bus terminal and town square. Jl. Merdeka, tel. (0366) 91179, US$5-10.

Homestay Dharmaputra: Near city center and ramshackle, but adequate for a night. Jl. Merdeka, no phone, US$3-5.

Bangli Inn: The newest and cleanest spot in town one block south of the bus terminal. Jl. Merdeka, tel. (0366) 91419, US$8-15.

EAST BALI

A lovely region of terraced ricefields and soaring mountains, eastern Bali offers some of the finest scenery, weather, and beaches on the island.

The entire region is dominated by mighty Gunung Agung, a sacred mountain which violently erupted during the closing years of the chaotic Sukarno regime in 1963. The final cataclysm postponed the Eka Dasa Rudra—an exorcism of evil which takes place only once every 100 years—until 1979, when the holy ceremony was finally completed. Today, the volcano quietly sleeps under the wary gaze of Balinese vulcanologists.

Though off the beaten track, eastern Bali offers enough natural beauty, history, and diving opportunities to keep many visitors busy for weeks.

KLUNGKUNG

After the Majapahit Empire of East Java fell to Muslim power in the 15th century, the royal court fled to Bali and reestablished itself at Gelgel, later transferring the capital to Klungkung in 1710. Of the eight Balinese rajadoms that ruled the island until conquest by the Dutch, it was the Gianyar and Klungkung empires that assumed the greatest territorial control.

The reign of the Gelgel Dynasty was also the Golden Age of Bali, when the arts of dance,

drama, music, and painting flourished as never before. In 1908 the Dutch mounted a military campaign against Klungkung in which the entire royal entourage chose collective suicide *puputan* rather than surrender.

Modern Klungkung is a dusty town without much character, though it merits a short visit to tour the Kerta Gosa and adjoining Royal Palace. Klungkung was renamed "Sukseskan" in 1992 to reflect its original title.

Kerta Gosa

Klungkung's greatest wonder is the ceiling of the Kerta Gosa, an ancient hall of justice first constructed in the late 1700s after the seat of power was transferred from Gelgel to Klungkung. Here, the all-powerful raja would sit with his Brahman elders to pass judgment in cases of murder, political conspiracy, and sacrilege.

After the 1908 fire destroyed most of the palace compound, the Dutch sponsored a series of renovations including a complete repainting on asbestos sheeting in the 1960s. Today the *bale's* walls and ceilings are covered in concentric murals, painted in the traditional *wayang* style, which depict the terrifying episodes due defendants after their deaths. The panels relate the fable of Bima and his two comical companions who venture into hell to rescue the soul of Bima's father.

KLUNGKUNG (SEMARAPURA)

Panels toward the top describe heaven and discovery of the waters of immortality.

For a pictorial survey and discussion of each panel, refer to Idanna Pucci's landmark work, *The Epic of Life.* Paintings inside the adjacent Bale Kambang ("Floating Palace") show Balinese astrology and scenes from the tale of *Pan Brayut.*

Accommodations

Klungkung has several hotels and *losmen* along the main road and near the bus terminal.

Ramayana Palace Hotel: Nine relatively clean rooms are found in the complex adjacent to the owner's house at the east end of Klungkung. Jl. Diponegoro, tel. (0366) 21044, US$8-15.

Bell Inn: A much less attractive but survivable alternative across the street from the Ramayana. Jl. Diponegoro, no phone, US$6-8.

BESAKIH

Besakih is the holiest site on Bali; the Mother Temple of Bali. Besakih dates from the 14th century and was built on a terraced site where prehistoric rites, ceremonies, and feasts once took place. The very complex architectural structure incorporates and venerates the holy Hindu trinity of Shiva, Vishnu, and Brahma through three main shrines, dozens of towering *merus*, and countless temples dedicated to all major figures in the Balinese pantheon.

Besakih lacks the architectural splendor of other Balinese temples, though the superb location and ungodly views can be unforgettable if the clouds haven't drifted in and obscured the site. However, you must bring your change purse, as every device imaginable by which tourists may be separated from their *rupiahs* is in operation: a desperate scene of hustlers, touts, beggars, and barking vendors.

Gunung Agung

Gunung Agung, Bali's highest and most sacred mountain, creates an imposing figure across the landscape of Bali and draws large numbers of hikers who wish to be on top for sunrise.

Guides recommended by the tourist office in Besakih can help with treks to the summit, but it's a dangerous and very exhausting hike. Most determined souls begin their attempt from Selat, a small village on the southern slopes from where a paved road leads all the way up to Pura Pasar Agung. From here, it's only a two or three hour trek to the lower edge of the crater rim. Guides can be contacted in Selat and Muncan, a few km west of Selat.

NUSA PENIDA AND LEMBONGAN

Nusa Penida, Nusa Lembongan, and Nusa Ceningan—three islands situated just south of Kusamba and within sight of Sanur—guarantee a welcome relief from the mass tourism of mainland Bali. Nusa Ceningan is little more than barren rock with little of great note, but Lembongan and Penida offer a rich combination of stark natural beauty, friendly villagers, and excellent surfing, scuba diving, and fishing.

Lembongan, not Penida, is the center of tourism for this small archipelago, largely because of the outstanding coral beds and three main reef breaks imaginatively named Shipwreck, Lacerations, and Playground.

Transportation

Both Penida and Lembongan can be reached by boat though the journey is not recommended in small boats when seas are rough.

From Padangbai: Modern twin-engined boats leave each morning from Padangbai and cost about 5,000Rp for Buyuk or Toyapakeh on Nusa Penida, from where *bemos* continue to *losmen* in Sampalan.

From Kusamba: Small local boats *(jukung)* depart daily from Kusamba and take almost two hours to reach Toyapakeh on Nusa Penida. You'll be accompanied by villagers bearing rice, oils, and fresh vegetables; figure on 2,500Rp.

From Sanur: Larger tourist boats cost 15,000Rp, depart daily from the north end of Sanur Beach near the Ananda Hotel, and take about two hours to Jungutbatu, the principal town on Nusa Lembongan. Departures are early mornings before 0900 and tickets can be purchased from a small office near the hotel.

From Jungutbatu, you'll need to walk one km north along the beach to reach the bungalows.

Nusa Lembongan Accommodations

Tourism is on the rise, but for the near future, the economy continues to revolve around cultivation of seaweed, which is processed into crackers and chips and exported to Japan, France, and Southeast Asia.

Jungutbau Beach: Over a dozen simple bungalows are now located on the beach just north of Jungutbatu. Some are simple homestays where you eat with the family, but most are standard places with clean rooms and common baths. Newer places with almost upscale restaurants and a/c rooms with private baths are now appearing here on Lembongan.

Bungalows under US$10 include Baruna,

Nusa Indah, Johnny's Inn, Main Ski Inn, Losmen Wayan, Agung's Lembongan Lodge, Ta Chi Cottages, and Tarsin Homestay.

More expensive options (over US$10) include Nusa Lembongan Bungalows and Puri Indah, which operates a reservation office on Jalan Pantai Legian in Kuta.

Mushroom Bay: Three km south of Jungutbau is an arching bay named after the offshore mushroom corals with several places to stay. Mushroom Beach Bungalows at the rocky north end has small but scenic chalets for US$8-12, while the ultra-elegant Waka Nusa Resort at the southern end of the bay features stylish cabanas for US$180-220.

PADANGBAI

Padangbai, a perfectly shaped and protected bay dotted with colorful one-eyed *prahus,* is the port town for ferries between Bali and Lombok. Direct ferry service from Benoa harbor to Lombok has somewhat reduced the appeal of Padangbai, though most Balinese and budget travelers continue to arrive to take the cheapest transport link to Lombok.

Goa Lawah, a bat cave between Klungkung and Padangbai, serves as one of Bali's nine most important temples and legendary home of a sacred dragon called Naga Basuki.

Accommodations

Several inexpensive bungalows are on the beach east of the pier and back from the beach in the middle of the small town. Walking east from the pier road you'll find the two-story Rai Beach Inn with rooms from US$10-40, Kerti Beach Inn which charges US$6-12, Padangbai Beach Inn at US$8-14, and Top Inn where simple bamboo rooms go for US$5-8.

Back from the beach is Homestay Dharm, Homestay Purba, Bagus Inn, and Pantai Ayu Homestay. All have rooms from US$5-10.

Ferry to Lombok

Large ferries depart Padangbai for Lembar harbor on Lombok every two hours from early morning until about 2200. The crossing takes four hours and costs 6,000Rp economy and 10,000Rp first class. Motorcycles cost an additional 7,000Rp.

INDONESIA

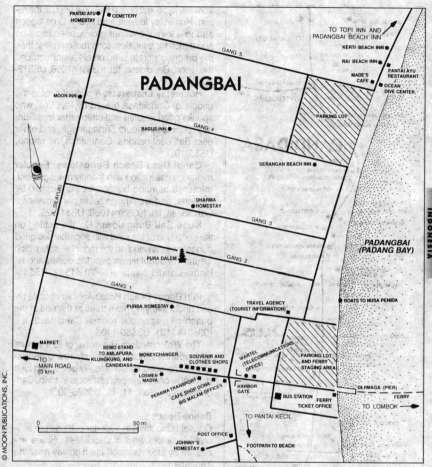

PANTAI AYU HOMESTAY • **CEMETERY**

TO TOPI INN AND
PADANGBAI BEACH INN

KERTI BEACH INN

RAI BEACH INN

PADANGBAI

MADE'S CAFE

PANTAI AYU RESTAURANT

OCEAN DIVE CENTER

MOON INN

GANG 5

PARKING LOT

BAGUS INN

GANG 4

JL. SILAYUKI

SERANGAN BEACH INN

DHARMA HOMESTAY

GANG 3

PADANGBAI (PADANG BAY)

PURA DALEM

GANG 2

GANG 1

BOATS TO NUSA PENIDA

PURBA HOMESTAY

TRAVEL AGENCY (TOURIST INFORMATION)

MARKET

BEMO STAND
TO AMLAPURA,
KLUNGKUNG, AND
CANDIDASA

MONEYCHANGER

TO
MAIN ROAD
(3 km)

SOUVENIR AND CLOTHES SHOPS

WARTEL (TELECOMMUNICATIONS) OFFICE

PARKING LOT AND FERRY STAGING AREA

LOSMEN MADYA

PERAMA TRANSPORT
CAFE SHOP DONA
BIS MALAM OFFICES

HARBOR GATE

DERMAGA (PIER)

FERRY

BUS STATION

FERRY TICKET OFFICE

TO LOMBOK

0   50 m

POST OFFICE

JOHNNY'S HOMESTAY

TO PANTAI KECIL

FOOTPATH TO BEACH

© MOON PUBLICATIONS, INC.

INDONESIA

CANDIDASA

Candidasa serves as the east-coast alternative to Kuta Beach with dozens of inexpensive bungalows and mid-priced hotels, cafes and restaurants, travel agencies, dive shops, money changers, postal agents, motorcycle rentals, bookshops, and most other travelers' necessities. The beach itself is almost non-existent, though the resort provides a convenient base for exploring the temples and ricefields of eastern Bali.

Candidasa takes its name from the local Shiva-Buddhist temple, established in 1181 and dedicated to Hatiri, the protector goddess of children.

Accommodations

Candidasa is a one-street town lined with dozens of *losmen* and hotels in all price ranges. Cheaper hotels are away from the beachfront, while more expensive hotels overlook the shoreline or are perched in the cliffs above town.

Homestay Ida: Many of Candidasa's better spots are located on the edge of town, removed

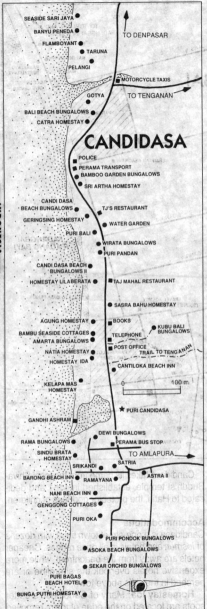

TO DENPASAR

TO TENGANAN

MOTORCYCLE TAXIS

CANDIDASA

POLICE
PERAMA TRANSPORT
BAMBOO GARDEN BUNGALOWS
SRI ARTHA HOMESTAY

SEASIDE SARI JAYA
BANYU PENEDA
FLAMBOYANT
TARUNA
PELANGI

GOTYA

BALI BEACH BUNGALOWS
CATRA HOMESTAY

CANDI DASA
BEACH BUNGALOWS
GERINGSING HOMESTAY
PURI BALI

TJ'S RESTAURANT
WATER GARDEN

WIRATA BUNGALOWS
PURI PANDAN

CANDI DASA BEACH
BUNGALOWS II
HOMESTAY LILABERATA

TAJ MAHAL RESTAURANT

SASRA BAHU HOMESTAY

AGUNG HOMESTAY
BAMBU SEASIDE COTTAGES
AMARTA BUNGALOWS
NATIA HOMESTAY
HOMESTAY IDA

BOOKS
TELEPHONE
POST OFFICE
KUBU BALI
BUNGALOWS
TRAIL TO TENGANAN

CANTILOKA BEACH INN

KELAPA MAS
HOMESTAY

0   100 m

GANDHI ASHRAM

★ PURI CANDIDASA

DEWI BUNGALOWS
RAMA BUNGALOWS
SINDU BRATA
HOMESTAY
PERAMA BUS STOP
TO AMLAPURA

SRIKANDI   SATRIA
BARONG BEACH INN   RAMAYANA   ASTRA II
NANI BEACH INN
GENGGONG COTTAGES
PURI OKA

PURI PONDOK BUNGALOWS
ASOKA BEACH BUNGALOWS
SEKAR ORCHID BUNGALOWS

PURI BAGAS
BEACH HOTEL
BUNGA PUTRI HOMESTAY

INDONESIA

© MOON PUBLICATIONS, INC.

from the hype and hustle that now engulfs the resort. Homestay Ida, situated near a large lagoon and in a lovely coconut grove, uses bamboo and thatch for bungalow construction rather than the dreary concrete piled on elsewhere around the resort. Candidasa, tel. (0363) 41096, US$12-20.

Homestay Lilaberata: A budget spot in the middle of Candidasa owned by Pak Lila, who speaks good English and often organizes Sunday tours to Amlapura, Tirtagangga, and other east Bali destinations. Candidasa, no phone, US$5-10.

Candi Dasa Beach Bungalows: Popular midrange destination with friendly management, attractive bamboo bungalows surrounded by gardens, and weekly *gamelan* performances. Candidasa, tel. (0363) 41066, US$10-25.

Kubu Bali Bungalows: Unique setting on the north side of the road with superbly designed bungalows elevated on the mountainside which insure wonderful views over the ocean and islands. Candidasa, tel. (0363) 41532, US$45-60.

Puri Bagus Beach Hotel: Another upscale resort under swaying palm trees at the end of the beach with spacious rooms. Candidasa, tel. (0363) 41131, US$80-140.

The Watergarden: The owner of TJ's in Kuta also operates this series of charming bungalows surrounded by streams, lily pools, and lush gardens—one of the prettiest spots in town. Candidasa, tel. (0363) 41540, US$75-90.

Balina Beach

Quieter bungalows in superior settings are several kilometers west of Candidasa. All are accessed by side roads off the highway near the Tenganan exit.

Balina Beach Bungalows: This basic but adequate resort serves as the scuba-diving center for the Candidasa region, including offshore dives and visits to Nusa Penida and shipwrecks on the north coast. Balina Beach, tel. (0363) 41002, US$35-60.

Puri Buitan: Simple, modern resort with oceanside pool and a/c chalets. Balina Beach, tel. (0363) 41021, US$35-75.

Amankila: East Bali's final word in luxury, situated above a private beach near Manggis, features 35 luxury pavilions set among landscaped grounds and superior suites with private salt-water swimming pools. Well-dressed visitors are welcome to enjoy lunch in their elegant and reasonably priced cafe. Manggis, tel. (0361) 771267, US$460-980.

Transportation
Candidasa is on the coastal road between Denpasar and Amlapura. Public buses reach Candidasa from the Batubulan terminal, but it's much quicker to take a direct tourist shuttle bus from Kuta, Ubud, Singaraja, or Lovina beach. Tourist shuttle buses cost twice that of public buses but you arrive in one-third the time and won't need to make changes in Batubulan or Klungkung.

TENGANAN

Tenganan, a small village west of Candidasa, is an original pre-Hindu settlement inhabited by the Bali Aga, aboriginal Balinese who settled the island long before the influx of immigrants from Java's decaying 16th-century Majapahit Empire. As with other megalithic towns, Tenganan is geometrically balanced with identical homes neatly facing each other across stone roads, and, like Trunyan to the northwest, the villagers once attempted to preserve their culture and way of life against mass tourism.

Looks like they gave up. Tenganan is now plastered with signs marked Gamelan Demonstration, Weaving Demonstration, and Please Come In. Yet the basic layout, totally different from that of any other community on Bali, remains, as do vestiges of their famous double-*ikat* textilework.

After paying your entrance fee and passing the souvenir shops, walk north past the wandering buffalo to visit *lontar* (palm-leaf script) artist Wratddhi Castra, and continue beyond the school to the path that leads six km to Candidasa.

To reach Tenganan, take a *bemo* to the turnoff and continue on the back of a waiting motorcycle.

AMLAPURA

Amlapura (formerly called Karangasem) once served as seat of one of the richest kingdoms of Bali. Established during the waning days of the

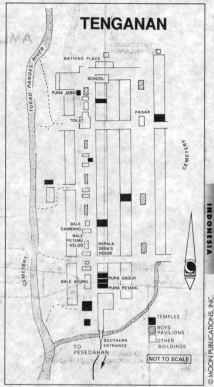

Gelgel Dynasty in the late 17th century, this rajadom rose to the pinnacle of its power in the 18th century but was devastated during Agung's monthlong eruption in 1963; traces of the catastrophe are still visible today in the western part of town.

Attractions
Puri Kangiana: Inside this enormous complex, which once functioned as the palace of the last raja, an air of slow-motion decay prevails: the fountains have stopped spouting and dragons and serpents sit stonily with wide-open mouths. A combination of European, Chinese, and Balinese architecture and interior design was used in this *puri's* construction, with the largest and most striking pavilion being the Edwardian-style Bale London.

AMLAPURA

TO
TIRTAGANGGA
AND SINGARAJA

TO
ABANG ALANG

TO
PURA BUKIT

HOSPITAL

PENJARA

TELEPHONE
OFFICE

GOVERNMENT OFFICES

JL. SULTAN AGUNG

SPORTSFIELD &
SWIMMING POOL

PURI KANGINAN
(PURI AGUNG)

JL. L. ALIT

TO RENDANG
AND KINTAMANI

LOSMEN
LAHAR
MAS

JL. GATOT
SUBROTO

POST
OFFICE

RM SEGAR

CLOCK TOWER

JL. HASANUDIN

HOMESTAY
SIDYA KARYA

BANK
PEMBANGUNAN
DAERAH

APOTIK

POS DAN GIRO

RM POJOK
RASA

JL. DIPONEGORO

MESJID

BEMO/BUS TERMINAL

PASAR

BANK RAKYAT
INDONESIA

RM SURABAYA

BEMO TO UJUNG

OJEK AND PASAR MALAM

CINEMA

TO CANDIDASA,
KLUNGKUNG, AND DENPASAR

POLICE STATION

0   200 m

TO UJUNG WATER PALACE

INDONESIA

© MOON PUBLICATIONS, INC.

Ujung Water Palace: Four km south of Amlapura are the remains of an old mock-European-style water palace surrounded by a moat largely destroyed by an earthquake in 1979. Today, children splash and farmers grow rice in the bathing pools: only your imagination can reconstruct the former glory.

Bemos to Ujung leave from the south end of Amlapura.

TIRTAGANGGA

Tirtagangga is among the prettiest and most relaxed places in all of Bali, a superb place to unwind and enjoy splendid scenery that unfolds in all directions. Tirtagangga ("Water of the

Ganges") technically refers to a water complex built in 1947 with corvée labor on the site of a sacred spring by the old raja of Amlapura. With its shallow pool, ornamental ponds, and pleasant weather, this is the perfect spot for family outings.

Hiking around Tirtagangga

Visitors are permitted to bathe in the ponds and in the formal swimming pool in the northwest corner, but come prepared for armies of exuberant schoolchildren.

Much better than the old baths is hiking through the fantastic scenery to remote villages almost completely untouched by the outside world. Simply pick a direction and go: north to Ababi, northwest to the Mahayana Buddhist colony at Budakling, west to the artist village of

Abianjero, all the way around the coastline to Singaraja.

Other possible destinations include the hillside village of Tanaharon, Tanah Lengis—known for its *angklung* orchestras—or the cattle-market town of Bebandam. Hiking around Tirtagangga is superb. *Losmen* owners in Tirtagangga can help with suggestions on specific hikes.

Amlapura to Rendang Scenery

Bali's most spectacular scenery isn't found around Ubud or high in the mountains, but rather along the narrow road which winds west from Amlapura toward Rendang. No matter how many photographs you've seen of the magical landscape, nothing prepares you for this journey.

Bemos are sporadic, so it's best to rent a motorcycle or car and allow as much time as possible. Highlights include the *salak* gardens at Sibetan, the almost-unbelievable views from Putung (have lunch at Pondok Bukit Putung), and the postcard-perfect rice terraces around Sideman and Iseh, former home of Walter Spies and Swiss painter Theo Meier.

Accommodations

Tirtagangga provides a variety of *losmen,* some with stunning views across east Bali.

Tirta Ayu Homestay: A six-bungalow homestay inside the water palace now managed by a descendant of the former raja. Very pleasant. Tirtagangga, tel. (0363) 21697, US$12-20.

Rijasa Homestay: *Bemos* from Amlapura stop at the intersection near this small but adequate place. Tirtagangga, tel. (0363) 21873, US$5-10.

Dhangin Taman Inn: An attractive spot where you can sit in the sun, gaze across the rice paddies, and pick up hiking tips from the owner, Wayan. Tirtagangga, tel. (0363) 22059, US$5-10.

Kusuma Jaya Inn: Tirtagangga's top choice (literally), situated at the summit of a very steep stairway, provides decent food, adequate lodging, and unforgettable views over endless ricefields. Tirtagangga, tel. (0363) 21250, US$8-15.

Prima Bamboo Inn: Another hilltop bungalow some 500 meters beyond Tirtagangga with simple cottages and outstanding views across the island. Tirtagangga, tel. (0363) 21316, US$6-12.

Transportation

Tirtagangga is on the main road and six km north of the Amlapura turnoff. Take any bus to Amlapura and change to another bus or *bemo* for the final stretch up to Tirtagangga. *Bemos* and a limited number of buses continue around the island to Tulamben and Singaraja.

AMED AND TULAMBEN

Bali's extreme eastern coast is attracting an increasing number of visitors, who come for the deserted beaches and superb diving over offshore corals and the wreck of an American cargo ship.

Amed

Due east of Culik are several small villages grouped together under the heading of Amed.

Accommodations: Kusumjaya Beach Inn in Cemelu, two km southeast of Amed, has well-constructed bungalows from US$12-25. Just down the road in Lipah is upscale Hidden Paradise Cottages with swimming pool, snorkeling gear, mountain bikes, and rooms with complimentary breakfast from US$35-80. Farther south along the coastal road is Vienna Beach Bungalows and Good Karma Inn where bamboo cottages cost US$10-20.

Transportation: Public transportation is available to Culik from Tirtagangga or Amlapura, but *bemos* are infrequent down to the coast and you may need to hire an *ojek* for about 2,000Rp.

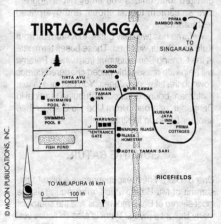

TIRTAGANGGA

PRIMA BAMBOO INN

TO SINGARAJA

GOOD KARMA

TIRTA AYU HOMESTAY

DHANGIN TAMAN INN · PURI SAWAH

SWIMMING POOL A

SWIMMING POOL B

WARUNGS

KUSUMA JAYA INN

PRIMA COTTAGES

ENTRANCE GATE

WARUNG RIJASA
RIJASA HOMESTAY

FISH POND

HOTEL TAMAN SARI

RICEFIELDS

TO AMLAPURA (6 km)

0   100 m

© MOON PUBLICATIONS, INC.

INDONESIA

Tulamben

Tulamben is chiefly visited by divers on day trips from Candidasa and Sanur, who come to explore the undersea wreck of the armed U.S. cargo ship, the *Liberty*, torpedoed by a Japanese submarine in January 1942.

Accommodations: Simple lodgings in the US$6-15 price range include Paradise Palm Beach Bungalows, Pondok Matahari just south of town, Gandu Mayu Bungalows near the bus stop, and Puri Madha right by the wreck, which lies in shallow waters 50 meters off the rocky beach.

Divers often stay at the upscale Mimpi Resort Bali where guests can qualify for their PADI certificates while staying in bungalows priced from US$45-150.

CENTRAL MOUNTAINS

Bali's spine of mountains provide a popular escape from the hotter lowlands in a setting where the climate is fresh and brisk, and there are great walks through the volcanic crater of Gunung Batur. At night the air is so clear you can see the moon sail over the volcano.

The Batur region, unfortunately, is overrun with money-hungry and aggressive salespeople who can easily spoil your visit to this magnificent destination. Don't stop for roadside touts who push tours and boat rides across the lake. The scene is worsened by the mandatory fees collected for admission to the Batur area, plus additional charges for cars, motorcycles, cameras, and video cameras.

Motorcycles should never be left unattended; store them with the *losmen* proprietor.

PENELOKAN

Penelokan means "Place to Look." Perched at 1,450 meters, this cool but messy village has several cafes and restaurants geared to tour groups which offer spectacular views across the crater. Vegetables thrive in the cooler climate, so you'll be able to enjoy fresh greens and luscious strawberries. The imposing Puri Selera, Caldera Batur, Gunawan, Puri Dewata, and Kintamani restaurants are good places to dine and escape the merchants who wave frantically from the road below.

A tourist office opposite the road down by the lake can help with tips on transportation, trekking, and places to stay.

Accommodations

Penelokan's dearth of hotels encourages most travelers to spend the night down on the lake in the village of Toya Bungkah. Warm clothing and blankets are essential if you plan to spend the night up here.

Lakeview Homestay: Very basic spot with claustrophobic cubicles and larger bungalows with private bath and hot water. Penelokan, tel. (0366) 51464, US$8-30.

Transportation

Most tour buses follow the main road via Tampaksiring, with pauses at the temples at Goa Gajah, Gunung Kawi, and Tirta Empul. Travelers with hired cars or motorcycles will enjoy the potholed but delightfully scenic road from Ubud to Peliatan, then through Tegal Lalang, Sebatu, and Pujung. Great scenery and no crowds. A third option, rarely explored, is the road from Bangli up to Kintamani.

Visiting Lake Batur and vicinity should be done with rented car or motorcycle rather than organized tour, unless you enjoy hyper-aggressive salesmen, tourist shops, and overpriced restaurants.

Perama has two daily buses to Kintamani from Kuta and Sanur via Ubud. These buses terminate at the Gunung Sari restaurant from where Perama will help with reasonably priced chartered *bemos* down to the lakeside villages. You can also take a Kintamani-bound bus from Batubulan terminal in Denpasar, or a *bemo* from Ubud to Gianyar then another *bemo* up to Kintamani.

GUNUNG BATUR

One of Bali's finest experiences is a hike to the summit of Mt. Batur, which, after Agung, is the most sacred of Bali's mountains and the source of many Balinese myths. Batur is also an active vol-

GUNUNG BATUR AND VICINITY

BALI SEA

TANJUNG GULAH

BONDALEM

TEJAKULA

TO AIR SANIH & SINGARAJA

LES

PENUKTUKAN

SAMBIRENTENG

TEMBOK

TO TULAMBEN & AMLAPURA

LUPAK

INDONESIA

SIAKIN

BLANDINGAN

GUNUNG PENULISAN
(1,745 m)

PURA TEGEH KORIPAN

PENULISAN

TO KUBUTAMBAHAN & SINGARAJA

PURA ULUN DANU BATUR

TOYA MAMPEH

PURA BUKIT MENTIK

GUNUNG BATUR
(1,717 m)

SONGAN

2 HOURS

2 HOURS

TOYA BUNGKAH

KUBAN

TRUNYAN

PURA JATI

KINTAMANI

HOTEL MIRANDA

PURA ULUN DANU

BATUR

POST OFFICE

GUNUNG SARI RESTAURANT

KUBUPENELOKAN

KINTAMANI RESTAURANT

DANAU BATUR

PURI SELERA RESTAURANT

PURI DEWATA RESTAURANT

GUNAWAN RESTAURANT

LAKEVIEW RESTAURANT AND HOMESTAY

PENELOKAN

TOURIST INFORMATION

ABANG

KEDISAN

GUNUNG ABANG
(2,152 m)

BUAHAN

PELUDU

BEYUNG GEDE

TO TAMPAKSARING & UBUD

TO UBUD

TO UBUD

TO BANGLI

TO RENDANG & BESAKIH

MOON

1 mi

1 km

© MOON PUBLICATIONS, INC.

cano that still bellows and erupts, throwing out showers of volcanic debris and glowing red in the night. Batur's eruption of 1917 destroyed 65,000 homes and 2,500 temples and forced the relocation of Batur village to a safer site on the ridge.

Climbing Mt. Batur
Arlina Bungalows and Jero Wijaya Tourist Services in Toya Bungkah can help with guides, which cost about 10,000Rp per group, but it's very simple to follow the signs and well-worn paths to the summit. Batur's bare slope is the easiest of Bali's volcanoes to climb because you can drive to its base and you don't have to struggle through vegetation on your way to its three craters.

There are several different approaches but the most popular is the stiff climb from Toya Bungkah and the shorter route from Purajati. After exploring the sandy middle crater and enjoying the panoramic views, return to Toya Bungkah or hike the back-side path toward Kintamani.

Trunyan and Lake Batur
Trunyan is an ancient Bali Aga village nestled compactly under a precipitous crater wall. Trunyan's austere old temple—a fossilized relic of aboriginal Balinese architecture—features a gigantic megalithic image believed to be the largest on Bali. The nearby cemetery in Kuban is morbid if somewhat intriguing.

The setting is spectacular, but overall it's a horrible tourist trap filled with hyper-aggressive hustlers who demand outrageous fees for everything from photography and temple entrances to visits to the cemetery.

Boat tours to Trunyan, the cemetery at Kuban, and the hot springs at Toya Bungkah cost about 10,000Rp per person in a group of four passengers from the fixed-price ticket office in Kedisan. Individuals can sometimes join large parties, often Indonesians on holiday, but a much more enjoyable option is to hike two or three hours around the shore from Kedisan.

Toya Bungkah (Tirta) Accommodations
Simple *losmen* are in Kedisan and Buahan but most visitors head directly to Toya Bungkah, right at lakeside. Hikers with limited time should watch for the sign near Purajati which announces Please follow white flag to Batur Volcano; a quickie shortcut.

Arlina Bungalows: Toya Bungkah has a half-dozen *losmen* under US$10, including this simple but helpful place on the left as your approach the grubby village. Toya Bungkah, tel. (0366) 51165, US$5-10.

Laguna Homestay: Basic but clean *losmen* on the edge of the lake. Toya Bungkah, tel. (0366) 51297, US$5-10.

Balai Seni Toyabungkah: The "World Headquarters for the International Association for Art and the Future" up the hill has rough but spacious bungalows managed by a professor from Jakarta. Toya Bungkah, tel. (0366) 51288, US$8-15.

Lakeside Cottages: Somewhat more luxurious digs just north of town. Toya Bungkah, tel. (0366) 51249, US$10-30.

Transportation
Private *bemo* drivers from Penelokan ask as high as 25,000Rp to take you down the paved road, but just wait patiently until a public *bemo* comes along and pay just 1,000Rp. When the weather permits, a great alternative is to hike down to the lake in about two hours and continue another hour to Toya Bungkah.

BATUR AND KINTAMANI

Batur and Kintamani are wind-blown market towns joined together and spread haphazardly along the road which hugs the outer rim of Gunung Batur. Local villagers might remind you of the Newars of Nepal in the way they dress and stare—traditional, turbaned, and always carrying their *parang* (machetes). Kintamani is also known for vegetables and fruits not found elsewhere on Bali and the sunrise markets held every three days.

Penulisan, eight km north, has the highest temple on Bali and spectacular views from the TV microwave station at the summit.

Accommodations
Several *losmen* are along the main road, but most are cold, cubicle-like, and damp-smelling joints only suited for shorts survivalists. Coming from Penelokan, you'll pass Pura Ulun Danu Batu before reaching the limited options near the center of town.

INDONESIA

Hotel Miranda: On the left side of the road just before Kintamani is a friendly but older *losmen* with decent rooms. Penelokan, tel. (0366) 51244, US$4-8.

BEDUGUL AND LAKE BRATAN

Bedugul is a friendly lakeside resort on the main road between Denpasar and Singaraja. Unlike Kintamani and Penelokan, Bedugul provides good hotels, warm restaurants, and outdoor activities from sailing to golf.

Attractions
From the *bemo* stop in Candi Kuning, walk down to Danau Bratan in order to take the mandatory photographs of picturesque Ulu Danu, a half-Hindu, half-Buddhist temple dedicated to Dewi Danau, the water goddess of the Balinese religion.

Canoes can be hired to paddle around the placid waters and visit caves dug by Indonesian slave laborers during WW II. Hikers can climb Gunung Catur in about three hours along a well-marked path and then return to circumnavigate the lake in the afternoon.

Also visit the sprawling botanic gardens and orchid gardens at Lila Graha, only 500 meters from the market. Ten km north of Lake Bratan are Lake Buyan and Tamblingan, two lovely spots from where trails lead to Munduk and the north coast.

Accommodations
Bedugul and Candi Kuning on the western shores of Lake Bratan have somewhat overpriced *losmen* and plenty of luxury hotels geared to the golfing crowd.

Strawbali Losmen: Small, six-room *losmen* and the only inexpensive spot near the lake. Bedugul, tel. (0368) 23467, US$8-12.

Bedugul Hotel: An older but decent hotel which serves as the lakeside water-sports center. Bedugul, tel. (0368) 21197, US$15-30.

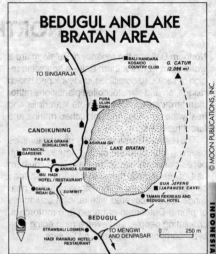

BEDUGUL AND LAKE BRATAN AREA

© MOON PUBLICATIONS, INC.

INDONESIA

Ashram Losmen: Simple concrete hotel with clean if overpriced rooms in a convenient location facing the lake. Canoes can be rented at reasonable rates at the nearby campground. Candi Kuning, tel. (0368) 21101, US$8-45.

Lila Graha Bungalows: A comfortable hotel across the road from the lake. Candi Kuning, tel. (0368) 21446, US$18-35.

Bali Handara Kosaido Country Club: An upscale resort with tennis courts, restaurants, Japanese spa, and an 18-hole championship golf course reported to be among the most scenic in Asia; the world's only course laid out inside an extinct volcanic crater. Pancasari, tel. (0362) 22646, US$80-420.

Transportation
Bedugul and Lake Bratan are on the main road between Denpasar and Singaraja. Buses leave hourly from the Ubung terminal in Denpasar and from the southern bus terminal in Singaraja. Perama also provides direct service from Kuta, Sanur, Ubud, and Singaraja.

NORTH BALI

Northern Bali and the regency of Buleleng are a world apart from southern Bali—a sprawling region of secluded coastlines, undeveloped beach resorts, an arid climate, coffee plantations rather than terraced ricefields, remote waterfalls and freshwater springs, and untouched marine and forest reserves.

The district also offers gaudily painted temples seething with baroque carved figures. Though not as classically rich as the Bali-Hindu southern half of the island, these extravagant shrines carved from soft pink sandstone quarried near Singaraja are covered with fanciful sculptures of plump Dutchmen cramped into motorcars, copulating people, and even a man riding a bicycle composed of leaves and flowers.

SINGARAJA

Bali's second largest city chiefly serves as a transit point for travelers heading west to the beaches at Lovina. With its suburban tree-lined avenues, rows of Chinese shophouses, and Muslim minarets, Singaraja still vaguely resembles a 19th-century colonial town and is populated by all of Bali's ethnic and religious minorities: Chinese, Bugis, Javanese, Malays, Hindus, and Arabs.

Few visitors stay in Singaraja, though the town provides an interesting afternoon of exploration from nearby Lovina Beach.

Attractions

Once the Dutch capital for all of Nusa Tenggara, Singaraja still boasts some fine old residences and colonial architecture of European design. One of the most noticeable is Kantor Bupati (formerly Hotel Singaraja), which loftily overlooks the whole city from the south end of Jalan Ngurah.

Gudung Kirtya, a manuscript library just down the street from Kantor Bupati, is a treasure trove holding thousands of rare and immensely valuable *lontar* epistles which relate the literature, mythology, medical science, folklore, religion, and history of Bali.

East of Singaraja

Temples in the north are among the most spectacular on Bali. Blessed with a soft pliable sandstone, northern sculptors were able to create super-exuberant tableaux of *rakasas,* comic-strip panels, effusive wildlife, hilarious sidebars on mass tourism, and mischievous figures taken from Hindu-Balinese mythology. Northern architects employ terraced bases which lead to squat stone buildings, rather than the courtyards of *merus* common in the south.

Most of the following temples can be quickly reached by rented motorcycle and *bemos* from Singaraja's eastern bus terminal.

Sangsit: Pura Beji, located about 500 meters down a side street in Sangsit, is an extraordinarily lavish *subak* temple that provides a brilliant example of the northern rococo style of carving, swarming with carved demons, *naga* snakes, *leyak* guardians, and stone vegetation growing in and out of the spellbinding gateways and terraces.

Jagaraja: Jagaraja Pura Dalem and a number of other temples on the road to Sawan feature panels profusely carved with great humor: madcap scenes of bicyclists, Balinese flying kites, dog-fighting airplanes, fishermen hooking a whale, bats, tigers, crabs clinging to the walls, and a long-nosed Dutchman being held up by a bandit with a horse pistol.

Sawan: Pura Jagaraja, two km south of Jagaraja, proves the Balinese fondness for caricature, masterfully represented here in bas-reliefs of corpulent Europeans in vintage Model Ts being robbed by armed bandits, aircraft falling from the sky into the sea, Dutch steamers being attacked by sea monsters, and mammoth fish swallowing the canoe of a kite flier.

Kubutambahan: Pura Maduwe Karang, about one km beyond the Kintamani turnoff, is one of northern Bali's largest and most elaborately carved temples. Steps lead through the courtyard into a second, inner section dominated by a magnificent stone pyramidlike wall richly embellished with ghouls, noblemen, soft pornography, a riot of leaves and tendrils, horrifying renditions of Durga, battle scenes from the

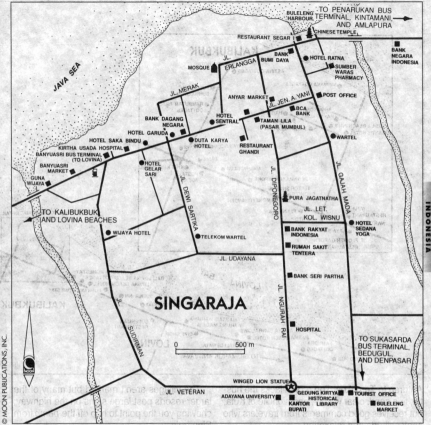

© MOON PUBLICATIONS, INC.

Ramayana, and—most famously—a one-meter-high relief of an official riding a floral bicycle.

East Coast: Beyond Kubutambahan the coast becomes dry, rough, and rather deserted. Yeh Sanih is a shady seaside spot with an enclosed natural swimming pool fed by underground springs. Tejakula, 35 km from Singaraja, is another bathing place with separate sections for *pria* and *wanita*.

Transportation

Singaraja has three bus terminals.

Buses from the Ubung terminal in Denpasar go to Sukasanda terminal in south Singaraja via Bedugul and Danau Bratan. *Bemos* shuttle up to

the Banyasri terminal, from where transport leaves for Lovina Beach. Buses and *bemos* from Amlapura and other east Bali towns reach Penarukan terminal two km east of Singaraja.

The Banyasri terminal on the west side of Singaraja has buses and *bemos* for Lovina Beach (30 minutes), Gilimanuk (two hours), and Surabaya (10 hours).

LOVINA BEACH

Lovina is the generic term for a number of small villages, beaches, and accommodation centers strung along the road west of Singaraja from

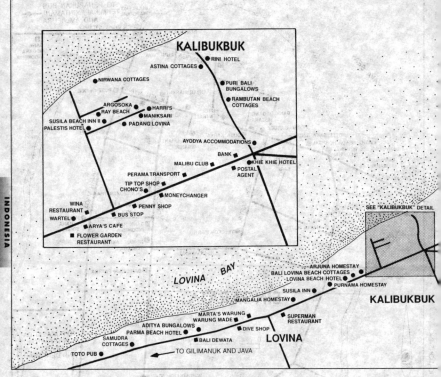

KALIBUKBUK
● RINI HOTEL
ASTINA COTTAGES ●
● NIRWANA COTTAGES
● PURI BALI BUNGALOWS
● RAMBUTAN BEACH COTTAGES
ARGOSOKA ●
RAY BEACH ● ● HARRI'S
● MANIKSARI
SUSILA BEACH INN II ● ● PADANG LOVINA
PALESTIS HOTEL ●
AYODYA ACCOMMODATIONS ●
BANK ●
MALIBU CLUB ● ● KHIE KHIE HOTEL
● POSTAL AGENT
PERAMA TRANSPORT ●
TIP TOP SHOP ●
CHONO'S ● ● MONEYCHANGER
● PENNY SHOP
WINA RESTAURANT ●
WARTEL ● ● BUS STOP
● ARYA'S CAFE
■ FLOWER GARDEN RESTAURANT
SEE "KALIBUKBUK" DETAIL

LOVINA BAY
ARJUNA HOMESTAY ●
BALI LOVINA BEACH COTTAGES ●
● LOVINA BEACH HOTEL
PURNAMA HOMESTAY ●
SUSILA INN ●
MANGALIA HOMESTAY ●
KALIBUKBUK
MARTA'S WARUNG ●
WARUNG MADE ●
● SUPERMAN RESTAURANT
ADITYA BUNGALOWS ●
PARMA BEACH HOTEL ● ● DIVE SHOP
SAMUDRA COTTAGES ●
● BALI DEWATA
LOVINA
TOTO PUB ● ← TO GILIMANUK AND JAVA

Anturan to Temukus. The region lacks the hustle, fine sand, clear waters, and nightlife of Kuta, but receives good comments from travelers who seek solitude and relaxation.

The most famous draw to Lovina isn't the mediocre sand or blazing sunsets but rather the schools of dolphins that cavort in the shallow waters just beyond the nearby coral beds. Early morning dolphin-spotting tours cost about 10,000Rp per person.

Anturan

Compared to the *losmen* and hotels in southern Bali, those at Lovina are simple places without the hype or hustle of Kuta or Sanur. Budget huts and mid-priced hotels are plentiful from Anturan (the village nearest Singaraja) to Temukus, though the largest concentration fills the middle near the town of Kalibukbuk.

The villages aren't marked but many of the larger resorts post large signs on the highway, showing you the point to hop off the *bemo* from Singaraja.

Baruna Beach Inn: Comfortable cottages with private baths, swimming pool, dive facilities, and restaurant overlooking the beach. Anturan, tel. (0362) 41745, US$20-50.

Puri Bedahulu: A newer place with spacious, clean rooms right on the beach. Anturan, tel. (0362) 41731, US$10-20.

Happy Beach Inn: Simple bamboo bungalows in a striking location adjacent to the ocean and surrounded by waving fields of rice. Anturan, no phone, US$5-10.

Bali Taman Beach Hotel: Popular upmarket resort with pool, gardens, and well-priced bungalows. Anturan, tel. (0362) 41126, US$25-60.

© MOON PUBLICATIONS, INC.

Sri Homestay: An old favorite with a fine beachside location next to the Bali Taman Beach Hotel. Anturan, no phone, US$5-10.

Jati Reef Bungalows: Concrete bungalows set in ricefields slightly back from the beach. Anturan, tel. (0362) 21952, US$8-20.

Kalibukbuk

Kalibukbuk is the main commercial center for Lovina with money changers, tourist office, Perama in the Hotel Perama, postal agents, a wartel, restaurants, and dozens of *losmen* in the US$5-20 price range.

Bemos from Singaraja stop at Nirwana Pub, near beachside bungalows and roadside hotels.

Banyualit Beach Inn: About one km before Kalibukbuk proper is this almost upscale inn with pool, gardens, and both fan-cooled and a/c rooms. Kalibukbuk, tel. (0362) 25889, US$15-35.

Ayodaya Accommodation: Roadside location, but a pleasant and relatively short walk through the ricefields to the beach. Kalibukbuk, no phone, US$5-10.

Rambutan Cottages: Seaside resort with pool, gardens, popular restaurant, and nicely furnished bungalows. Kalibukbuk, tel. (0362) 41388, US$15-45.

Angsoka Cottages: Two-story bungalows on one of the few roads connecting the highway with the beach. A lovely setting surrounded by tropical gardens. Kalibukbuk, tel. (0362) 41288, US$15-40.

Nirwana Cottages: Seaside location, plus big, clean rooms spread around a refreshing garden. Kalibukbuk, tel. (0362) 41288, US$10-30.

Lovina Beach Hotel: Top-end hotel with swimming pool, restaurant, bar, and 35 a/c rooms in two-story bungalows. Kalibukbuk, tel. (0362) 41473, US$15-65.

BOB RACE

A panel from the ceiling murals of Klungkung, painted in the wayang style, shows the horrors that await sinners. The scene to the left shows the punishment being inflicted on a man who tried to seduce his best friends' wives and his own sister; his genitals are being burned by a demon with a flaming torch. In the gory scene to the right, an enraged sow is savagely attacking a man who never married. Putting work above all human and spiritual values, he never had time for women, never married, and never had children—the most unpardonable sin of all. In vain, the man tries to tempt the sow away from his thigh by holding out nutmeg sprigs. These terrifying murals greatly influenced witnesses and defendants during hearings presided over by judges.

Lovina

Just across a narrow stream is the small village of Lovina, namesake to the entire region.

Aditya's Bungalows: Literally seven meters from the beach, Aditya's offers huts with common baths, plus newer bungalows with a/c and hot showers. Lovina, tel. (0362) 41059, US$20-55.

Samudra Beach Cottages: Quiet, remote, semiluxurious resort with both fan-cooled rooms and a/c bungalows just 10 meters from the beach, plus good food in the breezy restaurant. Lovina, (0362) 41571, US$10-35.

Transportation

Kalibukbuk is 10 km west of Singaraja. *Bemos* to Anturan, Kalibukbuk, and other Lovina towns leave from the Banyasri terminal in the west side of town. Travelers coming from south Bali by public transport will be dropped at the Sukasanda terminal in south Singaraja from where *bemos* shuttle across town to the Banyasi terminal.

NORTHWEST BALI

Northwest Bali remains a region almost completely untouched by mass tourism, though a steady trickle of visitors is now exploring the region between Singaraja and Gilimanuk.

The major attractions of western Buleleng are mainly located in the first 25 km west of Singaraja and in the hills that flank the ocean. Top draw in the far west is Bali Barat National Park near Gilimanuk.

Waterfalls

Singsing Air Terjun ("Daybreak Waterfalls") and the higher-elevation Singsing Air Dua are marked on the main road near Labuanhaji. Both are best visited during or immediately after the rainy season.

Brahma Asrama Vihara

Bali's only Buddhist monastery, 18 km west of Singaraja and four km south of Banjar Tega, is where resident *bhikkus* teach Theravadic breathing technique *(pranayama)* and "slow-walking meditation." Nearby thermal hot springs can be reached on foot in an hour, or take a motorcycle taxi from the Banjar Tega intersection.

Pura Pulaki

Pulaki, 48 km west of Singaraja and two km off the main road, features a dramatic temple overrun with monkeys and Indonesian tourists who come to honor Nirartha, a saintly Javanese priest who migrated to Bali in the 16th century.

Places to stay here include the budget Amandibali Bungalows with simple rooms from US$6-10 and the upscale Matahari Beach Resort which has a pool, private beach, dive facilities, and spacious bungalows for US$150-350.

Bali Barat National Park

The extreme northwest corner of Bali boasts the 77,000-hectare aquatic and nature preserve of Taman Nasional Bali Barat, gazetted in 1984 as one of the 10 national parks in Indonesia. Visitors can explore the forested hills, scrub acacia near the coast, and unspoilt reef along Teluk Terima and eastern bays.

Hiking and camping permits can be obtained at park headquarters offices in either Labuhan Lalang (12 km east of Gilimanuk) or Cekik, a few kilometers south of Gilimanuk. Mandatory guides cost US$5 per hour.

Accommodations: The only place to stay in the park is to camp near park headquarters at Cekik, but you must provide your own bedding, food, and water. The closest bungalows and hotels are in Gilimanuk and Pemuteran on the north coast.

Pulau Menjangan

Pulau Menjangan, a sanctuary island just north of Bali Barat National Park, ranks among Bali's premier scuba-diving and snorkeling locales. Dive shops in Kuta and Sanur organize tours to Menjangan but it's too far for a day-trip. A more sensible option is to contact one of the dive operators or travel agencies in Lovina.

Half-day excursions to Menjangan start from the visitor's center in Labuhan Lalang and cost around US$25 per person.

Gilimanuk

Gilimanuk at the far western tip of Bali is a decidedly grubby town where ferries depart for Java every 30 minutes around the clock. Few visitors pause here aside from those needing to overnight before making the short trip east to Bali Barat National Park and Pulau Menjangan.

Accommodations: Nirwana Losmen, near the *bemo* terminal, has acceptable rooms from US$5-10, while Lestari Homestay just east of town is the favorite spot for divers. Rooms here cost US$6-12.

SUMATRA

The magnificent island of Sumatra—with great lakes, steamy jungles, wildlife reserves, spectacular waterfalls, and remote tribes—vies with Sulawesi as the third most popular tourist destination in Indonesia.

The island is physically characterized by an unbroken mountain wall which marches down the entire western aspect and includes 93 volcanic peaks, three of which are still active. Sumatra has long been renowned for its wildlife such as Indian elephants, tapirs, tigers, clouded leopards, civets, bearded pigs, sun bears, proboscis monkeys, Sumatran rhinoceros, and a large free-ranging population of orangutans, plus thick jungle which still covers much of the jagged island.

Sumatra is also famed for its great diversity of tribes and numerous megalithic, aboriginal, and matriarchal societies—Indonesia's great ethnological goldmine.

GETTING THERE

From Penang

Sumatra can be approached from a variety of directions, but a popular and convenient option is to fly or ferry from Penang and then bus to Lake Toba and southward down to Bukittinggi.

Air: Malaysian Airlines Systems (MAS) and Sempati fly daily from Penang to Medan for about US$75 one-way or US$150 roundtrip, an inexpensive ticket that satisfies the "ticket out" requirement for an Indonesian visa.

By Sea: Sleek high-speed catamarans sail daily from Penang to Belawan (Sumatra's port on the Malacca Straits). The trip takes four hours and costs US$35-60 depending on class and the aftermath of the currency devaluation of 1997. Transportation from Belawan to Medan is included in your ferry ticket.

From Malaysia

Along with the Penang-Medan flights, MAS, Garuda, and Sempati offer flights to several cities in Sumatra.

MAS and Garuda fly daily from Kuala Lumpur to Medan (US$80), while Sempati does the same route at the same price three times weekly. Sempati also flies Kuala Lumpur-Padang (US$130) twice weekly.

Pelangi Air flies Ipoh-Medan (US$75) four times weekly, Malacca-Medan (US$110) thrice weekly, Kuala Lumpur-Padang (US$130) daily, Kuala Lumpur-Pekanbaru (US$110) daily, Penang-Banda Aceh (US$110) twice weekly, and Johor Bharu-Padang (US$110) thrice weekly. Pelangi offers 50% student discounts on standby fares and 25% student discounts for confirmed seats.

Malacca to Dumai

Travelers bound directly for Bukittinggi can use the twice-weekly ferry from Malacca (Melaka) to Dumai, a sleepy port town 158 km east of Pekanbaru. The fare is about US$40 and buses continue east to Pekanabaru and, eventually, Bukittinggi. Dumai is now a "no visa" entry point, so there's no need to obtain a visa from an Indonesian consulate.

From Singapore

Air: Singapore Airlines and Garuda Indonesia fly daily from Singapore to Medan and Pekanbaru, and three times weekly to Padang. Travelers heading to Sumatra from Europe or America should note that Singapore is closer than Jakarta to most Sumatran cities.

Boat: Less expensive—but also more of a hassle—than direct air connections from Singapore are sea routes through the Riau archipelago, the scattering of Indonesian islands immediately south of Singapore. Take the ferry from the World Trade Centre to Sekupang on Batam Island, from where boats leave daily until 1100 for Pekanbaru in southern Sumatra. For more information, see **Riau Islands.**

From Jakarta

Travelers can reach Sumatra from Jakarta by either air, land, or sea. Time permitting, buses barreling up the Trans-Sumatra highway are

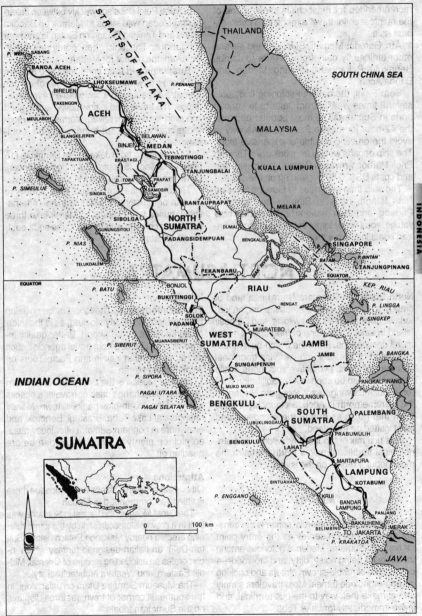

© MOON PUBLICATIONS, INC.

recommended for masochists seeking one of the quintessential travel experiences in Southeast Asia.

Air: Garuda, Merpati, Sempati, and several other airlines fly daily from Jakarta to Jambi, Bengkulu, Pekanbaru, Padang, Medan, and Banda Aceh.

Sea: Pelni, the national shipping line, sails several times weekly from Jakarta to various ports in Sumatra. The most popular option is the 42-hour journey to Padang, a fine way to avoid the grueling bus trip or expensive flight. The ship departs weekly from Jakarta's Tanjung Priok Harbor, arrives in Padang two days later, and costs US$20-60 depending on the class.

The ship then continues to Gunung Sitoli on Nias Island, back to Sibolga on Sumatra, Padang, and then to Jakarta. No matter how you go, you'll never forget the views of the Sumatran coastline, like a dream.

Several Pelni ships sail weekly between Jakarta and Medan with stops at Mentok on Bangka Island and Tanjung Pinang on Bintan Island near Singapore. The ship then continues up to Belawan, the harbor for Medan.

Bus: Improved road conditions and modern a/c buses now make overland travel across Sumatra a reasonably comfortable travel experience. The entire road is now paved and in good condition except after severe storms, when mudslides and washed-out bridges can be a nuisance.

Sample times from Jakarta are Bengkulu (15 hours), Padang (35 hours), Bukittinggi (40 hours), Lake Toba (56 hours), and Medan (60 hours).

Tickets can be purchased from agents in Jakarta or directly at the bus terminal. Alternatively, buses from Jakarta to Merak take three hours and connect with ferries to the southeastern tip of Sumatra.

NORTH SUMATRA

North Sumatra (Sumatera Utara) is a land of craggy volcanoes, high plateaus, plunging waterfalls, tropical jungle, rare wildlife, and Samosir Island in Lake Toba—one of Indonesia's major travel destinations. From the Dutch-built mountain resort of Brastagi you can visit traditional villages and climb two active volcanoes, while orangutans can be seen in a rehabilitation center at Bukit Lawang, reachable from Medan. In the extreme north is Aceh, a staunchly Islamic town that ranks as one of the friendliest and least visited on the island.

This rich mix of topography, wildlife, and ethnological traditions makes North Sumatra the most popular region on the island.

MEDAN

Sumatra's largest commercial center is the transportation hub which serves as the entry point for northern Sumatra. Medan is notorious among travelers for being noisy, dirty, and crowded—a crazy place of rubble-strewn streets and choking carbon-monoxide fumes. Most travelers simply arrive, make their way to the bus terminal, and leave immediately for Lake Toba.

Information
Tourist Information: The tourist office on Jalan Palang Merah is poorly stocked, as is the information counter at the airport. Better-quality information can be had from travel agencies such as Nitour on Jalan Yamin and Pacto Tours on Jalan Palang Merah.

Money: Medan is the best place in northern Sumatra to exchange cash or traveler's checks at any of the dozen-plus banks in town. Money changers at Lake Toba, Brastagi, Bohorok, and elsewhere in northern Sumatra offer lousy rates, so pick up plenty of rupiah in Medan before heading off.

Attractions
Other than a sultan's palace and a mosque there is little to recommended in Medan.

The Great Mosque, the largest in Sumatra, was built in a prewar Moroccan style by the same ruler who erected nearby Maimoon Palace (Istana Sultan Deli), an Italian-designed fantasy which incorporates an astounding mixture of Oriental, Middle Eastern, and Western architectural styles.

The Museum Sumatra Utara on Jalan Joni, in the southeast corner of town, features displays on the Sumatran tribals.

Surviving examples of Dutch-built rococo, art-deco, and art-nouveau architecture include Deli Maatschappij (now PPT Tobacco company), White Society Club (now Bank Negara), Hotel de Boer (now Hotel Dharma Deli), Grand Hotel Medan (now a bank), Kesawan Shopping Center, a Dutch church (Gareja Katedral), and Gubernoran, the imposing mansion of the former Dutch governor.

Budget Accommodations

Medan's *losmen* are hardly better than the town itself, though the scene is much improved from a decade ago.

Losmen Irama: Popular, grotty traveler's spot conveniently located in an alley across from the Hotel Danu Toba International. The managers can help with travel arrangements across Sumatra, especially to their home island of Nias. 1125 Jl. Palang Merah, tel. (061) 326416, US$4-10.

Hotel Zakia: Cleaner place south of city center near Masjid Raja with dorms and well-kept private rooms; breakfast is included. Jl. Sipiso Piso, tel. (061) 722413, US$3-10.

Sarah's Guesthouse: Another clean and friendly place south of city center with good vibes and helpful managers. Jl. Pertama 10, tel. (061) 743783, US$3-10.

Penginapan Taipan Nabaru: Cozy spot in an old Dutch home facing the Bobura River and adjacent to a public park and a Chinese temple. Quiet, clean, but a 20-minute walk from the center of Medan. Jl. Hang Tuah 6, tel. (061) 512155, US$4-10.

Sigura Gura Hotel: Good location next to the Garuda office, but best considered a second choice after Irama, Hotel Zakia, and Tapian Nabaru. Look for the sign: Cheap Hotel. 2 Jl. Suprapto, tel. (061) 323991, US$2-5.

Moderate Accommodations

Many mid-priced hotels are on or near Jalan Sisingamangaraja in the center of town.

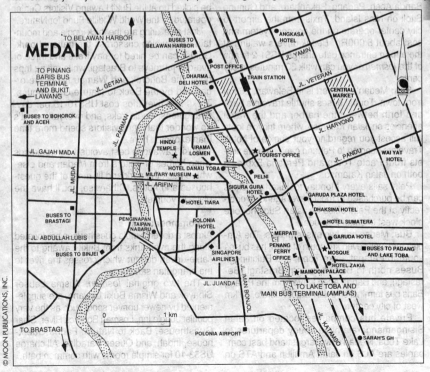

MEDAN

TO BELAWAN HARBOR

TO PINANG BARIS BUS TERMINAL AND BUKIT LAWANG

BUSES TO BOHOROK AND ACEH

JL. GETAH

JL. PARMAN

JL. GAJAH MADA

HINDU TEMPLE

JL. MUDA

IRAMA LOSMEN

HOTEL DANAU TOBA
MILITARY MUSEUM

JL. ARIFIN

BUSES TO BRASTAGI

PENGINAPAN TAIPAN NABARU

HOTEL TIARA

JL. ABDULLAH LUBIS

BUSES TO BINJEI

POLONIA HOTEL

SINGAPORE AIRLINES

TO BRASTAGI

0   1 km

POLONIA AIRPORT

BUSES TO BELAWAN HARBOR

POST OFFICE

DHARMA DELI HOTEL

JL. YAMIN

ANGKASA HOTEL

TRAIN STATION

JL. VETERAN

CENTRAL MARKET

JL. HARYONO

JL. PANDU

WAI YAT HOTEL

TOURIST OFFICE

PELNI

SIGURA GURA HOTEL

GARUDA PLAZA HOTEL

DHAKSINA HOTEL

HOTEL SUMATERA

GARUDA HOTEL

MERPATI

PENANG FERRY OFFICE

MOSQUE

BUSES TO PADANG AND LAKE TOBA

HOTEL ZAKIA

MAIMOON PALACE

JL. JUANDA

JL. IMAN BONJOL

TO LAKE TOBA AND MAIN BUS TERMINAL (AMPLAS)

JL. KATAMSO

SARAH'S GH

POLONIA AIRPORT

© MOON PUBLICATIONS, INC.

INDONESIA

Hotel Sumatera: A decent, renovated hotel some 400 meters from the Lake Toba bus terminal. The nearby Garuda and Dhaksina hotels have also been renovated. Jl. Sisingamangaraja 21, tel. (061) 324807, US$20-35.

Garuda Hotel: An enormous hotel next door to Hotel Sumatera with a/c rooms, two swimming pools, and a popular Chinese restaurant. Jl. Sisingamangaraja 23, tel. (061) 717733, US$30-65.

Danau Toba International Hotel: A four-star hotel and apartment complex in the heart of Medan, only five minutes from the airport, with 258 rooms, a Javanese restaurant, a fitness center, landscaped swimming pool, and banquet facilities. Jl. Imam Bonjol 17, tel. (061) 557000, US$95-180.

Transportation

Air: There are daily flights to Medan from Kuala Lumpur, Penang, Singapore, Jakarta, Denpasar, Banda Aceh, Padang, Pekanbaru, and Gunung Sitoli on Nias Island. Taxis from the airport to city center operate on the coupon system and cost about 8,000Rp. *Becak* drivers waiting at the airport entrance gate charge US$1-2 to any of the *losmen* or you can walk 30 minutes to city center.

Sea: Medan's seaport is in Belawan, 26 km from town. Tourist buses shuttle travelers back and forth between the harbor and the travel agencies on Jalan Katamso, where tricycle touts will accost you regarding your choice of hotel. Travelers heading to Penang can purchase tickets from Pacto Tours and Perdana Express, both on Jalan Katamso.

Pelni sails every Monday to Jakarta. Tickets can be purchased at most travel agencies or directly at the Pelni office on Jalan Sugiono, one block west of Jalan Pemuda.

Bus: Medan has two bus terminals. The Amplas terminal, seven km south of town, has buses south to Parapat, Lake Toba, and Bukittinggi. Buses north to Bukit Lawang, Brastagi (Berastagi), and Banda Aceh leave from the Pinang Baris bus terminal on Jalan Gatot Subroto, 10 km west of city center.

Private bus companies located on Jalan Sisingamangaraja have hourly departures to Lake Toba. Medan's two largest and best companies are ALS on Jalan Amuliun and ATS on Jalan Bintang. Many travelers go directly to the bus terminal or one of the private bus companies and depart immediately for Lake Toba rather than spending a single night in Medan.

BUKIT LAWANG

One of the world's three orangutan rehabilitation centers is inside Gunung Leuser National Park, 97 km northwest of Medan near the towns of Bohorok and Bukit Lawang. The center serves to preserve wild orangutans and rehabilitate specimens confiscated from private collectors or captured from poachers. Several orangutans are believed to have died during the fires of 1997, but you can expect to find over a dozen attending their twice-daily feedings of bananas and milk.

Visitors can watch feedings at 0800 and 1500 after obtaining a permit from the PHPA office in Bukit Lawang. Information on the orangutans can be picked up at the Bukit Lawang Visitors Center operated by the World Wildlife Fund for Nature.

Just as alluring are the thick jungle and mountain trails which crisscross the national park. Guides can be hired for day treks and three or five-day journeys to Brastagi, while rafting trips down the Bohorok and Wampu rivers are organized by the Back to Nature Guesthouse. Treks and river trips cost US$10-15 per day. Orangutans, jungle treks, and river rafting—it's no wonder that many visitors spend more time than expected here.

Bukit Lawang is best avoided on weekends when hordes of visitors from Medan and elsewhere pack the park and fill most of the guesthouses and hotels. Otherwise, you'll have the place to yourself.

Accommodations

Almost a dozen simple guesthouses are located along the riverbanks from Bukit Lawang to the cable-driven dugout which crosses the river to the orangutan sanctuary.

The two original *losmen,* Wisma Leuser Sibayak and Wisma Bukit Lawang, are supplemented by newer upriver spots such as the very popular Jungle Inn, Losmen Bohorok River, Sinar Guesthouse, Back to Nature, Farina Guesthouse, Indah, and Queen Paradise. All charge US$3-10 for simple rooms with common bath.

The only upscale place is Rindu Alam where a room with private bath, hot shower, and TV costs US$35-50.

Transportation
Buses to Bukit Lawang take three hours from Medan's Pinang Baris bus terminal. Direct tourist buses are available from Medan, Brastagi, and Lake Toba.

BANDA ACEH

The northernmost province of Sumatra and westernmost province of Indonesia is rarely visited by travelers because of its isolation and undeserved reputation for religious extremism. The truth is that Aceh ranks as one of the friendliest and safest spots on the island, plus it offers historic architecture, superlative beaches, and picturesque rural areas.

Attractions
First visit the tourist offices on Jalan Ujong Rimba and Jalan Chik Kuta Karang for maps, transportation details, and volunteer student guides.

Baitur Rahman Mosque: Aceh's premier attraction, in the center of town, was designed by an Italian architect and constructed 1879-81 by the Dutch to replace a mosque destroyed during the Aceh War. Behind the elaborate multiarched face, you'll see a splendid mixture of styles from Arabia, India, and Malaysia.

Gunongan: Constructed in the 17th century for the wife of an Islamic sultan, Aceh's former Taman Sari, or Pleasure Garden, provides an odd, almost surrealistic contrast to the concrete drabness of modern Aceh.

Kerkhof: Final resting spot for some 2,200 Dutch and Indonesian soldiers who died during the 30-year Acehnese resistance movement. Like a 19th-century Dutch Vietnam Memorial, the names of thousands interred have been engraved on the commemorative wall of the wrought-iron art-nouveau entranceway.

Aceh State Museum: A large three-story museum filled with displays of local artifacts, handicrafts, ceremonial clothing, and a reconstructed *adat* Rumah Aceh, former home of an Acehnese aristocrat.

Colonial Architecture: Near Lapangan Merdeka ("Freedom Square") are several historic edifices, including the White Society Club, the Grand Hotel, and the Dutch Tobacco Company.

Weh (Sabang) Island: Pulau Weh—more often called Sabang after the main town—is a small but striking island blessed with beautiful beaches flanked with swaying palms, caves filled with bats and birds, outstanding snorkeling and scuba diving, hot springs, and a vast tropical game reserve known for its monkeys, reptiles, and flying foxes. The tourist office in Banda Aceh publishes a very helpful brochure about the island.

Accommodations
Aceh has plenty of good *losmen* and hotels, though prices are somewhat higher than elsewhere in Indonesia. Four inexpensive *losmen* in the principal town of Sabang, but most travelers stay at Hotel Pulau Jaya on Jalan Umar, where clean rooms cost US$3-10. The owner can help with organized scuba-diving excursions, local treks, and homestays on other beaches.

Losmen Raya: Not the cheapest, but this old Dutch relic has fairly clean rooms, welcomes Westerners, and is conveniently located near Mesjid Raya. Jl. Ujong Rimba 30, tel. (0651) 21427, US$5-10.

Hotel Sri Budaya: Another budget place friendly to foreigners and with acceptable rooms. Jl. Majid Ibrahim 5, tel. (0651) 21751, US$5-10.

Medan Hotel: Decent mid-priced hotel with clean a/c rooms. Jl. Ahmad Yani 15, tel. (0651) 21501, US$15-35.

Wisma Prapat: Two-star hotel with both fan-cooled and a/c rooms plus a coffee shop, "banquet" facilities, and negotiable "grout" rates. Jl. Ahmad Yani 17, tel. (0361) 22159, US$10-45.

Kuala Tripa Hotel: Aceh's top-end hotel has the town's only disco, fitness center, and hotel swimming pool, which outside visitors can use for a modest entrance fee. Jl. Ujong Rimba 24, tel. (0361) 21455, US$55-95.

Transportation
Air: Garuda Indonesia flies twice daily from Medan, while Pelangi flies three times weekly from Kuala Lumpur and Penang. Taxis from the airport cost 16,000Rp to city center.

Bus: Buses from Medan take 8-12 hours to Seutul bus terminal on Jalan Teuku Umar in the south of Banda Aceh. *Bemos* and tricycles continue to city center.

Several bus companies have offices near the mosque on Jalan Mohammed Jam and can help with tickets to Medan and down the west coast of Sumatra to Calang (four hours), Meulaboh (five hours), and Tapaktuan (11 hours).

BANDA ACEH TO LAKE TOBA

A rugged journey can be made from Aceh to Lake Toba through the varied topography of north-central Sumatra.

Buses from Aceh reach Lake Tawar via Bureuen, though train enthusiasts might stop briefly in Sigli to view the colonial train station and its collection of antique locomotives.

Beautiful Lake Tawar and the town of Takingeun are great spots to unwind; inexpensive *losmen* are found near the marketplace and around the perimeter of the lake.

Blangkejeren to the south offers longhouses which once served as ancestral homes of the Gayo, former headhunters who fiercely resisted Dutch rule. Another entrance to Gunung Leuser National Park is near Tanah Merah, two km north of Kutacane.

Kutacane, a small market town known for its rice and potent cannabis, marks the division line between the Gayo homelands and Batak country. Buses continue south from Kutacane to Brastagi and Lake Toba.

BRASTAGI (BERASTAGI)

Brastagi is a cool and refreshing Dutch-built hill resort with great hiking, Batak and Karo villages, fields of European vegetables and fragrant flowers, and two volcanoes for determined hikers—Gunung Sinabung to the west and Gunung Sibayak to the north.

While in Brastagi, try the refreshing vitamin-rich *marquisa* juice, buffalo-milk yogurt, hot spiced ginger milk, and *babi panggang*, a traditional Batak meal of roast pork and sauce.

Attractions
Travelers often spend weeks exploring the tropical jungles, waterfalls, lakes, and volcanoes

near Brastagi. Just for inspiration, first hike up Gundaling Hill for fantastic views of the town, the steaming volcanoes of Sibayak and Singabung, and endless vistas of market gardens and forested hills. Most guesthouses provide adequate maps for hikers.

Gunung Sibayak: The 2,450-meter peak of Sibayak can be climbed in a single day with an early start from Brastagi. First, take a bus towards Medan and get off at Daulu Junction, nine km down the road. Then walk three km past

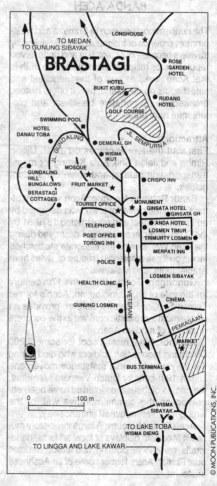

© MOON PUBLICATIONS, INC.

Danaulu to Semangat Gunung, then turn right up to the summit, where the belching crater and boiling turquoise-colored lake provide fascinating sights. Afterwards, soak in the medicinal hot sulfur springs near Radja Berne.

Mt. Singabung: Rarely climbed, Singabung takes at least two full days and requires a guide and an overnight stop in Singaranggalang.

Karo Towns: Several Karo villages near Kabanjahe such as Barusjahe and Lingga still have traditional, multi-family longhouses, which have largely disappeared from northern Sumatra. Another destination is Si Piso Piso Waterfalls, 25 km south of Kabanjahe near Tongging.

Accommodations

Inexpensive *losmen* are on the main street, while mid-level hotels are on Gundaling Hill, west of town with great views of Gunung Sibayak.

Wisma Sibayak: Brastagi's backpackers' center has dorms, private rooms, guestbooks with tons of tips, and further enlightenment from the owner who is an expert on Karo culture and regional histories. Jl. Udara 1, tel. (0628) 20953, US$3-12.

Losmen Sibayak Guesthouse: Handles the overflow from Wisma Sibayak. Jl. Veteran, tel. (0628) 20953, US$3-10.

Ginsata Hotel: Friendly, clean, and managed by Mr. Ginting, character and information source, as well as manager of the downstairs nasi padang cafe. Jl. Veteran 79, tel. (0628) 20901, US$5-10.

Ginsata Guesthouse: An old wooden villa that handles the overflow from Ginsata Hotel,

just around the corner. Jl. Veteran 81, tel. (0628) 20901, US$4-6.

Gundaling Hill Bungalows: Several other *losmen* and homestays on Gundaling Hill offer mid-priced rooms with views of Mt. Sibayak. Karo Hill, BIB, Miranda, and Kaliaga Bungalows are recommended. Jl. Gundaling, tel. (0628) 91586, US$5-15.

Hotel Bukit Kubu: You'll feel like a Dutch colonialist at this gracious hotel, located one km before town amidst a nine-hole golf course, with tennis courts and tremendous views of nearby volcanoes. Old-wing rooms are more romantic than new-wing additions. Jl. Sempurna 2, tel. (0628) 20832, US$20-65.

Hotel International Sibayak: Brastagi's newest and biggest hotel has a swimming pool, a gym, a disco, tennis courts, and 120 a/c rooms overlooking landscaped gardens. Jalan Merdeka, tel. (0628) 91301, US$60-120.

Transportation

Brastagi (also spelled Berastagi) nestles at the northern edge of the Karo Plateau, 68 km southwest of Medan at an elevation of 1,330 meters. Buses leave the main bus terminal in Medan every 15 minutes and take about two hours.

From Lake Toba, take a Medan-bound bus one hour to Siantar, then another bus three hours to Kabanjahe. A final minibus travels the last 12 km to Brastagi. The entire trip takes almost a full day, but the scenery is terrific.

Direct minibuses are quicker and booked by most guesthouses at Lake Toba.

LAKE TOBA

Lake Toba is one of the most spellbinding destinations in Indonesia. Surrounded on all sides by pine-covered beaches, steep mountain slopes, and forested hills, with Samosir Island sitting right in the middle, Toba is justifiably regarded as the chief draw of Sumatra and among the most idyllic and relaxing spots in the archipelago.

Some of the charm has been lost to a new hydroelectric dam which lowered the lake level, and the arrival of Western touches such as videos and noisy motorcycles, yet Toba remains a great place to unwind and recover from the hardships of overland travel across Sumatra.

PRAPAT

Prapat is the main town on the lake and principal embarkation point for ferries to Samosir in the middle of the lake. Once the exile point for Sukarno during the war for independence, Prapat today has grown into a busy tourist resort that caters to upscale travelers and Indonesian weekenders.

The town is divided between shops and hotels along the busy Trans-Sumatran Highway and quieter places near the ferry terminal. A small tourist office is just under the Batak Welcome

INDONESIA

MT. MELAS
(1941m)

TO BRASTAGI
AND MEDAN

SIGANANTANG

MEREK

SENBUDOLOK

TO BANGUNPURBA

MT. SILUATAN
(2457 m)

SIPISOPISO
WATERFALL

TIGARUNGGU

SIBAULANGI

HARANGAOL

LAKE
TOBA

MT. SIBARTONG
(2051 m)

TIGAN

TO ACEH VIA LAKE TAWAR

MALAU ISLAND

TAO
ISLAND

SIMANINDO

FERRY

SIDIKALANG

MT. SUHISULU
(1555 m)

PARBABA

SUHISHUHI

HUTARAJA

KASINGAHAN

PARTENGKOAN

TO
SINGKIT

BUHIT

SITUMORANG

HOT SPRINGS

PANGURURAN

LAKE
SIDIHONI

SIANTAR

TELE

RANGGURNI
HUTA

PANORAMIC VIEW

SIMBOLON

PALIPI

MT. ULUDARAT
(2157 m)

LAKE TOBA

HUTAGALUNG

0   10 km

MT. SOMPEAN
(1623 m)

TO BARUS AND SIBOLGA

DOLOK SANGGUL

DOLOK

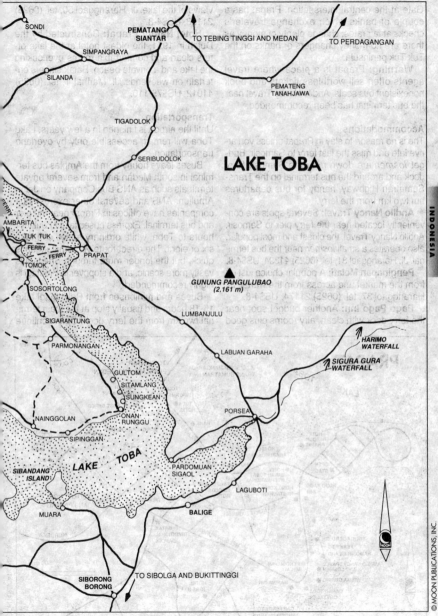

LAKE TOBA

SONDI

PEMATANG SIANTAR

SIMPANGRAYA

SILANDA

TO TEBING TINGGI AND MEDAN

TO PERDAGANGAN

PEMATENG TANAHJAWA

TIGADOLOK

SERIBUDOLOK

AMBARITA

TUK TUK

FERRY

FERRY

TOMOK

FERRY

PRAPAT

GUNUNG PANGULUBAO
(2,161 m)

SOSORTOLONG

SIGARANTUNG

LUMBANJULU

PARMONANGAN

HARIMO WATERFALL

GULTOM

SITAMLANG

SUNGKEAN

LABUAN GARAHA

SIGURA GURA WATERFALL

NAINGGOLAN

ONAN RUNGGU

SIPINGGAN

PORSEA

SIBANDANG ISLAND

LAKE TOBA

PARDOMUAN SIGAOL

LAGUBOTI

MUARA

BALIGE

TO SIBOLGA AND BUKITTINGGI

SIBORONG BORONG

INDONESIA

© MOON PUBLICATIONS, INC.

Gate at the central intersection. Prapat has a couple of banks which exchange traveler's checks at fair rates; change plenty of money as there are no money changers or banks on the Tuk Tuk peninsula.

Warning: Prapat is a place where travel agents often sell worthless tickets and book nonexistent bus seats. Andilo Nancy Travel near the bus terminal has been recommended.

Accommodations
The is no reason to stay in Prapat unless you arrive late and miss the last ferry to Samosir. Budget *losmen* are down near the Samosir ferry dock and around the bus terminal on the Trans-Sumatran Highway, handy for bus departures but two km from the ferry.

Andilo Nancy Travel: Several spots are conveniently located near the ferry pier to Samosir. Andilo Nancy Travel, the oldest and most popular, also operates a small *losmen* near the bus terminal. Jl. Haranggaol 31, tel. (0625) 41394, US$4-8.

Penginapan Melati: A popular choice just up from the market and across from the wartel. Jl. Haranggaol 37, tel. (0625) 21174, US$4-8.

Pago Pago Inn: Another budget spot near the ferry dock with clean, airy rooms plus good views of the lake. Jl. Haranggaol 50, tel. (0625) 21188, US$4-8.

Hotel Natour Prapat: Constructed by the Dutch in 1911, the oldest hotel at the lake offers clean and comfortable rooms overlooking the lake and a private beach. Batak singers entertain on weekends. Jl. Marihat 1, tel. (0625) 41012, US$75-110.

Transportation
Until the airport is finished in a few years, Lake Toba will remain accessible only by overland transportation.

Buses leave hourly from the Amplas bus terminal in south Medan and from several private terminals such as ANS Bus Company on Jalan Amuliun. ANS and several other express bus companies have offices in Prapat near the pier and bus terminal. Express buses take about four hours to Toba, while ordinary buses can take six or eight. The direct route via Simalungun is quick, but the longer route through Brastagi is vastly more scenic, and a stopover in Brastagi is highly recommended.

Buses and minibuses from Bukittinggi take 15-18 hours and usually stop at the main terminal two km from the ferry dock. *Oplet* continue

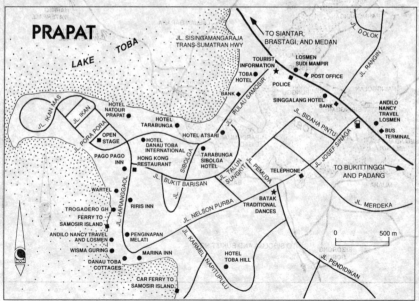

down to the harbor. Buses also leave Prapat for Sibolga (six hours) and Padang (20 hours).

Boats to Samosir: Boats shuttle back and forth between Prapat and several towns on Samosir daily from 0600 until around 1800. Departures are hourly and cost about 1,000Rp each way.

TOMOK

Ferries from Prapat generally go to Tomok, the main town on Samosir, before continuing up to Tuk Tuk. Most travelers head directly to Tuk Tuk and only visit Tomok on a day hike.

Attractions

Though there's little reason to stay in Tomok, it's a good place to bargain for handicrafts and view the old stone coffins and *adat* homes just off the main road. The chief attraction is the 200-year-old, boat-shaped sarcophagus of King Sidarbuta, surrounded by those of his descendants and by magnificent old banyan trees.

You might also attend Sunday church services to hear deep-throated Bataks praise Kristus and sing in full-volume strains.

Accommodations

Losmen and Batak-style homestays form a continuous line from Tomok to Ambarita, though the largest concentration flanks the Tuk Tuk peninsula. Most are similar in style and charge US$4-8 per room depending on facilities, such as common or private bath, and the age of the property. The farther you walk, the quieter it gets.

Roy's Losmen: Roy operates a simple *losmen* on the edge of town, three Batak houses near the lake, and a popular cafe in the center of town. Rooms cost US$3-6.

Toba Beach Hotel: Two km south of Tomok in the village of Parambatan is a fairly luxurious hotel with a lakeside restaurant for a pleasant splurge. Parambatan, tel. (0625) 41275, US$40-65.

TUK TUK

The principal destination on Samosir Island has over 50 small *losmen* and hotels, restaurants, and souvenir shops on a fairly scenic peninsula.

Hikes

Tuk Tuk, Tomok, and Ambarita to the north are starting points for hikes across Samosir Island. None are very difficult and trails are easy to follow, though guides are plentiful and you might enjoy the company of a local Batak. Bring along some raingear, warm clothes if you intend to overnight, small change, drinking water, and plenty of *kreteks* to offer as gifts. Trekking maps can be picked up at Carolina's and other guesthouses in Tuk Tuk.

Silakhosa Trek: A good warm-up is the short two-hour hike from Tomok to Silakhosa on the top of the cliff. The trail starts near the raja's tomb and heads past the souvenir stalls until it climbs up the steep cliff, where you can enjoy the views and a strong cup of Batak coffee before descending back to Tomok.

Cross-island Trek: The most popular trek on Samosir cuts right across the island from Ambarita or Tuk Tuk to the village of Pangururan on the west side of the island. Although many hikers start on the east coast, it's much better to take a *bemo* to Pangururan in the early morning and hike back toward Ambarita, since it's mostly downhill and you'll enjoy the scenery unfolding in front of you, not behind you! The trek takes about 10 hours and can be accomplished in a single day, though simple *losmen* and homestays are located along the way.

Pangururan: Trekkers can overnight in the 10-room Barat Guesthouse on Jalan Singamangaraja for US$3-6, or try the upmarket Hotel Wisata, where rooms cost US$4-15. Guides and porters can be hired in Pangururan, though the trail is relatively easy to follow in this direction.

There are two popular routes. The longer and more challenging option heads south along the main coastal road, then east about 16 km (three hours) past scenic Lake Sidihoni to the village of Ranggurni Huta. Homestays plus dinner here cost about US$4. The trail continues east across the island, past two primitive forest houses (Pasanggrahan I and II), and down the cliff to Sigarantung, Parmonangan, and finally Tomok.

The second route, shorter and more popular, leaves Pangururan and heads directly east to the village of Partungkoan (also called Dolok), where John's Accommodations charges US$4 for dinner and a room in a Batak chalet. The trail continues east down the mountain ridge to Ambarita.

SAMOSIR ISLAND

© MOON PUBLICATIONS, INC.

Accommodations

Tuk Tuk peninsula offers the island's best selection of low-priced accommodations, plus a handful of better resorts in the US$8-25 price range. With over 50 bungalows to choose from, the best strategy is to wander around and inspect a few places that fit your budget.

Carolina's: The most popular guesthouse on Samosir Island has its own pier, a private swimming cove, a bulletin board, an outstanding restaurant with fresh-baked breads, and all types of rooms from simple huts to luxurious Batak bungalows with a/c and hot water. Tuk Tuk, tel. (0625) 41520, Medan tel. (061) 326207, US$8-25.

Romlan: A handy alternative when Carolina's is filled; it's about mid-way up the peninsula and has a private jetty. Plenty of cheap and quiet places are farther north. Tuk Tuk, tel. (0625) 41557, US$4-10.

Samosir Cottages: Good budget to mid-priced resort with a small restaurant facing pine trees and weathered rocks. Room rates include continental breakfast and transport from Prapat. Tuk Tuk, tel. (0625) 41050, US$6-20.

Anju Cottages: Another spot with somewhat better rooms at the north end of the peninsula. Tuk Tuk, tel. (0625) 41358, US$6-20.

AMBARITA

Four km north of Tuk Tuk is an ancient stone village with flowered coves and old Batak houses. Samosir's largest settlement has a post office, a small hospital, and a market on Tuesdays near the boat dock.

Attractions

Batak houses in the old town face an archaeologically significant spot where the king of the Siallagan tribe once held judicial court with village elders. Those condemned to die were executed in a nearby field, though locals love to weave fancy tales to unsuspecting tourists. The one I heard was that captive enemies were beheaded on the stone slabs, diced up, and mixed with buffalo meat for a ritual village repast. An eerie, life-size stone figure sits in one chair—a silent witness to the rites once practiced by the Bataks.

Accommodations

Ambarita is isolated but a fine place to escape the crowds at Tuk Tuk.

Rohandy's: Batak homestay in a great location on its own miniature peninsula. Rooms cost US$3-6.

Barbara's: North of town with pool and cozy cafe. Ambarita, tel. (0625) 41230, US$3-10.

Gordon's: Two km beyond Ambarita en route to Simanindo, and near the flashy Sopotoba Hotel, you'll find a friendly little spot with cheap rooms in a quiet location. US$3-6.

Le Shangri-La: True escapists will probably love this isolated *losmen,* situated between Ambarita and Simanindo, near the village of Martahan. The owner is friendly and a gold mine of information on the region. Take a bus from Tomok or Tuk Tuk and look for the sign on the right. US$3-8.

SIMANINDO

Simanindo, a traditional village on the north tip of Samosir, 16 km from Ambarita, is chiefly visited for its boat building industry, offshore islands, and amazing Batak architecture.

Attractions

Superb examples of beautiful Batak homes are found all over the island, but none are as impressive as the former king's house in Simanindo, a large earthquake-proof structure which features elaborate carvings and sets of buffalo horns representing the 11 generations of the Sidarok rajas. Now a museum, the interior is filled with large Dutch and Chinese platters, spears, *kris,* carvings, witch-doctor charms, and *huda huda* horses once used in trance dances.

Flanking the king's residence are five large homes and smaller rice-storage barns which open onto a small pavilion of royal graves. Performances of life-size wooden puppets are given on weekends.

INDONESIA

WEST SUMATRA

West Sumatra stretches from Sibolga in the north to Padang in the south—a region of isolated villages, towering mountain ranges, and vast jungle bisected by the infamous Trans-Sumatra Highway. So rugged and unpredictable is this winding road that one of the chief interests of West Sumatra is the journey through it.

The legendary expedition has lost some of its horrors with improved highway maintenance, but overlanders must accept the inevitability of landslides, washed-out bridges, buses packed with everything from chickens to coffins, suicidal bus drivers, and endless Indonesian video movies played at full distorted volume. Medan to Padang takes 14-30 hours, depending on road conditions and how many times the driver stops for meals and *kreteks* (clove cigarettes). Overlanders sometimes overnight in Sibolga before continuing on to Nias.

Aside from the journey itself, West Sumatra's chief attractions are the spectacular landscapes, Minangkabau culture around Bukittinggi, and the remote island of Nias.

SIBOLGA

Sibolga chiefly serves as the embarcation point for boats to Nias and as an overnight pit stop on the grueling journey from Toba to Bukittinggi. The eastern approach to the port town of Sibolga is dramatic: the bus rounds a corner and abruptly plunges down a series of hairpin turns to the coast. Buses often make this descent at sunset; travelers who have mounted themselves on the roof will enjoy a spectacular experience.

Yet it is ironic that a town set in such a superb setting should turn out to be so uninspiring—Sibolga more closely resembles an exile point for political prisoners than a romantic ocean resort.

Accommodations

Self-appointed hotel touts and guides will appear at the *ekspres* bus terminal to direct you to the next available boat or one of Sibolga's fa-

mous *losmen*, which are grungy, noisy, and uniformly suffer from unpleasant owners.

Most travelers avoid Sibolga by catching the Nias boat, which departs nightly except Sundays around 2200.

Pantai Pandan, 12 km north, and Pantai Kalangan, one km south, are pleasant beaches to visit when boats are delayed or cancelled due to bad weather.

Hotel Pasar Baru: Sibolga's best place to crash has relatively friendly managers in a town known for its rapacious *becak* drivers and surly *losmen* owners. Jl. Imam Bonjol, tel. (0642) 22167, US$4-15.

Losmen Bando Kandung: Several inexpensive *losmen* are down near the Nias dock. Jl. Horas 142, tel. (0642) 21149, US$4-6.

Hidap Baru: Somewhat more expensive than the dives near the dock but probably worth the money. Jl. Suprapto 123, tel. (0642) 21957, US$5-15.

Hotel Tapian Nauli: Well-heeled or into Maughamesque colonial nostalgia? Try this upscale hotel in the north end of town. Jl. Let Parman 5, tel. (0642) 21116, US$14-22.

Hotel Wisata: Best in town with a seaside location and all a/c rooms. Jl. Katamso 140, tel. (0642) 23688, US$35-60.

Transportation

Sibolga lies off the main bus route between Danau Toba and Padang, but substandard buses make the journey from Prapat (six hours), Medan (11 hours), and Bukittinggi (12 hours). Most travelers opt for the faster, direct tourist minibuses from Prapat (four hours), Medan (nine hours), and Bukittinggi (10 hours). Tourist minibuses are about 40% more expensive than ordinary buses.

Boat to Nias Island
Ferries to both Gunung Sitoli and Teluk Dalam on Nias leave nightly except Sunday at 2000 from the Jalan Horas port. Tickets can be purchased directly at the dock or from local agents for a small service charge.

NIAS ISLAND

With its famous megalithic stone altars and furniture, spectacular traditional architecture, and complex religious rites, a trip to this fascinating island, 125 km southwest of Sibolga, is a journey into the past. About the size of Bali, Nias boasts a magnificent megalithic heroic culture which flourished well into the 20th century; headhunting and human sacrifice were still practiced as late as 1935.

Nias today is known for its traditional culture—which remains largely intact despite a century of contact with the outside world—as well as its thick jungle, near-impassable roads, and beaches blessed with some of the finest surf between Australia and India.

Transportation

Gunung Sitoli, on the northern tip, is Nias's largest town, but most travelers head directly to Teluk Dalam at the southern tip of the island, where most of the megalithic monuments and surfing beaches are located.

Air: Until an airport is constructed in the south, Nias's only air connection is on SMAC, which flies daily between Medan and Gunung Sitoli for about US$60. SMAC also flies between Padang and Gunung Sitoli on Wednesdays for US$50.

Bus: The road which connects Gunung Sitoli with Teluk Dalam via the central mountains is now paved but remains barely passable in the wet season when mudslides and washed-out bridges bring public transport to a halt. The less scenic but more tolerable road which skirts the east coast is now being improved and will soon replace the central road as the main conduit.

Boat: Ferries leave nightly at 2000 from Sibolga to Gunung Sitoli and Teluk Dalam, and take 10-12 hours to make the crossing.

Gunung Sitoli

The former Dutch administrative center and base for early German missionaries lacks charm but offers good walks to nearby villages with older homes. Traditional *rumah adat* with curious oval floor-plans still stand outside town in Hiliana and Hilimbawedesolo, 13 km south of Gunung Sitoli.

Gunung Sitoli has a small tourist office near the parade grounds, two banks which exchange traveler's checks at reasonable rates, and a Telekom office near the post office where you can make Home Country Direct phone calls.

Organized tours and treks can be arranged through the tourist office and Nias Megalithic Adventures at Miga Beach Bungalows.

Accommodations: Local *losmen* in town are nothing special but better places are five km south of town. Hotel Wisata, just opposite the pier, has fairly clean fan-cooled and a/c rooms for US$5-15. Hotel Gomo, one block south of the pier, has rooms in the same price range.

Most travelers head five km south of town to Wisma Soliga, where clean and spacious rooms cost US$6-15. The manager here can help with onward transportation and treks to nearby villages.

Miga Beach Bungalows, one km south of Wisma Soliga, is another option but somewhat more expensive at US$10-20. Both places can be reached by *oplet* or *becak* from city center.

Transportation: Buses to Teluk Dalam take four hours and leave from the bus terminal at the south end of town.

Teluk Dalam

Teluk Dalam, second-largest town on Nias, chiefly serves as the access point for Lagundri Beach, 12 km west. Lagundri can be reached with a *bemo* or hired motorcycle for US$1.

Traveler's checks can be exchanged at the bank on Jalan Ahmad Yani. Teluk Dalam has

a Telekom office on Jalan Pancasila and travel agents on Jalan Ahmad Yani which sell ferry tickets to Sibolga.

Accommodations: Nobody stays here, but if you need to overnight, Wisma Jamburae on the waterfront has simple rooms from US$4, while Hotel Ampera has larger rooms from US$10.

Lagundri Beach

Lagundri Bay served as the primary port of south Nias until the Krakatau eruption of 1883 wiped it out and the port was moved to Teluk Dalam (which means "Port of Peace"), leaving Lagundri to sleep on until it was discovered by Australian and American surfers in the mid-1970s.

Today this horseshoe-shaped bay consists of two fishing villages, which together form the Kuta and Legian of Nias. The surf at nearby Sorake Beach is almost legendary; much better than at Kuta, with waves breaking over three meters in hypnotically rhythmic patterns—an unreal world, like a dream. Surfing conditions are best from June to October while the remainder of the year brings in small waves perfect for beginners. A stage of the World Qualifying Series is held annually in June and July.

Accommodations: Over 40 *losmen* and a handful of upscale resorts flank the bay between the surfing spots on the west side and the less congested beaches in the east. Most charge a few dollars per room but expect guests to eat in their cafes to compensate for the bargain rates.

Places on Sorake Beach include the budget-priced Olayama, Sun Beach, and westerly Damai Beach Inn where simple huts cost US$2-5, and the somewhat upscale Sea Breeze Inn where larger bungalows go for US$5-10. Sorake Beach Resort around the headlands is geared to group tours with luxurious bungalows from US$50-100.

Bungalows closer to Lagundri attract non-surfers who prefer the better swimming conditions in the placid waters. Among the low-priced favorites are Risky, Magdalena, and Hassan's, while Lantana Inn captures the mid-level market with spacious bungalows priced from US$15-30.

Transportation: Ferries from Sibolga to Teluk Dalam are greeted by the standard assortment of motorcycle taxis, *bemos,* and trucks which depart immediately for Lagundri Beach. Travelers coming down from Gunung Sitoli should get off the bus at the crossroads midway between Teluk

Dalam and Lagundri, where motorcycles take passengers six km west to Lagundri.

Bawomataluo
The most important village architecturally in south Nias is renowned for its ancient homes festooned with superb carvings, high-roofed gables, and megalithic furniture scattered around the village courtyard. Top draw is the reconstructed *omo sebua* owned by the royal family but now converted into a museum raised on gigantic pillars and covered with exquisite wall carvings. Massive megaliths carved with great symbolism complete the scene.

Touristy to the extreme (don't even *ask* about stone jumping), Bawomataluo remains the singular attraction of south Nias. You can also hike down a stone staircase to the village of Orihili.

Bawomataluo, 15 km from Teluk Dalam, can be reached with public bus for about US$1.

Hilisimaetano
Sixteen km inland from Teluk Dalam on a good asphalt road is another traditional village with over 140 *adat* homes flanked by megaliths which line both sides of the broad stone-paved courtyard. Less popular than Bawomataluo; stone jumping is performed for tour groups on Saturday afternoons.

Bawomataluo-Hilisimaetano Hike
An outstanding one-day walk via a back path which passes through a number of traditional villages still filled with stone seats, memorial benches, and stairs of honor.

Orahill is the nicest town because of the relative absence of *"Allo Turi!"* Bawomataluo is best for tribal houses. Siwalawa is rather run-down. Onohondo is friendly, plus it has an inexpensive *losmen* for trekkers. Hilinawalo is the most traditional village, over 100 years old. Bawogosali is a pleasant and picturesque village, but Hilisimaetano is the worst for rascally kids. Just follow the stone path which connects all the villages on this 15-km walk.

BUKITTINGGI

The administrative and cultural center for the Minangkabau people, Bukittinggi is one of the loveliest, friendliest, and most relaxed towns in Sumatra—a real oasis after the rugged bus ride from Toba or Jakarta. There are musical taxis, pompadoured horse-carts, veiled schoolgirls, flower markets, good restaurants, and a wide selection of reasonable accommodations. Bukittinggi is also an excellent base to explore the nearby canyons, caves, equatorial lakes, hot springs, and traditional villages centered around Minangkabau architecture.

It can't be overstressed how important proper dress is in West Sumatra. The Minangkabau regard many travelers as impoverished hippies because of their unkempt appearance, saying that they lack *baso basi,* "good manners." Women should *always* remain well covered and never expose their shoulders or knees. Men should dress in long pants and clean shirts, rather than shorts or muscle fatigues. Modesty and respectable dress will improve goodwill and make your trip much more enjoyable.

Attractions
The tourist office near the clock tower has maps, brochures, and schedules of upcoming cultural events, and can help with organized tours of the countryside. Information can also be picked up from local bookstores and travel agencies. Traveler's checks can be exchanged at BNI Bank on Jalan Ahmad Yani and Bank Rakyat Indonesia near the clock tower.

Clock Tower: In the center of town and overlooking the market is Bukittinggi's Big Ben, constructed by the Dutch in 1827.

Bukittinggi Museum: Minangkabau culture is featured in the cluster of traditional houses which comprise the oldest museum in West Sumatra. Inside the two rice barns and communal living house are exhibits of resplendent wedding costumes, headdresses, musical instruments, bronzework, costumed mannequins, and architectural models of current and obsolete villages. The adjacent zoo is deplorable.

Fort de Kock: Erected by the Dutch in 1825, this site is best visited at sunset when giant fruit bats come out, looking like birds without tails. The site now serves as a public water supply.

Ngarai Canyon: On the southeast edge of town lies a four-km-long chasm with sheer rocky walls plunging down to the riverbed below. A two-km trail leads down to the river past Japa-

INDONESIA

nese tunnels and across to the silversmith village of Kota Gadang.

Budget Accommodations

Bukittinggi's cheap *losmen* on Jalan Ahmad Yani in the center of town charge US$3-6 for small but acceptable rooms. Be forewarned, however, that you are awakened each morning by the sounds of motorcycles, cars, and buses—ask for a room in the back.

Gangga Hotel: Walking down from the clock tower, the first rambling building on the right has decent rooms and, like most places in town, sells inexpensive 10-day tours to Siberut Island. Jl. Ahmad Yani 70, tel. (0752) 22967, US$4-6.

Wisma Tiga Balai: Top-of-the-hill *losmen* with very basic rooms at bargain prices. Jl. Ahmad Yani 100, tel. (0752) 21824, US$3-5.

Yany Hotel: An old colonial building with fairly clean rooms. The low-price cubicles are box-like, but the more expensive rooms include hot water and private bath. Jl. Ahmad Yani 101, tel. (0752) 22740, US$5-20.

Hotel Srikandi: This aging hotel offers fairly clean rooms with private baths and verandahs. Jl. Ahmad Yani 117, tel. (0752) 22984, US$6-10.

Moderate Accommodations

To beat the noise at somewhat higher prices, stay up near Fort de Kock.

Benteng Hotel: Great views and pleasant atmosphere make this a real find. Nearby Suwarni's Guesthouse is also recommended. Jl. Benteng 1, tel. (0725) 21115, US$15-25.

Lima's Hotel: Older but clean hotel removed from the traffic on Jalan Ahmad Yani. Jl. Kesehatan 34, tel. (0752) 22641, US$15-25.

Melia Pusako Hotel: The 1992 opening of this US$23-million-dollar hotel finally provided Bukittinggi with first-class accommodations, but it's poorly located three km east of town on the road to Payakumbuh. Jl. Sukarno-Hatta 7, tel. (0752) 32111, US$90-140.

Novotel Bukittinggi: Newest upscale resort with all the standard trimmings. Jl. Laras Datuk Bandara, tel. (0752) 35000, US$95-180.

Transportation

Bukittinggi's main bus terminal is three km south of town and reached by any *oplet* heading down Jalan Yamin. Arrivals from Toba and Pekanbaru should get off in the center of town near the clock tower rather than continue down to the bus terminal.

Bus tickets can be purchased directly from ANS, ALS, or Enggano bus companies on Jalan Pemuda or out at the Aur Kuning *terminal bis.* Bus destinations include Padang (two hours), Pekanbaru (five hours), Sibolga (11 hours), Danau Toba (13 hours), and Medan (18 hours).

VICINITY OF BUKITTINGGI

The countryside around Bukittinggi could keep you busy for weeks. Organized tours or chartered *bemos* are highly recommended—on your own you'll have long waits for public transport. Check with the guesthouses or travel agents in town.

Lake Maninjau

Known for its culture, remoteness, and beauty, this huge crater lake 34 km west of Bukittinggi is among the largest in the world—a wonder in itself. The ride out is just as incredibly scenic as the 610-meter drop to the lakeshore. Buses and *bemos* go direct from Bukittinggi, though a better alternative is to hike for six hours down from Lawang, a market village five km beyond Matur.

Accommodations: Lake Maninjau has over 20 inexpensive *losmen* and several upscale resorts with facilities for swimming, fishing, and boating. Amai Bungalows and Pillie Homestay some 200 meters south of the bus stop have decent rooms from US$3-6, while the more upscale Hotel Tandirih and Hotel Pasir Panjang Permai, both one km north of town, have rooms overlooking the lake from US$25-40.

Payakumbuh and Vicinity

Dozens of Minangkabau villages inhabited by traditional craftsmen and displaying horn-roofed homes are located outside Bukittinggi in countryside beautiful enough to stop your heart.

Payakumbuh, 33 km east of Bukittinggi, is larger than Bukittinggi and not as charming, but the surrounding landscape offers a spectacular blend of deep caves, icy waterfalls, broad canyons, blazing ricefields, megalithic stones carved by ancient peoples, and traditional villages largely unchanged by the 20th century.

Attractions: The village of Guguk, 13 km north of town, features an old village council house and over two dozen mysterious stone megaliths and menhirs profusely carved with symbolic figures. Grave sites? Magical talismans? Nobody knows.

Taram is a lovely traditional village just five km from Payakumbuh, while Balubus, 10 km from town, features a small museum and a long central avenue flanked by typical Minang housing. Nature lovers can also visit Harau Canyon (like a miniature Yosemite Valley, with four spectacular waterfalls and protected wildlife, a five-tiered waterfall at Burai, and limestone caves at Ngalan Indah).

Equator certificates (the equator is 37 km distant) are available from the local tourist office on Jalan Sudirman.

Accommodations: As a leading alternative to Bukittinggi, Payakumbuh now has several simple homestays and inexpensive hotels. Travelers usually stay at a cozy homestay called Mr. Wet's Place on Jalan Lingkungan, about four blocks east of the bus stop. Mr. Wet rents bikes, leads treks, tells fairly good jokes, and performs "marvelous magic tricks."

Wisma Bougainville on Jalan Sudirman and Wisma Flamboyan on Jalan Suryani have clean rooms for US$6-10.

Batu Sangkar and Vicinity

More attractive, and with greater attractions than Payakumbuh, is Batu Sangkar, 42 km southeast of Bukittinggi. Former capital of the Minangkabau nation and Dutch stronghold during their struggle against the Paderis, this town and its surrounding countryside are very special treasures—a real highlight of West Sumatra. The market is superb.

Attractions: Top draw is the famous Bali Janggo, a recently reconstructed Minangkabau royal palace filled with historical artifacts and valuable handicrafts. The palace is 10 km south of Batu Sangkar and adjacent to a striking modern mosque that almost floats in the heat. En route are two luxurious Minangkabau-style homes constructed by wealthy residents who now live in Jakarta.

Some of the oldest homes on Sumatra are still standing in the remote village of Balimbing; the best examples are down the side road behind the badly painted home at the town's entrance.

For a trip into the past, take a stroll through the ancient royal village of Pariangan on the slopes of Mt. Merapi, where people relax on the front steps as the volcano fumes above.

Mountaineers may want to climb Mt. Merapi starting from Sungai Puar on the southeast slope. This volcano is still deadly: two European tourists died in 1992 when the volcano suddenly began to spit lava and poisonous fumes, and several more tourists died on the mountain in 1997.

Lake Singkarak, one hour west of Batu Sangkar, is commercialized and rather unattractive.

Accommodations: Batu Sangkar is a great place to escape the tourists in Bukittinggi. Hotel Yoherma, a few blocks north of town center, is a clean, modern hotel with upscale rooms priced US$5-12. Hotel Pagarruyng across the street and nearby Parma Hotel are slightly cheaper. Kiambang Homestay on the same street costs just US$4-8.

PADANG

Padang, the provincial capital of West Sumatra, chiefly serves as a transit spot between Bukittinggi and southern Sumatra and as the arrival point for visitors coming by air or sea from Jakarta.

The West Sumatra tourist office is surprisingly helpful but closes at 1400 weekdays and 1230 on Saturday. Information about local sights can also be picked up from the Padang city tourist office on Jalan Samudra and Pacto tours on Jalan Tan Malaka.

Banks around town provide the usual money changing services, while Pacto serves as the representative for American Express.

Attractions

Adityawarman Museum offers informative exhibits on Minangkabau culture and the peoples of the Mentawai Islands, while the adjacent cultural center occasionally sponsors dance and *pencak silat* performances.

A popular walk leads south to the river and up Padang Hill via the Chinese cemetery; impressive views of the harbor. Farther south is Air Manis, a fishing village where boats can be hired to reach offshore islands.

The coastline south from Padang is extremely rugged and scenic, with pulse-stopping views from the highway as it twists over rocky ridges and curves past sandy coves. Travelers often escape Padang to spend a few days relaxing in the natural bay of Bungus, 23 km south or one hour by *oplet*. Bungus offers clean sand, bathtub-warm waters, and inexpensive *losmen:* the best reason to spend time in Padang.

Accommodations

Most travelers consider Padang simply a stepping-stone to Bukittinggi, but the town itself is surprisingly attractive and has decent hotels, professional travel services, and of course restaurants serving that famous Padang cuisine. Most of the hotels are in the center of town within easy walking distance of the bus terminal.

Hotel Benyamin: Travelers usually stay in one of the simple hotels near the bus terminal such as this one with fan-cooled rooms at the end of an alley near the Femina Hotel. Jl. Azizcham 15, tel. (0751) 22324, US$6-12.

Hotel Sriwijaya: Three blocks east of the bus terminal with small but adequate rooms in a quieter location. Jl. Alanglawas 24, tel. (0751) 23577, US$5-10.

Hang Tuah Hotel: Nearly opposite the bus terminal is a conveniently located hotel with spa-

PADANG

JL. PURUS III

NEW TIGA TIGA HOTEL

JL. PURUS II

JL. PURUS I

JL. OLO LADANG

ALDILLA HOTEL

JL. VETERAN

JL. BANDAR PURIS

JL. PASIR IX

JL. YANI

JL. KARTINI

ANGGEREK HOTEL

TO AIRPORT AND BUKITTINGGI

JL. JATI IV

JL. ABDULLAH MUIS

JL. JATI IV

JL. SUDIRMAN

WEST SUMATRA TOURIST OFFICE

WISMA MAYANG SARI

JL. RATULANGI

JL. TAN MALAKA

PACTO TOURS

JL. KOTO MABARK

JL. OLO

HOTEL JAKARTA

HOTEL GARUDA

MARKET

JL. AZIZ CHAN

TO SOUTH SUMATRA

TIGA TIGA HOTEL

MANDALA OFFICE

HOTEL CENDRAWASIH

JL. PEMUDA

JL. BANDAR OLO

JL. PASAR RAYA

HOTEL BENYAMIN MARKET

POST OFFICE

HOTEL PADANG

FEMINA HOTEL

HANG TUAH HOTEL

BUS TERMINAL

BEMO STATION

CITY HALL

TAXIS

POLICE

JL. HANG TUAH

DIPO INTERNATIONAL HOTEL

JL. YAMIN

AMUSEMENT PARK

TELEKOM

SRIWIJAYA HOTEL

JL. PANCASILA

MACHUDUN HOTEL

JL. IMAM BONJOL

JL. THAMPIN

TO SOLOK AND JAKARTA

CULTURAL CENTER

JL. DIPONEGORO

MARIANI HOTEL

JL. KANDUANG

JL. HILOGO

PROVINCIAL MUSEUM

HOTEL SEDONA

NATOUR MUARA HOTEL

HOTEL PANGERAN

JL. MONGISIDI

HOTEL HAYAM WURUK

JL. DOBI

CHINATOWN

JL. RAHMAN HAKIM

JL. GURUN

PADANG CITY TOURIST OFFICE

JL. COKROAMINOTO

JL. KANDUANG

CHINESE TEMPLE

JL. KELENTENG

JL. BATIPUH

ARAU RIVER

JL. NIPAH

JL. KARAM

JL. ARAU

BATANG ARAU

ESTUARY

SITI NURBAYA PARK

PADANG HILL

BOATS TO SIBERUT ISLAND

FERRY

PANTAI AIR MANIS

CHINESE CEMETERY

PADANG BEACH

STRAITS OF MENTAWI

0   200 m

N

MOON

INDONESIA

© MOON PUBLICATIONS, INC.

cious and fairly clean rooms. Jl. Pemuda 1, tel. (0751) 26556, US$10-25.

Dipo International Hotel: Best mid-priced hotel in town with all a/c rooms one block south of the bus terminal. Jl. Diponegoro 25, tel. (0751) 34261, US$20-35.

Femina Hotel: Another of Padang's numerous mid-priced hotels, Femina lies near the post office, Garuda, and central market with both fancooled and a/c rooms. Jl. Bagindo Chan 15, tel. (0751) 21950, US$15-30.

Wisma Mayang Sari: A friendly place in a former Dutch mansion where tourists sprawl over lawn chairs, writing postcards and gazing at what might have been a colonial garden. Jl. Sudirman 19, tel. (0751) 22647, US$18-35.

Hotel Sedona: Padang's best hotel with swimming pool, tennis courts, and restaurant popular with tour groups and the region's expatriate community. Jl. Bundo Kandung, tel. (0751) 37555, US$125-180.

Transportation

Padang—the transportation hub of West Sumatra—is halfway up Sumatra's west coast and three hours west of Bukittinggi.

Air: Merpati, Sempati, Silk Air, or Mandala fly daily from Jakarta, Medan, Palembang, Pekanbaru, Singapore, Kuala Lumpur, and Batam. SMAC flies every Wednesday to Gunung Sitoli on Pulau Nias.

Merpati, Pelangi Air, and SMAC are in Hotel Natour Muara on Jalan Gerja; Sempati is in Pangeran Beach Hotel on Jalan Juanda; and Silk Air is in the Hotel Hayam Waruk on the street of the same name.

Padang's Tabing Airport is nine km north of town on the Bukittinggi road. Taxis cost 10,000Rp to city center or walk to the road and hail an *oplet* or, better yet, a bus directly to Bukittinggi. You can reach the airport from town with bus 14A.

Ship to Nias and Jakarta: A Pelni ship departs every Friday from Padang's Teluk Bayur harbor for Gunung Sitoli on Pulau Nias. The ship then returns to Padang and leaves every Sunday for Jakarta, Semarang, and Pontianak. Fares are US$15-45 to Nias and US$30-80 to Jakarta depending on class. The Pelni ship to Jakarta is a very popular option since it's less exhausting than the bus and surprisingly comfortable with

clean beds and hot showers in superior classes. Deck-class passengers should grab a space early and be prepared to give English lessons to many of the very friendly passengers.

Teluk Bayur port is seven km south of town and served by *oplets.* Pelni tickets can be purchased at the harbor or from Ina Tour & Travel in the Dipo International Hotel.

Boat to Pulau Siberut: Boats to Siberut Island leave four times weekly from the pier at the south end of town in the Batang Arau River, also known as Sungai Muara.

Bus: Padang's bus terminal is centrally located near the budget hotels. Buses depart most frequently in the early morning and reach Bukittinggi (two hours), Pekanbaru (six hours), and Danau Toba (12-16 hours), and Jakarta (30-36 hours). Express bus companies with direct a/c services include ANS and ALS.

MENTAWI ISLANDS

The Mentawi Archipelago—Siberut, Sipora, and Pagai islands—comprises one of Indonesia's most complex geological, biological, and cultural puzzles. Separated almost a million years ago from the mainland of Sumatra, Mentawi has undergone a unique evolutionary divergence, giving rise to endemic forms of flora and fauna found nowhere else in Indonesia. And until quite recently, the people who lived in the jungles retained many of the stone-age traditions which disappeared generations ago from other regions of the nation.

Tourism, and deforestation in search of a fragrant resin called Gaharu, have transformed Mentawi to some degree, but much of the traditional lifestyles still survive in the villages away from the coastal plains.

Attractions

Siberut is the principal destination for most visitors to Mentawi. Muara Siberut in the south is the only town of any size and the only place with lodgings.

Most visitors take river trips and hike from Muara Siberut to Mentawi villages such as Tiap, two hours upriver, and Rokdok (Rogdog), five hours distant. Treks from Rokdok head to Madobag and Ugei, while another stop can be made at Siatanusa, a sago-producing village five hours away. Other villages include Madobak, six hours by boat, and Sakudai, two days of tough travel by boat and foot.

Organized Tours

Tourism is on the rise. Government officials estimate that annual tourist arrivals to Siberut rose from under 200 in 1988 to over 10,000 in 1997, and about 10% of all visitors to Bukittinggi now take an organized tour of Siberut. Villagers are accustomed to Westerners and anxious to separate you from your *rupiah;* expect to pay a reasonable amount for lodging, photos, and entrance into old homes.

A vast majority of visitors join a scheduled tour from Bukittinggi. Ten-day tours cost US$150-450 and include the boat from Padang, accommodations, meals, permits, and guide services. Most of the guesthouses and hotels in Bukittinggi sell tours and provide guestbooks with useful commentary, but check the credentials of your guide and his trekking experience before committing yourself to one of these fairly lengthy tours. Luxury tours priced from US$600 are sold by several travel agencies in Bukittinggi and Padang.

Accommodations

Travelers on organized tours are put up in local lodgings, often in homes of villagers where you sleep on hard wooden floors. Siberut's only lodging option is Syahruddin's Homestay in Muara Siberut, where decent rooms go for US$4-8.

Transportation

Boats operated by PT Rusco Lines depart Padang on Monday and Wednesday, while Mentawai Indah boats leave on Thursday and Saturday. Tickets can be purchased in advance from travel agents in Padang or directly at the Sungei Batang Arau pier. Boats take about 10 hours to reach Muara Siberut.

Roads are almost non-existent on Pulau Siberut and boats must be chartered to reach almost every destination—an expensive proposition which makes organized tours the most sensible way to see the islands.

SOUTH SUMATRA

South Sumatra is a wild, underpopulated district known for its oil wealth, large sluggish rivers which flow through highland plains, and ambitious *transmigrasi* resettlement projects. Aside from a limited number of historical and archaeological sites, there's little of great interest here.

Transportation

To avoid the experience of your life riding up through the fetid swamplands of South Sumatra, simply fly or take the Pelni ship from Jakarta to Padang.

Bus: Travel agents in Jakarta book reserved seats to Padang on modern Mercedes buses. There are many private bus companies, but the best are ALS and ANS. Direct service from Jakarta to Padang costs about US$30 and includes the ferry crossing from Java to Sumatra. Prices vary considerably; shop around.

Consider breaking your journey for a rest stop in Bengkulu, or at any of the other towns on the Trans-Sumatran Highway. Sungai Penuh near Lake Kerinci is a popular choice.

Ship: Pelni has two ships which leave Jakarta every week and take about two full days to reach Padang. Costs range from simple deck class at US$20 to luxurious first-class for US$50-80. Both ships are surprisingly modern vessels with hot showers, restaurants, and comfortable lounges.

PEKANBARU

Capital of Riau Province and the main city of oil-rich Riau Daratan, Pekanbaru is a clean, modern, and well-laid-out town on the Siak River and serves as the gateway to Southeast Asia's largest and richest oil fields. However, it's not what you'd expect from an oil city: it's unexpectedly friendly and easygoing.

Unfortunately, from a tourist's point of view, Pekanbaru is an unappealing destination with little of great interest. Most travelers who visit this river port do so for one reason: to take the ferry up the river to Batam Island and, finally, Singapore.

INDONESIA

Attractions

Grand Mosque: Pekanbaru's city mosque, with its bright onion dome, flanks the central church on Jalan Sheikh Burhanudin. To absorb the genuine flavor of the area, stroll around the fruit market and visit the sleazy harbor.

Siak Palace: The old royal palace at Siak Sri Indrapura was constructed in 1889 by the 11th of 12 sultans who ruled Siak from 1725 to 1945. From Pekanbaru, it's a two-hour downriver trip and three hours return by bus.

Accommodations

The booming economy, fueled by the local oil industry, means Pekanbaru is somewhat expensive, though budget *losmen* are plentiful around the bus terminal on Jalan Nangka. Several are geared to budget travelers and can help with boats to Batam or transportation to Bukittinggi and Lake Toba.

Poppie's Homestay: Popular place one block east of the bus terminal and about two km south of the port. Boat arrivals from Batam can call for a free pickup. Jl. Cempedak II, tel. (0761) 33863, US$3-6.

Tommy's Place: Another spot one block west of the bus terminal with helpful managers who can arrange Batam boat tickets for a small service charge. Gang Nantongga, tel. (0761) 33822, US$3-6.

Hotel Linda: Acceptable mid-range hotel just across the street from the bus terminal with both fan-cooled and a/c rooms. Jl. Nangka 133, tel. (0761) 36915, US$8-25.

Sinda Hotel: Another slightly better hotel near the bus terminal. Jl. Pepaya 73, tel. (0761) 23719, US$12-25.

Hotel Dyan Graha: Top hotel in Pekanbaru in the center of town one block east of Jalan Sudirman. Jl. Gatot Subroto 7, tel. (0761) 26851, US$65-110.

Transportation

Pekanbaru is 175 km northeast of Bukittinggi and 310 km west of Singapore.

Air: Garuda, Merpati, or Sempati connect Pekanbaru on a daily basis with Jakarta, Medan, Padang, Palembang, Singapore, Tanjung Pinang, and Batam. The airport is 10 km outside town and is served by taxis and *oplets* from the nearby highway.

Bus: Buses and minibuses depart several times daily from the bus terminal on Jalan Nangka for Bukittinggi (five hours) and Jakarta (35 hours).

Boat: Tickets to Batam can be purchased from local travel agencies and the guesthouses mentioned above. Boats depart daily in the early morning, cost US$18-25, and take about 10 hours to reach Singapore with a combination of bus transport and speedboat. Most speedboats pull into Batam around 1700, from where ferries immediately head off to the World Trade Centre in Singapore.

BENGKULU

Formerly known as Bencoolen, this historic coastal city of 70,000 has long been neglected by the tourism industry, largely because of its isolated location well off the Trans-Sumatran Highway.

Bengkulu, however, is a peaceful spot that once served as the center of British efforts to retain a toehold in Indonesia. The town was settled by the British in 1685 under the false impression that the best route to China was through the Sunda Straits. Bencoolen—a financial failure and "the most wretched place I ever beheld" according to Raffles, the final governor—was happily handed over to the Dutch in 1824, five years after Raffles fled Sumatra and founded Singapore. Today, it sleeps on.

Attractions

Fort Marlborough: Constructed from 1713 to 1719 by the British East India Company, Fort Marlborough remains the most formidable fort ever built by the British in the Orient. Other colonial reminders include a cupola-roofed memorial to a despised ex-governor and an old European cemetery dotted with the graves of British and Dutch sailors.

Sukarno's House: Sukarno, who distinguished himself early in his political career by his vocal opposition to colonial rule, was arrested by the Dutch on Java in 1933 and brought to Bengkulu in 1938, where he remained under house arrest until the Japanese arrived in 1941.

Provincial Museum: Bengkulu Museum Negeri, located south of town in an area called Padang Harapan, offers an extensive collection of prehistoric artifacts, bronze drums, traditional Engganese textiles, and most importantly, examples of highly regarded Bengkulu batiks called *kasin besuruh.*

Accommodations

Budget *losmen* are near Fort Marlborough, while better hotels are at the beach about two km south of the fort.

Losmen Samudera: Bengkulu's cheapest is right across the street from the fort but it's hot and noisy. Jl. Benteng, tel. (0736) 32912, US$3-5.

Wisma Balai Buntar: One block south of the fort and probably the best place in Bengkulu, this old Dutch villa has clean and spacious a/c rooms. Jl. Khadijah 122, tel. (0736) 21254, US$10-15.

Hotel Asia: Spotless a/c rooms with private bath and hot water in the center of town. Jl. Ahmad Yani 922, tel. (0736) 21901, US$15-25.

Horizon Hotel: Best in town on a fairly decent beach with a swimming pool and other upscale amenities. Jl. Pantai Nala 142, tel. (0736) 21722, US$60-90.

Transportation

Bengkulu is 110 km west of Lubuk Linggau, a junction town on the Trans-Sumatran Highway.

Air: Merpati flies daily from Jakarta and Palembang. The airport, 14 km south of town, can be reached with taxi or public *bemo* from the nearby highway. Merpati is in Hotel Samudera Dwinka on Jalan Sudirman.

Bus: Buses approach Bengkulu from several directions, though most conveniently from Lubuk Linggau on the Trans-Sumatran Highway. The main bus terminal is six km southeast of town. Buses go from here to Lubuk Linggau (four hours), Jakarta (24 hours), and Padang via Muko Muka (28 hours).

RIAU ISLANDS

Riau is a group of over 300 almost untouched islands that stretches south from Singapore across the South China Sea toward the giant landmasses of Sumatra and Kalimantan.

Batam—the most important island in Riau—serves as a popular weekend getaway for Singapore residents and also provides an intriguing backdoor approach to Sumatra. The island is abuzz with new projects: major hotels, marine clubs, dive operators, more golf courses, better ferry terminals, and an expanded airport to handle the growing crowds.

Transportation

Modern air-conditioned hovercraft and slower ferries to Batam and Bintan leave frequently throughout the day from the World Trade Centre in Singapore. Most go to, and terminate at, the Indonesian immigration checkpoint at Sekupang on Batam Island. The crossing takes 45 minutes.

After immigration formalities, you can stop at the money exchange counters and then walk one minute south to the domestic ferry terminal, from where speedboats depart to various destinations in Sumatra. The journey to Pekanbaru starts with a four-hour speedboat trip to Tanjung Buton on Sumatra, then a three-hour bus ride to Pekanbaru. This combination of speedboat and bus costs about US$20.

Important: Speedboats to Pekanbaru leave the domestic ferry terminal daily but service shuts down around 1000. Get an early start from Singapore unless you want to find yourself stranded in expensive, boring Batam.

Batam's recently extended Hang Nadim Airport handles connecting flights to Jakarta, Medan, Pekanbaru, and Pontianak. The flight to Jakarta costs US$100, a relatively economical way to reach Java from Singapore.

BATAM ISLAND

An island about two-thirds the size of Singapore, Batam has been developed into a major tourist destination with deluxe hotels, golf courses, and everything else craved by the overworked citizens of Singapore.

Sekupang

Ferries from Singapore dock at this bustling port town. If you miss the last boat to Sumatra, head into town by taxi or bus or continue to Pulau Bintan for less expensive accommodations.

Batam Fantasy Resort: This renovated and upgraded resort has 100 rooms with a restaurant, tennis courts, and a swimming pool. Tanjung Pinggir, tel. (0778) 322289, US$65-90.

Hilltop Hotel: On a hilltop behind town is this aptly named 64-room hotel, popular with rich Singaporeans who haunt the karaoke club and disco. 8 Jl. Sutami, tel. (0778) 322482, US$60-100.

Nagoya

Nagoya is a relatively new town built on reclaimed land less than a decade ago. Now the commercial and transportation hub of Batam, Nagoya is a slightly raucous place with modern hotels, dozens of excellent seafood restaurants, nightclubs, discos, massage parlors, duty-free shops, and hawker stalls that crowd the streets at night.

Accommodations in Nagoya are very expensive since most visitors are tourists, not travelers.

Budget Hotels: Inexpensive *losmen* under US$10 include several *penginapan* at Block C on Jalan Tenku Umar, about two km from town toward the post office. Penginapan Minang Jaya, Losmen Sederhana, and Wisma Chendra Wisata are survivable but badly overpriced compared to the average Indonesian dive.

Bukit Nagoya Hotel: A mid-priced hotel in the center of town with 32 a/c rooms. Jl. Sultan Abdul Rahman 1, tel. (0778) 352871, US$25-45.

Hotel Horizona: A decent alternative to the Bukit Nagoya. Jl. Rahman, tel. (0778) 457111, US$25-45.

Nongsa

Upmarket tourist developments are concentrated around the northeast corner of the island, where groves of coconut palms face a beautiful sandy beach. Upscale plans are afoot farther along at Telok Mata Ikan ("Fish Eye Bay"). After a day of lazing on the beach, enjoy a sunset dinner in Batu Besar, a fishing village eight km from Nongsa.

BATAM AND BINTAN ISLANDS

© MOON PUBLICATIONS, INC.

INDONESIA

Pelni ship to Bongka and Jakarta (Every 7 Days)

Ferry to Pulau Lingga

Ferry to Pulau Singkep

Ferry to Jambi

Ferry to Kuala Tungkal and Jambi

Ferries to Sumatra

10 mi

10 km

Turi Beach Resort: Upscale resort with 150 Balinese-style rooms, huge swimming pool, beach bar, windsurfing, Hobie Cats, and snorkeling, plus, you can see the lights of Singapore twinkling in the distance. Batu Ampar, tel. (0778) 310078, Singapore tel. (065) 273-5055, US$120-185.

Batam View Beach Resort: Facilities at this 196-room hotel include a swimming pool with sunken bar, four tennis courts, three restaurants, a private beach with yacht harbor, and an adjacent 18-hole golf course. Jalan Hang Lakir, tel. (0778) 322281, Singapore tel. (065) 235-4366, US$130-195.

BINTAN ISLAND

Bintan is the largest and most populous island in Riau, containing the capital and chief port town of Tanjung Pinang.

Situated on an important commercial sea lane, Bintan has long held strategic importance. Early kingdoms competed with the rulers of Temasek (Singapore) and Melaka for control of regional trade. The departure of the Portuguese from Melaka in the early 16th century marked the beginning of Riau's Golden Age: from 1530 to the end of the 18th century, Riau was the nucleus of the Malay civilization. Evidences of their glory can still be seen near Tanjung Pinang.

As on Batam, modern Bintan is also experiencing heady economic growth and enjoying a mini-tourism boom. An ambitious marine-tourism project has been announced by the Indonesian government, but for the present, Bintan remains a much more idyllic island than growth-intensive Batam.

Transportation

Speedboats to Pekanbaru generally leave from Batam and not Bintan, although a few speedboats do the trip from Tanjung Pinang with a stop at Sekupang on Batam.

Pelni has two ships which depart Bintan weekly for Jakarta. The KM *Rinjani* leaves Kijang in the southeastern corner of the island every Sunday and takes 28 hours to reach Jakarta. The MV *Samudera Jaya* leaves Tanjung Pinang every Thursday and does the crossing in a somewhat quicker 18 hours. Deck class on both ships costs about US$40.

The Pelni office is in Tanjung Pinang on Jalan Ketapang.

Tanjung Pinang

Tanjung Pinang is a Malay-Chinese trading town which spreads between a surprisingly modern commercial center and an older fishing village erected on rickety stilts. Travelers sometimes overnight here rather than in more expensive Batam, though the town can serve as a good base for exploring the nearby beaches, islands, and historical sights.

The markets, wharves, Chinese temples, mosques, and stilted houses at Pelantan 2 harbor are worth a look. Riau Kandil Museum, two km out of town on the road to Kijang, contains worthwhile collections of old *kris,* guns, antique brassware, genealogical charts, and most of the surviving *pusakas* (heirlooms) of the old Riau kingdoms.

Accommodations: Tanjung Pinang has plenty of accommodations in all price ranges. Budget travelers should look for signs marked Penginapan; the term *losmen* is not widely used in Riau. Homestays are also possible, but be extra cautious with your bags. Most of the inexpensive *penginapan* are in an alley between the wharf and the mosque.

Bong's Homestay: A very friendly homestay in the center of town, about two blocks from the ferry dock. Lorong Bintan II 20, US$4-8.

Johnny's Homestay: Gregarious and helpful Johnny often greets arrivals at the ferry pier, armed with the latest tips on travel connections to Java and Sumatra. Nearby Rommel Homestay handles the overflow. Lorong Bintan II 22, US$4-8.

Wisma Riau: A clean and comfortable, if somewhat older, hotel with fan-cooled and a/c rooms with private bath. Jalan Yusuf Kahar, tel. (0771) 21023, US$12-35.

Riau Holidays Indah: Upscale visitors often stay in this air-conditioned 50-room hotel built on stilts over the harbor. Great sunsets, but as Eric Oey points out in his fabulous guide to Sumatra, "The food is awful and the bar an insult to civilized drinking." Jl. Pelantar II 53, tel. (0771) 22644, US$28-60.

Nightlife: Revolves around cinemas, the night market near the wharf, and a pair of renowned "villages of joy": Batu Duabelas and Batu Enambelas, red-light districts located 12 km and 16 km (respectively) outside town toward Kawai.

Pulau Penyenget

Once the seat of power for the Riau-Johor Sultanate, Penyenget Island is the chief historical site in the archipelago. Boats from the Tanjung Pinang pier take 10 minutes and cost 500Rp. Upon arrival, turn right and walk toward the northwest corner of the island.

Highlights include the magnificent sulfur-yellow mosque which looks like something out of Disneyland, former palaces now under reconstruction, royal bathing places, ornate watchtowers, and a fine collection of burial pavilions.

Pantai Trikora

The eastern and southern coastlines of Bintan offer deserted beaches and excellent diving in

glass-clear water over beautiful coral reefs. The pristine beach at Trikora can be reached with public *bemo* or chartered taxi from Tanjung Pinang toward the airport at Kijang.

Offshore Mantang Island has a 15,000-ton British freighter sunk by the Japanese. Long, sandy white beaches fringed with coconut trees also stretch along the eastern coastline; Pantai Brakit has been recommended.

Accommodations: Accommodations range from simple huts to comfortable chalets. Yasin's Guesthouse near the village of Teluk Bakau has simple palm huts plus three daily meals for US$8-12. The adjacent Bukit Berbunga Cottages also provides a room and meals for US$8-12.

Trikor Beach Resort, one km north of the budget bungalows, costs US$40-60 for larger bungalows overlooking the very fine beach.

INDONESIA

NUSA TENGGARA

Stretching 1,500 km east from Lombok to Timor, Nusa Tenggara ("Southeastern Islands") offers the intrepid traveler a fascinating experience across three of Indonesia's most remote provinces: Nusa Tenggara Barat (Lombok and Sumbawa), Nusa Tenggara Timur (Komodo, Flores, the Solor and Alor archipelagoes, Sumba, and West Timor), and Timor Timur (East Timor).

Travel remains arduous and time-consuming, though Nusa Tenggara's lack of tourists and spectacular natural wonders ensure a welcome change from the commercialization of Bali and other Indonesian regions.

TRANSPORTATION

A decade ago, travel across Nusa Tenggara was a tiring and time-consuming experience due to the dearth of scheduled flights, abysmal roads which degenerated into muddy quagmires in the rainy season, and interisland boat service operated at the whim of the captain.

The situation has changed dramatically in recent years. Merpati and smaller airlines now link most of the provincial capitals with Bali, Jakarta, and other neighboring islands. Most of the roads have been surfaced (or resurfaced), and buses now race across the islands in record time. Pelni and other shipping lines operate boats between many ports and most islands are connected with dependable, daily inter-island ferry service.

Delays are inevitable and travelers should be prepared for unpunctual boats and crowded buses, but the horror stories of earlier days are largely a thing of the past.

Time: Travelers intent on visiting all the major islands of Nusa Tenggara should allow two or three weeks on their 60-day tourist visa. Those with less time will probably need to limit their experience to the major islands (Lombok, Komodo, and Flores are most likely) or utilize the services of Merpati to avoid lengthy overland travel.

A popular itinerary starting from Bali is by boat or air to Lombok, a bus across Sumbawa, a side trip to see the dragons of Komodo, a week or so enjoying the beaches and volcanoes on Flores, and finally a return flight from Flores to Bali (or Flores to Sulawesi).

Air

Merpati operates an extensive network of hops to provincial capitals across Nusa Tenggara. Routes are networked east from Bali and west from Kupang on Timor, the most common path being the route from Bali to Lombok, Sumbawa, Flores, and then down to Timor. A less-frequented route is the southeastern path from Bali to Sumba and then Timor.

Service from Bali to most destinations is on a near-daily basis, though Westerners generally head directly to Lombok, Labuhanbajo (the Komodo port) in western Flores, or Maumere on Flores. The most popular flights from Kupang are north to Flores or west to Sumba and finally Bali.

Fares are heavily subsidized by the Indonesian government and therefore relatively cheap, though bargain rates ensure that many flights are fully booked. Another problem is that reservations are difficult to confirm and published schedules are hardly worth the paper they are printed on. In most cases, airport delays, flight cancellations, and overbooked flights make bus transportation a much better bet on shorter routes.

Australia: Merpati flies twice weekly between Kupang on Timor and Darwin in Australia's Northern Territory, an excellent way to enter Indonesia and island-hop across Nusa Tenggara to Bali.

Kupang is a visa-free entry point and visitors arriving from Australia are automatically granted a 60-day visitor's permit. However, note that Australian visas are required of most nationalities going to Australia and Australian diplomatic offices are located only in Jakarta and on Bali, *not* on Timor.

Land

Travelers who stick to the main roads which cross Nusa Tenggara will have few problems, aside from portions of the Trans-Flores High-way, which are still under construction and subject to flooding during the rainy season from November to March. Otherwise, roads across Lombok, Sumbawa, Sumba, and Timor are fully surfaced and generally kept in good condition.

Buses are frequent and very inexpensive, though often packed to the gunwales with passengers and various forms of Indonesian wildlife. Tickets for reserved seats can be purchased in advance from your *losmen* manager or travel agents in larger towns.

To enjoy the scenery—which is, after all, the point of overland travel—request the front seat next to the driver or a window seat on the right side of the bus. Purchase these tickets from your *losmen* owner or arrive early at the bus terminal and snag a seat up front.

Several agencies on Bali now rent motorcycles by the month and allow visitors to travel the entire length of Nusa Tenggara with the aid of local ferries which carry motorcycles at minimal cost.

Chartered jeeps or *bemo* with driver cost US$40-60 per day, a reasonable fare when split by three or four passengers.

Sea

Nearly all the islands of Nusa Tenggara are connected by Pelni ships and local ferries which operate on various schedules.

Ferries: Boats leave Bali's Benoa and Padang-bai harbors several times daily for Lembar harbor on Lombok. Ferries leave Labuhan Lombok in eastern Lombok several times daily for western Sumbawa. A ferry departs daily in the early morning from Sape in eastern Sumbawa to Labunhanbajo in western Flores. Some services make a stop at Komodo in both directions. Roundtrip charter boats from Labuhanbajo to Komodo cost US$35-50 depending on your bargaining abilities.

Boat service from Flores to Sumba or Timor is sporadic, though the situation has improved in recent years. The best way to reach Sumba is a Merpati or Bouraq flight from Bali or Timor, though Merpati offers thrice-weekly service from Bima (Sumbawa) to Tambolaka on Sumba.

Pelni: Several Pelni passenger ships circulate around Nusa Tenggara weekly on circuitous paths between Surabaya (Java), Benoa (Bali), Lembar (Lombok), Bima (Sumbawa), Waingapu (Sumba), Ende (Flores), Kupang (Timor), Dili (Timor), Maumere (Flores), and Ujung Pandang (Sulawesi), and then back to Surabaya on the reverse route. The most useful connections are to Sumba from Bima and Ende and the overnight passage from Maumere to Ujung Pandang.

Pelni also sails monthly from Bima and Dili to Ujung Pandang, and from Dili to Ambon in the Malukus. Schedules can be checked at Pelni offices in most provincial capitals and at the docks.

LOMBOK

Comparisons with Bali are almost inevitable. Lombok's size is almost identical with that of its more famous neighbor, but the landscape is drier and, aside from Gunung Rinjani, less spectacular. Lombok has a cultural connection—some 85,000 Balinese live on the island—but most of the population are Sasak Muslims whose art and lifestyles are quite distinct from those of their Hindu neighbors. Despite being called the "Bali of three decades ago," Lombok is a unique destination that compensates for its lack of rich culture and lush topography with excellent beaches and opportunities for outdoor adventure.

Lombok is also a curious study in momentum. Despite its sparkling beaches and soaring mountains, the island remained an isolated destination almost completely unaffected by mass tourism until the early 1990s. Today, the island is firmly established on the tourist trail that runs east from Bali to Komodo and Flores. As part of the Indonesian government's policy to move tourism away from Bali, Lombok has witnessed a surge of hotel construction and beach resorts under the watchful eye of the Lombok Tourism Development Corporation. Upcoming projects include an international airport in the Batujai/Penujak area (south of Praya near Kuta Beach) and a 600-hectare planned resort along the five beautiful beaches of south Lombok.

Fortunately, until these projects get off the ground, Lombok will remain a destination where you can spend days traveling without seeing another Westerner—especially in the southern and northeastern regions.

Principle destinations are Senggigi Beach, the Gili Islands off the northwest coast, a climb up Gunung Rinjani, and the beaches near Kuta on the south coast.

Transportation

Lombok can be reached in 25 minutes by air from Bali's international airport, and in about four hours by boat from Padangbai harbor in east Bali. There's also an express boat service from Benoa harbor just south of Sanur Beach.

Air: Merpati flies 12 times daily from Bali to Lombok's Selaparang Airport, four km north of Mataram and six km east of Senggigi Beach. The fare is higher than boat transport, though the Lombok airport is much closer to Sengiggi and the Gili Islands than Lembar harbor.

Bemo and taxis waiting outside Selaparang Airport go to Mataram, Senggigi Beach, and the dock for the Gili Islands. Kuta Beach can be reached by *bemo* or bus from the Sweta bus terminal in Cakranegara, though direct service may be offered by the time you arrive in Lombok.

Sea: Ferries depart Padangbai harbor every two hours 0800-2000, cost US$4-6 depending on class, and take four or five hours. Morning ferries are recommended, since they dock at Lombok's Lembar harbor before nightfall; stay in Candidasa to make the early departures.

Mabua Express runs fast catamarans twice daily at 0800 and 1430 from Benoa harbor to Lembar and make the return from Lembar at 1130 and 1730. This convenient service takes just over two hours and costs US$15-25 depending on class. The more expensive tickets include transportation to Senggigi, Kuta, or the port for the Gili Islands.

Ferries depart hourly from Labuhan Lombok in east Lombok for Poto Tano on Sumbawa and take about two hours to make the crossing.

Lembar harbor, one hour south of Mataram, is served by *bemos* which rush you directly to your hotel or *losmen*. *Bemo* tickets are sold on the ferry. Special buses waiting at Lembar go to Labuhan Lombok, from where ferries continue east to Sumbawa.

Bus: Perama Transport offices in Kuta, Sanur, Ubud, Lovina, Candidasa, and Padangbai sell

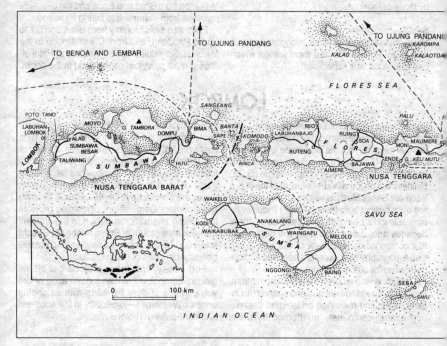

combination boat/bus tickets from Bali to most destinations on Lombok. This service costs more than public transport but eliminates the hassle of making *bemo* connections and eliminates the likelihood of finding yourself stranded in Mataram rather than finding yourself comfortably ensconced on the Gili Islands.

Getting Around: Attractions on Lombok are served by buses and *bemo* from the Sweta terminal. Official fares regulated by the local government are listed on a prominently displayed signboard.

An excellent alternative is to bring a motorcycle from Bali or rent one from the motorcycle owners on Jalan Gelantik in Mataram. Motorcycles cost US$5-7 per day depending on condition and engine displacement.

AMPENAN, MATARAM, AND CAKRANEGARA

The population and commercial center of Lombok encompasses three contiguous towns that stretch nine km east from the old harbor at Ampenan to the main bus terminal at Sweta. Ampenan, a colorful and run-down port town with a popular *losmen,* blends into Mataram, the regional capital with big banks and modern government offices, which blends into Cakranegara, the main business and hotel area.

Although most travelers head directly to Senggigi, the Gili Islands, or Kuta Beach, the tri-city region features a good regional museum, a handful of Balinese-style temples, antique shops, handicraft factories, horse races, and a colorful cattle market.

The following attractions and accommodations are shown on the enclosed map.

Information
The West Nusa Tenggara government tourist office on Jalan Langko in Mataram has few brochures in English but is run by a helpful and very friendly staff.

The Perama Transport office on Jalan Pejanggik provides general information and sells island tours, shuttle bus connections, treks to the

(continues on page 321)

TO UJUNG PANDANG   TO AMBON   MALUKU TENGGARA

NYATA

KEP. SOLOR   KOMBA   KEP. ALOR   WETAR   KISAR   MOA

LABAO   LARANTUKA   KALABAHI   KABIL   ALOR   ATAURO   BAUCAU   TUTUALA
ADONARA   LEMBATA   DILI   LOS PALOS
SOLOR   LEWOLEBA   BARANUSA   PANTAR   MANATUTO   ILIOMAN
WAIWERANG   LAMALERA   LIQUISA   E. TIMOR   VIKEKE

ATAPUPU   MAUBESSI

TIMOR   PANTE MAKASSAR   ATAMBUA   G. TATA MAI LUA   SAME   TIMOR TIMUR
NAIKLIU   KEFAMENANU   W. TIMOR
NIKI NIKI   SOE
CAMPLONG   KOLBANO   *TIMOR SEA*
SEMAU   KUPANG
ROTI   **NUSA TENGGARA**
NDAO   BAA

© MOON PUBLICATIONS, INC.

INDONESIA

INDONESIA

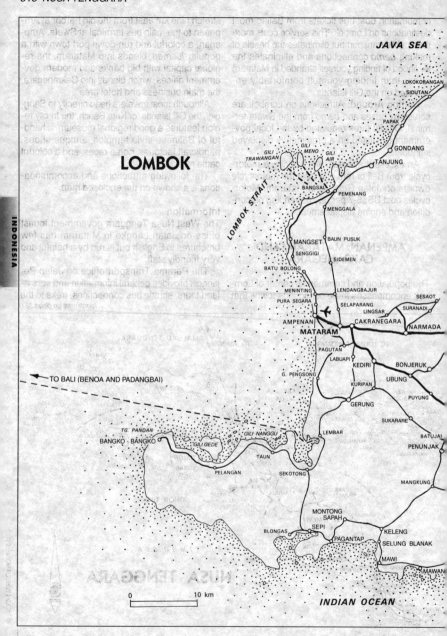

LOMBOK

JAVA SEA

LOKOKORANGAN
SIDUTAN
PAPAK
GONDANG
TANJUNG
GILI
TRAWANGAN
GILI
MENO
GILI
AIR
BANGSAL
PEMENANG
BANGSAL
MENGGALA
MANGSET
BAUN PUSUK
SENGGIGI
SIDEMEN
BATU BOLONG
LENDANGBAJUR
MENINTING
SELAPARANG
SESAOT
SURANADI
PURA SEGARA
LINGSAR
AMPENAN
CAKRANEGARA
NARMADA
MATARAM
PAGUTAN
LABUAPI
KEDIRI
BONJERUK
G. PENGSONG
KURIPAN
UBUNG
PUYUNG
GERUNG
SUKARARE
BATUJAI
TG. PANDAN
GILI NANGGU
LEMBAR
PENUNJAK
BANGKO - BANGKO
GILI GEDE
TAUN
MANGKUNG
PELANGAN
SEKOTONG
MONTONG
SAPAH
SEPI
KELENG
BLONGAS
PAGANTAP
SELUNG BLANAK
MAWI
MAWAN

LOMBOK STRAIT

TO BALI (BENOA AND PADANGBAI)

0   10 km

INDIAN OCEAN

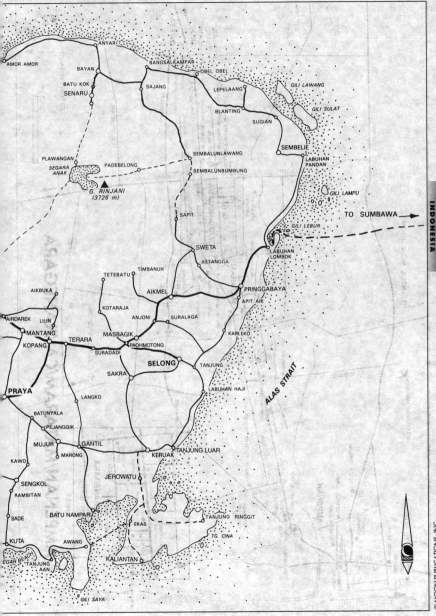

INDONESIA

TO SUMBAWA →

© MOON PUBLICATIONS, INC.

INDONESIA

AMPENAN/MATARAM/CAKRANEGARA

TO LINGSAR

TO SURADADI, TETEBATU, AND LABUHAN LOMBOK

SWETA

JL. TGH. FAISAL

JL. BRAWIJAYA

SWETA BUS TERMINAL

SWETA MARKET

JL. TUMPANG SARI

JL. CHARIL ANWAR

JL. LAU MESIR

TO PRAYA AND KUTA

1 km

0

TO LEMBAR

JL. JEN. SUDIRMAN

JL. GORA

SELAMAT RIYADI WEAVING

MAYURA WATER PALACE

PURA MERU

SARI BUNGA WEAVING

JL. ST. HASANUDIN

JL. GEDE NGURAH

SUKA HATI WEAVING

CAKRANEGARA

JL. SELAPARANG

JL. PANCA USAHA

JL. ISMAIL MARZUKI

SEE INSET

JL. JELANTIK GOSA

JL. PANJI ANOM

HOTEL KERTAYOGA

PERAMA TOUR AND TRAVEL

MATARAM

SAYONG GUEST COTTAGES

JL. SRIWIJAYA

JL. BUNG KARNO

TO BANGSAL AND G. RINJANI

TO SENABANG

JL. DR. SUTOMO

JL. HOS COKROAMINOTO

GOVERNOR'S OFFICE

GRAVE OF GENERAL VAN HAM

HOTEL HANDIKA

GRANADA HOTEL

JL. A. RAHMAN HAKIM

TO GUNUNG PENGSONG

IMMIGRATION

JL. DEWI SARTIKA

BRI

PEJANGGIK HOSPITAL

GARDEN HOUSE

LOSMEN RINJANI

JL. UDAYANA

CENTRAL POST OFFICE

SELAPARANG AIRPORT

BNI BANK INDONESIA

JL. PANCAWARGA

JL. AIRLANGGA

JL. PENDIDIKAN

LOMBOK POTTERY CENTER

JL. LANGKO

JL. MAJAPAHIT

TO SENGGIGI

JL. ADI SUCIPTO

LOSMEN TRIGUNA

AMPENAN

TOURIST OFFICE

POST OFFICE

JL. SUPRAPTO

WEST NUSA TENGGARA MUSEUM

BEMO TERMINAL

LOSMEN HORAS

LOSMEN ZAHIR

WARTEL

TELECOMMUNICATIONS OFFICE

PELNI

CHINESE CEMETERY

PURA SEGARA

BEMO STOP

CINEMA

JL. SALEH

SUNGKAR

LOSMEN PABEAN

INSET

JL. GEDE NGURAH

LOSMEN SRIKANDI

POST OFFICE

HOTEL PUSAKA

MERPATI OFFICE

BOURAQ OFFICE

CAKRANEGARA

JL. PANCA USAHA

BANK EXIM

HOTEL MATARAM

LOSMEN AYU

JL. ASTITI

JL. ISMAIL MARZUKI

SELAPARANG HOTEL

SEMPATI OFFICE

CILINAYA SHOPPING CENTER

LOSMEN

© MOON PUBLICATIONS, INC.

Lombok cattle traders

INDONESIA

summit of Gunung Rinjani, and Land-Sea Adventure tours to Komodo and Flores.

Attractions in Town
West Nusa Tenggara Museum: A useful introduction to the history and ethnographic variety of both Lombok and Sumbawa.

Pura Meru: Constructed by a Balinese king in 1720 and still the largest Balinese temple on Lombok, Pura Meru is arranged around three royal courtyards filled with over 30 multiroofed *meru* shrines. The central plaza features three *meru* dedicated to Shiva, Vishnu, and Brahma.

Mayura Water Palace: Cakranegara's former Balinese court was constructed in 1744 around a huge ceremonial pond complete with floating pavilion, still accessible by a narrow causeway.

Selamet Riady Weaving Factory: One block north of Mayura is one of Lombok's last remaining *ikat* factories, best visited 0800-1200.

Antiques: Both authentic and instant antiques are sold at Sudirman's Antiques opposite the former *bemo* station in Ampenan. His collection of business cards testifies to his longevity and worldwide fame.

Lombok Asli near the University of Mataram is also recommended for quality crafts at reasonable prices.

Cattle Market: A completely authentic cattle market is held every Sunday just outside Cakranegara; a photographer's dream.

Selakalas Racetrack: Horse races, jockeyed by young boys aged 6-12, are held on Sundays on Jalan Gora, just north of the cattle market.

Gunung Sari: A small town six km north of Mataram famed for its production of low-priced instant antiques.

Attractions outside Town
Gunung Pengsong: Some of Lombok's best panoramic views can be enjoyed from the Balinese temple constructed on this arid hill, about six km south of Mataram. Balinese festivals to honor rice goddess Dewi Sri are held here once each 210-day Balinese ceremonial calendar year.

Lingsar Temple: Lombok's most important temple—for both the Hindu Balinese and the local Sasaks who adhere to the Islamic Wetu Telu religion—was constructed in 1714 in a rich combination of Hindu, Balinese, and Islamic motifs. Both Balinese and Wetu Telu Sasaks worship together here, using different levels of the temple. Pura Lingsar is worn and faded but nevertheless the most impressive example of religious architecture on Lombok.

Lingsar is a few kilometers north of the main highway, midway between Cakranegara and Narmada. Direct *bemos* from Sweta terminal reach Lingsar and continue southeast to Narmada.

Narmada Water Palace: Constructed in 1805 by the Balinese raja of Mataram, the highly symbolic complex of Narmada, 10 km east of Cakranegara, encompasses a mixture of Balinese, Islamic, and Sasak architecture, combined with a miniature replica of the crater lake, Segara Anak, which fills the interior of Gunung Rinjani.

According to legend, the replica lake was constructed by the elderly king to more easily fulfill his religious obligations, but skeptics claim the old raja used the pools to spy on young maidens and select the loveliest to be his royal concubines.

Batu Kumbung: Four km north of Narmada is a small, rarely visited village known for its *gandrung* music ensemble and *kendang belek* dance groups. Some of the local women have revived the near-lost art of *ikat* weaving with backstrap looms. Pleasant walks can be made through the surrounding countryside. Villagers are shy but accustomed to Westerners.

Homestays are easy to find at US$3-4 per night; a rare opportunity to get off the tourist trail in Lombok.

Suranadi: One of the oldest and holiest temples on Lombok lies inside a pleasant garden noted for its restored Balinese-style baths and icy natural springs filled with sanctified eels. The temple can be combined with a hike through Taman Hutan Suranadi, a nature reserve and regional park located a few kilometers north en route to Sesaot.

Suranadi Hotel: Dutch visitors, perhaps seeking some colonial self-indulgence, often stay at this hotel, with its cracked tennis courts, dreary restaurant, and near-empty pool filled with gasping goldfish. Run-down nostalgia. P.O. Box 10, Narmada, tel. (0364) 23686, US$12-28.

Accommodations

Few visitors stay in town except to make onward travel connections and arrange a climb up Mt. Rinjani.

Wisma Triguna: The most popular *losmen* in the tri-city region features large three-bed rooms facing a noisy cobblestone courtyard. Proprietor Eddy Batubara rents cars, motorcycles, tents, and sleeping bags, and maintains an excellent information board and three-dimensional map of the Rinjani trek. Pak Eddy has arranged hundreds of all-inclusive three-day treks to the summit of Gunung Rinjani and helps with *bemo* to Lembar harbor (for Bali) and Labuhan Lombok (for Sumbawa). Other *losmen* in town such as Pabean, Zahir, Horas, and Angi Mammire are dumpy and noisy. Jl. Koperasi 76, Ampenan, tel. (0364) 31705, US$5-8.

Hotel Kertayoga: A very friendly, older hotel run by a Balinese family in a good location midway between Ampenan and Cakranegara. Jl. Pejanggik 64, Mataram, tel. (0364) 21775, US$6-15.

Astiti Guesthouse: Attractive gardens, excellent location, and spotless rooms at reasonable rates make this a good choice. Jl. Subak, Cakranegara, tel. (0364) 23670, US$6-15.

Granada Hotel: The tri-cities' top choice features 50 a/c rooms, a spacious restaurant, and a swimming pool surrounded by tropical jungle and a small zoo. Jalan Bung Karno, Mataram, tel. (0364) 22275, fax (0364) 23856, US$22-45.

Transportation

The Merpati office on Jalan Yos Sudarso in Ampenan handles bookings for both Merpati and Garuda. Sempati is in the Cilinaya shopping centre in Mataram, while Bouraq is in the Selaparang Hotel. Perama Transport is on Jalan Pejanggik.

Bemos from Sweta go to Lembar harbor, Labuhan Lombok for ferries to Sumbawa, Senggigi, Bayan on the north side of Gunung Rinjani, and Pemanang, from where boats leave for the Gili Islands. The *bemo* terminal in Ampenan has services to Senggigi, Pemanang, and Bayan.

SENGGIGI BEACH

Ten km north of Ampenan—past the horrendous Pertamina oil-storage tanks, delightful fishing boats with blue-checkered sails, a pink Balinese temple called Pura Segara, a smoking trash dump, and a weedy Chinese cemetery—lies Lombok's original beach resort.

Blessed with a long, curving stretch of sand and an expansive coral bed popular with skin and scuba divers, Senggigi is a great spot at which to relax and enjoy fabulous sunsets, despite the facts that the beach is somewhat narrow and covered with brownish sand and most of the clientele are upscale tourists on two-day escapes from Bali.

Senggigi hotels and *losmen* offer all possible amenities from money exchange to scuba packages and hiking programs up Rinjani. Batu Bolong temple, three km south of the beach, is the place for sunsets.

Accommodations

Most Senggigi hotels are aimed firmly at package tourists from Bali, though a handful of budget *losmen* are scattered along the highway near the south and north ends of the beach. After a decade of dormancy, Senggigi is exploding: 10 luxury hotels with over 6,000 rooms will open in the next few years, and by the turn of the century luxury hotels will probably line the entire highway from Batu Bolong to the town of Pemenang, over 20 km north.

Pondok Senggigi: Australian Ina and her Sasak husband, Tadjudin Nur, run Senggigi's popular travelers' center at the south end of the beach. The restaurant serves decent food and live entertainment is provided by local bands on weekends. Though often filled, Pondok Senggigi is a good place to start a search for other nearby *losmen*. Senggigi Beach, tel. (0364) 93273, US$10-20.

Pondok Sederhana: Another good budget spot some 300 meters north of Senggigi Losmen. Rooms are simple and share a common bathroom but are well located on a hillside with views toward the beach. Senggigi Beach, US$8-12.

Lina Cottages: Just opposite Pondok Sederhana is an excellent mid-priced choice situated directly on the beachfront with a/c rooms, decent restaurant, and friendly management. Senggigi Beach, tel. (0364) 93237, US$12-18.

Santai Cottages: Four km north of Senggigi is this idyllic little homestay facing a small but decent beach. Mangset, tel. (0364) 93038, US$10-15.

Windy Cottages: Another peaceful escape about five km north of Senggigi. Mangset, tel. (0364) 93191, US$15-20.

Senggigi Beach Hotel: An Aerowisata-owned (Garuda subsidiary) hotel and Lombok's first resort features water-sports facilities, restaurants, and a swimming pool amid 12 hectares of tropical gardens. Senggigi, tel. (0364) 93210, US$120-185.

Sheraton Senggigi Beach: The first Sheraton east of Bali. Senggigi, tel. (0364) 93333, US$180-265.

Transportation

Bemos from Sweta and Ampenan take about 30 minutes to reach Senggigi. Perama, Sunshine Tours, and other transport companies provide buses to Senggigi and connections for boats to the Gili Islands.

GILI ISLANDS

Three of Lombok's prettiest islands lie in the clear waters just off the northwest corner of the main island. All of the coral-fringed islands—Gili Air, Gili Meno, and Gili Trawangan—sport clean beaches filled with fluffy white sand, skin diving over shallow coral gardens, and dozens of inexpensive *losmen* skirting the pancake-flat landscapes.

The Gilis' spectacular combination of beach and water has made them an overwhelmingly popular travelers' escape since the mid-1970s—comparable on a smaller scale to Samui in Thailand, Boracay in the Philippines, and Tioman in Malaysia.

And yet, perhaps too popular. Like many other small beach resorts in Southeast Asia developed without proper government supervision, none of the Gilis have adequate supplies of fresh water, decent trash collection, septic tanks, sewage-treatment facilities, or dependable sources of electrical power aside from noisy generators. And not all problems originate with tourists: Local fishermen have dynamited most of the once-pristine coral beds into oblivion.

Popularity has other pitfalls. From early June to late September, when thousands of backpackers descend on the islands, it's almost impossible to find a room after 1000, and hundreds of bewildered new arrivals are forced to camp on the beach and search for rooms the following morning. And in a mercenary attempt to check free enterprise among local *losmen* owners, village councils now enforce "recommended" price minimums for all island huts. No matter how beautiful the environment, six bucks for a rudimentary bamboo shack with outside toilet, no fan, and minimal furniture is a bad deal by anybody's standards.

Visitors should also remember that the Gilis are conservative Muslim enclaves where indecent dress and behavior are considered completely scandalous. Swimsuits and cutoff shorts are acceptable on the tourist beaches, but visitors venturing into town should respect local customs and remain well covered from knee to neck.

Now that I've talked you out of visiting the Gilis, allow me to reiterate that the islands are spectacular places blessed with many charms—a welcome escape from the calculated confines of Bali. Crowded, but otherwise a genuine tropical escape.

Transportation

The Bangsal dock for the Gilis is 30 km north of town. With lucky connections, you'll be relaxing on the sand in less than three hours.

Bemo from Sweta bus terminal in Cakranegara, Rembiga terminal a few kilometers north of Mataram, and the airport head 27 km north to the town of Pemenang, from where *cidomo* continue one km down the road to Bangsal harbor. Groups can charter direct *bemo* from Mataram or Senggigi for US$8-10. Shuttle buses to Bangsal are operated by Perama Tours in Mataram and Senggigi.

Bangsal harbor is a sleepy place with several cafes such as Toko Basuki and Kon Tiki Bungalows, plus an official ticket outlet which sells fixed-price boat tickets to each island. Departures start in the morning and finish around sunset, but it's best to start early to find a room. All-day charters which visit the three islands and allow time for skin diving cost US$20-25.

There are regular boat connections between the islands so if you grow bored with Trawangan and want to experience Meno, you can make the short hop in the morning and return to Trawangan in the afternoon.

Money-exchange facilities are located on all the islands but rates are poor. Bring plenty of cash or expect to make frequent runs back to Mataram.

Gili Air

Which island to visit depends largely on whether you seek solitude or companionship, whether you prefer a large or a small island, and the importance of skin or scuba diving.

Gili Air, closest island to the mainland, is the smallest of the three Gilis (just 1.1 square km) but has the highest population: 1,000 people who make their living harvesting coconuts, fishing, raising livestock, and now through tourism. The island is perfectly flat and almost completely surrounded by a brilliant beach and a coral reef partially destroyed by dynamite.

Facilities on the island include a simple health clinic in the main village, a Perama office in Gili Indah Cottages which can help with travel plans and money exchange, and several dive shops, which rent gear and run scuba excursions to picturesque nearby reefs and submerged freshwater springs.

Accommodations: Most of the two-dozen *losmen* on Gili Air are scattered along the south coast near the harbor and the main fishing village. Most are similar in style—small rooms raised on stilts and sparsely furnished with two beds and rickety bamboo chairs—and charge US$5-8 depending on the number of included meals.

Budget choices on the south coast include Salabose Cottages, Lucky Cottages, Flying Dutchman, Anjani Bungalows, Bamboo Cottages, Pondok Gili Air, Kesuma Cottages, Bupati's, Resorta, and Sederhana Losmen. Similar digs on the east coast include Pino Cottages, Pondok Wisata Gita Gili, Santi Hans, Gili Air Cottages, and Coconut Cottages. North coast budget choices include Pondok Gusung Indah, Pondok Wisata Indah, Lombok Indah, Bunga Cottages, Matahari, and Hink Bungalows at the northwestern corner of the island.

Two superior operations at a higher price (US$15-40) are Gili Indah Cottages on the southernmost tip and Hotel Gili Air (formerly Hans Bungalows) at the extreme northern end. The remaining *losmen* are almost completely identical aside from cafe fare and whatever ambience they might offer in their gardens.

Gili Meno

Midway between Gili Air and Trawangan is teardrop-shaped Gili Meno, the middle-sized (1.5 square km) but least populated (350) and least developed of the three islands.

Meno has the smallest number of *losmen* due to its shortage of fresh water. Though tough on tourism, high groundwater salinity has benefited some residents, who harvest salt during the dry season in the lake near the west coast.

Accommodations: Meno's general lack of facilities and small number of *losmen* ensure a high degree of solitude at the cost of some minor inconveniences. Meno has about 10 bungalows scattered along the east coast and within walking distance of the pier at the southeastern corner.

Budget *losmen* which cost US$5-8 include Pondok Meno, Mallia's Child Bungalows, Rawa Indah, Fantastic Cottages, Janur Indah, Casablanca, and Pondok Santi on the north side of the island.

Better facilities at higher prices include the Blue Coral Bungalows on the north coast (best spot for divers), mid-priced Kontiki with attached bathrooms and a decent restaurant, and the upscale Bouganvil Resort, which has constructed a distillation plant to produce its own fresh water. Here, Balinese-style bungalows with a/c and private bathrooms cost US$45-65.

Gili Trawangan

Trawangan Island, the most distant and largest (3.5 square km) of the three islands, is home to over 700 fishermen who claim descent from the Bugis sailors of South Sulawesi. Trawangan briefly served as a penal colony in 1891 for some 350 Sasak rebels banished here by the raja of Lombok, and was later occupied during WW II by Japanese military forces who constructed two gun emplacements still standing on a southern hill.

Trawangan receives the most visitors for good reasons: plenty of *losmen* with decent facilities, money changers, a wartel, spectacular beaches, and the best coral beds in the region. Other draws include watching sunrises over Gunung Rinjani (Lombok) and sunsets over Gunung Agung (Bali)—but be careful: sunburns will arise all over your body. Trawangan is an extremely hot island with very little shade; bring suntan lotion or expect to be finely roasted.

Scuba rentals and dive excursions are arranged at Blue Marlin Dive Centre, Albatross Scuba Adventures, and Blue Coral.

Accommodations: All of Trawangan's several-dozen *losmen* and homestays are on the east or northeast coast. As with Meno and Air, most are simple huts with common bath priced US$6-8 depending on meal arrangements. Better chalets with private bath are dearer, while huts without meals included are somewhat less expensive.

Homestay owners wait for arrivals at the Trawangan pier. You can follow some engaging personality, take the recommendations of a previous visitor, or simply wander up the beach and inspect a few spots. Homestays in the middle sometimes have discos popular with singles, while couples often prefer the quieter places farther up the coast. Trawangan can be circumnavigated on foot in about five hours.

SOUTHWEST PENINSULA

Just south of Lembar harbor lie several excellent and completely untouched beaches, plus lovely coves dotted with tropical islands. Motorized outriggers from Lembar take you to Gili Genting and Gili Nanggu, where accommodations are available in simple bamboo bungalows. The village of Pelangan, 10 km west of Lembar, has another attractive beach and fairly good snorkeling.

Surfers often continue out to Bangko at the end of the road, where beach bungalows and simple *warungs* face the cliff and offshore breakers.

PRAYA AND VICINITY

Central and southern Lombok around the town of Praya form the island's tourist and handicraft center.

This is a journey through time, where entire villages of thatched palm have been constructed on hilltops to defend against human predators. Surrounding these Sasak villages are cultivated fields of *ubi kayu* and *ubi jalar*, types of sweet potatoes. Hilltop graveyards of tiny upright stones, like gnarly black toothpicks, remind one of Torajaland except that these are Muslim graves and not animist/Christian.

Market days rotate between villages to encourage intracity commerce. Larger markets worth attending include Praya (Saturday), Sengkol (Thursday), and Kuta (Sunday).

Tour buses make daily stops in most of the following villages, though otherwise these are peaceful towns relatively unaffected by mass tourism. Shoppers should check prices in advance in Mataram to avoid being overcharged at the source.

Sukarara is an Islamic weaving center known for its production of traditional *songket, lambung* (black blouses), *sarung,* and *selendang* (shawls). Many of the homes here are old-style Sasak dwellings elevated on wooden platforms and covered with thatched roofs. The people are friendly and discreet photography is acceptable.

Penujak

Six km south of Praya is a small village known for its production of *gerabah* pottery made from red clays, decorated with lizard and frog images, and then fired in the late afternoon in traditional kilns. Sasaks arrive to purchase immense water containers while tourists usually pick up small souvenir items such as handpainted flower vases and small water pitchers.

Pottery is also produced in several other nearby villages such as Kampung Tenandon, where more advanced firing equipment allows for greater delicacy in the pottery.

SADE (RAMBITAN)

Just south of Sengkol is a well-preserved Sasak village, which was declared a historic preservation area several years ago. Unlike many villages changed by modern improvements, Sade still has dozens of traditional homes constructed of thatch and bamboo, plus bonnet-capped *lumbung* (rice barns) which symbolize pre-Western Sasak culture.

Sade is now on every package tour, so expect some aggressive sales pitches from housewives and insistent young guides who demand a handful of *rupiah* for their services.

KUTA BEACH

Kuta Beach is the somewhat confusing name given to the coastline that stretches eight km east from Kuta village to Tanjung Aan. Southeast from Tanjung Aan lies the village of Grupuk and an Australian surfer spot known as "Desert Point." The scenery is spectacular and the beaches rank among the best in eastern Indonesia.

Along with the superb beaches and dazzling landscapes, Kuta is also known for a weeklong festival called Bau Nyale held each year on the full moon of the second lunar month (usually late February or early March). The event revolves around the reproductive cycle of a bottom-dwelling sea worm which local Sasaks have woven into a romantic legend and public drama that retells the tragic story of Princess Nyale and her broken heart.

Kuta itself is a long, narrow town where you can pick up supplies and wait patiently for *bemo* back to Sweta. The coastal road heads east to

the fabulous horseshoe-shaped bay at Tanjung Aan, where wealthy speculators from Jakarta have purchased most of the land in anticipation of a Balinese-style bonanza. But unlike the Balinese Kuta, the Lombok Tourism Development Corporation has organized a 600-hectare site near five contiguous beaches for the construction of almost 20 luxury hotels.

The road west from Kuta passes an amazing series of deserted beaches blessed with perfect sand and iridescent blue waters. After a few kilometers the road heads inland, but a side road leads south to the beach town of Air Goling and its offshore island of Nusa Tanjung.

West of Air Goling lie Mawun and Tampa, two fishing villages situated on arching bays of dazzling sand and crashing waves. The completion of the road from Tampa to Silungblanak will allow direct connection with the ferry harbor at Lembar.

Accommodations

Kuta has a good selection of budget *losmen* east of town, but many of the better beaches have been reserved for planned developments. While this sounds discouraging, tourism authorities have promised to monitor the hotels and keep major resorts at least 100 meters from the beach. In an unusual show of force several years ago, the Lombok Tourism Development Corporation closed a foreign-funded hotel constructed just 25 meters from the beach and forced the owners to dismantle the beachside chalets and move them back from the water. It seems apparent that while nobody wants to reproduce the sterility of Nusa Dua, neither do they want to see the messy hodgepodge which typifies the Kuta of Bali.

Simple hotels are located in Kuta town, but most *losmen* are along the hot and barren road which heads east to Tanjung Aan. All are very similar—just simple wooden huts—and identically priced at US$4-8 depending on whether you need shared or private bath. New bungalows are opening quickly but at present you choices include Rambutan Cottages, Wisma Segara Anak (with a booking office for Perama Transport), Pondok Sekar Kuning, Anda Cottages (money exchange services available), Rinjani Agung Beach Bungalows, and Cockatoo Cottages at the east end of the beach.

Several inexpensive bungalows and luxury hotels are under construction at Tanjung Aan and Grupuk, as well as west of Kuta toward Air Goling, Mawun, and Tampa.

Transportation
Direct *bemo* service from Sweta terminal to Praya is fairly frequent, though service south down to the beach remains sporadic, except during the high tourist seasons (summer and Christmas break). Local service from Praya to Kuta is now supplemented with private charters from the Praya *bemo* corner.

GUNUNG RINJANI

Famed for its great beauty and eerie isolation, Gunung Rinjani is the highest mountain in Indonesia outside Irian Jaya and the source of mystical inspiration for both the Muslim Sasaks, who sometimes follow a local religion called Wetu Telu, and the Balinese, who believe Rinjani

GUNUNG RINJANI

to be the home of departed spirits and highest possible seat of the gods. Both groups hike the mountain several times yearly to bathe in the thermal springs, honor local gods, and throw ritualistic golden ornaments into Lake Segara Anak, though full-moon evenings are the most popular excuses to climb Rinjani.

Resembling a tropical moonscape with iridescent lakes and smoking hot springs, the amazing panorama which spreads across the summit includes Gunung Rinjani (3,726 meters) on the east, Gunung Senkereang Jaya (2,900 meters) and Plawangan (2,687 meters) to the north, Gunung Buanmangge (2,894 meters) just southeast of the lake, and Gunung Barujari (2,375 meters), which dominates the lakeside peninsula.

All these volcanoes have erupted, collapsed, and showered sulfuric ash into multihued Segara Anak, a vast and impossibly elevated tropical lake which almost completely fills the inner caldera. These must have been memorable explosions: scientists estimate that the force necessary to create the half-dozen volcanoes—as well as form the kidney-shaped crater lake which fills much of the six- by eight-km caldera—was equal to 274 Hiroshima-strength atomic bombs. The result is a tropical landscape you'll never forget.

Independent Travel versus Group Tours
Local tourist officials estimate that well over 1,000 visitors annually hike toward the summit of Rinjani and spend a few days camping around and relaxing in the hot springs at Lake Segara. Although few trekkers bother to climb the actual summit (another tough day from the lake), the conquest of Rinjani remains one of Indonesia's unique experiences and certainly the most brilliant thing to do on Lombok.

Almost anybody in decent condition can make the climb, which is long and tiring but doesn't require any type of advanced mountaineering skills. Most hikers need three days and two nights for the roundtrip from Senaru (northern Lombok), including a descent to Lake Segara.

Escorted three-day tours from Wisma Triguna in Ampenan cost US$50-125 per person depending on the size of the party. Agencies in Mataram and Senggigi Beach such as Satriavi charge double. Even if you don't join a tour, Pak Eddy, the proprietor of Wisma Triguna in Ampenan, can help with trekking maps, advice, and fair-priced equipment rentals.

Most trekkers do Rinjani without the help of a guide, porter, or tour company, as the trail from Senaru is relatively easy to follow and dozens of other hikers are usually on the path. Though not absolutely necessary, guides are worth the modest expense since they know all the shortcuts, provide some entertaining insights, and help erect campsites and find fresh water. Guides and porters hired in Senaru charge US$4-6 per day, a reasonable fee that can be split among several hikers.

Rinjani should not be climbed during the Nov.-March rainy season or on full-moon evenings when hundreds of rowdy Indonesian teenagers crowd the lake. Bring along raingear, food, a flashlight, warm clothing, a sleeping bag or a thick blanket, a tent or a plastic tarp, a sleeping pad, fresh water, cooking equipment, matches, cigarettes for your guide, and a bottle of booze to warm the chilly evenings. Most supplies are available in Senaru but it's advisable to bring all possible provisions from Mataram.

The Trek

To Senaru: *Bemo* from Sweta terminal take three hours to reach the town of Anyar on the north coast of Lombok. From Anyar, it's three km east to the asphalted road which cuts off the main road and leads south to Batu Kok (four km) before terminating at Senaru (one more kilometer). The Anyar-to-Batu Kok hike—*very* long and tiring—should be avoided by flagging down a truck or finding a motorcycle taxi. No need killing yourself before you even reach the mountain.

Batu Kok and Senaru: Your final night prior to the climb can be spent in the small town of Batu Kok, where friendly homestays provide cheap beds, hot meals, up-to-date trekking information, weather predictions, sleeping bag and tent rentals, packed lunches, extra food and drink, plus guides and porters at reasonable rates. All *losmen* will be filled with trekkers who have just returned from the summit—your best resource for last-minute tips.

Current favorites include the Rinjani Homestay, managed by the local conservation official; Guru Bakti, which charges US$4-5 for room and two meals; Pondok Senaru; and Raden's Palace, operated by a former schoolteacher from Batu Kok.

One km uphill is Senaru, a traditional Sasak village of two-dozen thatched-roofed huts neatly arranged behind protective walls in near-perfect lines. Just beyond this fascinating village lies the trail to Rinjani.

Day One: This is the toughest day. To minimize late-afternoon heat, start before dawn and set a steady pace to reach Base Camp (Pos 3) well before sunset. A series of markers helps keep track of distances: Marker 200 denotes the Rinjani rim.

From Senaru (600 meters), Pos 1 (920 meters) takes about two hours of moderate hiking. Pos 2 Campsite (1,550 meters) at Marker 114 three hours from Pos 1 has a rudimentary shelter and water supply. Pos 3 Base Camp (2,100 meters) at Marker 185, two hours beyond Pos 2, has a water supply and a roofed sleeping platform where most hikers spend the night. Depending on your stamina, Batu Kok to Base Camp takes five to nine hours.

Day Two: Another long day but not as strenuous as the first. Depart from Base Camp at dawn to beat the heat and ensure clear views from the crater rim, perhaps all the way west to Gunung Agung on Bali and Sumbawa to the east. From the crater rim, it's another four to six hours slowly winding down the narrow and dangerous path which descends into the caldera and then along the slippery trail which circumnavigates the lake to the hot springs.

Lakeside campsites are poorly maintained and often crowded with locals, but the hot springs are a godsend after two tough days of trekking, and the surrealistic atmosphere of Lake Segara Anak ("Child of the Seas") is something quite remarkable.

Day Three: Most hikers need about eight hours to retrace their steps back to Batu Kok. To *possibly* enjoy clear views from Rinjani summit, you must leave before dawn and hike a short portion the previous morning to familiarize yourself with the poorly marked trail. Roundtrip up Rinjani takes a full day.

Sembalun Lawang: An interesting alternative to the familiar Batu Kok return is the eastern departure to Sembalun Lawang, a remote village in a spectacular valley connected to the outside world by a terrible road. The situation has probably changed since my 1987 motorcycle visit, when the villagers stared at me like I was from

Mars. Wisma Cemarasu in town has cheap rooms and can make arrangements with porters and guides.

TETEBATU

Once a Dutch hill resort favored by overheated colonialists, Tetebatu still provides sweeping views over southern Lombok and the opportunity to hire a guide and climb Mt. Rinjani from a completely unique approach. The town is small and hardly spectacular, but within a few kilometers are several good waterfalls, a monkey forest, and handicraft villages such as Kotaraja (blacksmiths), Loyok (bamboo and palm-leaf weavings), Rungkung (pottery), and Pringgasela (Sasak weavings).

Tetebatu is 42 km east of Mataram and five km north of Kotaraja on the cool slopes of Mt. Rinjani. To reach Tetebatu, first take a *bemo* from Sweta terminal to Pomotong (Paokmotong), a second north to Kotaraja, and a final *bemo* or horse-cart up the rocky road to Tetebatu.

Accommodations
Budget: Just south of town in the ricefields is Diwi Enjeni, Pondok Tetebatu, and Mekar Sari with bungalows from US$4-6, while east of town are a handful of somewhat more upscale places such as Green Ory Bungalows, Pondok Bulan, Cendrawasi Cottages, and Hakiki Cottages. Rooms out here go for US$5-10.

Soedjono Hotel: Tetebatu has long been known for this old colonial-style house, formerly the home of a doctor from Jakarta. Facilities include a swimming pool, a cafe with rice-terrace views, car and motorcycle rentals, trekking information, and over 25 bungalows in various conditions and prices. Tetebatu, tel. (0364) 22159, US$6-28.

Lendang Nangka
Lendang Nangka, a small but prosperous village seven km southeast of Tetebatu, is popular with backpackers who want to escape the standard tourist trail.

Radiah's Homestay: For over a decade, schoolteacher and town personality Haji Radiah has helped a steady stream of Westerners learn something about life in a traditional Sasak village by providing rooms, meals, maps, motorcycles, and cultural tidbits. Rooms with private bath and three good meals cost US$5-8.

LABUHAN LOMBOK

Labuhan Lombok is a sleepy Muslim town on a beautiful bay with fine views of Gunung Rinjani from the hill behind the harbor. Back in the days when boat service to Sumbawa was limited to a single early-morning departure, a steady stream of travelers would arrive in the late afternoon and spend the night in town.

Today, with hourly departures to Sumbawa daily 0600-2200, few travelers bother to explore the region or continue counterclockwise around the coast to the north shore. Actually, the most brilliant thing to do out here is the 16-km, five-hour hike from Pasugulan, north of Aikmel on the main highway, to the remote and untouched Sasak farming village of Sembalunbumbung.

Accommodations
Two simple *losmen* here help out the traveler who arrives late and misses the last ferry to Sumbawa. Losmen Dian Dutaku is right on the main road across from the post office, while Munwar Losmen is slightly down the road toward the ferry port. Both are cheap and acceptable for the night.

Transportation
Labuhan Lombok is 73 km east and two hours by bus from Sweta terminal in Cakranegara. The harbor and ferry ticket office are about two km north of town.

Ferries to Potu Tanu on Sumbawa leave hourly 0600-2200 and take about two hours to make the crossing. Bus tickets are sold on the ferry for onward connections to Taliway (one hour), Alas (one hour), Sumbawa Besar (two hours), and Bima (10 hours).

Most travelers leave Ampenan, Kuta, or the Gili Islands in the early morning hours to make a boat departure before noon. This allows you to reach Sumbawa Besar before nightfall.

SUMBAWA

Sumbawa—an island of rolling uplands, eroded foothills, and a volcanic mountain chain which extends east from Java all the way to Alor—divides itself into Sumbawa Besar in the west, where the locals speak a dialect of Sasak, and Bima in the east, where the language is closely related to those spoken on Flores and Sumba.

Most travelers hurry across the island and catch the first available ferry to Flores, though Sumbawa offers some stunning landscapes and a traditional culture largely undisturbed by mass tourism. Reset your watch: Sumbawa is one hour ahead of Java and Bali.

Transportation

Air: Merpati flies once daily from Denpasar to Sumbawa Besar for $35 and to Pale Belo airport south of Bima for $65. Merpati also flies to Bima from Bajawa, Ende, Labuhanbajo, and Ruteng (all on Flores), and to Tambolaka on Sumba.

Sea: Ferries depart Labuhan Lombok hourly each day 0600-2200 and take under two hours to reach Poto Tano, a fishing village 30 minutes south of Alas. Buses waiting at the Poto Tano harbor reach Sumbawa Besar in two hours and Bima in about eight.

Bus tickets for travel across Sumbawa can be purchased on the ferry from Lombok. Express bus companies on Lombok sell combination tickets from Sweta terminal to Sumbawa Besar, the town where most travelers spend their first night on the island.

SUMBAWA BESAR

West Sumbawa's largest town consists of little more than concrete shops, rough-looking *rumah makan,* and oversized government offices. Useful facilities include the Bank Negara on Jalan Kartini, a PHPA (national park) office on Jalan Garuda (information on Moyo Island), and a Pelni office on Jalan Wahidan.

Attractions

Sumbawa Besar's only notable tourist attraction is the wooden palace of the sultan, constructed in 1885 and partially restored a decade ago. Up until the mid-1970s, the wrinkled 100-year-old former wife of the sultan lived here. Today the *istana* is slowly being converted into a local museum, though most of the old treasures are

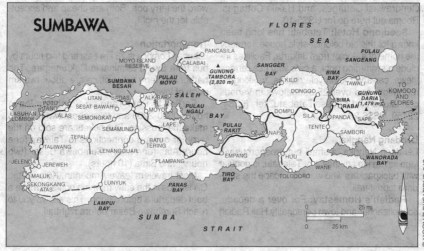

locked away in the Bala Kuning—the former home of the sultan's daughters.

Accommodations

The town is small enough to walk anywhere except to the harbor and to the airport. Several *losmen* are located on Jalan Hasanuddin, a five-minute walk south of the bus terminal and within earshot of the 0500 prayer call from the mosque.

Suci Losmen: Clean rooms and a pleasant courtyard but mighty close to the mosque. Jl. Hasanuddin 57, tel. (0371) 21589, US$6-8.

Hotel Tambora: The best hotel in town, a 15-minute walk west from the bus terminal, has a Chinese restaurant, travel agency, car rentals, local tours, and a small shop with local handicrafts. Managers are helpful to both group tours and backpackers, plus there's a useful map of Sumbawa mounted on the wall. This hotel has both fan-cooled and a/c rooms. Jl. Kebayan 2, tel. (0371) 21555, US$5-25.

Dewi Hotel: Second-best choice in town with spotless rooms. Jl. Hasanuddin 60, tel. (0371) 21170, US$5-25.

Kencana Beach Inn: The owners of Hotel Tambora also operate this seaside resort 12 km west of Sumbawa Besar with skin diving, fishing, and a good selection of Sumbawanese-style cottages—a fine place to escape the noise and dust of town. Pantai Karang Teruna, tel. (0371) 22555, US$25-60.

Transportation

Air: Brang Biji Airport is five minutes from the center of Sumbawa Besar. Merpati on Jalan Diponegoro can help with flights to Bali, Jakarta, Ujung Pandang, and Banjarmasin.

Bus: Buses to Poto Tano (harbor for Lombok) depart hourly from the Brang Bara terminal on Jalan Kaharuddin in the center of town and the main long-distance bus terminal five km northwest of city center.

Most buses to Bima (seven hours) depart from the Karang Dima long-distance bus terminal northwest of town but you might be able to pick up a bus at the more centrally located Brang Bara terminal. Buses also leave for Sape (eight hours). Best views are from the front seats near the driver and on the left side, which faces the northern coastline.

Hotel Tambora and local travel agencies sell combination bus/boat tickets all the way to Bali and east to Komodo.

GUNUNG TAMBORA

Bored with Indonesia? Need some excitement? Then climb one of the world's most dangerous volcanoes, Gunung Tambora. The massive 1815 eruption of Tambora—the most destructive and powerful in human history—was preceded for several years by dark, thick smoke which poured out of the crater. The rumblings and thundering grew more and more ominous. Finally, on 5 April, the volcano exploded with unbelievable fury: the blast shook Ternate and Surabaya, and in Batavia, 1250 km distant, Raffles marched his troops into the city to defend it against what he thought was a rebel attack.

The volcanic paroxysm reached its greatest magnitude the following week when the whole mountain turned into a body of liquid fire, creating thunder heard 1,775 km away on Sumatra and airborne ejecta which circled the globe and created the famous "year without summer" of 1816.

The human toll was staggering. Earthquakes, whirlwinds, and tsunamis caused by the collapse of the peak killed 12,000 people outright, while another 50,000 died of cholera, exposure, and starvation during the ensuing drought which devastated the whole of Nusa Tenggara. Tambora today is still considered a highly active and potentially deadly volcano.

Routes

The trail to the 2,851-meter summit of Gunung Tambora starts in the village of Pancasila, 15 km east of Calabai, a coastal logging town due west of the crater and opposite Moyo Island. Calabai can be reached by chartered boat from Sumbawa Besar or by bus from Soriutu, 20 km west of Dompu. Hikers must register with the police in Calabai and hire a guide in Pancasila. The roundtrip hike takes a minimum of three days.

HUU

Sumbawa's surfing scene centers on the village of Huu, 40 km south of Dompu on the southeast flank of Cempi Bay. Huu and its offshore breaks—Priscop, Nanga, Wall Peak, Lakey, the Pipes—were discovered in the late 1980s by Australian surfers who rode the empty waves and kept quiet about their newfound paradise.

In the early 1990s, however, several Australian surf companies constructed better lodges and organized surfing expeditions from Bali and Australia. Wealthy investors and hotel chains from Jakarta have recently sniffed around and purchased large tracts of land in anticipation of a major tourist boom. We'll see.

Huu is busiest during the southeast monsoons from June to September, when strong winds bring the largest waves.

Accommodations

Almost a dozen simple *losmen* have been constructed at Huu, plus there's a handful of moderately priced places with private bathrooms and larger bungalows facing the beach. Most of the simple spots cost US$6-8 daily, but this includes meals, drinks, and laundry services. Among the largest and most popular operations is the Mona Lisa, which features a good restaurant, volleyball courts, and 28 rooms in various price ranges.

Nearby options include the popular and well-managed Hotel Amangati, the far more basic Lakey Peak, and the original surf camp at Intan Lestari. Kabera Cottages and Periscopes also provide budget bungalows, while Prima Dona goes for the mid-level market with larger bungalows complete with TV and private baths. Rooms here cost US$8-20.

Transportation

Huu is very isolated and difficult to reach with public transport. Some attempt to reach the beach by bus or *bemo* from Dompu, but most surfers hire a taxi from the Bima airport and skip the hassle.

BIMA-RABA

Sumbawa's principal commercial and transportation center is a handy pit stop crowded with horse-drawn carts called "Ben Hurs" and smiling Muslim schoolgirls dressed in long skirts and brightly colored *rimpu*, the wraparound headscarves required by the Islamic Muhammadiyah

system. Residents are friendly but appreciate Western visitors who respect local etiquette and dress modestly.

Bima is Sumbawa's chief port, while Raba, a few km east, serves as the departure point for buses east to Sape, from where ferries continue to Komodo and Flores.

Town facilities include Bank Negara Indonesia on Jalan Sultan Hasanuddin, the Merpati office on Jalan Sukarno Hatta, and Pelni on Jalan Pelabuhan at the port.

Attractions

Sultan's Palace: The town's principal sight is the former palace, constructed in 1927 and now a small museum with a desultory collection of royal regalia. Dance rehearsals are held on Sunday mornings.

Views: Two small hills are worth climbing for religious monuments and views over Bima. Behind the bus terminal in the southwest corner of town is a small hill capped with a Hindu temple. Better bets are the excellent views and the grave of Bima's first sultan, Abdul Kahir, at the top of Dana Taraha, east of the bus terminal and south of Hotel Parewa.

Accommodations

Losmen are concentrated in city center near the old sultan's palace.

Hotel Lila Graha: Bima's most popular *losmen* is run by Balinese Ibu Sarini and her cheerful, mustachioed sergeant-major husband. The hotel is fairly clean, very noisy, and centrally located just 10 minutes from the bus terminal. Jl. Lombok 20, tel. (0371) 42740, US$4-20.

Wisma Komodo: Much quieter and for many travelers a superior choice over the Lila Graha, this government-run hotel near the *istana* features enormous rooms with several beds and private bath. Jl. Ibrahim 5, tel. (0371) 42070, US$4-6.

Hotel Parewa: A popular mid-priced hotel with a Chinese cafe, a helpful tour agency, and 24 spacious rooms; it's one km southeast of city center. Jl. Sukarno Hatta 40, tel. (0371) 42652, US$10-25.

Hotel Sanghyang: Opposite Wisma Komodo and once the town's swankiest hotel, but today nothing works and mosquitoes have taken over the largely abandoned hotel. Jl. Hasanuddin 6, tel. (0371) 42788, US$10-25.

Transportation

Air: The Merpati office, on Jalan Sukarno Hatta adjacent to Hotel Parewa, sells tickets to Bali, Yogyakarta, Jakarta, Ujung Pandang, and Timor. The airport is 15 km south of town.

Bus: Bima-Raba has two bus terminals. Buses west to Sumbawa Besar, Lombok, and Bali leave from the Bima bus terminal in the southwestern corner of the city. Departures are most frequent in the mornings before 1000 and in the evening from 1900 to 2000.

Buses east to Sape, the harbor for Komodo and Flores, take two hours and leave from Kumbe bus terminal in Raba, a 20-minute *bemo* ride east of Bima. It is difficult (often impossible) to find a bus which reaches Sape in time for the 0800 boat to Komodo and Flores. Fortunately, hotels and *losmen* in Bima sell combination bus/ boat tickets which do get you to Sape before the 0800 departure.

SAPE

Sape is a fishing village three km from the pier for Komodo and Flores. People here are friendly—a million "Hello Misters!"—and even the police smile at you. The PHPA office, about two km down the road toward the harbor, has little information on Komodo aside from some old weather charts and topographical maps. Sape has a post office but no bank; exchange plenty of money in Bima.

Accommodations

Many travelers overnight in one of Sape's *losmen* to guarantee a seat on the 0800 boat to Komodo and Flores. Places in town include Losmen Give with tiny, primitive rooms, Losmen Ratna Sari, and Losmen Friendship with the cleanest rooms of the three choices.

You can also stay adjacent to the harbor in Pelabuhan Sape, four km east of town, where Losmen Mutiara has inexpensive rooms facing the ferry terminus for Komodo and Flores.

Transportation

Ferries to Komodo and Labuhanbajo in Flores depart daily except Fridays at 0800 from Pelabuhan Sape, four km down the road from Sape town. The crossing takes six hours to Komodo and another four hours to Flores.

All ferries between Sumbawa and Flores make a brief stop at Komodo. Passengers do not disembark directly on Komodo but are transferred to smaller fishing boats which shuttle visitors to the beach.

KOMODO

One of the great wildlife regions of the world, this small archipelago nestled between Sumbawa and Flores is home of the Komodo dragon, perhaps a distant relative of carnivorous dinosaurs that thrived in tropical Asia 130 million years ago.

The giant monitor lizards—largest on Earth—remained a myth until the turn of this century when a Dutch army officer and curator of the Bogor Zoological Museum arrived to document the existence of *Varanus komodoensis.* Inhabiting the windswept island without any serious competing scavengers or predators, this solitary carnivore has achieved optimal size—up to three meters long with fearsome-looking jaws, forked tongue, sharp claws, and muscular legs to support the heavy body. The dragons have claimed several human victims, including an 84-year-old Swiss tourist in 1979, a 12-year-old boy in 1987, and Tony Wheeler in 1998 (just kidding).

Dragon Spotting

Komodo Island, part of the Indonesian national-park system, is administered by the PHPA from its office in Loh Liang. Visitors must register and pay a series of fees for entry permits, photography, and guides, which are mandatory to go anywhere on the island.

Komodo now attracts over 5,000 visitors annually, who generally arrive during the busy tourist months from June to September. The best time to visit is during the low season from April to June, or during the end of the dry season from September to December, when the dragons are the hungriest.

Dragon spotting is a fascinating but commercialized affair tightly controlled by the PHPA.

INDONESIA

Years ago, guides would lead you and a bait animal to the dragon-watching site at Banu Nggulung, about two km north of Loh Liang, string up the goat or a deer, then patiently wait until several of the beasts arrived for their afternoon feasts. But these organized feedings were halted several years ago, after the dragons began to behave more like trained dogs than wild creatures.

Today, dragon spotting is much chancier and increasing numbers of visitors are spotting nothing wilder than the chickens in the nearby fishing village. To successfully spot dragons, you'll need an experienced guide and be willing to wait patiently at the Banu Nggulung riverbed where many of the dragons come to drink and laze in the afternoon sun. Bring along a telephoto lens; visitors are kept well distanced from the dragons.

Afterward, guides can be hired to explore the interior of the island and climb up Gunung Ara, where you can enjoy great views across most of the island.

Accommodations

The PHPA administrative site of Loh Liang, a 30-minute walk north of Kampung Komodo, has one clean and spacious cabin with both dormitory and double rooms priced at US$4-6 per person. The attached cafe serves basic food and drink at fairly reasonable prices; bring extra supplies or survive on a steady diet of *nasi goreng* and *mee goreng*.

Transportation

Expensive guided tours are sold by the travel agents in Jakarta and Bali, but an overland trip isn't tough—it just requires an appreciation of *jam karet* ("rubber time").

Air: Hurried visitors can reach Komodo quickly with the Merpati flight from Bali to Labuhanbajo on the western tip of Flores. The flight costs US$90 and takes about three hours including a brief stop in Bima.

Alternatively, fly from Bali to Bima then take local transportation to Sape, from where ferries depart for Komodo daily except Friday at 0800.

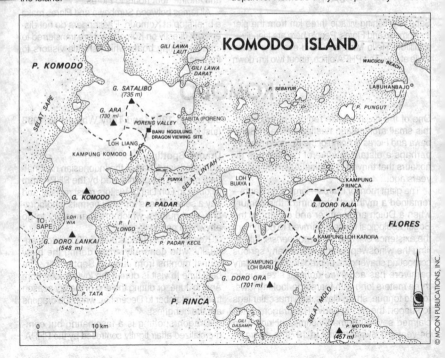

Sea: Ferries to Komodo depart Sape and Labuhanbajo daily except Friday at 0800. The trip takes about six hours from Sape and three hours from Labuhanbajo.

Travelers coming from Labuhanbajo often take one of the 5-7 day boat tours which cost US$95-125 depending on the transport company. A typical tour includes a day on Komodo, then a few days spent sailing along the north coast of Sumbawa with snorkeling stops on Pulau Satunda and Pulau Moyo. The boat trip terminates at Labuhan Lombok, from where buses continue west to Mataram and Lembar harbor for Bali.

FLORES

One of Indonesia's highlights, Flores is a remarkable island blessed with grandiose volcanoes, high mountain lakes, stretches of savannah, tropical deciduous forest, superb beaches, great scuba diving, and some of the finest ethnological regions in the archipelago. This alluring combination—traditional culture and great natural beauty—has made Flores *the* upcoming star of Indonesian tourism and the highlight of any visit to Nusa Tenggara.

History
Prior to the arrival of Western powers in the 16th century, Flores was occasionally visited by trading ships from China and the Majapahit Empire of Central Java. In 1544, a Portuguese explorer named Cabot arrived en route to the Spice Islands and christened the easternmost peninsula "Cabo das Flores" or "Cape of Flowers," though ironically the island has few flowers and was known to Javanese sailors as "Stone Island." Dominican priests sent by the Portuguese profoundly influenced local culture, and today many of the islanders have Portuguese names, practice old Portuguese customs and dances, and even *look* Portuguese. Flores, however, offered little of economic value to the Iberians aside from its function as a convenient stopover to the sandalwood forests of Timor.

The Portuguese era ended in 1859 when Dutch forces took over the island and brought in Jesuit and Franciscan priests who introduced other Christian denominations. Today, Flores is almost entirely Catholic. A native rebellion was crushed by the Dutch in 1907, but it wasn't until 1936 that they considered the island safe enough to be transferred from military to civilian control.

In December 1992, an earthquake measured at 7.5 on the Richter scale struck Flores and destroyed most of Maumere and Larantuka, killing over 3,000 Indonesians in a matter of minutes. The devastation was worst on the nearby island of Babi, where a gigantic, boiling hot, 20-meter tsunami swept over the island, leaving bodies hanging in trees and corpses floating in the once-tranquil bays.

Flores has recovered, though few residents will ever forget the quake of '92.

Transportation
Flores is a few hours by air from Bali, or several days of overlanding by bus and boat. The center of tourism on Flores is Maumere; visitors bound for Komodo should fly to Labuhanbajo.

Air: Merpati flies daily to Maumere from Bali (US$100), Ujung Pandang in Sulawesi (US$75), Kupang in Timor (US$45), and Bima in Sumbawa (US$50). Bouraq also flies from Bali to Maumere.

Merpati's flight from Bali to Labuhanbajo is difficult to book due to high demand, infrequent flights, small planes, and the unimproved landing field. Reserve early and reconfirm often. Merpati also serves Ruteng, Bajawa, and Larantuka from Ende, with connections to most towns in Indonesia.

Sea: The ferry schedule between Sape in Sumbawa and Labuhanbajo in Flores is listed above under "Sape." Several Pelni ships sail weekly from Ende to Kupang in Timor, and from Ende to Waingapu in Sumba.

Ferries depart Larantuka for Kupang several times weekly and a few services make brief stops in the Solor and Alor archipelagoes.

Land: Decades ago, few roads in Indonesia could compare with the Trans-Flores Highway, a 700-km nightmare of destroyed bridges, horrific mountain passes, and muddy quagmires which could delay you for several weeks.

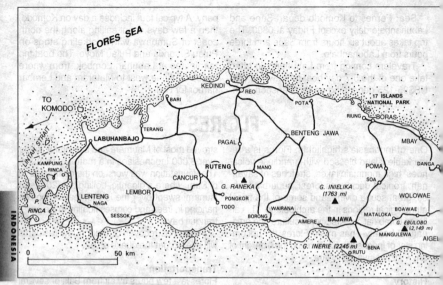

Today, the Trans-Flores Highway has been almost completely paved and, except during the rainy season from November to April, can be covered by bus in a few days. The only problem area is the stretch from Moni (Keli Mutu) to Maumere, which washes out during the rainy season and demands a long detour via the north-coast town of Kota Bharu.

The scenery across Flores is absolutely gorgeous. To best enjoy the vistas, ask your *losmen* owner to reserve a front seat next to the driver or a window seat on the south side of the bus. Travel distances and approximate times are Labuhanbajo-Ruteng (127 km, four hours), Ruteng-Bajawa (131 km, six hours), Bajawa-Ende (128 km, five hours), Ende-Moni (50 km, two hours), Moni-Maumere (99 km, four hours), and Maumere-Larantuka (138 km, four hours).

LABUHANBAJO

Labuhanbajo is a small fishing village perfectly situated on a lovely bay at the western tip of Flores. The town chiefly serves as the departure point for Komodo, though the beautiful islands and beaches are worth exploring in their own right.

Once well off the beaten track, Labuhanbajo is now visited by hundreds of Western tourists during the high season from June to September. Facilities include a Bank Rakyat Indonesia, a post office, a Merpati office at the airport, a health center, and a KSDA office for information on Komodo and Rinca islands.

Attractions

Snorkeling and sunbathing can hardly be recommended in Labuhanbajo, but within a few kilometers are deserted islands and superb beaches with clean white sand. Scuba dives are organized at several dive shops on the main road near the post office, while tour agencies organize visits to Batu Cermin ("Stone Mirror Cave"), whip fights in Kapar village (five km north), and a southern hillside sprinkled with petrified wood.

Bidadari Island: Serious divers head to the more distant islands of Tatawa, Sebayur Kecil, and Sebolan, but skin diving and lazing on the beach are recommended on Pulau Bidadari, just 20 minutes from Labuhanbajo.

Waecicu Beach: Twenty minutes by boat north of town is a long and clean beach with coral beds, several *losmen,* and the upscale Waecicu Beach Hotel.

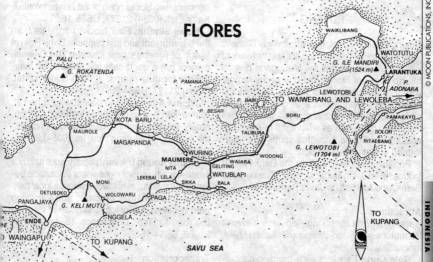

© MOON PUBLICATIONS, INC.

Batugosok Beach: Another excellent beach just 20 minutes from town. Take the Batugosaok Hotel boat.

Accommodations

Almost a dozen *losmen* and homestays line the main road, plus several mid-market hotels have been constructed on sandy beaches outside town.

Bajo Beach Hotel: The largest hotel in town arranges transportation to Komodo, scuba dives, and local tours, and has plenty of rooms in all price ranges, but bargain hard for the best prices. Jl. Sudarso, tel. (0385) 41009, US$3-20.

Mutiara Beach Hotel: Opposite the Bajo Beach Hotel and directly on the water is another favorite with clean rooms and harbor views from its popular cafe. Leo rents vehicles and arranges trips to Komodo but will try to squeeze every *rupiah* out of you. Jl. Sudarso, tel. (0385) 41039, US$3-8.

Gardena Hotel: Central location just off the main road with views of the harbor from some of the bungalows. Jl. Sudarso, tel. (0385) 41088, US$3-8.

Mitra Hotel: Popular and very clean spot in the south of town just past Bank Rakyat Indonesia. Jl. Sudarso, tel. (0385) 41003, US$3-8.

Weicucu Beach Hotel: Twenty minutes north of town by boat is a decent beach with several good *losmen* constructed in a simple but attractive Sumbawanese style. Waecucu also arranges tours to Komodo and might rent diving equipment. US$4-8.

Batu Gosok Beach Lodge: An upscale beach escape about 20 minutes from town with hotel boat. Labuhanbajo, tel. (0385) 41030, US$35-45.

Transportation

Air: Merpati flies several times weekly between Labuhanbajo and Ende, Ruteng, Bima, Mataram, and Denpasar. The Labuhanbajo airport is three km from town and the Merpati office is midway the distance.

Bus: Buses from the main terminal depart in the morning around 0700 for Ruteng (four hours), Bajawa (10 hours), and Ende (14 hours).

Boat: The ferry to Komodo and Sumbawa departs Labunhanbajo daily at 0800 except on Friday.

Pelni ships go from Labuhanbajo to Timor, Maluku, and Ujung Pandang on Sulawesi. Pelni schedules can be checked at the Pelni booking office on Jalan Sudarso just opposite the PHPA information booth.

RUTENG

Ruteng is a cool, neat, overwhelmingly Catholic town set amidst the scenic hills and network of valleys which comprise the Manggarai district, the rice bowl of Flores and one of the largest coffee-growing regions of Indonesia. The local Manggarai people speak a language unintelligible to other Floresians and still follow a few traditional rites such as whip fighting *(caci)*, an ancient homage to ancestral spirits often performed at Catholic weddings.

Facilities in Ruteng include the Bank Rakyat Indonesia on Jalan Sudarso, post office on Jalan Baruk, and Merpati on Jalan Pertiwi.

Attractions

Ruteng is great for hiking—endless views of beautiful lush-green *sawah* (ricefields), hills, mountains, and valleys.

Golo Curu: Excellent early-morning panoramas of Ruteng are best enjoyed from this hill about one km north of town, just past Wisma Agung I.

Gunung Ranaka: Southeast of Ruteng is an active volcano (2,400 meters) that can be climbed in about four hours from Robo. Alternatively, take a jeep to the top and hike the eight km down to Robo.

Lambaleda: A traditional Manggarai weaving village located 50 km northwest of Ruteng.

Pagal: Most Manggarai weaving villages are 21 km north of Ruteng near the village of Pagal on the road to Reo. The weaving season in Cibal Timur, two hours east of Pagal, is from May to October, while the weaving season in Compang, a few kilometers west of Golongorong (just north of Pagal), is from October to March. Samples of Manggarai *songket* and black *sarung* are sold in the Ruteng market.

Pongkor and Todo: Manggarai culture once centered on the traditional villages of Pongkor and Todo, 45 km southwest of Ruteng. Home to the last Manggarai rajas, these small villages still have a few circular conelike homes in the circular village, surrounded by circular ricefields divided into pie-shaped sections.

Accommodations

Hotel Dahlia: A clean and comfortable 30-room *losmen* with a popular cafe and friendly management, two blocks north of the bus terminal. Jl. Kartini, tel. (0384) 21377, US$5-15.

Hotel Sindha: Four blocks northeast from the bus terminal and just opposite Bank Rakyat is one of Ruteng's best *losmen*. The Chinese owners run a good cafe but sometimes overcharge for their rooms. Jl. Yos Sudarso, tel. (0384) 21197, US$4-20.

Wisma Agung II: The downtown *losmen* affiliated with Agung I is fairly clean but, unfortunately, located near the mosque—very noisy in the morning. Jl. Motang Rua, tel. (0384) 21835, US$4-8.

Wisma Agung I: A very popular spot run by a proprietor who spent eight years in Canada before returning to run his two *losmen,* a local bakery, a road-construction crew, and a thriving porn business. Quiet location north of town on the road to Reo. Jl. Waecos 10, tel. (0384) 21080, US$4-15.

Transportation

Air: Merpati flies daily to Ende (US$35), Bima (US$48), Kupang (US$65), and Bali (US$95).

Bus: Buses leave 0700-1000 to Labuhanbajo (four hours), Bajawa (five hours), and Ende (nine hours). Purchase tickets at the bus terminal, your *losmen,* or from the Bis Agogo travel agency adjacent to Losmen Ranaka.

BAJAWA

The most traditional areas of Flores and among the great natural wonders of Nusa Tenggara, Bajawa and the Bajawa Highlands are home to the Ngada people, who have retained many of their animistic beliefs despite conversion to Christianity in the early 20th century.

Sadly, most travelers hurry through the region on their way to Maumere and miss the richness of local culture and the spectacular scenery: brooding volcanoes looming over verdant *sawah,* stone megaliths abandoned in thick jungle, and male sacrificial posts *(ngadhu)* and accompanying female fertility shrines *(bhaga)* still honored in many villages.

Tradition also permeates many local festivals such as the Soa planting festival in September, the sacrificial Umamoni event in the fall, and the six-day celebration of Reba held in late December. Also, watch for boxing matches in which just the middle knuckles are used and partners steer their fighters from behind, like puppeteers.

Bajawa is a great place to learn about pre-Islamic, pretourism Indonesia.

Attractions

Buses from Ruteng pass through a spectacular array of immense volcanoes before arriving in the scenic but often chilly hill town of Bajawa. Guides to traditional villages charge about 20,000Rp per day and can help with introductions and insight into local cultures. All of the *losmen* and hotels in town have guides on call.

Ancestral Poles: According to Ngada tradition, the *ngadhu,* a carved wooden post crowned by a conical roof, and the *bhaga,* a little thatched house that represents female fertility, must always be aligned with the village cult house, royal tombs, and other megalithic structures. Two ancestral poles stand on Jalan Satsuitubu, in the south end of town.

Langa: Seven km south of Bajawa and just before Bena at the base of magnificent Gunung Inerie (2,245 meters) lies Langa, home to the six-day Reba ceremony and almost a dozen *ngadhu* and *bhaga.*

Bena: The finest traditional village near Bajawa features totem figures and megaliths in the town square, surrounded by Ngadanese bamboo dwellings and ritual houses topped by warriors wielding spears and *parangs.* Visitors must register and pay a small fee and can overnight in a simple guesthouse.

Gunung Inerie is an all-day expedition from Bena.

Wogo: The road from Bena continues clockwise through Jerebuu and Were to the *adat* village of Wogo, where the nearby village of Wogo Tua ("Old Wogo") features several large megaliths surrounded by grasses and bamboo.

Soa: Soa, 26 km north of Bajawa and constructed around a huge amphitheater with tiers of great megaliths, is known for its unusual festivals, annual deer hunts, and traditional boxing called *sagi.* Best visited for the colorful market held on Sunday evenings and Monday mornings.

Boawae: Forty-one km east of Bajawa lies the most famous *ikat*-weaving village in central Flores.

Accommodations

Bajawa has over a half-dozen *losmen* near the bus station, but in different directions.

Sunflower Homestay: Bajawa's original travelers' center, three blocks east of the market, compensates for its small rooms with a good restaurant, a useful wall map, and reliable information on nearby villages. Jl. Ahmad Yani, tel. (0384) 21236, US$3-8.

Hotel Korina: A small and friendly *losmen* that handles the overflow from nearby Sunflower Homestay. The owner provides excellent guide services to nearby villages. Jl. Ahmad Yani 81, tel. (0384) 21162, US$3-8.

Hotel Ariesta: A newer place with spotless rooms and relaxing atmosphere three blocks northwest of the market. Jl. Diponegoro, tel. (0384) 21292, US$6-10.

Elizabeth Kembang: Family homestay with friendly owners in a quiet location at the northern edge of town. Jl. Inerie, tel. (0384) 21223, US$3-10.

Hotel Dam: Actually another friendly homestay in a convenient location just one block southeast of the market. Jl. Pasar Rahmat, tel. (0384) 21145, US$6-8.

Hotel Kembang: Best hotel in town. Jl. Marta Dinata, tel. (0384) 21072, US$10-15.

Transportation

Air: Merpati flies from Bajawa to Bima and Ende, with onward connections to Sumbawa, Lombok, Bali, and Timor. The Merpati office is across from the market.

Bus: The long-distance bus terminal is three km east of town on the road to Ende. Buses depart early mornings for Labuhanbajo (10 hours), Ruteng (five hours), Ende (five hours), and Riung (three hours) on the north coast.

The *bemo* terminal in the center of town provides sporadic transport to nearby villages such as Soa, Mangulewa, Mataloko, Langa, Boawae, Bena, and Jerebuu.

RIUNG

Riung, on the north coast of Flores, offers some excellent beaches and snorkeling, and provides an opportunity of get off the Trans-Flores Highway, which snakes through the center of the island.

Attractions

Several dozen nearby islands reached by chartered boat are perfect places to daytrip with their brilliant sand and pristine coral beds. Hikers might want to climb Watujapi Hill for views over the Muslim fishing village of Riung and the offshore archipelago. Another draw to the region are the giant colored iguanas that can be spotted north of town near Torong Padang.

The PHPA office in the west side of town can help with island permits and snorkeling equipment, as can most of the guesthouses.

Accommodations

The newly completed road from Bajawa has increased tourism and brought almost a dozen small homestays and *losmen* to the once deserted village. Most places charge US$5-8 for decent rooms, sometimes overlooking the water. Hotel Iklas near the harbor in the Bugis stilt village and Homestay Tamari Beach are popular spots with friendly managers who can help arrange tours to nearby islands and iguana-spotting sites. Other choices scattered around town include Homestay Madone, Liberty Homestay, Homestay Florida Inn, and Homestay Riung.

Transportation

Riung can be reached by bus from Bajawa (three hours) and by direct bus from Ende (four hours) which leaves daily from the Ende Ndao bus terminal around 0600. Fishing boats sometimes take passengers on the eastward passage to Reo.

ENDE

Ende—the commercial center, political headquarters, and largest town on Flores—principally serves as a stopover en route to Keli Mutu and nearby *ikat*-weaving villages.

Attractions

Ende itself has little of great interest aside from the old port area and views of nearby volcanoes: Ebulobo to the west, Meja to the southeast, Ipi farther to the south.

Sukarno's House: Now a national shrine and museum, this cream-colored building on Jalan Dewantara was Sukarno's home during his exile in the 1930s.

Harbor: The new harbor, Pelabuhan Ipi, southeast of town past the airport, is where Pelni ships departs weekly. More intriguing are the docks and back alleys of Pelabuhan Ende, west of city center, where Bugis immigrants continue traditional boatbuilding techniques.

Nuabosi: Excellent views, a traditional clan house with sacrificial altar, and a gracious Dutch guesthouse can be enjoyed in this mountain town 10 km north of Ende.

Gunung Ipi: Ende's most impressive volcano can be climbed from the volcanology station in Tentandara, eight km south of town.

Accommodations

Ende has almost a dozen inexpensive *losmen* and several decent hotels. Many are clean and comfortable but subject to wake-up calls from town mosques.

Hotel Ikhlas: This curiously named *losmen* some 350 meters west of the airport is Ende's most popular travelers' center and information resource on local tours, bus schedules, sights, maps, and flights. Owner Djamal speaks good English and German. Jl. Ahmad Yani 5, tel. (0384) 21695, US$3-8.

Hotel Safari: A clean and well-organized *losmen* adjacent to the Ikhlas with both fan-cooled and a/c rooms. Jl. Ahmad Yani 3, tel. (0384) 21499, US$4-15.

Nirwana Hotel: Ende's best mid-priced *losmen*, just west of the Protestant church, has small but clean rooms with private bath and more luxurious rooms with a/c and TV. Jl. Pahlawan 29, tel. (0384) 21199, US$5-15.

Dewi Putra Hotel: Ende's largest and most luxurious hotel has over 40 spotless rooms and can help arrange roundtrip tours of Keli Mutu, plus visits to *ikat*-weaving villages. Jalan Dewantara, tel. (0384) 21685, US$8-25.

Transportation

Ende is second only to Maumere for transportation connections.

Air: Merpati stops daily in Ende on its Trans-Nusa Tenggara flight from Bali to Timor, with other stops in Mataram (Lombok), Bima (Sumbawa), Labuhanbajo, Ruteng, and Bajawa. The Bali flight takes just two hours over a distance that might require over a week by bus and boat. Reservations and reconfirmations are absolute-

INDONESIA

ly necessary. Merpati is on Jalan Nangka two blocks north of the airport.

Boat: Every other Saturday, the Pelni ship *Binaiya* departs from Pelabuhan Ipi (new harbor) to Kupang in Timor. After returning from Timor, the *Kelimutu* leaves the following Monday to Waingapu in Sumba.

Smaller ferries depart weekly for Sumba, Timor, Sabu, and various towns on the south coast of Flores. Inquire at the harbormaster office at Pelabuhan Ipi.

Bus: Buses west to Riung (four hours), Bajawa (five hours), Ruteng (nine hours), and Labuhanbajo (14 hours) leave from Terminal Ndao, two km northwest of town. Buses east to Keli Mutu (two hours) and Maumere (five hours) depart from Terminal Wolowana, four km northeast of town. Most *losmen* sell bus tickets which include pick-up from your hotel.

KELI MUTU

Keli Mutu is one of the more otherworldly sights in all of Indonesia, a volcanic cone filled with three lakes with different-colored waters and in constant state of flux as minerals leach in from the earth. Legend claims all three lakes are abodes of the dead: souls of sinners and sorcerers in the maroon lake, virgins and the pure of heart in the green, elderly in the blue.

Keli Mutu is best accessed by paved road from Moni (Mone), a small but attractive town 51 km northeast of Ende and 97 km west of Maumere. Guides are unnecessary, though it's important to reach the summit at dawn before the clouds roll in and ruin the views.

Transportation

The most convenient way to reach the crater is with minibuses and the Catholic mission truck, which departs at 0400 from Moni. Tickets are sold the previous night from most *losmen.* Other options from Moni include a tough 11-km hike, uncomfortable horseback rides, and expensive jeep rentals.

Bring warm clothing, a flashlight, hot drinks, snacks, and a sense of patience; the lakes are obscured by clouds over half the time.

After (hopefully) viewing the lakes, hike around the perimeter to escape the crowds, then hike down to Moni via the shortcut and continue to Maumere or Ende by bus.

MONI (MONE)

One of the finer aspects to Keli Mutu is an overnight in the nearby village and Catholic mission of Moni, 14 km northeast of the volcano. Blessed with the constant sound of running water and fantastic views of surrounding volcanoes, Moni provides a welcome relief from the monotonous towns of central Flores. The morning market attracts many of the local Lio people.

Attractions

Several traditional weaving villages are southeast of Moni and due south of Wolowaru. Take a morning truck or hike from Moni or Wolowaru. The 20-km roundtrip trek between Wolowaru and Nggela can be done in a single day.

Wolowaru: Twelve km east of Moni is a small town often used as a base for visits to the southern weaving villages. A cluster of old-style *rumah adat* with their high, steeply pitched roofs stands at the town entrance. The weekly market is on Saturday. Inexpensive *losmen* and homestays in Wolowaru include Losmen Kelimutu, Losmen Setia, and Losmen Hidaya. All charge US$2-4 for small rooms with common bath.

Jopu: Five km south of Wolowaru is an old-style Florinese village with steep-roofed *adat* houses and a distinctive Flemish-looking church, secluded in a valley with magnificent volcanoes on all sides. Weavers in Jopu produce a limited number of attractive *sarung ikat* but also inferior weavings colored with artificial dyes.

Wolonjita: Four km south of Jopu is another village with better *sarung* at slightly lower prices.

Nggela: Nggela is a well-known *ikat*-weaving village at the end of a terrible dirt road on a high cliff with views over the Sawu Sea. Nggela is famous for its use of hand-spun thread and natural dyes, though artificially dyed and mass-produced items are also sold by many of the 1,300 inhabitants.

The quality *ikat* and superb location perhaps compensates for the highly aggressive saleswomen who charge for photos and constantly wave their wares in your face. Approximate prices with firm bargaining are US$15-20 for an *ikat* shawl *(selendang)* and US$30-80 for an *ikat* sarong. Before arrival, check prices in Ende and at the Jawa Timur handicraft shop in Wolowaru.

Accommodations

The tourism boom on Flores has brought the linear village of Moni almost a dozen *losmen* and homestays which uniformly charge US$2-5 for rooms with common bath.

Market Hotels: On the main road, just opposite the market, are Homestay Daniel, Homestay Amina Moe, Homestay John, Homestay Friendly, Homestay Maria, and Losmen Nusa Bunga.

Wisma Kelimutu: Owned by and adjacent to the local Catholic mission is another popular spot with large, clean rooms and a good cafe.

Moni Sao Ria Wisata: Moni's top-end choice is about 1.5 km west of town on the road to Ende, near the turnoff to Keli Mutu. Rooms with private bath cost US$6-9.

MAUMERE

Within easy range of Maumere—the principal tourist destination on Flores—are superb beaches, some of the finest scuba diving in the country, traditional weaving villages, and spectacular topography from volcanoes to arid peninsulas.

Once the shining star of regional tourism, Maumere was almost completely destroyed in December 1992 by an earthquake that took over 3,000 lives and significantly altered the array of tourist services. Most facilities are now back in business, though town planners realigned some of the streets and relocated many of the *losmen* and other tourist facilities.

Maumere Attractions

Cathedral: Prior to the earthquake, Maumere's principal attraction was its large Catholic church filled with paintings of the Twelve Stations of the Cross, executed by a local artist in a distinctive Indonesian style. The cathedral was badly damaged in 1992 but has been faithfully reconstructed by local church authorities.

Market: A good place to search for thick Maumere blankets, but don't purchase ivory jewelry carved from old tusks—ivory cannot be imported to most Western countries.

Attractions near Maumere

Villages south and west of Maumere can be reached with local *bemo* or, better yet, rented motorcycles and cars.

Ladelero: Ladelero, 22 km southwest from Maumere on the road to Ende, is known for its large Catholic seminary and attached museum crammed with rare Florinese *ikat* from Sikka and Jopu, Chinese ceramics, old swords, and artifacts from other regions of Indonesia. The museum is open daily until 1400. A market is held two km past Ladelero at Nita until 1000 on Thursdays.

Sikka: An idyllic seaside location 27 km southwest of Maumere and a long tradition of distinctive Sikkanese *ikat* weaving make Sikka the most visited village near Maumere. Here, practically every house owns a primitive loom that spins popular motifs such as Dutch-influenced designs, plants, and cubist lizards—fertility symbols on Flores. Prices, however, are steep, and the saleswomen are both aggressive and mercenary. Sikka also has a fine church constructed by the Portuguese, who controlled most of Flores until the mid-18th century.

Geliting: Kewapandai district's largest market is held on Fridays in this seaside village, some 10 km east of Maumere on the road to Larantuka.

Accommodations

Losmen Wini Rae: An old favorite located slightly outside town and midway between the bus terminal and harbor. Choices include common or private bath, fan or a/c. Jl. Gajah Mada, tel. (0383) 388, US$3-8 fan, US$10-15 a/c.

Wisma Flora Jaya: Small quarters but friendly atmosphere, excellent food, and convenient location in the center of town just two blocks from the market: you'll have a great time with Mama Jo. Jl. Raja Don Thomas, tel. (0383) 333, US$3-8 fan, US$12-20 a/c.

Permata Sari Inn: Visitors arriving by air or with private transportation often stay at the Permata Sari, one km from the airport and two km outside city center. Clean rooms, friendly managers, seaside cafe, and excellent sunsets over a sandy black beach. 1 Jl. Sudirman, tel. (0383) 171, US$4-8 fan, US$10-15 a/c.

Losmen Beng Goan III: Prior to the earthquake, the Beng Goan operated two successful *losmen* near the market, plus a quieter, cleaner

INDONESIA

place two blocks south. Jl. Slamet Riyadi, tel. (0383) 283, US$3-8.

Gardena Hotel: A quiet and popular place three blocks east of the market and two blocks back from the bay. All rooms have attached baths and include complimentary breakfast. Guide services are available from Marsel Mitak. 5 Jl. Patirangga, tel. (0383) 21489, US$4-8 fan, US$12-16 a/c.

Maiwali Hotel: Maumere's best hotel has tennis courts, a bar, Chinese seafood restaurant, and a tour office that arranges *bemo* charters and escorted tours to Keli Mutu and nearby weaving villages. Jl. Raja Don Thomas, tel. (0383) 220, US$6-12 fan, US$15-25 a/c.

Transportation
Air: Merpati has daily flights to and from Bali (US$110), Kupang (US$40), Bima (US$60), and Ujung Pandang (US$70), with connections to Yogyakarta, Surabaya, and Jakarta.

Maumere's Wai Oti Airport, three km from town, is served by taxis and *bemo* from the Maumere-Larantuka road, about 600 meters from the airport.

Bus: Buses west to Ende leave from the Ende terminal, about 1.5 km south of city center. Buses east to Larantuka leave from the Waioti terminal, some three km east of town just past the airport turnoff. Departures are most frequent before noon; *losmen* owners can arrange pick-up at your hotel.

Sea: Pelni's *Kelimutu* leaves every other week for Ujung Pandang before returning to Maumere and heading east to Kalabahi (Alor) and, finally, Dili (Timor). Check with the Pelni office on Jalan Slamet Riyadi or with the harbormaster down at the dock.

Smaller shipping lines also sail to Timor, Alor, Solor, and Ujung Pandang.

WAIARA BEACH

Maumere's most popular beach resort and dive destination is 12 km east of town on the road to Larantuka. According to dive professionals, Maumere Bay—with its detached coral reefs, great diversity of ocean life, and world-class drop-offs—offers some of the finest diving in Indonesia. Diving, not the mediocre black-sand beach, is the main draw of Waiara.

Scuba Diving
The best visibility is during the dry season from March to November. Local dive operators have identified several dozen sites within the 40-km expanse of Maumere Bay, including over a dozen fairly good shore dives, superior coral gardens off Pulau Besar, cave diving near Pulau Babi, and best of all, the perfect corals and unlimited sealife at Pomana Besar Island and Gosong Bone Atoll.

Prior to the earthquake of Dec. 1992, Waiara Beach had two dive operators that provided rental equipment and dive boats. Both resorts were destroyed by the quake and tidal wave but intend to rebuild their properties and resume business by early 1994.

Sao Wisata: The most professional services were provided by Flores Sao Resort (Sao Wisata), a private company owned by a local politician who was granted guardianship over the local marine reserve. Sao Wisata operates a two-star hotel, conducts five-day NAUI certification courses, and runs a 25-knot catamaran and a liveaboard dive boat. All-inclusive dive packages (airport pick-up, accommodations, meals, and two dives per day) cost US$80-120 per day depending on room choice. Four-day eight-dive packages cost from US$300.

Sea World: Diving in Maumere began in the early 1970s after an Italian couple arrived to establish the first local dive club, then called Waiara Cottages. The operation was taken over several years ago by a local Roman Catholic foundation, which attempted to maintain the dive boat and scuba equipment in working condition. Sea World closed down after the earthquake but intends to reopen in the near future.

Accommodations
Waiara was leveled by the earthquake, though the two principal dive resorts will probably return, as will several of the inexpensive beachside bungalows that once lined the bay.

Sao Wisata: The premier dive operator has all-inclusive dive packages (described above), and less expensive packages for nondivers that cost from US$20 per day. 18 Jl. Don Thomas, Maumere, tel. (0383) 342. Jakarta headquarters: Borobudor Hotel, room 68, Jl. Lapangan, Banteng Selatan, Jakarta 10710, tel. (021) 380-5555, fax (021) 359741.

Sea World Resort: Sea World has always been the less-expensive alternative to Sao Wisata and will probably remain so after rebuilding. P.O. Box 3, Jl. Nai Noha, KM 13, Maumere, tel. (0383) 570, US$12-20.

LARANTUKA

Larantuka is an old Portuguese trading center where traces of the colonial era remain evident in the old stone and stucco houses, in the large-boned, Latin-featured inhabitants, in family names such as Monteiros and da Silva, and even in place-names such as Posto (the town's center). Strategically situated on sea routes used by Portuguese merchant sailors seeking to obtain sandalwood from Timor, the Portuguese-Catholic heritage also survives in its prayers recited in unintelligible Portuguese, Christmas and Good Friday processions, and much of the Iberian church architecture that survived the quake of 1992.

Larantuka chiefly serves as the embarkation point for the twice-weekly ferry to Timor and boats to the islands of the Solor and Alor archipelagoes. Town facilities include a Bank Rakyat that *doesn't* provide exchange services, a post office and tourist information center several kilometers north of town, and a Merpati office diagonally opposite the church.

Accommodations
Larantuka was badly damaged in the big quake, but the following *losmen* will probably be back in business by the time you arrive.

Rulies Hotel: The most popular travelers' place in town has good vibes and rooms with common or private bath. 40 Jl. Yos Sudarso, tel. (0383) 21198, US$3-8.

Trisna Hotel: A larger and slightly more luxurious spot adjacent to the Rulies. 38 Jl. Yos Sudarso, US$3-10.

Transportation
Air: Merpati flies once weekly to and from Kupang with a stop on the island of Lembata.

Sea: Ferries to Kupang leave twice weekly on Tuesday and Friday afternoons and return from Kupang on Monday and Thursday, the day after the flight arrives from Darwin.

Boats depart almost daily for the islands of the Solor archipelago. Check with the *syahbandar* office at the harbor or with the Pelni representative on Jalan Niaga. The new ferry dock is five km from town on the road to Maumere.

SOLOR AND ALOR

Separated from the larger islands by swift and narrow straits, the islands off the east coast of Flores are among the most traditional and untouched regions of Indonesia; a welcome escape from the tidal wave of mass tourism.

The Solor Archipelago includes Solor, Adonara, and Lembata, while the Alor Archipelago includes Pantar and Alor islands. Lembata and Alor—the two principal islands and the only ones with tourist facilities—receive a steady trickle of visitors throughout the year, but Western travelers should be prepared for tough travel conditions and rudimentary meals and accommodations. The rewards are friendly people, lovely scenery, and a fascinating travel experience for anyone interested in traditional Indonesian culture.

Visitors should bring along plenty of small bills since the entire region has only one exchange facility, in Kalabahi on Alor.

Transportation
Air: Merpati flies once weekly to Lewoleba (Lembata) from Larantuka and Kupang, before returning directly to Kupang. Merpati also flies several times weekly between Kupang and Kalabahi (Alor).

Sea: Ferries connect nearly all the islands on a daily basis. Boats from Larantuka head east to the nearby islands of Solor and Adonara. Boats continue from Waiwerang (Adonara) to Lewoleba. A weekly boat from Lewoleba reaches Kalabahi with overnight stops in Waiwerang and Balauring (northeast Lembata). A final ship continues from Kalabahi down to Kupang.

Pelni's *Kelimutu* sails every other week from Kalabahi to Maumere before returning to Kalabahi and continuing east to Dili and Kupang.

Adonara
Adonara is a Catholic island settled in the early 16th century by the Portuguese, though many of

the residents still follow animist practices and worship nature spirits under the firm gaze of Gunung Boleng (1,650 meters), which soars above the scrubby island.

Waiwerang: Boats from Larantuka cross the narrow channel to Wailebe or go directly to Waiwerang, largest town on the island. Market days are Monday and Thursday. Losmen Taufik and Losmen Tresna on the main road near the pier have rooms under US$3.

Solor

Once the rendezvous point for Portuguese sandalwood traders, and home to Dominican monks who built an impressive stone fortress, Solor today is a sleepy and rarely visited island known for its whaling village of Lamalera on the east coast and fortress ruins near Lohajong in the northeast corner. The principal township of Rita Ebang is served by boats from Larantuka.

Lembata

Lembata is a striking island of scrub grasslands, inland stands of eucalyptus trees, and open savannahs, inhabited by people with distinct dialects, customs, and beliefs in animism despite their conversion to Christianity. The main attractions are market day in the main town of Lewoleba, a climb up Gunung Ile Ape from the north coast, and the traditional whaling village of Lamalera in the far south.

Lewoleba: Served by boats from Larantuka, Lewoleba is best visited for the Monday market, which attracts thousands of people from across the archipelago. Losmen Rejeki is a friendly spot run by a young Chinese manager who can help with maps and advise on island walks. Motorcycles and cars can be rented here.

Gunung Ile Ape: North of Lewoleba is the most traditional region of the island: the towering pinnacle of Mt. Ile Ape (1,450 meters) can be climbed with local guides from the village of Lamaguete. Travelers can overnight by contacting the *kepala desa.*

Lamalera: Lamalera is one of the final whaling villages in Indonesia and among the last places on earth where people hunt whales from rudimentary boats, constructed without nails and propelled with sails of *gewang* palm. Unfortunately, whales are rare; only a dozen are speared each whaling season from May to October. A beachside house provides inexpensive rooms and meals.

Alor

Alor, 60 km north of Timor, has a population sharply divided between Islamic peoples living in the relatively narrow lowlands and a large number of indigenous ethnolinguistic groups residing in the mountainous interior. Chiefly known for its unique forms of *ikat* and bronze kettle drums called *moko,* Alor receives a grand total of about 30 tourists per year, mostly in July and August.

Kalabahi: Alor's main town serves as a base for visits to traditional villages such as Tapkala, 13 km east on a paved road, and Atimelang, described by Cora Dubois in her two-part ethnological tome, *The People of Alor.* An excellent three-km white-sand beach is found at Mali, 18 km north of Kalabahi.

Three *losmen* are in Kalabahi. Adi Dharma Hotel on the waterfront is run by an English teacher who is a goldmine of information about Alor. Nearby Hotel Melati, also on the waterfront, handles the overflow. Overflow? On Alor?

SUMBA

Outlying, dry, mostly barren Sumba is one of the most fascinating islands of Nusa Tenggara. Internationally known as the source of some of the most handsome *ikat* fabrics in Indonesia, Sumba is also famed as the breeding ground for the country's strongest horses, and for its ritual tribal life, flawlessly built high-peaked thatch-roofed villages, and mammoth sculptured stone tombs. Here you find an authentic ancient culture with none of the layers of Hinduism, Islam, or Christianity found elsewhere in Indonesia.

Sumba's premier tourist district is in the west near Waikabubak, where traditional culture remains apparent in megalithic gravesites, old homes covered with thatched roofing rather than galvanized steel, and age-old rituals, such as tribal war games *(pasola)* held every spring.

East Sumbanese highlights include textile villages south of Waingapu and deserted beaches with good surf.

Transportation

Situated south of Flores and midway between Sumbawa and Timor, Sumba is off the beaten path and somewhat removed from the standard Bali-to-Timor route. The most convenient access is by air from Bali, Kupang, or Bima. Aside from sea transport, Merpati from Bima is the least expensive way to reach the island.

Air: Sumba has two airports; the larger one is Mauhau Airport, six km outside Waingapu in East Sumba, and the other is Tambolaka airport, 42 km from Waikabubak in West Sumba.

Merpati flies daily to Waingapu from Bali (US$80) and Kupang (US$60), and three times weekly to Tambolaka from Bima (US$30) and Waingapu (US$28). The thrice-weekly Merpati schedule is Denpasar-Bima-Tambolaka-Waingapu-Kupang-return. Bouraq flies three times weekly Denpasar-Waingapu-Kupang-return.

Sea: Pelni's *Kelimutu* calls twice monthly at Waingapu on its Nusa Tenggara circuit: Padangbai-Lembar-Bima-Waingapu-Ende-Kupang-Dili-Kalabahi-Maumere-Ujung-Pandang-return. Smaller ships also sail from Ende to Waingapu.

Bus: Buses and minibuses take five or six hours to cover the 137-km paved road between Waingapu and Waikabubak. Outlying villages are served by a slow and crowded *bemo* network.

The ideal solution is a motorcycle (US$6) or chartered jeep (US$35-40) rented from any *losmen* or hotel. The jeep cost can be split between four or five passengers.

The *Pasola*

Sumba's premier event is a ritualistic tribal war held by hundreds of horsemen in various villages during February and March, shortly after the full moon and coinciding with the harvesting of a strange, multihued sea worm called the *nyale*. Essentially a violent and primeval jousting match between teams of horsemen brandishing long wooden spears and shields, the sometimes deadly *pasola* now attracts large crowds and even a few tour groups brought to the island specifically to witness the event. Exact dates and locations can be checked from any Indonesian tourist office.

Ikat

Visitors to Sumba are invariably met by hordes of *ikat* salesmen who quickly become tiresome with their insistent hawking of sarongs and Sumba blankets. Before opening your wallet, be patient and learn all you can about the process.

Fine *ikat* represents a colossal amount of human labor, and even in a poor society such as Sumba fabrics woven with fine threads and natural dyes rightly command stratospheric prices. Cylinder skirts for women *(lau)* and the sarong and shoulder mantle worn by men *(hinggi)* should cost US$25-100 if quickly woven with imported colored thread, synthetic dyes, and larger designs. However, fine ceremonial skirts woven with supplementary warp *(lau pahudu)* and blue-and-rust mantles *(hinggi kombu)* repeatedly dipped to ensure deep, saturated colors often cost US$250-1,000.

Visit the handicraft shop in the Sandlewood Hotel and weaving villages near Waingapu before you begin negotiations. Many salesmen start at two or three times the correct price, so bargain firmly but keep your sense of humor. Prices are about the same, but the selection is larger in Waingapu than in the nearby weaving villages.

WAINGAPU

Waingapu, principal port and district capital of East Sumba, is a sprawling commercial center of little note, but it's a useful base from which to explore the traditional weaving villages to the south and purchase East Sumbanese *ikat,* the finest in Nusa Tenggara.

Facilities include a Bank Rakyat with exchange services, a Merpati office on Jalan Ahmad Yani in the Elim Hotel, and a Pelni office down at the port.

Accommodations

Waingapu has two inexpensive *losmen* in the northern district near the harbor and four *losmen* one km south of the harbor near the bus terminal and the bank.

Hotel Lima Saudara: A popular spot near the waterfront; all rooms include private bath. 2 Jl. Wangametei, tel. 83, US$3-8.

Hotel Surabaya: An acceptable if noisy spot just opposite the bus terminal and supermarket. Motorcycle rentals cost US$6 per day. 2 Jl. El Tari, tel. 125, US$3-8.

Elim Hotel: An old but excellent-value hotel adjacent to the Merpati office and two blocks northeast of the bus terminal. All rooms include private bath. 73 Jl. Ahmad Yani, tel. 232, US$4-7 fan, US$12-20 a/c.

Sandlewood Hotel: Waingapu's best is this strangely misspelled hotel with a good restaurant and the largest selection of *ikat* on the island. All rooms include breakfast. 23 Jl. Panjaitan, tel. 199, US$5-8 fan, US$12-20 a/c.

VILLAGES NEAR WAINGAPU

Traditional East Sumbanese weaving villages are found near Waingapu, 65 km south near the town of Melolo, and along the southeastern coastline between Melolo and Baing.

Village Etiquette: Many villages now expect a donation of 1000-2000 *rupiah* to look around and take photographs. Independent travelers can make friends and possibly avoid fees by

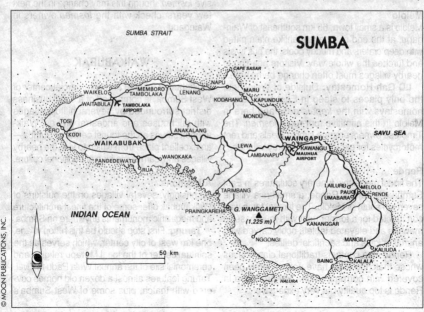

© MOON PUBLICATIONS, INC.

quickly offering small gifts of cigarettes or betel nut to the village headman, or whoever else appears to be important or collecting entry fees. A sensible approach is to keep your camera firmly packed away until you have established some kind of rapport with the villagers.

Hospitality, modest dress, and cultural sensitivity are traits highly prized by the Sumbanese, and guaranteed ways to insure a warm welcome for the next visitor.

Transportation: *Bemo* travel frequently from Waingapu to Melolo, but service to other villages is sporadic except on market days. The most efficient way to explore the following towns is with a rented motorcycle or a chartered vehicle from Waingapu.

Praliu

Praliu (two km from Waingapu), Lambanapu (eight km), and Kwangu (10 km) weave some of the most outstanding *ikat* on the island and provide one of the few places where visitors can watch the entire process, from preparation of the cotton to dyeing and the final weaving on backstrap looms. Prices are similar to Waingapu's and bargaining is essential.

Melolo

Melolo is a small town, 65 km southeast of Waingapu, at the end of a savannahlike plain pitted with deep craters and muddy pools; the bus twists and lurches the whole way. Visitors heading to nearby villages must often change *bemo* here.

LD Gah Homestay: Outside of Waingapu, the only places to sleep in East Sumba are homestays with the *kepala desa* and here in Melolo in this primitive four-room *losmen.* The Timorese owners prepare simple meals and rent motorcycles for exploring the nearby villages.

Rende

The finest megalithic funerary sculptures in East Sumba are here in Rende, a small raja village seven km south of Melolo. The largest tomb was constructed for a former ruler with four massive menhirs and elevated tablets richly carved with animal effigies and sacrificial deities.

Rende also contains traditional clan houses whose thatched roofs have unfortunately been covered with corrugated tin. *Ikat* produced in Rende is top quality but very expensive.

Umabara and Pau

Three km southwest of Melolo and reached by a dirt road just north of town is the dusty village of Umabara, known for its three surviving traditional huts and four megalithic tombs dedicated to the relatives of the present raja. Traditional *adat* homes are also found in nearby Pau.

South of Melolo

Farther south down the coast are several *ikat*-weaving villages and some excellent beaches now being discovered by surfers, divers, and fishermen.

Mangili: A well-known weaving village some 40 km south of Melolo near the larger village of Ngalu.

Kaliuda: Several km south of Ngallu and on the beach is another weaving village reputed to be among the best on Sumba, though most of the *ikat* is quickly purchased by merchants from Bali.

Kailala Beach: Five km before the road ends at Baing is a lovely beach with excellent surf, terrific game fishing, and a new luxury resort that specializes in deep-sea fishing and scuba diving. As of this writing, Kailala lacks inexpensive *losmen,* though this may change in the next few years; check with the *losmen* owners in Waingapu.

WAIKABUBAK

Waikabubak, capital and commercial center of West Sumba, is composed of a small business district surrounded by several hilltop villages with tall houses and ancestral graves. Waikabubak serves as the tourist center of Sumba—an excellent place from which to visit the nearby villages and learn something of traditional culture.

Attractions

Surprisingly, several villages on the outskirts of Waikabubak offer some of the finest architecture and megalithic monuments anywhere on Sumba.

Tarung: First stop should be this hilltop village, one km west of city center, which serves as the spiritual center of the local Marapu religion and ceremonial site of the annual Wula Padu festival. Tarung features almost a dozen old homes covered with thatch, plus some of West Sumba's most impressive gravesites. Many tombs are carved with crosses (symbolizing Christan conversion) and older ornaments such as buffalo heads (power), horses (a safe trip to heaven), and dogs (faithfulness).

Bondomaroto: Three km southeast of Waikabubak is another traditional village known for its strange megalithic carvings of sacred buffalo, and *ikat* weaving with backstrap looms.

Praijing: The trail opposite Bondomaroto leads to this lovely five-terraced village at the summit of a small hill. As elsewhere on Sumba, Praijing was constructed on a hilltop for defensive reasons and to resist the slave traders who frequently raided the island from Timor and Flores. Also, tombs are not built in remote graveyards outside town, but right in the center of the village; people here *live* with their dead.

Accommodations

Hotel Aloha: Waikabubak's travelers' center has clean rooms with complimentary breakfast, a popular cafe, motorcycle rentals, and plenty of current information on Sumbanese attractions. Jalan Gajah Mada, tel. 24, US$4-9.

Losmen Pelita: The cheapest local lodging is near the mosque; it's noisy but acceptable for a short stay. 2 Jl. Achmad Yani, tel. 104, US$2-6.

Hotel Manandang: A clean and relatively new hotel with budget rooms with common bath and better facilities with private bath and a/c. 4 Jl. Pemuda, tel. 197, US$6-10 fan, US$14-20 a/c.

Mona Lisa Hotel: Waikabubak's top-end choice has a fine restaurant and rooms fashioned after Sumbanese clan houses in an isolated location about three km northwest of city center. Jalan Adhyaksa, tel. 174, US$30-45.

Transportation

The easiest way to reach Waikabubak is by bus from Waingapu. Visitors arriving at the Tambolaka airport, about 42 km north of Waikabubak, can reach town with Merpati shuttle buses for US$1 or with chartered taxis that cost US$15-20.

EAST OF WAIKABUBAK

Anakalang

Twenty-two km east and one hour by *bemo* lies a busy village (Pasunga) known for its massive gravesite and oft-photographed tomb, conveniently situated right on the roadside. A paved road just opposite leads south to the next village.

Kabunduk

Beyond the central pathway is a small megalithic tomb topped by two carved horsemen, and an immense 30-ton slab (Resi Moni) under which the final raja of the Anakalang kingdom was buried in 1939.

Entrance fees paid to the *kepala desa* in Kapunduk (Matakakeri) should include admittance and photography of all nearby tombs. Visitors can overnight in the traditional house that faces the central altars; a rare opportunity to experience traditional Sumbanese life.

Lai Tarung

A dirt path west of Kapunduk heads up the hill to another village with numerous old graves and an elevated slab on which corpses once laid in state.

Gulabakul (Prai Bokul)

Two km south of Kapunduk is Sumba's largest and heaviest megalith, Umbu Sawola, a 70-ton monster erected in 1971 over the burial spot of Anakalang's richest raja.

SOUTH OF WAIKABUBAK

Wanokaka and Lamboya, two traditional regions south of Waikabubak, are famed for their annual *pasola*, stone tombs, and wonderful beaches popular with surfers and foreign hotel developers.

Paigoli

Just before Wanokaka Beach, where village priests sometimes gather *nyale* sea worms on *pasola* day, is a huge grave (Watu Kajiwa) fronted by one of the most famous tombstones on Sumba. Perhaps the oldest monument on the island, Watu Kajiwa is spectacularly carved with primitive yet powerful images of men, women, and nature.

Rua Beach

The long and sparkling beaches near Rua village and Tanjung Karosa to the west have been earmarked by the government for new hotels and other commercial enterprises. As of this writing,

INDONESIA

only the American-managed three-star Sumba Reef Lodge has opened, though surfers and backpackers can stay at several simple *losmen* owned by local fishermen.

The road continues west to an almost unending series of deserted beaches blessed with brilliantly pure white sand. Beyond Marosi Beach is Lemandunga, where *nyale* worms are gathered for the Labmoya *pasola,* followed by a surfers' spot at Pantai Patiala and a deserted beach called Pantai Dasang. The road to the following west-coast beaches may be completed by the time you arrive.

WEST OF WAIKABUBAK

Kodi is the westernmost district of Sumba, and Bonodokodi (Kodi), several kilometers east of the ocean, is the largest town. Spectacular beaches on the west coast are attracting a steady stream of travelers, who arrive to surf, dive, and enjoy the unhurried pace of life.

Pero
Also called Redakapal ("Ship Lookout"), Pantai Pero serves as the Australian surfers' center of activities for Sumba. The sand is great and the water is clear, plus there are plenty of other superb (and deserted) beaches to the south and to the north.

Accommodations: Several inexpensive *losmen* operated by Muslim fishermen are located at Pantai Pero. All charge US$4-6 for a room plus three meals. An Australian firm has started construction on what appears to be a fairly luxurious resort.

Transportation: Buses direct to Pero can be booked from most *losmen* in Waikabubak. Some buses stop in Kodi, from where you can hike down to Pantai Pero.

Pronobaroro
Two km south of Pero is a traditional village with the highest peaked roofs in all of Sumba, plus megalithic tombs and elaborate homes decorated with pig jaws and buffalo horns.

Ratenegaro
Three km south of Pronobaroro lies another intriguing hamlet separated by the Bonodokodi River from the tapered roofs of Wainyapu. Both villages face a fine beach blessed with sparkling waters and swaying palms.

TIMOR

After a long period of isolation, Timor once again receives a steady stream of visitors, mostly Australians, who enter via Kupang from Darwin. After picking up a 60-day entry stamp upon arrival at the airport, and a short holiday sightseeing around Kupang, most travelers then islandhop westward across Nusa Tenggara or fly directly to Bali.

Timor still suffers from lingering political disruptions, though most of the island is secure and visitors can travel safely from Kupang to Dili.

Warning: Malaria is an extremely serious problem, not only on Timor, but on all other islands in Nusa Tenggara. Visitors are *strongly* urged to take malaria pills, use repellent, and stay well covered in the evenings.

Transportation
Kupang is the transportation hub for the island and arrival point for visitors from Australia.

International Air: Merpati flies from Darwin in Australia's Northern Territory to Kupang on Wednesday and Saturday for A$220 one-way, A$380 return. No visa is required, as Kupang is now an official entry point, and travelers with sufficient funds do not need an onward ticket.

Note: Most travelers flying from Kupang to Darwin need an Australian visa, and Australian diplomatic offices are only located in Bali and Jakarta. Be sure to obtain your Australian visa *before* you begin the long journey from Bali to Timor.

Regional Air: A popular way to explore Nusa Tenggara is to fly from Bali to Kupang and then overland back to Bali. Merpati flies daily between Kupang and Dili (US$40), Maumere (US$40), Waingapu (US$60), Bajawa (US$65), Ujung Pandang (US$90), Bali (US$110), and Jakarta (US$200). Merpati also flies on a weekly basis to Tamboldka Airport, Sumba (US$85),

Alor (US$50), Lembata (US$45), Roti (US$25), and Savu (US$40).

Ship: Kupang's Tanau Harbor, seven km from the *bemo* terminal, is home base for two Pelni ships. The *Kelimutu* departs every two weeks on a Kupang-Dili-Kalabahi-Maumere-Ujung Pandang and return route. The *Kelimutu* then sails Kupang-Ende-Waingapu-Bima-Lombok-Bali-Surabaya-Banjarmasin and return.

More exotic ports are served by Pelni's newest ship, the *Tatamailau,* which sails monthly from Dili to Ambon and Banda (both in Maluku) before stopping at six ports in Irian Jaya; an inexpensive yet comfortable way to tour Indonesia's most remote provinces. The *Tatamailau* then returns to Dili and sails west to Ujung Pandang, Surabaya, Banjarmasin, Cirebon, and Pontianak. Schedules and fares can be checked with the Pelni office on Jalan Pahlawan in Kupang, opposite Fort Concordia.

Smaller ferries depart once or twice weekly to Roti, Savu, Kalabahi, and other remote islands in the Solor and Alor archipelagoes. The most useful service is the twice-weekly ferry from Kupang to Larantuka on Flores; this boat leaves the day after the flight arrives from Darwin. Contact Perum shipping agency on Jalan Cak Doko.

KUPANG

Kupang, the largest town in Nusa Tenggara, lies just 485 km from the coast of Australia—closer to Darwin than to Jakarta. Christianity is the dominant religion, but small minorities of Muslims, Hindu Balinese, and Chinese also live in Kupang, along with a veritable rainbow of races: Atoni, Rotinese, Savunese, Florinese, Kisarese, Adonese, Solorese, Ambonese, Javanese, Eurasians.

The Portuguese arrived on Timor in 1515, only three years after their conquest of Malacca, chiefly to harvest sandalwood and extract its aromatic oil. Seven years later, the survivors of Magellan's crew (Ferdinand was killed by Lapu Lapu in the Philippines) anchored off the island. The Dutch East Indies company seized Kupang in 1653 and established its military headquarters at Fort Concordia, while the Portuguese ran off and took East Timor. A final curious note was the arrival in 1789 of Captain Bligh after the disgruntled crew of the *Bounty* mutinied and forced Bligh to sail his rowboat from the Tongas to Kupang, across 3,816 nautical miles of open seas.

Kupang is a booming commercial center with all possible facilities, including a tourist office on Jalan Sukarno near the central *bemo* station, several banks, Garuda on Jalan Kohsasi, and Merpati on Jalan Sudirman adjacent to Hotel Flobamor.

Attractions

The historical Kupang described above has largely disappeared and been replaced with a messy assortment of concrete buildings and roads filled with the most nerve-wracking traffic east of Bali.

Museum: An excellent place to learn something about the complex history of Nusa Tenggara, though inconveniently located several kilometers east of city center; take *bemo* no. 4 from the downtown terminal. Open daily until 1600 except Fridays and Sundays.

Lasiana Beach: Pantai Lasiana, 11 km east of Kupang, is a deserted two-km-long beach with excellent sand and vendors on weekends.

Semau Island: Pulau Semau, a 45-square-km island visible from Kupang, offers some good snorkeling, decent beaches, an inland swimming pond, and a mid-priced hotel owned by Teddy's Bar in Kupang. Room, board, and transportation cost US$20-35.

Accommodations

Kupang has over a dozen inexpensive *losmen* widely spread across town, four one-star hotels, and a new three-star hotel opened in early 1993. *Losmen* touts waiting at the airport and harbor provide free transportation to many of the following hotels.

Backpackers: Kupang's most popular *losmen* is very basic but friendly and a good source of travel information, plus there's a natural swimming pool nearby. Located four km south of city center; take a no. 3 (three-lamp) *bemo* from the downtown terminal. 38 Jl. Kancil, US$2-3.

Eden Homestay: Another popular guesthouse just opposite the Backpackers. 6 Jl. Kancil. tel. (0391) 21921, US$2-3.

Fatuleu Homestay: A quiet, clean, and mosquito-free place with a beautiful garden and a

INDONESIA

friendly owner who speaks English and leads tours. Conveniently located in the center of town, just past the three-star Orchid Garden Hotel. 1 Jl. Fatuleu, tel. (0391) 31374, US$3-8.

Sea Breezes Homestay: Simple *losmen* in an excellent waterfront location adjacent to Teddy's Bar and just across from the downtown terminal. Jalan Ikan Tongkol, US$3-5.

Teddy's Bar: Although the proprietor no longer rents rooms, Teddy's—a hangout for ex-

pats—is an excellent place to arrange tours, find out about surfing packages to Roti, overnight on one of those gigantic fishing platforms *(bagan)* outside town, or just rent a motorcycle or a minivan. Jl. Ikan Tongkol, tel. (0391) 21142.

Clara's Hotel: Recommended seaside hotel operated by a former soldier (now a preacher) who speaks good English and leads tours for Natrabu. Great views and good food in the second-floor restaurant. Located about 1.5 km west

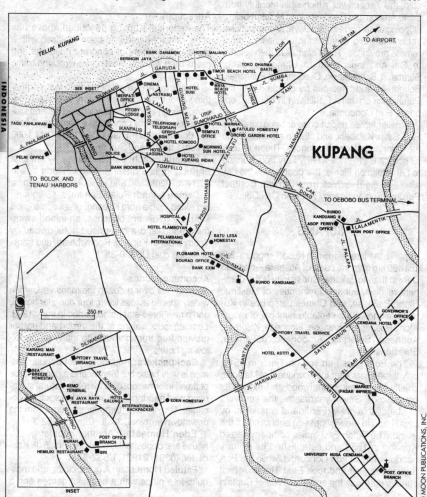

of town toward Tenau harbor. Jl. Pahlawan, tel. (0391) 22580, US$5-8 fan, US$12-16 a/c.

Hotel Flobamor II: Decent one-star hotel in the center of town next to the Merpati office. Popular with foreign project workers and long-term businessmen. 23 Jl. Sudirman, tel. (0391) 21346, US$25-50.

Orchid Garden Hotel: A three-star hotel with all possible amenities such as a pool, a business center, and a health club. 2 Jl. Fatuleu, tel. (0391) 21707, fax (0391) 31399, US$55-80.

Transportation

Air: Kupang's airport is 15 km east of city center and served by taxis for about US$4 per person. Arrivals can also hike 500 meters from the terminal and flag down a *bemo*.

Bus: Kupang's local bus and *bemo* terminal (Terminal Kota Kupang) is on the waterfront in the center of town. However, long-distance buses to Atambua, Dili, and other East Timor destinations depart from the Oebufu/Walikota Terminal in the east part of town near the museum. Take *bemo* no. 10.

Most travelers going to Dili overnight in Atambua, near the old border, about eight hours from Kupang. The most comfortable buses are operated by Natrabu on Jalan Gunung Mutis, two blocks southeast of Teddy's Bar.

Boat: Ships to Flores, Savu, Roti, Alor, and Sumba depart from the port of Tenau, eight km west of Kupang, reachable with *bemo* nos. 12 or 13 from the downtown "Terminal."

ROTI

Roti is a small but fascinating island known for its lontar cultivation and traditional culture, situated just 20 minutes by air west of Timor. Although not a part of Timor province, Roti is included here as a recommended side trip from Kupang.

The island is beautiful and almost completely untouched by tourists, except when the P&O Spice Island Cruise ship *Island Explorer* stops and disgorges several dozen wealthy foreign passengers. Aside from this scheduled disruption, the only visitors to bother with Roti are a handful of Australian surfers who have discovered the waves off southwest Roti. Surfing season is from April to October.

Transportation

Merpati's twice-weekly flight from Kupang to Baa takes just 20 minutes and costs US$24. Ferries depart Kupang for Olafulihaa (northeast corner) several times weekly and take about four hours. Both services are unreliable, disorganized, and subject to sudden cancellations.

Baa

The largest town on Roti has two mosques, a church, some government offices, no bank, and a colonial-style home once inhabited by a local raja.

Accommodations: Ricky's is a friendly spot with motorcycle rentals, tours, cold beer (order in advance), and simple but decent rooms for US$3-6. Two other joints handle the overflow.

Namberala (Dela)

Surfers' paradise is located at the southern end of Roti, where the road ends at Tanjung Bua. Waves are largest during the summer months when lefts break over an outside reef. Several simple *losmen* here charge US$4-6 per day with three meals. Alcohol is expensive; bring ample supply from Kupang.

Papela

Papela harbor in the far northeast corner is a spectacular combination of brilliant blue waters and an arching bay filled with bobbing boats. Fishermen here survive by gathering mother-of-pearl and sea cucumbers from the Australian coast; a fine place to relax for a few days.

Accommodations: Papela has several inexpensive *losmen* and homestays which cater to a steady trickle of international travelers. Best of the lot is Vonny's Homestay, operated by a Tasmanian lady who can help with tours, boat rentals, and travel tips on Roti.

SOE

Back to Timor. Most travelers overnight in Atambua, though chilly Soe, four hours and 110 km east of Kupang, might be an interesting stop if you have some extra time. Bill Dalton—mentor, guru, literary genius, and consummate bullshit artist—claims this is the richest area for travelers in West Timor.

Attractions

Traditional architecture survives in conical, steeply pitched homes called *lopo,* though the government encourages the Timorese to live in more modern styles. Market days provide the regional highlights: Niki Niki (Wednesday), Batu Putih (Sunday), and Oenlasi (Tuesday), the largest market in Soe District. Sandalwood carvings are produced in a small factory near Bank Rakyat.

Accommodations

Believe it or not, Soe has a half-dozen *losmen* and hotels.

Hotel Anda: An inexpensive place run by a multilingual couple from Roti who can help with local details. 5 Jl. Kartini, US$2-4.

Mahkota Plaza Hotel: Soe's best, just opposite the bus terminal, has a good restaurant and 20 clean rooms with private bath. Jl. Suharto, US$4-15.

ATAMBUA

Atambua is the largest town in central Timor and a useful place to overnight between Kupang and Dili.

Accommodations

Losmen Minang: An inexpensive and somewhat clean *losmen* near the bus terminal. 12 Jl. Sukarno, tel. (0391) 135, US$3-6 including breakfast.

Nusatara Hotel: Best value in town but often full. All rooms have attached bath and include breakfast. 22 Jl. Sukarno, tel. (0391) 117, US$4-8.

DILI

Dili and East Timor—"Tim Tim" or "Timor Timor"—were closed to international tourism from 1976 to 1989, until the Indonesian government thought it safe enough to open this former Portuguese colony to the outside world.

Dili made international headlines in 1989 when Pope John Paul II visited the town, and again in November 1991 when overzealous government troops fired on student demonstrators and killed dozens in a horrific bloodbath universally condemned by human-rights organizations.

Dili has a tourist office on Jalan Kaikoli, several banks with exchange facilities, and a Merpati/Garuda office on Jalan Avenida Bispo Medeiros. Indra Kelana agency on Jalan Kolmera is the local expert and the leading tour operator in East Timor.

Attractions

Dili will never win any awards for civic beauty, though the crumbling old stores near the waterfront and remnants of the Portuguese empire impart a vaguely Mediterranean atmosphere.

Liberation Monument: The spirit of Sukarno and Stalinist Realism survives in an aesthetically horrendous monument near the crafts center, dedicated to the annexation of East Timor into the Republic of Indonesia.

Catholic Cathedral: Another monument—largest church in all of Southeast Asia—constructed for and blessed during the 1989 visit of the Pope. Attend Sunday services, then lay a flower at the nearby graveyard.

Accommodations

Hotels in Dili are plentiful, though more expensive than elsewhere in Nusa Tenggara.

Wisma Taufiq: Decent budget place in a central location just one block back from the bay. Jl. Americao Thomas, tel. (0391) 22151, US$4-6.

Hotel Dili: An older hotel east of city center and facing the beach with acceptable rooms in the mid-priced level. Called "best value" or "run down" depending on the guidebook. 25 Jl. Sada Bandeira, tel. (0391) 21871, US$8-18.

Hotel Mahkota Timor: New three-story 100-room seafront hotel with upscale restaurant and business facilities. Jl. Alves Aldea, tel. (0391) 21283, US$32-55.

SULAWESI

Sit and stare at a large wall map of Sulawesi for a while and you'll see dragons, giraffes, spiders, orchids, even a headless octopus. Lying between Kalimantan and the Maluku Islands, Sulawesi (formerly known as Celebes) is Indonesia's third largest and second most popular tourist destination. An amazing diversity of societies exists here, with a distinct separation of old and new, traditional and modern within the many cultures themselves. Sulawesi also boasts some of the most remote jungle areas in the archipelago, with unusual flora and fauna and nearly unknown tribes.

Most travelers limit their visits to the Tana Toraja culture region in the south-central leg and the necessary stop in Ujung Pandang. The island's second most popular region is North Sulawesi (Sulawesi Utara), a beautiful land of vast coconut and clove plantations, active volcanoes, lakes, hot springs, ancient burial sites, picturesque villages, white-sand coral islands, and outstanding snorkeling and diving—considered some of the finest in Southeast Asia. For complete details, read Bill Dalton's *Indonesia Handbook*.

TRANSPORTATION

Getting There
Ujung Pandang (formerly Makassar) on the tip of the southwest peninsula is the major port of call and gateway to Sulawesi.

Air: Garuda and Merpati fly daily to Ujung Pandang from Jakarta, Surabaya, Denpasar, and other towns such as Balikpapan and Biak. Popular with travelers is the flight from Bali to Ujung Pandang and a return to Surabaya. Another option is traveling overland through Central Sulawesi to Manado, then flying back to Surabaya or east to Maluku or Irian Jaya.

Sea: All seven of the Pelni boats that shuttle around the archipelago stop in Ujung Pandang. The most popular choices are the MV *Rinjani* and the MV *Kerinci*. Both ships sail every other week from Surabaya and cost less than half the airfare.

Getting Around
The tortuously shaped island of Sulawesi can be toured by air, sea, or overland transportation.

Land: The southwest and northern peninsulas of Sulawesi have the best road systems, though one can now travel overland the whole length of the island. Roads are kept in good condition except during the monsoon season, when the route through Central Sulawesi turns into a muddy quagmire.

Air: Flying is the most expedient (though expensive) way to get around. Tana Toraja—the most popular destination on Sulawesi—can be reached direct three times daily from Jakarta, twice daily from Surabaya, and once daily from Biak, Denpasar, Medan, and Manado with Garuda International. Bouraq flies weekly from Balikpapan. These direct flights avoid having to spend a night in Ujung Pandang. Alternatively, Merpati has direct connections from Ujung Pandang to Tator (Tana Toraja) three times weekly from Ujung Pandang for about US$60 roundtrip. Flights land in Rantetaya, 14 km west of Makale and 32 km south of Rantepao; taxis and *bemos* continue into town.

Sea: Sulawesi has perhaps the best shipping services in all of Indonesia. Pelni's modern seacraft continually circle the island, stopping at Ujung Pandang, Pantoloan (Palu's port), Toli Toli, Kwandang, and Bitung (Manado's port). Sea connections are also made between Sulawesi and Kalimantan, Surabaya, Bali, Lombok, Sumbawa, and Maluku; see the Pelni route map in the Indonesia introduction.

INDONESIA

INDONESIA

SULAWESI

SULAWESI SEA

BORNEO

SANTIGI
TOLI-TOLI   LANU   BIAU
SIBOA   TOMINI
SABANG   TINOMBO

NORTH SULAWESI

MANADO
LIKUPANG
BITUNG
TONDANO
PIMPI   LOMBAGIN
KUANDANG   KOTAMOBAGU
MARISA   TILAMUTA   TALUDAA   DUMOGA
GORONTALO

EQUATOR

MAPAGA   TORIBULU
TG. KARANG
DONGGALA   PARIGI
PALU
PASANGKAYU
KAROSA   GIMPU
LORE LINDU
RESERVE

TOMINI
BAY

TOGIAN ISLANDS

SELAT WALEA

AMPANA

TOJO   BOALANG

POSO
TENTENA
D. POSO
PENDOLO

MALIK
TEKU
LUWUK
P'ALAM
P. PELENG

MALUKU SEA

**CENTRAL
SULAWESI**

BATUI
MOROWALI
RESERVE
KEMBANI
P. BANGKULU

P. TALIABU

EQUATOR

KOLONDALE   **TOLO BAY**

SOUTH SULAWESI
MESAMBA   WOLU
MAMUJU   BONEBONE
TALAPANG   RANTEPAO
MAMASA   MAKALE   PALOPO   TOLALA
CENRANA   POLEWALI
MAJENE   ENREKANG
PINRANG   SIWA
PANGKAJENE   SENGKANG-SOPPENG
PARE-PARE   D. TEMPE
SUMPANGBINANGAE   WATANGSOPPENG
BARU   WATAMPONE (BONE)
PANGKAJENE   BALANGNIPA
**UJUNG   MAROS   SINJAI
PANDANG**   MALINO   TANETTE
TAKALAR   BULUKUMBA
BANTAENG   BIRA
JENEPONTO

SAROAKO   D. MATANA   SOKITA
D. TOWUTI
MALILI   LABOTA
G. RANTEKOMBOLA
(3455 m)

**SOUTHEAST
SULAWESI**

MONDEODO

KENDARI
MONSE

KOLAKA
BAULA   BENUA

TOWARI

SAMAK   RAHA
PISING   P. MUNA
P. KABENA   BONE
MAWASANGKA   BAU BAU   PASARWAJO

P. BUTON

BENTENG   P. SELAYAR

P. BATUATA

P. TANAHJAMPA

P. KALAOTOA

0   100 km

BANDA SEA

© MOON PUBLICATIONS, INC.

SOUTHERN SULAWESI

This remarkable province offers spectacular limestone mountains, an almost endless coastline, huge shallow lakes, hot springs, caves and waterfalls, rare and exotic flora and fauna, Dutch fortress ruins, the age-old practice of *prahu* building, and fascinating cultures rich with unequaled ceremonies and festivals. The southern coastline and fishing villages are inhabited by the Muslim Bugis and Makassarese, while the interior mountains are home to the Christian Torajas, whose culture and architecture are the primary reasons to visit the island.

UJUNG PANDANG

Formerly known as Makassar, this bustling commercial, shipping, and government center constitutes a major air-sea crossroads between western and eastern Indonesia—the largest and busiest mercantile center in the eastern archipelago for almost 500 years. Ujung Pandang is a chaotic city that chiefly serves travelers as a transit point for Tana Toraja, though you will enjoy the sailing *prahus* and spectacularly beautiful sunsets over Makassar Bay.

Attractions

The tourist office (tel. 21142) is inconveniently located four km southeast of town. Tours around town and Tana Toraja can be arranged from Ramayana Travel on Jalan Anuang and from Pacto on Jalan Sudirman. Pacto also offers unique expeditions to the beaches of Southeast Sulawesi and the megaliths of Bada Valley in Central Sulawesi.

Fort Rotterdam: Within the walls of this once-crumbling fort are some of the finest examples of 17th-century Dutch colonial architecture in all of Indonesia. The spacious La Galigo Museum covers the ethnology of the region, with exhibits of ceramics, weaving technology, and miniature houses fashioned with extraordinary detail. The historical museum across the yard has fascinating photos, the famous Silkendang Buddha image, and a whole section devoted to the cultural heritage of the Goa Kingdom. Dance re-

hearsals take place in the nearby Conservatory of Performing Arts.

Boat Harbor: Ujung Pandang's finest sight is the row of handsome Bugis schooners docked in the harbors north of city center. Pelabuhan Paotere, north of Sukarno Harbor, has a handful of traditional *pinsis* whose designs haven't changed since the days of Genghis Khan.

Clara Bundt House: A refreshing escape from the squalor of Ujung Pandang can be found among the seashells and orchids inside the home of Clara and her German father.

Budget Accommodations

Hotels in the cheapest category around the port area tend to be either full or extremely barebones. The information counter at the airport has a list of hotels in all price ranges.

Ramayana Satrya Hotel: A popular if somewhat pricey 52-room hotel conveniently located on the road from the airport, near the Merpati office and the Liman Express bus stop and about two km east of the beach. The owners provide direct bus service to Wisma Maria in Rantepao. *Bemo* from the airport pass this hotel. 121 Jl. Bawakaraeng, P.O. Box 467, tel. (0411) 22165, US$7-16.

Hotel Purnama: A decent midtown hotel located just to the south of Fort Rotterdam. Like all other hotels in Ujung Pandang, the Purnama is overpriced, but it's well located for sunsets and inner-city explorations. 3 Jl. Pattimura, tel. (0411) 33830, US$5-10.

Hotel Nusantara: Good location in the north of town, but rooms are extremely simple. Hotel Murah across the street is also cheap but only survivable for one night. 103 Jl. Sarappo, tel. (0411) 33163, US$3-6.

Fortune Home: The former manager of the once-popular Mandar Inn has moved his operation one km south of Losari Beach, just below the city stadium. 19 Jl. Gagak, tel. (0411) 851496, US$4-8.

Moderate Accommodations

Pasanggrahan Makassar Hotel: A seaside hotel with 25 clean, breezy rooms and an ex-

INDONESIA

UJUNG PANDANG

TO HARBOR

JL. SERAM UJUNG

JL. BUTUNG

JL. SARAPPO

JAMESON SUPERMARKET

IMMIGRATION

HOTEL MURAH

HOTEL NUSANTARA

JL. BANDA

JL. BURU

DIPONEGORO TOMB

SOEKARNO HARBOR

JL. SANGIR

J L. DIPONEGORO

JL. LEMBE

JL. K.H. HASYIM

JL. MARTADINATA

JL. NUSANTARA

JL. SULAWESI

RAGAN

JL. TIMOR

MAKASSAR MALL

JL. K.H. RAMLI

HATTA HARBOR

JL. BALI

JL. SUMBA

LIMAN EXPRESS BUSES

JL. SERUI

JL. H.O.S. COKROAMINOTO

JL. IRIAN

JL. ANDALAS

JL. VETERAN

BOATS TO KAYANGAN ISLAND

LEGEND HOTEL

YASMIN HOTEL

CHINESE TEMPLE

HOTEL SENTRAL

JL. RIBURANE

JL. A. YANI

TAXIS

JL. BULUL SERAUNG

JL. MESJID RAYA

GARUDA

JL. UJUNG PANDANG

JL. SLAMET RYADI

JL. BALAI KOTA

FORT ROTTERDAM

POLICE

KAREBOSI SQUARE

BANK INDONESIA

HOTEL AMAN

BEMOS TO AND FROM AIRPORT

POST OFFICE

JL. KATAOLADINO

RAMAYANA SATRYA HOTEL

MERPATI AIRLINES

BENTENG HOTEL

JL. SUPRAATMAN

JL. THAMRIN

JL. KARTINI

JL. G. BAWAKARAENG

HOTEL MARLIN

LIMAN EXPRESS BUSES (MAIN OFFICE)

LOSARI BEACH INN

JL. PASAR

JL. IKAN

JL. PATTIMURA

HOTEL PURNAMA

MARANNU CITY HOTEL

JL. AMANAGAPPA

JL. JEND. SUDIRMAN

TO AIRPORT AND GOWA BUS TERMINAL

MAKASSAR GOLDEN HOTEL

CELEBES HOTEL

JL. SOMBA OPU

JL. BAUMASEPE

JL. INCE NURDIN

JL. SALAHUTU

LOSARI BEACH GUESTHOUSE

JL. ALI MALAKA

JL. KHAIRIL ANWAR

MAKASSAR CITY HOTEL

WISATA INN

NEW DELTA HOTEL

JL. SAWER GADING

JL. PENGHIBUR

JL. MOKTHAR LUFTHI

SAMIUN

JL. LATIMOJONG

THR AMUSEMENT PARK

PANTAI LOSARI

CLARA BUNDT ORCHID GARDENS

JL. HASANUDDIN

SOETOMO

HOTEL VICTORIA PANGHEGAR

JL. DATUMUSENG

JL. EMMY SAELAN

JL. DR.

JL. VETERAN

NOVOTEL HOTEL

PELNI OFFICE

TO SUNGUMINASA BUS TERMINAL

BOURAQ AIRLINES

JL. KENARI

JL. SADDANG

MANDALA AIRLINES

0   500 m

© MOON PUBLICATIONS, INC.

INDONESIA

cellent restaurant. Front rooms offer beautiful views of the harbor. Good value. 297 Jl. Somba Opu, tel. (0411) 85421, US$25-35.

Makassar Golden Hotel: Perfect waterfront location plus swimming pool, nightclub, and unforgettable sunsets from the Toraja-style terrace restaurant. The best in town. 52 Jl. Pasar Ikan, tel. (0411) 22208, US$65-90.

Transportation

Ujung Pandang's Hasanuddin Airport has all the usual facilities and is located 23 km from town. Taxis cost about US$5-8, or simply walk (or take a *becak* for 200Rp) 500 meters to the main road, then flag down a *bemo* and pay 1,000Rp all the way to main *bemo* station on Jalan Cokroaminoto near the Central Market.

Pelni docks at Pelabuhan Hatta, close to city center. Tickets to Surabaya, Kalimantan, and North Sulawesi can be purchased directly at the Pelni office, or from shipping agents which charge a small commission but save chasing around.

Within the city you can walk, bargain with a *becak* driver, attempt to decipher the *bemo* routes, or rent a taxi for US$40 per day.

Large buses from Ujung Pandang to Tana Toraja cost about 10,000Rp, leave daily at 0700, 1400, and 1900, and take 10-12 hours along a well-surfaced road. Liman Express is the best service; tickets can be purchased from the Marlin Hotel, opposite the Ramayana.

OTHER SOUTHERN DESTINATIONS

Few Westerners visit the following towns, though all provide an easy escape from the standard tourist trail between Ujung Pandang and Tana Toraja. Travel throughout the region is surprisingly easy along well-maintained roads that cut across spectacular landscapes. Buses to towns north and east of Ujung Pandang depart from Terminal Panaikan, a few kilometers outside town on the road to the airport. Buses to towns south of Ujung Pandang leave from Perumnas Todopuli Terminal, two km east of the tourist office.

One interesting route is south from Ujung Pandang along the southern coast to Bulukumba, then north to Watampone (Bone) and Singkang nestled in the foothills overlooking Lake Tempe, and finally Palopo, from where a

spectacular road heads southwest up to Tana Toraja. All these towns have simple hotels.

The Gowa Empire

Gowa and Tallo were two small kingdoms which united in the 16th century to form the powerful Makassar empire, which ruled much of southern Sulawesi until defeat by the Dutch and Bugis in 1669.

Remnants of royal tombs, graves, and palaces can be visited at Old Gowa (eight km southeast of Ujung Pandang), Tallo (three km north), and Sombaopu (seven km south), where a reconstructed former royal palace now serves as a museum and storehouse for recent excavations.

Bantimurung Falls

A deep limestone canyon, 41 km northeast of Ujung Pandang, attracts visitors for its spectacular waterfalls, lush tropical vegetation, and brilliantly colored butterflies once collected by the famous British naturalist Alfred Russel Wallace. Take a *bemo* to Maros, then another east toward Bone.

Five km west of Bantimurang are a series of limestone caves covered with rare and valuable prehistoric paintings dating back some 5,000 years. Both Bantimurang and the caves at Taman Purbakala Leang Leang are well signposted and charge modest admission fees.

Malino

On the lower slopes of Mount Bawa Kareng, 70 km southeast of Ujung Padang, lies a former Dutch hill resort with a great Sunday flower market and hikes to nearby waterfalls, river valleys, and, possibly, the summit of Mount Bawa Kareng. Bring warm clothing; at 1050 meters Malino can get chilly.

Bulukumba and Tana Beru

Traditional shipbuilding has declined dramatically since the early 1980s, though massive vessels are still constructed entirely by hand in several villages along the southern coastline.

Tana Beru, 174 km from Ujung Pandang and 28 km east of Bulukumba, is your best bet during the dry season from April to October. The nearby town of Bira, once the boatbuilding center for the region, now serves as the departure point for boats to Selayar Island. Ships are also constructed in the village of Ara, 13 km north of Bira.

INDONESIA

Losmen Sinar Jaya: An inexpensive *losmen* in Bulukumba. Bira also has a cheap *losmen* near its stunning white-sand beach. 4 Jl. Saw-erigading, US$2-4.

Selayar Island

Once an important island for its strategic location on the spice trail, Selayar is now visited for its beaches on the north side and a famous Dong Son drum kept at Bontobangun, three km south of the principal town of Benteng.

Ferries depart Bira daily at 1400, or take the 0700 bus from Ujung Pandang's Terminal Panax-ikan, which connects with the afternoon ferry.

Hotel Berlian: A Benteng hotel. US$4-6.

Watampone (Bone)

Once the strongest of all Bugis kingdoms, Watampone ruled much of the region until the late 17th century when British and Dutch de-stroyed the city in an effort to support the Makas-sarese empire.

Now a sleepy town some 180 km northeast of Ujung Pandang, Watampone is chiefly noted for its simple royal palace constructed in the 1930s to house the reinstated raja of Bone, an informative museum on the town square, and limestone caves at Gua Mampu (34 km north), considered the largest and most spectacular in South Sulawesi.

Wisma Bola Ridie: Watampone has plenty of decent hotels under US$10, including this ram-bling Dutch colonial structure, owned and oper-ated by a descendant of the last raja of Bone. 6 Jl. Merdeka, tel. (0421) 412, US$4-8.

Wattansoppeng (Soppeng)

Another former capital of the Bugis kingdom, Soppeng today is a very attractive town famous for its profuse orchid gardens, silk factories, to-bacco cured with palm sugar, cacao plantations, and millions of fruit bats which live peacefully in the town's trees.

Hotel Makmur: Clean spacious rooms with private bath. 104 Jl. Kemakmuran, US$4-8.

Singkang

Singkang, 192 km northeast of Ujung Pandang, is a sleepy town in a great hillside location over-looking shallow Lake Tempe.

Top draws are the views from the govern-ment resthouses across the square from the mosque, a thriving silk industry modeled on Thai techniques, and Bugis traditions such as dance and weddings recently revitalized by a deter-mined local princess.

Wisma Ayuni: Clean, spacious, high-ceilinged rooms in an old Dutch home. Jalan Puang Ri Maggalatung, US$2-4.

Hotel Apada: Somewhat expensive but the best place to experience traditional Bugis at-mosphere as promoted by a local aristocrat. Hotel Apada is one km from the lake. Jalan Duri-an, US$10-18.

Palopo

Palopo, 389 km northeast of Ujung Pandang but only three hours by bus from Rantepao, once served as the linchpin of the powerful Lawu king-dom. Also, it's the port from which enchained Torajan slaves were sold and shipped out to Java and Siam.

Palopo is noted for the various types of *prahu* docked to the long pier, magnificent panoramas across expansive Bone Bay, an ancient mosque opposite the post office, and a small museum in the house of a former raja of Luwu.

Wisma Kumda Indah: The most popular hotel in town has both fan-cooled and a/c rooms at reasonable rates. Jalan Opu Tosapaille, US$6-12

Palopo Hotel: Adjacent to the bus terminal. Rooms are ratty but acceptable for a single night. 11 Jl. Kelapa, US$3-8.

Pare Pare

Second-largest city and seaport of South Su-lawesi, 155 km north of Ujung Pandang, Pare Pare serves as a transportation center and stopover spot between Ujung Pandang and Tana Toraja.

Aside from the small Museum of Ethnology on the highway to Rantepao, most visitors stop here only to catch the daily boat to a Kalimantan port (Nunukan, Tarakan, Samarinda, or Balikpapan), or the thrice-weekly service to northern Sulawesi (Donggala, Toli Toli, and Manado). The latter ser-vices spare you the ordeal of overland travel across Central Sulawesi. In fact, the awful con-dition of roads through Central Sulawesi makes taking a boat to the northern peninsula an attrac-tive proposition; many travelers backtrack from Tana Toraja simply to avoid the journey.

Travel agents and shipping companies are plentiful near the bus terminal, at the harbor, and on the main street just up from the waterfront.

Hotel Gandaria: A clean and comfortable hotel with friendly, helpful managers, just five minutes from the bus terminal. Ask to see the proprietor's valuable collection of ritual objects and wedding costumes obtained from royal families. 171 Jl. Bau Masepe, tel. (0421) 21093, US$6-12.

Majene

Majene is a small, peaceful fishing and boat-building village on a stunning moon-shaped bay

about 80 km northwest of Pare Pare. The main activity is walking along the bay in the morning and exploring the nearby towns in the after-noon: Pangali-Ali, Cilallang, the ancient grave-yards at Ondongan and Salabose, and the silk-weaving villages of Tinamburng, Luaor, and es-pecially Pambusuang. Ibu Darmi Masud can help with directions.

Ibu Darmi Masud Homestay: Better than the rough *losmen* in the center of town is this friendly homestay near the harbor. 12 Jl. Amanna Wewang, Ujung Pandang reservations tel. (0411) 22482, US$3-6.

TANA TORAJA

The second most popular tourist destination in In-donesia, Tana Toraja is one of the country's most ruggedly magnificent regions—a high, fer-tile plateau buffered by green mountains which have protected traditional patterns of life and customs. The district is inhabited by proto-Malay peoples who, though largely Christianized in the early 20th-century by Dutch missionaries, con-tinue to honor their ancestors through a religion called Aluk Todol. Similar to the Batak and Mi-nangkabau of Sumatra, the Torajans are noted for their remarkable architecture, which features ship-shaped flying roofs and large panels elab-orately ornamented with geometric and animal motifs. But it is their frequent and highly ritualis-tic religious ceremonies—including rites of birth, marriage, and death—that attract increasing numbers of foreign visitors; Torajan funerals are considered among the most spectacular in Asia. This is a destination that deserves 10 days to two weeks to fully appreciate.

The principal towns of Rantepao and Makale serve as bases for extended multiday hikes in the surrounding countryside. Tana Toraja is best visited during the dry season from April to Octo-ber, when most of the burial and harvest festivals occur. Monsoons which sweep across the land from November to March ruin the roads but pro-vide an opportunity to escape the European and Japanese tour groups which flood the area in late summer. Funeral observers should dress conservatively, photograph with discretion, and bring along small gifts of cigarettes or rice for village dignitaries.

Attractions

Tana Toraja can be touristy in the busy sum-mer months, but once you're just a kilometer outside town, you're in a tropical Xanadu, peace-ful and beautiful. People ask you in for coffee and cigarettes, invite you to attend their cere-monies, and sometimes offer a room to over-night. Travelers should return the favor with a small present of food, betel nut, antibiotics, or cigarettes. Please don't give out candy; Tora-jans can hardly afford dental bills!

Villages near Rantepao can be reached with public *bemos* or hiked in a single day. *Bemos,* minibuses, and jeeps rented from *losmens* and the market cost about US$20-25 per day; a good deal for groups of people with limited time. Self-appointed guides can be hired everywhere at about US$5 per day, though their services are unnecessary for nearby hikes. Professional guides for multi-day treks can be hired from the tourist of-fice for US$10-20 per day for small groups.

Virtually anywhere in Torajaland you can spend the night in the *tongkonan,* or ask the *kepala kampung* (village chief) for help with ac-commodations. Always give the lady of the house US$2-3 for food and bring along small gifts for the village headman.

Getting There

Liman Express buses leave from their office on Jalan Laiya and pause near the Ramayana Hotel in Ujung Pandang daily at 0700, 1400, and 1900. Advance tickets can be purchased at the Hotel Marlin, just opposite the Ramayana.

Merpati flies three times weekly to the airport near Rantepao.

An interesting five-day journey is the trek from Ujung Pandang to Pare Pare, Polewali, Mamasa, Bittuang, and Rantepao. This adventurous route requires a good three days of hiking from Mamasa to Bittuang, from where buses continue to Makale.

MAKALE

Makale, an administrative center built by the Dutch in 1925, is the second-largest town in Tana Toraja. Few tourists stay here, though Makale—like Rantepao—can serve as a base for outstanding hikes.

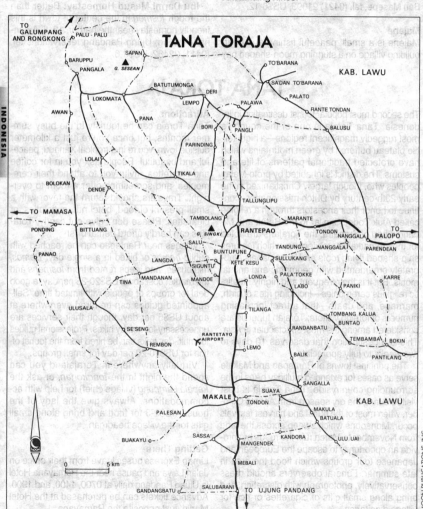

TANA TORAJA

Liman Express buses stop near the mosque in the middle of town. Minibuses up to Rantepao take about 45 minutes. Merpati flies from Ujung Pandang to Pongtiku Airport (12 km northwest of Makale) on Tuesday, Thursday, and Saturday.

Attractions

Guides can be picked up from the *losmen,* or simply orient yourself with the wall map in the Bupati Daerah building (2.5 km north of town) and wander off in any direction. Villagers throughout Tana Toraja are friendly, helpful, and accustomed to lost Westerners, though a basic understanding of Bahasa Indonesia will help. Buy a phrasebook and learn to use it!

East from Makale you'll find a row of *tau tau* effigies near Tondon (one km from Makale), caves with elaborately carved coffins near Suaya (six km), a king's *tongkonan* (house) that doubles as a museum in Buntukalando (8 km), minibuses to Makale at Sangalla (10 km), and hot springs at Makula (13 km).

Hikes west from Makale tend to be very long, but the scenery is spectacular and it's highly unlikely you'll see any other Westerners. First, take a *bemo* or walk to Rembon (12 km northwest), the swimming hole at Seseng (20 km), and finally to the market town of Bittuang (42 km). Both short and multi-day treks start from Bittuang. The 58-km trail to Mamasa takes three days, with luscious scenery of valleys, mountains, villages, and rice terraces. Another possibility is an eight-day trek from Bittuang back to Makale via the townships of Ponding, Pana, Nosu, Simbuang, Petarian, and Sanik.

Accommodations

Makale is a clean and pleasant town with a good selection of hotels on the half-dozen streets which form the city center.

Losmen Indra: Just south of the bus stop is a friendly spot, but prepare yourself for early-morning calls from the nearby mosque. Several other inexpensive *losmen* are along the main road. 11 Jl. Merdeka, tel. (0423) 22022, US$4-8.

Wisma Bungin: A modern hotel with spotlessly clean rooms at very fair prices. Recommended. 35 Jl. Pongtiku, tel. (0423) 22255, US$4-8.

Losmen Martha: At the far north end of Makale is a pleasant family-run place with cheap, quiet rooms. 75 Jl. Pongtiku, tel. (0423) 22011, US$3-6.

Marannu City Hotel: Tour groups usually stay at this hotel, five minutes from Makale and 15 minutes from the airport. Facilities include a swimming pool, tennis courts, and a 24-hour restaurant. 116 Jl. Pongtiku, tel. (0423) 22028, fax (0423) 22028, US$44-65.

RANTEPAO

Rantepao is a cool and pleasant town that serves as the focal point for tourism in Tana Toraja. Despite all the visitors who inundate it, and the heady air of rampant commercialism, Rantepao has remained a mellow town with lots of atmosphere. The tourist office on Jalan Pontigu offers useful hand-drawn maps, has schedules on upcoming funeral ceremonies, and can help arrange guides and charter *bemos.* Bank Rakyat near the town square cashes traveler's checks at good rates. Rantepao also has a post office, a long-distance phone center open 24 hours, a Merpati office, travel agencies, countless souvenir shops, and a fascinating market that peaks every six days.

Budget Accommodations

Rantepao offers dozens of budget *losmen* geared to travelers and a good selection of upscale hotels aimed at group tours. Rooms are scarce and reservations recommended from July to September; otherwise, they're plentiful and deeply discounted for longer stays.

Rantepao's cheapest places are on the main avenue of Jl. Mappanyuki near the mosque and the bus terminal. However, better and certainly quieter *losmen* and homestays are 10-15 minutes by *bemo* from the center of town. A sensible strategy is to follow a hotel tout from the bus terminal or wander the side streets and inspect a few places.

Wisma Maria I: An old favorite just two blocks from the center of town. Nice garden, boiled water, and direct service provided by Liman Express from Ujung Pandang—very convenient. Jalan Ratulangi, tel. (0423) 21165, US$5-15.

Wisma Monika: A travelers' special run by friendly folks with clean and quiet rooms. Jalan Ratulangi, tel. (0423) 21216, US$5-8.

Wisma Rosa: Perhaps the oldest *losmen* in town, with quiet rooms facing ricefields and a pleasant garden. North of town across the Sadan

RANTEPAO

TO SADAN (12 km) AND
PANGLI (7 km)

TO BORI

WISMA ROSA

WISMA MALITA

WISMA
SEDERHANA

WISMA
TIKALA
INDAH

TO TIKALA

WISMA NIRMALA

JL. ABDUL GANI

WISMA IRAMA

WISMA MONTON

TO TORAJA COTTAGES
AND PALOPO

WISMA LINDA

HOTEL
INDOGRACE

WISMA
SURYA

WISMA
WISATA

WISMA PALAWA

JL. DIPONEGORO

WISMA
SARLA

JL. BERINGIN

JL. KOSTAN

MARLIN INN

BATUMONGA
INN

JL. TAPPANG

WISMA
SURYA

JL. SAWEI GADING

MOSQUE ★

HOTEL VICTORIA

JL. PACUAN KUDA

JL. SAELANG

FLORA
LOSMEN

ALAM INDAH
BUSES

CHEZ
DODING INN

JL. NAGA

TOURIST OFFICE

WISMA
PURNAMA

JL. OLA RAGA

JL. MONGINSIDI

LIMAN BUSES

JL. LANDORUNDUN

BUSES

BANK

WISMA
RANTEPAO

JL. RATULANGI

HOTEL INDRA

RAINBOW
HOMESTAY

RAPA
HOMESTAY

POST OFFICE

JL. BUDI UTOMO

WISMA TE
BASS

WISMA
MARIA I

WISMA
MONIKA

PONDOK
WISATA

WISMA
MANGGALA

HERRON
INN

JL. PENANIAN

WISMA
MARTINI

SPORTS
FIELD ★

RAMAYANA
INN

JL. TAMAN BAHAGIA

JL. MERDEKA

WISMA ANATA

SADAN RIVER

HOSPITAL

JL. KARTIKA

JL. PATEKESU

TO SINKI AND
SINGUNTU

TO MAKALE, PIA'S POPPIES,
WISMA MARIA II, AND
MISSILIANA HOTEL

0   100 m

© MOON PUBLICATIONS, INC.

INDONESIA

River, a 10-minute walk from the bus terminal. Recommended. Jalan Pahlawan, tel. (0423) 21075, US$4-10.

Wisma Surya: Good place managed by Mrs. Ross Boby, tourist official at the Rantepao information center. Her brother leads tours at reasonable cost. 36 Jl. Kostan, tel. (0423) 21312, US$4-8.

Moderate Accommodations

Monton Guesthouse: Opened in July 1992 and highly recommended by many travelers, Monton is slightly outside town and just west of Wisma Irama. All rooms include private bath with hot showers. Proprietor Parubak once worked at the local tourist office and can help with trekking details. 14 Jl. Abdul Gani, tel. (0423) 21675, fax (0423) 21500, US$9-14.

Wisma Irama: A very beautiful and quiet hotel, which ranks among the better deals in town, offers both budget fan-cooled rooms and luxurious a/c rooms with private bath and hot showers. 18 Jl. Abdul Gani, tel. (0423) 21371, US$8-20.

Hotel Indra: Well run and conveniently located with three separate operations: economic Indra I with fan-cooled rooms, mid-priced Indra City Hotel, and upscale Indra II with a/c chalets facing a lovely garden and the Sadan River. 63 Jl. Landorundun, tel. (0423) 21163, fax (0423) 21500, US$6-32.

Pia's Poppies: Trendy Toraja-style resort with late-night disco, French restaurant, and great views over ricefields and mountains. South of town in Karassi. 27 Jalan Pongtiku, tel. (0423) 21156, US$10-25.

Luxury Accommodations

Top-end hotels are outside town toward Makale or Palopo.

Toraja Cottages: Four km northeast of Rantepao and near the Wednesday market is an upscale resort with a swimming pool, Torajan-style chalets, and the most popular nightclub in town. The luxury extension is called Toraja Prince. 4 Jl. Pakubalasalu, tel. (0423) 21089, fax (0423) 21369, US$40-60.

Missiliana Hotel: Three km south on the road to Makale is a 120-room two-star property designed for package tours, especially for European clients of Insatra and Ramayana Tours.

Jalan Batukangsi, tel. (0423) 21234, fax (0423) 21212, US$42-85.

Transportation

Rantepao is 328 km and eight hours by bus north of Ujung Pandang.

Air: Merpati departs daily from Ujung Pandang at 0900 and arrives at 0945 at the Rantetayo airport near Makale, 24 km south of Rantepao. Flights cost US$35 and depart daily, weather permitting, from Rantetayo at 1015. Merpati provides bus service into Rantepao.

Bus: Buses from Ujung Pandang take about eight hours and depart daily from the Panaikan bus terminal at 0700, 1300, and 1900. Tickets can be purchased in advance from several agencies such as Liman Expres on Jalan Laiya and Litha Company on Jl. Gunung Merapi. You can also take the next available bus or minibus from Panaikan bus terminal.

RANTEPAO VICINITY

South of Rantepao

Many of the following sites are within walking distance, but those closest to Rantepao can be super-touristy and thronged with kids asking for money and candy. Solo travelers will find themselves harassed less than those who join group tours. Distances from Rantepao are noted in kilometers.

Karasbik (1 km): Constructed in 1983 for a funeral, this horseshoe-shaped row of *rumah adat* is arranged around a group of megaliths.

Londa (8 km): Aside from their spectacular funeral ceremonies, Tana Torajans are also known for their cliff burial sites *(liang)*, carved wooden coffins *(erong)*, and rows of lifelike wooden effigies *(tau tau)* that represent the spirits of departed ancestors. Two of the more famous sites are located at Lemo and Londa, where the interconnecting passages and natural amphitheaters are stacked with old wooden coffins strategically arranged with skulls and bones. Guides with gaslamps take visitors through both caves for 1,000Rp; kids hold your hand until you give them something.

Tilanga (12 km): A beautiful three-km trail from the main road or from Lemo leads to this natural swimming pool with cool, clear water.

Lemo (12 km): The hanging graves at Lemo are among the best known in Tana Toraja. Peering down from the balconies are rows of wide-eyed *tau tau,* silent spectators best seen and photographed in the early-morning hours. Unfortunately, theft for the primitive art market has caused families to remove most effigies, and only a few figures remain.

Southeast of Rantepao

Keta Kesu (4 km): En route to the most touristy village near Rantepao you'll pass through Buntupune, a traditional enclave of *tongkonan,* rice barns, and the noteworthy home of Pong Maramba. Keta Kesu is a restored and highly commercialized village with handicraft shops, effigies, and a rotted wooden sign proclaiming Coffins.

Sullukang (6 km): A very old and secluded village with megaliths around a *rante* and statues seated in a run-down shack.

Palatoke (9 km): As at Lemo, Palatoke has a cliffside burial site, but no *tau tau.* This beautiful out-of-the-way site is tricky to find: consider hiring a young guide.

Buntao (16 km): A village with a *patane* (grave house) reached by infrequent truck or full-day hike from Rantepao. No signs, so just keep asking the way. Return via Nanggala or hike to Makale through Sangalla.

East of Rantepao

Marante (6 km): Located just off the road to Palopo, Marante is a mixture of traditional Torajan dwellings and wooden houses, with some coffins and *tau tau.*

Tandung (17 km): A spectacular area with pine forests, 18-meter-high stands of bamboo, and a gorgeous lake.

Nanggala (15 km): Situated in an area of pretty ricefields, Nanggala is a traditional village known for its large *tongkonan* and 14 rice barns—the best you'll see in Torajaland. From Nanggala, walk south over mountains past a coffee-growing region to Buntao.

Southwest of Rantepao

Singki Hill (1 km): Cross the river and hike up the overgrown trail for good views over Rantepao and surrounding landscapes.

Siguntu (6 km): A traditional village featuring a nobleman's house with remarkable carvings

and handsome rice barns. Adventurous hikers can continue west to Bittuang via Langda and Mandanan.

North of Rantepao

Pangli (8 km): Pangli is known for its house grave with a stone statue carved in the likeness of a dead man, a substitute for cliff burial sites. Pangli is also the source of a famous *tuak* (homemade beer).

Palawa (13 km): This traditional village has numerous *tongkonan* and rice barns decorated with *kerbau* horns. Palawa, built on rising terraces, reminds you of the spires of Gothic cathedrals. Also visit Palawa's Stonehenge-like circle of stones.

Sadan (16 km): Hyped as the weaving center of Torajaland, the cultural significance of Sadan is greatly exaggerated, though you might enjoy the palm toddy, *tuak sissing biang,* one bamboo full for 1,500Rp.

Deri (14 km): Clinging to the side of the mountain, Deri offers a hawk's-eye view into the valley and a mammoth black boulder with two carved graves.

Northwest of Rantepao

A six-day roundtrip trek can be made through seldom-visited villages using a combination of walking and vehicle transport. Rantepao to Batutumonga via Tikala and Pana is an 11-km full-day hike. Near Pana is an old set of cliff graves with some of the best *rante, liang,* and *tau tau* in Toraja. Graves here are painted black (representing death), yellow (life and blessings from the gods), white (purity), and red (human life). Near Batutumonga, visit the circle of 56 stones arranged amphitheater-fashion and the smithy fashioned from two huge bamboo bellows. A schoolteacher maintains a room in his house for travelers. From Batutumonga, hike to Pulu Pulu via Lokomata and Pangala or use the rugged trail past Gunung Sesean, highest mountain in Tana Toraja. The walk to Lokomata is recommended for its panoramic views—considered some of the best trekking in the region. Pulu Pulu to Awan is a 33-km 14-hour hike with a swim at Sulutallang, midway between Baruppu and Awan. Awan to Bittuang is another full day, with swimming in Bolokan. Return to Rantepao by truck or hike to Mamasa in three days.

INDONESIA

CENTRAL SULAWESI

The mountainous province of Sulawesi Tengah offers beautiful scenery, primitive tribes, ancient megaliths, sleepy port towns, vast stretches of coastline, fantastic diving on coral reefs, and unusual natural phenomena. Until recently this province was isolated, but now, with the completion of the Trans-Sulawesi Highway, a steady stream of determined adventurers are slowly wandering from Tana Toraja to Palu and onward to the northern town of Manado.

Sightseeing Highlights

Aside from the journey itself, the main attractions of Central Sulawesi are Lake Poso—perhaps the next Lake Toba—and the megaliths of the Bada, Besoa, and Napu valleys, some 40 km east of Lake Poso. Pendolo, a lovely town hugging the southern shores of Lake Poso, ranks as among the most idyllic and scenic destinations on Sulawesi. Also of interest is Lore Lindu National Park on the southern end of Palu Valley.

The rugged journey essentially ends in the town of Palu, the administrative capital and transportation hub for Central Sulawesi, from where you can reach northern Sulawesi by bus, boat, or plane. Many travelers simply visit Lake Poso and then return to Ujung Pandang.

Transportation

The Trans-Sulawesi Hwy. between Ujung Pandang and Palu was essentially finished in 1992, though some sections remain little more than muddy paths closed during the rainy season by landslides and the ever-encroaching jungle.

Rantepao to Lake Poso (245 km): The road from Rantepao to Wotu is fully surfaced and served by a steady stream of buses and minitrucks. The road deteriorates starting from Mangkutana, a few kilometers north of Wotu, and remains a muddy track strangled by jungle until it reaches Pendolo on the southern shore of Lake Poso. This is the worst, near-legendary, section of the highway.

During the dry season, Bina Wisata bus company in Rantepao operates twice-weekly bus service to Pendolo. The journey takes about 12 hours in favorable conditions but up to 30 hours during the rainy season. Alternatively, take a *bemo* from Rantepao to Palopo, another *bemo* to Mangkutana via Wotu, and a third *bemo* north to Pendolo. Simple *losmen* are located in all these towns.

Pendolo to Tentena (40 km): Although a fairly good road connects these two towns, most travelers take the ferry *Pamona,* which departs at 0600 and arrives in Tentena around 1100.

Tentena to Poso (57 km): As Tentena lacks the charm of Pendolo, most visitors immediately take a bus north to the small port town of Poso on the shores of Tomini Bay. Tentena to Poso takes two hours by bus.

Tentena to Bada Valley (60 km): The megaliths in Bada Valley are just 60 km west of Tentena, but the journey can take anywhere from eight hours to five days depending on road conditions. Jeeps leave from Tonusu, 10 km north of Tentena.

However, during bad weather an easier approach is from Gimpu, 99 km south of Palu along a surfaced road. Gimpu to Gintu (the main town in Bada Valley) takes two days by foot or on horseback.

Poso to Palu (220 km): Buses and minibuses from Poso to Palu take about eight hours on a decent road. Alternatively, exhausted travelers bound for Manado can take one of the thrice-weekly ships from Poso to Gorontalo in North Sulawesi. The journey takes two days with stops at various ports and in the Togian Islands. The bus from Gorontalo to Manado takes one day.

Palu to North Sulawesi: Garuda, Merpati, and Bouraq fly several times weekly to Gorontalo (US$60) and Manado (US$85). Pelni liners, the *Kerinci* and the *Kambuna,* sail weekly from Palu to various ports in North Sulawesi, plus other destinations such as the east coast of Kalimantan and Pare Pare in South Sulawesi.

The bus from Palu to Gorontalo takes almost two days on very rough roads. Gorontalo to Manado is another full day of bone-crunching travel.

MANGKUTANA

Mangkutana, a small village several kilometers north of Wotu, serves as the launching point for the ridiculously treacherous journey north to Lake Poso.

Toyota Land Cruisers leave when filled and take just six hours to Pendolo during the dry season. Wet-season delays such as destroyed bridges, landslides, and muddy trenches—which gladly swallow jeeps—can make this a two- or three-day journey.

Accommodations

Losmen in Mangkutana, such as Penginapan Sumber Urip and Penginapan Melati Mekar, charge US$2-3 per night. Several of the travel agencies will let you sleep for free in their *warung* if you are traveling with them the following day.

PENDOLO AND LAKE POSO

Pendolo, on the southern shore of Lake Poso, ranks as the most attractive and memorable destination in Central Sulawesi. Flanked by a wonderful lake surrounded by brilliant green hills, Pendolo has the potential to become the next Lake Toba, which almost certainly will happen once the road from Wotu is fully surfaced. For the present, however, Pendolo and Lake Poso remain sleepy paradises visited annually by only a few hundred backpackers.

Attractions

Lake Poso, called the "second-clearest lake in the world," guarantees a wonderful reward after the long and rough journey from Rantepao or Palu. Measuring about 37 km long and 13 km wide, Danau Poso is known for its indigenous fish species (especially the huge eels, which reach over two meters in length) and white sandy beaches which cover almost 75% of the coastline. The lake is also quite deep (440 meters) and situated at a refreshing elevation of 515 meters.

Boats can be chartered to visit Taipa village on the western shore, from where you can hike up to a promontory viewpoint and to lakeside Bancea Orchid Reserve, which raises over 50 plant species. A primitive track follows the western shore, but public transportation remains sporadic.

Accommodations

Almost a dozen simple *losmen* now line the lakeside. Losmen Wisata Masamda is typical, with simple rooms with shared bath for US$2-3 and rooms with private bath for US$4-5. Similar facilities are offered at Pondok Wisata Victory and the slightly more expensive Danau Poso Hotel farther up the lake.

TENTENA

Tentena is a small town in a lovely location on the north shore of Lake Poso. Once the home of headhunters, Tentena was Christianized in the early part of the 20th century by a Dutch Reformed Church missionary named Albertus Kruyt. Today, almost all the highland peoples are Christians who attend Sunday services in the whitewashed chapel.

The Pamona people who live around Lake Poso are distant relatives of the Torajans, but eastern Torajan culture is now extinct here. In fact, except for the enigmatic monoliths near Gintu and burial caves around Tentena, little remains in Central Sulawesi of pre-Christian culture.

Balai Buku, one-half km north of the docks, has books in Bahasa Indonesia about early missionary work in Sulawesi.

Attractions

Boat rides and caving are the main activities near Tentena. Among the more accessible caves is a rocky overhang just five minutes behind the church and Latea Caves, some 20 minutes behind town. Pamona Caves, near the Theological Institute and Poso River, has been cleared of skeletons but remains a pleasant place to relax and enjoy the views.

Accommodations

Tentena is more developed than Pendolo, with almost a dozen *losmen* and mid-priced hotels. The budget places are near the bus station or dock, while better hotels are nicely situated near the river and in the hills.

Penginapan Wisata Remaja: A decent place near the dock with simple, clean rooms. US$2-5.

Losmen Rio: Near the bus terminal, this rudimentary dive is only acceptable for one night. The adjacent *losmen* is just as bad. US$2-3.

Pamona Indah Hotel: A lakeside hotel with a good restaurant and near-luxury rooms with private bath. US$6-18.

INDONESIA

Hotel Nusantara: Overlooking the river and lake, the Nusantara offers fine rooms in all price categories. Budget rooms US$2-3, standard US$6-9, private bungalows US$9-12.

Panorama Hotel: Two km from the boat dock and up on the hill. Not only superb views, but Ibu feeds you like her long-lost starving child—the food is plentiful, fresh, and delicious. US$3-8.

POSO

A busy port town on the southern shore of Tomini Bay, Poso today serves mostly as a transit point for travelers heading northwest to Palu or sailing northeast to Gorontalo in North Sulawesi.

Accommodations
Most hotels and *losmen* are just north of the Poso River, which empties into Tomini Bay.

Anugrah Inn: Conveniently located near the bus terminal in the southern part of town, but far removed from the beach and the central business district. 1 Jl. Samosir, tel. (0451) 21820, US$5-8.

Penginapan Sulawesi: Basic but fairly clean rooms just north of the river. Friendly management. Jalan Salim, tel. (0451) 21294, US$2-3.

Hotel Bambu Jaya: The best in town is nicely situated right on the seashore just opposite Penginapan Sulawesi. Rooms are clean and comfortable. 105 Jl. Agus Salim, tel. (0451) 21570, US$6-8 fan, US$12-20 a/c.

Transportation
Those who depart Tentena very early in the morning can lunch in Poso, then catch an afternoon bus to Palu, arriving in the late evening. Along parts of this fairly well-surfaced road you might think you're in Bali—you pass Balinese *transmigrasi* villages filled with Balinese statues and rice offerings to Dewi Sri.

Pelni ships sail to Gorontalo in North Sulawesi every few days—a great way to avoid the long and painful bus journey. Schedules can be checked at the harbormaster's office on Jl. Pattimura and in the nearby Pelni office.

PALU

Palu is a rapidly growing commercial center and transportation hub in an attractive location at the south end of Palu Bay.

Attractions
Get maps and help with organizing a Bada Valley excursion from the Central Sulawesi Tourist Office on Jl. Cik Ditiro, five blocks east of the northernmost bridge.

Central Sulawesi Museum: Get a good introduction to the pre-Christian history of the region on Jl. Sapiri, six blocks southwest of the river. Exhibits include replicas of Bada Valley megaliths, bark cloth, and rare *ikat,* including the only Indonesian double *ikat* produced outside of Tenganan, Bali.

Traditional Dance: Live performances of local dance and theater are occasionally given in the Gedung Olah Seni (GONI) building on Jl. Muhammed Yamin in the eastern part of town.

Accommodations
Most of Palu's *losmen* and hotels are in the center of town just east of the Poso River. The noise can be ferocious; ask for a room in the rear.

Purnama Raya Hotel: Centrally located hotel with small but clean rooms. All include private bath. 4 Jl. Wahidin, tel. (0451) 23646, US$4-6.

Karsam Hotel: Fifteen minutes north of city center and about 100 meters from the beach is another acceptable hotel with decent rooms. 15 Jl. Suharso, tel. (0451) 21776, US$3-5.

New Dely Hotel: Good-value hotel near the tourist office and a 10-minute walk east from city center. 17 Jl. Tadulako, tel. (0451) 21037, US$7-9 fan, US$12-25 a/c.

Hotel Palu Beach: Palu's top-end hotel has gone to seed but compensates somewhat with sweeping views over the magnificent bay. Ask for a discount. 22 Jl. Raden Saleh, tel. (0451) 21126, US$20-30.

Transportation
Palu is a major transport hub for Central Sulawesi, with planes, boats, and buses to all possible destinations in Indonesia.

Air: Garuda, Merpati, and Bouraq fly to other destinations on Sulawesi (Ujung Pandang and Manado), plus Kalimantan (Balikpapan and Banjarmasin), Java (Jakarta, Yogyakarta, and Surabaya), and eastern Indonesia (Maluku and Irian Jaya).

INDONESIA

Boat: Three ports are north of Palu, but most departures are from Pantoloan, 35 km north of Palu. The Pelni ship *Kambuna* departs every other week from Pantoloan for Toli Toli and Bitung, the port for Manado. The ship then returns to Pantoloan and heads west to Kalimantan. Service to Kalimantan and Ujung Pandang is also provided by the *Tidar*. Pick up current schedules and tickets at the Pelni office on Jl. Gajah Mada.

Bus: All buses leave from the Besusu Terminal on Jl. Wahidin. Travel times are eight hours to Poso, two days to Gorontalo, and three days to Manado.

DONGGALA

Superb beaches are north of Palu near the town of Donggala. Once a powerful center of maritime trade, Donggala lost most of its importance when the regional capital was shifted to Palu after WW II and the shipping industry was transferred across the bay to Pantoloan.

Accommodations

Milano Beach Cottages: North of town on a great beach, this is a pleasant place with scuba-diving facilities, sailboat rentals, and rooms, plus meals. The German owner can be contacted via Milano Ice Cream shop on Jl. Hasanudin in Palu. US$7-12.

Wisma Rame: Back in town you'll find a clean place run by a very helpful Muslim. US$2-4.

LORE LINDU AND BADA VALLEY

Some 55 km south of Palu lies an immense national park chiefly visited for its ancient and utterly mysterious megalithic monuments, whose origins continue to baffle archaeologists. Carved from stone and eerily resembling the megaliths of Easter Island, these enigmatic monuments date back over 1000 years and provide a connection with megalithic cultures which once flourished on Nias and Sumba.

The tourist office and the PHPA office on Jl. Parman in Palu have information.

Transportation

Today, some two-dozen megaliths can be seen near the principal town of Gintu, a small village located just outside the southern boundary of the park. To reach Gintu, first take a bus or a taxi 100 km south from Palu to Gimpu, where a simple *losmen* is located on the main street.

From Gintu it's a two-day hike or horseback ride south to Gintu with an overnight stay at Moa. Gintu accommodations are limited to local homestays. Most of the ancient monuments can be visited in a single day, though a local guide will be necessary to find the widely scattered stones.

What a place: no English speakers, and except for occasional groups of Germans with a guide from Palu, no tourists. Real adventure in the heart of Sulawesi.

NORTH SULAWESI

A beautiful land of vast coconut and clove plantations, active volcanoes, lakes, hot springs, ancient burial sites, picturesque villages, white sand, coral islands, and outstanding snorkeling and diving, Sulawesi Utara comprises one of the most prosperous and spectacular regions in Indonesia.

The area has been embraced by scuba divers—who acclaim the diving as among the best in the world—but otherwise remains well off the beaten track for most Western travelers.

MANADO

The capital of North Sulawesi is a destination almost completely unlike any other in Indonesia: prosperous, progressive, and Protestant, a legacy of several centuries of Portuguese and Dutch domination. Right away you'll notice the strength of the middle class and the almost complete absence of extreme poverty. Manado typifies modern, upwardly mobile Indonesia—a jolt after all the squalor of the major islands; even the outlying towns are paradigms of order and cleanliness.

Attractions

Manado itself has little of great interest aside from its spectacular location around a broad bay flanked by three towering volcanoes. Most of the sights are located outside town in the mountains and designated nature reserves.

The tourist office, tel. 64299, unfortunately, is difficult to find, senselessly hidden away in an alley in the south of town off Jl. 17 Agustus. Try the tourist information center in the Bunaken Souvenir Shop on Jl. Sam Ratulangi.

Bunaken Sea Gardens: Top draw in North Sulawesi is the world-famous sea gardens located near Bunaken Island, some 30 minutes by boat north of Manado. Underwater walls, spectacular coral formations, deep caves, and a tremendous array of sealife attract a steady stream of divers from throughout the world.

Dives can be arranged at Murex, Nusantara Diving Center (the oldest in town), and Tirta Satwa Dive Resort in Malalayang. All provide dive masters, equipment, PADI courses, and accommodations in nearby beach chalets at very reasonable cost. Public boats at US$1 and inexpensive charters from US$12 leave from Toko Samudera Jaya in the Kuala Jengki market. Western dive operators such as Sea and See in San Francisco also conduct dive tours to Manado.

Sawangan Monuments: The most extensive collection of *waruga,* old pre-Christian tombs of ancestral Minahasans, is found in this small mountain town, 22 km southeast of Manado and three km south of Airmadidi. Hewn from single blocks of limestone, *waruga* are shaped like small Chinese temples with enormous roof-shaped covers, often lavishly decorated with intricate animal and anthropomorphic carvings. Colts leave from Manado's Paal 2 Terminal.

Mount Klabat: Just behind the police station in Airmadidi lies a well-worn trail that leads to the summit of Mt. Klabat, a dormant volcano that ranks as the highest peak (1,995 meters) in North Sulawesi. Summit climbs require almost 12 hours, so come prepared with enough gear to overnight or simply do half the mountain and enjoy the views.

Lake Tondano: The road continues south from Sawangan, past the unique Javanese-style Alfalah Mosque and Japanese caves used in WW II, until it reaches Tondano, an administrative center on the northern shore of Danau Tondano. Around the lake you'll find restaurants, boat rentals, hot springs, and a pottery village.

Tomohon and Mount Lokon: Next, head east to the hilltop village of Tomohon ("City of Flowers"), saddled between the twin volcanoes of Lokon on the northwest and Mahawu on the northeast. Explore the vegetable and flower markets and continue a few kilometers north to Kakaskasan, from where a two-hour hike leads to the summit of Mt. Lokon. Guides are unnecessary, but you'll need to register with the local *kepala desa.*

Kawangkoan Caves: More caves used by the Japanese during WW II are located three km north of Kawangkoan. Colts leave from Pasar Karombasan (Wanea Terminal) in Manado.

INDONESIA

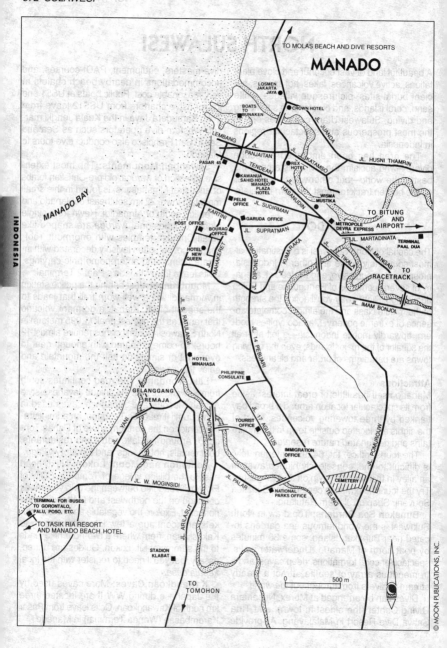

MANADO

TO MOLAS BEACH AND DIVE RESORTS

LOSMEN JAKARTA JAYA

BOATS TO BUNAKEN

CROWN HOTEL

JL. JUANDA

JL. LEMBANG

JL. PANJAITAN

JL. KATAMSO

JL. HUSNI THAMRIN

Pasar 45

JL. TENDEAN

REX HOTEL

KAWANUA SAHID HOTEL MANADO PLAZA HOTEL

JL. HASANUDIN

WISMA MUSTIKA

TO BITUNG AND AIRPORT

PELNI OFFICE

JL. SUDIRMAN

JL. KARTINI

GARUDA OFFICE

POST OFFICE

BOURAQ OFFICE

JL. SUPRATMAN

METROPOLE DEVRA EXPRESS

JL. MARTADINATA

TERMINAL PAAL DUA

HOTEL NEW QUEEN

JL. MAHAKERET

JL. KUMARAKA

JL. TIKALA

JL. MIANGAS

TO RACETRACK

JL. DIPONEGORO

JL. S. RATULANGI

JL. IMAM BONJOL

HOTEL MINAHASA

JL. 14 PEBUARI

PHILIPPINE CONSULATE

GELANGGANG REMAJA

JL. A. YANI

JL. PEMUDA

TOURIST OFFICE

JL. 17 AGUSTUS

IMMIGRATION OFFICE

JL. POMURROW

CEMETERY

JL. W. MOGINSIDI

JL. PALAR

JL. TELING

NATIONAL PARKS OFFICE

JL. ARILASUT

TERMINAL FOR BUSES TO GORONTALO, PALU, POSO, ETC.

TO TASIK RIA RESORT AND MANADO BEACH HOTEL

STADION KLABAT

TO TOMOHON

MANADO BAY

INDONESIA

0   500 m

© MOON PUBLICATIONS, INC.

Budget Accommodations

Manado is a progressive city with a good selection of hotels but only a limited number of budget *losmen.*

Hotel Kawanua: The best deal in town is often confused with the much more expensive Kawanua City Hotel, two blocks away. Ask for *"kecil"* (small) and you'll probably find this place. Clean, comfortable, and very friendly. Highly recommended. 40 Jl. Sudirman, tel. (0431) 63842, US$5-15.

Jakarta Jaya: Unlike most budget dives in Manado, this *losmen* is relatively clean and only a few blocks from the water, en route to the Ahlan Hotel. Room rates include a small breakfast. 25 Jl. Hasanudin, tel. (0431) 64330, US$3-4.

Moderate to Luxury Accommodations

Panorama Ridge: Somewhat outside town, but spotless rooms and fabulous views over Manado Bay make this good value for mid-level travelers. Jalan Tomohon Raya, tel. (0431) 51158, US$12-20.

Hotel Minahasa: Warm atmosphere in an old Dutch mansion. Highly recommended for the friendly vibes and helpful management. 199 Jl. Sam Ratulangi, tel. (0431) 62059, US$9-18.

Manado Beach Hotel: Manado's most luxurious resort is situated on beachfront property in Tasik Ria, a planned community 18 km south of Manado. Opened in late 1992, facilities at the 250-room resort include several restaurants, convention halls, tennis courts, and two pools facing a dazzling beach. P.O. Box 1030, tel. (0431) 67001, fax (0431) 67007, US$90-150.

Transportation

Manado is an international gateway city where entry-free visas can be approved on arrival.

Air: Manado has international connections via Jakarta with many European cities, plus Guam, Hong Kong, Tokyo, and Manila. Garuda and Merpati serve Jakarta, several cities on Kalimantan, and the remote islands of Maluku. Manado airport is seven km from town. Taxis cost US$4 or take an *oplet* to the center of town.

Boat: Manado's main port is located at Bitung, 47 km east of town. Pelni has two ships, the *Kabuna* and the *Umsini,* which sail from Jakarta via Surabaya, Ujung Pandang, and Pantoloan near Palu. Pelni boats from Poso terminate in

Gorontalo, from where buses continue east to Manado.

Bus: Certainly the most challenging way to reach Manado is by bus from Palu along the Trans-Sulawesi Highway. Although the highway has been "completed," it's difficult to connect with the far northeast tip of this rugged peninsula. The journey takes about two days from Palu to Gorontalo and another tough day to Manado along rough but passable roads.

Five bus and *bemo* terminals are scattered around Manado. Pasar 45 is the main *bemo* station. Calaca, just north of Pasar 45, serves the airport. Gorontalo Bus Terminal has buses to Gorontalo and Palu. Pasar Paal 2 has Colts to Bitung and Airmadidi. Pasar Karombasan serves Tondanao and Kawangkoan.

GORONTALO

Gorontalo, the second-largest city in North Sulawesi, is an attractive destination nicely situated at the confluence of Lake Limboto and three rivers that flow into the ocean.

Attractions

Gorontalo's varied mix of European history can be seen in splendid old Dutch architecture, such as the Hotel Saronde and the old public hospital, and Portuguese fortresses situated outside town.

Lake Limboto: Five km northwest of town in a fertile rice-growing area lies an immense yet incredibly shallow lake. Hire a *prahu* from boys to visit small lakeside fishing villages.

Otanaha Fortress: Exhilarating views over Lake Limboto compensate for the sad ruins of this old Portuguese fort.

Kwangdung: Some 65 km north of Gorontalo lies the sleepy hamlet of Kwangdung, the primary port for Gorontalo. The ruins of two Portuguese forts still stand on the outskirts of town, Benteng Ota Mas Udangan, which once faced the sea before the waters receded, and Benteng Oranje ("Orange Fort"), northeast of town on the road to Manado.

Accommodations

Most of Gorontalo's hotels and tourist services are concentrated in city center at the north end of town.

Penginapan Teluk Kau: A Dutch-built home with gigantic canopied double beds and high ceilings. Standards have fallen and the place badly needs renovation, but it's acceptable for one night. 42 Jl. Jenderal Parman, tel. (0435) 21511, US$4-6.

Hotel Wisata: Excellent-value hotel near the Merpati office with both fan and a/c rooms. 23 Jl. 19 Januari, tel. (0435) 21736, US$5-18.

Hotel Saronde: Another Dutch colonial villa converted into a hotel with large, comfortable rooms. 17 Jl. Walanda Maramis, tel. (0435) 21735, US$6-10 fan, US$12-16 a/c.

Hotel Saronde II: Attached to the old colonial building is the most upscale hotel in town. All rooms are a/c with private bath and hot water.

17 Jl. Walanda Maramis, tel. (0435) 21735, US$20-35.

Transportation
Air: Merpati and Bouraq fly daily to Manado and Palu, with same-day connections to Maluku, Kalimantan, Jakarta, Surabaya, and Bali. The Merpati office is in the Hotel Wisata on Jl. 19 Januari.

Bus: Buses from the central terminal on Jl. Ratulangi take about 12 hours to Manado and almost two days on a bad road to Palu.

Boat: Pelni's *Umsini* departs every other Monday morning for Bitung (Manado) and every other Monday for Ujung Pandang and Surabaya. Pelni and Gapsu, a smaller shipping line, have offices in town and at the Kwangtung harbor.

For every traveller who has any taste of his own, the only useful guide-book will be the one which he himself has written.

—ALDOUS HUXLEY,
ALONG THE ROAD

The theory I like best is that the rings of Saturn are composed entirely of lost airline baggage.

—MIKE RUSSELL

All travel is circular.

—PAUL THEROUX,
THE GREAT RAILWAY BAZAAR

LAOS

LAOS

*Travelers are fantasists, conjurers, seers—
and what they finally discover is
every round object is a crystal ball:
stone, teapot, the marvelous globe of the human eye.*

—GLADYS PARRISH

*Travel is at its best a solitary enterprise: to see, to
examine, to assess, you have to be alone and
unencumbered. Other people can mislead you; they
crowd your meandering impressions.*

—PAUL THEROUX

*I'm convinced that to maintain one's self on this
earth is not a hardship, but a pastime, if we will live
simply and wisely.*

—THOREAU

INTRODUCTION

The tiny landlocked nation of Laos—one of the remnants of "Old Asia"—has finally opened its borders to visitors from the outside world. An isolated region long called the "Land of a Million Elephants," Laos is now attempting to change its image from the Albania to the Shangri-La of Southeast Asia; it's a herculean though nonetheless conceivable task, thanks to the nation's central location, peaceful atmosphere, and almost completely untouched range of attractions.

Problems remain with rudimentary tourism facilities, overpriced government-controlled services, and the fact that most of the country remains off-limits or difficult to reach, but more than any other destination in Southeast Asia, Laos retains a remarkable feeling of serenity and timelessness. The time to visit is *now*.

THE LAND

Laos is among the most mountainous countries in Asia; over 90% of the land is low-lying but rugged forest-clad mountains. Slightly larger than Great Britain, the nation is comprised of two physiographic zones. Northern Laos includes several mountain ranges, the politically important Plain of Jars, and the Annamite Cordillera, which creates a formidable barrier between Laos and Vietnam. Southern Laos is characterized by the Mekong River, which traces the western perimeter, and the Boloven Plateau, situated at an average elevation of 1,100 meters.

The confusing knot of mountains which dominates much of the country and the primitive state of the roads make land travel extremely time-consuming. A prime example is Route 13, which connects Vientiane with Luang Prabang, the ancient capital 140 km to the north. Despite the fact that these are the two most important destinations in the country, Route 13 is little more than a rough dirt-and-concrete path so poorly maintained that scheduled bus service has never been attempted. The road is now being paved but continuing problems with insurgency groups mean that most internal transportation remains limited to air or river movement.

Climate

Laos is a subequatorial and monsoonal country with a wet season from June to November and dry

© MOON PUBLICATIONS, INC.

SIGHTSEEING HIGHLIGHTS

Travelers usually limit themselves to the primary destinations of Vientiane and Luang Prabang, plus side trips to nearby caves and a river journey down the Mekong. Visitors with more time might visit the Plain of Jars in northern Laos, Pakse and Wat Phu in the south, and other southern destinations such as Bolovens Plateau and the lower reaches of the Mekong River.

Vientiane

First stop for all visitors is Vientiane, a somnolent market town masquerading as the nation's capital. Formally called Vieng Chan by Laotians (Vientiane is a French-imposed term), Vientiane offers some bucolic charm but little of great interest aside from a handful of temples, French baguettes, and a sleepy atmosphere that entices (or bores) most visitors.

Luang Prabang

Laos's cultural highlight is this unsullied and sleepy village of great historical and artistic interest, 35 minutes by air north of Vientiane. The town of 50,000 is a treasure trove of splendid temples remarkably well preserved considering the political disruptions and benign neglect of recent years. Side trips from Luang Prabang include Pak Ou Caves—an ancient retreat packed with Buddha images—and journeys of varied lengths down the Mekong River.

Plain of Jars

One hour by air from Vientiane lie several small and undistinguished towns in an eerie landscape covered with bomb craters and several hundred stone funeral urns. The landscape is beautiful and the region offers a fascinating historical connection with the Vietnam War, though the unimpressive jars and steep cost of an organized tour have held tourism to a bare minimum.

Pakse and Wat Phu

Southern Laos opened for tourism in early 1992 and by late 1993 the government allowed foreign visitors in a half-dozen towns. Pakse, the largest town in the south and center of a former kingdom, chiefly serves as the jumping-off point for visits to the famed pre-Angkor Khmer ruins of Wat Phu, located near Champassak.

Bolovens Plateau

Adventure-travel groups often head directly to this plateau to enjoy jungle trekking, waterfalls, visits to tribal villages, and a spectacular river journey down the Kong River to Attapu Valley—the newest region to open in Laos.

season the remainder of the year. Rainfall during the monsoon season is heaviest in the higher elevations such as the Bolovens Plateau, which receives over 400 cm of annual precipitation.

The summer months from March to June are dry but extremely hot. Most visitors find the best travel season to be the cooler months from November to February, and not the hot season from March to June or the rainy season from June to November. Be prepared for cold weather in higher elevations such as the Plain of Jars and the Bolovens Plateau near Pakse.

HISTORY

The history of Laos is a record of almost continual tragedy. For centuries, the tiny country has been a pawn in the hands of more powerful neighbors, who coveted it for its strategic location between China to the north, Vietnam to the east, and Thailand to the southwest. Despite the gentle nature of the people, Laos has historically served as a mountainous battleground between warring Siamese and Vietnamese kingdoms, and more recently between the Americans and the Vietcong, who constructed much of their Ho Chi Minh Trail inside the national boundaries.

Though documentary records are nonexistent prior to the founding of the Lan Xang Kingdom in the 14th century, linguists and archaeologists believe that the Lao people began to migrate from southern China toward the Mekong River basin prior to the 10th century. The original inhabitants, Kha, were slowly displaced by the Tai peoples who filtered down and settled into Thailand, Burma, and Indochina.

The migratory process accelerated in the 13th century after Mongol invasions of southern China by Kublai Khan and widespread slave raids by the Han Chinese. Laos was raided by the Lanna Thai kingdom of Chiang Mai during the

11th century and by the Khmers during the 12th and fell under the suzerainty of the Sukothai Empire during the 13th century.

Lan Xang Kingdom

Recorded history and the unified nation of Laos began in 1353 under the leadership of Fa Ngum, a Lao prince who was raised in the Khmer courts of Angkor and married a Khmer princess for political gain. Considered the father of modern Laos, Fa Ngum was a visionary politician and talented warrior who, from 1353 to 1371, conquered most of present-day Laos and extended his Indo-Khmer civilization across the Mekong into north and northeastern Thailand. Fa Ngum also brought in Khmer missionaries from the empire of Angkor who introduced Theravada Buddhism as the state religion.

Fa Ngum—ruler of one of the largest territories in Southeast Asia—named his expansive holdings the Kingdom of Lan Xang, an epiphanous term which translates to "Kingdom of a Million Elephants." His widespread empire proved a resounding success. Aside from a half-century of Burmese rule (1574-1637), Lan Xang dominated Laos until 1713, when it split into the three separate kingdoms of Vientiane, Luang Prabang, and Champasak.

Other great leaders of the Lan Xang period included Samsenthai, who succeeded Fa Ngum and organized the nation along Siamese political lines, and Setthathirat, who is revered for bringing the Emerald Buddha to Vientiane in 1547 and successfully defending Laos from foreign aggression by Siamese and Burmese forces.

The Golden Age of Lan Xang occurred during the 60-year reign of King Souligna Vongsa, an enlightened leader who promoted Buddhism and established Vientiane as a center of regional intellectual brilliance. The death of Souligna in 1694 plunged the nation into a period of chaos and political domination by Vietnamese despots. In 1713 Laos split apart into three rival kingdoms and the glorious empire of Lan Xang ceased to exist.

The French Era

The fall of Lan Xang was followed by rule from three disparate kingdoms with divided loyalties. Luang Prabang under Souligna's grandson was chiefly aligned with China, Vientiane (properly called Vieng Chan) under Souligna's nephew was influenced by the Vietnamese empire at Hue, and Champasak in the south was largely controlled by the Siamese. However, the Siamese eventually proved their mettle by annexing Vientiane in 1826, Champasak in 1846, and Luang Prabang in 1885.

But Siamese designs were directly opposed to those of the French, who had established a so-called "protectorate" over most of Vietnam by the mid-19th century. Laos, in fact, was also a pawn in the territorial struggles between British forces expanding east from Burma and French forces moving west across Vietnam.

Events moved quickly. In 1886, the French established a vice-consul in Vientiane and by 1893 the Siamese officially recognized Laos as a French protectorate. French annexation was completed in 1907.

The French paid little attention to Laos except as a buffer zone between British economic zones to the west and their own colonial interests in Vietnam. Not much happened for the next 50 years; Laos remained a sleepy place almost completely unknown to the outside world. French diplomats stationed in Vientiane, however, considered themselves extraordinarily fortunate to be living in the land of lotus eaters.

In 1941, the Japanese took Indochina and, before their defeat in 1945, proclaimed Laos an independent nation. But France's refusal to leave Laos and grant true independence led to the rise of several anti-French movements, including the Lao Issara ("Free Lao") under the leadership of Prince Petsarath and the more radical Pathet Lao ("Lao Nation"), which joined forces with the communist Viet Minh of Vietnam in the early 1950s. Formal independence granted by the French in 1953 was soon followed by the defeat of French forces at Dien Bien Phu in 1954.

The Vietnam Era

A series of coalition governments—rightist, neutralists, and Pathet Lao representatives—attempted to run Laos until the early 1960s when the Vietnam War spilled over into the once-peaceful kingdom. From their bases in the northeast, the Pathet Lao fought the American-backed coalition government in Vientiane while supporting the Viet Minh in their struggle for national unification. To Western observers, Laos appeared destined to be the first "domino" to fall to communism, according to the political analogy first promulgated by Dwight Eisenhower.

By the mid-1960s, much of the Ho Chi Minh Trail supply line snaked through the Annamite Mountains of eastern Laos. Determined to stop communist Vietnamese forces, American bombers stationed in Thailand conducted secret saturation bombings of Pathet Lao strongholds in the northeast and along the entire length of the Ho Chi Minh Trail. It was an unprecedented campaign: more tonnage was dropped on Laos than on Germany during the entire history of WW II.

Despite the horrific onslaught, and a secret war financed by the CIA, Laos fell to the Pathet Lao shortly after the American withdrawal from Vietnam. On 23 August 1975, the Pathet Lao marched into Vientiane and took final control of the Kingdom of a Million Elephants. On 2 December 1975, the 600-year-old monarchy was abolished, opposition coalition leaders were ousted from the government, and Kaysone Phomvihane was appointed premier.

Pathet Lao

Following the 1975 takeover by the Pathet Lao, the former pro-Western and U.S.-supported government was replaced by the People's Democratic Republic of Laos, which followed a Marxist-Leninist philosophy modeled loosely after those in Vietnam and Cambodia. The government was headed by Kaysone Phomvihane, a son of a Vietnamese civil servant from Savannakhet who had led the Laotian Communist Party since its formation in 1955.

The Pathet Lao takeover was quite unlike the communist victories in South Vietnam and Cambodia. After years of venality, corruption, and political games manipulated by foreign powers, Laotians of many political stripes welcomed the Pathet Lao. Their bloodless coup showed them capable of imposing uniquely Laotian solutions, including a tolerance and lack of the aggressiveness that characterized the violent communist takeovers in neighboring countries. Even after abolishing the royal family, the Pathet Lao didn't execute the prince or demand the removal of the American diplomatic corps. Unfortunately, the Pathet Lao's homegrown solution also included the removal of thousands of political prisoners and intellectuals to reeducation camps, where many simply disappeared without a trace.

GOVERNMENT

Recent events have markedly changed the government. In March 1991 the Fifth Congress of the Lao People's Revolutionary Party (LPRP) voted for pro-market reforms and installed new leaders committed to *chin thanakan amai,* or "new thinking." The hammer-and-sickle motif was removed from the state emblem. By August 1991, even the hardline Kaysone had publicly announced the abandonment of a pure communist government in favor of a free-market economy, though he ruled out any real challenge to the party's monopoly on power. In November 1991, the U.S. agreed to upgrade relations and send an ambassador to Vientiane for the first time since the Pathet Lao took power in 1975.

Kaysone died in November 1991. His replacement, President Nouhak Phoumsavan, has been a Politburo member since the ruling LPRP was founded in 1955 and he was appointed the country's finance minister. Although also a hardline communist and close friend of Vietnam, Nouhak supports free-market reforms and has mounted a campaign to upgrade the country's relations with the outside world, particularly China and Thailand. The government is now headed by Nouhak, a secretary-general who serves as prime minister, and the LPRP, which is organized much like other communist parties, with a Central Committee headed by the Politburo.

Elections held in 1995 returned the familiar faces to positions of power.

ECONOMY

Laos is one of the world's poorest countries, with a gross national product ranked in the bottom 10 and an average annual income of just US$160. Over 80% of the population are farmers who primarily raise rice, cotton, maize, and cash crops such as coffee, tobacco, and cardamom. Opium is an important source of income in the Laotian portion of the Golden Triangle. The depressing wages in the public sector—government employees in Vientiane consider themselves lucky to make US$20 per month—has brought widespread corruption to every level of Lao society.

Much of the blame must be laid on the Pathet Lao who, after their victory in 1975, set about imposing a Stalinist system on the devastated economy: they collectivized farms, nationalized the tiny industrial base, and centralized control of prices and all other facets of the wounded economy. Their bloody campaign against intellectuals and political dissidents, combined with a mass exodus of the Laotian elite across the Mekong River to Thailand, stripped Laos of those who were most capable of restoring the economy and running the government. Since 1975, over 300,000 Laotians—roughly a tenth of the population—have fled to Thailand or emigrated to the United States.

However, the economy now seems to be improving, at least in Vientiane, where motorcycles, blue jeans, and consumer products from Thailand have flooded the local markets. Despite some recent crop failures and the abrupt loss of massive amounts of aid from the former Soviet Union, foreign economists estimate that the economy now grows at about 7% per year and that the inflation rate has dropped from stratospheric levels to just under 10%. Recent economic reforms have brought substantial foreign aid from United Nations agencies and major investments in the garment industry from Thai, Hong Kong, and Taiwanese companies. The deficit problem is finally being addressed. Overwhelming poverty still grips the countryside, but Laos now has an emerging entrepreneurial class in the urban areas and farmers welcome the opportunity to market their crops in a postsocialist economy.

THE PEOPLE

The people of Laos are divided by language, culture, and ethnographic background into four main cultural groups, which are subdivided into over 60 minority tribes which generally live in extremely isolated locations.

Lao Loum

The principal ethnic group in Laos accounts for about two-thirds of the national population and comprises most of the Laotians you will meet during your travels. The Lao Loum (also Lao Lum and Lao Lu) arrived from southern China sometime before the 10th century and slowly displaced the Lao Theung from the lowland valleys along the Mekong and its tributaries.

Lao Loum speak Laotian Tai, which is closely related to Thai, and are ethnically indistinguishable from the Lao Thais who inhabit the Issan Plateau of northeastern Thailand.

Lao Thai

Perhaps a subset of the Lao Loum, the Lao Thai are tribal minorities who have resisted assimilation into mainstream Lao society, chiefly by living in the highlands rather than the lowlands favored by the national majority.

The Lao Thai are divided into several groups conveniently distinguished by the color of the female dress: Red Tai, White Tai, and Black Tai. Lao Tai villages are often included with tours of southern Laos.

Lao Theung

The Lao Theung, better known as the Mon and Khmer, or Mon-Khmer, are seminomadic tribals who live mainly on mountain slopes throughout Laos. Although composed of perhaps some 60 ethnic groups, the lowland Lao often call them simply Kha, a derogatory term which translates as "Slave" and refers to their traditional role within ancient Lao society.

The more important subsets include the Khamu, who practice swidden agriculture and are mostly animists living in the north; the Akha, Alak, and Ta-Oy, who reside on the Bolovens Plateau in the south; and the Lamet, who are thought to be descendants of the earliest inhabitants of the country.

Lao Sung

The Lao Sung, or "High Lao," are tribal groups identical to the famous hilltribes of northern Thailand. Most migrated to Laos from southern China during the 18th and 19th centuries and today live in villages above 1,000 meters. Principal groups include the Hmong (formerly known as the Meo), the Yao (also called the Mien), the Lisu, and the Lahu. The Akha are often included in this group.

The Hmong are the largest group within the Lao Sung and certainly the most well-known to the outside world, chiefly because over 100,000 Hmong now live in the United States. The Hmong were originally recruited as mercenaries by the French colonialists in the final days of their struggle against the Pathet Lao. The Americans via the CIA subsequently trained and equipped thousands of Hmong to fight the Laotian communists under the command of their chief, a colorful rebel named Vung Pao who later fled to Thailand with his six wives and 29 children. Today, the remaining Hmong survive mainly by growing opium and exporting their product on horseback to the markets of Chiang Mai.

ON THE ROAD

GETTING THERE

By Air
Vientiane Wattay International Airport can be reached from Bangkok (US$100 one-way), Chiang Mai (US$80), Hanoi (US$80-100), Ho Chi Minh City (US$150-180), Phnom Penh (US$125-150), Singapore (US$350), Beijing, Kunming (US$100), Xishuangbanna, Guangzhou, Kuala Lumpur, Yangon (US$150), and Hong Kong on national airlines and Lao Aviation.

Bangkok to Vientiane costs US$100 one-way and US$190 roundtrip with Thai International and Lao Aviation. Bangkok Airways, in conjunction with Lanna Tours (a subsidiary of Diethelm Travel), has announced plans for weekly flights from Chiang Mai to Luang Prabang—the backend approach to Laos.

By Land from Thailand
Lao National Tourism Authority has opened the borders at several points with Thailand, Vietnam, and China. Lao visas, required for all these crossings, can be picked up from travel agents in towns on the Thai side.

Nong Khai: The first major crossing was at Nong Khai-Tha Deua over the Friendship Bridge which opened in 1994. Despite the promise, communications and transportation has been frustrated by measures that prevent the free flow of traffic between Nong Khai and Vientiane.

Chiang Khong: Foreigners can also cross the Mekong at Chiang Khong and enter Laos at Huay Xai, where a 250-km sealed road heads northeast to the Chinese border via Bokeo and Luang Nam Tha provinces. A bridge is now under construction at this site.

Chong Mek: Land entry is also permitted from Chong Mek, 76 km east of Ubon Ratchathani in northeastern Thailand. After crossing the Mekong, the road continues 52 km east to Pakse where it splits north to Savannakhet, east to Paksong and the Bolovens Plateau, and south to Champasak and the Khmer temple of Wat Phu.

Nakhon Phanom: River crossings are legal from Nakhon Phanom to Tha Kheak in south-central Laos.

Mukdahan: Ferries also cross from Mukdahan to Savannakhet where Highway 9 heads east to Vietnam (a legal border crossing), while Highway 13 goes north to Vientiane and south to Pakse and the Bolovens Plateau.

By Land from Vietnam
Foreign travelers can enter Laos at Lao Bao and continue past Sepon on Highway 9 to Savannakhet. Lao visas are required and should be obtained in Ho Chi Minh City or Hanoi.

Crossings from Dien Bien Phu, Vieng Xai, and Vinh are expected to open within a few years.

By Land from Cambodia
The border crossing from Thai Boei (Stung Treng Province) in Cambodia to Voen Kham in Champasak Province may open soon to Western travelers, probably after the completion of the American Development Bank highway from Voen Kham to Pakse.

By Land from China
Western travelers with Lao visas can enter Laos from China in the Mengla district of Luang Nam Tha Province. Lao border formalities are taken care of in Ban Boten.

The border crossing in Phong Saly Province is open to Chinese and Laotian citizens but closed to Western residents unless they can obtain written permission from a Lao consulate.

GETTING AROUND

Laos is a mountainous country with no railway, one seasonally navigable river (the Mekong), and some of the worst roads in the world. Lao Aviation handles all internal air traffic with flights originating or terminating at Wattay International Airport in Vientiane.

Air Transportation

Lao Aviation connects Vientiane with Luang Prabang (US$40 one-way), Phonsavan (Plain of Jars, US$35), Ban Huai Sai (US$ 65), Thakhek (US$50), Sayabuli (US$30), Xieng Khwang (US$55), Sam Neua (US$55), Savannakhet (US$60), Luang Nam Tha (US$60), Saravan (US$80), and Pakse (US$95). Other scheduled destinations include Muang Sai (US$50), Oudomxay, and Honeisay.

On domestic flights, Lao Aviation uses a patchwork of Soviet-built twin-prop Antonov 24s, Chinese-built 17-seater Y-12s, and French ATR-42s of more recent vintage.

Tourists are given priority over locals when booking flights but are charged double the local rate. Departures are often delayed for weather reasons or canceled due to lack of spare parts.

Land Transportation

Roads in Laos, to put it mildly, are terrible. For example, the 230-km journey from Vientiane to Luang Prabang along Route 13—the national north-south artery—takes only 35 minutes by air but 1-5 days on the tortuous mountain roads.

Route 13 is partially sealed but impassable during the rainy season when landslides close large swatches of the road. A more serious problem are the renegade bandits and opium warlords who attack truck convoys to kill passengers for their loot. A prominent French tour operator, Claude Vincent, was murdered in late 1996 when armed men fired on his minibus and killed Vincent and five of his staff. The insurgents appear to be disgruntled Hmong soldiers stationed along their old infiltration routes but now desperate for financial help after resources were cut off by Thailand and the C.I.A.

Route 13 from Vientiane to Luang Prabang is currently closed to Western visitors, but travelers are allowed to take Route 13 south to Savan-nakhet and Pakse. Roads are terrible and most visitors prefer to fly or use boats when possible.

River Transportation

The Mekong River is navigable from Luang Prabang all the way down to the Cambodian border but only when waters run high during the rainy season from June to November.

Luang Prabang to Vientiane is a popular three-day sail which costs US$6-12 and passes Tha Deua, Paklay, and Chiang Khong before reaching Vientiane—a romantic interlude once de rigueur with hippie backpackers in the late 1960s. Another recommended Mekong journey is from Pakse down to the Khmer temple of Wat Phu. Adventure travel types will also enjoy the rugged Sekong River which snakes through the gorgeous topography of the Bolovens Plateau in southern Laos.

VISAS

Business Visa

Thirty-day business visas can be obtained from Lao embassies or consulates when accompanied by a letter of invitation from a recognized Lao company, citizen, foreign mission, volunteer agency, or travel service which represents Lao Tourism. Permission must also be obtained from the Ministry of the Interior in Vientiane.

Tourist Visa

Tourist visas valid for 30 days can be obtained from most Lao embassies listed on the accompanying chart.

Lao embassies require an application in triplicate, three passport photos, and the visa fee which ranges from US$15-35 depending on the particular embassy.

Lao embassies are the most economical option, though the embassies which grant visas seem to change with the seasons. The Lao Embassy in Bangkok occasionally grants visas but other times refers applicants to an approved travel agent.

The new Lao Embassy in Khon Kaen issues visas in 48 hours and charges US$35 for Americans and most Europeans. The embassy is on Potisan Road past Bung Kaen Nakon Lake and Wat Pho Nontan.

The Lao government currently automatically grants visas to visitors arriving at the Vientiane

LAO EMBASSIES

Australia: 1 Dalman Crescent, O'Malley, Canberra; tel. (06) 286-4535; fax (06) 290-1910
Cambodia: 1517 Thanon Keomani, Phnom Penh; tel. 26441; fax 85523
France: 74 Avenue Raymond Poincare, Paris; tel. 4553-0298; fax 4727-5789
Germany: Am Lessing 6, Koenigwinter 1, Bonn; tel. 02 223-21501
Malaysia: 108 Jalan Damal, Kuala Lumpur; tel. 248-3895; fax 242-0334
Myanmar: NA1 Diplomatic Quarters, Fraser Rd., Yangon
Thailand: 520, 502/1 Soi Ramkhamhaeng 39, Bangkapi, Bangkok; tel. 539-6667; fax 539-6678
U.S.A.: 2222 S St. NW, Washington D.C., 20006; tel. (202) 667-0076; fax (202) 332-4923
Vietnam: 22 Tran Binh Trong, Hanoi; tel. 252271; 181 Hai Ba Trung, Ho Chi Minh City; tel. 299272

airport. Laos visas can also be picked up from travel agents in Bangkok and Nong Khai but check on additional service fees and the required wait. Travel agents ask US$50-100 to obtain Lao visas and can take anywhere from two days to a week.

Visa Extensions

Visas can be extended at US$1 per day at Lao immigration offices or US$3-5 a day from Lao travel agencies. Visitors who overstay their visa are charged US$5 per day at the immigration checkpoint upon departure.

Thai Visas

Thailand grants a 30-day permit to all Western visitors. Travelers who intend to stay more than 30 days should obtain a Thai visa at the Thai Embassy in Vientiane on Thanon Phon Kheng, northeast of the Pratuxai Monument. Visas cost 300B and requires three passport photos. The embassy is open weekdays 0900-1200 and 1400-1600.

TRAVEL PRACTICALITIES

Money

One US dollar equals roughly 900-1,000 kip (K). Thai baht is the preferred form of currency, while U.S. dollars are accepted in Vientiane and Luang Prabang.

Traveler's checks can be cashed in most larger towns while cash advances can be made at banks in Vientiane and Luang Prabang. Bring along plenty of small-denomination baht and a smaller supply of American dollars.

Prices here are quoted in relatively stable dollars rather than devaluating kip.

Health

Hospitals and medical facilities in Laos are poor and the country presents more health risks than westernized countries. Inoculations aren't required but immunizations are recommended against tetanus, polio, hepatitis, rabies, typhoid, and cholera. Malaria is common. Drink bottled water, and all food—especially fish and seafood—should be well cooked.

Business Hours

Government offices and banks are open weekdays 0800-1200 and 1400-1700. Museums and other state-regulated tourist attractions are open weekdays except Monday 0800-1130 and 1400-1630.

Laos is seven hours ahead of GMT. Vientiane at 1200 is 0100 in New York, 1500 in Sydney, and 0500 in London.

VIENTIANE

Vientiane—the national capital and administrative center of Laos—was constructed by the French on the site of Lan Xang, the ancient empire which once extended from southern China to northern Thailand. Vientiane today is a modern and unassuming town without the awe-inspiring sights of other Asian centers, but with a welcome sense of peace in a tranquil setting oddly perched on the banks of the muddy Mekong.

ATTRACTIONS

Vientiane, no special beauty, can be easily toured on foot or with a rented bicycle in a single day. Best activities are watching people in markets and contemplating the collision of Lao traditions with Western culture.

Revolutionary Museum: A distinctive white building with fascinating memorabilia about "imperialists" and the victory of the "people's revolution." Open Tuesday-Sunday 0800-1130 and 1400-1630.

Wat Mixai: Lao *wats* incorporate identical elements as those in Thailand though architectural terminology differs. Main ordination halls are *sim* rather than *bot*, secondary chapels are *hor sang pra* not *viharns*, stupas are called *that* not *chedi*, *chofas* equal *sofas*, while *nagas* are *nyaks*. Wat Mixai features verandahs of *sims* constructed in 19th-century Bangkok style.

Wat Hai Sok: A reconstructed Bangkok-style temple with soaring peak and multi-layered, uneven-numbered roofs.

Wat Ong Teu: Constructed in 1500 by King Setthathirat but reconstructed to enclose its immense Buddha flanked by Ramakien and Mahabharta murals.

Wat Impeng: Built several centuries ago, destroyed by Thai, Burmese, and Chinese armies, and later reconstructed with exquisite woodcarving and mosaic filigree.

Wat Chan: A remarkable bronze Buddha moved from the original temple after its destruction by Thai forces in 1827. Also, a solitary "Calling Rain" *mudra* Buddha inside the courtyard stupa.

Presidential Palace: Former royal palace that's now a reception hall for Nouhak Phoumsavan and closed to the public. Nouhak, along with other Pathet Lao leaders, live in Kilometer 6, an American-style suburb on the edge of Vientiane complete with ranch homes built by the United States during the Vietnam War.

Wat Sisaket: Wat Sisaket, constructed in 1818, remains the solitary temple to survive the Siamese destruction of 1827 with over 2,000 Buddhas encased in small niches and another 300 images sculpted in classic Lao style. Jataka murals and flowered ceilings inspired by Siamese prototypes in Ayuthaya grace the residence of the chief Buddhist *sangha* leader in Laos—an important religious site. Open Tues.-Sun. 0800-1130 and 1400-1630.

Wat Pra Keo: Wat Pra Keo (Phra Kaew or Pha Kaeo) was constructed in 1565 to house the Emerald Buddha presently installed in Bangkok's Wat Pra Keo. Today it features exquisite examples of Lao wood sculpture, Laotian interpretations of walking Buddhas from Sukothai, 16th-century doors carved with erotic Hindu images, multi-armed Khmer deities, and stone Dvaravati-style Buddhas among the oldest in the country. Open Tues.-Sun. 0800-1130 and 1400-1630.

That Dam: Vientiane's "Black Stupa" dates from the Lanna era (12th-14th centuries) and is known for its Chiang Saen stupas.

Markets: Morning Market (Talat Sao) is jammed throughout the day, Talat Khua Din is best for fresh produce and flowers, while Talat Tong Khan Kham, Vientiane's largest market, is liveliest in the early morning.

Pratuxai (Anousavari) Monument: Vientiane's oddest landmark, an Oriental-baroque monstrosity, was constructed with American cement intended for an airport runway but diverted to this ill-proportioned Arc de Triomphe. Sadly topped by an astonishing wedding-cake structure of Byzantine spires and Gothic gargoyles, the monument offers visitors a view out over Vientiane as it quietly disappears beneath the tropical foliage.

Pra That Luang: Pra That Luang (Great Sacred Stupa), erected in 1566 by King Setthathi-

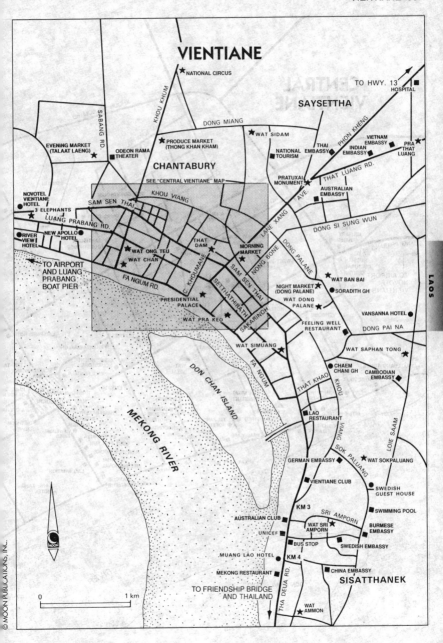

VIENTIANE

★ NATIONAL CIRCUS

TO HWY. 13
■ HOSPITAL

SAYSETTHA

DONG MIANG

KHOU KHUM

SABANG RD.

EVENING MARKET
(TALAAT LAENG) ★

★ WAT SIDAM

★ PRODUCE MARKET
(THONG KHAN KHAM)

ODEON RAMA
■ THEATER

CHANTABURY

PHON KHENG

● THAI
EMBASSY

● VIETNAM
EMBASSY

■ INDIAN
EMBASSY

★ PRA
THAT
LUANG

● NATIONAL
TOURISM

THAT LUANG RD.

SEE "CENTRAL VIENTIANE" MAP

PRATUXAI
MONUMENT ★

■ AUSTRALIAN
EMBASSY

KHOU VIANG

NOVOTEL
VIENTIANE
HOTEL ■

SAM SEN THAI

DONG SI SUNG WUN

3 ELEPHANTS ★

LUANG PRABANG RD.

RIVER
VIEW ■
HOTEL

● NEW APOLLO
HOTEL

LANE XANG AVE.

NONG BONE

DONG PALANE

THAT
DAM ★

★ WAT ONG TEU

● MORNING
MARKET

★ WAT CHAN

● WAT BAN BAI

★ NIGHT MARKET
(DONG PALANE)

● SORADITH GH

FA NGUM RD.

SAM SEN THAI

C. KHOUMANE

SETTHATHIRATH

WAT DONG
PALANE

● VANSANNA HOTEL

★ PRESIDENTIAL
PALACE

TO AIRPORT
AND LUANG
PRABANG
BOAT PIER

SAKARINOH

★ WAT PRA KEO

FEELING WELL
■ RESTAURANT

DONG PAI NA

★ WAT SIMUANG

★ WAT SAPHAN TONG

FA NGUM

THAT KHAO

● CHAEM
CHANI GH

■ CAMBODIAN
EMBASSY

DON CHAN ISLAND

KHOU VIANG

■ LAO
RESTAURANT

MEKONG RIVER

LOIE SAAM

SOK PALUANG

● GERMAN EMBASSY

★ WAT SOKPALUANG

■ VIENTIANE CLUB

● SWEDISH
GUEST HOUSE

KM 3

SRI AMPORN

■ SWIMMING POOL

■ AUSTRALIAN CLUB

★ WAT SRI
AMPORN

■ BURMESE
EMBASSY

■ UNICEF

■ BUS STOP

■ SWEDISH EMBASSY

MUANG LAO HOTEL

KM 4

THA DEUA RD.

■ CHINA EMBASSY

MEKONG RESTAURANT ■

SISATTHANEK

TO FRIENDSHIP BRIDGE
AND THAILAND

★ WAT
AMMON

0   1 km

LAOS

© MOON PUBLICATIONS, INC.

CENTRAL VIENTIANE

KHOUN BOULOM RD.

PHAI NAM RD.

DU PUITS RD.

CHAO ANOU ST.

PHNOM PENH RD.

SYRI GUESTHOUSE

STADIUM

VANNASINH GH

SAMSENTHAI RD.

HENG BOUN ST.

TENNIS CLUB

PUBLIC POOL

KHOUN BOULOM RD.

ANOU HOTEL

THAI MILITARY BANK

SANTISOUK GUESTHOUSE

LUANG PRABANG BLVD.

BAN HAY SOK RESTAURANT

FOSTER'S PUB

THAI FOOD

← TO AIRPORT, NOVOTEL VIENTIANE HOTEL

RUSSIAN CULTURAL CENTER

SWEET HOME BAKERY

REVOLUTIONARY MUSEUM

KY HUONG RD.

LANI #1 GUESTHOUSE

WAT INPENG

WAT HAY SOK

LE BAYOU

LAO PLAZA HOTEL

SAYSANA HOTEL

NOKEO KHOUMANE

LE VENDOME

LANG XANG TOURS

MANTRATURAT RD.

LAO-PARIS HOTEL

INPENG RD.

WAT ONG TU

SETTATHIRAT BLVD.

LAO TEXTILES

PHANTAVONG GH

THATLUANG TOURS

BANQUE SETTATHIRAT

GOVERNMENT BOOKSTORE

THE TA...

SODE TOUR

WAT MIXAI

FRANCOIS NGIN

BIKE RENTALS

SCANDINAVIAN BAKERY

NAM PHU GARDEN

PHORN THIP GUESTHOUSE

LAO AIR

THE FOUNTAIN

VAN MIXAI RESTAURANT

DHL (COURIER)

HEALTHY & FRESH BAKERY

NAM PHU SQUARE

L'OPERA

INTER HOTEL

WAT CHAN

LE BISTROT

DOUANG DEUANE HOTEL

INTER-LAO TOURISM

DIETHELM TRAVEL

NIGHT FOOD MARKET

TAI PAN HOTEL

AEROCONTACT ASIA

VIENTIANE TIMES

NANA CAFE

MIXAI GUESTHOUSE

LE SOURIYA

JUST FOR FUN

RAINTREE BOOKS

MIXAY CAFE

FA NGUM RD.

THAI INTERNATIONAL

LAO AVIATION

BANQUE EXTERIEUR

LANE XANG HOTEL

MEKONG

RIVER

DON CHAN ISLAND

LAOS

NOOC

0   200 m

TO PRATUXAI MONUMENT

ROYAL DOKMAIDENG HOTEL ●

SAYLOM ST.

LANE XANG BLVD.

BELMONT SETTHA ● PALACE HOTEL

LANI #2 ● GUESTHOUSE

KHOUN BOULOM RD.

PANGKHAM RD.

LAO ELYSEE GH ●

LANA TOUR ●   ● THAI FARMERS BANK

LAO NATIONAL ● TOURISM AUTHORITY

TOURIST AUTHORITY OF THAILAND ●

TNT (COURIER) ●

● HOTEL DAY INN

IMMIGRATION OFFICE ●

BANGKOK BANK ●

THE SALOON ●

SALA LUANG ● PRABANG RESTAURANT

THAT DAM ★

VIENTIANE ● COMMERCIAL BANK

MONEY-CHANGERS ●

HUA GUO ● GUESTHOUSE

BARTOLINI RD.

ASIAN PAVILION HOTEL ●

VIETNAMESE ● RESTAURANT

U.S. EMBASSY ●

DRY GOODS ●

TALAD SAO

MAHOSOT RD.

PHIMPHONE ● MINIMART

EKALATH METROPOLE HOTEL ●

KUALAO RESTAURANT ●

CHANTA KHOUMANE RD.

POST OFFICE ●

TALAD SAO (MORNING MARKET)

SIAM COMMERCIAL BANK ●

SIAM ● COMMERCIAL BANK

FOODSTALLS ●

KHUA DIN MARKET

KRUNG THAI BANK ●

BUS STATION ●

INTERNATIONAL FAX AND PHONE/TELECOM ●

TAXIS & JUMBOS ●

SETTIATHIRAT BLVD.

SAMSENTHAI RD.

GALLIENI RD.

KHOU VIANG

PRESIDENTIAL PALACE

● WAT SISAKET

WAT PRA KEO MUSEUM

FRENCH EMBASSY

CHURCH ✝

FA NGUM RD.

● MAHASOT HOSPITAL

LAOS

© MOON PUBLICATIONS, INC.

rat over an older Buddha relic site, now serves as Vientiane's most important religious site—a symbol of Lao sovereignty. Overall, less than impressive. Open Tues.-Sun. 0800-1130 and 1400-1630.

ACCOMMODATIONS

Vientiane has several dozen guesthouses and hotels in city center and south of town on the banks of the Mekong River priced US$5-15 (guesthouses) and US$20-60 (hotels).

Budget

Laotian guesthouses and budget hotels are somewhat overpriced but trends have improved dramatically in recent years.

Ministry of Culture and Information (MIC) Guesthouse: A fleabag with unclean rooms and little water pressure but the cheapest in town and centrally located one block west of Nam Phu Square. See "State Culture Guesthouse" on the Central Vientiane map. 11 Thanon Manthaturat, tel. 212362, US$3-10.

Hua Guo Guesthouse: A dozen spotless a/c rooms with western bathrooms and hot showers one block north of Nam Phu Square. 359 Thanon Samsenthai, tel. 216612, US$8-20.

Phantavong Guesthouse: Basic but clean rooms plus budget outdoor cafe a few doors north of MIC Guesthouse. 69 Thanon Manthaturat, tel. 214738, US$5-15.

Phorn Thip Guesthouse: Rambling old colonial house with spacious rooms, wooden floors, and genuine atmosphere; arrive early to secure a room. 72 Thanon Inpeng, tel. 217239, US$8-20.

Samsenthai Hotel: Geriatric place with enormous if somewhat ill-maintained rooms. 15 Thanon Manthaturat, tel. 216287, fax 212116, US$6-15.

Moderate

Discounts given for longer stays.

Syri Guesthouse: Colonial mansion in an excellent location with 15 spacious old-world rooms. Thanon Chao Anou, tel. 212682, fax 217251, US$15-25.

Lani 1 Guesthouse: Great location, beautiful gardens, comfortable a/c rooms, popular with long-term visitors and volunteer workers. 281 Thanon Setthathirat, tel. 216103, fax 215639, US$25-35.

Asian Pavilion Hotel: Formerly the Hotel Constellation immortalized in John Le Carre's novel *The Honourable Schoolboy,* the foreign gunrunners, opium dealers, gold smugglers, spies, mercenaries, and journalists have disappeared from the scene in this renovated hotel that still retains some of its old atmosphere. 379 Thanon Samsenthai, tel. 213430, fax 213432, US$26-45.

Anou Hotel: Refurbished hotel with cafe, disco-cabaret "animated by a Famous Live Band," and 50 a/c rooms with private baths and hot showers. 3 Thanon Heng Bun, tel. 213630, fax 213635, US$20-35.

Ekalath Metropole Hotel: Vietnamese-run hotel with 32 fan and a/c rooms plus the Melody Club disco. Thanon Samsenthai, tel. 213420, fax 222307, US$24-35.

La Parasol Blanca Hotel: Restored colonial mansion with bungalow accommodations set in pleasant gardens with a small pool. Lounge and Italian restaurant. Thanon Sidamdouan, tel. 216091, fax 214108, US$34-40.

Luxury

International standards are still lacking but the following hotels all feature a/c rooms with attached baths, minibars, and in-room satellite TV. Discount and corporate rates are available on request. The first three hotels are centrally located near the river, while the remainder are somewhat distant and require taxis to reach the center of Vientiane.

Tai Pan Hotel: Vientiane's best-value hotel is splendidly located a half block back from the river with a Thai restaurant, business center, function rooms, cocktail lounge, and 36 clean and well-appointed rooms complete with satellite TV, minibar, and IDD phone. 22/3 Thanon Francois Ngin, tel. 216906, fax 216223, US$55-70.

Lane Xang Hotel: Vientiane's venerable hotel—a disastrous monument to Soviet aesthetics—features a pool, tennis courts, sauna, and 109 rooms. Pleasant location facing the Mekong River. Thanon Fa Ngum, tel. 214102, fax 214108, US$50-100.

Lao Hotel Plaza: Big new 165-room hotel with pool, fitness center, business facilities, restaurants, and nightclub managed by a Thai hotel group. Good central location. 63 Thanon Samsenthai, tel. 213511, fax 213512, US$80-150.

Royal Dokmaideng Hotel: Five-story hotel near Pratuxai Monument with business center, pool, massage center, karaoke lounge, and Chinese nightclub. Thanon Lan Xang, tel. 214455, fax 214454, US$80-140.

River View Hotel: West of town, facing the river with small tree-enclosed swimming pool, rooftop cafe, and 32 a/c rooms plus suites with Mekong views. Thanon Fa Ngum, tel. 216224, fax 216232, US$40-75.

Novotel Vientiane: The former Belvedere Hotel, also west of town, attempts French style in its architecture, cafes, restaurant, pool, and 233 deluxe rooms in what was once a girl's school. Thanon Luang Prabang, KM2, tel. 213570, fax 213572, US$100-160.

New Apollo Hotel: West of town, a reincarnation of the old Santhiphab Hotel, now Thai-managed with an ostentatious Chinese restaurant and hostess nightclub. 69 Thanon Luang Prabang, tel. 213244, fax 214462, US$80-100.

RESTAURANTS

Vientiane's rising culinary aspirations are reflected in the tantalizing range of dishes served in a multitude of cross-cultural cafes and restaurants.

When the French departed Laos in 1953, they left behind their language, their legislative protocols, and best of all, their cuisine. Vientiane is a place where you can find baguettes and *pain au chocolat* along with fried rice, *tom yam kung,* and American fast food.

Night Markets: Lao specialties are best enjoyed from street vendors and night markets rather than restaurants, which usually serve Chinese or Thai fare. Vendors located on Hang Boun and Chao Anou serve bowls of steaming-hot noodles and *khao ji pate,* French bread stuffed with Laotian pate. Vendors also set up shop along Fa Ngum overlooking the river, north of the Mixai Restaurant, where they offer Lao staples such as *kai ping* and *laap.*

Mixay Cafe: Famous old open-sided cafe with decent food, pitchers of beer, and superb sunset views over the Mekong. Thanon Fa Ngum. Inexpensive.

Santisouk Restaurant: Also known by its pre-revolution name "Café La Pagode," Santisouk opens with Western breakfasts and serves cheap, tasty steaks at dinnertime in a/c comfort. 77 Thanon Noeko Koummane, tel. 215303. Inexpensive.

Thai Food: Very successful Thai cafe with all the fiery classics in a comfortable setting. Thanon Samsenthai. Inexpensive.

The Taj: North Indian dishes, tandoor, curries, breads, vegetarian specialties, and an all-

---

LAO FOOD

Similar to Thai cuisine, Lao meals revolve around heaps of glutinous rice, steaming vegetables, and freshwater fish spiced with lemongrass, chilies, tamarind, coconut milk, and other aromatic herbs such as marijuana, sold in the Morning Market as a cooking ingredient.

Staples: Fish *(paa),* chicken *(kai),* duck *(pet),* pork *(muu),* beef *(sin wua),* and vegetables *(phak).*

Condiments: As in Thailand, meals are often consumed with side dishes such as fish sauce *(nam paa),* hot chili sauce *(jaew),* and raw chilies *(mak phet).*

Rice and Noodles: Accompanying every Lao meal will be glutinous rice *(khao nio),* white rice *(khao jao),* flat rice noodles *(foe),* or thin white wheat noodles *(khao pun).*

Popular Lao/Thai Dishes

laap: raw meat marinated in lemon and chili; the national dish of Laos and northern Thailand

laap kai: raw marinated chicken

laap sin: raw marinated beef

phaneng kai: chicken stuffed with peanuts and coconut

kai ping: grilled chicken

kaeng kalami: cabbage-fish soup

tom yam paa: fish and lemongrass soup

paa beuk: giant Mekong catfish

kung ping: sautéed prawns

lao lao: white wine made from fermented rice

fanthong: red *lao lao*

you-can-eat luncheon buffet. 75 Thanon Pang Kham, tel. 212890. Inexpensive.

Le Souriya: Vientiane's classiest French restaurant offers upscale cuisine and fine wines in an elegant setting, owned by a former Hmong princess from Xieng Khouang. 31 Thanon Pang Kham, tel. 215887. Moderate.

Nam Phu Garden: Pleasant beer garden with a variety of Indian, Chinese, and Lao food served in an interior of white-washed walls and tables of smoked glass. French dishes include frog's legs Provençale and steak au poivre vert. Nam Phu Square, tel. 216775. Moderate.

SERVICES

Tourist Information

The LNTA and other groups may help with the latest travel news on Laos.

Tourist Office: The Lao National Tourism Authority (LNTA) has a few useless brochures and not much else. Thanon Lane Xang, tel. 212248, fax 212769.

Diethelm Travel: Southeast Asia's largest travel and tour agency serves as the representative of American Express and sells pricey if dependable tours of the country. Thanon Setthathirat, tel. 213833, fax 216294.

Inter-Lao Tourism: Private travel agency with helpful information desk and sensibly priced tours. Thanon Setthatihirat, tel. 214832, fax 216306.

Lane Xang Travel: Second largest travel agency in Laos. Thanon Pang Kham, tel. 212469, fax 215804.

AeroContact Asia: Tourism promotion company that publishes *Discover Laos* magazine every few months—good source of news and events, with current hotel listings. 23 Thanon Manthaturat, tel. 217294.

Books and Maps

Books and maps are best picked up before you arrive or in Vientiane at Raintree Bookstore.

Vientiane Guide: Annual guide published by the Women's International Group with an excellent annotated map; great for shopping tips. Sold at Raintree Books and better hotels.

State Geographic Service: Government agency with topo maps plastered all over the walls—point and the clerk will attempt to find it. One block west of Pratuxai Monument.

Raintree Bookstore: Vientiane's only English-language bookstore sells Thai newspapers, maps, used magazines and travel guides, and Lao-English dictionaries and phrasebooks. 25 Thanon Pangkham, tel. 217260.

National Library: Small English reading room with dated periodicals from the *Economist* to *Time*. Thanon Setthathirat, tel. 212452.

Embassies

Emergencies, visas for Southeast Asian destinations, and Lao visa extensions can be handled at the following offices. Most are open weekdays 0900-1200 and 1400-1630.

Visa Extensions: The Lao Immigration Office on Talat Sao and Lao National Tourism above LNTA can help extend Lao visas for US$3-5 per day. Many guesthouses and hotels also provide these services.

Western Embassies: Lost your passport? Need travel advice? Western embassies and consulates include the United States (Thanon Bartholonic, tel. 212581, fax 212584), Australia (Thanon Nehru, tel. 413610, fax 413805), France (Thanon Settathirat, tel. 215258), Germany (26 Thanon Sokpaluang, tel. 312111), and Sweden (Thanon Wat Nak, tel. 315018).

Southeast Asian Embassies: Visas for nearby countries can be picked up at the rep offices for Cambodia (Thanon Tha Dua, tel. 314952, fax 312584), India (Thanon That Luang, tel. 413802), Japan (Thanon Sisangvone, tel. 212632), Myanmar (Thanon Sokpaluang, tel. 312439), Thailand (Thanon Phon Kheng, tel. 214582), and Vietnam (60 Thanon That Luang, tel. 413400).

Communications

Communications within and beyond Laos remains a primitive mechanism slowly moving into the modern era.

Telephone: Overseas calls can be made from the Central Telephone Office on Thanon Setthathirat and from many hotels but first check service charges. To phone Laos, press 011 (the international access code), 856 (country code), the local area code, then the phone or fax number. The country code for Laos is 856. Lao area codes are Vientiane (21), Luang Prabang (71), Savannakhet (41), Pakse (31), and Tha Khaek

(52). Telephone numbers—even area codes—change frequently.

Mail: The GPO opposite the morning market provides mail, poste restante, and express mail services (EMS) but make sure you see them cancel the wondrous Lao stamps in person, or they might be recycled. Thanon Lan Xang, tel. 216425, open daily 0800-1700.

Couriers: International courier services are provided by DHL (52 Thanon Nokeo Kumman, tel. 216830, fax 214869) and TNT Express (Thanon Lan Xang, tel. 214361).

TRANSPORTATION

Air
Vientiane's Wattay International Airport, three km northwest of city center, can be reached by taxi (US$3-4) and by *samlor (tuk tuk)* for US$2.

Wattay Airport has been drastically remodeled and expanded to accommodate larger jets and increasing numbers of visitors who expect something approaching international standards. The airport now has cafes, tourist information booths, taxi stops, a few immigration or baggage custodians, and an exchange booth with decent rates—but you'll do better changing money at town markets.

Lao Aviation, Thai International, China Southern, and Aeroflot have offices in town. Departure tax is US$5.

Boat
River ferries and speedboats depart from Kao Liaw (Tha Heua Kao Liaw), nine km from downtown Vientiane, to Luang Prabang and Nong Khai in Thailand. Departures are irregular depending on the season and should be checked with guesthouses in Vientiane.

LUANG PRABANG

Luang Prabang—the historic, religious, and artistic capital of Laos—lies in a superb location on a promontory at the confluence of the Mekong and Khan Rivers with a dreamlike atmosphere not unlike some Indochinese Shangri-La.

Luang Prabang was established in 1353 by Fa Ngum as the royal capital of the first Lao Kingdom, Lan Xang, more romantically called the "Land of a Million Elephants." Previously the city served as a seat of early Thai-Lao kingdoms and a trading conduit between China and southern empires.

Luang Prabang remained the center of the Lan Xang Kingdom until 1563 when King Settathirat transferred the capital to Vieng Chan (Vientiane). Despite the move and subsequent fall of the Lan Xang Kingdom in 1694, Luang Prabang remained the source of monarchial power and spiritual headquarters well into the 20th century.

The French arrived in the late 19th century and took control of Luang Prabang after a succession of territorial treaties with the Siamese. Unlike in Vientiane, where the French imposed grand boulevards and French architecture, Luang Prabang was left alone as a sleepy escape for lotus eaters.

The Japanese occupation of Laos ended in 1945 with the arrival of French paratroopers, who once again declared Luang Prabang and Laos a French protectorate. However, French experiences in Vietnam and their ongoing problems with Algeria forced them to grant full sovereignty in 1953.

Luang Prabang remained a royal city until the Communist Pathet Lao takeover in 1975 and the elevation of Kaysone Phomvihane to the position of Prime Minister. The Pathet Lao immediately abolished the monarchy in Luang Prabang and established the Lao People's Democratic Republic (Lao PDR), which continues to rule the impoverished nation.

ATTRACTIONS

Central Attractions
The easygoing provincial town of Luang Prabang and its 30 intact temples clustered together around Mount Phousi (Phu Si) can be leisurely toured in two or three days.

Royal Palace Museum: Luang Prabang's major attraction, the former palace of Savang, was converted into a national museum soon

THE FINAL KING ~ SAVANG VATTHANA

The main drama of modern Luang Prabang centers around the fate of Savang Vatthana, the final king in a line of rulers that dates back to the empire of Lan Xang. Educated in Paris, Savang had a penchant for *Remembrances of Things Past* by Marcel Proust, and a classic white Ford Edsel that still sits in the royal palace garage. The king was also a devoted patron of Buddhism and a national patriot who cried over the terrible fate of his country.

Savang was initially named an "advisor" to the new Communist regime, but the government, fearing a coup built around the king but organized by insurgents in Thailand, sent the royal family into internal exile in Sam Neua Province in 1977. Sometime in the early 1980s the royal family (king, queen, and Crown Prince Vongsavang) perished in the jungle, though no one knows the details of their deaths, which the government only officially acknowledged to the outside world in 1989.

Curiously, the death of the final monarch has never been reported to the Laotian people, who are still told the great Lao-Orwellian euphemism: the king has "gone to the north" for "seminars."

after the disappearance of the king but still provides insight into regional history and the quirky collection habits of the final ruler of the 600-year-old dynasty. The most significant image of the numerous 15th- to 17th-century Buddha statues is a golden reproduction of the highly venerated Pra Bang, a 50-kilogram statue of Ceylonese origins brought to Luang Prabang in 1353 by King Fa Ngum. Pra Bang's arrival marks the introduction of Buddhism in Laos and inspired Fa Ngum to rename the city from Xieng Thong to Nakhon Luang Prabang—"Great City of the Big Buddha."

Wat Mai: Also called Wat Souvanna Phommaram, this five-roofed royal temple ranks among the most impressive edifices in Luang Prabang—the holiest as it once served as residence for the Supreme Patriarch of the Lao Buddhist *sangha*.

Mount Phousi: A magnificent site for panoramic views, sunsets over the Mekong, and experiencing the cultural-symbolic centerpiece of ancient Luang Prabang.

Wat Chomsi: A gold-spired stupa constructed in 1804 and now the starting point for a lovely candle-lit procession on Buddhist-Lao New Year.

Wat Tham Phousi: Small cave temple with several Buddhist images.

Wat Pra Buddhapat: Minor temple famed for its life-size three-meter-long footprint of the Buddha.

Wat Xieng Thong: Luang Prabang's crowning architectural achievement and among the most striking monuments in Southeast Asia, the "Golden City Temple," constructed in 1559 by King Setthathirat, features low, sweeping roofs overlapping in delicate yet complex patterns—a high point of Lao creativity with magnificent interior mosaics, richly decorated wooden columns, and coiffured ceiling embellished with dharma wheels. Auxiliary chapels behind the primary *sim* house extremely rare bronze reclining Buddhas and royal funeral sanctuary carved with erotic sculpture and filled with a grand 12-meter wooden hearse.

Wat Visunarot: Reconstructed in 1898, Wat Visounarot is noted for its vast collection of museum-quality Buddhas dating back 400 years which collectively represent one of the finest arrays of religious art in Laos. Fronting the *sim* is Thak Mak Mo (nicknamed Melon Stupa), a curious Sinhalese-style stupa constructed in 1504 by Queen Visounalat.

Wat Aham: Constructed in 1823, Wat Aham served as the residence of the supreme patriarch of the Lao Buddhist *sangha* but today sleeps on, visited only for its pair of spirit shrines under courtyard bodhi trees.

Wat That: Built in the 15th century, damaged during foreign invasions, restored at the beginning of this century, and renovated in the early 1990s with a multilayered roof, *sims* richly carved with Ramayana legends, and pillars ornamented with *nagas*—a fine example of traditional Luang Prabang style.

Wat That Luang: Royal mausoleum constructed in 1818 by King Manthaturat for the holy ashes of King Sisavang Vong, father of the final sovereign, now interred inside the golden stupa.

LUANG PRABANG

MEKONG RIVER

KHAN RIVER

LAOS

TO VIENTIANE

TO VIENTIANE

TO BAN HUAY SAI AND PAK OU CAVES

TO AIRPORT AND MEKONG SPEEDBOATS

TO BAN PHANOM AND SANTI CHEDI

TO KUANGSI FALLS (35 km)

TO VIENTIANE (385 km)

TO WATS

NAVIGATION OFFICE (BOATS TO MUANG NGOY)

CROSS-RIVER FERRY

SMALL-CRAFT DOCK (GOOD BOATS)/ LONG-DISTANCE FERRIES

ECOLE DES BEAUX ARTS (SCHOOL OF FINE ARTS)

SMALL BOAT RENTALS FOR PAK OU CAVES (TWO LOCATIONS)

WAT PAK KHAN

WAT XIENG THONG

WAT KHILI

AUBERGE CALAO

WAT SENE

VILLA SANTI

VILLA SANTI WING

DUANG CHAMPA RESTAURANT

DIETHELM TRAVEL AGENCY

KHEMKHANE GARDEN RESTAURANT

BOUASAVANH

BANEHOUS

MEKONG GH

PAPHAY GH

PHOUNSAB GH

WAT CHOMSI

CARGO BOAT DOCK

PALACE MUSEUM

MINISTRY OF CULTURE/ UN HERITAGE HOUSE

MOUNT PHOUSI

LAO RED CROSS (MASSAGE AND SAUNA)

WAT MAI

WAT AHAM

WAT VISOUN

IMMIGRATION OFFICE FOR FOREIGNERS

VISOUN RESTAURANT

'NEW' PRABANG HOTEL

LANE XANG BANK

DARA MARKET

RAMA HOTEL

VIRADESA GH

POTELECOM

PHOUSI HOTEL

WAT THAT

LUANG PRABANG TOURISM

MOUANG LUANG HOTEL

MOTORCYCLE RENTAL OFFICE

VIENG GH

YOUNG KHOUN RESTAURANT

VILLA VANVISA

FOUNTAIN

HOTEL SOUVANNA PHOUM

VANNIDA GH

BOUN GNING GH

WAT MANOROM

LAO AVIATION OFFICE

NAVIENGKHAM HOTEL

NAVIENGKHAM MARKET

PHOU VAO HOTEL

STADIUM

WAT THAT LUANG

SINXAY VILLA

MALEE RESTAURANT

MANGSUA HOTEL

MANOLUCK GH

KAYSONE PHOMVIHAN MONUMENT

300 m

0

300 m

© MOON PUBLICATIONS, INC.

Right Bank Temples

Temples situated across the Mekong—accessible by ferries from the pier opposite the Royal Palace Museum—are modest structures best visited for their timeless settings and senses of remoteness.

Wat Xieng Mene: Small temple constructed in the early 20th century, about one km north of the old royal cemetery.

Wat Chom Phet: Peaceful hilltop retreat with scenic views over the Mekong.

Wat Long Khoun: Once a royal retreat for kings of the Lan Xang Dynasty, Wat Long Khoun includes an older section in the back, which dates from the 18th century, and contemporary additions from the late 1930s. Some of the modern woodcarving is outstanding.

Wat Tham: A limestone cave temple complex filled with ancient Buddhas carved in Lao, Thai, and Burmese styles, as were the stupas and religious decorations which adorn exterior balustrades. Bring a flashlight to explore the unlit caves.

Pak Ou Caves

Some 25 km up the Mekong River lies one of the wonders of northern Laos: enormous limestone cliffs and a pair of sacred caves studded with thousands of wooden and gilded Buddha images, some dating back hundreds of years. According to legend, the caves were discovered in the 16th century by King Setthathirat, who commanded local artisans to fill them with their finest works, though most of the images were donated by devotees or monks. Many are carved in the distinctive Lao attitude of the Buddha "Calling for Rain": hands downward and palms turned inward.

The lower cave, Tham Thing, is reached by a stairway which continues left around the caves to the upper caves, Tham Phum. Both complexes once served as meditation retreats for monks who shared their quarters with powerful guardian spirits. Today the caves are visited in April by thousands of devotees during the Lao festival of Pimai. Bring a flashlight.

Xang Hai: The upstream journey passes itinerant gold panners, yellow mats spread with Lao watercress, and the village of Xang Hai (20 km upriver), where villagers use oil drums placed over charcoal fires to brew *lao lao,* a potent but very tasty moonshine whiskey distilled from fermented rice. Most boats stop for a quick shot, but it's best to drink *lao lao* straight (no chaser) and not diluted with unfiltered water.

Transportation: Boats from the pier in Luang Prabang take about two hours to the caves, one hour down, and charge about US$20 for the 10-person longtail.

ACCOMMODATIONS

Luang Prabang has an acute shortage of guesthouses and hotels but new facilities are under construction and many of the older, existing residences are being converted into classy digs for new arrivals.

Budget

Several decent places at somewhat lofty prices.

Boun Gning Guesthouse: Fairly new modern house with freshly scrubbed rooms, ceiling fans, and shared baths with hot water and western toilets. 109 Thanon Souvana Phouma, tel. 212274, US$6-8.

Rama Hotel: Modern three-story 33-room hotel with clean fan-cooled rooms and a cafe run by Madame Sayavong who rents bicycles and runs a "discotheque" with live bands on weekends. Ask for an upstairs room. Thanon Visunarot, tel. 212247, US$8-12.

Vannida Guesthouse: Old colonial mansion, former home to a Lao prince, with simple rooms, shared baths, and spacious dining room plus helpful owners who can advise on trekking and excursions to nearby caves and waterfalls. 87 Thanon Souvan Phouma, tel. 212374, US$8-15.

Vieng Keo Hotel: Ramshackle alternative with fine balcony and 10 fan-cooled rooms at unbeatable rates. Thanon Setthathirat, tel. 212271, US$4-10.

Moderate

Mid-range hotels generally offer fan rooms at bargain prices and a/c rooms as priced below.

Phousi Hotel: Central location just south of Phousi hill with interior restaurant, garden cafe, and upgraded a/c rooms with private baths and hot showers. Thanon Kitsirat Settahirat, tel. 212292, US$35-50.

Manoluck Hotel: Modern Lao-style hotel with 30 a/c rooms complete with TV, mini-fridge, and private bath with hot showers. Thanon Phu Wao, tel. 212250, fax 212508, US$25-45.

Muangsua Hotel: Warm guesthouse on the fringe of town with 20 a/c rooms, weekend disco, and popular cafe. Thanon Phu Wao, tel. 212263, US$15-25.

Luxury

Upscale facilities are limited but new hotels are opening as Southeast Asian hotel operators enter the Lao market.

Villa Santi: Former crown princess Khampha opened this 18-room, 130-year-old guesthouse a few years ago after the property was returned to her by the Lao government. Today the villa reflects its French-Lao heritage with the tasteful decorations and cozy upstairs cafe in each of the two wings. Thanon Sakkalin, tel. 212267, US$45-70.

Hotel Souvannaphoum: Another French colonial mansion restored to its former glory with 20 spacious balcony rooms, two grand suites, and three junior suites finely furnished and overlooking a garden restaurant serving classical Lao cuisine. Thanon Phothisarat, tel. 212200, US$65-100.

Phou Vao Hotel: Swiss and French-managed modern hotel on the crest of Phu Vao (Kite Hill) in the eastern edge of town with a bar, restaurant, the biggest pool in town, and 60 a/c rooms; rates depend on view. Thanon Phu Vao, tel./fax 212194, US$50-70.

SERVICES

Tourist Information

Luang Prabang Tourism on Thanon Phothisalat, Diethelm opposite Wat Sene, Lane Xang Travel near Dara Market, Inter-Lao Tourism at Hotel Souvannaphoum, and Southern Lao Travel arrange package tours, visits to hilltribe villages, guides, rental cars, upriver boats, and other services.

Post Office: The modern GPO on Thanon Phothisarath, opposite Phousi Hotel, is open weekdays 0830-1700 but its service is not reliable; packages should be mailed from Vientiane or Thailand.

Telephone: International calls can be made from the new telephone office near the GPO 0730-2200; cash only, no collect calls. Luang Prabang area code is 71.

Transportation

Luang Prabang is 230 km north of Vientiane and can be reached by air, boat, and road (conditions permitting).

Air: Lao Aviation daily flights from Vientiane cost US$50 one-way, US$90 roundtrip. Arrivals must check with the immigration officials for necessary stamps.

Road: The Lao government has paved and officially opened reopen the road to Vientiane. Travelers should remain vigilant along this Route 13, as problems with rebels have occurred near Vang Vieng. The route from Vientiane goes to Thalat (two hours), Nam Ngum reservoir ferry (two hours), then Vang Vieng (one hour), where travelers overnight and continue to Luang Prabang (12-15 hours) the following day.

River: Ferries depart several times weekly from Vientiane's northern jetty and take 2-5 days to reach Luang Prabang. Cost is US$6-20 per person. Speedboats are your best bet.

PLAIN OF JARS

The Plain of Jars in Xieng Khwang Province (also Xieng Kuouang and Xiang Khoang), some 200 km northeast of Vientiane and 130 km southeast of Luang Prabang, is a remote and rarely visited region famed for its mysterious stone urns scattered across the valley near the town of Phonsavan.

Xieng Khwang Province is also known for its horrific experience during the Vietnam War, when an estimated half-million tons of bombs were secretly dropped by Nixon during his covert war against the Pathet Lao. In the end, over two million tons of bombs were dropped on Laos—more than the total America tonnage used during WW II, and the end result was the 1975 victory of the Pathet Lao.

Xieng Khwang's unspectacular array of jars makes this region rather unpopular, though the refreshing scenery makes the province a worthwhile stop for travelers with money and time.

LAOS

PHONSAVAN

Xieng Khwang province lies in a lovely valley pocketed with thousands of craters—a moonlike landscape among rolling ricefields. Phonsavan has served as provincial capital since the annihilation of old Xieng Khwang.

Phonsavan, pop. 6,000, offers little of interest aside from the weekly market and a brief visit to a small Revolutionary Museum, three km south of town near the Hotel Auberge Plaine de Jarres. Most military memorabilia has been transferred to Vientiane though the remaining assortment of flags, uniforms, cluster bombs, and photographs may interest visitors intrigued with local military history. The museum is often locked and open only to tour groups.

Plain of Jars

Scattered across the plains 12 km southeast of Phonsavan are several hundred immense 2,000-year-old stone urns whose origins and purposes remain an enduring enigma. Some say the sandstone vessels once served as funeral encasements for nobility and royalty, but according to Lao legend they were constructed by giant ancestors for the production and storage of potent rice-based *lao lao*—the popular firewater of contemporary Laos.

Many jars remain intact despite the bombing raids of the Vietnam War, but the ravages of times are quickly taking effect. Dangerous ordnance remains a problem and visitors should take care exploring the region.

Accommodations

Several simple guesthouses and hotels have opened up in Phonsavan to cash in on the hordes of Western visitors once expected to deluge the district. But *farangs* have failed to arrive in sufficient numbers and some guesthouses have closed or sharply cut their rates.

Dok Khoune Guesthouse: Homestay experience with friendly family owners and freshly scrubbed rooms. Route 7, US$3-5.

Vieng Thong Guesthouse: Decent rooms, nightly party scene, and helpful owners who arrange Plain of Jars tours with their sturdy Land Rover. Route 7, US$3-5.

Muang Phuan Hotel: Basic but clean place

with rooms and private baths. Route 7, US$4-8.

Phu Doi Hotel: An overpriced, sterile, and gaudily painted hotel a few km southwest of town near Aroun May Bank. Thanon Phonsavan, US$12-18.

Auberge Plaine de Jarres: Relatively new hotel five km east of town sited on a Mount Pupadeng ridge with panoramic views, cozy cabins, generator until 2100, and restaurant warmed by a crackling fireplace. Route 7, US$30-50.

Transportation

Lao Aviation flies daily from Vientiane (US$80 roundtrip) and three times weekly from Luang Prabang (US$60 roundtrip).

Travelers can reach Phonsavan by road from Vientiane and Luang Prabang via Routes 13 and 7, but the grueling three-day trip cannot be recommended due to rebel Hmong attacks.

East to Vietnam: Route 7 leads 115 km east to the town of Nong Het near the Vietnamese border over sealed roads in fairly good condition. Foreigners may be allowed to enter Vietnam through this back door with proper paperwork and written permission from Laotian authorities.

Getting Around

Transport is a headache. A few private Land Rovers exist for hire but you'll most likely need to contact a local tour operator and join one of their escorted jeeps around the region. Lane Xang Travel near the market charges US$30-45 per day for jeep, driver, and guide. Tours to the Plain of Jars, Hmong villages, and Tham Phyu cave can be arranged at Inter-Lao Tourism on Thanon Phonsavan and Sodetour Travel on Route 7.

Taken together, visiting the Plain of Jars is an expensive proposition—US$80 roundtrip airfare, US$30-45 for jeep escort, and additional fees for hotels and meals. Package two-day, one-night tours from Vientiane cost US$150-200 depending on the number of passengers.

PHONSAVAN VICINITY

Xieng Khwang

Some tours also visit the former provincial capital of Xieng Khwang, 40 km south of Phonsavan and home to an ancient kingdom which predated even the Lan Xang Dynasty of Luang Prabang. Famed for its succulent oranges and peaches, moderate climate (elevation 1,000 meters), and distinctive style of religious architecture, Xieng Khwang was almost completely destroyed by American bombers in the early 1970s, then reconstructed and renamed Muang Khoune by the Pathet Lao.

Xieng Khwang today has little of great interest aside from its outstanding location in a magnificent valley and the tremendous amount of war material (bomb casings, tank parts, fuselages) cleverly incorporated into local construction projects. Tours usually visit a small hillside shrine and the ruined remains of 16th-century temples.

Xieng Khwang (pop. 10,000) has several simple hotels geared to local visitors and the occasional Western traveler. The town is generally visited on a full-day jeep tour from Phonsavan, 40 km north.

Muang Kham

Western travelers are also allowed to visit the town of Muang Kham, 53 km east of Phonsavan en route to the Vietnamese border.

Devastated during the war, Muang Kham has since been rebuilt with an ingenious combination of wood, mortar, and the war debris collected from the Plain of Jars and the Ho Chi Minh Trail. Muang Kham itself has little aesthetic appeal but the journey along Route 7 is superb, passing splendid valleys surrounded by towering limestone karsts. Tours stop at war sites and a Hmong village where bomb casings serve as picket fences.

Tam Phiu Cave: About five km north of town is one of the most poignant reminders of the futility of war—a large cave where hundreds of Laotians were killed during the bombing raids of March 1968.

Nong Het: Nong Het (Haet), a booming trade town on the Vietnamese border and some 60 km from Muang Kham, possibly serves as useful connection point with Vietnam and theoretically allows an overland circumnavigation of Indochina—Bangkok-Phnom Penh-Ho Chi Minh City-Hanoi-Vientiane-Bangkok.

SOUTHERN LAOS

Officially opened for tourism in 1992, southern Laos remains almost completely unexplored despite its great natural beauty, lush valleys, remote plateaus, and a famous temple constructed by the Khmers. Southern Laos is one of the newest regions for adventure travel in Southeast Asia.

Southern Laos is opening up. Individual travelers can now visit Savannakhet, Pakse, Champasak and the nearby temple of Wat Phu, Saravan, Paksong, Sekong, and Attapeu on the Bolovens Plateau, plus the Mekong River attractions in the deep south. Best of all, visitors can now enter by land via several northeastern Thai town such as Ubon Ratchathani, a direct route that makes regional tours far less expensive and time consuming than a few years ago.

SAVANNAKHET

Savannakhet, the commercial center and provincial capital of Savannakhet Province, lies on the banks of the Mekong just across from the Thai town of Mukdahan. Savannakhet has become

prosperous and ruthlessly mercantile thanks to its strategic location on Route 9—the highway that leads from Thailand to Danang in Vietnam—and its large community of Vietnamese and Chinese traders who vitalize the economy.

Attractions

Savannakhet has a pleasant riverside location, active markets, and several important monuments constructed by vassal kingdoms of Vientiane.

Savannakhet Provincial Museum on Thanon Khanthabouli houses dinosaur bones discovered east of the city and documentation of an ill-fated American-backed invasion of southern Laos by Vietnamese forces in 1971.

Talaat Yai (Large Market) is worth a wander as is Wat Sayaphum, Savannakhet's oldest and largest temple, on the banks of the Mekong River. Wat Lattana Langsi, another prominent landmark, is due east of the successful Savannakhet Chinese School.

That Ing Hang, Savannakhet's oldest religious structure and 12 km north of city center, was constructed in the 16th-century by a contemporary of King Setthathirat and today holds title as the most venerated monument in southern Laos.

Accommodations

Savannakhet should be considered a transit point though stranded travelers can overnight at the following guesthouses and hotels.

Sayamungkun Guesthouse: Colonial-style hotel with hardwood floors, elevated ceilings, and clean rooms with Western baths. 186 Thanon Rajsavongsuk, tel. 212426, US$4-10.

Hotel Santyphab: The backpacker's favorite with river views and cheap rooms with river views. Thanon Chaleunmuag, tel. 212177, US$3-5.

Savanbanhao Hotel: Two-story hotel with better quality rooms popular with package tour groups and independents who can afford to stay at the headquarters of Savannakhet Tourism. 644 Thanon Senna, tel. 212202, US$5-15.

Mekong Hotel: An old French-constructed hotel with charming, large, and decrepit rooms popular with patrons of the downstairs hostess bar. Thanon Tha Dua, tel. 212249, US$6-15.

Auberge du Paradis: Restored French villa with garden cafe and refurbished a/c rooms with hot showers. Thanon Kuvoravong, tel. 212445, US$25-35.

Nanhi Hotel: Top-end six-story high-rise with Chinese restaurant, karaoke lounge, pool, and spotless rooms. Thanon Latsavongsuek, tel. 212371, US$35-55.

Services

Savannakhet Tourism in the Savanbanhao Hotel, Lane Xang Travel on Thanon Ratsavongseuk opposite the market, and Sodetour on Thanon Kanvoravong can help with information and organize tours but have little to offer the independent traveler.

Traveler's checks and Visa card cash advances can be arranged at Lao May Bank two blocks east of the Mukdahan ferry terminal and at Banque Pour le Commerce Exterieur Lao opposite the central market.

The Vietnamese Consulate on Thanon Sisavangvong issues visas for crossings at Lao Bao; allow several days for processing.

Transportation

Savannakhet is 550 km southeast of Vientiane, just across the Mekong River from Mukdahan.

Air: Lao Aviation flies daily from Vientiane for US$60 one-way; office at the airport south of town.

Bus: Buses from the northern terminal head to Vientiane (12 hours), Pakse (four hours), Ta Khek (five hours), and Lao Bao (seven hours). Travelers with Vietnamese visas can catch buses to Danang (16 hours), Hue (12 hours), and Hanoi (72 hours). Departures are early morning (0400-0700) and passengers should arrive early to secure a seat.

Boat: River ferries depart from Vientiane during the rainy season July-November. River shuttles pass from Mukdahan daily 0800-1700.

To Vietnam: Travelers with Vietnamese visas can take a bus from Savannakhet to Lao Bao on the border and continue the following day to Hue in the south or Dong Hoi in the north. Vietnamese visas can be obtained in Savannakhet, Pakse, and Bangkok.

PAKSE (PAKXE)

Pakse, just across the Thai border from Ubon Ratchathani, is southern Lao's largest town and an important commercial crossroads between Vietnam, Cambodia, Laos, and Thailand.

Pakse once served as the regional headquarters for French occupation forces who left behind a handful of faded colonial buildings, and later as an independent Lao kingdom under the extravagant tutelage of Prince Boun Oum of Champasak. Boun Oum left for France shortly after the seizure of Vientiane by the Pathet Lao.

Pakse serves as the launching point for visits to Wat Phu and excursions to the scenic delights of the Bolovens Plateau.

Attractions

Pakse has a lively market and two curious pieces of architecture.

Boun Oum Palace: Constructed in the late 1960s by the last prince of Champasak, Pakse's "People's Palace" lords over the city as a monument to royal megalomania and the sheer madness of unrestrained extravagance. Prince Oum, the final royal ruler in southern Laos, initiated the 1,000-room six-story monstrosity in 1968, but construction stopped with his banishment in 1975. Today the structure has been converted into a deluxe 60-room hotel with an enormous ground-floor ballroom, dozens of stairways, and a former sixth-floor casino that once outraged the local citizens.

Wat Luang: Adjacent to the Sekong River, the oldest temple in Pakse was constructed in 1830 but renovated in 1990 with well-carved doors and a reconstructed exterior plastered with all the gaudy touches so loved by rural Buddhists.

Ban Saphay: Small village 11 km north of Pakse known for its production of *ikat* silk weavings and temple dating from the Angkor period.

Accommodations

Pakse hotels are near Wat Luang and the bus terminal.

Pakse Hotel: Older yellow behemoth offering clean, fan-cooled and a/c rooms with private bath. 112 Thanon 5, tel. 212131, US$5-15.

Phonsavan Hotel: Basic hotel near Wat Luang and Xedone River bridge with spartan rooms and shared baths. 294 Route 13, tel. 212842, US$4-6.

Suksamlan Hotel: Fairly new hotel featuring 24 clean, a/c rooms with private baths and hot showers, plus a popular Chinese restaurant. Thanon 10, tel. 212002, US$12-18.

Auberge Sala Champa Hotel: A 30-room former French-colonial hotel with bar and terrace, huge a/c rooms filled with period furniture, and newer facilities without the air of Old Asia. Thanon 10, tel. 212824, US$25-35.

Residence du Champa Hotel: Modern hotel two km east of town near the bus terminal with spotless a/c rooms and a popular dining hall. Route 13, tel. 212120, fax 212765, US$25-35.

Champasak Palace Hotel: The former Boun Oum Palace has been converted into a 60-room hotel on the banks of the Sedon River. Route 13, tel. 212263, fax 215636, US$40-60.

Transportation

Pakse is 640 km southeast of Vientiane.

Air: Lao Aviation daily flights from Vientiane cost US$100 one-way. Weekly flights are also made from Savannakhet (US$45), Don Khong (US$35), Attapeu (US$25), Salavan (US$30), and possibly from Phnom Penh (US$40).

Bus: Buses leave daily from the Thai border town of Chommeck, 76 km east of Ubon Ratchathani and take two hours to reach Pakse,

52 km east. Buses or trucks also go to Savannakhet (five hours), Champasak (two hours), Salavan (two hours), Sekong (six hours), Attapeu (eight hours), and Vientiane (18 hours).

Boat: Boats to Champassak leave at 0700 and 1200 and take about three hours.

CHAMPASAK AND WAT PHU

Champasak—the nearest town to Angkor-era Wat Phu—served as a Cambodian outpost during the 10th-13th centuries and was later ruled by the Lan Xang Empire in the 15th-17th centuries. After the demise of Lan Xang, Champasak (also spelled Champassak) remained an independent kingdom loosely affiliated with Vientiane until the Pathet Lao victory of 1975.

Wat Phu

The archaeological site of Wat Phu, eight km south of Champasak, is the most impressive Angkor-period structure in Laos and among the most significant pieces of architecture in Indochina.

History: Although its early history remains murky, some historians surmise that Wat Phu was an important religious site in the 6th-century Chen La empire of the Chams, who, from their nearby base at Sresthapura, ruled most of the lower Mekong until the rise of the Khmers. Sresthapura (Cesthapoura), now an army base, is five km north of Wat Phu.

Archaeologists believe that the present temple complex was begun in the late 11th century by Khmer King Suryavarman II, who later constructed his far more elaborate Angkor Wat in Cambodia. As such, Wat Phu predates and possibly served as the prototype for the architectural culmination of the Khmer civilization.

According to legend, the Hindu-Khmer king situated his temple at the foot of 1,400-meter-high Phu Pasak mountain because of the presence of a hilltop stone lingam, the symbol of Shiva and centerpiece of the Hindu-Khmer pantheon. Today, nobody can find the lingam and it takes great imagination to see the mountain as some enormous phallus.

Even after the Khmers moved their capital to Angkor, Wat Phu (also spelled Wat Phou and Wat Pou) remained an important religious sanctuary financially maintained by the Khmers until the last days of their Cambodian empire. The hillside temple was swallowed by the jungle after the fall of Angkor but rediscovered in 1866 by a French explorer named Francis Gaunier.

Some say that the Emerald Buddha enthroned in Bangkok is merely a copy, and that the true image lies buried in the jungle near Wat Phu.

The Complex: Wat Phu is approached via a pair of complementary reservoirs which symbolize earthly domains and, more practically, collect water for local irrigation projects.

Beyond the reservoirs, a long processional walkway—once flanked by undulating *nagas* and statues of other mythical animals—leads to the summit and its remarkably intact pavilions, libraries, and sanctuaries carved with superb images of the major themes of Hindu mythology: divine *asparas,* Vishnu dancing on the Sea of Milk, Indra mounted on his three-headed elephant, and Kala, the Hindu god of time and death.

Wat Phu has suffered from centuries of neglect and the devastating effects of a monsoonal climate. Renovations funded by UNESCO and the United Nations Development Program will disassemble the collapsing complex stone by stone and rebuild it over a concrete base and an underground drainage system, a US$10-million project that started a few years ago.

Transportation: Wat Phu, eight km south of Champasak, can be reached by hired jeep, taxi, or cyclos for about US$6 roundtrip. Wat Phu is referred to locally as Muang Kao, or "Old City." Wat Phu can be easily visited from Pakse in a single day. Buses and boats head down to Champasak where taxis or motorized cyclos leave for the ruins.

Accommodations

A solitary choice, and it's overpriced; most visitors tour Wat Phu from Pakse.

Hotel Sala Wat Phou: The former Champasak Hotel is currently the only option in town with fan rooms at US$12-18 and a/c rooms for US$18-24. Ask for a steep discount or overnight instead in Pakse.

Transportation

Champasak is 34 km south of Pakse and eight km north of Wat Phu. Buses from Pakse take one hour and terminate at the pier just opposite

Hotel Sala Wat Phou. A more pleasant option is the riverboat which leaves Pakse twice daily at 0700 and 1200.

BOLOVENS PLATEAU

Spread across the borders of Saravan, Champasak, Sekong, and Attapeu Provinces is an immensely fertile plateau rich with coffee, tea, and cardamom plantations developed by French plantation owners around the turn of the century. In fact, the route from Pakse to Paksong is referred to as the "Coffee Road," though finding a good cup of coffee around here is almost impossible.

The principal towns are Saravan, 150 km northeast of Pakse; Tad Lo, 30 km southwest of Saravan; Paksong, 60 km east of Pakse; Tha Teng, midway between Saravan and Paksong; and Attapeu in the southeastern corner of the country.

The Bolovens Plateau is both a beautiful region and an ethnological gold mine inhabited by over a dozen ethnic minorities, most of whom arrived in the late 1960s seeking safety from American air strikes on the Ho Chi Minh Trail to the east. Among the larger racial groups are Katou, Tayoi, Ngai, and Suk, along with traditional stocks of lowland Lao Loum—the principal ethnic group in Laos—and Mon-Khmer descendants called Lao Theung, semi-nomadic inhabitants of the Annamite Mountains to the east.

Saravan

Saravan, the capital of Saravan (also spelled Saravane or Salavan) Province, lies north of the lovely, almost ethereal, beauty of the Bolovens Plateau. Saravan serves as an access point to the region and to river journeys down the Sekong (also spelled Se Kong, Xedone, or Sedone) River gorge to magnificent Attapeu Valley through one of the more spectacular regions in the country.

Saravan itself was largely destroyed during the war and has little of interest aside from the market and a handful of colonial-era buildings that survived the bombing raids. Nong Bua Lake, 14 km east, is famed for its freshwater crocodiles, while Tumlan, 40 km north, features old longhouses and traditional textiles.

Lao Aviation flies twice weekly from Vientiane for US$95 and from Savannakhet for US$40.

Buses from Pakse take three hours over recently improved roads. Most travelers head directly to the lovely riverside retreat at Tad Lo.

Tad Lo

Set amid the tropical splendor of the Bolovens Plateau, some 90 km northeast of Pakse and 30 km southwest of Saravan, Tad Lo (also spelled Thad Lo, Tadlo, or Thadlo) is the perfect antidote for civilization—a utopian wonderland of natural swimming pools, crashing waterfalls, and ethnic villages within an easy day's hike.

Accommodations: Tad Lo is primarily visited by escorted tours and remains somewhat pricey. Tad Lo Resort, a government-run collection of riverside bungalows, charges U$10-25 but the two-room bungalows are comfortable and the open-air dining room is a tropical classic. The place has a Land Rover for private excursions and can arrange crashing jungle tours on lurching pachyderms. Reservations can be made with Sodetour in Pakse, tel. (031) 212725.

Somewhat less expensive facilities are offered at the Saise Guesthouse across the bridge but the modest savings are hardly worth the effort.

Transportation: Buses from Pakse take two hours to the Tad Lo halt, 30 km southwest of Saravan, where a one-km dirt road leads down to the river resorts.

Paksong

Paksong, 60 km east of Pakse, offers waterfalls, gorges, and tribal villages set amidst spectacular landscapes.

Tad Phan Waterfall: A 120-meter waterfall—one of the highest in Asia—cascades a few km west of Paksong near a hydroelectric dam that provides much of the power for southern Laos. Another set of nearby falls, Tad Lo, offers refreshing swims beneath the 10-meter falls.

Ban Houei Houne: Katou villages are known for traditional *ikat* weavings made with old backstrap looms by ethnic Annamite minorities of Vietnam.

Tha Teng

The Tha Teng district, 40 km south of Saravan, is known for its bracing climate, temperate fruits, and villages inhabited by Alak and Katu minorities still following traditional lifestyles. Among the more accessible villages are Ban Khian, an Alak settlement of Austro-Indonesian animists who to a large degree continue to live in grass-thatched huts arranged in circles and follow social beliefs based on shamans, spirits, and animal sacrifice.

Sekong River: River rafting trips leave Tha Teng early in the morning and head due east to the town of Ban Phom (near Sekong town), from where boats sail down through a magnificent gorge to fabulous Attapeu Valley—among the most scenic water journeys in Asia. Escorted tours arrange these boats but independent travelers can often join if space permits. Contact Sodetour in Pakse or inquire at Tad Lo Resort.

Attapeu

Lao's most remote and geographically stunning valley lies inside the "Emerald Triangle" intersection of Laos, Vietnam, and Cambodia.

Attapeu, officially Muang Samakhi Xai and the capital of Attapeu Province, served as the center of the Attapeu Dynasty from the 15th century until the empire's collapse and Cambodian conquest three centuries later.

Attapeu (also spelled Attapu) was largely destroyed in the late 1960s, though some evidence of its rich historical past survives in nearby Muang Khao. Wat Sathathrat, a 15th-century temple founded by a northern Lao king has been reconstructed several times in contemporary styles. Other excursions might include Lao Loum, Lao Theung, Taoy, or Alak villages.

Lao Tourism operates a government guesthouse with basic facilities from US$5, while the new Attapeu Hotel has upscale lodging from US$25.

A fairly decent road connects Attapeu with Pakse to the west and Saravan to the north. Buses leave mornings from Pakse, Saliva, and Sekong while boats leave from Sekong during the rainy season from July to December.

MEKONG ISLANDS

At the southern tip of Laos, 150 km south of Pakse, the Mekong River reaches a breadth of 14 km during the rainy season—the greatest width of the river during its 4,000-km course from the Tibetan Plateau to the South China

Sea. The river splits into dozens of snaking tributaries which create hundreds of islands—hence the Lao name for the district, Si Phan Don ("Four Thousand Islands").

Attractions

Don Khong, the largest of the islands at 8 by 15 km, serves as the base for exploring the region. Khong Island itself can be toured by bicycle, while day trips to Don Khone (Khone Island) and Khon Phapheng Falls, 35 km south, can be arranged through Souksan Guesthouse and Auberge Sala Don Khong Hotel.

Khong Island: Muang Khong, the largest town in the district, has a few worthwhile temples as do the two small villages at the southern tip of the island. Anyone who wants to escape the rat race will love the island: no telephones, cars, and no electricity—nothing to do but stare at the Mekong, ride a bicycle, or hike between the picturesque villages. By 2000, the island is pitch black and everyone has gone to sleep.

Boat Tours: Boats chartered from hotels or guesthouses on Don Khong head downriver to Khone Island where passengers are given a few hours to visit Li Phi Falls and the old French Bridge. The boat then heads to the mainland town of Ban Nakasong, where motorcycle taxis race down to Khon Phapheng Falls. Keep an eye out for rare freshwater dolphins, endangered animals due to the widespread use of nylon gill nets and explosives for fishing.

Khone Island: French expeditions moving upriver in the 1860s discovered that the Mekong was impassable near Don Khone and so constructed a narrow-gauge railway line to connect the southern and northern extremities of the island. A few rusting hulks of abandoned locomotives still litter the yards near the northern stone bridge that looks like it came from France.

All traces of the railway line have disappeared but the bed now serves as the only road on the island. Hike or ride a bicycle south across three original railway bridges that pass over deep gorges—a scary crossing of rotting planks resting on rusted tracks.

Hang Khone village is home to the Lao Dolphin Protection Project, an organization created by a young Canadian with the assistance of European and North American environmental groups.

At the western edge of the island are the cataracts of Taat Somphamit, also called Li Phi Falls.

Khon Phapheng Falls: The most beautiful set of cascades, the "Voice of the Mekong," is due east of Don Khon near the mainland village of Ban Thakho. While nothing like Niagara Falls, the broad cataract intrigues kayakers, who consider it midway between extreme difficulty and certain death.

Accommodations

Muang Khong has several pricey hotels geared to package tours and one or two guesthouses. The Auberge Sala Don Khong and Souksan Guesthouse offer spacious a/c rooms for US$30-45. Budget facilities include the Don Khong Guesthouse near the ferry landing and a dormitory at the Souksan Guesthouse.

Transportation

Khong Island, 120 km south of Pakse on Route 13, can occasionally be reached with Lao Aviation flights from Pakse for US$30. Passenger trucks leave Pakse daily at 0600 and take five hours to Don Khong. Ferries reach Don Khong but only during the rainy season when waters are sufficiently high.

From Don Khong, Route 13 continues south to the Cambodian border, where Laotians and Cambodians are allowed to cross the border. Tourism officials have announced plans to open this crossing to Western visitors—providing a convenient link between Pakse and Phnom Penh.

The modern reader of travelers' tales is a cautious fellow, not easily fooled. He is never misled by facts which do not assort with his knowledge. But he loves wonders. His faith in dragons, dog-headed men, bearded women, and mermaids is not what it used to be, but he will accept good substitutes.

—H.M. TOMLINSON,
THE FACE OF THE EARTH

He who travels fastest travels alone, but he who travels best travels with a companion, if not always a lover.

—PAUL FUSSELL,
ABROAD

It's not worthwhile to go around the world to count the cats in Zanzibar.

—PAUL THEROUX,
THE GREAT RAILWAY BAZAAR

MACAU

Travel, for too long, has been trivialized in the popular press and by the promoters of popular tours; it deserves better. It is an enduring subject of human concern, the essential requisite for a civilized life, perhaps the most effective tool for reducing foolish national pride and promoting a world view.

—ARTHUR FROMMER,
NEW WORLD OF TRAVEL

Travel broadens the mind.

—ANONYMOUS

Everybody in the world is a little mad.

—JOSEPH CONRAD,
THE SHADOW LINE

INTRODUCTION

A plaque outside the entrance to Monte Fortress proclaims "Stop! Take heed! Consider briefly the beautiful history of our country. Enter proudly and hold your head up high because you are a citizen of that country." Since those words were engraved in 1622, Macau has grown from an Iberian outpost on the southern coast of China into a modern city with industrialized parks, housing estates, and ambitious landfill projects to serve the next century. And yet, to a surprising degree, Macau, the inner Macau away from the landfill developments, remains a sleepy Portuguese town of cobbled streets and color-splashed architecture—a delightful land of grand mansions, magnificent churches, and romantic cafes.

THE LAND

Macau is located on the southeastern coast of China some 140 km southeast of Guangzhou and 60 km east of Hong Kong. Over 90% of the population lives on the peninsula with the remainder residing on the southern islands of Taipa and Coloane. The land is hilly with little arable acreage; much of the reclaimed land has been covered with housing projects, casinos, recreation areas, and the new airport just off Taipa Island.

The climate is subtropical and monsoonal, with cool-dry winters and hot-wet summers. Eighty percent of the total annual rainfall occurs during the summer rainy season, when the southwest monsoon blows up from the Indian Ocean bringing typhoons and high humidity. Winters can be very cold. Best times to visit are early spring and late fall when days are sunny but cool.

HISTORY

Shortly after Columbus made landfall on the Americas and well before other European nations arrived in strength, the Portuguese successfully exploited the navigational discoveries of Prince Henry to secure trading posts at Goa (1510), Malacca (1511), the Moluccas (1521), and Macau (1557). Macau was their final link in the chain of ports which allowed them to control trade between Europe and Asia by circumventing the Middle East and breaking Venice's iron grip on the Asian spice trade.

MACAU

Macau was founded after the Chinese ended direct trade between Japan and China. Portuguese merchants, recognizing the profit potential, soon began trading Chinese silks and porcelains for silver from Nagasaki and spices from India. China awarded Macau to the Portuguese in 1557.

Many feel that Macau became a Portuguese possession not from diplomacy or military campaigns but from the efforts of Jesuit priest Francis Xavier, the St. Paul of the Far East. Xavier had previously converted thousands to Christianity during his sojourns in Goa and Indonesia and, intrigued by reports about China and Japan, left Malacca in 1549 for the Japanese city of Kagoshima, where he worked until 1552. Xavier then sailed to Sheungchuen (80 km southwest of Macau), which served as his temporary base while waiting for Chinese approval to approach Macau. Xavier died on the island but his efforts had a great impact on the Portuguese government, which supported his missions to Macau and China.

The 1557-1640 period was a time of prosperity for Macau but decline for Portuguese power in Asia. Against all odds, Macau residents resisted the Spanish Crown and supported the Portuguese monarchy, a show of allegiance immortalized by an inscription over the Senate entrance which reads, "City of the Name of God, There is None More Loyal."

But loyalty wasn't enough. Dutch and English forces seeking control of the privileged location initiated a series of sea raids on the outpost including a 17th-century Dutch attack repulsed by a motley crew of Portuguese sailors, Jesuit priests, and African Bantu slaves. Portuguese influence ended in 1638 after they were expelled from Japan and lost their lucrative China-Macau-Japan trade monopoly. Their China trade monopoly ended in 1685 after the Chinese emperor opened Chinese ports to all Western nations.

Macau sputtered along an opium trading post until 1847, when Great Britain established Hong Kong and the remaining traders in Macau moved across the harbor to the British free-trade port. Since then, this sleepy Iberian backwater has survived on gambling, light industry, and tourism.

GOVERNMENT AND ECONOMY

Government

Macau is a Portuguese territory administered by a governor appointed by the president of Portugal and his 23-member Legislative Assembly, 16 elected and the remainder appointed by the governor. Portuguese rule (over 430 years) ends on 20 December 1999 when the colony reverts to Chinese rule and Macau becomes a Special Administrative Region with the same self-rule and freedoms guaranteed to Hong Kong.

Economy

Macau's biggest industry is gambling with over 80% of the gambling revenue generated by the Macau Tourism and Amusement Society (STDM), a government syndicate that operates Macau's nine casinos and racetracks. Each year almost five million Chinese from Hong Kong and curious mainland residents from Guangdong Province flock here to test their luck. Macau's remaining one million visitors include North Americans, Japanese, Southeast Asians, and Europeans, mostly attracted by a colonial history spanning the better part of five centuries and evidenced in its ornate Lusitanian churches, narrow cobbled alleyways, and sumptuous local cuisine.

Macau also produces garments, toys, artificial flowers, fireworks, and electronic goods, generally by companies headquartered in China, an economic situation that accounts for much of the local diffidence to the impending takeover.

MACAU CLIMATE

	JAN.	FEB.	MAR.	APR.	MAY	JUNE	JULY	AUG.	SEPT.	OCT.	NOV.	DEC.
Avg. Maximum C	20°	20°	21°	23°	28°	29°	31°	31°	30°	28°	25°	20°
Avg. Maximum F	68°	68°	70°	73°	82°	84°	88°	88°	86°	82°	77°	68°
Rainy Days	4	5	7	8	13	18	17	15	12	6	2	3

MACAU

CHINA

CHINA GATE

LING FONG TEMPLE

CANIDROME

MONG HA FORT

INNER HARBOR

OLD MARKET

KUAN IAN TONG TEMPLE

LIN KAI TEMPLE

LOU LIM GARDENS

RIQUEXO CAFE

CAMOES GARENS

CAMOES MUSEUM

CEMETERY

RESTORED HOUSES

SUN YAT-SEN HOUSE

ST. MICHEALS CEMETERY

COLLEGE OF PERPETUAL HELP

ST. PAULS

MONTE FORTRESS

ESTORIL HOTEL

GUIA FORTRESS

JAI ALAI

GRAND HOTEL

ROYAL HOTEL

MACAU FERRY TERMINAL

FLOATING CASINO

RESTAURANTS

CENTRAL HOTEL

HOTEL GUIA

LONDON HOTEL

MATSUYA HOTEL

KINGSWAY HOTEL

SENATE

TOURIST OFFICE

ST. AUGUSTINES

METROPOLE HOTEL

BEVERLY PLAZA HOTEL

NEW WORLD EMPEROR HOTEL

MANDARIN ORIENTAL HOTEL

DOM PEDRO

ST. LAWRENCE

SINTRA PRESIDENT HOTEL

HOLIDAY INN

GOVT. HOUSE

O PORTO INTERIOR RESTAURANT

LISBOA HOTEL & CASINO

MACAU CULTURAL CENTRE

RESTAURANTE LITORAL

RESTAURANTE A LORCHE

PENHA CHURCH

MARITIME MUSEUM

POUSADA RITZ HOTEL

BELA VISTA HOTEL

A MA TEMPLE

GOVERNOR'S RESIDENCE

BARRA HILL

NAM VAN LAKES

POUSADA SAO TIAGO (FORT BARRA)

NAM VAN LAKE

RESTORATION

PROJECT

MACAU-TAIPA BRIDGE

0   500 m

© MOON PUBLICATIONS, INC.

MACAU

THE PEOPLE

Almost 95% of Macau's 485,000 inhabitants are Chinese, followed by Portuguese, European, and Macanese. Most follow Chinese religions, but over 20,000 Roman Catholics are served by a dozen churches under the leadership of Monsignor Manuel Teixeira. In comparison, the Macau police set the number of gang members employed in drugs, prostitution, and loan sharking at 30,000.

Until the turnover in 1999, the most politically powerful group after the Portuguese will remain the Macanese, locally born citizens descended from Chinese-Portuguese marriages and educated in local Portuguese schools. Macanese serve as intermediaries between China and non-Chinese-speaking Portuguese administrators and fill most civil positions that require bilingual fluency.

ON THE ROAD

GETTING THERE

By Sea

Most visitors arrive from Hong Kong by ferry, departing from the Macau Ferry Terminal in Shun Tak Centre at 200 Connaught Road, Central, Hong Kong—a 15-minute walk west of Hong Kong's Star Ferry Terminal. Ferries also depart from the China Hong Kong Ferry Terminal in Tsimshatsui, Kowloon.

Advance reservations are advised on weekends and holidays; roundtrip tickets avoid delays on return passages. Departure tax is HK$26 from Hong Kong and 22 *patacas* from Macau.

Transport choices include a/c jetfoils (one hour, HK$100-140, tel. 2859-2222), 400-seat catamarans on foils, or "foil-cats" (50 minutes, HK$110-160, tel. 2859-2222), 300-passenger turbo-cats (one hour, HK$90-120, tel. 2789-5421), and slower HK ferries (90 minutes, HK$70-110, tel. 2815-3034). Almost 90% of the crossings are made on jetfoils with smaller numbers by foil-cats, turbo-cats, and tri-cats. Jumbo-cats and high-speed ferries were taken out of service a few years ago.

Ferries from Hong Kong move through the crowded harbor past Lantau and Cheung Chau islands before arrival at the Macau Jetfoil Terminal,

also called the Macau-Hong Kong Terminal.

First impressions of Macau are uniformly disappointing—an ugly landscape of faceless concrete structures and sterile gambling emporiums. Don't be discouraged, the beauty of Macau lies in its backstreets and not the atrocious landfill projects that have largely destroyed the charm of the old Outer Harbor.

The tourist office at the jetfoil terminal provides free brochures and a very useful map. Day visitors can check bags at the luggage office on the ground floor. There's no need to change money since Hong Kong dollars are welcome in Macau at approximately the same exchange rate.

Taxis and buses wait outside the terminal's front entrance. Twenty-five of Macau's three, four, and five-star hotels offer free transfer services, while most other hotels provide free or inexpensive transfers on request.

Buses 3 and 3A head past Hotel Lisboa and down Avenue Almeida Ribeiro to the floating casino and Inner Harbor.

By Air

Macau's new international airport opened in 1996 on a landfill project just east of Taipa Island. The US$500 million airport is capable of handling all wide-body aircraft capable of making nonstop flights from Europe and North

view over central Macau

FESTIVALS

Macau celebrates Chinese festivals, Catholic holidays, and special events such as the Macau Grand Prix. All together it adds up to over 25 official and semiofficial public holidays. Most of the religious festivals are movable feasts dated by the lunar calendar. Exact dates should be confirmed with the Macau Tourist Office. Chinese festivals are described in the Singapore and Hong Kong chapters. Only unique or exceptionally popular festivals are listed below.

February

Chinese New Year: While it's a quiet family affair in Hong Kong, the Macanese celebrate the new moon with fireworks, revelry, and nonstop gambling. At midnight the STDM director ritually places the first bet at the roulette wheel and then steps aside for the gamblers who throw money away at a furious rate, since many believe this the luckiest day of the year.

March

Feast of Our Lord of Passos: A candle-lit procession in which the image of Christ is slowly paraded from the Church of St. Augustine to the Macau Cathedral. One of the finest festivals in Macau.

April

Easter: Macau's 25,000 Christians celebrate with special masses in the Macau Cathedral.

Birthday of A Ma: The namesake of Macau (known as Tin Hau in Hong Kong) is honored by thousands of pilgrims, who bring offerings of food and incense to her temple near Barra Point. Taoist priests enter trances and perform magic rituals and self-mutilation.

Procession of Our Lady of Fatima: A Christian festival that commemorates the miraculous appearance of the Virgin Mary to three shepherd children over 80 years ago. Church dignitaries and veiled children carry images of the Virgin Mary through the streets.

June

Camoes Day: The famous Portuguese poet is honored with a military parade and pilgrimage to his grotto. The governor holds a party at his residence. Also known as Portugal Day.

Feast of St. Anthony: A procession starts from the Church of St. Anthony.

Feast of St. John the Baptist: A statue of the patron saint of Macau is taken from the Senate Chambers chapel and paraded around the City Square.

October

Republic Day: This public holiday marks the founding of the Portuguese Republic on 5 October 1910.

November

Macau Grand Prix: One of the world's premier motoring events. For over 40 years, movie stars and royalty have come to Macau to watch the world's fastest cars race through the winding Guia circuit. Other events include the Classic Car Event for nostalgia buffs, a Super Car Challenge, and the Motorcycle Grand Prix. Hotel reservations must be made well in advance.

December

Procession of Immaculate Conception: This procession of clergymen, bishops, and church members slowly winds through the cobbled lanes of Macau.

MACAU

America. The airport handled 1.2 million passengers in its first year of operation, two-thirds on the Macau-Taiwan route and one-fifth on Macau-China services.

Air Portugal and Sabena Airlines currently offer three weekly 16-hour flights from Lisbon and Brussels. Services within Asia are provided by Singapore Airlines, Thai International, Malaysia Airlines, Korean Airlines, China Northwest, China Northern, China Southern, and Macau's new flag carrier, Air Macau (NX).

Airport facilities include tourist information centers inside the baggage claim area and outside the customs area at the arrival level, restaurants and cafes, banks, postal services, travel agencies, and baggage storage. The Macau Hotels Association (MHA) operates a service counter that makes reservations at its 40 member hotels, which include three-star (US$46-124), four-star (US$53-139), and five-star (US$57-240) hotels. The MHA also operates a 24-hour MHA Hotline (tel. 703416) with repre-

MACAU TOURIST OFFICES

Australia: 449 Darling St., Balmain, Sydney, N.S.W. 2041; (02) 9555-7548

Canada: 10551 Shellbridge Way, Richmond, B.C. V6X 2W9, tel. (604) 231-9040
　　　　　13 Mountalan Ave., Toronto, Ontario, (416) 466-6552

France: 52 Champs Elysses, 75008 Paris, tel.(331) 4256-4551

Germany: Shafergasse 17, D-60313 Frankfurt-am-Main, tel.(49-69) 234094

Italy: Maffeo Pantaleoni 25, Rome 00191, tel.(396) 3630-9117

New Zealand: P.O. Box 42-165, Orakei, Auckland 5, tel.(64-9) 575-2700

Portugal: Avenida 5 de Outubro 115, 1050 Lisbon, tel.(3511) 793-6542

United Kingdom: 6 Sherlock Mews, Paddington St., London W1M3RH, tel.(071) 224-3390

U.S.A.: 3133 Lake Hollywood Dr., Los Angeles, CA 90078, tel.(800) 331-7150
　　　　70 Greenwich Ave, New York, NY 10011, tel.(212) 206-6828
　　　　P.O. Box 350, Kenilworth, IL 60043, tel.(847) 251-6241

sentatives speaking English, Cantonese, Mandarin, and Japanese.

Chinese immigration formalities will be handled at the passenger terminal after Macau changes hands in 1999.

All major hotels provide transportation; this can be booked in advance or arranged on arrival. Taxis are plentiful, air-conditioned, and metered. The airport bus AP1 leaves just outside the terminal every 15 minutes 0630-2300 and stops at major hotels.

Departure tax is M$80 to China and M$130 to other destinations.

GETTING AROUND

The most enjoyable way to discover the charms of surprisingly compact Macau is to slowly walk the back alleys and quiet neighborhoods and take a few taxis and bus rides to reach remote sights or the southern islands.

Taxis: Macau's distinctive black-and-cream taxis are abundant and reasonably priced, though few drivers understand English. Surcharges are five *patacas* to Taipa and 10 to Coloane; no surcharge on return trips.

Buses: Bus and minibus lines operate daily 0700-midnight and charge a flat fare of two *patacas* on the main island. The fare is 2.50 *pactacs* to Taipa, 3.20 *patacas* to Coloane, and four *patacas* to Hac Sa Beach; exact fare is required. The Macau tourist office publishes a useful brochure on bus routes to places of interest, and a bus

route summary is included on their free map.

Other Transport: Mokes—small, rag-topped jeeps—can be rented at Macau Mokes across from the jetfoil terminal, but at HK$475 a day are wildly expensive and very spartan for the tariff. Avis is in the Mandarin Oriental Hotel. Pedicabs and bicycles are fairly useless on Macau's cobblestoned roads over hills and through traffic.

TRAVEL PRACTICALITIES

Visas
Visas are not required by citizens of the United States, Australia, Canada, New Zealand, Germany, England, France, and most other European nations for stays up to 20 days.

Other nationals can obtain visas on arrival in Macau for HK$100 (individuals), HK$50 (children under 12), HK$200 (families), and HK$50 (tour groups).

Tourist Information
The Macau Tourist Information Bureau (MTIB) maintains branches at the new Hong Kong airport, Shun Tak Centre on the third floor just above the Macau Ferry Terminal (tel. 2540-8180), and at the Macau Jetfoil Terminal in Macau. Additional offices are at the Macau International Airport and many of the major sightseeing attractions in Macau. The main office is at 9 Largo do Senado, tel. 315566, fax 510104.

Macau Travel Talk provides tourism industry news while glossy *Welcome to Macau* is best for upcoming festivals and cultural events.

The Macau tourist office Web site address is turismo.macau.gov.mo. Several of the more upscale hotels also have Web sites where visitors can make reservations, often at special "Internet discount rates."

Maps

The complimentary map provided by the Macau tourist office is adequate for most visitors, but map junkies might want to pick up *Map of Macau and Zhuhai* (Universal Publications), *Map of Macau* (Jornal VA Kio), or *Streetwise Macau* (Eric Stone).

Money

The *pataca* (Ptc, ptc, MOP, or M$), the official unit of currency, has 100 *avos* per pataca. The

pataca, or "Macau dollar," is pegged to the Hong Kong dollar but worth about 3% less. Merchants gladly accept Hong Kong dollars and visitors on short stays and those who do not intend to make major purchases should use Hong Kong dollars rather than bother to convert to *patacas*.

Telephone

The international code for Macau is 853. Local calls are free from private phones and cost one *pataca* from public pay phones. Phone cards can be used for both local and international calls. Important telephone numbers include:

Tourist Office	315566
Directory Information	181
Emergency	999
Police	919

ATTRACTIONS

Southeast Asia's most romantic collection of historic churches, villas, and temples is situated within a cameo-sized country so compact that determined walkers can visit most of the highlights in a single day.

The following tour begins with a walk through the southern section and then moves north to the Chinese border. Visitors with limited time should start center stage with the Leal Senado, St. Paul's, and Old Protestant Cemetery, then walk south along the Praia Grande. The northern areas are industrialized and less inviting than the central or southern sections.

Whenever possible, wander the back alleys and avoid the roads along the Outer Harbor which face dismal concrete monstrosities that have mushroomed over the romantically named but seriously flawed Nam Van Lakes Reclamation Project.

SOUTH MACAU

Praia Grande

Long the favorite subject of painters and poets, this elegant esplanade is flanked to the right by a procession of colored stucco houses with balustraded balconies, carved architraves, frilled iron-

work, and inked shutters. Some buildings have been pulled down and replaced with modern structures, but enough remains of this "Gateway to the Mirror Bay" to make this a memorable walk.

To the right lies one of the great tragedies of modern times—the Nam Van Lakes Reclamation Project—an ill-conceived horror show that destroyed one of Asia's most idyllic bays in the name of residential and office developments. To Hong Kong's expatriate community, who has traditionally regarded Macau as a languorous refuge for recharging tired batteries, the enclave's recent transformation from quaint, exotic backwater to interminable building site is nothing short of a tragedy. Let's hope the ambitious plan will result in improved economic conditions, but the flavor of Old Macau has unquestionably been sacrificed to the God of Mammon.

Government House

Just beyond the Jorge Alvares statue is the salmon-pink Governor's Residence, a regal structure constructed in 1846 by Jose Tomas Aquino, the Portuguese architect who also designed Government House, St. Lawrence's Church, and the hermitage on Penha Hill. Among the features are exterior Corinthian columns, an interior grand staircase, and a reception hall decorated with ornately carved furniture and hand-painted blue tiles.

Bela Vista Hotel

This Victorian mansion, constructed in 1886 by the English captain of the HK-Macau Ferry, represents the best of Old Macau: the unhurried pace, natural elegance, and love of simpler times. Once a funky old fleabag hotel with sagging beds and erratic showers (the author stayed here in 1979), the Bela Vista has been renovated by the Mandarin Oriental hotel group into an exclusive boutique hotel with eight deluxe suites and a memorable terrace cafe overlooking the wonders of Nam Van Lakes.

Penha Hill

Penha Hill's immense bishop's residence (the "Bishops Palace") and adjacent Penha Church were founded in 1622, when Macau reigned as the center of Asian Catholicism from Japan to India. Dedicated to Notre Dame de France, Protector of Sailors, the present buildings date from 1935 and have been painted an unimaginative shade of gray. Beyond the parking lot lies a replica of the Lourdes Grotto and a souvenir stall with a hand-painted sign reading, From here we can see the nice view of China.

Pousada De Sao Tiago

Now a luxurious hotel, the former Fortaleza de Barra served as Macau's most important defensive position from 1629 until the harbor silted up in the 19th century and merchants moved over to Hong Kong.

After decades of neglect, Nuno Jorge, a local Macanese architect, restored the *pousada* with great imagination into Macau's first boutique hotel, Pousada de Sao Tiago. Step inside the cavelike entrance to visit 17th-century St. James Chapel, dedicated to the patron saint of the Portuguese army, and enjoy a Macanese lunch in the second-level restaurant.

A-Ma Temple

A-Ma Temple honors Tin Hau, the Queen of Heaven and Chinese Goddess of the Sea, with Tin Hau dressed in Chinese bride costume with strings of glass beads covering her face. Behind the main temple is a brightly painted rock with bas-reliefs of the Fukien junk that carried A-Ma to

Macau. Walk up the Path of Enlightenment to Kuan Yin temple, dedicated to the Buddhist Goddess of Mercy.

Maritime Museum

Opposite A-Ma Temple is an informative museum on seafaring with a model of Admiral Chang Ho's ship, maritime dioramas, models of modern Macau ferries, remains of Dutch vessels discovered during the excavation for the Macau airport, sextants and chronometers, Chinese garments, and two junks used by school groups and tour agencies.

CENTRAL MACAU

Church of Saint Lawrence

Macau, established by the Portuguese as a trading post and religious center for the Jesuits and Augustinians, witnessed the construction of many European-baroque churches that were later destroyed by fire or insensitively reconstructed in modern styles—but not the Church of Saint Lawrence. Largo De Santo Agostino features finely proportioned European towers painted in a Mediterranean scheme of cream and white, terracotta panels, and a Chinese-tiled roof—easily one of Macau's most beautiful churches.

Saint Joseph's Church

A confusing maze of classrooms and chapels founded by Jesuits in 1728 faces Saint Joseph's Church, home to Macau's most famous historian, priest, benefactor, and walking encyclopedia, Father Manuel Teixeira—an amazing individual who has almost single-handedly recorded the Asian heritage of Portugal in his 100-plus religious and secular literary treaties.

Dom Pedro V Theater

This mint-green, neo-classical gem, constructed in 1859, served as Asia's first Western playhouse and has been recently renovated to provide theater services for the nearby Club de Macau.

Saint Augustine Church

Constructed in 1586 by Filipino Augustinians and reconstructed in 1814, this baroque hall (Santo Agosinho) features a tremendous baroque altar displaying a life-sized statue of Jesus—a highly

CENTRAL MACAU

INNER HARBOR

TO CHINA

★ LIN KAI MIU TEMPLE

CAMOES GARDENS

TAI SOI MIU TEMPLE
★ OLD PROTESTANT CEMETERY

RUA COELHO DO AMARAL

ESTRADA DO REPOUSO

★ ST. MICHAELS CEMETERY

PALMISTS ★

RUA TARRAFEIRO

★ ST. ANTHONY CHURCH

RUA TOMAS VICIRA

RUA DE SAO PAULO

RUA BELCHIOR CARNEIRO

HOLIDAY HOTEL ●

★ ST. PAUL'S RUINS

RUA DA TERCENA

MONTE FORTRESS

RUA DAS ESTALAGENS

● EAST ASIA HOTEL
● GRAND HOTEL

MACAU - CANTON FERRY
PENINSULA HOTEL ■

RUA DE MONTE

RUA DOMINGOS

RUA DO CAMPO

● HOI KENG HOTEL

FLOATING CASINO ★

AVE. ALMEIDA RIBEIRO

RUA MERCADORES

BUSES TO CHINA

MASTERS HOTEL ■

■ RESTAURANTS

● HOU KONG HOTEL

CANTAO HOTEL ●

ST. DOMINIC CHURCH ★

RUA FELICIDADE

● VONG KONG HOSPEDARIA

SAFARI CAFE ● ● CENTRAL HOTEL

● LONDON HOTEL

TOURIST OFFICE

ST. DOMINIC CHURCH

★ HOLY HOUSE OF MERCY

★ CATHEDRAL   BOOKS ■

LEAL SENADO ★

GPO ■

★ ST. AUGUSTINE CHURCH

DOM PEDRO THEATER ★

RUA CENTRAL

VILA MENG MENG

● VALAI VILLA

VILA NAM TIN

VILA NAM PAN

★ ST. JOSEPHS CHURCH

● METROPOLE HOTEL

SOLMAR RESTAURANT

■ BUSES TO TAIPA AND COLOANE

MILITARY CLUB ■

RUA ANTONIO

RUA DA PRAIA GRANDE

NEW RECLAMATION

SINTRA HOTEL ●

AVE. HENRIQUE

AVE. SOARES

★ ST. LAWRENCE CHURCH

GOVERNMENT HOUSE

■ ESTRELA DO MAR RESTAURANT

POUSADA DE MACAU

TO BELA VISTA HOTEL

BANK OF CHINA ■

LISBOA HOTEL & CASINO ●

SHERATON (PROPOSED) ●

0   100 m

MACAU

© MOON PUBLICATIONS, INC.

tropical Iberian architecture

revered image solemnly paraded through the streets during Lent—and Christ on the cross, as well as an urn containing the right arm of Antonio Coelhos. Saint Augustine's Square (Largo de Santo Agostinho) has recently been paved with a Portuguese mosaic of wave-patterned tiles and installed with green lampposts reminiscent of the gas-light era.

Leal Senado

Largo do Senado (main town square) faces 18th-century Leal Senado (Loyal Senate), a classically proportioned building with a simple facade and a delicately carved wood, tile, and stone interior. The Portuguese entrance inscription describes Macau as "City of the Name of God. There is None More Loyal," an acknowledgment to Macanese loyalists who defiantly flew the Portuguese flag despite 60 years of 17th-century Spanish occupation.

An image on the wrought-iron gates depicts Queen Leonor, founder of Santa Casa de Misericordia, Asia's oldest medical welfare institution, while a walled garden features busts of Camoes (left) and Governor Amavel (right), and lovely blue-and-white tile friezes of flowers, dolphins, and cherubs. The upper Iberian Senate Chamber features heavily paneled walls and massive wooden chandeliers.

The adjacent Senate Library, constructed in 1926 and modeled after northern Portuguese libraries, features two inner chambers of carved wooden balconies and elaborate teak paneling,

considered masterpieces of Portuguese wood-carving.

Largo do Senado

Macau's old public square appears European thanks to its central fountain, arcaded buildings, and Santa Casa da Misericordia (Holy House of Mercy), a white plaster confection established in the 15th-century by nuns to serve widows, orphans, and lepers—the oldest Christian charity on the China coast. The Macau Tourism Information Bureau in the mustard-yellow building can help with maps and brochures, while the GPO on the second floor has a small philatelic museum.

Rua da Felicidade

Macau's "Street of Happiness" operated as a red-light and opium-den district until the late 1960s when it was cleaned up after pressure from the United Nations. During those days, Ian Fleming, creator of James Bond, described it as "one great and continuous street of pleasure." The three-storied opium dens and brothels of old have been transformed into Macau's "Restaurant Row," located very near the garish Floating Casino.

After experiencing the nostalgia of the main street, wander side streets filled with vegetable stalls, old women lounging in the sun, cranky rickshaw boys, streetside barbers, schoolkids in neat uniforms, and Chinese herbal stores which are often masterpieces of prewar Chinese architecture. The best is Loc Koc Teahouse, a seedy cafe popular for early-morning tea, dim sum, thick rice soups, and bird fanciers who gather under the high, rare, turn-of-the-century Chinese ceilings.

São Domingo Church

São Domingo, a beautiful 17th-century baroque church constructed by the Spanish Order of Dominicans, features three tiers of Ionic columns, shuttered windows, and surprisingly large doors which lead to a pastel interior and multitiered altar that almost exactly reproduces the shape of the exterior facade—one of Macau's great architectural masterpieces.

São Paulo Facade

São Paulo, one of Asia's finest monuments to Christianity, fuses Occidental and Oriental religious motifs in the great wall, now surrealistic with doors and windows that reveal nothing but open sky.

The center top pediment features a bronze dove (the Holy Spirit or Dove of Peace) surrounded by the sun, moon, and four stars—the fixed moment for the Immaculate Conception. Just below is Jesus surrounded by writhing vines, the nine instruments of the crucifixion, pincers, hammer, whip, crown of thorns, lance, Roman flag, ladder, and an angel with the inscription INRI.

On the third tier is the Virgin surrounded by Chinese peonies and Japanese chrysanthemums, which symbolizes Occidental and Oriental faiths; near the Virgin are six angels flanked by the Fountain of Eternal Life, a Portuguese ship, and a ghoulish figure that represents temptations of the flesh. Below are four Jesuit saints—Borgia, Loyola, Xavier, and Gonzaga—and an inscription over the doorway that reads Mater Dei (Mother of God).

Behind the facade is a series of glass-enclosed excavation pits with bones of Christian martyrs and a small museum with archaeological discoveries made during recent renovations of São Paulo.

Fortaleza do Monte

Monte Fortress, constructed by the Jesuits to fend off anticipated Dutch attacks, survives today as a museum (the former weather station) with views over Macau and old cannons aimed squarely at the Bank of China. The US$13 million partially submerged museum contains historical artifacts from 450 years of Portuguese-Chinese contact collected from government, churches, overseas Macanese communities, and private collectors. Exhibits are arranged around the Bright Period (1550-1750), Apogee and Decline (18th-19th centuries), and modern history.

Camoes Gardens

Luis Camoes was a Portuguese poet whose national epic Os Lusiadas relates the achievements of 16th-century Portuguese explorers but also served as a biting satire of Portugal's rich and powerful bureaucrats. This literary scandal incurred his banishment to Macau where he held the dismal post of Purveyor to the Dead in China. A bronze bust of Camoes with two stanzas from his famous work makes up the center of the park, which is popular with old men who like to play checkers as well as tourist-hustling fortune-tellers.

The nearby 18th-century historic structure of whitewashed stone and elegantly curved windows is the former Camoes Museum; it once served as Macau's principal museum until it was relocated to more spacious and secure facilities a few years ago. The old museum, now Casa Gardens, once acted as the British East India Company's presidential palace.

sermon in stone

Protestant Church and Cemetery

A well-tended burial site for common sailors and distinguished politicians near the former headquarters of the British East India Company, the cemetery contains the tombstones of artist George Chinnery, Henry Churchill (a distant relative of Winston Churchill), Robert Morrison (compiler of the first Chinese version of the Bible), Thomas Beale (opium king), and sailors who died from tragic if peculiar circumstances—history via epithets.

St. Michael's Cemetery

This Catholic cemetery features the lovely green-and-white St. Michael's Chapel, fascinating sculpture, and tombstones capped with angels, virgins, saints, and "grandfather bones"—picked clean and arranged to dry on the chapel's roof. The Chinese crypts to the right are embedded with somber photos and plastic flowers.

NORTH MACAU

Tourist Activities Centre

The tourist center near the ferry terminal has several worthwhile museums including the Wine Museum, which relates the story of Portuguese wine with a display of over 1,000 vintage bottles and a Madeira sample from 1815. Adjacent is the Grand Prix Museum showcasing formula-one race cars that won the Guia Grand Prix and award-winning production cars and motorcycles from other world-class events.

A Macau City Museum and Macau Arts Museum will open soon, perhaps in the Tourist Activities Centre.

Restoration Row

Dozens of three-story, yellow-and-red-brick structures dating from the 1920s with Palladian-style verandahs and graceful balconies have been carefully restored—one of Macau's first efforts toward architectural preservation.

Lou Lim Ioc Gardens

The traditions of Suzhou are reflected in these peaceful 19th-century gardens that combine classical European architecture with Chinese horticulture, funded by a wealthy Chinese merchant whose Victorian home to the rear now serves as a middle school.

Sun Yat-Sen Residence

The "Father of Modern China" and revolutionary hero of the 1911 Revolution, which toppled the Ching Dynasty, is honored in this elaborate Moorish structure erected near his former residence in Macau. Sun Yat-Sen was born in 1866 some 30 km north of Macau, attended Oahu College in Hawaii and Hong Kong University where he studied medicine, and later worked at Kiang Vu Hospital in Macau where he wrote, lectured, and organized protests against the corrupt Ching Dynasty. Sun served as provisional president of the new Chinese republic and founded the Kuomintang, the party which continues to rule Taiwan.

Macau-Taipa bridge

MACAU

Guia Fortress

Situated high atop Macau, Colina da Guia provides great views from its 17th-century Portuguese hermitage and Western-style lighthouse constructed in 1865—now the oldest on the China coast.

Kuan Iam Tong Temple

Macau's finest showcase of traditional Chinese art and architecture is dedicated to Kuan Iam (Kuan Yin), Buddhist Goddess of Mercy, with statues of present and future Buddhas, Tin Hau, and Marco Polo, noted by his bulbous nose and curly beard. To the rear is a courtyard with a stone table and four granite stools where the United States and China signed their first trade agreement.

Mong Ha Fortress

Constructed 1868 to protect against Chinese invasion, the fortress is reached via a long summit walk which passes the red-and-orange Institute of Tourism Education, designed by Lima Soares, and finishes at the weedy fortress. From the fortress, enjoy views over the harbor, markets, and fireworks factories.

China Border Gate

Macau's old border gate, which served for over a century as the crossing point into China, was replaced a few years ago with a modern facility better equipped to handle the increased traffic between the two countries—probably a moot point come 1999. The old Portas do Cerco now stands as a humble entrance to a small public park dedicated to Sun Yat-Sen—an honor that may not be well received by Beijing in 1999.

TAIPA ISLAND

Taipa—once a sleepy backwater populated by a handful of Chinese fishermen and junk builders who commuted to mainland Macau on ferries and sampans—has changed dramatically in recent years with the completion of the first Macau-Taipa bridge (1969), a second bridge (1989), and the Macau International Airport. The airport opened in 1996 on an eastern landfill project that almost connects Taipa with Coloane. A US$300 million China-Macau World Trade Centre has been proposed between Taipa and Coloane Islands; it would provide an international trade mart and entertainment complex with 10 hotels and Asian theme park. The project would include a rail link to Zhuhai and Guangzhou, making Macau an important economic link between China and the Western world.

Landfill projects, bridges, airports, and proposed world trade centers have ruined Taipa as a remote escape for the weary traveler, but the handful of cozy cafes and historic sights continue to make the island a worthwhile diversion for visitors with sufficient time.

Buses to Taipa and Coloane run down Avenue Almeida Ribeiro, easily picked up in front of Hotel Lisboa. Taxis cost M$40-50.

Attractions

The knoll at the Taipa end of the bridge features the controversial bas-relief Macau Monument (Os Calhau, or "Unformed Stones") which resembles a jumble of falling walls carved in a hopelessly outdated version of social realism. Just behind the swanky Hyatt Regency Macau

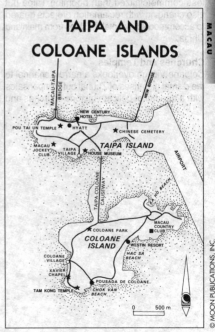

TAIPA AND COLOANE ISLANDS

MACAU-TAIPA BRIDGE

NEW BRIDGE

NEW CENTURY HOTEL

POU TAI UN TEMPLE ★ ★ HYATT

★ CHINESE CEMETERY

TAIPA ISLAND

MACAU JOCKEY CLUB ★ ★ TAIPA VILLAGE ★ HOUSE MUSEUM

AIRPORT

TAIPA-COLOANE CAUSEWAY

PA SA BEACH

COLOANE PARK ★

MACAU COUNTRY CLUB ■

COLOANE ISLAND

● WESTIN RESORT

HAC SA BEACH

COLOANE VILLAGE ★

XAVIER CHAPEL ★

POUSADA DE COLOANE ●

TAM KONG TEMPLE ★ CHOK VAN BEACH

0   500 m

© MOON PUBLICATIONS, INC.

MACAU

with its casino and restaurants is Po Tai Un Temple, a century-old Buddhist enclave that ranks among the finest in Macau.

Taipa Village deserves an hour or so to explore the narrow alleys flanked with peeling old buildings and religious structures such as the Pak Tai Temple, dating from the 1920s, and the century-old Lady of Carmel Church. From here, paths lead to the old Praia (waterfront) lined with restored Portuguese mansions and the Taipa House Museum, a re-creation of a typical early 20th-century Chinese mansion.

To the east is Macau Raceway and the requisite four-faced Buddha, which insures good luck, while to the west is the United Chinese Cemetery with a 10-meter high image of the Earth God and a sloping landscape of moongates and gravestones.

COLOANE ISLAND

Coloane, once the haunt of Chinese pirates, is less commercialized than booming Taipa but also changing with reclamation projects geared to accommodating container ships from mainland China.

Churches and Temples

Coloane Village overlooks a narrow channel to the dismal high-rises of Zhuhai but compensates with a handful of delicate historic churches and temples. Coloane square has been renovated with Portuguese limestone mosaics and cream-and-white cloisters that flank both sides of the nicely rectangular space.

Saint Francis Xavier chapel once enshrined the remains of Japanese Christians martyred at Nagasaki in 1597 and the humerus bone of Xavier, the founder of the Jesuit order who died on nearby Sheungchuen Island in 1552 while awaiting permission to enter China. No more. All bones were wisked away to São Paulo Museum when it opened a few years ago, but Father Ramon Manalo compensated by installing holy memorabilia and painting one of the alcoves with a psychedelic backdrop for the statues of Immaculate Conception and Immaculate Heart. Ramon, a fairly hip character, enjoys wearing T-shirts emblazoned Shalom Israel.

Tam Kong Temple on the outskirts of town features a two-meter whale bone carved like a dragon boat bearing the Eight Taoist Immortals.

Cheoc Van Beach and Hac Sa Beach are popular with locals on weekends but may be muddied by the Pearl River. The rec center has an Olympic-size swimming pool, roller-skating rink, tennis courts, and miniature golf course.

A final stop might be made at Lai Chi Wan village where a solitary boatbuilder continues to craft traditional Chinese junks without blueprints. Modern tools are used but body planks are still shaped over open fires and caulking is laid with traditional methods.

PRACTICALITIES

ACCOMMODATIONS

Macau has a wide selection of hotels in all price ranges; most are nearly empty during the week but filled on weekends with Hong Kong, Taiwanese, and mainland Chinese gamblers. Reservations are advised on weekends and holidays through Hong Kong booking offices and the hotel reservation agencies in Shun Tak Centre above the Hong Kong-Macau Ferry Terminal. Most agencies offer substantial discounts not available after arrival in Macau.

Budget—Central

Inexpensive accommodations are often claustrophobic, overpriced, and closed to Westerners since *vila, pensão* , and *hospedaria* owners fear communication difficulties with Westerners and prefer their regular customers of gamblers and young Chinese couples. Budget hotels are located in the Central district behind Sintra Hotel and west of the tourist office near the Inner Harbor—the place for the best selection and lowest prices.

Vila Nam Pan: The Nam Pan has fairly large rooms and accepts foreigners. 6 Avenida de Dom Joao, tel. 572289, M$150-220.

Vila Nam Tin: Clean and friendly. The small bright rooms have attached baths. 4 Travessa da Praia Grande, tel. 711212, M$320-400.

Vila Vai Lei: Friendly management and decent rooms at rock-bottom prices. 38 Avenida de Dom Jaoo, tel. 710199, M$160-240.

PenSão Nam In: Small but survivable rooms. 3 Travessa da Praia Grande, tel. 710024, M$220-280.

Vila Nam Kok: Bare-bones but adequate rooms. 95 Rua da Praia Grande, tel. 555523, M$200-250.

Vila Kam Loi: Almost friendly mangers and standard shoebox rooms. 34 Avenida do Infante d'Henrique, tel. 712561, M$200-250.

Vila Kimbo: Small, clean rooms. 57 Avenida do Infante d'Henrique, tel. 710010, M$180-240.

PenSão Ka Va: Superior location with well-priced rooms near the cathedral. 5 Calcada de São Joao, tel. 574022, M$240-280.

Holiday Hotel: Renovated building; not quite a hotel but with larger rooms. 36 Estrada do Repouso, tel. 361696, M$240-300.

Budget—Inner Harbor

Macau's least expensive guesthouses and hotels are west of city center near the Inner Harbor and Floating Casino. From the ferry terminal, take bus 3 or 3A to the far end of Avenue Ribeiro.

Cantao Hotel: Good location but noisy from paper-thin walls and open ceilings between rooms. 62 Rua da Guimaraes, tel. 922416, M$120-200.

Vong Kong Hospedaria: Moving downscale and less noisy with an owner who doesn't speak English but doesn't mind when you interrupt his mahjong game and walk up the tiled staircase to the carved cubicles. It's like a Charlie Chan movie set; you expect to find sultry women and old coolies smoking skinny pipes. 45 Rua da Lorchas, tel. 574061, M$80-140.

Vila Tong Nam: Another cheap dive with oodles of character. 31 Rua da Lorchas, tel. 937617, M$80-140.

Hoi Keng Hotel: Tucked away in one of the mazelike alleys, this is a decent place with slightly better rooms. 153 Rua da Guimaraes, tel. 572033, M$180-250.

London Hotel: Large quiet rooms with private baths in a rather strange location two blocks south of the Floating Casino. This is a real hotel with a lobby and dozing clerks at the front desk. 4 Praca Ponte Horta, tel. 937761, M$200-340. Big discounts on weekdays.

Diamond Hotel: Fairly new place with clean rooms. 11 Rua Nova do Comercio, tel. 923118, M$300-350.

Moderate—Inner Harbor

Several well-priced hotels are near the Floating Casino with hefty discounts during the week.

Peninsula Hotel: A newer 123-room hotel with clean a/c rooms, private bath, and harbor views from some rooms. Rua da Lorchas, tel. 318899, M$450-775.

Central Hotel: Macau's center of prostitution and opium was cleaned up in the 1950s and now offers somewhat shabby rooms but in a convenient location near Macau's sights and restaurants. 26 Avenida de Almeida Ribeiro, tel. 373888, M$250-340.

Grand Hotel: A 1930s-vintage hotel with clean and comfortable rooms opposite the Kam Pek Casino. 146 Avenida de Almeida Ribeiro, tel. 921111, M$420-480.

Macau Masters Hotel: New 75-room hotel overlooking Porto Interior with spacious a/c rooms still in decent condition. 162 Rua de Lorchas, tel. 937572, M$500-800.

Moderate—Central

Nothing competes with the gaudy Hotel Lisboa but many of the following hotels provide decent reasonably priced rooms near the gambling heart of central Macau.

Fortuna Hotel: Fairly new hotel with 368 a/c rooms with standard amenities, plus disco, karaoke lounge, and sauna. Rua da Cantao, tel. 786333, fax 786363, M$800-1,000.

Grandeur Hotel: Macau's tallest hotel topped by a revolving restaurant plus indoor swimming pool, gym, sauna, and karaoke lounge. 199 Rua de Pequim, tel. 781233, fax 781211, M$660-900.

Holiday Inn Macau: This trade name hotel has all the problems common to hotels in the area—rooms are perfectly adequate but the immediate surroundings are dominated by highrise quarters whose sheer ugliness cannot be adequately conveyed in print. 82-86 Rua de Pequim, tel. 783333, fax 782321, M$900-1,200.

Kingsway Hotel: Newish hotel with two restaurants, nightclub, and casino. Rua de Luis Gonzaga Gomes, tel. 702888, fax 702828, M$720-950.

New World Emperor: Reasonably priced 405-room hotel with shoeshine and lobby kiosk; however, it lacks a business center and swimming pool, and the "superb views of Macau's waterfront" referred to in the brochure are nothing of the kind. Perhaps to compensate for the infinitely depressing surroundings, individual travelers are offered 40% discounts on weekdays, 20% weekends. Rua de Xangai, tel. 781888, fax 782287, M$780-1,200.

Presidente Hotel: Full-on entertainment hotel with bar, disco, sauna, Café Cascais, and skylight nightclub. 355 Avenida da Amizade, tel. 553888, fax 552735, M$700-1,100.

Hotel Metropole: Owned and operated by the China Travel Service (CTS) with well-priced rooms, Chinese nightclub, and European restaurant. 63 Rua da Praia Grande, tel. 388166, fax 330890, M$550-900.

Hotel Sintra: Macau's favorite mad-kitsch Las Vegas icon offers a great location plus shows, bars, restaurants, casino, and coffee shop promoting well-priced weekend buffets. The East Wing rooms are far less tacky than the hotel's exterior might lead one to believe and ground-floor corridors are worked by teams of Russian hookers. Avenida de Dom Joao, tel. 710111, fax 510527, M$700-1,100.

Guia Macau: Remote location but posh rooms near Guia Fortress. 5 Estrada do Engenheiro Trigo, tel. 513888, fax 559822, M$550-950.

Matsuya Hotel: Another hillside hotel below Guia Fortress, recently renovated, with fine views from upper rooms. 5 Calcada de São Francisco, tel. 575466, M$550-800.

Luxury

Macau's top-end accommodations range from standard cookie-cutter hotels near the Inner Harbor to Portuguese *pousadas* and international resorts on Taipa and Coloane Islands.

Bela Vista: Perched hillside, the Bela Vista once ranked among the great, seedy, and romantic hotels of Southeast Asia with sagging beds, chipping paint, and undependable showers that dumped cold water on this travel writer in 1979. Today the hotel has been completely refurbished by the Mandarin Oriental Hotel group and offers only eight deluxe suites for well-heeled travelers. Pricey, but enjoy a cocktail on the verandah and gaze over the romantic horror show of Nam Van Lakes. 8 Rua do Comedador Kou Ho Neng, tel. 965333, fax 965588, M$2,400-4,800.

Hotel Lisboa: Macau's largest hotel-casino complex is also a tourist landmark because of its Las Vegas-styled roofline. Rooms are large, airconditioned, and equipped with color TVs; the favorite hotel for Chinese gamblers. Avenida da Amizade, tel. 577666, fax 567193, M$750-1200.

Pousada de São Tiago: Portuguese inn inside the ruins of the 17th-century Barra Fort, Macau's first boutique is in need of renovation but still a unique experience. Facilities include pool, restaurant, and 23 rooms furnished with Portuguese antiques and thick Chinese carpets.

MACAU

Avenida da Republica, tel. 378111, fax 552170, M$1,400-2,800.

Pousada Ritz: Modern, almost surrealistic hotel behind Bela Vista with spacious rooms, florist, indoor pool, sauna, restaurant, and service of Ritz standards. Rua da Boa Vista, tel. 339955, fax 317826, M$1,400-4,000.

Mandarin Oriental: Casino and top-flight amenities near landfill developments and bristling high-rises that threaten to obliterate the view of Guia fortress and lighthouse. Rooms are well-appointed and facilities include a business center, outdoor pool, health center, and five food and beverage outlets including Mezzaluna, an excellent new Italian restaurant. 956 Avenida da Amizade, tel. 567888, fax 594589, M$1,400-2,800.

New Century: Massive five-star 626-room hotel with ballroom, business center, massage, sauna, tennis, and five restaurants such as Caesar Terrace (grill) and Silver Court (Cantonese). Estrada Almirante Esparteiro, tel. 831111, fax 832222, M$1,400-2,800.

Hyatt Regency Macau: Mediterranean-style resort on Taipa Island with fitness center, sports facilities, restaurants, disco, casino, and decent rooms frequented by a loyal clientele of business and leisure travelers. Restaurants and recreational facilities are superb but the 326 rooms are neither large nor particularly well-appointed by current international standards. 2 Estrada Almirante, Taipa, tel. 831234, fax 830195, M$1,200-1,800.

Westin Resort: Farther out from city center on Coloane Island is this low-rise resort offering elegantly furnished rooms with smart bathrooms, large terraces, and the most complete sporting facilities on Macau—including an 18-hole, par 71 golf course. 1918 Estrada de Hac Sa, Coloane, tel. 871111, fax 871122, M$1,800-2,800.

RESTAURANTS

Portuguese-Macanese cuisine provides an exotic exploration into Portuguese, Chinese, and colonial cooking styles with dishes of hardy meat stews, seafood blended with tomatoes, potatoes, and olives, and fowl sautéed with prodigious doses of garlic.

Enjoy wine? Macau provides Portuguese wines, ports, brandies, sweet Mateus and dry Dao Vino Verde at exceptionally low prices. Bring a bottle back to Hong Kong. For daily specials, check local newspapers or wander Macau's "Restaurant Row"—Rua da Felicidade.

Macanese—Central Macau

As the 1999 Chinese takeover approaches, an increasing number of Portuguese and Macanese restaurants seem to appear, almost as a defiant last stand against the inevitable. Most of the following also serve European and Chinese dishes.

Café Safari: Central location near Leal Senado, established 1970, with set breakfasts and well-prepared Portuguese and Macanese dishes. 14 Patio do Cotovelo, tel. 322239, open daily 0900-0100. Inexpensive.

Afonso III: Busy cafe behind Leal Senado with daily set lunches and dinner specials. 11 Rua Central, tel. 586272. Inexpensive.

Fat Sui Lau: Fancy decor inside Macau's first Western restaurant (1903) but tasty Portuguese dishes at reasonable prices. Rua da Felicidade—Macau's original "Restaurant Row"—is a convenient venue to check out a variety of cafes and restaurants. 64 Rua da Felicidade., tel. 573585, open daily 1100-2300. Moderate.

Riguexo Cafe: This *very* basic cafe serves excellent home-cooked Portuguese lunches and early dinners in an odd location above Park 'n Shop. 69 Avenue Sidonia Pais, tel. 565655, open daily 1200-2100. Inexpensive.

Black Ship: A newcomer to the dining and nightlife scene with a cozy downstairs pub and upstairs Macanese restaurant with budget-priced luncheon buffets and weekend specials of Portuguese pies and stews, all served in an innovative environment at the edge of Penha Hill. Rua do Gamboa, tel. 934119. Inexpensive.

More Cheap Eats: The Venda de Cobra snake shop on Rua da Felicidade does a landmark business during the busy winter months, while inexpensive foodstalls are found on Rua da Lorchas near the Floating Casino.

Macanese—Outer Harbor

Many of Macau's oldest Macanese and Portuguese restaurants are situated along the curving boulevard that once ran along the historic Baia da Praia Grande. Although views have

MACAU

A PORTUGUESE MENU

bacalhau: codfish; the favorite seafood of the Portuguese

bacalhau guizado: Portuguese-style codfish stew

bacalhau a bras: codfish shredded and mixed with egg, potatoes, and olives

cabrito: grilled lamb served with chucks of peppers and chilies

caldo verde: potato puree with green vegetables sautéed in olive oil

camoroes: prawns

camoroes biri-biri: large crustaceans, peppered and barbecued over an open fire

carangue jos: crab

carne: beef

coelho: rabbit

feijoada: a traditional Brazilian stew of pork, spicy sausage, rice, and black beans

galinha: chicken

galinha a africanan: African chicken. Strips of chicken are marinated and spiced, then charcoal-broiled or baked in a *tandoori* oven. The classic Macanese dish.

galinha a Portuguesa: chicken baked with potatoes, onion, and eggs, and spiced with saffron, in a rich but mild curry sauce

minche: minced meat baked and sautéed with potatoes and onions

peixe: fish

Portuguese chicken stew: chicken in a delicious coconut and curry stock

sopa: soup

sopa de mariscos: seafood soup

sopa a alentejana: vegetable-and-meat soup

been largely sacrificed to the Nam Van Lakes Reclamation Project, the following cafes continue to offer unique dishes at reasonable prices.

Clube Militar: The pink-and-white colonial Military Club beside São Francisco Gardens has been exquisitely renovated and houses two bars and a restaurant, the latter open to the public with daily luncheon buffets and à la carte dinner selections. 795 Avenida da Praia Grande, tel. 714009. Moderate.

Praia Grande: Simple, elegant green-and-white cafe decorated with photos of old Macau;

it offers great views and unusual dishes such as seafood cataplana in clay bowl, mariscada in white wine, and sirloin fried in fresh cream and coffee sauce. 10 Praca Lobo d'Avila, tel. 973022, open daily 1800-2300. Moderate.

Solmar: Thirty-five years ago, Solmar opened on the Praia Grande to serve Portuguese expatriates and Macanese their favorite dishes in gloomy, well-worn ambiance. It's now cheerfully lighted, but the old paintings still hang on the walls. 11 Rua da Praia Grande, tel. 574391, open daily 1100-2030. Moderate.

Ze do Pipa: Rustic cafe ("Fat Chef") with mirrored walls and robust dishes such as stewed chicken livers and several versions of codfish favored by the predominately Portuguese clientele. 95 Rua da Praia Grande, tel. 372921, open daily except Tuesday 1200-2300. Moderate.

Henri's Gallery: Cozy restaurant fitted like a ship's cabin and known for its spicy giant prawns, baked African chicken, and Brazilian feijoada; much improved since Henri Vong returned from Canada. 4 Avenida da Republica, tel. 556251, open daily 1130-2300. Moderate.

Café Estrela do Mar: Near Henri's, this cafe serves up seafood, rabbit, and feijoada, but it's best to stick with soups and a bottle of wine. 11 Travessa do Paiva, tel. 322074, open daily 1100-2300. Moderate.

Bela Vista: A new chef has improved the food, which can be enjoyed in the antique-filled dining room or on the outside terrace. 8 Rua do Comendador Kou Ho Neng, tel. 965333, open daily 0700-1500 and 1900-2300. Expensive.

Macanese—Inner Harbor

As the Outer Harbor loses its atmosphere and views to landfill projects, many of the better restaurants to open in recent years have chosen the more scenic Inner Harbor toward A-Ma Temple and the Maritime Museum.

O Porto Interior: The first restaurant to open in the district combines Macanese home-cooking with upmarket decor. 259 Rua do Almirante Sergio, tel. 967770. Moderate.

Restaurante Littoral: Adjacent to O Porto Interior is another new, stylish Inner Harbor restaurant with Macanese and Portuguese cuisine served in the main dining area or the three private rooms to the rear. 261 Rua do Almirante Sergio, tel. 967878. Moderate.

Restaurante A Lorcha: The opening of the third stylish cafe in the Inner Harbor firmly shifted the focus of contemporary foodies in the direction of the old harbor and away from the aging kingpins facing the desolation of Praia Grande. 289 Rua do Almirante Sergio, tel. 313193, open daily 1200-1500 and 1900-2300. Moderate to Expensive.

Os Gatos: Macau's colonial-period Portuguese inn recently converted its cafe, bar, and terrace restaurant from French to Mediterranean style with an open kitchen, Italian ovens, white-marble counter, and dishes from Spain, Provence, Italy, Greece, and Portugal. Pousada de São Tiago, Avenida da Republica, tel. 968686. Moderate to Expensive.

Other Asian

Macau is known for its Macanese and Portuguese restaurants but other Asian specialties are provided at the following cafes.

Long Kei: Old Cantonese cafe with 359 dishes in the center of town near Leal Senado. 7 Largo do Leal Senado, tel. 573970, open daily 1100-2300. Inexpensive.

Nova Koka: Thai cafe catering to massage girls and other ladies working the prostitution rackets of Macau. Restaurante Thai on Rua Abreu Nunes and Bangkok Pochana at 31 Rua Ferreira do Amaral are similar—slow in the early evening but packed after 0200. 21 Rua Ferreira do Amaral, tel. 573288, open daily 1200-0600. Inexpensive.

Krauatheque: Another Thai cafe near Hotel Royal that, late at night, turns into a slightly made disco packed with roving Thai and Filipino girls. 11 Rua Henrique de Macedo, tel. 330448, open daily 1200-0600. Inexpensive.

Tropical House: Appears to be a juice bar but it's actually a Filipino restaurant on a street rapidly becoming an important food center for inexpensive ethnic cuisines. Dishes include Filipino pork sausages, lumpia, noodle dishes, and pork adobo. Travessa de São Domingos. Inexpensive.

Coloane Island

Macau's best Portuguese cafes and restaurants are considered those on the outer islands of Taipa and Coloane, with the latter island claiming the culinary crown. Taipa has suffered greatly from the new airport and other developments designed to make it the transportation capital of southern China.

Fernando's: Celebrated cafe that still knocks the socks off most other restaurants in the territory—and at rock-bottom prices. Try the signature clams in spicy black-bean sauce, spinach and sausage soup, grilled sardines, roast chicken, and pork knuckle stew with sausages and broad beans. 9 Praia Hac Sa, tel. 328531, open daily 1200-2130. Inexpensive.

Restaurante Cacarola: A charming dollhouse setting with rattan furniture, flower-sprigged curtains, and old wooden rafters painted a patriotic Portuguese green. Outstanding daily specials prepared by owners Mario Vale and his wife Luisa. 8 Rua das Gaivotas, tel. 882226, open daily 1230-2300. Moderate.

Balichao: Named after Macau's spicy shrimp paste but serving Portuguese and European dishes in a peaceful setting near the aviary of Coloane municipal park. Parque de Seac Pai Van Coloane, tel. 870098, open daily 1200-2300. Moderate.

Lord Stow's Bakery: Traditional Portuguese *pastelaria* run by an expatriate Englishman—an eccentric encounter on the edge of southern China. 1 Rua da Tassara, tel. 882534. Inexpensive.

Ven On Shop: Not really a cafe but rather an Aladdin's Cave crammed with toys, canned foods, swimming goggles, sweets, and an amazing selection of wines, ports, brandies, and liquors individually labeled by Mr. Veng On, who will provide a beautiful calligraphy receipt for your purchase upon request. Take your bottle to the beach and enjoy. Coloane Village.

NIGHTLIFE

Perhaps it was *Macau* the movie or the writings of Ian Fleming that glamorized Macau as a world of brothels, opium dens, and international spies but today nothing could be further from the truth. Aside from a few spiritless casinos, Macau is a fairly sleepy town best enjoyed after dusk with a bottle of vino in a quiet Portuguese cafe—not half bad.

Pubs

A few pubs have recently opened to provide locals and visitors with post-sunset diversions. None are very stable and may be closed/moved/abandoned by the time you arrive.

Pyretu's African Bar: Funky, lively, watering hole about five minutes by taxi from city center. Rua de Pedro Coutinho, tel. 581063.

Talker Pub: Another late-starting, in-vogue gathering spot for a handful of expatriates and the odd Western visitor. Rua de Pedro Coutinho, tel. 528975.

Black Ship: A few minutes walk from Leal Senado Square is a cozy, friendly pub with draft beer and weekend entertainment. Rua do Gamboa, tel. 934119.

Jazz Club: Jazz in Macau may not last but for the moment there's a small jazz venue tucked away in an alley behind Government House and Saint Lazarus Church. Rua da Alabardas, tel. 596014.

Adult Entertainment

Racy girlie shows are rather tame but a great deal of seedy activities take place in the massage parlors and Thai/Filipino cafes scattered around Hotel Royal on Estrade da Victoria.

Crazy Paris Show: Nightly Las Vegas-style revue staged by European dancers clad in little more than glitter and gold. Hotel Lisboa, tel. 377666, nightly at 2000 and 2130, M$200-250.

Skylight Nightclub: Low-key cabaret show followed by disco and dancing in the skylight lounge. Hotel Presidente, Avenida da Amizade, tel. 553888.

Massage: Thai and Filipino hostesses work those tired muscles in the massage parlors of the Lisboa, Sintra, and Estoril Hotels.

Snyper Bar: A pick-up joint run by a former soldier from the African wars. Calcada do Gaio.

Krautheque: This Thai cafe transforms later into a disco with roving Thai and Filipino prostitutes. 11 Rua Henrique de Macedo.

Gambling

Macau's casinos, greyhounds, harness racing, and jai alai annually bring in over US$500 mil-

lion—all controlled by Sociedade De Turismo e Diversoes de Macau (STDM), a government-licensed gambling syndicate which operates hotels, runs the world's largest fleet of hydrofoils, and largely supports the government of Macau. Profits are funneled back into social and welfare projects, low-income housing schemes, entertainment ventures, bridges, airports, and translating volumes of Portuguese laws into Chinese.

Casinos: Forget about extravagant architecture, glamorous crowds, and elegant shows—Macau's nine casinos are utilitarian structures filled with gamblers dressed in soiled sweaters and sloppy sports jackets whether at the 24-hour Hotel Lisboa casino or the luxurious casino in the Mandarin Oriental Hotel. Moving downscale, try the ornately decorated Floating Casino or Kam Pek Casino where upstairs gamblers once used wicker baskets to lower their bets and ignored the sign, Only risk what you can afford to lose.

Macau's casinos have Western games (blackjack, roulette, and slots—called "hungry tigers" by the Chinese), and Chinese games such as *fantan,* an extraordinarily simple and boring game played with a pile of porcelain buttons, and *dai sui,* (big and small), an equally obvious game played with three dice that relies more on luck than skill.

A word of warning. Macau casinos are home to professional card sharks who prey on Japanese and Western tourists who don't understand the odds: rather than the standard deck, a 40-card deck is used with twos, threes, and fours removed; the fewer cards guarantee higher hands and encourage amateurs to seriously overestimate the value of their hands. Poker is played for table stakes, making it easy for well-financed professionals with enormous arsenals of cash to easily force underfinanced amateurs to fold. And surly croupiers who encourage gamblers to make foolish bets often extort or automatically collect tips from winners.

Horse Racing: Punters gather at Taipa's 18,000-seat Macau Jockey Club (MJC) twice weekly starting at 1330 during the racing season, which now runs year-round with a one-month break. The season was recently expanded to help the MJC compete with Hong Kong racing tracks and it appears the strategy may finally help put MJC in better financial shape.

Greyhound Racing: The Canidrome features four weekly events starting at 2000 September-June. Computerized totalisators handle quinellas, trifectas, and six-ups bets. Foreign visitors can show their passport at the entrance and gain not only free admittance but also a complimentary beer according to chief manager Danny Osmund.

A journey is a person in itself; no two are alike. And all plans, safeguards, policies and coercion are fruitless. We find after years of struggle that we do not take a trip; a trip takes us.
—JOHN STEINBECK

I dislike feeling at home when I am abroad.
—GEORGE BERNARD SHAW

For my part, I travel not to go anywhere, but to go. I travel for travel's sake. The great affair is to move.
—ROBERT LOUIS STEVENSON

MACAU

MALAYSIA

Travel is fatal to prejudice, bigotry, and narrow-mindedness, and many of our people need it sorely on these accounts. Broad, wholesome, charitable views of men and things cannot be acquired by vegetating in one little corner of the earth all one's lifetime.

—MARK TWAIN,
THE INNOCENTS ABROAD

A good traveler is one who does not know where he is going to, and a perfect traveler does not know where he came from.

—LIN YU TANG

If you reject the food, ignore the customs, fear the religion and avoid the people, you might better stay home.

—JAMES MICHENER

INTRODUCTION

Perhaps it was the literature of Conrad or Maugham, Kipling or Wallace, or those old British films that formed our images of Malaysia: an exotic land of thick jungle and tropical rainforest filled with aboriginal headhunters, murderous pirates, man-eating tigers, and shaggy orangutans; a romantic crossroads of Asian trade lanes where White Rajahs sipped their evening *stengahs* on the edge of immense rubber plantations; an intoxicating colonial empire of ambitious traders, rugged planters, tin miners, sailors, government servants, and British administrators. While these early stories tell of a Malaysia now largely transformed by the West, the impression remains of a tropical hideaway full of adventure and excitement.

This reputation as an exotic destination attracts increasing numbers of Western tourists each year, yet Malaysia is also one of Southeast Asia's most affluent and progressive countries. The signs are everywhere. City youngsters are more interested in trendy fashions and progressive rock than top spinning or hand-stamped batik. A highway of American standards stretches along the west coast from Singapore to the edge of Thailand. And the steel-and-glass city of Kuala Lumpur hardly differs from Munich or Los Angeles.

While this modernization has watered down some of Malaysia's primitive appeal, it has also brought a well-ordered transportation system, excellent hotels, clean restaurants, and (wonder of wonders) tap water you can safely drink. Malaysia is exotic but comfortable, a delightful change after the poverty and rigors of travel in other Asian countries. Although the country admittedly offers few impressive temples or historic monuments, a great deal of traditional culture survives through the spectacular festivals of the Indian, Chinese, and Malay communities.

Malaysia is also a land of great natural beauty, from expansive national parks and river journeys to tropical jungles and deserted beaches. Beyond all these superb attractions, Malaysia has terrific food, classic architecture in the west coast cities, and a unique multiracial community which makes the country a fascinating political and social destination.

THE LAND

Situated in the very heart of Southeast Asia, Malaysia is geographically divided into two basic

RAINFALL IN MALAYSIA

Amounts are given in millimeters.

	JAN.	FEB.	MAR.	APR.	MAY	JUNE	JULY	AUG.	SEPT.	OCT.	NOV.	DEC.
Kuala Lumpur	168	145	213	302	179	129	112	132	167	270	259	225
Malacca	89	100	138	182	164	176	182	177	209	216	237	142
Penang	67	93	139	214	248	177	203	231	344	375	251	107
Kota Bharu	171	60	85	845	116	134	152	164	192	298	677	588
Kuantan	318	167	155	175	189	163	157	177	226	276	326	590
Kota Kinabalu	139	66	71	118	209	317	273	262	305	336	297	240
Kuching	664	532	334	289	256	200	191	209	274	335	339	466

areas: Peninsular Malaysia, the thin but bulbous piece of land that fattens out like one of Popeye's arms before being joined by the Johor Causeway to the island nation of Singapore, and East Malaysia, almost 1,000 km to the east. East (or Insular) Malaysia includes Sabah and Sarawak, the two Malaysian states which share the tropical island of Borneo with the Indonesian state of Kalimantan. Most of the country, except for the alluvial plain on the west coast of the peninsula, is mountainous and covered with tropical jungle. Although it appears to be a gigantic nation, Malaysia actually covers a total land area only slightly larger than New Mexico, or England without Wales.

Flora

As you might expect in a tropical land located between one and seven degrees north of the equator, the flora of Malaysia is luxurious and abundant. Dense tropical forests, estimated to be over 100 million years old, cover almost half the country. Among the 15,000 different species of plants which thrive in Malaysian jungles are over 5,000 kinds of trees, including prized hardwoods such as ebony, teak, and sandalwood. The most flamboyant flora are the flowering trees such as flame of the forest *(Delonix regia)* from Madagascar and the tulip tree *(Spathodea campanulata)* from West Africa.

Because of its immense forest reserves and aggressive logging policies, Malaysia is now one of the world's largest exporters of tropical hardwood. But as in Indonesia, Thailand, and the Philippines, the hardwood forests of Malaysia have been felled at a breathless—even reckless—pace. Environmental groups such as Friends of the Earth and senior officials in the Malaysian Forestry

Department claim that, at present rates of logging, most of the country's tropical rainforests will be gone by the year 2020. Allocation of timber concessions is a jealously guarded source of political and economic patronage, and unless international diplomacy can turn the tide, it appears certain that Malaysia will end up like the Philippines, a once-timber-rich country stripped of trees and now forced to import finished wood products.

Climate

Malaysia has a typical tropical climate with high temperatures, extreme humidity, and heavy rainfall during the two monsoon seasons. Total annual rainfall is relatively evenly distributed throughout the year, since the climate is somewhat moderated by the Indonesian island of Sumatra. The southwest monsoon from June to September brings intermittent but light rains to the west coast of Peninsular Malaysia. The northeast monsoon from November to February brings heavy rains and strong winds to the east coast. Roads and bridges are often washed out and week-long delays are commonplace. Check the weather forecasts and move to the west coast when rains become oppressive.

HISTORY

Due to its important geographical position on the trade lanes between Asia and Europe, Malaysia has been inundated by waves of conquerors, traders, and colonialists during its long and complicated history. First on the scene were the dark-skinned and kinky-haired Negritos who still live in the jungles of Peninsular Malaysia. These indigenous people were driven from the lowlands into the interior forest by Proto-Malays from southern China who arrived several millenia before Christ. Deutero-Malays, a more advanced people, arrived next, bringing their Iron and Bronze Age culture to the peninsula before continuing southward toward the Indonesian archipelago. These groups eventually merged to form the modern Malay communities of Indonesia, the Philippines, and Malaysia.

Malaysia entered recorded history during the early Christian Era, when much of Southeast Asia came under the influence of Indianized kingdoms such as the Dravidian states in Southern India and the Funanese Empire in the lower Mekong Delta. The decline and breakup of Funan in the 6th century led to the rise of the Mon Dvaravati Kingdom in Thailand and, more importantly to the history of Malaysia, the maritime empire of Srivijaya, centered near Palembang on Sumatra. Influenced by India but also

© MOON PUBLICATIONS, INC.

SIGHTSEEING HIGHLIGHTS

Malaysia's Tourist Development Corporation divides the country into four specific regions: Kuala Lumpur/Malacca, Penang/Langkawi, the east coast, and Sabah/Sarawak. A better division would be west coast, east coast, and Sabah/Sarawak, since most travelers arriving from Singapore or Thailand are limited by time constraints to one or possibly two of the three.

West Coast

Malaysia's most highly developed region is characterized by modern cities, efficient expressways, and a hard-working Chinese population intent on improving their financial standing. Penang is the most fascinating stop on the west coast, but other highlights include exploring the historic town of Malacca and the vibrant capital of Kuala Lumpur, relaxing at the former British hill resort of Cameron Highlands, and trekking through the rainforest of Taman Negara National Park.

Kuala Lumpur: Spruced up several years ago for an international travel symposium, the cosmopolitan city of Kuala Lumpur (KL) now resembles the futuristic but architecturally diverse city of Singapore. Highlights include the National Museum (perhaps the finest in all of Southeast Asia), Moorish architecture left behind by the British, spectacular modern architecture, and a vibrant Chinatown that becomes a fascinating street bazaar at sunset. Kuala Lumpur is a compact town that can be easily toured in a day or two.

Malacca: Melaka (Malaysian spelling), historical capital of Malaysia, has been occupied since the 15th century by Portuguese, Dutch, and British forces who left behind a selection of worthwhile forts and churches. Although the modern city has little charm, the old quarters' nostalgic architecture and sense of intimacy makes Malacca a worthwhile stop between Singapore and Kuala Lumpur.

Beaches: West coast islands such as Pulau Langkawi and Pulau Pangkor are attractive and have decent beaches, but hotel facilities, restaurants, and nightlife are better on the islands of southern Thailand. On the other hand, Langkawi is recommended for those visitors who seek solitude and want to get somewhat off the beaten track.

Cameron Highlands: Offering a pleasant escape from the oppressive heat of the coastal lowlands, Cameron and other former British hill resorts are ideal places to relax, read a good book, and wander through tea plantations. Cameron is the largest and most scenic of Malaysia's four hill resorts.

Taman Negara National Park: Situated midway between the coasts and accessible from Kuala Lumpur, Singapore, or Kuantan on the east coast, Malaysia's largest and most popular park offers river excursions, jungle trekking, and wildlife observatories. Tigers and wild elephants are rarely seen these days, although it's perhaps the easiest place in Asia to experience the wonders of a primeval tropical jungle.

Penang: This wonderfully eccentric and somewhat seedy old town is the premier tourist destination in Malaysia. Populated by Chinese, Tamils, and Malays, Penang is full of delightful character, charm, personality, great food, good beaches, romantic old hotels, elaborate temples, and fascinating architecture dating from the turn of the century. If you only have time for one stop on the west coast, make it Penang.

East Coast

The east coast of Peninsular Malaysia remains a relatively undisturbed and traditional land despite a pair of major highways which now link it with the west coast. This is where Malays, rather than Chinese, control the economy, where the call of Islam is stronger than that of Confucianism, and where a leisurely lifestyle is prized over material possessions. Large, modern towns such as Kota Bharu, Kuala Trengganu, and Kuantan have little to recommend them, but the pristine beaches and sleepy fishing villages almost completely untouched by mass tourism are worth visiting.

Two words of caution: Beaches are clean and untouristy, though not as spectacular as the hyperbole churned out by the local tourist office. Secondly, although the east coast is an extremely relaxing destination, single women and travelers in search of an escapist holiday should note that a resurgence of fundamentalist Islam has dramatically affected the mood and tolerance level on the east coast. This is especially critical in the conservative state of Trengganu, which is *not* the place to drink, find romance, or sunbathe in a skimpy bathing suit.

Tioman Island: Tioman is a large, lovely, densely forested island two hours by boat from Mersing. A first-class resort here has a golf course, plus a half-dozen inexpensive chalets strung along a fairly nice (but not great) beach. Restaurants are simple and nightlife is nonexistent, but the skin diving and jungle trekking are superb.

Cherating: Best choice for *kampong* atmosphere and privacy on the 710-km coastline that stretches from Singapore to Thailand is the secluded cove of Cherating. Club Med has constructed an outpost here but most visitors stay in simple wooden chalets set in a beautiful coconut grove. Cherating is a rising star, largely undiscovered by mass tourism yet popular enough to be fun.

Rantau Abang: One of the most impressive natural phenomena of Southeast Asia is the annual arrival of leatherback turtles at Rantau Abang from May to September. Visitors to the beach wait patiently at seaside cafes for one of the immense *Dermochels coriacea* to struggle up the steep beach to bury her eggs in a shallow hole, an eerie and unforgettable experience. Accommodations

range from inexpensive bungalows to some of the finest resorts on the east coast.

Marang: Home to Malay customs and traditions, the east coast is the ideal place to learn about Malay pastimes, arts, crafts, hobbies, sports, entertainments, value systems, and lifestyles. Most people live in small villages called *kampongs* and arrange their lives around the precepts of Islam. Although superbly idyllic and postcard beautiful, Malay *kampongs* are often difficult for Westerners to visit because of conservative attitudes and distrust of outsiders. Marang, however, one of the prettiest villages in Malaysia, is somewhat accustomed to curious outsiders and a reasonably good place to observe and experience life in a Malay *kampong.* Marang has several sets of inexpensive bungalows.

Perhentian Islands: Two stunning islands of crystalline sand and iridescent waters lie just off shore from Marang—the most impressive islands in all of Malaysia.

the first empire with Malay roots, Srivijaya became immensely powerful in the 8th century by controlling the Straits of Malacca, the remarkably narrow channel which funnels most of the trade between China and India. This Islamic empire fell five centuries later to the Majapahit Empire of Java, an expansionist dynasty which exerted strong cultural and political influence over the Malaysian Peninsula while balancing the territorial ambitions of the Thais at Ayuthaya.

Malacca (Melaka)

Modern Malaysian history began in 1401 when Paramesara, a refugee prince-consort from Palembang, fled Sumatra to Singapore and then Malacca, a small *orang laut* village with excellent harborage and an outstanding location between China, India, and the Indonesian Spice Islands. Malacca blossomed and soon became the center of Eastern commerce, diffusing Islam throughout Southeast Asia while controlling the legendary spice route which stretched from the Malukus to Europe. Traders met to exchange Chinese silks, Japanese gold, Banda pearls, Malaysian tin, Ming potteries, exotic feathers, and highly prized spices such as cloves, mace, nutmeg, and sandalwood. Early sultans adopted sensible open-trade policies and held duties at

attractively low levels, two smart moves which ensured continued vitality for the young port.

But greed and the Christian desire to confront the rising tide of Islam attracted European powers, notably the Portuguese, who, under the leadership of Alfonso de Albuquerque, had established a string of economic and military outposts from Africa to the Malukus. Anxious to compete with the Arab traders who had monopolized the spice trade since the Middle Ages, the Portuguese took Malacca in 1511. Early profits were encouraging, but sky-high duties, repressive taxes, and ill-conceived conversion attempts outraged the local population, who abandoned the city for friendlier ports. The city later fell to the Dutch, though they ignored the port in lieu of Jakarta, and finally to the British, who regarded Malacca as the poor stepsister to Penang and Singapore.

The British

Anxious to protect their lucrative tea and opium trade with China, the British East India Company, led by the young and ambitious Sir Francis Light, established a free-trade port on the jungle-covered island of Penang in 1786. Penang remained the region's major trading port until 1819, when Raffles established Sin-

MALAYSIA

gapore after obtaining the tiger-infested island from the sultan of Johor. The superb geographical location of Singapore and Raffles's enlightened leadership made the island an overnight success. Thousands of Chinese immigrants, merchants, and traders flooded the young city, anxious to escape the horrors of feudal China and hopefully make their fortunes in the New China. Singapore, Malacca, and Penang were combined to form the British Straits settlement in 1826. Singapore was declared capital of the British interests in 1832.

The late 19th and early 20th centuries were a period of great change for Malaysia. The European industrial revolution fueled the growth of tin and rubber industries, two dangerous and difficult enterprises which held little appeal to the local Malays. To keep their economic machinery in proper running order and fill labor shortages in tin mines and on rubber plantations, British colonialists actively encouraged thousands of Chinese and Indians to emigrate to Malaysia. This self-serving act profoundly changed the racial composition and political history of the country. In addition, local sultanates foolishly battled between themselves, enabling British authorities to gradually extend their suzerainty over the war-torn peninsula. British rule failed to create a modern nation-state, but peace was established, the economy boomed, and Malay political power was protected against the encroaching mercantilism of the Chinese. By the 1920s, all of Peninsular Malaysia had fallen under British control.

World War II

In a lightning attack which completely surprised Allied commanders in Southeast Asia, the Japanese army landed at Kota Bharu in December 1941. From there, they quickly drove their tanks and rode their bicycles toward Singapore, the so-called Gibraltar of the East. Impregnable Singapore fell to Japanese forces in only three months, an embarrassing debacle which forever smashed the myth of white superiority. Promising a Greater Asian Co-Prosperity Sphere, the Japanese occupied Malaya and immediately rounded up tens of thousands of Allied soldiers and civilians who were beaten, tortured, starved, and marched off to die in the construction of Siam's death railway.

Malays were also mistreated, but the worst cruelty was reserved for the Chinese, executed in shocking numbers by the Japanese Kempetai before being dumped into mass graveyards. Many fled into the jungles where they formed resistance units sympathetic to communist and Maoist ideology. After Hiroshima and the defeat of the Japanese, these communist freedom fighters initiated a violent counterrevolution against British occupation forces. The struggle finally ended in November 1989 when legendary communist leader Chin Peng, who had led the party since the late 1940s, agreed to give up his armed struggle and leave his jungle stronghold.

Independence

British agreements to grant total independence to the Malays after WW II were complicated by divisions of political power between the Chinese and Malays. The former were 19th-century immigrants who by then almost completely dominated the Malaysian economy, the latter the indigenous peoples who intensely feared the power of the Chinese. Realizing that British departure would leave both economic and political control in the hands of the Chinese, the once-disinterested Malays organized themselves into a political coalition determined to preserve Malay rights and privileges. Political power was ultimately secured by the Malays, but economic control was left with the Chinese, an unsatisfactory but seemingly irreversible situation which continues to the present day.

Malaya was granted independence in 1957 and changed its name to Malaysia in 1963 after Sabah and Sarawak agreed to join the new republic, a strategic move which helped maintain a Malay racial majority against the Chinese-dominated island of Singapore. This marriage was aborted in 1965 when Singapore was ejected from the new coalition on the grounds of political aggression. Racial tensions—always bubbling gently beneath the calm surface of Malaysian society—came to a boil in 1969 when 248 people died in racial riots and the government of Malaysia's first prime minister, Tunku Abdul Rahman, was toppled. This racial uprising also led to the creation of the New Economic Policy, a government program which seeks to restructure society and eliminate poverty among the indigenous Malays.

THE PEOPLE

Malaysia is a multiracial country with an estimated population of 18 million people. Eighty-two percent of the people live in Peninsular Malaysia, 10% in Sarawak, and 8% in Sabah. Malays comprise 48% of the population, the Chinese make up 35%, Indians 10%, and various indigenous tribal groups account for the balance. Although the largest racial group in the country, the Malays' less than 50% is a significant statistic in light of the political and economic equation. These races—Malay, Chinese, Indian, and tribals—have historically kept their distance from each other by following their own religions, doing different kinds of work, and living in separate communities. Incorporating this range of ethnic groups under one national flag has largely shaped Malaysia's political and economic structure, besides remaining an endless source of fascination to specialists on Asia.

Malays

Article 160 of the Malay constitution defines a Malay as a person who follows Islam, speaks Malay as the mother language, and conforms to Malay customs. Malays are of a mixed ethnic background, some having lived in the country for millennia while others are recent immigrants from Sumatra, Java, Sulawesi, Borneo, and other Indonesian islands. Malays, in fact, come from the same basic racial stock as people of the Philippines and Indonesia. A warm and extremely hospitable group with refined sensibilities and gracious manners, Malays typically live in rural villages and prefer the occupations of farmer and fisherman rather than urban businessman or entrepreneur.

Together with the Ibans, Kadazans, Melanaus, and other tribals living in East Malaysia, Malays constitute the Bumiputras, a government-recognized racial group. Being a "Son of the Soil" has great advantages. Most government positions are given to Bumis, 80% of university openings are reserved for them, job priority is enjoyed even when a Bumi is less qualified than a Chinese, low-cost loans are plentiful for Bumi businesses, and most government licenses are, by law, awarded to them. Statistics show that Malays hold 80% of all government executive

Malay market day

jobs, are granted 85% of all college scholarships, and receive 95% of all government land distributed to settlers. Malays can, at times, be somewhat defensive about their privileges, arguing that they were first in the country and were discriminated against by British colonialists who favored the Chinese and the Indians. Chinese, on the other hand, consider the Malays lazy, uneducated, and, perhaps worst of all, less than shrewd. Both Chinese and Indians resent the Malays' political domination and preferential treatment—especially the educational bias in favor of the Bumiputras—but largely accept these affirmative-action programs as necessary conditions for national peace and reconciliation.

Chinese

Malaysia's other large ethnic group is the Chinese, who arrived in large numbers in the late 19th century to work on the rubber plantations and in the tin mines. Between 1897 and 1927, when the disintegrating Manchu Dynasty could no longer enforce emigration restrictions, some

MALAYSIA

six million Chinese fled the twin scourges of war and famine to find their fortunes in Southeast Asia. Most of Malaysia's Chinese emigrated from Kwangtung and Fukien provinces, from the towns of Amoy, Swatow, and Canton.

Early immigrants settled into various lifestyle groupings: Babas, who descended from mixed Malay-Chinese marriages and developed a unique Sino-Malay culture; Straits Chinese who followed Chinese lifestyles modified by generations of life in Malaysia; and Straits-born Chinese who held to a culture as purely Chinese as possible. Together they formed microcosms of southern China as reflected in their various dialects, foods, marriage customs, funeral rites, and variety of religious and superstitious beliefs. Hokkiens became prosperous through trading and shopkeeping. Cantonese cleared the jungles, dug for tin, and tapped rubber. Rivalries between their various *tongs* (secret societies) were often violent and frightfully bloody, but peace was restored, and by the early 20th century the Chinese largely controlled the economy.

Today they drive the Mercedes in Penang, own the stately mansions in Kuala Lumpur, and keep the wheels turning in the gambling casinos at Genting Highlands. While Malays might consider them usurious moneylenders and tightfisted merchants, most would agree that the economic miracle of Malaysia is largely due to the admirable work ethic of the Chinese.

Race is a thorny and complex issue here in Malaysia, but it boils down to this: the Malays

control the political machinery and want more economic power, the Chinese control the economy and want more political power. As mentioned before, racial discrimination against the Chinese has become government policy supported by the New Economic Policy. But not everyone agrees that the Malays are an indigenous race; tribals roamed the peninsula long before the Malays arrived. Therefore, the Chinese claim, everybody's an immigrant—a line of logic that understandably infuriates the Malays.

Pragmatists to the extreme, Chinese generally accept Malay leadership in the political life of the country but deeply resent government meddlings in Chinese culture. The biggest clashes have revolved around the government's Bahasa Malaysia language policy, which seeks to unify the country by encouraging everyone to speak Malay. Tempers flared recently after non-Mandarin-speaking teachers were appointed to Chinese primary schools and the government banned Mandarin language courses from public universities. Discrimination is typically less obvious: a ban on the use of Chinese characters at a seafood festival in Johor State, university courses taught in Malay only, and the compulsory wearing of traditional Malay headdresses for non-Malay university graduates.

Indians

Malaysia's third-largest ethnic group was brought to the country by the British in the 19th century to work the rubber plantations. Most Indians are

Hindu marriage

AFFIRMATIVE ACTION ~ MALAY STYLE

Malaysia faces several economic challenges. Most serious is the uneven distribution of income between West and East Malaysia, between urban and rural residents, and most dramatically, between Malays and Chinese. As in nearly all other countries in Southeast Asia, the economy of Malaysia is controlled by the Chinese. UMNO Bharu and the Malay people are determined to change this equation through their New Economic Policy (NEP), an ambitious government program aimed at eradicating poverty and restructuring society through a more equitable distribution of the country's wealth. NEP's major goal is to increase Malay Bumiputra (literally "Sons of the Soil") ownership of shares in public limited companies. In 1971, foreigners owned 62% of the nation's corporate wealth, the Chinese controlled 36%, and the Bumiputra owned less than four percent.

As a result of the NEP, foreigners today have seen their corporate equity slashed to 30%, the Chinese have increased theirs to 50%, and the Malays hold some 20% of Malaysian equity. Although a dramatic improvement over 1970 levels, it remains far short of the 30% promised to Malays by 1990. Even this 20% figure is questionable, since many businesses transferred from Chinese to Malay ownership are only transactions that paper over continued Chinese control. The NEP has also come under a great deal of criticism from foreign corporations and Chinese entrepreneurs who say it discourages individual enterprise and institutionalizes widespread racial discrimination against the Chinese. Critics also charge that the NEP has primarily benefited well-connected Bumiputra, helping few of the poor Malays who still work in the ricefields.

Despite unending complaints and apparent shortcomings, the NEP has been extended past its 1990 deadline, since many powerful politicians believe it plays an important role as peacemaker between the races.

Dravidians from South India who speak Tamil, Telugu, or Malayalam, but Punjabis can be found in the larger cities working in railways, bureaucracies, and professional occupations. Most originally came from lower castes, economic and social classes which have largely disappeared in Malaysia through acculturation and intermarriage with locals.

Indigenous Peoples
Several other groups share Malaysia with the Malays, Chinese, and Indians. Largest of these *orang asli* ("original men") are the 40,000 Senoi or Sakai who live a seminomadic existence in the central foothills. Most are now Westernized and wear blue jeans rather than loincloths, though some continue to hunt with their traditional blowguns near the Cameron Highlands. The second-largest tribal group is the Jakun, Proto-Malays of the southern peninsula who have generally adopted a sedentary farming life. The northern regions of Peninsular Malaysia are home to Negritos or Semang, a short and kinky-haired people who continue their age-old nomadic hunting and gathering rituals, speak a Mon-Khmer language, and are respected by Malays for their prowess in witchcraft and magic.

Sabah and Sarawak are ethnological gold mines of Land Dayaks, Sea Dayaks, Punans, Bajaus, Muruts, and dozens of other small groups.

Islam in Malaysia
Islam is the state religion of Malaysia. Nearly all Malays are Sunni Muslims who follow the orthodox Shafie school of interpretation and five fundamental precepts of the Koran: profession of faith, daily prayer, religious alms to support the poor, a fast during Ramadan, and a pilgrimage to Mecca. Islam in Malaysia has important political and economic significance.

Symbolizing Malay supremacy over non-Bumiputras, it now permeates every level of society, culture, and political affiliation. UMNO maintains an image of an Islamic party in response to the nationwide increase of Islamic consciousness. Laws have been passed, an Islamic bank established, and a government-supported Islamic university now teaches traditional law. PAS, the opposition Party of Islam, which seeks to make Malaysia an Islamic state governed by an Islamic constitution and ruled by Islamic law, has made great strides in recent years. Although a radical party primarily supported by poor rural-based Malays, what began as the extremist

FESTIVALS

The multiracial and multireligious nation of Malaysia celebrates a staggering number of festivals, from Indian *pujas* to Chinese celebrations of the dead. All offer the visitor an excellent opportunity to discover something of Malaysia's rich and varied culture. Some festivals are national affairs held throughout the country, while others are confined to individual states. Most are connected with either Islam, Buddhism, Hinduism, or Chinese social dictums. Among the most memorable are the birthdays of the sultans, a rare chance to see traditional Malay performing arts. State holidays are fixed by the Western Gregorian calendar. Most religious festivals tend to float around the calendar since they are moveable feasts based on cycles of the moon; exact dates can be checked with the tourist office. Chinese and Hindu festivals are described in greater detail in the Singapore chapter, Buddhist festivals under Thailand.

January
Birthday of the Sultan of Kedah: 25 January. Aside from Sabah, Sarawak, and Penang, each state in Malaysia has a sultan who celebrates his birthday with great pageantry. East-coast venues provide outstanding opportunities to experience traditional Malay culture. Performances during the week-long festivities usually include *wayang kulit* (shadow puppets), *makyong* (traditional theater performed by females), *nogo* dance, and demonstrations of *pencak silat* (martial arts). Kite-flying, top-spinning, and bird-singing competitions are also held.

February
Federal Territory Day: 1 February. Kuala Lumpur's founding is marked with parades, cultural shows, and athletic competitions.

Thaipusam: A masochistic Hindu festival celebrated at Batu Caves near Kuala Lumpur and in Penang. Probably the most spectacular Hindu festival in Southeast Asia, Thaipusam is more fully described under Singapore Festivals.

Chinese New Year: Family visits, firecrackers, and shouts of "*Gung Hay Fah Choy*" are essential to the Chinese community. See the Singapore chapter.

Chap Goh Meh: Hokkiens celebrate this festival on the 15th and final day of the Chinese New Year.

Considered an excellent time to find a rich husband; you'll see lovely ladies dressed in extravagant gowns cruising around in flashy cars.

Chingay: Celebrated in Penang and Johor Bharu 22 days after the Chinese New Year. Acrobats and temple volunteers carry temple idols and enormous flags through the streets.

Genggulang Day: Animist New Year's celebration held by the *orang asli* in South Perak.

March
Birthday of the Sultan of Selangor: 8 March. Festivities, cultural performances, and prayers are held in the capital city of Alam and the royal town of Klang.

Melaka Week: Food festivals, cultural events, and decorative competitions are held during this week-long celebration.

Panguni Uttiram: This Hindu festival honors the celestial marriage of Lord Shiva to goddess Parvati with vegetarian meals and all-night prayer vigils.

Birthday of the Sultan of Kelantan: 30-31 March. Celebrated in Kota Bharu on the east coast. A rare opportunity to watch traditional Malay sports and performing arts such as *wayang kulit, pencak silat,* top spinning, and kite flying. Poetry competitions are held in the evenings.

April
Birthday of the Sultan of Johor: 8 April.

Birthday of the Sultan of Perak: 19 April. Celebrated in both Ipoh and the royal town of Kuala Kangsar.

Birthday of the Sultan of Trengganu: 30 April. Another outstanding east-coast celebration.

Kelantan Kite Festival: Enormous kites of all shapes and sizes are decorated with colored and shimmering paper before being sent aloft.

Ching Ming: Chinese visit and clean up the elaborate tombs of their ancestors during this celebration of the dead. See the Singapore chapter.

Sri Rama Navami: Rama is honored during this nine-day Hindu festival.

May
Hari Raya Puasa: An Islamic holiday which marks the end of the fasting month of Ramadan. Muslims pray in mosques and attend religious discussions.

Homes are opened to visits from relatives and friends.

Vesak Day: An important Buddhist festival which celebrates the birth, death, and enlightenment of Lord Buddha. Picturesque lantern processions encircle most Buddhist temples.

Penang Boat Races: International boat competitions are held between sleekly decorated dragon boats manned by 24 oarsmen, a *taikong* helmsman, and a gong beater.

Puja Pantai: A big and noisy beach festival held five km south of Kuala Trengganu. Originally a pagan celebration to ensure a successful rice harvest, it now revolves around rock bands and thunderous disco.

Kota Belud Festival (Sabah): Bajau dances, blowgun competitions, and horse-riding demonstrations are held in Kota Belud, 77 km from Kota Kinabalu. Sipitang holds a similar festival.

Kandazan Harvest Festival (Sabah): Ritualistic celebration of the rice harvest held annually by the indigenous Kandazans of Sabah. An enormous amount of *tapai* (rice wine) is drunk.

Dayak Festival (Sarawak): The Dayaks of Sarawak get into the spirit of spring with ritualistic animal sacrifices, war dances, cockfights, blowgun competitions, and the liberal consumption of *tuak*.

Kapit Festival (Sarawak): Cultural performances and a regatta are held in Sarawak's Seventh Division.

June

Birthday of the Sultan of Melaka: 10 June.

Fiesta of Saint Peter: 29 June. Christian fishermen's festival held at a Portuguese settlement near Malacca.

Kelantan Giant Drums Festival: Teams of *rebana ubi* pounders challenge each other in Kota Bharu. Judges award points for *lendik* (tone), *merdu* (sound), and *rentak lagu* (reverberation), in addition to the team's costumes and the decorations on their drums.

July

Birthday of the Governor of Sarawak: 7 July.

Birthday of the Governor of Penang: 16 July.

Birthday of the Sultan of Sembilan: 19 July.

Lumut Sea Carnival: The port town for Pangkor Island sponsors a boat procession, water sports, and the crowning of the Pesta Queen.

August

Krishna Festival: This Hindu festival marks the eighth reincarnation of Vishnu with dance and drama recalling the adventures of the blue-skinned lover and hero of the Mahabharata.

Koran Reading Competition: Held in Kuala Lumpur and televised throughout Malaysia.

Festival of the Hungry Ghosts: Chinese believe that once a year the gates of hell are opened and hungry ghosts are freed to roam around. Offerings of food, incense, and entertainment are made to appease these straying, destitute, and possibly bothersome ghosts. Chinese street opera can be seen in most west coast towns.

Hari Raya Haji: This Muslim holiday marks the occasion when pilgrims visit the holy black stone in Mecca.

Maal Hijrah: Islamic New Year's Day. Commemorates the journey of Mohammed from Medina to Mecca in 622.

Malacca Festival: Week-long celebration of kite flying, bird singing, top spinning, martial arts, boat races, windsurfing competitions, beauty pageants, and food fairs at the major hotels.

National Day: 31 August. Malaysia's independence is celebrated in Kuala Lumpur with parades, Chinese opera, traditional Malay dance, and Hindu drama.

September

Birthday of the Governor of Sabah: 10 September.

Birthday of the Sultan of Perlis: 25 September.

Firewalking Festival: Hindus race across beds of burning coals to prove their devotion.

October

Birthday of the Sultan of Pahang: 24 October.

Deepavali: Hindu festival celebrating the victory of Rama over Rawana, good over evil, wisdom over ignorance.

Moon Cake Festival: Marks the overthrow of the Mongol overlords in feudal China. Lanterns are lit, women pray to the goddess of the moon, and everyone enjoys heavy cakes made from egg and lotus seed.

Festival of the Nine Emperors: The nine kings of ancient China are honored with Chinese opera and some spirited firewalking. A grand procession is held on the ninth day of the ninth moon to commemorate the return of the gods to heaven.

MALAYSIA

FESTIVALS
(continued)

Navarathri: Young Hindu girls dress up as the goddess Kali to honor their virginity. Hindu organizations in Kuala Lumpur stage Hindu dance and drama.

November

Mohammed's Birthday: Muslims celebrate Mohammed's birthday with prayers, religious lectures, and recitations of the Koran.

Kuan Yin's Birthday: The Chinese goddess of mercy celebrates her birthday four times a year.

December

Penang Festival: December is carnival time in Penang. Highlights include decorated floats, an international film festival, Indian and Chinese theater, boat races, and sports competitions.

Feast of St. Francis Xavier: The Catholics of Malacca honor their patron saint with a religious procession.

Malaysian Islamic Youth Movement in the '70s has now gained respectability with the Malaysian middle class. No longer are *dakwah* (proselytizing Muslims) limited to nonconformist youth or students disappointed by economic inequality brought on by Western capitalism.

The rise of right-wing Islam is most apparent on the east coast where women wear black robes and remain veiled in *purdah,* while *dakwah* of the hard-line Darul Arqam community can be seen with their long black robes, green headgear, and trademark goatees hanging from their chins. And despite many middle-class Malays being disturbed by these developments, few dare speak out for fear of being labeled anti-Islam, infidel, or *murtad* (deviant within the faith). Travelers should remember that Islam is one of the five sensitive subjects whose special position must not be questioned and which are protected under the Sedition Act.

Under pressures from the ultraconservative PAS and Islamic student organizations, the legal trend in Malaysia has been one of gradual and officially sponsored adherence to the stricter tenets of *shariah* (Islamic) law. The Non-Islamic Religions Act of 1988—a measure which forbids conversion attempts on behalf of any religion except Islam—was used to arrest Christian missionaries who proselytize among Muslims. A major constitutional amendment the same year ended the rights of the civil bench to overrule a *shariah* court decision. Legislation has also been proposed to require Malay women to cover all but their hands and faces in public. Punishment

administered by Islamic *shariah* courts seems extraordinarily harsh by Western standards: whippings for the consumption of alcohol, *khalwat* (close proximity between the sexes), and *zina* (illicit sex); the amputation of thieves' hands; the stoning to death of adulterers; the crucifixion of murderers. Worldwide press was given to a 1987 case in which a young man was whipped six times with a cane for drinking liquor and committing *khalwat* . . . in a Kota Bharu restaurant. Islamic law currently applies to Muslims only, but political pressure to enforce *shariah* laws uniformly on all people has frightened both the Chinese and Indian communities.

ARTS AND CRAFTS

Batik

The ancient art of fabric printing using wax-resistant dyes still survives along the east coast and in a limited number of factories near Kuala Lumpur and Penang. Malaysian styles tend to be more modern and experimental than Indonesian designs. East coast batiks typically favor dense and bright colors of reds, greens, and blacks, while Penang *sarongs* are usually dyed in softer colors of blues and browns. As elsewhere in Southeast Asia, batik can either be stamped by machines in long rolls or hand-stamped in 12-meter lengths with metal blocks called *japs.* Shopping for batik is somewhat tricky, but a few guidelines will help. The finest batik is paper thin, retains a slight aroma from

MOVIES FILMED IN MALAYSIA

South Pacific: Tioman, a beautiful island off the east coast of Peninsular Malaysia, was used as a backdrop for the Rogers and Hammerstein musical. You'll recognize the distinctive twin mountains as you approach by hovercraft from Kuantan. Other scenes in *South Pacific* were filmed on nearby Malaysian atolls and on the Hawaiian island of Kauai.

Farewell to the King: Nick Nolte played the king of the Dayaks in this 1989 flick filmed in the rainforests of Borneo. Spectacular photography, but Nick's Dayak dialogues, subtitled for Westerners, are silly.

Tong Tana: A Journey to the Heart of Borneo: A 1990 Swedish-produced documentary about a Swiss citizen, Bruno Manser, and his legendary protest against the reckless depletion of Borneo's 160 million-year-old hardwood rainforests.

Beyond Rangoon: A John Boorman film based on the 1989 anti-government protests in Myanmar and the rise to prominence of Aung San Suu Kyi. The gripping 1995 drama was filmed in Malaysia, despite the protests of the Burmese government, which called it "a hostile act."

the natural astringents used in the aftertreatment, and is hand painted with a copper instrument called a *janting*. Don't buy batik printed on only one side; this has been mass-produced by a textile-printing process.

Songket

Malaysia's cloth of gold is a distinctive fabric made from fine silk or cotton interwoven with imitation gold or silver threads. Patterns are reproduced from Islamic designs of Arabic calligraphy and geometric designs of plant life such as the petals of the *chempaka* flower. Rarely seen in ordinary wear, *songket* shows up during religious ceremonies and *akad nikah* marriage ceremonies. As you might expect, this time-consuming craft is very expensive. Other decoration techniques include gilded needlework used for military epaulettes and pressed gold-leaf designs called *telepuk*.

Pewterware

Malaysia enjoys a reputation for producing some of the finest pewterware in the world. Pewter is made from tin, with token amounts of antimony and copper added to give more strength. The resulting 97% alloy can be cast, hammered, and stretched into beer mugs, sake cups, and a wide range of kitchen implements. Malaysia's largest and most famous pewtermaker is in Selangor near Kuala Lumpur.

Silverware

Malaysia's finest silverwork comes from Selangor Pewter and from the town of Sireh near Kota Bharu in the state of Trengganu. Currently out of vogue but fascinating nevertheless are silver chastity discs displayed in the National Museum.

Pottery

Malaysian pottery is hardly famous, though there is a surprisingly good selection. Chinese-style pottery in utilitarian designs is produced by Aw Eng Kwang Pottery at Air Hitam, 120 km north of Johor Bharu. Peninsular Malaysia's most distinctive potteries are the stunning black pots of Perak made by the Labu people of Lenggong, Kepala Bendang, and Pulau Tiga. Ochre pots are made in Kelantan, but the most sought-after potteries are those produced by the indigenous peoples of Sabah and Sarawak. Decorated with traditional tribal designs, the hand-applied decorations often feature Sarawak hunters, Murut dancers, and stylized dragons from the Kayah tribes.

MALAYSIA

ON THE ROAD

GETTING THERE

Air

Malaysian Airlines (MAS) flies five times weekly from Los Angeles to Kuala Lumpur with a stopover in Hong Kong. MAS also serves Kuala Lumpur from Australia, New Zealand, and Europe.

From Thailand

Air: Malaysia can be reached from Thailand by air, train, bus, or shared taxi. Both Thai International and MAS fly from Bangkok, Phuket, and Hat Yai to Penang and Kuala Lumpur. The Phuket-Penang flight is reasonably priced and saves a full day of hard bus travel.

Train: Trains operate daily between Bangkok and Butterworth, the terminus town just across from the island of Penang. The train then continues south to Kuala Lumpur and finally Singapore. Schedules change frequently; accurate departure times and fares can be checked with tourist departments or stationmasters in Thailand. The express is comfortable and offers good scenery, but some restrictions apply. For example, only first and second classes are available. In addition, supplemental charges for air-conditioning, superior classes, and sleeping berths make the express much more expensive than ordinary trains or buses.

Trains can also be taken from Hat Yai in southern Thailand to Sungei Golok at the border of the east coast. Travelers then get off the train, walk across the border into Malaysia, and continue by bus to Kota Bharu. More details on border crossings are found in the Penang and Kota Bharu sections.

Sea: Modern ships and ferries depart daily for Langkawi from Satun in southern Thailand. Service may also be available from Phuket.

Bus: Buses from Hat Yai head down to Penang and Kuala Lumpur. Direct bus service is also available from Phuket, Ko Samui, and Surat Thani.

Share Taxis: Share taxis—lumbering old Mercedes—are fast, comfortable, cozy, fun, and memorable since you might share the space with traveling salesmen, schoolgirls, Koranic scholars, or turbanned Sikhs. Share taxis leave daily from Hat Yai guesthouses.

From Singapore

Train: Almost a dozen trains ranging from ordinary to express coaches leave daily from the Singapore train station on Keppel Road. Departures can be checked at the Singapore Tourist Office or at the railway station.

Bus: Buses leave from the open-air bus terminal at Lavender Road and Kallang Bahru near Little India. Buses also leave from the Golden Mile Complex on Beach Road. Departure schedules and prices are listed in the Singapore chapter. An inexpensive alternative to long-distance buses is public bus 170 from Queen Street to the Johor Bharu bus terminal, from where buses fan out to most Malaysian towns.

MALAYSIAN DIPLOMATIC OFFICES

Australia: 7 Perth Ave., Canberra, ACT 2600, tel. (06) 273-1543

Canada: 60 Boteler St., Ottawa, Ontario K1N 8Y7, tel. (613) 237-5182

France: 2 Bis rue Benouville, 75116 Paris, tel. 4553-1185

Germany: Mittelstrasse 43, 5300 Bonn 2, tel. (0228) 37680306

Japan: 20-16 Nanpeidai-cho, Shibuya-ku, Tokyo 150, tel. 3476-3840

New Zealand: 10 Washington Ave., Brooklyn, Wellington, tel. (04) 385-2349

United Kingdom: 45 Belgrave Square, London SWIX 8QT, tel. (0171) 235-8033

U.S.A.: 2401 Massachusetts Ave. NW, Washington, D.C. 20008, tel. (202) 328-2700

SUGGESTED TIMETABLES FOR MALAYSIA

AREA	2 WEEKS	3 WEEKS	4 WEEKS	8 WEEKS
Penang Island	1 week	1 week	1 week	1 week
Kuala Lumpur	2 days	2 days	2 days	2 days
Hill Resorts	3 days	3 day	3 days	3 days
Malacca	2 days	2 days	2 days	2 days
East Coast	—	1 week	2 weeks	2 weeks
Sabah/Sarawak	—	—	—	4 weeks

Share Taxis: Share taxis can be booked at budget hostels and through taxi services.

From Indonesia
Air: Garuda Indonesia and Malaysia Airlines serve Kuala Lumpur from Jakarta, Denpasar, and several towns in Sumatra. The most popular connection is the daily flight from Medan to Penang, a ticket which also satisfies the "ticket-out" requirements for Indonesian entry permits.

Sea: Ferries to Penang leave daily from Belawan, a port near Medan in northern Sumatra. Boats also cross from Dumai in central Sumatra to Malacca. More adventurous types might consider the boat from Pekanbaru to Singapore. Further details are discussed in the Singapore chapter.

GETTING AROUND

Air
Malaysia Airlines Systems (MAS) and its subsidiary, Pelangi Air, operate all international and domestic routes within the country. MAS flights within Peninsular Malaysia are rarely necessary, thanks to the country's excellent network of buses, trains, and taxis. Pelangi serves less-frequented destinations such as Tioman Island.

MAS offers all the standard discounts such as advance-purchase, night fares, student prices, and family fares. Departure tax on international flights is RM40 and RM5 for domestic flights. The airport tax for flights between Malaysia and Singapore or Brunei is RM20.

Train
Trains on Peninsular Malaysia present a wonderful alternative to crowded buses. Service is rea-

sonably frequent, prices are moderate (comparable to a/c buses), and the scenery is superb. Trains are also safer, saner, and offer a great deal more legroom. Best of all, trains provide endless opportunities to meet people, wander around, gaze out the window, read a book, and simply enjoy the nostalgia unique to this kind of travel.

Peninsular Malaysia has two train lines: west coast service from Singapore to Thailand and an east coast line from Gemas to Kota Bharu. The privatized national railway company, KTM (Keretapi Tanah Melayu) sells various rail passes, but these are of little use to visitors due to limited lines.

Trains come in several classes and types. Ordinary trains and mail coaches in second and third classes only stop at every station and are very slow. The Ekspres Sinaran and the Ekspres Rakyat (People's Express) in a/c or fan coaches are much faster and only slightly pricier than ordinary trains. Unless you have a great deal of time, these are the ones to take. Supplemental charges are collected for sleeping berths. Timetables can be picked up from stationmasters in Singapore and Kuala Lumpur.

Bus
Bus transport on Peninsular Malaysia is fast, frequent, and fairly comfortable on short hauls. Most destinations are served by deluxe a/c coaches complete with smiling hostesses, complimentary soft drinks, and freezing air-conditioning. Ordinary buses serve most of the same routes, plus all the smaller towns off the beaten track. Dozens of bus companies operate in Malaysia but the largest is MARA, the Malaysian government service which usually operates from centrally located terminals.

MALAYSIAN TOURIST OFFICES OVERSEAS

Australia: 65 York St., Sydney, NSW 2000, tel. (02) 9299-4441
56 William St., Perth 6000, tel. (09) 481-0400
Canada: 830 Burrard St., Vancouver, BC V6Z 2K4, tel. (604) 689-8899
France: 29 Rue des Pyramides, 75001 Paris, tel. (01) 4397-4171
Germany: Rossmarkt 11, 60311 Frankfurt Am Main, tel. (069) 283782
Hong Kong: 47-50 Gloucester Rd., Hong Kong, tel. 2528-5810
Japan: 3-4 Nihombashi-Hongokucho, Chuo-ku, Tokyo 103, tel. (03) 3279-3081
Singapore: 10 Collyer Quay, Ocean Building, tel. (02) 532-6321
Thailand: 315 Silom Rd., Bangkok 10500, tel. (02) 236-7606
United Kingdom: 57 Trafalgar Square, London WC2N 5DU, tel. (0171) 930-7932
U.S.A.: 818 West 7th St., Suite 804, Los Angeles, CA 90017, tel. (213) 689-9702
595 Madison Ave., Suite 1800, New York, NY 10022, tel. (212) 754-1113

Share Taxis

Another convenient way to travel around Malaysia is by share taxis, comfortable and fast Mercedes-Benzes which cost about the same as second-class trains or a/c buses. Share taxis from Johor Bharu to Kuala Lumpur, Kuala Lumpur to Penang, and Penang to Kota Bharu can be found waiting near bus or train stations, and leave when filled with five passengers. They're fast and exciting as drivers pass wildly on blind curves and roar through crowded streets at breathtaking speeds. Unless you have nerves of steel, it's best to sit securely in the back seat and ignore the driver's appalling lack of sense.

TRAVEL PRACTICALITIES

Visas

Visas are unnecessary for most visitors to Malaysia. Citizens of the United States, Australia, New Zealand, and most European nations are normally granted a one-month visitor's permit upon arrival. Two months are given on request and granted automatically to those who arrive by air. Extensions up to three months can be obtained at state capitals and the immigration office in Kuala Lumpur.

Tourist Information

Tourism Malaysia, also known as the Malaysia Tourism Promotion Board (MTPB), offers a wide selection of fairly useful maps and brochures. More detailed information is provided by state tourist promotion organizations, which are listed under each respective city within Malaysia.

Maps

Complimentary maps from Tourism Malaysia are fairly useful, but the best maps of Malaysia, Johor Bharu, Kuala Lumpur, Melaka, and Penang are produced by Periplus Editions from their office in Singapore. Periplus maps are widely available in Malaysia and Singapore and can be ordered from Moon Publications.

Money

The Malaysian *ringgit* (RM), sometimes called the Malaysian dollar, is divided into 100 *sen* or cents. The *ringgit* currently trades at US$1 to RM2.50.

The *ringgit* has declined against the Singapore dollar to a point where these two currencies

INTERNATIONAL CLOCK FOR MALAYSIA

San Francisco	-16
New York	-13
London	-8
Paris	-7
Sydney	+3

AREA CODES IN MALAYSIA

To dial Malaysia from the United States, first dial the international access code (011), the country code for Malaysia (60), the area code (without the zero; that's for local long-distance calls), and then the local number. For example, to call a number in Kuala Lumpur, dial 011-60-2-xxx-xxxx.

The international access number for calling *out* of Malaysia is 007.

Cameron Highlands	05
Ipoh	05
Johor Bharu	07
Kota Bharu	09
Kota Kinabalu	088
Kuala Lumpur	03
Kuala Trengganu	09
Kuantan	09
Kuching	082
Langkawi	04
Malacca	06
Penang	04
Singapore	02
Taiping	05

are no longer interchangeable. Malaysian merchants will happily accept Singapore currency at even exchange rates, but you'll be giving up at least 25% in the transaction.

Visa and MasterCard are widely accepted and can be used for cash advances from ATMs and most banks.

Government Hours

Malaysia is an Islamic nation with varying government hours depending on the particular state. Government hours throughout most of the country are 0800-1245 and 1400-1615 Mon.-Fri., 0800-1245 on Saturday, closed Sunday. Government hours in the Islamic states of Kelantan, Trengganu, Kedah, Perlis, and Johor are Sat.-Wed. 0800-1245 and 1400-1615, 0800-1245 on Thursday, and closed on Friday, the Muslim holy day.

Caution

In Malaysia, *dadah* (drugs) mean death. Despite pleas for mercy from the Australian and British governments, two Australians caught with 180 grams of heroin at the Penang airport in 1983 were hanged for trafficking under Malaysia's strict drug laws. Ten foreigners have been executed since drugs became a hanging offense in 1975. Over 120 people (including 20 foreigners) are currently facing death and another 70 are serving long jail terms. While many were merely pawns in corporate drug-smuggling games, the Malaysian Dangerous Drugs Act demands the death sentence purely on the quantity of drugs found and not on culpability.

There is little distinction between soft and hard drugs; holding a few joints is almost as serious as carrying large quantities of heroin. Drugs are sold by rickshaw drivers and hotel clerks, but remember that most drug busts are the result of tip-offs from dealers who pick up sizable cash rewards. When in Malaysia, just say no.

MALAYSIA

PENINSULAR MALAYSIA ~ WEST COAST

JOHOR TO KUALA LUMPUR

The east and west coasts of Peninsular Malaysia are differentiated by their unique histories, peoples, cuisines, weather, architecture, crafts, religious traditions, political leanings, and cultural attractions.

The east coast is home to easygoing Malays who follow Islam and earn their livings as fishermen or farmers. Progress has arrived with the opening of new roads and discoveries of oil and natural gas, but much of the region remains a timeless world of sleepy fishing villages, deserted beaches, minarets, and colorful weekend markets filled with exotic fruits, smelly fish, woven baskets, and batik sarongs.

West coast towns and cities, on the other hand, are mostly populated by hard-working Chinese who prefer more entrepreneurial pursuits like shopkeeping and trading. An enclave of energy and excitement, the pace of west coast life is cranked up several notches beyond typical Asian levels. While the east coast is more relaxing and has better beaches, the west offers more in the way of historical sights, religious architecture, vibrant night markets, and topographic variety.

JOHOR BHARU

Johor Bharu (also spelled Johore Baru and Johor Bahru) is the administrative and royal capital of the state of Johor. Situated just across the causeway from Singapore, this city of 750,000 people is one of the country's richest and most Westernized, a fact largely attributed to Sultan Abu Bakar. This strong-willed, English-educated maharaja established his capital at the small fishing village of Tanjung Petri in 1866, changed the name to Johor Bharu (New Johor), initiated an ambitious building program, and then successfully kept the sultanate free of foreign domination and British economic exploitation during his 33-year reign.

Attractions

Most travelers simply race through Johor Bharu en route to Malacca or Kuala Lumpur, but those with the time might walk along the waterfront to the following attractions.

Royal Abu Bakar Museum: Johor's Istana Besar (Grand Palace) was built in 1866 in Victorian English style, the favorite architectural motif of this admitted Anglophile. The palace, overlooking the sea, is set amid 50 hectares of lush tropical gardens with a Japanese teahouse and a small zoo. The north wing of the palace houses a throne room and a museum with collections of court dresses, weapons, the famous Ellenborough centerpiece, and other state regalia. Open daily 0900-1700. Admission for foreigners is a hefty US$7, but worth the tariff—this is the finest sultanate museum in the country.

Sultan Abu Bakar Mosque: This white Victorian building at the top of a small hill about a block beyond the Istana commands a panoramic view of the Johor Straits and Singapore housing projects. The foundation stone was laid in 1892 by Abu Bakar who died before completion of the architectural gem in 1900.

Istana Bukit Serene: Five km west of downtown, the modern waterside palace and residence of the present sultan of Johor is crowned by a 32-meter tower, Johor's most distinctive landmark.

Accommodations

Few Western visitors stay in Johor, although inexpensive hotels can be found near the train, taxi, and bus stations in the center of town.

Footloose Homestay: A friendly and peaceful homestay about 15 minutes west of the train

PENINSULAR MALAYSIA

station. 4 Jalan Ismail, tel. (07) 224-2881, RM12-24.

Hotel JB: Acceptable low-end hotel one block southwest of the train station. 80 Jalan Wong Ah Fook, tel. (07) 223-4788, RM55-75.

City View Hotel: Good value mid-level hotel one block west of the train station. 16 Jalan Station, tel. (07) 224-9291, RM90-120.

Putri Pan Pacific Hotel: Top end hotels include the Holiday Inn, two km north of city center, the Hyatt Regency, three km west, and this first-class hotel in the center of town two blocks west of the train station. Jalan Salim, tel. (07) 223-3333, fax 223-6622, RM280-340.

Transportation

From Singapore, bus 170 departs quarter hour from the Ban San bus terminal on Queen Street, within walking distance of Bencoolen Street dorms. The Johor Bharu Express leaves every 30 minutes from the terminus on Rochor Road. Both buses pass through immigration and continue to Larkin bus terminal in Johor, five km north of city center.

Johor Bharu, a major transportation hub, offers frequent departures of buses, taxis, trains, and planes—all at significantly lower prices than similar transport from Singapore.

Share taxis depart from the taxi stand on Jalan Trus and the new taxi center adjacent to the Larkin bus terminal. Johor Bharu's ferry terminal, two km east of the Causeway, provides ferry services to Changi Point in Singapore and Batam and Bintan islands in Indonesia. The Johor Bharu airport, 20 km north of town, can be reached by bus shuttle from the MAS office or taxi for RM25.

MALACCA

Few cities in Southeast Asia can match Malacca (Melaka in Bahasa Malaya) in history or antiquity. For hundreds of years, the Portuguese, Dutch, and British fought for Malacca's strategic position on the Straits of Malacca and its incalculable wealth generated from the Asian silk and spice trades.

WEST COAST HIGHLIGHTS

The most important sights on the west coast are the futuristic city of Kuala Lumpur, the small historic town of Malacca, beaches at Pangkor and Langkawi, the relaxing hill resort of Cameron Highlands, Taman Negara National Park, and Penang, the premier travel destination in Peninsular Malaysia. Travelers with additional time might visit one or more of the following attractions.

Fraser's Hill
Deserted during the week, this small old British hill resort is packed on weekends, when wealthy businessmen arrive with their families to play golf and tennis and relax in luxury condos which have sprouted in the cool mountain air.

Ipoh
Ipoh's rich past is recalled through its stately colonial architecture, its magnificent Perak homes, and elegant Chinese shophouses in the old quarter. It's delightfully free of tourist hype and hustle (you'll be the only Westerner in town), and you can get a quick impression with a three- or four-hour walking tour starting from the bus or train station. Ipoh has dozens of hotels in all price ranges.

Kuala Kangsar
Perak State's old royal capital is famous for the Ubudiah Mosque, perhaps the most beautiful example of Islamic architecture in Malaysia. Other attractions include a small but informative museum and the magnificent Iskandariah Palace, constructed in a unique art-deco-Saracenic style. Kuala Kangsar is a worthwhile and relatively easy three-hour stop between Ipoh and Penang.

Taiping
One of the prettiest little towns on the west coast, Taiping is an ideal spot to wander around, soak up the '30s atmosphere, enjoy some tasty Chinese food, check out the museum's ethnological artifacts, and experience Malaysia slightly off the beaten track.

Maxwell Hill
Bukit Larut is a small and unpretentious former tea plantation and hill station with pleasant hiking trails, flower gardens, romantic old bungalows, and spectacular views across the Straits of Malacca. Maxwell Hill provides a good alternative to the more developed hill resorts at Genting Highlands and Cameron Highlands.

MALAYSIA

MALACCA (MELAKA)

TO SINGAPORE

TO PORTUGUESE SETTLEMENT

CHENG HO

JALAN

JALAN PARAMESWARA

JALAN THAMBY ABDULLAH

0.5 km

0

MY PLACE GUESTHOUSE

KANCIL

SUNNY'S INN

MERDEKA

AMY HOMESTAY

ROBIN'S NEST

SD GUESTHOUSE

TRAVELLER'S LODGE

JALAN

JALAN

PARK

CHINA HILL

EASTERN HERITAGE GUESTHOUSE

APPLE GUESTHOUSE

ABDULLAH

TEMENGGONG

JALAN BANDA

INDEPENDENCE MUSEUM

SANTIAGO GATE

MALACCA SULTANATE PALACE MUSEUM

PARK

MAHKOTA PARADE SHOPPING COMPLEX

MAJESTIC HOTEL

MALACCA RENAISSANCE HOTEL

EMPEROR HOTEL

CENTRAL HOTEL

JALAN BENDAHARA

JALAN BUGARAYA

RESTORAN VAZHAI ELAI

ORANGUTAN ART GALLERY

CHRIST CHURCH

THE STADTHUYS

ST. PAUL'S CHURCH

ISLAMIC MUSEUM

TOURIST OFFICE

GLUTTON'S CORNER

MAHKOTA SQUARE

CENTURY MAHKOTA HOTEL MELAKA

TO ZOO, MINI MALAYSIA MINI ASEAN AND NORTH-SOUTH HIGHWAY

CHONG HO HOTEL

EXPRESS BUS TERMINAL

TAXIS

LOCAL BUS TERMINAL

IMMIGRATION

CHENG HOON TENG TEMPLE

KAMPONG KLING MOSQUE

BABA NYONYA HERITAGE MUSEUM

HEEREN HOUSE

MARITIME MUSEUM

NAVY MUSEUM

FERRIES TO DUMAI

STRAITS

OF

MALACCA

JALAN KUBU

SRI POYATHA VINAYAGAR MOORTHI TEMPLE

CHEE SWEE CHENG MANSION

BABA HOUSE HOTEL

TO TANJUNG KLING AND PORT DICKSON

MALAYSIA

© MOON PUBLICATIONS, INC.

Malacca is also something of a paradox. Although six centuries of colonization, warfare, and political intrigue left behind a rich historical legacy, few impressive monuments remain aside from some colorful Dutch architecture. This is the legacy of conquerors who successively demolished their predecessors' heritage. The Portuguese dismantled Islamic mosques and royal palaces to build their military forts and churches. Then, nearly all Portuguese architecture was destroyed during subsequent Dutch assaults or pulled down when the British finally took Malacca. Still, the handful of surviving European buildings, Chinese temples, and old Malaccan terrace houses makes this city one of Malaysia's leading destinations.

History

At the beginning of the 15th century, Malacca was little more than a small cluster of fishing huts located at the confluence of a narrow muddy river. To the south was Temasik (ancient Singapore), a small but successful trading port ruled by Sumatran Prince Parameswara, who endured almost constant attack by hostile Thai and Indonesian forces who sought to control the Straits of Malacca and its lucrative spice trade. After final destruction by Thai forces, Parameswara took his Islamic court and fled north to a small fishing village of sea pirates and shady *melaka* tress.

It was an inauspicious beginning. But this was the era of spices, when European consumers were willing to pay fabulous sums for Indonesian condiments used to flavor and preserve meats during their long, cold winters. Profits were enormous; 45 Spanish dollars of spice in the Malukus would bring over $1,800 in Venice. This trade had long been controlled by Arab and Indian traders who stopped to rest, barter, and store their goods in Malacca between the monsoons. Paramesara organized the port, lowered taxes, built warehouses, and, with the blessings of the powerful Chinese court in Peking, turned Malacca into one of the world's great trading emporiums.

Mastery of the lucrative spice trade belonged to the nation that controlled the Malukus and held the Malacca Straits, a situation nicely described by Tome Pires: "Whoever is Lord of Malacca has his hands on the throat of Venice." To break the stranglehold of Arab traders and possibly convert some heathens to Christianity, the Portuguese sailed east while Columbus sailed west. Malacca fell to the Portuguese in 1511 when Alfonso de Albuquerque, governor of Portuguese India, sailed into Malacca with a fleet of 18 ships and 800 Portuguese soldiers. He found the ruling sultanate opulent and strongheaded, yet decadent and unable to protect its fragile empire. Albuquerque quickly took the city and massacred all who would not convert to Christianity; in a fit of rage, he then tore down all Muslim mosques and royal palaces. Most traders fled south to Johor or across the channel to Aceh, where they reestablished their trading port. The Portuguese then raised taxes to extortionate levels, a foolish act which marked the end of the port's short but glorious reign as center for Asian trade.

Malacca then passed between various European nations for the next several centuries. After a terrible five-month seige by the Dutch in 1641, which almost completely destroyed the city, Malacca was rebuilt in the image of a Dutch mercantile town. Most of the town's most memorable architecture dates from this period. But authorities in Amsterdam lost interest after discovering that trade winds would carry their spice ships directly from Java to the Cape of Good Hope. By the time Malacca fell to the English East India Company in 1824, the harbor had silted up and most of the trade had moved to Singapore.

One enduring legend centers around the lost fortunes of early Islamic rulers, who once measured their wealth in 200-kg bars of gold. According to ancient chronicles, several tons of gold were stashed away by various sultans and the wealthy Chinese traders of early Malacca—an enormous haul that somehow disappeared and has never been recovered. It is unlikely that the final Islamic rulers were able to remove such a staggering amount of gold and Portuguese conquerors never admitted to finding the cache. New light was shed on the mystery a few years ago when foreign marine salvagers discovered Albuquerque's flagship, the *Flor de la Mar*, buried off the coast of Malacca, perhaps carrying with it the plundered treasure of the final sultanate. Dozens of gold coins and bars were unearthed but most of the missing fortune may yet remain buried somewhere at the bottom of the Malacca Straits.

Christ Church

Small and compact Malacca can be easily seen on foot in a single day. Begin your walking tour at the Tourist Information Center and then walk across to Malacca's "Red Square," a collection of salmon-colored buildings that forms the finest Dutch architecture in Malaysia. Finest of the assemblage is the bright red church built in 1753 for the Dutch Reform Church but now used by the Anglicans. The sanctuary bears many Dutch characteristics: massive walls of thick brick built over plinths of red granite, a roof of Dutch tiles, heavy roundheaded windows, and louvers topped with fan-shaped decorations. The interior is especially rich in detail: massive ceiling beams cut from a single tree, a collection of antique silverware behind the altar, handcarved pews, a brass Bible rest dated *Anno 1773*, and most striking, the old Portuguese, Dutch, and Armenian tombstones set into the floor.

The small park in front holds the marble Queen Victoria Fountain and a beautifully proportioned clock tower donated by a wealthy Chinese merchant. Local Chinese who remember Japanese brutality during WW II were upset when the old English clock was replaced by a Seiko model. Trishaw drivers can be hired here.

The Stadthuys

Malacca's old city hall, constructed by the Dutch between 1641 and 1669, stands as their oldest surviving building in the East. Originally used as the residence of Dutch governors and their retinue, the Stadthuys now serves as a museum divided into history, ethnography, and literature sections. Open daily 0900-1800.

Outside the Stadthuys are embankment walls embedded with memorial plaques to the United East India Company, Queen Victoria's Diamond Jubilee, the first king of Portugal, and the Makara Stone, an ancient Hindu relic in the shape of a stone fish with an elephant head—now the symbol of Malacca. Indonesian *prahus* and wily old sailors smoking *kreteks* sometimes hang out at the pier at the mouth of the Malacca River.

St. Paul's Church

St. Paul's Hill was once covered with Portuguese homes, churches, and shops, enclosed by the three-meter-thick walls of the A Famosa Fortress. One of the few buildings spared destruction by

European powers was St. Paul's, constructed in 1590 by Jesuit missionaries who had previously hosted famous Jesuit missionary St. Francis Xavier. Xavier's corpse was interred here for several months after his death near Macau; his crypt in the rear is covered with wire mesh and a marble statue of the saint stands in the front.

After Malacca fell to the Dutch, St. Paul's was converted into a fortress and the roof was pulled down to allow for military extensions. In 1753 the hill was converted into a burial ground for Dutch notables. Among the 36 unbelievably large tombstones are Latin, Dutch, and Portuguese inscriptions describing the lives of the second bishop of Japan, the captain of Malacca, and various wives and children of local merchants. St. Paul's is also a popular spot for local artists to display their works and chat with Western visitors.

Santiago Gate

This badly blackened stone gate is all that remains of the great 16th-century Portuguese fortress, A Famosa (The Famous). Soon after his conquest of Malacca in 1511, Albuquerque ordered the construction of the walled city as a bastion of Portuguese power and symbol of the nation's predominance in Southeast Asia. Hundreds of slaves and war prisoners tore down local mosques and Muslim tombs for the building brick used to construct a Portuguese castle, two palaces, five churches, and hundreds of homes. After being badly damaged in a Dutch attack, the gate was renovated and ironically replastered with the VOC Dutch crest, dated "Anno 1670." The fort was finally demolished by the British, who only spared Santiago Gate (Gate of St. James) at the insistence of Southeast Asia's first architectural preservationist, Sir Stamford Raffles.

Independence Museum

Mementos of Malaysia's struggle for independence are exhibited inside the former Melaka Club, constructed 1911 by local British planters who installed a library, a cabaret, several bars, and a billiards room. One of the early visitors was Somerset Maugham, who wrote "it is a spacious but shabby building: it has an air of neglect . . . in the morning you may find a couple of planters who have come in from their estates on business and are drinking gin-slings before starting back."

Malacca Sultanate Palace Museum

A reconstruction of the palace of Sultan Mansur (1459-1477) from descriptions found in the *Malay Annals* with first-class exhibits such as lifelike re-creations of Malaccan court life and Malaysian weddings. Also on display are artifacts from every era of Malacca's turbulent past—ancient *batu hidup* stones which reputedly grow with age, the Islamic tombstone of Sultan Mansur Shah, Ming porcelain, Portuguese costumes, Dutch silverware, *nonya* wedding dresses, Malay *krises*, and English sepia-toned photographs. Open daily 0900-1800.

The adjacent old Protestant cemetery holds intriguing Dutch and English headstones that relate sad stories of death in the tropics; memorials to Lt. Harding, killed during the Nanking War; Rachel Milne and her two children, dead from disease; and John Kidd, the doomed captain of the *Morning Star*.

Jalan Tun Tan Cheng Lock

Walk back to the tourist office and cross the bridge to Malacca's old Chinatown, a crosshatch of narrow streets far more fascinating than any historical attractions. Best of all are the people: beaming Malay schoolgirls with heads tightly wrapped in white shawls, heavy Tamil women draped in polyester saris, serious young men on their way to the nearest mosque, Chinese shopkeepers anxiously peddling antiques, old *nonya* ladies dressed in the traditional *sarong kebaya*, pasty tourists being peddled around by sweating rickshaw drivers. The range of emporiums is equally fascinating: coffin carvers with shamrock-shaped repositories, Chinese herbalists who cure fatigue with shark's fin, Indian sari vendors, rubber mills ingeniously situated inside automobile garages, bird sellers up a cheerful alley.

Walk across the bridge, turn left, then continue down Jalan Tun Tan Cheng Lock, once known as Heeren Street and nicknamed Millionaires Row after the lavish Peranakan ancestral homes that flank both sides of the narrow street. Many are decorated with canopies of Chinese tiles, porcelain dragons and flowers, and elaborately carved double doors which open onto interiors furnished with blackwood chairs fashioned after Chinese and Dutch designs.

Baba Nonya Heritage Museum: A privately operated museum inside a Peranakan home

constructed 1896 by millionaire rubber planter Chang Cheng Siew. Open daily 1000-1230 and 1430-1630; the admission fee includes an informative 45-minute tour.

Chee Swee Cheng Mansion: The magnificent Chee House at 117 Jalan Tun Tan Cheng Lock, constructed 1906 by a Eurasian architect, incorporates Chinese and European elements in a classic example of Straits Chinese architecture. Once the Dutch Embassy, today it's a private residence for descendants of the founder of the Overseas Chinese Bank. Another elaborate building decorated with carved deer stands three blocks farther west at number 167.

Cheng Hoon Teng Temple

The "Temple of the Green Merciful Clouds," one of Malaysia's oldest and finest examples of traditional Chinese temple architecture, has served as the center for the Chinese community since it was founded in 1646 by Kapitan China Lee Wei King. The finely proportioned front entrance features two guardian lions, which symbolize filial piety, and moon windows opening into the first courtyard. Inside the spacious main hall are several statues such as a 75-centimeter solid bronze image of Kuan Yin, Man Cho Po (Guardian of Fishermen), and red-faced Kwan Ti, the God of War and Justice. Note the wooden support beams carved with jolly Chinese and fat Europeans and the beautiful lacquer tables as well as the elaborate woodcarvings behind the altars. Halls to the rear honor Confucius and all the Dutch-designated leaders of the Chinese community.

Kampong Kling Mosque

A lovely little mosque and one of the few that modestly dressed Westerners can visit without harassment from indignant Muslims. It was constructed 1868 in a unique Sumatran-Chinese design with distinctive towers shaped somewhat like Chinese pagodas. The stunning interior features Portuguese and British glazed tiles, Victorian chandeliers, and an Islamic wooden floral ceiling—a tasteful integration that makes Kampong Kling among Malacca's finest gems.

Sri Poyatha Vinayagar Moorthi Temple

This colorful Hindu temple constructed 1781 enshrines a black stone image of Vinayagar (also known as Subramaniam), the Hindu deity with a human body and four hands but with the head of an elephant. Although disfigured by an ugly wire fence, the temple's wild color combinations make for some unusual photographs.

The Orangutan House is also worth a visit for its eclectic range of alternative art pieces by Charles Cham and rather graphic T-shirts promoting Malaysian rubber as the world's leading component of condoms.

Other Attractions
The following may be of interest to visitors with extra time.

China Hill: Bukit China, a huge Chinese graveyard hill about two km southeast of the tourist office, holds over 13,000 burial plots whose elevated location blocks the winds of evil and gives the spirits an unobstructed view of their descendants. As the oldest and largest Chinese graveyard outside China, this weedy hill offers great views and another sidelight into Malaccan history. The *Malay Annals* relates that in 1459 the Malaccan sultan accepted a Chinese bride from Emperor Yung Lo of the Ming Dynasty to cement close economic agreements. In return, the sultan bestowed this hill to his young bride and her 500 handmaidens. This historic exchange ensured Malaccan safety and almost guaranteed great economic power. The modest temple at the base of the hill has a dirty but famous well which, according to legend, will ensure the return of any visitor who drinks its waters; it's more likely you will die from pollution.

Portuguese Settlement: Three km east of city center is a small community of some 500 Eurasians of Portuguese-Malay descent who speak a medieval dialect called Cristao (surprisingly similar to 16th-century Portuguese) and celebrate all the familiar Christian holidays. Sounds intriguing but the place more closely resembles a low-income housing project.

Tanjung Kling: A fairly nice beach 10 km northwest of Malacca with several mid-level and luxurious hotels for visitors who would rather stay at the beach than in town.

Air Keroh: Some 15 km north of Malacca near the North-South Highway are several tourist attractions such as a small zoo, crocodile farm, and two theme parks (Taman Mini Malaysia and Taman ASEAN) with reconstructions of traditional Malay homes from all 13 states: Malac-

can long-roofed, Johor five-roofed, Kadazan, and Iban longhouse. Take bus 19 from the local bus terminal.

Budget Accommodations
Malacca has an excellent range of budget guesthouses in an area known as Taman Melaka Raya, a landfill project just east of the massive Mahkota Square reclamation project.

Bus arrivals are invariably met by hordes of frantic, shouting, pushing, sweating rickshaw drivers who desperately wave mimeographed sheets and photo albums of their hostels. Although a rude introduction to what is otherwise a pleasant town, the drivers are helpful and friendly. A taxi or trishaw should cost RM5 or take bus 17 from the local bus terminal.

Traveller's Lodge: One of Malacca's first backpacker venues features decent rooms and a rooftop garden in a modern and clean apartment building. 214B Taman Melaka Raya, tel. (06) 245-3319, RM7 dorm, RM15-30 private room.

Amy Homestay: Another clean and friendly homestay that draws raves from its steady stream of visitors. 156B Taman Melaka Raya, tel. (06) 245-8816, RM7 dorm, RM15-30 private room.

Melaka Youth Hostel: Spotless hostel with both ordinary and a/c dorm rooms. 341 Taman Melaka Raya, tel. (06) 282-7915, RM8-15.

Also located in Taman Melaka Raya are other popular guesthouses such as Robin's Nest, Sunny's Inn, SD Guesthouse, Kancil, and My Place Guesthouse.

Apple Guesthouse: Fairly new operation with clean rooms on a quiet back alley. 24 Lorong Banda Kaba, tel. (06) 667-8744, RM7 dorm, RM15-30 private room.

Eastern Heritage Guesthouse: A neoclassical building constructed 1918 near Bukit China with heaps of character but rather ordinary rooms. 8 Jalan Bukit China, tel. (06) 283-3026, RM7 dorm, RM15-30 private room.

Chong Hoe: Although not really a travelers' center, Chong Hoe can be recommended for its authentic atmosphere and great location in the center of Chinatown; Malacca's cleanest and cheapest Chinese-style hotel. 26 Jalan Tukang Emas, tel. (06) 282-6102, RM20-40.

Majestic Hotel: An aging Chinese hotel with carved wooden swing doors and a timeless bar— almost a colonial classic but the less expensive

MALAYSIA

rooms are hardly larger than shoeboxes. 188 Jalan Bunga Raya, tel. (06) 282-2455, RM20-40.

Moderate Accommodations

Malacca has several modern hotels in the mid-level price range but the following options provide a degree of charm and character not found in newer facilities.

Heeren House: Superb location in a well-restored godown with six a/c rooms overlooking the Malacca River plus a cozy Peranakan cafe and bakery on the ground floor. 1 Jalan Tun Tan Cheng Lock, tel. (06) 281-4241, fax 281-4239, RM100-140.

Baba House: Several old Peranakan homes have been converted into a 42-room hotel with a magnificent if strangely configured lobby. The more expensive upstairs rooms are quite pleasant but the inexpensive rooms to the rear often lack windows and have been filled with cheap, tacky furnishings. 125-127 Jalan Tun Tan Cheng Lock, tel. (06) 281-1216, fax 281-1217, RM70-120.

Luxury Accommodations

Malacca hoteliers in the luxury category face an uncertain future with the recent opening of the 617-room Century Mahkota Hotel Melaka, the 250-room Pan Pacific Melaka, and the 300-room Equatorial Hotel. The Malacca Hotel Association recently noted that occupancy rates had fallen below 50% and no recovery is expected for several years. All this means that most of the following hotels will gladly offer steep discounts off their rack rates upon request by walk-in customers.

Malacca Renaissance Hotel: Malacca entered the major leagues almost a decade ago with the opening of this 24-story hotel at the top end of town which features several restaurants, health center, squash courts, disco, and a small pool on the ninth floor. Jalan Bendahara, tel. (06) 284-8888, fax 284-9269, RM340-460.

Emperor Hotel: Locally owned hotel offers steeply discounted rooms (30-60%), happy hour specials in the cocktail lounge, and whatever else helps fill rooms. 123 Jalan Munshi Abdullah, tel. (06) 284-0777, fax 283-8989, RM250-350.

Tanjung Kling Accommodations

Several new luxurious hotels have opened on this uninspiring stretch of sand facing the choppy waters of the Malacca Straits. Most of the inexpensive

guesthouses and motels have closed down as Tanjung Kling attempts to move upscale.

Klebang Beach Resort: Modern, relatively new 46-room hotel with pool, restaurant, and spotless a/c rooms. Tanjung Kling Km 9, tel. (06) 315-2588, RM160-200.

Shah's Beach Resort: A longtime favorite with 50 deluxe rustic chalets, pool, tennis courts, and Malay/Western restaurant. Tanjung Kling Km 9, tel. (06) 315-2120, fax 315-2088, RM120-160.

Riviera Bay Resort: Flashy new 450-room resort with pool, tennis courts, cafes and restaurants, karaoke, and sports center. Tanjung Kling Km 10, tel. (06) 315-1111, fax 315-3333, RM350-500.

Mutiara Malacca Beach Resort: Another huge new hotel with all possible facilities facing a rather narrow, brownish strip of sand. Tanjung Kling Km 12, tel. (06) 518518, fax 517517, RM240-500.

Restaurants

Malacca has dozens of cafes and restaurants serving outstanding yet inexpensive Chinese, Malay, Indian, Nonya, and Portuguese dishes.

Glutton's Corner: The best selection of budget cafes is along Jalan Taman Merdeka opposite the Mahkota reclamation project, which pushed the shoreline back several blocks from its historic tracings. Merchants are somewhat aggressive about finding customers but selection ranges from creamy oyster omelettes to succulent sea bass steamed in fish stock. Bunga Raya at number 40 serves barbecued Sri Lankan crab, sambal prawns, and steamed lobster in black bean sauce under the careful supervision of manager "Madam Fatso." No joke.

Foodstalls: Inexpensive foodstalls can also be found on Jalan Bendahara opposite the decrepit Central Hotel, and near the produce market on Jalan Kee Ann.

Mahkota Parade Shopping Complex: Western fast food, basement supermarket, and a spotless food court on the first floor. Inexpensive.

Lucky Famous Restaurant: Popular Chinese spot with extensive menu near the guesthouses of Taman Melaka Raya. Best visited with a large group of fellow travelers. 578 Taman Melaka Raya, tel. (06) 284-0031. Inexpensive.

Restoran Vazhai Elai: Authentic down-home banana leaf cafe serving Halal South Indian vegetarian specialties. 42 Jalan Munshi Abdullah, tel. (06) 283-1607. Inexpensive.

Restoran Veni: Well-prepared vegetarian and non-vegetarian Indian dishes. 34 Jalan Temenggong, tel. (06) 284-9570. Inexpensive.

More Indian Cafes: Sri Lakshmi Vilas and adjacent Sri Krishna Bavan at the south end of Jalan Bendahara serve tasty fresh *parathas* accompanied by thick mutton curries. Inexpensive.

Restoran San Pedro: Malacca's Portuguese settlement, three km southeast of city center, features several rustic cafes that serve Portuguese seafood dishes along with jugs of cold beer and memorabilia from the Portuguese era. Cultural performances are held outside in front of the nearby Restoran de Lisbon Saturday evenings starting at 2030. 4 Aranjo Rd., tel. (06) 284-5734.

Transportation

Long-distance buses leave from the terminal on Jalan Tun Ali for Kuala Lumpur, Singapore, Penang, and other Malaysian destinations. The taxi stand is 50 meters up the road near the local bus terminal. Share taxis depart when filled, are fast, and cost about 50% more than a/c buses.

Malacca's nearest train terminus is in Tampin, 40 km north of town. A small airport is at Batu Berendam, 10 km from town, from where Pelangi Air flies to Kuala Lumpur, Singapore, Ipoh, and Medan and Pekan Bharu on Sumatra.

Malacca-Dumai (Sumatra) ferries leave daily at 0800, take four hours, and cost RM80 one-way to the Sumatran gateway for Medan and Lake Toba. Purchase tickets one day in advance.

SEREMBAN

Seremban, the capital of Negri Sembilan (Nine States), is known as the "Minangkabau state" for its concentration of west Sumatran settlers who traditionally honored a matrilineal society based on

Sumatran *adat* laws; all property belonged to female rather than male offspring. Minangkabau means "buffalo horns"—a term perhaps taken from the Minangkabau's feisty nature, their legendary origins, or their magnificent homes capped with distinctive horn-shaped roofs.

Attractions

Seremban attracts few visitors though it's a pleasant enough place with decent hotels and several worthy attractions.

Lake Gardens: Seremban's centrally located twin lakes provide weekend cultural performances, an imposing State Secretariat Building at the north end, and a modern Disneyesque mosque with nine columns symbolizing the nine original states of Negri Sembilan.

Taman Seni Budaya Negeri: Seremban's Arts and Cultural Park features the Muzium Negeri (State Museum), constructed to resemble a Minangkabau palace and two Minangkabau houses built in the 1860s without nails as a gift from the sultan to his engaged daughters. The complex is three km west of the bus station on the road to Kuala Lumpur.

Colonial Architecture: British flair comes full force at the Gothic-style Catholic church, the restrained Methodist church, and impressively colonial King George V school a few blocks south of city center.

Accommodations

Hotels are somewhat overpriced even by Malaysian standards. Hotel Nam Yong and the Oriental Hotel on Jalan Tuanku Munawir offer rudimentary rooms starting at RM25, while better digs are found at the Carlton Star Hotel where a/c rooms cost RM60-80.

Top-end hotels include the Minangkabau-style Tasik overlooking Lake Gardens (RM100-150), Seri Malaysia Hotel in the same price range but one km west of city center, and Allson Klana Resort to the east with Seremban's best facilities priced at RM280-350.

KUALA LUMPUR

Romantically named after the muddy Klang and Gombak rivers, Kuala Lumpur (Muddy Estuary) has unfairly gained a reputation as just another faceless Southeast Asian city best avoided by Western travelers. While the metropolis admittedly has less to offer than Bangkok or Singapore, it is surprisingly rich with graceful architecture that reflects its ethnic diversity: Tudor edifices, Saracenic railway stations and office buildings, smoky Chinese temples filled with gigantic joss sticks, wildly painted Indian temples dedicated to multi-armed gods, gleaming Islamic mosques, and most unexpectedly, some of Southeast Asia's most impressive modern skyscrapers.

KL (its popular nickname) also boasts an outstanding museum and an exceptionally vibrant night market in Chinatown. Also intriguing are the divergent races who live together with little outward signs of racial tension. Kuala Lumpur isn't a major destination, but to skip this clean, safe, and historically significant city is to miss a look at modern Malaysia.

History

Kuala Lumpur, one of the youngest cities in Southeast Asia, hides a turbulent history reminiscent of a gunslinger town from the American Wild West. KL sprang to life in the 1850s after two mining chiefs, Raja Jumaat and Raja Abdullah, persuaded Chinese miners to prospect for tin in Klang Valley, a dozen kilometers beyond the rich mines of Lukut. It was a treacherous undertaking: only 18 of the original 87 Hakka miners who poled up the Klang River survived the first month. But enormous tin deposits were uncovered and a tremendous mining town was constructed only to be almost completely destroyed by devastating civil wars between rival secret societies and contentious Malay chiefs.

In walked Yap Ah Loy, a ruthless but energetic Hakka who rose to the position of "Kapitan China" and restored order by offering 50 silver dollars for each hooligan's head. Yap almost single-handedly transformed Kuala Lumpur—a filthy, disease-ridden mining camp with wide-open brothels, opium dens, and enormous gambling halls—into the leading commerical center of the Malayan Peninsula.

Attracted by the economic vitality, British officials transferred their headquarters from nearby Port Klang to Kuala Lumpur in 1880 and, under the leadership of Frank Swettenham, widened streets and built an array of delightfully imaginative Moorish-styled government offices.

ATTRACTIONS

Kuala Lumpur is compact; most of the following attractions are within easy walking distance of city center. The biggest challenge facing walkers is traffic—busy highways often divide attractions. Crossovers and walkways exist but are almost impossible to find. A good map is essential and the best is produced by Periplus. The following attractions are described in a suggested walking order.

The Colonial Core

After young timber-and-atap KL was destroyed by fire in the late-19th century, architects turned to fire-resistant brick structures, which now comprise the historic monuments of modern Kuala Lumpur. The City Hall, State Secretariat, and Railway Station were all designed by British colonial engineers from 1894 to 1910.

These ambitious young designers borrowed English Tudor, Persian Arabesque, and Indian Saracenic styles to create something quite unique. Leading architects included A.C. Norman, who looked to North Indian Mogul traditions, and A.B. Hubbard, who favored the artistry of Islam. Both fused golden domes, soaring minarets, graceful Islamic archways, and spiraling stairways into remarkable statements that remain Kuala Lumpur's greatest attraction—despite the arrival of observation towers and high-rise oil buildings.

Jame Mosque: Start your walking tour at the red-and-white Masjid Jame (Friday Mosque), nestled among coconut palms at the exact spot where KL was founded. Designed by Hubbard in 1909 after a North Indian mosque, this en-

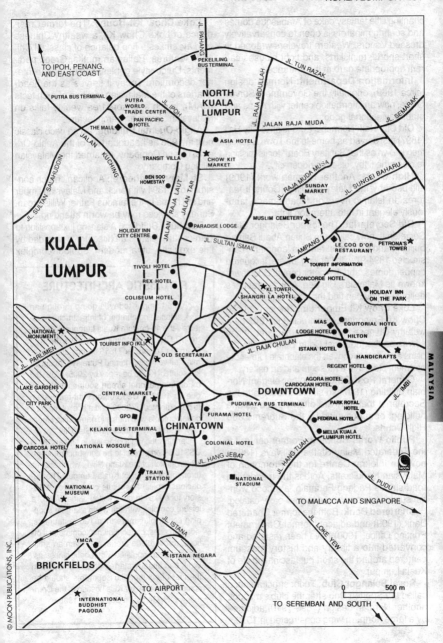

KUALA LUMPUR

NORTH KUALA LUMPUR

DOWNTOWN

CHINATOWN

BRICKFIELDS

TO IPOH, PENANG, AND EAST COAST

PUTRA BUS TERMINAL
PUTRA WORLD TRADE CENTER
THE MALL
PAN PACIFIC HOTEL
ASIA HOTEL
TRANSIT VILLA
CHOW KIT MARKET
BEN SOO HOMESTAY
PARADISE LODGE
HOLIDAY INN CITY CENTRE
TIVOLI HOTEL
REX HOTEL
COLISEUM HOTEL
NATIONAL MONUMENT
TOURIST INFO (KL)
OLD SECRETARIAT
LAKE GARDENS
CITY PARK
CENTRAL MARKET
GPO
KELANG BUS TERMINAL
CARCOSA HOTEL
NATIONAL MOSQUE
COLONIAL HOTEL
TRAIN STATION
NATIONAL MUSEUM
NATIONAL STADIUM
YMCA
ISTANA NEGARA
INTERNATIONAL BUDDHIST PAGODA

SUNDAY MARKET
MUSLIM CEMETERY
LE COQ D'OR RESTAURANT
PETRONA'S TOWER
TOURIST INFORMATION
CONCORDE HOTEL
HOLIDAY INN ON THE PARK
KL TOWER
SHANGRI LA HOTEL
MAS
EQUITORIAL HOTEL
LODGE HOTEL
HILTON
ISTANA HOTEL
HANDICRAFTS
REGENT HOTEL
AGORA HOTEL
CARDOGAN HOTEL
PARK ROYAL HOTEL
FEDERAL HOTEL
MELIA KUALA LUMPUR HOTEL
PUDURAYA BUS TERMINAL
FURAMA HOTEL

JL. PAHANG
PEKELILING BUS TERMINAL
JL. TUN RAZAK
JL. RAJA ABDULLAH
JALAN RAJA MUDA
JL. SEMARAK
JALAN KUCHING
JL. IPOH
JALAN RAJA LAUT
JALAN TAR
JL. RAJA MUDA MUSA
JL. SUNGEI BAHARU
JL. SULTAN SALAHUDDIN
JL. SULTAN ISMAIL
JL. AMPANG
JL. PARLIMEN
JL. RAJA CHULAN
JL. HANG JEBAT
JL. HANG TUAH
JL. PUDU
JL. IMBI
JL. ISTANA
JL. LOKE YEW

TO MALACCA AND SINGAPORE
TO SEREMBAN AND SOUTH
TO AIRPORT

MALAYSIA

MOON

0   500 m

© MOON PUBLICATIONS, INC.

chanting little fantasy cake of Arabesque domes and soaring minarets is open to conservatively dressed visitors. Western travelers wrapped in short-shorts, miniskirts, and tight blouses can rent appropriate garb at the entrance.

Information Department: Norman design (circa 1909), originally the Government Survey Office, now an information center with maps and other navigational goods.

Old City Hall: Norman's Euro-Islamic City Hall (1897) first served as home to the Town Council, then known as the "Sanitary Board" for its mission to clean the filthy, disease-ridden city.

High Court: Another Norman work (1909) still used by the Malaysian High Court; it features an Islamic riverside façade made fabulously elegant in late afternoon light.

Old Secretariat: The former Selangor State Secretariat, now called the Sultan Abdul Samad building and KL's most famous landmark, constructed 1894-97 with flanking towers, lacquered copper domes, and 43-meter central clocktower known as Malaysia's Big Ben. A photographer's delight—if you can find the right angle.

Loke Chow Kit Emporium: The former Loke Chow Kit Emporium, constructed in 1905 by a wealthy Chinese clothing manufacturer, today serves as the Industrial Court Building; though plans are afloat to convert the elaborate former department store into a museum and art gallery.

General Post Office: Another elegant Norman building (1897) so similar in design to the Secretariat that they are often viewed as one building; both occupied by the Supreme and High Courts.

Public Works Building: Former center for the Federated Malay States Railways (1896); now the Infokrat Centre for the Promotion of Malaysian Handicrafts. Across the maddening road stands Padang Fountain, a rococo wonder supposedly purchased by mail-order catalog.

Chartered Bank: Both the former Chartered Bank (1909) and adjacent former Government Printing Office (1900) have been restored and converted into a library and history museum centered around the short but fascinating life of Kuala Lumpur.

Royal Selangor Club: Tudor structure once called the Spotted Dog after the club's mascot; another Norman-design (1890-1910) adjoined by a large northern wing constructed in 1970.

Loke Chow Kit House: The former residence of Loke Chow Kit, a wealthy Chinese *towkay,* strikes a fine balance of classical Chinese features, Palladian motifs, Greek pediments, Dutch-style gables, and European interior decoration. Today it serves as the headquarters of the Malaysian Institute of Architects (PAM), which sponsors free weekly talks on Malaysian history and architecture.

Anglo-Oriental Building: An art deco classic built in 1936 as headquarters of the Anglo-Oriental Mining Company, renamed the Malaysian Mining Company.

St. Mary's Cathedral: Anglican church constructed in 1894 with brick and Malaysian timber and still home to the famous Father Willis organ. Sunday services may be worth attending.

Dayabumi Building: A startling juxtaposition to 19th-century Islamic architecture is provided by this exquisite, ultra-modern, 36-floor complex

---

FUTURISTIC ARCHITECTURE

Kuala Lumpur today is going through an astonishing number of infrastructure projects—the 40-hectare Kuala Lumpur City Centre (KLCC) project which includes the twin Petronas Towers; an US$8 billion national administrative capital named Putrajaya (about 25 km south of KL) to be ready by 2005; a US$3.6 billion international airport southeast of town due for 1998; a US$3 billion light-rail system to be completed by 2000; and a host of multiuse developments with futuristic names like Linear City, Vision City, and Berjaya Star City.

Certainly the most intriguing is Linear City, a US$10 billion project to be constructed over a 12-km stretch of the Klang River, which snakes through the center of Kuala Lumpur. The audacious project has as its centerpiece a 10-story tube-like structure called "Giga World," a leisure complex with the world's largest shopping center plus more than 100 restaurants, video arcades, condominiums, commercial offices, a rollerblade arena, and even an artificial rainforest populated with robotic dinosaurs. Work has already started on Linear City and the first of six modular segments should be completed in time for KL's hosting of the Commonwealth Games in September 1998.

MALAYSIA

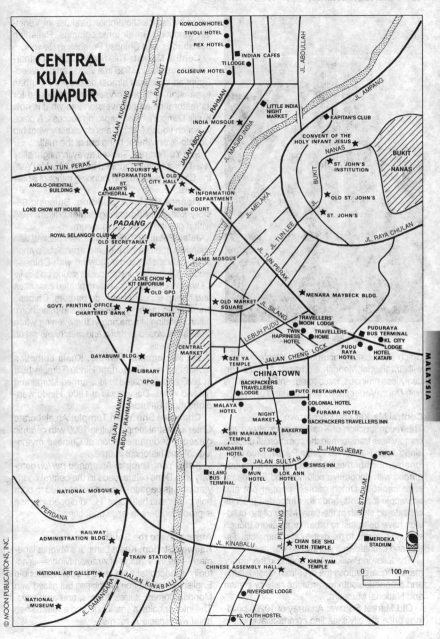

CENTRAL KUALA LUMPUR

KOWLOON HOTEL
TIVOLI HOTEL
REX HOTEL
INDIAN CAFES
TI LODGE
COLISEUM HOTEL

JL. ABDULLAH

JL. AMPANG

LITTLE INDIA NIGHT MARKET

INDIA MOSQUE

KAPITAN'S CLUB

CONVENT OF THE HOLY INFANT JESUS

BUKIT NANAS

BUKIT NANAS

JALAN KUCHING

JALAN ABDUL

JL. RAJA LAUT

RAHMAN

JL. MASJID INDIA

JALAN TUN PERAK

TOURIST INFORMATION

ST. JOHN'S INSTITUTION

OLD CITY HALL

ST. MARY'S CATHEDRAL

ANGLO-ORIENTAL BUILDING

INFORMATION DEPARTMENT

OLD ST. JOHN'S

LOKE CHOW KIT HOUSE

HIGH COURT

JL. MELAKA

ST. JOHN'S

JL. RAYA CHULAN

PADANG

ROYAL SELANGOR CLUB

OLD SECRETARIAT

JAME MOSQUE

JL. TUN LEE

JL. TUN PERAK

LOKE CHOW KIT EMPORIUM

OLD GPO

MENARA MAYBECK BLDG.

GOVT. PRINTING OFFICE
CHARTERED BANK

INFOKRAT

OLD MARKET SQUARE

JL. SILANG

TRAVELLERS' MOON LODGE

PUDURAYA BUS TERMINAL

LEBUH PUDU

TWIN HAPPINESS HOTEL

TRAVELLERS HOME

KL CITY LODGE

DAYABUMI BLDG.

CENTRAL MARKET

JALAN CHENG LOCK

PUDU RAYA HOTEL

HOTEL KATARI

LIBRARY

SZE YA TEMPLE

GPO

CHINATOWN

JALAN TUANKU

ABDUL RAHMAN

BACKPACKERS TRAVELLERS LODGE

FUTO RESTAURANT

MALAYA HOTEL

NIGHT MARKET

COLONIAL HOTEL

FURAMA HOTEL

SRI MARIAMMAN TEMPLE

BAKERY

BACKPACKERS TRAVELLERS INN

MANDARIN HOTEL

CT GH

JL. HANG JEBAT

YWCA

JALAN SULTAN

SWISS INN

NATIONAL MOSQUE

KLANG BUS TERMINAL

MUN HOTEL

LOK ANN HOTEL

JL. PERDANA

RAILWAY ADMINISTRATION BLDG.

JL. KINABALU

JL. PETALING

JL. STADIUM

CHAN SEE SHU YUEN TEMPLE

MERDEKA STADIUM

TRAIN STATION

NATIONAL ART GALLERY

JALAN KINABALU

CHINESE ASSEMBLY HALL

KHUN YAM TEMPLE

0   100 m

NATIONAL MUSEUM

JL. DAMANSARA

RIVERSIDE LODGE

KL YOUTH HOSTEL

MALAYSIA

© MOON PUBLICATIONS, INC.

modern Islamic architecture

which successfully incorporates Western styles with traditional Moorish elements. And it's certainly less ominous, foreboding, and evil than the twin Darth-Vader spires of Petronas Towers.

Central Market and Chinatown

The reconstruction of Kuala Lumpur after 19th-century fires transformed the commercial districts along Jalan Bandar and Jalan Petaling into fashionable neighborhoods filled with shophouses graced with decorative columns and European-style capitols, Dutch gables, pepper pot and pineapple topknots, and other imported touches considered stylish at the time. Many of the buildings have been lost to urban renovation, though enough remains to make the old commercial district and Chinatown a worthwhile wander.

The following walking tour begins in the former market square across the river from Masjid Jame and proceeds south towards the railway station and National Museum.

Old Market Square: An array of 1920s buildings once the city's leading commercial enclave noted by its eclectic architectural use of Venetian windows, Greek Ionic columns, Palladian balustrades, and Chinese Peranakan tilework.

Central Market: This restored produce market constructed in 1935 in a vague art deco/neo-Egyptian style was almost destroyed for urban expansion until preservationists petitioned for its restoration and conversion into what is now Kuala Lumpur's most surprising success. A place to watch young Malaysians do exactly what hip kids do everywhere: hang out at the mall.

Sze Ya Temple: Tucked away in a tight alley is a Taoist temple founded in 1882 by Mr. Yap, the Chinese warlord and founding father of Kuala Lumpur.

Menara Maybank Building: Stunning 58-story *kris*-shaped banking center built in 1988 with a ground floor coin museum.

Jalan Petaling: Chinatown street packed with shoppers, merchants, pavement palmists, python soup cafes, shops overflowing with Chinese wedding dresses, roasted ducks strung up like little wagons, hawkers peddling pirated cassettes and cheap shoes, streetside barbers, Chinese pharmacies pushing deer antler and rhino horn. Jalan Petaling is amazing in the evening when streets are closed to traffic and merchants set up their foodstalls.

Sri Mariamman Temple: Kuala Lumpur's oldest and most important Hindu Temple built in 1887 and dedicated to four-armed Murga and his two wives. Daily *pujas* at 1800; Hindu weddings most Saturdays.

Chan See Shu Yuen Temple: An elaborate Chan ancestral temple built in 1906 with ceramic glazed roof ornamentation of Chinese mythological and historical figures.

Khun Yam Temple: An arched *pai lou* gateway with Doric pillars leads to the central courtyard and its pagoda-shaped ovens used to burn holy paper and hell notes. Hand-dipped incense is produced here in large quantities.

Attractions to the South

Railway Station: Kuala Lumpur's favorite landmark—the very image of *Arabian Nights*—is actually a functional train shed modeled after old English glass-and-iron prototypes but gilded with Moorish domes, spires, turrets, and archways. The interior holds a small cafe and a refurbished hotel with spacious rooms.

Nearby sights include the Malayan Railway Administration Headquarters, National Art Gallery, and National Mosque.

National Museum: One of Southeast Asia's finest museums and repository for the country's historic and artistic wealth. Unlike other Asian museums, Musium Negara provides extraordinarily imaginative dioramas and theme shows that bring Malaysian culture to life: a life-sized Malay wedding, collections of Southeast Asian puppets, circumcision tools, Islamic grave markers, Peranakan displays, Malay games. . . even Lat cartoons! The history gallery has Srivijaya bronzes, the famous Trengganu stone, Martaban jars, and an "amok catcher" used to capture Malays run "amok," while the Gold Room offers precious *krises* and the decidedly curious "modesty discs." Upstairs exhibits range from Malaysian rock lyrics to live shadow theater, all chosen by Dato Shahrum, the wonderfully innovative director who deservedly won for his efforts Asia's prestigious Magsaysay Award.

Lake Gardens: Kuala Lumpur's green-belt area features the National Monument sculpted by the same artist responsible for the Iwo Jima Memorial (you'll notice the resemblance), Parliament House, and natural sights such as an orchid garden, butterfly park, and deer park. An afternoon cocktail at the Carcosa Seri Negara Hotel is recommended for visitors with hired transportation.

International Buddhist Pagoda: A modern Indian-style stupa south of city center filled with replicas of Buddhas and pagodas.

Attractions to the North

India Mosque: Muslim Indian mosque and headquarters for Jammah Tabligh, Malaysia's fundamentalist Islamic missionary body whose 30,000 missionaries wear *baju Melayu* (Pakistani attire) and sport untrimmed moustaches and beards. Nearby are paraphernalia shops hawking woven hairpieces and Korans, Hindu street barbers, *sari* emporiums, and sidewalk portrait painters.

Attractions to the East

Jalan Ampang: Kuala Lumpur's former millionaire's row features several impressive mansions such as the once-seedy Bok House, now Le Coq d'Or, (worth visiting for the elaborately tiled bathrooms) and nostalgic Chan Chin Moo House. A path heads north through a pretty cemetery to Pasar Minggu (Sunday Market).

Jalan Bukit Nanas: Noteworthy Gothic and neo-Classical buildings include St. John's Church (1886), St. John's Institution (1908), and Convent of the Holy Infant Jesus (1912).

Kuala Lumpur Tower: Menara Kuala Lumpur, at 421 meters, ranks as the third highest observation tower in the world and the most expensive at RM270 million. The 11-level tower head, opened in 1996 and modeled after a Malaysian *gasing* (spinning top), houses telecommunication stations, a revolving restaurant which takes an hour to complete the cycle, and an observation platform served by four speedy lifts (22 km/h). Admission is RM8 adult, RM3 children under 12. Open daily 1000-2200.

Attractions near Kuala Lumpur

Batu Caves: Popular side trip 13 km north of town with limestone caves filled with life-sized sculptures of Lord Muruga and other garishly painted Hindu deities made even more bizarre by theatrical colored lights. Batu Caves comes alive at Thaipusam, when thousands of Hindus gather to honor Lord Subramaniam. Take minibus 11 from Central Market or bus 70 from the stop outside Bangkok Bank in Chinatown. The 30-

MALAYSIA

PETRONAS TOWERS

In 1997 Malaysia claimed title as the country with the world's tallest building—Petronas Towers, which houses the national oil company. But is this American-designed tower the largest structure in the world and has Petronas Towers seized the title from Chicago's Sears Tower? It all depends on spires.

Petronas measures 1,483 feet to the top of its spire, while Sears Tower does not include its spires in total height. Do spires really count when measuring height? Most architectural firms measure building height from ground level to top floor elevation and disregard superfluous spires and transmission antennas. By that standard, Sears Tower remains the tallest structure in the world at 1,454 feet and 110 floors, putting Petronas in second place with 1,224 feet and 88 floors.

minute rides passes some of the world's largest and ugliest open-pit tin mines.

Templar Park: A 500-hectare national park 10 km beyond Batu Caves with well-marked pathways that wind past cascading streams, bathing pools, and tropical foliage. Take bus 66 from Puduraya bus terminal.

Genting Highlands: Hillside gambling resort with hotels, golf courses, jungle trails, and casinos packed with Chinese gamblers testing their karma—Malaysia's sole place to play blackjack, craps, and Chinese games such as *tai sai*. Gaming parlors here give some of the lowest payout ratios in the world. Genting, 56 km from Kuala Lumpur, can be reached by bus from Puduraya terminal.

ACCOMMODATIONS

Budget—Chinatown

Kuala Lumpur has a good selection of inexpensive guesthouses and Chinese hotels with dorm beds and private rooms, common baths, and travel services that book buses, trains, and organized tours to nearby attractions. Most are basic and somewhat overpriced but adequate for a night or two. The following are in Chinatown or the old shopping district a few blocks north.

Backpackers Travellers Inn: Convenient Chinatown location, spotless rooms, and friendly management make this a popular place. 60 Jalan Sultan, tel. (03) 238-2473, RM8-12 dorm, RM25-70 private room.

Backpackers Travellers Lodge: Another Chinatown guesthouse with common lounging area and general travel services. 158 Jalan Lee, tel. (03) 201-0889, RM8-10 dorm, RM25-60 private room.

Travellers' Moon Lodge: Popular guesthouse with helpful management by Fred, Cletus, and May. 36 Jalan Silang, tel. (03) 230-6601, RM8-10 dorm, RM20-30 private room.

Twin Happiness Hotel: Newly renovated hotel with well-furnished rooms and helpful proprietors. 44 Jalan Silang, tel. (03) 238-7667, RM8-10 dorm, RM40-55 private room.

Travellers Home: No dorms but fairly large and clean rooms. 46C Jalan Siliang, tel. (03) 230-6601, RM25-30 private room.

KL City Lodge: An inexpensive but somewhat rough hotel opposite the bus terminal. 16A Jalan Pudu Lama, tel. (03) 230-5275, RM10 dorm, RM25-35 private room.

Riverside Lodge: Spotless rooms in a quiet location east of the railway station about 10 minutes south of Chinatown. 80 Jalan Rotan, tel. (03) 201-1210, RM8-10 dorm, RM25-40 private room.

Kuala Lumpur Youth Hostel: Modern, clean, four-story a/c hostel with 84 dorm beds, TV lounge, dining area, and tour services. Larger and more comfortable than most KL guesthouses. 21 Jalan Kampung Attap, tel. (03) 230-6870, RM12-15.

YMCA: Quality rooms but an inconvenient location well south of city center. 95 Jalan Kandang Kerbau, tel. (03) 274-1439, RM40-90 for an a/c room with TV and private bath.

Colonial Hotel: Venerable Chinese hotel with winding hallways, teetering staircases, creaky old men wandering around, and small, clean rooms where you can hear your neighbor cough through open-walled partitions. Atmosphere . . . of sorts. 39-43 Jalan Sultan, tel. (03) 238-0336, RM25-35.

Others in Chinatown: Jalan Sultan has several other cheap but *very* seedy Chinese hotels such as the Lee Mun and the Sun Kong. Ask for a room away from the street. Rooms with fan and common bath start at RM20, a/c doubles with private bath are RM35-45.

Budget—North

The following guesthouses and old hotels offer an escape from the congestion and noise of Chinatown.

Ben Soo Homestay: Small but friendly homestay run by helpful Ben Soo in his mother's house—a genuine homestay which provides complimentary breakfast for all guests. Call Ben's cell phone at (010) 332-7013 for free transport from the bus terminal or train station. 61B Front, 2nd floor, Jalan Tiong Nam, tel. (03) 291-8096, RM10 dorm, RM25-35 private room.

Paradise Lodge: Small 10-room hotel two km north of downtown run by a friendly Indian "manageress." 319-1 Jalan Tuanku Abdul Rahman, tel. (03) 292-2872, RM25-45.

Coliseum Hotel: Famous old hotel somewhat seedy but rooms are spacious and common baths are kept fairly clean. The ground floor restaurant and bar, once frequented by Somerset Maugham and other notable novelists, still serves some of the best steaks in town. 100 Jalan Tuanku Abdul Rahman, tel. (03) 292-6270, RM25-35.

Tivoli Hotel: A convenient and similar alternative to the often filled Coliseum Hotel with enormous rooms, chipping paint, sagging beds, and the ubiquitous washbasin. 136-138 Jalan Tuanku Abdul Rahman, tel. (03) 292-4108, RM25-40.

Moderate

Both older properties and newer mid-market hotels can be found in Chinatown, north along Jalan Tuanku Abdul Rahman, and east in Kuala Lumpur's so-called "golden triangle." The oversupply of hotel rooms means that discounts are often given upon request at the front counter.

Hotel Puduraya: A fairly new 200-room highrise tower hotel conveniently located above the Puduraya bus terminal with restaurant, health club, gym, and acceptable if somewhat faded rooms. Puduraya Bus Terminal, 4th floor; tel. (03) 232-1000, fax 230-5567, RM120-140.

Hotel Katari: Just across from Puduraya bus terminal is another good-value hotel with Makana Coffeehouse and 100 mid-level a/c rooms with TV and in-house videos. 38 Jalan Pudu, tel. (03) 201-7777, fax 201-7911, RM120-180.

Hotel Furama: High-rise Chinatown hotel with decent rooms at fair prices. Jalan Sultan, tel. (03) 230-1777, fax 230-2110, RM130-160.

Swiss Inn: New Chinatown hotel with spacious, clean rooms plus popular coffee shop and nightclub with live bands. 62 Jalan Sultan, tel. (03) 232-3333, fax 201-6699, RM140-180.

Heritage Hotel: Kuala Lumpur's famous train station features a newly refurbished hotel with Malay restaurant, cocktail lounge, and a/c rooms with TV and private bath. Jalan Sultan Hishamuddin, tel. (03) 273-5588, fax 273-2842, RM180-240.

Luxury

Top-end hotels are located in the "golden triangle" district filled with shopping centers and rush-hour traffic jams beyond belief.

Shangri-La: Rated among the leading hotels in the country with three restaurants (Japanese, Cantonese, and European), health club, semi-

circular pool, nightclub, and the largest rooms in town. 11 Jalan Sultan Ismail, tel. (03) 232-2388, fax 230-1514, RM550-700.

Regent: KL's popular luxury property provides 542 luxurious guestrooms with panoramic views, five restaurants, four bars, and a beautiful swimming pool. 160 Jalan Bukit Bintang, tel. (03) 241-8000, fax 242-1441, RM550-700.

Pan Pacific: The best option for convention and exhibition delegates for its location next to the Putra World Trade Centre. Jalan Putra, tel. (03) 442-5555, fax 441-7236, RM380-460.

Mandarin Oriental: Situated in the new Kuala Lumpur City Centre project near Petronas Towers is KL's newest deluxe property, a 628-room hotel with several food and beverage outlets, the city's largest ballroom, comprehensive business center, health club, pool, and tennis courts. KLCC, tel. (03) 232-4422, fax 232-4487, RM650-900.

Carcosa Seri Negara: A spectacular pair of fully restored colonial mansions set on 450 acres of landscaped gardens, five minutes from city center, under the management of AmanResorts—the premier boutique inventor of Southeast Asia. The Carcosa once served as residence of Sir Frank Swettenham, British advisor to the Sultan of Perak, while Seri Negara housed the Governor of the Straits Settlements. Tasik Perdana, tel. (03) 282-1888, fax 282-7888, U.S. reservations (800) 447-7462, RM950-2,800.

RESTAURANTS

Night Markets

Kuala Lumpur's most memorable evening dining experience is Chinatown along Jalan Petaling, which comes alive after sunset with foodstalls serving steamboat chili crab, steamed prawns, and *bah kut teh* (pork ribs with rice) and small cafes and corner stalls serving inexpensive claypots and delicious *lo han kuo,* an ice-cold drink made from boiled *longan* and sugar.

Night food markets are also found on Jalan Masjid India two blocks north of the mosque and around Chow Kit Market north of city center. Pasar Minggu (Sunday Market) in Kampong Bharu actually operates on Saturday evenings, but it's a disappointing experience with tacky souvenir stalls and mediocre food. Jalan Tu-

MALAYSIA

anku Abdul Rahman on Saturday evenings is closed to traffic and packed with shoppers and food vendors—a great scene.

Indian

Little India near Masjid India just north of city center has plenty of foodstalls and simple cafes that serve Indian dishes at rock bottom prices. More formal settings include Bangles Restaurant at 60 Jalan Tuanku Abdul Rahman and nearby Shiraz Hotel cafe at 1 Jalan Medan Tuanku for Pakistani meals. Omar Khayam next door serves Mogul and vegetarian dishes.

Several South Indian vegetarian cafes can be found in the Brickfields area near the YMCA, two km south of city center. Banana-leaf shops serving vegetarian *murtabaks* and curried dishes include Devi Annapoorna on Lorong Maarof, a non-profit venture run by volunteers from the Temple of Fine Arts.

Other Asian

Chinese is the most common but the following Thai, Nonya, and Malay restaurants may provide a welcome change from Cantonese fare.

Kapitan's Club: Classy Nonya restaurant in a restored shophouse with reasonably priced Peranakan entrees plus a selection of Chinese and Western dishes. 35 Jalan Ampang, tel. (03) 201-0242. Moderate.

Barn Thai: Thai dishes served in a pleasant spot decorated with Thai handicrafts and antiques plus jazz performances starting nightly around 2300. 370 Jalan Tun Razak, tel. (03) 244-6699. Moderate.

Restoran Seri Melayu: Cultural performances plus either set or buffet Malay meals served in a 500-seat hall built to resemble a wooden sultanate palace. 1 Jalan Conlay, tel. (03) 245-1833. Moderate.

Bon Ton: Marble tabletops and club chairs in a colonial bungalow-cafe, now a popular haunt of expatriates and upscale Malaysians in search of simple home-cooked Malay and international cuisine. Reservations recommended. 7 Jalan Kia Peng, tel. (03) 241-3614. Moderate.

Western

Along with the fast food outlets scattered around the city, KL has a few unique restaurants with charm and character plus Western cafes that transform themselves into nightclubs as the evening progresses.

Coliseum Hotel: A 70-year-old institution famed for its outstanding sizzling, pepper, and sirloin steaks served by elderly Hainanese waiters almost as old as the hotel itself. 98-100 Jalan Tuanku Abdul Rahman, tel. (03) 292-6270. Moderate.

Le Coq d'Or: Former mansion residence of a wealthy Chinese merchant, Le Coq d'Or provides a touch of colonial charm with its lofty ceilings, Italian marble statues, oil paintings in gilt frames, and airy dining rooms ventilated by fans powered by reconditioned DC-3 engines. Set lunches are economical or you can go for the big splurge and try their beef fondue, chicken breast with cognac, or steak à la Luciano. 121 Jalan Ampang, tel. (03) 261-9732. Moderate to Expensive.

The Jump: Tex Mex food served in a kitschy but popular nightclub where dancing to house music starts around 2300. 241 Jalan Tun Razak, tel. (03) 245-0046. Moderate.

Yellow Cafe: Romantically decked-out cafe open all night with a Continental menu plus a large selection of seafood dishes. 237 Jalan Bukit Bintang, tel. (03) 245-9935. Moderate.

CULTURE CLASH IN KUALA LUMPUR

Anyone who wanders around central KL or spends any time in the Central Market will discover the underbelly of Malaysian society: the heavy-metal world of the *kutus*. Literally meaning "lice" in Malay, *kutus* are young Malaysian rockers who have rejected the increasing Islamic fundamentalism of Malaysian society and embraced the rebellious signs of the Western world—punk music, black leather jackets, safety pins and chains. While not a remarkable form of rebellion, *kutu* culture and their "decadent" rock music are considered direct challenges to conservative Muslim lifestyles and the Malaysian government, which has banned rock concerts by subversives such as Michael Jackson. All this censorship has done little to change the tide. Today, *kutu* culture and *kutu* rock bands are immensely popular, adding another intriguing insight into the wildly divergent worlds of contemporary Malaysia.

MALAYSIA

TRAVEL PRACTICALITIES

Tourist Information

Tourism Malaysia headquarters, tel. (03) 441-1295, Putra World Trade Center in the north of town is open Mon.-Fri. 0830-1645, Saturday 0830-1300.

More convenient is the Malaysia Tourist Information Centre, tel. (03) 242-3929, inside a former colonial mansion at 109 Jalan Ampang in KL's "golden triangle." Along with the tourist information counter, facilities include a MAS reservation desk, money changer, bus bookings, national parks counter, Telekom office, restaurant, audiovisual shows, and cultural performances most afternoons and some evenings.

Travel information can also be picked up at the Kuala Lumpur Tourist Association, tel. (03) 238-1832, at 3 Jalan Sultan Hishamuddin next to the National Art Gallery, and at their branches in the train station and airport.

Services

Immigration: Malaysian visas can be extended at the immigration office, tel. (03) 255-5077, on Jalan Semantan, one km west of Lake Gardens. Most foreign diplomatic offices are open weekdays 0900-1600.

Mail: The General Post Office in the Dayabumi Complex at 9 Jalan Sultan Hishamuddin is open daily except Sunday 0800-1800. American Express cardholders can receive mail at AMEX, MAS Bldg., 2nd floor, P.O. Box 12269, Kuala Lumpur 50772.

Taman Negara: Information and reservations from the Malaysia Tourist Information Centre on Jalan Ampang.

Travel Agents: Best budget agency is MSL Travel, tel. (03) 442-4722, 66 Jalan Putra next to the Grand Central Hotel.

Telephone: Overseas calls can be made from the Malaysia Tourist Information Centre on Jalan Ampang 0900-2100 and from the Telekom office on Jalan Raja Chulan around the clock.

TRANSPORTATION

Subang Airport

Kuala Lumpur's Subang Airport, 22 km from city center, has a post office, left-luggage service, international phones, and tourist information office open daily 0900-2300. Taxis operate on a coupon system and cost RM25-30. Blue bus #47 costs RM2, runs every 30 minutes, and terminates at Klang bus terminal in Chinatown.

Subang Airport will be served by a high-speed express rail link by December 1999. This new system will connect the airport with Brickfields in Kuala Lumpur in 30 minutes for an estimated RM32. Travelers will also be able to go through airport formalities, including baggage check-in and customs clearance, at the KL Sentral station in Brickfields.

Bus

Puduraya Bus Terminal near Chinatown is the departure and arrival point for most long-distance buses and share taxis. Dozens of bus companies are located inside the confusing terminal; inquire first at the tourist information booth at the main entrance.

Klang bus terminal in Chinatown has buses to Shah Alam, Klang, and Subang Airport.

Buses to Taman Negara depart from Pekililing bus terminal, tel. (03) 442-1256, north of town on Jalan Tun Razak.

Train

Trains to Singapore, Butterworth, and Thailand leave several times daily from the station on Jalan Sultan Hishamuddin. The information counter can provide schedules, rates, and information on student discounts, rail passes, and express services to Bangkok.

Share Taxis

Share taxis leave from Puduraya bus terminal one floor above bus level. Fares are about 50% higher than a/c bus service.

MALAYSIA

KUALA LUMPUR TO PENANG

TAMAN NEGARA

Straddling a mountain range that escaped glaciation, Taman Negara (National Park) ranks among the world's oldest tropical rainforests—over 130 million years old. Visitors can hike through dense jungle on well-marked trails, overnight in a wildlife hut, fish, enjoy whitewater rafting, and in general, escape the concrete jungles of modern Malaysia. Wildlife sightings are extremely rare but the powerful beauty of the rainforest makes Taman Negara a very special destination.

Rainforest Walks

Hiking paths are easy to follow with maps provided by local rangers, but it's best to pick up superior maps in Kuala Lumpur from the tourist office or local bookstores. Many of the trails were originally mapped and marked by Australian naturalist Ken Rubeli, who has campaigned since 1974 to stop road and dam construction in the park.

A popular half-day hike leads 4.5 km to the summit of Bukit Teresek, then on to the salt lick at Tabing or the cooling cascades of Lata Berkoh, past immense nest ferns that sprout from tree trunks, exquisite hanging necklaces of red flowers that smell like rotting flesh to draw insects, and trilobite beetles protected by their reddish armor. You might hear calls from the "perfect octave" bird. From either stop, trails descend to the Tahan River, where boats head downriver to Kuala Tahan.

Another marvelous hike that provides a unique perspective of the rainforest is along the newly constructed Canopy Walk, two km from park headquarters. Taman Negara's most ambitious hike is up to the summit of 2,187-meter Gunung Tahan, the loftiest peak in Peninsular Malaysia.

Wildlife such as sambar, barking deer, boar, and small cats can sometimes be seen from observation hides that overlook salt licks within the park. Bring drinking water, flashlight, high-speed film, and plenty of patience.

River Trips

Riverboats offer several reasonably priced excursions, with the most popular stretch being the 13-km journey down Tembiling River to Kuala Trenggan over a series of seven swirling rapids. Trenggan Lodge, has 10 bungalows privately managed by Taman Negara Resort. Kuala Kenyam is 90 minutes farther through the huge primeval rainforest filled with chattering birds and *orang asli* settlements.

Another public riverboat heads to Bimbun Belau and Bumbun Yong.

Accommodations

Resorts, A-frame chalets, and dorms are available in a half-dozen spots along the Tembiling River.

Kuala Tahan: Park headquarters is a surprising jungle town set with mown lawns, manicured gardens, generator-powered electricity, restaurants, and several privately operated lodging options including top-end a/c chalets for RM120-200, dormitory beds at RM18, and campsites for RM2 per person.

Dining choices include the reasonably priced Teresek Café and the more upscale Tahan Restaurant offering both à la carte and buffet selections.

Reservations can be made directly at park headquarters, tel. (09) 266-3500, fax 266-1500, and in Kuala Lumpur at their sales office in Hotel Istana, 73 Jalan Raja Chulan, tel. (03) 245-5585. Reservations should be made several days in advance during the week and several weeks ahead for weekend and holiday visits.

Kampung Kuala Tahan: The small village directly across the river from park headquarters has far less expensive if somewhat grotty accommodations and dining facilities. Liang Hostel and Tembeling Hotel have dorm rooms from RM10, while Pakwarin Chalets and Teresek View Village rent A-frame huts from RM30-60. Three floating restaurants moored in the sandbars serve inexpensive and tasty meals.

Nusa Camp: The increasing popularity of Taman Negara has made park headquarters a somewhat hectic scene during the high season from April to August, and many visitors prefer to escape the crowds by heading to Nusa Camp, 15 minutes up the Tembeling River from Kuala Tahan, where dorm beds cost RM10 and A-frames are RM45-80. Reservations can be made at their Jerantut office at the bus terminal, the Kuala Tembeling office near the jetty, and their Kuala Lumpur office, tel. (03) 264-3929, in the Malaysia Tourist Information Centre on Jalan Ampang.

Kuala Trenggan: Some 40 minutes upriver from Kuala Tahan is the luxurious 10-room Trenggan Lodge with deluxe facilities from RM120.

Kuala Keniam: Ten minutes past Kuala Trenggan is another luxury property with rooms from RM130.

Kuala Perkai: An isolated lodge two hours on foot past Kuala Keniam with rustic huts from RM8, operated by the Wildlife Department and often filled with fishermen. Reservations should be made in advance at park headquarters.

Services

Services are in short supply in Taman Negara and frugal travelers would be wise to bring plenty of currency and useful supplies such as food, drink, and sheets if you intend to overnight in a budget hostel.

Money: The reception desk in Kuala Tahan will cash traveler's checks but rates are poor.

Telephone: Calls can be made at the reception desk but expect stiff access fees.

Equipment Rentals: The resort office in Kuala Tahan rents two-person tents at RM8 per day, four-person tents for RM16, sleeping bags RM3, backpacks RM3-6, as well as stoves, fuel, and other camping equipment for the survival impaired.

Supplies: Bring a long-sleeved shirt, long pants, bug repellent, swimwear, antibiotic ointment, flashlight, high-speed film, extra food, and if possible, sleeping sheets, fishing rods, and other camping equipment. Food here is almost three times the cost of food elsewhere in Malaysia.

When to Go: Taman Negara is relatively dry from March to September but uncomfortably wet during the rainy season from mid-November to February.

Transportation

Taman Negara is 60 km from Kuala Tembeling, 76 km from Jerantut, and eight hours from Kuala Lumpur, almost impossible to reach in a single day—most travelers overnight in Jerantut.

Kuala Lumpur: Buses from Pekililing bus terminal in Kuala Lumpur take five hours to Jerantut, where another bus takes 45 minutes to Kuala Tembeling. Boats to the park leave Kuala Tembeling daily at 0900 and 1400 and take three hours to park headquarters or Nusa Camp, depending on your preference.

Public buses from Kuala Lumpur rarely connect with afternoon boat departures, but private transport arranged via KL guesthouses insures one-day travel to park headquarters—no need to overnight in the less-than-fascinating metropolis of Jerantut.

Singapore: The most convenient departure leaves Singapore at 2100 and arrives Jerantut dawn where waiting vans continue to Kuala Tembeling and boats head up to park headquarters. Trains stop midway between Jerantut and Kuala Lipis at Tembeling Halt—a romantic, old-time service on its way to extinction.

Kota Bharu: The morning train from Kota Bharu misses the afternoon boat and travelers should expect to overnight in Jerantut or Kuala Lipis.

Boat Ride: Boats leave Tembeling daily at 0900 and 1400, take three hours on the 60-km chug, and pass thick *merbau* jungle of immense root systems, liana water vines, kingfishers, hornbills, and *orang asli* settlements.

Jerantut

Travelers who need to overnight in Jerantut will find plenty of decent accommodations at reasonable prices. The Nusa Camp office at the bus terminal can help with reservations while inexpensive supplies should be picked up at local supermarkets.

Hotel Chett Fatt: Popular spot with fan and a/c rooms opposite the bus terminal. Jalan Jerantut, tel. (09) 266-5805, RM15-45.

Jerantut Resthouse: Superior rooms plus cafe, organized tours to Taman Negara, and helpful management; 10-15 minutes south of the bus and train stations. Jalan Sultan, tel. (09) 266-4488, RM8 dorm, RM22-60 private room.

MALAYSIA

FRASER'S HILL

Fraser's Hill is a small golf resort named after an English adventurer who operated a mule train, gambling hall, and opium den here around the turn of the century. Activities include hiking, bird-watching, and playing golf.

Accommodations

Fraser's Hill is a family destination popular with expatriates on weekends and almost deserted during the week when room rates are highly negotiable. Most accommodations can be booked through Fraser's Hill Development Corporation, tel. (09) 362-2201, and reservations are recommended on weekends and holidays, and during peak season from April to December.

Corona Nursery Youth Hostel: Hostel two km east of the golf course with lounge, kitchen, and basic rooms. Jalan Valley, tel. (09) 362-2225, RM10-15.

Gap House: Old bungalow eight km south of town in a quiet location with large if somewhat rudimentary rooms. Jalan Gap, tel. (09) 362-2201, RM40-60.

Puncak Inn: Adjacent to the bus stop with acceptable but certainly overpriced rooms. Jalan Gap, tel. (09) 362-2255, RM60-90.

Merlin Fraser's Hill: Modern 109-room resort near the golf course with restaurant, disco, bicycle rentals, and money exchange facilities. Jalan Lady Guillemard, tel. (09) 362-2300, RM180-240.

Transportation

Take a bus or taxi from Puduraya terminal to Kuala Kubu Bharu (KKB), 62 km north of Kuala Lumpur, then another bus or taxi to the resort. Alternately, take a public bus from KKB to the Gap, then try hitching eight km to Fraser's Hill.

CAMERON HIGHLANDS

Cameron Highlands, 200 km north of Kuala Lumpur, is Malaysia's premier hill resort and the best place to relax between the urban experiences of Kuala Lumpur and Penang—a world of British flavor, Tudor lodgings, manicured flower gardens, tea estates, rose gardens, and jungle hikes along well-marked paths.

Attractions

Hikes can be made to Parit and Robinson falls, up to the summit of Gunung Beremban, and to tea plantations such as those south of Tanah Rata. Cameron's famous 18-hole naturally air-conditioned golf course may seem inviting until you consider the roughs so radical that ball boys need to dive into towering grasses for lost balls.

Accommodations

Abundant guesthouses provide inexpensive rooms, bus reservations, and tourist information to the trickle of visitors who make the trek off the North-South Highway.

Bala's Holiday Chalets: Cameron's original hostel features rabbit warrens of tiny rooms, hidden bathrooms, lukewarm showers, and an expensive cafe with unbeatable patio cafe views; it's a 20-minute hike from Tanah Rata. Jalan Tanah Rata, tel. (05) 491-1660, RM9 dorm, RM15-40 private room.

Father's Guesthouse: Former monastic habitat with monastic yet comfortable rooms plus hot showers, budget meals, and tons of information in a convenient location just south of town. Jalan Tanah Rata, tel. (05) 491-2484, RM6-8 dorm, RM20-30 private room.

Twin Pines Chalet: Central location, cheap, and clean dorms plus rooms with private bath—one of the best budget spots in town. 2 Jalan Mentigi, tel. (05) 491-2169, RM8 dorm, RM20-30 private room.

Smokehouse: Tudor mansion opposite the golf course worth a photo or a meal, even if you can't afford the tariff. Jalan Golf Course, tel. (05) 491-1214, RM360-420.

Merlin Inn: Upscale 60-room hotel. Jalan Tanah Rata, tel. (05) 491-1205, RM280-260.

Services

All services are available in Tanah Rata.

Tourist Office: A small tourist office in town can help with local information and hiking tips.

Money: Traveler's checks can be exchanged at the Hong Kong Bank and May Bank on the main road.

Mail: The post office on the main road near the Oriental Hotel is open Mon.-Sat. 0800-1630.

CAMERON HIGHLANDS

★ BOH SUNGEI PALAS TEA ESTATE
★ ROSE GARDENS
★ MARKET

G. BRINCHANG (2,032 m)

★ BUTTERFLY FARM
■ STRAWBERRY FARM

● BRINCHANG
★ ROSE GARDENS

★ STRAWBERRY PARK RESORT

SAM PO TEMPLE ★

● MERLIN INN RESORT
♦ CLUBHOUSE

CAMERON GOLF LINKS

2

G. PERDAN (1,576 m)
● YE OLD SMOKEHOUSE

12

10
11

G. JASPAR (1,696 m)

3

G. BEREMBAN (1,841 m)

● BALA'S CHALETS

PARIT WATERFALL

4

5

11

TANAH RATA

★ MOSQUE

7

● HOTELS
★ CLOCK TOWER

CHURCH ★
● MARDI

FATHER GH
● BUS AND TAXI

TWIN PINES CHALET ●

13

ROBINSON WATERFALL

G. MENTIGA (1,563 m)

9A

BHARAT TEA ESTATE ★

14

9

ROBINSON FALLS POWER STATION ■

TO BOH TEA ESTATE 8 km →

0   1 km

TO TAPAH 52 km

HABU

GUNONG EMAS TEA ESTATE ★

MALAYSIA

© MOON PUBLICATIONS, INC.

Transportation

Cameron Highlands can be reached from Kuala Lumpur by bus from the Puduraya terminal mornings before 1000. Buses from Cameron can be booked at most guesthouses and hotels in Tanah Rata.

IPOH

Ipoh, capital of Perak State, is a predominately Chinese town founded in 1884 after tin discoveries in nearby Kinta Valley attracted thousands of Chinese miners who later created "millionaires' town" for their early 20th-century mansions and colonial estates. Ipoh today still recalls its rich heritage through its architecture, Perak homes of gingerbread molding, and elegant Chinese shophouses embellished with Peranakan tilework—memorable ambiance refreshingly free of tourists and well worth a short walking tour from the train or bus station.

Attractions

Railway Station: An elegant whitewashed edifice constructed 1917; now a nostalgic hotel with immense dining rooms once described by Paul Theroux as a place with "skeletons in every closet and a register thick with the pseudonyms of adulterers."

British Structures: British 1920's architecture includes the Ipoh Town Hall with its colonnaded wings and Palladian façade, City Hall flanked by a modern state mosque and colonial High Court, Ipoh Club, Saint Michael's School, and India Mosque.

Old Ipoh: Ipoh's old town west of muddy Kinta River offers remarkable Peranakan and Chinese architecture gilded with rococo scrollwork, pompous Palladian porticoes, and multihued peacocks inlaid along Jalan Treacher and Panglima.

Tengah Mosque: A surprising gem, also called Masjid Panglima Kinta, near shophouses and cafes serving famous Ipoh *kway toew* and well-named Bomba Fire Station on Jalan Sultan Idris Shah.

Attractions near Ipoh

Visitors with extra time might visit the following sights.

Kelly's Castle: Mysterious mansion buried under jungle vegetation constructed in the 1920s by a wealthy Scottish rubber planter, William Kelly Smith, who died suddenly and left the folly to his widow. The partially restored castle, 12 km south of Ipoh, can be reached by bus to Batu Gajah.

Cave Temples: Buddhist caves are off the trunk road both north and south of Ipoh and can be quickly toured. Sam Po, five km south of Ipoh, features vegetarian cafes, turtle pond, and the largest Buddhist monasteries in Malaysia. Perak Tong, 6.5 km north of Ipoh, provides more thrills with some 100 murals and new paintings added weekly.

Accommodations

YMCA: Ipoh's YMCA is somewhat distant from the center of town but it's clean, friendly, and very quiet. Grab a taxi or take a bus from the city bus terminal. Rooms are air-conditioned with private bath. 211 Jalan Raja Musa Aziz, tel. (05) 254-0809, RM12-15 dorm, RM45-65 private rooms.

Rex Hotel: Another simple but survivable Chinese hotel with clerks and furnishings from the '20s. Jalan Sultan Iskandar Shah near the Kinta River, tel. (05) 254-0093, RM20-25.

Embassy Hotel: Most of Ipoh's inexpensive hotels are located in the business quarter near the traffic circle at the south end of Jalan Chamberlain. This is also Ipoh's noisy nightlife and restaurant center so ask for a room away from the street. The Embassy is the first in a line of hotels which includes the Hollywood, the City, the Cathay, the Beauty, the Kowloon, and the Winner. 35 Jalan Yussuf, tel. (05) 254-9496, RM25-45.

Majestic (Station) Hotel: This colonial relic in the north end of Ipoh has 34 enormous but musty a/c rooms each with private bath, separate sitting room, TV, and refrigerator. Tons of atmosphere together with the smells of mold. Club Road, tel. (05) 255-5605, RM100-150. Rooms are often discounted 30-40%.

Excelsior Hotel: Ipoh's former leading hotel has 133 a/c rooms, a comfortable coffee shop, and small lounge with live entertainment. 43 Jalan Clarke, tel. (05) 253-6666, RM180-240.

Royal Casuarina: Ipoh's finest hotel is located five minutes outside town in a residential neighborhood near the race course. 217 rooms,

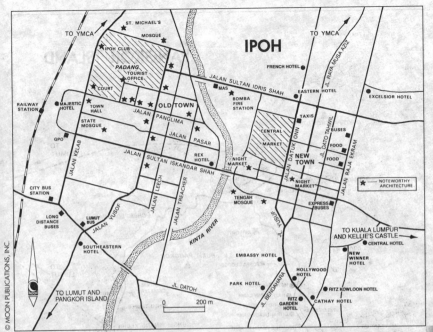

Ipoh map

TO YMCA
ST. MICHAEL'S
MOSQUE
IPOH
TO YMCA
IPOH CLUB
PADANG
TOURIST OFFICE
FRENCH HOTEL
JL. RAYA MUSA AZIZ
COURT
JALAN SULTAN IDRIS SHAH
MAS
EASTERN HOTEL
EXCELSIOR HOTEL
RAILWAY STATION
MAJESTIC HOTEL
TOWN HALL
OLD TOWN
BOMBA FIRE STATION
STATE MOSQUE
JALAN PANGLIMA
TAXIS
BUSES
GPO
JALAN PASAR
CENTRAL MARKET
NEW TOWN
FOOD
JL. DATO TAHWIL
JALAN RAJA EKRAM
FOOD
JALAN KELAB
REX HOTEL
NIGHT MARKET
JALAN DATUK ONN
NOTEWORTHY ARCHITECTURE
JALAN SULTAN ISKANDAR SHAH
NIGHT MARKET
CITY BUS STATION
JALAN LEECH
JALAN TREACHER
TENGAH MOSQUE
LONG DISTANCE BUSES
LUMUT BUS
EXPRESS BUSES
JALAN YUSOF
KINTA RIVER
JL. YUSOF
TO KUALA LUMPUR AND KELLIE'S CASTLE
CENTRAL HOTEL
SOUTHEASTERN HOTEL
NEW WINNER HOTEL
EMBASSY HOTEL
HOLLYWOOD HOTEL
TO LUMUT AND PANGKOR ISLAND
JL. DATOH
PARK HOTEL
JL. BENDAHARA
RITZ GARDEN HOTEL
RITZ KOWLOON HOTEL
CATHAY HOTEL
0   200 m

© MOON PUBLICATIONS, INC.

16 suites, huge swimming pool. 18 Jalan Gopeng, tel. (05) 250-5555, RM200-250.

Leaving Ipoh

Ipoh has three bus terminals located around the same intersection. Private operators will usually approach and help you find the next available bus. Buses to Kuala Lumpur, Butterworth, Singapore, and other interstate destinations leave from the terminal behind the big modern building. Bus offices are on the ground floor.

Buses to Lumut (the town for ferries to Pangkor Island) leave hourly from the same terminal complex and from the smaller station across the road. Buses to Kuala Kangsar and Taiping leave from the local bus terminal.

PANGKOR ISLAND

Located 88 km southwest of Ipoh off the coast from Lumut, Pulau Pangkor (Pulau is Bahasa Malaysia for "Island") is a jungle-clad island with long beaches and clear waters. Accommodation ranges from moderately priced shacks for students to expensive resorts for wealthy Malaysians.

Attractions

Although the beaches have been marred with seaborne trash and unattractive huts, a day's excursion around the island can still be recommended since the island is actually a stunning mix of thick jungle, deserted beaches, and idyllic Malay fishing villages. The entire island can be circled in four hours on funky bikes rented from most guesthouses. Check the brakes (there are some terrifying hills on the east coast) and head north past the superb beaches of Teluk Ketapang and Coral Bay, which can be reached by dirt path through strange trees. These two beaches are ideal spots for western women to escape Muslim voyeurs, provided you lie outside their lines of sight.

The Pan Pacific Pangkor Resort at the northwest corner charges a hefty RM40 admission charge for day-trippers; consequently it's the cleanest beach on the island. Pedal your bike over the steep hills to the commercial develop-

MALAYSIA

PANGKOR ISLAND

TUKUN I.

BUKIT PANGKOR UTARA

TO LUMUT

BELANGA BAY

TELOK DALAM

PAN PACIFIC RESORT

TELOK DALAM

CHEMPEDAK BAY

AIRPORT

BUKIT PANGKOR

TO LUMUT

CORAL BAY

FOREST LODGE

GIAN I.

NIPAH BAY VILLA

NAZRI NIPAH CAMP

CHINESE CEMETERY

BOTTLE HOUSE

PANGKOR INDAH

HINDU TEMPLE

TELUK NIPAH

CORAL BEACH CAMP

MENTANGOR I.

HORNBILL BEACH RESORT

SUNGEI PINANG KECHIL

DUTCH TOMB

TORTOISE HILL

SUNGEI PINANG BESAR

TORTOISE BAY

PANGKOR VILLAGE

KHOO HOLIDAY RESORT

FISHERMAN'S RESTAURANT

POLICE

POST OFFICE

PANGKOR VILLAGE BEACH RESORT

PANGKOR ANCHOR

PANGKOR CAMP

BOGAK BEACH RESTHOUSE

SRI BAYU RESORT

DUTCH FORT

SEA VIEW HOTEL

CARVED ROCK

GEDONG BAY

PANGKOR LAUT

TELOK GEDONG

PANGKOR PARADISE VILLAGE

EMERALD BAY

PANGKOR YACHT CLUB

PANGKOR LAUT RESORT

0   1 km

MOON

© MOON PUBLICATIONS, INC.

MALAYSIA

ments of the east coast to see the Chinese and Muslim cemeteries, boatbuilders, and an amazing house decorated with Heineken bottles.

The nondescript town of Sungai Pinang Besar has several good seafood restaurants. Continue through Pangkor Village past the immense jackfruit tree wrapped with protective coverings to the old Dutch Fort constructed in 1670 as an outpost to store tin and protect against Malay pirates. The abandoned fort has been carefully restored by Musium Negara. About 30 meters from the fort is a large boulder known as Batu Bersurat and inscribed *Ifcralo 1743,* with carvings of a tiger and a child. The rock is intriguing but nobody knows the exact meaning . . . tiger eats Dutch child?

Accommodations—Pasir Bogak

Pangkor's mid-level and luxury hotels are concentrated on Pasir Bogak, while the island's few remaining budget places are to the north on Teluk Nipah.

Pangkor Anchor: Pangkor's oldest backpackers' stop run by Mrs. Wong, chief information source on Pangkor Island. Pasir Bogak, tel. (05) 695-1363, RM12-20 for basic A-frame huts with mattresses on the floors.

Pangkor Village Beach Resort: Tents, huts, and upscale chalets at the west end of the beach. Pasir Bogak, tel. (05) 685-2227, RM15 tents, RM40-50 huts, RM120-150 a/c chalets.

Khoo's Holiday Resort: Pangkor's original backpackers' homestay has been developed into an uncreative collection of towering concrete buildings—Motel 6 standards on such a lovely island? Pasir Bogak, tel. (05) 685-1164, RM60-90 fan, RM100-150 a/c.

Sea View Hotel: The southern end of Pasir Bogak has several overpriced and poorly maintained hotels which face the beach. Best of the lot is this nondescript place that compensates with a pleasant restaurant. Pasir Bogak, tel. (05) 685-1605, RM120-160 a/c chalets.

Sri Bayu Beach Resort: This $2.5 million development includes a dormitory, 48 chalets, a swimming pool, tennis courts, and a small marina. Pasir Bogak, tel. (05) 685-1929, RM300-450.

Accommodations—Teluk Nipah

Nazri Nipah Hut: A short walk up from the beach with a garden cafe popular with travelers. Teluk Nipah, tel. (05) 685-2014, RM20-50.

Coral Beach Camp: Another inexpensive lodging with rudimentary A-frame huts and some larger chalets. Teluk Nipah, tel. (05) 685-2711, RM25-50.

Hornbill Beach Resort: Comfortable mid-level hotel at the southern end of the beach. Teluk Nipah, tel. (05) 685-2005, RM120-150.

Nipah Bay Villa: Another luxury property at the northern end of the beach. Teluk Nipah, tel. (05) 685-2198, RM140-180.

Accommodations—Elsewhere

Pan Pacific Resort Pangkor: Pangkor's finest sand and amenities are at Teluk Belanga (Golden Sands) Beach at the northwest corner. Facilities include a beautiful swimming pool with bar, a small golf course, water sports, and three restaurants. Six daily direct ferries from Lumut. Teluk Belanga, tel. (05) 685-1339, RM300-550.

Pangkor Laut Resort: Pangkor's other first-class resort is on Pangkor Laut, a 500-acre privately owned island just west of Pangkor with some 180 individual bungalows designed in traditional Malay fashion with *atap* roofs and open-air verandahs. Pangkor Laut, tel. (05) 669-1100, fax 669-1200, RM575-940.

Getting There

Ferries to Pangkor leave from Lumut, a small town served by bus and taxi from Ipoh, Taiping, Kuala Lumpur, Butterworth, and once daily from Cameron Highlands. Buses leave Ipoh hourly from the Lumut terminal and from the larger bus terminal across the street.

Ferries from Lumut to Pangkor leave every 30 minutes 0800-1930, sail past Russian tankers, and stop briefly at Sungai Pinang Kechil before continuing to Pangkor. Stay on the boat until the last stop.

Taxis can be hired for the short ride to Pasir Bogak; buses are infrequent.

KUALA KANGSAR

Perak State's former royal capital has enough outstanding architecture to make for a worthwhile three-hour stop between Ipoh and Penang. Leave your bags at the bus terminal and walk through the market, across the bridge, and along the muddy Perak River to the following sights.

MALAYSIA

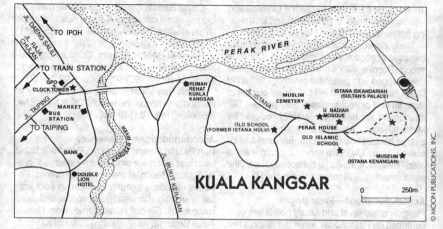

MALAYSIA

Former Malay College: The long, hot walk is finally rewarded by a magnificent, crumbling colonial mansion which now serves as a local school. Everyone smiles at you as you wander around.

Muslim Cemetery: The royal burial grounds and small marble mausoleum at Bukit Chandan are lovely and informative; both ancient and modern Muslim graves show a wide range of burial arrangements. Although nobody else will be there, visitors should be well dressed.

Ubudiah Mosque: Appearing like a vision from the Arabian Nights, this byzantine wonder is widely regarded as the most beautiful mosque in all of Malaysia. The Ubudiah was designed by an English engineer and constructed between 1913 and 1917 on orders of Idris Murshidul, the 28th Sultan of Perak. Across the road are a wonderful old Islamic school and elevated Perak homes with gingerbread moldings.

Iskandariah Palace: This magnificent Saracenic edifice was built in 1930 in an art-deco-Islamic style to replace the former palace, and underwent a major face-lift in 1984 for the coronation of the 34th sultan of Perak. It is unfortunately closed to the public. Views are best from the rear but decent photos are almost impossible.

Former Royal Palace and Museum: Situated down the road to the right, the elaborate Istana Kenangan (Palace of Memory) was constructed in traditional Malay style without the use of nails. Looks like a scene from *Alice in Wonderland*. Interior displays and interesting photographs relate Perak's colorful history.

Accommodations

Double Lion Hotel: Centrally located hotel with fan-cooled and a/c rooms. 74 Jalan Kangsar, tel. (05) 776-1010, RM20-35.

Rumah Rehat Kuala Kangsar: Refurbished resthouse on the road to Ubadiah Mosque. Jalan Istana, tel. (05) 776-3872, RM60-100.

TAIPING

Taiping's history goes back to the middle of the 19th century when the discovery of rich tin deposits attracted thousand of Chinese laborers to the fever-ridden mining camps of Larut. After warfare broke out between the rival secret societies of Hai San (Hakka) and Ghee Hin (Cantonese), British authorities stepped in and restored order; they wisely renamed the wild mining town Taiping, City of Everlasting Peace. Modern Taiping is an attractive little town of Peranakan shophouses and residences dating from the 1920s and '30s.

Attractions

Lake Gardens: Taiping's most famous landmark is the garden laid out in 1890 over an abandoned tin pit by an Indian mine inspector named Captain Akwhi. A small zoo is located on the grounds of the 80-hectare park.

State Museum: A small but well-presented collection of historical photographs and ethnological artifacts is displayed in Malaysia's oldest museum. Open daily 0900-1700; closed Fridays 1200-1430.

Ling Nam Temple: Chinese temple on Station Street with hundreds of gold-plated antiques imported from China during the last century.

Accommodations

Town Resthouse: Taiping's less expensive resthouse, located near the train station, formerly served as the governor's residence and today provides 10 creaky rooms with private baths. 101 Jalan Stesyen Taiping, tel. (05) 808-8482, RM20-35.

New Resthouse: Minangkabau-Roman resthouse on a hill overlooking Lake Garden, a 45-minute walk from the station or short taxi ride. Jalan Sultan Mansor, tel. (05) 807-2044, RM30-45.

Other Budget Hotels: Taiping has over a dozen inexpensive Chinese hotels in the RM20-30 range, including the Wah Bee at 62 Jalan Kota and the Town Hotel on the same street.

MAXWELL HILL

Rising up directly behind the Taiping Lake Gardens, the former tea plantation of Bukit Larut is the oldest and least developed hill resort in Peninsular Malaysia. Maxwell is blessedly free of flashy casinos and trendy golf courses but rather offers hiking trails, flowers blooming in well-tended gardens, and a handful of fine old bungalows with superb views across Taiping to the Straits of Malacca.

Access to the resort is along a one-way road which winds up the 1,372-meter hill through some 72 hairpin turns. Land Rovers leave hourly from the foot of the hill near Taiping Lake Gardens, make a midway stop at the Tea Garden House, and then continue up to the bungalows.

Accommodations

Accommodations are available at a number of bungalows and resthouses, including Bukit Larut Guesthouse (formerly Maxwell Resthouse) at 1,036 meters and Gunung Hijau Resthouse (formerly Speedy Resthouse) at 1,113 meters. Both cost RM15-20.

Rumah Beringin (Watson Bungalow) at 1,036 meters and Rumah Cempaka (Hugh Low Bungalow) at 1,139 meters cost RM60-80 for large eight-man cabins. Bookings can be made by calling the Officer in Charge from the Land Rover station in Taiping.

PENANG

Penang Island, with its urban center of Georgetown, is Malaysia's most popular tourist destination. And for good reason. Unlike most other Asian towns, which have lost their distinctive identities through modernization and urban development, Penang has stayed wonderfully nostalgic by retaining its old architecture, narrow alleyways, extravagant temples, lively street markets, authentic ethnic neighborhoods, and, perhaps most importantly, its gracious sense of disorder. Much of the island is so unchanged from the late 19th century that you could imagine Conrad or Kipling sailing in on a broad-masted ship or sipping coffee in a small cafe. Penang is great—don't miss it.

History

Penang opened to the outside world in 1786 when Sir Francis Light negotiated with the sultan of Kedah to make the island a tax-free and duty-free entrepôt for British traders. According to legend, the adventurer and visionary ex-navy man from Suffolk encouraged the clearing of the thick jungle by firing cannons filled with gold and silver coins into the island's undergrowth. Local Malays and Indian *sepoys* quickly cleared a small area on the Isle of Betel Nuts and erected a small wooden stockade on the present site of Fort Cornwallis. Georgetown's population grew rapidly and the city boomed as immigrants and traders arrived from China, South India, and Indonesia. But Light's policy of free trade failed to bring in enough revenue to support the adventure, and Penang began a slow but steady decline after Light's death from malaria in 1794. Penang had fallen on hard times by the time Raffles established Singapore in 1819. In 1826, the island was joined with Malacca and Singapore to form the Straits Settlement; six years later the capital was moved to Singapore.

TIKUS
ISLAND

MUKA HEAD
LIGHTHOUSE
USM MARINE
RESEARCH
KERACUT BEACH
TELUK BAHANG

BATU
FERRINGHI
TANJUNG
BUNGAH
TANJUNG
TOKONG

CHANGE
BUS
HERE
★ BUTTERFLY
FARM
★ TELUK BAHANG
RESERVE
★ BOTANICAL
GARDENS
BAGAN JERMAL

★ RECREATIONAL
FOREST
PENANG
HILL
★

★ DURIAN ORCHARDS
STATE
MOSQUE
GEORGETOWN

ACEH
★ TITI
KRAWANG
POOLS
FUNICULAR RAILWAY

ANDAMAN
SEA
SUNGAI
PINANG
HITAM RESERVOIR
AYER ITAM
JELUTUNG
FERRY
BUS,
TRAIN,
TAXI
STATIONS

RUSA
★ CLOVE
ORCHARDS
★ KEK LOK SI
TEMPLE
GULUGUR

★ BALIK
PULAU
RESERVE
CHANGE
BUS
HERE
USM

BALIK
PULAU
★ BUKIT
RELAU
RESERVE
PENANG BRIDGE

BURUNG
PEKAN GENTING
BUTTERWORTH

BETONG
ISLAND
RELAU
★ SNAKE
TEMPLE

BETONG
SUNGAI ARA
JERESAK
ISLAND

GERTAK
SANGGUL
★ BUKIT
GEMURUH RESERVE
PENARA
BAYAN LIPIS
TELUK
KUMBAR
★ PENANG
AIRPORT
BATU
MAUNG

BAKAR
KAPUR

RIMAU
ISLAND

PENANG ISLAND

0   2 km

© MOON PUBLICATIONS, INC.

Penang sputtered along without much fanfare except for a brief revival during the rubber boom of the early 20th century. Most of the island's extravagant mansions and Peranakan shops date from this period.

Penang in the late 1960s lay smack in the middle of the hippie trail, the overland odyssey that stretched from Europe to Southeast Asia. Like Kuta and Kathmandu, Penang was a comfortable place to rest up, purchase a cheap airline ticket, enjoy some good food, and get high on cheap weed. Opium dens were commonplace. Batu Ferringhi, the main tourist beach on the island, enjoyed a near legendary reputation as an untouched stretch of sand where inexpensive bamboo huts could be rented for a few dollars and nudity rarely caused more than a shrug among the locals, who regarded the foreign invasion as just another colorful bit of local history. Those days ended in the early '70s after developers and international consortiums moved in to claim the beach and authorities began deporting longhairs from their grass shacks; passports were stamped with the acronym for "Suspected Hippie: In Transit."

Although Penang is less wide-open these days, it's far more liberal than most of Malaysia. Perhaps this is because it's the only state dominated by Chinese, who generally have a live-and-let-live attitude. Or maybe it's the politics: Penang is the only state controlled by the opposition Gerankan Party, a political phenomenon that continues to astonish most observers, who had expected UMNO to quickly recontrol the rebellious island. While hard to quantify, it seems that much of Penang's great appeal comes from its easygoing attitude toward Westerners, the immense likeability of its people, and its unique attractions, described below.

ATTRACTIONS

Street names in Penang are somewhat confusing since many are now being Malaysianized (street is now *lebuh,* road is *jalan,* lane is *lorong,* avenue is *lebuhraya*) and renamed (Rope Walk is now Jalan Pintal Tali, Northam Road is Jalan Sultan Ahmad Shah, Green Lane is Jalan Mesjid Negeri). Furthermore, the Chinese community uses another set of names which describes the streets in historical terms such as Noodle Maker Street, Malay Cemetery Street, and Bean Curd Street. When in doubt, try all three versions: English, Chinese, and Bahasa.

Fort Cornwallis and the *Padang*
A good spot to begin a walking tour of Penang is the central *padang* (parade grounds) surrounded by handsome late-Victorian memorials to Penang's colonial past. The Penang Tourist Association on Jalan Tun Syed Shed, tel. 366665, and the adjacent TDC office have glossy brochures and the useful publication *Penang for the Visitor.* Named after the governor of Bengal, Fort Cornwallis was built 1808-10, reputedly on the spot where Captain Light first landed. Protruding from the renovated fort are iron cannons retrieved by the British from pirates who took them from the Johor sultanate, once a Dutch protectorate. One cannon, the famous phallic Seri Rambai, is believed to bring fertility to childless women who place flowers in its big barrel.

Next to the fort, traffic circles around the King Edward Circus Clock Tower donated to the city by a Penang millionaire in honor of Queen Victoria's Diamond Jubilee. The imposing lime-washed City Hall constructed in 1897 stands at the far end of the *padang.* The old High Court building and St. George's Church complete the British colonial arrangement of Military, Government, and Commerce—with Religion discreetly tucked away in the background.

St. George's Church
This magnificent neo-Greek edifice on Farquhar Street was built with convict labor between 1817 and 1810 as the oldest Anglican church in Southeast Asia. Designed by the artist-captain R. Smith, the Palladian structure of Doric columns and pillars cost the East India Company the sizable sum of 60,000 English pounds. The building has remained unaltered except for the gabled portico which overlays the original flat roof. A circular and curiously empty monument to Francis Light stands on the front lawn.

Penang Museum and Art Gallery
Inside the peeling building which once was the oldest English school east of the Suez is a marvelous collection of old photographs, etchings, and artifacts illustrating the tumultuous history of Penang. The Chinese bridal chamber and de-

GEORGETOWN

MTPB
PENANG TOURIST OFFICE
SWETTENHAM PIER
UNION
FORT CORNWALLIS
IMMIGRATION
BISHOP
GPO
OLD RAIL STATION
ISLAND BUS TERMINAL
BUTTERWORTH FERRY TERMINAL
PADANG
CITY HALL
CATHAY PACIFIC
GEREJA
CHINA
CITY BUS TERMINAL
CHEW JETTY
CATHEDRAL
MUSEUM
CHURCH
KUAN YIN TEMPLE
QUEEN
PITT
HINDU TEMPLE
KING
PASAR
PINANG
RAILWAY BOOKING OFFICE
TAXI STAND & SRI NEGARA BUSES
KHOON LEONG JETTY
EASTERN AND ORIENTAL HOTEL
CITY BAYVIEW HOTEL
CHINESE MANSION
CATHAY HOTEL
LOVE LANE
CAMPBELL
KHOO KONGSI
MUNTRI ROAD
ENG AUN HOTEL
CHULIA ROAD
KAPITAN KLING MOSQUE
CARNARVON
MELAYU MOSQUE
PENGKALAN WELD
VICTORIA
PANTAI
ENGLISH CEMETERY
PEKING HOTEL
NEW CHINA HOTEL
LEITH ROAD
SWISS HOTEL
FOOD STALLS
ROPE
CINTRA
FOOD STALLS
KIMBERLEY
PRANGIN
SINGAPORE AIRLINES
MALABAR
JALAN ARGYLL
CENTRAL MARKET
KOMTAR CENTRE
SHANGRI LA HOTEL
MAGAZINE
JALAN HUTTON
MAS
PENANG ROAD
HOTEL GRAND CONTINENTAL
PARAMOUNT HOTEL
YEAP LEONG HUT HOMESTEAD
#48
SHERATON INN
JALAN BURMA
TELEPHONE
GAMA SHOPPING CENTRE
FOOD STALLS
WOODVILLE
GURNEY DRIVE
JALAN SULTAN AHMED SHAH
EMBASSY HOTEL
ANSON ROAD
SALVATION ARMY BOYS HOME
FOOD STALLS
THAI INTERNATIONAL
JALAN MACALISTER
JALAN BURMA
JALAN LOGAN
CHINESE MEN'S CLUB
TO YMCA, THAI CONSULATE
PENANG BUDDHIST ASSOC.
JALAN KERAMAT
JALAN PANGKOR

500 m
0

MALAYSIA

© MOON PUBLICATIONS, INC.

Padang Parade

scriptions of *tong* warfare are intriguing, but the highlight might be the air-conditioned rooms which offer blessed relief from the sweltering heat. Open 0900-1700 daily, closed Fridays 1215-1445.

Cheong Fat Tze Mansion
Between 1860 and 1880 at least five mansions modeled after Ching Dynasty homes were constructed in Malaysia by wealthy Chinese merchants. Aside from the House of Tan Yeok Nee in Singapore, the sole surviving example of this imperial style of architecture is the Penang residence of Teo Tau Siat. Teo was a prosperous rice merchant who built separate courtyards and rooms for the sons and wives of his nine future generations.

The complex is surrounded by 10-foot walls with two signed entrances which warn off curious visitors. Flanking the central chamber are two side halls with discolored walls which have taken on a wonderful patina from the elements. Note the porcelain shards and decorative plaster work which have been modeled under the gabled roof. A quick photo from the front lawn is OK, but visitors are not allowed inside the private residence with its ancestral hall, spiral staircase, courtyards supported by Corinthian iron pillars, and sitting halls embellished with ornamental screens.

Old Christian Cemetery
This Protestant and Roman Catholic cemetery shaded by lovely frangipani trees is where the body of Captain Light lies buried among other European settlers. Light's archaic tombstone is on the left as you enter from Farquhar Street.

Muntri Street
Malaysia's finest collection of Chinese shophouses with Peranakan details is found on Muntri and Stewart streets between Penang and Pitt roads. The lovely tilework, richly carved doorways, and extravagant decorative molding make this street one of Asia's architectural goldmines—a must-see for any visitor to Penang.

Formerly the home to a thriving Eurasian community of Babas and Nonyas, this idyllic alley also features several superb Chinese-association buildings constructed on traditional Chinese floorplans—especially fascinating at dusk as the lights flicker on and residents socialize on the five-foot walkways. A public toddy shop, popular with Indian rickshaw drivers and budget travelers looking for a cheap buzz, is located on the right side of Pasar just before Pitt Street; it opens an hour before sunset.

Kuan Yin Temple
Constructed in 1800 by the Hokkien and Cantonese community on a site given to them in perpetuity by the British government, this small and unassuming temple is the spiritual heart and soul of Penang's Chinese community. Although the temple is relatively plain by Chinese standards, it seems perennially crowded with devotees who burn immense towers of incense and make offerings to Kuan Yin, the beloved Buddhist God-

dess of Mercy. Puppet shows are given on her birthday three times yearly on the 19th days of the Chinese 2nd, 6th, and 9th moons.

Sri Mariamman Temple

Although Penang is essentially a Chinese city, it has always had a sizable community of Indians who originally immigrated to work as policemen, soldiers, clerks, and laborers on rubber plantations. Many settled on Queen Street near the government offices and inadvertently created an ethnic buffer zone between the colonial rulers and the Chinese merchants. These racially divided neighborhoods were identified by their street names: China Street for the Chinese, Chulia Street for the Southwest Indian Muslim traders, Acheh Street for Sumatran merchants, Malay Street for the indigenous Muslim population. Racial boundaries are now somewhat blurred, but to a surprising degree Little India still thrives along Queen and adjacent side streets. Religious centerpiece for the Hindu community is the modest temple built in 1883 and dedicated to Lord Subramaniam.

Kapitan Kling Mosque

As if to compete with the Chinese and Indian temples in the neighborhood, this arabesque monument was built in 1801 by Cauder Mohideen, Kapitan of the Indian-Muslim community. (Kapitan was the name given to the powerful headman through which the colonial administration governed the Chinese and Indian communities. Kling is slang for South Indians, particularly the Tamils.)

This dome-shaped and ochre-painted mosque replaced an earlier attap structure erected in 1786 by the Havidars, Jemadars, and Indian Sepoys attached to the British East India Company. Well-dressed visitors are welcome to walk along the cool marble floors of the mosque, which serves the religious needs of Indian Muslims and Jawi Pekan, descendants of mixed Malay and Indian Muslim marriages. Nearby Acheh Street has a modest Malay Mosque with a curious Egyptian-style minaret kept locked and closed to the public.

Khoo Kongsi

Located up a small side street called Cannon Square stands the most elaborately decorated building in Penang and possibly the whole of Malaysia. Built in 1906 in the style of a miniature imperial palace, this clanhouse of the Khoo descendants literally drips with stucco dragons, ceramic flowers, and fantastic mythological guardians. It also symbolizes and embodies an important tradition in Chinese culture in which the extended family becomes a major element in the life of the Chinese immigrant; this isn't a temple but headquarters for a *kongsi*—a clan organization and benevolent society which extends spiritual and financial help to all people with the same surname.

Ancestor worship is inextricably interwoven with this Confucian concept as shown by the memorial tablets in the right room. The center room has an altar for the worship of the Khoo's tutelary deity, Tua Sai Yeah, while the room on the left contains plaques honoring distinguished living members and an image of Tua Peh Kong, God of Prosperity. Across the square is a dusty but finely carved stage for opera and theater performances. The interior of the Khoo Kongsi is open Monday-Friday 0900-1700 and Saturdays 0900-1300 by pass from the adjacent clan office. Photos of the shady exterior are best at sunset.

Komtar Centre

Penang's latest monument is the 65-story Kompleks Tun Abdul Razak, which bills itself as the tallest building in Malaysia. Within the US$115-million circular tower are several shopping centers, an office of the Malaysian Airlines System, and most of the island's government offices. There's a useful tourist office on the second floor and a convenient bus terminal in the basement. The observatory on the 58th floor has spectacular views over Georgetown's sea of red-tiled roofs.

Residential Walking Tour

Some of Penang's greatest architectural attractions are the magnificent Sino-colonial mansions constructed during the early 20th century by wealthy rubber and tin barons. Some have decayed in tropical mildew but others have been well maintained at great expense by local families. Most are located west of downtown and can be easily visited by trishaw or rented bicycle or on foot. The following walking tour starts at Penang Road and Campbell Street and takes three or four hours.

Komtar view

Jalan Hutton: Several attractive Peranakan shophouses stand on Nagore Lane just before the Merlin Hotel. Just opposite the Merlin is a large mansion which has been tastefully converted into a Kentucky Fried Chicken.

Jalan Anson and Jalan Logan: Walk down Anson Street past the Pro-Am Snooker Hall and turn right on Logan Street. Alternatively, make a detour to visit the spacious Penang Buddhist Association. Several fine old homes grace shady Logan Street, such as the Salvation Army Boys' Home at number 8A and the Chinese Men's Club at number 34. Walk across Perak Street and along Dunn Street past a dozen identical bungalows dating from the 1920s with hanging reed curtains wrapped around the porches. Turn right on Peel and continue walking under the row of stately royal palms to Perak and Jalan Burmah.

Bangkok Lane: An exceptionally fine set of terrace houses stands on this small street.

Wat Chayamangkalaram: This Thai-style temple is chiefly known for its enormous 33-meter reclining Buddha, which combines Thai, Burmese, and Chinese religious motifs. The curious fusion is symbolized by the dual entrances with Buddhist *nagas* left, Chinese dragons right, and the interior, which has Buddha statues right and Chinese deities left. Visit the small Burmese temple just across the street and then walk down Burma Lane to the waterfront.

Gurney Drive: Bordered by swaying casuarina trees, this is an ideal spot to enjoy a late lunch from one of the hawkers who set up their portable stalls alongside the promenade.

Northam Road: East toward town is Northam Road, now renamed Sultan Ahmed Shah. Often dubbed Millionaire's Row, this is where wealthy Chinese merchants, rubber barons, and powerful colonial administrators built the most extravagant mansions in all of Penang. Some have kept their colonial nametags such as Woodville and Soonstead, while others have been rechristened with Chinese titles such as the magnificent Yeap Leong Huat Homestead. The equally impressive Runnymede, site of the former residence of Sir Stamford Raffles which was torn down in 1901, presently houses the 2nd Infantry Division of the Malaysian Army. Hopefully someone will save the abandoned Metropole Hotel before it collides with the wrecker's ball. Continue down Northam to end your tour with a cocktail inside the famous E & O Hotel.

Botanical Gardens

This 30-hectare garden at the end of Waterfall Road some eight km west of town has hundreds of exotic and indigenous plant species, plus a gaggle of inquisitive rhesus monkeys whose chatterings and unabashed begging are always amusing. Take City Council bus 7 from the Weld Quay Bus Terminal one block from the Ferry Building.

Penang Hill

Barely one year after Captain Francis Light arrived in Penang, he instructed his *sepoys* to

MALAYSIA

build a trail to the top of Penang Hill, 830 meters above sea level. Finding the temperate climate more agreeable than the malarial lowlands, British colonialists constructed a hill resort complete with English bungalows and vegetable gardens. In 1923 a railway line was built to the peak, where spectacular panoramic views spread across Penang to the coastal stretches of the mainland. Sunsets are magical as the lights blink on and twinkle in steamy Georgetown.

Trams leave every half-hour 0630-2130 from the terminus near the village of Ayer Itam. Take Green Bus 91 from the Jalan Prangin Bus Terminal near the Komtar building to Ayer Itam, where City Council bus 8 continues up to the tram terminus. From the summit it is possible to hike down Waterfall Road and reach the Botanical Gardens in about three hours.

Kek Lok Si Temple

Malaysia's largest Buddhist temple complex is dominated by the 30-meter Pagoda of 10,000 Buddhas, whose unique architectural style combines a Chinese base, Thai middle tiers, and a golden Burmese stupa on top. The resulting mishmash is inelegant but less irritating than the aggressive salesmen who work the continuous sprawl of souvenir shops that flank the long entrance walk. The only way to avoid the hustle is to arrive in the late afternoon after the busloads of tourists have returned to Georgetown. Take Green Bus 91 from the main terminal on Jalan Prangin near the Komtar building to Ayer Itam.

Around the Island

Penang is a beautiful island of tumbling waterfalls, miles of forest, idyllic *padi* fields, and quaint fishing villages of wooden Malay *kampung* houses elevated on rickety stilts. To do the 75-km circular route in a single day, an early start is recommended. A rented car or motorcycle is preferable to public buses since many of the fishing villages and beaches are located on side roads and inaccessible without private transportation. Bus travelers should begin with Yellow Bus 83 to the Snake Temple. The same bus continues on to Balik Pulau, where Yellow Bus 76 continues north to Teluk Bahang. Blue buses return to Georgetown with a quick change in Tanjung Bunga.

Snake Temple: Dedicated to the Taoist deity Chor Soo Kong, the Temple of the Azure Cloud is known for its venomous Wagler pit vipers kept harmlessly dazed by the intoxicating fumes curling up from the burning joss sticks. This popular tourist stop is quite ordinary aside from the sleepy snakes.

Balik Pulau: After passing through industrial estates, the Penang Free Trade Zone, the turnoff for the notorious RM850-million white elephant Penang Bridge, the Penang International Airport, and spice plantations of clove and nutmeg, the bus lurches to a halt in the pleasant rural town of Balik Pulau. Yellow Bus 76 continues north past turnoffs for Malay fishing villages, durian plantations, freshwater pools at Titi Krawang, the Forest Recreation Park, an orchid farm, and the Penang Butterfly Farm, which claims the world's largest collection of lepidopterous insects.

Teluk Bahang: The newly opened and immense five-star Penang Mutiara Hotel has dramatically changed the sleepy atmosphere of this small and mostly undeveloped fishing village situated at the northwest corner of Penang. Inexpensive accommodations are available at Rama's Homestay off the main intersection toward the water. Rama's son will probably find you. Hikers might enjoy tramping through the Muka Head Forest Reserve. The trail starts at the beach and soon divides into two forks. The path right leads to the USM Marine Research Station and an hour later reaches the lighthouse and beach at Muka Head. The left trail winds through the forest to the public campsites at deserted Keracut Beach, also called Monkey Beach because of the colony of monkeys that comes down to play in the sand.

Batu Ferringhi

Penang's best beaches are found along the north shore about 15 km from Georgetown. The entire coastline is broken into a series of small coves with private beaches except for a singular stretch of sand nicknamed Batu Ferringhi (Foreigner's Rock). During the late '60s this was home to legions of hippie backpackers—until the infamous police raids of the early '70s forced the freaks northward to the more tolerant islands of Phuket and Ko Samui.

Batu Ferringhi today only welcomes travelers with enough cash to afford the plush first-class hotels that overhang the beach. Some say the police did the freaks a favor: the coarse sand and murky water at Batu Ferringhi don't compare with the sand and sea at Thai beach resorts. Although the atmosphere is artificial and disappointing (there is little reason to day-trip out here from Georgetown), the jagged hills and the swaying palms over the beach remain quite attractive. Also, hotel rates have remained low from over-building and perennially high vacancy rates.

ACCOMMODATIONS

Budget

Travelers will be pleasantly surprised at the hotel situation in Penang. Unlike many other cities in Southeast Asia, Penang has a good selection of clean Chinese hotels with high ceilings, swishing ceiling fans, and, of course, old Chinese men sitting around in their underwear. Most of Penang's budget hotels in the RM15-30 range are located in Chinatown along Lebuh Chulia and adjacent side streets, a 10-minute walk or RM3 rickshaw ride from the ferry terminal. Middle-priced hotels in the RM30-70 range are around the corner on Penang Road, while most of Penang's luxury hotels are located at Batu Ferringhi Beach.

Eng Aun and Swiss Hotels: Penang's two most popular budget hotels are simple, clean, and quiet since they are nicely situated back from the road. Other facilities include travel services and inexpensive restaurants with decent food and friendly vibes. The old men who hang around the office and sleep in the hallways are the owners. Both hotels are often filled by early afternoon, especially during the high travel season from November to March and during August. Eng Aung Hotel, 380 Chulia St., tel. (04) 261-2333. Swiss Hotel, 431 Chulia St., tel. (04) 262-0133. Both charge RM15-25.

Other Budget Hotels: A quick stroll along Lebuh Chulia, Lorong Cinta (Love Lane), and Lebuh Leith will uncover another two-dozen budget hotels of varying standards. Most charge RM15-30 for rooms with fan and common bath. Couples should ask for a single room, which often has a bed large enough for two people. Super-budget travelers might try the dorms at the Tye Ann on Lebuh Chulia or the Wan Hai Hotel around the corner on Love Lane.

YMCA: Penang's coed Y is located about 20 minutes from Chinatown in a quiet residential neighborhood near the Thai Embassy. Take bus No. 7 from the jetty or Komtar. All rooms have telephones and attached baths. 211 Jalan Macalister, tel. (04) 228-2211, fax 229-5869, RM35-80.

Moderate

Penang Road Hotels: Penang's middle-priced hotels in the RM35-80 range are located on Penang Road between the waterfront and Chi-

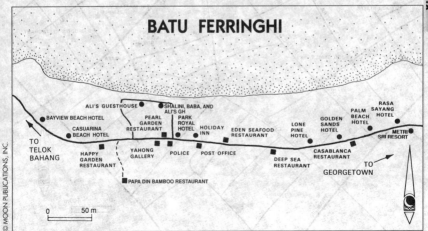

BATU FERRINGHI

TO TELOK BAHANG

ALI'S GUESTHOUSE
BAYVIEW BEACH HOTEL
CASUARINA BEACH HOTEL
HAPPY GARDEN RESTAURANT
SHALINI, BABA, AND ALI'S GH
PEARL GARDEN RESTAURANT
PARK ROYAL HOTEL
HOLIDAY INN
YAHONG GALLERY
POLICE
PAPA DIN BAMBOO RESTAURANT
POST OFFICE
EDEN SEAFOOD RESTAURANT
LONE PINE HOTEL
DEEP SEA RESTAURANT
GOLDEN SANDS HOTEL
PALM BEACH HOTEL
RASA SAYANG HOTEL
CASABLANCA RESTAURANT
METRI SRI RESORT
TO GEORGETOWN

0   50 m

© MOON PUBLICATIONS, INC.

MALAYSIA

CENTRAL GEORGETOWN (PENANG)

SULTAN AHMED SHAH

JL. FARQUHAR

EASTERN AND ORIENTAL
HOTEL (E & O)

ENGLISH
CEMETERY

BRITISH COUNCIL

LEITH

JL. TUN
SYET SHAH

JL. GREENHALL

CITY BAYVIEW HOTEL

ART GALLERY

JL. LEITH

CONTINENTAL

LIGHT

MALAYSIA

CHINESE MANSION

WALDORF

JL. SRI BAHARI

PEKING

FEDERAL

NEW CHINA

CATHAY

HIGH COURT
BUILDING

WHITE
HOUSE
HOTEL

MERCHANT
HOTEL

TOWN HOUSE

LUM FONG

MODERN

PENANG MUSEUM

JL. ARGYIL

LOVE LANE

TEONG WAH

JL. FARQUHAR

ORIENTAL

JL. MUNTRI

ST. GEORGE'S
CHURCH

JL. DATO KOYAH

LUM THEAN

JL. CHULIA

CHUNG KING

JL. STEWART

JL. PITT

WAN HAI

QUEEN

FOOD STALLS

ENG AUN

KUAN YIN
TEMPLE

JL. HUTTON

SWISS

PING SENG

JL. MALABAR

YENG KENG

NOBLE

JL. CHINA

JL. KING

PENANG

TAJ CAFE

NAM WAH

TYE ANN

TODDY SHOP

BROADWAY HOTEL

CAMPBELL

JL. CARNARVON

JL. CHULIA

SRI MARIAMMAN
TEMPLE

JL. PASARI

CINTRA

FOOD STALLS

KAPITAN
KLING
MOSQUE

DAWOOD'S RESTAURANT

JL. KANGSAR

KIMBERLEY

FOOD STALLS

JL. PINTAL TALI

PLAZA

JL. PENANG

JL. ROPE

JL. ACEH

JL. CHULIA

JL. PANTAI

JL. HONG KONG

CARNARVON

PITT

JL. MELAYU

MALAY
MOSQUE

KHOO
KONGSI

PRANGIN

0   100m

MooN

© MOON PUBLICATIONS, INC.

MALAYSIA

natown. Most rooms are air-conditioned with private bath and basic Motel 6 furniture. Comfortable a/c doubles were RM50-80 at the Peking, White House, and Federal, while the more luxurious Oriental and Continental had a/c doubles for just RM90-120.

Cathay Hotel: Similar but superior to the Eng Aun and the Swiss, this delightful old Chinese hotel has large and well-furnished rooms with air-conditioning, private baths, and hot showers. With an exterior paint job and a spacious lobby that evoke the 1920s, this is the hotel for couples looking for atmosphere at an affordable price. 15 Leith Street, tel. (04) 262-6271, RM50-70.

Luxury
Eastern and Oriental Hotel: Constructed in 1885 by the Sarkie Brothers of Raffles fame, Penang's Grand Dame is one of Southeast Asia's great colonial hotels. Although it needs some refurbishing, anyone who appreciates nostalgic old-world atmosphere will love this waterfront hotel. 10 Farquhar Street, tel. (04) 263-0630, fax (04) 263-4833, RM150-250.

Shangri-La Hotel: Downtown Penang entered the modern age with the opening of this towering 18-story hotel in 1986. Swimming pool, health club, and business center, adjacent to the Komtar building. Jalan Magazine, tel. (04) 262-2622, fax 262-6526, RM340-500.

Batu Ferringhi Hotels: Penang's most popular beach is lined with eight international hotels that have all the standard amenities, such as restaurants, swimming pools, and water-sports activities. Rooms at the Casuarina Beach Hotel, the Golden Sands, the Holiday Inn, the Pan Pacific, and the Rasa Sayang start at RM220, while the less luxurious Ferringhi Beach and Lone Pine offer rooms from RM140. The Penang Mutiara, a five-star hotel managed by the Mandarin Group from Singapore, offers rooms on Ferringhi's only private beach. Budget rooms from RM20 are found at Ali's Guesthouse and the White House Hotel located in the village at the west end of the beach.

FOOD

Penang's multiracial population has given it one of Asia's most diverse and exciting ranges of foods. Rivaling Singapore in terms of affordability and variety, the city's food emporiums offer everything from Malaysian *nasi lemak* and Chinese *kuay teow* to Nonya *kerabu* and Indian *nasi kandar*. Most restaurants and foodstalls serve the Chinese and Indian dishes described in the "Singapore" chapter, but the island's great culinary discovery is Malay cuisine, a wonderful mixture of spicy Indonesian peanut sauces, rich Thai coconut milks, and fiery Indian curries with fresh vegetables and succulent meats. Malay cuisine is typically limited to home cooking and therefore difficult to find but worth seeking out.

Penang has countless places to eat from simple cafes to expensive restaurants, but streetside foodstalls provide the island's great culinary adventure. First-time visitors sometimes dismiss hawker food as unclean, assuming that any meal served on a rickety aluminum table at the edge of a busy street must be inferior to those in a first-class restaurant.

Nothing could be further from the truth. If a steady queue of Mercedes-Benzes waiting for noodle soup is any indication, hawker food provides stiff competition for many of Penang's best restaurants. Hawker food is popular for several reasons. Large congregations of foodstalls in a singular location ensure a greater array of foods than in any single restaurant. Secondly, since there is virtually no overhead, prices are low—a filling meal can be served for RM3 to RM6 in most cases. But perhaps most importantly, food-stall dining is a great way to meet people; al fresco dining is one of Penang's great social events.

Ordering from a hawker stall can sometimes be confusing in Southeast Asia, but you won't have much trouble here in Penang. The simplest method is to wander around a group of stalls and point to whatever looks best. To aid both visitors and locals, many of the foodstalls have put up plastic signs that list their specialties. Owners often speak some rough English and are often happy to explain their dishes to confused strangers. Conversations might be limited to baby talk, but you will probably find the people of Penang (including hawkers) both friendly and helpful . . . especially when they stand to make a small profit. Serious eaters should purchase *Hawkers Galore: A Guide to Penang Hawker Food*, which describes with color photographs the island's most popular street dishes.

A HAWKER MENU

ayam goreng: Malay-style fried chicken

ban chian koay: a sweet Indian pancake of rice flour, coconut milk, eggs, and sugar cooked in an earthenware pot. Ground peanuts and sesame are sprinkled on top.

cendol: a cold dessert made from pandan-flavored green noodles, palm sugar, and coconut milk. This weird-looking dish vaguely resembles green worm soup.

chok: thick rice porridge garnished with shredded chicken, spring onions, and sliced ginger. Although this dish sounds extremely boring, it can be superb when prepared by a talented cook.

curry kapitan: an Indonesian specialty of curried chicken with chunks of red onions, chilies, and yellow ginger saut—ed in coconut oil, sugar, and lemon juice; best prepared in the Indian cafes across from the Sri Mariamman Temple

curry mee: Noodle soup made with curry paste, coconut milk, sliced clams, shrimps, and dried bean cake; sometimes garnished with cockles, pig's blood, and mint leaves; moderately spicy.

enchee kabin: marinated and deep-fried chicken served with rice and piquant sauce. This Nonya specialty fuses Malay sauces with Chinese cooking techniques.

gado gado: Indonesian salad of blanched vegetables such as potatoes, cabbage, beans, and sprouts covered with a rich and spicy peanut-coconut sauce. Prawn crackers *(krupok)* are also served.

Hainanese chicken rice: Singapore's classic dish of roast chicken, ginger, spring onion, and cucumber served with lightly oiled rice and garlic chili sauce is also very popular in Penang.

Hokkien prawn mee: rich and very spicy soup made from pork ribs, prawns, round rice noodles, and ground chilies. Exudes a great fragrance after being slowly stewed for several hours.

ice kachang: Malay snowcone made from colorful sweet red beans, corn, jelly, and fruit buried under thick syrup. Evaporated milk and ice cream are sometimes added. Delicious on a hot day.

ikan bilis: fried whitebait or anchovies served as an appetizer with *nasi lemak*. Crunchy, salty, strong, and addictive with daily intake.

ikan sadin: canned sardines in tomato sauce

kari ayam: curry chicken

kerang: fried cockles

kueh mueh: traditional Nonya desserts made from tapioca, glutinous rice, and sago, and flavored with *gula melaka*, coconut milk, or pandan juice. Tables filled with these vibrantly colored desserts are dazzling sights.

kuay teow: char (fried) *kuay teow* are flat white rice noodles fried in a black bean sauce together with eggs, clams, prawns, cockles, and bean sprouts. *Kuay teow* is the classic pasta dish of Penang.

laksa: thick rice noodle soup served in a tangy broth made from fish stock, onions, lemon grass, and tamarind juice. Penang or *asam* (sour) *laksa* has a sharp and slightly sour flavor in contrast to the creamy and mild Singapore version. *Laksa lemak* (also called *siam laksa*) is a sweeter, richer, and somewhat spicier version. Both are outstanding.

lok lok: Penang's version of the traditional steamboat. Hawker stalls display a variety of meats and vegetables on colored skewers which indicate price. Just walk up, select a stick, and drop it in the boiling water for a few seconds. The skewer is then dipped into a dish of rich spicy sauce and quickly eaten. *Lok lok*, sensibly enough, means "dip dip."

lontong: vegetables and fried rice cakes covered with coconut gravy. A simple but delicious Malaysian snack.

lor bak: deep-fried meat wrapped in a crispy vegetable skin. The same hawker stall will also serve deep-fried prawns, octopus fritters, crispy pigs' ears, hundred-year-old eggs, and fried stingray served with glutinous chili sauce.

mee: Chinese yellow wheat noodles can be prepared in literally hundreds of ways: *mee java* is noodles in a tomato soup (often made from Del Monte catsup), *mee rebus* is noodles with eggs and prawns in a tasty brown gravy, *mee goreng* is fried noodles without gravy, *mee siam* is fried rice vermicelli with chili in a thin gravy, *mee hoon* is threadlike white rice noodles in mixed sauces.

nasi: *Nasi* is Malay for "cooked rice." Rice can also be prepared in limitless ways: *nasi goreng* is fried rice, *nasi padang* is rice prepared in a cooking style associated with the Minangkabau people of Western Sumatra, *nasi kandar* is an Indian Muslim rice dish with a variety of curries.

MALAYSIA

nasi lemak: rice cooked in coconut milk and pandan leaves served with tasty tidbits such as prawn fritters marinated in tamarind juice, chilies with lime, sliced fruit, and crunchy anchovies. Just point through the window to whatever looks inviting and it will be piled on the plate. This traditional Malay breakfast is now sold at hawker's stalls throughout the day.

ngau lam: dark and spicy noodle soup cooked with meats, vegetables, a generous dose of black pepper, and a dash of cloves. First decide which noodles you prefer: *mee, meehon,* or *kuay teow,* and then point out what ingredients you want in your soup. This can also be left to the discretion of the chef. A Chinese dish also popular with Malays.

o chien: oyster omelette cooked with onions and sweet potatoes

popiah: spring rolls stuffed with pork, prawns, fried bean curd, and beans. The *popiah* (thin pancake) is first spread with black bean, plum, or *hoi sin* sauce with chili before being carefully wrapped around the mixture. Very tasty.

rendang: spicy Indonesian curries served with beef or chicken

rojak: a spicy fruit-and-vegetable salad mixed with a black sauce of sugar, chilies, and *hoi sin.* The unripened assemblage is then garnished with ground peanuts and served in a take-away plastic bag.

roti jala: traditional Malay pancakes made by swirling thin egg batter from a punctured can of condensed milk onto a sizzling griddle. The lacy creation is normally eaten with a mild chicken curry.

sambal: fiery chili sauce used in Malay and Indonesian cooking

satay: Skewers of chicken, beef, or lamb are first seasoned in a medley of spices and then slowly grilled over a charcoal fire. Malay *satay* is served with peanut sauce, while the Chinese version is made with pork and served with sweet potato-chili sauce.

sayor: Malay for "vegetables"

soto ayam: soto is soup, *ayam* is chicken. *Soto ayam* is spiced chicken soup with vegetables and potatoes.

sotong: cuttlefish

tahu goreng: deep-fried beancurd covered with pungent peanut sauce

tahu lemak: beancurd cooked in coconut-milk curry

telor goreng: fried eggs

udang sambal: prawns fried in *sambal* hot sauce

Hawker Locations

Chulia at Carnarvon Road: Hawker food is sold throughout the day at several locations; most are within easy walking distance of Chinatown. This collection of foodstalls is conveniently located in the middle of Penang's cheap hotel section. Unlike most of the other hawker areas, which operate evenings only, Carnarvon Road is best visited in the early morning. Try the tasty Malay breakfast called *nasi lemak.*

Kimberley at Cintra Road: Chinatown's largest collection of hawker stalls branches off from this intersection. More foodstalls set up in the evenings on Tamil Lane, just off Penang Road one block north of Kimberley, and along Malabar Lane at Penang Road.

Komtar Centre: Several popular hawker centers are located diagonally opposite and to the west of Penang's tallest building. The entire sidewalk in front of the GAMA Department Store on Jalan Brick Kiln is taken up with hawkers, as are those on the west side of Jalan MacAlister and farther afield on Lorong Selamat.

Gurney Drive: Because of its prime location next to the sea and its almost endless selection of stalls, Gurney Drive is considered the premier hawker center on Penang. Activity is minimal during the day but after sunset the mile-long promenade comes alive with countless hawkers who unload their portable furniture and fire up the woks. A rickshaw from Chinatown to Gurney Drive is RM4.

Night Market: Almost as popular as Gurney Drive is the roving night market which changes locations every two weeks. Local residents and the tourist office will know the current venue.

Toddy Shop

Toddy is palm wine made from the fermented juice of unopened fronds. Tappers climb the trees in the morning and sell the pungent beverage to shops which operate under a government license. The milky broth is popular with Indian rickshaw drivers and budget travelers who gather in the late afternoon at the toddy shop on Lorong Pasar, off Lebuh Pitt near the Kuan Yin Temple. Bring your own cup and ignore the drug dealers.

TRAVEL PRACTICALITIES

Arrival

Airport: Penang's Bayan Lepas International Airport is 16 km south of Georgetown and 35 km from Batu Ferringhi Beach. Penang is served by flights from Kuala Lumpur, Singapore, Bangkok, Hat Yai, Medan, and Madras. The MTPB has a small information booth in the lobby. Airport taxis use a coupon system and cost RM20 to the city, RM30 to Batu Ferringhi. Yellow Bus 83 leaves hourly from the airport and reaches Weld Quay in an hour.

Bus, Train, and Taxi: Most buses, trains, and taxis bound for Penang terminate in Butterworth, a small town just across the straits from Georgetown. The rebuilt Butterworth-Penang ferry opposite the terminal operates 24 hours. On arrival in Butterworth you can take a trishaw or walk to most hotels in 15 minutes.

Getting Around

Bus: Penang has five bus companies which operate from three different terminals. Routes are displayed on signboards and ticket collectors can advise on fares and destinations. The Blue, Yellow, and Green buses all leave from Pengkalan Weld, next to the ferry terminal.

Blue bus No. 93 goes to the north side of the island including Batu Ferringhi and Teluk Bahang. Yellow bus No. 66 goes to the Snake Temple, Bayan Lepas, Ayer Itam, and Balik Pulau. Lim Seng bus No. 91 goes to Ayer Itam.

City buses (called Juara) leave from the Lebuh Victoria Terminal across from the ferry terminal and go to various city destinations. Useful routes include bus No. 7 to the Botanical Gardens and the YMCA, bus No. 1 to Ayer Itam and Kek Lok Si Temple, and bus No. 8 from Ayer Itam to the Penang Hill Railway.

Trishaws: Three-wheeled manpowered vehicles called *lancas* in Penang average about RM2 per kilometer or RM6-8 per hour. Some of the Tamil and Chinese drivers are very knowledgeable about sightseeing attractions, but rates should be agreed on before boarding.

Bicycles and Motorcycles: Bikes can be rented from several of the budget hotels and bookstores on Jalan Chulia. Ambitious types can circle the island in a single day. Motorcycles cost RM20-25 daily from the same locations and from roadside stands in Batu Ferringhi.

Taxis: Penang taxis do *not* use their meters. Drivers are supposed to charge fixed rates based on city zones but most ask whatever they think they can get. Fares should be agreed on in advance. Sample fares from Georgetown are RM15 to Batu Ferringhi, RM10 to the Botanical Gardens, RM10 to Penang Hill, RM15 to the Snake Temple, and RM20 to the airport.

Services

Tourist Offices: The Penang Tourist Association, tel. (04) 281-6665, on Jalan Tun Shed Barakbah near Fort Cornwallis gives away some useful publications such as *Penang for the Visitor* and *This Month in Penang.* Tourism Malaysia, tel. (04) 262-0066, is in the same building.

Foreign Consulates: Ten countries maintain consular representatives in Penang, but the most useful is the Royal Thai Consulate at 1 Ayeh Rajah Road, tel. (04) 282-8029. Take bus 7 or walk there in 45 minutes on the residential walking tour described above. The Indonesian Consulate is at 467 Jalan Burmah, tel. (04) 25162. Both consulates are open weekdays 0900-1200 and hopelessly disorganized. Let a travel agency pick up your visa unless you actually enjoy bureaucratic hassles and want to waste half a day.

General Post Office: Penang's GPO on Lebuh Downing is open daily except Sundays 0800-1800.

Telephone: International phone calls can be made around the clock from the telegraph office on Lebuh Downing and from the Penang International Airport daily 0800-2030. Penang area code is 04.

Leaving Penang

Air: Penang's international airport can be reached by taxi in 30 minutes or in one hour by Yellow Bus 83 from the Pengkalan Weld Bus Terminal near the ferry.

Bus: Penang's bus terminal is next to the ferry terminal in Butterworth but many buses also leave from the basement of the Komtar Centre. Most departures are in the morning before 0900 and in the evening 1800-2000.

Buses to Kota Bharu depart twice daily at 0900 and 2100. For Tioman Island, take the 1600 bus to Johor Bharu, the 0600 bus from Johor to Mersing, and the noon ferry to Tioman. Buses leave several times daily for Hat Yai, Krabi, Ko Samui, and Phuket in Thailand.

Travel agents on Jalan Chulia can book reserved seats on most buses.

Train: Penang's railway station is located in Butterworth. For bookings or information, call the railway booking office at the ferry terminal (tel. 04-261-0290) or the Butterworth station (tel. 04-334-7962).

Share Taxis: Malaysia's fastest and most hair-raising forms of transport are share taxis which leave next to the ferry terminal in Butterworth. Because they avoid delays at the border, share taxis provide a speedy way to reach Thailand. Fares are about 50% higher than those for non-a/c buses.

Ferry to Sumatra: Ferries leave Penang for Belawan—near Medan on Sumatra—five days a week and take 15 hours to cross the straits. Reclining chairs and private cabins can be booked at the two ferry offices adjacent to the tourist office.

Getting to Thailand

Air: You can fly or take the train, bus, or a share taxi from Penang to Thailand. There is little reason to fly from Penang to Hat Yai (unless you want to explore the deep south), but the Penang-Phuket flight is reasonably priced and saves two full days of very hard bus travel. Penang-Phuket-Bangkok is somewhat cheaper than a direct Penang-Bangkok ticket.

Train: Ordinary trains do not run from Butterworth to Hat Yai. Travelers must take the International Express which departs at 1340 and arrives in Hat Yai at 1640 and Bangkok at 0830 the next morning.

Bus: Buses can be taken from Penang to Thailand, but you should only take a bus that goes *directly* to Hat Yai, Phuket, Krabi, or Ko Samui. Tickets are available from travel agents in Penang. Do not take passage on a bus that terminates at the Malaysian border town of Changlun, since Sadao, the nearest Thai border town, is 20 km distant and can only be reached by hitchhiking.

Share Taxi: One of the best ways to reach Hat Yai is by fast and comfortable share taxi. These lumbering old Mercedes make the crossing in record time since they avoid the border crossing formalities that delay train and bus travelers. Share taxis can be picked up just outside the bus terminal in Butterworth, leave when filled, and cost about 50% more than non-a/c buses. They can also be chartered from travel agents in Georgetown.

LANGKAWI ISLAND

ALOR SETAR

Northwest Malaysia is, for most visitors, a lush and green land glanced at from the window of their speeding bus or train. Alor Setar, the provincial capital of Malaysia's richest rice-growing region, offers a hybrid Thai-Malay culture and some uniquely stylized architecture grouped around the Padang Besar.

Attractions

Most famous of the curious buildings is the Moorish-styled Masjid Zahir, which some consider the most beautiful mosque in Malaysia. The octagonal Balai Nobat (Hall of Drums), just opposite, holds the *nobat,* a Malay royal orchestra of drums, gongs, and *napori* trumpets. Constructed in 1898, the Thai-colonial Balai Besar down the road is now used for royal ceremonial functions such as the Sultan's Birthday. The State Museum on Jalan Bakar Bata has a small collection of artifacts from nearby archaeological excavations. The Wednesday market is held daily.

Accommodations

Most hotels are near the bus and taxi stations.

Station Hotel: Inexpensive hotel directly above the bus terminal and across the street from the train station. 74 Jalan Langgar, tel. (04) 733-3786, RM18-26.

Yuan Fang Hotel: Another cheap option one block down the street from the bus terminal. 97 Jalan Langgar, tel. (04) 733-1376, RM18-28.

LANGKAWI ISLAND

TO SATUN (THAILAND)

CERITA CAVE

PANTAI RHU

LANGGUN ISLAND

TO PENANG

TELUK BURAU

BLACK SAND BEACH

JETTY LALANG

DATAI

TEMURUN FALLS CROCODILE FARM

HOT SPRINGS

PERANGIN FALLS

DAGN

PANTAI KOK

SEVEN WELLS

LUBUK PARK

GUNUNG RAYA

KISAP

TELUK NIBONG

TERIANG

BURNT RICE FIELDS

ULU MELAKA

BUKIT PUTIH

MASURI TOMB

KUAH

TIMUN ISLAND

GOLF

JETTY

KEDEWANG

MALUT

LANGKAWI ISLAND RESORT

REBOK ISLAND

PANTAI CENANG

TEMONYONG

BANGAN NYORO

TO KUALA PERLIS

PANTAI TENGAH

TUBA ISLAND

BRAS BASAH ISLAND

LANGSIR CAVE

WILDLIFE PARK

SINGA BESAR ISLAND

DAYANG BUNTING LAKE

DAYANG BUNTING ISLAND

TO KUALA KEDAH

0   5 km

MALAYSIA

© MOON PUBLICATIONS, INC.

LANGKAWI ISLAND

Once remote and unspoiled, these sparkling islands in northwestern Malaysia have become the most popular beach destination in the country. Langkawi—an archipelago of 99 islands—romantically calls itself the Legendary Islands after the colorful tales surrounding its history; one claims the islands were cursed for seven generations by a Malay princess unjustly executed for adultery.

To promote tourism, the government has paved roads, declared Langkawi a duty-free port, pro-

vided loans for local resort development, and opened an international airport. Today, over one million Malaysians, Singaporeans, and other Asians annually arrive to fill the hotels and resorts during the high season from November to January. Otherwise, the island is largely deserted and hotels often slash rates to fill rooms. Light monsoons sprinkle the island between June and October; better beach weather is found on the east coast.

Government offices and banks on Langkawi follow Islamic hours: closed Friday, open half a day on Saturday, and Sunday is an ordinary business day.

Attractions

Langkawi, from which the archipelago takes its name, is an enormous island twice the size of Penang. Organized tours are probably the easiest and quickest way to see the island, although motorcycles can be rented from many hotels and shops in Kuah. Buses circle the island several times daily, but schedules are erratic and service sometimes ends in the early afternoon. Taxis cost RM50-75 per day—a good deal for larger groups. The following tour goes counterclockwise from Kuah.

Kuah: Aside from a picturesque mosque and duty-free shops, not much of interest detains travelers in this booming port town.

Durian Perangin Waterfall: The road north from Kuah passes through serene landscapes of ricefields, rubber plantations, coconut farms, and sleepy Malay villages tucked away under thick jungle. A small sign near Sungai Itau, some nine km from Kuah, marks the turnoff for the cascading falls best seen at the end of the monsoon season. The Telaga Hotsprings (Air Panas), 13 km from Kuah, have been renovated into a rather disappointing tourist trap complete with 200-seat theater restaurant, commercialized hot springs, and a range of cultural displays.

Pantai Hitam: Langkawi's unimpressive Black Sand Beach is believed to be colored by floating streaks of tin oxides.

Telaga Tujuh: Although the term translates to "Seven Wells," it's really a freshwater stream cascading down through a series of seven bathing pools.

Kuah

The ferry from Kuala Perlis arrives in Kuah ("Gravy"), which takes its name from a legendary nuptial fight in which the gravy pot landed where the town grew up. Kuah is a convenient spot for shopping but most travelers head directly to the beaches at Pantai Cenang, Pantai Tengah, and Pantai Kok. Taxis from the pier head into town or directly to the beaches.

Tourism Malaysia has an information booth at the jetty and a larger office in town.

Pantai Cenang

Langkawi's most popular beach provides a fairly attractive two-km stretch of sand virtually blanketed by a nonstop line of mid-priced chalets and hotels. Most are somewhat overpriced but bargains can be negotiated except during the busy winter months of December and January.

To reach Pantai Cenang from Kuah, take a bus to Temonyong or hire a taxi for RM10-15. The following spots are described from north to south.

Sandy Beach Hotel: Perhaps the island's most popular resting spot for budget travelers, Sandy's has bicycles and boats for hire and a small outdoor canteen for tasty Thai meals. Pantai Cenang, tel. (04) 955-1308, RM35-80.

AB Motel: Several budget spots are south of Sandy Beach Hotel near the rocky overpass to Pantai Tengah. Venerable AB Motel needs work but remains a popular choice. Pantai Cenang, tel. (04) 955-1300, RM30-55.

Semarak Beach Resort: Adjacent to Sandy Beach Hotel with attractive chalets at reasonable cost. Pantai Cenang, tel. (04) 955-1377, RM90-140.

Pelangi Beach Resort: Luxury 350-room property at the north end of the beach with all possible amenities. Pantai Cenang, tel. (04) 955-1001, RM340-480.

Pantai Tengah

Tengah Beach, just south from Pantai Cenang, has several budget guesthouses and a few upscale hotels facing a decent beach.

Budget Chalets: Low-end choices include the Green Hill Beach Motel, Tanjung Mali Beach Motel, Sugar Sands, and Charlie's. All offer basic chalets for RM35-50.

Sunset Beach Resort: Good mid-range place with simple a/c units and more luxurious chalets near the beach. Pantai Tengah, tel. (04) 955-2285, RM50-110.

Langkawi Holiday Villa: The southern tip of Langkawi is taken by this 258-room luxury resort with its two swimming pools, tennis courts, and convention facilities. Pantai Tengah, tel. (04) 955-1704, fax 955-1504, RM240-360.

Pantai Kok

A few inexpensive chalets survive on what is possibly the most attractive beach on Langkawi, though upscale resorts are slowly taking over the bay and the planned golf course will drive the last of the budget chalets off to more remote beaches. Most facilities are located between the

MALAYSIA

north end of the bay, Teluk Burau, and the southern tip, known as Teluk Nibong.

Country Beach Motel: Dead center on the beach is an old favorite with a popular restaurant, motorcycle rentals, and both fan-cooled and air-conditioned rooms. Other nearby cheapies—all scheduled for demolition within a few years—include the Mila Beach Motel, Dayang Beach Resort, Pantai Kok Motel, and the Coral Beach Motel. Pantai Kok, tel. (04) 955-1212, RM30-65.

The Last Resort: One of the better spots, operated by a Brit expat and his Malay wife, at the north end near luxurious Burau Bay Resort. Prices are moderate and the layout is less cramped than other budget places. Pantai Kok, tel. (04) 955-1046, RM35-60.

Sheraton Langkawi Resort: The early 1990s saw a construction frenzy that brought Langkawi a half-dozen resorts, including this luxurious outpost at Teluk Nibong. Pantai Kok, tel. (04) 955-1901, fax 955-1968, RM280-450.

North Coast

Pantai Datai and Pantai Rhu (Casuarina Beach) on the north shore offer some of Langkawi's finest sand and perfect solitude, but only luxury resorts have been constructed on these privately owned beaches.

Radisson Tanjung Rhu Hotel: After a long financial struggle, Radisson took over and then renovated this huge white elephant which now features a swimming pool, several restaurants, and endless water sports. Pantai Rhu, tel. (04) 959-1091, RM340-420.

Datai Langkawi: Langkawi's most exclusive resort tucked away in a small bay on the northwestern corner of the island. Teluk Datai, tel. (04) 959-2500, fax 959-2600, RM680-860.

Getting There

Langkawi is 30 km off the coast from Kuala Perlis, 51 km from Kuala Kedah, and 109 km north of Penang.

Air: MAS flies daily from Penang, Kuala Lumpur, and Singapore. The international airport is very close to the beaches, reached by taxis which operate at fixed rates on the coupon system.

From Kuala Perlis: Take a bus from Penang or Thailand to Kangar, followed by a shared taxi to Kuala Perlis. Ferries leave Kuala Perlis hourly and take an hour to reach Langkawi.

From Kuala Kedah: Hourly ferry service is also provided from Kuala Kedah near Alor Setar.

From Satun: Daily ferry service is provided from Satun to Langkawi, though the service is irregular and subject to cancellation. Check with the budget guesthouses in Hat Yai, Krabi, or Phuket before heading down to Satun.

MALAYSIA

PENINSULAR MALAYSIA ~ EAST COAST

The charms of the east coast are largely the result of geography. Isolated by the jungle-clad Barisan Mountains, which run the length of the peninsula, the east coast is a land of small villages, verdant ricefields, and fleets of bobbing fishing boats moored in blue lagoons. Unlike the west coast with its modern architecture and bustling cities filled with hard-working Chinese, the east coast is a sleepy place where life moves at a delightfully slow pace. Most residents are laid-back Malays who follow Islam and make their livings from fishing or farming. Cross-peninsula highways have brought modernization, and oil rigs and petroleum refineries have marred some of the coastline, yet much of the east coast remains an idyllic region of sun-drenched beaches, funky *kampongs* of stilted houses, and gentle people whose gracious lifestyles haven't changed much in recent times.

Two caveats: East coast beaches are clean and untouristy but not as stunning or well developed as those in southern Thailand. Secondly, single women and travelers looking for an escapist holiday should note that fundamentalist Islam has dramatically affected the mood and tolerance level on the east coast. Except for a few isolated beaches and offshore islands which offer some privacy from outraged locals, this is *not* the place to drink, find romance, or sunbathe in a skimpy bathing suit.

Transportation

A paved and well-maintained road skirts the coast from Singapore up to the Thai border just north of Kota Bharu. Other useful roads include the east-west highway across the top of the peninsula and the newly completed central highway which parallels the railway line between Johor Bharu and Kota Bharu. A steady stream of local buses rumbles along the coastal road and independent travelers should have little trouble flagging one down.

Transportation terminals in the larger towns are usually located on the main highway, at a strategic intersection, or adjacent to the central marketplace. Share taxis are also available for about 50% more than ordinary buses. Hitchhiking is relatively easy (but not guaranteed) and a good way to meet a traveling salesman. Roads are flat and bicyclists will enjoy the ride aside from the constant stream of traffic. MAS flies from Kuala Lumpur to Kota Bharu, Kuantan, and Kuala Trengganu.

Travel Practicalities

Travel can be difficult or impossible during the monsoon season from November to January, when rivers flood and roads disappear under mountains of water. Read the newspapers carefully and travel the west coast during monsoons.

Banking Hours: The Muslim weekend falls on Thursday and Friday in the states of Kelantan and Trengganu. Banks are open until 1130 on Thursday, closed all day on Friday, but open 1000-1500 on Saturday and Sunday.

Festivals: East coast celebrations from April to June are good opportunities to watch top spinning, kite flying, shadow-puppet plays, traditional dance, and boat races. The birthdays of the sultan of Kelantan (late March) and Trengganu (late April) are lively events, while cultural activities take place throughout the year in Kota Bharu.

Shopping: Malaysia's best selection of handicrafts is found on the east coast. Each state produces its own specialties. The Kelantanese of Kota Bharu produce outstanding silver filigree work, gold-thread needlework known as *songket*, and some truly exquisite paper kites. Trengganu artisans are known for their colorful hand-stamped batik and woodcarvings of intricate figureheads for fishing boats. Each town has a number of handicraft shops, often located somewhat outside the city limits; tourist offices can advise on nearby handicraft villages.

Behavior and Dress Codes

The east coast is the most conservative Muslim region in Malaysia and visitors must take this

EAST COAST HIGHLIGHTS

Top draws are the beaches, islands, villages, handicrafts, festivals, and the annual migration of the leatherback turtles. Recommended destinations include Tioman Island, Cherating beach, and the fishing village of Marang.

Towns

Urban centers such as Kota Bharu, Kuala Trengganu, and Kuantan are monotonous and disappointing places with little of interest except for the colorful local markets. The best one is in Kota Bharu, where dozens of brightly clad ladies sell their goods in a tiered emporium under wonderfully diffused lighting.

Beaches

The 710-km coastline from Thailand to Singapore is a nearly continuous stretch of sand interrupted only occasionally by rocky headlands or muddy estuaries which ooze their reddish waters into the turquoise sea. Although less impressive than the beaches of Thailand or the Philippines, many visitors love the sleepy pace and the lack of commercial development. These beaches are also superior to those on the west coast. Most beaches provide accommodations but for privacy and rural ambience I'd recommend Cherating, a lovely and relatively unde-

veloped beach with simple bungalows standing under the swaying palm trees.

Islands

Serious beachcombers will also want to visit several of the superb islands that sparkle in the sunshine off the coast from Mersing. Tioman once served as the backdrop for the 1950s film *South Pacific* and has been called among the world's 10 most beautiful islands. Accommodations range from an international-standard hotel with golf course to a dozen budget bungalows facing crystal-clear waters.

To the north and reached by fishing boats from Besut and Marang are the absolutely stunning islands of Kapas, Perhentian, and Redang with simple huts, mid-priced bungalows, and an increasing number of luxury resorts.

Villages

Malay *kampongs* are worth a quick visit since they are perhaps the cleanest and most picturesque villages in all of Southeast Asia. Remember, however, that this is the Bible Belt of Muslim Malaysia; conservative residents place great importance on modest dress and proper behavior. Shorts and bathing suits are completely inappropriate when wandering around an Islamic village.

into account and act in accordance with Malay traditions. Some of the best beaches are now closed to Westerners, who have offended local sensibilities with immodest dress such as shorts and bathing suits. Beaches next to Malay *kampongs* are generally off-limits. Best locations for sunbathing without upsetting the locals are at Cherating, Teluk Chempedak near Kuantan, and offshore islands such as Tioman. Shorts and halter tops are considered offensive dress in all urban areas, where visitors should wear long pants or full-length skirts. Women must be especially careful about this. Visitors to mosques must also be well covered. Public consumption of alcohol can be risky outside of protected tourist enclaves.

There's more: smoking is discouraged, public displays of affection are considered scandalous, and it is inadvisable to show any disrespect toward the sultan. Possession of drugs can bring

heavy fines, jail terms, or execution. While Muslim laws against indecency, alcohol, and close contact between persons of the opposite sex may seem harsh to Westerners on holiday, to disregard them could bring serious consequences.

MERSING

The small fishing town of Mersing is the departure point for boats to Tioman and other nearby islands. There is little of interest here except for a mosque overlooking the town and the small flotilla of fishing boats constructed with hulls in the distinctive style of Trengganu.

Accommodations

Most of Mersing's inexpensive Chinese hotels can be found by walking east toward the pier.

Boredom can be relieved with a movie at the nearby Union Theater.

Embassy Hotel: A popular backpackers' hotel and rendezvous spot despite the loud TV and somewhat expensive dishes in the cafe. Friendly managers. 2 Jl. Ismail, tel. (07) 799-1301, RM25-35.

Sheikh Tourist Agency: Sulaiman Aziz's place just opposite the post office toward the dock is another dependable backpackers' spot that doubles as a tourist agency. 1B Jl. Abu Bakar, tel. (07) 799-3767, RM6 dorm.

Mersing Merlin Inn: Mersing's top-end choice with all a/c rooms and swimming pool is two km outside town. Endau Rd., tel. (07) 799-1312, RM110-120.

Getting There

Avoid spending a night in Mersing by arriving in time to catch the noon boat to Tioman. An early bus from Kuantan and the 0900 bus from Singapore might arrive in time. An early start is essential from Kuala Lumpur since buses take about five hours. Most buses stop at the roundabout opposite the Restoran Malaysia, which sells bus tickets and tasty Indian food. To reach the ferry pier, walk east through Mersing to the boat offices.

TIOMAN ISLAND AND VICINITY

When James Michener described Bali Hai in his *Tales of the South Pacific* as an island paradise of sandy beaches, clear blue waters, and beautiful brown people, he never anticipated that moviemakers would one day search for the mythical island. The quest ended when Tioman was selected as the mysterious Bali Hai for Rogers and Hammerstein's musical *South Pacific*.

Located in the South China Sea off the eastern coast of Peninsular Malaysia, the teardrop-shaped and surprisingly undeveloped island achieved further fame when Geneva-based Magnum Press declared Tioman to be one of the world's 10 most beautiful islands. While Tioman certainly isn't in that rarefied class, it offers some fairly good beaches, clear waters filled with corals and colorful fish, and a spectacular jungle that climbs up soaring mountain walls.

ATTRACTIONS

West Coast Hike

Pulau Tioman, with its towering rock spires, thick jungles, and wealth of flora and fauna, provides ideal hiking opportunities for anyone interested in nature and wildlife.

The most famous rock formations are the twin peaks of Nenek Sri Mukut and Bau Sirau, which figured prominently in the film *South Pacific*. From the central pier at Tekek, hike south past Tioman Island Resort to a deserted stretch

of beach which rates among the best on the island. A small trail just beyond the hazardous but scenic 18-hole golf course leads over the hill

TIOMAN ISLAND

TULAI ISLAND

SALANG

BERUS DALAM

SOUTH CHINA SEA

PENUBA

ABC HUTS

BATANG PIER — KARINI PLACE

TO MERSING ← NAZRI'S BUNGALOWS

DUNGUNG

BUNGALOWS

TEKEK PIER — MOSQUE

RENGIS ISLAND AIRPORT

GOLF COURSE — BERJAVA IMPERIAL RESORT

BUNUT

JUARA PIER

G. ANGIN (831 m)

PAYA

GENTING PIER — GENTING

G. KAJANG (1,038 m)

NIPAH

MUKUT ASAH

ASAH PIER

0   2 km

© MOON PUBLICATIONS, INC.

MALAYSIA

to another long, fine beach flanked by swaying palms and large boulders set in clear waters. Across the bamboo bridge and over a steep hill is a small Malay fishing village, Kampong Paya, where an unmarked track leads to the summit of Gunung Kajang.

The seashore path north of Tekek winds past Ayer Batang Beach (where the best budget bungalows are located) and ends at Salang Beach about two hours farther north.

Cross-Island Hike

Tioman's most spectacular hike is the trans-island trail which starts near the mosque in Kampong Tekek and climbs over the mountains to Kampong Juara. The well-marked trail passes freshwater pools, waterfalls, and a rubber plantation. Allow two or three hours for this trek. Kampong Juara has several cafes and bungalows set on a beautiful beach.

Diving: Perhaps the most compelling reason to visit Tioman is to experience the underwater world. Waters immediately offshore have little to offer, but several of the nearby islands are rich in tropical fish and corals. Pulau Rengis, a minuscule island a few hundred meters offshore from the beach, is the easiest of these islands to dive. Snorkelers can also view the coral-encrusted wreck of a Japanese warship near Mukut and explore the underwater caves around Pulau Cebeh. The reefs at Tulai, Sepoy, and Labas islands have also been recommended. Dive trips can be arranged through the Tioman Island Resort, Samudra Swiss Cottages on Tekek Beach, and Ben's Diving Center on Salang Beach.

ACCOMMODATIONS

Tekek Beach

Tioman's central beach is taken over by Berjaya Imperial Beach Resort (former Tioman Island Resort), tel. (09) 414-5445, where standard a/c rooms with private baths are RM280-340.

To the north of the pier are a dozen unnamed bungalows with simple rooms in the RM15-25 price range. Unfortunately, none of these bungalows have been built with any imagination and all are disappointing when compared with similar efforts at Thai beaches. Best of the group are the two large brown bungalows owned by Rahim and Rahman. Most travelers skip these joints and head north to the less expensive huts at Ayer Batang.

Ayer Batang

The fine white sand and sense of seclusion of Ayer Batang (Air Batang) have made it the most popular backpackers' beach on Tioman. The A-frame huts are extremely basic—just mattresses on the floor and few offer electricity but only cost RM15-30 depending on the season, how long you plan to stay, the mood of the owner, and your bargaining ability.

Nazri's Bungalows just south of the jetty is situated on good sand, offers water sports, and has upscale chalets from RM40-80, but it's often filled because of proximity to the pier. North of the jetty is Tioman House, Kartini Place, Rinda House, and the recommended ABC Bungalows at the extreme northern end of the beach—worth the 20-minute walk. Boats from Mersing first stop at the Telek Jetty and then continue up to Ayer Batang Jetty.

Salang Beach

The small fishing village on the northwest corner of Tioman has excellent diving and an outstanding beach. Accommodations and diving gear are available at Ben's Diving Center, Bidin's Guest House, and Abidin Bungalows. South of the jetty you'll find Khalid's Place, Nora's Chalets, and Zaid's, which have chalets for RM20-45. Indah Salang, Salang Beach Resort, and Ella's have similar chalets for RM20-45 and a/c chalets for RM80-100. The newest addition, Strawberry Park Island Resort, has three restaurants, water sports facilities, and 150 rooms priced from US$110.

Most boats from Mersing continue to Salang after stops at the Tekek and Ayer Batang piers.

Juara

The settlement on the east side of Tioman has a handful of basic huts for RM10-15 such as Din's Sunrise, Ali Awang's, and Sammy Hussein's, though many of the older huts have been torn down and replaced with larger chalets in the RM15-30 price range.

GETTING THERE

Air

Silk Air and Pelangi Air fly daily to Tioman from Singapore for US$100. Pelangi Air also serves Tioman daily from Kuala Lumpur and Kuantan. There's also a daily catamaran service from the World Trade Centre in Singapore to Tioman.

Boat

Tioman is 43 nautical miles from Mersing and can be reached in about two hours with express boats which depart Mersing daily 1100-1500, depending on the tides. The fare is RM25 and discounts are provided on roundtrip tickets. The Mersing Pier and ticket offices are located at the far end of town.

OTHER ISLANDS NEAR TIOMAN

Rawa Island

Rawa is the most developed of the islands that dot the waters near Mersing. Opened in 1971, Rawa Island Safari Resort, tel. (07) 799-1204, is run by a member of the Johor royal family who provides visitors with activities such as windsurfing, canoeing, fishing, sunbathing, and skin diving, though little remains of the coral beds.

Accommodations in comfortable chalets cost RM110-190. Bookings can be made at the office at the Mersing pier.

Babi Besar Island

Larger and closer to the mainland than Rawa, this sparkling island has a few cheap bungalows such as White Sand Beach Resort and Sun Dancer at RM40-60 per person and several small resorts built in traditional Malay style. Both Radin Island Resort, tel. (07) 799-4152, and Hillside Chalet Island Resort, tel. (07) 799-4831, provide a/c bungalows from RM140-200.

Boats to Pulau Babi Besar from Mersing cost RM30-35 return. Like other nearby islands, Babi Besar gets crowded on weekends and closes down during the monsoon season from November to January.

Tinggi Island

Pulau Tinggi's unmistakable conical silhouette once earned it the nickname of "General Hat's Island" from passing Chinese sailors—a magnificent volcanic peak of sheer granite walls plunging into a deep blue sea; the interior jungle is home to screeching monkeys, pythons, and brilliantly plumed birds that can be trained to mimic the human voice with extraordinary precision. The island is so beautiful that some say an image of Tinggi was superimposed over a scene filmed on Tioman for the movie *South Pacific*.

Few budget spots remain although local families in Tinggi's main village sometimes provide basic accommodations in thatched *attap* huts hanging over the water. Luxury resorts such as Tinggi Island Resort, tel. (07) 799-4451, Apil Beauty Island, tel. (07) 799-4355, and Nadia's Inn Tropical Resort, tel. (07) 799-5582, cost RM100-450. Boats chartered from the Tourist Boat Association at Mersing jetty take about two hours and cost RM50 return.

Sibu Island

Some eight km west of Tinggi and reached in two hours from Mersing, Pulau Sibu is the perfect spot for travelers who enjoy squeaky white sand, skin diving, jungle treks, windsurfing, and a degree of solitude. The island also has a wide selection of accommodations from mid-priced chalets to upscale resorts.

The O&H Kampung Huts, tel. (07) 799-3125, has basic facilities for RM20-50, while the more upscale Sea Gypsy Village Resort, tel. (07) 223-1493, located on an exquisite crescent-shaped beach has luxury chalets from RM160-220. Other choices include Sibu Island Resort, tel. (07) 223-1188, and Sibu Island Cabanas, tel. (07) 331-7216, from RM100-160.

MALAYSIA

CENTRAL COAST ~ KUANTAN TO KOTA BHARU

KUANTAN

Situated midway up the east coast at the mouth of a muddy river, this gritty Chinese business town has little to offer most visitors, who head directly to the nearby beach resort of Teluk Chempedak.

Attractions

Kuantan attractions include a Muslim dinner at a waterfront cafe, the night market on Jalan Mahkota, and a ferry ride across the river to a Malay *kampong*. Kuantan is also the center for Pahang's numerous cottage industries, such as woven silks, pandan-leaf baskets, wood pieces carved by *orang asli,* silver filigree jewelry, dara jade necklaces, and handpainted batiks. The handicraft center at Teluk Chempedak has a good selection.

Attractions near Kuantan include Lake Chini, picturesque during the summer months when it is blanketed with a brilliant carpet of red and white lotuses, the Buddhist Cave at Sungai Lembing with its immense reclining image, the touristy fishing village of Beserah, and Chendor Beach, where loggerhead turtles lumber ashore during the summer months.

The Pahang State Tourist Office in the Kompleks Terantum, Kuantan's 22-story shopping and office complex, can help with transportation details.

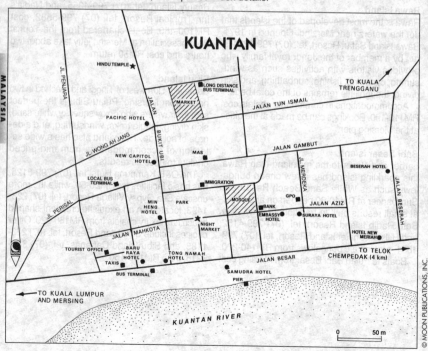

© MOON PUBLICATIONS, INC.

Accommodations

Kuantan is a compact town and most of the hotels are within walking distance of the bus terminal. Several inexpensive Chinese hotels are down near the waterfront.

Tong Nam Ah Hotel: Small but adequate rooms in the center of town; ask for a quiet room in the rear. Jalan Besar, tel. (09) 513-5204, RM15-20.

Min Heng Hotel: Another budget spot with a touch of exterior charm. Jalan Mahkota, tel. (09) 513-5885, RM15-20.

Hotel New Meriah: Somewhat better place with private baths plus hot water. 142 Jalan Telok Sisek, tel. (09) 525-5433, RM22-35.

Hotel Pacific: Upscale hotel away from the traffic and one block southwest of the long-distance bus terminal. 60 Jalan Bukit Ubi, tel. (09) 514-1980, RM70-95.

TELUK CHEMPEDAK

Kuantan's big draw is the beach at Teluk Chempedak, about five km north of town.

The road leading down to the beach is lined with gaudy Chinese restaurants, sleazy bars, and tourist shops selling T-shirts and cheap sunglasses: a discouraging introduction to what is otherwise a fairly pleasant place. Busloads of Malays picnic under the trees and patronize the handicraft stalls next to the parking lot. The small beach is often crowded on weekends because of its easy accessibility to Kuantan. Much more attractive and often completely deserted are the beaches at Methodist and Pelindong bays, reached with a leisurely 30-minute hike through the peninsula forest.

Accommodations

Most Western visitors at Teluk Chempedak are conventioneers from Singapore or Kuala Lumpur who need a few days of relaxation before returning home. Teluk Chempedak can be reached from Kuantan by taxi or bus 39 from the local bus terminal on Jalan Mahkota.

Homestays: Unusual options are the homestays in the street behind the Hillview Hotel. Most charge RM15-25; look for a Room to Let sign. Homestays at the top of the street are in good shape but the vandalized houses at the

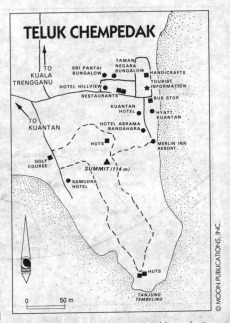

bottom of the road vaguely resemble a ghetto housing project.

Hotel Kuantan: A fairly good if somewhat overpriced hotel just opposite the Hyatt with both fan-cooled and a/c rooms. Teluk Chempedak, tel. (09) 513-0026, RM45-80.

Samudra Beach Hotel: Teluk's best midpriced hotel is across the peninsula near the golf course. Teluk Chempedak, tel. (09) 513-5933, RM70-95.

Hyatt Kuantan: High-end resort with all standard amenities, even a small wooden junk once used by Vietnamese refugees but now converted into a beach bar. What will the marketing director dream up next? Teluk Chempedak, tel. (09) 513-1234, RM240-320.

CHERATING

This beautiful sweeping beach about 45 km north of Kuantan is among the most popular stops, along with Tioman, Perhentian Island, and Kota Bharu. The sand is nothing special but the idyllic setting and attractive bungalows make this an

© MOON PUBLICATIONS, INC.

MALAYSIA

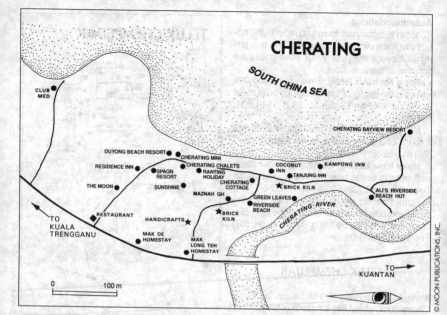

CHERATING

SOUTH CHINA SEA

CLUB MED

CHERATING BAYVIEW RESORT

DUYONG BEACH RESORT — CHERATING MINI
RESIDENCE INN — CHERATING CHALETS
SPAGN RESORT — RANTING HOLIDAY
THE MOON — SUNSHINE
COCONUT INN — KAMPONG INN
TANJUNG INN
CHERATING COTTAGE
BRICK KILN
MAZNAH GH
ALI'S RIVERSIDE BEACH HUT
GREEN LEAVES
RIVERSIDE BEACH
BRICK KILN
RESTAURANT — HANDICRAFTS

CHERATING RIVER

TO KUALA TRENGGANU

MAK DE HOMESTAY
MAK LONG TEH HOMESTAY

TO KUANTAN →

0   100 m

© MOON PUBLICATIONS, INC.

MALAYSIA

outstanding place to relax for a few days . . . or weeks. Cherating is also one of the few beaches in Malaysia where Westerners can wear swimsuits without fear of offending Muslim sensibilities.

The jutting hill to the north separates Cherating Beach from Southeast Asia's first Club Med and, farther north, Chendor Beach where turtles sometimes arrive to lay their eggs. Aside from making sidetrips to Tasik Chini or Pandan Falls, there isn't much to do at Cherating but loaf, wander around the beach looking for sand crabs, and perhaps inspect the old and collapsing brick kilns. Cherating is an idyllic and perfectly relaxing destination.

Accommodations

Cherating is quickly expanding as local entrepreneurs open new bungalows and restaurants on a near-weekly basis. Accommodations range from basic A-frame huts in the RM10-15 price range to chalets with private baths for RM25-60; many represent excellent value. Upscale resorts in the RM80-250 range can also be found at Cherating.

Mak Long Teh Homestay: Teh Ahmad, or Mak Long Teh, pioneered the idea of village ac-

commodations for tourists over 20 years ago and today continue to provide guests with Malay hospitality in an authentic *kampong* home. Cherating, tel. (09) 581-3290, RM12-15 including meals.

Mak De Homestay: Another memorable homestay somewhat marred by the noise from the nearby highway. Cherating, tel. (09) 581-1316, RM12-15 including meals.

Coconut Inn: A quick walk along the narrow road uncovers some real gems, but perhaps the best choice is this lovely Malay house facing the arching bay. Cherating, tel. (09) 581-3199, RM15-35.

Other Budget Chalets: Kampong Inn has decent rooms from RM15-30, brown Cherating Indah features individual porches and tables, and Ali's Riverside Beach Hut at the end of the road offers clean bungalows and views over the Cherating River for RM20-60.

Club Mediterranee: Club Med to the north was constructed on a public beach, technically open to day guests despite the heavy presence of guards. Facilities include a conference center, restaurants, and extensive sports facilities. Cherating, tel. (09) 591131, US$600-900 per week.

Transportation

All buses between Kuantan and Kuala Trengganu roar past Cherating, but from Kuantan it's best to take the gray-and-red bus marked "Kemaman." Ask to be dropped at Mak Long Teh Homestay.

RANTAU ABANG

Not all visitors to the east coast come to lie on the beach and improve their tans. Some must attend to more important matters. One of the world's most impressive natural phenomena is the annual migration and struggle of leatherback turtles onto the narrow beach at Rantau Abang. Each year between May and September, hundreds of these rare and remarkable creatures instinctively return here to nest and ensure the survival of their species. The 20-km stretch of beach near Rantau Abang plays an important role in this story; although leatherbacks spawn at some 12 locations worldwide, only Surinam in the Western Hemisphere and Rantau Abang are considered important in their yearly ritual. Of the eight species of sea turtles in the world, giant leatherbacks *(Dermochels coriacea)*, green turtles *(Chelonia mydas)*, olive ridleys *(Lepidochelys olivacea)*, and hawkbills *(Eretmochelys imbricata)* are all known to nest in Malaysia. But leatherbacks are unquestionably the largest and most famous—the *Guinness Book of World Records* cites a monster which measured almost three meters and tipped the scales at over 1,000 kilos! In the reptile world only the estuarine crocodile and the Komodo dragon compare in sheer physical size.

Leatherback Spotting

Turtle watching is a rewarding but exhausting experience since the female turtle prefers nocturnal cover for her egging expeditions. Although it plays havoc on a good night's sleep, you must join the crowds and wait patiently in a seashore restaurant. Rantau Abang's beaches are divided and tendered to licensed egg collectors, who are authorized to collect entrance fees to their enclosed beaches. Fee collectors can be recognized by certified identification tags from the Fisheries Department. Turtle watching is free along the stretch of beach controlled by the government near the Rantau Abang Visitor's Center.

Turtles are most numerous in late August when the reptiles swim ashore from midnight to early morning. Relax with your *paratha* and *roti bakar* until someone sounds the alarm. Everyone then races down the beach and gathers in the eerie darkness to watch the creature silently struggle up the steep beach. It is like a King Kong movie as the primeval dinosaur lumbers past the silent crowds, patiently digs a dummy hole to fool the predators, and then laboriously lays 50-100 eggs in her final hole. Tears of exhaustion slowly drip from her eyes. A licensed egg collector keeps the crowd quiet and prevents any possible disturbances while he gathers the eggs under the watchful eye of the Fisheries Department. After he departs, spectators take photos, kick sand, and ride the frightened animal.

Unfortunately, a decline in the turtle population continues despite the best efforts of the

---

LEATHERBACK TURTLES ~ ON THE BRINK OF EXTINCTION

Leatherbacks are an endangered species. Annual landings have declined from over 10,000 in the early 1950s to less than 600 in recent years. Predators such as hawks and lizards capture many of the newly hatched turtles as they scurry from beach to ocean, but the most serious threat is man. As with rhino horns and tigers' paws, some misguided people believe leatherback eggs to be an aphrodisiac worth exorbitant prices. It's incredibly tragic that despite the near-complete extinction of the species and the pleas of the World Wildlife Fund, sale and consumption of the rubbery, Ping-Pong ball-sized eggs is still legal in Malaysia! Fortunately, the situation isn't hopeless. Under pressure from international and local environmental groups, the government recently gazetted Rantau Abang as a turtle sanctuary and now purchases 100% of all collected turtle eggs. These are then incubated in protected sand nests for 56 days before the young hatchlings are released to the sea. The situation remains critical, but with increased local awareness and tough legal measures it might be possible to save the magnificent reptiles from extinction.

government and concerned naturalists. Today, less than a few dozen turtles are sighted anywhere along the east coast of Malaysia and few visitors now bother to stop at these once-famous turtle nesting grounds.

Accommodations

Two inexpensive bungalows are located on the beach within walking distance of the turtles and the Turtle Information Center, while a trio of better resorts is within a few kilometers.

Awang's Beach Bungalows: Pak Awang almost single-handedly started local tourism in 1959 when he constructed the first rustic dormitory at Rantau Abang. The manager can help arrange tours to nearby Pulau Kapas, Sekayu Waterfall, and the night market at Kuala Dungun. Rantau Abang, tel. (09) 844-3500, RM15-20.

Ishmail Beach Resort: Similar facilities adjacent to Awang's. Rantau Abang, tel. (09) 844-1054, RM10-30.

Dahimah's Guesthouse: A clean and quiet alternative to the tourist center is provided at this popular guesthouse one km south toward Dungun, on the west side of the Abang River. All rooms have private baths; the more expensive chalets are a/c with hot showers. Rantau Abang, tel. (09) 983-5057, RM30-50.

Merantau Inn: The middle price gap is filled by this older resort located a few kilometers south of the visitor center. Kuala Abang, tel. (09) 844-1131, RM45-120.

Tanjong Jara Beach Hotel: The top-end choice, six km south of the Turtle Center and 13 km north of Kuala Dungun, has 100 luxurious rooms spread across 76 acres. Best of all, the hotel has a seven-km beach stretching between two headlands virtually to itself. Mile 8 Jalan Dungun, tel. (09) 844-1801, RM260-480.

MARANG

Situated 15 km south of Kuala Trengganu on the estuary of a wide river, the splendid fishing village of Marang offers a rare opportunity to observe local Malay lifestyles and enjoy one of the finest beaches in the region. The setting is ridiculously picturesque: quaint little houses elevated on stilts surround a pure blue lagoon speckled with colorful fishing boats. Wide-eyed children smile shyly at the visitor while older residents go about their business of drying squid and fish in the blazing sun. Despite its superb location and fine beach, Marang remains almost completely untouched by tourism.

Attractions

Kampong Walk: Westerners are welcome to wander around the small village north of the river,

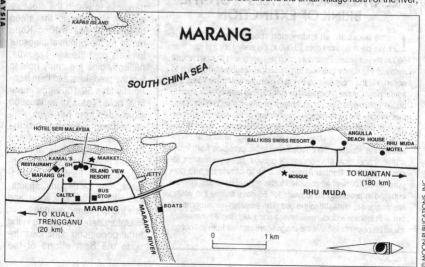

© MOON PUBLICATIONS, INC.

MALAYSIA

but local customs must be observed. All visitors should remain well covered. Shorts and revealing tops are considered scandalous dress in the village and bathing suits can only be worn on the beaches directly fronting the tourist bungalows.

Marang River: Day-long voyages up the muddy Marang can be arranged through most bungalows. Boats typically leave in the early morning and return by sunset with wildlife stops and lunch at Kuala Mesta some 50 km upriver. Charters and motorized self-drive boats are also available.

Kapas Island

Scattered offshore from Marang and Kuala Trengganu are several islands with pristine beaches and submerged coral beds rich with tropical marinelife. Kapas, six km from Marang, has a succession of deserted beaches joined at low tide, a bat cave, monitor lizards, and excellent snorkeling on the backside of adjacent Gemai Island. Kapas is a day-trip for most visitors, although you can sleep on the beach or stay in a basic chalet or more upscale resort. Bring food, drink, and mosquito net if you plan to camp out.

Accommodations: Pulau Kapas now has a half-dozen places to stay. The least expensive spots are Zaki Beach Chalet, tel. (09) 612-0258, where rooms cost RM15-30, and Mak Cik Gemuk Beach Resort, tel. (09) 618-1221, which charges RM20-50. A good mid-priced choice is Kapas Garden Resort where rooms with private baths cost RM45-60.

The island's high-end resort is Primula Kapas Island Village Resort where deluxe bungalows cost RM120-260. Facilities include water sports, restaurant, and swimming pool. Contact the Pantai Primula Hotel in Kuala Trengganu for details.

Transportation: Kapas can be reached by speedboat from the Marang pier for RM10. The island gets crowded on Thursdays and Fridays when Muslim day-trippers pack Kapas.

Marang Accommodations

The broad Marang River separates the small commercial district to the north from the village of Kampong Rhu Muda, two km to the south.

Kamal's Guesthouse: Marang's original guesthouse has been serving the needs of budget travelers for over a decade. The owner, Kamaruzaman, arranges excursions up the Marang

River and out to Kapas Island. Marang, tel. (09) 618-2181, RM5-15.

Marang Guesthouse: Popular spot and one of the best guesthouses on the east coast with excellent restaurant and locally made batiks. 132-133 Bandar Marang, tel. (09) 618-2132, RM15-45.

Hotel Seri Malaysia: Marang hit the big time a few years ago with the construction of this modern hotel overlooking the lagoon—the first development geared exclusively to attact tourists rather than travelers. Marang, tel. (09) 618-2889, RM90-140.

Rhu Muda Accommodations

Places here tend to cater to families and couples rather than backpackers.

Angulla Beach House Resort: A reasonably attractive resort though individual chalets are overpriced and the place badly needs some landscaping. Bargain for a room. Km 20, Kampong Rhu Muda, tel. (09) 618-2403, RM50-95.

Bell Kiss Swiss Resort: Better value is found at this adjacent resort. Note: Both resorts in Rhu Muda are surrounded by protective fences and visitors are strongly advised to safeguard their valuables. Incidents of theft, rock throwing, and tire slashing by scandalized locals have been reported. Lot 212 Jalan Pantai, Marang, tel. (09) 618-1579, RM25-50.

Transportation

Marang is 15 km south of Kuala Trengganu and 23 km north of Rantau Abang. From the south, take any bus heading north and get off in Rhu Muda, or near the bridge for Marang guesthouses. From Kuala Trengganu bus station, take a bus marked, Marang, or Kg. Rhu Muda, depending on your destination.

KUALA TRENGGANU

Kuala Trengganu, seat of the sultan and capital of the state of Trengganu, is a once-sleepy fishing village now being transformed by its recently found oil wealth into a modern city.

Tourism Malaysia is inconveniently located at the far end of Jalan Sultan Zainal Abidin, while the less useful Trengganu State Tourism Office is near the GPO in the center of town.

Attractions

Rather than impressive architecture or historical monuments, Trengganu's top draws are the nearby beaches, tropical islands, and traditional handicrafts.

Market: A well-organized but impersonal and dark market best experienced in the early morning hours—durians are downstairs, handicrafts upstairs. Nearby Jalan Bandar has some fine wooden buildings.

Old Sultan's Palace: A curious French-style *istana* constructed in 1903 to replace the burned Green Palace with tapered roofs and wooden windows embellished with intricately carved Koranic inscriptions. The State Mosque stands on the adjacent corner.

Duyong Besar Island: The estuary of the Trengganu River has several islands which are home to Malay fishermen and boatbuilders who fashion traditional and modern crafts. Ferries to

Duyong Besar leave from the jetty near the taxi stand. Boats can also be hired for upriver trips to Kampong Pulau Rusa, whose occupants are famous for the quality of their *songket* weavings.

Accommodations

Kuala Trengganu has two backpackers' hostels, plus a half-dozen hotels in the low to middle price range in the center of town.

Ping Anchorage Homestay: The best guesthouse in town offers a wonderful rooftop cafe, dorms and private rooms, and organized tours to nearby attractions. 77A Jalan Dato Isaac, tel. (09) 622-0851, RM5 dorm, RM12-25 private room.

Triple A Guesthouse: Another budget spot in the center of town near the central market. Jalan Bandar, tel. (09) 622-7372, RM5-10 dorm, RM12-18 private room.

Awi's Yellow House: A rustic waterside guesthouse in a traditional village on the shipbuilding is-

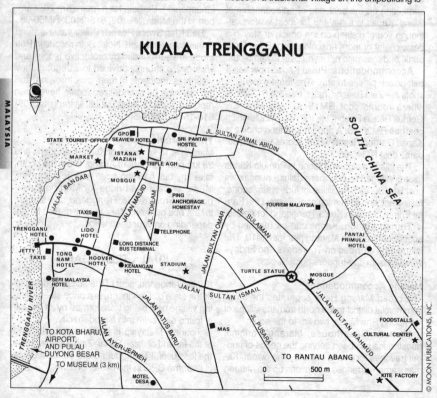

KUALA TRENGGANU

© MOON PUBLICATIONS, INC.

land of Duyong Besar; a great spot to escape city life and *relax*. From Kota Bharu, get off the bus at the enormous new bridge that spans the Trengganu River. From Kuala Trengganu, take a Duyong bus from the local bus terminal or a ferry from the jetty. 3576 Duyong Besar, tel. (09) 633-1741, RM5 dorm, RM10-25 private room.

Seaview Hotel: Good mid-priced hotel in the center of town with both fan-cooled and a/c rooms with private baths. 18A Jalan Masjid Abidin, tel. (09) 622-1911, RM20-55.

Pantai Primula Hotel: Kuala Trengganu's only luxury hotel with swimming pool, water sports facilities, and three restaurants facing a fairly good beach. Jalan Persinggahan, tel. (09) 622-2100, RM180-280.

Transportation

Kuala Trengganu is 76 km north of Kuala Dungun and 142 km south of Kota Bharu. A new transnational highway now connects Kuala Trengganu with Gua Musang (Taman Negara National Park) in the center of the country and Ipoh on the west coast.

Long-distance and local buses leave from the main bus terminal on Jalan Masjid Abidin. The taxi station is just across the street.

MERANG AND REDANG ISLAND

Traveling north from Kuala Trengganu, the road leaves the coast and passes through a rich to-bacco- and rice-growing region. Side roads reach the coastal villages of Merang (not Marang) and Besut, where boats depart for several beautiful islands. Most have been declared protected marine parks to prevent fishing and coral collection and all offer clean beaches and crystal-clear waters filled with varied marine life, sponges, and coral beds.

Boat service to Pulau Redang is most frequent on the Muslim weekends of Thursdays and Fridays. Organized snorkeling and scuba dives can be arranged at the Pantai Primula Hotel in Kuala Trengganu.

Merang

Merang, another idyllic fishing village located on a long stretch of clean, white sand, is also the departure point for boats to Pulau Redang and other smaller islands.

Accommodations: Razak's Kampung House and Naughty Dragon's Green Planet Homestay in the center of town have simple but acceptable rooms from RM15. Both spots can help with boats to Redang Island.

Transportation: Merang can be somewhat difficult to reach as there are few public buses that follow the narrow coastal road; most buses race along the main highway, which connects Kuala Trengganu and Kota Bharu. From Kuala Trengganu, take a bus toward Penarik and alight at Merang. Alternatively, take a share taxi or one of the more frequent minivans direct to Merang.

From the north, take a bus to the Penarik turnoff at Permaisuri, another bus to Penarik,

cheaper by the dozen

and a share taxi to Merang. A quicker alternative is to charter a taxi from Permaisuri.

Redang Island

Pulau Redang, 50 km from Trengganu and 30 km from Merang, is actually an archipelago of over 25 small islands known for its pure beaches, spectacular coves, and outstanding diving over vast expanses of coral beds. Long a secret of nature lovers, change arrived suddenly in 1993 with the construction of an immense resort bitterly opposed by Malaysian environmental groups such as the Malaysian Nature Society. Redang Island Resort now covers almost 25% of the main island with a four-story 250-room hotel, dozens of chalets, and, almost unbelievably, an 18-hole golf course constructed over landfilled mangrove swamps.

First port of call is the small but orderly fishing village of Kampung Puala Redang, where last-minute supplies are available from the general store. Activities include skin diving among the hard and soft corals, jungle hiking, and swimming in the crystal-clear bay at Teluk Dalam.

Accommodations: Accommodation on Redang is limited to camping at Teluk Kalong, the very expensive Redang Island Resort, or Dahlan Beach Chalets, owned and operated by a tour and dive operator from Kuala Trengganu.

Transportation: Boat service from Merang to Pulau Redang is sporadic and it's best to arrange an organized tour with Ping Anchorage in Kuala Trengganu.

PERHENTIAN ISLAND

The twin islands of Perhentian Besar (Big Perhentian or the "Big Island") and Perhentian Kecil (Small Perhentian or the "Small Island"), 21 km off the coast from Kuala Besut, are outstanding warm-water destinations considered among the most beautiful islands in all of Malaysia. Both islands are accessed from Kuala Besut.

Kuala Besut

Kuala Besut, a rather run-down fishing village with lots of odor and little charm, is the departure point for boats to the Perhentian Islands.

Accommodations: Several inexpensive guesthouses are found in the center of town a block or two from the Perhentian pier. Coco Hut Chalet, tel. (09) 687-2085, provides very basic rooms from RM10-15, while Nam Hotel covers the mid-range with fan-cooled and a/c rooms from RM35-50. Both places sell boat tickets to the Perhentians.

Transportation: From Kuala Trengganu, take a bus to Jerteh and then another bus direct to Kuala Besut. From Kota Bharu, take a bus to Pasir Puteh and then continue by bus to Kuala Besut. Share taxis from Jerteh or Pasir Puteh are much quicker than waiting for one of the infrequent buses. Quickest of all are share taxis direct from Kota Bharu or Kuala Trengganu.

Perhentian Besar

Shaped almost exactly like Australia, Perhentian Besar is due for some big changes as developers arrive to construct larger resorts and transportation wizards dream of hydrofoils and, believe it or not, even an airport. Still, the Big Island remains a place you wouldn't mind being shipwrecked for several weeks . . . if not months.

Aside from lazing on the beach, visitors can join snorkeling trips organized by most of the guesthouses on both islands. Scuba dive shops located on both islands provide basic PADI certification courses plus other water sports activities such as windsurfing and sailing.

The south side of the island is dominated by the large bay of Teluk Dalam which enclosed a two-km stretch of white sand. The western end of the bay runs into the headlands of Batu Lepir, which features a small white Fisheries Department and a low light tower. The west side is comprised of a series of small, sandy bays interrupted by low headlands formed by enormous granite boulders. Separating the two islands is a calm body of water perfect for snorkeling.

Just north of promontory Tanjung Genting lies the stunning soft white sand of Telok Pauh ("wild mango bay") and shallow waters blessed with outstanding corals. Continuing northeast around the island is one final bay, Pasir Tiga Ruang, as yet undeveloped and still a nesting site for turtles. Turtles also arrive at remote Teluk Tukas at the southeastern extremity of the island.

Accommodations: Both islands now offer over a dozen inexpensive guesthouses and chalets, which cost RM15-30 depending on the condition of the huts and the season; expect big discounts during the rainy months. Camping is free on both islands but bring plenty of food, water, and other necessities.

Perhentian Island Resort, tel. (010) 901-0100, (03) 244-8530 in Kuala Lumpur, takes over a stunning cove on the northwestern side of the island and features individual chalets with either overhead fans from RM120 or a/c from RM240-320.

Perhentian Besar's budget places are on the west side of the island facing the narrow straits that separate Perhentian Besar from Perhentian Kecil. Most charge RM20-30 but an increasing number are tearing down the older huts and replacing them with larger chalets in the RM35-60 price range.

At the north end of the beach you'll find the somewhat upscale **Coral View Island Resort,** tel. (09) 691-0943, with larger chalets outfitted with private baths from RM25-60. Heading south along the arching beach are the less expensive Mama's Place, Cozy Chalet (tel. 09-691-0090), Coco Hut, Samudin, ABC Chlaets, Ibi Huts, and Abdul's Chalets, which proudly claims to be "where dreams become reality"—as opposed to Perhentian Island Resort, which boasts to be "where reality becomes fantasy." Apparently, somebody's been eating mushrooms again.

Camping is permitted at the south end of the beach just beyond the Government Resthouse.

The island's third accommodation center is the large and relatively uncrowded beach on the southern side of the island which makes up Teluk Dalam, nicknamed Flora Bay. The three main chalet operations—Flora Bay Chalets, tel. (011) 987-7266, Fauna Bay Chalets, and D'Laguna Chalets, tel. (09) 691-0105—provide basic huts from RM20-30 and larger chalets with fans or a/c from RM40-85.

Transportation: Boats from Kuala Besut leave in the morning, return in the late afternoon, and cost around RM15 one-way. Passengers are dropped at the beach of their choice; smaller boats shuttle between the two islands.

Perhentian Kecil

Dewdrop-shaped Perhentian Kecil, the smaller of the two Perhentian Islands, has long served as the main backpackers' destination with outstanding sand around Pasir Panjang (Long Beach) on the eastern side and smaller stretches of equally inviting sand at Pasir Petani to the south and Coral Bay to the west. Long Beach provides most of the guesthouses but it's only a 15-minute walk across the narrow waist of the island to Coral Bay and then a 90-minute hike south to Pasir Petani and another 20 minutes east to Perhentian village.

The island's popularity sometimes means packed-out chalets and some travelers prefer lodging in the less hectic atmosphere on Perhentian Besar.

Accommodations: Long Beach boasts several very decent budget accommodations, including Moonlight Chalets located at the northern end of the bay, Matahari Chalets in the center near the trailhead to Coral Bay, Cottage Huts also in the center with a popular beachside cafe, basic but very quiet Chempaka Chalets at the southern end of the beach, and Rock Garden elevated above the beach across a rocky headlands.

Coral Bay on the west side of Perhentian Kecil is a much smaller beach than Long Beach, but serves as a great spot for sunsets and hikes south to a series of tiny, untouched coves. Among the budget options are Coral Bay Chalets, Aur Bay Chalets, and Rajawali Chalets (tel. 09-691-0818), which provide both basic huts from RM20 and larger, more comfortable chalets from RM35-55.

A few chalets are also found along the southern coast en route to the small administrative village of Kampong Perhentian (Kampong Pasir Hantu), which has a few small shops for supplies plus foodstalls, school, and mosque. Mira Chalets is a one hour hike south of Coral Bay, while Pleasure Chalets and Pasir Petani Village are your final two options on the southern coast, some 30 minutes east of Mira Chalets. All three chalets have basic rooms from RM20 while Mira Chalets also offers larger bungalows from RM35-50.

MALAYSIA

KOTA BHARU AND VICINITY

Tucked away at the northeastern corner of the peninsula some 24 km from the Thai border, Kota Bharu (also spelled Baru), the state capital of Kelantan State, is considered the heartland of traditional Malaysian culture. While the city is physically indistinguishable from most other Asian cities constructed of concrete and cinderblock, it remains the best place in Malaysia to see shadow puppets, kite flying, top spinning, and other Malay games. It is also somewhat of a handicrafts center with a handful of shops producing fine batiks, silverware, brasswork, and woodcarvings.

The Kota Bharu tourist office, tel. (09) 748-5534, on Jalan Sultan Ibrahim just south of the clock tower is friendly and can help with directions to nearby handicraft villages.

Note that banks and most government offices are closed on Thursday afternoons and Fridays but open Saturdays and Sundays.

Thai visas can be obtained 0900-1230 and 1430-1600 Sunday-Thursday at the Royal Thai Consulate, tel. (09) 744-0867, at 4426 Jalan Pengkalan Chepa.

ATTRACTIONS

Sights in town are limited to several historic buildings clustered together near Merdeka Square, a few blocks south of the commercial center.

Central Market
A good place to begin your walking tour is at this modern market where scores of brightly clad women gossip, chew betel nut, and display their rambutans, mangosteens, pandan mats, and batiks in the open-air emporium. Constructed like a theater with two stories of balconies that overlook the vegetable center court, this fabulous market is perfectly lit by the filtered sunlight which radiates through the glass ceiling. This is Malaysia's most colorful market . . . a photographer's dream.

Royal Museums
Istana Jahar (Royal Customs Museum): The superb craftsmanship of the Kelantanese is ev-ident on this eclectic architectural marvel which harmoniously combines Dutch-Javanese and Asian styles. Originally the residence of the Sultans, this century-old building now serves as a Royal Museum with a small but worthwhile collection of royal costumes and regalia and a startling variety of swords and antique daggers. The museum is open daily except Wednesdays.

Istana Batu (Royal Museum): Just up the road is Istana Batu, constructed in 1939, the residence of the crown prince until 1969 when it was donated to the state and converted into the Royal Museum. After viewing the royal memorabilia, wander across the street and visit the Handicraft Market for a quick overview of local crafts.

Istana Balai Besar: The Palace with the Large Audience Hall was built in 1844 and still serves as a venue for coronations and royal weddings. Inside is a Throne Room, the State Legislative Assembly Hall, and an elaborately carved Royal Barge used once in 1900 for a kingly pleasure cruise on the Kelantan River.

Merdeka Square Museums
The State Mosque on the far side of the park was constructed in 1926 in a European-Saracenic style similar to that of the Abu Bakar Mosque in Johor Bharu. The adjacent State Religious Council Building was built at the same time to foster Islamic development and progress in Kelantan. Today it serves as the Islamic Museum to reflect the pervasiveness of Islam in Kelantan.

Also note the former Hong Kong and Shanghai Bank, constructed 1912 as the first brick building in Kelantan. It later served as the headquarters for Japanese occupation troops after they landed at a nearby beach on 7 December 1941. Today, it houses the World War II Memorial Museum with photographic reminders of the Japanese invasion.

Kelantan Cultural Center (Gelanggang Seni)
Shows featuring *wayang kulit* (shadow plays), *gasing uri* (top spinning), *rebana ubi* (giant drums), *wau* (kite flying), *silat* (a martial art), *ker-*

KOTA BHARU

KITE MAKER

TO BEACH OF PASSIONATE LOVE (BUS 10, 28)

★ BATIK & SONGKET STORES

JALAN ZAINAB

POST OFFICE

JALAN MERBAU

KB GARDEN HOSTEL

JOHNTY'S GH

★ ROYAL MUSEUM

STAR HOSTEL

SAFAR INN

IDEAL TRAVELLER'S HOUSE

ISLAMIC MUSEUM (HONG KONG AND SHANGHAI BANK)

★ STATE MOSQUE

PANTAI HOSTEL

RESTAURANTS

ROYAL CUSTOMS MUSEUM

MERDEKA SQUARE

JUITA INN

ISTANA BALAI BESAR

JL. PINTU PONG

TO AIRPORT →

INDAH HOTEL

CENTRAL MARKET

MUMMY'S R.I.P. HITEC HOSTEL

BUS 10 TO BEACH

NORTH MALAYSIA HOTEL

JL. TENGKU CHIK

THAI CONSULATE

TEMENGONG HOTEL

JL. TOK HAKIM

NIGHT MARKET ★

FRIENDLY GH

ZECK GH

RAINBOW GH

KENCANA HOTEL

TAMAN SEKEBUN BUNGA

BUS TERMINAL

YEE GH

JALAN PENGKALAN CHEPA

FAMILY GARDEN GH

OLD MARKET

JL. LAMA

JL. TEMENGGONG

TAXIS

JL. CHE SU

JL. PATI

MURNI HOTEL

PARK

JL. DUSAN RAYA

HOTEL ANSAR

JL. DOKTOR

BATIK STORES

CLOCK TOWER

MAS

★ STATE MUSEUM

JALAN HOSPITAL

TOURIST INFORMATION

STADIUM

FOOD STALLS

JL. SULTANAH IBRAHIM

CULTURAL CENTER ★

JALAN BAYAM

MENORA GH

IMMIGRATION

GPO

PERDANA HOTEL

★ ISTANA KOTA LAMA

JALAN MAHMUD

TO WAKAF BARU TRAIN STATION (BUS 19)

REBANA HOUSE

★ SILVERSMITHS

IRAMA HOTEL

0   100 m

JL. SULTANAH

BUSES TO PENANG & KUALA LUMPUR

JL. HAMZAH

TO PENANG, THAI BORDER AND RANTAU PANJANG (BUS 29)

LANGGAR BUS TERMINAL (KL PENANG, KUANTAN, AND SINGAPORE)

JALAN PASIR PUTEH

JL. DUSAN MUDA

STATE OFFICES

TO KUALA KRAI (BUS 5)

TO KUALA TRENGGANU, KUALA LUMPUR (BUS 3)

KELANTAN RIVER

MALAYSIA

© MOON PUBLICATIONS, INC.

tok (coconut orchestra), and Kelantanese dance are performed several times weekly at the Gelanggang Seni on Jalan Sultan Mahmud across from the Hotel Perdana. While the shows are performed by amateurs, this is probably the single best place in Malaysia to enjoy such a diversity of traditional Malay performing arts. The tourist office has performance schedules and can advise on upcoming festivals.

Handicraft Shops
Many of Kota Bharu's weavers, silversmiths, and kite makers are located along the road which runs north to the Pantai Cahaya Bulan (PCB) or Moonlight Beach, a decent stretch of sand once known as Pantai Cinta Berahu or Beach of Passionate Love. Perhaps the most unusual shop is Tukang Wau Bulan, where Nik Abdullah sells his technicolor kites.

Take bus 10 and be prepared to do some walking between showrooms. A better idea is to rent a bicycle as the showrooms are spread over a six-km stretch of road.

Night Market
One of the great pleasures of Kota Bharu is grazing at the evening food market, with its dazzling variety of dishes at rock-bottom prices. Some specialties to look for include *nasi dagang* (unpolished glutinous rice served with coconut milk and fish or chicken), *kerutup ayam* (curry chicken), *solok lada* (steamed stuffed chilies), *gulai ikan tongkol* (curried bluefin tuna), and the popular Kelantanese specialty *ayam percik* (charcoal-grilled chicken). While Malaysians are generally noted for their fiery-hot recipes, Kelantan dishes are often sweetened with sugar and a coconut sauce called *lemak*. Dieters should be forewarned about the delicious array of sweets, cakes, and other caloric desserts.

ATTRACTIONS NEAR KOTA BHARU

Beaches
The Kelantanese, true romantics at heart, have given the nearby beaches some unforgettable names. Pantai Cinta Berahu (Beach of Passionate Love) some nine km north of Kota Bharu is superbly named, although it is highly unlikely you will witness any open displays of romance here in the heartland of Islamic Malaysia. Actually, the beach was renamed Pantai Cahaya Bulan (PCB or Moonlight Beach) a few years ago so as not to upset Muslim sensibilites.

Other well-named but ordinary beaches near Kota Bharu include Pantai Kuda (Horse Beach), Pantai Bisikan (Whispering Breeze), and Pantai Irama (Beach of Melody). Pantai Dasar Sabak, 13 km from town, is where Japanese troops first stormed ashore to conquer Malaya and then ride their bicycles down the coastal road to Singapore.

Wat Photiviharn
While Kota Bharu's population might be predominately Muslim, several Buddhist temples are situated in the region including Wat Photiviharn, which claims to hold the largest reclining Buddha in Southeast Asia. Not so, since the 70-meter image in Rangoon and the 46-meter statue at Wat Po in Bangkok are both larger than the 40-meter specimen at Wat Photiviharn.

Wat Photiviharn is located in Kampung Jambu, 12 km north of Kota Bharu towards Tumpat. Take bus No 19 or 27 to Chabang Empat and then walk 3.5 km along the southwesterly road to Kampung Jambu.

Kelantan River Trip
Bus 5 leaves Kota Bharu at 0745 and arrives in Kuala Krai around 0930. The 1030 boat from Kuala Krai to Kuala Balah takes another two hours. Kuala Balah makes for an intriguing overnight destination at a local resthouse. The following morning you can take a bus to Jeli near the Thai border and then return by bus back to Kota Bharu. You could also just take the early morning boat back to Kuala Krai and a final boat to Kota Bahru.

An alternative from Kuala Krai is to get off at Dabong, a small town a few km before Kuala Balah and directly on the rail line that heads back to Kota Bharu. From Dabong you can either return to Kuala Krai on the 1345 train or spend the night in the Government Rest House and explore the nearby Gua Ikan (Fish Cave) on the main road, some three km east of Dabong. You can also trek to the Jelawang Waterfall across the river toward Jeli.

MALAYSIA

ACCOMMODATIONS

Budget

Kota Bharu has a good selection of inexpensive guesthouses with dorm beds in the RM4-6 range and private rooms with either common or private baths for RM8-20. Most provide free tea, often have bicycles for loan or hire, and sport notebooks spread around the lobbies which provide useful tips for off-the-beaten-track destinations near Kota Bharu and beyond.

Ideal Traveller's House: Kang Sam Chuan's private home is probably the best spot in town since it's tucked away in a quiet neighborhood and well removed from the noise of Kota Bharu. Also, the owners are helpful and it's conveniently located near the night market and bus station. Last time I stayed here the place was overrun with Italian "fruitarians"! 3954 Jalan Kebun Sultan, tel. (09) 744-2246, RM8-25.

Yee Guesthouse: Clean, comfortable, and well-located guesthouse run by Mr. Yee, among the friendliest people in town. Ask for a quiet room in the back. 1872B Jalan Padang Garong, tel. (09) 744-1944, RM8-20.

Town Guesthouse: Town, somewhat outside town and cursed with a fairly grungy exterior, has decent rooms and a very popular rooftop cafe with views over the KB greenbelts. Ask for Anuar Yusoff. 4959B Jalan Pengkalan Chepa, tel. (09) 748-5192, RM8-20.

Mummy's Hitec Hostel: Mummy, once one of the most colorful characters in Malaysia, died a few years ago but her cramped hotel on the outskirts of town continues to offers good vibes . . . if you enjoy all-night parties in the living room. The Thai Consulate and the Rainbow Guest House, a hippie crash pad with little furniture but plenty of bad art, are located across the street. Take buses 4, 8, or 9 from the bus terminal. 4398B Jalan Pengkalan Chepa, tel. (09) 748-7803, RM8-15.

Family Garden Guesthouse: Just across from Mummy's and up a short street is another popular spot fashioned out of a traditional wooden Malay house. All rooms have fans and windows and the owner sells transportation tickets to Perhentian for RM30 roundtrip. 4945-D Lorong Islah Lama, tel. (09) 747-5763, RM5-20.

Rebana House: Enjoy Malay *kampong* life at this graceful little house just 10 minutes from the bus terminal. The owner, world traveler and "Culture Man" Mr. Pok Jak, can help with travel and shopping advice. 1218 Hadapan Istana Kota Lama, no phone, RM8-15.

Johnty's Guesthouse: Very popular place often filled by early afternoon; the overflow wanders off to nearby KB Garden Hostel or Star Hostel. Jalan Dusan Raya, tel. (09) 747-8677, RM6-15.

Moderate

Once almost the exclusive haunt of budget travelers, Kota Bharu has opened up with several new mid-range hotels in recent years, largely catering to couples and other travelers who crave a bit of privacy and modern comforts. All of the following have a/c rooms with private baths and hot showers.

Safar Inn: Good location north of the central market and near Kota Bharu's half-dozen museums. Jalan Temmengong, tel. (09) 747-8000, RM55-85.

Hotel Ansar: Right downtown and somewhat plagued with traffic noise but still a handy location and fairly decent facilities. Jalan Che Su, tel. (09) 747-4000, RM70-90.

Kencana Inn: Older but well maintained hotel in the center of town just opposite the Hong Kong Bank. Jalan Padang Garong, tel. (09) 744-7994, RM70-95.

Hotel Pendana: The best in town with pool, tennis courts, and a/c restaurants. Jalan Sultan Mahmud, tel. (09) 748-5000, RM180-280.

TRANSPORTATION

Air

Malaysia Airlines serves Kota Bharu from Kuala Lumpur, Penang, and Alor Setar. Their office, tel. (09) 744-7000, is opposite the clock tower on Jalan Gajah Mati.

Bus

The central bus terminal for nearby destinations including most east coast towns is located just opposite the night market. Buses to Kuala Trengganu and Kuantan depart every two hours.

Long distance buses to Penang, Kuala Lumpur, and Singapore leave from the two long-distance bus terminals in the south of town. State-run SKMK buses leave from the Langgar bus station on Jalan Pasir Puteh, while private company buses leave from the so-called "External" bus station on Jalan Hamzah, formerly called the Mara bus terminal.

SKMK buses to Johor Bharu, Kuala Lumpur, and Singapore leave daily at 2000. SKMK buses to Butterworth and Penang leave daily at 1000 and 2000. Departure schedules are subject to change and should be double-checked at your guesthouse or tourist office.

Train

The Kota Bharu train station is located across the Kelantan River in the town of Wakaf Bharu. Take bus 19 or 27 from the central bus terminal.

The train passes through spectacular jungle and can be used to comfortably reach Taman Negara National Park, Kuala Lumpur, or Singapore. There are several daily departures but the early morning ordinary train is probably best since it allows you to see some of the interior jungle. Evening departures are best if you're in a hurry to reach Singapore, while the afternoon departure is recommended for Jerantut, the access point for Taman Negara.

Visitors heading to the park generally must spend a night at the local resthouse in Jerantut and proceed the following morning to Tembeling Halt for the noontime boat trip to park headquarters. The train reaches Kuala Lumpur and

Singapore the next day after a change of trains in Gemas. Schedules change frequently and departure times should be checked with the tourist office.

Getting to Thailand

Bus 29B departs on the hour from the central bus terminal for the Malaysian border town of Rantau Panjang. You then follow the crowds and walk along the train tracks to the Thai border town of Sungai Golok where you have your passport stamped. Trishaws to the train station cost RM3-5.

Hat Yai, Surat Thani (for Ko Samui) and Bangkok are served by trains which depart Sungai Golok at 0600, 1000, and 1055; the last departure is an express train.

If you miss the 1055 train to Hat Yai and Bangkok, walk down the hot and dusty main street to the Valentine Hotel from where buses depart for Hat Yai daily until around 1500. You can also try the nearby share taxi stand for transportation to Hat Yai, Yala, or Narathiwat.

Ko Samui in 24 Hours

Take bus 29B at 0800 to Rantau Panjang, change money, walk across the bridge to Sungai Golok, and have your passport stamped. The 1055 express train arrives in Surat Thani at 2100. Take a bus or a taxi down to the harbor and catch the night ferry to Ko Samui which leaves at 2300. The ferry pulls into Samui at the crack of dawn.

EAST MALAYSIA

SARAWAK

Borneo brings to mind the mysterious tropical island that framed the human dramas and adventure stories of Joseph Conrad: a world of impenetrable rainforests filled with vibrant flora and fauna, friendly yet dangerous natives fond of headhunting, a visionary white society that ruled Sarawak during the heady years of the White Rajahs.

Time has passed and the realities of modern Borneo may not be quite as romantic as the legends of the past. In all but the most remote villages you will find teenagers wearing Rambo T-shirts, tribal families gathered around battery-operated TV sets, and small shops selling kung-fu videos, music cassettes, and electronic calculators.

Despite these changes, Borneo remains a rugged land where you can explore upriver villages where several generations of families share a common household, climb through immense caves, and tramp across some of the finest national parks in all of Southeast Asia. The world of Conrad may be drawing to an end in the romantically named "Land of the Hornbills," but the lingering aura of mystery and adventure still makes Borneo a unique and memorable destination.

The Land

The state of Sarawak stretches some 700 km along the northwestern coast of the tropical island of Borneo, third largest in the world. Borneo is actually the old name for the island now parceled into four political subdivisions. Kalimantan is the Indonesian state, which comprises the lower two-thirds of the island. Brunei is an independent oil-rich sultanate wedged between the Malaysian states on the northern coastline. Both Sarawak and Sabah are former British Crown Colonies which merged with Malaya in 1963 to form the Federation of Malaysia.

Climate

Sarawak is a tropical country with two seasons. The northeast monsoon from November to February brings heavy rains which flood coastal towns and reduce most roads to muddy and impassable quagmires. The southwest monsoon during the summer months is less wet. Best time to visit Sarawak is from April to July, when the skies are clear and rivers remain high enough for journeys into the interior. Upriver journeys are difficult from July to November, when many rivers become too shallow for boats. Sarawak's best festivals (harvest celebrations) take place during May and early June.

TRANSPORTATION

Getting There

Air: MAS has daily flights to Kuching from Singapore, Johor Bharu, and from Kuala Lumpur. The 1997 collapse of the Malaysian currency means you can save a great deal (20-40%) on tickets purchased in Malaysia with Malaysian *ringgit* rather than in Singapore with highly inflated Singapore dollars. Don't fly from Singapore—fly from Johor Bharu or Kuala Lumpur.

MAS tickets can also be purchased with Malaysian dollars in Singapore at the MAS office; you then take a special bus to the Johor Bharu airport and fly to Kuching at a big discount.

Other discounts available from MAS include special night flights and 14-day advance-purchase tickets. Discounts are also given to students and groups of three or more who purchase tickets at least one week in advance.

MAS and Merpati also fly twice weekly to Kuching from Pontianak in Indonesian Kalimantan. Pontianak is now a visa-free entry point to Indonesia.

Getting Around

Air: Malaysia Airlines operates a comprehensive network of services linking most urban and interior centers in Sarawak. Prices are reasonable since flights are heavily subsidized by the Malaysian government. Current schedules can

SABAH, SARAWAK, AND BRUNEI

PHILIPPINES

SULU SEA

Turtle Islands

Kudat

Kota Belud

Mount Kinabalu N.P.

Mount Kinabalu (4,101 m)

Poring Hot Springs

Ranau

Sandakan

Gomantong Caves

Sepilok Orangutan Sanctuary

Lahad Datu

Sibutu Island

Sipidan Island

Semporna

Tawau

SULAWESI SEA

SABAH

Tambunan

Keningau

Tenom

Sipitang

Merapok

Lawas

Penampang

Papar

Beaufort

Labuan Island

Kota Kinabalu

Mempakul

Bandar Seri Begawan

Long Semado

Gunung Mulu N.P.

Bareo

Long Lellang

Io Matoh

Long Murum

Rumah Kulit

Timbang B.

BRUNEI

Seria

Kuala Belait

Lumut

Miri

Marudi

Tutoh R.

Baram R.

Long Akah

KALIMANTAN (INDONESIA)

Bunut Lake

Niah Caves N.P.

Batu Niah

Bintulu

Kemena R.

Belaga

Rajang R.

Baleh R.

Kapit

Kanowit

SARAWAK

Similajau N.P.

SOUTH CHINA SEA

Sibu

Sarikei

Saratok

Bandar Sri Aman (Simanggang)

Kuching

Bako N.P.

Serikin

Sematan

Lundu

100 km

© MOON PUBLICATIONS, INC.

MALAYSIA

SARAWAK HIGHLIGHTS

Kuching

The economic and geographic isolation of Sarawak's capital city has helped Kuching retain some of its old charm and character. The city offers evocative architecture, a nearby beach resort and national park, and an outstanding museum where you can learn the fascinating story of the Brooke Dynasty, which ruled the state for over a century. Kuching is one of Malaysia's most romantic towns—an excellent introduction to Sarawak.

Skrang River

Only outside Kuching do the particular flavors of Sarawak begin to assert themselves. The nearest opportunity to see tribal people who still live in sprawling, stilt-raised apartments called longhouses is along the Skrang River, a five-hour bus ride from Kuching. A visit to a jungle-surrounded longhouse to experience communal living, war dances, ceremonial dresses, and peer at a dusty collection of skulls is perhaps the single greatest attraction in Borneo.

Although the Skrang River has become somewhat commercialized in recent years because of its easy accessibility to Kuching, the longhouses are genuine, and traditional tribal lifestyles resume after the tourists have returned to their hotels. Overnight visits can be arranged by travel agents in Kuching.

Rejang River

When compared to the longhouses on the Skrang, those on the Rejang River are less touristy and more authentic but also more time-consuming and expensive to reach. Don't expect to find something from Conrad's *Heart of Darkness;* as Sarawak's commercial lifeline, the wide and muddy Rejang River is surprisingly busy with timber boats stacked with precious cargo and air-conditioned express boats that entertain passengers with the latest videos. Though the Rejang is firmly rooted in the 20th century, it remains the best river trip in east Malaysia.

Niah Caves

Niah National Park near Miri encompasses over 3,000 hectares of forest, vast limestone formations, and the Great Niah Cave, one of the most important archaeological sites in Southeast Asia. The forest department maintains a comfortable and inexpensive hostel here. Journeys are also possible up the Baram River to remote interior towns.

Gunung Mulu National Park

This recently opened park is known for its impressive landscapes and an extensive underground cave system, reputedly one of the largest and longest in the world. The river journey from Marudi to park headquarters takes a full day.

MALAYSIA

---

be checked in the *Borneo Post* or by calling MAS in Kuching, Sibu, Bintulu, or Miri.

Most flights are heavily booked and advance reservations are recommended. If you don't have a reservation, go to the airport and ask to be put on the waiting list. Overbooking is so common that most waiting-list passengers get seats.

Land: Overland transportation, once slow and tedious, has improved dramatically in recent years with the completion of the paved road from Kuching to the Brunei border. Today, scheduled buses cover the entire stretch and travelers no longer need to suffer the travails of the old trans-Sarawak highway. Estimated bus journey times are: Kuching-Sibu (5-6 hours), Sibu-Bintulu (three hours), Bintulu-Niah Caves (two hours), Niah Caves-Miri (two hours), and Miri-Brunei border (two hours).

The Kuching Tourist Office has a schedule of current bus departures.

The only highway section worth skipping is from Kuching to Sibu, a winding road through mediocre scenery with far too many stops in small villages. Most travelers continue to use the high-speed passenger ferries that do the trip in a tolerable 3.5-4 hours.

Boat: Much of Sarawak is a flat, swampy, and monotonous coastline bisected by a network of muddy rivers which wind up to the interior (called the *ulu*). Before the arrival of aircraft, rivers served as the region's sole communication and transportation network. Today, most rivers can be explored with boats ranging from primitive dugouts to high-speed cruisers known as *ekspres*.

In some cases, you will have to choose between regularly scheduled commercial boats and expensive private charters although commercial boat service—both affordable and dependable—can be found on most rivers, especially along the lower reaches. Commercial *ekspres* boats operate around the year Sibu-Kapit (2-3 hours) and Kuala Baram-Maurdi (two hours). During the rainy season when rivers run high, additional *ekspres* services include Kapit-Belaga (six hours), Marudi-Kuala Apoh (two hours), and Kuala Apoh-Long Terawan (two hours). Schedules are listed in the *Borneo Post*.

Chartered boats, on the other hand, are often your only choice during midweek in the deep *ulu*. Charters can be extremely expensive unless you share expenses with a large group of 8-12 people. Worse yet is the amount of time wasted hanging around some dirty little town, waiting for the next boat. Bring a good book.

TRAVEL PRACTICALITIES

Visas and Special Permits
Both Sarawak and Sabah have their own immigration controls but restrictions have been noticeably relaxed in recent years. Visitors arriving on international or domestic flights are given a one-month travel permit upon arrival. These permits can sometimes be extended at immigrations offices in Kuching and Miri.

Special permits are technically required to visit many interior towns and national parks. In reality, few travelers bother to obtain these permits which are rarely, if ever, checked. Permits for national parks are sold directly at the park, so it's no longer necessary to visit park headquarters in the larger towns or Kuching.

Costs
Travel in both Sarawak and Sabah is more expensive than on peninsular Malaysia since most merchandise must be imported from the mainland. Meals, transport, and other necessities generally run 20-30% higher than on the mainland.

The hotel situation can be tricky. Aside from dormitories in Kuching and the national parks, rooms often cost 30-50% than their mainland counterparts. Budget travelers should be prepared to spend a minimum of RM25-35 for a basic double with fan and shared bathroom.

Time
Sufficient time should be allotted for sightseeing and the inevitable transportation delays. A minimum of one month is needed to travel overland from Kuching to Kota Kinabalu with a journey up the Rejang River, visits to several national parks, a few days in Brunei, and the climb to the summit of Mt. Kinabalu. Two weeks is enough if you use air transport.

KUCHING

Kuching, provincial and administrative capital of Sarawak, is one of the more attractive and fascinating towns in Malaysia. Situated on the Sarawak River 32 km from the sea, Kuching has largely escaped rampant modernization and retained a degree of charm due to its historical and economic isolation from mainland Southeast Asia. An aura of past colonial splendor lingers on: Anglo-Oriental mansions slowly chip and fade in the tropical heat, ferns grow from roof gutters, and rows of Chinese shophouses fight a losing battle against time and the elements.

Kuching also shows change: modern subdivisions that uncannily resemble the urban sprawl of Los Angeles, Malay and Chinese yuppies who network at the San Francisco Grill House, and daily traffic jams of Toyotas and Nissans that clog downtown bottlenecks. Despite the contemporary culture, much of the town remains an open-air museum that recalls the colorful history of rule under the White Rajahs.

Attractions
Sarawak Museum: This internationally renowned museum is home to a staggering collection of Bornean archaeological and ethnological artifacts, as well as natural-history specimens gathered by the famous naturalist and co-founder of the theory of evolution, Sir Alfred Russell Wallace. Within its walls are Sarawak tribal weapons, indigenous tools, weavings, woodcarvings, burial paraphernalia, and other cultural oddities that form an excellent introduction to the flora, fauna, and tribal groups of Borneo. This fascinating and somewhat eclectic assemblage was masterminded by Rajah Charles Brooke, with encouragement from Wallace, who visited Sarawak in 1854-56. In 1880, Brooke commissioned his

END OF THE RAINFORESTS

The controversy surrounding commercial logging in the rainforests of Sarawak has intensified from a national to an international issue in recent years. Malaysia is the world's largest exporter of tropical-hardwood logs, most of which are harvested from Sarawak. Malaysia's largest state reaps almost RM2 billion yearly from hardwood exports. Almost 80% of the timber is sold to Japan, a small nation that consumes three times as much timber per head as Western Europe and eight times as much as the United States. Regardless of who ultimately consumes the timber, tropical rainforests remain an essential link in the world's ecosystem: they modulate our climate by precipitating rain; they provide plentiful sources of food and give us 40% of our medicines; they ensure stability of soil masses, and they provide refuge for millions of species of wildlife.

The situation in Sarawak has become increasingly grim since the late '70s when logging companies were awarded large concessions by government officials. The Malaysian environmentalist group, Sahabat Alam Malaysia (SAM), estimates that 76 hectares of Malaysian forest are cut down each hour, and that if commercial logging continues at the same rate, 30% of Sarawak's forest will be destroyed in the next 10 years. The long-term impact, they contend, will be ecological disaster. Reports from the World Bank, the United Nations, and international conservation groups such as the Rainforest Action Network estimate that the complete destruction of Southeast Asia's rainforests will be a fait accompli within 50 years. Even senior officials in the Forest Department concede that unless the political will is found to sharply curtail logging, Malaysia will end up like the Philippines—a country once rich with tropical forests, now forced to import timber.

Blame is usually laid on shifting agriculturalists (tribals who farm with slash-and-burn techniques) and international logging companies. Other factors include a soaring population that needs land and food, the necessity for developing countries to raise hard cash, and the simple fact that the logging industry provides jobs. Yet the environmental consequences remain monumental. Critics charge that the lack of effective controls stems from the thick tangle of political patronage that revolves around the granting of the state's 320 timber licenses. Most of Sarawak's largest logging concessions are held by senior government officials such as prime ministers and retired state governors. The conflict of interest is astounding: Sarawak's minister of the environment and tourism (whose job it is to protect the environment and encourage tourism) is also the owner of Limbang Trading, one of the largest and most successful logging consortiums in Sarawak. He's publicly stated that selective logging practices rather than large-scale reforestation projects will save the rainforests, a rationale that finds little support among environmentalists, who find natural reforestation a failed pipe dream. The bottom line is that so long as the political machinery is controlled by those who profit from logging, there is little hope for the rainforests of Malaysia.

Much of the world's press coverage about the Sarawak situation has centered on the struggle of the Penan tribespeople to save their ancestral homelands from indiscriminate logging. Under a scheme adopted by the state government, over one million acres of Sarawak's rainforests are to be cleared and replaced with rubber and cacao plantations. The nomadic Penans and other Dayaks such as the Kayans will then be resettled in townships and offered employment on these plantations. Understandably enough, the Penans are opposed to the plan. They have instead demanded that logging be completely halted in their homelands near the Baram River and that compensation be paid for land already cleared of forest. To dramatize their situation, human barricades have been formed to blockade the logging trucks, an action which found a great deal of sympathy and support from Malaysian public and international environmentalist groups. The Penans, clad in little more than loincloths and beads, then traveled to Kuala Lumpur to ask for government assistance in their struggle against the logging companies. The Malaysian government responded with the Forest Ordinance, which decreed stiff fines and lengthy jail sentences for anyone caught obstructing logging operations. In November 1987, the Malaysian government arrested 43 Penan leaders and placed Harrison Ngau, tribal activist and director of Malaysia's Friends of the Earth, under house arrest. In January 1989, in the largest demonstration to date, 125 tribespeople were arrested. Trials, fines, and imprisonment face the Penans of Borneo.

MALAYSIA

KUCHING

TO PENDING WHARF,
MARINE BASE WHARF

★ KAPIT HOTEL

JL. PADUNGAN

★ PERUMAL HINDU TEMPLE

SARAWAK PLAZA ■

HOLIDAY INN ■

MAS ■

JL. SONG THIAN CHEOK

BORNEO EXCURSION
TRAVEL ■

DRAGON
AIR ●
● SINGAPORE
AIRLINES

JL. PADUNGAN

JL. TUNKU ABDUL RAHMAN

FORT
MARGHARITA ★

SHELL
STATION ●

● KUCHING
HILTON

METROPOLE HOTEL ●

JL. MATHIES

SELAMAT
HOTEL ●

JL. BAN HOCK

● TUA PEK
KONG TEMPLE

● KUCHING
HOTEL

● METROPOLE INN

JL. TABUAN

SARAWAK RIVER

SIN HWA
TRAVEL ●

BORNEO HOTEL
B&B INN ■

TO AIRPORT,
IMMIGRATION,
AND STATE OFFICES

★ HONG SAN
TEMPLE

JL. TEMPLE

● BORNEO
ADVENTURE

SARAWAK
HOUSE ●

★ FATA HOTEL

JL. MAIN BAZZAR

JL. CARPENTER

ANGLICAN HOSTEL

★ ISTANA

ANGLICAN
CHURCH

JL. McDOUGHALL

JL. RESERVOIR TEMPLE

SARAWAK TOURIST
ASSOCIATION OFFICE ■

● COURTHOUSE

GPO ■

MALAYSIA

BUSES ■
★ HINDU MOSQUE

PADANG MERDEKA

● AURORA HOTEL

■ KIA HIN HOTEL

JL. BARRACK

JL. INDIA

OLD MUSEUM ★

■ TAXIS

ELECTRA
HOUSE ■

JL. MESSJID

NEW MUSEUM ★

JL. TUN ABANG OPENG

0   100 m

★ SIKH
TEMPLE

SARAWAK TOURIST
INFORMATION CENTRE ■

CHIAN LIAN
LONG BUSES ■
PETRA JAYA
BUSES ■

MARKET ●

TO CIVIC
CENTER

STC BUSES ■

TO SUNDAY MARKET,
INDONESIAN CONSULATE,
AND NATIONAL PARKS OFFICE

★ STATE MOSQUE

JL. JAWA

© MOON PUBLICATIONS, INC.

French valet to design the building, which, when completed in 1891, perhaps not surprisingly resembled a French chateau in Normandy style. Open daily except Fridays 0900-1800. Free.

Downtown: The historic center along the waterfront near the Pangkalan Batu Boat Ferry has several fine survivors of former days. Constructed in 1874, the old Courthouse with its oversized verandah and landmark clock tower was designed to impress the people with its sense of permanence. The English Renaissance fortress known as the Square Tower originally served as a prison before being converted into a local dance hall. Constructed in an imposing Neoclassical style with Corinthian columns and ornamented friezes, Kuching's General Post Office is one of the few buildings erected by Vyner Brooke, the third and final rajah, who ceded Sarawak to Britain in 1946 despite protests by his subjects. Almost directly opposite is a graceful and distinctive three-story building nicknamed the Pavilion.

Kuching's best shopping venue is the Sunday market on Jalan Satok, packed with housewives, Chinese farmers, and tribal peoples. The market is in full swing on both Saturday nights and Sunday mornings 0600-1300.

Istana: Sarawak is divided by the Sarawak River into the south city, with the museum, hotels, and commercial and residential areas, and the north city with the new Petra Jaya Ministerial Complex and two historical landmarks constructed by Charles Brooke. The Istana features a style similar to British houses in Java during Stamford Raffles's governorship with crenellated towers which date from the 1880s. The decaying Istana (also spelled Astana), or Palace, was the official residence for Charles, who succeeded his Uncle James and served as the second Rajah of Borneo from 1868 to 1917. Currently closed to the public, the complex serves as official residence of Sarawak's governor and can be seen clearly from the opposite riverbank.

Fort Margharita: Named after Ranee Margaret, wife of the second White Rajah, this fort was constructed in 1879 to guard against attack by maurauding bands of pirates. In later years it served as headquarters for the paramilitry Sarawak Rangers before being converted into a Military Museum. Ironically, the only occasion when the fort came under attack was on 19 De-

cember 1941, when the Japanese bombed Kuching. While the building is an outstanding example of British colonial architecture, the most famous sight is the six laughing skulls kept hanging in the watchtower. Believed to have been collected in battle by an Undup warrior in the late 18th century, legend has it that laughter was heard coming from the skulls while in transit to the museum. Enter the room with caution. The old fort is reached by *tambang* ferry from Pangkalan Batu near the Sarawak Tourist Association Building.

Budget Accommodations

B & B Inn: Best budget spot in town and a useful source of updated travel information on Borneo. 30 Jalan Tabuan, tel. (082) 237366, RM14 dorm, RM22-35 private room.

Anglican Hostel: When the B & B Inn is filled, you might try this clean and comfortable hostel which is technically reserved for church visitors but welcomes travelers on a space-available basis. Located on the hill behind St. Thomas's Anglican Church. tel. (082) 414027, RM18-35.

Kuching Hotel: Chinese hotel near city center with adequate rooms with fan and common bath. 6 Jalan Temple, tel. (082) 413985, RM18-25.

Moderate and Luxury Accommodations

Metropole Inn Hotel: Large hotel with clean rooms and friendly management. 22 Jalan Green Hill, tel. (082) 412561, RM40-60.

Fata Hotel: Another mid-range hotel with decent sized rooms; all with private baths and hot showers. Jalan McDougall, tel. (082) 248111, RM60-80.

Holiday Inn: Kuching's first international hotel is located on the banks of the Sarawak River, within easy walking distance of sights and shopping. 320 rooms, swimming pool, fitness center. Jalan Tunku Abdul Rahman, tel. (082) 423111, RM240-380 double.

Kuching Hilton: Kuching's newest hotel offers 322 rooms fronting the river, five food and beverage outlets, and sports facilities. Jalan Tunku Abdul Rahman, tel. (082) 248200, RM340-560.

Holiday Inn Damai Beach: Sarawak's number-one beach resort is located on Santubong Beach, 32 km north of Kuching. Windsurfing, trekking, 18-hole Trent Jones golf course, and

MALAYSIA

over 200 chalets and studios surrounded by beach and mountains. Damai Beach, tel. (082) 846999, RM280-420.

Services

Tourist Information: The Sarawak Tourist Association (STA), tel. (082) 240620, on Main Bazaar Road is your best source of information for travel in Sarawak. They also have a small kiosk at the airport. Another useful source is the Sarawak Tourist Information Centre, tel. (082) 410942, at Padang Merdeka.

National Parks: Information and advance room reservations for Bako, Niah, and Gunung Mulu national parks can be made at the National Parks & Wildlife Office, tel. (082) 248088, at Padang Merdeka.

Visa Extensions: Malaysian visas and permits can be extended at the Malaysian immigration office in the State Government Complex on Jalan Simpang Tiga, three km south of town en route to the airport. Open Monday-Friday 0900-1630 and Saturdays 0900-1200. Take blue CCL buses 6 or 17 from the bus stop near the State Mosque.

Indonesian Visa: The Indonesian Consulate, tel. (038) 241734, at 5A Jalan Pisang can be reached with bus No 5A or 6. Most Indonesian towns are now visa-free entry points, including Pontianak.

Getting Around: Most local buses are operated by the privately owned Chian Lian Long (CLL) Motor Vehicle Company. Useful routes include Jalan Mosque to the State Government Complex on bus No 6 or 17, Jalan Satok to the Police Marine Base Wharf via bus No 17 or 19; Jalan Tunku Abdul Rahman to Bintawa Wharf with bus No 16.

Maps: Periplus maps of Sabah and Sarawak can be purchased at the Mohamed Yahia bookshop in the basement of Sarawak Plaza. Their outlet inside the Holiday Inn also sells Periplus maps and other books on Borneo.

Leaving Kuching

Air: The MAS office, tel. (082) 244144, on Jalan Song Thian Cheok, has a variety of flights and tickets including ordinary, discounted early-morning flights, and even cheaper advance-purchase tickets. MAS flies to over 20 small towns in Sarawak and Sabah. Singapore Airlines, tel.

(082) 240266, is in the Ang Chang building on Jalan Tunku Abdul Rahman. MAS and Merpati have flights several times weekly to Pontianak, Kalimantan and onward to Jakarta.

Bus: Long-distance buses to southwest Sarawak operated by the Sarawak Transport Company (STC) leave from their long-distance bus terminal on Jalan Jawa near the river. Petra Jaya buses to Bako National Park and Damai leave from Lebuh Khoo Hun Yeang. Most buses for Sarikei, Bintulu, and Miri leave from the Regional Express Bus Terminal on Jalan Penrissen, five km east of town.

The road from Kuching to Sibu is fully paved but there's little reason to travel overland unless you are going up the Skrang River; most travelers take a high-speed boat from Kuching to Sibu.

Boat: Speedy launches from Kuching to Sibu leave from the jetty in Pending, six km east of city center. Operated by Ekspres Pertama, Concorde Marine, and Ekspres Bahagia, the Kuching-Sibu boat ride takes about four hours and costs RM28-35 depending on the class. Tickets should be purchased one day in advance from a travel agency or boat representative office in Kuching. Tickets are also sold on the boat; take bus No 17 or 19 from the market on Main Bazaar Road.

KUCHING VICINITY

Bako National Park

Sarawak's two most famous attractions are river journeys with longhouse visits and a few days spent exploring one of the region's national parks. Bako's 2,742 hectares are set on a sandstone plateau covered with open scrub and mangrove swamps thick with exotic vegetation such as epiphytic ferns, heath forests, and several species of carnivorous plants including bladderworts and giant pitcher plants. Wildlife includes silver leaf monkeys, water monitor lizards, and the bizarre long-nosed proboscis monkey, native only to Borneo.

Bako isn't as rugged as Gunung Mulu nor as famous as Niah Caves, but it's easy to reach from Kuching and offers over 30 km of organized trails from short walks to exhausting all-day treks. Maps and other details can be obtained at park headquarters.

Accommodations: Resthouses, equipped with cooking facilities and beds, cost RM40 per room. Reservations and permits should be obtained in advance at the Sarawak Tourist Information Center in Kuching.

Transportation: Bako, 37 km from Kuching, can be reached with bus No 6 to Kampung Bako, from where private boats can be chartered onward to the park. A 10-person boat costs RM25-30.

Semonggok Wildlife Rehabilitation Sanctuary

This animal refuge 22 km from Kuching is where orangutans, hornbills, and monkeys rescued from captivity are trained for reentry into the jungle. Permits must be obtained in advance from the Sarawak Tourist Information Centre in Kuching.

Semonggok can be reached in 45 minutes with bus No 6 to the Forest Department Nursery followed by a 30-minute hike through the rainforest.

Santubong and Dumai

Kuching's leading beach resort is 32 km north of Kuching at the mouth of the Sarawak River. The sand is rather ordinary (better beaches are west at Sematan) but the fishing village is picturesque and the setting spectacular.

Santubong was an important trading center from the 7th to 13th centuries, as shown by the Chinese and Hindu rock carvings and artifacts unearthed by archaeologists. Of the notable rock carvings located along the small river, Sungai Jaong, the most intriguing is the human figure carved spread-eagle with Kenyah headdress. This rock is situated up the road toward Kuching about two km beyond the *kampong*. Turn right after the second coconut farm and follow the stream about 200 meters, or ask locals for *batu gambir*.

The Sarawak Cultural Village has been set up to help preserve the states' rich cultural heritage. Half-day organized programs start daily at 0900 and 1400; one-hour cultural performances daily at 1130 and 1630.

Holiday Inn Damai Beach Resort: Upscale resort for the well-heeled traveler. Damai Beach, tel. (082) 846999, RM240-360.

Transportation: Take bus No 2B from Kuching or the private shuttle from the Holiday Inn Kuching.

SKRANG RIVER

Sarawak's classic adventure is visiting several Iban (Sea Dayak) or Bidayuh longhouses scattered upriver in the *ulu*. The area immediately near Kuching has several badly commercialized longhouses that can be quickly visited by frantic group tours.

Although the most pristine longhouses are those in the upper reaches of the Rejang River, visitors with limited time can still experience authentic longhouses on the nearby Skrang. Excellent two- and three-day tours organized by travel agencies in Kuching begin with a four-hour drive through rubber and pepper plantations before the one-hour upstream journey in native longboats. The Skrang is much smaller than the Rejang and in many ways seems more mysterious with its hanging vines and harrowing rapids.

You will quickly discover that the Ibans are a warm and slightly outrageous group of people who perform their dances with what appears to be genuine enthusiasm. Iban hospitality revolves around singing, dancing, and the consumption of prodigious quantities of *tuak*. It's rude to refuse!

After a night in the longhouse, tours either return to Kuching the following morning or continue upriver to visit another longhouse. While package tours of the Skrang are somewhat expensive and contrived, they avoid the hassles of independent travel.

SRI AMAN

Formerly called Simmanggang, this backwoods town is where Charles Brooke spent some time before becoming the rajah of Sarawak. During his short tenure he constructed Fort Alice in 1864 to control the fierce Skrang Ibans.

As in most towns in Borneo, there is little of interest here except for arranging a journey up the Skrang River; self-guided river trips are possible but difficult. Public boats, most numerous on weekends and holidays, are the cheapest forms of transport. Otherwise, it will be necessary to charter a private boat or accept an invitation from a local Iban. The cost can be estimated by asking how many tanks of gas (each tank holds about 20 liters or five gallons) are required to reach the longhouse, then multiplying by the cost of the gas. It is customary to pay an additional RM25 one-way for the boatman and another RM15 for the bowman, who watches for dangerous rocks.

Accommodations: Travelers stranded in Sri Aman can stay at either the Alishan or Taiwan hotels on Jalan Council or the Sum Sum or Hoover hotels on Club Road. Rates range RM25-40 depending on hotel facilities and room size.

Transportation: STC buses go hourly from Kuching to Sri Aman.

SIBU

Situated 130 km from the sea on the right bank of the Rejang River, Sibu (formerly called Maling) is the second-largest town in Sarawak and gateway for journeys up the Rejang River.

Most travelers spend the night in town and leave the following morning, but with a few extra hours you might visit the central market, where Hokkien shopkeepers bargain with Iban tribesmen over cassettes and polyester shirts, and then wander through the Chinese temple by the docks.

Accommodations

Hotels in Sibu are mostly run-down and overpriced, but staying in one is a necessary evil before heading upriver the following day.

Hoover House: Sibu's cheapest and cleanest spot is a revamped colonial house adjacent to the Methodist Primary School. 22 Jalan Pulau, tel. (084) 332973, RM10-12.

Today Hotel: Travelers turned away from the oft-filled Hoover House often stay at this decent hotel with a/c rooms five blocks back from the waterfront. 40 Jalan Kampung Nyabor, tel. (084) 336499, RM25-35.

River View Hotel: A mid-priced hotel with a/c rooms, private baths, and TV. Good value and conveniently located just opposite the bus terminal. 65 Mission Rd., tel. (084) 334419, RM30-50.

Premier Hotel: Best in town. Jalan Kampung Nyabor, tel. (084) 323222, RM120-180.

Leaving Sibu

To Kuching: Express boats leave daily 0700-1000 from the Sarikei Wharf, cost RM30-35 depending on class, and take four hours with a change of boats in Sarikei.

MAS, located on Kampung Nyabor Road opposite the Premier Hotel, flies several times daily to Kuching.

To Bintulu and Miri: Buses leave several times daily and take about four hours to Bintulu, although most travelers take an early morning a/c bus straight through to Miri (7-8 hours). MAS flights to Bintulu, Miri, and other interior towns should be booked in advance before exploring the Rejang River.

Up The Rejang River: Speedy, ultramodern boats equipped with action videos and blasting stereos depart hourly 0600-1200 from the wharf on Jalan Peng Loong and take 2-3 hours to reach Kapit. Stops en route include Kanowit, the town where Charles Brooke built a fort to suppress headhunting, and Song, where dozens of Japanese lost their heads while promising the New Asia Co-Prosperity Sphere. The skeptical Ibans were delighted when British commanders gave permission to resume their headhunting. The boat continues to Belaga during the rainy season when rivers run high.

REJANG RIVER

Travelers hungry for a bit of the Byronesque will discover a journey up the Rejang River—the same river that inspired Conrad to write *Lord Jim*—to be one of the most rewarding travel experiences in Sarawak. The main attractions are jungle trekking, local tribespeople, and a few days of residence in an Iban longhouse.

Enjoying the scenery and watching people barter in the Kapit Market is fun and simple, but visiting a longhouse is no easy task. In recent years, great numbers of visitors have arrived, walked up to a longhouse, and expected to be welcomed with open arms. While the Iban remain a warm group of people with a near-legendary reputation for hospitality, their patience has been pushed to the limit and some have become unenthusiastic about strangers knocking on their front doors. This is not to say that longhouse visits are impossible, but without a formal invitation it takes a great deal of guts to front up, smile, and walk in. Brave souls should first seek permission to enter, park their shoes at the door, and then ask to see the *tuai rumah* (headman) in Iban longhouses or *tua rumah* or *tua kampong* elsewhere.

Travelers' experiences vary dramatically. Sometimes you are completely ignored, meals are served to you in a lonely room, and items mysteriously disappear from your backpack. At other times you are welcomed as a long-lost relative who is feted with food and *tuak* before being wished a fond farewell by the entire village. Travelers determined to experience longhouse living should bring along small gifts such as beer, cigarettes, food, medicines like *tiga kaki*, shirts, batiks, large sealed containers, and Indonesian sarongs as gifts or for bartering. Presents should be given to the headman, who will distribute the goods evenly. Earplugs are also a good idea to muffle the grunting pigs, howling dogs, and crowing roosters that live underneath the floor.

Longhouses near Kapit are somewhat commercialized but more authentic examples can be visited up the river toward Belaga. Ask townspeople, boat drivers, and other travelers for recommendations, but double-check prices for transport, beer, and other luxuries before accepting anybody's "generous" offer.

KAPIT

Tiny Kapit is the final trading post of the mighty Rejang River, 250 muddy and winding kilometers up from the sea. No roads link Kapit with the outside world—the only feasible way to reach this back-of-beyond town is by airplane or riverboat. Kapit sits on a two-square-km clearing which forms a perfect place to relax and watch Ibans land their dugouts and sell their fruit, peppercorns, and cocoa to Chinese brokers, the commercial kingpins of the *ulu*.

Permits to travel beyond Kapit should be obtained from the Pejabat Am office on the first floor of the State Government Complex. Kapit has several banks which change money at fair rates. MAS is one block back from the jetty.

Attractions

Sights include Fort Sylvia, built by the Brookes in 1880, and a pair of waterfalls. Sungai Seraman is a one-hour hike across the Rejang River. Bukit

Garam is 30 minutes by taxi and then a 45-minute hike. Try hitching on the weekends.

Kapit is also a convenient base for exploring nearby jungle and villages. Most travelers visit the longhouses on the Rejang River en route to Belaga, but closer longhouses are situated up the Baleh River. Try Rumah Temonggong Jugah and Long Agat, home of the late Temmonggong Koh. Both impressive longhouses have small museums in the headman's *bilek* (room), although they are now somewhat spoiled from tourists and commercial film crews. The perfect book to bring along is *Into the Heart of Borneo* by Redmond O'Hanlon, a humorous account of his 1983 journey up the Baleh to climb Mount Tiban and "re-discover the Borneo rhinoceros."

Accommodations

Like most other upriver towns, Kapit has several cheap hotels that double as brothels and a few mid-priced places for traveling businesspeople and a steady trickle of tourists.

Kapit Rejang Hotel: One of the few decent cheap hotels is about 300 meters down from the jetty near a traffic roundabout. The Rejang has a variety of rooms in all sizes, with varied decor, and available with or without fan, a/c, or private baths. 28 Jalan Temenggong Jugah, tel. (084) 796709, RM18-35.

New Rejang Inn: The owners of the Rejang also operate this annex about 50 meters from the jetty. Rooms are clean, all with a/c, and include private baths, hot showers, and TV. 104 Jalan Teo Chow Beng, tel. (084) 796600, RM45-60.

Ark Hill Hotel: The lumber and dam business beyond Bintulu has brought several hotels to Kapit, including this place three blocks to the right of the jetty. All rooms are a/c with private bath. 1 Jalan Tiga, tel. (084) 796168, RM40-50.

Hotel Meligai: Kapit's top-end choice, north of the jetty in the direction of the airport, features a lobby photo of the famous Iban chief, Temmonggang Koh. 34 Jalan Airport, tel. (084) 796611, RM50-80.

Transportation

MAS flies several times weekly from Kapit to Sibu and Belaga. If you plan to travel upriver from Kapit to Sibu or Belaga, be sure to make reservations before you begin the river trip or

MALAYSIA

run the risk of being stranded for days on end in these wonderfully boring towns.

Boats downriver to Sibu leave hourly 0600-1200. Boats upriver to Belaga take 6-8 hours and leave daily except during the dry season, when shallow waters and dangerous rapids prevent commercial boat service.

BELAGA

Kapit is now somewhat civilized. Belaga, on the other hand, is a real *ulu* town where most of the Kenyahs and Kayans go barefoot and sport tattoos. Sights include the elaborate carvings at Mr. Ong's shop and the hilltop tomb of the late Temenggong Matu Puso.

Accommodations
Belaga's small selection of hotels are to the right of the *Borneo Post* sign.

Belaga Hotel: The travelers' favorite offers both fan-cooled and a/c rooms with private bath. Jalan Belaga, tel. (084) 461244, RM15-40.

Bee Lian Hotel: Older hotel with adequate rooms. Jalan Belaga, tel. (084) 461416, RM15-35.

Going Upriver
Permission for upriver travel should be obtained from the District Officer and police who may restrict the length of your journey to Bakun Rapids, one hour upriver. This technicality doesn't necessarily stop onward travel, but it waives all government responsibility.

Express boats during the rainy season to upriver towns and longhouses are most plentiful on weekends: Wong Jawa in two hours, Ukit in a full day. Scalpers may be your only choice during the week. Prices are determined by the number of gallons or tanks needed to reach your destination. It takes two tanks to Long Murum or eight tanks to Ukit. Other passengers (including friends and relatives of the boatmen) should be expected to share the cost.

Trekking from Belaga
An intriguing possibility when leaving Belaga is to hike over the watershed to Bintulu during the dry season—a 2-3 day hike depending on your route. It also saves backtracking to Sibu and covers

some new territory. Trekking agencies which offer guide services are now established in Bintulu, although guides are generally unnecessary.

The quick route involves a short boat ride, some hiking, and a jeep down to Bintulu. A slower but more varied route is upriver to the Tiban Rapids where you alight and hike several hours along a good path to circumvent the rapids. A second boat goes to the next longhouse, where you spend the night. Tubau, the town on the Kemana River midway between Belaga and Bintulu, can be reached by hiking over the hills or hitching a ride with logging trucks. You can stay in Tubau with local school teachers. Boats from Tubau to Bintulu take three hours.

BINTULU

The discovery of large natural-gas reserves near Bintulu in the late 1970s transformed the once-sleepy coastal village into a modern boomtown filled with pipe fitters and migrant laborers. Today, the economic expansion continues with the arrival of another immense liquefied-natural-gas plant at Kidurong (second largest in the world) and the enlargement of the deep-water port in the same region.

Attractions
Bintulu is a modern town with little of interest except for the remnants of a fishing village on the banks of the Kemana River, an attractive mosque opened in 1988, and the blue-roofed produce market down at the riverfront. The remainder of the attractions are outside of town, such as the Kemana River and Similajau National Park, 20 km north.

The Bintulu Welcome Centre and Similajau Adventure Tours are in the BDA building on Jalan Sommerville.

Accommodations
Oil wealth has transformed Bintulu into one of Malaysia's more expensive towns. Bintulu's cheapest spots are bare-bones cubicles, perhaps acceptable for a single night. Most are located on the waterfront road near the jetty and bus terminal.

Capitol Hotel: Somewhat less depressing than most options is this aging hotel a few blocks west of the bus terminal. Keppel Rd., tel. (086) 334667, RM15-45.

Duong Hotel: Simple but clean hotel with both fan-cooled and a/c rooms one block northeast of the Plaza Hotel. 20 New Commercial Centre, tel. (086) 336698, RM10-30.

Dragon Inn: Another inexpensive hotel right behind the Plaza Hotel. Jalan Abang Galau, tel. (086) 334223, RM20-35.

Kamena Hotel: Refurbished hotel with spiffy a/c rooms. 78 Keppel Road, tel. (086) 331533, RM55-70.

Plaza Hotel: Top-end choice is the luxurious L-shaped hotel just opposite the waterfront bus terminal. 116 Jalan Abang Galau, tel. (086) 335111, fax 332742, RM160-280.

Transportation

Bintulu is 360 km from Kuching.

MAS flies several times daily from Kuching, Sibu, Miri, and Kota Kinabalu. The airport is incongruously located on the outskirts of town, a 10-15 minute walk from most hotels.

Bintulu's main bus terminal is in the center of town about five blocks back from the jetty. The main bus companies are Syarikat Bas Suria and Rejang Transport. Buses to Batu Niah (Niah Caves) and Miri leave hourly 0700-1800 and take two hours to Niah Caves and four hours to Miri. Buses to Sibu leave five times daily 0600-1500.

NIAH CAVES

Niah Caves ranks among the most popular and memorable stops in all of Borneo. The limestone caves were discovered in the 1870s by British naturalist and explorer A. Hart Everett, but the real significance of the caves remained unknown until 1954, when anthropologists from Kuching's Sarawak Museum excavated evidence of man's existence in Borneo dating back some 40,000 years. The discovery of the skull of a young *Homo sapiens* startled the world's scientific community by challenging the theory that mankind's ancestors originated in the Near East and progressively migrated to the Far East. Later excavations of Chinese porcelains and stone tools from the Paleolithic and Neolithic periods led anthropologists to conclude that the caves were inhabited from 40,000 B.C. up to A.D. 1400. The most spectacular discovery was the Painted Cave, an ancient burial chamber filled with red haematite rock paintings, spirit offerings, and elaborately carved Ships of the Dead complete with skeletal remains.

The caves are also a geological wonder. The Great Cave alone covers an area of over 11 hectares—large enough to fit 26 football fields—which makes it one of the largest single chambers in the world. Beyond the Great Cave is an intricate network of grottoes which extend right through the 394-meter limestone massif known as Gunung Subis.

Just as fascinating is the collection of edible bird's nests which form the expensive ingredient in the Chinese delicacy, bird's-nest soup. Twice yearly in the spring and fall, licensed collectors scale rickety 60-meter bamboo poles to scrape the ceilings of the precious clumps of twigs and congealed bird saliva. And how precious! Top-quality first-regurgitation nests can command over RM1,000 per kilo. Another unusual activity is the collection of bat and bird guano by native Ibans who sell the droppings as fertilizer to nearby pepper plantations.

The caves are approached by a four-km trek through dense jungle across an elevated plankway. Visitors are encouraged to wander off the path and explore the virgin lowland rainforest filled with long-tailed macaques, hornbills, and Rajah Brooke butterflies. Another outstanding natural phenomenon is the mad flight of millions of swiftlets and bats through the cave entrance at sunset.

Accommodations

The national park operates a visitor's hostel at Pangkalan Lubang, directly opposite the river and plankway to the cave entrance. You can also pick up your permits for the cave at park headquarters.

Dorm beds cost RM10, while four-man chalets cost RM60 per night. Air-conditioned VIP chalets cost RM200. Bedding, cooking utensils, toilets, showers, and refrigerators are provided. The visitor's hostel also has a cafe or you can purchase provisions at a shop just outside the park.

Advance bookings at the national park office in Kuching or Miri are unnecessary during the week but advisable on weekends, when locals pack the hostel. If you can't get a place in the dorm or a private chalet, the town of Batu Niah, three km from the visitor's hostel, has several hotels with rooms from RM25-80.

Getting There
From Bintulu: Direct buses from Bintulu to Batu Niah leave eight times daily 0600-1600 and take two hours. Do not take the direct Bintulu-Miri bus as it bypasses Batu Niah and you must either walk or hitch the remaining eight km to Batu Niah.

From Batu Niah, you can walk to the park in 45 minutes, hire a taxi for RM10, or take a quick boat ride through the thick rainforest—certainly the most pleasant way to reach park headquarters.

From Miri: Direct buses from Miri to Batu Niah leave six times daily 0600-1600 and take two hours. Once again, do not take the direct Miri-Bintulu bus which bypasses Batu Niah.

MIRI

The administrative capital of the Fourth District is an oil boomtown with a wide range of hotels, karaoke clubs, bars, and pricey restaurants.

Most travelers simply pause long enough to make transportation connections to Brunei, Niah Caves, or Gunung Mulu National Park and obtain the necessary permits at the National Parks Office (tel. 085-436637) on Jalan Raja, the road behind the mosque toward Brunei. The Land & Survey Office sells detailed maps of Sarawak.

Pick up information on Gunung Mulu National Park at several tour agencies, such as Borneo Adventure, tel. (085) 414935, in the Pacific Orient Hotel on Jalan Brooke or Tropical Adventure, tel. (085) 419337, at 228 Jalan Maju.

Accommodations
Most local hotels are expensive and often filled on a semipermanent basis with oil and timber workers.

Tai Tong Lodging House: Cheapest of the lot is this rudimentary Chinese hotel, near the riverfront and opposite the Chinese temple. 26 Jalan China, tel. (085) 411072, RM8 dorm, RM28-55 private room.

Fairland Inn: A well-priced hotel just behind the town square with clean a/c rooms and attached baths. Jalan Raya, tel. (085) 413981, RM30-45.

Hotel Plaza Regency: Miri also has a handful of midrange hotels such as this newish spot just outside town on the road toward Brunei. 47 Jalan Brooke, tel. (085) 413113, RM65-125.

Transportation
MAS flies daily to Kuching, Bintulu, Kota Kinabalu, and almost a dozen smaller towns such as Marudi, Bareo, Long Lellang, Long Seridan, Limbang, Labuan, Lawas, and Sibu.

Buses leave from the terminal behind the Park Hotel and Wisma Pelita Tunku shopping complex to Bintulu, Batu Niah (the town near Niah Caves), and Sibu. Tickets can be purchased in advance from the Syarikat Bas Suira across from the bus terminal.

Getting to Brunei
Miri Belait Transport Company has six buses daily to Kuala Belait, the first town in Brunei. After crossing a few rivers and racing along the beach past monkeys and oil platforms, you pass through customs and immigration before arriving in Kuala Belait about three hours later. Delays at river crossings can be avoided by taking your gear off the bus and walking to the front of the line. Drivers often give rides to Western travelers, or you can cross the river by boat and then hitchhike.

From Kuala Belait you should immediately take a bus to Seria and then onward to Bandar Seri Begawan. Traveler's checks can be changed at the bank in Kuala Belait. The entire stretch can be covered in a single day.

A quicker option is to take a private minibus to Bandar Seri Begawan for RM30; try Miri-Sibu Express at the bus terminal.

BARAM RIVER AND THE INTERIOR

Miri is the starting point for trips up the Baram River and the remote longhouses of the Kayan and Kenyah. The entire region is a cultural feast and less exploited than the Skrang or Rejang Rivers.

Marudi
This Christianized trading post is a pleasant change from the red-light districts of the oil boomtowns.

Buses leave Miri hourly for Kuala Baram, the town toward Brunei at the mouth of the Baram River. Launches equipped with video machines and blasting stereos leave Kuala Baram hourly 0800-1400 and take about three hours to reach Marudi.

The Grand Hotel, tel. (085) 755711, on Marudi Bazaar has a few ordinary rooms from RM16 and a/c rooms from RM35-55; the manager is a good source of travel information.

Permits for interior travel can be picked up from the district officer located in Fort Hose, constructed in 1901 and named after the last of the Rajah's Residents.

Upriver Towns

Multi-day river journeys are possible to the villages and longhouses scattered along the Baram and Tinjar Rivers. Hustlers in Marudi will ask "*Mau pergi ulu?*" ("Going upcountry?"), but expensive private charters should be a last resort.

Sarawak's seventh national park is located at Logan Bunut, a picturesque lake on the Tinjar River a few km beyond the town of Long Teru. Regular launches up the Baram River to the town of Long Lama leave several times each morning and take four hours.

Accommodations: Long Lama's hotels include the obvious Long Lama Hotel, where dirty rooms cost RM18-25. Much cleaner and friendlier is the Telang Usan Hotel. Turn left, walk down to the bazaar, and follow the paved lane on the right.

Transportation: Local guide Yup Po Kiuk at the Yak Radio Shop leads expensive tours and can advise on nearby longhouses. An express boat from Long Lama to the 50-door Kayan longhouse at Long Miri takes about two hours. Also served by ordinary river taxis are Long Akah and Long San, where the Christian Church has been completely carved with Kenyah art. Lio Matah is another day's journey upriver.

Interior Towns

MAS flies Twin Otters from Miri and Marudi to Bario and other interior towns. Flights are actually more economical than paying for chartered boats and getting ripped off by greedy boatmen.

The most popular upcountry destination is Bario, a small town set in the Kelabit Highlands near the Indonesian border. MAS flights are usually met by Ngimet Ayu, who operates a lodging house. The entire region is covered with hiking trails through valleys and across mountains dotted with longhouses. Guest books are filled with recent travelers' accounts and suggestions for treks.

One of the best hikes is west to Pa Umur to see their ancient stone called *batu narit,* to Pa Lungan, and to the large Murut settlement at Ba Kelalan. Visitors are welcome to stay in most longhouses but presents of food, canned sardines, frozen meat from Marudi, sweets, sugar, medicines such as panadol, and batik sarongs are expected.

GUNUNG MULU NATIONAL PARK

Among the largest and most magnificent parks in Borneo, Gunung Mulu is famed for its extensive underground system of caves, rich flora and fauna, and magnificent topography of towering mountains and jutting limestone pinnacles. A great deal of excitement was generated among speleologists in 1980 when an expedition uncovered the world's largest cave, the Sarawak Chamber, which according to the *Guinness Book of World Records* is spacious enough to hold Carlsbad Caverns and Lav Verna Caves in France with room to spare.

Other spectacular chambers include the Deer Cave, which boasts the world's largest cave entrance, and Clearwater Cave, which ranks as the longest cave in Southeast Asia at over 62 kilometers. All are filled with impressive stalactites and stalagmites (hanging down and rising upwards, respectively) and home to wildlife such as *Tadarida plicata* bats, snakes, white crabs, and swiftlets which find their ways in the dark by making clicking noises and listening for the echoes. Deer, Lang's, Clearwater, and Wind Caves are open to visitors but others may be closed for safety reasons.

Other activities in the park include a three- to five-day hike to the summit of Gunung Mulu and visits to Penan settlements.

Accommodations

The National Park Service operates two hostels which have 20 dorm beds at RM10 per person. Two-person chalets cost RM120 and VIP resthouses go for RM160. Cooking facilities, drinking water, and blankets are provided. A small canteen provides meals and sells basic supplies but extra food should be packed in.

Several hotels and almost a dozen small guesthouses owned by tour companies are located outside the park entrance. Top-end choice is the Royal Mulu Resort, tel. (085) 421122, with swimming pool, satellite TV, and a/c rooms from RM180-500. The guesthouses owned and operated by Borneo Adventure, Tropical Adventure, and Seridan Mulu will accept independent travelers when not filled with their organized tours.

Permits and Fees

Permits and room reservations must be arranged in advance from a travel agency or the National Parks and Wildlife Office in Miri. You will probably be refused admittance if you show up without a reservation.

Although it is possible to visit Gunung Mulu as an independent traveler, the onslaught of admission and guide fees makes an organized tour a sensible proposition. Borneo Adventure, Tropical Adventure, and other agencies in Miri organize 3-7 day visits at reasonable rates.

Independent travelers will face the following charges. Guides are required to explore each cave and charge RM25-40 per group. Guides are also required for trekking trips, such as the Pinnacles trek which costs RM350. Boats must be hired to reach most caves and charters are not cheap: RM85-250 depending on the cave. As an example, Clearwater Cave requires a boat charter (RM85) and guide (RM40) for a total of RM125 to visit a single cave—a hefty sum for solo travelers or couples but a much more reasonable fee when split by a party of five people.

For this reason, it's best to check into group tours or organize a small group of fellow travelers to share expenses. Individual travelers and couples who cannot hook up with a large group will probably find Mulu prohibitively expensive.

Transportation

Most visitors now fly from Miri to Gunung Mulu (RM70 one-way; three flights daily), and return downriver to Miri. It's still possible to reach Gunung Mulu with a combination of bus and boat, but the daily air service has almost killed off this much slower alternative.

SABAH

Sabah, the former British Crown Colony, occupies the northeastern tip of Borneo, the isolated island famous for its dense jungles, tribes, wildlife, and soaring mountains. Nicknamed the Land Below the Wind (since it lies south of the Southeast Asian typhoon belt), Sabah is a wonderland for the outdoor adventurer. Its 1,448 kilometers of coastline are flecked with technicolor coral reefs and tiny archipelagos of tropical islands washed by the warm South China and Sulu seas. Dominating the terrain is 4,101-meter Mount Kinabalu, the highest peak in Southeast Asia and one of Asia's most popular climbs. Sandankan's world famous orangutan sanctuary attracts a steady stream of Western visitors.

Rivers snake past the tribal homelands of Kadazans, Bajaus, and Muruts, who cling to ancient customs while carefully stepping into the 20th century. Other peoples include Chinese

merchants, Malay immigrants from the Peninsula, Filipinos from the Sulu Archipelago, and Indonesians up from Kalimantan.

Good beaches, clean seas, swift rivers, soaring mountains, profuse wildlife, friendly people, and large tracts of unspoiled jungle await the discerning traveler. Short of a trip to Africa or interior South America, Sabah is one of the world's best adventure-travel destinations.

And yet very few people come here. Apart from tourist centers such as Mount Kinabalu, it is unlikely that you will see more than a handful of Western visitors. Some are discouraged by the higher cost of travel, although reasonably priced accommodations can now be found in the more popular destinations. It's when you get off the beaten track that prices begin to climb, though most visitors will find Sabah only slightly more expensive than travel in mainland Malaysia.

Visas and Permits

Both Sabah and Sarawak are semiautonomous states and have their own immigration controls, largely to regulate the influx of mainlanders to the island rather than to control the movements of Western visitors.

Westerners are given one-month permits, which can be extended at immigration offices in larger towns. Permits are unnecessary for interior travel but reservations are required for some of the national parks.

TRANSPORTATION

Getting There

Air: MAS flies daily to Kota Kinabalu from Singapore, Kuala Lumpur, and Johor Bharu. The cheapest fares are 14-day advance-purchase tickets and night flights from Johor Bharu. To encourage traffic from Singapore, MAS provides complimentary bus service from its Singapore office to Johor Bharu airport. Economy night flights are also available from Kuala Lumpur.

MAS and Cathay Pacific fly three times weekly from Hong Kong.

MAS and Philippine Airlines fly daily from Manila to Kota Kinabalu. Visitors traveling south from the Philippines might find this an intriguing route: Manila to Kota Kinabalu, overland to Kuching, south to Pontianak by air or land, down to Jakarta by ship or air, and onward to Bali.

Getting Around

Air: MAS flies from Kota Kinabalu to Bintulu (twice daily), Brunei (three times weekly), Kuching (seven daily), Labuan (five daily), Lahad Datu (four daily), Miri (six daily), Sandakan (five daily), and Tawau (five daily). Smaller towns include Limbang (twice weekly), Lawas (weekly), and Kudat (twice weekly).

Flights around Sabah are reasonably priced but often booked solid, especially on weekends and holidays. On the other hand, multiple bookings are so common that MAS often discovers its fully booked flights leaving with empty seats. Best strategy for filled flights is to simply arrive early at the airport and put your name on the waiting list; in most cases you'll fly.

Land: Buses, minibuses, and Land Rovers run along paved roads that now cover most of Sabah. Travel is quick; the 400-km stretch from

---

SABAH HIGHLIGHTS

Adventure Travel

River rafting, mountain climbing, and scuba diving on Sabah are among the finest in Southeast Asia. All the navigable rivers have recently been graded from Class I (easy) to Class VI (expert). Novices can try their luck on the Papar River (Classes I and II) and the Kadamaian River near Kota Belud (Classes II and III). Serious enthusiasts can challenge themselves on the Padas River, a Class-IV excursion through the spectacular Tenom Gorge.

Scuba diving is also spectacular. Dive locations include Tunku Abdul Rahman (TAR) Marine Park near Kota Kinabalu and a tiny island called Sipadan, in the southeast of the state. TAR Marine Park is adequate for beginners, but experts compare the proliferation of marine life and the towering coral walls of Sipadan to the Maldives and the best of Australia's Great Barrier.

Kota Kinabalu

Completely destroyed during WW II, the capital of Sabah is a bustling commercial enclave with little

charm or character. Top draw is the offshore group of islands, which offer good beaches and attractive coral beds. KK (the common abbreviation for Kota Kinabalu) is a convenient place for visas, permits, transportation arrangements, and one of Sabah's few places with good restaurants.

Mount Kinabalu

Sabah's most famous attraction is the immense sawtooth mountain which ranks as the highest peak between New Guinea and Myanmar. Kinabalu can be climbed in two days by almost anyone in good physical condition. The surrounding national park is a naturalist's wonderland of waterfalls, rivers, and spectacular flora and fauna such as bizarre pitcher plants and the famous rafflesia.

Orangutan Sanctuary

Sandakan, another nondescript town, boasts the Sepilok Orangutan Sanctuary—one of the world's few places where orangutans can be observed in their natural habitat.

Kota Kinabalu to Sandakan can be covered in a single day. Travel times are Beaufort (two hours), Keningau (2.5 hours), Kota Belud (two hours), Kudat (three hours), Lawas (five hours), Papar (one hour), Ranau (two hours), Sandakan (six hours), Tenon (four hours), and Tuaran (45 minutes).

Share taxis also head out to most destinations and cost 25-35% more than public buses.

KOTA KINABALU

Known as Jesselton prior to 1963, Kota Kinabalu is a relatively modern and undistinguished city constructed over the ruins of the original town destroyed during WW II. Lacking Kuching's charm or character, KK is also a destination plagued by bad luck: during the late 19th century it was pillaged and burned by pirates so many times that local inhabitants nicknamed their town Api! Api! ("Fire! Fire!"). Postwar reconstruction has created a faceless place, although it offers some good restaurants and is a convenient place to extend visas and make reservations for Mt. Kinabalu.

Attractions
State Mosque: Splendid example of contemporary Islamic architecture and a worthwhile visit on Friday afternoons when the faithful gather for services. Situated south of downtown toward Tanjung Aru, the modernistic Arabian fantasy was designed in 1977 by an Italian architectural firm. Take the red bus from Jalan Tunku Abdul Rahman.

Sabah Museum: KK's impressive repository for Sabah's ethnological treasures located near the State Museum in a trio of modern buildings modeled after Rungus and Murut longhouses. Galleries display collections of tribal artifacts, contemporary handicrafts, dioramas on natural history, Chinese ceramics, and exhibitions on Sabah's indigenous peoples. Also visit the science center, the art gallery, and the theater where the slide show *Sabah, The Land Below the Wind* is given twice daily. The museum is open daily except Fridays 1000-1800. Take the red bus from Jalan Tunku Abdul Rahman and get off near the mosque, then climb the hill opposite the State Secretariat.

Tanjung Aru Beach: The satellite town of Tanjung Aru, eight km south and 10 minutes from the airport, has a passable beach and Sabah's premier resort hotel, nicely set on 23 acres of landscaped gardens. Shangri-La Tanjung Aru Resort, tel. (088) 225800, RM380-650. Take the red bus signposted Beach from Jalan Tunku Abdul Rahman.

Tunku Abdul Rahman National Park: Just offshore from Kota Kinabalu are five attractive and popular islands with sheltered bays, clear waters, and protected coral beds. Pulau Gaya, the largest island of the group, has 20 km of graded nature trails through mangrove swamps and tropical forests filled with wild rattan, tristana trees, rhizophora with distinctive aerial roots, nibong palms used as *attap* for old-fashioned roofing, and exotic birds such as pied hornbills and megapodes. Several agencies run daily tours.

The most popular and developed island in the park is Pulau Sapi, which has a sandy beach and clear waters. Pulau Mamutik is a relatively unspoiled island with a resthouse; make reservations from the Sabah Parks Office in Kota Kinabalu. Pulau Manukan is being developed for campers while Pulau Sulug remains the most distant and least visited of the islands.

Camping is permissible on all islands. Basic cooking and washing facilities are provided, but visitors should bring proper gear and food supplies. Gaya and Sapi islands are just offshore, while the last three are closer to Tanjung Aru.

All can be reached by shuttle boats from the Tanjung Aru Beach marina and by private charter from the jetty in front of the Hyatt Kinabalu. Boat service is frequent on weekends. Return fares are RM15-20 depending on the island.

Services
Tourist Information: Sabah Tourism Promotion Corporation, tel. (088) 218620, at 51 Jalan Raya, can help with transportation schedules, upcoming festivals, and weekly markets *(tamus)*. Tourism Malaysia, tel. (088) 211732, in the Wing Onn Life building is also helpful.

National Parks: The Sabah Parks Office, tel. (088) 211585, on Jalan Tun Fuad Stephens one block west of the tourist office, makes reservations for rooms at Kinabalu National Park, Tunku Abdul Rahman, Poring Hot Springs, Pulau Tiga, and Turtle Islands National Park. Reservations for

KOTA KINABALU

TO KOTA BELUD, MT. KINABALU, AND SANDAKAN

TO SIGNAL HILL

SOUTH CHINA SEA

■ BRITISH AIR

JL. TUN FUAD STEPHENS

■ TOURISM MALAYSIA

■ SABAH TOURIST OFFICE

■ WISMA SABAH

● HOTEL CAPITAL

WISMA MERDEKA

■ SINGAPORE AIR

AUSTRALIA PLACE

● NA BALU LODGE

● SINGAPORE AIR

● HOTEL NAM XING

■ BUSES TO KOTA BELUD AND KUDAT

BOATS TO OFFSHORE ISLANDS

HYATT KINABALU

JL. SALLEH SULONG

■ BUSES TO BEAUFORT, KENINGAU, AND TENOM

● BILAL HOTEL

JL. HAJI SAMAN

JL. PANTAI

JL. GAYA

SEGAMA COMPLEX

LONG BUS STAND

● HOLIDAY HOTEL

CENTRAL MARKET

● POST OFFICE

● PADANG

■ BUSES TO KENINGAU, PAPAR, RANAU, MT. KINABALU, SANDAKAN

★ ISTANA

JL. CHONG VUN

TAXIS

BUS STOP

■ BANK NEGARA

● HIGH COURT

JL. PADANG

JL. TUN RAZAK

NIGHT MARKET ★

■ BUSES TO AIRPORT, LIKAS, AND BEAUFORT LORONG JESSELTON

● TRAVELLER'S RESTHOUSE

● CENTRAL HOTEL

PUTERA HOTEL ●

● DIAMOND INN

JL. TUNGKU ABDUL RAHMAN

■ SABAH PARKS OFFICE

A
B
C
D SINSURAN
E COMPLEX
F
G
H
I
J

● PINE BAY HOTEL

■ IMMIGRATION

● ASIA HOTEL, HOTEL PERTAMA

● HOTEL FORTUNE

BANDARAN BERJAYA

K L

M N

NIGHT MARKET ★

● HOTEL RAKYAT

● ISLAMIC HOTEL

● RUBY INN

JL. TUGU

■ API TOURS

JL. TUN FUAD STEPHENS

JL. DUA PULUH

SOUTH COASTAL HIGHWAY

JL. LAMAN DIKI

● SHIRAZ RESTAURANT

TO AIRPORT, TRAIN STATION, BEAUFORT, MUSEUM, TANJUNG ARU

CENTRE POINT

SEDCO COMPLEX

0   25 m

© MOON PUBLICATIONS, INC.

MALAYSIA

Mt. Kinabalu should be made well in advance, especially during weekends when it seems like half the population of KK sets out to conquer the mountain.

Visas: Malaysian immigration, tel. (088) 216711, on the 4th floor of the Government Complex just off Jalan Tunku Abdul Rahman can extend visas. The Indonesian Consulate, tel. (088) 219110, is on Jalan Karamunsing.

Adventure Travel Companies: Best bets are Borneo Divers, tel. (088) 222226, on the ground floor of Wisma Sabah; Api Tours, tel. (088) 221233, in Wisma Sabah; and Borneo Eco Tours, tel. (088) 234005, at 6 Sadong Jaya.

Budget Accommodations

Traveller's Resthouse: Noisy but centrally located, very popular spot near the parks office and night market. Sinsuran Complex, Block L, 3rd floor, tel. (088) 224264, RM15-20 dorm, RM25-45 private room.

Borneo Wildlife Youth Hostel: Another inner city budget option adjacent to the Traveller's Resthouse. Sinsuaran Complex, Block L, 3rd floor, tel. (088) 213668, RM15-20 dorm, RM25-35 private room.

Na Balu Lodge: Downtown guesthouse but somewhat removed from the grimy city core. Jalan Bakau, tel. (088) 262281, RM15-20 dorm.

Jack's Bed & Breakfast: Pleasant location one km south of town near the State Mosque. Jalan Karamunsing, 17 Block B, tel. (088) 232367, RM18-20 dorm.

Farida's Bed & Breakfast: Several clean and quiet guesthouses geared to travelers are located in Kampung Likas, six km north of city center. The former Cecilia's B&B continues to serve a steady stream of backpackers who appreciate the quiet location and wonderful meals prepared by the owners. 413 Jalan Saga, Likas, tel. (088) 35733, fax 236902, RM12-18 private room.

Moderate and Luxury Accommodations

Hotel Rakyat: The cleanest of KK's inexpensive hotels. Block I, Sinsuran Complex, tel. (088) 211100, RM30-60.

Full Hua Hotel: KK has over a dozen hotels in the RM50-75 range for a/c doubles with attached baths. Some serve the short-time trade but most are clean and safe. 14 Jalan Tugu, tel. (088) 234950, RM55-70.

Hyatt Kinabalu: Located in the heart of town along the waterfront with several restaurants and a swimming pool overlooking the South China Sea. Jalan Datuk Salleh Sulong, tel. (088) 221234, fax 218909, RM340-420.

Shangri-La Tanjung Aru Resort: High-end property right on the beach facing the marine park. Tanung Aru Beach, tel. (088) 225800, fax 217155, RM380-650.

Leaving Kota Kinabalu

Air: Kota Kinabalu airport in Tanjung Aru, eight km south of town, can be reached by taxi or red Putatan bus from Jalan Tunku Abdul Rahman. Taxis from the airport to town operate on the coupon system at fixed fares. MAS and other airlines fly to Singapore, Kuala Lumpur, Johor Bharu, Manila, Hong Kong, Kuching, and Bandar Seri Begawan.

Bus: Kota Kinabalu has three stops where buses, minibuses, Land Rovers, and share taxis depart for destinations in Sabah. Locations are shown on the map. Minibuses are somewhat more expensive than buses but are also faster and more comfortable.

Departures for nearby towns such as Beaufort and Kota Belud are plentiful up until 1400. Service to distant towns such as Sandakan usually ends around 0800 or 0900. Visitors going to Kinabalu National Park can take any bus or minibus bound for Ranau or Sandakan and get off at park headquarters.

Train: A slow moving but very colorful train connects Kota Kinabalu with Tenom in the east, passing through spectacular scenery between Beaufort and Tenom as it passes along the Papas River. The journey from Kota Kinabalu follows the coastline and offers little visual interest; most travelers take a minibus to Beaufort and then join the train for the 1.5 hour ride to Tenom.

Reservations can be made in Kota Kinabalu at the Tanjung Aru train station or immediately upon arrival in Beaufort at the funky old station just across the grassy field. Both diesels and superior railcars connect Beaufort with Tenom. Daily departures are 0825 (railcar), 1050 (diesel), 1200 (railcar), 1330 (diesel), 1550 (railcar).

Getting to Brunei

Aside from air connections, travelers need to use a combination of land and sea transportation to reach Brunei since no roads connect Kota Kinabalu with Bandar Seri Begawan. With an early start it's possible to reach Brunei in a single day.

Labuan Island Route: Buses and taxis directly to Labuan leave from the bus stand on Jalan Balai Polis in Kota Kinabalu. Otherwise, take one of the three daily ferries from the pier behind the Hyatt Hotel. Departures are at 0800, 1000, 1300, and 1500.

Ferries continue from Labuan to Menumbok daily at 0800 and 1300. Launches from Labuan to Bandar Seri Begawan leave several times daily and take two hours.

Sipitang-Lawas Route: The road west from Beaufort passes through Sipitang and Merapok before grinding to a halt in the one-horse town of Lawas. Ferries from Lawas to Bandar Seri Begawan leave twice daily at varying times and take two hours. To avoid getting stuck in Lawas, it's important to double-check schedules before leaving Beaufort. Lawas has a Government Resthouse if you miss the last boat to Brunei.

PENAMPANG AND PAPAR

Kadazans, the members of the ethnic group which forms one-third of Sabah's population, make their homes in the towns near Penampang 13 km south of Kota Kinabalu. These agriculturalists are known for their handicrafts, harvest dances called *sumazau,* and ritualistic exorcisms known as *monogit.* Progress is changing the character of the region, although several small and beautiful Kadazan villages with palm-thatched houses elevated on stilts are still found in the countryside.

Sights in town includes historic St. Michael's Church, Kadazan graveyards, and the so-called House of Skulls, where spiritual ceremonies are held to appease the 42 skull spirits. Penampang holds its weekly market every Saturday morning.

Papar, a modern Kadazan village 38 km south of Kota Kinabalu, holds its *tamu* on Sundays. Buses to both towns leave Kota Kinabalu from the terminal behind the GPO.

BEAUFORT

A quaint market town constructed on stilts to escape the annual flooding of the Padas River and chiefly visited to attend the Saturday market or catch the train to Tenom.

Trains leave Beaufort several times daily as listed under Kota Kinabalu. The two-hour journey along the banks of the Padas River passes through gorgeous countryside while crossing the Crocker Range into the heart of the Padas Gorge.

Reservations should be made immediately upon arrival in Beaufort. Seats are generally available during the week but trains may be filled on weekends or midweek market days. In that event, you can return to Kota Kinabalu or overnight at one of the hotels in Beaufort.

The Hotel Beaufort, tel. (087) 211911, and the Beaufort Inn, tel. (087) 211232, both have rooms for RM30-40.

LABUAN ISLAND

Pulau Labuan is a Federal Territory near Sabah's westernmost point, known for its skin diving and duty-free shopping. The island once served as a base for 17th-century pirates, a British trading post, and a Japanese surrender site at the end of WW II.

Sights include an orchid farm and the Commonwealth War Cemetery three km from the principal town of Victoria. Labuan is otherwise a dull and expensive destination, even by Borneo standards, and most travelers simply pass through without a pause on their way to Brunei.

Three of the cheaper hotels—Pantai View, tel. (087) 411339, Hotel Sri Villa, tel. (087) 416369, and Melati Inn, tel. (087) 416307—are almost side-by-side along Jalan Okk Awang Besar, but even the smallest rooms cost RM40-50.

TENOM

South of Kota Kinabalu lies Murut country, a timber territory inhabited by Murut tribals who have largely given up their traditional lifestyles for jobs in timber factories and now wear blue jeans and T-shirts rather than tribal dress. Although the countryside of jungle and farmland remains quite beautiful, most towns lack character except for Tenom, which has retained some of its old world charm. There's also rubber plantations and the Cocoa Research Center just outside town.

MALAYSIA

Most visitors arrive in Tenom on the train from Beaufort, as described above. The region's few remaining Murut longhouses can be reached with the aid of local guides.

Accommodations include the Sabah Hotel, tel. (087) 735534, across from the Standard Chartered Bank with clean rooms from RM25-30, and the newer Hotel Sri Jaya, tel. (087) 735669, with a/c rooms from RM35-50.

TUARAN AND KOTA BELUD

Several towns famous for their *tamus* (weekly markets) are located slightly north of Kota Kinabalu.

Tuaran: Tuaran, a small town 30 minutes north of Kota Kinabalu, holds its market every Sunday morning. From Tuaran a visit can be made to the nearby Bajau fishing village of Mengkabong, constructed on stilts, where sampans remain the chief mode of transportation. Mengkabong is worth a detour, although some residents have become disturbingly aggressive about their salesmanship.

Kota Belud: The most famous Sabah *tamu* is the Sunday market held in Kota Belud, a sleepy town 77 km north of Kota Kinabalu, an event attended by Malay housewives, Chinese merchants, Kadazans, and Bajaus, who might turn up on their small horses fitted with bells and colorful caparisons for dramatic effect.

From Kota Belud, you can continue north to Kudat or backtrack to Tamparuli, where buses head east to Kinabalu National Park.

KINABALU NATIONAL PARK

Soaring 4,101 meters (13,445 feet) into the clear blue skies of northern Borneo, the sacred mountain of Kinabalu is the highest point between the Himalayas and the snowcapped massif of Mount Wilhelmina in Irian Jaya. The chief attraction is a two-day climb to the summit of the sawtooth mountain, still revered by native Kadazans as Aki Nabalu or "Home of the Departed Spirits."

Apart from the magnificent topography, the 767-square-km national park is home to an extraordinary range of flora and fauna, some found nowhere else in the world. Botanists claim that half the plants growing above the 1,500-meter level are unique to the mountain, although close relatives are found in the highlands of New Guinea, Australia, and New Zealand. Over 800 species of orchids and 500 species of birds live in the park. Among the more famous plants are the rare and endangered rafflesia, whose bloom can reach a meter in diameter, and the more common genus of bizarre carnivorous plants known as *Nepenthes* because of their pitcher-plant shapes.

The park also has something for history buffs: the Kundasang War Memorial, which honors the 2,400 Allied POWs who died on the 11-month death march from Sandakan to the foothills of Mount Kinabalu.

The Climb

The two-day trek can be accomplished by most people in good health, although it requires some preparation. Permission to climb Kinabalu *must* be obtained in advance from the Sabah Parks Office in Kota Kinabalu. Guides are also required at RM25-30 per group; this expense can be shared by joining a large group at park headquarters or directly at the gate checkpoint near the power station. Porters are optional.

The weather is changeable and nighttime temperatures often fall below freezing—bring along proper raingear and an extra set of warm clothing packed in plastic bags. Other necessities include a flashlight, toilet paper, adhesive bandages, kerosene, and food. Mountain huts are equipped with bunks, mattresses, sleeping bags, blankets, kerosene stoves, and cooking facilities. Also attend the naturalist programs at park headquarters and read Susan Kacobson's *Kinabalu Park*, available at the headquarters.

The hike begins with a one-hour walk or a 15-minute drive from park headquarters at 1,585 meters to the power station at 1,890 meters. Security guards here check for the mandatory guide. Guideless hikers should arrive early enough to beat the guard or ask to join a registered group.

The first leg of the climb passes through montane and rhododendron forests to Carson's Falls, where water bottles can be refilled. The trail continues to the first shelter at 2000 meters and then through a zone of Low's pitcher plants, named after the British colonial officer who first climbed the mountain in 1851. The trail climbs past swaying bamboo forests, several sets of primitive huts, and finally the Layang Layang Camp, three hours from the summit at an elevation of 3,359 meters. Most exhausted hikers collapse here, but hardy types can continue another 90 minutes to the new huts at Laban Rata that complement the older huts farther up at Sayat Sayat. Fully equipped with hot water, heaters, and a restaurant, the Laban Rata Huts can accomodate over 70 persons in dormitories. Beds cost RM25 per person at Laban Rata Guesthouse but only RM10 at the Panar Laban, Gunting Lagandan, and Sayat Sayat huts.

The following morning it's up to the summit where, weather permitting, a spectacular sunrise and magnificent views are the final rewards. Since rainstorms and thick clouds often obscure views by 0900, some hikers hedge their bets by booking two nights at Layang Layang or Sayat Sayat. The return hike takes about six hours. Anyone wishing to soak in the hot tubs at Poring Hot Springs that same evening must catch the last minibus to Ranau, which passes park headquarters around 1430.

Accommodations

Park Headquarters has a wide range of accommodations from inexpensive dormitories to comfortable but expensive bungalows. Room reservations must be made in advance at the Sabah Parks office in Kota Kinabalu. Weekends and holidays are extremely busy, but reserving a bed during the week is easy.

Dorm beds in the old and new hostels cost RM10 per person. Both hostels are equipped with bedding, cooking facilities, and fireplaces. Private cabins cost RM50-150 for a double room with private bath. There are two restaurants and a provisions store with food, drink, hiking supplies, and equipment rentals.

Park rangers conduct daily walking tours of the nearby trails and give informative slide shows in the evenings. While a hike to the summit is the top attraction at Kinabalu National Park, a few days exploring the caves, waterfalls, and surrounding forests are also recommended.

Getting There

Any bus or minibus going to Ranau or Sandakan can drop you at park headquarters. Direct minibuses leave three times daily before 1300 from the bus station on Jalan Balai Polis in Kota Kinabalu. Land Rovers are available for a few extra dollars. Both take about two hours. Coming from the *tamu* in Kota Belud, you should transfer to a Sandakan-bound minibus in Tamparuli rather than return to Kota Kinabalu.

Poring Hot Springs

Poring Hot Springs, 43 km from park headquarters, are sulphur baths first developed by Japanese soldiers during WW II with both the hot- and cold-water baths nicely set in landscaped gardens surrounded by tropical jungle interlaced with winding trails to waterfalls, caves, and bamboo forests.

Accommodations cost RM10 per person in large dormitories.

Poring is a great place to relax after conquering Mount Kinabalu, but to reach the springs the same evening you must catch the final Ranau-bound minibus, which passes park headquarters around 1430. Ranau, a small town on the KK-Sandakan highway, about 18 km south of the springs, is a transit point since most travelers head off immediately to the springs.

Buses and minivans from Ranau to Poring are plentiful on weekends and holidays but somewhat scarce during the week. You might need to hitchhike or hire a taxi for RM15-20.

Accommodation in Ranau includes the Ranau Hotel, tel. (088) 875351, and Hotel Kinabalu, tel. (088) 876028, where rooms cost RM30-60.

SANDAKAN

Sandakan lies approximately 386 km from Kota Kinabalu, on the east coast of Sabah facing the Sulu Sea. Formerly the capital of North Borneo, Sandakan was completely destroyed by the Japanese during WW II but quickly rebuilt afterward by Chinese entrepreneurs. It served as center for the state's booming timber industry until the mid-'80s when overlogging finally exhausted the resource in the district: the devastation is painfully obvious on the bus ride from Ranau to Sandakan.

The Sabah Parks Office, tel. (089) 273453, is in Wisma Khoo Siak Chiew at the northeastern end of town. They issue permits for visits to Turtle Islands National Park (Taman Pulau Penya). Permits for Gomantong Caves are issued at the Wildlife office, tel. (089) 666550, at Batu 7, some 11 km west of town. The immigration office is also out here at Batu 7.

Sepilok Orangutan Rehabilitation Centre

Its name literally translating to people of the jungle, the humanlike orangutan was once hunted by the great British naturalist, Sir Alfred Wallace, who reported that the red-haired beasts were especially fond of . . . durians! Today the gentle animal is an endangered species largely because its natural habitat has been destroyed by logging.

Sepilok, 25 km from Sandakan, is home to one of the world's four orangutan sanctuaries designed to reintroduce into the jungle those animals captured in logging camps or kept illegally as pets. Other protected wildlife such as gibbons, macaques, Malay sun bears, and wild cats are also brought to Sepilok and eventually coaxed back into the jungle.

The park is open daily 0900-1600; orangutans are fed daily at 0900 and 1400 from two elevated platforms in the middle of the jungle. Orangutan spotting is strictly a matter of luck: sometimes a half-dozen young animals will appear for their breakfast of milk and bananas, while on other days attendance is zero. Other park attractions include jungle hiking through mangrove forests, waterfalls, swimming pools, and educational programs sponsored by park rangers.

Permits are unnecessary to visit the reserve. Sepilok can be reached on the blue bus marked Sepilok Batu 14, which leaves mornings from the bus terminal located at the waterfront at the west end of the vegetable market in Sandakan. Buses marked Sepilok Batu 16, 17, and 30 will drop you at the junction two km from park headquarters.

Turtle Islands National Park

Pulau Penyu National Park, 40 km north of Sandakan, consists of three islands (Selingan, Bakungan, and Gulisan) and their surrounding coral reefs. Egg-laden green and hawksbill turtles come here between August and October to nest in the warm sand. Hatcheries are open to the public.

Turtle Islands is not a day-trip from Sandakan and requires an overnight stay in the Sabah Parks Chalet on Pulau Selingan. Rooms cost RM30-60 per person in rustic cabins and RM150 for private two-person chalets. Reservations must be made at the Sabah Parks Office in Sandakan.

Few travelers visit the sanctuary, since there is no regular boat service and only large groups can afford to charter a boat for the three-hour journey. Boat transfers and guided tours are best arranged through tour operators and the parks office.

Gomantong Caves

Sandakan's third major attraction is the enormous network of caverns famous for their edible bird's nests. Similar to the more accessible caves at Niah, thousands of swiftlets called *burong layang layang* spin their phlegm baskets inside the immense limestone cliffs. Harvests are conducted several times a year by skilled collectors of the Orang Sungeti tribe, natives of the nearby Kinabatangan River area.

Permits must be obtained from the Wildlife office in Sandakan.

Gomantong is across the bay some 24 km south of Sandakan. Visitors can take a boat across the bay and then a 16-km Land Rover ride—a difficult and expensive journey best arranged through travel agents.

Accommodations

The hotel situation in Sandakan has improved somewhat in recent years for budget travelers.

Uncle Tan's: Best inexpensive place is 29 km from Sandakan; ask the bus driver to drop you there. Tan arranges budget trips to Sepilok sanctuary and Turtle Islands. Batu 17, tel. (089) 531917, RM20-25.

Traveler's Rest Hostel: Back in town, this hostel has dorm beds, private rooms, and reasonably priced tours to Sepilok Rehabilitation Centre and Turtle Islands. Bandar Ramai Ramai, Block E, tel. (089) 216454, RM14-25.

Mayfair Hotel: Decent place with clean a/c rooms and private baths. 24 Jalan Pryer, tel. (089) 219855, RM32-45.

Hotel London: Best value mid-priced hotel near the Sabah Parks office. Jalan Empat, tel. (089) 216371, RM40-50.

Sandakan Renaissance Hotel: Top-end hotel north of town with swimming pool and view restaurant. Jalan Utara, tel. (089) 213299, RM280-360.

LAHAD DATU

This prosperous Chinese town of 20,000 people receives the few visitors going from Tawau to Tarakan in Kalimantan.

Sipadan Island

Boats can be chartered to explore the offshore islands near Semporna, an old Bajau town three hours south of Lahad Datu. Formed from an arc of land which once rimmed a volcanic crater, these stunning islands are inhabited by seafaring Bajaus who live over the water in pilehouses or in traditional Bajau boats called *lipa lipa.*

The coral beds at Sipadan are reputedly some of the finest in Southeast Asia, but the expense makes Sipadan almost exclusively a diver's destination. Borneo Divers in Kota Kinabalu can help with tour packages and diving arrangements. Figure on US$150-250 per day from Kota Kinabalu including transportation, meals, lodging, and two dives per day.

Accommodations and Transportation

Lahad Datu has several hotels in the RM35-40 price range, such as Hotel Venus, tel. (089) 781900, near the Ocean Hotel in the center of town.

Buses and minibuses for Lahad Datu leave from the bus terminal near the Federal Hotel in Sandakan. From Sandakan, allow four hours to Lahad Datu and seven hours to Tawau. MAS flies daily to Lahad Datu and Tawau.

TAWAU

Tawau, a small commercial center at the southeastern border of Sabah, mainly serves as a transit point for Indonesian Borneo. Visas can be picked up at the Indonesian consulate on Jalan Apas; a better idea is to pick up your visa in Kota Kinabalu and avoid this hopelessly disorganized office.

Tawau has several hotels in the RM25-30 range on Jalan Stephen Tan, three blocks east of the bus terminal, near the central market.

Getting to Indonesia

Although time-consuming and expensive, it is legal to enter or exit Tarakan (Indonesia) from Tawau. Note that Tarakan is not a recognized visa-free entry port for Indonesia and that all visitors must obtain an Indonesian visa in advance from an Indonesian consulate.

MAS flies to Tarakan on Monday and Friday, while Bouraq flies on Tuesday, Thursday, and Saturday. Boats from Tawau to Nunukan, a small Indonesian fishing town just across the border, leave Tawau each morning around 0800. Another boat continues south to Tarakan.

MALAYSIA

Homesickness is one of the traveler's ailments, and so is loneliness. Fear—of strangers, of being embarrassed, of threats to personal safety—is the traveler's usual, if often unadmitted, companion. The sensitive traveler will also feel a degree of guilt at his alienation from ordinary people.

—PAUL FUSSELL,
THE NORTON BOOK OF TRAVEL

The real meaning of travel, like that of a conversation by the fireside, is the discovery of oneself through contact with other people, and its condition is self-commitment in the dialogue.

—PAUL TOURNIER,
THE MEANING OF PERSONS

Fish and visitors stink in 3 days.

—BENJAMIN FRANKLIN

MYANMAR (BURMA)

Of the gladdest moments in human life, methinks, is the departure upon a distant journey into unknown lands. Shaking off with one mighty effort the fetters of Habit, the leaden weight of Routine, the cloak of many Cares and the slavery of Home, man feels once more happy.

—RICHARD BURTON,
JOURNAL

The man who wishes to wrest something from Destiny must venture into that perilous margin-country where the norms of Society count for nothing and the demands and guarantees of the group are no longer valid. He must travel to where the police have no sway, to the limits of physical resistance and the far point of physical and moral suffering.

—CLAUDE LÉVI-STRAUSS,
TRISTES TROPIQUES

Pasteurized and homogenized cultures are not what take us abroad.

—PICO IYER,
VIDEO NIGHT IN KATHMANDU

INTRODUCTION

Myanmar (Burma) is one of the most isolated and exotic countries in the world, a land of gentle charm where timelessness and the quest for Buddhist nirvana fly in the face of Western efficiency and capitalistic wealth. The government has opened the country to tourism and extended visa entry to four weeks, but progress has come slowly to this intriguing land. Myanmar remains primitive, untamed, and extraordinarily memorable—"quite unlike any land you will ever know," said Kipling, who also wrote, "in all the world there is no place like Burma."

Myanmar is a destination for travelers rather than tourists, and a country best seen in retrospect. Only *after* the ordeal of rushing around, packing and unpacking, waiting for transportation, and dealing with one of the world's most medieval bureaucracies can you begin to love the country. Yet your recollections of magnificent temples and delightful people will captivate you as with no other country in Southeast Asia. How much can you absorb in just 30 days? Only enough to know that you *must* return.

Myanmar What?

Burma has officially changed its name to Myanmar (MEE-en-ma), the name of the capital from Rangoon to Yangon ("End of the Enemy"), and Pagan to Bagan. The predominant nationality and official language are now called Myanmar, the national airline is Myanmar Airways International (MAI), and Tourist Burma goes by Myanmar Travel and Tours (MTT). The "r," added by the British, is silent so most titles are pronounced MEE-an-ma rather than MEE-an-mar.

Government authorities say the changes are meant to better reflect Burma's ethnic diversity and provide Romanized spellings more phonetically in tune with local pronunciations, while minorities claim that the rename is yet another historical distortion by the military junta. Minorities prefer the more inclusive, colloquial "Bama," later corrupted by the British to Burma.

Although not widely adopted by the international press, Myanmar's new nomenclature is used throughout the country, and in this book with former names in parentheses. The "Destination Names" chart will help decipher maps, brochures, and other publications from the MTT.

Should You Go?

Groups opposed to Myanmar tourism—Free Burma Coalition (www.freeburma.org), Human Rights Watch (hrwnyc@hrw.org), Withdrawal

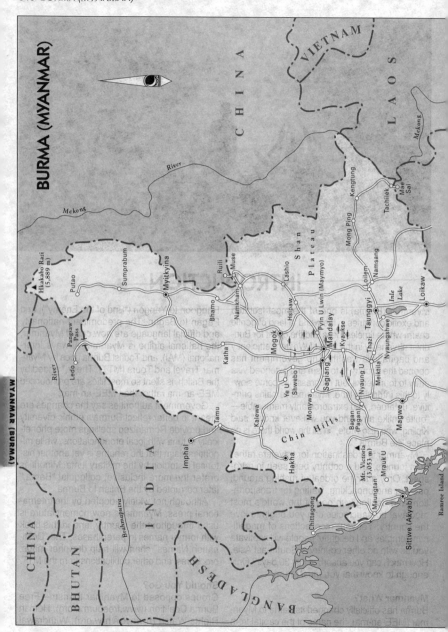

BURMA (MYANMAR)

CHINA

VIETNAM

L A O S

C H I N A

Mekong

River

Mekong

Hkakabo Razi
(5,889 m)

Putao

Sumprabum

Pangsau
Pass

Ledo

Myitkyina

Bhamo

Ruili Muse

Namtham

Lashio

Katha

Mogok

Hsipaw

Pyin U Lwin (Maymyo)

S h a n

P l a t e a u

Mong Ping

Kengtung

Namsang

Loilem

Mae
Sai

Tachilek

Mandalay

Kyaukse

Thazi

Taunggyi

Inle
Lake

Nyaungshwe

Loikaw

Tamu

Kalewa

Ye U
Shwebo

Monywa

Sagiang

Nyaung U

Meiktila

Magwe

Imphal

I N D I A

Brahmaputra

C H I N A

BHUTAN

BANGLADESH

Hakha

Bagan
(Pagan)

C h i n   H i l l s

Mt. Victoria
(3,053 m)

Maungtaw

Mrauk U

Chittagong

Sittwe (Akyab)

Ramree Island

MYANMAR (BURMA)

CAMBODIA

THAILAND

Gulf of Thailand

BANGKOK

Three Pagodas Pass

Mae Sot
Myawaddy
Kawkareik
Thanbyuzayat
Ye
Palaw
Myeik
Kawthoung

Paan
Thaton
Kyaikto
Kyaikkami
Mawlamyine (Moulmein)
Kyaikkami (Amherst)
Dawei (Tavoy)
Mergui
Mergui Archipelago

Pasawng
Taungup
Taunggoo
Pyay (Prome)
Tharrawaddy
Padaung
Bago (Pegu)
YANGON (RANGOON)
Pathein (Bassein)
Chaungtha
Ngapali
Thandwe (Sandoway)
Cheduba Island

Gulf of Martaban

Andaman Sea

Bay of Bengal

Andaman Islands (India)

DESTINATION NAMES

OLD NAME   NEW NAME

100 mi
100 km

MYANMAR (BURMA)

© MOON PUBLICATIONS, INC.

from Burma (frde@igc.org), Open Institute (burma@sorosny.org), and others—argue that most tourist dollars go into Slorc (State Law and Order Restoration Council, the ruling regime) pockets and are used to purchase weapons for the suppression of minority groups and control of the general population. The travel boycott movement—an echo of the strategy used against South Africa during apartheid—points out that Slorc and family members of former dictator General Ne Win maintain economic interests in Myanmar International Airlines and the Strand, New World, Nawarat, Mya Yeik Nyo, and Inya Lake Hotels. Stephen Law, son of former drug warlord Khun Sa, is said to launder opium profits through his Rangoon Traders Hotel, an upscale high-rise partially funded by the Singapore government.

These groups also object to tourism projects such as the dredging of Mandalay Palace moat, improved railway lines, and construction of the new Bassein airport which use unpaid, forced "slave labor" that essentially benefits the murderous regime in Yangon. Slorc has also confiscated land for golf courses and beach resorts, and bulldozed entire towns for tourism facilities and foreign-financed hotels.

The leading opponent to Myanmar tourism is Aung San Suu Kyi, the freely elected but detained civilian leader who says tourism legitimizes the Slorc regime that holds power despite her overwhelming victory in the 1990 elections. Her beliefs are supported by many travel agencies such as Himalayan Kingdoms and Student Travel Australia (STA), which dropped tours to the country in late 1996.

The campaign to derail "Visit Myanmar 1996" proved wildly successful as anticipated visitor arrivals dropped from 500,000 to well under 200,000 and local wags dubbed the failed project "Visit Malar Year" ("Not Coming Year").

There are, of course, travel agencies, tour companies, and publishing organizations that argue in favor of tourism to Myanmar; these hold that tourism can be a powerful force for political and economic change since it spreads ideals of freedom and democracy, and distributes wealth among the common citizens. Travel companies on this side of the fence include Mountain Travel Sobek, Abercrombie & Kent, Geographic Expeditions (former Inner Asia), Eastern & Orient Express (the *Road to Mandalay* ship) and Radisson Seven Seas.

Not many approve of the Slorc regime, yet many travelers would still like to visit Myanmar without financially supporting one of the world's most despicable military dictatorships. One compromise suggested by an anti-government group concludes, "Tourists should not engage in activities that will only benefit Slorc's coffers, but those who wish to publicize the plight of the Burmese people are encouraged to utilize Slorc's more relaxed tourist policies." Travelers can visit the country but minimize Slorc income by spending dollars at the local level, such as on privately owned guesthouses, cafes, hired cars, markets, tour guides, and other small-scale entrepreneurs.

Rather than exclusively patronizing expensive tourist hotels, restaurants, and tour companies milked by Slorc, spend as much money as possible in guesthouses and cafes generally free of Slorc fingers. Responsible tourism means to travel like a local, depend on the local economy, and avoid the gaudy excesses of Western tourism.

DESTINATION NAMES

FORMER NAME	NEW NAME
Akyab	Sittwe
Amherst	Kyaikkami
Arakan	Rakhine
Bassein	Pathein
Irrawaddy River	Ayeyarwady River
Mandalay	no change
Martaban	Mottama
Maymyo	Pyin U Lwin
Mergui	Myeik
Moulmein	Mawlamyine
Pagan	Bagan
Pegu	Bago
Prome	Pyi
Rangoon	Yangon
Sandoway	Thandwe
Syriam	Thanlyin
Taunggyi	no change
Tavoy	Dawei
Salween River	Thanlwin River
Sittang River	Sittoung River

MYANMAR (BURMA)

SIGHTSEEING HIGHLIGHTS

Principal Destinations

Most visitors to Myanmar visit the capital city of Yangon (Rangoon), Mandalay to the north, the world-famous temples at Bagan (Pagan), and perhaps a stop at lovely Inle Lake.

Yangon: Yangon's top attraction, magnificent Shwedagon Pagoda, ranks among the world's great Buddhist monuments, an unforgettable spectacle at twilight. Yangon has little else of interest though it's amazing to see what 50 years of total neglect will do to what was once one of the most prosperous cities in Asia.

Mandalay: Mandalay served as the final Burmese capital during the 18th and 19th centuries and, to a certain degree, still retains the easygoing charms of an earlier day. Several fascinating temples and monasteries are worth visiting, although not everybody is impressed with the dust and heat and modern structures which have replaced most of the older neighborhoods destroyed by fire over the decades.

Bagan: Bagan (Pagan), a magnificent array of 12th-century ruins in central Myanmar, ranks among the world's premier archaeological sites—unquestionably a must-see for every visitor to the country.

Inle Lake: Travelers jaded with archaeology and old temples may prefer the splendid environment of Inle Lake, an idyllic lake retreat amid the foothills of eastern Myanmar.

Sidetrips

Sidetrips to temples, former capitals, and old British hill stations can be made from Yangon, Mandalay, Bagan, and Inle Lake.

Bago: Eighty km northeast of Yangon lies Bago (Pegu), an old Mon capital famed for its fabulous Shwemawdaw Pagoda—just as impressive as the

Shwedagon. Together with other nearby temples, Bago proves an outstanding day-trip from Yangon.

Mandalay Vicinity: Mandalay excursions visit the Mingun pagoda, Ava, Sagaing, and Amarapura—three sleepy towns that briefly served as upper Burmese capitals during the 18th century. Most of the secular architecture has been lost but the remaining temples, pagodas, and monasteries are fascinating.

Pyin U Lwin (Maymyo): Two hours east of Mandalay is a former British hill station famed for its picturesque location, brisk climate, market, and colonial reminders. Pyin U Lwin needs an overnight from Mandalay but can be a day-trip for hurried travelers.

Mount Popa: A dramatic mountain near Bagan, center for *nat* worship, and an easy, brief stopover from Bagan to Thazi.

Inle Lake Vicinity: Kalaw, a former British hill resort, and the 10,000 Buddhas of Pindaya Caves are popular excursions from Inle Lake.

Remote Destinations

Myanmar's four-week visas make it possible to explore regions untouched since the end of World War II—a fleeting moment at best.

Visiting these new frontiers is not as easy as the government would like you to believe. While the government claims most regions open to tourism, destinations beyond Yangon, Mandalay, Bagan, and Inle Lake often require permits from the Ministry of Hotels and Tourism. Tour groups (package tours) are favored but FITs (Foreign Independent Travelers) are allowed into most districts with a permit. See "Visas and Travel Permits" in the text for more information.

MYANMAR (BURMA)

THE LAND

Myanmar, shaped somewhat like a hexagonal kite with a dangling tail, is surrounded by rugged mountains on three borders which has kept the country politically and culturally isolated from the outside world. A central basin divides itself into a fertile rice-growing region of lower Myanmar and a dry, desert-like central region topped by a confusing knot of mountains that soar to over 6,000 meters. The northern mountains run

from China southwest to Myanmar where they disappear under the sea and reappear as the Andaman Islands, the counterpart to the Ayeyarwady River (Sanskrit for River of Refreshment), popularized by Kipling as the "Road to Mandalay" and his "River of Lost Footsteps."

The tropical forests which once covered half of Myanmar have been badly exploited by the Burmese National Timber Corporation which has sold logging licenses to Thai consortiums and some fear that Burmese teak may be gone within a few decades.

YANGON'S CLIMATE

	JAN.	FEB.	MAR.	APR.	MAY	JUNE	JULY	AUG.	SEPT.	OCT.	NOV.	DEC.
Avg. Maximum C	32°	33°	36°	36°	33°	30°	29°	29°	30°	31°	31°	31°
Avg. Maximum F	90°	92°	96°	96°	92°	86°	84°	84°	86°	88°	88°	88°
Rainy Days	0	0	1	2	14	23	26	25	20	10	3	1

Myanmar is hot. Temperatures March-June soar to 45° C (115° F), making vacations feel like Dante's Inferno. Winter months are cooler while summer monsoons drench coastal regions with rain. Temperatures drop to tolerable levels during monsoons though humidity levels hover near 100%.

HISTORY

Surrounded by towering mountain walls that encircle the country like an iron horseshoe, Myanmar has always been an isolated and insular region.

The early Christian Era saw four races migrate south from Tibet into Myanmar including the Pyu, a mysterious race that practiced syncretic Theravada Buddhism and animism and settled in south-central Myanmar near Prome. Next were the Mons, a highly civilized and cultured race with profound influence on the Bagan Burmese, who were firmly entrenched near Bago prior to the arrival of the Burmans in the 7th-9th centuries. The Mons were followed by Burmans who fled Tibet and settled in central Myanmar near Bagan, and Shans (Tai or Thai), who fled Mongol invasions of Nanchao and settled along the Thai-Myanmar border. These four Mongoloid-Chinese races waged almost continual warfare with brief periods of peace and unity.

Bagan (1044-1287)

Myanmar's first empire centered on the Ayeyarwady River among dry and dusty plains under the leadership of King Anawrahta, an ambitious leader who had conquered the Mons and transported their retinue of artists, philosophers, and religious leaders back to his isolated capital. Mons made profound contributions to Burmese culture—craftsmen taught Burmese their skills,

religious leaders spread Theravadism and Pali language, architects designed temples and stupas which remain among the wonders of Asia. Bagan later fell to an envious Kublai Khan who demanded tribute and marched on the city.

After Bagan fell, Myanmar split into confusing kingdoms whose histories are dizzying kaleidoscopes of peace and warfare. Shans ruled upper Myanmar from Ava while Burmans founded Toungoo in central Myanmar. Mons set up camp at Bago where they traded with Malacca. The Burmese conquered the Shans and captured Bago from the Mons in the 16th century; the capital wandered until Alaungpaya ("Future Buddha") reorganized Burmese forces and destroyed the Mons at Bago. During his eight-year reign (1752-1760), Alaungpaya founded the Konbaung dynasty which ruled Myanmar from Rakhine to Tenasserim until British conquest in 1885.

British Occupation

Territorial conflicts led to the British-Burmese war of 1824 during which Assam, Rakhine (Arakan), and Tenasserim were annexed by the British. Burmese-British relations deteriorated under the rule of Bagan Min (1846-1853); after European traders protested the extortionate behavior of Yangon Burmese officials, British forces deposed the religious-minded but temperamental Mindon Min (1853-1878). An expansionist governor-general, Lord Dalhouse, annexed lower Myanmar including Yangon in 1852 and the rich Ayeyarwady delta was cleared of mangrove forests, carved into extensive rice plantations, and soon ranked among the world's most productive rice-growing regions. Yet wealth went to British firms and Indian moneylenders while locals descended into abject poverty. Mindon of Ava modernized what little remained of his medieval country but Myanmar fell to British forces in 1886.

Independence

Wealthy offspring of the Burmese during the early 20th century were educated in London and proselytized on capitalism and democracy, ideals these future leaders of an independent Burma brought home. The Young Men's Buddhist Association (YMBA) and Thakins (Thirty Comrades), led by Aung San, U Nu, and Ne Win, organized student and worker strikes geared toward the socialist and fascist philosophies popular in 1930s Japan. Aung San, political activist and father of modern Myanmar, moved to Japan where he received military training from sympathetic Japanese leaders.

Japanese forces captured Myanmar in 1941 accompanied by Thakins, who were given token control of the country. Although the Japanese promised an Asian Co-Prosperity Sphere based on equality and brotherhood, they soon alienated the local population with their insulting behavior, sadistic treatment, and slaughter of innocent civilians by the dreaded *kempatai*. Yangon Cemetery holds over 27,000 soldiers and civilians killed by Japanese through forced labor, torture, and starvation.

Burma is remembered by Allied heroes such as "Vinegar" Joe Stilwell, Chennault and his Flying Tigers, and Merrill's Marauders—covered in detail in Barbara Tuchman's *Stilwell and the American Experience in China.* After the war turned against Japanese interests, Burmese leaders turned to British forces who later granted immunity from postwar prosecution.

Independence occurred at 0420, 4 January 1948—an auspicious hour determined by Burmese astrologers. Charismatic Aung San took control but was soon murdered by gunmen hired by Burmese right-wing politicians. Successor U Nu was helpless as economic and political collapse erupted into warring of communists, Karens, and dissident followers of Aung San against the newly formed government. To appease warring factions, U Nu established separate, semiautonomous states for minorities.

In 1962 General Ne Win led a coup d'état against U Nu and established a military dictatorship which succeeded in slowing the revolution but at a high cost: suspended constitutions, nationalized industries, and total censorship.

Ah, Yes, a Kind and Gentle Land

1988 was the year that Myanmar exploded. Early rumblings started in 1987 after the government declared large-denomination bank notes worthless and ordinary people awoke to discover their money fit only for lighting cheroots. The wave broke in March 1988 after minor student brawls escalated into the first major antigovernment demonstrations since 1974; dozens of protesters were massacred by the dreaded Lon Htein secret police and 41 people suffocated inside police vans. During a second wave of violence on 21 June, an estimated 100-120 students and monks were cut down by the secret police, universities were closed, army reinforcements were sent to Yangon, and students occupied Shwedagon.

MYANMAR (BURMA)

the perils of independent travel

Ne Win resigned but, incredibly, Sein Lwin—the man responsible for the brutality of earlier months—was appointed chief of state and party leader. Outrage was immediate. By early August hundreds of thousands of Burmese were marching through Yangon and, true to form, Sein Lwin responded with unprecedented brutality—soldiers shot unarmed demonstrators and massacred nurses and doctors inside the confines of the Yangon General Hospital. An estimated 1,000-3,000 people were killed during the brutal repression which finally ended on 12 August.

On 13 August Sein Lwin resigned and was replaced by Dr. Maung Maung, a Western-educated lawyer who promised reforms. The demonstrations grew larger. Over 500,000 people marched on 24 August, clapping and cheering in the belief that the country was about to return to democracy and "People Power." The dream died on 18 September when the Myanmar Army seized control of the government, declared martial law, and ordered troops to fire on demonstrators.

Then, the impossible happened. After decades of misrule, free and fair elections were held and Burma's military junta suffered a humiliating defeat in the general elections of May 1990. The National League for Democracy (NLD) won almost 90% of the 485 votes in the new National Assembly and the government announced that it would relinquish power once the new constitution was approved. But the government soon nullified the elections, put most NLD leaders in jail, and placed Aung San Suu Kyi, the daughter of Burmese independence hero Aung San, under house arrest.

A New Leader

In October 1991, Aung San Suu Kyi (pronounced Ahn Sahn Soo Chee) was awarded the Nobel Peace Prize by Norway's Nobel Committee, who called her struggle "one of the world's most extraordinary examples of civil courage." She remained under house arrest in her simple home near Inya Lake. In February 1993, six Nobel Peace Prize winners—the Dalai Lama, Archbishop Desmond Tutu, the former president of Costa Rica, and others—gathered in Thailand to call for the release of Aung San Suu Kyi. The following year, ex-dictator Ne Win left for medical treatment in Singapore, one of the few countries in the world that has publicly kowtowed to the Slorc regime.

After six years of resisting worldwide opinion, Slorc suddenly released Aung San Suu Kyi from house arrest in July 1995, a day before the U.S. Congress was scheduled to debate the banning of all economic contacts with Myanmar. Then the Slorc campaign to settle the decades-old conflicts with ethnic resistance groups started to find accords as major players signed peace agreements with the Yangon regime—the opium-producing Mon-Khmer Wa (signed in 1989), the ethnic Chinese drug-trafficking Kokang (1990), opium-centerpiece Shan States (1995), Tibeto-Burman Kachin (1993), Karen (1996), the two-million Mons (1995), and the last holdouts, the Karenni, who signed an agreement with Slorc in 1996. All groups agreed to cease-fires on the condition that they could keep their weapons and maintain semiautonomous status with rights to continue their traditional forms of income, often smuggling of antiques and the cultivation of opium.

The fate of the National League for Democracy (NLD) worsened in 1996 as hundreds of NLD members were arrested and new laws were passed to limit the constitutional freedoms of the freely elected party. In June 1996, a European diplomat died in jail after being arrested for operating phones and faxes without government permission and in October 1996 over 1,000 activists and students were detained by the Slorc regime after a series of street protests.

GOVERNMENT

Myanmar is a single-party socialist government run by a prime minister, his nine-man cabinet, and National Unity Party (NUP) under the State Law and Order Restoration Council (Slorc), which finally dropped Ne Win's "Burmese Way to Socialism"—an isolationist and xenophobic political philosophy which combined the Marxist and Fabian thinking popular during the 1930s.

Ne Win's (Slorc) Road to Socialism proved to be the Road to Nowhere. Ne Win, as with other leaders in Southeast Asia, remained in power for several decades (he retired in 1989) but, unlike his compatriots, he drove his country to the brink of economic collapse, a stunning accomplishment considering that Myanmar is rich in gems and timber and was once the world's leading rice exporter. "Everything in this country is sliding down into a pit," says a Myanmar observer, "the only question is whether the pit has a bottom."

Ne Win is among the world's most idiosyncratic leaders—a self-proclaimed Buddhist and devoted family man married five times including a union with a granddaughter of King Thibaw, the last monarch of Burma. Ne Win believes himself a descendant of the old Konbaung Dynasty. In a country without any national parks, his love affair with golf has brought the country over 25 golf courses. Even more bizarre is his abiding belief in the powers of astrology, mysticism, and

numerology. It is said he personally ordered the introduction of odd 45- and 90-*kyat* banknotes since both numbers are divisible by nine, his lucky number, and that the renaming of Burma to Myanmar was done under his belief that an indigenous term would prevent the wholesale Westernization of his country, a name change announced on 27 May, an auspicious day since two plus seven equals nine.

Ne Win's astrologer once told him he would only reach nirvana if he married a girl from Rakhine, shot his own image in the mirror, and bathed himself in blood. He's assumed to have completed all three rituals.

OPIUM KING KHUN SA

Myanmar's leading export isn't teak, gems, or oil . . . it's opium. The Golden Triangle—an isolated area of 75,000 square miles wedged between Myanmar, China, Laos, and Thailand—annually produces over 2,000 tons of opium and over 70% of the world's illicit heroin supply, mostly exported through Thailand to the West where the profits are mind-boggling. One poppy field produces 2,000 kilos of raw opium which is heated in water, distilled with lime fertilizer and ammonia to produce morphine, fused with acetic anhydride to produce heroin, and then smuggled into Thailand where it brings US$25,000 per kilo. Heroin in the west wholesales per kilo for over US$200,000 *before* being cut six times by street dealers. The final tally: one kilo

of raw Burmese opium eventually brings US$2.5 million; a single square mile of Burmese land can yield heroin worth US$50-200 million. Small wonder the hilltribes refuse to grow peanuts.

The mastermind of Myanmar's opium industry has long been Khun Sa (a.k.a. Chang Chi-fu), a half-Chinese half-Shan warlord widely regarded as one of the world's most prolific drug dealers . . . right up there with the Mafia and the Medellin cartel. Khun Sa first came to the attention of the world's press in 1967 when he launched the Opium War and wrestled control of the lucrative trade from the remnants of Chiang Kai-Shek's Nationalist Chinese Army. After capture by Myanmar forces and time in a Yangon prison, his private army (the Shan States Army) kidnapped two Soviet doctors as hostages and by 1978 Khun Sa controlled almost 80% of Myanmar's opium trade.

Capturing Khun Sa proved impossible. The U.S. government once offered US$25,000 for his head, but Khun Sa countered by offering payments for the murder of Americans in Chiang Mai. He was also a media manipulator who met frequently with the press, including a 1989 visit by Tom Jarrell of ABC-TV.

Khun Sa finally signed a "peace accord" with the Myanmar government in 1996 and now lives in a comfortable Yangon estate where he conducts business in hotels, tour companies, travel agencies, and other enterprises in cooperation with the ruling regime. It is also assumed he keeps his hand in the opium and methamphetamine monopoly, which continues to profit the Slorc regime.

MYANMAR (BURMA)

ECONOMY

Thirty years after embarking on its misguided road to socialism, Myanmar has joined North Korea and the Philippines on Asia's short list of foreign-debt defaulters. Ne Win's (Slorc) dead-end policies have led to nothing but economic collapse. Per-capita income of less than US$200 is somewhere between that of Botswana and Bangladesh. An unmanageable US$4.2-billion foreign debt gobbles up some 90% of export earnings while foreign reserves are barely enough to run the country for two weeks. With its vast reserves of teak, minerals, and oil, Myanmar is potentially one of Asia's richest countries, and yet, a country once able to feed most of Southeast Asia now faces the specter of its first food shortages since WW II. The Myanmar government was forced to reappraise its backward economic policies and ask the United Nations to classify it as a "Least Developed Country." Sadly, permission was granted. Myanmar has devolved into Southeast Asia's wounded isolation patient.

It must also be said that Myanmar's economic failure has spared the country the horrors of uncontrolled development. You won't find too many faceless high-rises, industrial pollution, or gaudy billboards filling the countryside. Pure, peaceful, and perhaps the most untouched country in the world, but at a heavy price. Public transportation is often creaky buses that

began life on the Burma Road during WW II. Hotels are rich in colonial atmosphere but elevators are busted and showers have lives of their own. Myanmar's retreat from the West has preserved family and religious traditions but has given new and painful meaning to the phrase "shared poverty"—a fascination at the cost of human suffering.

THE PEOPLE

An ethnographical map of Myanmar shows a bewildering patchwork of peoples divided into dozens of ethnic groups speaking a veritable tower of babble. Two-thirds of Myanmar's 40 million residents are Burmans while the remainder are Indian, Chinese, or part of a minority group. Walk down the street in Yangon and the kaleidoscopic range hits you: Burmans with dark brown skin and almond-shaped eyes, Tamil women in brightly colored saris, Chinese with light skin and Asiatic eyelids. Go to Inle Lake and you'll find Shans in winding turbans and baggy blue pants, Karens in rough-hewn red-and-white dresses, Paduangs with heavy necklaces of brass rings. To the north are rebellious Kachins, Wa, and Naga.

Burmans have been called the "Irish of Asia" because of their lively and genial but sometimes contentious nature. The term "Burman" traditionally has referred to the predominant ethnic group, while "Burmese" means all peoples liv-

Karenni culture week

FESTIVALS

Myanmar's Buddhist festivals follow the lunar calendar and take place on full-moon nights during the dry season. National holidays are fixed on the Gregorian calendar and take place on the same date each year.

January: Burmese independence is celebrated in the wee hours of the morning—an annoyance for diplomats required to be on hand for the celebration. Yangon holds a military parade. *Zat pwes* (special festivals that combine music, dance, and dramatics) and sporting events take place throughout the country.

February: Union Day happens on 12 February; this state holiday honors ethnic groups with a week-long celebration of dance, drama, and sporting events at Yangon's Royal Lake

March: Farmers' Day on 2 March honors the working classes, Resistance Day on 27 March is Armed Forces Day, while the Shwedagon Festival on the full moon of the final month in the Buddhist calendar marks the enshrinement of eight sacred Buddha hairs in Shwedagon Pagoda more than 2,500 years ago.

April: Thingyan Festival on the full moon of the first Buddhist month is a water-throwing festival—Buddha images are sprinkled with water and everyone else (especially visitors) are mercilessly drenched with squirt guns, water buckets, and hoses.

May: The birth, death, and enlightenment of Buddha happens on the full moon of the second month—the holiest of all Buddhist holidays.

June: Mount Popa Nat Festival on the full moon of the third month honors unseen spirits and provides a chance to see *nat kadaw,* a trance dance performed by possessed villagers.

July: Dhammasetkya on the full moon of the fourth month commemorates Buddha's first sermon after his enlightenment and the beginning of Buddhist Lent—a popular time for young men to enter the priesthood.

August: Taungbyon Nat Festival on the full moon of the fifth month is a seven-day festival of dancing, drinking, and music in Taungbyon, 20 km north of Mandalay.

September: Inle Lake Boat Festival on the full moon of the sixth month insures a spectacular sporting and religious time held in Nyaungshwe during which five Buddha images from Paung Daw Pagoda are placed on royal barges and ceremonially pulled around the lake by leg rowers.

October: The end of Buddhist Lent on the full moon of the seventh month, also called the Festival of Lights, celebrates the Buddha's return from heaven and the end of the rainy season when young monks return home.

November: Tazaung Daing Festival on the full moon of the eighth month features homes illuminated with votive candles, handmade lanterns, and unmarried women who weave new robes for monks.

December: Nat Festivals on the full moon of the ninth month honor spirits with trance dances performed by transvestites and *nat kadaws* (spirit wives), professional prophetesses considered married to insatiably polygamistic *nats.*

ing within national boundaries. Burmese males typically wrap themselves in a plain or checkered *longyi* tied directly in front and don a Western T-shirt or a short, tight-fitting jacket of Chinese design known as an *ingyi*. On formal occasions, men add a *gaungbaung* or turban of brightly colored strips of silk wrapped around a small wicker basket balanced on the head. Ladies prefer flowered *longyi* tied seductively on the hip.

Burmese society is remarkably free of class and caste distinctions. Burmese women enjoy equal opportunities to education, full property rights, and maintain almost complete control of family money matters and choice of partner.

ON THE ROAD

GETTING THERE

Air

Most visitors arrive by air at Yangon International Airport, served from Bangkok by Thai International (daily; US$230 roundtrip), Myanmar Airways International (daily; US$220 roundtrip), and Biman Bangladesh (once weekly; US$160-200). Thai International is by far the most dependable airline but travelers heading west to Bangladesh might consider the weekly Bangkok-Yangon-Dhaka flight with Biman Bangladesh. Myanmar Airways International (MAI) should only be regarded as a last resort due to safety concerns.

Flights are also available from Singapore on Silk Air and MAI (daily; US$250 roundtrip), Kuala Lumpur on Malaysian Airlines and MAI (daily; US$250 roundtrip), and Hong Kong on Cathay Pacific and MAI (three times weekly; US$280 roundtrip). Air China flies once a week from Kunming to Yangon.

Onward tickets should be reconfirmed at the airport or at an airline office in Yangon. A departure tax of US$6, payable in dollars or FECs, is collected at the airport prior to your departing flight.

Airport Arrival

Airport formalities can be time consuming but those who arrive first can generally get through the airport in 20-30 minutes. Visitors must first stop at immigration and then customs where a form must be completed that lists all valuables such as electronics, cameras, and jewelry.

After picking up luggage from the conveyor belt, visitors are expected to stop at the Foreign Exchange Certificate (FEC) counter and exchange US$300 for 300 FECs, used for payment at hotels, airlines, and trains. FECs are useful and can be easily exchanged into *kyat* or U.S. dollars—there's little reason to avoid this exchange requirement.

Travelers who would rather not make this exchange can often slip past the FEC counter or request that a smaller amount be exchanged. Burmese officials at the airport appear rather unconcerned about this exchange requirement since you'll probably need to purchase some FECs at some point to pay for officially approved hotel rooms or government-regulated transportation such as internal flights or the express train from Yangon to Mandalay.

Other Entry Points

A few alternatives exist from the standard flight from Bangkok.

From Mae Sai: Western visitors can enter Myanmar from Mae Sai in northern Thailand and then travel 163 km north to Kengtung, the provincial capital of Shan State. Locals and Westerners with proper permits can continue north to the Chinese border and continue to Kunming. Another road heads west from Kengtung, to Taunggyi but remains off-limits since it passes through opium country.

Other Thailand Entries: Three Pagodas Pass west of Kanchanaburi remains closed to Westerners, though Thai and Myanmar officials have discussed opening this land crossing when roads have been sealed. Mae Sot, farther north along the Thai border, is open to local traders but currently closed to foreign tourists.

From China: Entry can also be made from Kunming (China) via the Chinese border town of Ruili to Muse in Myanmar's Shan State. Travelers must join an organized tour in Kunming or make arrangements in advance with a travel agency abroad. The Chinese side has been paved and largely straightened out over the last few years. Hotels and guesthouses are located in both Ruili (China) and Muse (Myanmar) but all demand Chinese Yuan and won't accept U.S. dollars. The road from Muse to Lashio is in poor condition as it follows the original path of the Burma Road, constructed by the Americans during World War II.

Lashio has several guesthouses and a few new hotels under construction. Most travelers continue south to Pyin U Lwin (Maymyo) by train, passing over the impressive Gokteik viaduct. The four-day package tour from Ruili to Maymyo costs US$500-900; independent travel may be permitted in the next few years.

GETTING AROUND

Air
Internal flights are provided by Myanmar Airways (MA), the government-subsidized airline, and Air Mandalay (AM), a relatively new private airline with superior airplanes and expatriate pilots.

Myanmar Airways: MA flies daily between Yangon, Mandalay, Bagan (Nyaung O airport), and Inle Lake (Heho airport). MA also serves remote destinations such as Loikaw, Sittwe (Akyab) Myitkyina, and Myeik (Mergui). Schedules change often and flights are subject to cancellation. Tickets can only be purchased inside the country and payment must be made with Foreign Exchange Certificates (FECs) or U.S. dollars cash (no traveler's checks).

Air Mandalay: A welcome alternative to Myanmar Air is Air Mandalay, which provides punctual departures on comfortable, clean planes flown by a professional staff. The fleet— a joint venture between the government and a Singapore-based aviation company—comprises new ATR 72-210 carriers upgraded in France for a capacity of 66 passengers.

Air Mandalay tickets between Yangon, Mandalay, Bagan, Sandoway, and Heho (Inle Lake) can be booked in Bangkok, Singapore, and Yangon. AM intends to soon provide international connections from Thailand, Malaysia, Singapore, and Hong Kong.

Air Mandalay is 20-30% more expensive than Myanmar Airways, though most visitors feel the improved level of safety and dependable departures are worth the extra fee.

Train
Trains are slow and crowded but provide more comfort and scenery than buses and are certainly cheaper than planes. Trains connect Yangon with Mandalay (the most popular route) and continue north to Myitkyina in Kachin State and Lashio in northern Shan State. From Yangon, trains also head to Pathein (Bassein) and Kyaikto via Bago (Pegu). A new train service is now available from Mandalay to Bagan.

See Yangon for more information on departures from Yangon to Mandalay, Bagan, and Inle Lake.

city bus at Mandalay Hill

Buses
For dozens of years, tour groups were shuttled around in large and comfortable buses while independent travelers were relegated to broken-down buses and packed Datsun pickups— nightmares on wheels packed to the gunwales with cargo and passengers. Fortunately, this situation changed a few years ago with the privatization of the tourism industry.

Private a/c express buses now provide speedy and comfortable service between all the primary tourist destinations. Best of all, tickets can be purchased with local currency instead of dollars or FECs, a situation which makes bus transportation far more economical than by train or plane.

Hired Car
Cars and jeeps can be hired at US$200-350 per week plus gasoline, a great deal that provides flexibility and comfort at a reasonable cost. Drivers can be found around most hotels and guest-houses in Yangon. Be sure to settle all details in

MYANMAR (BURMA)

advance—such as sites to visit and any possible additional costs—and find a driver who speaks good English, knows the country, and has made many extensive excursions.

Motorcycles can be rented from several dealers in Yangon at US$10-20 per day.

River

The river trip from Mandalay to Bagan remains one of the great travel experiences of Myanmar—a drifting journey through ancient Burma past forgotten villages inhabited by people almost completely untouched by the modern world. Ferries, both local and tourist, depart Mandalay twice weekly (Sunday and Thursday) at daybreak, stop briefly at a few small villages to unload vegetables, and arrive just north of Bagan after sunset. The experience is *highly recommended*.

Further travel downriver to Yangon is time-consuming (1-2 days), but also inexpensive and almost completely free of Western tourists. The ferry goes to Pyi where guesthouse owners often greet arrivals. Downriver travel from Pyi may be restricted depending on river conditions but visitors can always catch the overnight train to Yangon.

Other boat trips include Yangon-Bassein, Yangon-Syriam, and Mandalay-Mingun on rickety local craft.

Travelers with bucks can also take the Road to Mandalay river cruise from Mandalay to Bagan operated by Eastern & Orient Express. The five-day tour (US$2,000-3,500) can be reserved in the U.S. (tel. 800-524-2420), U.K. (tel. 928-6000), Australia (tel. 02-232-7499), France (tel. 4562-0069), and Germany (tel. 211-162106).

VISAS AND TRAVEL PERMITS

Visas

Myanmar now grants 28-day tourist visas. Visa applications require three passport-sized photos and cost US$15-20. Most embassies and consulates process the visa application in a single day.

Visas can be extended for an additional 30 days for US$30-40 at the discretion of immigration departments in larger towns. Visitors who overstay their visa are generally fined US$3 per day at the airport.

Travel Permits

Travel permits are not required for the standard tourist destinations of Yangon, Mandalay, Bagan, Inle Lake and most other spots near these tourist sites. Travel elsewhere in Myanmar technically requires a permit issued from the tourist office in Yangon or from an approved travel agency. Permits are free but may require the services of a hired guide.

The situation varies from destination to destination—some places are on the "travel permit" list but can be reached without possession of this permit. Other places, such as Mawlamyin, may require travel permits one week but be off the list the following week. Even the tourist office seems confused about the situation, but they seem to err on the side of safety and claim that almost all destinations outside the tourist quadrangle require permits.

It appears that destinations easily reached with public land transportation and located in relatively safe districts can be visited without a travel permit. Although the tourist office may claim the area requires a travel permit and hired guide, many travelers simply head off toward the destination and try their luck.

Travel permits are required for remote destinations near insurgency movements and for places reached only by air, such as Myitkyina, Loikaw, Dawei, and Myeik (Mergui).

Customs

Visitors are permitted the duty-free import of one quart of liquor, 400 cigarettes, and a 500-ml bottle of perfume or cologne. All electronics and other Western valuables must be declared on arrival and taken out of the country on departure.

MONEY

Myanmar operates with three currencies—Myanmar *kyat,* Foreign Exchange Certificates (FECs), and U.S. dollars.

Kyat

The Myanmar *kyat* (pronounced chat), the national currency, is divided into 100 *pya* with banknotes from K1 to K500. All currency should read "Central Bank of Myanmar" rather than the now useless "Union of Burma Bank."

BURMESE LANGUAGE

The people of Myanmar speak over 80 different languages divided into the three linguistic classes of Tibeto-Burman, Mon-Khmer, and Thai-Chinese. The Burmese alphabet has 32 consonants, eight vowels, and four diphthongs. It's a tonal language similar to Thai or Chinese, and like Chinese and Thai, it can easily trip up the beginning student. The script is a curious but delightful track of bubbles taken from the Pali script of South India. English is widely understood by educated Burmese and older citizens who remember the days of the Raj. However, simple courtesies such as special forms of address are always appreciated. *U* (pronounced "oo") is the respectful term for uncle. *Maung* refers to young males but can also be an expression of humility. *Ma* is used for all females up to middle age. *Daw* is used for adult women regardless of marital status.

how are you?—*maa yeh laa?*
I'm fine—*maa bah dai*
good morning—*min ga la baa*

thank you—*kyai zoo tin baa dai*
goodbye—*pyan dor mai*
excuse me—*kwin pyu baa*
do you understand?—*kin bar nar lai tha laa*
I don't understand—*chun note nar ma lai boo*
where is . . . ?— . . . *beh mah lai?*
bus stop—*bas car hmat tine*
railway station—*bu dar yon*
police station—*yeh sa khan*
hospital—*say yon*
how much?—*bah lout lai*
too much—*myar dai*
drinking water—*thow yea*
beef/chicken/fish—*ah meh tar/beh tar/ngar*
mutton/pork/rice—*seik tar/wet tar/san*
1, 2, 3,—*tit/nit/thone*
4, 5, 6,—*lay/ngar/chak*
7, 8, 9, 10,—*kun nit/shit/ko/ta sair*
100—*ta yar*

The official exchange rate is 5.5 *kyat* per dollar while the black market exchange rate hovers around K300 per dollar—a ridiculous spread designed to fleece foreign investors. With the introduction of Foreign Exchange Certificates, Western visitors no longer need to worry about this situation and certainly never need exchange dollars at the absurdly low rate.

Kyat are used to purchase items in small markets, cafes, local transportation, and other venues unsupervised by the government.

Foreign Exchange Certificates

Myanmar's secondary form of legal currency is Foreign Exchange Certificates (FECs), which serve as a substitute for U.S. dollars. FECs are equal in value to U.S. dollars and can be legally used as currency anywhere in the country. Ordinary citizens are permitted to possess, trade, and accept FECs, unlike U.S. dollars which remain a restricted currency. FECs are also freely convertible into *kyat* at free-market exchange rates.

FECs can be purchased upon arrival at the Yangon airport and later at tourist offices, the Central Bank of Myanmar, Foreign Trade Bank, and state-owned hotels. The purchase can be made with U.S. dollars or British pounds sterling in the form of cash, traveler's checks, or credit cards. Australian dollars are not accepted. Exchange rates are fairly uniform from the outlets mentioned above, though some travelers report that better rates are offered at the Central Market in Yangon.

FECs or U.S. dollars are required at most hotels and guesthouses, airlines, and larger souvenir stores and will be needed for airline and train tickets.

U.S. Dollars

The dollar is a "restricted currency" off-limits to most citizens and legally accepted only by licensed establishments such as hotels and airlines. In reality, many merchants will accept dollars since U.S. currency can be used to purchase foreign goods unavailable with *kyat* and FECs.

Bring along a supply of small-denomination dollars to help in emergency situations and to maximize return with independent merchants.

MYANMAR (BURMA)

Credit Cards

Visa, MasterCard, American Express, and Diners Club are accepted at a few hotels and travel agencies in Yangon and Mandalay. They are also honored by Air Mandalay and for cash advances at the Foreign Trade Bank in Yangon. High service charges are prohibitive, and the limited acceptance makes using credit cards a dicey bet in the near term.

TRAVEL PRACTICALITIES

Tourist Information

Myanmar Travels and Tours (MTT), formerly known as Tourist Burma, is at 77 Sule Pagoda Road, tel. (01) 278376, fax 289588, near Sule Pagoda in Yangon. Branch offices are located in Mandalay, Bagan, Taunggyi, Sittwe, and Sandoway. MTT has a few outdated brochures and maps and largely exists to sell expensive tours to unsuspecting tourists.

The decline of the MTT is due to the privatization of the tourism industry which resulted in the creation of hundreds of new travel agencies, most of which provide superior services at better prices. Today there are very few reasons to visit the MTT offices aside from purchasing an express train ticket between Yangon and Mandalay or an express boat ticket from Mandalay to Bagan.

Communications

Mail service from Myanmar is unreliable, though postcards and aerograms seem to arrive without major problems. Important packages should be sent via private services in Yangon such as DHL and Mercury Air Cargo.

International and domestic phone calls can be made from Central Telephone & Telegraph (CTT) offices located in larger towns. The country code for Myanmar is 95. Area codes include Yangon (01), Bago (052), Lashio (082), Kengtung (101), Meiktila (064), Monywa (071), Myitkyina (074), Pathein (042), Pyin U Lwin (085), Sagaing (072), Sittwe (043), Taunggyi (081), and Tangoo (054). Yangon city phone numbers changed from five to six digits in 1996, adding a two, five, or six to the old number.

Health

Myanmar is the only country in Southeast Asia where visitors *should* worry about their health. Nausea and diarrhea combined with high heat and primitive tourist facilities can quickly make your vacation an unforgettable ordeal. Eat and drink with extreme caution. Only bottled water, soft drinks, or Mandalay beer should be consumed. Keep the diet simple and safe; avoid dairy products, uncooked vegetables, rich sauces, and spicy dishes. Do not assume that the best hotels or restaurants are okay. Use malaria pills and bring a strong antidiarrheal such as Pepto-Bismol.

YANGON (RANGOON)

A decaying colonial city of 3.5 million—one of Asia's most fascinating relics—probably best described by what it does *not* have: traffic jams, fast-food restaurants, freeways, smog, hordes of tourists, flashy discos, or businessmen in three-piece suits. Yangon still reflects the eastern romance of Conrad and Kipling, a place where little effort had been made to improve or even maintain its appearances since the British left in 1948.

Everything rests in a fine state of decay: palm trees poke through the sidewalks, patches of jungle threaten to swallow much of the city, and buildings remained unpainted for decades. Yangon's infamous platoon of old taxis has been replaced with modern vehicles but many of the buses remain antiquated wrecks held together with wire and glue. In all the world there is no place like Myanmar.

ATTRACTIONS

Myanmar temples and pagodas are sacred no matter their condition and Western visitors are expected to respect Buddhist traditions. Dress conservatively. *Shorts are inappropriate.* Males should wear long pants and a clean shirt, while females should keep well covered. Sandals are better than shoes since footwear must be removed and a shoulder bag for slippers, camera, and water bottle may prove useful.

YANGON (RANGOON)

- NARAWAT CONCORDE HOTEL
- TO AIRPORT
- PHILIPPINES EMBASSY ◆
- MAHA PASAN CAVE ★
- KABA AYE PAGODA ★
- NEW WORLD INYA LAKE HOTEL

INYA LAKE

KABA AYE PAGODA RD.

YANGON UNIVERSITY

- AUNG SAN SUU KYI
- SEDONA HOTEL ●
- SALA THAI RESTAURANT ★
- ARMY CLUB ★
- MAHASI MEDITATION CENTER ●
- HSIMMALAIK BUS TERMINAL (TO BAGO, PATHEIN, KYAIKTO)
- DIETHELM TRAVEL ●
- MYA YEIK NYO HOTEL ●
- CHAUK HTAT GYI PAGODA ★
- NIGHT MARKET ★
- PAN SEA HOTEL ●
- LIBERTY HOTEL ●
- KEMENDINE TRAIN STATION ●
- COMFORT HOTEL ●
- VIETNAM EMBASSY ◆
- NGA HTAT GYI PAGODA ★

PROME RD.

KEMENDINE

- ROYAL HOTEL ●
- SAVOY HOTEL ●
- MARTYR MAUSOLEUM ★
- BAGAN INN ●
- FAME INN ●
- MALAYSIA EMBASSY ◆
- KOE HTAT GYI PAGODA ★
- RESISTANCE PARK
- SHWEDAGON PAGODA ★
- KANDAWGYI HOTEL ●
- KARAWEIK RESTAURANT ★
- PAKISTAN EMBASSY ◆
- THAI EMBASSY ◆
- CRYSTAL PALACE HOTEL ●
- MAHA WIZAYA PAGODA ★
- SUMMIT PARKVIEW HOTEL ●
- ZOO
- SHANGRI-LA HOTEL ●
- CHINA EMBASSY ◆
- MINGALA MARKET ■

ROYAL LAKE

- MUSIC AND DRAMA SCHOOL ★
- THAMADA HOTEL ●
- SAKANTHA HOTEL ●
- TRAIN STATION
- AUNG SAN ST.
- MARKET ★
- DAGON HOTEL ●
- ANAWRAHTA ST.
- MAHABANDOOLA ST.
- SULE PAGODA ★
- MTT ■
- GARDEN GH ■
- YWCA ●
- YMCA ●
- MUSEUM ★
- STRAND HOTEL ● GPO ■
- MERCHANT ST.

YANGON RIVER

0 _____ 1 km

- BOTATAUNG PAGODA ★
- STRAND RD.

© MOON PUBLICATIONS, INC.

MYANMAR (BURMA)

Shwedagon Pagoda

This "Great Pyramid of Fire," which rises like "a sudden hope in the dark night of the soul," towers as the world's most impressive Buddhist shrine—a must-see for all visitors to the country. Situated on Singuttara Hill five km north of city center, Shwedagon rises dramatically above Royal Lake to provide the spiritual heart and soul of Myanmar—a magical fantasy land of countless shrines, pagodas, and holy images that dazzle visitors as well as the endless streams of pilgrims who believe eight sacred Buddha hairs and relics of three previous Buddhas are enshrined within. Shwedagon is best visited late afternoons when temperatures drop and pilgrims' activities increase.

Shwedagon is usually approached up a stairway flanked by a pair of grinning *leographs* or *chinthes,* Myanmar mythological offspring from lions and dogs. Shoes must be checked before climbing the stairway filled with stalls of nirvana goods, headdresses, religious tomes, packages of gold leaf, *thanaka* cosmetics, and marionettes.

At the top you leave the gloom and plunge into one of the world's most brilliant spectacles. Here is the Shwedagon, a Buddhist fantasyland of dazzling golden spires, mysterious images of Buddha, and cheerful *nats,* extraordinary temples of imaginative design, all the magic and mystery conjured up by the Orient. During the cooler parts of the day, hundreds of saffron-clad monks and devotees constantly circle the central pagoda in clockwise fashion.

Dominating the spectacle is the magnificent golden pagoda soaring over 100 meters into the clear blue sky. Burmese royalty over the last five centuries has donated tons of gold and thousands of precious stones. Today the pagoda is entirely sheathed in gold leaf and studded with a remarkable 20,912 bricks of *solid* gold. The tip is set with over 10,000 diamonds, rubies, and sapphires, topped by a gigantic 76-carat diamond.

Open daily 24 hours. Admission is US$5, which includes an elevator ride up to stupa level.

Sule Pagoda

Sule Pagoda served as city center after the British arranged Yangon's grid-street system in the late-19th century around the tallest structure in town—this eight-sided pagoda which attracts a few pilgrims, fortune-tellers, and spirit

SHWEDAGON PAGODA

1. southern stairway
2. Shwedagon Pagoda
3. Temple of the Konagamana Buddha
4. Planetary Post for Mercury
5. Chinese Prayer Pavilion
6. Planetary Post for Saturn
7. Student Commemorative Monument
8. Guardian Nat of Shwedagon
9. Arakanese Pavilion
10. Reclining Buddha
11. Chinese Merchants Pavilion
12. Mai Lamu and King of the Nats
13. Temple of the Kassapa Buddha
14. Two Pice Pavilion
15. western staircase
16. small pavilion
17. small pavilion
18. Planetary Post for Jupiter
19. Planetary Post for Rahu
20. Pagoda of the Eight Weekdays
21. Maha Gandha Bell
22. Assembly Hall
23. Miracle Buddha
24. northwest corner pagoda
25. Wish-granting Spot
26. Chinese Prayer Hall
27. Buddha's Footprint Pavilion
28. northern stairway
29. Library of the Zediyingana Society
30. Sandawdwin Pavilion
31. Temple of the Gautama Buddha
32. Planetary Post for Venus
33. Mahabodi Pagoda
34. gilded pagoda
35. Kannaze Pavilion
36. Shin Itzagona Pavilion
37. Naungdawgyi Pagoda
38. carved pavilion
39. Maha Tissada Bell
40. Planetary Post for the Sun
41. Replica of the Hti
42. Replica of the Lotus Bud
43. Tawagu Buddha
44. Temple of the Kakusandha Buddha
45. eastern staircase
46. Planetary Post for the Moon
47. U Nyo Pavilion
48. Hintha Prayer Pillar
49. Planetary Post for Mars
50. Bodhi Tree with Buddha
51. Shwedagon Museum

SHWEDAGON PAGODA

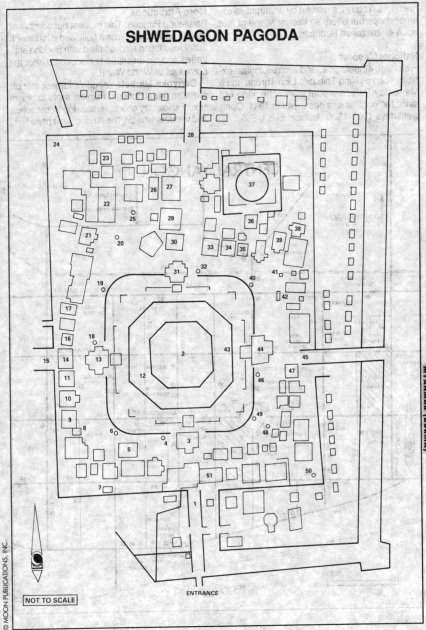

MYANMAR (BURMA)

© MOON PUBLICATIONS, INC.

NOT TO SCALE

ENTRANCE

mediums. Today it's marred by unattractive exterior shops but offers an interior scene of four neon-emblazoned Buddhas.

National Museum

Historical, ethnological, and archaeological exhibits such as King Thibaw's Lion Throne and a Mandalay Palace model worth checking out since the original was destroyed in 1944. Open weekdays 1000-1500. Admission is US$5.

More Attractions

Botataung Pagoda: This modest but somewhat unique pagoda features a hollowed interior with dusty meditation alcoves filled with Buddha statuettes and old inscriptions discovered after the bombings of World War II.

Bogyoke Market: Yangon's largest market provides herbal lotions, magical roots to revive sexual spirits, dry goods, textiles, foods, cassettes, and vendors who cry "Best price, best price."

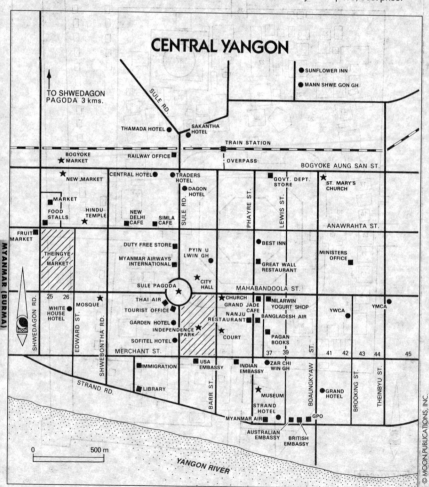

CENTRAL YANGON

Chauk Htat Gyi Pagoda: An open-air shed over a 70-meter reclining Buddha with nicely painted face and feet inscribed with the 108 sacred symbols of Buddhist enlightenment.

Mae La Mu Pagoda: *Nat* monuments and gaudy statues north of Yangon—a deserted and run-down joint somewhat like Hong Kong's Tiger Balm Gardens

Kaba Aye Pagoda: Modern, nondescript pagoda constructed in 1954.

Ah Lain Nga Sint Pagoda: Somewhat intriguing pagoda (1950s) in wedding-cake style with Chinese towers, Muslim minarets, and messy museum with plaster elephants and some antique radios.

ACCOMMODATIONS

Once notorious for its poor quality and limited supply of hotels and guesthouses, Yangon added many new facilities after government restrictions against private hotel ownership were dropped in the early 1990s. The government Web site (www.myanmar.com) lists almost 100 hotels including a dozen newly opened or recently renovated hotels such as the Central Floating Hotel, Kandawgyi Palace, Nawarat Concorde, Ramada, Sofitel, Savoy, Sedona Yangon, Summit Parkview, and Traders Hotel.

Prices are higher than elsewhere in Southeast Asia, but the glut of rooms will probably bring rates down to more reasonable levels in the near future. Payment must be made with either US dollars or FECs.

Budget

Yangon's inexpensive guesthouses and hotels are overpriced by Asian standards and generally in poor condition with rudimentary cubicles priced US$8-15. Bargaining may bring down the price, especially if you offer to skip the simple breakfast, often included in the tariff.

Dagon Hotel: An old favorite just a short walk north of the tourist office. Scheduled for renovation and may reopen under a new name. 256 Sule Pagoda, tel. (01) 289354, US$12-20.

Garden Hotel: Run-down, poorly maintained, and noisy but conveniently located near the tourist office. Another old timer possibly due for renovation or closure. Sule Pagoda Rd., tel. 271140, US$10-20.

Pyin U Lwin Guesthouse: Small featureless rooms redeemed by fairly clean common showers and friendly managers. 183 Mahabandoola Garden St., tel. (01) 274005, US$10-15.

Sunflower Inn: North of the train station—a 15-minute walk from the tourist office—you'll find a very clean place run by helpful Indian owners. 1 Pho Kya Rd., tel. (01) 276503, US$15-20.

White House Hotel: Small, popular 10-room guesthouse a few blocks west of the tourist office. 69/71 Konzaydan St., tel. (01) 271522, US$10-12.

YMCA: Run-down but friendly spot with 20 creaky rooms, baggage storage facilities, and an inexpensive cafe. Admits both men and women. Closed for renovation but expected to reopen soon. 263 Mahabandoola St., tel. (01) 294109, fax 296848, US$8-10.

Moderate—Central

Moderate hotels near city center include small renovated guesthouses and modern high-rise hotels geared to tourists and budget-minded business travelers.

Best Inn: Popular hotel with clean a/c rooms in the center of town two blocks east of the tourist office. 96/98 Pansodan St., tel. (01) 286058, fax 286058, US$45-65.

Central Hotel: Opened in 1997; convenient location with simple, clean, a/c rooms plus decent Cantonese restaurant. 335 Bogyoke Aung San St., tel. (01) 278472, fax 272324, US$60-100.

Euro-Asia Hotel: Modern high-rise hotel two km east of city center with seven floors of clean a/c rooms with private bath, mini-fridge, and TV. 374 Strand Rd., Botataung, tel. (01) 296731, fax 289960, US$30-50.

Lai Lai Hotel: Tall, narrow, newish hotel two km west of city center in Yangon's Chinatown (Lanmadaw district) with a/c rooms, satellite TV, and complimentary breakfast. 783 Mahabandoola Rd., tel. (01) 227878, fax 225913, US$35-55.

Thamada Hotel: Older hotel now privately managed with spacious if somewhat sterile socialist-era rooms in a fairly handy location one block north of the train station. Renovated in 1997 with refurbished bar, restaurant, and deli. 690 Sule Pagoda Rd., tel. (01) 271477, US$65-90.

Three Seasons Hotel: Small but well-maintained property with homey atmosphere, traditional-style a/c rooms with private bath, about two km east of city center. 83/85 52nd St., Pazungdaung, tel. (01) 293304, fax 297946, US$40-65.

MYANMAR (BURMA)

Moderate—North

North of city center you'll find several new hotels and a few residences converted into cozy guesthouses—either modern homes or refurbished colonial mansions.

Bagan Inn: Three modern residences converted into a well-decorated hotel a few blocks north of Kandawgyi Lake. 29 Natmauk Lane, tel. (01) 550489, fax 549660, US$40-70.

Liberty Hotel: Two-story colonial mansion with parquet floors, high ceilings, floral wallpaper, bright green carpets, spacious rooms and a modern annex plus coffee shop some 15 minutes north of city center. 343 Pyay Rd., tel. (01) 530050, fax 524144, US$45-60.

Royal Hotel: Converted mansion just north of Shwedagon with spacious, well-furnished rooms without the sound and fury of downtown hotels. 140 Dhammazedi Rd., tel. (01) 284695, fax 524158, US$40-60.

RESTAURANTS

Burmese

Burmese meals generally consist of rice with sides of curried fish, chicken, or vegetables plus the national side dish *ngapi*, a strong-smelling fish paste. Best bets are thick fish-and-noodle soup *(mohinga)*, clear vegetable soup *(hingyo)*, superb Burmese tea leaf salad, and rice seasoned with coconut. Burmese food is enjoyable in households but disappointing in most cafes and restaurants which serve bland curries, mysterious soups, and foul drinks.

Mandalay beer is great on a hot day . . . if the brewery isn't broken down, out of hops, or short on bottle caps.

Aung Thuka: Simple cafe with dozens of pots filled with outstanding Burmese curries and vegetarian dishes. 17 1st St., no phone. Open daily 1000-1900. Inexpensive.

Hla Myanmar: Another authentic Burmese cafe with elemental yet elegant dishes served from cooking pots. 27 5th St., Bahan, tel. (01) 526822. Open daily 1000-1900. Inexpensive.

Hi Top Cafe: Standard Burmese fare enhanced by excellent evening views of Shwedagon. 235 Pyay (Prome) Rd., tel. (01) 220003. Inexpensive.

Bamboo House: Considered among the best Burmese restaurants in Yangon. 3 Thapye Nyo Street northwest of the Shwedagon Pagoda. Take a taxi. Moderate.

Street Stalls: Burmese vendors gather near the YMCA. Bo Galay Bazaar Street. Inexpensive.

Asian

Chinese is Yangon's most common Asian cuisine but you'll also find a few Thai and Indian cafes hidden away in the back alleys.

Sala Thai: Teak Thai-style building with comprehensive menu and tables set indoors or outside around a small pond. 56 Sayasan Rd., Bahan, tel. (01) 548661. Moderate.

New Delhi Restaurant: Wide selection of Indian dishes both vegetarian and non-vegetarian. Anawrahta at 29th Street. Inexpensive.

Kandawgyi Hotel: Cozy lakeside setting with excellent Burmese, Chinese, and Thai specialties plus weekend Burmese music and dance. Kanyeiktha Road. Moderate.

YMCA: An old favorite under renovation with budget Chinese and Indian dishes served buffet style on the main floor.

Palace Restaurant: Perhaps the best Chinese restaurant in Yangon. Sichuan or Hokkien specialties are expensive but portions are generous. 84 37th St., near Merchant Street. Moderate.

Nilarwin Cold Drink and Yogurt Shop: Conveniently located near the center of town and a good place for fruit shakes and dairy products. Clean, friendly, and a hangout for Burmese searching for Western goods. 337 Mahabandoola Street. Inexpensive.

SHOPPING

Myanmar has relatively little to offer the shopper aside from a few handicrafts such as lacquerware, Shan shoulder bags, and antique puppets. Like elsewhere in Asia, handicrafts are least expensive at the point of origin. You can save a bundle by using black-market currency or swapping your shirts, cassettes, and ballpoint pens. Among the better buys are lacquerware tables and chests from Bagan. Shan shoulder bags are cheapest in the Inle Lake region.

Longyi collectors may want to pick up and then wear the Burmese sarong while traveling around the country. Males wear solids or plaids; ladies wear colorful splashes of tropical flowers. The Burmese will love you for it. Whackin' great che-

MYANMAR (BURMA)

roots are sold by toothy ladies at incredibly low prices. Pay for one and you get a month's supply. Most of the old 19th-century wooden puppets once sold at Shwedagon have now been purchased by antique dealers from Bangkok.

Myanmar's most famous products are precious gems such as rubies, emeralds, and sapphires. Westerners can legally buy precious stones only at the Diplomatic Store in Yangon. Prices are high, and unless you are an expert gemologist, *don't buy gems in Myanmar.* Street stones are just clever Japanese synthetics that convincingly scratch glass.

Where to Shop
Bogyoke Market: Myanmar's largest marketplace has a good selection of handicrafts sold by aggressive touts. Bring Western goods for trading and bargain firmly.

Diplomatic Store: This government-operated store near the tourist office has a poor selection of overpriced handicrafts. Shop first in Bagan and Inle and leave the Diplomatic Store for last-minute purchases.

Other Markets: Yangon's Chinese market is at the intersection of Lanmadaw and Mahabandoola. The Indian Market is on 26th Street just off Anawrahta. Both are worth a quick look, although there isn't much worth buying.

Shwedagon Pagoda: The bizarre bazaar on the southern stairway is packed with bronze Buddhas, tattoo instruments, newly manufactured puppets, and other religious paraphernalia. The most intriguing shopping opportunity in Myanmar.

Bookstores: U Ba Kyi's Bagan Book House in the narrow alley at 100 37th Street has a surprisingly good selection of books for sale and he actively purchases any books on Myanmar or Southeast Asia. Other bookstores include Theingi Maw Book Shop at 355 Maung Taulay Street and the street stalls on Sule Pagoda Road.

PRACTICALITIES

Tourist Information
The main office of Myanmar Travel and Tours (MTT, the former Tourist Burma) is at 77 Sule Pagoda Road in the center of Yangon. MTT arranges tours, sells maps, and changes money in the back office but has little useful travel information aside from a handful of brochures. The office is open daily 0800-2000.

Diplomatic Offices
Yangon can be a handy place to pick up visas for neighboring countries since diplomatic offices are generally very quick and visas can often be purchased with black-market currency. The more popular diplomatic offices are shown on the map; most are open weekdays 1000-1500.

Communications
The GPO at the corner of Strand and Aung Kyaw roads is open weekdays 0930-1630, but mail service is not reliable.

International phone calls can be made from the Central Telephone & Telegraph (CTT) office at the corner of Pansodan and Mahabandoola streets on weekdays from 0800-1600 and weekends 0900-1400. The area code for Yangon is 01. Service is erratic but this is probably the best place in the country to attempt an international call.

Myanmar has two English-language newspapers, the *Working People's Daily* and the *Guardian,* both published by the Peoples Printing and Publishing Works and carefully monitored by the Press Scrutiny Agency.

Myanmar Broadcasting has three English-language radio programs which compete with foreign broadcasts such as the BBC.

Myanmar is six hours *and 30 minutes* ahead of Greenwich mean time . . . Yangon is 30 minutes behind Bangkok standard time! You might want to set your watch back.

Medical Services
Emergency medical attention is best obtained abroad or at the Diplomatic Hospital (tel. 650149) on Kyaikkasan Road near Royal Lake.

GETTING AROUND

Taxis
Chartered taxis are a great way to tour Yangon, but beware of drivers charging outrageous fares. Taxis should cost around US$25 for a full day of touring or US$3-4 per hour. One-way fares should be about US$1-2 depending on the distance. Taxis wait outside the better hotels and licensed vehicles are marked with red plates.

MYANMAR (BURMA)

Buses

Yangon has over 40 bus routes served by older carriages packed to the gunwales and new Japanese models that provide a modicum of comfort. Routes are confusing but the helpful employees in the MTT office are happy to write out bus numbers in Burmese script.

LEAVING YANGON

Air

Internal flights are provided by Myanmar Airways (MA), the government-subsidized airline, and Air Mandalay (AM), a relatively new private airline with superior airplanes and expatriate pilots. See the Introduction for more information on Myanmar Airways (MA) and Air Mandalay, a welcome alternative to MA. Air Mandalay is 20-30% more expensive than Myanmar Airways, though most visitors feel the improved level of safety and dependable departures are worth the extra fee.

Train

Trains are slow and crowded but provide more comfort and scenery than buses and are cheaper than planes. Trains connect Yangon with Mandalay (the most popular route) and continue north to Myitkyina in Kachin State and Lashio in northern Shan State. From Yangon, trains also head to Pathein (Bassein) and Kyaikto via Bago (Pegu).

The Yangon-Mandalay train takes 15-18 hours to complete the 718-km trip with departures at 0600, 1700, 1930, and 2100. Since the countryside is dry and somewhat monotonous, most travelers take one of the nightly express trains which offer reclining seats in first class. Ordinary class condemns you to extremely uncomfortable wooden seats. Sleepers can be reserved though they are in short supply.

Visitors heading to Bagan from Yangon can take a train to Thazi and continue to Bagan by bus or Datsun pickup. Those heading to Inle Lake (Taunggyi) can take the train to Thazi, then a rugged seven-hour bus ride to Taunggyi. Trains cost US$30 to Mandalay and US$27 to Thazi.

Tickets must be purchased from the Yangon tourist office or the "Foreigner Ticket Centre" at the train station. The tourist office accepts Visa, MasterCard, and American Express. Tickets purchased at other railway stations generally require payment in FECs or U.S. dollars but travelers should first attempt to pay with Burmese *kyat*.

Train windows should be kept closed while leaving Yangon unless you enjoy buckets of water thrown by laughing schoolkids.

Buses

For dozens of years, tour groups were shuttled around in large and comfortable buses while independent travelers were relegated to broken-down buses and packed Datsun pickups—nightmares on wheels packed to the gunwales with cargo and passengers. Fortunately, this situation changed a few years ago with the privatization of the tourism industry.

Private a/c express buses now provide speedy, comfortable service between all the primary tourist destinations. Best of all, tickets can be purchased with local currency rather than with dollars or FECs, a situation which makes bus transportation far more economical than by train or plane.

Most buses to northern destinations leave from the Highway Bus Centre just southwest of the airport in Mingaladon. Private buses are about twice the cost of public buses but provide greater comfort and are generally much quicker. Travelers without a bus reservation can arrive at the Highway Bus Centre early in the morning and check with any of the bus offices, which are grouped according to destination.

Bus tickets can also be purchased in advance from bus offices located downtown such as Rainbow Express at 96/98 Pansodan St., Skyline Express at 284 Seikkantha St., Trade Express at 9 Yawmingyi Street in Dagon, and Myanmar Arrow Express at 19/25 Aung San Stadium. Most bus companies provide shuttle from your hotel to the bus terminal.

Buses to Bago, Pathein, and Kyaikyo leave from the Hsimmalaik Bus Centre in northwest Yangon a few blocks west of Inya Lake near the Hledan Railway Station.

MYANMAR (BURMA)

VICINITY OF YANGON

THANLYIN (SYRIAM) AND KYAUKTAN

Syriam (now called Thanlyin), just across the river from Yangon, was a major European trading post during the 15th and 16th centuries. The city was established by a Portuguese adventurer named De Brito soon after his gang of mercenaries sacked Bago in 1599. Initially it appeared that the De Brito and the Portuguese were about to establish a colonial outpost in lower Myanmar, but reinforcements from Goa were not forthcoming, and Syriam fell to the Burmese in 1613. Sentenced to death, it is said that De Brito survived for three days after a sharpened stake was driven through his vital organs.

Syriam today is little more than a sleepy backwater blessed with Myanmar's largest oil refinery and the People's Brewery. Buses and trucks reach Thanlyin from a halt on Sule Pagoda Road opposite City Hall.

Kyauktan Pagoda

Twelve km south of Thanlyin and situated on a small island is the Kyauktan Pagoda (Ye Le Paya Pagoda), with temple murals and sacred catfish kept fat by devout pilgrims. Buses from Syriam take about 30 minutes.

BAGO (PEGU)

Bago, ancient capital of Myanmar and storehouse of Myanmar culture, is a fascinating side trip just 80 km northeast of Yangon. The city was established by King Byinnya, who had transferred his Talaing capital from Martaban in 1365. Hamsawaddy kings during the next three centuries erected dozens of monuments which survive today as the city's major monuments.

In 1541 the Toungoo Dynasty annexed Bago to create Myanmar's second capital before the city was visited in the 16th century by Europeans who described it as the most impressive city in Asia. Constant warfare bankrupted the dynasty. Bago was razed by the ruler of Toungoo in 1599 but enjoyed another brief era of glory as a 17th-century Mon kingdom before being finally destroyed by King Alaungpaya in 1757. Bago today is a modestly sized town with some of the more impressive monuments in Myanmar.

Attractions

Shwemawdaw Pagoda: Soaring to over 110 meters and loftier even than Yangon's Shwedagon, Bagan's magnificent "Great Gold God Pagoda" is among the most venerated and impressive monuments in Southeast Asia. Mythological *chinthe* guard the cool passageways filled with religious souvenirs and fading murals. As at Shwedagon, the terrace is crowded with pilgrims who pray at the planetary posts and make offerings to *nat* and Buddha images. Shwemawdaw alone makes the journey to Bago worthwhile.

pilgrim at Shwedagon

MYANMAR (BURMA)

Maha Kalyani Sima: All of the following are located about three km east of Shwemawdaw. Trishaws can be hired but it's an interesting walk through town and across the Bago River. Continue one km further and then walk north of the main road. Reconstructed Maha Kalyani Sima now serves as a Buddhist ordination hall for hundreds of monks. Pali and Mon tablets to the east are inscribed with histories of Myanmar's trading policies with Sri Lanka and India.

Shwethalyaung Buddha: Constructed in 994 by King Migadippa, this enormous image was abandoned to the jungle until being uncovered in 1881 by British engineers. Many consider the 55-meter reclining image the most lifelike and beautiful in the country.

Mahazedi Pagoda: The great stupa to the north was constructed in 1560 to enshrine a replica of the Buddha's tooth brought from Sri Lanka. Formerly damaged by earthquakes but recently reconstructed. Good panoramic views from the top.

Shwegugale Pagoda: 64 Buddha images encircle the dark interior.

Kyaikpun Pagoda: Constructed in 1476 by King Dhammazedi, this quartet of 30-meter seated Buddhas represents the four historical Buddhas; to the north is Gautama, Konagamana faces south, Kakusandha is east, and the destroyed image of Kassapa once faced to the west. Located four km south of Bago, about 100 meters off the road to Yangon.

Shwegugyi Pagoda: This cluster of ruined monuments was originally built by Dhammazedi after the original prototype in Bodgaya. Located in Payathonzu Village about one km farther toward Yangon.

Accommodations

Several hotels and guesthouses are clustered near the train station on the west side of the Bago River.

Emperor Hotel: A surprisingly large and relatively clean hotel on the main street a few steps east of the train station. Yangon-Mandalay Rd., tel. (052) 21349, US$10-15.

San Francisco Guesthouse: Another acceptable choice near the train station with somewhat smaller but less expensive rooms. Yangon-Mandalay Rd., tel. (052) 21362, US$6-15.

Shwewahtun Hotel: About one km east along the main road just past the Bogyoke Aung San Statue. Yangon-Mandalay Rd., tel. (052) 21263, US$10-20.

Hin Tha Guesthouse: Budget spot near the Shwemawdaw Pagoda. Shwemawdaw Pagoda Rd., tel. (052) 21990, US$5-10.

Getting There

Bago is 80 km northeast of Yangon and is probably best visited with a hired taxi from Yangon, but be sure to agree on the price and all attractions to be visited.

Buses leave Yangon hourly from Latha Street and stop at the Bago bus terminal about one km south of town center. Bago can also be visited on the train back from Mandalay. The station isn't signposted but passengers will point out where to jump off the slowly moving train. Trishaws can be hired at the train station.

SOUTHEAST OF YANGON

KYAIKTIYO

Myanmar's most popular pilgrimage center is the holy rock at Kyaiktiyo, about 160 km east of Yangon. After reaching the base of the mountain at Kinpun, a small town on the Yangon-Mawlamyin train line, it's a five-hour hike up the winding trail to the golden-sheathed, hti-capped boulder which hangs precariously over a deep canyon.

This trek is best accomplished during the dry season and on full-moon evenings from October to May. The summit has sleeping huts, shrines, and cafes.

Accommodations

Mt. Kyaikto Hotel: Most visitors spend the night at the top of the mountain in this overpriced hotel which offers simple bamboo huts and rudimentary rooms overlooking a panoramic valley. US$10-25.

Kyaikto Hotel: Back in town at the base of the mountain is another rough hotel with grungy rooms and cold water showers. US$10-15.

THE ARTS OF MYANMAR

As in other Indianized countries in Southeast Asia, Burmese art received its source of inspiration from older Indian traditions. Prior to the rise of Bagan in the 11th century, the 7th-century Pyu kingdoms of Halin and Sri Kshetra created Indian-derived sculpture of Mahayanic images, funerary urns, and great cylindrical stupas. The western Mons in the lower Ayeyarwady also constructed heavy and graceless temples with narrow, fretted windows and interior frescoes of Theravada inspiration. After the Chinese destroyed the Pyu in 832, Burman immigrants began to settle near Bagan. It was here, during the reign of King Anawrahta, that captive Mon architects and craftsmen constructed a magnificent empire of 5,000 pagodas and temples filled with images and frescoes.

Bagan and the Golden Age of Burmese Arts ended in 1287. The succeeding four centuries were periods of warfare; Burmese arts did not emerge from this period of political instability until the kingdom of Ava was established in 1636. This was the second chance for Burmese arts. After the defeat of the Thais in 1767, royal Siamese dancers were brought back to Ava, where Thai classical *khon* and *lakhon* were used to form the basis of modern Burmese dance. The final century of the Konbaung Dynasty (1783-1885) witnessed a resurgence of architecture, sculpture, and *zat gyi* (masked dance-drama) sponsored by the courts of Amarapura and Mandalay. Artistic creation died when British colonial rule ended state sponsorship and royal patronage.

Burmese Theater

Burmese dance-drama, marionette plays, spirit-medium dances, and classical masked dance are among Southeast Asia's most charming and likeable forms of the performing arts. Best are the *zat pwes*

held during temple festivals and village fairs. Starting in the evening around 2100 and finishing just before sunrise, this "people's theater" combines unrestrained dance and melodramatic action with Punch-and-Judy comedy and exuberant music. Among the 100 performers who parade across the stage are a dozen clowns who keep the audience howling with their wild antics. Stories are taken from Buddhist Jatakas, which recount early incarnations of Buddha, or from Indian epics such as the Ramayana. Stories set in classical periods of Burmese history are also popular. But rather than the serious retelling of old Buddhist or Hindu legends, Burmese theater is extraordinarily lively, warm, and full of good humor, and reflects the friendly personality of its people. If you enjoy the Burmese disposition, then you will love their theater. Dramatics are backed by a Burmese *saing* orchestra similar to Indonesian *gamelan* but with an additional circle of nine tuned drums and a 13-string harp. Although the music is atonal and based on the pentatonic scale, it ranks second only to Indonesian *gamelan* in terms of beauty and appeal.

Unfortunately, with only a 15-day visa and the disorganized state of Myanmar's tourist industry, it can be very difficult to find a performance. You must ask everyone from hotel employees to cigarette salesmen. Performances are generally held on temple grounds under a full moon night during the dry season from October to May. Visitors interested in *zat pwe* should arrange their visits to coincide with a full moon and then look for the makeshift bamboo stages on the grounds of Buddhist temples. Nightly dance performances in Yangon's Karaweik Restaurant are touristy but still highly recommended for the superb costumes and outstanding technique. Burmese puppet shows can be seen in Bagan.

MYANMAR (BURMA)

Transportation

Kyaiktiyo is a vaguely legal destination which may or may not require a permit from the authorities in Yangon. Buses leave Yangon from the Highway Bus Centre near the airport and take about eight hours along a rough road. Permits may be checked on this bus route.

The permit situation and lengthy journey make Bago a preferable departure point for Kyaiktiyo. A train leaves Bago for Kyaiktiyo daily at 0430 and takes three hours to reach Kinpun at the base of

the mountain. Permits are rarely checked on the train but may be checked at the trailhead. Visitors without permits are generally charged an additional US$5 above the US$4 admission fee.

MAWLAMYIN (MOULMEIN)

Kipling probably was referring to the Kyaikthanlan Pagoda when he wrote "By the old Moulmein Pagoda, looking lazy at the sea," but given his powers of imagination it is possible that he wrote the lines while having tea aboard his tramp steamer. In any event, the former Moulmein remains a far more idyllic and authentic experience than the more progressive cities of Yangon and Mandalay.

Mawlamyin appears to be an open destination and few visitors have been required to produce a permit, though this should be checked with the MTT prior to departure from Yangon.

Attractions

East of city center along a cragged ridge are five pagodas and monasteries constructed in Mon and later styles of Burmese architecture.

Chief draw is the stupendous Kyaikthanlan Pagoda, the tallest and most romantically situated stupa in the former teak exporting center. The nearby Mahamuni Pagoda features Mon-style buildings linked by covered brick walkways. More contemporary is Seindon Mibabya Kyaung, a century-old monastery once favored by the queen of King Mindon Min. Aung Theikdi, a silver and gold-plated chedi, completes the parade of monuments which overlook the city.

Back in town, the main attraction is the Mon Cultural Museum dedicated to the indigenous peoples of the region. South of Mawlamyin is a large Allied war cemetery and the beach resort of Amherst once popular with British colonialists.

Accommodations

Few travelers visit Mawlamyin which means that accommodations are limited to a few overpriced hotels and guesthouses which change ownership and location with the seasons.

Mawlamyin Hotel: Best digs in town with well-maintained bungalows in the northwestern corner of town. Mottama Rd., tel. (032) 22560, US$45-65.

Breeze Rest House: Simple homestay with dorms and basic rooms at reasonable prices. 6 Strand Rd., US$4-10.

Transportation

Myanmar Airways flies twice weekly from Yangon for US$65-75 and once weekly from Mandalay for US$75-85.

Buses from Yangon take around 12 hours and terminate in Mottama, just across the river from Mawlamyin. A more comfortable option are the twice daily express trains which take eight hours and cost US$8 in upper class.

MANDALAY

Myanmar's second-largest city is one of the most romantic place-names in the English language. Whether it was Kipling's famous verse about those flying fish on the Road to Mandalay or that old Bob Hope movie, this sprawling city has an image that most tourist-promotion departments would kill for.

Mandalay is the cultural heart of Myanmar, where the most refined dance and music traditions survive and where Burmese is spoken in its purest form. Although much of the city was destroyed during WW II, surviving monasteries and temples stand as some of the finest wooden structures in the country.

Nearby attractions include several former capitals with splendid secular and religious architecture, tremendous pagodas, and a British hill resort with a fascinating market and a nostalgic colonial hotel. Some complain about the hot climate and are disappointed with the monotonous modern architecture, but most visitors leave satisfied with their brief look at Myanmar's northern city.

History

Mandalay takes its name from Mandalay Hill, which according to legend was climbed by the Buddha, who pointed across the plains and prophesied that a magnificent city would be built on the 2,400th anniversary of his birth. Much of the region remained a deserted plain until about 2,400 years later when King Bagan Min (1845-1852) established the capital of his Konbaung Dynasty in nearby Amarapura. Dynamic but headstrong and fond of grandiose construction projects, Bagan Min financed his building mania by killing his rich subjects, collecting their fortunes, and forcing the remainder of his citizenry to work on his mad projects. British irritation with the bloody reign of Bagan Min resulted in the systematic dismemberment of lower Myanmar.

AYEYARWADDY RIVER

MANDALAY

MANDALAY HILL

KYTHODAW PAGODA

KYAUKTAWGYI PAGODA

SANDAMUNI PAGODA

MOAT

ATUMASHI MONASTERY

ROYAL PALACE

SHWENANDAW MONASTERY

KING MINDON'S MAUSOLEUM

PALACE RECONSTRUCTION

MUSIC AND DRAMA SCHOOL

C ROAD

24 ROAD
GPO
SHWEKYIMYINT PAGODA
25 ROAD
26 ROAD
MUSEUM

INWA HOTEL

TO MINGUN BOAT

NYLON ICE CREAM BAR

EINDAWYA PAGODA

ZEGYO MARKET

27 ROAD

28 ROAD

MANDALAY HOTEL
MANDALAY NEW HOTEL

MYA MANDALA HOTEL
MARIONNETES

TOO TOO RESTAURANT

POPA 1 HOTEL

HONEY GARDEN RESTAURANT

SILVER CLOUD HOTEL

29 ROAD

SETKYATHIHA PAGODA
30 ROAD
31 ROAD

RAILWAY STATION

32 ROAD

TEXAS BAR

33 ROAD

PALACE HOTEL

79 ROAD

34 ROAD

35A ROAD

SHANGHAI HOTEL

SEA HOTEL

TO PYIN U LWIN (MAYMYO)

TO BAGAN BOAT

84 ROAD
83 ROAD
82 ROAD
81 ROAD
80 ROAD

SHWEINBIN MONASTERY

TIGER HOTEL

KINWUN MONASTERY

BUDDHA MAKERS

TO AMARAPURA, AVA AND SAGAING

MAHA MUNI PAGODA

TO AIRPORT

MOON

0   400 m

MYANMAR (BURMA)

© MOON PUBLICATIONS, INC.

Following the embarrassing fiasco of the second Anglo-Burmese war, Bagan Min was deposed by his half-brother Mindon Min (1852-1878), who, according to the tradition of the time, moved his capital to a new location determined by Brahmanic court astrologers. To please the Brahmin priests and fulfill the 2,400-year-old prophecy of the Buddha, Mindon Min ordered his capital transferred from Amarapura to Mandalay in 1860. As a devoutly religious leader who believed he had truly reached Buddhist enlightenment, Mindon Min was determined to make his Golden City the new center of Buddhist teachings. Among his religious achievements was the convocation of the Fifth Buddhist Council in 1879, which recited and engraved the complete Buddhist Tripitaka on the marble slabs at Kythodaw Pagoda. While regarded by the British as a welcome change from his nutty predecessors, Mindon was also a ruler plagued by royalist rebellions, archaic court traditions that forced all British envoys to remove their shoes in his presence, and medieval traditions that scandalized the Western world. When the foundations of his royal palace were laid in 1858, three people were buried *alive* under each gatehouse, plus one more under each corner of the palace wall. Four more victims were entombed under the Lion Throne. A total of 52 terrifying deaths were ordered in the belief that the trapped spirits would continue to guard the city from ruinous plagues and foreign invaders.

Mindon Min was succeeded after his death in 1878 by young King Thibaw and his strong-willed queen. Thibaw made international headlines and shocked the world when he and his domineering queen systematically ordered 80 of their closest friends and relatives massacred to discourage royal rebellion. London newspapers reported that the murders were committed during a noisy three-day *pwe* to drown out the screams. According to royal protocol, each victim was placed in a red velvet bag and respectfully beaten to death; princes by light blows on the back of the neck and princesses on the throat. Mandalay's foreign colony had hardly recovered from this horrific display when royal court astrologers demanded the sacrifice of an additional 600 people to stop a smallpox epidemic; 100 were to be foreigners.

Mass roundups were ordered and a wave of terror seized the city. Wholesale evacuation quickly followed as thousands of terrified Burmese packed onto whatever paddle wheelers were leaving the city. Massacres and Thibaw's political overtures toward the French proved to be the final straws for the British, who ordered warships up the Ayeyarwady. Mandalay was captured on 29 November 1885, and the final Burmese kingdom came to an crashing end.

ATTRACTIONS

Burmese temples and pagodas are considered sacred. All visitors are expected to respect Buddhist tradition and dress conservatively. *Shorts are inappropriate when visiting Buddhist shrines.* Long pants and a clean shirt should be worn by males. Women must be well covered. Sandals are better than shoes since all footwear must be removed before entering temples.

All major sightseeing attractions now carry admission fees of US$2-4, a source of complaint for the MTT which administers the tourist attractions. The only way to avoid these fees is to arrive before 0700 or after the guards go home at 1700.

Mandalay Hill

This dry and dusty 236-meter hill with its 1,729 steps is where most visitors start their tour of Mandalay. Three covered stairways wind their way up to the summit, though most visitors climb up the southern staircase guarded by two gigantic *chinthe*. This long but relatively easy climb takes about two hours and passes Buddha images, dozing monks, souvenir stalls, astrologers, and beautiful Burmese women languorously smoking cheroots.

Halfway up are the Pershawar Relics, perhaps the world's only authentic bones of the Buddha. According to Buddhist legend, after his cremation his bones were enshrined under eight stupas located in India. Three centuries later the chambers were opened by King Ashoka, who distributed the holy relics to various Buddhist strongholds. Finally, in 1908 a British Museum curator named Dr. Spooner uncovered some of the bones in Pershawar. These were presented to the Burmese Buddhist Society who placed them on Mandalay Hill. Incredibly, the shrine is almost completely ignored.

Farther up the mountain is the gold-plated Shweyattaw Buddha, whose standing and pointing pose uniquely commemorates the legendary visit and prophecy of the Buddha. Difficult to photograph because of cramped quarters and poor lighting. Views from the summit over the misty Shan hills and Ayeyarwady plain are impressive on crisp mornings but disappointing on hot and hazy afternoons.

Kyauktawgyi and Sandamuni Pagodas
Constructed in 1878 by King Mindon, Kyauktawgyi is chiefly noted for its seated Buddha carved from a single block of Sagyin marble so monstrous that 10,000 men labored almost two weeks to drag it here from the banks of the Ayeyarwady. King Mindon himself instructed the sculptors as to the shaping of the face but as one writer put it, "His pious zeal was greater than his artistic talent for the image, like the building which shelters it, is exceedingly ugly." You will, however, be impressed by the psychedelic neon halo. Fabulous. Surrounding the shrine are the 80 disciples of Buddha, 20 on a side.

The whitewashed pagoda of Sandamuni was constructed over the graves of the royal family members killed during the palace rebellion of 1866. Spread across the pagoda grounds are some 1,774 stone monoliths inscribed with commentaries on the Buddhist Pali Canon.

Kythodaw Pagoda
Built in 1857 by King Mindon, the central pagoda is modeled after the Shwezigon in Bagan and surrounded by a collection of 729 stone slabs inscribed with the complete Buddhist Tripitaka. After Mindon's Fifth Great Buddhist Council of 1879 corrected the sacred Pali texts, a team of 2,400 monks spent six months reciting the entire canon nonstop. Afterward it took stonecutters another six years to carve the world's largest book of man-sized pages protected by individual pagodas. The foyer is now modernized with coin-operated puppet machines where for a few *pya* you can listen to a calliope melody as the puppets gyrate.

Atumashi Monastery
European visitors of the 19th century described this monastery as the most magnificent build-

ing in Mandalay. Although the pagoda, its four sets of priceless Tripitaka, and its colossal figure of Gautama tragically burned down in 1892, the sculpted foundations and stairways still hint at the former magnificence of the building. Photos of the pagoda prior to its destruction can be seen in the nearby Shwenandaw Kyaung Monastery.

Shwenandaw Monastery
This magnificently carved wooden monastery is all that remains of King Mindon's Royal Palace, which was destroyed during WW II. Shwenandaw originally served as the apartment of King Mindon and his chief queen until his death in 1878. His successor, King Thibaw, considered the building haunted by Mindon's ghost and ordered it disassembled and moved to the present location in 1880.

Today it's considered Myanmar's single most outstanding example of 19th-century woodcarving and a must-see for all visitors to Mandalay. Supporting the monastery are dozens of fantastically carved *nagas*. Embellishments surrounding the doors and windows are masterpieces of the woodcarver's art. Inside the cool and dark interior are legions of antique clocks and religious art donated by pilgrims.

State School of Music and Drama
This Performing Arts School on East Moat Road occasionally sponsors public performances. Visitors are welcome to visit the facilities during regular school hours. Myanmar Travel and Tours has details . . . maybe.

Mandalay Fort and Royal Palace
King Mindon's "Center of the Universe" constructed 1859 to serve as the final capital for Burmese kings, a magnificent city-within-a-city replete with Glass Palace and its Water-Feast Throne, a richly decorated monastery where King Thibaw served his priesthood, and an observatory tower where Queen Supayalat helplessly watched British troops enter Mandalay. The palace served as Fort Dufferin during British colonial occupation.

Great efforts were made by Lord Curzon to protect this absolutely unique example of old Burmese palace architecture, but tragedy struck on 20 March 1945, when, despite all possible precautions, British air raids against Japanese

MYANMAR (BURMA)

emplacements ignited fires which completely leveled the palace. For many years, all that remained were the massive walls, dilapidated towers, and a poorly restored tomb of King Mindon.

Then in the mid-1990s, the government began a reconstruction project based on photographic records, plans, and drawings kept at the Department of Archaeology. Today the ferroconcrete re-creation has brought back the principal buildings including the Lion Throne Room, adjoining audience halls, and the treasury.

Shwekyimyint Pagoda

This pagoda northeast of Zegyo Market was established in the 12th century by Prince Minshinzaw, the exiled son of Bagan's King Alaungsithu (1112-1167). As such it significantly predates the founding of Mandalay in the 19th century. The central Buddha image enshrined by Prince Minshinzaw is noteworthy, but the adjacent rabbit warren of pagodas, plaster tableaux, and antiquated mechanical games is modern and somewhat garish.

Eindawya Pagoda

The outstanding proportions and brilliant glaze of this pagoda make it the finest religious edifice in Mandalay. Eindawya was constructed in 1847 by King Mindon to mark the site where he resided before ascending the throne. Inside is a beautiful Buddha image cut from chalcedony, a sparkling combination of quartz and opal. To find this beautiful pagoda follow the unmarked lane that runs west from the market, or walk down 26th toward the river and turn left at the big yellow building.

Setkyathiha Pagoda

This pagoda is known for the five-meter bronze Buddha cast in 1823 at Ava and taken to Mandalay in 1884 during the third Anglo-Burmese war. Even more impressive than the image is the wild electronic halo which alternately spins clockwise and counterclockwise before radiating outwards. This mind-blowing display wins the *Southeast Asia Handbook* Award for Best Special Effects. The courtyard is also worth a wander to see the tableaux telling of the birth, temptations, and enlightenment of the Buddha, and a *bodhi* tree planted by U Nu. To the right of the south gate is an immense reproduction of the hanging golden rock at Kyaiktiyo.

Star Wars *meets the Buddha*

Monasteries and Traditional Crafts

Visitors interested in 19th-century Burmese woodcarving should ask their trishaw driver to stop at the Shweinbin Monastery south of 35th Road and Kinwun Monastery across the Shweta Canal near 41st Road. This neighborhood is a beehive of traditional Burmese handicrafts. Most cottage industries operate from private homes but trishaw drivers know the locations. The hereditary occupation of gold-leaf production is especially interesting to watch. After being melted down, the gold is pounded into extremely thin sheets, pressed between oiled bamboo paper, and sold to worshipers who press the micro-thin leaves onto images of the Buddha.

Other traditional crafts include ivory carving, silk weaving, puppet carving, production of musical instruments, and Buddha-image carving near Maha Muni Pagoda. Other outlying areas for traditional crafts include Amarapura for silk weaving, Ywataung near Sagaing for silversmiths, and Kyithunkyat near Amarapura for bronze- and brassworkers.

Mahamuni Pagoda

Also known as the Rakhine Pagoda from its area of origin. Burmese believe the principal image to be one of only five exact likenesses made during Sakyamuni's lifetime. So highly revered is the image that gold leaf applied by pilgrims has almost completely obliterated all detail—Buddha becomes the Blob. Visitors are welcome to take photographs.

Stacked somewhat haphazardly in the outer courtyard are six famous bronze Khmer sculptures which originally guarded the entrance to Angkor Wat. First hauled off to Ayuthaya by the Thais in 1431, the magical images were then taken to Bago by the Mons in 1564, hauled off to Rakhine in 1600, and finally delivered to Mandalay in 1784. Devotees believe the images can cure illnesses when rubbed on the appropriate spot. Gastrointestinal problems seem common. The courtyard also has inscription stones, a five-ton gong, and a curio museum filled with life-sized statues of Burmese kings.

ACCOMMODATIONS

Budget

Dozens of guesthouses have opened in recent years in the center of town near the main bus terminal and pickup truck halts for Maymyo and other nearby towns. Most offer small, simple rooms with either common or private baths and are priced from US$6-15.

Royal Guesthouse: Popular spot with fairly clean rooms a few blocks north of the Zegyo Market and Central bus terminal. 41 25th St., tel. (02) 22905, US$5-15.

Garden Hotel: Another centrally located hotel with rooms in all price ranges depending on facilities. 174 83rd St., tel. (02) 25184, US$6-25.

Sabai Phyu Guesthouse: Well-maintained modern option just off B Road. 58 81st St., tel. (02) 25377, US$6-15.

Moderate

Mandalay Swan Hotel: Mandalay's former top hotel has 60 rooms with private baths, a strangely deserted restaurant with mediocre Western food, and an upstairs bar that is positively grim. MTT and a money changer are in the lobby. 26th at 68th St., tel. (02) 22499, US$45-85.

Mya Mandala Hotel: This friendly hotel just around the corner from the Mandalay has 50 spacious a/c rooms with attached bathrooms, an outdoor patio, comfortable restaurant, pool and lounge where you can watch Burmese TV on Sunday afternoons. 27th at 69th St., tel. (02) 21283, US$40-55.

Unity Hotel: Downtown hotel with clean a/c rooms furnished with TV, phones, and refrigerators. 27th at 82nd St., tel. (02) 28862, fax 33467, US$45-60.

Luxury

Sedona Mandalay Hotel: New 247-room hotel just south of the former Royal Palace. Facilities include a pool, tennis courts, business center, Planter's Lounge, and Bellini Italian Restaurant. 26th at 66th St., tel. (02) 36488, fax 36499, US$180-240.

Novotel Mandalay: New property situated at the base of Mandalay Hill. Oo Boke Taw Quarter, tel. (02) 356388, fax 35639, US$165-280.

RESTAURANTS

Hotel food may be disappointing but Mandalay has boomed in recent years with dozens of new cafes serving excellent Chinese, Shan, Burmese, and Indian dishes.

Too Too: An old favorite with traditional Burmese dishes served in simple surroundings. 27th St. between 74th and 75th Streets.

Sakantha: Upscale Burmese restaurant with indoor dining and a cooler outdoor garden venue. 72nd St. between 27th and 28th Streets.

Pyigyimon Royal Barge: Reproduction of an old royal barge opposite the Mandalay Swan Hotel with dance and marionettes in the evenings. 26th at 66th Sts., tel. (02) 26779.

Thai Yai: Shan and Burmese specialties served near the Classic and Thailand Hotels. 84th at 23rd Street.

Mann Restaurant: One of Mandalay's most popular Chinese restaurants one block northeast of Zegyo Market. 83rd between 25th and 26th Streets.

Honey Garden Restaurant: Upscale Chinese restaurant in a garden setting with individual dining cabanas. Nicely illuminated in the evenings. 70th at 29th St., tel. (02) 24098.

MYANMAR (BURMA)

Nylon Ice Cream Bar: An oddly named but venerable cafe with safe-to-eat ice cream and Burmese snacks. 176 83rd Street.

Texas Bar: What would Mandalay be without the obligatory Western cafe serving burgers and shakes amid Burmese cowboy decor? 243 80th St. between 31st and 32nd Sts., tel. (02) 24681.

TRANSPORTATION

Air
Myanmar Airways and Air Mandalay fly daily from Yangon to Mandalay. Air Mandalay has announced plans to serve Mandalay from Chiang Mai, Thailand.

A new international airport is now under construction in Tada U township and is expected to be completed by 2001.

Train
Express trains depart Yangon several times daily and take about 14 hours to reach Mandalay. Be sure to take an express train—not the local service—and reserve a reclining seat in first class. Train arrivals in Mandalay are sometimes met by tourism officials who check passports. The trishaw drivers who wait just outside the station charge honest rates to the hotel of your choice.

Trains depart Mandalay daily for Myitkyina, Monywa, and Lashio.

Bus
Private buses from the Highway Bus Centre in Yangon usually take 12-14 hours to Mandalay

and charge US$8-12 depending on the amenities on the bus.

Buses and pick-up trucks depart Mandalay for Bagan, Inle Lake, Lashio, Meiktila, Monywa, and other destinations from the main bus terminal at the corner of 26th and 82nd Streets. Several private bus and pick-up companies also provide transport services from other locations such as 23rd St. near the Classic Hotel, along 25th between 85th and 86th Streets, and at 83rd and 27th Streets.

Guesthouse owners can usually advise on the latest schedules and often help make reservations with private transport companies.

Boat
Purchase boat tickets to Bagan in advance from the Inland Water Transport office at the Gawwein Jetty, at the western terminus of 35th Street.

Getting Around
Mandalay is surprisingly spread out—don't even think about walking around. Considering the extraordinary heat the only practical way to see the sights is with hired trishaw, horse-drawn *tonga,* or bicycle rental. A full-day visit by trishaw to the three main pagoda areas at the base of Mandalay Hill and several others near the center of town should cost US$3-5. Bicycles can be rented from several guesthouses in the center of town.

Buses are also possible: bus 1 to the Mahamuni Pagoda, buses 4 and 5 to Mandalay Hill, and bus 8 to Mahamuni Pagoda, Amarapura, and Ava.

VICINITY OF MANDALAY

AMARAPURA

Located near Mandalay are three ancient cities— Amarapura, Ava, and Sagaing—which once served as capitals for the final Burmese dynasty.

Founded by King Bodawpaya in 1783 to succeed Ava, Amarapura ("City of Immortals") served as capital of upper Myanmar until 1850 when King Mindon moved to Mandalay. As was customary, most of the important wooden monasteries and royal palaces were disas-

sembled and hauled off to the new location. Today, little of Amarapura's royal architecture remains intact, although the two surviving pagodas are worth visiting.

Attractions
Royal Palace Ruins: Most of Amarapura's wooden palace was transferred to Mandalay or subsequently pulled down by the British for road construction. Still standing are the four corner pagodas, a dilapidated watchtower, a rectangular record office, the masonry treasury, and a

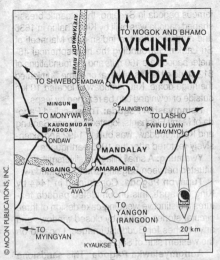

TO MOGOK AND BHAMO

VICINITY OF MANDALAY

AYEYARWADDY RIVER

TO SHWEBO MADAYA

MINGUN

TO MONYWA

KAUNG MUD AW PAGODA

ONDAW

SAGAING

AVA

TO MYINGYAN

KYAUKSE

TO YANGON (RANGOON)

MANDALAY

AMARAPURA

TAUNGBYON

TO LASHIO

PWIN U LWIN (MAYMYO)

MOON

0   20 km

© MOON PUBLICATIONS, INC.

pair of royal tombs where King Bodawpaya and his grandson King Bagyidaw are buried.

Patodawgyi Pagoda: Constructed in 1820 by King Bagyidaw just outside the city walls, this well-proportioned stupa is one of the largest of its kind in Myanmar. Marble panels on three lower terraces are illustrated with scenes from the Jataka tales; good views from the upper terraces.

U Bien Bridge: This two-century-old bridge was constructed by mayor U Bien with teak planks salvaged from the royal city of Ava. The 1.2-km hike across the Taung Thaman lake is hot and tiring but the pagoda on the opposite side is worth the effort.

Kyauktawgyi Pagoda: This impressive replica of the Ananda Pagoda at the far end of U Bien Bridge was constructed in 1847 by King Bagan Min. An immense Buddha cut from green Sagyin jade dominates the interior, which is adorned with frescoes of Burmese nobility, Europeans, zodiac charts, and religious symbolism.

Silk Weaving: Amarapura is Myanmar's center for cotton and silk weaving. Visitors can watch *longyi* weaving in private homes or at the State Cooperative on the main street.

Getting There

Take a pickup truck or bus No. 8 from the corner of 84th and 29th Streets and get off when you see the palace walls on your left and the pagoda on your right. Better yet, organize a group and hire a taxi for the day to tour all three destinations.

AVA

After the destruction of the Kingdom of Bagan, Ava emerged as the new capital of the Burmese kings. Formerly known as Ratnapura ("City of Gems"), Ava was founded in 1364 by King Thadominbya and remained the capital of upper Myanmar for almost 400 years. During this turbulent era, Ava was attacked and conquered in turn by the Mons from Bago and the Burmans from Toungoo. After a disastrous earthquake in 1838 leveled most of the city, the capital was shifted to Amarapura. Today most of the wooden architecture has rotted away and the palace grounds have been plowed for crops, but a few sights are worth visiting.

Attractions

Royal Palace: The Nanmyin Watchtower or "Leaning Tower of Ava" bears testimony to the destructive power of the 1838 earthquake, which almost completely leveled the city. This 27-meter campanile and some city walls are all that remain of King Thadominbya's royal palace.

Maha Aungmye Bonzan Monastery: Constructed in 1818 of stone rather than teak, this outstanding building has fortunately survived the fires and earthquakes that typically destroy wooden monasteries. Note the multiple roofs and wealth of ornamentation on this masonry monastery.

Judson Memorial: The Reverend Adoniram Judson and his wife Ann were American Baptist missionaries in the late 1800s who compiled the first Anglo-Burmese Bible and converted a large number of Burmese to Christianity. Both were briefly held prisoner in Ava. Ann eventually died from fever; Judson was tortured but eventually released to complete his translation work.

Getting There

Take a pickup truck or bus No. 8 from the corner of 84th and 29th Streets in Mandalay and get off just before the Ava Bridge. You can also take bus No. 8 from Amarapura. Walk down to the Myitnage River and take the ferry that crosses to Ava. Another ferry crosses the Ayeyarwady from Ava to Sagaing.

MYANMAR (BURMA)

MYANMAR (BURMA)

SAGAING

Founded in 1315 as a Shan capital, Sagaing served as the capital of upper Myanmar for 60 years. Unlike Amarapura and Ava, Sagaing remains a living city filled with hundreds of pagodas, stupas, caves, and monasteries that attract thousands of monks. Sagaing is typically visited on an organized day tour, although it is possible to overnight in a Buddhist monastery.

Attractions

Thabyedan Fort: Burmese forces mounted their final resistance here against British forces during the third Anglo-Burmese War. This dilapidated fort is located just across the Ava Bridge.

Sagaing Hill: Most of Sagaing's active monasteries are located on this hot and dusty hill. Best views are from Soon U Ponya Pagoda just behind the town of Sagaing.

Kaungmudaw Pagoda: Considered the most

a whackin' great cheroot

famous pagoda in Sagaing, this gigantic breast-shaped pagoda was built by King Thalun in 1636 and modeled after the Indian-style Mahaceti of Sri Lanka. Surrounding the hemispherical 46-meter pagoda are 160 *nats* and the foundations of 812 stone oil lamps which at one time illuminated the huge dome. Kaungmudaw is located 10 km outside of town and can be reached by jeeps.

Hsinmyashin Pagoda: The so-called Pagoda of Many Elephants, located between Sagaing and Kaungmudaw, was built in 1492 and extensively restored after the 1955 earthquake.

Ywataung: A small village of silversmiths also situated between Sagaing and Kaungmudaw.

Tupayon Pagoda: Constructed in 1444 by King Narapati, this uncompleted pagoda features a distinctive wedding-cake design of three circular stories marked by closed windows and anvil niches for Buddhist images. Located on the western side of Sagaing.

Aungmyelawka Pagoda: This sandstone pagoda was built in 1783 by King Bodawpaya, who had it fashioned after the Shwezigon Pagoda in Bagan. Located on the riverfront near the Tupayon.

MINGUN

Mingun is home to the world's largest uncracked bell and the world's greatest brickwork foundation, which, if completed, would have supported the largest pagoda in the world. Both were the ideas of King Bodawpaya, the mad king who conquered Rakhine in 1785 to bring back the venerated Mahamuni and 20,000 slaves to work his megalomaniac building projects. Bodawpaya began his reign of terror with the slaughter of all possible rivals, including the royal family, his generals, their families, and all their servants.

He later punished a traitor by killing every single living thing in the village—human beings, animals, fruit trees, and standing crops. His disastrous and costly campaigns against the Siamese were financed by tax collection so ruthless that his tax records became known as the Doomsday Book.

Attractions

Mingun Bell: Cast in 1790 at the insistence of King Bodawpaya, this iron monster weighs almost 90 tons and is nearly five meters across, second in size and weight only to the cracked bell of Moscow. After completion, the tyrannical king ordered the bronzesmith killed to prevent him from re-creating his masterpiece. Crawl inside and let one of the local boys give it a good ring.

Mingun Pagoda: Convinced that he was the reincarnation of the Buddha, Bodawpaya began construction on his monstrous pagoda in 1790. Some 20,000 Rakhineese slaves worked on his mad project until 1797, when the project was abandoned due to economic and political exhaustion. Nothing on this scale had been attempted since the Egyptian pyramids, and as with the monuments of the pharaohs, the drain on human manpower was so great that society cracked. Entire villages fled into the jungle to escape forced labor. An earthquake in 1838 rent the gigantic cube with fantastic fissures and collapsed the upper section into the treasure vault filled with thousands of gold and silver images, precious stones, and even a soda machine which the crazy king had imported from England. The present pagoda is only one-third the intended size but even in this ruined state it remains a very impressive pile of rock. A pair of ruined *chinthe* guard the entrance.

Settawya Pagoda: Inside the small building, about 10 minutes south of the pagoda, is a Buddha footprint and an attractive seated Buddha backed by a gold-leaf standing Buddha.

Mingun Pagoda Model: This scale model just beyond the Settawya shows what the pagoda would have looked like if completed; enormous but not terribly graceful.

Hsinbyume Pagoda: The layout of this lovely pagoda is based on Buddhist cosmology which places the mythical Mount Meru in the center of seven waving chains of mountains. Hsinbyume lacks detailed carvings and has little of artistic interest, but it's kept nicely whitewashed and offers some good views from the top. The path south from the bell to this pagoda is home to some amazing old Buddhist nuns who cheerfully collect alms, smoke cigars, and pose for photographs.

Getting There

Riverboats leave Mandalay's 26th Street pier hourly until early afternoon. Boatmen often sell tickets on board, making it possible to avoid the overpriced ticket from the tourist office. Mingun is a full-day trip, so start early and remember that

the last boat returns to Mandalay at 1600.

This one-hour ride is a crowded, hot, but fascinating journey past graceful sailboats and immense rafts made of teak. A short stop is made at a muddy village before finally reaching Mingun. Walk straight ahead through the tea stands and Buddhist infirmary to the big bell. Mingun Pagoda is to the left. About 200 meters farther south is the Settawya Pagoda and finally the scale model of the pagoda. The Hsinbyume Pagoda is about 300 meters north of the bell.

PYIN U LWIN (MAYMYO)

Located on the edge of the Shan Plateau about 67 km northeast of Mandalay, this former British hill station is a great place to escape the searing heat of the lowlands and relax in an old English hotel. Pyin U Lwin was established in 1886 by Col. May of the 5th Bengal Infantry Regiment as a summer retreat for British colonials stationed in Mandalay.

Despite 40 years of neglect, Pyin U Lwin retains the broad avenues, carefully tended vegetable gardens, and classically designed churches favored by the British. Sightseeing highlights include a fascinating morning market attended by Shan tribespeople, miniature stagecoaches which serve as local taxis, and a timeless atmosphere little changed from the days of Kipling.

The Burma Road

Pyin U Lwin is also the beginning of the famous Burma Road, which once served as supply route between the Americans and the beleaguered forces of Chiang Kai-shek. With the invasion of China by the Japanese in the 1930s and the retreat of Chiang's forces to Kunming, the Americans decided to construct a road to supply Chiang's resistance movement against Japanese forces. Winding 800 km through some of the world's densest jungle, the Burma Road took three grueling years and the services of some 40,000 laborers to complete before being seized by the Japanese.

The Allies then began an airlift of military hardware across the Hump, a treacherous line of 6,000-meter mountains which eventually claimed over 600 planes and the lives of some 1,000 pilots. One ridge became so littered with wreckage that pilots nicknamed it Aluminum-Plated Mountain.

Allied forces in 1944 constructed the Stilwell Road, which connected northern Burma to Ledo in India. Both the Stilwell and Burma Roads were abandoned after the war and have presumably returned to jungle.

Paul Theroux's *Great Railway Bazaar* has an amusing account of his attempt to travel the Burma Road.

Attractions

Pyin U Lwin Market: Each morning dozens of ethnic groups from the Shan states can be seen shopping in this fascinating bazaar. Among the sights are farmers in distinctive fan-shaped hats, young monks collecting alms, and turbaned ladies shopping for English produce such as cabbages, cauliflower, and ripe strawberries.

Stagecoaches: Lined up just alongside the bazaar are a half-dozen miniature coaches that resemble transport of the American Wild West. These 19th-century carriages can be hired to tour outlying attractions for about K30 per hour. Pyin U Lwin also has some amazing buses constructed entirely of wood.

Botanical Gardens: This 432-acre garden is located about one km south of town.

Waterfalls: Pwe Kauk Waterfall is located about eight km north of town and is fairly easy to reach. The more spectacular Anisakan Waterfall is 10 km west on the road to Mandalay.

Accommodations

Although the majority of visitors heads directly to the Candacraig Hotel, almost a dozen guest-houses and hotels are now licensed to accept Western travelers.

Golden Dream Hotel: Budget place near Purcell Tower with fairly clean rooms. 42/43 Mandalay-Lashio Rd., tel. (085) 22142, US$5-8.

Ruby Guesthouse: Right in the center of town; rooms in various sizes with either common or private bath. 54 Mandalay-Lashio Rd., tel. (085) 22494, US$5-20.

Candacraig Hotel: Colonial-style hotel and among the best reasons to overnight in Pyin U Lwin. Originally constructed in 1906 as a chummery for the staff of the Bombay-Burmah Trading Company and ungraciously renamed the Thiri Myaing Hotel by tourism officials, the Candacraig is located about five blocks up the hill from the center of town. Enjoy a roaring fire in the evening and their British dinner of meat and potatoes. Large and funky rooms; the place needs some work but still retains more atmosphere than most spots in Southeast Asia. Anawrahta Rd., tel. (085) 22112, US$12-30.

Getting There

Japanese pickups leave Mandalay hourly between 0700 and 1500 from several different locations including the main bus terminal. Allow three hours to wind through the 22 hairpin turns and several stops for radiator water and snacks. As these trucks are always packed out, arrive early and secure a seat in the front for better views and extra legroom. Jeeps returning to Mandalay leave from the main road just down from the clock tower.

BAGAN

The mysterious and magnificent ruins of Bagan comprise one of the world's great archaeological sites. Although most of the original 5,000 monuments have been reduced to great piles of rubble, the remaining 50 or so temples still bear witness to the amazing construction frenzy that seized this area during the 11th and 12th centuries. Bagan is one of the wonders of the world and the major highlight of any visit to Myanmar.

History

The traditional date of the foundation of Bagan is 849, but the actual Golden Age began in the 11th century after King Anawrahta (1044-1077) ascended the throne and became the 42nd ruler of the Bagan Dynasty. Considered the greatest of all Burmese kings, Anawrahta conquered and united most of Myanmar while seeking a new religion to replace the decadent Tantric practices and Ari *naga* worship popular at the time. Tradition has it that Shan Arahan, a Buddhist monk from the Mon capital of Thaton, visited Anawrahta in the 11th century and converted him to Theravada Buddhism. Impressed by the logical rationalism of his newfound religion, Anawrahta requested a copy of the Tripi-

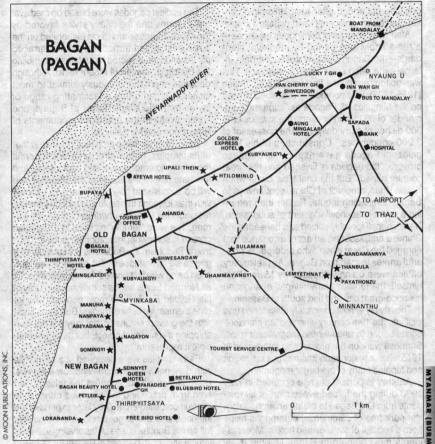

BAGAN (PAGAN)

AYEYARWADDY RIVER

BOAT FROM MANDALAY

LUCKY 7 GH ○ NYAUNG U

PAN CHERRY GH ● INN WAH GH
SHWEZIGON ■ BUS TO MANDALAY

AUNG
MINGALAR ★ SAPADA
HOTEL ■ BANK

GOLDEN
EXPRESS ● HOSPITAL
HOTEL

KUBYAUKGYI

UPALI THEIN ★

● AYEYAR HOTEL ★ HTILOMINLO

TO AIRPORT

BUPAYA ★

TOURIST
OFFICE ★ ANANDA TO THAZI

OLD BAGAN

★ BAGAN ★ SULAMANI
HOTEL

THIRIPYITSAYA ★ NANDAMANNYA
HOTEL ★ SHWESANDAW ★ THANBULA

MINGLAZEDI ★ ★ DHAMMAYANGYI LEMYETHNAT ★ PAYATHONZU
KUBYAUKGYI

MANUHA ★ ○ MYINKABA ● MINNANTHU

NANPAYA ★

ABEYADANA ★

NAGAYON ★

SOMINGYI ★ TOURIST SERVICE CENTRE ■

NEW BAGAN

SEINNYET
QUEEN
HOTEL

BAGAN BEAUTY HOTEL ■ BETELNUT
PETLEIK ★ PARADISE
GH ● BLUEBIRD HOTEL

○ THIRIPYITSAYA

LOKANANDA ★ ● FREE BIRD HOTEL 0   1 km

© MOON PUBLICATIONS, INC.

taka from the Mon king of Thaton. After King Manuha refused to share his sacred books with the northern barbarians, an angry Anawrahta sacked Thaton and hauled 30 elephant-loads of the Tripitaka back to Bagan. For good measure he also dragged along Manuha and his entire retinue of Mon architects, artisans, scholars, linguists, theologians, and the entire population of 30,000 souls. So impressed was Anawrahta with Mon culture and spiritual traditions that he quickly adopted their alphabet, religion, and artistic models.

Anawrahta's son, King Kyanzittha (1084-1112), intensified construction of Mon-style mon-

uments during Bagan's so-called Golden Age of Monument Builders. Over the period of 28 years, Kyanzittha undertook the restoration of the Mahabodi Temple at Bodgaya and constructed his architectural masterpiece, the Ananda Temple. Kyanzittha's successor, Alaungsithu (1112-1167), continued building works of merit and authored the famous quadrilingual inscription at the Kubyaukgyi Temple. The discovery in 1911 of this Rosetta Stone of Myanmar inscribed in four languages (Pyu, Mon, Burmese, and Pali) helped provide the key to understanding the Pyu language and the chronology of the early Bagan kings. Temple construction continued with Nara-

MYANMAR (BURMA)

patisithu but ended after King Htilominlo constructed his magnificent Gawdawpalin Temple.

After two centuries of continuous existence—a remarkably long period by medieval standards—the Bagan Dynasty collapsed from internal exhaustion and corrupt monarchies. This was epitomized by the final king, Narathihapati (1256-1287), who pompously described himself on the Mingalazedi Pagoda as "supreme commander of 36 million soldiers, the swallower of 300 dishes of curry daily, and the possessor of 3,000 concubines." Construction of his Mingalazedi Pagoda gave rise to the Burmese proverb, "the pagoda is finished and the great country ruined." But the final blow came when Kublai Khan, emperor of China, sent envoys to Bagan demanding tribute. Rather than returning a suitable acknowledgment of submission, Narathihapati foolishly seized and beheaded the Chinese ambassador, an act of arrogance that enraged the Great Khan, who ordered his powerful armies to march on Bagan. As preliminary battles were being witnessed by Marco Polo himself, the terrified Narathihapati abandoned his once-great city and fled south to Bassein.

The city lay almost completely abandoned until well into the 19th century when British archaeologists began to uncover the magnificent ruins. Burmese work on the project was interrupted in 1975 when a major earthquake struck the region and toppled many of the larger monuments.

Another important change occurred in May 1990 during the forced evacuation of all residents from Old Bagan to create an archaeological park free of commercial enterprises aside from a handful of state-owned hotels. Most residents moved south to Bagan Myothit (New Bagan) or east to the small village of Nyaung U where they set up new guesthouses, cafes, and handicraft centers.

Architectural Styles

Buddhist monuments in Bagan fall into two basic styles: pagodas and temples. Pagodas (also called stupas, *chedis*, *zedis*, *ceityas*, and *dagobas*) are solid, bell-shaped structures raised on series of terraces and crowned by golden finials known as *hti*. These serve as monuments of commemoration and each usually entombs a relic of the Buddha such as a sacred hair or a piece of bone.

The earliest pagodas were based on medieval Indian forms and the heavy styles favored by the Mons. Burmese architects elaborated on the basic design and turned the simple terraced plinths into virtual sacred mountains resembling the Buddhist Heaven of Mount Meru. Although pagodas seem monotonously similar to most visitors, Bagan offers a fascinating range of styles from the simple forms of Bupaya and Ngakyawena to the grandiose monuments of Shwezigon and Mingalazedi.

Bagan's other basic architectural style is that of its temples, hollow structures which permit the pilgrim to enter a dark and cool interior and meditate before the image of the Buddha. You will be surprised at how much Bagan's temples with their towering transepts and moody corridors resemble the Gothic cathedrals of medieval Europe. The word "temple" as used in a Christian context is somewhat inappropriate since in Theravada Buddhism the Buddha is not considered a god to be "worshipped" but rather an enlightened being who is "honored" for his teachings. Or as Norman Lewis writes somewhat cynically in his *Golden Earth,* "Like most peoples who incline themselves before images, Buddhists insist with the gravest emphasis that they are not worshipping the material object, but the great principle it represents."

Early temples were designed in a Mon style with dark hallways and small narrow windows. Burmese architects adopted the false ribbed arch from preceding Indian styles rather than the true corbelled arch. They later expanded the interior and added larger windows to let the light fall on the Buddha image. A fascinating variety of temple styles can be seen in Bagan: those based on North Indian models such as Ananda, others from Central India such as Mahabodi, and those based on South Indian styles such as Gawadapalin and Sulamani. Bagan also boasts a handful of unusual structures, such as the Pitakat Taik Library and Upali Thein Ordination Hall, which simulate in stone the architectural forms of wood.

Murals and terra-cotta tiles are also worth special attention. Many temple interiors are covered with superb murals which represent a treasure house of classical Burmese art. Some are reminiscent of eastern Indian Buddhist manuscript styles, others show delightful scenes of everyday Burmese life complete with bored clerks, laughing children, and lusty courtesans. Many of the finest murals have been tragically painted over by less talented artists, completely whitewashed out of existence, or stolen and sold to foreign art collectors. Those temples with original murals are often locked to guard against such vandalism, but a young villager or groundskeeper with the key will admit you for a small fee. Another strategy is to join a tour or at least keep an eye out for their bus.

The beautiful exterior walls fitted with glazed terra-cotta tiles often depict the Buddhist Jataka tales, stories of previous incarnations of the Buddha. Tiles come in two styles: the enameled green tiles which show Chinese influence such as those at Ananda and Shwezigon, and the red baked clay tiles of South Indian influence such as those at Petleik Pagoda. Repeated heavy gilding and repainting has destroyed many tiles but those at Mingalazedi and in Minnanthu are still in good condition.

OLD BAGAN MONUMENTS

All Myanmar temples and pagodas are considered sacred. Visitors are expected to respect Buddhist tradition and dress conservatively. Shorts are inappropriate when visiting religious shrines. Males should wear long pants and a clean shirt; females should wear clothing which keeps them keep well covered.

Before exploring the ruins, visit the Bagan Museum for a useful introduction to the architecture and sculpture of the region. The Yangon tourist office sells the *Pictorial Guide to Bagan* and the *Tourist Myanmar Map of Bagan*. The entrance fee into the Bagan Archaeological Zone is US$10.

Visitors with only a day or two should limit themselves to the important monuments near Bagan village. Travelers with more time can get farther afield with either bicycle or horse-drawn cart. Bullock carts are romantic, but as Sir George Scott wrote, "The unlucky passenger shortly discovers that there are bones in parts of his body where previously he had imagined all was soft."

Bicycles are the perfect answer: cheap, comfortable, and fast. Carefully check the bike's condition. All of Bagan's monuments can be reached by bicycle except for those far south of Thiripyitsaya because of the sandy roads. No matter what, sunsets should be enjoyed from the pinnacle of any of the taller monuments which allow sunset visitors. Less ambitious visitors might substitute a cold drink on the verandah of the Thiripyitsaya Hotel.

Saraba Gateway
The following monuments are described in a clockwise fashion starting from the tourist office. Saraba (Tharaba) Gateway, the only surviving relic of the 9th-century city built by King Pyinbya (846-878), is flanked by a pair of masonry shrines holding sibling *nats*. To the left is Min

MYANMAR (BURMA)

the author and friends

Mahagiri, nicknamed Mr. Handsome, and to the right is his sister Shwemyethana, also known as Golden Face. Both died tragically (or possibly incestuously) in a fire and remain among the most popular of Burmese spirits.

An attractive monastery lies to the left of the path leading to the Ananda Temple. This rarely visited building features some superb wood-carvings, which the young monks will be delighted to show you. Have a cup of tea with the old abbot.

Ananda Temple

Bagan's most famous monument is one of the region's few active Buddhist temples. Ananda was constructed by Kyanzittha in 1091 in the shape of a perfect Greek cross bisected by four gabled vestibules. The overall effect is of a gigantic white wedding cake standing atop the red soil of Bagan. Rising above the diminishing terraces is a golden spire or *sikhara* adapted from the temples of India, and then a bell-shaped pagoda of Burmese design. No one is allowed to climb this temple.

Enshrined at the end of each corridor are four colossal standing Buddhas with hands raised in the pose of dispelling fear. Lighted mysteriously

from concealed apertures in the vaulted ceiling, each represents one of the four previous Buddhas; Gautama is at the west. The western sanctum enshrines a life-sized statue of Kyanzittha and the monk Shin Arahan who converted the king to Theravada Buddhism. Ornamenting the exterior base are glazed terra-cotta tiles which have been badly disfigured with heavy-handed whitewashing, but check those squatting griffins with multiple penises.

Thatbyinnyu Temple

This 61-meter monument is the tallest temple in Bagan and an excellent place to view the sunset. Thatbyinnyu was built during the 12th century by King Alaungsithu, who was responsible for many of the Mon-style temples in Bagan. Despite the heavy mass of two cubes piled on top of each other, the architect also created a soaring effect with his use of corner stupas mounted on the terraces and the flamboyant arch-pediments that point skyward.

Hidden in the circumambulatory corridor around the central mass is a narrow set of stairs that leads up to the Buddha image seated on the upper floor. Another set of stairs leads to

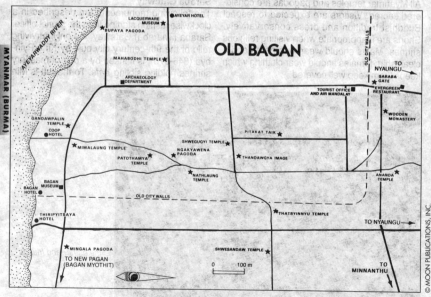

OLD BAGAN

Ananda by Kyanzitha

the uppermost terrace, where the sunsets are especially spectacular.

Shwesandaw Pagoda

Somewhat of a side trip from the central area, this whitewashed pagoda was built by King Anawrahta soon after his conquest of Thaton in 1057. Of all stupas in Bagan, the Shwesandaw is the most perfectly balanced with its five diminishing terraces that complement the cylindrical stupa resting on an octagonal platform. Bisected by well-defined stairways, the terraces have an eerie resemblance to the Central American temples of Incan and Mayan design.

Located on the grounds is the 11th-century **Shinbintalyaung,** a nondescript brick shed which houses an 18-meter recumbent image of the Buddha. The image has been defaced but note the well-preserved tree-of-life fresco surrounded by Balinese-style figures.

Thandawgya Image

This six-meter Buddha located back from the central area was constructed from brick and plaster in 1284 by King Narathihapati. The roof has collapsed and it appears that his belly has been excavated by treasure hunters.

Shwegugyi Temple

This small but finely proportioned temple was built by Alaungsithu in 1131 in a surprisingly light and airy style. Mounted on a high brick platform, this little gem has some exquisite stucco carvings, including finely molded birds on the west doorway. The interior has a pair of inscribed stone slabs which poetically tell the history of the temple.

Pitakat Taik Library

Although this building is often overlooked by visitors to Bagan, it has great historical and architectural significance. After King Anawrahta conquered the Mon kingdom of Thaton he brought back 30 elephant-loads of prized Buddhist scriptures, an event that established Bagan as one of the more important cultural and political powers in Southeast Asia. The precious scriptures were stored in this library. Significantly, this building replicates in stone the styles which were commonly built of wood and have long since disappeared.

Nathlaung Temple

This badly deteriorated temple, dedicated to Vishnu, remains the only surviving Hindu sanctuary in Bagan. The outer wall has 10 niches holding seven of the avatars of Vishnu. Three images in poor condition are found in the cool interior, which once held a Vishnu riding his *garuda* prior to its removal to Berlin's Dahlem Museum.

Patothamya Temple

This small 11th-century temple is typical of Mon-influenced architecture—single storied and set low to the ground with dark corridors dimly lit by narrow windows. Patothamya is kept locked to protect the mural paintings with Mon inscriptions.

Mimalaung Temple

Built by King Narapatisithu in 1174, this small square temple is surmounted by multiple roofs which have been insensitively reconstructed with ferroconcrete.

Gawadapawlin Temple

Constructed by Narapatisithu (1174-1211) in an architectural style similar to that of Thatbyinnyu, this massive temple was badly damaged during the disastrous 1975 earthquake, which struck 225 of the 2,217 Bagan monuments officially registered by the Burmese archaeological department. Afterward the Burmese government embarked on a project to fortify the monuments with funds provided by the U.N. Development Program. European earthquake engineers who studied the problem recommended that the bonding capacity of the old mortar be strengthened by cement injection and steel ties. You can see the startling results on the reconstructed *sikhara,* which soars to 55 meters. Another popular place for sunsets despite the obnoxious electronic loudspeaker.

Bupaya Pagoda

Once used as a navigation aid for passing ships, this stupa stands on the banks of the Ayeyarwady above circular rows of crenellated terraces. The antiquity of this pagoda is indicated by the bulbous shape, as opposed to the tall and tapering forms of later periods. It is, however, a complete re-creation, since the original structure collapsed into the river during the 1975 earthquake. Boats can be hired below to cross the Ayeyarwady.

Mahabodi Temple

Constructed by Nantaungmya (1124-1174) after the original in Bodgaya, this unique Gupta-period temple is typical of Central Indian styles rather than traditional Burmese designs. Some intriguing statuary lies scattered among the weeds in the back yard.

MONUMENTS TOWARD NYAUNG U

The following monuments are located along the paved road that connects Bagan with the village of Nyaung U. A three- or four-hour bicycle journey can be made from Bagan to Nyaung U, stopping at Upali Thein, Htilominlo, Shwezigon, and Sapada Pagoda before returning on the southern paved road past Kubyaukgyi Temple. The sense of isolation and complete stillness makes this a powerful and memorable travel experience.

Upali Thein Ordination Hall

Similar to the Pitakat Taik, this attractive Buddhist hall has great importance since it replicates in stone the wooden architecture from the 13th century. Influenced by South Indian prototypes, the exterior design and treatment of carved stone somewhat resembles the 7th-century seaside temples of Mahabalipuram. Interior frescoes from the early 18th century are kept locked to prevent vandalism.

Htilominlo Temple

This impressive temple was erected by King Nantaungmya to commemorate his ordination into the Buddhist priesthood. Of special note are the decorative friezes and exquisite stucco carvings which survive on the false exterior columns. Several are capped by strange creatures set with bulging eyes and dangling tongues, mythological animals which inexplicably resemble those in Bali. Four Buddha figures of recent construction face the cardinal points on the ground floor, although inscribed horoscopes found at the east entrance are more intriguing.

Shwezigon Pagoda

This golden stupa is one of Myanmar's most venerated since it enshrines a cornucopia of Buddha relics, including the Buddha's frontlet bone obtained by King Anawrahta, his collarbone from Sri Kshetra, and a duplicate of the Tooth of Kandy from Sri Lanka. Anawrahta began construction of this temple to fuse indigenous *nat* worship with his newfound faith. The project was finished by subsequent kings after Anawrahta was gored to death by a mad bull in 1077.

Important artistic features include the enameled plaques around the terrace which depict Jataka tales and the four Gupta-style Buddhas standing in the entrance chambers. Also note the *nat* images riding mythical animals in the building at the northeast corner. As at other famous pagodas in Myanmar, the grounds are filled with weird and wonderful oddities that range from the sublime to the ridiculous. Toward the east are a revolving coin-toss *hti,* which grants wishes to pilgrims with good aim, and several gaudy dioramas which show the Buddha calmly facing raging animals and earthly temptations.

Sapada Pagoda

This modest brick stupa is considered a landmark in the history of Buddhism. During the 12th century a Burmese monk named Sapada from Bassein journeyed to Sri Lanka for ordination into the Sinhalese form of Theravada Buddhism. Afterward he returned to Bagan to establish the pure form of Buddhism and construct this pagoda. The most distinctive feature is the cubical relic chamber mounted above rather than buried beneath the bell.

MYANMAR (BURMA)

Kubyaukgyi (Gubyaukgyi) Temple

Featuring a distinctive spire of Indian Gupta style, the chief features of this small 13th-century temple are the outstanding frescoes painted on the interior walls. Because many were stolen by German art collectors in the late 19th century, the interior is kept locked to protect the remaining frescoes. Local attendants might have keys, although you can still peer through the steel bars for a partial view.

MONUMENTS TOWARD MINNANTHU

Roads from Bagan village to Minnanthu are unpaved but passable by bicycle. It's a strange but memorable journey to pedal out here on a hot afternoon.

Dhammayangyi Temple

Constructed during the short but bloody reign of King Narathu (1167-1170), this massive shrine is chiefly known for its outstanding exterior brickwork. The floor plan of this temple is similar to Ananda's, but the interior circumambulatory passage has been mysteriously blocked with brick. Note the unusual set of double Buddhas in the west entrance.

This temple is very popular for sunsets, but finding your way to the top can be difficult. Children playing at the entrance will show you the narrow and claustrophobic stairway located at the southeast corner of the ground floor. Take careful note of the route or risk getting lost on the way back down. Forget the way and the kids will laugh at you.

Sulamani Temple

Constructed in 1181 by King Narapatisithu, this important temple heralded the final period of temple construction. The monument consists of two stories ornamented with parapets and stupas with four porches facing the cardinal points. The exterior lacks the impressive brickwork of Dhammayangyi, but 18th-century frescoes located on the interior of the southern walls are fascinating. The requisite Buddhas are there, but it is the ordinary scenes of everyday Burmese life that project such warmth. Note that almost everyone seems to be smiling behind the protective wire screen.

Minnanthu Village

The following four temples are located just east of Minnanthu village, about 20 minutes by bicycle beyond Sulamani. Allow an hour to pedal here from Bagan. The road is well marked and you won't have any problem with heavy sand. These modest little temples are chiefly known for their superb interior frescoes, which are always locked. The village of Minnanthu has a small lake to the left and a group of houses to the right. Stop here and ask for the young girl who keeps the keys to the temples. Mg Aung Lin, a popular guide, and the girl with the temple keys both expect a small tip or present.

Lemyethnat Temple: This neglected temple immediately on your left has a shocking example of priceless frescoes carelessly splattered over with whitewash.

Payathonzu Temple: This triple temple farther to the right features vaulted corridors joined together by narrow passageways. Each little gem is capped by a *sikhara* modeled after Orrisian prototypes. The interior vaults are covered with exquisite and well-preserved frescoes of Mahayanist and Tantric character. Extraordinary mythical monsters, animals, and human figures are cleverly woven among floral motifs.

Thanbula Temple: Constructed in 1255 by the wife of King Uzana, this small shrine features some outstanding murals in the circumambulatory corridor.

Nandamannya Temple: This final temple contains the finest frescoes in Minnanthu. Behind the temple is a subterranean monk's retreat which welcomes visitors.

MONUMENTS SOUTH

The following temples are located on both sides of the road which parallels the river. Bicyclists can follow the dirt road as far as the Nanpaya Temple, but beyond that the sand becomes too thick.

Mingalazedi Pagoda

Although this pagoda was constructed in 1284 just a few years before Bagan was abandoned, the basic shape is almost identical to that of the Shwezigon constructed two centuries earlier. Mingalazedi is chiefly noted for the outstanding

MYANMAR (BURMA)

terra-cotta tiles embedded on the steep terraces. Some of these unglazed tiles have been stolen or badly defaced by art collectors, but a large number are still extant in fine condition. The groundskeeper will unlock the gate for you and there is no admission charge.

Kubyaukgyi (Gubyaukgyi) Temple
Constructed in 1113 by Rajakumar, son of Kyanzittha, this small Mon-style temple is noted for the frescoes that cover the inner sanctum and surrounding corridors. The central mural relates the 547 Jatakas in nine rows, of which Buddha's descent from Tavatimsa is considered the most important. Orthodox Theravada paintings predominate, but a 10-handed Mahayana bodhisattva is also painted on the outer porch. Note, too, the unusual stone windows cut with geometrical designs.

Kubyaukgyi is where the Myazedi stone was discovered, the Rosetta Stone of Myanmar which enabled linguists to decipher the ancient Pyu language. Kubyaukgyi is kept locked but someone in Myinkaba village will open it for a small tip.

Myinkaba Village
On your left as you enter the village is a small lacquerware store which sells ice-cold drinks and "instant antique" terra-cotta tiles. Myinkaba has an active lacquerware industry and is a good place to trade your Western goods for lacquerware.

Manuha Temple
In 1057 King Anawrahta conquered the southern capital of Thaton and brought back King Manuha and his royal court. Manuha was exiled south to Myinkaba, where he was allowed to build this temple in 1059. The exterior is dull, but some say that the claustrophobic interior with its cramped Buddhas is an allegorical representation of the captive king's mental distress. Visitors can climb the narrow stairs in the rear and peer down on the sitting image. Although the story is intriguing, the temple is ugly and has little architectural or sculptural merit.

Nanpaya Temple
Located just behind the Manuha Temple is this well-preserved monument with distinctive arch

pediments and Mon-style perforated stone windows. The interior has four stone pillars carved with outstanding hanging floral designs and rare bas-relief figures of Brahma holding lotus flowers. Archaeologists believe this temple may have been a Hindu shrine before being converted to Manuha's prison. Nanpaya is kept locked to prevent damage, but young boys usually have the key.

Abeyadana Temple
Visitors on bicycles will find the road too thick with sand to proceed south of Nanpaya. Abeyadana is a Mon-style temple constructed by King Kyanzittha to commemorate the loyalty of his wife Abeyadana. The northern porch, pierced by three entrances constructed from true rather than false arches, leads to the inner sanctum, which is filled with paintings inspired by Bagan's three major religions: Theravada Buddhism, Mahayana Buddhism, and Hinduism. Mahayanist figures of bodhisattvas cover the outer walls of the corridor while the inner walls are painted with small circular panels of Brahmanic gods and terrifying Tantric images. Porch panels illustrate Jataka scenes with Mon script.

Nagayon Temple
According to legend, this Mon-style temple was also constructed by King Kyanzittha on the spot where he was miraculously protected by a giant naga snake. The locked interior contains a huge standing Buddha flanked by two smaller Buddha images, plus a large number of niches filled with Buddha images. Unlike Abeyadana Temple (mentioned above), this temple contains mural paintings devoted solely to Theravada Buddhism.

Somingyi Monastery
Very few of Bagan's wooden monasteries have survived centuries of weather and fire. Somingyi, once a residential college for young monks, is a rare example of a brick monastery.

Seinnyet Ama Temple and Pagoda
The temple is of standard design with multiple terraces and a sikhara supported by a square basement. The embellished stupa has some finely carved lions on the second terrace. Both face each other within a walled enclosure

BAGAN MARIONETTES

Although *yokthe pwe* (Burmese marionette theater) has been popular since the 17th century, today it's lost favor with the Burmese and is rarely performed outside temple festivals. Foreign visitors are fortunate to have marionette theaters in Bagan. Performances are frequently given at the Thiripyitsaya Hotel and at the Evergreen Restaurant near Saraba Gate.

During the 45-minute show, the master puppeteer and his assistant manipulate 28 puppets hanging from a dozen strings, recite poetry, and extemporaneously add dialogue that ranges from humorous to bawdy. Taken from the Jatakas or the Ramayana, the stories include colorful characters, from heroic princes and their lovely princesses to Brahmanic priests, corrupt officials, and slapstick clowns. You will especially enjoy the flying sorcerers and the extraordinarily realistic galloping horses.

East and West Petleik Pagodas

These two pagodas hold what are considered to be the finest existing terra-cotta plaques in Bagan. Constructed during the 11th century, the lower portions of both pagodas were buried under dirt and debris. When excavated in 1905, archaeologists discovered 550 Jataka plaques in excellent condition. These unglazed panels described and labeled in traditional Pali script are in far better condition than the glazed plaques at Ananda and Shwezigon. Vaulted corridors have been reconstructed to protect the plaques.

ACCOMMODATIONS

Old Bagan

Prior to the political disruptions of late 1980s, almost a dozen inexpensive guesthouses lined the narrow road that bisects what is now called Old Bagan. Then, in a fit of politically motivated anger, the Burmese government demolished all the guesthouses and forced the residents south to Bagan Myothit (New Bagan) and east to Nyaung U, where they established a second round of guesthouses and mid-level hotels.

Today, a few hotels are still located within Old Bagan overlooking the Ayeyarwady River.

Co-operative Hotel: Least expensive place in Old Bagan with scruffy rooms but handy location near museums and major monuments. Old Bagan, US$6-20.

Ayeyar Hotel: Former Irra Inn recently spiffed up but still a somewhat dreary place aside from its spacious lawns and riverside location. Old Bagan, tel. (01) 95156 in Yangon, US$18-45.

Bagan Hotel: Privately owned and fairly cheerful hotel with a choice of fan or a/c rooms in the main building and superior chalets overlooking the river. Old Bagan, tel. (101) 12, US$18-45.

Thiripyitsaya Hotel: Modern resort hotel, government-owned, with 36 a/c rooms overlooking the Ayeyarwady plus decent restaurant, verandah bar with sunset view, and pool open to outside guests for a modest fee. Old Bagan, tel. (101) 89000, US$45-80.

Bagan Myothit (New Bagan)

Three km south of Old Bagan lies the boom town of New Bagan where over a dozen guesthouses have opened since the government eased restrictions against private hotel ownership. Most provide complimentary breakfasts.

Queen Hotel: Simple rooms and attached baths in the north end of town. New Bagan, US$12-25.

Bagan Beauty Hotel: Center of town location with acceptable rooms and shared baths. New Bagan, US$6-12.

Myathida Hotel: Family-owned guesthouse with clean if somewhat spartan rooms. Bicycle rentals. New Bagan, US$6-10.

Paradise Guesthouse: Among the first to open in town and still quite popular. New Bagan, US$8-20.

Palm Hotel: Tucked away in the northeastern corner of town amid crumbling pagodas—one of the most tranquil and pleasant places in Bagan. 9 Thamudarit Ward, New Bagan, tel. (01) 90589 in Yangon, US$12-28.

Free Bird Hotel: Also located east of town with heaps of atmosphere and decent rooms. Khaye St., New Bagan, tel. (01) 94941 in Yangon, US$12-32.

Blue Bird Hotel: Your third choice east of town and somewhat south near Yeosin Creek. New Bagan, tel. (01) 21515 in Yangon, US$12-24.

MYANMAR (BURMA)

Nyaung U

Five kilometers east of Old Bagan lies the dusty town of Nyaung U with market, bus terminal, and a dozen guesthouses and mid-level hotels located near town or on the road toward Old Bagan.

Inn Wa Guesthouse: Small but popular guesthouse just opposite the market near the center of town. Nyaung U, US$6-12.

May Kha Lar Guesthouse: Another centrally located guesthouse featuring simple rooms with common baths. Nyaung U, US$6-12.

Royal Guesthouse: Cozy place down the road near the entrance to Shwezigon Pagoda. Bagan-Nyaung U Rd., tel. (101) 285, US$6-12.

Golden Village Inn: Newer place with fan-cooled and a/c rooms just south of Shwezigon near the proposed Bagan Golf Course. Anawrahta Rd., US$12-28.

Aung Mingalar Hotel: Handy location near Shwezigon Pagoda and Green Peace cafe not to mention the only cinema in town. All rooms a/c with private bath. Bagan-Nyaung U Rd., tel. (101) 64, US$25-45.

Golden Express Hotel: Two km east and almost midway between Old Bagan and Nyaung U is a mid-level hotel with budget fan rooms and more expensive a/c chalets. Bagan-Nyaung U Rd., tel. (101) 37, US$10-45.

SHOPPING

Lacquerware

Bagan is known for its lacquerware produced in the form of boxes, bowls, *sadaik* manuscript chests, and traditional objects such as *kunit* (betel-nut boxes), *lahpetok* (receptacle boxes divided into pie-shaped sections), *hseileik taung* (cheroot boxes), and *bu* (storage containers for *ngapi* fish paste).

The finer products are shaped over a fine bamboo frame, covered with tree lacquer, and then painted with black lacquer resin derived from the *Melanorrhoea usitata* tree. Bagan lacquer is famous for a unique style of incised decoration called *yun*, in which the carved patterns are filled with coloring matter of either red, yellow, or green. The entire process can take several months to complete. For an excellent introduction visit the **Bagan Lacquerware School and Museum** on the road to the Ayeyar Hotel.

TRANSPORTATION

Air

Myanmar Airways and Air Mandalay fly daily to Nyaung U Airport from Yangon, Mandalay, and Heho near Inle Lake.

BUDDHA AND THE *NATS*

Myanmar is perhaps the most profoundly Buddhist country in the world. Over 85% of the population follows the precepts of Theravadism. Monks of all ages in all shades of yellow and orange robes are seen everywhere. Each morning some half-million monks silently walk the streets with their begging bowls, giving residents the opportunity to improve their karma. Another 100,000 have permanently joined the Noble Order of the Yellow Robe.

And yet there is more to Burmese religion than just monks and Buddhism. Underlying Myanmar's Theravadism is an animist substratum of nature spirits, ghosts, and departed ancestors who control the weather, health, luck, future, life, and death. The average Burmese honors the Buddha but keeps an abiding sense of fear and respect for the all-powerful 37 *nats*. As with the Chinese practice of ancestor veneration, the Burmese propitiate *nats* to prevent the great trouble they cause when ignored. And like the saints of the Catholic Church, *nats* boast magical powers that can be called on in time of need. Soothsayers, magicians, and mediums all invoke their spirits to cure disease and foretell the future. *Nats* are also similar to Thai *phi* in that most are derivations of historical figures *(dewas)* taken from ancient Hindu mythology. As in Thailand, small spirit houses are nailed to buildings and trees, while *nat* images, with oversized ears and bulbous noses, figure prominently in almost every Buddhist temple. *Nat* veneration continues to form the bedrock of Burmese religion, despite arguments against it made by King Anawrahta of Bagan in the 12th century, King Mindon in the 19th century, and U Nu and Ne Win in modern times.

MYANMAR (BURMA)

Train

A direct train connection recently opened from Mandalay to Bagan but there remains no direct train link to Yangon. Trains from Yangon take 12 hours to Thazi from where Japanese mini-trucks and buses depart for Bagan from the bus terminal some 150 meters from the train station.

Trains leave Mandalay at 2230 and arrive in Bagan at 0530 the next morning.

Bus

Private a/c buses depart in the early morning hours from the long distance bus terminal in Yangon near the airport and take 12-15 hours to reach Bagan.

Private a/c buses with videos and cold drinks depart several times weekly from the main bus terminal in Mandalay and take 8-12 hours to reach Bagan. Bagan Express near Shwezigon Pagoda in Nyaung U arranges bus transport to Yangon, Mandalay, and Inle Lake. Both ordinary and a/c buses are available.

Other options include uncomfortable pickups and chartered taxis from Yangon, Mandalay, or Inle Lake.

Boat

Among the most memorable journeys in Southeast Asia is the riverboat from Mandalay to Bagan—a timeless adventure past simple villages inhabited by people almost completely untouched by the outside world for several decades.

Passenger ferries depart Mandalay at 0530 twice weekly on Thursday and Sunday and arrives that evening in Bagan 1730-2000. The cost is US$10 deck class and US$30 cabin. Tickets must be purchased from the tourist office in Mandalay.

The ordinary ferry which departs daily except Thursday and Sunday costs US$2-4 depending on the class. This slower boat takes 24-30 hours to reach Bagan and stops overnight in the Pakkaku, where travelers can stay at the Myayatanar Inn. Bagan is a two-hour ferry ride the following morning.

Travelers can sleep on the ferry the night before departure and save the cost of the hotel room in Mandalay.

MOUNT POPA

This 1,518-meter peak some 50 km from Bagan is the official home of Myanmar's *nats*—a collection of 37 magical spirits both feared and honored by Myanmar citizens. The dusty village of Popa situated at the base of the sugarloaf mountain has souvenir stalls, several basic but adequate restaurants, and hostels for pilgrims.

Main attraction is the *nat* museum constructed in 1925, which holds 37 life-size *nat* statues sculpted from teak by a Mandalay craftsman. Thousands of Burmese gather here twice yearly to honor the spirits and attend the festivals. The one-hour climb to the summit passes the Min Mahagiri Shrine, dedicated to Mr. Handsome and Miss Golden Face, the two most beloved *nats* in Myanmar cosmology.

Popa can be visited on a side trip from Bagan (look for notices in the tourist office) or as a brief stop en route to Thazi. Accommodations are available in the monastery.

MYANMAR (BURMA)

INLE LAKE AND VICINITY

One of the most picturesque spots in Southeast Asia, Inle Lake and the surrounding region is an outstanding alternative to the historical attractions of Bagan and Mandalay. Surrounded by lovely blue mountains, this idyllic lake is home to the Intha people, who live in stilted villages and farm floating islands created from mud and reed. They are also known for their curious technique of rowing slender crafts with a single leg wrapped around the oar.

Although Inle is the most famous attraction, the region also offers Taunggyi and Kalaw, two former British hill stations with cool weather and colorful markets visited by Shan tribals, plus Pindaya Caves to the north of Kalaw, filled with thousands of Buddhist images.

Orientation

Place-names at Inle can be confusing. Taunggyi, the largest town in the region, has the main tourist office, the largest marketplace, and the only first-class hotel in the region. Heho airport is 25 km west of Taunggyi. The train terminus is at Shwenyaung, 12 km north of the lake and almost midway between Taunggyi and Heho.

Nyaungshwe, situated on the northern shore of Inle Lake, has a small tourist office, money-exchange facilities, and several inexpensive guesthouses; probably the most convenient place to stay when time is limited.

TRANSPORTATION

Air

Both Myanmar Airways and Air Mandalay fly to Heho Airport from Yangon and Mandalay several times weekly. Both minitrucks and buses go from Heho to Shwenyaung, from where pickups continue south to the lake.

Train

Express trains from Yangon take 10-14 hours to Thazi from where minitrucks and buses depart for Taunggyi when filled. Travelers who wish to go directly to the lake and save two hours of unnecessary travel should get off at Shwenyaung and take a bus to Nyaungshwe.

The train from Thazi to Shwenyaung takes a full day but passes through spectacular scenery and is certainly more comfortable than trucks and buses which are generally crammed to the rafters.

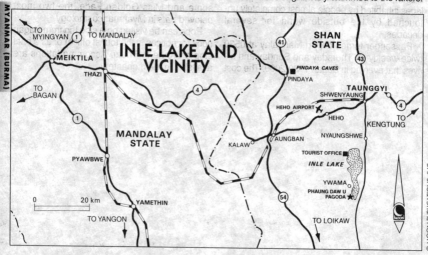

MYANMAR (BURMA)

© MOON PUBLICATIONS, INC.

Bus

Few travelers make the long bus journey from Yangon, though the trip is somewhat bearable from Mandalay and Bagan.

Buses and minitrucks depart early morning from the main bus terminal in Mandalay and take 10-12 hours to reach Shwenyaung and Taunggyi.

Several bus and minitruck companies offer direct services from Bagan to Shwenyaung and Taunggyi, generally leaving Nyaung U around 0400 and arriving at Shwenyaung in the late afternoon.

KALAW

Former British hill station, on the edge of the Shan Plateau about 70 km west of Taunggyi, blessed with a cooler climate and old Tudor houses spread among the tall pine trees—a worthwhile stop for travelers with extra time.

Highlights include the Kalaw Market with its Shan, Padaung, and Pa O people who attend the bazaar which rotates every five days between Taunggyi, Kalaw, Pindaya, Heho, and Aungban. Other attractions include Thein Tong Pagoda overlooking the main road and the glittering Dama Yan Thi Pagoda near the market. The Kalaw Hotel and local tourist office can help with treks to nearby Padaung villages such as Ta Yaw, Shwe Mine Phone, and Pein Ne Pin.

Accommodations
Kalaw Hotel: About one km south of town center is this romantic Tudor-style lodge constructed in 1906 for British officers on holiday and now highly regarded for its nightly dinners of Burmese and English fare. Kalaw Rd., tel. (01) 60563 in Yangon, US$15-45.

Pineland Inn: Center of town with basic but fairly clean rooms. Thazi-Taunggyi Rd., US$5-8.

Parami Hotel: Another centrally located guesthouse with common baths and hot showers. Merchant Rd., US$8-12.

PINDAYA CAVES

Small town some 45 km north of Kalaw known for its limestone caves filled with thousands of gilded Buddha images. The scenic road from Kalaw via Aungban passes Pa O and Danu villages before arriving in Pindaya, chiefly inhabited by Taungyos. Cave entrance on the ridge overlooking the lake can be reached by hired jeep or via a covered walkway. To the northwest are Padah Lin Caves, with Neolithic wall paintings of bison, elephants, and human figures.

Accommodations
Diamond Eagle Guesthouse: A quasi-legal guesthouse near the lake with small if survivable rooms. Shwemin Paya Rd., US$10-14.

Pindaya Hotel: Midway between Pindaya and the caves and facing the lake is the only authorized place to stay. Shwemin Paya Rd., tel. (01) 21425 in Yangon, US$24-40.

TAUNGGYI

Spread across the wooded foothills above Inle Lake is this cool and colorful former British hill resort founded by Sir James George Scott who, under his pseudonym of Shway Yoe, wrote his classic work *The Burman, His Life and Notions*. Situated at a bracing 878 meters, Taunggyi serves as the capital of Shan State and as an important economic pipeline for goods smuggled from Thailand.

Attractions
Chief draw is Taunggyi Market, held once every five days, and a convenient venue to watch local hilltribes who arrive in their traditional costumes. An introduction to the 30-plus ethnic groups of the Shan Plateau can be found inside the Shan State Museum near the Taunggyi Hotel. You can also enjoy the views from Yat Taw Me Pagoda on the top of the hill just west of St. George Anglican Church.

Accommodations
Perhaps since Western visitors are not permitted to travel beyond Taunggyi, the bustling trading post offers few guesthouses or hotels open to foreign travelers.

May Khu Guesthouse: An old backpackers' favorite just west of the main road and one block south of the market. US$10.

Khemarat Guesthouse: Best value guesthouse in town a few hundred meters west of the main street in the northwest residential corner of town. 4 Bogyoke Aung San Rd., US$8-18.

Taunggyi Hotel: Best in town with 56 spacious rooms at Taunggyi's south end just east of the Shan Museum. The tourist office and moneychanging facilities are located here. Tower Rd., tel. (081) 21127, US$30-65.

NYAUNGSHWE (YAUNGHWE)

Small town at the northern end of Inle Lake which serves as the primary accommodation center and launching point for boat tours of the lake.

Nyaungshwe, one of some 200-odd Intha settlements constructed around the lake, features several small but worthwhile pagodas and the small Shan Palace Museum in the northeast corner of town. The tourist office at the canal arranges boat tours of Inle Lake and collects the US$3 entry fee.

Accommodations

Almost a dozen guesthouses opened a few years ago after the government eased restrictions on private ownership.

Joy Hotel: Popular budget spot on the access canal a few blocks west of the central market. US$6-15.

Shwe Hintha Guesthouse: Another basic lodge across the street from the access canal and flanked by several boat landings. US$5-12.

Golden Express Hotel: Mid-range hotel four blocks east of the canal with spacious fan-cooled rooms and private baths with hot water—almost a necessity during the cold winter months. 19 Phaungdawpyan Rd., US$25-50.

Hupin Hotel: One block west of the market is another mid-range hotel with rooftop restaurant and utilitarian rooms with hot showers. 10-66 Kan Tar Quarter, tel. (081) 21374 in Taunggyi, US$20-45.

INLE LAKE

Inle Lake—one of the most dazzling and magical places in Asia—has long served as the home to the Intha ("Sons of the Lake"), a Mon people who migrated here centuries ago from the southeastern regions of Myanmar. This clever and relatively prosperous race of people literally farms the lake by cultivating floating gardens and fishing with enormous conical traps—a brilliant concept of manufacturing land which has made them justifiably famous throughout Southeast Asia.

First the rubbery tubes of water hyacinths and rushes are woven together into gigantic mats. Incredibly fertile mud is then dredged from the bottom of the lake and dumped on the mat to form instant land. When the layer of humus is deep enough to allow farming but not so heavy as to sink, the floating garden is towed to the owner's home and pegged to the lake floor with long bamboo staves, thereby disproving Will Rogers' axiom, "Buy land, they ain't making it anymore."

These remarkable people have also developed an eccentric method of fishing while rowing with one leg wrapped around the oar. Although this storklike style of rowing appears peculiar and overly dramatic, it effectively leaves one hand free for holding the net while maneuvering through the water hyacinths. When the fisherman spots a sizable shoal of fish in the shallow and crystal-clear water, he drops the huge trap and pushes it home with his leg. The ensnared fish are then speared at his leisure through a hole in the top of the cage.

Touring the Lake

Visitors can tour the lake by private boat or government crafts operated by the tourist office. Prices range 800-1,500 *kyat* per boatload and the typical five-hour tour includes stops for lunch, shopping, and sightseeing.

The boat trip passes floating gardens, wildlife, leg rowers, and fishermen before reaching the picturesque village of Ywama, where once every five days a small but colorful floating market is held along the largest canal. Visitors are also taken to the highly revered Phaung Daw U Pagoda with its five tiny and shapeless Buddha images which, according to legend, were brought from Malaysia by King Alaungsithu in the 12th century. Having proved their miraculous powers, they are now transported around the lake on a gilded royal barge each fall during the annual Karaweik Celebration.

Besides being successful farmers and fishermen, the Intha are also talented craftsmen who produce famous Shan shoulder bags, thick Shan *longyis*, conical hats called *khamouts*, and delicate silverware.

An alternative to the somewhat rushed and commercialized boat tour is a canoe trip along the canals near Nyaungshwe.

The glamour of the East had cast its spell upon him; the mystery of lands in which no white man had set foot since the beginning of things had fired his imagination; the itch of travel was upon him, goading him to restlessness.

—HUGH CLIFFORD,
THE STORY OF EXPLORATION

Travel can hardly ever fail to wreak a transformation of some sort, great or small, and for better or for worse, in the situation of the traveller.

—CLAUDE LÉVI-STRAUSS,
TRISTES TROPIQUES

Every man carries within himself a world made up of all that he has seen and loved; and it is to this world that he returns incessantly, though he may pass through, and seem to inhabit, a world quite foreign to it.

—CHATEAUBRIAND,
VOYAGE EN ITALIE

MYANMAR (BURMA)

>

THE PHILIPPINES

Diego Gutieres, first Pilot who went to the Phillippinas, reports of many strange things: If there bee any Paradise upon earth, it is in that countrey, and addeth, that sitting under a tree, you shal have such sweet smells, with such great content and pleasure, that you shall remember nothing, neither wife, nor children, nor have any kinde of appetite to eate nor drinke.

—HENRY HAWKS (1572)
NAVIGATIONS OF ENGLISH NATIONS

When I wish to be misinformed about a country, I ask a man who has lived there thirty years.

—LORD PALMERSTON,
THE IMPERIAL IDEA

Three hundred years in the convent and fifty years in Hollywood.

—ANONYMOUS

INTRODUCTION

The Philippines is the undiscovered paradise of Southeast Asia. Blessed with over 7,000 sun-drenched islands, this tropical wonderland has just about everything needed for a superb vacation: exquisite white-sand beaches fringed with gently swaying palm trees, unparalleled scuba diving, volcanoes for mountaineers, classic baroque cathedrals, vast expanses of verdant ricefields, outstanding nightlife, and the most enthusiastic festivals in Asia. The Philippines is also an outstanding travel bargain since it offers some of the region's lowest prices for accommodation, food, and transportation—chiefly due to the currency devaluation of 1997.

With all this, you might expect the country to be crowded with visitors and overrun with tour groups. Surprisingly, most of the country remains virtually untouched by mass tourism, giving adventurous travelers the opportunity to easily get off the beaten track.

But what really separates the Philippines from the rest of Asia is the people, whose warmth and enthusiasm are legendary throughout the East. Seldom will you meet such hospitable people—so ready to smile, joke, laugh, and make friends with Western visitors. Perhaps

because of their long association with Spain, Filipinos are emotional and passionate about life in a way that seems more Latin than Asian. And because of their American ties, communication is easy since most Filipinos speak some form of English, whether American slang or homegrown pidgin. They're also a talented race of people. Music fans will be happy to learn that Filipinos, for reasons endlessly debated, are unquestionably Asia's most gifted singers, musicians, dancers, and entertainers.

If you believe that the most important travel experience is to make friends and learn about people, rather than just tour temples and museums, then the Philippines is your country.

THE LAND

Surrounded by the Philippine Sea to the east, the South China Sea to the west, and the Sulawesi Sea to the south, the 7,109 islands of the Philippines spill like a diamond necklace from northern Batanes to the Sulu Archipelago. This widely scattered archipelago is divided into four major groups. The largest and most important is Luzon.

PHILIPPINES

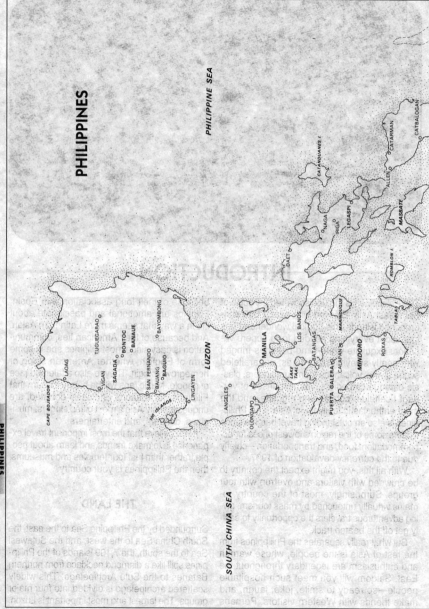

PHILIPPINES

PHILIPPINE SEA

SOUTH CHINA SEA

LUZON

MANILA

CAPE BOJEADOR
LAOAG
VIGAN
TUGUEGARAO
BONTOC
SAGADA
BANAUE
BAYOMBONG
SAN FERNANDO
BAGUIO
100 ISLANDS
LINGAYEN
ANGELES
OLONGAPO
BATANGAS
LOS BANOS
LAKE TAAL
PUERTA GALERA
CALAPAN
MINDORO
ROXAS
TABLAS
ROMBLON I.
MARINDUQUE
MARBATE
MASBATE
LEGASPI
IRIGA
NAGA
DAET
CATANDUANES I.
CATARMAN
CATBALOGAN
ALLEN

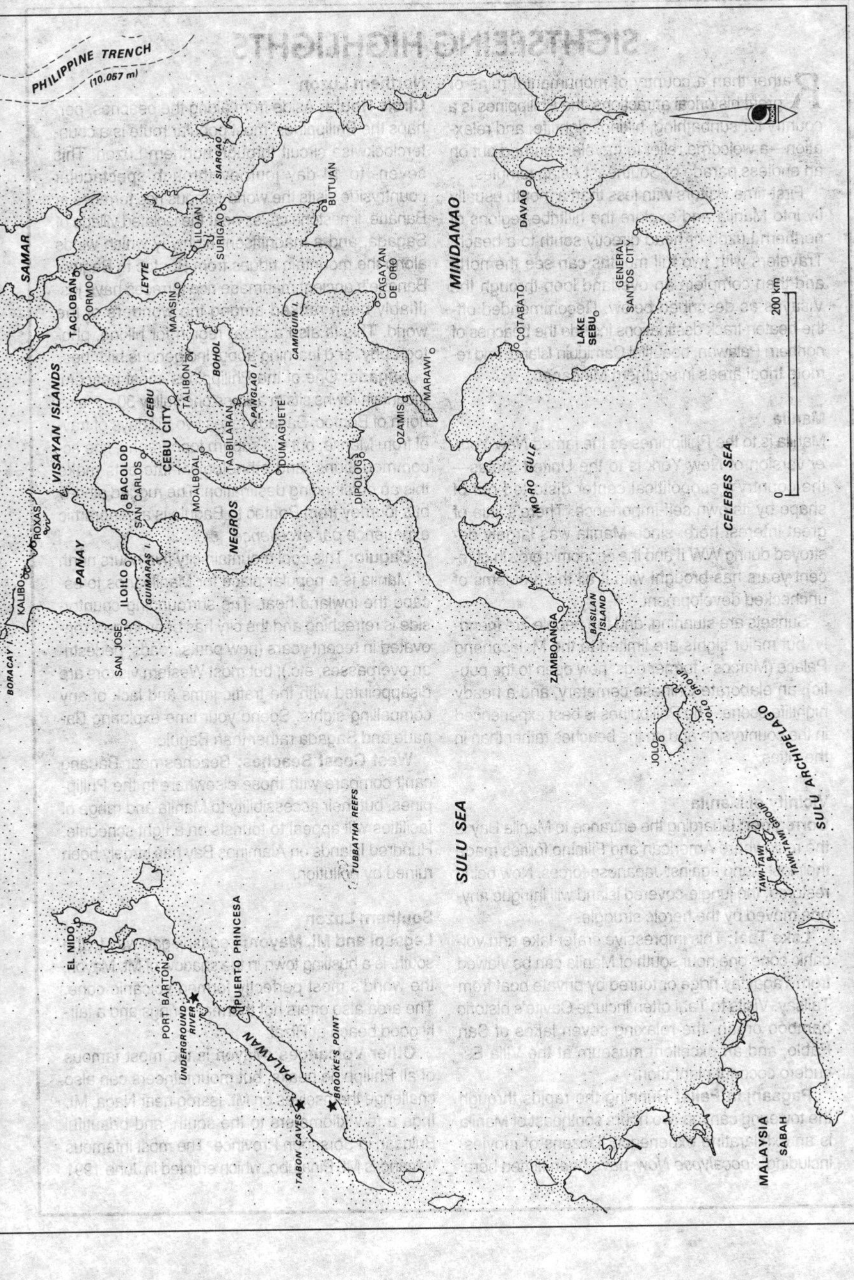

PHILIPPINE TRENCH
(10,057 m)

SAMAR

VISAYAN ISLANDS

PANAY

KALIBO
BORACAY
ROXAS
ILOILO
SAN JOSE
GUIMARAS

NEGROS
BACOLOD
SAN CARLOS
MOALBOAL
DUMAGUETE

CEBU
CEBU CITY
TAGBILARAN
PANGLAO
BOHOL
TALIBON

LEYTE
TACLOBAN
ORMOC
MAASIN

SIARGAO
SURIGAO
BUTUAN
CAGAYAN DE ORO
CAMIGUIN I.
MARAWI
DIPOLOG
OZAMIS

MINDANAO

DAVAO
GENERAL SANTOS CITY
COTABATO
LAKE SEBU
MORO GULF

CELEBES SEA

ZAMBOANGA
BASILAN ISLAND

JOLO GROUP
JOLO

SULU SEA

SULU ARCHIPELAGO

TAWI-TAWI GROUP
TAWI-TAWI

MALAYSIA
SABAH

PALAWAN
EL NIDO
PORT BARTON
PUERTO PRINCESA
UNDERGROUND RIVER
BROOKE'S POINT
TABON CAVES
TUBBATAHA REEFS

200 km
0

PHILIPPINES

© MOON PUBLICATIONS, INC.

SIGHTSEEING HIGHLIGHTS

Rather than a country of monumental ruins or great historical attractions, the Philippines is a country for sunbathing, hiking, nightlife, and relaxation—a welcome relief to travelers burned out on an endless parade of Southeast Asian temples.

First-time visitors with less than a month usually fly into Manila and explore the hilltribe regions of northern Luzon or head directly south to a beach. Travelers with two full months can see the north and then complete an overland loop through the Visayas as described below. Recommended off-the-beaten-track destinations include the beaches of northern Palawan, beautiful Camiguin Island, and remote tribal areas in southern Mindanao.

Manila

Manila is to the Philippines as the famed *New Yorker* version of New York is to the United States—the country's ecopolitical center distorted out of shape by its own self-importance. There's little of great interest here, since Manila was largely destroyed during WW II and the economic growth of recent years has brought with it all the problems of unchecked development.

Sunsets are stunning, and the people are friendly, but major sights are limited to the Malacañang Palace (Marcos's former digs, now open to the public), an elaborate Chinese cemetery, and a heady nightlife scene. The Philippines is best experienced in the countryside and on the beaches rather than in the cities.

Vicinity of Manila

Corregidor: Guarding the entrance to Manila Bay is the rock where American and Filipino forces made their last stand against Japanese forces. Now being restored, the jungle-covered island will intrigue anyone moved by the heroic struggle.

Lake Taal: This impressive crater lake and volcanic cone one hour south of Manila can be viewed from Tagaytay ridge or toured by private boat from Talisay. Visits to Taal often include Cavite's historic bamboo organ, the relaxing seven lakes of San Pablo, and an excellent museum at the Villa Escudero coconut plantation.

Pagsanjan Falls: Running the rapids through the towering canyon two hours southeast of Manila is an exhilarating experience. Dozens of movies, including *Apocalypse Now,* have been filmed here.

Northern Luzon

Circle Route: Aside from along the beaches, perhaps the Philippines' most popular route is a counterclockwise circuit through northern Luzon. This seven- to 14-day journey through spectacular countryside visits the world-famous rice terraces at Banaue, limestone caves near the isolated village of Sagada, and a magnificent highway which winds along the mountain ridges from Bontoc to Baguio. Banaue's ancient manmade rice terraces have justifiably been ranked among the wonders of the world. This is also a great region for hiking, photography, and learning about indigenous hilltribes.

Sagada: One of the Philippines' most peaceful mountain towns sits in a limestone valley 30 minutes north of Bontoc. Sagada takes two full days of travel from Manila, but the superb topography, fine accommodations, and ethnological interests make this an outstanding destination. The rugged all-day bus journey from Bontoc to Baguio is a panoramic experience *par excellence.*

Baguio: This cool mountain city five hours north of Manila is a popular place for Manileanos to escape the lowland heat. The surrounding countryside is refreshing and has been largely renovated in recent years (new parks, roads, pedestrian overpasses, etc.), but most Western visitors are disappointed with the traffic jams and lack of any compelling sights. Spend your time exploring Banaue and Sagada rather than Baguio.

West Coast Beaches: Beaches near Bauang can't compare with those elsewhere in the Philippines, but their accessibility to Manila and range of facilities will appeal to tourists on a tight schedule. Hundred Islands on Alaminos Bay has largely been ruined by pollution.

Southern Luzon

Legaspi and Mt. Mayon: Legaspi, gateway to the south, is a bustling town in the shadow of Mt. Mayon, the world's most perfectly formed volcanic cone. The area also offers hot thermal springs and a fairly good beach at Rizal.

Other Volcanoes: Mayon is the most famous of all Philippine peaks, but mountaineers can also challenge themselves on Mt. Isarog near Naga, Mt. Iriga a few kilometers to the south, and beautiful Bulusan in Sorsogon Province. The most infamous volcano is Mt. Pinatubo, which erupted in June 1991 and forced the closure of American-run Clark Air Force Base. Climbing this famous peak is one of the newest and most popular outdoor activities in the country.

Other Islands
Bohol: One of the prettiest but least visited islands in the Visayas is known for outstanding Spanish churches, crystalline beaches on nearby Panglao Island, and the eerie geological formations known as the Chocolate Hills. Travel logistics make Bohol an easy side trip from Cebu.

Boracay: The spectacular expanse of crystalline sand, clear waters, and swaying coconut palms have deservedly made Boracay the most famous beach resort in the Philippines. Facilities range from simple nipa-palm bungalows to first-class resorts with air-conditioned chalets, windsurfing, sailing, and entertainment from sunsets to folk music. And after years of unchecked development, the government is finally doing something about the water pollution and lack of sanitation facilities.

Cebu: Cebu City, economic and cultural hub of the Visayan Islands, is a convenient base for exploring the beaches, churches, and diving areas of the central Philippines. Visitors short on time can fly directly to Cebu and make side trips to Bohol, the nearby beaches on Mactan and Moalboal, and then continue west across Negros and Panay to Boracay. Cebu City has good restaurants, great festivals, lively nightlife, and historical attractions connected with the Spanish era.

Mindanao: Travelers not discouraged by the remoteness and political disruptions of Mindanao will discover Muslim townships little changed in generations, some of the country's last remaining stands of tropical forests, and isolated pockets of tribal culture. Camiguin, north of Cagayan de Oro, is a superb island with great beaches and few tourists. Lake Sebu, west of General Santos City in southern Mindanao, is the idyllic homeland of the traditional T'boli people. Islamic lifestyles continue near Marawi City and in the Sulu Archipelago. Davao and "exotic" Zamboanga are modern towns with little of charm or interest.

Mindoro: Puerto Galera on Mindoro Island is an immensely popular beach resort only five hours from Manila. Although haphazard development has ruined some of the region, scuba diving remains outstanding and the more remote beaches remain inviting.

Negros: Top draws are the ancient steam trains that haul cane on sugar plantations near Bacolod. Train enthusiasts come from all over the world to photograph and ride the rare German and British steamers.

Palawan: Long considered the final frontier of the Philippines, Palawan in recent years has been attracting increasing number of travelers who want to get off the beaten track and enjoy some of the best beaches and diving in the country. Highlights include topographic wonders near Puerto Princesa, underground caves near Port Barton, anthropological discoveries at Tabon, and the spectacular scuba diving at El Nido. Travel conditions remain primitive, but accommodations and restaurants are plentiful and cheap.

Palawan is unquestionably the finest destination in the Philippines.

Panay: Spanish churches modified with Filipino designs are the highlights of Iloilo, capital of Panay. Other draws include Sicogon Island and the annual Ati Atihan festival in Kalibo.

Samar and Leyte: Waterfalls and historical ties to WW II are the main attractions here. Frequent interisland buses and boats connect Samar and Leyte with Luzon and the lower Visayas.

Routes
Visitors with limited time should fly directly from Manila to the beach or island of their choice. Travelers with more time (6-8 weeks) might take a more leisurely approach with an overland journey through northern Luzon and then around the central Visayan Islands. The more leisurely trip can be done in either direction starting from, and with a return to, Manila, with a combination of boats and public buses.

The clockwise route first visits Legaspi and Mt. Mayon in southern Luzon before continuing south through Samar and Leyte to Cebu. Bohol can be toured between Leyte and Cebu or as an easy backtrack from Cebu. The journey continues west across Negros and Panay to Boracay. Then it's north to Mindoro and the beaches at Puerto Galera before returning to Manila. More travel details under "Islands to the South."

Those with less time who want to see the real highlights should fly from Manila to Palawan and then spend a few days or weeks relaxing on the beaches at Sabang, El Nido, or south of Puerto Princessa.

PHILIPPINES

home to Tagalog-speaking Filipinos and site of Manila. The best beaches and diving are found in the Visayas, the string of islands situated between Luzon and Mindanao. To the south is the rarely visited but culturally rich island of Mindanao. To the west is snakelike Palawan, a remote destination almost a world unto itself.

Problems in Paradise

The rich volcanic soil and heavy rainfall of the Philippines has blessed it with an exotic and varied plant life, from flowering plants to hardwoods such as the Philippine mahogany. At one time, most of the country was covered with mangrove swamps and tropical forests filled with spectacular wildlife.

But unchecked population growth and reckless logging have seriously depleted the once-plentiful tropical forests and killed most of the wildlife. Resource specialists chart a staggering rate of destruction. When independence was achieved in 1946, over 30 million hectares—almost three-quarters of the land—was covered with tropical hardwoods and drier *molave* forests. Last year it stood at less than five million hectares. Calling it among the highest rates of deforestation in the world, the Asian Development Bank estimates that at present levels the Philippines will be completely stripped bare in less than two decades.

The devastation has aroused the passions of both international environmentalists and the local Catholic Church, which recently ranked it as a more serious threat than political instability and economic stagnation. Loggers, of course, bear much of the blame, but deforestation is mostly due to skyrocketing population growth and destructive slash-and-burn farming techniques of the landless poor. Solutions have been proposed by environmental groups such as the World Wildlife Fund and Manila-based Haribon Foundation, but unless action is quickly taken the outlook for the Filipino environment remains grim.

Climate

The Philippines is a tropical land with high temperatures and extreme humidity along with heavy rainfall during the summer monsoons. Temperature varies with altitude but not latitude; if it's hot in Zamboanga it will be just as uncomfortable in Manila.

The country has three seasons. Winter months from November through February are hot and dry but pleasant. The extraordinarily hot summer months from March through June can be devastating to first-time visitors. Travel during the rainy season from June to October is difficult but enjoyable because of the green landscapes and cooler temperatures. Rainfall and typhoons hit the east coast during the summer months.

Best time to visit the Philippines is during the dry and slightly cooler period from November to April.

HISTORY

Filipino history is unique in Asia. Early inhabitants of the archipelago were dark-skinned Negritos and brown-skinned Malays who had emigrated across land bridges from Indonesia and mainland Southeast Asia. Chinese, Indian, and Arab traders began arriving in large numbers sometime after A.D. 1000. Animism, the native religion of the lowland agriculturalists, fell in the 14th century to Islam, which arrived from Brunei and quickly spread north to Manila.

Though the pre-Hispanic Philippines served as an important trading crossroads for Chinese and Indonesian merchants, it failed to develop into a unified nation with a sense of insular cohesion. Life remained loosely organized around tribal vil-

PHILIPPINES

MANILA'S CLIMATE

	JAN.	FEB.	MAR.	APR.	MAY	JUNE	JULY	AUG.	SEPT.	OCT.	NOV.	DEC.
Avg. Maximum C	29°	31°	33°	34°	33°	33°	31°	31°	31°	31°	30°	29°
Avg. Maximum F	84°	88°	92°	94°	92°	92°	88°	88°	88°	88°	86°	84°
Rainy Days	6	3	4	4	12	17	24	23	22	19	14	11

lages *(barangays)* ruled by hereditary chieftains *(datus)* who had rejected the Hindu and Buddhist cultural influences that dominated the balance of Southeast Asia. Expansive empires were never constructed; sophisticated economies never developed; great heroes and political leaders never rose to unify the vast archipelago.

This lack of an evocative past prior to the arrival of the Spanish is of great significance to modern Filipino history. Filipino scholars searching for their cultural identity are often frustrated by historical records which seem scant when compared to the other countries of Southeast Asia. The paucity of data has inspired some historians to romanticize the past and create false legends about mythological characters. More importantly, the lack of history has sapped national self-confidence and weakened the search for political unity.

All this was exacerbated by the arrival of Spanish *conquistadores* and American colonialists who brought with them their Western religion, artforms, political models, and value systems. This long and destructive period of foreign rule—the so-called 300 years in a Spanish convent and 50 years in Hollywood—has created an Asian contradiction: the Philippines, gateway to Asia, is essentially a highly Westernized country populated by a Christian majority that speaks English.

Spanish Rule

Filipino history, at least in written form, begins with the arrival of Ferdinand Magellan in 1521. Assigned by the Spanish Crown to discover a western route to the Spice Islands of Indonesia, the Portuguese explorer instead stumbled across the Philippines, where he befriended the raja of Cebu and converted hundreds of islanders to the Spanish faith. Considering his great feats of exploration and diplomacy, it is ironic that Magellan foolishly got involved with tribal politics and was killed by Lapu Lapu, a petty chieftain now immortalized as the first Filipino to resist foreign rule. Magellan's ship eventually returned to Spain loaded with valuable spices, thereby recovering the expense of the three-year expedition and successfully completing the first circumnavigation of the world.

Another Spanish explorer, Legaspi, annexed the islands in 1565 and named them "Filipinas" in honor of King Philip of Spain. Legaspi moved his army and capital from Cebu to Manila, where

Spanish military and religious power continued to rule for 327 years. Catholic friars proceeded to convert most of the population to Christianity—except for the Muslims of Mindanao and the mountain tribals of northern Luzon.

From an economic standpoint, however, the Philippines was a failure. Without revenues from the Sino-Mexican galleon trade—Chinese silks exchanged for Mexican silver via the trading entrepot of Manila—the colony would have collapsed long before the Americans took control in the early 20th century.

The Philippine Revolution

Spain continued to rule the Philippines without serious opposition until the late 19th century, when Filipino leaders began agitating for greater political control. The struggle for independence gained worldwide press in 1872 after several Filipino priests were brazenly executed by the Spanish authorities for leading a small revolt in Cavite.

Three Filipinos soon emerged as leaders of the revolution. The most dynamic was Jose Rizal, the Filipino-Chinese national hero who founded the Propaganda Movement and inspired the masses with his passionate poetry. Andres Bonifacio formed the radical Katipunan Society, while Emilio Aguinaldo served as Bonifacio's revolutionary captain. The Spanish made their biggest blunder in 1896 when they publicly executed Rizal after a farcical trial, thereby creating the revolution's first martyr and inadvertently uniting the educated classes *(illustrados)* and the revolutionaries.

Inspired by the martyrdom and fiery writings of Rizal, Bonifacio organized armed resistance against Spanish rule but was executed by Aguinaldo during a bitter power struggle. Aguinaldo eventually proved himself a figure of great power but also a ruthless leader who ambushed his rivals and made a long series of grave political blunders. His moment of glory arrived on 12 June 1898, when he unfurled a flag and declared his country a sovereign state. The Philippines had become Asia's first country to declare independence from European colonialism.

American Rule

Filipino independence seemed assured when the Spanish-American War erupted in 1898 and Dewey's warships steamed from Hong Kong to

PHILIPPINES

Manila under the war cry, "Remember the *Maine* and to Hell with Spain."

But the promise of Filipino statehood proved short-lived. Despite the painful conflict of American democracy and colonial rule, and an American Senate which almost rejected the war prize, the Spanish-American Treaty of Paris ceded the Philippines, Puerto Rico, and Guam to the U.S. in return for $20 million. The Filipinos felt deeply betrayed. Fighting immediately erupted between American troops and Filipino rebels who rejected President McKinley's policy of Manifest Destiny. It was a horrible war in which over 200,000 Filipinos were killed. The revolution sputtered to an end in 1901 when Aguinaldo was captured and most of the educated *illustrados* joined the new government.

Under McKinley's policy of benevolent assimilation, American leadership over the next five decades proved itself somewhat more enlightened than Spanish rule. Huge sums were spent on infrastructure and health. Perhaps most significant were the American ideals of political democracy and other less tangible manifestations such as dress, purchasing preferences, and hierarchy of social values. English was introduced as the medium of instruction in an attempt to bind together the disparate linguistic and religious groups.

By the time the Americans left five decades later, American cultural imperialism—from language to mass marketing—was inexorably ingrained in Filipino consciousness.

World War II

The American timetable for Filipino independence was disrupted in December 1941, two days after Pearl Harbor, when Japanese forces bombed Clark Air Base and began their fateful march toward Manila. Filipino-American troops under the leadership of General Douglas MacArthur retreated to Corregidor island, where they mounted a valiant but futile last stand. MacArthur subsequently fled to Australia, where he proclaimed "I shall return," while the remaining 80,000 POWs endured the Bataan Death March, a five-day ordeal in which over 10,000 soldiers died from torture, starvation, and beatings.

MacArthur fulfilled his promise on 20 October 1944, when he beached at Leyte to begin the reconquest of Luzon. Blinded by their national-

istic fervor, Japanese forces retreated to Manila's historic city of Intramuros and refused to surrender, a tragic decision that cost the lives of over 100,000 Filipino civilians and forced the near-complete destruction of Manila. Although the brutal Japanese occupation was deeply resented by most Filipinos, it also broke prewar colonial bonds and inspired the Filipinos to take their place in the new Asian consciousness.

The Marcos Era

America's colonial experience came to a close on 4 July 1946, when Manuel Roxas, the nation's first president, proclaimed Filipino independence. The ensuing two decades were a traumatic period of mounting political anarchy, economic chaos, and increasing concentration of wealth in the hands of a few. Leftist insurgencies flourished in central Luzon, while Muslim secessionist movements plagued the south.

Into this firestorm came Ferdinand Marcos, a brilliant and charismatic lawyer who took the presidency in 1965. Marcos at first enjoyed widespread and genuine popularity as he constructed schools, roads, and telecommunications systems while attempting to deal with the Philippines' chronic social and economic problems. But corruption, lawlessness, and civil disorder worsened.

Legally barred from serving a third term, Marcos declared martial law in 1972, dissolved the congress, and rewrote the constitution. He also jailed hundreds of political opposition leaders, including Benigno Aquino, who had been considered a virtual shoo-in to win the 1973 presidential election.

As the new supreme godfather, Marcos proceeded to establish a nation-strangling network of nepotism and cronyism that made his friends and relatives grotesquely rich. His wife Imelda was appointed governor of Manila, with a nonaccountable budget of US$200 million. Her brother became governor of Leyte, Marcos's cousin was made chief of staff of the armed forces, his golfing buddy was awarded control of the nation's largest construction company, and other cronies were given control of the sugar and coconut industries. The level of graft was breathtaking even by generous Filipino standards.

By the time Marcos fled the country in 1986, he had become neither the longest-reigning nor the most dictatorial leader in Southeast Asia.

He had, instead, become the world's biggest crook: the country was bankrupt, the people's standard of living had collapsed, and Marcos had salted away an estimated US$10 *billion* in Swiss bank accounts.

The Aquino Era

Political opposition to the Marcos regime galvanized after Benigno Aquino was assassinated by the Philippine military in August 1983. General Fabian Ver, a close friend and trusted ally of Marcos, was arrested and interrogated during a carefully staged 10-month trial which ended with the conviction of a lone dead gunman. The country exploded.

Threatened by widespread political demonstrations, Marcos suddenly called for "snap" presidential elections to settle the question of national leadership. Benigno's widow, Corazon Aquino, a political neophyte with little experience and an election machinery that resembled a Filipino Woodstock, disproved the maxim that Filipinos lack the willpower to depose evil dictators.

Despite widespread vote buying, intimidation by goons, and voter disenfranchisement that characterized the dirtiest election in Philippine history, Marcos lost the referendum and was forced to flee the country in February 1986. Left behind were his dialysis machines, Ouija boards, half-eaten tins of caviar, a collection of crystals and power pyramids, and a basement filled with Imelda's gowns, furs, and 3,000 pairs of shoes including disco sprinters equipped with rechargeable lights in the heels. With People Power versus the Forces of Evil as the theme, Marcos was the loser in a stunning victory that set off political reform throughout the rest of Asia.

GOVERNMENT

The Philippines is a constitutional republic with a presidency and a National Assembly comprised of a House of Representatives and a Senate. An extraordinarily complex constitution, which passed a few years ago, limits the president to a term of six years, restricts presidential power, guarantees human rights, and attempts to legislate morality with restrictions on birth control and abortion.

Aquino's miracle, engineered by the Filipino people and military forces commanded by

Ramos, was a magical moment in Philippine history. But the housewife from Tarlac soon discovered that political honeymoons are difficult to sustain. Democracy was restored and a painfully long-winded "freedom" constitution passed, but economic problems centered on land reform and massive foreign debt continued to pile up. Marcos's vast fortune has eluded the Presidential Commission on Good Government, and the anticipated flood of post-revolution foreign aid and investment slowed to a trickle.

The Ramos Era

On 11 May 1992, democratic elections brought new national leadership under the helm of Fidel Ramos, the former military leader who received critical endorsement from Corazon Aquino. In accepting President Ramos, Filipinos voted soundly against Marcos crony Eduardo Conjuangco in an obvious vote against authoritarianism. They voted strongly against Ramon Mitra, in a demonstration against the politics of patronage which dominates Philippine society, but voted in large numbers for antigraft crusader Miriam Santiago as they registered their contempt for corrupt public officials. The litany of losers perhaps told more about contemporary Filipino society than the election of a bespectacled West Point graduate who co-led the February 1986 revolt.

Ramos brought great change to the Philippines by opening the economy to Western investors. Ramos's three-tiered cabinet of military leaders, corporate technocrats, and professional politicians pulled the Philippines out of its economic malaise and returned it to healthy levels not seen since the 1950s.

In national elections held in May 1998, Filipinos elected one-time B-movie film star and Vice President Joseph Estrada to the presidency. The general elections were among the country's most peaceful in recent history.

ECONOMY

News on the Filipino economy has improved in recent years. With the fall of Marcos and increased investments from local and foreign entrepreneurs, a sense of confidence has returned

FILIPINO CUSTOMS

Something of a false veneer lies over the people and culture of the Philippines. Things seem so familiar that many Western visitors are easily lulled into misguided complacency, thinking that what has been borrowed from the West has been absorbed into the inner core of Filipino society. This is a mistake. Filipino customs and beliefs are surprisingly different from Western values. The following might help avoid misunderstandings while traveling around the country.

Body Language: Filipinos are masters at cleverly using their eyes, lips, and hands to convey a wide range of messages. Eyebrow talk is perhaps the most obvious. Raised eyebrows and a smile indicate a silent "hello" or "yes" to your question. Fixed, hard eye contact between males is an aggressive gesture best avoided. Ladies often purse their lips and nod their heads to indicate direction. The proper method to summon somebody is with a downward wave, not with a skyward wave and call. If the waiter doesn't respond, a soft *psssst* will do the trick.

Spoken Language: Filipinos place great emphasis on polite language and gentle conversation. They also desire to keep peace and please Western visitors. Since admitting ignorance to a question brings shame, most Filipinos instead answer "yes" or venture their best guesses. Be forewarned that the Filipino "yes" can mean "yes," "maybe," "no," "OK," or "I don't know," depending on the spirit in which it was given. Euphemism is often used to maintain smooth interpersonal relations. Voice tone is always soft and gentle. Direct questions should be avoided. Before asking for directions, it would be polite to ask, "Excuse me, but may I ask you a question?" Filipinos, surprisingly, can also be blunt. Inquiries about your occupation, income, size of family, and how much you paid for your hotel room and camera are used to evaluate your social standing as well as just to make friendly conversation. No harm intended.

Nicknames: Most Filipinos have Spanish-sounding first and surnames. These Hispanic titles were only adopted in 1849 after a decree issued by the Spanish governor forced all Filipinos to take a Western surname for bureaucratic reasons. And yet, when you ask for somebody's name, it's just as likely to be a nickname such as Peachy, Ding Dong, Tingles, Pinky, Toytoy, or Ballsy. Filipinos love nicknames since they make people feel closer and add a degree of informality.

Hiya: Filipino values, often a marriage of Western values borrowed from Catholicism and Eastern

---

to the country. The economy is now growing at six to eight percent, a welcome reverse from the declining figures of the early '80s.

But the recovery faces serious obstacles. A World Bank report claims that over 30 million of the country's 70 million live in absolute poverty and that the situation has worsened during the past three decades. Among ASEAN nations, the Philippines has the highest level of poverty and the lowest calorie supply per capita. Furthermore, real wages have steadily dropped since 1960 and almost 60% of the population is either under- or unemployed. It is painfully obvious to even the most casual traveler that little of the urban economic recovery has filtered down to the impoverished *barrios.*

These dismal statistics are especially discouraging since the Philippines lies within one of the most economically dynamic regions in the world. The country was once, in fact, the shining star of Southeast Asia, boasting the region's highest growth rates from 1950 to 1960. By 1980 it had fallen to dead last.

What went wrong? The World Bank reports that on a macroeconomic level, more than 50% of the gross national product is wasted in a hopeless attempt to reduce a staggering foreign debt of almost US$30 billion. On a microeconomic level are the factors of declining agricultural productivity, lack of crop diversity, and unequal ownership of basic assets. The country has long relied on a narrow base of commodity exports such as sugar, coconuts, minerals, and forest products.

Unequal distribution of land and income is another problem. Studies show that moneyed mestizos of Spanish-Filipino or Chinese-Filipino blood make up less than 20% of the population but earn over 50% of the nation's total income. A Manila University study once claimed that most of the Filipino economy is controlled by a mere 60 mestizo families. And despite decades of land reform, land ownership patterns remain badly values shared by other Southeast Asian peoples, are typified by *hiya,* the Tagalog term for "shame." Perhaps the most powerful glue of Filipino society, the desire to obey the rules of society and not rock the boat keeps most Filipinos from showing anger or displeasure. Western visitors should control their emotions and keep a sense of *hiya.*

Amor Propio: Closely tied to the notion of "shame" is the Oriental notion of "face," or *amor propio,* literally "love of self." There are endless ways to lose face: arguing, being publically criticized, performing degrading labor, or not knowing the answer to a question. Preserving self-esteem is often why Filipinos just smile to your strange questions; that's better than admitting ignorance. Publicly criticizing or arguing with a Filipino should be avoided since this is a direct attack on his *amor propio.* Many Filipino males will fight for the preservation of their pride and *amor propio.*

Pakikisama: Filipinos strongly believe in sharing, camaraderie, and the ability to get along with others. Fitting in is more important than standing out. *Pakikisama* is also the reason why Filipinos spontaneously invite strangers in for dinner, quickly reach for the check in restaurants, and are willing to loan almost anything to anybody with little hope of recovery. It's also why they never publicly disagree with each other and think it's strange that

Westerners travel alone. "Where is your companion?"—the constant inquiry to solo travelers—really means "What on earth did you do to deserve such an awful fate?"

Utan Na Loob: Reciprocal relationships and the need to repay debts of gratitude are other important components to Filipino society. Many relationships begin with a small gift, which must be repaid later with interest. The cycle escalates for a period of years or generations until a highly complex web of interdependencies has been created. Both Marcos and Aquino used *utan na loob* to create their political dynasties. Wealthy industrialists are often connected through this cycle. Western travelers who accept Filipino generosity also accept the principle of repayment.

Compadrazco: The Roman Catholic concept of standing as godfather to a child during baptism is another important element in Filipino life. This ritual creates powerful bonds of obligation not only between godfather and godchild but also between godfather and the child's parents. Since godfathers often provide financial support, jobs, and upward social mobility to their godchildren, parents will search out their wealthiest friend or relative to accept this religious obligation. Western visitors are sometimes invited to act as godfathers, but obligations should be carefully considered.

skewed. The Philippines has Asia's highest percentage of landless tenant farmers and the situation is getting worse; landless agriculturalists have grown from 10% in the '50s to an estimated 30-35% today. Land reform—by far the most controversial and emotional subject in the country—got another push under Ramos, but few experts believe agrarian reform will improve productivity or encourage the agricultural diversification that the country so desperately needs.

But the country's most pressing problem is the frightening population explosion. Filipinos have increased from 19 million in 1948 to over 70 million today. The population will soar past 100 million in another 20 years. This unchecked growth devastates the environment, threatens political stability, and keeps most Filipinos mired in absolute poverty. Simply no more land is left for population growth. Farmland population density is already higher than in Indonesia and nearly twice that of Thailand.

Stopgap measures have been proposed by the World Bank to try to slow the annual rate of growth from the current 2.4-2.8% to 2% by the year 2000, but birth control and abortion are controversial subjects in the staunchly Catholic Philippines. The fact remains that unless strong action is quickly taken, all economic gains will simply be absorbed by the rapidly growing population.

THE PEOPLE

The Filipinos
And now for some more encouraging news. What separates the Philippines from the rest of Southeast Asia is the people—undisputedly the most charming, enthusiastic, and open in Asia. It might take years to make friends with a Chinese, but the Filipino becomes a close partner within minutes. Their hospitality is direct and honest, their smiles are warm and spontaneous,

PHILIPPINES

And, as you will soon notice on arrival in Manila, Filipinos are easy to relate to since most speak some English, attend Christian churches, and follow Western music and fashion trends as closely as anyone in the world.

Filipinos are a unified race of people racially related to Malaysians and Indonesians. To this Malay stock has been added rich transfusions of Chinese, Indian, Spanish, and American blood, producing offspring such as Filipino-Spanish creoles and Filipino-Chinese mestizos. It's been a good marriage; racial tensions are rare.

Filipinos are sometimes classified into 10 major cultural groups based on either language or religion. Eight of the nine groups are Christians who differ little except for their dialects. Filipinos also have their own peculiar set of strengths and weaknesses as once described in a public report called the "Moral Recovery Program."

It's an interesting list. Weaknesses were given as a lack of discipline, initiative, self-analysis, and self-reflection, plus extreme personalism, fatalism (bahalana), and the kanya-kanya (blame somebody else) syndrome. Their strengths were listed as their sensitivity to people's feelings, sense of humor and flexibility, strong family loyalties, and the ability to survive daily hardships. Whatever the truth of these findings, Filipinos certainly are a fascinating race of people.

The Chinese

Chinese and Filipino-Chinese mestizos form the single most influential racial group in the Philippines. It is hard to overstate their contributions to the history of the country. Chinese traders were active in the archipelago well before the arrival of Islam from Brunei and Christianity from Spain. Chinese merchants later dominated the immensely lucrative Spanish galleon trade, while Chinese craftsmen and artisans constructed most of Manila's churches, roads, and homes.

Although periodically massacred or expelled by the Spanish, who feared their economic acumen, the Chinese have survived to gain almost complete control of the Filipino economy through hard work, intelligence, personal sacrifice, and the acceptance of extraordinarily thin profit margins. Many have married Filipino women. Their offspring, mixed-blood mestizos, now dominate the economy, in place of the once-powerful Filipino-Spanish families. Today they are involved

in virtually every major segment of the economy, from small *sari sari* stores to international mining and manufacturing consortiums.

However, not everything is fine in the Filipino-Chinese community. As elsewhere in Southeast Asia, there is the problem of Chinese assimilation into local society. While many Chinese have attempted to please the locals by adopting Filipino surnames and converting to Christianity, others continue to extol their cultural superiority by keeping their Chineseness through dress codes, private schools, newspapers, and other lifestyle choices. Interpreted by many as a rejection of Filipino culture, this nonconformity has nurtured strong anti-Sinitic feelings among less fortunate Filipinos.

Some call them the Jews of Asia, an impolite but perhaps valid comparison based on Chinese socio-religious differences and economic successes in the face of government-sanctioned persecution and discrimination. It was, in fact, only in 1975 that Marcos eased the naturalization criteria and made it possible for the Chinese to obtain Filipino citizenship. Despite this offer, it is estimated that today only 40% of the nation's 2.1 million Chinese have opted for naturalization.

Muslims

The Philippines' only large non-Christian Malay group is the Muslims who live throughout southern Mindanao and the Sulu Archipelago. Followers of Islam are divided into five major and five minor subgroups based on language and cultural background. All have resisted being assimilated into the Philippine nation, whether under Spanish, American, or Filipino control.

The latest skirmish was the Muslim secessionist war, which engulfed Mindanao from 1973 to 1979. After claiming at least 50,000 lives and involving two-thirds of the Filipino army, an uneasy truce was arranged between the central government and the Moro National Liberation Front. Despite a large degree of self-rule, however, Muslims remain an unsatisfied group that resents the political and economic domination of the Christian majority.

Cultural Minorities

Perhaps the most colorful and fascinating groups in the Philippines are the designated cultural minorities who inhabit the mountainous interiors

SPEAKING THE LANGUAGE

Over 70 dialects and 11 major languages are spoken throughout the Philippines. The most widely used languages include Tagalog, based on the Malay language and spoken by over 10 million residents of central Luzon, and the Cebuano language spoken by almost 20 million Visayans. Other languages include Ilocano spoken in northwest Luzon, Bicolano in southern Luzon, Pangasinese in northwestern Luzon, and Hiligaynon in Panay and eastern Negros.

The national language is Pilipino, a variation of Tagalog, although English continues to serve as the lingua franca of the archipelago. This odd situation is a legacy of American rule, when foreign educators established their language as the medium of instruction in all public schools. Today, Pilipino is being promoted over English for reasons of national pride, but most Filipinos continue to speak a heady melange of English, Pilipino, a regional dialect, and Taglish, a bizarre mixture of Tagalog and American slang. The universality of English ensures that basic conversations are possible with almost everybody from college students to loinclothed tribespeople.

Of course, peeling off a few phrases of Tagalog or Pilipino will help to establish your rapport and impress your hosts. It also helps save money. The language is complex in structure but easy to speak since most words are pronounced exactly as spelled. Important exceptions are consonants spoken with a Spanish inflection (Jose is pronounced as Ho-say), stretched out double consonants (*ng* is nang), double vowels pronounced as two syllables (Lake Taal is Lake Ta-al, maalam is ma-alam), and the interchangeability of *F* and *P* (as in Pilipino and Filipino). A few useful words and phrases:

Conversation
greetings—*mabuhay*
good morning—*magandang umaga po*
good evening—*magandang gabi po*
goodbye—*paalam na po*
please/thank you—*paki/salamat po*
you're welcome—*wala pong anuman*
yes/no—*oo/hindi*
How are you?—*Kumusta po sila?*
What is your name?—*Anong pangalan mo?*
How old are you?—*Ilang taon ka na?*

Where do you live?—*Saan po kayo nakatira?*
Where are you from?—*Taga saan ka?*
What is your job?—*Anong tarbaho mo?*
How much do you make?—*Magkano ang iyong suweldo?*
Are you married?—*May asawa ba?*
How many children?—*Ilan ang anak mo?*
You are beautiful!—*Maganda ka!*
I love you.—*Mahal kita.*
Where are you going?—*Saan ka pupunta?*
I am going to . . .—*upunta ako sa . . .*
no problem—*walang problema*
never mind—*hindi bale*

Bargaining
do you have . . . ?—*meron ba kayong . . . ?*
Where is a cheap hotel?—*Saan may murang hotel?*
How much is this?—*Magkano ito?*
too expensive!—*masyadong mahal!*
anything cheaper?—*mayroon bang mas mura?*
Where is my change?—*Nasaan ang sukli ko?*
It doesn't matter—*Bahalana.*

Numbers
1, 2, 3—*isa, dalawa, tatlo*
4, 5, 6—*apat, lima, anim*
7, 8, 9, 100—*pito, walo, siyam, sampu*
11, 12—*labing isa, labing dalawa*
20, 30—*dalawampu, tatlumpu*
40, 50—*apatnapu, limampu*
100, 1000—*isang daan, isanglibo*

Getting Around
How do I get to . . . ?—*Paano ang pagpunta sa . . . ?*
Where is the bus stop?—*Saan ang hintayan ng bus?*
Which bus is for Manila?—*Aling bus ang papuntang Manila?*
What town is this?—*Anong bayan ito?*
I want to go to Manila.—*Gusto kong pumunta sa Manila.*
I need . . .—*kailangan ko ng . . .*
bathroom—*banyo*
bus station—*istasyon ng bus*
police station—*istasyon ng polise*
village/town/city—*barrio/bayan/lungsod*
hill/mountain—*burol/bundok*

PHILIPPINES

and rainforests of many Filipino islands. Most practice slash-and-burn or wet-rice cultivation and follow a syncretic religion which mixes elements of animism and Christianity. Although long considered by the Filipinos as dangerous and primitive, today they are respected for their ethnic diversity and encouraged to maintain their distinctive lifestyles.

The most famous groups live among the rice terraces of northern Luzon near Banaue, Bontoc, and Sagada. Most are now quite Westernized, preferring blue jeans to loincloths and aluminum roofs to thatched, but enough traditional culture and natural beauty remain to make this an outstanding travel destination.

More authentic and less Westernized tribes are found in interior Mindoro, southern Mindanao, and Palawan. Problems of transportation and accessibility make these difficult journeys, although Lake Sebu in Mindanao has recently been attracting increasing numbers of determined travelers.

ON THE ROAD

GETTING THERE

Air

Ninoy Aquino International Airport, 12 km from downtown Manila, is served by over 150 flights a week from all major Western and Asian cities. By air, Manila is 90 minutes from Hong Kong, two hours and 40 minutes from Bangkok, three hours from Singapore, seven hours from Sydney, 17 hours from San Francisco, and 19 hours from Europe.

Visitors intending to spend most of the time in the Visayas can avoid Manila by inquiring about direct flights to Cebu. Travelers coming from Borneo or Indonesia should check on air connections from Kota Kinabalu to Zamboanga, and Manado to Davao. The latter is currently served twice weekly by Bouraq.

All travelers are strongly advised to buy roundtrip tickets before arriving in Manila. Discount travel agencies in the Philippines are scarce and price competition between travel agents is minimal. Bucket shops in Tokyo, Hong Kong, Bangkok, and Singapore often beat Manila rates by 25-40% on both one-way and roundtrip tickets.

American travelers will find the latest discount fares listed in the Sunday travel supplements of the *San Francisco Examiner, Los Angeles Times, New York Times,* and other large metropolitan newspapers. Discounted roundtrip fares from the U.S. west coast to Manila are currently US$725-900.

GETTING AROUND

Air

Philippine Airlines (PAL) operates domestic flights to over 40 destinations throughout the country. Fares on a per-kilometer basis are among the lowest in the world; it is estimated that 60-70% of domestic routes are run below cost as a social obligation to far-flung communities.

PAL internal flights are made even cheaper by discount programs offered on night flights and to seniors, groups, and students with a valid ISIC card. Props are slightly cheaper than jets, and internal flights are even cheaper when you fly in the early morning or late at night.

Because internal air travel is so cheap, domestic flights are often fully booked, especially during holidays and on weekends. You'll save time and money by booking all flights in advance. PAL's waiting-list system operates on a first-come, first-served basis, starting when the check-in counter opens or at midnight at larger airports.

PAL isn't the only airline in the country. Services to both major and minor destinations are also offered by Air Ads, Air Philippines, Asian Spirit, Cebu Pacific, Grand Air, Pacific Airways, SE Air, and Soriano Aviation.

The departure tax is P500 in Manila, P400 in Cebu City, and P200 in Davao.

Ship

Boat travel in the Philippines will be a necessity for most travelers who spend any amount of time in the country. Several shipping lines provide service between Manila and most larger cities on a near-daily basis, but the largest company by far is the newly formed WG&A, an amalgamated company formed by the merger of Williams, Gothong, and Aboitiz lines. All of their ships—named Superferry 1, Superferry 2, etc.—are safe and comfortable.

Shipping lines advertise their routes, schedules, and prices in most newspapers. Reservations are difficult to make over the phone but tickets can be purchased in advance from travel agencies or directly at the pier a few hours before departure. If you're going deck class, arrive early for the best beds.

Sea travel is slow but considerably cheaper than flying. Air-conditioned cabins for two, four, six, or eight persons come equipped with private bathrooms and catered dining. Cabins are about twice as expensive as third-class cots but only half the price of ordinary airfare. First-class air-conditioned dormitories cost 50% more than third class.

By far the cheapest way to travel is on third-class cots spread across the deck or down below

PHILIPPINES

FESTIVALS

Few countries in Southeast Asia offer as many superb festivals as the Philippines. Each year, over 40,000 *barangays*—the smallest political divisions in the archipelago—sponsor fiestas to honor the local patron saints, commemorate historical events, or simply throw a party for friends and relatives. Fiestas are a time for renewal of friendships and communal homecomings, a chance to honor prominent citizens and crown beauty queens, to enjoy a weekend of music, or for religious piety, cockfights, lavish balls, and unparalleled hospitality.

Most are small affairs centered in the village square, but others have grown into major events which merit national and even international attention. Whether small or large, all keep the Filipino calendar packed with an endless array of colorful and *enthusiastic* events. Though most festivals revolve around Christianity and therefore run the risk of becoming solemn, Filipinos eagerly add elements of pagan animism, Latin *machismo,* Hollywood glitz, *Star Wars* technology, sexuality, homespun humor, and natural gaiety to the religious pageantry. The results are a stunning riot of color and music with all the solemnity of Carnival in Rio.

Attending a Filipino festival is often an unforgettable experience. Some of the more famous events are described below. Most are dated by the Western calendar and occur on fixed dates. The tourist office in Manila has the latest schedule.

January

Black Nazarene Procession: Manila's Quiapo district honors its centuries-old Black Nazarene image on 9 January with a mammoth *carroza* (gilded carriage) procession and nightly dramas. Filipinos believe that whosoever shoulders the carriage or touches the image will be cured of sickness and forgiven of all sins.

Mardi Gras: The Philippines' three most outrageous Mardi Gras festivals take place in the Visayas on the third weekend. None is actually a Mardi Gras celebration, but all look, sound, and feel like their South American cousins. Taken from a pagan festival which commemorates the legendary barter of Panay between Negroid *atis* and seafaring Malays, the unforgettable spectacle occurs simultaneously in Kalibo (Panay Island) where it is called Ati Atihan, in Cebu City where it goes by Sinulog, and in Iloilo where it's called Dinagyang. Each honors the image of Santo Nino, the infant Christ and patron saint considered the most powerful of all Filipino miracle icons. A stately but moving religious procession is held on Friday evening.

On the following day is a riotous parade of drummers, dancers, and thousands of Filipinos outlandishly dressed in animal skins, tribal spears, plastic plumage, bamboo plants, Spanish dresses, T'boli weavings, and NPA uniforms. Participants might be soot-stained Rambos, new-age zombies, African warriors, Cory clones, bar girls, or stoned

carnival in Cebu

astronauts. It's an unforgettable mixture of Carnival in Rio, Mardi Gras in New Orleans, and Halloween in San Francisco.

February

People Power Anniversary: On 22 February 1986, Defense Minister Enrile and General Ramos announced to a transfixed audience that Filipino forces stationed at Camp Aguinaldo had broken from the government of Ferdinand Marcos and thrown their support toward Cory Aquino. It was electrifying news. Today, the historic event is celebrated with day-long festivities where it all began in Quezon City on Epifanio De Los Santos Highway (EDSA).

March

Palm Sunday: The Sunday before Easter begins the week-long series of solemn processions, *canaculos* (a distinctly Filipino Passion play), *pabasas* (chanting of the gospels), *pasyons* (reading of the liturgies), and reenactments of the Last Supper.

Good Friday: Holy Week climaxes on Good Friday rather than Easter Sunday since Filipinos emphasize the penitence rather than the joy of Easter. This is the day that flagellants, bare to the waist and wearing a crown of leaves, atone for past sins by beating themselves bloody with glass-spiked leather whips. Even more electrifying are the crucifixions that take place in San Pedros, 50 km north of Manila, where several Filipinos allow themselves to be nailed to the cross, hoisted above the crowds, and hung crucified until they faint.

Easter: The final day of Holy Week is marked by *salubong*, a glittering procession of devotees who honor the reunion of Mary and Christ with prayers, chants, and waving masses of plaited palm fronds. Total darkness rules inside the church until midnight, when the priest lights the *paschal* candle.

Moriones Festival: Perhaps the most spectacular of all the week's rituals is the passion play held in Boac on Marinduque Island, 580 km south of Manila. From Ash Wednesday to Easter Sunday, hundreds of Moriones dressed as Roman centurions wander the streets and reenact popular Biblical stories. The most popular legend surrounds Longinus, a Roman soldier whose eyesight was miraculously restored by a spilled drop of Christ's blood. After converting to Christianity, Longinus was arrested, tried, and executed by Pontius Pilate. This curious mixture of Christian history, animism, and local mythology has enough gore and passion to guarantee a spectacular weekend of entertainment.

April

Bataan Day: A parade of Filipino soldiers and American veterans honors those who fell at Corregidor and during the Bataan Death March. One of 11 national holidays celebrated in the Philippines. 9 April.

Magellan's Landing: The historical event of 27 April 1521 is faithfully reenacted on the beach at Mactan near Cebu. A fluvial procession of decorated *bancas* is followed by the planting of the cross and the baptism of tribal chieftain Humabon and his wife.

May

Santacruzan: May is a busy month for springtime festivals, but the most universal is the Santa Cruz de Mayo, a nine-day evening procession reenacting St. Helena's and Prince Constantine's search for the Santa Cruz ("True Cross of Christ"). Essentially a parade of Filipina beauties and their consorts, the basic cast of characters has been embellished with Methuselah, Negritos, Muslims, cherubs, and even the Queen of Sheba.

Pahiyas: San Isidro Labrador, patron saint of farmers, is honored throughout the country on 15 May with an afternoon procession past gaily decorated homes. Farmers provide a visual catalogue of their livelihood by transforming their homes into veritable hanging gardens, complete with chandeliers of vegetables, duck eggs, live fowl, rice cakes, cigarette boxes, and leaves colored with rice paste.

June

Independence Day: On 12 June 1898, 97 Filipinos and one American signed an announcement that promised the Filipino people freedom from Spanish rule and national sovereignty. Fifty years later, Truman declared Philippine independence on 4 July 1946, but Filipinos prefer to celebrate the occasion on 12 June. Major festivities are held on the Luneta in Manila.

Pig Parade: 24 June is much less serious. This day honors St. John the Baptist with a bizarre Parada ng Lechon in Balayan, Batangas, south of Manila. This procession features dozens of freshly roasted and glazed pigs protected by raincoats to minimize baptism by beer, and barbed wire to discourage hungry spectators.

(continues on next page)

PHILIPPINES

FESTIVALS
(continued)

July
Pagoda Sa Wawa: Decorated *bancas* and a colorful Pagoda on the Water form a fluvial procession to honor the Holy Cross of Wawa. Held on the first Sunday in July in Bocaue, 27 km north of Manila.

Mountain Province Festivals: Cultural minorities in northern Luzon honor their gods and ancestors with movable feasts dated by animist calendars. The Grand Canao, now promoted as a major tourist attraction, brings together various indigenous cultures for a spectacular weekend of dancing, singing, and recitation of tribal epics. It's also celebrated in November or December as a fall harvest festival.

August
Festival of the Performing Arts: The Department of Tourism and Cultural Center in Manila sponsor a month-long festival of the nation's top singers, dancers, and dramatists.

Davao Fruit Festival: The second-largest city in the Philippines celebrates the ripening of durians, orchids, and other aromatics with agricultural exhibits and a Miss Durian competition.

Giants of Lucban: During the Lucban town fiesta on 19 August, residents proudly parade their leering collection of *gigantes* (five-meter giants) and *unanos* (dwarves) constructed from papier-m—ch—wrapped over bamboo frames. *Gigantes* also feature in January's Mardi Gras festivals.

September
Penafrancia Festival: The Virgin of Penafrancia, patron saint of Naga City, is honored on the third weekend of September with one of the most spectacular fluvial parades in the country. Even typhoons

and a major bridge collapse in 1973 failed to discourage local devotees.

October
MassKara: Bacolod's charter-day celebration is one of the best fall festivals in the Philippines, conceived in 1980 to dramatize the Negrenses' happy spirit. Bacolenos by the thousands now make music and parade through the streets garbed in Mardi Gras-like costumes made of *nipa*, bamboo, cogon grass, and palm.

November
Day of the Dead: Filipinos celebrate their *Undas* or All Soul's Day at local graveyards with 24-hour vigils complete with votive candles, flowers, and blaring transistor radios.

December
Lantern Festival: Christmas is celebrated in the town of San Fernando, one hour north of Manila, with a spectacular display of native lanterns consisting of a bamboo interior skeleton covered with a tightly stretched translucent paper skin. Ranging in size from small stars to gigantic flatbed monsters, many have been ingeniously wired with hundreds of electric lights for dazzling and kaleidoscopic light shows.

Christmas: The Filipino Christmas season is reputedly the longest in the world, beginning with a series of predawn masses on 16 December and stretching to the Feast of the Three Kings on 6 January. Highlights include the Panunuluyan or Maytinis passion play as performed in Bulacan and Cavite and the Feast of the Three Kings celebrated with theater on Marinduque Island.

the water line. Deck passengers enjoy better air circulation but sometimes get wet during rainstorms. Be advised that third-class "deluxe" ensures a reserved bed, an absolute necessity unless you want to fight for floor space with "ordinary" passengers.

Interisland journeys over 12 hours usually include simple meals of rice and fish in third class and more elaborate meals in first and cabin classes. Bring along extra food and drink to supplement the supplies available at the canteen.

Warning: Be extremely cautious about sea travel during bad weather and holidays. Some Filipino ships are dangerously overloaded, poorly maintained, and lack life vests and lifeboats. Shipping disasters such as the 1987 sinking of the *Dona Paz*, in which over 3,000 passengers died, have cleaned up the industry to a certain degree, but travelers should always exercise caution.

More dangerous than the large ships are smaller crafts and outriggers such as the MV *Jem*, which sank a few years ago en route from

Looc to the resort island of Boracay. Never board an outrigger at night, during bad weather, or when it looks overloaded.

Fast Ferries

"Fast ferries" are certainly the most welcome addition to the transportation scene in the Philippines. These are relatively small, high-powered, and very speedy watercraft that quickly zip between most of the islands in the Visayas and cut travel times down by at least 50% from the days of slow ships.

It's amazing the number of connections these ferries can provide, including some very obscure routes such as from Dumaguete on Negros to Siquijor Island. Fast ferries leave several times daily from most towns in the Visayas and Mindanao including Cebu City, Dumaguete, Iloilo, Bacolod, Tagbilaran, Ormoc, Dipolog, Dapitan, Cagayan de Oro, Tubigon, and Surigao.

Bus

Public buses connect most towns in the Philippines along a fairly good network of roads. Major routes are served by air-conditioned buses, while rural destinations are limited to minivans, overloaded jeepneys, and colorful rattletraps better suited for museums of indigenous psychedelia.

Bus service is fast, frequent, and cheap but nowhere near as luxurious or dependable as in Thailand or Malaysia.

Recommending specific buses is difficult since the Filipino bus industry is spread across dozens of companies that compete in a market neither dominated by a state monopoly nor by a handful of powerful transportation companies. The larger and more dependable bus companies in Luzon include Pantranco, Philtranco, and BLTB—three companies that make direct connections to their final destinations with a minimum of stops.

Tickets with reserved seats can be purchased in advance from these companies. Otherwise, tickets are purchased directly at the terminal for the next available departure. Fares on rural buses are collected toward the end of the journey.

Other Transport

Jeepneys: Lavishly decorated with metallic reflectors, streamers, gyrating iron horses, pulsating lightbulbs, cheeky nameplates like "Virgin Busters," and Jesus statues that flash in rhythm with the music, jeepneys are obviously more than just the Filipino substitute for intra-city buses. They symbolize the clash of Asian sensibilities with Western consumerism, folk art with utilitarianism, and cold machinery with Filipino passion. More extravagant examples mix religious iconography and Western hedonism into something almost beyond description.

Most Filipinos, of course, regard them simply as uncomfortable but convenient forms of public transportation found in nearly all towns throughout the archipelago. More information under **Manila.**

Taxis: Taxis are only of importance in Manila and larger towns such as Cebu, Baguio, and Davao. Most are metered and rates are low—provided the meter is correctly calibrated. Unmarked vehicles and taxis with inoperable meters should not be taken unless you are absolutely sure of the correct fare and make a firm agreement with the driver in advance.

TRAVEL PRACTICALITIES

Visas

Visitors to the Philippines may enter the country without a visa and stay for up to 21 days provided they hold an onward ticket. Visitors who arrive without a visa but would like to stay longer than the initial 21 days must obtain a visa waiver from an immigration office in Manila, Cebu City, or Angeles. In Manila, this office is on Magallanes Drive near the General Post Office. This waiver allows a stay of up to 59 days and costs P500.

However, it is *strongly* advised that you obtain a visa in advance from a Filipino embassy or consulate since a visit to Manila's immigration department is something of a Kafkaesque experience.

Visa Extensions

Extensions beyond the 59-day limit can be obtained with proper application and payment of an Alien Head Tax, legal research fees, Alien Certificate of Registration fees, and extension fees charged on a monthly basis. A number of travel agencies will handle the extension process for a modest service fee, or check with Malate Pensionne in Manila.

PHILIPPINES

PHILIPPINES DIPLOMATIC OFFICES

Australia: 1 Moonah Place Yarralumla, Canberra, tel. (06) 273-2535

Canada: 130 Albert St. #606, Ottawa, tel. (613) 233-1121

France: 5 Faubourg Saint Honore, Paris 75009, tel. (01) 4265-0234

Germany: Argelanderstrasse 5300, Bonn, tel. 213071

Hong Kong: 21F Regent Center, 88 Queen's Rd., tel. (01) 810-0770

Indonesia: 6 Jalan Iman Bonjol, Jakarta, tel. 314-9319

Japan: 11-24 Nampeidai Machi, Shibuya-ku, Tokyo, tel. (03) 3496-6555

Malaysia: 1 Jalan Changkat Kia Peng, Kuala Lumpur, tel. 248-4233

New Zealand: New Hobson St., Wellington, tel. (04) 472-9921

Singapore: 20 Nassim Rd., tel. 737-3977

Thailand: 760 Sukhumvit Rd., Bangkok, tel. 391-0008

United Kingdom: 17 Albemarle St., London WIX 7HA, tel. (0171) 499-5443

U.S.A.: 1617 Massachusetts Ave., Washington, D.C. 20036, tel. (202) 467-9300
447 Sutter St., San Francisco, CA 94118, tel. (415) 433-6666

Visitors who would like to stay longer than six months must secure a Certificate for Temporary Visitors.

Tourist Information

The Department of Tourism (DOT) is the government agency responsible for tourism: general information, licensing of travel agents and tour operators, classifying hotels, and international promotion. The DOT maintains both overseas and domestic field offices with the head office located in the imposing Tourism Building on Agrifina Circle in Manila. An information center is also found at the Manila airport.

Employees are extremely personable and anxious to help, but there is a perennial shortage of reliable, printed information. Your best bet is to visit their offices and ask to speak to the most knowledgeable person in the office. The Manila DOT information desk has some very sharp employees whose expertise makes up for the lack of printed material.

Maps

The patchwork arrangement of the Philippines makes a good map absolutely essential. National maps provided by the Department of Tourism (DOT) are sketchy, although they do have a useful map of Manila and Makati.

Best national map is the 1:1,000,000-scale *Roadmap of the Philippines* published by the National Bookstore and sold in most bookstores in Manila. The Nelles Verlag *Philippines* map is also worthwhile.

Detailed topographic maps of individual provinces can be purchased at the Bureau of Coast and Geodetic Survey offices in Manila, Cebu City, Cagayan de Oro, and many other larger towns. Neither the *Petron Map of the Philippines* nor the *Mobil Philippine Travel Map* are worth purchasing.

Currency

The unit of currency is the peso (Tagalog *piso*), symbolized by a capital P with two horizontal lines through the top. The peso, a floating currency divided into 100 centavos, has fluctuated between 35-40 per dollar since the currency crisis of 1997. Further devaluation is expected, although the peso has not fallen as much as the Thai *baht* and other Southeast Asian currencies.

Exchange facilities are available at banks, major hotels, and authorized exchange dealers who chiefly operate along Mabini Street in Manila. All offer varying exchange rates, the worst at facilities in luxury hotels and the best from the money changers on Mabini Street. Banks are somewhere in the middle.

The Filipino exchange system is full of perils. Rates are unregulated and vary somewhat from dealer to dealer. It's important to shop around and compare rates before changing large amounts of currency. Remember that cash is king in the Philippines. American currency guarantees the highest rates, especially larger bills such as $50s and $100s. Smaller bills such as $20s are often discounted 5-10% below the highest rate.

Traveler's checks can be problematical. They can be cashed at major banks and American Express offices, but only at slightly lower rates than cash. Besides being a time-consuming ordeal, cashing a traveler's check in the provinces can be difficult, if not impossible. Passports and purchase receipts are required to cash traveler's checks. To get the highest possible rate and avoid ordeals at the bank, bring US$100 bills with you rather than relying solely on traveler's checks.

Currency declaration on arrival is unnecessary. Pesos can be reexchanged for dollars at the airport but an official receipt may be required.

Warning: Never attempt to change money on the street. Manila has dozens of street money changers who with the use of accomplices and phony policemen prey on unsuspecting travelers. It is virtually impossible for street vendors to legitimately offer a higher rate than licensed money changers. Remember: All street changers are professional con artists.

Cash Advances

Running out of money in the Philippines is another tricky problem. There are no ATMs that

---

PHILIPPINES TOURIST OFFICES

OVERSEAS

Australia: Highmount House, 122 Castlereagh St., Sydney 2000, tel. (02) 9267-2695

France: 3 Faubourg Saint Honrore, Paris 75009, tel. (01) 4265-0134

Germany: Kaissestrasse 15, 60311 Frankfurt am Main, tel. (069) 208-9395

Hong Kong: United Centre, 95 Queensway Rd., Central, tel. (05) 2866-6471

Japan: 11-24 Nampeidai Machi, Shibuya-ku, Tokyo, tel. (03) 3464-3630

Singapore: 20 Nassim Rd., Singapore, tel. (02) 235-2184

United Kingdom: 17 Albemarle St., London WIX 7HA, tel. (0171) 499-5443

U.S.A.: 3660 Wilshire Blvd. #285, Los Angeles, CA 90010, tel. (213) 487-4527
447 Sutter St., #507, San Francisco, CA 94108, tel. (415) 956-4060
556 Fifth Ave., New York, NY 10036, tel. (212) 575-7915

DOMESTIC

Bacolod: City Plaza, Bacolod, Negros, tel. (034) 29021

Baguio: Tourism Building, Governor Pack Rd., Baguio, Luzon, tel. (074) 442-7014

Cagayan de Oro: Pelaez Sports Complex, Velez St., Cagayan de Oro, Mindanao, tel. (08822) 723696

Cebu City: GMC Plaza Building, Plaza Independencia, Cebu City, Cebu, tel. (032) 91503

Cotabato: Elizabeth Tan Building, Cotabato, Mindanao, tel. (064) 211110

Davao: Magsaysay Park Complex, Davao, Mindanao, tel. (082) 221-6798

Iloilo: Tourism Complex, Bonifacio Drive, Iloilo, Panay, tel. (033) 270245

Legaspi: Penaranda Park, Albay District, Legaspi, Luzon, tel. (05221) 44492

Manila: DOT Headquarters, Rizal Park, Manila, Luzon, tel. (02) 523-8411

San Fernando (La Union): Matanag Justice Hall, General Luna St., San Fernando, Luzon, tel. (072) 412098

San Fernando (Pampanga): Paskuhan Village, San Fernando, Luzon, tel. (045) 961-2665

Tacloban: Children's Park, Senator Enage St., Tacloban, Leyte, tel. (053) 321-2048

Tuguegarao: Tuguegarao Supermarket, Tuguegarao, Luzon, tel. (078) 844-1621

Zamboanga: Lantaka Hotel, Valderroza St., Zamboanga, Mindanao, tel. (062) 991-0218

PHILIPPINES AREA CODES

Manila. 2
Bacolod 34
Baguio. 74
Cebu City 32
Davao 82
Iloilo 33
Tarlac 452
Zamboanga 62

gladly spit out money to cash-strapped tourists. Fortunately, cash advances with your Visa or MasterCard can be quickly obtained at any branch of the Equitable Bank. Equitable has branches in almost every town in the country. Cash advances can also be picked up in a limited number of traveler's hotels such as the Swagman chain. Another strategy is to visit any of the casinos in the country and use your Visa or MasterCard for a quick advance.

Telephone
The Philippine telephone network is operated by the Philippine Long Distance Telephone Company (PLDT) and community telephone systems in the provinces.

Local Calls: Domestic calls can be made from public pay phones and private businesses for two pesos. Domestic long-distance calls can be made by dialing 0 and then the area code. Dial 109 for operator-assisted domestic long distance. A few of the more useful area codes are listed in the "Philippines Area Codes" chart.

International Calls: Overseas calls and faxes can be made to the Philippines from the United States by dialing the international access code

INTERNATIONAL CLOCK FOR THE PHILIPPINES

San Francisco . . . . +16
New York . . . . +13
Chicago . . . . +14
London . . . . +8
Paris . . . . +7
Sydney . . . . -2

(011), then the country code for the Philippines (63), then the city code, followed by the local phone number. For example, to call a hotel in Manila, dial 011, 63, 2, and then the local hotel number. The area code for Manila is 02; drop the zero when you dial Manila from overseas.

Rates from the Philippines are set in U.S. dollars by the government. A three-minute station-to-station call during the daytime to the U.S. costs US$9 plus US$3 for each additional minute. You can save money by making a quick call and having your friend return the call station-to-station.

The international access code for making phone calls *from* the Philippines is 00.

FOOD AND DRINK

Filipino food is an intriguing blend of Malaysian, Chinese, Spanish, and—most importantly—American cuisines. You'll quickly discover—perhaps to your dismay—that hamburgers, hot dogs, and omelettes are popular throughout the country. You'll also discover that Filipino attempts at Western food have been less than successful.

Rather than sticking with poorly prepared Western food, try native dishes such as *adobo* and *kare kare* served in the smaller cafes, or street food such as *lugaw* and steamed corn. Filipino food has great range but admittedly isn't popular with everybody. Critics have charged that native dishes often lack the complexity and refinement of other Southeast Asian cuisines and that sauces tend to be heavy or greasy and unimaginative. On the other hand, many dishes compensate with a freshness and simplicity that accentuate the natural flavors.

Eating in the Philippines is inexpensive, though travelers can economize further by patronizing *turo turo* (point point) restaurants and the inexpensive street stalls. Also worth seeking out are *kamayan* restaurants, which serve native dishes on banana leaves without the use of silverware. Ordering in most restaurants is easy since menus are printed in English and service personnel speak some English.

Note that many dishes are described simply by their method of cooking: any item stewed in vinegar and garlic is called *adobo,* sour soups are *sinigang,* food sautéed with tomatoes is *pangat,* food cooked in blood is *dinuguan,* and anything raw is *kilawin.* The Philippines also has one of Asia's largest selections of tropical fruits. Be sure to try a *guabano!*

Popular Filipino Dishes

adobo: a distinctive stew made from pork or chicken marinated in vinegar, garlic, soy sauce, and sugar. One of the most popular dishes in the country

afritada: beef served Spanish style in a rich tomato sauce with olives, green peas, chopped potatoes, and slivered green peppers

asado: meat marinated in *kalamansi* juice and soy sauce, then fried and served with marinade and cubed potatoes, tomatoes, and onions

aso: dog. Popular in northern Luzon among the hilltribes.

baboy: pork

balut: fertilized but unhatched duck eggs incubated 17 days, then boiled and eaten. One of the more bizarre delicacies in the world. Filipinos believe that *baluts* ensure virility and fertility plus have aphrodisiac qualities. Novices should ask for the more mature *balut sa puti.* The proper technique is to pick the top off the shell, suck out the juice, shell completely, add vinegar and salt, and pop the crunchy fellow into your mouth. Several beers make this easier.

bangus: bony but delicious milkfish. Bred locally in fishponds.

bibingka: sweet rice cakes with coconut milk and white cheese

buko: young green coconut

calamares: squid

carne: beef

chicharon: fried pork rinds. Look for the expensive but superb rinds heavily cut with pork meat.

crispy pata: pigs' feet and forelegs fried golden brown, served with soy sauce, garlic, and *kalamansi* juice. Although most Westerners find this dish much too fatty, the crispy skin and accompanying sauce are delicious.

dinuguan: pork and intestines stewed in a rich, dark blood sauce. A mild but surprisingly tasty dish.

ginatan: anything cooked in coconut milk

gulay: vegetables

halo halo: a colorful dessert of shaved ice, colored sweets, white beans, corn, cubed fruits, and evaporated milk

hito: catfish

inihaw: Anything broiled over a charcoal fire is called *inihaw* or *ihaw.*

kare kare: beef, oxtail, or pig knuckles served in a spicy peanut sauce with rice and vegetables

kilawin: raw fish marinated in *kalamansi* juice, vinegar, and onions

lapu-lapu: rock bass

adobong pusit: cuttlefish soup with coconut milk and vinegar

lechon: roast suckling pig served with thick liver sauce. A traditional fiesta specialty.

lumpia: Filipino egg rolls

maise: steamed corn

mami: noodle soup with chicken, beef, or fish

manok: chicken

pancit: noodles prepared in several styles. Canton is egg noodles with meat and vegetables, *guisado* and *malabon* are thin rice noodles, *molo* is Chinese dumplings fried with garlic and meats.

pochero: beef and spicy sausage mixed with vegetables

pusit: cuttlefish

shrimp rebosado: baked shrimp

siopao: Chinese pork buns

sinigang: sour and delicious soup flavored with tamarind, lemon, and *calamansi.* This Filipino bouillabaisse is made from any kind of meat, fish, or shellfish, with tomatoes, radishes, and *kangkong* leaves added for flavor.

suman: long fingers of sweet rice wrapped in coconut leaves

tabala: raw oysters marinated in *calamansi* and garlic

tahong: steamed or baked mussels

tapa: a simple breakfast dish of dried beef and onions

Drinks

Filipino beer is among the finest and cheapest in the East. Longtime leader San Miguel is now being challenged by several new brews such as the lighter Carlsberg and less expensive Manila beer. Five-year-old Tanduay rum and locally pro-

PHILIPPINES

duced gins and vodkas are all first-class spirits. Prices are ridiculously cheap at P30-45 per liter. Filipino wines, on the other hand, are sweet and unappealing. Fortunately for the wine drinker, good-quality California wines are available at reasonable prices from duty-free shops in Manila.

Residents outside the larger towns often drink homebrews such as *tuba* and *tapey* rather than the more expensive beers or liquors. Both are only 12-18 proof but pack a deadly wallop with effects similar to that of tequila. *Tuba* is made by extracting the sap from either *nipa* palms or the tops of young coconut palms. When drunk immediately after gathering, the yellow liquid is slightly sweet and palatable. Overnight fermenting turns the gentle firewater into something bitter and much more potent. Experts claim they can judge the hours of fermentation by the color alone.

Lambanog is boiled *tuba* distilled in the true Kentucky moonshine manner. *Tapey* is an alcoholic beverage made from rice or corn popular with the hilltribes of northern Luzon. *Basi*, a homemade wine from Ilocos Norte, is made from crushed sugarcane juice compounded with barks and berries.

CAUTIONS

While most Filipinos are completely trustworthy and sincere about their interests in foreign visitors, a small percentage of the population are professional con artists who make their living by defrauding Western tourists. Caution must be exercised at all times.

The good news is that fraud and theft in the Philippines are almost exclusively nonviolent encounters where the racketeer uses his wit and charm rather than weapons or physical threats. The bad news is that con artists are as thick as fleas in certain areas, such as Manila's Ermita District, Baguio, and many of the popular beach resorts.

You *must* be careful about everybody who approaches you—no matter their appearance or the believability of their story. Thieves come in all shapes and sizes: kids hanging out on the street corner, matronly housewives, clean-cut students, lovely ladies, and elderly gentlemen dressed in three-piece suits.

My favorite story is of a German attorney who met two middle-aged ladies at Sunday church services in Manila. They offered a tour of the city and lunch followed by an afternoon film in a darkened theater. One of the women went for Cokes, which the German later recalled as tasting slightly strange. Three hours later he awoke from his drug stupor stripped of his watch, camera, traveler's checks, and other valuables. A few of the more common tricks are listed below.

Alerts

The Come On: "Do you remember me . . . ?" should be an instant tip-off that you're being set up for fraud. The con artist usually claims that he met you at airport customs or immigration, drove your taxi, or knows a common friend. If you actually respond to such a ridiculous line, you're well on your way to being drugged, mugged, or invited in for a friendly game of cards.

Money Changers: As pointed out above under "Currency," all money changers working the streets are professional con artists who pass counterfeit bills and shortchange unsuspecting Westerners.

Pickpockets: Razor-blade artists work their trade on crowded buses and jeepneys. Child street vendors often distract their victims by waving their merchandise in front of the victim's face while another grabs the bag. Avoid people hiding their hands under newspapers and keep your valuables pressed closely against your stomach while in crowds.

Knock-out Drugs: Invitations for coffee or beer should in most cases be declined. Friendly strangers who offer free drinks may also be offering complimentary servings of Ativan, a potent drug that quickly leaves the victim helplessly dazed or completely unconscious. *Beware:* knock-out drugs are *extremely* common in the Philippines.

Card Games: One of the most popular cons involves a friendly game of cards. It begins when a well-dressed Filipino approaches a tourist and claims his cousin is a card dealer in the local casino. He then promises that great sums of money can be earned with the cooperation of a willing foreigner. To set the stage, a game is arranged at his house using a phony bankroll. After being taught the signals and winning a dozen straight games, the tourist feels very con-

MOVIES FILMED IN THE PHILIPPINES

Too Late the Hero: Cliff Robertson, Michael Caine, and Toshiro Mifune star in this 1970 release shot in Boracay in the late 1960s. A rare chance to see the Philippine's most famous island without all the guesthouses, hotels, condominiums, and golf courses.

Apocalypse Now: The helicopter scenes in Francis Ford Coppola's 1979 masterpiece were filmed at Balera Bay, while the climactic explosion of Kurtz's Cambodian temple was staged on the riverbanks near Pagsanhan Falls. Tribal dance scenes were performed by the Ifugaos of Banaue. Coppola's ex-wife subsequently wrote an intriguing book about their problems with typhoons and clashing personalities.

Platoon: Most of this Academy Award-winning film was filmed in the Philippines.

An Officer and a Gentleman: Richard Gere and Debra Winger star in this 1982 love story whose early parts were filmed in Olongapo.

The Year of Living Dangerously: One of the best films about contemporary politics in the region was filmed in the Philippines in 1983 after Indonesian authorities refused to allow the Australian director to complete the film on location.

Missing in Action: All of the *Missing in Action* films, 1984-1988, starring Chuck Norris were filmed in the Philippines.

Born On The Fourth Of July: Ron Kovic's autobiographical novel was largely filmed in the northern Philippine province of Ilocos Norte. While there in 1989, director Oliver Stone and star Tom Cruise stayed in the Fort Ilocandia Resort Hotel, built by the Marcoses to house guests for the 1983 wedding of their daughter Irene. Stone summed it up: "I have been all over the Far East, and the Philippines has the most natural wonders. The people give their hearts to you; it's like being in the old pirate country in the Caribbean."

Fortunes of War: A 1994 film set in Thailand and Cambodia but acutally shot in the Philippines at Subic Bay; cameo appearance by Martin Sheen.

---

fident about the arrangement. Suddenly, a wealthy Chinese gambler arrives for a casual afternoon game. The game goes well with the provided bankroll until the stakes grow alarmingly large and the tourist is forced to use his personal funds to cover the pot. This, of course, is the final hand where all those carefully rehearsed signals fail.

Other Cons: Be sure to retrieve *all* your luggage from the trunk of your taxi. Better yet, carry your gear with you in the rear seat. Inspect your room very carefully for trap doors in the closets and unlocked windows. Never leave valuables unattended in your hotel room. Valuables should instead be checked in hotel safes or in safe-deposit boxes at large banks for a nominal fee. Avoid dark alleys or rough sections of town after dark.

Drugs: The Philippines has a major problem with a drug called *shabu,* a smokeable methamphetamine that sends users on a racing high. Though relatively cheap at US$25-50 a gram, *shabu* is also a very addictive drug that seems to have permeated Filipino society to its very core—now considered the country's most serious problem ahead of crime, violence, and political corruption.

PHILIPPINES

LUZON

MANILA

Metro Manila, a conurbation of four cities and 13 municipalities, is not only the hub of Filipino politics and national economics, it also sets the pace in entertainment, culture, communications, and religion. From its humble beginnings on the banks of the Pasig River, today's city of 10 million residents has spread haphazardly across 636 square kilometers from Manila Bay toward the Pacific Ocean. Like most other Asian cities, Manila is actually a maze of villages tied together with highways, shopping centers, neon signs, and urban sprawl.

It's a world of startling contrasts: international hotels that charge a daily rate in excess of the annual income of most Filipinos; miles of slums where people survive without electricity or running water; elegant suburbs where the Filipino elite live behind protective walls; smoking garbage pits where thousands survive by recycling the waste of others; exclusive nightclubs where jet-setters sip properly chilled champagne and discuss the latest fashions; burned-out hotels that face one of the world's most romantic harbors. Manila is alive and pulsating, confusing and exciting, one of Asia's most perplexing destinations.

Though the city boasts some of Asia's best nightlife and a handful of worthwhile sights, Manila lacks the anticipated exotic charm and historical flavor because of its near complete destruction at the end of WW II. The following attractions can be quickly toured on foot and by public transport before heading off to the mountains and beaches.

The city is divided into several distinct neighborhoods. Hotels, restaurants, and most nightlife are located in the tourist sections of Ermita and Malate, just south of Rizal Park where the main tourist office is situated. Intramuros, the old historic quarter north of Rizal Park, can be reached on foot, but public transport is necessary to reach more distant destinations. Rizal Park, the Chinese cemetery, and the financial center of Makati are worth visiting.

ATTRACTIONS

Ermita and Malate

Once a Muslim fishing village and later a wealthy residential neighborhood for leading Tagalog families, Ermita and Malate are the heart of Manila's tourist belt. A handful of large colonial-style homes still stand, but most have given way to hotels, antique shops, and bars set along M.H. del Pilar and Mabini streets.

Malate Church: A convenient spot to begin your walking tour is at this highly ornate church constructed in 1773 to replace the original Augustinian structure. The austere interior makes a strong contrast with the romantic facade of Spanish-Muslim balusters and Mexican baroque columns. Rajah Sulayman Park just opposite has several good seafood restaurants, *calesa* drivers, and a statue of the Muslim sultan who ruled Manila prior to the Spanish era.

Mabini Street: Many of Manila's better antique shops are located along this chaotic street filled with money changers, hustlers, inexpensive pensions, touts who "remember you from immigration," and quality restaurants. The Manila Zoo and the Metropolitan Museum, with its changing exhibits and a money display, are south of Malate.

Adriatico Circle is where the smart set drinks espresso amid gentrified homes converted into cafes, bistros, and gay nightclubs. San Andreas Market offers an outstanding albeit expensive selection of fresh fruits including durians and guabanos. The romantic old Spanish cemetery of Paco Park, a block from UN and Taft Avenues, is where famous patriots are interred in three rows of burial niches. A popular spot for Sunday weddings and chamber music performances.

Rizal Park

Manila's 58-hectare green lung, also known as the Luneta, is an excellent place to wander, photograph the balloon vendors, and watch people

PHILIPPINES

ERMITA AND MALATE

RIZAL PARK

TO MANILA HOTEL

TO INTRAMUROS

ROXAS BOULEVARD

ALHAMBRA

National Library ★

★ DEPARTMENT OF TOURISM (DOT)

KALAW

★ Museo Pambata

UNITED NATIONS

McDONALD'S ● HOLIDAY INN

■ EQUITABLE BANK

UN AVENUE STATION

TO TRAIN STATION →

TAFT AVENUE

■ U.S. EMBASSY

■ SWAGMAN HOTEL

PIZZA HUT

FLORES

OROSA

BOCOBO

■ BARRIO FIESTA RESTAURANT

● PENSION FILIPINAS

LA CORONA HOTEL

SHAKEY'S PIZZA

ARQUIZA

★ PACO PARK

● PARK HOTEL

THE POOL ■
ISEYA HOTEL ●

DEL PILAR

ROYAL PALM HOTEL

■ KAYMAYAN RESTAURANT

PADRE FAURA

ERMITA

GUERNICA'S RESTAURANT ■

GUERRERO

MABINI

● AIDA'S ■ MABINI PENSION

SANTA MONICA

■ ROBINSON DEPARTMENT STORE

GENERAL HOSPITAL ■

ROSIE'S DINER ■

● CENTRE POINT HOTEL

SALAS

ADRIATICO

SOLDADO

■ PHILIPPINE AIRLINES

● SANTOS PENSION

● MANILA MIDTOWN HOTEL

PEDRO GIL

PEDRO GIL STATION ■

PALM PLAZA HOTEL ●

■ ZAMBOANGA RESTAURANT

SHERATON MARINA ■

● MANILA DIAMOND HOTEL

● PAN PACIFIC HOTEL

MALVAR

PENSION NATIVIDAD ●

DEL PILAR

MANILA BAY

OROSA

LEON GUINTO

AGONCILLO

SAN MARCELINO

● EPISODE CAFE

NAKPIL

■ INSOMNIA CAFE

■ CAFE CARIBANA

HOBBIT HOUSE ●

MALATE PENSION ■

■ GUERNICA'S RESTAURANT

REMEDIOS

■ CAFE ADRIATICO

● ROYAL PLAZA HOTEL

★ MALATE CHURCH

● CAFE 1900

JAZZ BOX ■

BOCOBO

ADRIATICO

TAFT AVENUE

ARISTOCRAT RESTAURANT ■

■ W G & A

MALATE

SAN ANDRES

MABINI

● SOFITEL GRAND HOTEL

QUIRINO STATION ◉

● ADMIRAL HOTEL

■ MY FATHER'S MOUSTACHE

CAROLINA

QUIRINO AVENUE

TO AIRPORT

★ MANILA ZOO

← TO HARRISON PLAZA

0   200 m

PHILIPPINES

© MOON PUBLICATIONS, INC.

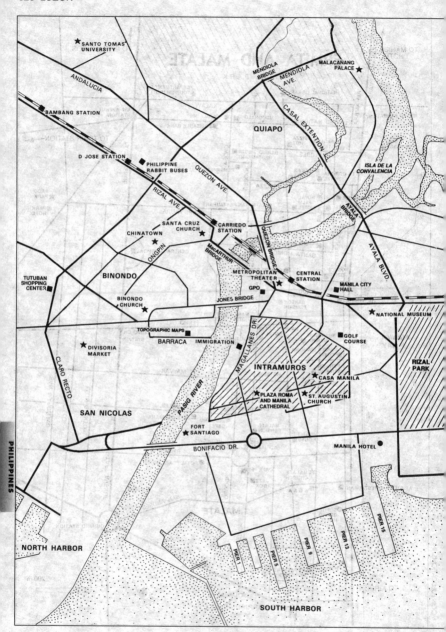

PHILIPPINES

CENTRAL MANILA

PACO TRAIN STATION

PACO

PACO PARK AND CEMETERY

SAN MARCELINO

KANSAS

AGONCILLO

LEON GUINTO

UN AVENUE STATION

ERMITA

TAFT AVE.

PEDRO GIL STATION

INDIANA

VASQUES

GUERRERO

OROSA

BOCOBO

ADRIATICO

Manila Midtown Hotel

MALATE PENSION

MABINI

DEL PILAR

SHERATON MARINA

ROXAS BLVD.

US EMBASSY

HARBOR CRUISE

TO MAKATI

SOUTH SUPER HIGHWAY

QUIRINO

REMEDIOS

QUIRINO STATION

VITO CRUZ STATION

MALATE

TO AIRPORT

PADRE FAURA

PEDRO GIL

MALVAR

NAKPIL

SAN ANDREAS

VITO CRUZ

MALATE CHURCH

PASAY

CENTURY PARK SHERATON

★ **Manila Zoo**

Harrison Plaza Shopping Center

AMBASSADOR HOTEL

SOFITEL HOTEL

METROPOLITAN MUSEUM ★

TRADERS HOTEL

VIXENS

Manila Yacht Club

CORREGIDOR HOVERCRAFT

MANILA BAY

CULTURAL CENTER ★

CONVENTION CENTER ★

FOLK ARTS CENTER ★

COCONUT PALACE ★

WESTIN PHILIPPINE PLAZA HOTEL ★

KALAW

UNITED NATIONS

★ **TOURIST OFFICE**

0   500 m

PHILIPPINES

© MOON PUBLICATIONS, INC.

parade in the early-evening hours. Points of interest include a planetarium where free cultural events are held every Sunday evening, Chinese and Japanese gardens, a restaurant operated by deaf and mute waiters, the National Library, which briefly starred in *The Year of Living Dangerously, balut* vendors, elderly Chinese practicing tai chi, and a giant topographic map which floods during the rainy season and dries into a dust bowl during the summer months.

The tourist office on the ground floor of the imposing Tourist Building offers maps, sightseeing ideas, and other travel information.

Rizal Park is named after the great Filipino patriot whose remains are enshrined under a towering obelisk guarded around the clock by stern sentries. Translations of Rizal's famous poem "Mi Ultimo Adios" can be read on bronze plaques near the monument, though you'll need to be fluent in either Spanish or Tagalog. An English version can be read at Fort Santiago in Intramuros. The nearby National Museum has a disappointing collection of religious objects and botanical specimens but an impressive room on Filipino cultural minorities.

Intramuros

Manila's famous walled city, one of the finest examples of medieval fortress architecture outside Europe, served as the political and cultural capital of Manila from its founding by the Spanish in the 16th century until its near-complete destruction by Allied forces in 1945. The physical elimination of Intramuros—one of the great tragedies of the Pacific War—took less than 30 days and cost the lives of more than 1,000 Americans, 16,000 Japanese, and almost 100,000 Filipino civilians. In the end, over a dozen churches, three convents, two cathedrals, 13 chapels, and two universities constructed in a rich Hispano-Filipino style were reduced to a great heap of rubble and creeping vegetation.

Sadly neglected and badly run-down, Intramuros today has little of exceptional interest, although the following attractions and a walk along the ramparts of the reconstructed walls can be recommended.

St. Augustine Church: Built in 1599 as the headquarters for the Augustinian order in Asia, this stone seminary was the only religious edifice to survive the destruction of Intramuros. An extensive collection of colonial religious art including valuable *santos, carrozas,* and antique books is housed in the museum on the ground floor.

Manila Cathedral: Farther along is the modern home of Cardinal Sin, the outspoken and controversial archbishop of Manila. Earlier cathedrals destroyed by fires, typhoons, and earthquakes were replaced in 1958 by this Romanesque-Byzantine building, noted for its bronze doors, which depict the cathedral's history and stained-glass windows with religious symbolism unique to the Philippines.

Fort Santiago: Strategically located near the mouth of the muddy Pasig River is one of the best historical attractions in town. Constructed on the site of the original Malay stockade, the century-old garrison served Spanish and Japanese forces as a diabolical prison in which the lower dungeons flooded at high tide, killing all those incarcerated below. The main entrance off Aduna Street faces an attractive plaza where soldiers sometimes parade past a row of antique automobiles rusting in Bastion San Francisco. The Rizal Museum inside the old barracks is where Rizal wrote his moving "Mi Ultimo Adios" before being executed at dawn in Rizal Park.

North of the Pasig River

Quiapo: Manila is a city cut in half by the Pasig River. South of the river are the walled city of Intramuros, the tourist enclaves of Ermita and Malate, and the financial district of Makati. North is the heart of old Manila, a world of crowded alleys, Chinese temples, mosques, stinking canals, chaotic markets, *calesas,* slums, and churches.

Religious life revolves around the Quiapo Church and its Shrine of the Black Nazarene, one of the most famous religious images in the country. The long and hot 20-minute walk from the church to Malacañang Palace passes a gold-domed mosque, an outdoor brass market, and beautiful old buildings overlooking the muddy Pasig.

Malacañang Palace: Since its construction in 1802, Malacañang has served as a country home for Spanish aristocracy, American generals, and, most significantly, Marcos and Imelda. When they fled the country in 1986, they took with them much of the national treasury but left behind the remnants of a reign of extraordinary self-delusion, indulgence, and vulgarity.

PHILIPPINES

The building once held memorabilia of the Marcos dynasty—including Mrs. Marcos's 3,000 pairs of shoes—but all this was removed several years ago and today only a few rather disappointing photographs of former presidents remain. No longer worth the trouble to visit.

Chinatown: Straddling Quiapo and Tondo is Binondo, a modern crowded commercial center which serves as home for many of Manila's Philippine-born Chinese. A wander down the main street of Ongpin will turn up some interesting restaurants, temples, godowns, mahjong parlors, acupuncture clinics, and Chinese pharmacists.

Chinese Cemetery: Manila's most unusual attraction is the eccentric 54-hectare cemetery located near the junction of Rizal and Aurora avenues. Behind the yellow exterior walls embedded with over 10,000 burial niches for the poor are hundreds of massive mausoleums complete with furniture, air-conditioned kitchens, and tiled bathrooms. These two-story memorials serve both to honor the deceased and to prove the economic success of the Chinese community. Take a jeepney marked Monumento or Caloocan City, or the Metro Rail to R. Papa Station.

Other Attractions
Cultural Center of the Philippines: Designed by Filipino architect Leandro Locsin, this magnificent collection of ultramodern buildings comprises some of the best contemporary architecture in Southeast Asia. The CCP houses a Cultural Center designed in classical opera-house tradition with curving staircases and glass chandeliers, a vast Folk Arts Theater where beauty pageants and cultural performances are staged, the Parthenon-like Manila Film Center, Museum of Philippine Culture, and the Coconut Palace.

Makati: Approximately 10 km southeast of Ermita, this planned community of international banks, air-conditioned shopping centers, embassies, expensive restaurants, five-star hotels, and ritzy nightclubs is the most modern and wealthy suburb in the Philippines. Highlights include the Ayala Museum with its collection of ethnic art and historical dioramas, Makati Commercial Center, and the American Cemetery, which holds the remains of over 17,000 American and Allied troops who perished during WW II.

ACCOMMODATIONS

Budget
Budget accommodations under P400 are found in the tourist belt of Ermita and Malate, but most are cramped, dirty, and noisy. You must spend P500-600 to find a decent room with fan and common bath and P750-1,200 for an a/c room. Manila is not a cheap place to stay, so if you're on a tight budget, it's best to leave the city as soon as possible.

A good starting spot is Malate Pensionne on Adriatico Street. If it's filled, you can drop your bag in the lobby and start your search for another place.

Malate Pensionne: Manila's largest and most popular pension house has the enclosed Portico Café for people watching, Glasshouse, Sidebar, useful information board, harried but patient employees, and well-maintained rooms in all price ranges—the best budget to mid-priced place in Manila. Their business center can help with long-distance phone calls and visa extensions. Bar girls are not allowed inside the rooms. Tell Mila that Carl sent you. 1771 Adriatico St., tel. (02) 523-83044, info@mpensionne.com.ph, P150-200 dorm, P350-990 private rooms.

Shoshana Pension House: Bare-bones but very cheap place just down the alley from Malate Pensionne. 1776 Adriatico St., tel. (02) 524-6512, P250-350.

Pension Natividad: Receives good reviews from travelers and is fairly new, clean, and safe, although it looks intimidating from the outside. 1690 del Pilar, tel. (02) 521-0524, P150-180 dorm, P500-800 private rooms.

Joward's Pension House: Small but acceptable rooms just across from the Midtown Hotel. 1726 Adriatico St., tel. (02) 521-4845, P320-550.

Santos Pension: An old favorite now run down but with cheap rooms and a completely depressing lobby. 1540 Mabini St., tel. (02) 523-4896, P300-600.

Midtown Inn: Just above the Midtown Inn Diner with small but survivable rooms. 551 Padre Faura, tel. (02) 525-1403, P425-800.

Tropical Mansion Hotel: Rough but inexpensive place with discounted monthly rates. 1242 Bocobo St., tel. (02) 521-2639, P550-950.

PHILIPPINES

Moderate

Cherry Lodge Apartelle: Short-time hotel with 10% discount on monthly stays. 550 Jorge Bocobo St., tel. (02) 524-7631, P800-1,200.

Swagman Hotel: This small Australian hotel, which caters to bachelors on holiday, offers good vibes and ice-cold beer plus friendly, helpful personnel. Swagman has daily bus service to Angeles, Subic, La Union, and Baguio. 411 Flores St., tel. (02) 523-8541, P1,300-2,000.

Hotel Soriente: A modern, clean, 35-room hotel on a quiet side street with negotiable rates during the low season. 545 Flores St., tel. (02) 523-9480, P900-1,400.

RESTAURANTS

Filipino

Plenty of Western fast food joints in Manila, but native Filipino cuisine should also be tried. The cheaper ones are often *turo turo* (point point) style, which lets you point to whatever looks best, a convenient way to select something without blindly ordering off the menu. These are plentiful along Del Pilar and Mabini streets. Also worth searching out are *kamayan* restaurants, which serve Filipino fare on banana leafs without the use of silverware. It's hand to mouth in these places!

Barrio Fiesta: The country's largest chain of restaurants specializing in native Filipino cuisine is famous for its *kare kare, inihaw na bangus,* and crispy *pata.* There are two outlets in Ermita, one on Orosa at Arkansas and another on United Nations just west of Del Pilar. Moderate.

Aristocrat: Filipino seafood and international specialities served in a large, informal restaurant. Try *alimango* (crabs wrapped in banana leaves), chicken honey, and *maliputo,* a locally raised freshwater fish. Open 24 hours. 432 San Andreas at Roxas Boulevard. Moderate.

Buffets: Luncheon buffets at five-star hotels are one of Manila's best bargains. Although largely a Western smorgasbord, a selection of native dishes will also be included. Prices range from P300-500 at the Midtown, Silahis, and Manila Pavilion Hotels.

Western

Hula Hut: Rosie's Diner on the corner and the Hula Hut behind the Blue Hawaii serve great burgers, steaks, and daily specials from an extensive menu. The place was closed on my last visit but may reopen soon. 1427 Del Pilar. Inexpensive.

Aida's: Local specialties and ice-cold beer served at rock-bottom prices to locals, streetwalkers, and the occasional tourist. Del Pilar at Santa Monica Street. Inexpensive.

Iseya Hotel: Escape the belching jeepneys and street hustlers by riding the elevator to this patio restaurant on the sixth floor of the Iseya. Tasty fare, inexpensive beer, and daily specials served around the clock. 457 Padre Faura at Del Pilar Street. Moderate.

Shakey's: The pizza is overpriced and lousy, but the place is air-conditioned and comfortable. Rock bands entertain in the evening at the Mabini branch. Rock 'n' roll in a pizzeria? Only in the Philippines! Mabini at Arquiza Street. Moderate.

Juri's Grand Cafe: Upscale Dutch cafe and European watering hole popular with Brits and Aussies; look for the giant, comical, wooden waiter figure out front. 1320 Del Pilar Street. Moderate.

Endangered Species: Classy and very hip place with trendy bar and popular restaurant serving steak and seafood specialties. 1834 Del Pilar Street. Moderate.

Remidios Circle Bistros: Manila's trendy neighborhood for espressos, art talk, and nouvelle cuisine is centered around Rotary Circle in Malate. All of the following cafes are somewhat expensive but a refreshing change from pizzas and yet another pot of *adobo.*

Names and locations change with the seasons, but the most popular venues currently are the North American Beef Company, Blue Café, Insomnia Café, Café Iguana, and Café Caribana on Julio Nakpil Street. A block south near Remidios Circle you'll find Café Adriatico, Racks Ribs, Patio Guernica, Camp Gourmet, Dean Street Café, Penguin Café, Café 1900, and Bistro Remedios. Heading down Adriatico Street is Jazzbox, Larry's Café, and Remember Café.

Bistro Remedios offers first-class Filipino dishes including *dinengdeng* from Ilocos, *pancit molo* from Iloilo, and *kamansing bukid* from Pampangna. Patio Guernica serves Spanish specialties like *paella, lengua,* and *callos.*

ENTERTAINMENT

Nightclubs

Zamboanga Restaurant: Several restaurants put on nightly dinner shows for their guests. Dinner plus show runs P350-600. 1619 Adriatico Street.

Hobbit House: Manila's nightlife includes more than dinner shows and cultural revues. The Hobbit House, one of the most popular small nightclubs in town, features Mexican food and live folk music by some of the country's top performers, such as Freddy Aguilar. Food and drinks are served by dwarf waiters. 1801 Mabini at Remedios Street.

My Father's Moustache: Another small nightclub with folk musicians and modest cover charge. 2144 Del Pilar near Quirino.

Guernica's: Spanish guitar and regional dishes like *gambas* and *calamares* served in a peaceful restaurant in operation over 30 years. 1325 Del Pilar.

Remedios Circle Clubs: Trendy and chic bistros include all the cafes listed above under Western restaurants. Many have entertainment or drag shows and sometimes collect a modest cover charge on weekends or for special events.

Girlie Bars

Manila's nightclubs, bars, and strip joints once located along Del Pilar and Mabini streets in the heart of the tourist district were closed down several years ago by the ever-vigilant Mayor Alfredo Lim—a blow that devastated the local tourism industry and almost completely destroyed the once-famous tourist quarter. Boarded-up doorways, burned-out nightclubs, and scores of homeless squatters are the legacy of Mr. Lim, a puritanical mayor who never bothered to close the prostitution dens in Chinatown, Quezon City, and other districts under his command. To add insult to injury, Lim once publicly referred to the Australian, British, and American owners of the nightclubs as "white monkeys," a racist comment that spoke volumes about his Chinese roots.

Many of the nightclub owners packed up their bags and headed south a few kilometers to the neighboring town of Pasay where they reopened their clubs along Roxas Boulevard and in the so-called Edsa Entertainment Complex.

Vagabond Niteclub: The old spirit of Ermita lives on in this immensely popular nightclub packed with expats and tourists every night of the week. 2102 Roxas Boulevard.

Edsa Entertainment Complex: Somewhat sterile and overpriced but the most concentrated collection of girlie nightclubs in the country. The most popular clubs include the infamous Firehouse, My Fair Club, Esperanza (a hostess club), Pitstop with car decor, and the Cotton Club (the former Australian Club).

Makati: A small go-go scene survives on Burgos Street just outside the perimeter of the Makati district. Prices are high and there's little competition between clubs since most venues (Dimples, Papillon, Friday's, Rascals, and Ivory) are owned and operated by a single individual. Go early and take advantage of happy hour.

SHOPPING

Handicrafts are the best buys in the Philippines. This is *not* the place to buy electronics or other imported goods, but rather woodcarvings, shell items, rattanware, and tribal art.

Manila has a great selection but, as elsewhere in Southeast Asia, prices will be much lower in the area of origin. For example, woodcarvings, guitars, and brassware are cheapest in Baguio, Cebu, and Mindanao, so save your major purchases for provincial markets.

Bargaining is *de rigueur* except in large department stores. Always ask for the "best price" before making your first counter offer. Note that Filipino merchants do not discount prices as sharply as in Indonesia, although you should be able to save 20-30% on most purchases.

Ermita: Manila's main shopping area for tourists has just about everything possible—from finely carved *santos* to gaudy pop paintings on black velvet. Mabini Street at the north end has over a dozen handicraft and curio stores such as Terry's, Likha, and Via and Antica. T'boli Arts is stocked with beaded necklaces, belts, clothing, and utilitarian items woven from T'boli *nalak*. Tesoro's across the street at 1325 Mabini is one of Manila's largest handicraft emporiums. Mandaya weavings from Mindanao can be purchased from Godilla in the nearby Dabaw Etnika Weaving Center.

PHILIPPINES

Intramuros: Many of the better antique and handicrafts stores in Manila are located in Makati and the walled city of Intramuros. El Amanecer at 744 Calle de Palario (General Luna Street) sports three floors of Philippine arts and crafts, including Silahis for weavings, Bob Lane's Chang Rong Gallery for antique basketry, and Galeria de las Islas for paintings and Filipiniana books. The Barrio San Luis complex on the same street has a half-dozen emporiums, including Santamaria Arts for pottery and Capricci for antique jewelry. Casa Manila opposite San Augustin is also worth touring.

SERVICES

Travel Information

The Department of Tourism (DOT) in the monstrous edifice in Rizal Park has a limited supply of printed information but plenty of knowledgeable employees. Open daily 0800-1800.

Travel Agencies: Manila has several expat clubs which provide travel information and tour services. Swagman on Flores Street sells air tickets, arranges visa extensions, and operates resorts around the country. They now have over 20 travel agencies throughout the Philippines.

Money: Most independent but licensed money changers are located on Mabini Street in Ermita. Cash advances on your Visa or MasterCard are only possible at the Equitable Bank. They also cash traveler's checks at reasonable rates.

Visas

Visitors intending to stay in the Philippines more than 21 days should obtain a visa *before* arrival. Extensions can be made at the Department of Immigration on Magallanes Drive in Intramuros near the General Post Office but it's quite a time-consuming hassle. The best strategy is to let someone else—such as Malate Pensionne—take care of this formality.

Extensions can also be picked up in Angeles and Cebu City. Foreign embassies are located in Makati. Hours vary but most are open 0800-1200.

Maps

The free map of Manila, Makati, and Intramuros provided by the Tourist Office is excellent, although greater detail is provided in the *City Map of Manila* published and distributed by National Bookstore.

Detailed topographic maps and nautical guides can be purchased at Namria (formerly the Bureau of Coast and Geodetic Survey) on Baracca Street in San Nicolas. Various publications are given away at hotels and nightclubs in Ermita such as the touristy *What's On in Manila* for nightclub acts and the outstanding *Expat,* which provides a steady stream of relevant news, gossip, and restaurant reviews.

Bookstores

Ermita has several small but well-stocked bookstores for literature on the Philippines and other travel destinations. Solidaridad Books, a friendly shop on Padre Faura at Adriatico owned by Philippine novelist Francisco Sionil Jose, specializes in revolutionary political literature. National Bookstore in Makati has the widest selection of books in the country, while Bookmark (also in Makati) specializes in books on the Philippines.

Communications and Media

Mail: Registered letters, telegrams, and parcels can be mailed from the General Post Office near the river in Intramuros. Poste restante operates from a separate counter. The GPO is open daily 0800-1700 except Sundays 0800-1200. Mail can also be sent from the uncrowded Rizal Park post office across from the Manila Hotel.

Telephone: International phone calls can be made from most hotels and from PLDT and BayanTel offices located around the city. Public phones are a rarity in the Philippines and most local calls are made from shops and restaurants.

Electricity: 220 volts in rural areas and either 110 or 220 volts in most cities. Portable radios burn out if the voltage isn't set correctly!

Media: Manila has about 20 morning dailies including the *Manila Bulletin* with the largest classified section. Other papers include *Malaya, Daily Inquirer, Chronicle,* and *Star.*

Cinema: Movies are a great bargain in the Philippines. For just a few pesos you can disappear into an ice-cold theater and enjoy first-run American films. Recommended local films produced in recent years include Lino Brocka's *Bayan Ko* and *Manila in the Claws of Darkness,*

Ishmael Bernal's graphic *Manila by Night,* and the acclaimed *Perfumed Nightmare* by Kidlat Tahimik. These, of course, are rarely seen since local audiences prefer soap operas and violence, plus films starring Kris Aquino, daughter of the former president.

TRANSPORTATION

Airport Arrival

Manila International Airport is 12 km from city center. After immigration and customs you can pick up tourist information at the DOT counter and change money at the bank outlets. Rates are good; ask for small change for the cab drivers and don't get freaked out by the enormous crowd of Filipinos waiting for friends and relatives.

Getting from the airport to your hotel without getting ripped off is difficult, but not impossible. Buses leave from the main road some 200 km from the airport terminal, but most visitors take a taxi to avoid getting lost.

All taxis in Manila are metered but few taxi drivers use their meter. The airport has a taxi counter where you can purchase taxi coupons to any hotel, but this service is badly overpriced at P300-500 per destination.

Ignore all the taxi touts who will pounce on you the moment you enter the airport lobby or exit any door. Instead, walk up the stairs to the departure level, head out the front door, and wait for a taxi to let off passengers. There's also a small taxi halt about 30 meters to the right of the door where the taxis miraculously use their meter. The correct fare to any hotel in Ermita or Makati is P80-100, but you should figure on P100 after including a small tip.

Whether you use the taxi stand or flag down an arriving taxi, confirm with the driver that the meter is working properly and tell him you know the correct fare should be around P100. Do not get inside any taxi that refuses to use the meter or claims the meter is broken—cheating tourists is a major industry among taxi drivers in Manila.

Some drivers will try to renegotiate the fare as they roar down Roxas Boulevard, or illegally attempt to collect individual fares from each passenger. Don't fall for these tricks. If you have a problem, keep quiet until you arrive at your hotel and have unloaded your baggage. Take your gear inside the hotel and explain to the front desk that your taxi driver is attempting to cheat you. Another strategy is to unload your bags, drop them in the lobby, and then return to the taxi and pay the driver a flat fee of P100.

Baggage should be carried inside the cab or carefully watched while it's being loaded in the trunk.

Getting Around

Taxis: Metered taxis in Manila are about the cheapest in Southeast Asia when operating properly with well-calibrated meters. Fares average just over P10 per kilometer. There are some problems, however. Cab drivers waiting at the airport and near tourist hotels often claim their meters are broken and then attempt to negotiate flat fees. Always confirm that the meter is operating before getting into any cab.

Jeepneys: To take jeepneys around Manila you must learn a few important place-names. Signs above the driver and on the side refer to either a major suburb such as Cubao or Quiapo, an important landmark such as Monumento, or a major street such as Ayala Street in Makati.

Jeepneys going south along Del Pilar or Taft Avenues are marked either Libertad, Baclaran, Vito Cruz, or Pasay. These are useful for reaching the Cultural Center, the Philippine Village, and the zoo.

Jeepneys going north along Mabini or Taft are marked Quiapo, Santa Cruz, Divisoria, Blumentritt, or Monumento. All northbound jeepneys pass the Lawton bus terminal and GPO before passing over the Pasig River to Quiapo and Chinatown. The fare is P2 for shorter distances and P2-8 for longer journeys. In most cases, you just hand the driver P2.

Front seats are the most highly prized since you can actually see where you are going. Drivers stop on demand when you hiss, rap on the roof, or call out *para* or *bayad*. Blasting disco music was mercifully banned in jeepneys a few years ago but the flashing Christs and cheeky slogans carry on.

Buses: Buses also display their destinations on the front and sides. Most buses follow a circular route from Taft Avenue in Ermita out to Makati, up EDSA highway to Quezon City, then south to Quiapo before returning to Ermita. Also vice-versa.

PHILIPPINES

Light Rail Transit: Manila's Metrorail or LRT is a fast and comfortable way to reach Baclaran in south Manila, for the Philtranco and Victory Liner bus terminals, and to go north to Victory Liner and Philippine Rabbit bus terminals. The LRT also reaches Quiapo and the Chinese Cemetery. When time is important, take the LRT.

Leaving Manila

By Air: International flights leave from the Ninoy Aquino International Airport (NAIA) while domestic flights leave from the domestic terminal about two km away.

Philippine Airlines in the PAL building on Legaspi Street in Makati is as perpetually crowded as its branch office on Roxas Boulevard in Ermita. There's also a PAL office inside the Manila Hotel and the Intercontinental in Makati. Most of the smaller, newer domestic airlines have offices at the domestic terminal.

A metered taxi from Ermita or Makati to NAIA or the domestic terminal should cost P100-120.

Airport departure tax for international flights is P500.

By Bus

Manila has eight major bus companies and several bus terminals located on the outskirts of town.

It's impossible to catch a long-distance bus from Ermita or Makati; you'll need to first take a taxi or bus to one of the outlying bus terminals.

Philippine Rabbit (Santa Cruz): Buses to central and northwestern Luzon including Angeles, Baguio, and the La Union beaches. 819 Oroquieta, Santa Cruz. Take a jeepney on Mabini marked Monumento or Metrorail to D Jose Station.

Philippine Rabbit (Caloocan): Buses to central and northwestern Luzon including Angeles, San Fernando, and Vigan. Rizal Avenue Extension at 2nd Avenue. Take Monumento jeepney or Metrorail to R Papa Station.

Victory Liner (Caloocan): Buses to central Luzon including Olongapo, Alaminos, and Dagupan. 713 Rizal Avenue Extension, Caloocan (near the Bonifacio Monument). Take Monumento jeepney or Metrorail to North Terminal.

BLTB: Buses to southern Luzon including Santa Cruz (for Pagsanjan Falls), Tagaytay, Nasugbu, Batangas, Naga, and Legaspi. Edsa, Pasay City. Take a taxi or Metrorail to Edsa Station and walk east.

Philtranco: Buses to southern Luzon, Samar, and Leyte. It's even possible (though suicidal) to take a direct 44-hour bus to Davao City in southern Mindanao. Edsa, Pasay City. Take a taxi or Metrorail to the Edsa Station.

AROUND MANILA

While the most popular destinations on Luzon are the Banaue rice terraces and the mountain towns of Bontoc and Sagada, several places of interest are close enough to Manila to be visited on shorter excursions. Travel agents in Ermita organize tours, but independent travelers will have little trouble reaching the following attractions by bus.

The five provinces south of Manila—Cavite, Laguna, Batangas, Rizal, and Quezon—are now united in an ambitious economic plan called Calabarzon, an international effort planned by a Japanese agency in cooperation with Filipino industries. The tourism sector includes two new national parks, an amazing amount of development near Lake Taal, and overdue improvements to beach and scuba-diving facilities in Cavite and Batangas provinces.

Routes

Corregidor, the famous organ at Las Pinas, and the Sarao jeepney factory are half-day visits, while the provinces south of Manila are best experienced on longer journeys.

A popular three- to five-day tour begins with a visit to Las Pinas Church and the nearby Sarao jeepney factory before continuing down to Tagaytay and Lake Taal. Accommodations are available on the volcanic ridge at Tagaytay and down at Talisay at the lakeside. Alternatively, after enjoying the views for a few hours and possibly descending down to lake level, local transport can be taken down to the beaches near Anilao or over to San Pablo, where a youth hostel overlooks beautiful Sampaloc Lake.

Within striking distance of San Pablo are the expensive private resort of Hidden Valley and an excellent museum at Villa Escudero. Hidden Valley is overrated, but the museum and park at Villa Escudero are highly recommended. Buses continue northeast to Pagsanjan for budget accommodations and river rides early the following morning.

Travelers with more time might spend a night at one of the hot-spring resorts between Los Banos and Calamba before trekking up Mt. Makiling. The return to Manila by bus takes about two hours. Otherwise, backtrack to Batangas City and take a boat across to Mindoro Island.

CORREGIDOR ISLAND

Guarding the entrance to Manila Bay is the tadpole-shaped "Rock" where American and Filipino forces made their final stand against the Japanese forces in 1942. After five months of constant bombing, the May 1942 surrender was followed by the infamous Bataan Death March, in which over 10,000 POWs died from beatings and executions.

Corregidor today is an eerie place of destroyed bunkers, mile-long barracks, and rusting batteries being swallowed through jungle vegetation. Visitors can wander through a museum with photographs of prewar Corregidor, see a Pacific memorial to those who died in the struggle, and walk around Malinta Tunnel where Douglas MacArthur, President Quezon, and General Wainwright once survived the intense shelling.

Accommodations
Corregidor accommodations are handled by the Corregidor Foundation in the DOT building in Rizal Park. Choices include the 31-room Corregidor Hotel where rooms cost from P2,200 and the Corregidor Youth Hostel, which charges P250 for a dorm bed.

Transportation
Corregidor tours are somewhat expensive. Escorted tours arranged by Sun Cruises cost P900 and leave daily at 0800 from the ferry terminal adjacent to the Cultural Center. These tours include roundtrip hovercraft transport and a four-hour sightseeing tour by bus. The light and sound show inside the Malinta Tunnel costs an extra P150.

Every Sunday a slower but perhaps more comfortable boat—the *Tennessee Walker*—leaves from the Manila Hotel dock and does a 12-hour Corregidor tour with buffet breakfast and lunch for P850. The *Tennessee Walker*, a converted oil tanker (guaranteed unsinkable), also does dinner cruises nightly at 1930 for P600 per person. Contact the Manila Hotel for reservations.

LAS PINAS ORGAN

The world's only bamboo organ can be seen in the San Jose parish church in Las Pinas. Constructed by Father Diego Cera in 1817-22, the organ fell into disuse for almost a century until 1973 when Hans Gerd Klais, a German organ specialist, had it rebuilt in Bonn. Today the famous 3.5-ton Balik organ and its 832 bamboo and 130 metal pipes can be heard during Sunday services and sometimes during the day 0900-1100 and 1400-1600. Organ music tapes are sold in the gift shop.

Transportation
To reach Las Pinas, 12 km south of Rizal Park, take any bus on Taft Ave. marked "Zapote" or "Cavite" and ask the driver to drop you near the church. Public buses continue south to the Sarao jeepney factory and to Lake Taal.

SARAO JEEPNEY FACTORY

Three km south of Las Pinas in the town of Zapote is the Sarao Motors jeepney factory, where decorative bodies are mounted on Japanese frames for Manila's wild wagons. The operation began in 1953 when Leonardo Sarao saw the potential for converting American jeeps left behind after WW II into public-transportation vehicles. Sarao stretched the jeep chassis so that 10 people could be packed inside and then added the colorful paint job that somehow typifies what is most exuberant about the Filipino lifestyle. Today, the factory and its 450 employees crank out about 1,500 jeepneys per year, each costing about US$8,000.

Tourists are welcome to wander around and watch the workmen; closed Sundays.

TAGAYTAY

Perched on a ridge 686 meters above sea level, Tagaytay City (City?), a sprawling collection of homes and shops, offers a spectacular vista over one of the world's most scenic volcanoes. Today, the views, the lake, and the volcano form one of Luzon's most popular tourist destinations.

Tagaytay is being developed into a tourism center with a greatly expanded Taal Vista Lodge, casino, 400-room Hyatt Hotel, condominiums, and perhaps a cable-car ride from the ridge down to the shores of Lake Taal.

Attractions

Tagaytay's big draws are the views over Lake Taal and the fresh air, though a visit to the Palace in the Sky is worth the effort.

Palace in the Sky: One of the more remarkable sights near Tagaytay is this magnificently situated, partially completed, and never-occupied home of ex-dictator Ferdinand Marcos. Now called People's Park in the Sky, the rather amazing history of this ill-fated project is related on a signpost erected near the front entrance. The Palace briefly made newspaper headlines in May '89 when a helicopter used in filming a Chuck Norris movie crashed into a nearby ravine, killing four people. Early mornings guarantee limitless views from Manila to Batangas and Corregidor.

The palace is up a winding road five km east of Taal Vista Lodge. It's too far to walk, but jeepneys can be hired at the Tagaytay road junction.

Accommodations

Tagaytay has several hotels and a few guesthouses on the ridge overlooking Taal Lake.

Taal Vista Lodge: Tagaytay's leading hotel is also the best place for views, photographs, and lunch. Cultural shows are given on weekends. Tagaytay, tel. (096) 413-1223, P2,200-2,800.

Villa Adelaida: A less expensive hotel with pool and restaurant several kilometers east of the Taal Vista Lodge in the suburb of Foggy Heights. Barangay Sungay, tel. (096) 413-1175, P850-1,200.

La Montana Resort: Dorm beds plus budget priced rooms. Tagaytay, tel. (096) 378-6011, P80-550.

Private Homes: The market across the road from the Taal Vista Lodge can help with accommodations in private homes, but they also suffer from a rip-off-the-tourist mentality. The lack of reasonably priced accommodation forces many budget travelers back to Manila by nightfall or on to San Pablo, Pagsanjan, or nearby beach resorts.

Transportation

Tagaytay is 60 km south of Manila and can be reached in 90 minutes by BLTB bus from Pasay City. Look for a bus marked "Nasugbu."

parade pause

PHILIPPINES

TALISAY AND LAKE TAAL

Taal is one of the Philippines's most active volcanoes and also one of the deadliest. An explosion in 1911 killed over 1,300 people while another eruption in 1965 destroyed several villages and killed hundreds more. More recently, an eruption in 1992 forced the evacuation of thousands from the interior islands to more secure locations at Talisay and Tagaytay.

The topography is somewhat complicated, but Taal itself is an enormous caldera filled by a vast lake in which sits Volcano Island and its two cones: an extinct one on the northwest filled with cold water heavy with sulfuric acid, and an active cone on the southwest which occasionally belches forth sulfuric fumes and spits out ash. The principal town on the north shore is Talisay.

The volcanic inner island can be visited by hiring a *banca* and guide in Talisay and nearby towns (Banga, Balas, Leynes) on the north shore or San Nicolas on the southwest. Rates and all services must be firmly negotiated in advance, but figure on about P500-750 for boat, gasoline, and guide services. It's a common tactic of boatmen to demand additional money for gasoline once you're in the middle of the lake.

Accommodations
Rosalina's Place: Simple place at the intersection of the descending and lakeside roads. The owner can help with boat rentals and volcano tours. Banga, tel. (0973) 373-6066, P250-400.

Milo's Paradise: Family-run with large rooms, swimming pool, and knowledgeable owners. Balas, tel. (097) 372-0318, P650-950.

Taal Lake Guesthouse: Budget option midway between Tagaytay and Talisay. Leynes, tel. (0973) 373-6066, P300-500.

Transportation
Lake Taal can be reached from several directions, but the easiest route is by minitruck down from the road junction on Tagaytay Ridge, a steep and extremely winding journey. What a ride! You can also go direct from Manila with any BLTB bus marked Batangas. Get off in Tanauan and catch another bus or jeepney west down to Talisay.

The lake can be reached by bus from Pagsanjan via Los Banos, Calamba, and Tanauan.

SAN PABLO

This small town, famous for its seven crater lakes formed eons ago by volcanic activity, also serves as a convenient base for visiting the nearby attractions of Hidden Valley and Villa Escudero.

Attractions
Sampaloc Lake, directly behind City Hall, is the most accessible body of water in the vicinity. An early-evening stroll along the circular road will uncover floating fishpens surrounded by narrow bamboo rafts used by the fishermen, fields of cultivated water hyacinths, and the Kamayan Dagat Restaurant, which serves Chinese dishes and fish specialties made of tilapia raised in the nearby pens. Filipinos relaxing in outdoor cafes are happy to share shots of the local brew and chat with visitors. San Pablo's other six lakes, all located outside of town, are difficult to reach without private transportation.

Hidden Valley Springs: This 44-hectare private resort four km north of Alaminos offers picnic tables, hot springs dammed into artificial swimming pools, a small waterfall, and concrete paths leading through jungle thick with the massively buttressed trunks of huge dipterocarps. Hidden Valley is pleasant but touristy, certainly not worth the stiff P1,400 admission fee.

Villa Escudero: One of the finest collections of arts and crafts in the Philippines can be seen in the superb museum at Villa Escudero, a private coconut plantation south of San Pablo. The late Don Arsenio Escudero was an incurable collector of almost everything: stuffed birds, silver spoons, coins, tanks and cannons, Filipino costumes, and magical amulets that stop bullets. On a more serious side, his large museum also displays a wide range of religious artifacts such as priceless *santos,* silver altars from well-known churches, and lovely Chinese celadons.

After touring the museum, you can take a leisurely ride on a *carabao* cart and do a few laps in the icy swimming pool. Bring your swimsuit. Admission is P500. Villa Escudero is 10 km south of San Pablo. Take a jeepney from San Pablo to the park entrance and walk one km through the coconut groves.

San Pablo to Pagsanjan Falls

Between San Pablo and the falls at Pagsanjan are several worthwhile sights.

Nagcarlan: Fifteen km east of San Pablo is an old town with unusual residential architecture, a fine church dating from 1752, and a circular cemetery much like Manila's Paco Cemetery. Worth a quick stop.

Majayjay: The historic and largely untouched town of Majayjay a few kilometers south of the main road from Sambat is dominated by a monumental three-story church built between 1711 and 1730. Having survived all subsequent earthquakes, it remains the oldest religious structure in the country and an outstanding example of Philippine colonial baroque architecture.

Bridge of Whims: Also visit the Puenta del Capricho ("Bridge of Whims") five km from Majayjay. Constructed in the 1850s by a parish priest using forced labor, this huge stone bridge was partially destroyed in the film Apocalypse Now.

Accommodations

San Pablo has several inexpensive hotels in town, but it makes sense to stay near the lake and enjoy the views.

Sampaloc Lake Youth Hostel: San Pablo's best value is this clean and friendly hostel in a quiet residential neighborhood overlooking the lake. From the church, walk down Schetelig Street and turn left at the YH sign. Efarca Village, tel. (093) 344-3448, P120-180.

Villa Escudero: Spacious cottages in a coconut grove plus three meals a day. Villa Escudero, tel. (02) 521-0830, P2,000-3,400.

Transportation

San Pablo is 87 km from Manila and can be reached in two hours with any BLTB, Philtranco, or Superlines bus heading toward Lucena, Daet, Naga, or Legaspi. All stop in San Pablo. From Pagsanjan, take a jeepney to Santa Cruz followed by another to San Pablo.

PAGSANJAN

Shooting the rapids at Pagsanjan (pronounced Pak-SAN-han) is a popular outing from Manila. Bancas, which are pushed, pulled, and paddled by any of Pagsanjan's 1,200 licensed banceros,

can be hired at local hotels or at the upriver Pagsanjan Falls Lodge. Fees are P500 per two-person boat and boatmen expect tips of P100-200 per person; ignore pushy banceros who plead for larger tips by bragging about the generosity of other customers.

The journey begins in dugouts towed by motorized bancas which noisily roar through the canyon walls hung with curtains of mosses, lianas, orchids, and begonias, past wispy waterfalls and chattering monkeys armed with coconuts. A local tourist office now stands on the site of the Indochinese temple constructed for and then dramatically destroyed in Coppola's 1975-76 Apocalypse Now. Other scenes filmed along the riverbanks have appeared in Platoon and several of Chuck Norris's war sagas, and the infamous helicopter accident that killed Vic Morrow and three children during the filming of The Twilight Zone. Vietnamese village film sets, complete with watchtowers and red flags, seem to have become permanent fixtures up here.

Eventually, the motorized bancas disconnect and the remaining 14 rapids are hurdled up to 30-meter Magdapio Falls, which thunders into an icy pool. For a few additional pesos, you can get yourself drenched on a raft guided along fixed wires. Bring a plastic bag for your camera.

The only way to avoid tour groups who flood the river by late morning is to spend a night in Pagsanjan and do an early-morning river run. Whatever you do, avoid weekends, when the river resembles Disneyland.

Accommodations

Most budget accommodations are on Garcia Street alongside the river.

Willy Flores's Place: A longtime favorite operated by postman Willy, his wife Pacita, and their boatman son, Noli, all of whom can advise on nearby hiking, swimming, dancing, and weekend cockfights. Also on the same street, but somewhat more expensive, is Pagsanjan Village Hotel and Riverside Bungalows. 821 Garcia St., no phone, P150-420.

Pagsanjan Youth Hostel: A peaceful but somewhat difficult place to find. Walk across the river, turn right, and look for the AYH sign. 237 General Luna St., tel. (049) 645-2347, P100-200.

Camino Real Hotel: Best choice in the mid-priced range is this modest but very clean hotel on the main street near the bridge. 39 Rizal St., tel. (049) 645-2086, P550-850.

La Corona de Pagsanjan: An upscale lodge with three swimming pools, restaurant, and deck with views over the river. Pinagsanjan, tel. (0912) 306-9766, P1,500-2,400.

Transportation
Buses to Santa Cruz leave from the Lawton bus terminal near City Hall. BLTB in Pasay City also serves Santa Cruz. Jeepneys continue from Santa Cruz to Pagsanjan. Ignore the tricycle drivers and watch your belongings as this is a *very* popular route for professional pickpockets and bag slashers.

From Pagsanjan, you can return to Manila via Santa Cruz or go directly to San Pablo, Lake Taal, Tagaytay, or Batangas for Mindoro, or head south toward Legaspi.

MOUNTAIN PROVINCES

Northern Luzon's varied topography, cultural minorities, beaches, and amazing rice terraces have made it one of the country's most popular destinations. Several weeks would be necessary to explore the more remote regions, but a quick loop through the central Mountain Province can be completed in 7-14 days with public transportation.

A recommended counterclockwise loop visits the Banaue rice terraces and the lovely mountain town of Sagada before passing through Baguio on the return to Manila. This covers the highlights of northern Luzon, although those with more time might detour to the beaches on the west coast.

Another bit of advice: contrary to tourist office promotions and the generally held belief of many Filipinos, Sagada and Banaue are far more pleasant and intriguing destinations than the congested city of Baguio.

ANGELES CITY

Angeles City, former home to Clark Air Force Base, is 82 km north of Manila on the highway to Baguio. Prior to the eruption of Mt. Pinatubo in 1991, Angeles was home to the largest U.S. military installation outside the continental United States.

Parasitically surrounding the fences of the abandoned air base are dozens of bars, nightclubs, restaurants, souvenir shops, and short-term hotels that once served the needs of the enlisted military personnel and now serve the same needs of visiting Western males. In fact, most of Manila's flesh trade moved here in the mid-1990s after the purges of Mayor Lim.

Along with the roaring sex trade, the main attraction in the region is trekking to the summit of Mt. Pinatubo. Escorted hikes are put together by several hotels and travel agencies in town.

Accommodations
Angeles has some of the best-priced hotels in the country with dozens of places in the P500-800 price range. Most are located along the road that skirts the former American airbase.

New Liberty Hotel: Inexpensive option off MacArthur Highway a short stroll from the go-go bars and nightclubs. Spacious grounds, swimming pool. Coching Alley, tel. (045) 602-5896, P250-600.

Tropicana Resort Hotel: Clean hotel with Mistys Nighclub and reasonably priced a/c rooms. 151 Fields Ave., tel. (045) 785-1822, P500-900.

Phoenix Hotel: Very well maintained hotel with swimming pool, soccer matches on the tube, and friendly managers. 810 Malabanias Rd., tel. (045) 888-2195, P600-900.

Sunset Garden: American-style motel with large swimming pool and breezy restaurant popular with visiting Australians and German travel writers. Malabanas Rd., tel. (045) 888-2312, P400-700.

Transportation
Philippine Rabbit buses from Rizal Avenue in Manila stop in downtown Angeles a few kilometers from the hotels and nightclubs. Jeepneys shuttle from the bus terminal to the hotels on MacArthur Highway.

Direct air-conditioned coaches depart daily from the Swagman Hotel in Ermita—somewhat more expensive than Rabbit buses, but *much* more convenient. There's no obligation to stay at a Swagman hotel.

Buses back to Manila, up to Baguio, and over to Olongapo can be picked up where MacArthur Highway intersects the road to the Dau Expressway, just beyond McDonald's and the old tourist office on your left.

OLONGAPO AND SUBIC

Perhaps without exaggeration, Olongapo—the town nearest the former naval base at Subic—once claimed to be the entertainment capital of the Philippines. Lined along the main thoroughfare of Magsaysay Drive were dozens of clubs featuring the widest possible selections of live musical entertainment, from country and western to heavy metal, and new wave, ska, reggae, and rap.

But after the Americans left the 5,000-man Subic naval base in 1992, Olongapo and Subic reverted back to very quiet places chiefly known for their duty-free shopping, wreck diving, and

beach resorts both north and south of town. Most visitors head directly to Barrio Barretto, a beach resort four km north of Olongapo.

Barrio Barretto has almost 20 hotels and a handful of nightclubs that attempt to keep alive the old spirit of Olongapo.

Accommodations
Rooms have been plentiful since the closure of Subic Naval Base.

Ram's Inn: A budget option two blocks down Rizal Avenue from the Victory bus terminal. 765 Rizal Ave., tel. (047) 222-3481, P150-350.

Subic Bay Garden Inn: A Barrio Barretto hotel with all a/c rooms. National Highway, tel. (047) 222-4550, P400-750.

Halfmoon Hotel: One of the best in town with pool and landscaped gardens. National Highway, tel. (047) 222-4987, P800-1,500.

Transportation
Victory Liner serves Olongapo from Manila and Angeles. Jeepneys continue from Olongapo north to Barrio Barretto.

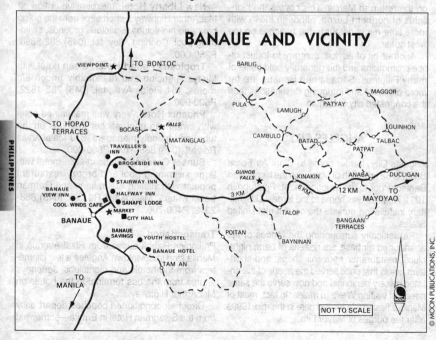

BANAUE AND VICINITY

VIEWPOINT ★ TO BONTOC
TO HOPAO TERRACES
BOCAS ★ FALLS
MATANGLAG
TRAVELLER'S INN
BROOKSIDE INN
STAIRWAY INN
BANAUE VIEW INN ● HALFWAY INN
COOL WINDS CAFE ● SANAFE LODGE
★ MARKET
BANAUE ■ CITY HALL
BANAUE SAVINGS
● YOUTH HOSTEL
● BANAUE HOTEL
TAM AN
TO MANILA

BARLIG
PULA MAGGOR
LAMUGH PATYAY
CAMBULO GUINHON
BATAD TALBAC
PATPAT
GUIHOB FALLS ★
3 KM KINAKIN ANABA DUCLIGAN
6 KM 12 KM TO MAYOYAO
TALOP
BANGAAN TERRACES
POITAN
BAYNINAN

NOT TO SCALE

© MOON PUBLICATIONS, INC.

PHILIPPINES

BANAUE

The manmade rice terraces at Banaue are among the top draws in the Philippines. Although rice-terrace culture is practiced throughout most of Southeast Asia, those near Banaue are incomparable in terms of magnitude and daring—soaring wonders carved from the sides of mountains over 2,000 years ago. Today they form vast amphitheaters cleverly irrigated by manmade waterfalls that gently cascade down the terraced walls. Laid end to end, these handcarved walls would stretch around the world; the total amount of stone used exceeds that in the pyramids of Egypt.

Aside from the spectacular topography, Banaue provides hiking amid stunning scenery, tribal handicrafts, and native villages still somewhat off the beaten track.

Attractions

Banaue: Banaue town is an unimaginative square surrounded by handicraft shops, cafes, and inexpensive pensions down the road. The Saturday market is worth attending, although only the elderly continue to wear traditional clothing.

Traveler's checks can be cashed at the Banaue Hotel and several guesthouses, but rates are poor; it's best to arrive with a healthy supply of pesos. The local tourist office sells maps and can advise on the correct jeepney fares to nearby villages. Visit the small but informative museum inside the Banaue View Inn.

Banaue Rice Terraces: The finest views are from the viewpoint four km up the Banaue-Bontoc road. You can hike up the road or wander through the terraces via Bocus village. Banaue is most spectacular in the fall after the rains, when the ricefields are a brilliant green. Hiking during the summer months is difficult because of heavy rains and thick mud. Guides are only necessary for hikes beyond Batad and prices should be agreed upon in advance.

Bocus and Matanglag: This half-day hike passes through the woodcarving and weaving village of Bocus before arriving in Matanglag, a bronzesmith center where fertility pendants were cast until recently using the lost-wax method.

Tam An and Poitan: This short trek beginning just behind the Banaue Hotel includes the touristy weaving village of Tam An and Poitan, where several traditional Ifugao houses with *cogon* roofs still stand.

Batad: Batad's magnificent amphitheater of rice terraces, 12 km east of Banaue, is one of the highlights of the region. Jeepneys can be chartered to the drop-off point for those who intend to return the same day. Hikers are met at the cafes overlooking Batad by guides, although their assistance is unnecessary for visiting Batad and making short hikes. Homestays are located in Batad and Cambulo to the west.

It's a two-hour hike from Batad to Cambulo and five additional hours back to Banaue. Alternative treks from Batad include a three-day hike to Talboc, Maggor, and Patyay. With proper supplies such as raingear, food, water, flashlight, and a guide you can also hike from Cambulo to Banaue via Pula and the Banaue viewpoint.

Accommodations

Banaue has a dozen small hotels and pensions and an upscale hotel operated by the Philippine Tourism Authority.

Budget Guesthouses: Pensions at the top of the hill such as Sanafe Lodge, Valgreg Hotel, People's Lodge, Green View Lodge, and Wonder Lodge are slightly more expensive than those at the bottom such as the Cozy Nook Inn, Halfway Lodge, Stairway Lodge, Brookside, and popular Traveller's Inn, a favorite of veteran traveler and art collector David Howard. Few of these places take advantage of the potential views but all are perfectly adequate for a night or two. Prices average P75-180.

Banaue Youth Hostel: The hostel adjacent to the Banaue Hotel costs P150 but is clean and you can use the Banaue Hotel swimming pool.

Banaue View Inn: An excellent choice for a few additional pesos is the clean and friendly lodge about 100 meters up the road toward Bontoc. Banaue-Bontoc Highway, tel. (074) 386-4078, P100 dorm, P400-500 private room.

Banaue Hotel: Top-end choice for group tours and unsuspecting tourists afraid of travelers' hostels. Nonguests can use the pool for P20. Banaue, tel. (074) 386-4087, P1,400-2,000.

Transportation

Banaue is 348 km from Manila, 44 km from Bontoc, and 220 km from Baguio.

PHILIPPINES

Manila: Pantranco buses leave from their Quezon City terminal several times daily 0730-1000. Alternatively, take a Pantranco or Dangwa bus to Solano (toward Cagayan Valley) and then the connection to Banaue.

Bontoc: Buses to Bontoc leave from the market daily 0500-0900. If you miss an early departure, buses pass the historical marker by the main road 1100-1300. The ride is magnificent.

Baguio: Buses to Banaue depart daily 0600-0800 from the Baguio bus terminal and take about eight hours via the less scenic southern route through San Jose and Bayombong.

A better option is the early-morning bus from Baguio to Bontoc, which snakes along the almost unbelievable Halsema mountain highway, one of the more spectacular roads in Southeast Asia. Direct connections from Baguio to Banaue are possible, though nearly all travelers take a connecting bus from Bontoc up to Sagada.

BONTOC

Though the provincial capital of Mountain Province is an important junction for travelers passing from Banaue to Baguio, the town itself has little aesthetic appeal. A few attractions are worth visiting, plus traveler's checks can be cashed at good rates from the Philippine National Bank north of the town square.

A word of caution about Bontoc. Despite the modern facade of concrete shops and corrugated roofs, you should remember that Bontoc is a very conservative town. Do not take photographs of the people without first asking permission. Bathing in the river at sunset is a pleasant experience, but you must remain well covered to avoid serious problems.

Bontoc is also a town in a remarkable state of transition: old women dressed in traditional costume with snake-bone ornaments in their hair make a startling contrast to young kids with cheeky T-shirts and thumping ghetto blasters. It is painfully obvious in Bontoc that Igorot tribal culture is quickly coming to an end.

Attractions

Bontoc Museum: This small but well-presented museum adjacent to the Roman Catholic church provides a useful overview of the arts and crafts of the three major tribes of the Cordillera: Ifu-

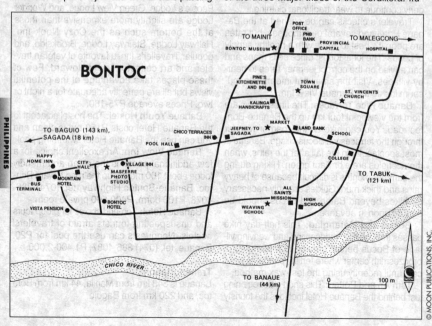

BONTOC

TO MAINIT

POST OFFICE
PNB BANK
PROVINCIAL CAPITAL

TO MALEGCONG

BONTOC MUSEUM

HOSPITAL

PINE'S KITCHENETTE AND INN

TOWN SQUARE

ST. VINCENT'S CHURCH

KALINGA HANDICRAFTS

MARKET

TO BAGUIO (143 km),
SAGADA (18 km)

JEEPNEY TO SAGADA

LAND BANK

SCHOOL

CHICO TERRACES INN

POOL HALL

HAPPY HOME INN

CITY HALL

VILLAGE INN

MASFERRE PHOTO STUDIO

COLLEGE

BUS TERMINAL

MOUNTAIN HOTEL

BONTOC HOTEL

ALL SAINTS MISSION

HIGH SCHOOL

TO TABUK (121 km)

VISTA PENSION

WEAVING SCHOOL

CHICO RIVER

TO BANAUE (44 km)

0   100 m

© MOON PUBLICATIONS, INC.

PHILIPPINES

gao, Bontoc, and Kalinga. Backyard displays include an authentic *ato* where elders assembled and a claustrophobic *ulog* where young unmarried girls once resided. Neither custom continues today. The tiny Kalinga handicraft shop just below the museum sells both genuine antiques and modern reproductions.

Malincong Rice Terraces: The region's finest terraces are located directly behind the enormous hill that looms over Bontoc. A near-vertical hiking trail is plainly visible from town (the trail begins a few blocks beyond the PNB), but an easier strategy is to take the 0700 jeepney to Mainit, where you can soak in the hot springs before hiking back to Bontoc via Malincong. Guides and jeeps can be hired at Pines Kitchenette.

Kalinga Province: The road going northeast from Bontoc passes directly through the ancestral homeland of the Kalingas, former headhunters who have traditionally resisted all forms of outside interference. A controversial plan to flood the Chico River Valley a decade ago for a monstrous hydroelectric dam worsened relations between the Kalingas and the Manila government and dramatically increased local popularity of the communist NPA. Law and order have been restored and visitors should encounter few problems.

Most travelers take the 1300 bus from Bontoc to Tinglayan and then hire guides to lead them to smaller, more remote villages. A circular loop leads from Tinglayan to Tulgueo, and then on to Dananao, Sumadel, Malango, and then back to Tinglayan via the main road.

Accommodations

The isolation of Bontoc has limited accommodations to a few simple inns and one slightly better hotel.

Happy Home Inn: Bontoc's best budget choice is the rudimentary inn just opposite the Dangwa bus terminal. The water supply is sporadic, but owner David Yawan is most helpful with directions and advice.

Other Budget Inns: Mountain Hotel, Chico Terrace, and Village Inn are also inexpensive, though the owners aren't as helpful as David at Happy Home.

Pine's Kitchenette and Inn: Bontoc's top-end choice has a fairly good restaurant and clean rooms with common bath from P100-350.

Transportation

Bontoc is 44 km from Banaue, 143 km from Baguio, and 18 km down the hill from Sagada. Most travelers only overnight in Bontoc en route to Sagada, though the town makes a convenient base from which to explore the surrounding countryside.

Public transportation in spots like Bontoc is subject to delays, cancellations, and early departures depending on the whims of the driver and the capacity of the vehicle. In other words, buses and jeepneys arrive at irregular hours and leave whenever packed to capacity.

Sagada: With those caveats in mind, Skyland buses to Sagada leave daily at 0900 and 1500. Jeepneys to Sagada leave in the morning around 0800 and in the early afternoon around 1300.

Banaue: Dangwa buses to Banaue depart once daily around 0800. A jeepney from Baguio en route to Banaue passes through Bontoc sometime between noon and 1400.

Baguio: Dangwa buses to Baguio leave hourly 0600-0900 and take a full day to reach Baguio. Seats on the left provide the best views.

Kalinga: Jeepneys from Manila to Bugnay and the Kalinga region pass through Bontoc between 1300 and 1400.

SAGADA

Situated 18 km from and 600 meters above Bontoc, this small village hides itself amid spectacular limestone pinnacles and tall pines that sway in the cool mountain air. One of the most beautiful landscapes in the country, Sagada is also famous for its Igorot burial caves, vast subterranean caverns filled with limestone drippings and black rivers, crashing waterfalls, impressive rice terraces, colorful tribal weavings, and almost endless possibilities for hiking and mountain climbing. It's also a great place just to relax in the brilliant sunshine.

Besides all this, Sagada offers some of the finest accommodations and food in the country. Small wonder that it has become a favorite destination for world travelers.

Attractions

Maps and further information on Sagada's sights can be picked up at the guesthouses and pen-

PHILIPPINES

SAGADA-BONTOC REGION

▲ 1,904 m

MAINIT

GUINAANG

MALINCONG
RICE
TERRACES ★

AGUID

FEDILSAN
WATERFALL

DALICON

SABEAN

AMBAGUIO
GUEDAY

PIDE
FEDILSAN

BANGAAN

AGAWA

TANULON

BALITIAN CREEK

AGAWA
FALLS

BESAO

RIDGE TRAIL TO MT. SIPITAN

BIG
BOKONG
FALLS

BAANG
TERRACES ★

TO TABUK

NABANIG

LITTLE BOKONG
FALLS

TETEPAN

AMLUSONG RIVER

PAYEO

LAKE
DANUM

KILONG

BONTOC

BASAO

SAGADA

ANTADAO

BANGUITA

RIDGE TRAIL

DANTAY

TO BANAUE

AMBASING

★ LUMIANG CAVE
★ SUMAGING CAVE

CHICO RIVER

▲ 1,981 m

SUYO

ALAB

ANKILENG

BALILI

▲ 1,889 m

NAKAGANG

TACCONG

MALITEP

TAPAO

BAGNEN

IDATA

▲ 1,923 m

GONOGON

BILA

MAGGON

BAUKO

SABANGAN

TO BAGUIO

0   10 km

© MOON PUBLICATIONS, INC.

PHILIPPINES

sions. Few of the following attractions are marked but most can be found by asking the locals for directions. Guides are also plentiful and jeeps can be hired for longer journeys. U.S. dollars can be exchanged at the Rural Bank of Sagada.

St. Mary's Church and Echo Valley: Episcopalian missionaries arrived in Sagada in 1904 to convert the locals and construct this oversized church. Beyond the church and graveyard on Mt. Calvary is a beautiful and mysterious limestone canyon with caves and hanging coffins. Fifteen minutes southeast from the center of Sagada.

Sagada Weavers: One of the few places in the Philippines to watch backstrap-loom weavers slowly create colorful blankets, shawls, skirts, shoulder bags, and wallets. Prices are very reasonable. Weavings are also sold at the Sagada Cooperative. Nearby Masferre Studios sells old b/w photos. Fifteen minutes east.

Matangkib Cave and Underground River: Follow the cement path between the big boulders to a narrow limestone valley with hanging coffins near an underground river. As with many of the caves near Sagada, a guide and proper equipment are necessary for proper exploration. Twenty minutes east.

Bokong Falls: Take the trail between the houses beyond Sagada Weaving and follow the river. The larger falls one km beyond Little Bokong Falls have better swimming. Forty minutes north.

Ambasing Hanging Coffins: Local tribespeople have traditionally interred their dead in coffins hung high in remote caves to prevent the cadavers from being consumed by wild animals. The coffins beyond Ambasing (take the left fork) are easy to reach but a respectful attitude should be kept in all Igorot graveyards. Thirty minutes south.

Sumaging Big Cave: Look for the concrete steps to the left. Guides are necessary to explore the Kings Palace, the Dance Hall, and the Swimming Pool inside this vast subterranean world. Mr. Jacinto at the hospital has been leading amateur spelunkers for over 40 years. Guides and groups often gather at 0900 at the Shamrock. **Warning:** Caving here is very dangerous because of vertical plunges and rocks covered with slippery bat scat. No coffins. Forty minutes south.

Farther South: Longer hikes beyond Sumaging pass Balangagand Cave (left at the waiting shed) before reaching Suyo and Ankileng in about three hours. Villages beyond Suyo include Data; Bagnen, with bathing streams and good views over the valley; and the pottery villages of Bila, Bauko, and Maggor.

West of Sagada: The road west of Sagada leads to a viewpoint in 30 minutes, Lake Danum in about one hour, the *carabao* trail up to Mt. Sipitan in two hours, Agawa Falls in three hours, and the stone agricultural calendar at Gueday in about four hours. A full day of hiking.

North of Sagada: Sagada's most spectacular waterfall is located three hours north at Fedilisan, a 30-minute hike down from Bangaan. Bring your swimsuit for the icy pools. A downstream suspension bridge leads to a higher falls with more pools. The distinctively rocky Tanulon and Baang Rice Terraces, situated near the Amlusong River, are also accessible from the Sagada-Bangaan road. Jeeps can be taken from Sagada, although it's a wonderful all-day hike starting from Masferre Photo Studios.

East of Sagada: Walk down the road toward Bontoc, turn left at the village, and hike down through Kilong to the Tetepan Pools and Hanging Bridge across the Amlusong River. From Tetepan return to the road, hike north along the river to the Baang Rice Terraces, or continue across the river to Mainit, Guinaang, Malincong rice terraces, and eventually, Bontoc.

Accommodations

Places to stay in Sagada are superb value: recently constructed and still quite clean, crisp linens, wonderful views from the windows, candlelight dinners, fireplaces, buckets of hot water, freshly baked breads, and friendly management. Most charge P75-150 per person.

Masferre's Guesthouse: For over a decade Julia welcomed visitors with her singing, wholesome cooking, and advice on sightseeing. Julia's has now been renamed Masferre's, but it remains a cozy place with great views. A useful map is mounted in the dining room. Masferre's is located in an unmarked tin building just below the bus stop and Shamrock Cafe. Dinner is served by reservation only.

Mapiyaaw Sagada Pension: Sagada's best homestay is located 15 minutes from the center of town; ask the bus driver to drop you there en route from Bontoc. Two fireplaces, a lounge, and several floors of rooms in various prices. Somewhat isolated but a wonderful place with super vibes.

St. Joseph's Resthouse: Sagada's original pension is often the only place in town serving dinner during the slow season. Bring a flashlight or fall off the narrow stone path. Managed by the Episcopalian sisters.

Olahbinan Resthouse: The only place in town that has rooms with attached baths. P100-500.

Transportation

Skyland Motors operates direct buses from Banaue to Sagada, leaving around sunrise or when-ever filled. Direct buses are much better than attempting a connection in Bontoc. From Sagada, Skyland buses and jeepneys rumble down to Bontoc mornings around 0600 and again at noon.

Dangwa Tranco and Lizardo Motors operate buses to Baguio daily at dawn. Sit on the right side for the best views.

BONTOC TO BAGUIO

The eye-popping Halsema Highway, which winds between Baguio and Bontoc, is one of the most spectacular drives in Southeast Asia, rivaled only by the Taroko Gorge on Taiwan. Orig-

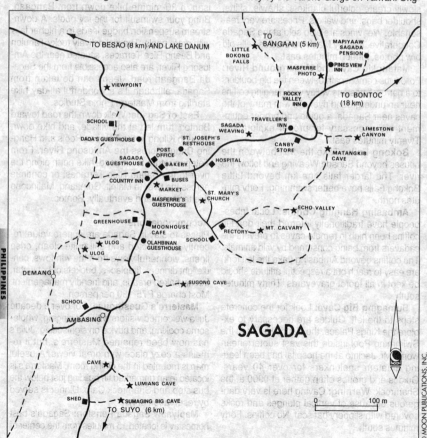

SAGADA

© MOON PUBLICATIONS, INC.

inally constructed by American gold miners in the early 1900s, this twisting, turning, and pot-holed road rises steadily from Baguio until it literally disappears into the clouds a few kilometers beyond La Trinidad. Breathtaking views over the valleys are possible whenever the fog and clouds blow away. Although most travelers travel directly from Bontoc to Baguio, several worthwhile points of interest are en route.

Mt. Data Lodge: This resort operated by the Philippine government offers tranquility, panoramic views, and evenings around the fireplace. Comfortable rooms start at P700.

Kabayan: This Ibaloi town, situated in a wide valley off the Halsema Highway, is noted for its aromatic Arabian coffee and centuries-old mummies discovered in nearby burial caves. Unfortunately, many of the mummies have been stolen and the remainder are off-limits to the public. Dangwa Transport serves Kabayan from Baguio and Bontoc.

Mount Pulog: The second-highest peak in the Philippines can be climbed between October and May via a good trail starting at the Ellet Bridge, midway between Kabayan and Bokod. Guides can be hired in Ellet *barangay*, where most hikers spend the first night. Camp the second night on the plateau below the summit before hiking the summit for a frigid sunrise. Weather is unpredictable; bring warm and waterproof clothing.

BAGUIO

Baguio, cool summer capital of the Philippines, nestles in the Central Cordilleras at a height of 1,524 meters above sea level. Originally developed by the Americans and architect Daniel Burnham as a mountain retreat from lowland heat, Baguio later played a pivotal role in WW II, taking bombs in 1941 and serving as the surrender site for General Yamashita in 1945.

Baguio was devastated by a major earthquake in 1990, but the city has been largely reconstructed with new pedestrian overpasses and landscaped gardens. The invigorating climate, parks, and sprawling marketplace annually attract thousands of visitors, even though the big-city atmosphere and Westernized flavor make it less inviting than Banaue or Sagada.

Note that Baguio is extremely crowded on holidays and much wetter than the lowlands. Avoid the rainy season from June to October.

Cash advances on Visa or MasterCard can be picked up at the Equitable Bank on Magsaysay Avenue.

Attractions

Tourist Office: A useful map showing the sights outside the city center can be picked up at the tourist office on Governor Pack Road. Open daily 0900-1700.

City Market: Baguio's bewildering public market overflows with a wide variety of temperate fruits and vegetables packed into narrow aisles named Broccoli Alley, Tomato Lane, etc. Stalls along Magsaysay Avenue and the adjacent Marhalika Shopping Complex peddle ethnic arts such as snake-bone headdresses and wooden *bulols,* but prices are much lower in Sagada and Banaue. Photographs are best in the open-air street markets to the rear.

Baguio Cathedral: Constructed in the '30s and modeled on a church in Saigon, Baguio's most famous landmark overlooks the city and Mt. Santo Thomas, highest peak in Benguet Province.

St. Louis Silver Shop: Exquisite and reasonably priced silverwork is meticulously crafted here by the students of St. Louis University.

Easter School Weaving: Conventional lowland looms and backstrap models favored by the mountain people produce some of the country's most famous weavings in this shop managed by the Episcopalian missionaries. Located outside town. Take a jeepney marked Guisad from Kayang Street near City Hall.

Camp John Hays: Facilities at this former rest-and-recreation center for the American Air Force include a movie theater, tennis courts, a golf course, a swimming pool, a formal restaurant, and a cozy bar overlooking the 19th tee. The camp was returned to the Philippine government in 1991 and closed to the public in 1997 for redevelopment and condominium construction. It's scheduled to reopen in 2001.

Faith Healers: Baguio is a center for healers who barehandedly excise tumors from trusting patients without leaving a scar. Among eight healers listed by the tourist office is Ramon Jun Labo, owner of the Nagoya Inn on Naguillian Road.

PHILIPPINES

CENTRAL BAGUIO

- EQUITABLE BANK

CITY HALL

MOUNT CREST HOTEL

ALBERTO'S AND KUSINA NI IMA RESTAURANT

SWAGMAN ATTIC HOTEL

CAFE BY THE RUINS

50'S DINER

PRESSBY'S CHICKEN

PEEK-A-BOO DISCO

MARKET

SPIRIT DISCO

FOOD STALLS

BENGUET PINE TOURIST INN

CAFÉ TERIA

DANGWA AND LEZARDO BUSES

BURNHAM

FOOD STALLS

INFO KIOSK

Lake

BAGUIO GOODWILL LODGE

PNB

COZY NOOK

BENGUET PRIME HOTEL

ST. LOUIS SILVER SHOP

AVIS

PAL

P A R K

SWISS BAKER

BAGUIO CATHEDRAL

SHAKEY'S

BARRIO FIESTA

SONGS MUSIC GALLERY

BADEN POWELL HOUSE

POST OFFICE

DAGUPAN & PARTIS BUSES

PHILIPPINE RABBIT BUSES

VICTORY LINER BUSES

TOURST OFFICE

UNIVERSITY OF THE PHILIPPINES

0   200 yds

0   200 m

© MOON PUBLICATIONS, INC.

PHILIPPINES

Accommodations

Benguet Pine Tourist Inn: Somewhat isolated with hardly an inspiring lobby, but rooms are fairly clean and it's away from the noise of downtown Baguio. You can book rooms in Manila at the Ermita Tourist Inn on Mabini Street. 82 Chanum St., tel. (074) 442-7325, P275-600.

Baguio Goodwill Lodge: Basic but right in the center of town. 58 Session Rd., tel. (074) 442-6634, P220-500.

Baden Powell House: Moderately priced hotels are plentiful near the top of Session Road including this old favorite near the Victory, Dagupan, and Pantranco buses. 26 Governor Pack Rd., tel. (074) 442-5836, P210 dorm (free breakfast), P850-1,200 private room.

Swagman Attic Hotel: An Aussie-owned hotel with reasonably priced a/c rooms, 24-hour pub, and international restaurant near Baguio's modest nightlife. 90 Abanao St., tel. (074) 442-5139, P800-1,200.

Mount Crest Hotel: Good spot for mid-level travelers with Café Legarda piano bar on the main floor. Legard St., tel. (074) 442-3324, P1,200-1,800.

Restaurants

Session Road: Most of Baguio's restaurants are located along Session Road. Filipino food is served at Barrio Fiesta, Sizzling Plate, and Tahanang Pilipino. Familiar Western dishes are dished out at Shakey's, Jughead, and Baguio Chicken House. The Mandarin on Assumption Road is a popular Chinese cafe with well-prepared Cantonese dishes.

Swiss Baker: This clean and comfortable cafe serves fresh breads, daily specials, and "bottomless" cups of native coffee. Prices are somewhat high but it's a great place to relax after shopping and sightseeing. Session Road. Moderate.

Cafe by the Ruins: Just across from Baguio City Hall and owned by an anthropologist, two journalists, and a visual artist, this eclectic restaurant features such unusual entrees as fish roe pâté, Ifugao chicken stewed with salted pork, and river eel harvested from rice terraces. Try their homemade *tapuey* (rice wine)—tasty but *very* potent. 25 Chuntug Street. Moderate.

Kusina ni Ima: Filipino and Western dishes served along with Kapampangan specialties.

Legarda Road, across the street from the Mount Crest Hotel. Moderate.

Pressby's Chicken: Look for the large, rotating racks of chicken in the front window just a few doors down from Swagman Attic Hotel. 84 Abanao Street. Moderate.

50's Diner: American diner with burgers, shakes, and appropriately dressed waitresses. 88 Abanao Street. Moderate.

Nightlife

Folk and Karaoke Clubs: Baguio's nightlife is evenly divided between karaoke clubs that cater to university students and high-volume nightclubs pumping out disco and rock. Popular folk/karaoke clubs include Cozy Nook Restaurant on Assumption and Songs Music Gallery on Session Road. Cafe by the Ruins mentioned above has installed an improvised bamboo stage for poetry readings, traditional dance, folk singers, and impromptu theater performances.

Abanao Street: Several of Baguio's low- to medium-quality nightclubs are located along Abanao Street, such as Peek-a-boo Disco and an unnamed atrocity across the street. Café Teria has live music and plenty of freelancers on the prowl.

Live Music: Much better is Spirit, a beautiful nightclub in a converted mansion situated a few blocks from Abanao Street. The modest cover charge includes the first cocktail.

Baguio's most popular spot for live bands is Alberto's which has no cover charge and features two or three bands each night. Alberto's is at the corner of Legarda and Carino Streets just across from the Mount Crest Hotel.

Transportation

Baguio is 250 km north of Manila and 143 km south of Bontoc.

Air: PAL flies twice daily from Manila to the Baguio airport, eight km from downtown Baguio. Baguio is also served several times weekly by Asian Spirit. The flight costs P1,000 and takes 35 minutes. The PAL office is in the Padilla Building on Harrison Road.

Bus: Baguio is a six-hour bus ride from Manila. Philippine Rabbit, Victory Liner, Dangwa Tranco, and Dagupan have buses from Manila, although Victory Liner seems to have the most frequent departures.

PHILIPPINES

Dangwa Tranco has four buses daily to Bontoc between 0600 and 1000, one daily bus to Banaue at 0630, and a daily service to Kabayan at 1000. Buses from the terminal on Magsaysay Avenue also serve Vigan and other coastal destinations several times daily 0600-1800.

NORTHWEST COAST

HUNDRED ISLANDS

Scattered off the coast near the town of Lucap are dozens of coral islets bizarrely eroded into formations resembling giant toadstools and dome-shaped spaceships. Numerous legends are attached to the islands: tears of a lovelorn giant, mermaids once lived here, etc. Top draws are underwater caves, marinelife, and small sandy beaches tucked away on several of the islands—although none compare with those in the Visayas. Snorkeling, unfortunately, is mediocre since the waters are often murky and most of the coral beds have been destroyed by dynamite fishing.

Boat Tours
Six-person *bancas* from the park office at the Lucap pier charge P275-300 per boatload for a full-day tour. Most go directly to Quezon Island, where the boatman waits while you sunbathe and snorkel before touring the other islands on the return to Lucap. Dive equipment can be rented from shops in Lucap.

Accommodations
Hotel rates in Lucap vary according to the season and day of the week; bargaining works during the week but won't bring much results on weekends.

Kilometer One Tourist Lodge: As you might guess, an inexpensive tourist lodge one km back from the beach. Lucap, no phone, P150-250.

Gloria's Cottages: Basic but acceptable for a single night in the center of town. Lucap, no phone, P150-250.

Ocean View Lodge: A better place just opposite Gloria's. Lucap, tel. (0912) 320-5579, P250-750.

Transportation
Philippine Rabbit and Dagupan bus lines have buses to Alaminos from their terminals in Manila. Dagupan and Byron buses serve Alaminos from Baguio. You can also reach Alaminos with Philippine Rabbit buses from the Dau interchange near Angeles.

Tricycles cost P10 out to Lucap and the boat terminal for Hundred Islands.

BAUANG (LA UNION) BEACHES

The beaches between Bauang (to the south) and San Fernando (to the north) are hardly spectacular—the sand is brown and the diving is secondary—but many people love this area for its authentic Filipino atmosphere and near complete lack of Western tourists. The convenient location near Manila and Baguio helps keep this area alive plus many of the expats who operate resorts here enjoy their distance from more commercialized resorts such as Boracay and Puerto Gallera.

San Fernando, a large town a few km north of the Bauang beaches, has little of interest but you might want to visit the tourist office inside city hall and the nearby museum.

The proper is address is Paringao at Bauang in La Union Province.

Attractions
The long beach here may not be as impressive as elsewhere in the Philippines, but the local flavor perhaps more than compensates. People here are friendly and the odd Westerner walking down the beach is something almost special. You'll pass fishermen working on their boats, gaggles of kids splashing in the water, and plenty of families who are more than happy to pose for photographs.

After dark, there's several small go-go clubs with dancing girls and happy hours; these include Tramps in the Koala Hotel, Stiletto's in the Southern Palms Hotel, and Footlights across the highway. Strange as it sounds, these might be the three best dance bars in the country.

There's also a low-end but entertaining Filipino nightlife center a few kilometers north at Poro Point, a former American naval base.

Accommodations

Over 20 beach resorts are located between Bauang and San Fernando. Most raise their prices somewhat on weekends but generally you can find a well-maintained bungalow for P600-1,200.

Bali Hai Beach Resort Popular resort with small but well-sited pool and open-air restaurant with all the standard fixins. Be sure to ask about the saga of "Dead Fred." Bauang, tel. (072) 412504, e-mail: balihai@net.com.

Coconut Grove: Great looking spot with swimming pool and landscaped grounds plus lawn-bowling venue for all the Brits and Aussies. Bauang, tel. (072) 414276, P900-1,400.

Cabana Beach Resort: Rooms are just OK but the pool is about the best in this neighborhood. Bauang, tel. (072) 412824, P900-1,200.

China Sea Beach Resort: Solid cottages plus one of the few dive shops in La Union. Bauang, tel. (072) 414821, e-mail: chinasea@net.com.

Hideaway: Good budget spot about a 20-minute walk north of the central beach; friendly managers and good vibes. 1312 Baccuit Norte, Bauang, tel. (0912) 311-2421, P350-550.

Koala Motel: Another cheap place in a good location near all the nightclubs and the center of the beach. Bauang, tel. (072) 242-0863, P250-450.

Transportation

Bauang is 260 km north of Manila and 60 km west of Baguio. Philippine Rabbit and several other bus lines take six or seven hours from Manila. You can also catch buses from the Dau interchange in Angeles. Travelers coming from Hundred Islands must change buses in Dagupan.

Philippine Rabbit connects Bauang with Baguio several times daily, a scenic and winding journey down from the mountains.

VIGAN

Vigan, the capital of Ilocos Sur Province, was founded in 1572 by the grandson of Legaspi, who constructed the city in a style similar to that of Intramuros. Mercifully spared the destruction of WW II, Vigan remains a museum city with some of the best-preserved examples of Spanish colonial architecture in the Philippines.

The town and coastline to the north are also rich in Spanish domestic architecture and massive baroque churches constructed in a distinctive "earthquake" motif. One shouldn't, however, expect the great architecture of Avila or Burgos, since the Spaniards in the Philippines never achieved the degree of excellence they reached in their homeland. Nevertheless, Vigan and its nearby beaches and mountains make Ilocos Sur an eminently worthwhile destination.

Attractions

The Colonial Quarter: Modernization has arrived to some degree, but a leisurely walk through the old section still reveals cobblestone alleys, a baroque cathedral guarded by Chinese *fu* dogs, clip-clopping *calesas,* and mestizo mansions erected in the 18th century by wealthy Chinese traders.

Ayala Museum: The former residence of Jose Burgos now displays Burgos memorabilia, period rooms, a fine collection of Ilocano and Tingguian artifacts, and a 14-painting series depicting events of the Basi Revolt.

Crisologo Museum: A small but interesting museum with Spanish-era artifacts and memorials to Governor Crisologo, assassinated in 1970 inside the Vigan Cathedral. The furniture upstairs is beautiful.

Vicinty of Vigan and Laoag

Magsingal: The cream-and-white church in Magsingal, 13 km north of Vigan, is fitted with ornate baroque *retablos* carved of *molave* wood without nails. Note the incongruous pair of pregnant mermaids amid the religious imagery.

Badoc: Badoc's small but massively buttressed blue-and-cream church houses a statue of the Virgin Mary which locals claim washed ashore from China seven centuries ago. The reconstructed home of Juan Luna, an important 19th-century Filipino painter, is now a museum containing memorabilia, antique furniture, and reproductions of his paintings.

Batac: The sleepy town of Batac—the ancestral home of the Marcos family—is where Josefa Marcos (Ferdinand's mother) is displayed

PHILIPPINES

in an open casket. The upstairs Marcos Museum holds dozens of phony war medals, genealogical trees, vintage campaign literature, and 23 life-size Marcos mannequins.

Paoay: The Philippines' most famous "earthquake" church stands in this prosperous town, situated four km west of Batac. Designed and constructed by Filipinos in 1704, it's a remarkable piece of architecture that mixes both Asian and Western styles: massive flying buttresses and crenellations influenced by the Majapajit culture of Indonesia, exterior staircases that lead nowhere, cantilevered facades carved with Chinese emblems of coral and limestone, a separate three-story watchtower used as a lookout by the Katipuneros during the Philippine Revolution.

Like most other Ilocano religious architecture, the Paoay church is characterized by thick walls heavily buttressed to resist earthquake damage (hence the terminology), finials shaped like urns or pyramids, and Augustinian markings such as a transfixed heart and tasseled hats. The overall effect is one of simplicity and strength, one of the triumphs of Filipino architecture.

Sarrat: The former home of Ferdinand Marcos, eight km west of Laoag, is a small town radically transformed by the power and wealth of the deposed president. Sarrat features a Marcos Museum, a church where his daughter Irene was married in 1983 (5,000 guests, food for 100,000, estimated cost US$10 million), an airport large enough to handle jumbo jets, and the magnificently deserted 126-room Fort Ilocandia Hotel . . . another of his famous white elephants. The hotel was used by Tom Cruise and Oliver Stone during the 1989 filming of *Born On The Fourth Of July.*

Pagudpud: The spectacular drive north from Laoag—the so-called "Riviera of the North"— passes magnificent coastline, deserted beaches, coves, corals, and pounding surf. The region's finest expanse of pure white sand is at Saud Beach, five km east of Pagudpud.

Accommodations

Overnighting in Vigan is recommended, since the town best reveals its soul in the early-morning hours.

Grandpa's Inn: The backpackers' favorite is eight blocks east of the Philippine Rabbit bus terminal at the intersection of Bonifacio and Quirino streets. 1 Bonifacio St., tel. (077) 722-2118, P150-500.

Vigan Hotel: Another budget option two blocks west of St. Paul's Cathedral and in a quiet neighborhood near the river. Burgos St., tel. (077) 722-3001, P275-700.

Aniceto Mansion: A restored Spanish-era hotel with inexpensive fan-cooled rooms and much more expensive a/c rooms with TVs and private baths. 1 Crisolog St., tel. (077) 722-2383, P200-800.

Cordillera Inn: An overpriced but stylish colonial-style inn three blocks east of the bus terminal. 29 Crisologo St., tel. (077) 722-2526, P900-1,200.

Transportation

Vigan is 407 km north of Manila and 196 km northwest of Baguio. Direct bus service is available from Manila, though most travelers stop at Baguio or the beaches near Bauang before reaching Vigan. Buses from the plaza in San Fernando take about two hours to Vigan.

Buses to Manila, Baguio, and points north leave from the bus terminal on General Luna Street in the center of town and from the terminal on Quezon Avenue.

SOUTHERN LUZON

The Bicol region of southern Luzon, formed by four contiguous provinces and the islands of Catanduanes and Masbate, is known for its smoking volcanoes, hot springs, boiling lakes, caves, deserted beaches, *abaca* crafts, violent typhoons which devastate the region with depressing regularity, and spicy food typified by the small chili pepper dubbed the "Bicol Express."

Sightseeing Highlights

Bicolandia's greatest attraction is the perfectly symmetrical Mt. Mayon near Legaspi, but travelers with extra time and a sense of *bahala na* might also explore the beaches near Daet, soak in the hot springs at Tiwi, or do a side trip to Catanduanes or Masbate. Rizal Beach is also recommended, while Naga City's Penafrancia

Festival held in September is considered one of the best in the Philippines.

Bicol also offers some excellent climbs. Mountaineers can challenge themselves on Mt. Isarog 15 km east of Naga, Mt. Iriga farther south, or the still-active and dangerous Mt. Mayon. Mount Bulusan near the southern tip is another possible trek.

Transportation
Bus service along the main highway from Manila to Legaspi is straightforward, provided by several bus companies which depart from the terminal on Edsa in Pasay City. You can take an overnight bus to Legaspi or do a shorter day segment to one of the closer towns.

An interesting alternative is to take the only train service in the Philippines from the Manila train station to Naga, and then continue to Legaspi by bus. The train is primitive, uncrowded, and slow but it's something quite unusual to experience this fading dinosaur. Go in the so-called first class and you'll be seated in a reclining seat that probably provides a better night of sleep than seats in most buses.

DAET AND SAN MIGUEL BAY

Daet (pronounced di-et), 350 km south of Manila, is the access point for several attractive beaches and an island resort operated by an Australian tour company.

Attractions
The best mainland beach near Daet is at Bagasbas, five km from town. Another natural draw is Libmanan Caves, a complex of 19 caves dripping with stalactites and stalagmites one km off the highway between Sipocot and Naga City.

Independent travelers can cross San Miguel Bay by taking an early-morning jeepney from Daet to Mercedes, from where a *banca* leaves around 1000 for Takal on the opposite side of the bay. Simple accommodations are available in Takal from a German/Filipina couple who collect books on Filipiniana.

Boats continue from nearby Siruma down to Bagacay near Naga City. Further information on San Miguel Bay and other attractions near Daet can be picked up in the Karilagan Hotel.

Accommodations
Most travelers only pass through Daet en route to San Miguel Bay or the Australian resort on Apuao Grande Island.

Karilagan Hotel: A clean and popular hotel in the center of Daet. 22 Moreno St., tel. (054) 721-2314, P150-750.

Apuao Grande Island Resort: An Australian-managed resort with clean and comfortable *nipa* bungalows facing a dazzling beach, a restaurant, a bar, and water sports such as windsurfing, Hobie Cat sailing, and jet-skiing. Rooms cost P250-700.

The island is reached from the town of Mercedes, but most visitors make reservations and transportation arrangements through Swagman Hotel in Ermita.

NAGA

Naga, a busy commercial enclave in the shadow of Mt. Isarog, is chiefly known for its fluvial Penafrancia Festival held in late September, and for the amazing number of No Jaywalking signs around town.

Sights include the black Nazarene inside the Spanish-Romanesque Naga Cathedral and the highly venerated Virgin image inside the modern Penafrancia shrine across the river. Nearby Mt. Isarog can be climbed in two days from Hiwakloy *barangay* between Ocampo and Tiganon on the east side of the volcano. Naga is also the access point for Weinert's Guesthouse.

Accommodations
Rodson Palace Inn: Budget option two blocks north of the town plaza. Burgos St., tel. (054) 739828, P100-380.

Fiesta Hotel: Another simple place in the center of town near the central market. Caceres St., tel. (054) 811-1787, P150-400.

Grand Imperial Hotel: Naga's best hotel operated by the local tourist representative. Burgos St., tel. (054) 736534, P650-900.

Weinert's Guesthouse Pacific: Seaside resort near Sagnay, northeast of Naga. Sagnay, tel. (054) 454-7001, P400-1,200.

Transportation
PAL's daily flight from Manila takes one hour. Buses from the Edsa Highway in Manila take

PHILIPPINES

nine hours, two hours from Daet, and two hours from Legaspi. The Naga bus terminal is three km south of city center; jeepneys shuttle into town.

LEGASPI

Albay's provincial capital lies in the shadows of Mt. Mayon, perhaps the world's most perfectly formed volcanic cone. No matter how many photos you've seen, nothing prepares you for the symmetrical peak, which visually, symbolically, geographically, and historically dominates southern Luzon.

Legaspi itself has little of interest, although it makes an ideal base for explorations of the region's thermal attractions, boiling mud lakes, caves, and gray-sand beaches.

Legaspi's tourist office is west of town in the suburb of Albay. Take a jeepney toward Daraga. Visa and MasterCard cash advances are possible at the Equitable Bank on Rizal Street.

Mayon Volcano
Sleepy and peaceful Mayon suddenly erupted in early 1993, killing over 60 residents who were farming on the slopes of the scenic volcano. All hikers must make advance arrangements through the tourist office in Albay. The hike takes two days and costs US$80 for two people, though less expensive guides and porters can sometimes be hired in Buyuhan. Do not underestimate this volcano: It's an extremely difficult and dangerous climb up crumbling ash and vertical cliffs through high winds, icy fog, and sudden rainstorms.

The standard route begins with a jeepney ride to Buyuhan, from where a dry riverbed gradually climbs up to Camp One at 800 meters and then Camp Two at 1,463 meters. The following morning begins with a rugged five-hour scramble to the top where, weather permitting, views extend from the Catanduanes to Sorsogon.

Those who wish to experience a midlevel climb without the expense and physical hardships should try the northwestern Buang Trail. Take a jeepney to Tabaco and then another to the Mt. Mayon National Park entrance at Buang. From here, it's an eight-km hike up the zigzag asphalt road to the abandoned Mayon Vista Lodge and Mayon Volcanic Observatory and Museum. Large groups can charter a jeepney from Tabaco. The mountain trail from the observatory is hazardous and difficult to follow without a guide.

Attractions
Cagsawa Ruins: Mayon's powers of destruction are best appreciated at the ruined church of this village buried under the violent eruption of 1814. According to local folklore, over 200 peasants and wealthy Spanish citizens took refuge in the church, only to perish under tons of rock and volcanic ash.

PHILIPPINES

Mayon and Cagasaw ruins

LEGASPI

TO AIRPORT

LAKANDULA ST.

TO TABACO AND TIWI HOT SPRINGS

SIPING ST.

CALTEX

■ PAAYAHAYAN SEAFOOD RESTAURANT

● ALBAY HOTEL

GOV. FORBES ST.

BLTB BUSES ■

CASABLANCA HOTEL ■

■ FIRE STATION

■ BARS

PENARANDA ST.

ALBAY GULF

■ SHELL AND AMDG BUSES

MOSQUE ★ RAMON SANTOS ST.

■ WAYWAY RESTAURANT

ALONZO ST.

● CATALINA'S LODGING

AGUINALDO ST.

RIZAL PARK ★

● REX HOTEL

PEKING LODGE ●

LA TRINIDAD HOTEL

■ BANK

WENDEE'S PASTRIES ●

MAYON HOTEL ●

RIZAL ST.

■ PAL

LCC DEPARTMENT STORE

● SHANGRILA RESTAURANT

ELIZONDO ST.

TO AIRPORT AND MAIN BUS TERMINAL

JEEPNEY TERMINAL

■ JB BUSES

GILBERT

QUEZON AVE.

IMPERIAL ST.

FRUIT MARKET ●

TELEPHONE ■

● BAYAN TEL

ALLIED BANK ●

ROSAL ST.

POST OFFICE ■

■ EXECUTIVE TOURIST INN

IMPERIAL ST.

EQUITABLE BANK ●

● DHL

ILANG ILANG ST.

● VICTORIA HOTEL

WHARF

MAGNOLIA ST.

● LEGASPI PLAZA HOTEL

TANCHULING INTERNATIONAL HOUSE ●

JASMIN ST.

● FISHING VILLAGE ★

GUMAMELA ST.

RIZAL ST.

CAMIA ST.

TO TOURIST OFFICE, ALBAY, MANILA

N

0   100 m

KAPUNTUKAN HILL

PHILIPPINES

© MOON PUBLICATIONS, INC.

Jeepneys from the market toward Camalig pass the Cagsawa sign. You can also catch a jeepney in Locin (formerly Daraga).

Caves: Several large limestone caves are 10 km south of Camalig near the *barrio* of Cotmon. Alfredo Nieva guides visitors through Hoyop Hoyopan Cave where Neolithic remains were discovered in 1972, and Calabidongan Cave two km farther south. More caves are 10 km southwest of Camalig near Pariaan.

Tabaco: Tabaco, 28 km north of Legaspi, is a center for Bicol *abaca* weaving and metalcraft. Ferries to Catanduanes Island leave mornings around 1100.

Tiwi: Eleven km beyond Tabaco, Tiwi offers the striking Sinimbahan ruins and some very mediocre hot springs three km north behind the old youth hostel. Not worth the effort.

Accommodations
Most of Legaspi's cheap and run-down hotels are in the center of town along Penaranda and Rizal streets. None will inspire you to spend any time relaxing in Legaspi, though you really should try the spicy fried peanuts sold on the sidewalks.

Catalina's Lodging House: A small but friendly hotel with decent rooms. 96 Penaranda, tel. (05221) 223593, P100-450.

Hotel Xandra: Another budget option in the center of town. Penaranda St., tel. (05221) 22688, P100-340.

Tanchuling International House: Large and clean rooms, plus views of Mayon from the rooftop, five minutes south of town. Jasmin St., tel. (05221) 22747, P300-600.

La Trinidad Hotel: Legaspi's former leading hotel is centrally located and reasonably priced. Rizal St., tel. (05221) 22951, P800-1,100.

Albay Hotel: Best in town; opened 1996 a few blocks north of city center. 88 Penaranda St., tel. (05221) 243640, P1,200-1,800.

Transportation
Legaspi is 545 km south of Manila.

Manila: PAL and Air Philippines fly daily between Manila and Legaspi. Buses to Manila and points south leave from the various bus terminals scattered around town: BLTB at the north end of Penaranda St., JB Bicol Express in central Penaranda St., and Philtranco a few blocks west of downtown.

Local Transport: Jeepneys to Tabaco and Tiwi leave north of the public market. Minibuses and jeepneys to Albay, Casagwa, and Camalig leave west of the market.

To Samar: Travelers heading south to Samar should take a very early-morning bus or jeepney to Matnog, since ferry service across to Samar ends around 1300. Allow about four hours to Matnog, including time-consuming changes in Sorsogon or Irosin.

Buses from Manila pass through Legaspi several times daily but tend to be filled with passengers. Philtranco provides direct bus service from Legaspi to Catbalogan and Tacbalogan on a space-available basis, a useful service that saves time and hassle. You might also check with BLTB and JB Bicol Express.

SORSOGON AND RIZAL BEACH

Sorsogon province at the southern end of Luzon may not be the "Switzerland of the Orient" (an overstatement invented by a former governor), but the district features the impressive Mt. Bulusan and a fairly decent stretch of sand at Rizal Beach.

It's almost impossible to climb Mt. Bulusan without the help of a guide, but a visit to Bulusan Lake just south of the volcanic cone may be worth the effort; a paved trail follows the perimeter of the lake. Rizal Beach has brownish sand, and is long, broad, and almost completely deserted except on weekends.

Accommodations
Dalisay Lodge: Budget hotel in Sorsogon. 182 Peralta St., tel. (056) 211-1330, P100-200.

Fernando's Hideaway: The best in Sorsogon at the north end of town, owned and operated by the mayor's wife who also serves as the local tourism representative. Pareja St., tel. (056) 211-1573, P600-850.

Rizal Beach Resort: Two-story motel with empty pool and rooms from dorms to a/c suites. Rizal Beach, tel. (056) 211-1056, P360-800.

MATNOG

Matnog is the departure point for ferries across to Samar. Ferries leave Matnog daily 0900-1300 except during typhoons when all services are cancelled. Matnog has several restaurants and a host of government buildings often used by stranded travelers for an overnight stay.

Transportation

To reach Matnog before the final ferry departure at 1300, it's important to depart from Legaspi early in the morning. The bus trip takes about four hours from Legaspi to Matnog. You can take a Philtranco bus from Legaspi or attempt to join an express bus coming down from Manila

on a space-available basis. Otherwise, take a bus to Irosin (the last major town in Sorsogon Province), then continue south to Matnog by jeepney.

Accommodations

One inexpensive lodge is located in Matnog, though it's best to spend the night in Legaspi or at Rizal Beach and arrive in time to catch an early-morning boat to Samar. If you miss the ferry to Samar, you should backtrack and spend the night in Irosin.

ISLANDS TO THE SOUTH

The southern islands of the Philippines—the Visayas, Mindanao, and Palawan—comprise a necklace dripping with crystalline beaches, soaring volcanoes, brilliant green coconut plantations, and some of the finest coral reefs in Southeast Asia.

Most of the islands are tightly packed together in the Visayan group between Luzon and the sprawling island of Mindanao. Palawan, shaped like a shark pointing toward Borneo, offers travelers a chance to get off the beaten track and experience what is unquestionably the most beautiful island in all the Philippines.

ROUTES AROUND THE VISAYAS

Visitors short on time should take advantage of inexpensive PAL domestic flights and travel directly to the island or beach of their choice. Those with more time and enough patience to deal with irregular boat departures can tour the Visayas on the following circuit. Boat connections between most islands are inexpensive and frequent—except from Boracay to Mindoro where there exists no formal shipping service.

Allow about one month to complete the following route and longer if you plan to explore the national parks or really unwind on the beaches. The Visayan loop can be completed in either a clockwise or a counterclockwise direction, but the clockwise route is perhaps a better choice since it saves Boracay and Mindoro for the final stretches. Palawan and Mindanao could be side trips from the Visayas or separate destinations starting from Manila.

Manila To Samar: Transportation is straightforward from Manila to Legaspi, but somewhat problematical from Matnog at the southern end of Luzon to Samar on Leyte, since ferry service ends around 1300. An early start from Legaspi is necessary to avoid getting stranded in Matnog.

Samar To Cebu: Both air-conditioned and ordinary buses wind along the scenic road that skirts the west coast of Samar to Tacloban in Leyte. Fast ferries depart several times daily from Ormoc to Cebu City. Boat service from Leyte (Bato) to Bohol is undependable and most travelers go to Cebu and then backtrack to Bohol.

Cebu To Boracay: Cebu City to Bacolod can be completed in a single day with an early start. Alternatively, you could take a fast ferry from Cebu City directly to Dumaguete and then continue around the sugar island by bus. Bacolod is a good place to pause if transportation bogs down.

Fast ferries go several times daily from Bacolod to Iloilo on Panay, from where buses continue north to Kalibo. Outriggers constantly dart from Caticlan, two hours north of Kalibo, over to Boracay. Iloilo to Boracay can be done in a single day of steady travel. Direct flights from Cebu to Kalibo are useful for those anxious to reach Boracay.

Boracay To Mindoro: Because of high winds and rough waters, this is often the stretch that fouls an otherwise trouble-free journey. Outriggers occasionally leave from Boracay to southern Mindoro, but most travelers sail north to Tablas before continuing west to Mindoro. This crossing should only be attempted on clear days. Alternatives when the weather looks bad are flying from Kalibo to Manila or backtracking to Iloilo. Palawan can be reached by boats from Iloilo.

Mindoro To Manila: Several small boats leave in the mornings from Puerto Galera to Batangas on Luzon. Buses connect from Batangas to Manila.

BOHOL

Bohol, a relatively small island resting in the center of the Visayan archipelago, has much to offer in terms of history and natural attractions. The island was first visited in 1563 by Magellan's crew, which fled Cebu after the death of its leader. In 1565 Legaspi brought the island under Spanish rule by sealing a historic blood compact with a native chieftain named Datu Sikatuna. Major rebellions against Spanish rule broke out in 1622 and 1744, followed by a revolt against American occupation in 1901.

Bohol today is a sleepy place with great beaches and scuba diving, the famous geological formations nicknamed the Chocolate Hills, and some of the finest Spanish colonial church architecture in the Philippines.

Most travelers reach Bohol by fast ferry from Cebu City and proceed immediately across to Panglao Island to enjoy the beaches and scuba diving. Buses from Tagbilaran reach the Chocolate Hills in the center of the island and continue around the island through towns dominated by magnificent Spanish churches.

Scuba Diving

Bohol is one of the most popular diving spots in the Philippines. At least a half dozen dive shops are located on Panglao Island, just south of Bohol. All shops rent equipment and most offer PADI or NAUI certification courses along with advanced dive classes.

Other popular dive areas around Bohol include Pamilican Island near Baclayon and Cabilao Island off Looc.

TRANSPORTATION

From Cebu

Fast ferries depart several times daily from Cebu City for Tagbilaran, the capitol of Bohol. There's no need to make a reservation in Cebu City; just go down to the ferry terminal and wait for the next departing boat.

The fast ferry takes 90 minutes to Tagbilaran. You then can take a motorized tricycle or jeepney down to Panglao Island. Another op-

tion is to hire a taxi at a fixed fare (P200-250) or call one of the metered taxi companies located in Tagbilaran (P180-220).

Ships also connect Cebu City with Tubigon and Talibon but most travelers head directly for Tagbilaran and Panglao.

From Other Islands

Fast ferries serve Tagbilaran from Cagayan de Oro (Mindanao) and from Dumaguete (Negros) once daily.

Getting Around

Buses from Tagbilaran leave hourly for all Bohol destinations, including the Chocolate Hills at Carmen. It's a long but pleasant walk from the highway turnoff to the Chocolate Hills Lodge. Additional service to Carmen is provided by buses and jeepneys departing from the rear of the public marketplace.

Buses from Tagbilaran to Alona Beach on Panglao leave several times daily until 1700. Also check out Tagbilaran's tricycles, which have been cheerfully emblazoned with religious slogans.

Leaving

PAL flies twice daily from Bohol to Cebu City. There's also large ships several times weekly from Tagbilaran to Manila.

Fast ferries depart Tagbilaran for Cebu City several times daily and take about 90 minutes in a/c comfort. Small ferries leave Tubigon for Cebu several times daily.

TAGBILARAN

The provincial capital, principal port, and commercial center of Bohol is simply a stepping-stone to nearby beaches, churches, and other attractions. There is little reason to stay here.

Attractions near Tagbilaran

Baclayon Church: Constructed in 1595 by Jesuit missionaries, the Baclayon church, seven km east of town, is the oldest stone church in the

PHILIPPINES

ISLAND-BY-ISLAND HIGHLIGHTS

Bohol

Sandwiched between Cebu and Leyte is Bohol, among the more attractive islands in the Visayas with its colonial architecture, beautiful beaches on nearby Panglao Island, and eerie geological formations known as the Chocolate Hills.

Boracay

Boracay, a small island just north of Panay, has long served as the premier beach destination in the Philippines. Once known only to a few backpackers, Boracay today has hundreds of bungalows, dozens of first-class hotels, a championship golf course, condominiums across the north end of the island, raging nightclubs, prostitutes, superb sunsets, decent diving, and cafes and restaurants facing one of the world's most dazzling beaches.

Camiguin

Travelers who dislike crowds and commercialization may enjoy this idyllic little island just off the north coast of Mindanao. Camiguin's isolation and good—but not great—beaches have made it a favored stop for travelers discouraged by the scene at Mindoro and Boracay.

Cebu

The Visayan hub of commerce and transportation has a few good beaches around the island and a handful of historical attractions in the capital of Cebu City, where restaurants, nightlife, and shopping are second only to Manila.

The remainder of the island is a mixed bag. Typhoons have damaged the once-brilliant coral beds on the west coast, but the relatively protected beaches on the southeastern coastline are still in good condition. Mactan Island beaches are mediocre and only recommended for tourists on tight schedules. One of the upcoming stars of Cebu tourism is Malapascua Island just off the north end of Cebu—a beautiful island with stunning beaches and none of the commercialization that has overtaken many other islands, such as Boracay.

Leyte

Noted for its historical ties to General MacArthur and WW II, Leyte chiefly serves as a transit point for overlanders traveling from Samar to Cebu. The island's natural attractions such as national parks, waterfalls, and offshore islands can be reached with public transportation but only with great difficulty from Ormoc and the principal town of Tacloban.

Mindanao

The Philippines' second largest island is a world of contrasts: modern cities only hours from animist cultures, Christian fundamentalists and traditional Muslims, capitalist warlords battling with communist insurgents—a feudal but progressive land with all the strengths and weaknesses of Filipino society. Mindanao also has natural wonders such as the country's highest mountains, thick rainforests, swampy lowlands, and isolated beaches rarely visited by Westerners, plus it's home to dozens of distinct tribes whose traditional lifestyles remain much less affected than those of northern Luzon.

Highlights include the T'boli tribal area at Lake Sebu, a climb to the summit of Mt. Apo, and the beautiful islands around Surigao. Davao and Zamboanga serve as important transit points, although neither has any strong aesthetic appeal.

Mindanao is also, unfortunately, an island troubled by Muslim resistance groups near Cotabato City and the Sulu Islands south of Zamboanga. Otherwise, Mindanao is safe.

Mindoro

A trip to the country's seventh-largest island is synonymous with a sojourn at Puerto Galera, a beach resort five hours distant from Manila. Situated on an outstandingly beautiful harbor beneath soaring green mountains, it's a vision of paradise partially marred with hastily built cottages and other signs of unplanned development.

And yet, Mindoro can still be recommended for its relatively undeveloped beaches to the west and its untouched interior. Mindoro is also an important connection on the overland/oversea route from Manila to Boracay.

Negros

The sugar island of the Philippines is worth visiting for its volcano and beach resorts south of Dumaguete, as well as its antique sugar trains near the capital city of Bacolod. Dumaguete is also the departure point for ordinary boats and fast ferries to

Siquijor, a small but very beautiful island visible in the distance from Dumaguete.

Palawan
The Philippines' final frontier features the finest beaches, diving, and natural wonders in the country. Transportation is rugged, but inexpensive hotels and restaurants are plentiful. Key attractions include the diving and surrealistic landscapes at El Nido, topographic curiosities such as the underground caves near Port Barton, and the beaches at Sabang, Port Barton, and south of Puerto Princesa. This is an island where days turn to weeks, weeks to months. In fact, many travelers are now bypassing Boracay and heading directly to Palawan after touring the mountain provinces of northern Luzon.

Panay
Shaped somewhat like a triangular kite fluttering between Negros and Mindoro, Panay's chief draws are the outstanding churches in Iloilo and the January festivals which celebrate the original pact between the indigenous *atis* and the *datus* from Borneo. Most travelers rush directly from Negros to Boracay or vice-versa, but those with extra time should explore Iloilo and some of the nearby beaches and islands.

Samar
The third-largest island in the Philippines serves as a stepping stone between Luzon and points south. A few surf resorts are located on the rarely visited eastern coast.

Philippines. Although currently under restoration and sometimes closed, the painted ceilings, intricately carved altar, and small museum of religious relics can be toured by request. At least one million pesos worth of religious objects were carted away from the church in 1997—the ninth recorded time that the museum had been burglarized over a span of two decades. All of the thefts remain unsolved.

Tontonon Falls: Swimming is possible in the stream but not underneath the 10-meter falls at the hydroelectric station beyond Loboc.

Punta Cruz Watchtower: The ancient fortress near Maribujoc west of Tagbilaran once served as the island's stronghold against Muslim pirates.

Tarsiers: Bohol is also known for its tarsiers, miniature primates with large gogglelike eyes and long tufted nonprehensile tails. Related to lemurs and considered the smallest monkeys in the world, they are said to be so gentle that they cry themselves to death in captivity.

Accommodations
Most of the hotels are grouped together near the city center, though few travelers stay in Tagbilaran unless they miss the last jeepney out to Panglao.

Tagbilaran Vista Lodge: Cheap and centrally located. 12 Lesage St., (038) 411-3072, P80-350.

LTS Lodge: Probably the best budget- to middle-priced choice in town. Garcia Ave., tel. (038) 411-3310, P100-450.

Chriscentville Pension House: New place featuring spotlessly clean a/c rooms with private baths and cable TV. Gallares St., tel. (038) 411-4029, P550-900.

PANGLAO ISLAND

Bohol's finest beaches—and some of the best sand in this section of the Visayas—are on the southeastern coast of Panglao Island, where a wonderful combination of dazzling sand, swaying palms, warm waters, and colorful corals have made the island one of the premier beach destinations in the central Visayas.

All this beauty has not been lost on Manila's tourism officials who have announced a 20-year plan for tourism, in cooperation with the United Nations Development Program and the private sector. The main goal is ecotourism on Palawan, the relatively untouched island of Panglao, and Samal, another tropical island near Davao.

Panglao has a half-dozen beaches in various states of development but nearby all the bungalows and dive shops are at Alona Beach on the southwestern corner. Just over the rocky headlands to the east is an immense stretch of dazzling sand that has just one place to stay—the decidedly upscale Bohol Beach Club.

Alona Beach
Alona Beach caters almost exclusively to the scuba diving crowd; few budget travelers can af-

PHILIPPINES

ford the fare for accommodations and bungalow owners have little interest in catering to low-end visitors.

Accommodations: Most bungalows at Alona charge P600-900 for a fan-cooled room and P1,200-1,500 for a/c suites. Many places now quote rates in U.S. dollars and you can expect this trend to continue with the continued devaluation of the peso.

Lodges include Alona Kew right where the road meets the beach, and then, heading east, Sea Quest, Pyramid Resort, Alonaville, Planet Mars (rooms from P300), and Peter's at the end of the beach. A few hundred meters farther east is Alona Tropicana, the overpriced Crystal Coast, and the superbly isolated and eclectically decorated Bananaland, a great place to escape the scuba frenzy that washes over most of Alona Beach.

Heading west from Alona Kew you'll find Playa Blanca, Swiss Bamboo Bungalows, Casa Nova, and Kalipayan Resort up on the hilltop.

Scuba: Scuba dives can be arranged through several dive shops such as the two largest operations—Atlantis Dive Center (run by Kurt and Thomas) and Sea Quest. Note that snorkeling is possible at Alona but much better on the southwest coast at Cervera Shoal and adjacent islands.

Bohol Beach

A few kilometers east of Alona Beach is an amazing stretch of pure white sand with only one hotel, the expensive and often deserted Bohol Beach Club. Facilities include a swimming pool, a spa, tennis courts, water-sports facilities, and 40 individual bungalows for US$80-140.

The magnificent beach will probably remain sadly abandoned and lifeless until small-scale entrepreneurs are allowed to construct some less expensive bungalows.

Transportation

JG Express buses from the bus terminal on Butalid Street leave several times daily until 1700. Late arrivals in Tagbilaran can hire a motorized tricycle or call for a metered taxi.

Buses marked "Panglao" go to Panglao town near Doljo Beach and do not connect directly with Alona Beach. Buses marked "Panglao-Tauala" follow the southern coastline and stop in Alona before continuing on to Panglao town.

CHOCOLATE HILLS

Bohol's most famous and mysterious draws are the hundreds of perfectly cone-shaped mounds located 55 km northeast of Tagbilaran and five km before the town of Carmen. These enigmatic and otherworldly hillocks were either formed by prehistoric, submarine volcanic eruptions followed by sea erosion or, more romantically, they are the teardrops of a grief-stricken giant. Eric Von Daniken, in his book *Chariots of the Gods,* theorized that they were formed by extraterrestrials, a somewhat believable notion on a full moon night or weirdly misty morning.

Accommodations

The Chocolate Hills Resort, magnificently situated on top of a giant chocolate kiss, charges P100 for dorm beds and P250-480 for private cottages.

Transportation

Both Arples Line and St. Joseph buses serve Carmen. Look for the Coca-Cola sign, which marks the turnoff to the Chocolate Hills Resort. For a great experience, arrive at the junction after sunset, hike in the darkness to the resort, and wake early for one of the world's most surreal sunrises.

JAO ISLAND

Jao (pronounced how) Island is an isolated and relaxing little island situated off the northeast coast of Bohol. Beaches are nonexistent and most of the coral beds have been destroyed by typhoons, but there's an air of tranquility and fine walks are possible through native villages famous for their *nipa* weavings.

Accommodations

Laguna Escondido Resort and Yacht Haven, managed by a crusty old German-Canadian sailor who entertains his guests with tales of Pacific crossings, charges P100 for dorm beds and P300-350 for private cottages. Food here is much better than the average Filipino fare.

PHILIPPINES

Transportation

Talibon can be reached by buses from Tagbilaran and the Chocolate Hills. Regular boats from Talibon to Jao Island leave several times daily. Jao Island is a place for quiet conversation and long books.

BORACAY

Once an isolated island known only to backpackers and world travelers, Boracay today is deservedly the most popular beach resort in the Philippines. The reasons are obvious: sand as fine and white as talcum powder, dazzling aquamarine waters, soaring coconut trees that hang over the beaches like in a scene from *South Pacific*, lonely coves, epic sunsets, plus some of the finest accommodations in the country.

But all is not well in paradise. Despite the growth of tourism, government agencies—both local and national—failed to construct waste treatment plants or even to pipe in fresh water for human consumption. For over two decades, waste water was pumped into the bay and trash was simply pushed into giant landfills. The result has been that the once pristine waters are polluted almost beyond redemption.

Another problem was that the local *barangay* officials sold over 400 tricycle permits to local residents, giving them a wealth of votes-in-pocket but also cursing the island with a ridiculous supply of noisy, polluting machines that buzz incessantly up and down the solitary road that runs from the south to the north end of the island.

Another nail in the coffin was the transformation of the northern third of the island into a wonderland of condominiums and swimming pools surrounding an 18-hole golf course—exactly what most people don't want to find in a tropical resort.

Then, in 1997, the minister of the environment stated in a public address that Boracay was an environmental disaster area. No kidding. After a great deal of soul searching, and a dip in the waters by Tourism Minister Mina Gabor, Manila finally announced that something would be done to save Boracay. This new plan, approved in late 1997, promises to bring fresh water from a new dam on Panay, a wastewater-treatment plant, and garbage-collection services to the immensely popular island.

If the government fails to take action on the very serious problems facing Boracay, I'd say skip the island and head directly to Palawan.

From Manila by Air

There are literally dozens of slow ways to reach Boracay but only one fast way: fly. PAL and Air Philippines fly several times daily for P1,200-1,400 to Kalibo from where buses take two hours to Caticlan. Pumpboats shuttle constantly from Caticlan across the narrow straits to White Sand Beach.

Warning: A serious bottleneck exists between Manila and Boracay. Flights between Manila and Kalibo are perpetually filled during the high season from November to May. To avoid getting stranded in Boracay (not half bad), you should make roundtrip reservations well in advance.

Alternatively, Asian Spirit, Pacific Airways, and Seair have direct flights from Manila to the small landing strip at Caticlan for P1,600-1,800. The first two airlines fly three times daily to Caticlan while Seair flies once daily.

Services

Boracay is a well-developed resort island with all possible facilities. There's a small but helpful tourist office in the Oro Beach Resort near Boat Station Two.

Money: Cash and traveler's checks can be changed at the Boracay Tourist Center in the middle of White Beach near Red Coconut Resort. The Boracay Tourist Center also has international phone services, both incoming and outgoing faxes, a postal office, a booking agency for all airlines, hotel reservations throughout the Philippines, safety deposit boxes, drugstore, one-hour photo processing service, and a bulletin board with some very interesting ads posted by local expats (stuff for sale, upcoming events, etc.). The Boracay Tourist Center will also help with money transfers and will give Visa and MasterCard cash advances with a seven percent service charge.

Cash and traveler's checks can also be exchanged at the three Allied Bank branches scattered around White Sand Beach.

PHILIPPINES

BORACAY

PUNTA-INA BEACH

YAPAK BEACH

BAT CAVES

ILIG ILIGAN BEACH

PUKA SHELL BEACH

SANTOYO BEACH

BUNYUGAN BEACH

CLUB PANOLY HOTEL

FIL-ESTATE CONDOMINIUMS

LAPU-LAPU BEACH

PUNTA BUNGA BEACH

PINAUNGAN

SIBUYAN SEA

GOLF COURSE

DINIWID BEACH

TYROL

PEARL OF THE PACIFIC
BEACHCOMBER

BALABAG

BULABOG

BOAT STATION

BOAT STATION 1

GALAXY

RED COCONUT

BULABOG BEACH

BASURA BAR

MANGO RAY

SUMMER PLACE

BOAT STATION 2

TIROL

LORENZO'S

MANGAYAD VILLAGE

TITAY'S

SULU

BOAT STATION

TOLOBHAN

TRAVELLER'S BAR

BARRACUDA

SAND BAR

BOAT STATION 3

ANGOL

BANTUD

BOAT STATION

MALABONOT

MANOC MANOC BEACH

TABLAS STRAIT

YACHT CLUB

MANOC MANOC
BOAT STATION

CAGBAN BEACH

TO KALIBO

CATICLAN

AIRPORT

SAN VIRAY

MALAY

PANAY

© MOON PUBLICATIONS, INC.

PHILIPPINES

MOON

0   1 km

Telephone: International and domestic phone calls can be made from most resorts and from the Boracay Tourist Center, Pantelco Business Center in Balabag, and BayanTel at the south end of the beach.

Post Office: A small post office is in Balabag just behind the basketball court.

Visa Extensions: Visa extensions are handled by Swagman Travel with several offices along the main beach.

Hospital: Emergency medical care is best at the Tirol Hospital on the main road near Green Hill Cottages. Serious problems will require evacuation to Kalibo or Manila.

Accommodations

Boracay's bungalows and resorts are among the finest in Southeast Asia—clean, comfortable, and well priced. At last count, Boracay had over 300 lodging operations with some 4,500 rooms.

Most accommodations are on the west side of the island along White Sand Beach. This four-km stretch of pure-white sand has three villages that serve as general reference points—Balabag in the north (Boat Station One), Mang-gayad in the middle (Boat Station Two), and Angol in the south (Boat Station Three).

Inexpensive bungalows average P300-600 during the low season from June through October and double that fare during the high months from November to June. Most of the budget places are at the south end of the beach in Angol near Boat Station Three.

Mid-priced bungalows cost P600-1,000; the middle of the beach (Manggayad at Boat Station Two) is your best bet for something in this price range.

Luxury resorts are mainly found from the middle to the top of the beach (Balabag at Boat Station One) facing some of the best sand on the island.

There's little reason to make any specific recommendation, since most places are in good condition and generally charge an appropriate rate for their facilities. A good strategy is to have the boatman drop you somewhere in the center of the beach (ask for Boat Station Two) and then begin your bungalow search. If you're really on a budget, Boat Station One is the place to be dropped.

CAMIGUIN ISLAND

Camiguin is a picturesque volcanic island situated off the north coast of Mindanao favored by travelers searching for an alternative to Boracay. Although the beaches are rocky and less inviting than those found elsewhere in the Philippines, the island compensates with magnificent natural scenery, seven soaring volcanoes, tiny offshore islets with good coral, hot and cold soda-water springs, crashing waterfalls, and very friendly people. Accommodations are cheap and plentiful.

Transportation

Camiguin is reached with a ferry from Balingoan in northern Mindanao (two hours east of Cagayan de Oro) to Binoni on Camiguin. Ferries leave eight times daily and take 90 minutes to make the crossing. Jeepneys continue to the provincial capital of Mambajao.

The fastest way to reach Cagayan de Oro is with a fast ferry from either Cebu City or Du-maguete. Buses leave frequently from the Cagayan de Oro bus terminal for Balingoan.

Also, direct ferries leave Cagayan de Oro several times weekly at 0800.

MAMBAJAO

The provincial capital of Camiguin is the island's main accommodation center and a good base for exploring the nearby beaches and waterfalls. The small tourist information center in the municipal hall across from the church has information on skin diving and climbing Mt. Hibok. The Philippine National Bank cashes traveler's checks.

Attractions in town include some old Spanish homes, Tia's antique collection, and the NACIDA Handicraft Center, which sells locally made baskets. Mambajao cleverly derives its name from *mamhaw* (let's eat breakfast) and *bajao* (leftover boiled rice).

PHILIPPINES

Attractions near Mambajao

The best way to explore the island is with a bicycle or motorcycle rented from one of the guesthouses in Mambajao.

Katibawasan Falls: Beautiful 50-meter waterfalls plunge into an icy pool surrounded by lush vegetation and wild monkeys five km south of Mambajao. Take a *motorella* to Pandan and follow the trail.

Ardent Hot Springs: Visit this natural stone pool with 40-degree waters in the early morning, late at night, or on rainy days. Three km south of Kugita.

Hibok Hibok Volcano: In 1951 Camiguin's most active volcano erupted without warning, belching hot gases and absorbing so much oxygen that over 2,000 people instantly died from asphyxiation. Now dormant, 1,600-meter Hibok Hibok can easily be climbed in a single day during the dry season from November to May, but you'll need to hire a guide in Mambajao.

Accommodations

Inexpensive pensions are located in town and on the beaches a few kilometers west.

Tia's Pension House adjacent to the town hall and RJ Pension House on Neri Street have singles for P80-220. Both rent bikes, motorcycles, and offers tips on sightseeing. Tia also manages some beachside cottages a few minutes outside town. Across from Tia's Cottages are Shoreline Cottages for P200-250.

More accommodations are situated in small *barrios* west of Mambajao. First stop is at Turtles Nest Cottages in Kugita, three km west of town. The remainder of the places are described below under Agoho, Bug-ong, and Yumbing.

AROUND THE ISLAND

Camiguin's 65-km road can be circumnavigated with a combination of bus, jeepney, and tricycles called *motorellas.* An alternative for groups is to charter a private jeepney for sightseeing; the local term is *pakyaw.* Motorcycles and bicycles can be hired from guesthouses and private individuals.

The standard clockwise route begins with an early-morning bus or jeepney from Mambajao towards Binone and Catarman. Touring the remainder of the island from Catarman to Mambajao requires a tricycle ride to Bonbon, a long but scenic walk to Naasag, and a final tricycle ride back to Mambajao. Get an early start and allow a full day for sightseeing.

The traveler's center is just west of Mambajao at Bug-ong, Agoho, and Yumbing.

Mahinog

Facing a rocky beach and Magsaysay Island (also known as Mantigue Island) is the Western-style Mychellin Beach Resort, where clean rooms with private baths cost P250 double. Mychellin, three km south of Mahinog, rents motorcycles and diving gear and can arrange boat trips across to Mantigue.

Binoni

Binoni is where the ferry from Mindanao docks. About two km south of Binoni is Taguines Lagoon, an artificial lake, where you can stay at the J&A Fishpen Lodge for P300-600. Their restaurant serves fresh fish raised in private ponds.

Guinsiliban

Behind the elementary school is a 300-year-old watchtower used by the Spanish as a lookout against Moro pirates. Ferries to Cagayan de Oro depart from Guinsiliban several times weekly.

Cantarman

Camiguin's second-largest town was established by the Spanish in 1871 after the eruption of Mt. Vulcan Daan (Old Camiguin Volcano) destroyed their settlement at Bonbon. The region's chief draws are the Santo Nino Springs and nearby 25-meter Tuwasan Falls. A circular route to both attractions begins 500 meters north of Cantarman.

Fishermen's Friend Resort, two km south of town, has simple rooms with private baths for P450-600.

Bonbon

Signs of volcanic destruction are plentiful just north of Bonbon: San Roque Church constructed by the Augustinians in the early 17th century and now largely buried from the eruption, a submerged graveyard only visible at extreme low tide, black lava falling into the ocean. Tricycles connect Cantarman and Bonbon but you'll need to walk the remaining five km to Naasag.

Tangub Hot Springs is where dozens of volcanic springs form bathing pools whose temperatures are regulated by the rising and falling of the ocean tides. Thus, the water's cool at high tide, too hot at low tide, and agreeably warm at mid-tide.

Agoho, Bug-ong and Yumbing

These three small villages—five to seven km west of Mambajao—are where most travelers stay on Camiguin.

Bungalows in Agoho (five km west of town) include Camiguin Seaside Lodge, Morning Glory Cottages, Paradise Palm Pension House, Caves Resort, and Payag Cottages. All have simple but acceptable rooms from P100-450.

Jasmine by the Sea Beach Resort in nearby Bug-ong (six km west of town) has dive facilities and rooms from P300-500.

Finally, Paras Beach Resort in Yumbing (seven km west) has decidedly upscale rooms from P1,200-2,800, plus a swimming pool, restaurant, and dive shop.

CEBU

Residents of Cebu like to boast about their province and city: oldest university, church, and street in the country; more cathedrals and historical attractions than anywhere else; best beaches and the finest climate; coral reefs and aquamarine waters that rank among the tops in the country; freshest beer and rum (San Miguel and Tanduay are located here); most beautiful women; sweetest mangoes and creamiest *guabanos*.

Shaped somewhat like a giant snake that evenly divides the Visayas in half, Cebu is also an economic miracle that disproves the notion that prosperity never reaches the underdeveloped hinterlands. Credit for growth rates which have recently far outstripped those in Manila goes to Chinese-Filipino entrepreneurs, who comprise less than 15% of the population but, as elsewhere throughout Asia, almost completely dominate the local economy.

Scuba Diving

Cebu is the center for diving throughout the Visayan archipelago. Dive resorts with compressors, divemasters, and fully equipped boats are located throughout the island, but those on Mactan near Cebu City are the most convenient. Diving at Mactan includes the coral reefs surrounding the Olangos and the double-barriers reef at Caubian Island.

Cebu's second-largest dive site is at Moalboal on the southwestern coastline. Though shoreline corals were wiped out several years ago by a powerful typhoon, excellent reefs remain around the Pescadores and the luxurious Japanese-owned resort island of Badian. Moalboal has inexpensive accommodations.

Other diving is possible north of Cebu City and on Bantayan and Gato Islands off the northwestern tip of Cebu.

TRANSPORTATION

Air

Cebu is the transportation hub of the Philippines. PAL, Air Philippines, and most other domestic airlines have daily service from Manila and other Visayan islands. International travelers should inquire about direct charters from America, Europe, Hong Kong, and Japan—a convenient approach that avoids having to mess with Manila.

City center can be reached from the airport on hourly shuttle buses or metered taxis, which cost P100-150 including the bridge toll.

Ship

Cebu is served by large passenger ships from Manila and by fast ferries from Tagbilaran on Bohol; Ormoc and Maasin on Leyte; Dumaguete on Negros; and Cagayan de Oro, Iligan, and Ozamis on Mindanao.

Fast ferry service is also available from Cebu City to Bantayan Island—a convenient if somewhat expensive option that avoids a long and grinding bus ride.

Bus

Buses departing to Negros, Bohol, and southern Cebu destinations such as Moalboal and Argao leave Cebu City from the southern bus terminal

PHILIPPINES

on Rizal Avenue. Special direct services include the a/c Ceres Liner buses to Bacolod daily at 0600, Ceres Liner buses to Tagbilaran at 0800 and 1400, and ABC buses to Dumaguete at noon.

Bus touts will direct you, but try to get on a bus that looks almost filled and ready to leave. Otherwise it's a long wait in the sweltering heat.

Buses to Bacolod leave daily from the Rajah Hotel. Buses to northern Cebu leave from the northern bus terminal at Cuenco and Maxilom streets, and from the closer Rough Rider terminal at Cuenco and Padilla.

CEBU CITY

The oldest and second-largest city in the Philippines is a friendly place without the overpowering pace and urban headaches of Manila. Cebu offers some historical landmarks connected with the Spanish era, good restaurants, a wide range of accommodations, and nightlife second only to that of Manila. More importantly, Cebu is a convenient base from which to explore the beaches and islands in the Visayas.

The city is divided between the older and somewhat congested downtown section near Colon Street and the newer uptown neighborhood around Fuenta or Osmena circles.

Attractions
Fort San Pedro: Cebu's Department of Tourism is located inside one of the oldest forts in the Philippines. The triangular bastion, founded by Legaspi in 1565, served for several centuries as a lookout for Muslim marauders and later as a garrison for Cebuano rebels captured during Spanish occupation. Later reincarnations included an American military camp, a city zoo, and a private nightclub.

Magellan's Cross: Cebu's most important historical landmark stands inside an unimposing kiosk near the city cathedral. Some say the *tindalo* wood case protects the original cross raised in 1521 by Magellan to commemorate the archipelago's first encounter with Christianity. Finely painted frescoes on the ceiling relate the conversion of Rajah Humabon, his queen, and their 800 followers.

Basilica of Santo Niño: A small chapel in the rear of the oldest church in the Philippines houses the 30-cm image of Santo Niño de Cebu or Infant Jesus, one of the most powerful and revered icons in the Philippines. The adjacent basilica displays a rich collection of religious art and artifacts.

University of San Carlos Museum: Highlights of this small but worthwhile museum include a pair of mounted Philippine eagles and amazing giant crabs that climb coconut trees. Founded by the Jesuits in 1595, U.S.C. is now operated by the Societes Divini Verdi, a German Catholic order once popular in Southeast Asia.

Casa Gorodo Museum: The restored residence of Cebu's first Filipino bishop offers a rare glimpse into the lifestyle of a wealthy 19th-century trader. Difficult to find but highly recommended for its timeless atmosphere.

Beverly Hills Taoist Temple: Situated six km from downtown in the wealthy Chinese suburb of Beverly Hills stands a gaudy red-and-green temple dedicated to the teachings of philosopher Lao Tzu. Mystics predict the future and pick lottery numbers on Wednesdays and Sundays. Take a taxi or jeepney marked Lahug. Wealthy homes further remind you of Los Angeles and not the Philippines.

Mactan Island
One of the easiest excursions from Cebu City is across the bridge to Mactan Island, where the beaches are unspectacular but the diving and the handicraft industries are worthwhile diversions. Mactan is also known for its guitar production and memorial to Lapu Lapu, the tribal chieftain who killed Magellan in a minor dispute and is now honored as the first Filipino to repulse foreign aggression.

Accommodations: Most of Mactan's accommodations are upscale resorts set along the rocky and grayish strip of sand near Maribago and Marigondon beaches. Most places start at US$120 per night and cater almost exclusively to wealthy Filipinos and Western businessmen.

Budget Accommodations
Ruftan Pension: Cebu's most popular travelers' center has paper-thin walls but rooms are clean and the restaurant is a good place to meet other backpackers. Managers Fina and Jose offer advice and give discounts to Peace Corps volunteers. Legaspi St., tel. (032) 79138, P175-380.

PHILIPPINES

CEBU CITY

CAPITOL
MAYFLOWER PENSION

ESCARIO

BOULEVARD
RESTAURANT

DON JOSE

CHRISTINA ST.

JASMIN
PENSION

OSMENA

RIZAL MUSEUM ★

GALI
PENSION

PARK PLACE
HOTEL AND
AIRPORT BUSES

CEBU GRAND
HOTEL, PAL

CEBU MIDTOWN HOTEL

TO BEVERLY
HILLS, CEBU
PLAZA HOTEL
THAI AIR,
MALAYSIAN AIR

ROBINSON'S SHOPPING CENTER
THOMAS
COOK
KAN IRAG HOTEL

NATIONAL BOOKS

RUSTAN'S

NIGHTCLUBS

VIENNA
COFFEE
HOUSE

JASMINE PENSION

IGLESIA NI
CRISTO CHURCH

SINGUBA RESTAURANT

SHAKEY'S

ST. MORITZ HOTEL
AND BAR

GORDO AVE.

DIPLOMAT
HOTEL

JOVEL'S PENSION

ARBEL'S PENSION

MORBAI MAPS

YMCA

RAMOS ST.

BOOKMARK

ABC BUSES

TO AYALA CENTER →

JAKOSALEM ST.

CAFE ADRIATICO

GENERAL MAXIMO AVE.

RIZAL AVE.

OSMENA BLVD.
JONES BLVD.)

TEO FIL
PENSION

DEL ROSARIO

SOUTHERN BUS
TERMINAL

SANCIANGKO

UNIVERSITY OF SAN
CARLOS MUSEUM ★

NORTHERN BUS
TERMINAL (FORMER)

OUR PLACE

COLON ST.

PETE'S KITCHEN

HOTEL DE
MERCEDES

STARDUST
BAR

MAGALLANES

POST
OFFICE

PADILLA

CARBON
MARKET ★

MANZALILI

GAISANO

CASA
GORODO
MUSEUM ★

TO SM CITY AND NEW
NORTHERN BUS TERMINAL →

BRIONES

PLARIDEL

OSMENA BLVD.

JAKOSALEM

RUFTAN
PENSION

GULLAS

CUENCO

GONZALES

PAL

BASILICA
OF SANTO
NIÑO CHURCH

CEBU
CATHEDRAL

PATRIA DE CEBU
PENSION

MAXIMO AVE.
(MANGO AVE.)

CITY HALL AND PNB

MAGELLAN'S
CROSS

LAPU LAPU

BURGOS

TOURIST OFFICE

EDDIE'S LOG CABIN

INDEPENDENCE
SQUARE

MACARTHUR BLVD.

ARELLANO BLVD.

FORT
SAN
PEDRO

LEGASPI

QUEZON BLVD.

PIER 4

PIER 3

PIER 2

PIER 1

CEBU HARBOR

IMMIGRATION

GPO

0   500 m

© MOON PUBLICATIONS, INC.

PHILIPPINES

Patria de Cebu: Catholic run place with simple but clean rooms. Burgos St., tel. (032) 72084, P150-250.

Arbel's Pension House: Small but adequate rooms in a quiet location off the main road. 57 East Jones (Osmena) St., tel. (032) 253-5303, P200-500.

Verbena Pension House: Another inexpensive to moderate pension northeast of Osmena Circle. 584 Garcia St., tel. (032) 253-3430, P390-480.

Jasmin Pension: Upper Cebu is convenient for shopping, dining, and nightlife near Fuenta Circle. The Jasmin and nearby Loreta Pension (once voted the cleanest pension in Cebu) are good choices. 395 Osmena Blvd., tel. (032) 253-3757, P370-500.

Teo-Fel Pension House: Thirty a/c rooms with private baths plus restaurant, room service, and other perks not found in most budget hotels. 4 Junquera Extension, tel. (032) 253-2482, P350-700.

Century Hotel: An old creaking hotel with countless rooms in a convenient downtown location. Pelaez St., tel. (032) 255-1341, P350-600.

Moderate Accommodations

Hotel de Mercedes: Downtown hotel with reasonably priced if somewhat scruffy rooms. 7 Pelaez St., tel. (032) 253-1105, P600-1,100.

Kan Irag Hotel: An old favorite with funky but acceptable rooms tucked away on a quieter street near Osmena Circle. Ramos St., tel. (032) 253-6935, P750-1,200.

St. Moritz Hotel: A better name than the hotel itself but popular with visiting Europeans who pack the pub in the evenings. Gorodo Ave., tel. (032) 231-1148, P1,200-1,800.

Montebello Hotel: Spanish atmosphere, swimming pool, and attractive gardens but a long distance from downtown or Osmena Circle. Gorodo Avenue, tel. (032) 231-3681, US$40-80.

Cebu Plaza Hotel: Cebu's first five-star hotel has breathtaking views but is inconveniently located about eight km out of town. Lahug, tel. (032) 231-2064, US$120-200.

Restaurants

Eddie's Log Cabin: Cebu's attachment to foreign expats is best experienced in this Western tavern owned by the American Cherokee contractor who made his fortune developing Beverly Hills . . . Cebu, not Los Angeles. Great sizzling steaks, salads, and homemade pies. Briones Street near Plaza Independenzia. Moderate.

Our Place: The most popular expat gathering venue in town with friendly hostesses and American and European grub at moderate prices. Don't be alarmed by the narrow staircase or general dereliction of the neighborhood. Pelaez Street.

Gaisano Cafeteria: Modern and clean downtown restaurant with tasty Filipino specialties. Nearby Pete's Kitchen is also recommended; both are inexpensive.

Robinson's Shopping Center: This modern complex near Fuenta Osmena Circle has three clean and comfortable restaurants, Sizzling Plate on the ground floor, Maxim's Coffee Shop on the second, and the luxurious Lotus Garden for Chinese specialties on the fourth. Good places to cool off from the searing heat. Moderate.

Charlie's: Jazz club and restaurant with delicious *calamansi* and mango daiquiris. 171 Ramos Street. Somewhat expensive unless you go during happy hour 1700-1900.

Vienna Coffee House: Lousy cappuccino and pricey cakes but well stocked with current newspapers and German publications such as *Der Spiegel*. Mango Avenue. Moderate.

Cafe Adriatico: Upscale and trendy cafe in an old Cebuano home; excellent coffee and cozy atmosphere. Ramos Street. Moderate.

Nightlife

Entertainment in Cebu is divided between the low-end bars downtown and the classier places uptown along Osmena Boulevard and Maxilom Avenue.

Live Music: Charlie's Jazz Club on Ramos Street offers some of the best music in town, plus delicious daiquiris in a Casablanca atmosphere. The Boulevard on upper Osmena Boulevard and Shakey's on Maxilom Avenue are popular rock 'n' roll clubs. Raunchy and very loud bands blast away at Gaw Central Square on Colon Street. Hot Gossip Disco in Robinson's Shopping Center is Cebu's upscale nightclub.

Go-go Bars: St. Moritz, Cebu's hottest girlie bar, is located near the Magellan Hotel. The Club on Mango Avenue is basic but friendly and inexpensive. Our Place is modest but the best

PHILIPPINES

place in downtown Cebu. The Stardust on Magallanes is a wild taxi hall and cabaret which has been entertaining Filipino males for several generations. Only for the brave.

Services

Information: The Department of Tourism in the GMC Building on Plaza Independencia near Fort San Pedro is more helpful than most other DOT offices. Their service counter at the Mactan International Airport can help with hotel reservations and transportation into the city.

Money: Traveler's checks and cash can be exchanged at all the usual banks and with money changers outside the post office and around Independence Square. American Express is at the Ayala Center in Cebu Business Park, while Thomas Cook is in the Metrobank Plaza on Osmena Boulevard.

Cash advances on Visa and MasterCard can be picked up at the Equitable Bank on Port Center Avenue adjacent to SM City in the failed Reclamation Area—city fathers thought this gigantic landfill project would someday be the location of a new supercity, but as you can see, the vast acreage now looks like the city dump.

Mail: The GPO is near Plaza Independencia and branch offices are on Briones Street, Colon Street, and at the University of San Carlos on Del Rosario Street.

Transportation

PAL has an uptown office on Maxilom Avenue and a downtown center on Osmena Boulevard. Other international airlines and travel agents are near the Magellan Hotel and on Ramos Street.

Buses to the airport leave hourly from Osmena Boulevard near Robinson's. Buses to Negros, Bohol, Panay, and southern Cebu leave from the southern bus terminal on Rizal Avenue. Buses to northern Cebu leave from the northern bus terminal on Cuenco Avenue and from the terminal near the post office.

BANTAYAN ISLAND

Bantayan Island, off the northwestern tip of Cebu, offers excellent diving and some of the most spectacular beaches in the region, especially along the southern coastline between Santa Fe

and Maricaban. The island's superb combination of sun, sand, and sea will probably make it a major destination in the coming years.

Accommodations

Basic hotels are located in Bantayan, the island's largest town, in Santa Fe, the third largest, and at several beaches near Santa Fe.

Santa Fe Beach Resort: A large and well-developed resort with a cafe, Windsurfers, outrigger rentals, and boat charters to nearby islands and coral reefs. The resort is in Talisay, a few kilometers north of Santa Fe pier. Santa Fe, Cebu tel. 211339 or 82548, P300-400 fan, P900-1,500 a/c doubles.

Kota Beach Resort: Another popular resort, one km south of Santa Fe and three km from the new airport, where the sand and waters are absolutely dazzling. Santa Fe, Cebu, tel. 75101, fax 53748, US$15-25 fan, US$36-45 a/c.

Admiral Lodging: Basic accommodation in the town of Bantayan. The Arriola family can advise on inexpensive accommodations on Bantayan. 21-23 Rizal Ave., tel. 215692, P80-300 fan, P450-500 a/c.

Transportation

Bantayan Island is 138 km northwest of Cebu City and 24 km from Hagnaya port near San Remigio.

Air: Pacific Air flies daily from Cebu City to the Santa Fe Airport.

Bus and Boat: To reach Bantayan in a single day, take either the 0600 a/c or 0500 ordinary bus from the North Bus Terminal in Cebu City to Hagnaya wharf, from where a regular public ferry departs daily at 0930 and reaches Bantayan in one hour. Late arrivals can take the night ferry, which leaves around 2130.

Ferries back to the mainland depart Santa Fe at 0600 and 0700 and connect with buses leaving at 0715 and 1300.

To Negros: Public ferries also shuttle from Bantayan across to Cadiz on Negros, a convenient route which avoids some backtracking.

SANTANDAR

Cebu's longest white-sand beach is at the southern tip of Cebu near the village of Liloan, two km south of Santandar. The beach is fairly attractive, offshore diving is good, and scuba excursions can be arranged to Sumilon and Apo islands.

Accommodations

Manureva Beach Resort: Jean Pierre Franck's isolated but lovely resort boasts a dive center, motorcycle rentals, and sailboards. The resort also organizes big game-fishing expeditions. Santandar, tel. 16001, US$12-24 fan, US$25-50 a/c. Pierre cooks great French meals. Ask him about his postcard business.

Transportation

Santandar can be reached in a few hours with hourly ABC bus from the Southern Bus Terminal in Cebu City. It's a spectacular ride on a recently repaved highway.

MOALBOAL

Panagsama Beach, situated at the edge of a rocky promontory some 90 km southwest of Cebu and five km from Moalboal, remains a popular travelers' destination despite the tragic destruction of its beaches and offshore coral gardens by Typhoon Nitong in 1984. Locals say the tides were at their very lowest when the 280-km/h winds virtually sandblasted the once-famous coral beds to oblivion. The remaining beaches are rocky and unpleasant except for a narrow strip of sand just north of the expensive Moalboal Reef Club.

The scruffy town suffers from a general lack of urban planning, and an overabundance of barking dogs, and hustling schoolchildren, although the underwater buttresses and coral-studded reefs around Pescador Island remain popular with scuba divers. Saavedra Dive Center charges US$25 per dive including equipment or US$200 for a five-day PADI-certification program. Other dive centers include Ocean Safari,

run by Nelson Abenido; Visaya Divers; and Philippine Dive and Tour.

Accommodations and Transportation

Rooms and private cottages average P100-250 depending on facilities. Pacita's Bungalows to the left of the Coke sign is a popular place despite the lack of sand and sad shape of the huts. Norma's, Nanita's, Calypso, Cora's, and Pacifico Cottages are similarly priced.

Moalboal's two best lodging options are Sumisid Dive Lodge, which costs US$10-25, and the Moalboal Reef Club for US$25-50. Both include full board.

Moalboal can be reached in three hours by ABC bus from Cebu's southern bus terminal. Philippine Eagle goes direct at noon. Buses terminate in Moalboal, from where tricycles cost P10-15 out to Panagsama Beach.

SOUTH OF MOALBOAL

Badian Island Resort

Tremendous coral reefs untouched by the ravages of dynamite fishing are situated near the only deluxe resort in western Cebu. Amenities include a swimming pool, a restaurant, and equipment for water sports. Badian, Cebu, tel. 61306, US$120-200.

Kawasan Falls

Two lovely waterfalls with natural swimming pools and simple huts for overnighters are located west of Matutinao. Alight at the Matutinao bridge and hike 30 minutes west through the beautiful river canyon. Matutinao also has a simple restaurant and hotel.

Transport to Dumaguete

Good alternatives to the standard ferry from Toledo on Cebu to San Carlos on Negros are the hourly boats from San Sebastian and Bato to Tampi near Dumaguete. Run to the jeepney or you'll be stranded.

LEYTE

Though visited only by overlanders passing from Luzon to Cebu, the island of Leyte has played a key role in Filipino history. In 1521 Magellan formed a blood compact with a local chieftain and subsequently held the first Christian Mass in Southeast Asia. Leyte was also the site of MacArthur's triumphant return at the end of WW II.

More recently, Tolosa—a small town slightly south of Tacloban—received international attention and a great deal of economic gain for being the birthplace of Imelda "Shoe Princess" Marcos. Aside from these historical sidelights, Leyte has a handful of beautiful but rarely visited national parks and some isolated islands perfect for the visitor who wants to get off the beaten track.

TRANSPORTATION

Traveling across Leyte is rather straightforward. Travelers can reach Tacloban from Legaspi in a single nonstop day, provided they catch the morning ferry from Matnog on Luzon to Allen on Samar. Tacloban to Ormoc takes two hours by bus. Most travelers then catch a boat from Ormoc to Cebu City. Other departure options include flying with PAL, daily boats from Tacloban to Surigao in northeastern Mindanao, the twice-weekly ferry from Maasin to Surigao, and sporadic ferries from Maasin to Ubay on Bohol. Schedules should be checked with the tourist office in Tacloban.

TACLOBAN

Leyte is an island both physically and psychologically divided by the central mountain range. The capital city of the eastern seaboard is home to the Waray people, who speak a local dialect and survive by raising coconuts. Ormoc, the economic and cultural center of western Leyte, is populated by Cebuanos who speak Cebuano, raise sugar, and regard Cebu City as their spiritual homeland. Tacloban itself is a medium-size deep-water port with a lively market but a limited number of sights.

Attractions

The tourist office in the Children's Park at the north end of town has maps and other useful information.

Walking Tours: Their walking tour passes the Provincial Capitol, whose murals recall Magellan and MacArthur, the Price Mansion, where MacArthur once lived, and the anthropological museum in the Divine World University.

Heritage Museum: Top draw, however, is the Santo Nino Shrine and Heritage Museum on Calle Real two km south of downtown. On the site where the young and hungry Imelda once lived, the former first lady constructed a monument to her extravagance, self-importance, and appalling bad taste. The interior sports a baby Jesus surrounded by disco lights, a framed image of the Madonna done with pearls splashed across crimson velvet, and guest rooms for her friends instead of side altars. This audacious monument proves that Imelda not only matched but exceeded her husband's attempts to recast their personal histories in a more favorable light.

Attractions outside Town

Tacloban's other draws are outside of the town.

Red Beach: The MacArthur monument at Red Beach, seven km south of Tacloban just before the town of Palo, can be reached on jeepneys leaving from the harbor stand. Like MacArthur, the images are larger than life.

Sohoton Park: Tacloban's other big attraction is actually located across the Leyte Gulf in Samar, although access is easiest from Tacloban. Sohoton National Park offers tropical jungle, waterfalls, and deep caves best explored during low tides. Take a jeepney from the harbor to Basey where forestry officials can help hire boats and guides to explore the park. A day visit is too rushed; plan on spending the night inside the park with the rangers.

Tolosa: Imelda fans might also visit Tolosa, 24 km south, where the Olot presidential beach resort was completely stripped after the fall of Marcos. Olot today is in ruins; the swimming pool is now home to frogs and mosquitos rather than the rich and powerful.

Accommodations

Most of Tacloban's inexpensive hotels in the P50-150 range are along Romualdez St. a few blocks from the bus and jeepney stop.

San Juanico Travel Lodge: Low-end choices in Tacloban aren't very clean, but for an overnight crash try this spot in the center of town. 104 Justic Romualdez St., tel. 321-3221, P60-100.

Leyte State College House: A clean and comfortable student-run hostel, about five blocks south of Romualdez at the corner of Paterno and Santa Cruz streets. All rooms are a/c. 1 Paterno St., tel. 321-3175, P120-200.

Tacloban Village Inn: One of the few decent hotels in Tacloban after the 1992 closure of the upscale Leyte Park Hotel. Facilities include a "disco pad, adequate parking space," and a "Love Taxi." Veteranos St., tel. 321-2926, P180-300 a/c.

Services

Traveler's checks can be cashed at the PNB on Romualdez Street. PAL offices are located at the airport and in the Hotel Village Inn on Imelda Avenue. Buses and jeepneys to destinations on Leyte leave from the terminal between the market and the harbor. Philtranco, Ceres Liner, and Bachelor Express bus terminals are on Real Street.

BILIRAN ISLAND

Formerly called Panamo, 495-square-km Biliran Island can be reached on a direct bus from Tacloban to Naval, the main town. Naval has a few simple pensions such as the LM—or try the popular Agta Beach Resort three km north of Almeria. Boats leave Naval daily for Gigantan and Maripipi islands for secluded beaches and great snorkeling. Both islands have simple accommodations.

Other adventures near Caibiran on the east coast include bathing in sulfur springs at Mainit, the clear waterfalls at Tumalistis, and trekking to the summit of 1,178-meter Biliran Volcano. Guides can be hired from the mayor.

ORMOC

Ormoc, the main port and commercial center for western Leyte, chiefly serves as the departure point for ships to Cebu and as a base for exploring the nearby national parks.

Attractions

Attractions include the wharf and the market, the remains of an old bridge near City Hall, the Zaldibar Museum, a Japanese peace memorial, and Pura Beach, 12 km distant. Farther afield is Tungonan Hot Springs, with a swimming pool and thermogeyser projects, and Leyte National Park, with its sunken volcanic lake said to be the haunt of giant eels. Hikers might enjoy the 50-km Leyte Nature Trail, which begins near Ormoc.

Accommodations

Most of Ormoc's hotels are within walking distance of the bus terminal and the shipping port.

Eddie's Inn: Simple but clean rooms in a small hotel about four blocks from the bus terminal. Rizal St., tel. 2499, P60-100.

Pongos Hotel: A somewhat more expensive but cleaner choice located down near the wharf. Bonifacio St., tel. 2482, P80-120 fan, P150-220 a/c.

Don Felipe Hotel: Ormoc's top-end choice is also near the wharf. The hotel is divided into an inexpensive annex and the main building with more expensive rooms. Bonifacio St., tel. 2460, P60-100 fan, P150-420 a/c.

Transportation

PAL flies twice weekly from Ormoc to Cebu City. Ships to Cebu City depart nightly around 2200 and take about six hours.

PHILIPPINES

MINDANAO

The second largest island in the Philippines is considered by many Filipinos to be the Wild South—a mysterious and exotic land of high mountains and impenetrable rainforest peopled by intransigent Muslims and pagan hilltribes. In reality, Mindanao is three-quarters Christian and largely developed with towns, roads, and other signs of urban progress. Its role as a meeting ground for Christians and Muslims has brought problems of political assimilation, but the island is also replete with natural wonders, diverse cultures, and dozens of minorities who remain less modernized than those in northern Luzon.

Highlights on Mindanao include the beautiful offshore islands near Surigao on the northeastern corner of the island, and a climb to the summit of Mt. Apo near Davao. Visitors interested in cultural minorities should visit Lake Sebu, one of the prettiest and least visited regions in the country. Davao and Zamboanga are nondescript cities with few sights of particular interest, though both serve as gateways to more exotic destinations.

Most of Mindanao is relatively safe for Western visitors, but travelers should check with local tourist officials or embassies before traveling through the Lake Lanao region and the Sulu Archipelago south of Zamboanga.

Transportation

PAL, Air Philippines, and other regional airlines serves major cities in Mindanao from both Manila and Cebu. Visitors who are short on time but would like to see a specific region such as Lake Sebu, Marawi, or Sulu should fly directly to the nearest airport and proceed by bus or jeepney.

Several north-coast ports are served by shipping lines and fast ferries from Visayan cities such as Cebu, Tacloban, and Dumaguete. Cebu City has the most connections, though fast ferries from Leyte, Samar, Negros, and Panay are convenient for travelers coming down from those islands.

Routes

Buses that link the main cities rarely travel at night, making early-morning departures a necessity for longer journeys. Express buses with nonstop or five-stop signs are the quickest and well worth a few extra pesos.

The easiest loop around Mindanao covers the northern coastline with that all-important visit to Camiguin Island near Cagayan de Oro. First, take a ferry from Maasin or Liloan in southern Leyte to Surigao in northeastern Mindanao and spend a few days relaxing on Siargao Island. Then return to Surigao and head west along the coast, passing through Butuan, to Balingoan where boats make the crossing to Camiguin.

After Camiguin, return to Balingoan and continue by bus west to Cagayan de Oro and Iligan before finishing up at Dapitan and Dipolog. From here, you can take a fast ferry back to Cebu, Negros, or Siquijor Island.

A longer circuit involves a bus down to Davao City, then another bus west to General Santos City and Koronadel, from where jeepneys bounce the rough road to Lake Sebu. Then it's north to Marawi and west through Pagadian to Zamboanga. This very long journey can be shortened with flights between larger towns.

SURIGAO AND SIARGAO ISLAND

Situated on a hook-shaped peninsula at the northeastern corner of Mindanao, Surigao mainly serves as the launching point for visits to the beautiful group of islands just off the mainland. The town's focal point is the plaza where you'll find a small tourist office.

Siargao Island

Surigao's top draw is the group of islands scattered to the east. Siargao, the largest island, has become a surfer's paradise with large breaks on the eastern side of the island from July to November. The island came of age in 1996 with the inauguration of the Siargao Surfing Cup, an event which placed the Philippines on the international surfing trail.

Dapa is the principal town while General Luna serves as the surfing camp, a short walk from the 10 documented surf breaks just north of town.

Transportation: Boats to Dapa on Siargao Island leave in the early morning 0800-1100 from the pier at the southern end of Borromeo Street in Surigao. Jeepneys continue 14 km to the town of General Luna, where accommodations are found in beachside nipa huts.

General Luna also serves as gateway to several small islands such as Guyam, Dako, and La Janoza. Snorkeling is reportedly superb near Suyangan.

Accommodations: Most visitors head straight to General Luna or to Union on the southern coast. In the General Luna vicinity you'll find almost a dozen simple bungalows with rooms from P150-300 including BRC Beach Resort, Maite's Beach Resort, Jade Star Lodge, Siargao Pension House, and Pisangan Beach Resort. More expensive places in the P300-800 price range include the Green Room, Tuason Point, and Siargao Pacific Beach Resort.

At Union between Dapa and General Luna you'll find another beautiful, sandy beach with several inexpensive places to stay including the popular Latitude 9 Beach Resort.

Accommodations

It's best to head straight out to Siargao Island, but there's plenty of places if you get stuck in Surigao.

Garcia Hotel: Inexpensive place just south of the town plaza. 311 San Nicolas St., tel. (086) 231-7881, P75-550.

Leomondee Hotel: Newer hotel on the main road a few blocks east of town. Borromeo St., tel. (086) 232-7334, P200-600.

Tavern Hotel: An old favorite with musty rooms but a good location right on the waterfront. Borromeo St., tel. (086) 231-7301, P140-750.

Transportation

PAL flies to Surigao from Manila three times weekly and from Cebu City four times weekly. Waterjet fast ferries leave Cebu City four times weekly and take 3.5 hours to Surigao, including a stop in Maasin in southern Leyte. You can also catch buses from any of the north coast towns such as Cagayan de Oro or from Davao via Butuan.

Buses from Surigao to Davao and Cagayan de Oro leave from the small bus terminal on the main road a few blocks east of city center.

BUTUAN

Butuan is a junction town where the highway coming up from Davao terminates and splits east to Surigao and west to Camiguin Island and Cagayan de Oro. Not much to see here but you might need to overnight if your travel plans include Davao or if you miss the final buses heading east or west.

Accommodations

The bus terminal is outside town and you'll need to catch a jeepney into city center. Otherwise, coming from Surigao, hop off the bus when you see the town plaza or cathedral.

Hensonly Plaza Hotel: An old and somewhat frightening hotel but with acceptable rooms for a single night. San Francisco St., tel. (085) 225-1340, P120-450.

Emerald Villa Hotel: Marginally better option just around the corner and opposite the Echelon Plaza Hotel. Villanueva St., tel. (085) 225-2141, P350-650.

Hotel Karaga: Modern upscale hotel near La Terazza Cuisine and Weegool's Grill Haus. Montilla Blvd., tel. (085) 242-8387, P600-1,400.

BALINGOAN

Balingoan is the small town between Butuan and Cagayan de Oro from where ferries depart hourly 0800-1400 to Camiguin Island.

Accommodations

If you miss the last ferry to Camiguin, you'll need to overnight in Balingoan at Lingaya's Pension House, Balingoan Pension House, or Balingoan Hotel where rooms go for P125-300.

CAGAYAN DE ORO

The provincial capital and commercial center of Misamis Oriental is mainly a transit point for visitors heading west to Camiguin or south toward Marawi and Davao.

Attractions

Sights around town include the Maranao and Bukidnon artifacts at Xavier University on Corrales Avenue in the southeast corner of town. Outside town are the Huluga Caves, where ancient Chinese shards were unearthed, Macahambus Cave, where Filipino revolutionaries defeated American forces in 1900, and the Del Monte pineapple plantation for guided tours. A tourist office is in the Sports Complex on Velez Avenue.

Accommodations

Lodgers Inn: Bare bones place in the center of town just west of the Excelsior Hotel. Yacapin St., tel. (088) 824-1131, P125-300.

Sampaguita Hotel: Old and basic hotel also in the center of town one block west of Velez Street with both fan-cooled and a/c rooms. Borja St., tel. (088) 872-2640, P250-500.

Excelsior Hotel: Good location plus 56 decent a/c rooms with private baths and color TV. Velez St., tel. 752748 (88) P500-950.

Dynasty Court Hotel: Best in town with an a/c lobby for overheated travelers. Hayes St., tel. (088) 872-7908, P850-1,600.

Transportation

Cagayan's bus terminal is northeast of town near the Cogon market; jeepneys heading into city center are marked Divisoria or Velez Street. Jeepneys also go from the bus terminal out to the pier for ships to Manila and Camiguin Island.

DIPOLOG AND DAPITAN

Dipolog sometimes serves as an arrival point for travelers coming down from Cebu.

Attractions

The town's only draw is nearby Dapitan, where Filipino patriot Jose Rizal was exiled from 1892 to 1896 after his satirical and nationalistic novels offended Spanish officials. Deported to this isolated town in an attempt to kill his revolutionary fervor, Rizal was soon captivated by the people, tranquility, and simple beauty of the region. It's still a lovely place with its old St. James Church and Iberian plaza surrounded by raintrees. Residents have honored their favorite son with a small museum and tree-lined lanes named after his novels, poems, and Irish wife.

Accommodations

Ranillo's Pension House: Clean rooms and friendly management in Dipolog. Bonifacio St., tel. (065) 415-3536, P100-350.

Ramos Hotel: Another budget place in the center of town. Magsaysay St., tel. (065) 415-3299, P150-500.

CL Inn: Best in town with all a/c rooms. Rizal Ave., tel. (065) 415-3491, P450-900.

Dakak Park Beach Resort: Luxurious resort with a 750-meter beach, 100 a/c cottages, tennis courts, swimming pool, and dive facilities. Dakak Bay, tel. (02) 721-8164 in Manila, US$100-240.

DAVAO CITY

Davao City, a modern commercial center located in south Mindanao, is the Philippines' third most populous city after Manila and Cebu, its gerrymandered boundaries give it a greater land area than any other city in the country, and it's home to the nation's sweetest durians. Although unremarkable by most standards, Davao lacks the congestion of Zamboanga, plus it exudes a refreshing atmosphere of growth and success.

Services

The tourist office in Magsaysay Park has information on nearby beaches and islands, plus will advise on treks to Mt. Apo. You can extend visas at the Immigration Office in the Antwel Building near Magsaysay Park and get Visa or MasterCard cash advances from Equitable Bank.

Attractions

Sights around town include the largest Buddhist temple on Mindanao, handicraft shops with outstanding Mandaya weavings, and the small museum and Dabaw Etnika handicraft shop at the Davao Insular Hotel.

Don't miss the wonderful durian monument erected by the Durian Appreciation Society in Magsaysay Park near the wharf. Durian season runs from March to June; otherwise try the candy or dried preserves sold at the Madrazo Fruit Center.

Samal Island

Across the straits and due east of Davao is an immense island of blazing sand and aquamarine waters which, until recently, remained quite

PHILIPPINES

unspoiled. Samal's best beach is Paradise Island Beach on the west-central coast near the towns of Kaputian and Tigala. Samal has several small resorts and the upscale Pearl Farm Beach Resort with 30 a/c bungalows elevated over the clear waters and priced from US$150 per night.

Boats to Samal Island depart from several piers, including the downtown wharf and the Davao Insular Hotel pier.

Mount Apo National Park

Mount Apo, situated 40 km southwest of Davao, is at 2,954 meters the highest mountain in the Philippines and a naturalist's wonderland with lakes, waterfalls, hot springs, and steam vents emitting sulfuric gases. Fauna slowly changes from virgin rainforest thick with giant mahoganies to windswept grasses, while wildlife ranges from the endangered Philippine eagle to tiny falconets.

The four- to five-day climb can be started from either Digos, Kidapawan, or New Israel near Bulatukan. The Davao Tourist Office will help with recommended gear, guides, and routes. Guides and porters can also be hired directly at less cost in Kidapawan and New Israel. The hiking season is from March to May.

Accommodations

Budget hotels are located downtown on San Pedro, Pelayo, and Pichon Streets.

El Gusto Family Lodge: The travelers' favorite is clean, reasonably quiet, and centrally located. 51 Pichon St., tel. (082) 227-3622, P150-300.

Le Mirage Family Lodge: Another inexpensive place in the center of town. San Pedro St., tel. (082) 221-4334, P150-300.

Downtown Home Inn: Small but inexpensive place tucked away in the downtown shopping district across from Smokey's Café. San Pedro St., tel. (082) 226-2180, P350-600.

Aljem's Inn: Good mid-priced place in the center of town near the bars and nightclubs along Anda Street. Pichon St., tel. (082) 221-3060, P650-1,050.

Hotel Galleria: Fancy looking place in the northwestern corner of town behind Gaisano shopping center. Duterte St., tel. (082) 221-2480, P900-1,500.

Apo View Hotel: Best in town with swimming pool, several restaurants, and lively nightclub. Camus St., tel. (082) 221-6430, US$60-120.

Davao durian monument

Transportation

Davao's airport is in Lanang about 12 km northeast of the city proper. Take a metered taxi into town or take a tricycle to the highway and hail a jeepney marked San Pedro.

Philtranco, Ceres Liner, and Bachelor Express buses leave from the Ecoland Terminal across the bridge, east of town, toward the Ecoland nightclub complex on MacArthur Highway.

LAKE SEBU

Sebu, a picturesque lake surrounded by verdant green foothills in the heartland of South Cotabato, is an excellent place to see what's left of the nation's cultural minorities. Beyond that, it's a fine region for hiking and relaxation in the clear, crisp mountain air. Highly recommended.

Inhabiting the Tiraray Highlands bounded by Surallah, Kiamba, and Polomok are some 200,000 T'boli people whose women are famed

PHILIPPINES

for their skills in *abaca* weaving, intricate brass-work belts, and ornamental combs.

Guides can be hired to explore the foothills and possibly visit the more distant tribes of Manobos and Mansakas. Some say the Tasaday are a four-day hike due west, but others claim it's a 30-minute motorcycle ride.

Don't miss the Saturday market: a photographer's dream.

As this region is at the southern reaches of Muslim-controlled provinces, and there have been reports of separatist activities, check with local tourism officials before heading off to Lake Sebu and points north such as Lake Marawi and Cotabato.

Accommodations

Bao Baay Village Inn: Right on the lakeside is a spot where the hotel owner and "Honorable Vice Mayor," Bao Baay, can help with boat rentals and offer advice on trekking, caves, waterfalls, and forest resorts. P125-350.

Lakeview Tourist Lodge: Good location near the market and lake. P50-150.

Hillside View Park & Tourist Lodge: Another lakeside lodge with simple yet clean rooms. P50-150.

Transportation

Lake Sebu is in the Alah Valley, south of Koronadel and the nearby village of Surallah. Buses from Davao reach General Santos City and continue on to Koronadel, from where jeepneys head down to Surallah and then up to the lake. The last jeepney leaves around 1500.

Travel time from Davao is about eight hours.

ZAMBOANGA

Southeast Asia is blessed with a handful of place-names so evocative that most tourist offices would kill for them: Mandalay, Borneo, Bandung, and Zamboanga. These destinations sometimes live up to their reputations, which isn't the case with Zamboanga, a hot and congested city filled with ugly concrete buildings, movie posters, tawdry nightclubs, and narrow streets crowded with blasting motorcycles.

Apparently, few travel writers actually come down here to do their research. Recent articles have described the city as "the garden of the Philippines" . . . "a provincial town where the pace of life is slow and unhurried" . . . "the heart of the intriguing exotica of Muslim-land."

Hardly. Less than a third of the population are Muslims and signs of Islam barely extend beyond the fishing slum of Rio Hondo. Colorful *vintas,* primitive sailing crafts which once served as the symbols of exotic Zamboanga, have largely disappeared from local waters.

The main reason to visit Zamboanga is to travel down through the Sulu Archipelago, which, despite reassurances given by local tourism officials, is a risky adventure.

The tourist office is in the Lantaka Hotel where you can lunch and enjoy cocktails at sunset.

Attractions

Wharf: First stop should be the open-air market near the wharf, where enormous fish are weighed, cleaned, and hauled into pickup trucks. Durians of enormous size cost only P20 during the hot summer months.

Fort Pilar: A nicely restored old Spanish fort which has been incongruously capped with a highly revered shrine dedicated to Our Lady of the Pilar.

Rio Hondo: Beyond the military checkpoint and aluminum mosque—one of the most photographed scenes in the south—stands the Muslim fishing community of Rio Hondo. People are friendly and it's perfectly safe to wander around this government-constructed housing project . . . but watch out for gaps in the planking!

Outside Town: Beyond Zamboanga are Santa Cruz Island, Pasonanca Park with a sequestered hotel, a few Badjao fishing villages, and penal farms where inmates sell their woodcarvings.

Sulu Archipelago

The string of islands that stretches from Zamboanga down to Borneo is home to dozens of Muslim groups who have resisted foreign control since the arrival of the Spanish. Sulu is rarely visited by Westerners since it lies almost completely off the beaten track. It's pure virgin country—something that can't be said of most of Southeast Asia.

But there have been problems. Muslim groups such the Moro National Liberation Front (MNLF) and the Moro Islamic Liberation Front (MILF)

PHILIPPINES

seem to grab hostages solely for ransom, rather than for political revenge as with the NPA. Anyone traveling in the region should check carefully with tourism officials and embassies regarding the current political situation.

You'll get all sorts of opinions. Everybody in Manila will tell you it's extremely dangerous, but then few people in Manila have ever been this far south. Tourist officials in Zamboanga claim that most areas are now relatively safe if you stick to the larger towns, stay indoors after dark, and travel only with large groups.

Accommodations

Atilano's Pension House: A good escape from the noise, on a small alley just off the former Pasonanca Road. Major Jaldon St., tel. (062) 991-0784, P150-350.

L'Mirage Pension House: Another pension house with both fan-cooled and a/c rooms. Mayor Jaldon St., tel. (062) 991-3962, P180-420.

Paradise Pension House: Bridging the middle gap is this newish spot with clean rooms and friendly management. Barcelona St., tel. (062) 991-3465, P500-750.

Lantaka Hotel: Zamboanga's best hotel with swimming pool and wonderful waterfront location. Valderroza St., tel. (062) 991-2033, P950-2,200.

Transportation

PAL flies daily to Zamboanga from Manila, Cebu, and several towns on Mindanao. The airport is three km from city center; take a taxi or jeepney marked Canelar.

Ships connect Zamboanga with Cotabato, Dipolog, General Santos City, Pagadian, and Manila. The tourist office can help with shiping schedules.

MINDORO

A visit to Mindoro is almost synonymous with a sojourn at Puerto Galera, the closest good beach near Manila. The remainder of Mindoro is largely unexplored, though the breathtaking mountains, thick jungles, remote beaches, and cultural minorities offer endless possibilities for the adventurous traveler.

Scuba Diving

Mindoro's easy accessibility and well-preserved marine environment have made it one of the top dive locations in the Philippines. Among the highlights are the coral gardens situated off Long Beach; the famous shark cave near Escarceo Point; and the wrecks of a Japanese ship near the Boulders, a Spanish galleon near Verde Island, and another Spanish wreck in the Manila Channel (only discovered in 1983).

Puerto Galera is also the launching point for dives to renowned Apo Reef, a 30-square-km reef off the west coast of Mindoro. Professional dive shops which can help with equipment rentals, boats, guides, and PADI certification include Capt'n Greggs on Sabang Beach, El Galleon on Small La Laguna Beach, and Reef Raiders on Big La Laguna Beach.

Transportation

Ferries leave daily around noon from Batangas to Puerto Galera. The easiest way to make the connection is on private a/c buses leaving at 0900 from the Centrepoint Hotel in Manila. The cost is P350 and arrival time in Puerto Galera is about 1400. A half-price alternative is an early morning (0700-0800) BLTB bus from Pasay direct to the ferry dock in Batangas.

Jeepneys waiting in Puerto Galera go in two directions: east to the busy beaches at Sabang and La Laguna or west to the relatively peaceful beach of White Sand. Sabang is best for scuba divers and party animals searching for bars and discos. White Sand is best for long walks, sunsets, and quiet evenings in simple restaurants.

Heading south by bus from Puerto Gallera is scenic but somewhat time consuming: Puerto Gallera-Calapan (two hours), Calapan-Roxas (four hours), Roxas-Bulalacao (two hours), Bu-lalacao-San Jose (four hours), and San Jose-Pandan Island (four hours).

Transportation to Boracay

Mindoro also serves as a transit point for visitors going to Boracay.

The most popular route is by boat from Roxas in southeastern Mindoro across to Tablas Island, from where *bancas* continue down to Boracay. There's also a direct boat service from Roxas to Boracay—twice weekly during the low season and almost daily during the busy months from December to June.

Although a somewhat dangerous journey due to unexpected storms, the Roxas-Boracay route allows you to enjoy the beaches at both Puerto Galera and Boracay with a minimum of back-tracking. The tourist office in Puerto Galera has the latest schedules for boats from Roxas and other towns on Mindoro.

PUERTO GALERA

Six hours south of Manila is this famous travelers' scene and tourist haunt set along a stunning harbor speckled with superb beaches and secluded coves. The magnificent wall of mountains that rises from the ocean and towers over the bay adds a wonderful sense of mystery and grandeur to the scene.

Puerto Galera Town

The beautiful harbor at Puerto Galera has evolved from a 10th-century entrepôt of Chinese junks and Indian *prahus* to ferries and *bancas* filled with travelers, tourists, and Filipinos. Accommodations are found in town but there's little reason to stay here unless you plan on catching a very early-morning ferry back to Batangas. It's best to immediately take a jeepney east to Sabang or west to White Beach.

Puerto Galera has a small but useful tourist office near the pier and a Swagman travel office near the Puerto Galera Resort Hotel. International phone calls can be made at reasonable prices at the BayanTel office just up from the

PHILIPPINES

PUERTO GALERA

VERDE ISLAND PASSAGE

TO BATANGAS

LONG BEACH
MEDIO ISLAND
COCO BEACH
LA LAGUNA BEACH
SABANG BEACH
LIGHTHOUSE
BOQUETE ISLAND
HALIKE BEACH
BALATEROS COVE
SINANDIEAN
TAMARAW BEACH
WHITE BEACH
BAYANAN BEACH
TALIPANAN BEACH
MINOLO BAY
SAN ISIDRO
BALATERO
MARKOE COVE
PUERTO GALERA
TALIPANAN WATERFALL
ENCENADA BEACH
BALETE BEACH
HUNDORA BEACH
TABINAY BEACH
DULANGAN BEACH
HOT SPRINGS
TABINAY
TO CALAPAN
DULANGAN

0   1 km

© MOON PUBLICATIONS, INC.

pier, while traveler's checks can be cashed at the First Allied Savings Bank just opposite BayanTel.

Sabang and La Laguna Beaches
Once an idyllic beach reached only by chartered *banca,* Sabang and nearby La Laguna beaches are now fully developed resort areas with hotels, bungalows, restaurants, discos, nightclubs, girlie bars, money changers, a pharmacy, general goods stores, and plenty of dive shops. Most of the visitors here are either scuba divers or bachelors down from Manila with Filipina girlfriends in tow.

Sabang is the main beach where you'll find the nightlife and most of the dive shops. Big La Laguna and Small La Laguna beaches to the east are somewhat quieter and have better sand. From these beaches it's a 10-15 minute walk to Sabang.

Sabang Beach: Sabang is a mid-market destination with most resorts now in the P500-1,500 price range. A handful of simple bungalows priced P250-500 are in the east side of Sabang, past the Sunset Disco (a girlie dance bar) and a pool hall. Cathy's Cottages, At-Can's Inn, VIP Lodge, Juling's Place, Seashore Lodge, and Sea Breeze Vista Lodge have rooms from P250-500.

Resorts in the middle of the beach and to the west tend to be more expensive but sometimes have a few low-end bungalows tucked away for the budget traveler. Places in the P500-1,500 price range include Capt'n Gregg Resort, Red Coral Cottages, Atlantic Resort Hotel, Angelyn Beach Resort, Paradise Inn, Kokomo Inn, and Lopez Lodge.

Small La Laguna Beach: The beach then turns to black sand and rock and ends at the Point Bar where Asia Divers has their headquarters. Heading around the point, you'll arrive at Small La Laguna, where mid-priced accommodations include El Galleon Resort, Sunsplash Resort, Havana Moon Resort, Sha Che Inn, Portofino, and Carlo's Inn. Little La Laguna also has outlets for Swagman Travel and Action Divers.

Big La Laguna Beach: You then climb some steps over a small cliff (visit the viewpoint) and arrive at Big La Laguna, which has the best sand at Sabang plus some great swimming in pure-blue waters. Nothing cheap up here but spots in the P500-1,500 price range include Cataquis, El Oro Resort, La Laguna Beach Club, Fernando's, Lory's Cottages, and Millers Corner at the end of the beach.

White Beach

White Beach (also called San Isidro Beach) is the quieter and more relaxed alternative to the commercialized frenzy of Sabang Beach. Diving is poor and the water is often too rough for swimming, but the sand is abundant and the sunsets great.

Unfortunately, most of the small bungalows tucked away under the coconut trees were constructed with little imagination and very few have been maintained over the last decade. And prior to the devaluation of the peso in 1997, all were badly overpriced when compared to similar facilities in Thailand or Indonesia. Prices are more reasonable today (if inflation doesn't wreck the equation) but you'll never really love these concrete cubicles.

You'll need to mention a specific cottage to the jeepney driver or you'll be let out near Jenny's Store at the far western end of the beach.

Accommodations: Cottages, lodges, inns, and huts in the P500-800 price range include (from east to west) South of the Border Resort, Arco Baleno Cottages, Mylah's Nipa Huts, Delgado's Cottages, Estrella's Resort, Warren's Seaview, Majesty Lodge, Peter's Inn, Traveller's Beach Delight Cottages, Buena Lynn's Lodgin, White Beach Nipa Huts (all concrete . . . not a nipa palm in sight), White Beach Lodge, Grace Lodge, Cherry's Inn, Lodger's Nook, and Summer Connection.

Tucked away back from the beach under a wonderful grove of palm trees is Villa Luisa Lodging, Julie's Store, and White Beach Disco.

ROXAS CITY

Roxas is an important connection for travelers going down to Boracay. A wide variety of boats reach Boracay but only large and safe vessels should be taken. Do not take small outriggers or attempt the crossing during rough weather or after nightfall, since the Tablas Straits are extremely dangerous.

Some boats go directly to Boracay while others go via Tablas. In most cases, you'll need to overnight in Roxas and perhaps the interim island before continuing to Boracay. The tourist office in Puerto Galera has current schedules.

Accommodations

Accommodations in town include the Hotel Dannarosa with rooms from P100-200 and the nearby Santo Nino Hotel with fan-cooled or a/c rooms from P120-500. Some travelers prefer to stay on the beach at Catalina's Resort some two km from town where simple rooms cost P100-250.

NEGROS

Shaped like a boot in the heart of the Visayan archipelago, this elongated island serves as an important stepping-stone for travelers island-hopping between Boracay and Cebu. Negros is a friendly island with some historical sights, a soaring volcano for mountaineers, and wonderful old steam trains that draw rail enthusiasts from all over the world.

The island is made even more fascinating by the intricate web of political and economic forces that sweep across the land. As the undisputed center of the Filipino sugar industry, Negros has been riding a dangerous roller coaster since the late 19th century. While prices were high during the 1960s and '70s, thousands of migrant workers flooded northern Negros to cut the cane and earn a good living. Everybody seemed to prosper: field workers had plenty to eat, a handful of Chinese-mestizo hacienda owners became fabulously wealthy, and Bacolod was known as the city with the nation's highest number of Mercedes limousines.

But the devastating collapse of sugar prices in the early '80s led to social and economic turmoil, widespread poverty, and malnutrition reminiscent of an African famine. It also brought calls for land reform, the rise of militant Catholic priests who openly supported the demands of the communists, and the emergence of private militias organized by wealthy landowners to protect their financial interests. To the intense embarrassment of local officials, Negros became center stage for television crews and foreign politicians who dubbed it the "Ethiopia of the Philippines." The beleaguered island also became a leading prop in the morality play against Ferdinand Marcos.

Today it's a somewhat better scene here in "Sugarlandia." A small rise in domestic sugar prices has helped keep some of the mills open, although Victoria Mills was forced into bankruptcy several years ago and continues to operate under receivership.

Through all this, the Negrenese have kept their enthusiasm for life and acceptance of *bahala na . . .* what will be, will be.

Transportation

Air: PAL flies daily from Manila and Cebu City to Bacolod and Dumaguete.

From Cebu: The easiest way to reach Negros from Cebu City is with the daily fast ferry which zips you across the waters to Dumaguete on the southeastern corner of the island. You can overnight here, look around the next day, and continue by bus around the island to Bacolod.

Another option is the direct a/c bus which departs Cebu City each morning from the central bus terminal and heads directly to Bacolod. Otherwise, take a bus to Toledo City and then a ferry to San Carlos on Negros.

Travelers in Moalboal might take the ferry from San Sebastian to San Jose or Tampi near Dumaguete before continuing around the island.

From Panay Fast ferries leave Iloilo daily for Bacolod.

BACOLOD

Bacolod is a comparatively affluent city with a thriving commercial center, friendly people, and level sidewalks thanks to the 1981 visit of the pope. It's also the site of the famous MassKara Festival, an October Mardi Gras bash that ranks as one of the liveliest events in the Philippines.

Buses from Cebu arrive at the northern bus terminal, from where jeepneys marked Libertad continue to city center. Metered taxis can be hailed at the fast ferry harbor and at the northern bus terminal.

The tourist office is in the town square.

Attractions

Bacolod makes a good base for exploring the nearby sugar mills and national parks. Sights around town are limited to the century-old San Sebastian Cathedral near the park and San Virgen Chapel outside town, known for its collage mural of almost 100,000 shells. The best place to visit is the Negros Museum inside the former provincial capitol where excellent displays relate local history.

Iron Dinosaurs

Perhaps the most intriguing sights on the island of Negros are the antique steam trains which haul sugarcane on the plantations near Bacolod. Originally manufactured in America, Germany, and England shortly after the turn of the century, these extremely rare "Iron Dinosaurs" now attract a steady stream of railway enthusiasts who come to photograph and ride the trains during the cutting season from September to May. Many have been retired but stationmasters can arrange rides whenever the locomotives are in action.

Victoria Mills: The world's largest integrated sugar mill and refinery offers more than just old trains. Just as fascinating is a guided tour

Iron Dinosaurs at Victoria Mills

PHILIPPINES

Map of Bacolod showing streets and landmarks:

L'FISHER HOTEL

PENSION BACOLOD

CERES BUSES

11th ST.

BACOLOD

6th ST.

NEGROS SHIPPING LINE

NORTHERN BUS TERMINAL

NEGROS MUSEUM

McDONALDS

TO WHARF

SAN JUAN ST.

GATUSIAO ST.

LACSON ST.

TO SANTE FE

EL CAMINO RESTAURANT

RECLAMATION AREA

BURGOS ST.

GALO ST.

MANOKAN COUNTRY

LAS ROCAS HOTEL

CEBU PACIFIC AIR

RIZAL ST.

MABINI ST.

HILADO ST.

LOPEZ JAENA ST.

CATHEDRAL

TITA'S PIER 7

TOURIST OFFICE

PLAZA

LOCSIN ST.

BASCON HOTEL

GONZAGA ST.

SEA BREEZE HOTEL

PNB

MARKET

BEST INN

LUZURIAGA ST.

CITY HALL

GPO

HALILI INN

ANG SINGBA RESTAURANT

SAN SEBASTIAN ST.

PALM INN

STAR PLUS PENSION

EQUITABLE BANK

ROSARIO ST.

RIZAL SCHOOL

LIBERTAD ST.

JEEPNEYS TO MAMBUCAL

ESTER PENSION

SEN YENG RESTAURANT

SPORTS COMPLEX

SOUTHERN BUS TERMINAL

CASA NOBLE

ROYAL EXPRESS BUSES

ARANETA ST.

LIZARES ST.

TO MAMBUCAL

ROXAS AVES.

LECHON FOODSTALLS

CHURCH

D&B PENSION

FAMILY PENSION

REGENCY PLAZA TOURIST INN

TO AIRPORT

BACOLOD CONVENTION HOTEL

LUPIT RIVER

MAGSAYSAY AVE.

GOLDENFIELD ENTERTAINMENT COMPLEX

0   50 km

PHILIPPINES

© MOON PUBLICATIONS, INC.

of the mill, a look at the Filipino company town, and the St. Joseph Chapel where an angry, psychedelic Christ glares down on the huddled masses. Victoria's 400 km of track are worked by modern diesels and about a dozen steams, including German Henschels dating from 1924-30, a Baldwin, and a '24 Bagnall imported from the Fanling railhead in Hong Kong. Visitors are welcome to walk down the tracks and inspect the repair yard. Buses from Bacolod reach the main intersection, from where jeepneys continue to the mill compound.

Hawaiian Mills: Midway between Bacolod and Victoria Mills, and two km north of Silay, stands another mill with a handful of old steam engines which operate at sporadic schedules. Apart from a single '29 Henschel, all trains are Baldwins dated 1916-1928.

La Carlotta Mills: Most of the remaining steams from the closed Ma Ao Mill have been transferred to La Carlotta Mills, 50 km south of Bacolod. La Carlotta has 10 Baldwins, a Porter dating from 1912, and two '21 Alcos. Most engines are either dead or in poor condition.

Mambucal and Mt. Kanlaon

Nestled at the base of Mt. Kanlaon is a modest hill resort originally constructed by the Americans as an escape from the lowland heat of Bacolod. Mambucal is somewhat neglected and run-down, though the seven waterfalls, trails through thick forest, and views from the nearby Salesian Lodge are outstanding. The sprawling lodge with rooms from P150-400 overlooks a greenish boat pond.

Mambucal is also the starting point for hikes to 2,465-meter Mt. Kanlaon, seventh highest peak in the Philippines. Guides and porters can be hired from the tourist office in Bacolod or directly in Mambucal. Allow two or three days during the dry hiking season from March to May.

The quickest approach is from Masulog west of Kanlaon City, but for a much more scenic travel experience take the longer trail from Mambucal. This well-marked route leads to a nature center and campsite in Margaha Valley, from where you approach the summit the following morning. Kanlaon is capped by two craters, a dormant cone sometimes used as a protected campsite and an active crater hissing with noisome sulfuric vents.

The volcano last erupted in 1996, killing two Filipinos and a British national who served as a volunteer at the Coral Cay conservation project.

Accommodations

Bacolod has plenty of hotels, but the inexpensive pensions are some of the grungiest lodgings in the country.

Ester Pension: Convenient location a few blocks south of city center. Araneta St., tel. (034) 432-3526, P150-300.

Star Plus Pension House: Small, fairly new place with both fan-cooled and a/c rooms three blocks south of the town plaza. Lacson St., tel. (034) 433-2948, P200-400.

Family Pension: Budget spot with minimalistic, rough rooms a few blocks south of town. 123 Lascon St., tel. (034) 438-1211, P150-300.

Regency Plaza Tourist Inn: Good mid-priced hotel in the south of town near Family Pension. Lacson St., tel. (034) 433-1458, P550-700.

Bacolod Pension Plaza: Another new mid-priced option just east of the town plaza. Cuadra St., tel. (034) 433-2203, P600-800.

Sea Breeze Hotel: An old but well-located hotel overlooking the failed reclamation area. San Juna St., tel. (034) 432-4571, P700-950.

DUMAGUETE CITY

The provincial capital of Negros Oriental is a small town almost completely dominated by Silliman University, a Protestant school founded 1901 in a peculiar design somewhat reminiscent of 19th-century southern U.S. architecture. Today it has over 20,000 students and dozens of American professors.

Attractions

Top draw is the Silliman Anthropological Museum for artifacts, ethnic weavings, and sorcery instruments from Siquijor Island. Also of interest is a walk along the waterfront and the old Spanish watchtower on Al Fonseo Street across from the central park.

Outside town there's mediocre beaches to the north and much better beaches heading south. Dumaguete also serves as the jumping-off point to outstanding dive sites near Siquijor, Apo Island, and Sumilon Island in southern Cebu.

PHILIPPINES

Accommodations

Jo's Lodging: Bare-bones but acceptable student crash pad just south of the university. Silliman Ave., tel. (035) 225-4412, P100-220.

Opena's Hotel: Clean and quiet hotel one block north of city center in the heart of the university district. Katada St., tel. (035) 225-0595, P150-500.

O.K. Pensionne House: Modern pension with decent rooms in a quiet neighborhood a few blocks south of city center. Santa Rosa St., tel. (035) 225-5925, P275-650.

Al Mar Hotel: Older hotel right on the beach with spacious if somewhat funky rooms. Rizal Blvd., tel. (035) 225-2567, P240-600.

Bethel Guesthouse: Big, modern, and immaculately clean hotel right on the beach with spotless cafe on the ground floor; best choice in town. Rizal Blvd., tel. (035) 225-2000, P450-900.

Kookoo's Nest Beach Resort: Several relaxing beach resorts are some 40 km south of Dumaguete, including this attractive operation with seven cottages, sunset views, two-km offshore reef, and dive shop. Take a bus south to Zamboangita then hire a motorcycle taxi. Tambulo Bay, US$4-20.

SIQUIJOR ISLAND

Twenty km offshore from the southeast tip of Negros lies Siquijor, the smallest province in the Philippines. Filipinos associate the island with images of voodoo and bizarre rituals, but there are also some sandy beaches, good snorkeling, and an undeveloped rural environment. Dive companies stop here since the island is blessed with coral reefs largely undamaged by dynamite fishing.

Larena is the main port and Siquijor town is the provincial capital, but most visitors head directly to the fine beaches at Sandugan, six km northeast of Larena, or Paliton, at the westernmost tip of the island.

Transportation

Fast ferries connect Siquijor with Dumaguete twice daily and once daily from Cebu City. There's also twice weekly fast ferries from Plaridel on Mindanao.

Accommodations

Larena: A sleepy little port town where you stay at the Larena Pension House or Luisa and Son's Lodge for P100-250.

Siquijor: Several resorts are within a few km of the provincial capital such as Beach Garden Hotel in Catalinan (one km west of town), Dondeezco Beach Resort in Dumanhug (two km west), and Tikarol Beach Resort in Candanay (three km east). All charge P250-500 for decent bungalows facing a white sand beach.

Sandugan Beach: Six km northeast of Larena is a long, peaceful beach with decent sand, excellent diving, and almost a dozen resorts priced P300-600 such as Islander's Paradise Beach, Kiwi Dive Resort, Casa del Playa Beach Resort, and Hidden Paradise.

Paliton Beach: Not far from San Jose is another fine beach with a few simple bungalows such as Sunset Beach Resort and Paliton Beach Resort. Both have rooms from P200-350. Two km south of San Juan in Tubod you'll find the San Juan Coco Grove Beach Resort with swimming pool, restaurant, jeepney rentals, and a/c rooms with "private marble bath" from P650-1,200.

PALAWAN

Situated not far off the northwest tip of Borneo, Palawan is an isolated and mountainous island covered with tropical rainforests inhabited by primitive tribes and some of the last remaining wildlife in the Philippines.

Although many places of interest exist on the main island, the star attraction is undoubtedly El Nido on the northeast coast. Here, cataclysmic geological upheavals have left Bacuit Bay studded with a remarkable collection of limestone pinnacles and dazzling white beaches—scuba diving here is considered about the best in Southeast Asia.

Other natural attractions include the Underground River, Tabon Caves, and pristine beaches at Sabang and Port Barton (northwestern coast), near Roxas and Taytay (northeastern coast), and south of Puerto Princesa.

PHILIPPINES

While Palawan has its drawbacks—such as terrible roads and limited accommodations—these are more than compensated for by the unspoiled beauty of the land and sea.

Scuba Diving

The vast potential of scuba diving in the Philippines is best at the coral beds and offshore islands around Palawan. It is said that the underwater shelf surrounding the island contains almost 60% of the archipelago's coral reefs.

Most divers head directly for El Nido, where dive shops can arrange equipment rentals, dive boats, and certification courses at very reasonable prices. Dives can also be arranged in Puerto Princesa with several dive shops and at the northern islands such as Busuanga and Cuyo.

Transportation

Air: PAL, Air Philippines, and Grand Air fly daily from Manila to Puerto Princesa. Pacific Airways and Air Ads fly daily from Manila to Busuanga. Soriano Aviation flies daily from Manila to a small airstrip near El Nido. Pacific Airways flies three times weekly from Manila to Cuyo Island. PAL flies twice weekly from Cebu City and Iloilo to Puerto Princesa.

Ship: WG&A and Sulpicio sail once weekly from Manila to Puerto Princesa, a 24-hour journey which costs P450-750 depending on the class.

Milagrosa sails once weekly from Iloilo to Puerto Princesa. The passage takes in about 40 islands and includes a stop at Cuyo Island.

Getting Around

Transportation on Palawan is quite good heading south from Puerto Princesa, but rough going north since the all-weather road from Puerto Princesa to El Nido remains on the drawing boards. At present, it's a fairly easy bus or jeepney ride to Sabang and Port Barton on the west coast, where many travelers continue by public or chartered boat up to El Nido. This is probably the best way to reach El Nido.

From Sabang or Port Barton, you can also return to Roxas and continue north to Taytay and onward to El Nido with a combination of bus, jeepney, and possibly the boat from Liminongcong

Buses and jeepneys from Puerto Princesa to Taytay takes eight or nine hours along a very rough and dusty road. From Taytay, you can catch a jeepney in the very early morning for the extremely dangerous ride over mountain ridges to El Nido—not a journey for the faint of heart.

An alternative route from Taytay to El Nido is to take the boat from a dock west of Taytay to the surprisingly prosperous town of Liminongcong (superb scenery) and continue to El Nido with a final boat.

Bus journey times from Puerto Princesa heading north are to Roxas (four hours), Sabang (five hours), Port Barton (six hours), Taytay (nine hours), and El Nido (12-18 hours).

Boat Excursions

The sheer number of islands and rudimentary state of land transportation makes boat travel around Palawan an appealing way to explore the island. It's also the perfect way to enjoy scuba diving around northern Palawan and Tubbataha reef.

A typical 10-day excursion from Puerto Princesa heads north to Coco Loco Island, Elephant Island, and Flowers Island before circling around northern Palawan and continuing south to El Nido, Sabang, and the Underground River. Boat operators are also talking about treks into rainforest jungle north of Taytay and spending a few nights sleeping on deserted beaches near Busuanga.

The same boat might also do exclusive dive tours to El Nido, Busuanga, and Tubbataha reef.

Queen Anne Divers and *Moonshadow,* two Swiss-managed boats, offer these northern Palawan tours and dive excursions each year from December to April. The northern Palawan tours designed for non-divers (or occasional divers) costs US$50 per day and includes boat trip, onboard accommodations, all meals, and transfers. Dives are not included on "tours" but cost an additional US$15 per dive.

Dive trips with equipment and two daily dives cost US$500-650 (five days), US$700-900 (seven days), US$1,100 (nine days), and US$1,350 (15 days). You can contact both *Queen Anne Divers* and *Moonshadow* at Trattoria Inn, 353 Rizal Ave., Puerto Princesa, e-mail: trattori@pal-onl.com.

The success of *Queen Anne Divers* and *Moonshadow* has not gone unnoticed on Palawan and other resorts and travel agencies are now getting into the same business. First off the block is Coco Loco Resort in conjunction with their travel agency in Puerto Princesa. Their 5-10 day tours from Coco Loco Resort near Roxas to Sabang and El Nido are on their 25-meter trimaran *(banca)*, the MBC *Serena*. These tours are designed for non-divers and include fishing, snokeling, beach barbecues, and camping on deserted beaches. You can contact them at Palawan Tourist Travel & Tours, Rizal Ave., Puerto Princesa, e-mail: cocoloco@pal-onl.com.

Another option is Discovery Cruises, an upscale cruise around the islands of northern Palawan at US$250-300 per night. More information from their office in the Shangri-La Hotel on Ayala Avenue in Manila.

PUERTO PRINCESA

Puerto Princesa, a large town set along magnificent Honda Bay, will probably be your first stop in Palawan. The town lacks charm but it's a good place to obtain current travel information and take care of housekeeping chores (exchanging money, etc.) before heading off into the wilds of Palawan.

Services

The city tourist office is at the airport, while the provincial tourist office is in the capitol building on Rizal Avenue.

Money: Traveler's checks and cash can be exchanged at the Philippine National Bank and at several money changers on Rizal Avenue. *Warning:* Exchange facilities elsewhere in Palawan are extremely limited and it's a wise idea to change plenty of money in Puerto Princesa. Otherwise, you might go broke in some deserted hamlet or find yourself at the mercy of merciless money changers.

Telephone: International phone calls are best made at the BayanTel office on Rizal Avenue.

Attractions

Sights around town are limited to the colorful market and a twin-spired cathedral. Tribal handicrafts can be purchased at Macawili Ethnic Shop near the market and at Karla's on Rizal Avenue.

Iwahig Penal Colony: Twenty-three km south of town is a prison without bars where some 4,000 inmates farm, fish, and earn pocket money selling handicrafts to visitors. Within the 37,000-hectare settlement are several rivers with swimming pools, sulfur springs, and a butterfly habitat.

Honda Bay: Outstanding diving in shallow waters can be enjoyed in the bay and among the islands 10 km north of Puerto Princesa, near the gateway town of Tagburos. Take a jeepney from the market toward Lourdes Harbor, alight at the Caltex tank, and walk toward the water. Day tours are organized by several travel agencies in Puerto Princesa.

Places to stay include Yayen's Bungalows, Starfish Sandbar Resort, and Meara Marina Island Resort where bungalows cost P500-800.

Accommodations

Over 20 guesthouses and hotels are located in Puerto Princesa.

Duchess Pension: Popular spot but a bit of a hike from the center of town. 107 Valencia St., tel. (048) 433-2873, P100-250.

Abelardo's Pension: A cozy homestay owned and operated by the very friendly Remedio "Nene" Dizon. 63 Manga St., tel. (048) 433-2049, P150-500.

Puerto Pension: Perhaps the most popular budget place in town with small but comfortable rooms made from natural materials rather than concrete. 35 Malvar St., tel. (048) 433-2969, P175-550.

Trattoria Inn: The best place in town with spotlessly clean rooms, friendly mangers, cozy bar, and wildly popular restaurant in the back. 353 Rizal Ave., tel. (048) 433-2719, e-mail: trattori@pal-onl.com.

Transportation

Buses heading north to Sabang, Port Barton, Roxas, Taytay, and El Nido leave from the Puerto Royal Bus terminal on Malvar Street one block west of the market. This must be the filthiest bus halt in the Philippines and the buses aren't much better. You're better off waiting for a departing bus rather than jumping on the first big jeepney that lumbers out of this godforsaken terminal.

Buses south leave from the equally disorganized bus terminal on Malvar Street near the Shell station, a few blocks east of the market.

Jeepney and bus trips to Sabang are organized by many of the guesthouses and travel agencies on Rizal Avenue.

SOUTHERN PALAWAN

Most travelers head north for El Nido although a fair number of excellent beaches and tropical islands are also found in the south.

Tabon Caves

Southern Palawan's most important draw is the Tabon Caves, where fossilized remains of neolithic man were discovered in the early 1960s. Tabon is reached from Quezon, a five-hour bus ride from Puerto Princesa. Guides can be hired from the national museum in Quezon, though the caves will probably only interest visitors with a serious interest in anthropology.

More alluring are the islands and beaches. The most accessible beach is the Tabon Village Resort on Tabon Beach, five km north of town, where attractive cottages cost P200. Also of interest are the offshore islands of Tamlagun and Palm, where a pair of Westerners have set some *nipa* huts.

SABANG

The Underground River

The submerged river in Saint Paul's National Park is among the longest underground rivers in the world; boats can navigate almost half of its eight-km length. The Underground River can also be approached from Port Barton with outriggers for about P800. The tourist office has information, or ask other travelers in Puerto Princesa. Stay at St. Paul National Park for P50-80.

PORT BARTON

A fairly good beach and outstanding snorkeling at Port Barton have deservedly made it one of the more popular destinations on Palawan. Hikers can wander the lovely beaches to the south and trek to the inland waterfall to the north. Outriggers can be chartered to snorkel the coral beds surrounding Albagin and Exotica islands,

while larger boats can be hired to the Underground Caves and up to El Nido at fixed rates maintained by a local trade union.

San Vicente, 20 km north of Port Barton, has another great beach just across the peninsula.

Accommodations

Port Barton has over a half-dozen modest resorts which charge P60-100 for basic *nipa* huts and P150-250 for better bungalows with private baths.

Port Barton: Beachside choices include Elsa's Beach House, El Bosero Inn, Paradiso Beach Resort, Shangri La Beach Resort, and Swissipilli Cottages.

Capsalay Island: Slightly north of Port Barton is a dazzling island with a set of cottages called Manta Ray Resort. Managed by Paola Sani and Tizianna, Manta Ray offers great vibes and some of the best Italian cuisine east of Venice. Contact Manta Ray Resort at 66 Valencia St., Puerto Princesa, tel. 2609, US$60-75.

ROXAS

Roxas is a small fishing village fronted by several offshore islands.

Accommodations

Roxas: Bungalows in town include Gordon's, Gemalain's Inn operated by Mr. Rodriguez, and Rover's Luncheonette, which, sensibly enough, doubles as a cafe. Rooms here cost P50-80.

Pandan Island: Coco Loco Island Resort is an Italian-operated resort with sailboats, snorkeling, diving, sailboards, and 30 cottages priced at P150-220.

TAYTAY

Taytay is a very picturesque town at the northern end of the road from Puerto Princesa. Although a track continues north to El Nido, this is the last town of any size where you can stock up on basic supplies. Taytay has an outlet of the Palawan Bank, a post office, two pharmacies, a BayanTel office across from the school, and an old Spanish fort worth a quick wander.

Accommodations

Pem's Pension House near the 300-year-old Church of Santa Monica has huts and bungalows from P100-650. You might find better value at Rainbow Country Lodging two blocks east or Publico's International Guesthouse a bit farther, where decent rooms cost P100-250.

Island Resorts

Two very distinct resorts are situated in scenic Taytay Bay. Club Noah Isabelle is a stunning place with cabañas elevated over a lagoon; it's priced from US$175-250.

Farther out into the bay is Flowers Island Resort—a tropical wonderland constructed by a Frenchman and his Filipino wife. Rooms with three meals daily cost P1,200-1,500; obtain more information from Pem's Pension in Taytay.

Liminangcong

Liminangcong is a surprisingly properous fishing town on the west coast of Palawan midway between Taytay and El Nido. Travelers passing through this town on their way to El Nido may find themselves stranded if the weather turns foul and boatmen refuse to complete the hazardous crossing. A road now connects Liminangcong with Taytay but most traffic continues to move by water.

Accommodations in town include Puerto Paraiso Inn and Ann's Lodging House at the south end of town where rooms cost P100-150. Kaver's Inn in the center of town has small but clean rooms from P250-500.

Transportation

Taytay is 215 km north of Puerto Princesa and can be reached in 9 or 10 grueling hours by bus or jeepney departing from the bus terminal on Malvar Street. One or two jeepneys depart daily in the early morning hours and take three or four hours to El Nido.

Visitors heading to Club Noah Isabella generally fly from Manila to Sandoval Airport in the north end of Taytay Bay.

Six km west of Taytay is Agpay boat station (sometimes called Embarcadero), where large outriggers leave several times daily for Liminangcong, en route to El Nido. Direct boat service from Agpay to El Nido is provided during the high season from December to April.

EL NIDO

Talcum-powder beaches fringed with coconut palms, vast coral reefs teeming with an astonishing variety of fish, and spectacular limestone mountains soaring vertically from clear turquoise waters have made El Nido one of the most visually stunning destinations in the Philippines. The area's extremely remote location makes it both expensive and time-consuming to reach, a double-edged sword that also helps preserve the fragile environment.

Highlights include the beaches on Inabuyatan Island and coral reefs surrounding Tapituan and Matinloc islands. Dives and certification programs can be arranged with Willie and Nora at Bacuit Dive Shop. El Nido is a place where days turn to weeks and weeks into months.

Accommodations in Town

El Nido, the picturesque village nestled at the base of sheer limestone cliffs, serves as the main backpackers' center and launching point for dive trips throughout the Bacuit Archipelago. Accommodations are available at almost a dozen homestays. Note that El Nido lacks a bank, so bring plenty of pesos or greenback dollars.

Austria Guesthouse: Prospero Austria opened his lovely homestay in 1985 when backpackers began drifting into the region and has since maintained one of the most popular spots in northern Palawan. The homestay is about 100 meters from the wharf. Rooms cost P40-80.

Other Homestays: Mr. Ellis Lim in the green house near the water tower has rooms in the same price range, as does Manuel and Susan Jenato's across from the dive shop and Judge Paloma's next to the jetty.

Slightly more expensive are the newer guesthouses such as Lally Beach Cottage and Bay View Inn, where rooms with private baths cost P60-120.

Island Accommodations

Resorts within Bacuit Bay tend to be elegant but very expensive because of higher construction costs and supply problems with water and energy. As of this writing only two islands have been developed, though permits have been granted for another half-dozen island resorts near El Nido.

PHILIPPINES

Pangalusian Island Resort: Some 15 km southwest of El Nido lies a dazzling island where a Scotsman named Jack Gordon has opened a small resort and cafe with dive facilities. A cottage with full board costs US$45-60 per day.

El Nido Resort: One of the most exclusive resorts in the country and among Asia's most stunning natural destinations is this exclusive hideaway on Miniloc Island, 10 km southwest of El Nido. Contact Hotel Nikko, Edsa Highway, Manila, tel. 818-2623, fax 818-4127, US$180-300.

Transportation

El Nido is in northwestern Palawan, some 180 km from Puerto Princesa and 320 km southwest of Manila. The poor condition of the roads makes it necessary to either fly or take a boat for a portion of the journey.

Air: Ten Knots Air (tel. 812-0671) flies daily from Manila to El Nido for US$180 roundtrip.

PAL flies daily to Puerto Princesa, from where Pacific Air Charter (Manila tel. 832-2731) operates commuter flights to El Nido, Coron, and Roxas. Aerolift flies four times weekly from Manila to Puerto Princesa.

Ship: Several shipping lines serve various destinations on Palawan from Manila and the Visayas. Palawan Shipping Line sails twice monthly from Manila via Panay, Sulpicio sails weekly from Manila, while Ascuncion Shipping has three ships to Palawan with intriguing stops in the northern islands of Cuyo, Culion, and Lubang.

Land: Several Puerto Royale buses depart the Puerto Princesa market daily from 0500 to 0700 and reach Roxas about five hours later. Jeepneys continue from Roxas north to Tabuan, from where outriggers sail up to El Nido via Liminangcong. Boatmen charge about P1,000 for a 10-man outrigger; P100 per person. It's a spectacular journey.

PANAY

This triangular-shaped island is justifiably famous for its fine old Spanish churches, the resort island of Boracay, and highly charged Mardi Gras festivals held in January. Celebrating the original pact made between Muslim *datus* from Borneo and Panay Negritos, the festivals take place in all four provincial capitals. Kalibo's Ati Atihan is the most renowned and impressive, but the festivals at Dinagyang in Iloilo, Harlaran in Roxas, and Binirayan in San Jose de Buenavista are just as lively and much less commercialized—like attending Carnival in Bahia rather than Rio.

Panay is also known for its friendly people, the Ilonggos, who welcome visitors with *hapit anay* (come in) and speak a languorous and seductive dialect which rises sharply at the end to make statements sound like questions.

Transportation

By Air: PAL, Air Philippines, or other smaller airlines fly daily from Manila to Kalibo, Roxas City, and Iloilo City, plus there are connections from Puerto Princesa, Cebu City, and other Visayan towns.

The most popular connection is to Kalibo, from where buses and *bancas* reach Boracay in about three hours. If Manila-Kalibo is fully

booked, fly to Roxas and continue by bus. Return tickets should be booked well in advance and reconfirmed upon arrival in Kalibo.

By Ship: Fast ferries connect Bacolod on Negros with Iloilo several times daily. Larger ships from Manila go to Iloilo and New Washington, a small port on the northern coast of Panay. Also, a weekly ship sails from Palawan to Iloilo.

Connections are also possible between Boracay and Mindoro. See Boracay and Mindoro for more information on this approach to Boracay.

Getting Around

Ceres Liner operates a comfortable fleet of buses on Panay. Buses from Iloilo to Roxas take about four hours, plus another two to Kalibo. Ceres buses depart Iloilo mornings 0700-1200 direct to Boracay. You can also take faster minibuses to Kalibo and Boracay from the minibus halt just south of the bus terminal in Iloilo. With an early start you'll be on the beach by late afternoon.

ILOILO

Iloilo, one of the more attractive towns in the Visayas, makes a good base for exploring the

PHILIPPINES

nearby churches, beaches, and islands. The curious name was given to the original settlement by Spanish conquistadors as an abbreviation for the original name of Ilong Ilong.

Attractions
The tourist office is in a massive new building at the far end of Bonifacio Drive just past the museum and very near the river.

Iloilo Museum: Panay's rich heritage is best seen in the Museo de Iloilo on Bonifacio Street. The small but worthwhile collection ranges from anthropological artifacts and jewelry excavated from pre-Spanish burial sites to British knockoffs, WW II memorabilia, and some outstanding *santos,* including a magnificent reclining Jesus.

Around Town: Downtown Iloilo is an odd mixture of ungainly shophouses covered with grit and attractive wooden architecture dating from the 1920s and '30s; Iloilo was apparently once a very prosperous town. Native coffee and local weavings are sold in the colorful central market.

Attractions near Iloilo
Jaro: The suburbs of Iloilo are rich with historic Spanish architecture and romantic Antillean houses. Jaro, an elite residential center three km south of Iloilo, is known for its Gothic-style cathedral and hand-embroidered *pina* and *jusi* fabrics. Streets fanning from the plaza are lined with the mansions of wealthy sugar barons and Hispano-Filipino elite.

Molo: Even more impressive is the outstanding church in Molo, a wealthy Chinese quarter three km west of Iloilo. Constructed in the 1870s of coral rock, the twin towers and Gothic Renaissance exterior now form a striking Panay landmark. Antiques are sold at several stores and private homes.

Guimaras Island: The large island south of Iloilo offers beaches, caves, waterfalls, springs, villages, and intriguing spiritual encounters. Ferries to Jordan depart hourly from the post office. Climb Holy Mountain for good views and then continue by jeepney to the Bayani Resort near Buenavista for a narrow sandy beach, a pool, hiking, and *nipa* cottages with views of Iloilo from P900. Other possible stays include the private island of Isla Naburot, owned by Alice Saldana, and a German-owned beach resort on

Nagarao Island near San Isidro. The tourist office has more information.

Miagao: Forty km west of Iloilo stands a unique fortress-church which ranks as one of the most impressive works of architecture in the Philippines. Originally completed in 1797, the massive honey-colored sandstone monument has been repeatedly restored following damage by revolution, fire, and earthquake. Note the dissimilar towers—the first priest-foreman died before his work was completed. The superbly carved facade is a wild impressionistic collage of St. Christopher with Jesus and tropical botanical motifs: palms, papaya trees, scalloped arches, and fruiting guava trees. Reminds you of Gaudi's animistic cathedral in Barcelona or St. Paul's in Macau.

Accommodations
Most of the better pensions and hotels are a few blocks north of city center.

Family Pension House: A clean place but with small, dark rooms and a treehouse cafe for

PHILIPPINES

ILOILO

BOATS TO BUENAVISTA

TRANS ASIA

BOATS TO JORDAN

FT. SAN PEDRO DR.

FORT SAN PEDRO

DURAN ST.

SULPICIO

DE LA RAMA ST.

ZAMORA ST.

GENERAL HUGHES ST.

NEGROS LINES

WG&A

FAST FERRIES TO BACOLOD

SAN JOSE CHURCH

PLAZA

PNB

QUIRINO-LOPEZ ST.

BOATS TO GUIMARAS ISLAND

RIZAL ST.

RIVER

ILOILO

GPO

SHAKEYS

BASA ST.

UNIVERSITY OF ILOILO

ILOILO STRAIT

CAPITOL

MUSEUM

TOURIST OFFICE

YMCA

IZNART ST.

CENTERCON HOTEL

BAYAN TEL

CENTRAL MARKET

THE CASTLE

SUPERMARKET

AMIGO TERRACE HOTEL

NEGROS SHIPS

TO JARO

RIVER QUEEN HOTEL

PNB

SHOEMART

CINEMA

VALERIA ST.

CHINESE TEMPLE

EROS PENSION

TAVERN PUB

CAESAR DISCO

QUEZON ST.

FAMILY PENSION

EQUITABLE BANK

AIR PHILIPPINES

DE LEON ST.

PENSION DEL CARMEN AND MANFRED'S INN

MABINI ST.

MARKET

UNIVERSITY OF ST. AGUSTINE

FUENTES ST.

GENERAL LUNA ST.

JALANDON ST.

LEDESMA ST.

MINIBUSES

BUSES TO KALIBO

DELGADO ST.

RIZAL ST.

SARABIA MANOR HOTEL

HIGHWAY 10 RESTAURANT

3rd SPOT RESTAURANT

WEST AVE.

HOSPITAL

TO AIRPORT AND JARO

OCEAN CITY RESTAURANT

HOTEL DEL RIO

TO MOLO AND CERES BUS TERMINAL

0   250 m

PHILIPPINES

© MOON PUBLICATIONS, INC.

breakfast and nighttime entertainment. General Luna St., tel. (033) 270070, P180-700.

Hotel Centercon: Tucked away in a strange alley is this old hotel with acceptable if somewhat worn rooms. Basa St., tel. (033) 73431, P150-520.

River Queen Hotel: The hotel near the museum looks touristy, but rooms are large and fairly clean plus there's a great patio for dining near the river. Bonifacio Dr., tel. (033) 76667, P240-550.

Iloilo Midtown Hotel: Good, new mid-range hotel just off the main drag in the center of town. 888 Yulo St., tel. (033) 336-8888, P800-1,200.

Amigo Terrace Hotel: Iloilo's top-end choice has recently renovated rooms, swimming pool, and cozy cafe. Iznart St., tel. (033) 335-0908, P1,200-2,400.

Transportation

Fast ferries from Bacolod (Bullet Express and Sea Angels) dock a few blocks from city center. You can walk to most hotels or flag down a taxi or jeepney on the main road.

Buses to Roxas, Kalibo, and Caticlan leave from the intersection of Mabini and Ledesma streets. Luxury Ceres buses leave from two blocks south on Rizal Avenue.

Ferries to Guimaras Island leave from several different locations along the wharf. A primitive boat leaves for Palawan via Cuyo Island twice weekly on Monday and Thursday. Ships to Manila leave from the main wharf near Fort San Pedro.

KALIBO

Most visitors come for the annual Ati Atihan festival—Kalibo is otherwise just another transit town. Buses connect the Kalibo airport with Boracay. Be sure to reconfirm your return flight before leaving the airport.

Accommodations

Gervy's Lodge: Simple but acceptable place in the center of town, one block east of Pastrana Park. Pastrana St., tel. (036) 662-1166, P100-200.

Garcia Legaspi Mansion: Clean mid-level hotel on the main road to Boracay. Roxas Ave., tel. (036) 662-3251, P350-950.

Hibiscus Hotel: Best in town with small pool, cafe, and landscape gardens some 15 minutes east of city center. 5600 Andagao St., tel. (036) 268-4093, P900-1,400.

SAMAR

The second largest island in the Visayas mainly serves as a stepping-stone between Luzon and Leyte. Its outstanding attraction, Sohoton National Park, is most easily reached from Tacloban on Leyte.

Transportation

Ferries cross at least twice a day between Matnog and Allen. The most convenient connection is on direct Philtranco buses from Legaspi to Catbalogan and Tacloban. As these buses are often filled with passengers coming down from Manila, independent travelers should get an early start to connect with the ferry from Matnog. It's a spectacular ride through vast coconut plantations along the coast from Allen to Catbalogan.

Travel time from Allen to Tacloban is seven hours with direct Philtranco bus.

CATBALOGAN

Another sleepy little town with little of interest except for transportation connections and as an overnight stop between southern Luzon and Leyte.

Accommodations

Fortune Hotel: Decent place in the north end of town near the Landmark Bank. Del Rosario St., tel. (055) 72344, P120-500.

Catbalogan Travelers Lodge: Simple, friendly new spot two blocks back from the main road. Rizal St., no phone, P80-250.

Kikay's Hotel: Rough, but decent alternative to other budget hotels in town. San Bartolome St., tel. (055) 71188, P120-250.

PHILIPPINES

Transportation

Buses from Allen take about four hours to Catbalogan, which means you'll probably need to spend the night in this one-horse town. Several small bus halts are scattered around town including the Philtranco terminal on San Bartolome Street in the north of town, Eagle Star buses on San Roque Street three blocks back from Del Rosario Street, and a small bus terminal at the corner of Allen and San Francisco Streets.

> *Journeys, like artists, are born and not made.*
> *A thousand differing circumstances contribute to them,*
> *few of them willed or determined by the will—*
> *whatever we may think.*
>
> —LAWRENCE DURRELL,
> *BITTER LEMONS*

> *Traveling is not just seeing the new;*
> *it is also leaving behind.*
> *Not just opening doors;*
> *also closing them behind you, never to return.*
> *But the place you have left forever,*
> *is always there for you to see whenever you shut your eye.*
> *And the cities you see most clearly at night,*
> *are the cities you have left,*
> *and will never see again.*
>
> —JAN MYRDAL,
> *THE SILK ROAD*

> *I sought trains; I found passengers.*
>
> —PAUL THEROUX,
> *THE GREAT RAILWAY BAZAAR*

SINGAPORE

Every trip we take deposits us at the same forking of the paths: it can be a shortcut to alienation— removed from our home and distanced from our immediate surroundings, we can afford to be contemptuous of both; or it can be a voyage into renewal, as, leaving our selves and posts at home, and traveling light, we recover our innocence abroad.

—PICO IYER,
VIDEO NIGHT IN KATHMANDU

The first condition of right thought is right sensation— the first condition of understanding a foreign country is to smell it . . . .

—T.S. ELIOT

Life is short; live it up.

—NIKITA KRUSHCHEV

INTRODUCTION

The Malay Chronicles relate that the Prince of Palembang, who claimed direct descent from Alexandar the Great, landed at this Srivijayan trading post in the 13th century and encountered a strange animal, "very swift and beautiful, body bright red, head jet black, breast of white, and larger than a he-goat." Although it was most likely a wild tiger, the Prince called it a lion, and Temasek the "Sea Town" became Singa Pura the "Lion City." Another story explains that this Sanskrit name actually derives from a sect of Bhairava Buddhism dominant at the 14th-century Majapahit courts whose Javanese priests adopted the lion motif as their religious symbol. Other 14th-century towns such as Singosari in East Java and Singaraja on North Bali used the term and it's possible that Singapore was the third of Southeast Asia's Lion Cities.

From its humble beginnings as a distended backwater of pirates and traders, this Chinese city-state of almost three million inhabitants has grown into one of the great success stories of Southeast Asia. Blessed with few natural resources except for its strategic location and a hard-working population, this futuristic metropolis enjoys the highest standard of living in Asia after Japan. With few slums, minimal unemployment, and little crime, Singapore excels as a post-industrial urban miracle that graciously lacks such exotica as colorful slums, the mañana syndrome, 10-year-old shoeshine boys, and rampant bribery . . . all the romantic anachronisms that make Southeast Asia so fascinating to visit but so hellish to inhabit.

It is also quite possibly the most downright beautiful modern metropolis in the world. While many Asian cities are ugly, chaotic nightmares of faceless ferroconcrete boxes and hopeless traffic jams, Singapore is so clean and green that it richly deserves its self-proclaimed title of Garden City. Although the soaring skyscrapers and air-conditioned shopping centers bear little resemblance to the romantic port of Conrad or Kipling—and some visitors are disappointed with the concrete canyons and Instant Asia mentality—those who prefer safety and cleanliness with a touch of the Orient will find Singapore a refreshing change from the hardships of other Southeast Asian countries.

SINGAPORE

MALAYSIA

Johor Bahru

Straits

JOHOR
CAUSEWAY

ADMIRALTY RD.

Sembawang

Woodlands

Sarimbun
Reservoir

Kranji
Reservoir

SELETAR

SINGAPORE ZOO
& NIGHT SAFARI

Sunge
Seletar
Reservoir

Murai
Reservoir

BUKIT

Seletar
Reservoir

SEMBAWANG RD.

YISHUN AVE

EXPY

WOODLANDS

Johor

Straits

EXPY

TIMAH

Poyan
Reservoir

KRANJI

Peirce
Reservoir

LIM CHU KANG RD.

PAN-ISLAND

EXPY

Tengah
Reservoir

PAN-ISLAND

Bukit
Timah

RD.

MacRitchie
Reservoir

EXPY

PAN-ISLAND

ASIA PACIFIC
BREWERIES

JALAN

AHMAD

Jurong

IBRAHIM

BUKIT

EXPY

Holland
Village

TIMAH

BOTANIC
GARDENS

RD.

Tuas

JURONG
BIRD PARK

PIONEER
RD.

ORCHARD

RD.

AYER

WEST

COAST

RAJAH

EXPY

TRAIN
STATION

Pulau
Merlimou

Pulau
Sraya

HWY

Mt. Faber

WORLD TRADE
CENTRE

Krepel Harbor

CABLE
CAR

Pulau
Ayer Chawan

Pulau
Sakra

Pulau
Ayer Meribau

Sebarok

Sentosa
Island

Pulau Buran
Darat

St. John's
Island

Pulau
Ular

Pulau
Busing

Channel

Sisters
Island

Pulau
Hantu

Pulau
Bukum

Pulau
Sudong

Pulau
Sebarok

Pulau
Semakau

Pulau
Sakeng

Pulau
Pawai

Pulau
Senang

To Batam & Bintan

SINGAPORE

© MOON PUBLICATIONS, INC.

To Desaru

MALAYSIA

★ MASAI

MALAYSIA

Pulau
Seletar

PASIR
GUDANG

Johor

Punggol
Point

SELETAR
AIRPORT

Pulau
Serangoon

Pulau
Ubin

Pulau
Tekong
Kechil

Pulau
Tekong

Punggol

Pulau
Katam

Serangoon

TAMPINES

Pasir
Ris

Changi

EXPY.

Kelong
Loyang

CHANGI FERRY
TERMINAL

UPPER SERANGOON

Tampines

CHANGI
INTERNATIONAL
AIRPORT

CENTRAL

Bedok
Reservoir

EXPY.

RD.

PAN-ISLAND

Bedok

EXPY.

RD.

CHANGI COAST RD.

CHANGI

RD.

EAST COAST RD.

TANAH MERAH
FERRY TERMINAL

PKWY.

Geylang

COAST

MOUNTBATTEN
RD.

Katong

EAST

SINGAPORE ISLAND

Pulau
Renggit

Straits   of   Singapore

Kusu
Island

Lazarus
Island

0   4 mi

0   4 km

To Batam & Bintan

SINGAPORE

SINGAPORE'S CLIMATE

	JAN.	FEB.	MAR.	APR.	MAY	JUNE	JULY	AUG.	SEPT.	OCT.	NOV.	DEC.
Avg. Maximum C	30°	31°	31°	31°	32°	31°	31°	31°	31°	31°	31°	31°
Avg. Maximum F	86°	88°	88°	88°	90°	88°	88°	88°	88°	88°	88°	88°
Rainy Days	17	11	14	15	15	13	13	14	14	16	18	19

THE LAND

Singapore is a diamond-shaped island of 618 square km just across the causeway from Malaysia and one degree north of the equator. To the south is Java and to the west Sumatra, perhaps visible on a clear day. The main island and some 54 smaller islets have an undramatic topography with two-thirds of the land lying less than 15 meters above sea level. The highest elevations are nothing more than foothills. Although Singapore has no important mineral or oil deposits and the soil is of poor quality, its deepwater anchorage and natural harbor on the Straits of Malacca have helped make it the region's leading shipping and commercial center.

Singapore is also a predominately urbanized country with little remaining wildlife or untended flora. Most of the tropical foliage that once covered the island has been completely cleared, although about 5% of the land remains forested and carefully preserved in the Bukit Timah Nature Reserve. You won't find untamed jungles or wild tigers, but you will find some of Asia's finest flora and fauna in its amazing parks and gardens. For example, over 2,000 varieties of orchids grow in the Mandai Orchid Gardens. Singapore Botanic Gardens, considered second in Asia only to Bogor's famous park, boasts one of the finest collections of tropical palms in the world. Best of all, the nearby Singapore Zoological Gardens has been designed in a sympathetic open-style architecture that won't make you pity the animals. Finally, the Jurong Bird Park boasts a gigantic five-acre walk-in flight aviary with thousands of brilliantly colored birds. Here in Singapore, flora and fauna have made their peace with the urban jungle.

HISTORY

Singapore's geographical location should have made for a long and important history, but prior to the development of the city by the British in the 19th century it was little more than a sleepy backwater ignored by both local and distant powers. Early records indicate that its thick mangrove swamps once served as refuge for marauding pirates and dumping ground for the remains of their victims. Colonists from Palembang in Sumatra arrived in 1287 and established a small fishing village later known as Singa Pura. Marco Polo possibly stopped here in 1284 on his voyage from China to Italy. At various times this isolated seaport was controlled by the Sumatran empire of Srivijaya and the Cholas from South India before being destroyed in 1376 by the Majapahit empire of East Java.

Raffles

Singapore's modern history dates from 1819, when Sir Thomas Raffles of the East India Company stepped ashore to establish his great commercial emporium. Explorer, entrepreneur, politician, naturalist, historian, and visionary, Raffles ranks as one of the most important figures in modern Southeast Asia history. Originally he searched for a new trading post for the British, who had left the Indonesian archipelago after a territorial tradeoff with the Dutch. Neither Malacca nor Penang was proving too successful and Raffles was anxious to establish a free port which could control the sea route through the Malaccan Straits.

Recognizing the geographic superiority of Singapore over Penang, Raffles claimed the island and founded the city after a little political maneuvering with the local sultans. His policy of free trade and strong British discipline was greeted enthusiastically by the Chinese and Muslim merchants. Singapore rapidly eclipsed other British ports and was soon designated capital of the Straits Settlements. During his nine months in Singapore, Raffles proved his humanity by abolishing slavery and gambling but also his racist notions by creating a city plan that carefully segregated the Chinese, Malays, and Indians into separate communities.

But disaster soon struck the great colonialist. Within a few years his children would be dead from tropical diseases and a fire would tragically destroy his invaluable records. Raffles was ordered back to England to face a lawsuit brought by his ingracious employer, the East India Company, who somehow considered him derelict in his duties. It was a terrible end for one of Britain's greatest visionaries, who, despite his impressive contributions to the British Empire, died in London a poor and despondent man at the age of forty-five.

World War II

Singapore continued to prosper as Chinese merchants planted pepper and gambier and then harvested a fortune. British acquisition of Hong Kong in 1842 and the opening of the Suez Canal in 1869 also fueled the growth of the city. Singapore came of age at the dawn of the automobile era when a British botanist, affectionately known as "Mad Ridley," persuaded Malayan coffee growers to try cultivating and processing a strange elastic product known as rubber. It was a raging success. By the early 20th century, Singapore, once an island of tigers and pirates, had become the region's leading economic power.

Singapore hummed along until February 1942 when it fell to the invading Japanese forces. More than just a massive fiasco with both tragic and comic overtones, the fall of Singapore heralded the end of British imperial influence in the Far East. Confident of their military superiority, the British had made Singapore their center of Asian naval power. Two powerful battleships were stationed in her harbor and massive 15-inch guns were installed on Sentosa Island pointing south.

Both proved flawed. On 8 December the Japanese began their military offensive by destroying the American fleet at Pearl Harbor and invading Hong Kong and the Philippines. Forces were simultaneously landed in southern Thailand and northern Malaya near Kota Bharu. British confidence in their "impregnable fortress" crumbled two days later when Japanese torpedo bombers sank both the *Repulse* and the *Prince of Wales* off Kuantan in the South China Sea. The Japanese commandeered bicycles, peddled down the Malay Peninsula, and easily took Singapore. It was a disaster, not only the largest capitulation in British history, but also a mammoth bluff by Japanese forces short on supplies and outnumbered almost three to one by British troops.

Three years of horror ensued. An estimated 25,000-50,000 Chinese were marched to the beaches and executed or tortured to death by the Japanese Kempeitai for being too Western. Almost 30,000 Allied POWs were held in Changi Prison, an ordeal described by author James Clavell in his novel *King Rat,* and then marched to Thailand where thousands died constructing the bridge over the River Kwai. The carnage was complete. By the time the Japanese surrendered to Lord Mountbatten in 1945, it is said that over 100,000 civilians had perished from starvation, torture, or execution at the hands of their Japanese liberators.

Yet Singapore had mixed reactions after the surrender of Japan. While everyone was relieved that the occupation was over, few now believed that the British were either invincible or infallible. When Britain offered to dissolve the Straits Settlements it raised a very thorny question: should Singapore and Malaysia be united in a single country? Census figures indicated that Chinese would outnumber Malays in the new nation. Fearing both economic and racial domination by the Chinese, Malaysian leaders soon formed political parties that opposed the merger. Sympathizing with their plight, the British merged Malacca, Penang, and nine Malay states into the Federation of Malaya. Singapore was made a separate Crown Colony, a compromise that left Singapore for the Chinese and Malaya for the Malays.

Lee Kuan Yew

In 1955 a young Cambridge-educated attorney named Lee Kuan Yew and a small group of lawyers, journalists, and teachers organized the People's Action Party (PAP). Their rallying cry was *"Merdeka"* (Independence) and "Merger with Malaya." In a daring move calculated to attract Chinese-speaking immigrants generally ig-

SINGAPORE

nored by conventional political parties, Lee made peace with the Communists and allowed his grass-roots party to be almost entirely dominated by leftists. His strong anti-colonial and pro-labor line proved very popular with the proletariat classes and his determination to create an independent state whose citizens would owe loyalty to the nation rather than separate communal groups brought him a respectable showing in the 1955 election and a complete mandate in 1959. Lee then consolidated his power, ended his marriage of convenience with the Communists, and forged ahead with the political entity that has ruled Singapore since 1961.

Fearing that his young country could not survive without the natural resources of Malaya, Lee insisted on a united Singapore-Malaya nation. This merger became feasible after the Malay-dominated states of Sabah and Sarawak agreed to join the new nation, thereby ensuring a plurality for the Malays. But it was soon apparent that the marriage of '63 was doomed to failure. Sukarno of Indonesia denounced the merger as a neocolonialist plot and formally launched his confused policy of konfrontasi. World leaders feared that Singapore's militant trade unions would transform the island state into the Cuba of Southeast Asia.

Most seriously, Malay leadership in Kuala Lumpur felt its sovereignty threatened when Lee's party attempted to become a national force rather than just a localized Singapore party. The Malays had assumed the Chinese in Singapore would remain merchants and steer clear of political power. But after the PAP became the leading opposition party to the Malay UMNO party,

RESTORATION OF THE PAST

Singapore, the most popular stop in Southeast Asia, hosts over seven million annual visitors who spent over S$12 billion per year, almost 6% of the country's gross domestic product. Westerners flock to Singapore because it's a safe and clean city with excellent restaurants and some of the best themed attractions in Asia, if not the world.

Singapore has changed dramatically over the last few decades. After years of relentless urban development, the romantic city of Kipling and Maugham lost much of its soul to anonymous skyscrapers and air-conditioned shopping centers. As one leading guidebook states, "Physically, many parts of Singapore are so modern as to persuade you that the city has had no history."

Singapore's Chinatown—once one of the architectural goldmines of Southeast Asia—was reduced to a few neglected streets towered over by faceless housing projects and massive shopping centers. Thousands of irreplaceable Chinese homes dating from the 1920s and traditional Malay fishing villages were also leveled as were Singapore's famous night markets, which were closed down for reasons of hygiene. The destruction of old Singapore was a tragic mistake.

Few residents opposed the early destruction of Chinatown aside from a few young Chinese architects who disputed government claims that the old structures were unfit for human habitation and that

preservation efforts were impractical from an economic standpoint. The government certainly didn't recognize the importance of old Singapore as shown by the Preservation of Monuments Act—a government decree formulated to save historically important buildings—which gazetted less than 20 buildings over a period of two decades. Some critics even claim that the preservation agency responsible for saving Singapore's architectural heritage actually destroyed more sites than it saved.

It wasn't until hotel occupancy rates plummeted in the mid-1980s that the government finally enacted a conservation and restoration plan. Despite the late start, enough extravagant architecture survived to make conservation efforts a worthwhile project. In 1987, the government launched an ambitious and costly program designed to attract the support of private investors through various tax incentives. The program proved a remarkable success as entire neighborhoods were saved from destruction, including the districts of Boat Quay and Tanjung Pagar. Some restoration projects, such as Clarke Quay and Little India Arcade, were less successful in terms of authenticity while others were dismal failures such as the poorly executed revival of world-famous Bugis Street. Despite a few miscalculated moves, the government must be complimented for the enormous amount of time, energy, and resources poured into saving the final vestiges of old Singapore.

FESTIVALS

January

Ponggal: A Hindu harvest festival celebrated by Tamils in both temples and homes. Colorful greeting cards and presents are exchanged. Enormous pots of boiled rice and vegetarian delicacies are consumed at temples. Check Perumal Temple on Serangoon Road.

International Kite Festival: Malay moon kites, Thai fighting kites, and Chinese dragon kites are judged for beauty and aerial height.

Thaipusam: An Indian festival of human endurance and self-sacrifice, considered among the most spectacular in all of Southeast Asia. Entranced devotees at the Perumal Temple prove their devotion to Subramaniam by shoving metal skewers through the skin of their forehead, cheeks, and tongues. Other instruments are jammed through the body and hung with fruits. The ritual culminates when a massive spiked cage *(kavadi)* is lowered onto the shoulders to pierce the chest and back with sharp metal spikes. Devotees then carry the burden in a three-km procession to the Chettiar Temple on Tank Road.

February

Chinese New Year: The most important social, moral, and personal festival of the year. A time for spiritual renewal, family reunions, and social harmony. The old are honored with mandarin oranges while the young receive red envelopes filled with lucky money called *hong bao* in Singapore and *lai see* in Hong Kong. All debts are settled and salaried workers receive year-end bonuses. Miniature peach trees symbolizing good luck are exchanged. Everybody calls out *"gung hay fah choi,"* or "good luck making money." Clothes are purchased, houses cleaned, and calligraphers paint messages of good luck on red banners. A special salad of raw fish and 20 vegetables is prepared. The image of the Kitchen God (a deity who reports everybody's activities to the Jade Emperor) is courted with special candies, sweet wine, hell money, and dabs of sticky opium to seal the lips against speaking evil. After the bribe, he's taken outside and burned. Images of the Door Gods and the God of Wealth are replaced. The weeks' activities are climaxed with a dragon parade.

Lantern Festival (Yuen Siu): Chinese New Year ends with displays of brightly painted lanterns hung in windows and doorways. Ancestral halls are filled with finely crafted lanterns while auctions raise thousands for charities.

Chingay Processio: Chinese New Year also ends with a mad and crazy parade of stiltwalkers, snapping lions, bejeweled Indian dancers, cute pom-pom girls, Malay wedding couples, and armies of roller skaters. Volunteers carry giant flags over three stories high. One of the best parades in Singapore.

March

Birthday of Kuan Yin: One of the most popular figures in Chinese mythology, the Buddhist Goddess of Mercy is honored on her birthday in the second moon, date of enlightenment in the sixth, and date of death in the ninth.

Monkey God's Birthday: The Monkey God is a celebrated and beloved rascal who made himself indestructible and acquired miraculous powers after sneaking into heaven and stealing the Peaches of Immortality. During the temple ceremony in his honor, Taoist priests enter a trance to allow his spirit to enter their bodies. The medium then jumps around, scratches his armpit, howls, slashes himself with sharp knives, and scrawls magical symbols on scraps of paper. Frenzied efforts are made to grab these papers since some consider them winning lottery numbers. Chinese opera and puppet plays are performed in the courtyard. The Monkey God is honored twice yearly at the temples on Eng Hoon and Cummings streets.

April

Ching Ming: This important Chinese festival pays homage to departed ancestors. Families visit ancestral graves to perform traditional rites, clean weedy tombstones, repaint the inscriptions, and burn incense sticks and red candles. After the formalities, this "clear and bright" occasion often assumes the air of a lively party with blaring music, food, and games. Ching Ming is held on spring equinox and best seen—but never photographed—in the cemeteries along Upper Thomson and Lornie Road.

Songkran: Both a Buddhist religious holiday and a wet and wild water festival where absolutely everybody is drenched by water balloons, fire hoses, and buckets of colored water. On a more sedate note,

(continues on next page)

SINGAPORE

FESTIVALS

(continued)

this is the occasion when the sun enters the first month of the Buddhist New Year. Rites are performed in the Buddhist temple on Jalan Bukit Merah and at the Saptha Puchaniyaram Temple on Holland Road. Wrap your camera in plastic and don't forget your water pistol.

May

Birthday of Tin Hau: This popular festival honors the Sea Goddess, who walks on water, calms the seas, and ensures a bountiful catch. According to popular legend, Miss Tin was a 10th-century historical figure who lived on a small island near Hong Kong. During a terrible storm at sea, she miraculously saved her two brothers but lost her life while attempting to rescue her father. After centuries of veneration she was officially canonized by the Chinese court and promoted to Queen of Heaven in the 17th century. Today she is honored by the local fishermen in both Singapore and Hong Kong, who decorate their boats for a seaborne parade.

Birthday of the Third Prince: This festival honors the miracle-working child-god who rides on the wheels of wind and fire. Entranced temple mediums slash themselves with swords and use blood from their tongues to write magical charms. A street procession of stiltwalkers, dragon dancers, and Chinese musicians follows. Check Leng Hyam Twoi Temple on Clarke Street at North Boat Quay.

Tam Kung Festival: Honors the second patron saint of the boat people. Celebrated in both Hong Kong and Singapore.

Vesak Day: Commemorates the birth, death, and enlightenment of Buddha. Devotees visit Buddhist temples to burn candles and offer donations. Best experienced at Temple of 1000 Lights on Race Course Road.

June

Dragon Boat Festival: Commemorates the tragic death of Wat Yuen, a 3rd-century government official who drowned himself to protest the injustice and corruption of Manchurian government. In symbolic recreation of the event, a colorful regatta of elegantly decorated boats races off the shore of the East Coast Parkway. Dragon boats are brought to life during a temple ceremony called "opening the light" in which each eye is painted with blood from a brown chicken. Sexes compete separately: *yang*-powered dragon boats are raced by the men while the women race *yin*-fueled Phoenix Dragons.

Ramadan: Muslim holy month during which neither food nor water may pass the devotee's lips in daylight hours. Mosques are filled with worshippers who fulfill their religious obligations. Sultan Mosque is surrounded by foodstalls selling *halal* specialties.

July

Hari Raya Puasa: The end of Ramadan fast is marked by elaborate thanksgiving feasts in Muslim homes. Kampong Glam is the center for Singapore activities.

Enlightenment of Kuan Yin: Although the Buddhist Goddess of Mercy was originally a male deity from Tibetan Mahayana Buddhism, she miraculously changed gender when adopted by the Chinese. This immensely popular figure is honored three times yearly.

August

National Day: Singapore's Independence Day on 9 August is celebrated with a parade of school floats, military bands, and masses of flag wavers. Tickets to the event are available from the tourist office.

Festival of the Hungry Ghosts: A one-month celebration somewhat similar to Halloween. Chinese believe that the Gates of Hell are opened once a year to release restless and hungry spirits who died without proper funeral preparations. Ignored and troublesome, these disgruntled spirits must be placated with offerings of money, feasts, and free entertainment from Chinese opera and puppet shows. Life-sized paper models of *shiu yi* are burned in the streets before Taai Si Wong—the mythological figure who watches and records the whole event and then reports back to the Jade Emperor—is thrown on the bonfire, signaling the completion of earthly duties. This spectacular festival is an excellent time to witness Chinese street opera.

Market Festival: An extension of the Festival of the Hungry Ghosts. Local merchants offer food and free Chinese opera at temporary *matshed* constructions.

September

Navarathri Festival: This Hindu festival honors the consorts of the triumvirate of Brahma, Vishnu, and Shiva. The first three days are devoted to Durga (Shiva's mistress), the next three to Lakshmi (Goddess of Wealth and consort of Vishnu), and the last three to Saraswati (Goddess of Music and lover of Brahma). Classical Indian dance is performed nightly at the Chettiar Temple on Tank Road. A grand procession with a silver horse is held on the final day.

Mooncake Festival: Commemorates a 14th-century revolution during which Chinese patriots passed revolutionary messages hidden inside special cakes and lanterns were used to signal the beginning of the revolution. Singapore shops sell heavy and bitter cakes *(yuet bang)* stuffed with sweet lotus seeds and eggs. The Mooncake Festival has other names: Moon and Lantern Festival in Singapore, Mid-autumn and Harvest Festival in Hong Kong.

October

Thimithi Festival: Hindu firewalking festival held at the Sri Mariamman Temple in Chinatown. A huge pit filled with fiery embers is sprinted across by devotees. Hot, crowded, and as fascinating as India herself.

Festival of the Emperor Gods: Celebration honoring the nine powerful Chinese gods whose spiritually possessed images are carried through the streets. Mediums enter trances in the temples. Another excellent opportunity to enjoy Chinese street opera. Celebrated on the ninth day of the ninth moon, a doubly auspicious date since Chinese astrologers consider nine the male principle in Chinese cosmology. Best seen at the Chinese temples on Upper Serangoon Road and at Lorong Tai Seng.

Chung Yeung: Festival of Autumn Remembrance. Chinese honor their departed ancestors twice yearly: in the spring with Ching Ming and in the fall with Chung Yeung.

Birthday of Confucius: The famous sage and teacher is honored with ceremonies in local temples and at Confucius societies.

Death of Kuan Yin: The Buddhist Goddess of Mercy is honored once again.

November

Deepavali: This Hindu festival celebrates Rama's victory over the demon King Ravana and the return of Lakshmi to the earth. Thousands of tiny oil lamps make Deepavali one of the most enchanting of all Hindu festivals.

---

radical Muslim elements demanded the ouster of Singapore from the new republic. Singapore was unceremoniously booted out of the republic and Lee's dream of a united Malaysia ended after a short 23-month honeymoon.

Recent News

Lee Kuan Yew stepped down in 1990 after serving as the nation's sole prime minister since 1959. His successor, Goh Chok Tong, has presided over a revitalized administration that has worked to create a "kinder and gentler" nation under the watchful eye of LKY, who now serves as senior minister.

The People's Action Party once again won the general elections in 1997, carrying 63.5% of the total vote and taking 81 of 83 seats in Parliament. Today the most powerful members of the cabinet are Senior Minister Lee Kuan Yew and his son, Lee Hsien Long, who served as a brigadier general in the army before assuming the position of sole deputy minister in 1993. Lee Hsien Loon, known locally as B.G. Lee, is widely considered the heir-apparent to the current leadership of Singapore despite a 1993 bout with cancer that briefly threatened to derail his career.

THE PEOPLE

If one-quarter of the world's population is Chinese, Singapore is just the opposite. Three-quarters of the population is Chinese and the remaining one-quarter Malay, Indian, and European. Most Singaporean Chinese are descendents of poor and uneducated South Chinese laborers who fled the grinding hunger and corruption of 19th- and early 20th-century China. Arriving as indentured laborers obligated to work off their passage, most would quickly join a clan house, a type of mutual-assistance society which helped people from a similar district or who shared a common last name. Others fell into

SINGAPORE

CHINESE FESTIVALS BY THE LUNAR CALENDAR

Moon 1	Chinese New Year	Day 1
	Birthday of the God of Wealth	Days 2 and 3
	Lantern Festival	Day 15
Moon 2	Birthday of Hung Shing Kung	Day 13
	Birthday of Kuan Yin	Day 19
Moon 3	Ching Ming Festival	Spring Solstice
	Birthday of Tin Hau	Day 23
Moon 4	Birthday of Buddha	Day 8
	Birthday of Tam Kung	Day 8
Moon 5	Dragon Boat Festival	Day 5
Moon 6	Birthday of Hau Wong	Day 6
	Enlightenment of Kuan Yin	Day 19
Moon 7	Festival for the Hungry Ghosts	Day 15
Moon 8	Mid-autumn or Moon Festival	Day 15
	Birthday of the Monkey God	Day 16
	Birthday of Confucius	Day 27
Moon 9	Chung Yeung	Day 9
	Death of Kuan Yin	Day 19
Moon 10	Birthday of Tat Moh	Day 5
Moon 11	Chung Yeung	Winter Solstice
Moon 12	Kitchen God Festival	Day 24

the secret societies which ran the gambling emporiums, opium dens, and brothels. Also imported were their beliefs in ancestor worship and the religious doctrines of Buddhism, Taoism, and Confucianism.

Hailing from all regions of China, Singaporeans today differ between themselves physically, linguistically, culturally, and by choice of profession. Hokkiens from Southern Fukien province, who comprise 40% of the population (the largest Chinese group in Singapore), are the country's most economically successful ethnic group. Displaying a touch of chauvinism, Hokkiens regard themselves as the republic's best group. Teochews from the Swatow region in Kwangtung form 20% of the population. Many Teochews

have chosen to be fishermen. Cantonese from Hong Kong, who make up 17% of the population, gravitate toward professions in the arts, crafts, and restaurant industries. Hakkas and Hainanese, who form some 10% of the population, tend to work as manual laborers.

Peranakans (Straits Chinese) are one of the most intriguing groups in Singapore. This distinct social group came into being after mainland Chinese government prohibitions against the emigration of females forced many of the early Chinese settlers to intermarry with the local Malay women. Speaking a Malay-Chinese patois, Peranakan men (Babas) and women (Nonyas) developed a rich and elegant subculture which tastefully combined Chinese, Malay, and English customs. Ladies, for example, wore Malay dresses but held their hair with Chinese hairpins. Men dressed in Chinese fashions but took up such nontraditional activities as cricket, polo, and high tea. Peranakans were smart, hardworking, and politically sophisticated. They became commercially successful by adopting British business customs and acting as compradores between British administrators and China-born immigrants. After amassing great wealth, Peranakans fled the ghettos of Chinatown to wealthy suburbs of baroque homes and broad boulevards.

Peranakans eventually melded into mainstream society, and today, as a separate group with a distinctive culture, have largely disappeared from modern Singapore. But you'll still find Peranakan foodstalls, Nonya wedding ceremonies, and museum displays of Peranakan culture during your visit to Singapore.

ON THE ROAD

GETTING THERE

From Malaysia

Most travelers arrive by bus or train from Kuala Lumpur or by bus from the east coast of Peninsular Malaysia.

Malaysian Airlines flies to Singapore daily from Kuala Lumpur, Penang, Langkawi, Kuantan, Kuching, and Kota Kinabalu in East Malaysia. Silk Air provides flights to Singapore from Tioman Island (daily), Kuantan (three times weekly), and Langkawi (three times weekly). Pelangi Air provides daily service from Melaka, Ipoh, Tioman, and Pangkor Island. All flights arrive at Changi airport except for those originating from or departing to Tioman and Pangkor Islands.

Air tickets are much cheaper in Malaysia due to the widening gap between the Malaysian *ringgit* and the Singapore dollar—the *ringgit* continues to decline in value compared to the Singapore dollar and therefore has stronger purchasing power vis-à-vis foreign currencies.

Passengers flying from Singapore to a destination within Malaysia such as Penang, Kuching, or Kota Kinabalu, can save 20-35% by flying from Johor Bharu rather than Singapore. To make arrangements, contact the Malaysian Airlines office in the Singapore Shopping Centre, 190 Clemenceau Ave., tel. 336-6777. MAS also provides a direct bus service from the Novotel Orchid Hotel at 214 Dunearn Road to the Johor Bharu Airport.

From Indonesia

Singapore can be reached by air from almost a dozen cities in Indonesia and by ship from several ports.

Air: Garuda, Singapore Airlines, and a number of other international carriers fly daily to Singapore from Jakarta for US$80-120 one way and US$160-200 roundtrip, and from Bali for US$180-240 one way and US$340-480 round trip.

Garuda provides direct service to Singapore from Medan, Padang, Palembang, and Pekanbaru on Sumatra, Surabaya on Java, and Pontianak on Kalimantan. As with Malaysian Air-lines, Garuda is a lower cost carrier than Singapore and travelers can economize by flying Garuda for domestic flights. Some travelers find it economical to take a ferry to Batam, a resort island just 30 minutes south of Singapore, and take Garuda to Kalimantan and Pekanbaru rather than a direct Garuda flight from Changi Airport. It's also cheaper to fly from Sumatra to Batam and continue up to Singapore by ferry.

Sea: Singapore can be reached indirectly from Indonesia via several unusual routes. There is no direct service to Singapore from main ports such as Jakarta and coastal Sumatra, but ships sail from these ports to the islands of the Riau Archipelago—Bantam and Bintan—just south of Singapore from where ferries continue up to Singapore.

The most popular option is the speedboat from Pekanbaru in Sumatra to Sepukang on Batam. The speedboat departs daily around 0700 and takes five hours to reach Batam. Another option is to take a bus from Jambi in Sumatra to either Tembilahan or Kuala Tungkal, from where boats take four or five hours to Batam.

Pelni's KM *Lawit* leaves either Jakarta or Belawan every two weeks and stops at Tanjung Pinang on Bintam, from where ferries take about two hours to reach Singapore.

POINTS OF ARRIVAL

Singapore Airport

The Arrival Hall just beyond baggage claim has telecommunication offices, shops, restaurants, and other useful services for arrivals or transit passengers.

Left Luggage: Left luggage costs S$3 per bag for the first day and S$4 per day thereafter.

Hotel Reservations: The free hotel reservation counter operated by the Singapore Hotel Association is open daily 0700-2300 and requires a S$10 deposit which is applied to the price of the room. The hotel counter can make reservations at almost every hotel except for the dormitories in the Bencoolen Street area. Discounts are often provided at the better hotels.

SINGAPORE

Telecommunications: Singapore Telecom offices provide postal, telephone, fax, and telegram services. Visitors can make international calls through their own country operator and charge calls on a collect-call basis on Country Direct Phones, or dial 161 to make collect calls through a Singapore operator. Local calls require a 10 cent coin or the use of a Singapore Telecom phonecard.

Banks: Banks and money changers, which provide exactly the same exchange rates as those in town, are open daily around the clock.

Car Rentals: Avis and Sintat Rental provide chauffeur-driven cars and self-drive cars for visitors with international driver's licences. Both offices are open daily 0700-2300.

Transit Hotels: Transit Hotels are located within the transit area of both terminals. The rooms are leased on a six-hour basis for S$42-64 depending on the size of the room. Passengers can use the hotels' bathing facilities with soap, shampoo, and towel for just S$5, or use the gym or sauna for just S$10. Use of the pool facilities including towel rental costs S$11.

Free City Tours: Passengers in transit with at least four hours to kill can take a free two-hour coach city tour of Chinatown, Little India, the Colonial Center, Singapore waterfront, and business district. Tours depart daily at 1030 (for flight departures after 1400), 1430 (departures after 1800), 1630 (departures after 2000), and 1900 (departures after 2130). Register at Free City Tour Counters in the departure lounges of both terminals.

Restaurants: There are almost 20 restaurants inside the two terminals including McDonalds, Le Cafe, and Sze Chuan Garden Restaurant in Terminal 1 and Sakura, Spice Express, and A&W inside Terminal 2. The least expensive meals are in the basement Food Centre beneath Terminal 1; take the elevator next to McDonalds.

From Airport to Hotel

Arrivals can take a taxi, Airbus, or public bus to selected city hotels.

Taxis: Metered taxis waiting immediately outside both terminals take about 20 minutes and cost about S$15 during the day to reach most hotels in the center of town. Drivers are entitled to collect a S$3 sucharge for service from the airport (not to the airport) and an additional 50% on fares between midnight and 0600. These addi-

tional charges do not appear on the meter but will be added by the driver.

Airbus: Airbuses operate daily 0620-0030 at an average frequency of 20 minutes and cost S$5 for adults and S$3 for children. You may pay the exact fare directly on the bus or purchase a ticket in advance from the Airbus counters in both arrival halls.

Airbus 1 stops at the Albert Court Hotel and hotels on Scotts Road before reaching the hotels on Tanglin Road to the north of Orchard Road.

Airbus 2 stops at the Inter-Continental Hotel and then the Allson Hotel on Victoria Street, three blocks from the budget guesthouses on Bencoolen Street. The bus continues to the hotels in the Central District, the YMCA, and hotels along Orchard Road before stopping at the Bencoolen Hotel, just a few doors down from the budget guesthouses.

Airbus 3 serves the luxury hotels near the Suntec Convention Center such as the Marina Mandarin, Pan Pacific, Ritz Carlton, Oriental, Westin Stamford, and the Raffles.

Public Bus: Public buses leave from the basement levels of both terminals daily 0600-midnight and cost S$1.30 into town. Exact change is required.

Bus 16 and 16E stop at Raffles City near the Raffles Hotel and at guesthouses a few blocks away on Beach Road, and then stop at the National Museum near the budget guesthouses on Bencoolen Street, YMCA, and inexpensive hotels. The bus heads up Penang Road, Somerset Road, and Orchard Boulevard. When heading back to the airport, catch bus 16 on Orchard or Bras Basah Road near Bencoolen Street.

Arrival by Bus

Buses from Malaysia stop at one of three terminals in Singapore. Buses arriving from Malaysia first stop at the Singapore immigration checkpoint just over the causeway which connects the two countries. Visitors must get off the bus and go through immigration and customs procedures. You then reboard the first available bus into town—be sure to take all belongings off the bus.

Ban San Terminal: Many buses from Johor Bharu and other destinations on the west coast of Peninsular Malaysia arrive at the Ban San Terminal at the junction of Queen and Arab Streets. The budget guesthouses on Bencoolen

Street are about a 10-minute walk down Queen Street or Rochor Canal Road. Travelers can also grab a taxi from the adjacent taxi stand or walk five minutes to the Bugis MRT station, three blocks away at the intersection of Rochor Road and Victoria Street.

Lavender Street Terminal: Some buses from elsewhere in Malaysia and Thailand terminate at the old bus station at the corner of Lavender Street and Kallang Bahru, in the far end of Little India and a 10-minute walk from the Lavender MRT station.

New Terminal: The old bus terminal on Lavender Street is currently relocating to a new location on Crawford Street between North Bridge and Beach roads, about one block south of the Lavender MRT station. Arrivals heading to the budget guesthouses on Bencoolen Street can take the MRT from Lavender to the Bugis MRT station and then walk six blocks or hail a cab on North Bridge Road.

Arrival by Train

Trains from Malaysia terminate at the Singapore Railway Station on Keppel Road, southwest of Chinatown. There are immigration and custom offices at the cavernous train station constructed in 1932 and renovated in 1990 with the launch of the Eastern & Oriental Express. Be sure to have your passport stamped by both Malaysia and Singapore officials to avoid any problems later in your journey. Call the train station at 222-5165 for fare and schedule information.

The station has showers, luggage storage for S$1 per day per bag, phones, cafes, and shops that sell phone cards and maps of Singapore.

Taxis wait outside the train station. Alternatively, you can walk about 15 minutes to the Tanjong Pagar MRT station by following Keppel Road (under the Ayer Rajah Expressway) and turning left up Anson Road. Buses from the train station include bus 97 to Tanjong Pagar MRT station and on to Selegie and Serangoon roads, bus 20 to Beach Road, and bus 148 to Serangoon Road.

GETTING AROUND

Singapore is compact and most neighborhoods are best reached and explored on foot. Public transportation is only necessary to reach destinations outside the city center or for cross-town journeys.

Taxis: Taxis in Singapore are metered and honest. Basic rates are reasonable, though surcharges for airport pick-up, baggage, travel in the restricted city center, and late-night travel can add up. Empty cabs have blue lights. Downtown, taxis can only be hailed at designated taxi stands.

Buses: Buses are a great way to get around Singapore. Intercity fares are 50 cents to S$1 depending on the distance. Routes are listed in the Singapore Bus Guide available from local bookstores. Buses range from red-and-gray SBS

asleep at the wheel

INTERNATIONAL CLOCK FOR SINGAPORE

San Francisco	-16
New York	-13
London	-8
Paris	-7
Rome	-7
Sydney	+3

buses to one-man operations which require exact change. Explorer Bus Tickets allow you to board any Singapore or Trans-Island Bus and then break your journey as often as you wish; a convenient way to explore the island without a pocket of change.

MRT: Singapore's S$5 billion 67-km Mass Transit System has two main lines. The north-south circular line runs around the island while

the east-west line connects Pasir Ris near the airport to Boon Lay beyond Jurong. Trains operate 0600-midnight and fares range from 50 cents to S$1.80.

Trishaws: A handful of the old rickshaws that have always congregated in the early evening near the Raffles and across from the National Museum still survives to serve the tourist trade. Daytime rides might be nerve-wracking, but late-night rides through Chinatown and Little India are worthwhile. Prices are negotiable, but figure on S$10-15 per hour. Trishaw drivers know the underside of Singapore.

TRAVEL PRACTICALITIES

Visas

Visas are not required for stays up to 90 days for Americans and citizens of most European countries. A 14-day permit is granted on arrival. Ex-

SINGAPORE TOURIST OFFICES

Australia: Level 11, AWA Building, 47 York St., Sydney NSW 2000, tel. (02) 290-2888, fax (02) 290-2555

Australia: 16 St. Georges Terrace, 8th floor, Perth 6000, tel. (09) 325-8578, fax (09) 221-3864

Canada: 121 King Street West, Suite 1000, Toronto, Ontario M5H 3T9, tel. (416) 363-8898, fax (416) 363-5752

France: 2 Place du Palais Royal, 75044 Paris, tel. (01) 4297-1616, fax (01) 4297-1617

Germany: Hochstrasse 35-37, 60313 Frankfurt, tel. (069) 920-7720, fax (069) 297-8922

Hong Kong: Central Plaza, Suite 2003, 18 Harbour Rd., Wanchai, tel. (852) 2598-9290, fax (852) 2598-1040

Italy: Corso Plebisciti 15, 20129 Milano, tel. (02) 7000-3981, fax (02) 738-1032

Japan: Yamato Seimei, 1 Chome, 1-7 Uchisaiwai-cho, Chiyoda-ku, Tokyo 100, tel. (03) 593-33388, fax (03) 359-11480

New Zealand: 43 High St., 3rd floor, Auckland, tel. (09) 358-1191, fax (09) 358-1196

Switzerland: Hochstrasse 48, CH 8044 Zurich, tel. (01) 252-5454, fax (01) 252-5303

Thailand: Alma Link Bldg., Soi Chidlom, Ploenchit, Bangkok 10330, tel. (02) 252-9879, fax (02) 254-8535

United Kingdom: Carrington House, 126-130 Regent St., London W1R 5FE, tel. (0171) 437-0033, fax (0171) 734-2191

U.S.A.: 180 North Stetson Ave., Suite 1450, Chicago, IL 60601, tel. (312) 938-1888, fax 938-0086
590 Fifth Ave., 12th Floor, New York, NY 10036, tel. (212) 302-4861, fax 302-4801
8484 Wilshire Blvd., Suite 510, Beverly Hills, CA 90211, tel. (213) 852-1901, fax 852-0129

**IMPORTANT
TELEPHONE NUMBERS**

Ambulance, Fire.	995
Directory Assistance	103
International Calls.	104
Malaysia Call	109
Tourist Information.	(800) 738-3778
Flight Information	541-8590
Taxi	452-5555
Immigration	532-2877
Police	999

tensions may be obtained at the Immigration Department (tel. 532-2877) at 95 South Bridge Road.

Tourist Information

The Singapore Tourist Promotion Board (STPB) has an outlet on the second floor of the shopping arcade behind the Raffles Hotel, tel. (800) 334-1335, open daily 0830-2000. Their headquarters moved a few years ago from Raffles City to the north end of Orchard Road near the Traders Hotel at 1 Orchard Spring Lane, tel. (800) 738-3778.

Maps

Complimentary maps include the *Map of Singapore* from the tourist office and *Singapore Visitor Map* with excellent details on neighborhoods and shopping centers. The best overall map is the Periplus Singapore Island and City Map.

Money

The Singapore dollar (S$) is divided into 100 cents. Exchange rates currently range S$1.50-1.80 per U.S. dollar. After the currency crisis of 1997, Malaysian currency is rarely accepted in Singapore and will only be accepted at very poor exchange rates.

Post Offices

Letters and packages can be mailed from the General Post Office on Fullerton Road and from branch offices in Raffles City and on Orchard Road. Offices are open daily 0800-1800 except Sundays. The computerized Poste Restante at the GPO wins *Southeast Asia Handbook's* Award for Best Poste Restante in Asia. To win Best GPO they must add a packing service similar to that of the Bangkok GPO.

Telephones

International phone calls, telegrams, and telexes can be made 24 hours daily from the GPO. Rates are low compared to most Asian countries. Overseas calls can easily be made from many public phones with the use of a locally purchased phone card.

International calls to Singapore (from America, Europe, etc.) can be made by dialing 011 (international access code), 65 (country code for Singapore), followed by the local phone number.

ATTRACTIONS

While modern Singapore may at first more closely resemble a tropical Manhattan than an Oriental oasis, a closer look uncovers a good deal of history that still remains between the concrete towers. Landmark buildings—especially those of religious character—have been preserved, while some sections of the older neighborhoods have been spared the wrecking ball. In the late 1980s an ambitious preservation plan was launched to save some of the old buildings and help revitalize the tourist trade.

The modern layout of Singapore is essentially the city plan of Raffles. During his visit in 1822, Raffles discovered his young settlement had grown into a jumble of disorderly shacks and streets. Raffles ordered planning committees to divide the town into distinct neighborhoods based on commercial and racial guidelines. Government buildings and churches were placed around the *padang,* commerce and boat quays near the mouth of the river, *godowns* farther upriver. To ensure racial harmony, Raffles gave the land south of the river to the Chinese, who subdivided their neighborhood into enclaves for each dialect group. Hokkien merchants took the land along the coast, Teochew food merchants settled near the river, Cantonese and Hakka took residence in the narrow lanes and alleys between

SINGAPORE

SINGAPORE

SINGAPORE CITY

Upper
Orchard
Road

Lower
Orchard
Road

Little
India

Colonial
Singapore

Arab
Quarter

Marina
East

Marina
South

Marina
City
Park

Marina
Bay

Financial
District

Chinatown

Tanjong
Pagar

Pearl Hill
Park

Havelock
Road

Fort
Canning
Park

Istana
Grounds

Java
Park

Farrer
Park

Botanic
Gardens

Suntec
Convention
Center

Marina
Center

Raffles
Place

Marina
Bay

To World Trade Centre,
Sentosa & Jurong

To West Singapore
& Jurong

Mt. Faber ▲

© MOON PUBLICATIONS, INC.

0.5 mi
0.5 km

LAVENDER STREET
BUS TERMINAL

BUS TERMINAL
(THAILAND)

BAN SAN BUS
TERMINAL

U.S.
EMBASSY

SINGAPORE TOURIST
PROMOTION BOARD
HEADQUARTERS

INDONESIAN
EMBASSY

SINGAPORE
TRAIN STATION

TANJONG PAGAR

DHOBY
GHAUT

NEWTON

OUTRAM
PARK

RAFFLES PLACE

CITY
HALL

To Airport

To Airport

the coast and river. Indians were given High Street but later moved out to Serangoon Road. Muslims settled in the *kampong* around Arab Street near the Sultan Mosque. The prime land along Beach Road and the central Esplanade was claimed by the British. Raffles's plan also included five-foot covered walkways to "ensure regularity and conformity."

Cultural assimilation and urban resettlement have somewhat blurred the lines, but to a surprising degree Singapore still retains these ethnic divisions. The juxtaposition of these cultures and their neighborhoods remains Singapore's greatest attraction. The following section is divided into convenient walking tours through Colonial Singapore, Chinatown, Little India, and the Muslim Quarter.

COLONIAL SINGAPORE

Raffles reserved the prized land on the waterfront and east of the river for the British. Around the large recreational square originally known as the Esplanade, British architects constructed government buildings, hotels, sports clubs, and churches in the then-popular Palladian style of architecture. Many of the early buildings were designed by architect George Coleman, a 31-year-old Irishman who had consulted with Raffles on the 1822-23 Town Plan. As Town Surveyor, Coleman successfully combined Palladian styles with tropical modifications such as shady verandahs and louvered windows. Some of his finest architecture, such as the Armenian Church, the Caldwell House, and the Maxwell House, still stands. Coleman's house was unfortunately demolished in 1969 for the Peninsula Hotel and Shopping Center.

Singapore's other great architect was Alfred John Bidwell, an Englishman who had previously worked on the Saracenic-style Government Secretariat in Kuala Lumpur. Bidwell's neo-Renaissance buildings include the main wing of the Raffles Hotel, the Goodwood Hotel, the Stamford House, St. Joseph's Church, the Singapore Cricket Club, and the Victoria Theater and Memorial Hall. Together, Coleman and Bidwell created the finest colonial architecture in the East.

The following walking tour begins from Orchard Road and proceeds south toward the waterfront. Allow a full day or start from the National Museum and see the highlights in a few hours.

Botanic Gardens

Considered second in Asia only to the Bogor Gardens on Java. Visitors can tour the Herbarium, the experimental Orchid Garden, and the plantation where "Mad Ridley" began his experiments with the rubber tree. Ridley's discovery of a way to tap rubber without killing the tree eventually revolutionized the economies of Singapore and Malaysia.

Open daily 0500-2300; allow yourself a full day to appreciate the wonders of this magnificent park.

Emerald Hill

This remarkable series of 150 prewar homes and shophouses was Singapore's first effort to preserve its endangered architecture. Also known as terrace or Malacca houses, these Chinese-baroque/Palladian residences were constructed between 1918 and 1930 by Peranakan Chinese who fused neoclassical European designs with Chinese features such as raised floors, gabled walls, and pier bases. Exteriors were painted in pastel shades inspired by the soft hues of Peranakan porcelains. Note the plaster motifs sculpted to resemble the embroidery of the *nonya sarong kebaya* and the intricately carved *pintu pagar* (fence door) that allowed ventilation but ensured privacy. Interiors were furnished with vintage clocks, teak furniture, and ancestral altars. Most buildings are closed to the public except for the Peranakan Museum, which provides a good if somewhat expensive look at traditional furnishings. Also visit the Peranakan exhibit in the National Museum.

Tan Yeok Nee Mansion

This classically styled Chinese house was constructed in 1885 by a wealthy Teochew merchant who made his fortune growing gambier and pepper. The building, with its massive granite pillars imported from China, was badly damaged by the Japanese Army during the war but later restored by the Salvation Army. Listed as a national monument in 1974, Tan's home has been closed for several years and its fate is unclear.

To Little India

To Ban San
Bus Terminal

To Arab
Quarter

BUTIK TIMAH RD.

BUTIK TIMAH RD.

SUNGEI

OPHIR

MADERSAN L.

MACKENZIE RD.

ROCHOR CANAL RD.

JOHOR ST.

CLYDE

JEDDAH

ALBERT ST.

ROCHOR

FRASIER

MOUNT EMILY RD.

PRINSEP ST.

BUGIS STREET

Mount Emily
Park

PRINSEP CT.

NOORDIN LN.

BUGIS MRT

BUGIS

ROCHOR ST.

TAN QUEE LAN ST.

FARQUHAR

UPPER WILKIE RD.

SHORT ST.

CHENG YAN PL.

BUGIS JUNCTION

LIANG SEAH ST.

WILKIE RD.

MIDDLE RD.

KUAN YIN TEMPLE

MANILA PL.

SEEGIE ST.

KRISHNA TEMPLE

VICTORIA ST.

BEACH RD.

SOPHIA RD.

PRINSEP ST.

BENCOOLEN ST.

WATERLOO ST.

QUEEN ST.

RD.

PURVIS ST.

MOUNT SOPIA RD.

KIRK TER.

BRAS BASAH RD.

BAIN ST.

MAGHAIN ABOTH SYNAGOGUE

CHURCH OF ST. PETER AND PAUL

CASHIN ST.

SEAH ST.

HANDY RD.

Bras Basah Park

SINGAPORE ART MUSEUM

BRIDGE RD.

RAFFLES HOTEL

OLDHAM LN.

ORCHARD RD.

BASAH

PENANG RD.

DHOBY GHAUT MRT

Istana Park

NATIONAL MUSEUM

CATHEDRAL OF THE GOOD SHEPHERD

WESTIN PLAZA HOTEL

War Memorial Park

CANNING RISE

WESLEY METHODIST CHURCH

CONVENT OF THE HOLY INFANT JESUS

RAFFLES CITY

CLEMENCEAU AVE.

PENANG LN.

CANNING WALK

DRAMA CENTRE

STAMFORD RD.

WESTIN STAMFORD HOTEL

PERCIVAL RD.

FORT ENTRANCE

CANNING RISE

MPH BUILDING

CITY HALL MRT

TAN KIM SENG FOUNTAIN

OXLEY RISE

Fort

CEMETERY

SUBSTATION

STAMFORD HOUSE

SINGAPORE REC. CLUB

SINGAPORE COMMAND AND STAFF COLLEGE

FORT CANNING CENTRE

CHINESE CHAMBER OF COMMERCE

CONNAUGHT

OLD FORT AND BUNKERS

ASIAN CIVILIZATIONS MUSEUM

ST. ANDREWS CATHEDRAL

The

Canning

Fort Canning Reservoir

SINGAPORE PHILATELIC MUSEUM

ARMENIAN CHURCH

COLEMAN ST.

COLOMBO CT.

CITY HALL

LIM BO SENG MEMORIAL

Park

MASONIC HALL

NORTH BRIDGE RD.

ST. ANDREWS RD.

Padang

CENTRAL FIRE STATION

HIGH ST.

SUPREME COURT

SINGAPORE CRICKET CLUB

RIVER VALLEY RD.

PARLIAMENT HOUSE

Clarke Quay

ELGIN BRIDGE

PEDESTRIAN MALL

EMPRESS PLACE BLDG.

VICTORIA THEATRE

UNITY ST.

NORTH BOAT QUAY RD.

RIVERSIDE GALLERIA

River

RAFFLES LANDING PLACE

Boat Quay

CLEMENCEAU BRIDGE

The Riverfront

SOUTH BOAT QUAY RD.

Singapore River

TEWCHEW ST.

CARPENTER ST.

PEDESTRIAN MALL

SULTAN

CIRCULAR RD.

HONG KONG ST.

MERCHANT RD.

CANAL RD.

N. CANAL RD.

BATTERY

Chinatown

SINGAPORE

© MOON PUBLICATIONS, INC.

COLONIAL SINGAPORE

To New Bus Terminal

To Airport

To Airport

REPUBLIC AVE.

RD.

RD.

NICOLL

East Coast

Park

EAST COAST PKWY

Marina
East

VIRTUAL
REALITY PARK

FOUNTAIN
TERRACE

SUNTEC CITY
TOWER

CENTENNIAL
TOWER

CONRAD
INTL.

SUNTEC
CONVENTION
CENTRE

MILLENNIA
WALK

MILLENNIA
TOWER

BLVD.

RAFFLES

PAN
PACIFIC

RAFFLES

RITZ
CARLTON

MARINA
MANDARIN

THE
ORIENTAL

AVE.

RAFFLES

MARINA
SQUARE

MOO

Marina

MARINA WAY

Marina
South

THE
MERLION

FULLERTON

Marina

Bay

Marina

City

MARINA PARK DR.

MARINA PKWY

EAST COAST PKWY

SINGAPORE

ST.

RD.

0   0.2 mi

0   0.2 km

Park

To West Singapore & Jurong

Chettiar Hindu Temple

This extravagant temple is dedicated to the Hindu god Subramaniam, son of Shiva and protector of celestial devas. The highly refined architecture reflects the wealth and refined taste of the Chettiars, a successful caste of moneylenders from South India. Balancing the wildly painted 23-meter *gopuram* (entrance) packed with gods and goddesses is a massive wooden door carved with 72 lotus flowers. Though the interior is somewhat cold and impersonal, don't miss the extravagant drainage spouts and ceiling of etched glasswork which filters the falling light. Best visited during *puja* (prayer) hours in the early morning or sunset hours.

Fort Canning Park

Once known as Bukit Larangan ("Forbidden Hill") by Malays who believed it haunted by ghosts of ancient Singa Pura. Some say the hill was once covered with Malay palaces and royal courts, though excavations haven't uncovered any evidence. From the Chettiar Temple, follow the path up to the remains of the old fort, constructed in 1861 by the British. Only the gate remains after demolition in 1907 made way for the reservoir.

Down below you'll find the *kermat* (holy tomb) of Sultan Iskandar Shah, last ruler of ancient Singa Pura. Elderly Malays often stand guard. Evocative cemetery plaques are mounted in walls at the bottom of the hill. Coleman is here, and Raffles himself requested to be buried here so that his bones "would mix with the ashes of Malayan kings."

Presbyterian Church

This small but elegant church constructed in 1877 is noted for its balanced facade of mixed architectural styles, including a Serlian motif flanked by square porticos and double Ionic columns. Revived by Palladio, this Romanesque treatment was enthusiastically adopted by amateur architects throughout the British Empire. Note the smaller but identical arrangement above and below the baroque scrollwork curling up from the entablature. Further details on the historical plaque.

National Museum

Originally opened as the Raffles Museum in 1887, Singapore's National Museum is both a good museum with a well-displayed collection of historical and ethnological artifacts and an excellent example of British colonial architecture. Of special note is the painted silver dome, so difficult to erect that it is said it literally drove the contractor mad. The History of Singapore Gallery has 20 historical dioramas. Audiovisual shows are given in the small auditorium.

Don't miss the Straits Chinese Gallery and its superb collection of Peranakan fabrics, costumes, furniture, and a bridal chamber with an ornamented Chinese wedding bed. Upstairs

art lovers at the museum

SINGAPORE

the future and the past

are Chinese puppets, the famous 387-piece Haw Par Jade Collection (considered one of the finest in Southeast Asia), and the Trade Ceramics Gallery with its educational descriptions. Downstairs in the rear (easy to miss) you'll find a cramped gallery packed with Southeast Asian artifacts.

Open daily except Monday 0900-1730; admission S$4. Tours are given weekdays at 1100.

Singapore Art Museum

The former St. Joseph's Institution has been magnificently restored and converted into the finest modern art museum in Southeast Asia, a must-see for lovers of contemporary art from Singapore, Malaysia, the Philippines, Indonesia, and Thailand. Open daily except Monday 0900-1730; admission $3.

Cathedral of the Good Shepherd

Designed by amateur architect Denis McSwiney and constructed 1843-1846, this classical cathedral has a basilican ground plan and six porticoed entrances derived from Coleman's Palladian themes. Later additions included the tower, the spire, and three bays.

Convent of the Infant Holy Jesus

This fine 19th-century French Gothic Revival convent designed 1890 by Father Nain, a Catholic priest who also worked on St. Joseph's Institution, has also been completely renovated and restored and now houses an art gallery, boutiques, and several restaurants including the 400-seat Stars Singapore, created by San Francisco chef Jeremiah Tower.

Armenian Church

The church of St. Gregory the Illuminator, Singapore's oldest ecclesiastical structure, was constructed in 1835 for the colony's 5,000 Armenians, who fled warfare between the Russians and the Turks. Considered the finest work of Coleman, who borrowed heavily from James Gibbs's *Book of Architecture* and his St. Martin in the Fields. Although the Armenian community was prosperous and influential in early Singapore, 20th-century emigration has left but a handful of Armenians to attend Sunday services. Just opposite are the photogenic Chinese Chamber of Commerce and the Central Fire Station.

Raffles Hotel

No visit to Singapore is complete without a stop at the splendid hotel that is "quite possibly more famous than Singapore itself." The Raffles was constructed in a French Renaissance style by the Sarkies brothers, three shrewd Armenians who also ran the Strand in Rangoon and the E&O in Penang. Early guests included Joseph Conrad and Rudyard Kipling, who wrote, ". . . Raffles Hotel, where the food is excellent as the rooms are bad. Let the traveller take note. Feed at Raffles and sleep at the Hotel de l'Europe." Tigran Sarkies wisely edited the verse to "Feed at the Raffles, where the food is excellent," omitting the part about the rooms.

The hotel is also known for tigers under the billiard table and being home to the infamous Singapore Sling, a revolting combination of gin, cherry herring, Cointreau, Benedictine, pineapple, lime juice, and Angostura bitters. Later additions in the '60s and '70s failed to preserve architectural themes and the hotel was com-

SINGAPORE

pleted reconstructed several years ago with mixed results.

Raffles City

Convenient shopping venue with exchange facilities, post office, and a well-stocked bookstore on the second floor. The cocktail lounge on the top floor of the attached Westin Singapore offers mind-blowing views across most of Singapore Island.

St. Andrew's Cathedral

This English Gothic Anglican church was designed by Coleman but rebuilt in 1853 by an amateur architect named MacPherson. Costs were minimal since as superintendent of convicts MacPherson had a steady source of cheap labor. Inside the soaring interior are stained-glass windows and plaster walls covered with Madras *chunam* made from egg white, shell lime, and sugar. The original church bell, donated by the daughter of Paul Revere, is now kept in the National Museum. Marble and brass memorial plaques are embedded in the walls and floors.

The Padang

Raffles in 1819 saw little more than thick mangrove swamps and a patch of green nicknamed Raffles Plain or the Esplanade. Today the Padang (Malay for central lawn) is surrounded by government buildings, churches, and private sports clubs. At one end lies the Singapore Cricket Club, constructed in 1877 as the city's all-white sports club, while at the other end is the recently constructed Singapore Recreation Club.

City Hall and Supreme Court

To the north stands the 1926 neoclassical City Hall, where during WW II the British surrendered to the Japanese. Three years later the Japanese presented their swords to Mountbatten. The equally imposing Supreme Court was built in 1937 on the site of the now-demolished Hotel de l'Europe.

Victoria Theatre and Memorial Hall

As noted earlier, Raffles himself dictated that the government buildings should be located on the north side of the Singapore River. Today these imperial buildings in Palladian, Gothic,

Victorian, neo-Renaissance, and neoclassical styles form the political and historical heart of modern Singapore. Focal points include the Victoria Theater and Memorial Hall, which serves as home for the Singapore Symphony. Designed by architect Bidwell in 1905, this hybrid of classical and Renaissance elements is capped by an elegant clocktower, which strengthens the symmetry and acts as a city landmark. A bronze statue of Raffles stands in front.

The adjacent Empress Place has been converted into a museum showcasing historical and cultural relics from the People's Republic of China. Parliament House to the rear marks the spot where Raffles first landed and met the Malay sultan who vacated his residence for the British. A copy of the Raffles statue stands on the riverbank.

Financial District

Across the iron girders of Cavenagh Bridge you'll find the gray-faced General Post Office, designed by Keyes and Dowdeswell as the final expression of classical architecture. Clifford Pier is where boats depart for harbor and island cruises. Change Alley, Singapore's original mall, has been leveled and octagonal Telok Ayer Food Market, a Victorian whimsy constructed in 1894 from cast-iron ribbing imported from England, has been ruined by careless redevelopment.

CHINATOWN

When Raffles landed in Singapore, he discovered a small Chinese business community firmly established along the banks of the Singapore River. Raffles assigned separate streets to each Chinese group: Hokkiens from Fukien settled along Amoy Street, Teochews from Swatow and Cantonese from Hong Kong in other areas. Clubs and clan associations *(kongsi)* aided those who shared common family names or hailed from the same regions. Others joined secret societies *(tongs)* which controlled the loan sharking, gambling, prostitution, and drug trade. Although outlawed by the British government, these societies remained influential until the Japanese occupation put an end to their power.

Chinatown thrived until the '50s, when young Singaporeans began fleeing the crowded tenement houses for modern housing complexes in the suburbs. Only the elderly or poor remained behind. Rent control kept living expenses low, but refurbishing became so expensive that properties were routinely neglected and fell into serious disrepair. Considered an unsalvageable anachronism by the '70s, Chinatown seemed doomed to destruction until an economic slowdown forced the government to come up with an ambitious preservation plan. The following walking tour begins at the Elgin Bridge and makes a clockwise circle through the better sections.

Wak Hai Cheng Bio Temple

Mornings are the best time to visit Chinatown. Begin your tour with a Malay breakfast in the Empress Food Center before crossing Elgin Bridge and walking down Boat Quay Road. The juxtaposition of old *godowns* and soaring skyscrapers forms one of Singapore's great sights. Turn right at the modern Overseas Chinese Banking Center to the Temple of the Calm Ocean on Phillip Street. Built in 1855 by Teochew Chinese fishermen for the Goddess of the Sea, this temple once bordered the waterfront before land reclamation pushed back the sea. Note the intricate roof carvings and finely carved interior ceiling beams.

Fuk Tak Chi Temple

This small but fascinating Shenist temple was built by Hakka and Cantonese immigrants who dedicated it to Toa Peh Kong, Chinese God of Wealth and Protector of the Poor. His image is depicted in mourner's sackcloth or as a bearded Hokkien sailor. Much of the temple's interest comes from its links with Taoism, the mystical and magical folk religion of the poor. Inside you'll find papier-mâché horses, magical figures used in trance ceremonies, and an altar filled with strange religious icons.

Nagore Durga Mosque

Though sadly neglected, this lime-green mosque built in 1830 by Tamil Muslims displays a curious marriage of disparate architectural styles: fluted Corinthian columns, half-moon fans, a pieced Islamic balustrade, Chinese towers, and Islamic minarets being attacked by tropical plantlife. Farther on you'll pass the modest Al Abrar Mosque constructed in 1855 by *chulias* Muslims from South India.

Thian Hok Keng Temple

Singapore's oldest Chinese temple is also the most spectacular in the city. Constructed in 1841 by the Hokkiens and dedicated to the Goddess of the Sea, the Temple of Heavenly Happiness is also a treasure trove of Chinese craftsmanship. Of special note are the door guardians, elaborate roof brackets which support the roof, and intricately carved granite pillars imported from China. All were carefully integrated into a spatial arrangement to balance the forces of *yin* and *yang*. Beyond the 19th-century courtyard stands the principal temple with images of Tin Hau and other gods whose mouths have been sealed with tobacco tar (formerly opium). Smaller pavilions to the rear are filled with ancestor tablets and images of Kuan Yin.

Amoy and Club Streets

Black flags stenciled in gold with mystical trigrams indicate the homes of Chinese mediums who communicate via seances with departed ancestors and wandering ghosts. Walk slowly around China, Chin Chew, Nanking and Hokkien streets . . . one of the most authentic sections left in old Chinatown. Return to Club Street (named for the trade guilds once located here) to watch idol carvers kept busy carving miniature gods and goddesses. Then walk up Club to the inclined terrain of Ann Siang Hill and South Bridge Road.

Sago, Tanjong Pagar, and Neil Roads

Sago Road was once a busy brothel district named after the factories that extracted starch from the trunk of the sago palm. Before being torn down a decade ago for redevelopment, Sago was where elderly Chinese came to die in Death Houses. Today it's just an empty lot most likely haunted by ghosts waiting for the return of prospective developers. A few surviving funeral stores on Sago still make paper reproductions of cars, houses, and yachts to be burned at funerals. Walk south to the Maxwell Food Center and the V-shaped Jinrickshaw Building wedged at the intersection. Designed in 1913 by Swan and MacLaren, this strategically placed building acts as a strong anchor between the older shophouses of Chinatown and the restored terrace homes on Tanjong Pagar and Neil Roads—the largest block of Straits Chinese shophouses in Singapore.

SINGAPORE

Chinatown Center

The intersection of Trengganu and Smith streets is the heart of old Chinatown. Before street merchants were relocated in 1973 into faceless shopping complexes, this neighborhood dazzled the visitor with its vegetable stalls, roving food hawkers, and itinerant vendors selling everything from live snakes to counterfeit Rolexes.

Although largely destroyed by urban redevelopment, it's still an active and colorful neighborhood with dozens of fascinating shops. Smith Street is best for Chinese teas, porcelain, beaded slippers, jade, bonsai trees, incense dolls, dried lizards, medicines, and haircuts. Temple Street merchants deal in paper effigies, *tai chi* shoes, and soy sauce. Look for the Chinese medical hall.

Pagoda Street, once filled with opium dens and the center for Singapore's slave trade, is now lined with tailor shops. Mosque Street is famous for Teochew restaurants and old tea houses little changed from the '20s. Try the duck soup with salted vegetables, black chicken soup, Teochew *muay,* roast pig, and sweet yam paste.

Sri Mariamman Hindu Temple

Sri Mariamman was first constructed from *attap* and timber but expanded in 1842 by an Indian merchant named Naraina Pillai. Dedicated to the Mother Goddess Devi, this temple shows the three principal elements of Dravidian architecture: an interior shrine *(vimanam)* covered by a decorated dome, an assembly hall *(madapam)* used for prayers, and an entrance tower *(gopuram)* covered with brightly painted gods and goddesses. Prayer services are announced by wailing Indian clarinets, crashing cymbals, and the frenzied beating of drums. The nearby Jamae Mosque was built in 1835 by Muslim *chulias.*

Thong Chai Medical Institution

Named after the Cantonese theaters that once lined the road, Wayang Street features an extremely rare medical clinic constructed in traditional Chinese style. Cloud-shaped gables and glazed green tiles cap what is now an antique store. Several old warehouses (godowns) still stand along North Boat Quay Road.

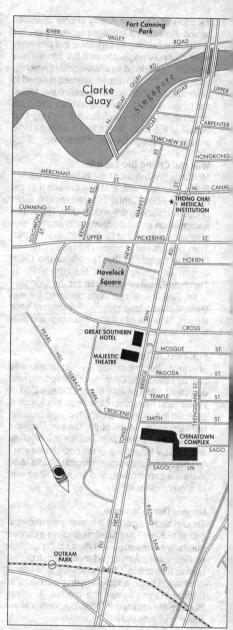

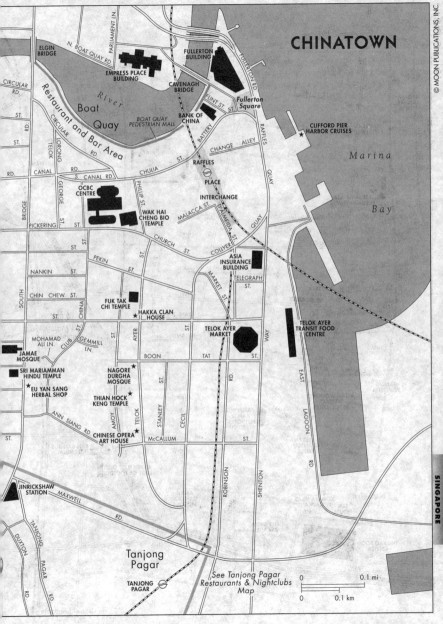

CHINATOWN

Marina

Bay

ELGIN
BRIDGE

N. BOAT QUAY RD.

PARLIAMENT LN.

FULLERTON
BUILDING

EMPRESS PLACE
BUILDING

CAVENAGH
BRIDGE

River

Boat
Quay

Restaurant and Bar Area

BOAT QUAY
PEDESTRIAN MALL

BANK OF
CHINA

FLINT ST.

Fullerton
Square

FULLERTON RD.

CLIFFORD PIER
HARBOR CRUISES

CIRCULAR
RD.

ST.

ST.

RD.

BRIDGE

TELOK

LORONG

CIRCULAR

CANAL

GEORGE

RD.

ST.

ST.

PICKERING

S. CANAL RD.

OCBC
CENTRE

PHILLIP

ST.

CHULIA

ST.

BATTERY

ST.

CHANGE ALLEY

RAFFLES
PLACE

INTERCHANGE

WAK HAI
CHENG BIO
TEMPLE

MALACCA ST.

CHURCH

ST.

ST.

D'ALMEIDA ST.

COLLYER

RAFFLES

QUAY

QUAY

PEKIN

ST.

ST.

NANKIN

ST.

CHIN CHEW ST.

ST.

SOUTH

ST.

CHINA

FUK TAK
CHI TEMPLE

HAKKA CLAN
HOUSE

ASIA
INSURANCE
BUILDING

TELEGRAPH
ST.

MARKET

ST.

TELOK AYER
MARKET

TELOK AYER
TRANSIT FOOD
CENTRE

MOHAMAD
ALI LN.

JAMAE
MOSQUE

CLUB

GEMMILL
LN.

ST.

AYER

ST.

BOON

TAT

ST.

ST.

WAY

EAST

SRI MARIAMMAN
HINDU TEMPLE

EU YAN SANG
HERBAL SHOP

ANN SIANG RD.

NAGORE
DURGHA
MOSQUE

THIAN HOCK
KENG TEMPLE

AMOY

TELOK

STANLEY

ST.

CECIL

ST.

ST.

RD.

LAGOON

RD.

CHINESE OPERA
ART HOUSE

McCALLUM

ST.

JINRICKSHAW
STATION

MAXWELL

RD.

ROBINSON

SHENTON

Tanjong
Pagar

TANJONG
PAGAR

TANJONG
PAGAR

DUXTON

RD.

RD.

See Tanjong Pagar
Restaurants & Nightclubs
Map

0   0.1 mi

0   0.1 km

© MOON PUBLICATIONS, INC.

SINGAPORE

© MOON PUBLICATIONS, INC.

SINGAPORE

LAVENDER

LAVENDER STREET
BUS TERMINAL

SERANGOON RD.

RD.

RD.

BEATTY RD.

FOCH RD.

HAMILTON RD.

CAVEN RD.

AVE.

HORNE ST.

PENHAS RD.

LEONG
SAN SEE
TEMPLE ★

★ TEMPLE OF
1,000 LIGHTS

RD.

STURDEE

Jalan Besar
Stadium

GEORGE

FRENCH RD.

JELLICOE RD.

LAVENDER
MRT

TASSENSOHN RD.

PETAIN

JALAN

TYRMITT

RD.

SRI SRINIVASA
PERUMAL TEMPLE

New World
Park

PLUMER RD.

RD.

KITCHENER

RD.

JALAN

MALABAR
MOSQUE ★

Old Malay
Cemetery

OWENS

COURSE

RD.

BURMAH RD.

BIRCH RD.

ROBERTS LN.

KINTA RD.

SAM LEONG RD.

MAUDE RD.

TOWNSEND

KING

RD.

MUSTAFA
CENTER

LEMBU RD.

SYED

ALWI

JALAN BERSEH

DESKER

RD.

KELANTAN LN.

RACE COURSE LN.

ROWELL LN.

BABOO RD.

HINDOO RD.

NORRIS RD.

BESAR

KELANTAN LN.

GANDHI
MEMORIAL ★

ASIAN WOMEN'S
WELFARE
ASSOCIATION

VEERASAMY

KLANG LN.

KAMPONG
KAPOR
METHODIST
CHURCH

RD.

VICTORIA

ROCHOR CANAL RD.

ROTAN LN.

WELD RD.

WELD RD.

ARAB

RACE

CHANDER RD.

BELILIOS LN.

★ SRI VEERAMA
KALIAMMAN
TEMPLE

CUFF

WELD

PERAK

RD.

TAXIS

BAN SAN BUS
TERMINAL

UPPER DICKSON RD.

DICKSON

CHURCH OF OUR
LADY OF LOURDES

SUNGEI

QUEEN ST.

KERABAU RD.

TAN ★
HOUSE

KOMALA VILAS
RESTAURANT ▼

DUNLOP

MADRAS ST.

ST.

ABDUL
GAFFOOR
MOSQUE

ST.

ROCHOR

BUFFALO

CAMPBELL LN.

MAYO ST.

★ LITTLE INDIA
ARCADE

BENCOOLEN ST.

ZHUJIAO FOOD
CENTER

CLIVE ST.

SUNGEI ST.

CANAL RD.

PRINSEP ST.

BUGIS
MRT

BUTIK TIMAH RD.

ROCHOR

SHORT ST.

BUTIK TIMAH RD.

ALBERT

MACKENZIE RD.

To Central Singapore

LITTLE INDIA

Serangoon Road is Singapore's "Little India." Originally brought here as indentured workers to clear the jungles and drain the swamps, the 200,000 Indians of Singapore now influence the country far beyond their modest numbers. Most are from the south but others include Coromandel Muslims *(chulias)*, Malabar Muslims *(kakaks)*, North Indians *(Bengalis)*, Malayali from Kerala, Sikhs from the Punjab, and Orang Bombays from Gujarat.

Like the Chinese, the Indians also grouped together according to religion, state of origin, and choice of occupation. Tamils settled along Serangoon Road and moved into white-collar occupations. Sikhs, Sindhis, and Gujaratis took High Street and found work as textile merchants, tailors, and policemen. Intermarriage between Indian Muslims and Malays produced a class called the Jawi Peranakans. The most powerful and highly visible caste is that of the Chettiars, wealthy moneylenders from Madras who have financed many of the city's most elaborate temples.

Singapore's Little India is an outstanding place to experience the exotic sights, sounds, and smells of India. The heart lies in the small alleys near at the western end of Serangoon Road. Streets farther east have been redeveloped and lost much of their charm, though the outstanding architecture on Jalan Besar and Petain Road is worth visiting.

The Center

Start your tour with a meal in the Zhujiao Food Center, a simple building erected after the unfortunate destruction of the beautiful Thekka Market. Small alleys across Serangoon Road form what is most authentic and fascinating about the neighborhood. Walk slowly to enjoy the aromas, sitar music drifting from record stores, hefty women wrapped in polyester saris, cowboy beer bars with swinging doors, garland weavers, pungent spice shops, goldsmiths, turbaned Sikhs, street barbers, and grinning Tamils pouring glasses of steaming *chai*.

Walk a street ten times and it looks different every time. Buffalo Road is where Chettiar moneylenders patiently wait for customers. Don't let the modest surroundings fool you; these men are rich! Lunch is best at Komala Vilas Restau-

SINGAPORE

Hindu god in Little India

Kaliamman Chettiar Temple: Although rarely mentioned in most tourist publications, this flamboyant temple offers some of Singapore's most impressive Hindu statuary and murals.

Sakya Muni Buddha Gaya Temple: The Temple of 1000 Lights is noted for its gaudy 15-meter, 300-ton Buddha image with an oversized nose and elephantine ears. Spin the fortune-telling wheel on the left.

Leong San See Temple: This recently renovated temple was constructed in 1926 for the worship of Kuan Yin and other Buddhist bodhisattvas. To the rear is a spacious courtyard filled with countless ancestral tablets.

Petain Road

Designed in the '30s by a British architect named Jackson, the Chinese-baroque homes on Petain Road are perhaps the most impressive and intact group left in Singapore. Among the remarkable details are Corinthian pilasters, Chinese-inspired bas-reliefs under the second-story windows, Malay-fretted eaves, and glazed ceramic tiles designed with peony flowers, chrysanthemums,

rant or the upscale restaurants on Race Course Road. Cuff Road has several more cafes.

Sri Verama Kaliamman Temple
The Bengalis constructed this temple in 1881 and dedicated it to Kali, the goddess of death and destruction. The brightly illuminated Coke machine which stands in front seems to strangely complement the wildly cavorting gods. Pause at the neglected Gandhi Memorial Hall and continue walking down Serangoon to the noteworthy shophouses on Roberts and Owens roads. Many are occupied by bachelors who pay S$10 monthly to sleep on the floors in shifts.

Temples to the East
Perumal Temple: The 20-meter *raja gopuram* is decorated with polychromed reincarnations of Vishnu, the main deity of the temple. Originally constructed in 1855 and reworked by South Indian sculptors in 1970, this is the starting point of the Thaipusam procession, which ends at the Chettiar Temple on Tank Road.

SINGAPORE

Muslim tailor

roses, and birds. Also worth visiting is the Lee An Leng Bird Shop on Jalan Besar.

Jalan Besar

Jalan Besar features more superb Chinese-baroque architecture. Of special interest are the nine shophouses on Syed Alwi Road (nos. 61-69) with their oval-shaped windows surrounded by bowtie moldings, and the two shophouses on Syed Alwi (nos. 77-78) set with elaborate window architraves and European tiles.

Another highlight is the flamboyant pair at the junction of Jalan Besar and Veerasamy Road. These three-story wonders are enduring reminders of Singapore's rich architectural heritage. The Garut Road "Thieves'" Market has more motorcycle parts and shrink-wrapped radios than thieves. Final stop is the Abdul Gafoor Mosque, which fuses Islamic arches with Roman columns. The dilapidated remains of the original mosque stand on Mayo Street.

ARAB STREET

Sultan Mosque

Between Bencoolen and Arab streets you might visit the Kwan Yin Temple and try a durian at the colorful fruit market on Queen Street. The medium temple on Johore Road displays Taoist trance daggers and magical images whose mouths have been sealed with tobacco. Top draw in Singapore's Muslim quarter is the Sultan Mosque, a Saracenic building designed in 1924 by Swan and MacLaren with onion-shaped domes, four-corner minarets, pointed trefoils, and cinquefoil arches over the balconies. Modestly dressed tourists may enter the mosque via the rear entrance on Muscat Street. Inexpensive cafes on North Bridge Road serve tasty *murtabaks* and *biryanis*.

Back Streets and the Sultan's Palace

North Bridge Road passes herbalists, perfume shops, and Islamic supply stores to Sultan Road. Turn right and walk past Alsagoff Arab School to Hajjah Fatimah Mosque, which was designed by a British architect in 1846 for a wealthy Malaccan-born lady. Pahang Street has traditional stonecutters and blacksmiths. Istana Kampong Glam, at the end of the alley, is the former palace

of the sultan. Constructed around 1836 and influenced by architect Coleman, this modest house is scheduled for renovation and possible conversion into a Malay cultural complex. To the left is an impressive bungalow once occupied by Malay royalty.

Arab Street

Bussorah and Kandahar streets are excellent streets to wander and purchase prayer rugs, Korans, and ginger drinks called *sarabat*. Shops on Arab Street are packed with imported batiks, Indonesian brasswork, fragrant basketware, exotic perfumes, jewelry, traditional medicines, and *barang haji*—everything required for a pilgrimage to Mecca. A fine change from the air-conditioned shopping centers of Orchard Road.

WEST SINGAPORE ATTRACTIONS

Singapore Zoo

The best zoo in Asia. Over 2,000 animals including rare and endangered species live in this open-air zoo situated by the Seletar Reservoir. Unlike most Asian zoos, this one uses natural barriers instead of iron bars and impersonal cages. Animals include Sumatran orangutans, Thai elephants, Malaysian tigers, and small Komodo dragons. Arrive by 0900 for breakfast with the orangutans. Animal shows throughout the day.

The newest twist here is the amazing Night Safari, the world's first and only nighttime safari park where visitors can watch nocturnal animals going about their active nightlives undisturbed.

The zoo is open daily 0830-1830; admission S$10. Night Safari is open daily 1930-midnight and is best visited after 2100 when the crowds have thinned. The adjacent Mandai Orchid Gardens are easily visited. Take the MRT to Ang Mo Kio and then SBS bus 138.

Jurong Bird Park

This 20-hectare park, one of Singapore's best attractions, boasts the world's largest collection of Southeast Asian birds inside a gigantic aviary, and the Nocturnal House which cleverly uses modern technology to turn day into night. Bird shows at 1030 and 1500. Arrive before 0900 for buffet breakfast in the songbird ter-

SINGAPORE

city view of the Padang

race, but avoid the weekends, when it's jammed with Singaporeans.

Just across the street is Jurong Crocodile Paradise with some 3,000 crocodiles doing all the familiar wrestling and feeding routines.

Jurong Bird Park is open daily 0900-1800; admission S$9. The crocodile park costs S$6. Take the MRT to Boon Lay station, then SBS bus 194 or 251 from the interchange.

Haw Par Villa

Tiger Balm Gardens has recently been redeveloped and expanded into a multimillion-dollar Chinese mythological theme park with lasers, robotronics, an artisans village, boat rides through the world of Chinese spirits, and a hologram-studded journey with the Monkey God. Designed by the same people responsible for Knott's Berry Farm and Lotte Theme Park in Seoul, but a somewhat tacky place on the verge of bankruptcy.

Open daily 0900-1800; admission S$16. Take the MRT to Buona Vista, then bus 200 to Pasir Panjang Road.

Sentosa Island

A multimillion-dollar leisure and recreation resort with an artificial swimming lagoon, wax displays, a butterfly park, two beaches, a golf course, a roller-skating rink, musical fountains, a maritime museum, and an underwater world with see-through tunnels. Recent additions include an 11-story Merlion Statue and Images of

Singapore including Pioneers of Singapore, the Surrender Chambers, and Festivals of Singapore—a very informative and worthwhile attraction.

Open daily 0600-midnight but most attractions operate 0900-1900. Admission is S$6 but a better deal is the Sentosa Saver ticket for S$14 which includes admission to most of the better attractions.

Chinese and Japanese Gardens

The 14-hectare Chinese Gardens in Jurong are decorated with miniature temples, pagodas, arched bridges, and lakes surrounded by wispy willows. The adjacent Japanese Gardens are the largest outside Japan.

Open daily 0900-1800; admission S$4 for both gardens. Take the MRT to Lakeside station.

Tang Dynasty Village

Singapore's largest theme park attempts to re-create the most famous era in China's history—the 7th-century peak of the Tang Dynasty centered in the ancient capital city of Xian—with architectural reproductions of the Imperial Palace, housing estates, and an underground chamber filled with more than 1,000 replicas of Xian's famed terra-cotta warriors. Despite the promise, this is another themed attraction on the verge of bankruptcy.

Open daily 0900-2000; admission S$16. Take the MRT to Lakeside station and walk south.

ACCOMMODATIONS

The rise of Singapore to the economic centerpiece of Southeast Asia has been accompanied by a remarkable growth in the number of hotels to serve almost seven million annual visitors—over three times the population of the country.

Prices: Singapore's hotels are not the bargains of old days but have risen sharply due to continuing high occupancy rates and a steadily rising local currency. Average prices of over S$400 for luxury accommodations and S$250-350 for moderate hotels are now on par with New York and Tokyo and surpass all other Southeast Asian capitals except for Hong Kong. So-called budget hotels average S$150-200 and even the YMCA charges almost S$100 for clean but basic rooms.

Fortunately for the budget traveler, Singapore also has dozens of inexpensive guesthouses—chiefly on Bencoolen Street and Beach Road—where dormitory beds cost under S$10 and private rooms average S$25-45. The term "guesthouse" is a bit of a misnomer since most are actually residential flats or office buildings in which several floors have been converted into makeshift hotels comprised of a rabbit warren of dormitory rooms and private rooms.

Most guesthouse rooms under S$30 are tiny, sparsely furnished, and often divided by paper-thin partitions which make for less than ideal conditions. Rooms over S$30, however, tend to be larger, quieter, and include a/c and perhaps a small television.

Districts: Singapore's hotels are located in several districts. The largest concentration of hotels are on Orchard Road, the main tourist belt and home to most of the country's upscale shopping centers. Central Singapore—the district between Chinatown and Little India—has most of the guesthouses and moderately priced hotels and is ideally located within walking distance of both ethnic neighborhoods and the colonial attractions near the Singapore River. Chinatown has few hotels except for a handful near the business district and a trio of boutique hotels in restored buildings. Little India has a few guesthouses and hotels almost exclusively geared to Indian travelers and the occasional iconoclastic traveler who really wants to explore one of central Singapore's most interesting yet least visited neighborhoods.

BUDGET

Bencoolen Street Guesthouses

Bencoolen Street has served as the backpackers' center since the early 1970s when several guesthouses opened in the buildings between Bras Basah Road and Albert Street. Most of the places have dorm beds in fan-cooled rooms for S$7-8 and S$8-10 in a/c rooms depending on the number of beds. They also offer private fan-cooled rooms for S$20-30 and a/c rooms for S$35-50 depending on the size of the room and amenities such as private baths and televisions.

Bencoolen Street has a few old Chinese hotels which may appeal to travelers who seek privacy and dislike the congested atmosphere of budget guesthouses.

Peony Mansions: One of Singapore's largest and oldest collection of guesthouses are located in the seven-story Peony Mansions at 46-52 Bencoolen just across the street from the Bencoolen Hotel. Three different guesthouses operate dorms and private rooms on all floors of the building.

Peony Mansions has a furniture store on the ground level and no signs indicating the location of the entrance to the guesthouses. You need to walk around to the back and take the elevator to one of the three guesthouses.

Lee Traveler's Club: The largest guesthouse in Peony Mansions has dorms and fan-cooled rooms in the standard ranges, plus a variety of a/c rooms with common or private bathrooms. Bus tickets to Malaysia can be purchased at the front desk and laundry services cost S$6 per load. Lights must be turned out shortly after midnight. 46-52 Bencoolen St., 7th floor, tel. (65) 338-3149 or 336-5509, S$8-10 dorm, S$20-60 private rooms.

Peony Mansions Travellers Lodge: The building's original guesthouse, established in 1971, has 28 rooms on several floors and a re-

SINGAPORE

ception area on the 4th floor decorated with statues of Christ, Sai Baba, and Blind Justice. Also known as Green Mansions, this guesthouse has laundry services and provides complimentary breakfast to all travelers staying in their facilities. 46-52 Bencoolen St., 4th floor, tel. (65) 338-5638, fax 339-1471, S$8-10 dorm, S$25-60 private rooms.

Latin House: The smallest of the three guesthouses inside Peony Mansions is somewhat cheaper than the others and provides a complimentary locker and coffee at the reception desk.

46-53 Bencoolen St., 3rd floor, tel. (65) 339-6308, S$7-10 dorm, S$20-50 private rooms.

Bencoolen House Homestay: Just across the street from Peony Mansions and wedged between the Strand and Bencoolen hotels is another older building with dorms and private rooms on the upper floors reached with an incredibly small elevator. The 22 rooms are reasonably clean and preferred by many travelers over those in Peony Mansions. 27 Bencoolen St., 7th floor, tel. (65) 337-3734 or 338-1206, fax 292-6000, S$7-10 dorm, S$20-50 private rooms.

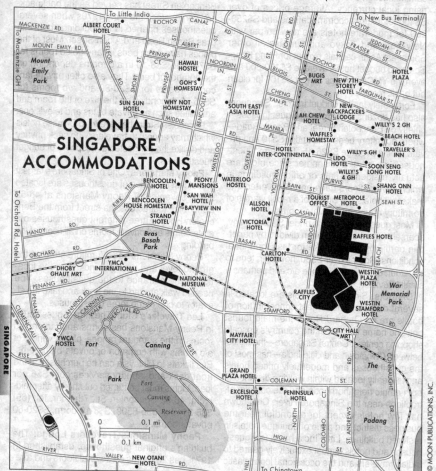

COLONIAL SINGAPORE ACCOMMODATIONS

© MOON PUBLICATIONS, INC.

Why Not Homestay: Another longtime travelers' favorite with a cozy cafe on the ground floor and dozens of small but bearable rooms on the upper floors. 127 Bencoolen St., tel. (65) 338-8838, S$10-12 a/c dorms, S$25-50 private rooms.

Goh's Homestay: The original Goh's Homestay at 173 Bencoolen—the place where the author first met Moon Publications founder Bill Dalton in 1979—has been closed for reconstruction but the name lives on in the adjacent building, which sadly lacks an elevator and requires a hike up an incredibly long flight of stairs. The trudge is worth the effort since rooms are very clean if windowless and all dormitory rooms are air-conditioned if somewhat expensive. Goh's is worth a few extra dollars. 169-D Bencoolen St., 4th floor, tel. (65) 339-6561, fax 339-8606, S$12 a/c dorm, S$30-60 private rooms.

Hawaii Hostel: Same building as Goh's and less of a hike since the reception is located on the second floor. Rooms are small, clean, and include a/c plus guests receive complimentary breakfast. 171-B Bencoolen St., 2nd floor, tel. (65) 338-4187, S$30-50 private rooms.

Guesthouses near Bencoolen Street

Several decent guesthouses are located near Bencoolen Street.

Waterloo Hostel: A centrally located Catholic-run hostel with immaculate a/c rooms furnished with telephone, television, and small refrigerators. Facilities include complimentary breakfast, safe deposit boxes, and laundry services. 55 Waterloo St., 4th floor, tel. (65) 336-6555, fax 336-2160, S$60-75 private rooms.

Mackenzie Guesthouse: Although somewhat distant, the friendly owners and homey atmosphere make this popular with many travelers. 114A Mackenzie St., tel. (65) 334-4980, S$6-9 dorm, S$20-45 private rooms.

Budget Hotels near Bencoolen Street

Very few of the old Chinese hotels which once dotted this neighborhood have survived two decades of urban development.

San Wah Hotel: Bencoolen's inexpensive old-style Chinese hotels are chiefly a memory of the past but the remaining units offer simple but clean rooms with an old-world atmosphere. Chow Yoke San, owner of the San Wah for over 50 years, provides a nice touch with his ancestral

photographs posted on the interior walls. 36 Bencoolen St., tel. (65) 336-2428, S$45-55 private rooms.

Sun Sun Hotel: A well-restored 1928 building with a memorable confectionery on the ground floor and 17 spotlessly clean rooms with common baths. 260 Middle Rd., tel. (65) 338-4911, S$40-55.

South East Asia Hotel: Right next door to a lively Buddhist temple is a venerable but well-maintained Chinese hotel with a vegetarian cafe on the ground floor and 51 clean a/c rooms with attached baths in the more expensive units. Somewhat claustrophobic but a great location and friendly management. 190 Waterloo St., tel. (65) 338-2394, fax 338-3480, S$70-90.

New 7th Storey Hotel: Once the tallest hotel in the district, this venerable block of concrete deceptively holds 38 clean and comfortable rooms with a/c, TV, telephone, and attached baths in the more expensive units. 229 Rochor Rd., tel. (65) 337-0251, fax 334-3550, S$60-85.

Victoria Hotel: Moderately priced a/c rooms with either common or private baths in a handy location near several good food centers. 87 Victoria St., tel. (65) 338-2381, fax 334-4853, S$65-90.

Beach Road Guesthouses

Beach Road near Liang Seah Street and Middle Road has the second largest concentration of guesthouses in Singapore in an unrestored neighborhood just a few blocks from the Raffles Hotel. The first three guesthouses described below are located in the Fu Yuen Building at 75 Beach Road.

Das Travellers Inn: The first guesthouse in the area has frayed after years of use but offers some of the cheapest dorms and private rooms in Singapore. 87 Beach Rd., 4th floor, tel. (65) 338-7460, S$7-10 dorm, S$20-45 private rooms.

Lee Guesthouse: Affiliated with the guesthouse on Bencoolen Street, this counterpart also has fairly clean rooms plus a comfortable communal lounging area. 75 Beach Rd., 6th floor, tel. (65) 335-5490, S$7-10 dorms, S$25-45 private rooms.

Willy's Guesthouse: The third choice in the Fu Yuen Building has a few private rooms and dormitory beds in the common sitting area. 75 Beach Rd., 4th floor, tel. (65) 337-0916, S$7-

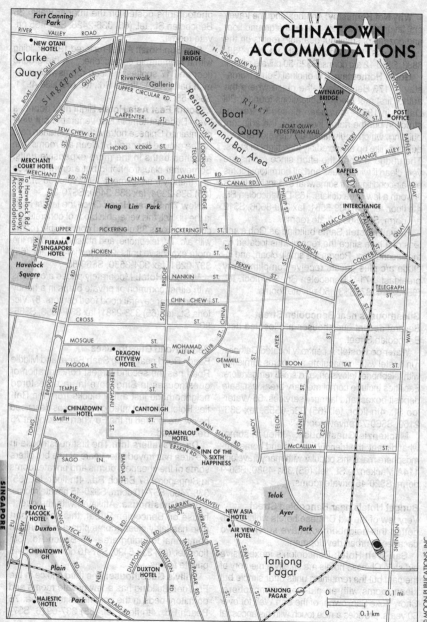

CHINATOWN
ACCOMMODATIONS

© MOON PUBLICATIONS, INC.

10 dorm, S$25-35 private rooms. Willy's also has two other nearby guesthouses with similar prices at 101 Beach Road and around the corner on Liang Seah Street.

Willy's Guesthouse 4: Willy's latest outlet has a/c dorms and private rooms, storage facilities, and laundry services in a location about 400 meters from the Raffles Hotel. 41 Middle Rd., tel. (65) 334-6498, S$8-10 dorm, S$28-38 private rooms.

New Backpackers Lodge: Tucked away in a narrow alley between Beach and North Bridge Roads is a surprisingly friendly little guesthouse with inexpensive rooms, over 20 dorm beds, and complimentary breakfast until noon. The sitting area is cozy to say the least. 18A Liang Seah St., tel. (65) 293-5251, S$7-10 dorm, S$20-30 private rooms.

Waffles Homestay: The final guesthouse in the area is located in an older building across the street from the Inter-continental Hotel and the Bugis Junction shopping complex. Waffles was originally called the Raffles Homestay until a copyright lawsuit was filed by the Raffles Hotel—as if anybody could possibly confuse the two properties. 490 North Bridge Rd., 2nd floor, tel. (65) 334-1608, S$7-10 dorm, S$25-40 private rooms.

Beach Road Hotels

The old and inexpensive Chinese hotels near Beach Road are simple places typically set with Wild West swinging doors, period furniture, shuttered windows, and airy rooms far more spacious than in the nearby guesthouses. None of the following hotels offer dormitory beds.

Ah Chew Hotel: A 14-room relic run by elderly men who lounge around the lobby in their T-shirts and shorts. Rooms are large if sparsely furnished and include a common bath down the hall. 496 North Bridge Rd., tel. (65) 337-5285, S$25-35.

Lido Hotel: A clean and friendly Chinese hotel with friendly management and spacious rooms at bargain prices. 54 Middle Rd., tel. (65) 337-1872, S$25-35.

Shang Onn Hotel: Just two minutes from the Raffles Hotel and a million miles in terms of atmosphere is this quaint relic with green-shuttered windows and 10 reasonably priced rooms. 37 Beach Rd., tel. (65) 338-4153, fax 338-5818, S$35-55.

Soon Seng Long Hotel: The final old Chinese hotel in the area provides spacious rooms with minimal furniture and common baths in the hallway. 26 Middle Rd., tel. (65) 337-6318, S$30-40.

Chinatown

Most of Chinatown's inexpensive guesthouses and hotels are located at the far end of the district near the railway station and Tanjong Pagar MRT station.

Chinatown Guesthouse: Friendly managers and an unusual location but dorms and private rooms are cramped and minimally furnished. 325-D New Bridge Rd., 5th Floor, tel. (65) 220-0671, S$8 dorm, S$30-40 private rooms.

Canton Guesthouse: A renovated prewar shophouse in the heart of Chinatown with carpeted a/c dorms and cozy but comfortable rooms. 42 Smith St., tel. (65) 323-1275, S$8-10 dorm, S$35-55 private rooms.

Chinatown YMCA: The Metropolitan YMCA International Centre near the train station provides a convenient layover for travelers scheduled for early morning departures. 70 Palmer Rd., tel. (65) 222-4666, S$15 dorm, S$35-55 private rooms.

Majestic Hotel: Set on a street lined with old Malaccan shophouses and homes, the Majestic provides a quiet escape from the average tourist enclave and presents good value in its clean, a/c rooms. 31-37 Bukit Pasoh Rd., tel. (65) 222-3377, fax 223-0907, S$50-80.

New Asia Hotel: The New Asia and adjacent Air View Hotel are run-down hotels not worth their bargain rates. 2 Peck Seah St., tel. (65) 221-1861, fax 223-9002, S$55-70.

Little India

The following guesthouses and budget hotels are within a few blocks of the Little India Arcade.

Bencoolen Junction Travellers Lodge: The latest branch of the Why Not Homestay on Bencoolen Street lacks personality and charm but provides inexpensive dorm beds and a limited number of private rooms with shared facilities. Just opposite the Sim Lim Towers. 35A Jalan Besar, tel. (65) 293-7287, $S7-9 dorm, S$20-25 private room.

Boon Wah Boarding House: A renovated small Chinese hotel with 37 small but clean a/c rooms furnished with TV and attached bath-

SINGAPORE

rooms. The hotel faces Jalan Besar but the entrance is around the corner on Dunlop Street. 43A Jalan Besar Rd., tel. (65) 299-1466, fax 294-2176, S$65-80.

Lodging House: Cheap boarding house favored by male Sri Lankan immigrants on temporary work assignments. The owners are somewhat reluctant to welcome foreign visitors though this may be a rather unique place to overnight. 13A Upper Dickson Rd., tel. (65) 299-3354, S$18-30.

Little India Guesthouse: Tidy and well-run small hotel with an Indian clientele but also willing to admit the odd Western traveler. Rooms with fans are small but immaculate and include a

TV and decent furniture. 3 Veerasamy Rd., tel. (65) 294-2866, fax 298-4866, S$38-62.

Kerbau Hotel: Simple but clean place in a perfect location near all the "fish-head curry" restaurants on Race Course Road. 54-62 Kerbau Rd., tel. (65) 297-6668, fax 297-6669, S$45-65.

Ali's Nest Guesthouse: This small but friendly spot near the Broadway Hotel has tiny rooms but free breakfast, coffee, hot showers, and sun deck all day long. 23 Roberts Lane, tel. (065) 291-2938, S$6-8 dorm, S$20-25 private rooms.

Marajan Lodge: The offshoot of the New Backpacker's Lodge near Beach Road has both fan-cooled and a/c dorms plus a few small but clean rooms. 30 Roberts Lane, tel. (65) 293-5251, S$7-9 dorm, S$20-30 private rooms.

Palace Hotel: Few Westerners venture up to the northern end of Jalan Besar near the Lavender Street bus terminal, though this ancient place has spacious, clean rooms at very reasonable prices. 407A Lavender St., tel. (65) 298-3108, S$25-35.

Guesthouses to Avoid: Guesthouses and inexpensive hotels which cater primarily to Indians and Sri Lankans and are cool to Western visitors include the **Fook Leong Guesthouse, Friendly Guesthouse, Hoe Pin Hotel, Kam Leng Hotel,** and **Nan Yong Hotel.**

Orchard Road

Guesthouses occasionally open up in private apartments and public housing estates where owners decide to pull in a little extra money as unlicensed innkeepers. Their status appears to be overlooked by authorities unless neighbors complain about the foot traffic or noise and then they are told to follow the rules and close their doors to guests.

These floating guesthouses, which seem to pop up mainly

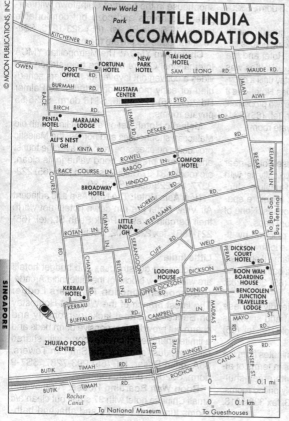

© MOON PUBLICATIONS, INC.

LITTLE INDIA ACCOMMODATIONS

New World Park

KITCHENER RD.

OWEN

POST OFFICE

FORTUNA HOTEL

NEW PARK HOTEL

TAI HOE HOTEL

SAM LEONG RD.

MAUDE RD.

BURMAH RD.

MUSTAFA CENTER

SYED

JALAN ALWI

RACE

BIRCH RD.

PENTA HOTEL

MARAJAN LODGE

LEMBU RD.

DESKER

RD.

ALI'S NEST GH

KINTA RD.

ROWELL

LN.

COMFORT HOTEL

RACE COURSE LN.

BABOO

KELANTAN LN.

BESAR

HINDOO

BROADWAY HOTEL

NORRIS

RD.

KLANG LN.

VEERASAMY

LITTLE INDIA GH

SERANGOON RD.

To Ban San Bus Terminal

ROTAN LN.

CUFF RD.

WELD

RD.

PERAK

DICKSON COURT HOTEL

CHANDER RD.

BELILIOS LN.

LODGING HOUSE

DICKSON

BOON WAH BOARDING HOUSE

KERBAU HOTEL

UPPER DICKSON RD.

DUNLOP AVE.

BENCOOLEN JUNCTION TRAVELLERS LODGE

KERBAU RD.

CAMPBELL

LN.

MADRAS ST.

MAYO ST.

BUFFALO RD.

ZHUJIAO FOOD CENTRE

CLIVE

SUNGEI

RD.

CANAL RD.

PRINSEP ST.

BUTIK TIMAH RD.

ROCHOR

0   0.1 mi

BUTIK TIMAH RD.

Rochor Canal

0   0.1 km

To National Museum

To Guesthouses

SINGAPORE

BOTANIC GARDENS

HOTEL PREMIER

OMNI - MARCO POLO HOTEL

POST OFFICE

ANA HOTEL

BURMA EMBASSY

NEW ZEALAND EMBASSY

PHILIPPINE EMBASSY

LADYHILL HOTEL

JAPAN EMBASSY

RELC INTERNATIONAL HOUSE

METROPOLITAN YMCA TANGLIN CENTRE

SHANGRI-LA HOTEL

REGENT

BOULEVARD HOTEL

ORCHARD PARADE HOTEL

HILTON

ORCHARD HOTEL

BALMORAL RD.

SLOANE COURT HOTEL

GARDEN HOTEL

V.I.P. HOTEL

ORCHARD ROAD

NEGARA HOTEL

THAI EMBASSY

PATERSON RD.

STEVENS BLVD.

ROYAL HOLIDAY INN

SCOTTS RD.

ORCHARD RD. MTR

DYNASTY HOTEL

HYATT REGENCY

GOODWOOD HOTEL

SCOTTS RD.

ASIA HOTEL

SHERATON TOWERS

MELIA AT SCOTTS

GRANGE RD.

ORCHARD BLVD.

ORCHARD RD.

YORK HOTEL

ELIZABETH HOTEL

NEWTON MTR

INDIAN EMBASSY

CROWN PRINCE HOTEL

CAIRNHILL HOTEL

NEWTON FOOD CIRCUS

CLEMENCEAU RD.

RIVER VALLEY RD.

MANDARIN HOTEL

SOMERSET MTR

CASABLANCA RESTAURANT

PHOENIX HOTEL

EMERALD HILL RD.

MADAM LIM'S PLACE

BIBIS RESTAURANT

PERANAKAN PLACE

CUPPAGE CENTER

CAVENAGH RD.

MITRE HOTEL

SAXOPHONE JAZZ CLUB

EXETER RD.

JACKS TRAVELODGE

LLOYD HOUSE

MERIDIEN

HOLIDAY INN PARK VIEW

ISTANA

GRAND CENTRAL HOTEL

SUPREME HOTEL

0   250 m

COCKPIT HOTEL

HONG SONG SEE TEMPLE

HOUSE OF TAN YEOK NEE

IMPERIAL HOTEL

BUKIT TIMAH RD.

CHETTIAR TEMPLE

YWCA

FORT CANNING

POST OFFICE

DHOBY GHAUT MTR

YMCA

© MOON PUBLICATIONS, INC.

SINGAPORE

in apartment complexes near Orchard Road and Chinatown, are worth seeking out since the rooms are uniformly spotless and visitors have a rare opportunity to experience Singapore in an authentic family setting. Word of mouth is the best way to find out about these places.

Madam Lim's Place: A recent example of a quasi-legal homestay is this three-room operation in the Cavenagh Garden complex. Clean, quiet, and very comfortable. Call first and inquire about reservations or referrals to other similar homestays currently in operation. To reach Madam Lim's, walk to the end of Cuppage Road, cross the Central Freeway on the pedestrian footbridge, and walk left up to the apartment complex. Cavenagh Rd., Cavenagh Block 73, 3rd floor, tel. (65) 737-4600, S$10 dorm, S$40-75 private rooms.

Mitre Hotel: A colonial relic in decline favored by oil rig workers who frequent the shabby downstairs bar and ruminate on the past. Weedy gardens, slowly turning overhead fans, and rough rooms for the brave only make the Mitre a Conradesque experience. May be condemned in the near future; call first to confirm its existence. 145 Killiney Rd., tel. (65) 737-3811, S$25-40.

Metropolitan YMCA Tanglin Centre: Just a 15-minute walk from Scotts Road and situated in a quiet neighborhood of large homes and stylish apartment complexes, this 94-room YMCA features a swimming pool, downstairs gym supervised by an American fitness instructor, two squash courts, and a budget cafe with set meals at bargain prices. Reservations should be made in advance. 60 Stevens Rd., tel. (65) 737-7775, fax 235-5528, S$60-100.

MODERATE

Bencoolen Street Area

Two Y's and four inexpensive hotels make this convenient hunting grounds for mid-level travelers.

YMCA International House: One of the best low-priced hotels in town is centrally located between Orchard Road and the sights in Central Singapore. All rooms have a/c, private bath, telephone, and color TV. Facilities include a restaurant, rooftop swimming pool, billiards room, squash and badminton courts, and fitness club.

This place is somewhat expensive but very popular with large groups of students. Advance reservations are suggested. 1 Orchard Rd., tel. (65) 337-3444, fax 337-3140, S$20 dorm, S$75-110.

YWCA Hostel: A small hostel a few blocks away from the YMCA International House has recently reopened after renovations and now welcomes single women, couples, and families. Rooms are immaculate and the atmosphere is far less hectic than the sister property down the road. 6/8 Fort Canning Rd., tel. (65) 336-3150, fax 737-2804, S$25 dorm, S$65-100.

Bencoolen Hotel: An older hotel in a good location with rooftop garden restaurant and 86 clean if somewhat unimaginative rooms in need of renovation. Room rates are negotiable at the front desk. 47 Bencoolen St., tel. (65) 336-0822, fax 336-2250, S$85-120.

Strand Hotel: Adjacent to the Bencoolen Hotel is another inexpensive hotel with simple but clean rooms fitted with color televisions and IDD telephones. 25 Bencoolen St., tel. (65) 338-1866, fax 336-3149, S$95-130.

Bayview Inn: The finest hotel on Bencoolen Street has a rooftop restaurant, cozy cafe on the ground floor, and very comfortable rooms. 30 Bencoolen St., tel. (65) 337-2882, fax 338-2880, S$130-160.

Hotels near Bencoolen Street

Two almost upscale hotels, one cheap place, and one of Singapore's finest boutique hotels are located within a few blocks of Bencoolen Street.

Albert Court Hotel: An eight-story boutique hotel restored and expanded as part of a government master plan to realize the Albert Street corridor. Everything about this hotel is wonderful—the superbly decorated lobby, the intimate Peranakan cafe, and the spotless rooms furnished with antique re-creations. Highly recommended. 180 Albert St., tel. (65) 339-3939, fax 339-3252, S$180-280.

Allson Hotel: A convenient location near Raffles City and modern rooms set with rosewood furniture make this hotel a popular choice for mid-level visitors and business travelers watching their expense accounts. 101 Victoria St., tel. (65) 336-2526, fax 334-0631, S$220-280.

Landmark Mercure Hotel: Situated somewhat outside the central district and on the edge of the Arab district is this yellowish landmark that keeps prices low to fill the well appointed rooms. Facilities include a business center, health club, and swimming pool. 390 Victoria St., tel. (65) 297-2828, fax 298-2038, S$200-280.

Beach Road Area

Several moderately priced hotels are located closer to the action.

Carlton Hotel: Upscale hotel located at the crossroads of the financial, shopping, and convention districts of Singapore and just a stone's throw from the historic Raffles Hotel and the Singapore Asian Art Museum. All rooms feature bay windows, a writing desk, and IDD telephones adjacent to the bed and in the bathroom. Facilities include a business center, fitness center, swimming pool, and several restaurants serving international, Cantonese, and local dishes. 76 Bras Basah Rd., tel. (65) 338-8333, fax 339-6866, S$280-380.

Beach Hotel: A new and almost budget hotel with immaculate if small a/c rooms furnished with telephone, television, and private baths. Strictly a utilitarian place with low prices but without restaurants or other facilities provided by most hotels. 95 Beach Rd., tel. (65) 336-7712, fax 336-7712, S$100-140.

Metropole Hotel: The "Economic Business Hotel" just behind the Raffles Hotel is perhaps the best value mid-priced hotel in Singapore. Rooms are simple but clean and superb meals are available from the ground-floor coffee house and the well-known Imperial Herbal Restaurant on the third floor. Recommended. 41 Seah St., tel. (65) 336-3611, fax 339-3610, S$140-180.

Chinatown

Dragon Cityview Hotel: The gentrification of Chinatown includes the conversion of many old shophouses into renovated hotels fitted with modern amenities but without the additional facilities—pools, fitness centers, restaurants—provided by most other hotels in Singapore. The humble little Dragon Cityview Hotel in the heart of Chinatown features mid-sized and perfectly clean a/c rooms with TV, attached bath, and mini-refrigerator. 18 Mosque St., tel. (65) 223-9228, fax 221-8198, S$120-160.

Damenlou Hotel: Tucked away on a lovely lane among an outstanding row of restored shophouses, the Damenlou Hotel features a stunning exterior and 12 nicely appointed rooms that have been tragically modernized rather than restored to their original condition. 12 Ann Siang Rd., tel. (65) 221-1900, fax 225-8500, S$110-140.

Inn of the Sixth Happiness: Singapore's first boutique hotel opened in 1991 near Tanjong Pagar after the renovation of 14 shophouses into this 48-room hotel—named after the 1958 Paramount film starring Ingrid Bergman which related the true-life story of a young Chinese idealist. Rosewood furniture, porcelain lamps, Chinese wedding beds of impractical proportions for Westerners, and blackwood opium beds in the Antique Suites should have insured a superb hotel experience. Unfortunately, most of the rooms are windowless, uncomfortably small, and noisy due to thin walls. Too bad. 9-37 Erskine Rd., tel. (65) 223-3266, fax 223-7951, S$160-380.

Royal Peacock Hotel: Chinatown's newest boutique hotel opened in 1996 on Keong Saik Road in a historic former red-light district known as the "poor man's brothel" until just a few years ago. Today the hotel celebrates its racy past with decadent red curtains, purple carpets, large beds, gilded mirrors, and a bar called the Butterfly. 55 Keong Saik Rd., tel. (65) 223-3522, fax 221-1770, S$160-200.

Chinatown Hotel: Another new mid-range property, slightly off the beaten path in a former red-light district now renovated into a neighborhood of cute Peranakan shophouses and cozy cafes. 12-16 Teck Lim Rd., tel. (65) 225-5166, fax 225-3912, S$140-180.

Duxton Hotel: The Duxton Hotel, superbly sited in the heart of Tanjong Pagar, features 50 gorgeous rooms tastefully decorated with colonial and Peranakan furnishings, many with louvered windows overlooking the adjacent park and arching walkways. Many say the attached restaurant, L'Aigle d'Or, rates as the finest French restaurant in Singapore. Highly recommended. 83 Duxton Rd., tel. (65) 227-7678, tax 227-1232, S$340-550.

Orchard Road

Two surprisingly well-priced hotels flank the lower end of Orchard Road near the Somerset MRT station.

SINGAPORE

Cairnhill Hotel: A former apartment block on a fine hillside location at the top of Emerald Hill Road and a 10-minute walk down to Orchard Road. The non-descript exterior hides 220 clean and comfortable rooms providing views over downtown Singapore. 19 Cairnhill Circle, tel. (65) 734-6622, fax 235-5598, S$180-220.

Cockpit Hotel: Renamed several decades ago due to its popularity with airline crews, the Cockpit was reconstructed with pseudo-colonial decor in 1972 when the hotel hosted Queen Elizabeth II—her suite has since been converted into a boardroom. The somewhat unsightly hotel dramatically sited on Oxley Rise has 176 adequate a/c rooms at bargain prices. 115 Penang Rd., tel. (65) 737-9111, fax 737-3105, S$180-260.

Grand Central Hotel: A featureless concrete box not very grand but centrally located behind Le Meridien Hotel on Orchard Road. 22 Cavenagh Rd., tel. (65) 737-9944, fax 733-3175, S$170-220.

Lloyd's Inn: This modern hotel offers perfectly clean a/c rooms with private baths. Lloyd's lacks facilities except for a small cafe but compensates with an ideal location in a quiet neighborhood just five minutes from Orchard Road. 2 Lloyd Rd., tel. (65)737-7309, fax 737-7847, S$90-120.

Supreme Hotel: Budget hotel—actually called the Hotel Supreme—surprisingly located at the lower end of Orchard Road just behind Le Meridien and very near the Holiday Inn Park View. 15 Kramat Rd., tel. (65) 737-8333, fax 733-7404, S$95-150.

Royal Hotel: Though inconveniently located across Bukit Timah Road beyond the former, much-lamented Newton Circus Food Centre, the Royal provides spacious rooms with all essentials at bargain rates. The Newton MRT station is within walking distance but taxis are necessary for any further ventures. 36 Newton Rd., tel. (65) 2553-4411, fax 253-8668, S$150-220.

Sloane Court Hotel: Sloane Court, Garden, and VIP hotels are clustered together in a prime residential area on Balmoral Road, a 15-minute walk from Anderson or Scotts at Stevens roads. Sloane Court is a pseudo-Tudor style motel with 32 a/c rooms with TVs and private baths. 17 Balmoral Rd., tel. (65) 235-3311, fax 733-9041, S$100-140.

VIP Hotel: Just beyond Sloane Court is another moderately priced hotel with swimming pool, restaurant, and attractive a/c rooms fitted with minibars, TVs, and private baths. Good value. 5 Balmoral Crescent, tel. (65) 235-4277, fax 235-2824, S$120-145.

Garden Hotel: The most expensive hotel of the three on Balmoral Road features modern, clean rooms and upscale facilities such as pool, business center, conference halls, and health club. 14 Balmoral Rd., tel. (65) 235-3344, fax 235-9730, S$180-240.

RELC International House: The headquarters of the Regional Language Centre (RELC) serves both as a conference center for local universities and budget hotel for visiting scholars and Western tourists. Rooms are spotless if simply furnished and include attached baths, TVs, minibars, and private balconies that overlook the quiet neighborhood just behind the Shangri-La. 30 Orange Grove Rd., tel. (65) 737-9044, fax 733-9976, S$130-175.

Hotel Premier: This older property just beyond the ANA Hotels was formerly owned by the Singapore Hotel Association (SHATEC), who used the restaurant to provide hands-on training for their students. In 1996, SHATEC moved to a new location and opened the Rosette Restaurant, which continues to serve inexpensive meals prepared by food and beverage students. 22 Nassim Hill Rd., tel. (65) 733-9811, fax 733-5595, S$120-140.

RESTAURANTS

Time to eat *lah*. Singaporeans' love of food is more than just a passing fancy—it's an obsession that inspires both enthusiasm and reverence. Singapore's reputation as the food capital of Asia is credited to its multiracial society, which cooks up everything from Peking duck and Penang *laksa* to Indian curries and Malaysian *mee*. Selection is beguilingly diverse and gives gastronomically curious travelers a rare chance to try a bewildering variety of Asian specialties.

ORCHARD ROAD

Food Courts

Cuppage Centre: The most popular food center near Orchard Road is located on the third floor of a parking complex just behind Centrepoint. Somewhat hectic around lunchtime but fairly quiet in the evenings until it closes down around 2100. 55 Cuppage Road.

Emerald Food Court: Tucked away in the basement of the Orchard Emerald shopping center is a spotless food emporium with the usual Chinese, Indian, and Muslim fare plus fruit and dessert stands for a final sugar rush. 218 Orchard Road.

Scotts Picnic Food Court: The most upscale food court near Orchard Road has dozens of vendors in a restaurant setting serving the widest possible range of both Asian and International dishes at very reasonable prices. Scotts Shopping Center, 6 Scotts Road.

Botanic Gardens: Taman Serasi at the entrance to the Botanic Gardens is known for its *roti john* served with outstanding chili sauce and the stall with fresh soursop juice. Cluny at Napier Road.

Cantonese

Crystal Jade Palace: Restaurant chain known for its roasted goose, double-boiled shark's-fin soup thickened with crab roe and Yunnan ham, stewed eel with salty vegetables, baked live prawns, and deep-fried mango ice cream. Moderate. Ngee Ann City #04-19, 391 Orchard Rd., tel. (65) 735-2388.

Fook Yuen: Fancy yet moderately priced place known for its dim sum *(dian xin)* such as *siew mai* (pork and shrimp dumplings), *char siew soh* (barbecued pork pastry), deep-fried crab claws, and pan-fried garoupa roll with mango. Moderate. Paragon, 290 Orchard Road #03-08, tel. (65) 235-2211.

Grand City: Chefs from Hong Kong provide the creamy restaurant with Cantonese specialties such as roast suckling pig, creamy orange shark's-fin soup with fresh crab meat, blackened beef in a yams nest, and glutinous rice dumplings filled with mashed sesame seed. Also try the cold lobster salad and golden crispy chicken. Moderate. Cathay Building, 11 Dhoby Ghaut #07-04, tel. (65) 338-3622.

Lingzhi Vegetarian: Veggie fans on a moderate budget will enjoy this tastefully decorated place with all-natural hits such as braised spinach soup thickened with bamboo fungus and black moss, mushroom and seaweed salad served with peach segments, and fried tofu in a sauce of sliced mushrooms over a bed of sautéed spinach. Moderate. Orchard Towers #B1-17, 400 Orchard Rd., tel. (65) 734-3788.

Royal Garden: Rather simple place near the Dhoby Ghaut MRT with set lunches and dinner specialties from lobster sashimi to sliced goose meat marinated in soy sauce. Moderate. Park Mall #04-02, 9 Penang Rd., tel. (65) 538-1888.

Sichuan

Chinatown: An unusual setting of red brick walls and hanging lanterns provides the venue for unusual Sichuan (Szechuan) dishes including deep-fried *soon hock* (fish) with soy sauce and abalone sautéed in oyster sauce with broccoli. An inexpensive buffet is available at both lunch and dinner. Moderate. Imperial Hotel, 1 Jalan Rumbia, tel. (65) 737-1666.

Si Chuan Tou Hua: Sichuan Tou Hua ("Sichuan bean flower") restaurant is an offshoot of the original located in Beijing, owned and operated by a division of the Sichuan provincial government. Considered so authentic that officials at the Chinese Embassy in Singapore recommend this venue over all other

SINGAPORE

TASTE OF SINGAPORE

CHINESE

bak kut teh: pork soup highly seasoned with garlic and chilies

bee hoon: rice vermicelli often used in *laksa*

bird's-nest soup: thick soup made from boiled swiftlet nests and barley sugar. An expensive delicacy; more than just regurgitated bird saliva.

carrot cake: giant white radishes steamed and fried in egg, garlic, and chili

char kway teow: fried noodles and clams in a black bean sauce

char siew fan: barbecued pork with rice and sliced cucumber

chicken rice: boiled chicken served over rice steamed in chicken stock. The popular Hainanese version is served with chili-ginger sauce.

chwe chia pow: translucent pork buns filled with prawns, beans, and turnips

claypot rice: baked rice served with Chinese sausages, salted fish, diced chicken, vegetables, and duck

congee: rice porridge

foo yong hai: crab-meat omelette

hokkien mee: thick yellow noodles and vermicelli fried with prawns and pork in a rich sauce

kway teow: flat white rice noodles, also called *hors fun*

mee: spaghetti-like yellow noodles made from wheat flour

mee pok: flat noodles made with wheat and egg, often dusted with flour

mee suah: long noodles kept in dried form

mi fun: rice vermicelli

moi: porridge

or luak: oyster omelette

or chian: oyster omelette

popiah: spring rolls filled with meats, sweet black paste, and vegetables

pow: steamed pasty buns filled with pork in a sweet sauce, chicken sautéed in garlic, sweet red bean paste, or sweet lotus seed

rojak: salad of bean sprouts, pineapple, white turnip, and fried bean cake tossed in a peanut and shrimp paste; the Chinese version of *gado gado*

shark's-fin soup: thick and expensive glutinous soup made from boiled shark fins

steamboat: Chinese fondue. Thinly sliced meats and vegetables are cooked individually at the table in a clear broth. Called Mongolian hot pot in Hong Kong.

swee kow: prawn dumpling soup

tahu pok: stuffed and barbecued bean cakes served with shrimp paste

tung hoon: transparent noodles made from mung beans

yong tau foo: Hakka eggplant and bean curd stuffed with fish paste and minced meat, served in a thick stock

INDIAN

biryani: steamed yellow rice with chicken and saffron

chapati: flat unleavened bread made from wholemeal flour

fishhead curry: red snapper in a fiery curry gravy; Singapore's most famous Indian dish

kambing: thick mutton soup served with French bread

kway teow goreng: Indian-style fried noodles

murtabak: fried bread filled with minced mutton and egg and served with a small side dish of curry sauce. Watching the *murtabak* man is half the fun of ordering this delicious bread.

papadum: deep-fried lentil bread usually dipped in curry sauces

paratha: flaky Indian bread fried in oil and served with curry sauce

rojak: fried prawns, potatoes, and bean curd served with sweet curry sauce

roti: bread

MALAY

ayam goreng: Malay fried chicken

gado gado: vegetable salad covered with a peanut and coconut sauce. Served with prawn crackers. A favorite dish of both Malays and Indonesians.

ikan bilis: fried and crunchy anchovies. Served with *nasi lemak*.

ikan sadin: canned sardines in tomato sauce

kari ayam: curry chicken

kerang: fried cockles

lontong: vegetables and rice cakes covered with coconut gravy. One of Singapore's classic dishes. Superb.

mee rebus: Malay noodle soup in a rich and spicy sauce

nasi goreng: fried rice

nasi lemak: Malaysian breakfast. Combination plate of coconut rice, *ikan bilis*, peanuts, and sautéed vegetables. Probably an acquired taste but addictive once you become accustomed to it.

nasi padang: Sumatran style of buffet dining. A dozen individual dishes are brought to your table and laid out for your selection. You pay only for those that you eat. Most Singaporeans just point out a dish in the front window.

rendang: Indonesian-style curry served with beef or chicken. Very spicy.

sambal: fiery chili sauce liberally used in Malay cooking

satay: skewers of chicken, beef, or lamb grilled over charcoal and served with peanut sauce

sayor: Malay for vegetables

soto ayam: spiced chicken soup with vegetables and potatoes

sotong: cuttlefish

tahu goreng: deep-fried bean curd covered with pungent peanut sauce

tahu lemak: bean curd cooked in coconut- milk curry

telor goreng: fried eggs

udang sambal: prawns fried in a sambal hot sauce

NONYA (PERANAKAN)

kueh pie tee: vegetarian won tons

laksa: noodle soup highly spiced with coconut, chilies, and aromatic spices. A classic dish of Singapore.

mee siam: rice vermicelli fried with chili and prawns. Served in a sweet-sour thin gravy.

Peranakan kueh: Nonya sweet rice cakes flavored with coconut and palm sugar

poh piah: vegetarian rice cakes

DRINKS AND DESSERTS

bubor chacha: dessert made from sweet potato and tapioca boiled in coconut milk. Served either hot or cold.

bubor hitan: black glutinous rice covered with hot coconut milk

chendol: iced coconut milk and palm-sugar syrup

goreng pisang: banana fritters

ice kachang: shaved-ice dessert served with syrup, evaporated milk, and jellies

tahu chui: soybean milk

choices in Singapore including top-rated Cantonese and Hokkien restaurants. Moderate. United Square #B1-55, 101 Thomson Rd., tel. (65) 251-2733.

Magic of Chongqing Hot Pot: An odd name but one of the least expensive Sichuan restaurants in Singapore, designed to resemble a Chinese village inn with lanterns set against worn walls and floors pebbled with cement. Each table houses a gas stove where patrons can watch their dinners rise to a boil and then dip their meat, vegetable, and seafood selections into a sesame oil sauce. The extensive set menus at lunch and dinner allow unlimited servings of over 40 dishes. Moderate. Tanglin Shopping Centre #04-06, 19 Tanglin Rd., tel. (65) 734-8135.

Teochew and Hunan

Charming Garden: A simply furnished restaurant serving mildly seasoned Hunanese specialties such as steam minced pigeon soup, red tilapia fish covered with crispy soy bean crumbs, and beef tenderloin in a rich pepper sauce. Diners who seek spicier fare can try the Sichuan dishes adapted from the Phoenix restaurant. Moderate. Novotel Inn, 214 Dunearn Rd., tel. (65) 251-8149.

Teochew City Seafood: Seafood specialties in this unpretentious cafe include steamed cold crab served with pungent sauce, fried crayfish garnished with chives and chilies, and shark's-fin soup served in a light broth. The restaurant also serves meat dishes from goose to venison. Inexpensive. Centrepoint #05-16, 176 Orchard Rd., tel. (65) 733-3338.

SINGAPORE

Malay and Indonesian

Aziza's: One of Singapore's first Malay restaurants rather than outdoor cafes or hawker stalls is this narrow shophouse on Emerald Hill just a few steps up from Orchard Road. Aziza's should be credited for spreading the word about Malay cooking, though years of media coverage has marginalized the food and turned the place into a tourist cliché with spotty, overpriced dishes. Moderate. 36 Emerald Hill Rd., tel. (65) 235-1130.

Bintang Timur: One of the earlier Indonesian restaurants in Singapore (1983) features all the classic dishes from the archipelago such as *satay goreng, satay udang, ukop belanga,* and *ayam lemak* plus, for dessert, icy *chendol* and durian *serawa*—glutinous rice covered with durian sauce thickened with brown sugar. *Enak!* Moderate. Far East Plaza #02-08, 14 Scotts Rd., tel. (65) 235-4539.

Cahaya Murni Halal Muslim: Here's something unique, a Muslim *hala* cafe that serves both Malay and Chinese dishes daily 0900-2100. Perpetually packed but worth the wait for a table. Inexpensive. Far East Plaza #05-91, tel. (65) 734-8434.

Nonya and Baba: Situated a few blocks from Orchard Road is a highly regarded and simply furnished cafe that serves the authentic food of the Peranakans—the female Babas and their Nonya husbands. Highlights include *buak kelauak ayam, otak otak, satay ayam, babi pongtay, ayam buah keluak,* and *bakwan kepiting.* Inexpensive. 262 River Valley Rd., tel. (65) 734-1382.

Nusa Indah: A simple yet pleasing interior decorated with Indonesian paintings mounted on support piers covered with polished burlwood. Featured dishes include *tahu telor, kepala ikan, ikan pepes, sambal udang, ayam panggang, terong belado,* and, of course, *ayam goreng*—fried chicken. Moderate. Wisma Atria #02-18, 435 Orchard Rd., tel. (65) 738-7719.

Ramayana: Not much atmosphere but good Indonesian dishes at reasonable prices. Try the chicken in a thick coconut sauce, mutton curry, *gado gado, otak otak,* or a large portion of *nasi goreng.* Moderate. Singapura Plaza #07-01, 68 Orchard Rd., tel. (65) 338-3579.

Sanur: Waitresses clad in batik sarongs and piped-in Javanese pop music add to the atmosphere of this simply decorated cafe in one of Singapore's most popular shopping centers. All the favorites but be sure to try the *tahu telur,* fried bean curd and eggs topped with black soy sauce—a towering silky wonder that critics consider the finest in all of Singapore. Moderate. Centrepoint #04-17, 176 Orchard Rd., tel. (65) 734-2192.

Sukmaindra: Singapore's most elegant and overmarbled Muslim restaurant actually features Malay, Bruneian, and Indonesian specialties including *sambal goreng tahu tempeh, ayam masak merah, kambing korma, asam kepala ikan,* and *bekara panggang,* grilled lobster marinated in a pungent herbal sauce. Moderate. Royal Holiday Inn Crowne Plaza #03-10, 25 Scotts Rd., tel. (65) 731-7988.

Thai

Baan Thai: Elegantly decorated restaurant furnished with teak carvings, Thai Buddhas, Burmese wall decorations, and other art objects including a display case of *khon* masks used in traditional Thai drama. All the classic Thai dishes are prepared here with great imagination by chefs formerly employed at the famed Bussaracum restaurant in Bangkok. Moderate. Ngee Ann City #04-23, 391 Orchard Rd., tel. (65) 735-5562.

Cuppage Thai Food: An alfresco cafe under the leafy trees of Cuppage Terrace with decent Thai food served at authentic Thai temperatures—hot—except for the *tom yam kung* (prawn soup) which has been toned down. A convenient place to build up a thirst for drinks at nearby Saxophone. Inexpensive. 49 Cuppage Terrace, tel. (65) 734-1116.

Patara Fine Thai: Classy setting with marble tables, cane chairs, and a green decor carried through to the Thai celadon ceramics. Owned by a Thai female entrepreneur from Bangkok, Patara lists its specialties as chicken wrapped in pandan leaf, seafood galangal in coconut cream, prawn and chicken curry, Thai salads, an enormous serving of *tom yam* flavored with tomato and lemon grass. The staff dressed in Thai costumes provides a nice touch. Moderate. Tanglin Mall #03-14, 163 Tanglin Rd., tel. (65) 737-0818.

Indian

Bombay Meadowlands: South Indian vegetarian dishes prepared with care in this unpretentious cafe near the Orchard Parade Hotel. The chef uses very little chili but dishes can be spiced up on request. Try the inexpensive daily luncheon buffet. Moderate. Tanglin Shopping Centre #B1-01, 19 Tanglin Rd., tel. (65) 235-2712.

Maharani: Consistently voted one of Singapore's top Indian restaurants, Maharani is actually one of the earliest Indian restaurants on Orchard Road and a modestly decorated place despite its reputation. Recommended dishes include chicken *tikka, palak paneer,* mutton *moghlai,* and *malai kofta* curry. Moderate. Far East Plaza #05-36, 14 Scotts Rd., tel. (65) 235-8840.

Mumtaz Mahal: Another mid-level Indian restaurant popular with businesspeople and locals seeking quality food at sensible prices. House specialties include a crayfish *marsala* covered with tomato puree and chilies, a vegetarian dish called *navarathan jalfarazei* somewhat like *palak paneer,* and a well-seasoned *mumtaz murgh* kebab. Moderate. Far East Plaza #05-22, 14 Scotts Rd., tel. (65) 732-2754.

Orchard Maharajah: Set in a two-story Peranakan shophouse, this North Indian restaurant serves quality dishes in the 20-seat main dining room and specializes in tandoori in the 40-seat Maharajah room on the upper floor. Try the fish *mumtaz* stuffed with minced mutton, almonds, and eggs; *bhutti kebab,* boneless lamb marinated in yogurt and papaya; *tandoori pomfret;* or *murgh nawabi,* a creamy chicken dish prepared with cashew nuts, raisins, and fresh cream. Moderate. 25 Cuppage Terrace, tel. (65) 732-6331.

River Valley (Sin Guan): Small Indian-Muslim *nasi* stall marked as River Valley Restaurant on the street sign but Sin Guan above the front door. Try the traditional *nasi lemak* for breakfast or the fried chicken with vegetables and *rendang* for lunch. Inexpensive. 221 River Valley Road.

Roti John: Roti John, concocted by a Malay hawker and named after one of his British military customers, is a bread *(roti)* dish stuffed with egg, chopped peppers, onions, and secret spices and then grilled to lip-smacking perfection. Singaporeans acknowledge that chef Shukor at the food center opposite the Botanic Gardens is the Roti John king, plus he puts out a "damn solid" homemade chili sauce. Inexpensive. Taman Serasi Food Centre, Cluny at Napier Road.

Samy's Curry Restaurant: For something completely unique, grab a taxi to this old British Army mess hall now used as a civil service clubhouse on the grounds of the Ministry of Defense. Absolutely no interior decor at the Dempsy Club but the South Indian curry dishes, which are served on banana leaves rather than plates, are absolutely authentic and incredibly cheap—S\$3 for vegetarians and S\$5 for chicken, mutton, squid, or other meat dishes. Samy's is just past the Botanic Gardens. Inexpensive. Singapore Civil Service Club House, Block 25, Dempsey Rd., tel. (65) 472-2080.

Italian

Pete's Place: Cozy basement trattoria with brick walls and checked tablecloths which remains immensely popular despite its rank as the oldest Italian restaurant in Singapore. You can watch chefs baking pizzas in the wood-burning oven located in the open kitchen or visit the pasta station where the chef whips up quick pasta dishes. Salad bar, set lunches, and Sunday brunches. Moderate. Hyatt Regency, 10/12 Scotts Rd., tel. (65) 738-1234.

Spageddies: A concept restaurant that combines lively Italian decor with classic dishes served in enormous portions. Moderate. Tanglin Mall #02-22, 163 Tanglin Rd., tel. (65) 733-5519.

Mediterranean and Spanish

Goya: Spanish restaurant with sangria, tapas, paella, *pescado à la Sal* (baked salted seabass), *fidegua* (vermicelli paella), *cochnillo* (roast sucking pig), and *paletilla de cordero asado* (roast lamb "Segovia style"). Atmosphere provided by Goya reprints and a glass wall that provides views over a landscaped garden. Moderate. Melia at Scotts, 45 Scotts Rd., tel. (65) 732-5885.

Possumus Cafe: A Mediterranean cafe with Spanish chicken, prawn *croquetas,* marble pork ribs, *knecht* burger, and dishes suggested by local food aficionados as approved by chef Conchi Kaibel, a Spanish restaurant consultant previously employed in Kenya, Hong Kong, and Manila. Vegetarians will enjoy the seafood tofu fettucine. Moderate. Pacific Plaza, 21 Scotts Rd., tel. (65) 735-9518.

Tapas: Spanish cafe and bar with tasty tidbits such as fresh oysters topped with tomato and vodka, crab and brandy tart covered with melted manchego cheese, meat empadillas, and fried chicken wings à la Spain. Tapas also has a sunken dance floor with live rock music after 2230 when the singles crowd arrives to suck up

SINGAPORE

sangria and margaritas. Moderate. Omni Marco Polo, 247 Tanglin Rd., tel. (65) 474-7141.

Continental
Angus House: A minimalist cafe with sleek black furniture and clean tiled floors that serves beef dishes and other continental fare in a Japanese style. Moderate. Ngee Ann City #04-25, 391 Orchard Rd., tel. (65) 735-6015.

Fosters: Steaks, "farmhouse fare," and Devonshire cream tea served with hot scones and sandwiches daily 1500-1800 for S$10. Moderate. Specialist Centre #02-38, 277 Orchard Rd., tel. (65) 737-8939.

Poolside: Take a break from the shopping and try a salade Niçoise or club sandwich at this swimming pool surrounded by palms and surprisingly lush gardens. Barbecue lunch on Sunday and Mongolian buffets served nightly. Moderate. Hyatt Regency, 10/12 Scotts Rd., tel. (65) 738-1234.

Rosette: SHATEC (Singapore Hotel Association Training & Educational Centre) runs this sensibly priced restaurant as a training ground for service employees. Continental lunches cost S$14-18, while a four-course set dinner runs S$25. Moderate. 22-24 Orchard Rd. #02-00, tel. (65) 339-6115.

North American
Chico n' Charlie's: One of Singapore's first Mexican restaurants serves all the standard south-of-the-border dishes plus American-sized portions of ribs and steaks. Lunch specials include an unlimited soup and salad buffet for S$10 or S$12 with a main course. Sunday buffet brunch costs just S$18—one of the least expensive brunches near Orchard Road. Moderate. Liat Towers #05-01, 541 Orchard Rd., tel. (65) 734-1753.

Aunt Stella's: Pastry shop decorated in a Pennsylvania style with freshly baked cookies, pies, cakes, and rich coffees. Inexpensive. Ngee Ann City #B2-08, 391 Orchard Rd., tel. (65) 735-1395.

Café Cafe: This New York Italian-style cafe in the Time bookshop features paper-wrapped beer chicken in herbs, pasta with prawns in a paprika sauce, and a variety of pizzas. Inexpensive. Plaza Singapura #03-45, 68 Orchard Rd., tel. (65) 339-9459.

Chili's: One of many American chain restaurants in Singapore with all the standard dishes served in generous portions plus indulgent desserts such as frozen cookie pies served with creamy yogurt and chocolate sauce. Moderate. Orchard Parade Hotel, 1 Tanglin Rd., tel. (65) 735-1322.

Dan Ryan's Chicago Grill: American fare with huge portions of deep-fried onion rings, New England clam chowder, salads, steaks, barbecued pork ribs, hickory smoked pork chops, and New York cheesecake voted among the best in Singapore. The decor follows a 1930s'-Chicago theme with piped-in big band melodies and the crooning of Frank Sinatra. Moderate. Tanglin Place #B1-01, 91 Tanglin Rd., tel. (65) 738-2800.

DKNY Cafe: A sleek nosh counter and modish boutique decorated in a minimalist black-and-white theme with sandwiches served on onion rye, foccacia, or bagel. Try the hot pastrami or grilled pepper chicken sandwich. Inexpensive. Palais Renaissance #01-03, 390 Orchard Rd., tel. (65) 733-4226.

Hard Rock Cafe: Carnivores appreciate the burgers, ribs, gigantic sandwiches, the infamous hickory-smoked "pig" sandwich, Singapore Samosas (for the tourists), and steaks served here, while vegetarians will appreciate the "south of the border" salad, papaya seafood salad, a man-sized veggie sandwich, and a meatless garden burger made from mushrooms, onions, grains, and low-fat cheese. All this is served amid acres of rock memorabilia in the first Hard Rock Cafe to open in Asia and a frequent winner of the STPB's Most Popular Nightclub award. Moderate. 50 Cuscaden Rd., tel. (65) 235-5232.

Island Cafe: Exhausted shoppers can drop their bags in this homey cafe and try the fresh salmon burger, spicy Thai fried rice, or black pepper crab. Inexpensive. Ngee Ann City #03-09, 391 Orchard Rd., tel. (65) 735-6213.

McDonald's: Only mentioned because it claims to hold the world's record for most Big Macs served on opening day—45,000. Inexpensive. Shaw House #05-11, 350 Orchard Rd., tel. (65) 735-7108.

Planet Hollywood: The world's largest outlet of the restaurant/nightclub chain associated with Arnie, Bruce, and Demi opened in early 1997 on the site of the former Galeries Lafayette. With a seating capacity of more than 350 and occupying an impressive 18,000 square feet, the new theme restaurant—the 32nd in the world—is designed to give the Hard Rock Cafe down the street a run for its money. The menu lists Chinese pot stickers stuffed with turkey, pastas, salads, pizzas, smoked meats and fish, and Arnold's own wiernerschnitzel apple strudel—all accompanied by ear-splitting music. Moderate. Liat Towers #02-02, 541 Orchard Rd., tel. (65) 733-5339.

Silver Spoon: A long-time favorite with well-prepared set lunches both Western and Asian, plus a decent range of à la carte selections. Park Mall #B1-05, 9 Penang Rd., tel. (65) 337-8838.

TGI Friday's: American standards, Tex-Mex specialties, a garden burger for vegetarians, and decadent mud pies for chocoholics. Fine views and plenty of sunlight inside the two-story glass-enclosed building opposite Dhoby Ghaut MRT. Moderate. The Glass House, 9 Penang Rd., tel. (65) 334-7811.

Tony Roma's: Rib house offering a selection of sauces such as "special recipe" and "Carolina honey" plus the standard assortment of burgers, steaks, and combo plates. Moderate. Orchard Hotel, 442 Orchard Rd., tel. (65) 738-8600.

COLONIAL SINGAPORE

Food Courts
Ground rules for eating in food courts are fairly simple. Diners can sit anywhere and are not obligated to patronize any particular stall. You may order soup from one stall, drinks from another, and desserts from a third. Table sharing is the rule and you pay when served. Be aware that some vendors can be pushy about finding customers; don't be talked into ordering anything you really don't want.

Albert Court Mall: A new and fashionable food center with a dozen outlets on the site of the deeply missed Albert Street night market. Choices include Chocho's Peranakan Café, Diva North Indian, Hillman Seafood Garden, Straits Café, Taste of South India, the Beer Garden, and American fast food from Burger King to Kentucky Fried Chicken. 180 Albert Street.

Blanco Food Court: Blanco Court, poor cousin across the road from Bugis Junction, has a dozen hawker stalls on the poorly signposted third and fourth floors that serve all the standards at very low prices. Kim Kee Fish Porridge is known for its fresh mackerel porridge with pork and egg omelette. 588 North Bridge Road.

Bras Basah Food Centre: Somewhat downscale but one of the few food centers that stays open all night. Stamford Road near the National Library.

Bugis Junction: Central Singapore's newest and flashiest food center occupies the entire basement of the Seiyu department store. Along with American chains and local favorites like Loy Kee Chicken Rice are some unusual venues such as Thai Kitchen for *tom yam* soup, Shanghai Zhu Jian Fen, Hup Lee Claypot, and Sizzling Steamboat for the Taiwanese classic. 290 Victoria Street.

Empress Place: Simple but pleasant spot to enjoy a bite before crossing Cavenagh Bridge to Boat Quay and Chinatown. Empress Place Museum.

Funan Centre: The computer shopping headquarters for Singapore also has a half-dozen restaurants in the basement including Mooi Chin Palace for Hainanese dishes. 109 North Bridge Road.

Golden Mile Food Centre: Way out on Beach Road near the Lavender MRT station is a rarely visited by quite interesting food court frequented by Malays from the nearby Arab Quarter, old *tongkang* men from the days when there was an unloading pier at the mouth of the Kallang River, young heavy metal rockers who bring along their "dolly birds," and dozens of Thai workers and young Thai girls who cross over the road from Who Hup shopping center, also known as "Little Thailand." This unusual range of people means unique dishes are available such as shark liver pie, "crystal" dumplings filled with turnip or red bean paste, peanut rice balls in peanut soup, soup *tulang* made from mutton bones in a tomato-chili sauce, and Thai dishes washed down with fiery Mekong whiskey purchased from the stalls across the street. Beach Road at Crawford Street.

High Street Food Centre: Buried deep within a shopping center better known as a haunt for Russian sailors is a modest collection of stalls including Tai Wah, known for its tasty pork noodle soup. 1 North Bridge Road.

SINGAPORE

Hill Street Food Centre: Office workers pack this venerable sidewalk spot for its *bah ku teh, lor mee,* and excellent Hainanese chicken rice with liver. 30 Hill Street.

Paradiz Food Center: A clean and modern food center in an air-conditioned basement with a wide selection of Chinese, Indian, and Malay stalls including Li Ying for *char kueh teow,* Kiat Heng for fish noodle soup, Shereena for Indian dishes, and Xiang Xiang for rice vermicelli in satay sauce. Convenient location for Bencoolen Street backpackers. Selegie at Prinsep Streets.

Cantonese

Fatty's Wing Seong: Jovial Fatty, once the hawker king of old Albert Street, moved his operation into this undistinguished shopping complex soon after the government closed down all street stalls in the early 1980s. Dishes are well prepared and speedily served in this perpetually crowded cafe. Inexpensive. Albert Complex #01-33, Albert St., tel. (65) 338-1087.

Grand City: Large and very popular restaurant done up in gold and ostentatious red with an extensive dim sum selection and excellent en-

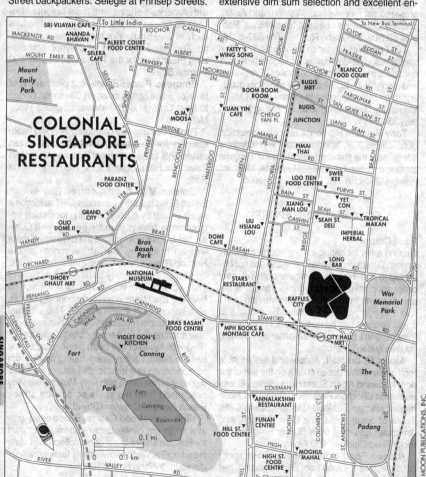

COLONIAL SINGAPORE RESTAURANTS

© MOON PUBLICATIONS, INC.

trees such as cold lobster salad, monk jumps over the wall, abalone and asparagus in oyster sauce, and king prawns vermicelli in a spicy curry sauce. Expensive. Cathay Building #07-04, 11 Dhoby Ghaut, tel. (65) 338-3622.

Imperial Herbal: Simply furnished and immensely popular place that specializes in herbal dishes created to balance your yin and yang. Diners can select from the descriptive menu or consult with an in-house physician who might recommend fried egg whites with scallops to improve the complexion, *lingzhi* soup which is "good for your organs," *gui fei* tonic soup with black chicken to maintain your youth, deep-fried scorpions with minced prawns to help with arthritis, or crispy black ants on shredded potato to clear the mind. Moderate. Metropole Hotel, 3rd floor, 41 Seah St., tel. (65) 337-0491.

Kwan Yim: Rustic vegetarian cafe in the South-East Asia Hotel adjacent to the immense Kuan Yin temple. Inexpensive. 190 Waterloo St., tel. (65) 338-2394.

Loo Tien Food Centre: Great place to dine alfresco in the late evening, or squeeze past the potted plants and find a table inside the restaurant nicely sited near the Raffles. A popular seafood and beer spot open nightly until 0300. Moderate. 2 Purvis St., tel. (65) 336-7981.

Xiang Man Lou: Ignore the ostentatious decor and you'll find excellent Cantonese dishes listed on its extensive menu. Convenient for night owls since it serves nightly until 0330. Moderate. Bras Basah Complex #01-79, Bridge at Bain St., tel. (65) 338-7885.

Shanghai and Sichuan

Sichuan food is based on hot peppers, salty bean paste, and plenty of garlic. Their most famous dishes are chili prawns and smoked duck, which is marinated in Chinese wine for 24 hours, steamed for two hours, and then smoked over a charcoal fire sprinkled with camphor wood chips and red tea leaves—it's the aromatic tea leaves that give the duck its distinctive taste.

Chungking Chinese Szechuan: A clean and elegant new addition to the restaurant scene without the fish tanks and gaudy red lanterns common to many upscale Chinese places. Despite its name, the restaurant offers a very comprehensive menu including shark's fin with Mandarin chili sauce, smoked chicken (a highly unusual dish),

eight vegetarian selections, and chilled almond bean curd for dessert. Moderate. Bugis Junction #02-53, 200 Victoria St., tel. (65) 334-8840.

Esquire Kitchen: Shanghai and Sichuan dishes served à la carte and on set menus at both lunch and dinner. Moderate. Bras Basah Complex #02-01, North Bridge Rd., tel. (65) 336-1802.

Shanghai Palace: Cantonese, Sichuan, and Shanghainese favorites such as drunken chicken in wine sauce, hot and sour soups, and fish and bean curd served in baked clay pots. Moderate. Excelsior Hotel, 5 Coleman St., tel. (65) 339-3428.

Hainan

Good Family: Chef Huang claims the secret to perfect chicken rice is a meaty bird with thin skin slaughtered between 35 and 40 days of age. Along with the classic steamed chicken dish served with garlic chili sauce, the Good Family hawker stall prepares roast chicken, marinated pork, and sweet-and-sour chicken feet ("phoenix claws") cooked Thai style, all served with rice steamed with ginger and spring onions. Inexpensive. Tropical Makan Food Palace, Beach Centre, 15 Beach Road.

Loy Kee Chicken Rice: One of the most successful Hainanese chicken rice vendors in Singapore now has eight outlets including this new operation in Bugis Junction. Loy Kee also serves vegetables with oyster sauce, pork congee, and something listed on the menu as "spare parts." Inexpensive. Bugis Junction #B1-01, tel. (65) 334-5422.

Mooi Chin Palace: A venerable 60-year-old cafe that relocated a few years ago into this modern complex filled with computer shops. It still serves Hainanese classics in a tony setting of glass and aluminum. Moderate. Funan Centre #B1-03, tel. (65) 339-7766.

Swee Kee: Venerable colonial coffee shop famed for its succulent chicken rice served with sliced cucumber and sauces of ginger, chilies, and soy. Inexpensive. 51 Middle Rd., tel. (65) 338-5551.

Tien Seng Curry: Some 40 years ago a Hainanese fellow called "Fatso" invented something called "scissors curry rice" after his habit of trimming the pork chops with an old pair of scissors. His only dishes were homemade fish cakes, pork chop and braised pork belly pounded with a mallet, chicken wing curry, and stewed cabbage with fried eggs—all drenched in two types of curries and pork gravy. Fatso later went bankrupt from his gambling habit but his dishes live on in this simple hawker stall in the HDB block just north of Bugis MRT station. Inexpensive. 450 Victoria Street.

Yet Con: Another old favorite that competes with Swee Kee for the title of best chicken rice in this part of town. The menu also lists steamboat fondues cooked at the table and crispy roast pork served with pickled cabbage and black bean sauce. Inexpensive. 25 Purvis St., tel. (65) 337-6819.

Indian

Aangan: North Indian vegetarian and nonvegetarian restaurant serving *palak panner, makhmoli tikka, rashmi kabob,* and mutton curry in the renovated shopping center. Funan Centre #04-05, 109 North Bridge Rd., tel. (65) 334-4125.

Ananda Bhavan: Simple cafe in existence since 1924 in a prewar shophouse half camouflaged by stalls selling Indian cassettes and cheap clothing. The vegetarian dishes are of Tamil Nadu or Kerala origin and are served without utensils on a bed of rice accompanied by chutneys and curries. Inexpensive. 219 Selegie Rd., tel. (65) 336-3891.

Annalakshmi: A sumptuous north and south vegetarian Indian restaurant run by Kala Mandhir, an Indian religious and cultural organization located in the adjacent building. Many of the staff are volunteers who dress in traditional garb and serve all the classic dishes including a variety of breads and curried stews. Moderate. Excelsior Hotel, 5 Coleman St., tel. (65) 339-9993.

Moghul Mahal: Elegant yet lively restaurant serving North Indian specialties since 1984. Try the *paneer makni,* cottage cheese in spinach; *brinjal bharta,* roasted eggplant drenched in tomato-garlic; and *rogan gosh,* stewed mutton served in a rich gravy. Moderate. Colombo Court #01-11, 1 North Bridge Rd., tel. (65) 338-6907.

O.M. Moosa: Muslim cafe next to the Why Not Guesthouse with quick and excellent chicken *murtaba, bryani,* and *roti prata* served with delicious curry sauces. Popular with the Bencoolen crowd and open around the clock. 129 Bencoolen Street.

Selera Cafe: Rarely visited by Westerners but very popular with locals who come for the curry puffs and other Indian/Chinese delicacies. The Selera and adjacent Rex Restaurant are located in a neighborhood largely unchanged since the 1920s. Inexpensive. 15 Mackenzie Rd., tel. (65) 338-5687.

Sri Vijayah: Another bare-bones vegetarian cafe popular with backpackers, Tamil workers, and health-conscious students attending the nearby art college. Meals are served on banana leaves and eaten by hand. Inexpensive. 229 Selegie Rd., tel. (65) 336-1748.

Taste of South India: Fast-food Indian cafe with fish-head curry, chicken *bryani,* and mutton *marsala.* Not much atmosphere but you can dine outdoors on the patio under the palms. Albert Court #01-03, 180 Albert St., tel. (65) 334-5157.

Thai

Coca: Unpretentious cafe serving Thai appetizers, soups, and entrees plus Chinese dishes since 1957. Their steamboat luncheon special includes beef, chicken, pork, and all possible varieties of seafood and shellfish. Moderate. Concourse #02-28, 298 Beach Rd., tel. (65) 295-3611.

Pimai Thai: Singapore's first restaurant to serve "royal" Thai cuisine provides equally elegant surroundings of polished wooden walls, antique ceramics, and light classical Thai music floating across the sunken dining area. Specialties include grilled beef salad flavored with lemon juice and paprika, crab legs dipped in a coconut milk sauce, and deep-fried pomfret served with mango sauce. Moderate. Hotel Inter-Continental, 80 Middle Rd., tel. (65) 431-1064.

Pornping Thai: Located in a distant shopping complex known as "Little India" are dozens of unique hawker stalls and this almost elegant seafood restaurant serving huge portions of fish in plum sauce, claypot crabs, and Thai fish cakes with vermicelli. Golden Mile Complex #01-96, 5001 Beach Rd., tel. (65) 298-5016.

Malay and Indonesian

Bintang Timur: This Malay-Indonesian restaurant serves familiar staples at this location and at their outlet on the second floor of the Far East Plaza shopping center. Moderate. Landmark Mercure Hotel, 390 Victoria St., tel. (65) 299-2996.

Chocho's: Peranakan specialties such as *bakwan kepiting, papaya titek, jantung pisang, itek sio,* and *ayam alia* created by the great grandmother (Chocho) or the present owners. One of the few Peranakan restaurants in Singapore. Moderate. Albert Court #01-23, 180 Albert St., tel. (65) 337-3283.

Rendezvous: *Nasi padang* cafe serving *rendangs, sambals,* and Padang delights in a comfortable, modern setting but without the charm and character of its former location in an old shophouse near the National Museum. Moderate. Raffles City #02-19, 252 North Bridge Rd., tel. (65) 339-7508.

Sari Jaya: Creative setting furnished with Indonesian batiks and artifacts and a popular spot for *satay, tahu telur, keplal ikan assam, udang baker,* and *ayam goreng* polished off with *es teller* or *es delima. Bagus.* Moderate. Metro Plaza #02-22, 750 Beach Rd., tel. (65) 297-2282.

Western

Bar and Billiard Room: The finest place to dine in the Raffles Hotel is also the most historic (the last tiger in Singapore was shot under the billiards table) as well as the most authentic—this is the only original building left on the reconstructed site. Dinners are nothing special but the lunch buffets and Sunday brunches include a vast array of high-quality dishes such as smoked salmon, wild mushroom salad, beef carpaccio, prawn and dill weed salad, clams, marinated scallops, and main entrees from lamb chops to steamed sea bass—all served in a truly wonderful setting right from the days of Conrad and Kipling. Their lunch buffet is highly recommended. Raffles Hotel, 1 Beach Rd., tel. (65) 331-1746.

Compass Rose: Sure it's pricey, but the commanding views from the top of the world's tallest hotel are truly spectacular. The continental menu varies from lobster and scallops served in a garlic-pepper sauce to champagne and mandarin orange zabaglione. Three- or four-course dinner costs S$75/S$95, buffet lunch S$45, high-tea buffet S$24. Snacks are served 1430-1730. Expensive. Westin Stamford, 2 Stamford Rd., tel. (65) 431-5707.

Deli France: Singapore's largest chain of croissant and coffee shops has over 30 outlets serving fresh-baked breads along with a variety of coffees. Inexpensive. Capitol Building #01-03, 11 Stamford Rd., tel. (65) 334-1645.

Doc Cheng's: The Hawaiian-born chef trained in French cuisine blends Eastern and Western traditions in his creative ensemble of sun-dried tomato *naan* with mango chutney, ginger tiramisu, seaweed scallops, Tahitian crabmeat soup, and banana shrimp pizza. The quirky room is decorated with the oddball sayings of the mysterious Doctor Cheng—a wealthy Chinese rubber trader who was supposedly a close friend of Mad Ridley, the rubber tree king of Singapore. Moderate. Raffles Arcade #02-02, 1 Beach Rd., tel. (65) 337-1886.

Dome Cafe: Trendy hangout fitted with Italian decor and done up in black, black, black. Still, the sandwiches and coffees are well prepared and the crowd is something beyond the standard Singapore look. Singapore Art Museum, Bras Basah Rd., tel. (65) 339-8511.

Long Bar: One of the most cynical and calculated tourist rip-off joints in Singapore, this tacky re-creation of the original Long Bar now resembles an American imitation of a colonial Denny's—complete with schlocky fans and bartenders who insist you throw your peanuts on the floor. Under no circumstance should any sane visitor go here and order a Singapore Sling unless they want to be known as the *ah beng* of the Western world. As *San Fransico Chronicle* columnist Herb Caen once noted, the snack food includes "French fries and tortilla chips with Velvetta sauce." He also noted that "misspelling Velveeta only makes it worse, if possible." Moderate. Raffles Hotel, 1 Beach Rd., tel. (65) 337-1886.

Montage Cafe: Cozy little cafe located in Singapore's largest bookstore serving homemade carrot soup and cleverly named dishes such as Salmon Rushtea. Buy a book and then relax over a leisurely lunch. Inexpensive. MPH Bookstore, 71 Stamford Rd., tel. (65) 334-1963.

Olio Dome II: One of many branches; this one draws a young and stylish crowd that dines here after taking in a movie in the downstairs theater. Asian, continental, and Australian fare. Moderate. Cathay Picturehouse #02-00, 6 Handy Rd., tel. (65) 339-8511.

Olive Tree: Mediterranean cuisine from Morocco, Lebanon, Spain, Greece, and France is served in this high-vaulted restaurant marked

SINGAPORE

by a series of imported olive trees. Elegant furnishings and sophisticated food make this a welcome relief from the hawker stalls and gaudy Chinese emporiums that characterize much of Singapore dining. Moderate. Hotel Inter-Continental, 80 Middle Rd., tel. (65) 338-7600.

Prego: An immensely nouvelle-cuisine Italian restaurant with stylish yet casual decor and creative dishes sold at reasonable prices. Among the favorites are *fettuccine al Nero con granchio e asparagi* (squid ink fettuccini served with crab and asparagus), *raviolo aperto con gamberi e capesante* (prawns, scallops, eggplant and zucchini in a white cream sauce), and *filetto d'orata e capesante* (roasted snapper with scallops, spinach, and deep fried mushrooms). Moderate. Westin Plaza, 2 Stamford Rd., tel. (65) 338-8585.

Seah Street Deli: Singapore's only Jewish delicatessen provides welcome relief from colonial artifacts and the country's endless onslaught of shopping centers by offering classics as potato "knish upon a star," the familiar "lox, stock and bagel," and mysterious items like "Ike and Tina Turner" and "Marshall with maalox." Bagels, mountainous pastrami-and-rye sandwiches, and irreverent menus make this a welcome relief

from colonial indigestion. Raffles Arcade, 328 North Bridge Rd., tel. (65) 337-1886.

Stars: Chef Jeremaih Tower of San Francisco opened this nouvelle-cuisine restaurant in late 1996 in the renovated, former Convent of the Holy Infant Jesus. As with his previous effort on Victoria Peak in Hong Kong, the menu emphasizes fresh and light ingredients arranged with great creativity, California style. Expensive. 30 Victoria Street #01-18, tel. (65) 332-1033.

Tiffin Room: The white walls, high ceilings, and rotating brass fans in this small dining room distract tourists from the bland if plentiful tiffins offered throughout the day. An elegant setting but the unimaginative fare is aimed squarely at moneyed travelers afraid of an authentic Asian experience. Expensive. Raffles Hotel, 1 Beach Rd., tel. (65) 337-1886.

BOAT QUAY

Boat Quay, once the haunt of working stevedores and Chinese coolies, has now been transformed into a harbor front recreation area and fashionable eating place for Singapore's increasingly cosmopolitan population.

Boat Quay has also transformed the eating habits of Singaporeans who, until quite recently, shunned alfresco dining as suitable only for peasants who couldn't afford to patronize a/c restaurants. But the Boat Quay restoration of the early 1990s suddenly made it fashionable to sit outdoors and shoot the breeze with friends while draining jugs of cold Tiger beer and tucking into three-cheese pizzas. It was deja vu all over again—the return of the dining styles once common in the night markets of Chinatown and along Albert Street near the Bencoolen backpacker lodges.

Western

Al Dente Trattoria: Owner Anthony Wong serves seafood antipasti, grilled salmon dosed with olive pesto, al dente pastas, and pizzas baked in a wood-fired oven for that smoky Italian touch. Moderate. 70 Boat Quay, tel. (65) 536-5366.

Café@BoatQuay: Coffee and snacks and Sun workstations for Internet access at S$10 per hour. Inexpensive. 82 Boat Quay, tel. (65) 230-0140, http://smedia.com.sg/café.

Chili's: American chain with American-sized portions of ribs, steaks, salads, sandwiches, and Mexican favorites. Moderate. 74 Boat Quay, tel. (65) 538-4577.

Coco Carib: New spot serving Caribbean and South American dishes in a lively setting. Moderate. 42 Boat Quay, tel. (65) 435-1800.

Coffee Club: Drop in for house coffee roasted at their head office or spring for the Blue Mountain special at S$15 per cup. Patrons can choose to sip their coffee by the river or on the second or third floors. Inexpensive. 52 Boat Quay, tel. (65) 538-0061.

Culture Club: Another new venue with Asian and Western dishes served in a decidedly unusual "cultural" atmosphere. Moderate. 39 Boat Quay, tel. (65) 536-2471.

Dada: Enchiladas, fajitas, shepherd's pie, and English roast beef served in a restaurant cum music bar with three floors of entertainment near the Elgin Bridge. Inexpensive. 79 Boat Quay, tel. (65) 538-8979.

Escobar: A modest selection of bar snacks and simple entrees but worth visiting for the superb music, which ranges from world beat to Brazilian samba. Inexpensive. 37 Boat Quay, tel. (65) 536-6696.

Good Life: Named after a BBC sitcom of some 20 years ago is Singapore's first macrobiotic restaurant serving pastas, soups, and salads in a wholesome atmosphere. Inexpensive. 36 Boat Quay, tel. (65) 533-0534.

Gourmet Bistro: Dine outdoors on the comfortable wooden cane chairs and try the lunch special, set dinner, or steak-and-seafood fondue that serves parties of two. Then it's crêpes suzette or Gran Marnier soufflé for dessert. Moderate. 35 Boat Quay, tel. (65) 534-4318.

Harry's: Singapore's best night spot of the year serves as a watering hole for the financial community as well as tourists who can join the well-dressed young execs on the ground floor bar or wander upstairs to the light and airy dining room, which has hanging ferns, murals of old Boat Quay, and a small bar and lounge area. The menu lists seafood gumbo and shrimp romulade as an appetizer, entrees including cajun chicken and fried prawns, and desserts such as bread and mango pudding. And while you dine, you can ask the concierge to make concert bookings, send urgent documents via DHL or FedEx, or call a London Cab for a ride back to your hotel. Moderate. 28 Boat Quay, tel. (65) 538-3029.

Hot Stones Dinosaur: The curious name refers to the cooking method in which steaks, chicken, and seafood are grilled tableside on alpine rocks heated to 200° F. Diners can also opt for the crispy fried calamari served with homemade tartar sauce or the surf-and-turf combo platter while gazing at the dinosaur that peers from an upper window. Moderate. 53 Boat Quay, tel. (65) 534-5188.

Louis' Oyster Bar: Spiffy black-and-white interior festooned with mirrors and Satchmo photos, and serving oysters in a half-dozen styles and entrees from oxtail stew to prawns stewed in creole sauce. The major S$50 splurge is the "high society" platter—crayfish, crab, mussels, oysters, and prawns accompanied by three sauces and sides of salad and bread. Moderate. 36 Boat Quay, tel. (65) 533-0534.

Luna Luna Trattoria: Right in the thick of the action is a trattoria and "cafe art gallery" serving Italian seafood soups, oysters baked with spinach and cheese Florentine style, fetuccine with oysters and artichokes, and the house specialty of salmon baked in a tangy Dijon mustard sauce. Moderate. 31 Boat Quay, tel. (65) 538-2030.

SINGAPORE

Moomba: Contemporary Australian cuisine has hit Singapore in the form of a chic new eatery decorated with aboriginal art, didgeridoos, and contemporary Australian paintings commissioned by the restaurant. Among the nouvelle dishes are fresh yabbies—quintessential Australian shellfish—served with a basil butter sauce, roast kangaroo salad, and crab cappuccino soup. Moderate. 52 Circular Rd., tel. (65) 438-0141.

Molly Malone's: Singapore's first Irish pub serves traditional fare like bangers, roast beef, steak and kidney pie, Irish stew, and cottage pie and cabbage; it's all washed down with Kilkeeny beer in the second-floor dining hall. Irish musicians entertain in the evenings. Moderate. 42 Circular Rd., tel. (65) 536-2046.

Movenpick: Swiss restaurant chain with Alpine decor and dishes from English pie to Swiss fondue. Moderate. 39 Boat Quay, tel. (65) 538-8200.

Pasta Fresca: A rather tacky chain restaurant with cafeteria furnishings and bad Italian art on the walls. Moderate. 30 Boat Quay, tel. (65) 532-4920.

Singapore Town Club: The second oldest private club in Singapore (1861) is open only to members for lunch, but welcomes the public at dinner. On the menu are baked camembert with cranberry sauce and gazpacho as appetizers, and crispy duck with rambutans and Batavia chicken as main courses. A refined place with private club atmosphere. Moderate. 44 Boat Quay, tel. (65) 532-2189.

Sizzling Rock: Perhaps following the lead of its successful neighbor, Hot Rocks Dinosaur, Sizzling Rock serves steak, chicken, and seafood on blazing hot rocks that maintain their heat for over an hour. 51 Boat Quay, tel. (65) 534-2531.

Asian

Gina's Peranakan: Malay, Indonesian, and Peranakan dishes like *ayam buah keluak,* (chicken in tamarind), *asam pedas,* (claypot chicken in a spicy sour sauce), *bakwan kepiting,* (minced pork and crabmeat soup), and Nonya *otak otak* (minced fish paste barbecued in banana leaf). Moderate. 49 Boat Quay, tel. (65) 538-7876.

House of Sundanese Food: A new incarnation of an inexpensive but highly praised fam-ily-run restaurant which has moved upmarket from the original shophouse on East Coast Road in suburban Katong. Here you can feast on the aromatic, spicy cuisine of Bandung in western Java—*satay,* barbecued seafood, and vegetable salads tossed with garlic, chili, lime, and peanut sauce. Moderate. 55 Boat Quay, tel. (65) 534-3775.

Khazana: Northwest Indian cuisine served in an Indian palace atmosphere with Rajasthani carved furniture and antique oil lamps. Try the marinated leg of lamb flamed at the table or Punjabi boneless chicken served in a butter-yogurt sauce or opt for one of the multitude of vegetarian dishes. Moderate. 61 Boat Quay, tel. (65) 534-4166.

Kinara: The exotic, imaginative interior decor brings to mind Rajasthan: antique carved screens and tables and chairs rescued from a pre-Raj mansion by Parvinder Singh, the proprietor who also runs an interior design consulting firm. Menu specialties are centered around Punjabi dishes served alfresco by the river and in the two a/c floors of this renovated shophouse. Moderate. 57 Boat Quay, tel. (65) 533-0412.

Royal Bengal: The elegant colonial look and interesting sepia photographs do not compensate for the surprisingly bland food that has been toned down so as not to offend the casual tourist. Ask the waiter to turn up the fire and try the mutton *rara* served in a rich gravy, ginger marsala lamb chop, or chicken tandoori served on a flaming sword. Expensive. 72 Boat Quay, tel. (65) 538-4327.

Sukothai: Named after the ancient capital of the Thai kingdom, Sukothai provides an elegant decor highlighted by illuminated Buddha statues and a menu with both familiar Thai fare and unusual dishes such as dried fish salad with shredded mangoes and preserved olive and fresh lemon in claypot. Arrive early for dinner to secure a window table on the third floor for the best views of the river. Moderate. 47 Boat Quay, tel. (65) 538-2422.

Superbowl—The Art of Eating Congee: A surprisingly popular restaurant that specializes in 47 varieties of rice porridge—big steaming bowls of rice porridge—along with Cantonese and Hunanese meat and seafood items. Owner Jeannie Lau decorated her cafe as a 1930s Shanghai noodle shop with rosewood back-to-back cubicles, marble-topped tables, wood paneling on the walls, and checkered tiles on the floor. After the cafe became an instant hit, Lau went on to open the Magic of Chong Qing Hot Pot on Orchard Road and the Potato Museum in Suntec City. Inexpensive. 80 Boat Quay, tel. (65) 538-6066.

Tinsel Moon: A fairly new Cantonese restaurant with decent steamed sea bass in black bean sauce and fried spareribs with tangy orange sauce. Moderate. 47 Circular Rd., tel. (65) 536-9919.

Warung Wayan: The former River Palace restaurant has shifted gears and brought in a chef from Bali who whips up all the familiar Javanese dishes but almost completely avoids the question of authentic Balinese cooking, just like nearly all the restaurants on the island itself. Moderate. 50 Boat Quay, tel. (65) 538-3889.

CLARKE QUAY

Western
J.P. Bastiani: Clarke Quay's most acclaimed dining venue has shifted culinary emphasis with the departure of French chef Thierry Lalanne and the arrival of American John Beriker who previously worked for Wolfgang Puck at Spago in Hollywood. Beriker has combined traditional Mediterranean cuisine with nouvelle California influences to produce artistic towers almost too beautiful to consume. House specialties include crispy soft-shelled crabs eaten whole, baked chicken stuffed with mushrooms and served with sweet shallot sauce, and wild mushroom ravioli with sun-dried tomato pesto. A Friday night buffet for S$45 includes unlimited servings of three red and three white wines from the restaurant's extensive wine cellar. Moderate. Merchants Court #01-12, 3A River Rd., tel. (65) 433-0156.

Key Largo: An oyster bar and seafood restaurant with rough ceiling rafters, red-tile floor, bentwood chairs, and the requisite Bogey posters and movie stills mounted on the walls. Diners can start with a choice of over 10 oyster varieties, then move on to oven-baked trout stuffed with lobster mousse and doused with a crayfish cream sauce, or grilled lamb chops stuffed with oysters and pan-fried mushrooms. Moderate.

Traders Market 301-01, 3E East River Valley Rd., tel. (65) 334-4055.

Asian
Four Seasons: Certainly not the famous hotel but a garishly lit fruit emporium dedicated to the king of fruits—the infamous, malodorous, yet delectable durian. Durians here are served plain, baked in faux pastry puffs, pounded into silvery puddings, wrapped in feathery pancakes, or boiled in coconut and served with thick cream over crushed ice. Quite unique. Inexpensive. Traders Market #01-14, 3D River Valley Rd., tel. (65) 336-1821.

Satay Club: After the original Satay Club near the Padang waterfront was torn down to make way for the Nicoll Highway extension and the Esplanade performing arts center, 27 former vendors were invited to set up stalls in the walkways of Clarke Quay or elsewhere on the island or accept a cash grant of S$15,000. Six took the money and retired while most of the remainder moved to other food courts in Singapore. Those who elected to move to Clarke Quay have fared badly. The sterile atmosphere is a world removed from that of the original. R.I.P. Satay Club. Inexpensive. Read Street near the River Valley Road taxi stand.

Thanying: Thanying ("noble lady") serves up *tom yam* soup garnished with two juicy prawns and other familiar favorites in a beautiful teak-paneled dining room overlooking the Singapore River. The original outlet is located in the nearby Amara Hotel. Moderate. Shophouse Row #01-14, 3D River Valley Rd., tel. (65) 336-1821.

Tongkangs: Several traditional Chinese barges have been refurbished and now serve Cantonese and Hokkien dishes along with pub food and live folk music. Moderate. Hawkers Alley, 3D River Valley Road.

Yunnan Kitchen : One of the few Yunnanese restaurants in Singapore serves unusual dishes such as *guoqiao* ("crossing the bridge") vermicelli with chicken, scallops, or prawns, and braised chicken smoked over *pu er* tea leaves, which impart an exceptional taste. The Matsutake mushrooms, a house specialty promoted as a cure for diabetes and cancer, are bland. Moderate. Merchants Court #01-09, 3A River Valley Rd., tel. (65) 338-3001.

SINGAPORE

CHINATOWN

Food Centers

Chinatown Complex Food Centre: Two floors of foodstalls in a monstrous housing and shopping complex which, when constructed in the early 1980s, almost single-handedly destroyed the character of old Chinatown. Sago at Trengganu Street.

Maxwell Food Centre: By far the best food center in Chinatown is this large open-air complex near the start of Tanjong Pagar, filled with almost 100 food vendors. Perhaps not the cleanest place but a big favorite with Singaporeans who arrive from all parts of the country. Recommended stalls include the "pig trotter" joint facing the surfaced carpark, another one selling excellent claypot rice, and the *hun chi beng* stall where customers are invited to fry their own Chinese pastries. Just inside the Maxwell Street entrance is Hajmeer Kwaja Muslim foodstall which sells tasty chicken, mutton, and sardine *murtabaks*, fried in 60 seconds on a flat circular griddle and then served with curry sauce and cucumbers. South Bridge at Maxwell Road.

People's Park Food Centre: Right behind People's Park Complex is a sad collection of stalls surrounded by huge slabs of concrete and high-rise housing estates. Eu Tong Sen Street.

Cantonese

Happy Realm Vegetarian: All natural cafe serving tofu baked with curried vegetables; emerald fresh soup; and the "robe of honor," to help you find a sound mind. Inexpensive. Pearl Centre #03-16, 100 Eu Tong Sen St., tel. (65) 222-6141.

Lee Tong Kee: Try their "executive" set lunch with oyster chicken, bean sprouts with *kai chong, hor fun,* wonton soup, and homemade barley—all for just S$10. Inexpensive. 278 South Bridge Rd., tel. (65) 223-1896.

Majestic Restaurant: The cafe in the old Majestic Hotel serves a variety of Cantonese standards and whole roasted suckling pig as their pricey specialty. Moderate. 31-37 Bukit Pasoh Rd., tel. (65) 223-5111.

Mouth Restaurant: Popular, classy spot for nouvelle Cantonese dishes and dim sum, served daily 1100-1630. Moderate. Chinatown Point #02-01, 133 New Bridge Rd., tel. (65) 534-4233.

New Nam Thong Tea House: Situated above a prewar shophouse is a rustic and colorful teahouse serving early morning dim sum, *congee, char siao pow, siao mai,* and other assorted finger food enjoyed by the congregation of old men who gather to read the Chinese newspapers. Dim sum is served daily 0530-0900 and 1100-1430. A newer and less atmospheric outlet is at 181 New Bridge Road. Inexpensive. 8-10A Smith St., tel. (65) 223-4229.

Tai Tong Hoi Kee: Old fashioned cafe on a newly renovated street serving traditional dim sum daily 0500-1900. Inexpensive. 2-3 Mosque St., tel. (65) 223-3484.

Tiong Shian Porridge: Famous old place serving *congee* laced with your choice of fish head, pork, century eggs, or cuttle fish plus braised kidney with stir-fried vegetables and Hainanese chicken rice. Open daily 0700-0200. Inexpensive. 265 New Bridge Rd., tel. (65) 221-1596.

Tong Heng: Serves the best *kai tan tahk* (Cantonese egg tarts) in Chinatown—sweet, rich, and sticky. Inexpensive. 285 South Bridge Rd., tel. (65) 223-3649.

Tung Lok Sharks Fin Restaurant: The luxurious setting featuring a priceless collection of Chinese paintings and calligraphy compliments the highly regarded cuisine, which ranges from nouvelle dim sum to the house specialty of braised shark's fin in a delicate consommé. Expensive. Liang Court Complex #04-07, 177 River Valley Rd., tel. (65) 336-6022.

933 Salt-Baked Chicken: Simple cafe with noodle and porridge dishes plus a salted baked chicken marinated in medicinal herbs to improve your health. Chickens are sold whole, half, or in a set meal. Inexpensive. 192 South Bridge Rd., tel. (65) 323-8933.

Teochew and Hokkien

Ban Seng: Traditional charcoal-baked dishes include roasted crayfish with garlic and shallots, steamed carp with sour plums, braised goose with chili sauce, sea cucumbers stuffed with mushrooms, and a mashed yam dessert known as *oh nee.* Inexpensive. 79 New Bridge Rd., tel. (65) 533-1471.

Beng Hiang: An old favorite in a restored shophouse known for its Hokkien *kwa huay* (liver appetizers), *ngo hiang* (pork and prawn rolls) served with sweet plum sauce, *ha cho* (prawn

SINGAPORE

CHINATOWN RESTAURANTS

See Boat Quay Restaurants & Nightclubs Map

Fort Canning Park

RIVER VALLEY ROAD

Clarke Quay

Singapore

N. BOAT QUAY RD.

N. BOAT QUAY RD.

ELGIN BRIDGE

▼ VIOLET OON'S KITCHEN

▼ RAJAH INN

Riverwalk Galleria

UPPER CIRCULAR RD.

ELLENBOROUGH FOOD CENTRE

CARPENTER ST.

Boat Quay

River

EMPRESS PLACE FOOD CENTRE

CAVENAGH BRIDGE

FLINT ST.

FULLERTON RD.

POST OFFICE

LIANG KEE

TEW CHEW ST.

HONG KONG ST.

Restaurant and Bar Area

CIRCULAR RD.

TELOK AYER LORONG

BOAT QUAY PEDESTRIAN MALL

BATTERY ST.

CHANGE ALLEY

RED LANTERN REVOLVING RESTAURANT

RAFFLES QUAY

MERCHANT RD.

MARKET ST.

BAN SENG

N. CANAL RD.

CANAL RD.

GEORGE ST.

S. CANAL RD.

CHULIA ST.

RAFFLES PLACE

BENG THIN HOON KEE RESTAURANT

PHILLIP ST.

INTERCHANGE

MALACCA ST.

CHURCH ST.

D'ALMEIDA ST.

COLLYER QUAY

Hong Lim Park

UPPER PICKERING ST.

PICKERING ST.

PICKERING ST.

Havelock Square

NEW BRIDGE RD.

SOUTH BRIDGE RD.

HOKIEN ST.

NANKIN ST.

CHIN CHEW ST.

PEKIN ST.

CHINA ST.

MARKET ST.

TELEGRAPH ST.

▼ MOUTH RESTAURANT

NEW NAM THONG TEA HOUSE

CROSS ST.

933 SALT-BAKED CHICKEN

CLUB ST.

BENG HIANG

AYER ST.

WAY

▼ LAU PA SAT

PEOPLE'S PARK FOOD CENTRE

CHUI WAH LIN

CHINA VILLAGE

MOSQUE ST. STEAMBOAT HOUSE

GEMMILL LN.

HUAT KEE

BOON TAT ST.

DOME CAFE

TAI TONG HOI KEE

PAGODA ST.

MOSQUE ST.

TELOK AYER ST.

BEE HEONG CAFE

STANLEY ST.

CECIL ST.

BANGKOK GARDEN

TEMPLE ST.

TRENGGANU ST.

NEW NAM THONG TEA HOUSE

TONG HENG

AMOY ST.

CECIL GOURMET CORNER

BANJARA

SMITH ST.

BEAUJOLAIS WINE BAR

ANN SIANG RD.

McCALLUM ST.

TIONG BAHRU RD.

LEE TONG KEE CAFE

FROTHY TEA SHOP

ERSKIN RD.

TIONG SHIAN PORRIDGE

SAGO LN.

SAGO ST.

BANDA ST.

CHINATOWN COMPLEX FOOD CENTRE

NOBLE HOUSE

HAPPY REALM VEGETARIAN

MYSORE SOUTH INDIAN

KRETA AYER RD.

MAXWELL FOOD CENTRE

MAXWELL RD.

Telok Ayer Park

SHENTON WAY

▼ TASVEE

Duxton

KEONG SAIK RD.

TECK LIM RD.

MURRAY TER. FOOD ALLEY

MURRAY TER.

TANJONG PAGAR RD.

TUAS ST.

Plain

NEIL RD.

DUXTON HILL

DUXTON RD.

Tanjong Pagar

TANJONG PAGAR

▼ VIOLET OON'S KITCHEN

Park

CRAIG RD.

0   0.1 mi

0   0.1 km

See Tanjong Pagar Restaurants & Nightclubs Map

© MOON PUBLICATIONS, INC.

SINGAPORE

dumplings), *kong bak* (grilled pig's feet), and roasted suckling pig. Moderate. 112-116 Amoy St., tel. (65) 221-6684.

Chiu Garden: Combination restaurant-karaoke pub with 10-person set meals of Swatow dim sum, double-boiled soup, sliced abalone with spinach, chicken and pomegranate scallops, steamed fish in bean sauce, and sweetened green beans with water chestnuts. Moderate. Pearl Centre #03-19, 100 Eu Tong St., tel. (65) 323-9088.

Chui Wah Lin: Traditional old shophouse with precooked Teochew dishes displayed in containers, a convenient arrangement since the owners speak little English but understand the point-and-choose ordering method. Inexpensive. 49 Mosque St., tel. (65) 221-3305.

Huat Kee: Hokkien cafe on a trendy street serving dim sum and à la carte entrees daily 1100-1430 and 1800-2200. Inexpensive. 76 Amoy St., tel. (65) 323-1344.

Liang Kee: This finely sited cafe facing the Singapore River features superior oyster omelettes cooked without the use of arrowroot, tasty fish soup, *haw chor* (prawn and liver fritters), and other seafood items. From the second floor of the converted HDB flat, you gaze across to the commercialized hubbub of Clarke Quay. Inexpensive. HDB Block 1 #02-40, 1 Teochew St., tel. (65) 534-1029.

Mosque Street Steamboat House: Lively late-night joint where diners cook their own meals on individual woks set over propane heaters. Open daily 0700-1400. Inexpensive. 44 Mosque St., tel. (65) 222-9560.

Indian

Banjara: Owner Kumar Thirupathi not only serves his native Punjabi favorites but also the food of Delhi and Rajastan, adapted from his years of experience in Singapore's Omar Khayam and Delhi restaurants. *Methi* fish is a favorite, fetched from the seafood wet markets of nearby Chinatown. Moderate. 66 Smith St., tel. (65) 323-7657.

Mysore South Indian: "Lucky" Singh and his three partners chose a central location for their successful restaurant. In addition to Tamil staples, they serve north Indian classics such as tandoori. The glass-enclosed cafeteria setting has little charm, but the food is full of great flavors. Moderate. 49 Kreta Ayer Rd., tel. (65) 323-5474.

Tasvee: The first Indian restaurant in Chinatown has been wooing customers for almost a decade with its *paratas* and *murtabaks* stuffed with pork, beef, or marinated chicken. The emphasis is on Muslim dishes served around-the-clock under swishing fans. Predominately Chinese crowd. Moderate. 323 New Bridge Rd., tel. (65) 323-9911.

Indonesian and Polynesian

Kintamani: Named after the wind-swept village on a volcano top in Bali, Kintamani offers classic Javanese dishes during their impressive luncheon buffet and at dinner when items must be ordered à la carte. Moderate. Apollo Hotel, 405 Havelock Rd., tel. (65) 733-2081.

Rajah Inn: A spacious and gaily decorated restaurant with bentwood chairs wrapped in batik and elaborately set tables, some of which face the Singapore River. Popular dishes include fish head curry and Indonesian classics—*tahu telor, asam udang,* and *sambal goreng ayam.* Moderate. Riverwalk Galleria #B1-38, 20 Upper Circular Rd., tel. (65) 538-2088.

Trader Vic's: This famous San Francisco-based restaurant closed several years ago in the U.S., but has franchised their Polynesian concept around the world including this exotic venue known for its crab Rangoon, bongo bongo soup, barbecued Norwegian salmon, and Indonesian rack of lamb. The weekend buffets are quite popular. Moderate. New Otani Hotel, 177 River Valley Rd., tel. (65) 338-3333.

TANJONG PAGAR

Of note in this district is **Murray Terrace,** Singapore's original "food alley" and one of the first major restoration projects to be attempted in the country. A sign explains some of the background of this important turning point in local efforts to preserve some of Singapore's past. For over a decade, Murray Terrace thrived as a popular collection of simple, unpretentious cafes serving a variety of Asian cuisines. In recent years, however, competition from newer venues in Tanjong Pagar has hurt business and today the owners appear somewhat anxious to pull in customers. None of this should dissuade you since most of the restaurants continue to provide de-

SINGAPORE

cent food at fair prices. Many of Murray Terrace's cafes are listed below.

Chinese

Chinatown Garden Seafood: Tanjong Pagar's celebrated Jinrikshaw Station now houses a Cantonese seafood restaurant open for lunch and dinner, 1800-0400—perfect for the hungry night owl. Moderate. 1 Neil Rd., tel. (65) 223-1813.

Delicious Kitchen: Utilitarian restaurant serving Teochew dishes such as baked claypot chicken in bean sauce, fish rolls with julienned vegetables, and steamed prawns with a cute bird decoration. Inexpensive. 30-32 Tanjong Pagar Rd., tel. (65) 226-0607.

Dynasty Garden: Tanjong Pagar's most expensive Chinese restaurant is located in a renovated prewar shophouse decorated to resemble an imperial courtyard with all the requisite splashes of red and glittering chandeliers. Among the more unusual dishes are lobster sashimi, pepper fried Sri Lankan crab, and the "all hands meal" for which diners are given plastic gloves to use when diving hands-first into platters of prawns, crabs, chicken, cuttlefish, and tempura vegetables all served on banana leaves. Expensive. 40-42 Craig Rd., tel. (65) 224-1725.

Fatty Ox Hong Kong Roast Duck: This Hong Kong-style cafe serves roast suckling pig along with *tai yeh* chicken and *jing ling* duck. Inexpensive. Murray Terrace, 10 Murray St., tel. (65) 222-0923.

Liang Kee Tew Chew: Teochew favorites and seafood specials such as steamed pomfret and crab dipped in a pungent *sambal* sauce. Inexpensive. Murray Terrace, 16 Murray St., tel. (65) 225-5145.

Loke Who Yuen Vegetarian: Simple vegetarian fare served in a unassuming coffee shop. Inexpensive. 20 Tanjong Pagar Rd., tel. (65) 221-2912.

Mitzi's Cantonese: Rudimentary family-run cafe with zero atmosphere but tasty chicken in prawn paste, fried pig trotters (intestines, etc.), and almond soup for dessert. Inexpensive. Murray Terrace, 24-26 Murray St., tel. (65) 222-0929.

Moi Kong Hakka: For over 50 years this basic food house has churned out unpretentious Hakka favorites like prawns fried in red wine, braised pork in a rich dark soy sauce, and yam starch fried with preserved vegetables. Inexpensive. Murray Terrace, 22 Murray St., tel. (65) 221-7758.

Aun Zhong Eating House: Coffee shop specializing in the food of northern China. Inexpensive. 21 Neil Rd., tel. (65) 221-3060.

Sang Yong Shark's Fin: Another basic Cantonese restaurant with bargain set lunches and dinners starting at S$12 and a 38-dish lunch or dinner buffet for just S$16. Inexpensive. 81 Tanjong Pagar Rd., tel. (65) 323-7883.

Tian Jin: The place for Beijing beet noodles and other northern Chinese wheat-based delights such as *guo tie* (pan fried dumplings), pancakes stuffed with meat and chives, and *cheng up bing* (green onion pie). Inexpensive. 18 Tanjong Pagar Rd., tel. (65) 221-5148.

Yan Hong Kee: Cheap Hokkien cafe serving thick rice porridges and other basic fare. Inexpensive. 72 Tanjong Pagar Rd., tel. (65) 223-5275.

Peranakan

Blue Ginger: Designer Ed Poole has created a modern and sophisticated interior graced with Peranakan-style lamps imported from Spain and walls painted in shades of pastel. The delicately seasoned Nonya dishes include a pork meatball soup with bamboo shoots, steamed sea bass topped with preserved bean paste, noodles laced with lily buds and sweet bean curd, and the classic Peranakan dish, *ayam buah keluak* (fish with unstuffed black nuts). Inexpensive. 97 Tanjong Pagar Rd., tel. (65) 222-3828.

Violet Oon's Kitchen: Violet Oon is Singapore's best-known food critic and advocate of Peranakan cuisine, which is served in her main restaurant on Bukit Pasoh and her newer outlets in Holland Village, Bugis Junction, Victoria Theatre, Kallang Theatre, and the Drama Centre on Fort Canning Hill. Aside from running her cafes, Violet stars in a TV cooking series, tours the world to promote the Singapore Food Festival, and supervises her *Food Paper,* covering the Singapore culinary scene.

Violet Oon's Kitchen fills an immaculately renovated shophouse set with Western art prints and simple cane chairs over burnished hardwood floors. Popular with the artsy crowd, diners can try set menus at lunch and dinner or opt for à la carte specials such as outstanding Nonya *laksa* and *popiah* spring rolls garnished with prawn and crab. Also offered are Violet's famed shepherd's pie and a fabulous dessert called *bo-bo cha-cha*—palm sugar sauce over crushed ice mixed with sweet yam and other delicate morsels. Inexpensive. 11 Bukit Pasoh Rd., tel. (65) 226-3225

Indian

Jaggi's North Indian: Somewhat outside the Tanjong Pagar neighborhood in the H.L.Y Eating House opposite the I.B.M Towers are several Indian fast-food cafes with excellent curries and steaming breads at rock-bottom prices. Inexpensive. Tanjong Pagar Complex, Keppel Road.

Moti Mahal: Waiters at this upscale restaurant terrorize the streets for customers, who when snared are taken to the front door and shown a *Far Eastern Economic Review* quote proclaiming Moti Mahal "one of the best Indian restaurants anywhere." The food doesn't live up to that lofty description but it's decent if you can handle the pretentious attitude of the waiters—and you can quote me on that. Moderate. Murray Terrace, 18 Murray St., tel. (65) 221-4338.

Malay and Indonesian

Cumi Bali Nasi Padang: Formerly the Pagi Sore Nasi Padang, Cumi Bali Nasi Padang serves Indonesian, Balinese, and fiery Padang mouth-burners from Sumatra. Inexpensive. 20 Duxton Rd., tel. (65) 221-6936.

Mount Faber Nasi Lemak: Cozy cafe featuring banana-leaf *nasi lemak* plus side dishes of fried chicken wings, anchovies, and *otak*. Open until the wee hours of the morning. Inexpensive. 47 Kreta Ayer Road.

Musa Muslim: Convenient corner spot for Muslim *roti prata* and *teh tarek* served around the clock. Inexpensive. 2 Murray St., tel. (65) 226-2393.

Thai

Oriental Thai Inn: Enjoy the 36-dish Thai buffet for just S$13/18 (lunch/dinner) or try the "new generation claypot super sharksfin" soup for S$20. Inexpensive. 97 Duxton Rd., tel. (65) 323-5016.

Rama Thai Sharksfin: One of several restaurants that serve Thai-style shark's-fin soup. Moderate. 81 Tanjong Pagar Rd., tel. (65) 222-6626.

Siamese Fins: A classy polished-wood restaurant with award-winning braised shark's-fin soup, baked crab claws with vermicelli, and sautéed gooseweb. An outdoor signboard displays photos of the dishes. Moderate. 45 Craig Rd., tel. (65) 227-9759.

Siang World Thai: Clean cafe serving *tom yum*, Thai chili crab, olive rice, baby *kai lan*, and prawn cakes with pineapple rice. Inexpensive. Murray Terrace, 14 Murray St., tel. (65) 227-8983.

Thanying: Thanying ("noble lady"), considered among the best Thai restaurants in Singapore, serves *tom yam* soup garnished with two juicy prawns, an exquisite Thai chicken-and-prawn salad, and other classics of royal Thai cuisine. Another branch of the restaurant, perhaps more convenient, is located in a beautiful teak-paneled room at Clarke Quay overlooking the Singapore River. Moderate. Amara Hotel, 165 Tanjong Pagar Rd., tel. (65) 222-4688.

Tea Houses

Hua Tuo Guan: Just down from Jinriksha is a renovated shophouse that serves herbal teas, iced plum juices, and medicinal desserts to cure what ails you. Quick shots of bitter herbal 24 or sweet herbal 5 are dispensed from two huge brass and copper urns out front, while desserts and other medicinal teas are served inside. 22 Tanjong Pagar Rd., tel. (65) 222-4854.

Tea Chapter: This rustic second-floor teahouse features small booths and a variety of teas ranging from simple green, black, and herbal brews to gourmet strains that you can sniff over before consumption. Rare 100-year-old teas and expensive tea sets are sold; teas cost S$6-15 depending on the brew. Tea Chapter was visited by Queen Elizabeth in 1989 and, as you might expect, walls are plastered with photos of the occasion. 11A Neil Rd., tel. (65) 226-1175.

Yixing Xuan: For a more elegant tea experience, try this ground floor place a few doors down from Tea Chapter. Yixing Xuan (Relaxing Home) is ideal for Western visitors since the proprietors, Vincent Low and C.K. Loh, are English-educated Chinese accustomed to dealing with people untrained in the art of tea drinking. Inside this reconstructed teahouse is a tea artifact center and tea cafe set with rosewood tables in private vestibules. Most teas are imported from the Taiwanese Lu Yu Tea company, which awards recognized diplomas in "teaology." None of this seems to matter to the artists and calligraphers who meet here weekly to drink tea, recite

Chinese poetry, and sometimes even belt out Italian arias. 23-25 Neil Rd., tel. (65) 224-6961.

Yi Pao Er Hong Frothy Tea: A kitschy joint with over 50 Taiwanese teas blended with fruit juices to make beverages like Frothy Green Pearl—an unsettling combination of 12 teas with milk, cane sugar, and sago palm juice. As for food, the menu lists "floss toast" and "eel rice" and if that's not enough, the room has been decorated in a weird mishmash of painted fans, miniature trains, and silly Taiwanese toys. 183 South Bridge Rd., tel. (65) 323-1040.

Western

Da Paolo: Small restaurant in need of a facelift but still serving rich homemade pastas with cuttlefish or crabmeat and classic osso bucco swimming in rich cremolada sauce. Moderate. 66 Tanjong Pagar Rd., tel. (65) 224-7081.

Duxton Deli and Wine Bar: Escape the crowds at this higher elevation cafe decorated with mirrors and marble, red tiles and bentwood, and serving sandwiches and light entrees in the dining area or outside on the pleasant terrace. Inexpensive. 21 Duxton Hill Rd., tel. (65) 227-7716.

Fratini La Trattoria: Italian country atmosphere with high ceilings and artwork provided by owner Gabriel Fratini. Skip the eggplant and carpaccio appetizers and order the seafood soup with clams and mussels. Popular entrees are illustrated on the menu and include sea bass in white wine and tortellini with ham and mushrooms in creamy white sauce. Moderate. 51 Neil Rd., tel. (65) 323-2088.

L'Aigle d'Or: Among the finest French restaurants in Singapore is this fabulously expensive venue affiliated with the famed restaurant of the same name in Paris. Bookings can be difficult so call well in advance. Expensive. Duxton Hotel, 83 Duxton Rd., tel. (65) 227-7678.

Le Bistro Neuf: Trendy avant-garde bistro with an original menu of duck breast in pistachio sauce, stingray, quail, eggplant in béchamel, and steaks smothered with braised artichokes— all created by a chef formerly affiliated with the Shangri-La Hotel. Moderate. 9 Duxton Hill, tel. (65) 221-2837.

Pasta Brava: Peranakan decor, friendly staff, and a sensible way to order your pasta: select one of eight pastas (pennette, fusilli, linguine,

etc.) and then the sauce (carbonara, vongole, puttanesca, etc.). Beyond the pasta entrees are osso bucco flavored with lemon zest, pork chops flamed with white wine, and chicken breast stuffed with prosciutto and mozzarella. Moderate. 11 Craig Rd., tel. (65) 227-7550.

LITTLE INDIA

Vegetarian

Komala Vilas: Singapore's most famous vegetarian cafe provides light meals on the ground floor, though most Westerners head upstairs to grab a table near the window or duck into the small a/c private room. Almost 60 years in the business, Komala Vilas continues to serve unlimited helpings of delicious South Indian vegetarian dishes on fresh banana leaves with sides of chutney, *dahl*, and *dosai*. The mainly Indian clientele eat with their hands, though utensils are available upon request. Afterwards, use the sink to wash up and be sure to purchase a few sweets at the counter downstairs as a take-away delight. Excellent food—one of the best cultural experiences in Singapore. Don't miss Komala Vilas. Inexpensive. 76 Serangoon Rd., tel. (65) 293-6980.

Little India Arcade: To the rear of this recently renovated arcade is Hastings Food Court with a dozen small cafes serving curries, tiffins, vegetarian snacks, and Malay dishes in a clean but somewhat sterile environment. Open daily 0930-2300. Inexpensive. 48 Serangoon Road.

Madras New Woodlands: Clean a/c cafeteria serving both south and north Indian vegetarian dishes including the *thali* set meal—the classic all-you-can-eat onslaught of steamed rice, curried vegetables, *dhal*, *sambal*, *rasam* (hot and sour soup), and *papadums.* For S$2 more you can dig into their V.I.P *thali*, which ups the condiment count. Diners are expected to share tables during busy periods. Inexpensive. 12-14 Upper Dickson Rd., tel. (65) 297-1594.

Maharaja Kitchen: An Indian rickshaw greets diners at this cafe with extra hot South Indian fare during lunch and northern dishes added in the evenings; try the garlic fish. Inexpensive. 42 Veerasamy Rd., tel. (65) 299-3321.

Sella Vilas: Decent but inferior copy of Komala Vilas. Inexpensive. 60 Serangoon Rd., tel. (65) 298-9866.

SINGAPORE

Yamabuta Seafood: New place claiming to be Singapore's first macrobiotic restaurant. No msg and preservatives used. All seafood is collected from "unpolluted" waters, then dispatched to nirvana by immersion in icy water. Mr. Yamabuta, the owner who lives upstairs, also serves fresh oysters, crabs, and sushi accompanied by brown rice, sea salt, and filtered water. Inexpensive. 73 Dunlop St., tel. (65) 297-7388.

Muslim and North Indian

Sasural: Narrow two-story shophouse with pleasant outdoor dining and a gaily decorated interior that sets it apart from the standard cafe in Little India. Sasural (In-laws Residence) serves homemade Punjabi chicken, curried lamb, plus a selection of vegetarian entrees called "mock meat curry." Attractive place with superior food. Inexpensive. 39 Campbell Lane, tel. (65) 336-9100.

Thye Cheng: Four bearded Bengalis work this Muslim foodstall known for its hand-cooked breads, minced mutton in curry, and two unusual dishes—brain omelettes with garlic, ginger, and tomato and curried green wood pigeons. Somewhere between the size of a large sparrow and a young chicken, these gamey little creatures are only available when supplies arrive from Malaysia; otherwise ordinary quails are substituted. Inexpensive. 168-170 Serangoon Rd., tel. (65) 293-3507.

Zhujiao Food Centre: Has dozens of ethnic foodstalls serving Chinese, Indian, and Malay dishes at rock-bottom prices. Inexpensive. 1 Serangoon Road.

Delhi: Considered the finest North Indian restaurant in Little India and among the most reasonably priced in Singapore, Delhi specializes in tandoori meat and fishes first marinated in wine, baked in a traditional clay oven, and served with a choice of over a dozen varieties of bread. Set meals are available daily. Dinner reservations are required though the overflow is handled at their nearby Deli Pub and an outlet in the Broadway Hotel. Moderate. 60 Race Course Rd., tel. (65) 296-4585.

Mahraj Tandoori: Same range of dishes in less elegant surroundings. Moderate. 52 Race Course Rd., tel. (65) 299-9364.

Maharajah's Tandor: Another Maharaj/Maharaja/Maharajah restaurant serving tandor/tandoor/tandoori dishes fit only for royalty. Moderate. 70 Race Course Rd., tel. (65) 293-0865.

Nur Jehan: Another contender on "curry alley" in the heavyweight North Indian division. Chef

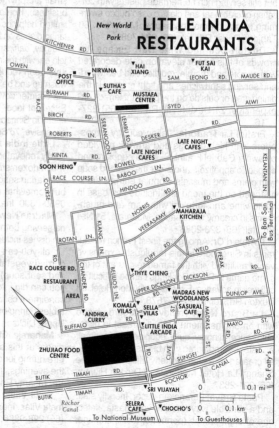

LITTLE INDIA RESTAURANTS

© MOON PUBLICATIONS, INC.

Singh has worked some of the best Indian restaurants in Singapore so you can be assured of high standards in this unassuming restaurant. Moderate. 66 Race Course Rd., tel. (65) 292-8033.

Fish Head Curry Houses

The following restaurants compete between themselves for the coveted title of "best fish head curry in Singapore," an award presented each year during competitions sponsored by the Singapore Food Festival. In this dish, the head of a large fish (usually red snapper) is cooked tender in a pot of bubbling curry and then served on a banana leaf with one enormous eye staring straight at the customer. Accompanied by steaming *marsala* or *biryani* rice, eggplant, okra, two *papadam,* and a range of chutneys and yogurts, fish-head curry costs S$22-28 but will feed at

least two people. The eye is considered a delicacy though no one minds if you cover the glutinous ball with a dab of curried okra.

Banana Leaf Apolo: Serves one of the best fish-head curries in Singapore along with a wide selection of South Indian dishes, all on fresh banana leaves and seasoned with prodigious amounts of chili. Inexpensive. 56-58 Race Course Rd., tel. (65) 293-8682.

Muthu's Curry: Famous fish-head curry cafe but visitors squeamish about handling fish heads the size of a football can opt for the chicken or mutton curries, fried flower crab, squid, or prawns served on banana leaves in a comfortable a/c setting. À la carte entrees cost just S$6-9. Muthu's has won the "best fish head curry in Singapore" award several times. Inexpensive. 78 Race Course Rd., tel. (65) 293-7029.

ENTERTAINMENT

CLASSICAL

Hotel Shows

Several hotels and amusement parks put on cultural shows that might include a Chinese lion dance and acrobats, Indian *bharat natyam,* snake charmers, Malay *bersilat,* and a demonstration of a Peranakan wedding. Current venues should be checked in *Singapore Visitor* or *Singapore This Week.*

Raffles Hotel: Two multimedia shows about Raffles and the history of Singapore. Seah Street Entrance, tel. (65) 331-1732, S$10.

Singha Inn Restaurant: An "Instant Asia" show nightly at 1900 with buffet dinner. 920 East Coast Rd., tel. (65) 345-1111, S$35-45.

Tang Dynasty City: Chinese dancers and acrobats during the buffet lunch from noon to 1300. 2 Yuan Ching Rd., tel. (65) 261-1116, S$25-30.

Sentosa Island: Asian Village at Sentosa presents a 30-minute traditional dance show in

Instant Asia reviews

SINGAPORE

the Thai Pavilion daily at 1015 and 1115 and a 30-minute dinner show nightly at 1830. Sentosa Island, tel. (65) 222-9339, S$5 morning show, S$15-20 dinner show.

Drama

Singapore's most dynamic form of performing arts is theater and drama as performed by over 30 companies, ranging from ethnic troupes to avant-garde ensembles.

Act 3: Singapore's first professional theater company works to promote drama among the youth through workshops, productions, and tours. 126 Cairnhill Rd., tel. (65) 734-9090, fax 736-1196.

The Necessary Stage: One of Singapore's more popular forms of drama are original plays translated from Chinese to English and vice versa. Past performances include Michael Chiang's *Private Parts* and Stella Kon's *Emily of Emerald Hill.* TNS performs both English and Chinese plays at the Drama Centre on Canning Rise. 126 Cairnhill Rd., tel. (65) 738-6355, fax 732-2931.

TheatreWorks: Singapore's first professional English-language drama company fuses Western and Eastern traditions in its critically acclaimed productions such as *Beauty World,* an upbeat musical produced in 1988, and *Mortal Sins,* a dark and emotional 1995 musical about artistic censorship and nostalgia for simpler times. Fort Canning Centre, tel. (65) 338-4077, fax 338-8297.

NIGHTLIFE

Singapore has far more nightlife than most visitors assume thanks to some 500-plus venues with alcohol licenses and an entertainment industry that generates an estimated S$700 million in income each year. The latest trend seems to be the all-in-one nightclub, which includes the standard flashing-lights disco plus a selection of smaller lounges, cafes, wine bars, jazz cellars, and private karaoke rooms. Orchard Road still has the largest concentration of nightclubs in Singapore, though many new clubs have opened along Boat Quay, Tanjong Pagar, and Robertson Quay.

Orchard Road

Studebaker's: Singapore has all the popular international nightclubs—Hard Rock Café, Planet Hollywood, TGIF—including now an outlet of Australian-based Studebaker's in Pacific Plaza. Decorated in a Thai style with an eclectic collection of bronze sculptures, Studebaker's attracts an elite crowd of models, visiting movie stars, and royalty. The cover charge of S$17/20 female and S$20/25 male on weekdays/weekends includes one drink. Ladies' night on Wednesday includes unlimited drinks for females. Pacific Plaza, 9 Scotts Rd., 12th floor, tel. (65) 736-0006.

Sparks: Sparks is a sprawling 35,000-foot art deco emporium of shiny black and gold with mirrors, lasers, and three entertainment venues aimed at distinct audiences. The disco features live music as well as DJs and attracts a younger and more demographically diverse crowd than Studebaker's or Velvet Underground. Cover and first drink charges are S$15 weekdays, S$20-30 weekends. Happy hour admission charges are S$8 from 1700-2000. Ngee Ann City, 391 Orchard Rd., 8th floor, tel. (65) 735-6133.

Fabrice's World Music Bar: World music from Africa, Spain, India, and the Middle East found its first home in Singapore at this watering hole. The carpets, masks, and artifacts from Indonesia provide a suitable ethnic flavor. Bands range from the flamenco guitars of the Matadors to salsa from the Cha Cha Cha Cuban Boys. Cover charge S$17 weekdays, S$22 weekends after 2200. Open 1900-0300; happy hour 1900-2000. Marriott Hotel, 320 Orchard Rd., tel. (65) 738-8887.

Fire: Three levels of entertainment appealing to a predominantly teenage crowd. The downstairs nightclub serves as a disco, while Singapore hard rock bands work the upstairs venues. Cover ranges S$12-25. Open 1700-0300; happy hour 1700-2000. Orchard Plaza #04-19, tel. (65) 235-0155.

Top Ten: Another cavernous nightclub with light shows, terraced seating around the stage and dance floor, and live bands both local and foreign. This converted movie theater is mostly patronized by expatriates and roving ladies who sip cocktails beneath a huge mural of the New York skyline. Orchard Towers #04-35, 400 Orchard Rd., tel. (65) 732-3077.

SINGAPORE

Ginivy: This country-and-western nightclub to the rear of Orchard Towers features a decent house band and loads of Thai and Indonesian girls offering more than polite conversation. Orchard Towers Rear Block #02-11, 1 Claymore Rd., tel. (65) 734-1748.

Hotline: Their ad says it all: "Headbangers will definitely bang their heads off and bemused [sic] by heavy metal and rock music whenever the Pryamid Band climbs on stage." For a real trip, try the Sunday tea dance 1300-1800 when hundreds of Filipino maids and expats on the prowl pack this 350-person basement nightclub. Ming Arcade #B2-01, 21 Cuscaden Rd., tel. (65) 734-6604.

Planet Hollywood: Singapore's latest addition to the nightlife scene is the world's largest Planet Hollywood, which opened in 1997 on the former site of Galerie Lafayette. The 18,000-square-foot restaurant and nightclub serves dinner until around 1030, when bands take to the stage or a DJ spins CDs for your dancing pleasure. 541 Orchard Rd #02-02., tel. (65) 733-5339.

Hard Rock Cafe: The first HRC to open in Asia starts live music around 2230 after the diners are finished. HRC has often received the STPB "best night club of the year" award. HPL House #02-01, 50 Cuscaden Rd., tel. (65) 235-5232.

Anywhere: This difficult-to-find nightclub features resident band Tania, a group that has entertained expats and locals for over a decade with a mix of rock, reggae, and R&B. A lively place without attitude and one of the best party spots in town. Open until 0200 weekdays, 0300 weekends, happy hour 1800-2030. Tanglin Shopping Centre, 4th floor, tel. (65) 734-8223.

Brannigan's: A jam-packed watering hole and pick-up joint popular with expats and single ladies who practice mating rituals while the house band knocks out top-40 covers. Sample prices are S$9 a beer, S$10 cocktails, and S$32 a pitcher of beer. Hyatt Regency, 10/12 Scotts Rd., tel. (65) 738-1234.

Saxophone: Live blues, rock, and jazz in intimate surroundings at Cuppage Center just off Orchard Road. Saxophone is a great place to hang out but seating is limited and it can be impossible to find a cocktail waitress in the mad crush. This outdoor cafe with pricey French meals and pricey cocktails was the first club opened by Fabrice de Barsy, the Belgian who later opened Fabrice's World Music Bar and the now-defunct Ka. Be sure to check his vintage anti-long hair sign in the bar. 23 Cuppage Terrace, tel. (65) 235-8385.

Excalibur Olde Englysche Pub: A cozy English/Aussie pub favored by expats and locals for its continual happy hour prices and wide selection of beers. Tanglin Shopping Centre #B1-06, 19 Tanglin Rd., tel. (65) 732-8093.

5 Emerald Hill: A cozy bar and cafe popular with expatriates, the advertising crowd, and sarong party girls who will talk to anyone with a good opening line. The upstairs bar features impromptu jazz gigs from local musicians such as Spencer Goh and his pals. Try the pizza number five with sausage and jalapeño peppers. 5 Emerald Hill Rd., tel. (65) 732-0818.

Que Pasa Wine Bar: The classiest of a trio of Emerald Hill cafes is this wine-and-tapas bar favored by fashionable Ralph Lauren suits and cute sarong girls outfitted in strappy camisole dresses and jellied sandals. 7 Emerald Hill Rd., tel. (65) 235-6626.

Ice Cold Beer: A simple little watering hole with red-cushioned bar seats, hundreds of beers, dart tournaments, and a little movie room upstairs showing the latest videos. 9 Emerald Hill Rd., tel. (65) 735-9929.

Central Singapore
Scandals: The classiest nightclub in this part of town attracts the same trendy crowd that frequents Fabrice's and Studebaker's on Orchard Road. Same hours and cover charges as similar clubs. Westin Plaza Hotel, 2 Stamford Rd., tel. (65) 338-8585.

Compass Rose: The best views in Singapore are from this tony nightclub and cafe on the 70th floor of Southeast Asia's tallest hotel. Most of the island can be surveyed through windows that reach from floor to ceiling. Open 1100-0100; happy hour 1730-2030. Minimum S$15 charge per person after 2030. Westin Stamford Hotel, 2 Stamford Rd., tel. (65) 338-8585.

Somerset: Classy and spacious lounge that features top-notch American and European jazz artists—one of the few jazz venues in Singapore. Westin Plaza Hotel, 2 Stamford Plaza, tel. (65) 338-8585.

Long Bar: A tacky tourist trap hidden away on the third floor past the shopping arcade and

SINGAPORE

other superficialities that accompanied the re-construction of the Raffles Hotel. Closely resembles a Hungry Tiger or old Sambo's restaurant. Raffles Hotel, 1 Beach Rd., tel. (65) 337-1886.

Elvis at the Concourse: A nightclub in the basement of the vast Concourse shopping arcade that attracts an international crowd looking for a party. Formerly located in Tanjong Pagar, this mini-museum to the king plays all types of music from the 1950s including Jerry Lee Lewis and Chuck Berry. Half-priced drinks during happy hour 1600-2030. The Concourse, 298 Beach Road #B1-13, tel. (65) 299-0451.

Lot, Stock & Barrel Pub: Tucked away in an alley adjacent to the Raffles are several old shophouses occupied by a few Chinese Clan Associations, a Chinese medicine shop, and this cozy, unpretentious bar and cafe with wooden doors and French green windows. A popular place for a game of pool, darts, or to have a beer while listening to oldies from the jukebox. 29 Seah St., tel. (65) 338-5540.

Boom Boom Room: Tucked away on the second floor of a re-created entertainment complex is the only vestige of old Bugis Street—the former transvestite haunt torn down in the early 1980s to make way for Bugis Junction shopping center. The red-curtained cabaret room features two shows nightly with a mix of song, dance, and Singlish humor by cross-dresser Kumar. Due to the show's shallowness and predictability, this is merely a third-rate imitation of the original acts of old Bugis Street. 3 New Bugis St., #02-04, tel. (65) 339-8187.

Boat Quay

Harry's Quayside: The definitive bankers hangout opened in August 1992, making it the grand-daddy among social establishments at Boat Quay. Harry's has followed the tradition of Harry McElhone, the founder of Harry's in Paris and inventor of the Bloody Mary, by inventing the Bank Breaker in honor of Nick Leeson. Harry's in Singapore also claims to be the first bar in the world with a fully operational concierge service, which can book reservations for restaurants, concerts, London cabs, golfing, and scuba diving. 28 Boat Quay, tel. (65) 538-3029.

Escobar: A lively Latin-American bar and restaurant with quick bar snacks and the hip sounds of Latino world beat. Some of the best

music on the quay. 37 Boat Quay, tel. (65) 536-6697.

Tommorrow's Piano Bar: Upstairs on the third floor is a cozy escape from the quayside crowds with snacks and relaxing piano music. 66 Boat Quay, tel. (65) 534-5316.

Shoreline II Pub: British and Singaporean pub food plus a variety of rock and blues classics. 69 Boat Quay, tel. (65) 532-1166.

Big Ben Pub: Big Ben and the adjacent Nineties Pub are re-creations of British pubs; both just past the poorly stocked BookWorld. 77 Boat Quay, tel. (65) 538-6310.

Molly Malone's: Singapore's first Irish pub opened a few years ago right behind Boat Quay in a three-story building painted a suitable shade of Irish green. The first floor bar serves finger food and Guinness while live traditional Irish folk music can be enjoyed on the second floor. A private club called The Office takes up the top floor. 42 Circular Rd., tel. (65) 536-2046.

Off Quay Bar: An upstairs venue with jazz bands jamming until the early morning hours. 36A Boat Quay, tel. (65) 534-4800.

Zappa Rock Bar: A newer joint with the sounds of modern rock and the recorded classics of Frank Zappa. 45 Boat Quay, tel. (65) 532-5633.

Riverbank: Sit outside and enjoy the recorded music or head to the second floor for karaoke or the third for live bands and comedy acts. 68 Boat Quay, tel. (65) 538-1135.

Dada Music Bar: Recorded tunes on the first-floor Rebel Bar, karaoke in the second-floor Gallery KTV, and excellent live bands in the Loft on the top floor. 79 Boat Quay, tel. (65) 538-8979.

Zouk: Zouk is a place apart, where people break conventions and experiment with new forms of music, style, fashion, and theater. Crowds of up to 3,000 pack the dance floor—lost in the music which pulsates with an endless techno world beat. Zouk is located near the River View Hotel. Open 1800-0300. Velvet Underground cover charge S$20/25 females, S$20/30 males weekdays/weekends. Weekend cover charge in the disco is S$12 before 2100. 17-21 Jiak Kim St., tel. (65) 738-2988, www.zoukclub.com.sg.

Tanjong Pagar

Lone Star Bar: The best country-western bar in Singapore features a free jukebox holding the largest collection of country-western records in the country. Try the Mexican Martini, La Casa Especial, and Texas Cherry Bombs—cherries soaked in rum. 54 Tanjong Pagar Rd., tel. (65) 225-5844.

JJ Maloney Pub: A beautifully furnished three-story a/c pub featuring 200 kinds of beer (Tiger on tap), live bands on the ground floor, German restaurant and games on the second, and karaoke on the top. Classy and comfortable. Open 1500-0200. 58 Duxton Rd., tel. (65) 225-6225.

Moon: One of the latest additions to the neighborhood is this spacey nightclub decorated with a Gothic interior of illuminated gargoyles and twisted wrought iron tables. Early evening entertainment is provided by lounge acts while house music, acid jazz, trance, and reggae music is piped in after 2300. Open daily except Sunday 1800-0100. 62 Tanjong Pagar Rd., tel. (65) 324-2911.

Cable Car Saloon: San Franciscans may want to pop into this narrow pub dedicated to all the icons of Baghdad-by-the-Bay. Nice photos but nobody in The City throws peanut shells on the floor. 2 Duxton Hill Rd., tel. (65) 223-3366.

Nightshift: Housed in a completely unique yellow-and-green building set back from the street is this somewhat suspicious nightclub with karaoke on the second floor and live entertainment downstairs that ranges from light rock to a six-piece all-female Filipino band. New Paper once voted this the number one pub in Singapore; worth a shot for the adventurous. 39 Craig Rd., tel. (65) 225-7010.

SHOPPING

Singapore enjoys a reputation as a shoppers' haven though bargains have largely disappeared due to inflation, soaring wages and the strength of the Singapore dollar.

ORCHARD ROAD

Singapore's "Golden Mile" runs along a tree-lined boulevard flanked on both sides by humongous department stores, vast shopping complexes bisected by elevators and escalators, and upscale boutiques designed for the privileged classes.

Tanglin Shopping Centre

Singapore's largest concentration of Asian antique shops is located in this older and somewhat funky complex adjacent to the Orchard Parade Hotel. Long patronized by Western tourists and expatriate residents, an amazing range of both new and old antiques can be discovered in the rectangular hallways of this centrally located complex.

Most of the galleries are located on the second and third floors, although you'll find a few shops on the ground floor and downstairs such as the Arts Centre, Moon Gate, Tzen Gallery, and Renee Hoy Fine Arts for Asian furniture and Oriental decor.

Highlights on the second floor include B C Antiques, Kensoon Asiatic Art, Jul Antiques, Polar Arts of Asia, Tang Horse, Tiepolo, Timepiece Antiques, Yong Lin, and Mata-Hari Antiques for arts and collectibles from Southeast Asia. Certainly the most fascinating shop is Antiques of the Orient, which claims to have the largest collection of antique maps of Southeast Asia in the world.

Lucky Plaza

This confusing rabbit warren of narrow lanes choked with miniscule shops selling every manner of bric-a-brac rates as one of the most popular shopping venues on Orchard Road. While Singaporeans may enjoy gazing at overpriced designer merchandise, when it comes to spending money, their *kaisuism* leads them to this hotchpotch bazaar in search of bargain-priced goods.

Ngee Ann City

Gotham City landed on Orchard Road in 1994 with the completion of this massive, brooding building comprised of two monolithic office towers and a six-floor shopping complex anchored by the Japanese retail Godzilla, Takashimaya. Tang's Studio on the second, third, and fourth floors of Tower B offers similar products as Takashimaya but with a local theme.

Centrepoint

This one-stop, compact shopping center is one of the liveliest complexes on Orchard Road and one of the few filled with practical shops within the lifestyle constraints of ordinary human beings. Robinson's department store, the anchor tenant, has enjoyed a reputation for quality merchandise at reasonable prices since it began operations in 1858. The hectic little place also has stores specializing in music, casual clothing, electronics, furnishings, sporting goods, and outlets of Times and MPH books.

COLONIAL SINGAPORE

Raffles City

Raffles City—an aluminum sphere and multilevel shopping complex designed by architect I.M. Pei—houses two hotels, several restaurants, and one department store, as well as dozens of specialty shops in the upper arcades overlooking the atrium. The spacious atrium is often used for special events, music concerts, and art exhibitions. Services inside Raffles City include a post office and DBS Bank on the first floor and a well-stocked outlet of Times Books on the second.

Bugis Junction

Singapore's most unique shopping center is situated between the Hotel Inter-Continental on Middle Road and the Bugis Street MRT station at Rochor Road. This fairly new complex features four re-created streets flanked by pseudo-shophouses, all enclosed within a soaring a/c atrium. Rather than the standard combination of concrete walls and shiny escalators, Bugis Junction feels somewhat like the traditional shopping districts that once existed in Chinatown and Central Singapore.

Sim Lim Square

Just across Rochor Canal from Little India and taking up an entire city block is an older shopping complex known for its good deals on electronics, stereos, CD players, cameras, and video equipment. Merchants here can often undercut the prices of Orchard Road but shoppers should bargain hard and be wary of fraudulent merchandise, altered receipts, and international guarantees.

Stanford House

One of Singapore's classiest sources of interior furnishings and home accessories is the beautifully restored building at Stamford Road and Hill Street. Originally constructed in 1904 and reborn in 1994, this Victorian-style building houses shops specializing in home decor, period furniture re-creations, art objects, and Asian antiques. Stanford House also has a photography studio and cozy cafe on the third floor.

Funan Centre

Singapore's computer center features over 80 computer shops selling all possible arrays of hardware and software at competitive prices. The seven-story pinkish building holds the huge Challenger department store, which takes up an entire level, and Tokyu, a major Japanese outlet, as well as smaller shops filled with books, music, watches, souvenirs, and jewelry .

Marina Square

Singapore's largest shopping complex sprawls over an area the size of seven football fields in the Marina district near the Pan Pacific and Oriental hotels. Anchored by a Metro and a K-Mart department store, this subterranean world includes over 200 smaller shops, several cinemas and amusement parks, dozens of cafes and restaurants, and hordes of teenagers who can help you when you get lost in the confusing maze of corridors and windowless atriums.

SPECIALITY SHOPS

Antiques

Singapore's location in the heart of Southeast Asia makes it a convenient center for one-stop shopping for antiques from all regions of Southeast Asia. Bear in mind, however, that prices can be 2-5 times higher than in their country of origin. Bronze statues that sell for US$500 in Bangkok can fetch US$1,000-1,500 here in Singapore and markups on Indonesian artifacts can be even higher, often 5-10 times the prices in Ubud and Yogyakarta. Serious collectors would be wise to pick up a copy of *Antiques, Arts & Crafts in Singapore* by Anne Jones from most Times or MPH bookstores in Singapore. Although published in 1988, the illustrations and photographs are worth the cover price alone.

Babazar Design: Adjacent to Centrepoint on Orchard Road and situated in a row of restored shophouses is an old favorite loaded with few antiques but plenty of reproduction furniture, vintage clothes, contemporary art, fashionable jewelry, assorted curios, and souvenirs. 31-35 Cuppage Terrace, tel. (65) 235-7866.

National Museum Shop: Fine selection of reproductions of ceramic bowls and sculpture fired in the kilns of China, Thailand, and Singapore as well as ethnic jewelry, contemporary Indonesian artwork, and lacquerware from Burma. 53 Armenian Street.

Raffles Arcade: Tiepolo Premier Antiques and Tomlinson Antique House on the second floor are aimed at Southeast Asian and Indian antiques while Renaissance Antique Gallery on the same floor specializes in rare Angkor sculpture. Two other top-notch outlets include Doeloe Ethnic Arts for collectible textiles and Boutique Chinoiserie, featuring a broad range of Asian objets d'art and modern reproductions. 1 Beach Road.

Art

Singapore has jumped into the international art market with the opening of the Singapore Art Museum, Asian Civilizations Museum, and the conversion of the Singapore National Museum to the Singapore History Museum. Art galleries have been cropping up in Singapore over the last few years, featuring modern Western art and works produced from Southeast Asian artists.

Notices the Gallery: A successful gallery that exhibits and sells works by both Asian and Western artists such as Lensman Stefano and Indonesian painter Krijono. Four Seasons Hotel #01-08, 190 Orchard Blvd., tel. (65) 734-1110.

Tanglin Shopping Centre: Although most dealers in this shopping complex specialize in antiques, several concentrate on local artists; these places include Sun Craft Gallery, which opened in 1975 and Tzen Gallery, which deals in the works of famous Chinese painters from the late 19th century as well as contemporary masters. 19 Tanglin Road.

Art Forum: Artists from Singapore and Southeast Asia are represented in this gallery, which was established in 1970 as one of the first in the country. Raya Gallery is also located in the same building. 82 Cairnhill Rd., tel. (65) 737-3448, fax 732-0298.

Art Focus: Deals mainly in local original works of art as well as limited edition prints and ceramics. Decor Arts Gallerie on the third floor sells originals, limited editions, sculpture, and prints. Centrepoint #05-07, 176 Orchard Rd., tel. (65) 733-8337, fax 732-0448.

Macassar Singapore: Classy new gallery featuring Asian and European artists such as the French oil painter Marc Rambeau. Stamford House #03-04, Stamford Rd., tel. (65) 338-8888.

Atrium Gallery: One of Singapore's most exclusive art galleries specializes in upcoming regional artists including Malaysian favorite Ahmad Kahlid Yusof who is best known for his *Alif Ba Ta* series on Arab-Islamic calligraphy. Marina Mandarin Hotel, 6 Raffles Blvd., tel. (65) 338-3388.

Riverwalk Galleria: Over a dozen art dealers are located in this modern shopping complex, which overlooks the Singapore River on the edge of Chinatown. Asia Artist Gallery on the third floor has been actively promoting Asian artists through exhibitions and the publication of its magazine, *Asian Artists,* since its opening in 1993. 20 Upper Circular Road.

Chinatown Point: The huge complex just opposite People's Park Centre has another small concentration of art dealers who form part of the Singapore Handicraft Centre. Art Gallery 3 on the third floor deals in watercolors, Chinese brush paintings, old jade pieces, pottery, and Buddha images from Nepal and Tibet. 133 New Bridge Road.

Books

Singapore has an excellent selection of English-language books including titles about Singapore and Southeast Asia that are not distributed abroad.

MPH Books: The largest and most comfortable bookstore in Singapore is located near the National Museum and Raffles City in the heart of the old colonial district. Titles on Singapore and the region are displayed just inside the entrance while travel guides are located to the rear of the main floor. 71-77 Stamford Rd., tel. (65) 336-3633 or 334-0592.

Times Books: Singapore's largest book publisher has over a dozen stores spread around the country and several conveniently located

SINGAPORE

near city center including outlets in Raffles City, Centrepoint and Lucky Plaza on Orchard Road, Columbo Court near City Hall, Holland Village, Changi Airport, and the World Trade Centre.

Select Books: Singapore's largest selection of books on Southeast Asia is found in this cozy bookstore which also doubles as an important publishing house and distributor of rare Asian imprints. Carries everything from travel guides to academic studies rarely carried by Times or MPH. Tanglin Shopping Centre #03-15, 19 Tanglin Rd., tel. (65) 732-1515, fax 736-0855.

Tower Books: Excellent bookstore with hard-to-find periodicals and Singapore's largest selection of CDs. Pacific Plaza, 13 Scotts Rd., tel. (65) 731-1166.

Bras Basah Complex: Bookshops in this older building cater primarily to students but also carry general stock on art, computers, and regional history. Popular Books has the largest selection followed by Big Bookshop, Knowledge Books, Pacific Books, Sunlight Book Centre, Union Book Company, and Art Books on the third floor. 231 North Bridge Road.

I have always had a fanatic belief that travel enriched individual lives, increased the community's prosperity, raised a nation's living standards, opened political barriers, and most important, functioned as the most effective eye-opener between different cultures. We in the travel business are a lucky lot to be in such a useful, joyful, and peaceful endeavor.

—EUGENE FODOR,
CONDÉ NAST TRAVELER

People generally think of travel in terms of displacement in space, but a long journey exists simultaneously in space, in time, and in the social hierarchy . . . Travel can hardly ever fail to wreak a transformation of some sort, great or small, and for better or for worse, in the situation of the traveller.

—CLAUDE LÉVI-STRAUSS,
TRISTES TROPIQUES

Do not be amazed by the true dragon.

—DOGEN ZENJI,
FUKANZAZENJI

SINGAPORE

THAILAND

THAILAND

> In traveling: a man must carry knowledge with him, if
> he would bring home knowledge.
>
> —James Boswell,
> *Life of Samuel Johnson*

> There are only three things which make life worth
> living: to be writing a tolerably good book, to be in a
> dinner party for six, and to be traveling south with
> someone whom your conscience permits you to love.
>
> —Cyril Connolly,
> *A Romantic Friendship*

> A good holiday is one spent among people whose notions
> of time are vaguer than yours.
>
> —J.B. Priestley

INTRODUCTION

For most Westerners, Thailand's image as an Eastern paradise perhaps derives from *The King And I* and sobriquets bestowed by creative copywriters—Land of Smiles, Land of the Free, The Most Exotic Country in Asia. While the hyperbole is somewhat excessive, Thailand unquestionably deserves its accolade as one of the world's premier vacation destinations. Annual tourist arrivals have exploded in the last decade from under one million to over seven million for excellent reasons: superb archaeological sites, glittering temples, lively nightlife, outstanding shopping, superlative culture, exuberant festivals, and culinary treasures to delight even the most demanding gourmet. Thailand is also blessed with an incredibly varied range of natural attractions: expansive national parks, fertile plains, remote jungles, pristine beaches washed by turquoise waters, and tropical islands bathed in endless sunshine.

All this is perfectly complemented by the Thai people, who have graciously preserved the traditions of a unique culture while embracing the conveniences of modern living. Perhaps because of their religion and belief in *chai yen* (cool heart) and *sanuk* (life is a pleasure!), Thais display an extraordinary sense of serenity, courtesy, humor, and well-being. More than anything else, it is the people that make Thailand such a wonderful place to visit.

HISTORY

Thailand's earliest recorded inhabitants were Buddhist Mons who formed the loosely knit Dvaravati kingdom in the Chao Praya basin from the 6th to 11th centuries. From the 8th to 12th centuries, Hindu Khmers expanded westward from Kampuchea and absorbed the Mons into their powerful empire. Mons today have largely disappeared in Thailand, although a sizable Mon community still exists in Myanmar. The Thai (Tai) people arrived later; two theories speculate as to their origins. Most believe they migrated from southern China during the 11th and 12th centuries and settled among the Khmers and Mons already residing in the central plains. Others argue that Neolithic cave settlements near Kanchanaburi and recent discoveries of a 6,000-year-old Bronze culture at Ban Chiang prove that the Thais preceded the Mons and Khmers.

THAILAND

© MOON PUBLICATIONS, INC.

Sukothai Period, 1220-1378

The brief but brilliant kingdom of Sukothai marks the true beginning of the Thai nation and remains to this day a source of great pride. While Sukothai's preeminence lasted less than 200 years, it gave rise to uniquely personified forms of architecture, sculpture, and even political structure. Under the leadership of King Ramkamheng (1278-1318), revered today as the father of Thailand, Sukothai fused Khmer and Mon traditions into a dynamic kingdom that ruled Southeast Asia from Laos to Malaysia. Military power and economic prosperity allowed the development of highly refined artistic achievements, including the world-renowned Sawankalok celadon and Buddha styles of great creativity and sensitivity. Ramkamheng's successors were less ambitious; by the late 14th century Sukothai had become a vassal state of upsurgent Ayuthaya.

Ayuthaya Period, 1378-1767

Sukothai's gradual decline was followed by the rise of Ayuthaya. Within a century of its founding by an ambitious Tai prince from U Thong, this riverine capital had become a major military power and the grandest city in Southeast Asia. Western visitors who arrived during the 16th and 17th centuries described Ayuthaya as a splendid metropolis with a population larger than London's. Among the *farangs* (foreigners) was Constantine Phaulkon, a Greek adventurer who rose to great power in the court of King Narai. After he attempted but failed to convert the king to Christianity, a palace rebellion broke out in which Phaulkon was executed and all Westerners expelled. It was during this period of self-imposed isolation that Ayuthaya created its own golden age of arts and architecture. This came to an end after the Burmese became jealous of their wealth and mounted a series of military campaigns against the city. In 1763 the Burmese attacked, and after two years of resistance they had slaughtered most of the population and burned the city to the ground. Not only did they destroy the artistic and literary heritage of Ayuthaya, they also pulled down many of the magnificent Buddhist temples and reliquaries—an act of horror which still profoundly shocks the Thais.

Bangkok Period, 1767-Present

The destruction of Ayuthaya was a devastating setback. But with typical Thai resilience, an ambitious half-Chinese soldier named Taksin rallied the nation and established a new capital in Thonburi, a sleepy fishing village just across the river from modern Bangkok. Within 10 years Taksin drove the Burmese from Thailand and expanded Siamese sovereignty from Chiang Mai to the deep south. As the son of a Chinese tax collector, Taksin repopulated the country with Teochew Chinese trade merchants, whose taxes provided significant revenue for the fledgling state. But the strain of long years of warfare took its toll, and Taksin apparently went insane with delusions of grandeur and paranoia. After imagining himself an incarnate Buddha, Taksin was executed in the manner prescribed for royalty: placed in a velvet sack and beaten to death with a sandalwood club.

Word of the coup d'etat eventually reached General Chakri, a popular Thai military leader on expedition in Cambodia. Chakri was called back to Thonburi and crowned King Rama I, first ruler of the dynasty which continues to the present day. Fearful of attack by Burmese forces, Rama I transferred his capital across the river to present-day Bangkok and attempted to re-create the former magnificence of Ayuthaya with the construction of royal temples and palaces. The city continued to be called Bangkok by Western mapmakers, but Rama I renamed it a multisyllabled Sanskrit moniker abbreviated as Krung Thep ("City of Angels"). Rama II (1809-1824), an outstanding poet, is chiefly remembered as the author of the Thai Ramayana. The British defeat of the Burmese during the reign of Rama III (1824-1851) allowed the Thais to expand their national boundaries to Malaysia, Laos, and Vietnam.

The King and I

Thailand's modern phase begins with King Mongkut (Rama V, 1851-1868), better known to the Western world as the autocratic despot in *The King and I*. Mongkut was actually an enlightened ruler whose imaginative diplomacy kept Thailand free from the European colonial expansionism that swallowed Myanmar, Malaysia, and French Indochina. During his 25 years of monkhood prior to being crowned Rama V,

THAILAND

SIGHTSEEING HIGHLIGHTS

Bangkok

Thailand's rich and kaleidoscopic tapestry of tourist attractions is enough to keep most visitors busy for months, though a single region could be explored well in a month. Visitors generally arrive by air at Bangkok, a chaotic and unnerving metropolis of immense traffic jams and modern high-rises. Appalled by the problems, many travelers make the mistake of pausing only long enough to buy a plane ticket and then moving out as quickly as possible. While Bangkok is certainly an urban planner's nightmare, it is also home to dozens of dazzling Buddhist temples, outstanding restaurants, superb shopping, and one of the liveliest nightlife scenes in the world. You will also be surprised at the vitality and friendliness of many of its eight million residents . . . if you survive the heat and congestion.

Vicinity of Bangkok

It may sound implausible, but enough historical monuments, beaches, and natural wonders are located within a 200-km radius of Bangkok to keep most visitors busy for weeks, if not months.

Pattaya: Thailand's eastern seaboard boasts several highly developed beach resorts, of which Pattaya is the most famous. One of the largest beach resorts in Asia, this low-powered Riviera of the East annually attracts over a million pleasure-seekers for its breathtaking range of water sports, restaurants, and legendary nightlife. Lively, chaotic, exciting, polluted, highly commercialized, and tacky, Pattaya in the past catered almost exclusively to military personnel or single businessmen who filled the bars and nightclubs. Today the resort appeals primarily to families, with attractions such as zoos, botanical gardens, and water parks for the kiddies. Although the beaches are inferior to those of Phuket or Samui, the proximity to Bangkok makes it convenient for visitors with limited time.

Ko Samet: To escape the high-rise development of Pattaya, many travelers continue eastward to this *kris*-shaped island south of Rayong. The beaches here are fairly good (though they can't compare with those in the deep south), and facilities are limited to simple bungalows and small restaurants that shut down at sunset.

Nakhon Pathom: Often visited on a day-trip from Bangkok or as a brief stop en route to Kanchanaburi, this small town one hour west of Bangkok is home to the world's tallest Buddhist monument.

Damnern Saduak: Thailand's most authentic floating market, two hours south of Bangkok, is much less commercialized than the artificial floating bazaar in Bangkok. Avoid an organized tour but rather see it yourself with an early start.

Kanchanaburi: This beautiful and relaxing region, three hours east of Bangkok, offers inexpensive floating guesthouses, refreshing waterfalls, hiking, and cool caves filled with Buddhas. Highly recommended for history buffs (the Bridge over the River Kwai is located here), nature lovers, and anyone annoyed with Bangkok's traffic jams.

Ayuthaya: For over 400 years the riverine-island town of Ayuthaya, two hours north of Bangkok, served as the second royal capital of Thailand. Though largely destroyed by the Burmese in 1767, many of the restored architectural ruins provide eloquent testimony to the splendor of Thailand's most powerful empire. Ayuthaya and Sukothai are Thailand's largest and most impressive archaeological sites.

Lopburi: Lopburi is a minor destination with modest Khmer ruins and an old summer capital for Ayuthayan kings that makes a convenient stopover en route to the Northeast.

Khao Yai National Park: Thailand's most popular park, four hours northeast of Bangkok, boasts a dozen hiking trails, refreshing waterfalls, and protected wildlife such as elephants and hornbills. Another popular stop en route to the Khmer monuments of the Northeast.

Central Thailand

Sukothai: In 1238 the Thai people proclaimed their independence from Khmer suzerainty and founded Sukothai, the first truly independent Thai capital. For over a century Sukothai ruled the region and created a Golden Age of Thai Arts that left behind a treasure trove of outstanding temples, stupas, and elegant Buddhas. Most of the ruins have been restored and surrounded by manicured gardens and refreshing pools. A brief visit to *both* Ayuthaya and Sukothai is highly recommended for visitors interested in Thai architecture or history.

Si Satchanalai and Kamphang Phet: Satellite towns of Sukothai with architecture dating from the 13th and 14th centuries. Both can be visited as side trips from Sukothai.

Northern Thailand

Chiang Mai: With its wealth of cultural and historical attractions, superb shopping, great food,

THAILAND

friendly people, and delightful weather, Chiang Mai deservedly ranks as one of Thailand's leading tourist destinations. Unlike many Asian cities, which have lost their charm and character from unmanageable growth, this city of one million residents has graciously preserved many of its lovely teak homes and tree-shaded roads. Chiang Mai also serves as a convenient base for trekking into the countryside, touring the infamous Golden Triangle area, and visiting the historic towns of Lamphun and Lampang.

Hilltribes: Living in the remote highlands near the Thai-Myanmar-Laos borders are shifting agriculturalists who cling to ancient lifestyles despite encroaching Westernization and assimilation efforts by the Thai government. An organized trek of five to 10 days is a unique and memorable experience.

Mae Hong Son: The Shangri-La atmosphere of this small but quickly growing village near the Burmese border attracts travelers who want to get slightly off the beaten track. A better bet is the village of Pai, midway between Chiang Mai and Mae Hong Son (less tourists).

Golden Triangle: For over 20 years a steady stream of travelers has bused from Chiang Mai to Thaton, floated down the Kok River to Chiang Rai, and then continued up to Chiang Saen—the real heart of the Golden Triangle. Today, opium production has largely shifted to Laos and Myanmar, and tour buses are more common than drug warlords—don't expect a Wild West atmosphere.

Northeastern Thailand

The sprawling plateau bordered by Laos and Cambodia is Thailand's forgotten destination. Known locally as the Issan, the dry and rugged northeast is home to a boisterous people with a distinctive culture, a handful of impressive Khmer temples, and several worthwhile national parks. Otherwise, there is little of great interest—save this region for last.

Korat: Nakon Ratchasima is an undistinguished city which serves as the gateway to the Khmer temples and national parks of the northeast.

Khmer Monuments: Once under the suzerainty of the Khmers, the northeast today offers several impressive stone castles erected by the Cambodians to honor their gods and kings. Two of the most impressive are at Phimai and Phanom Rung near Korat, a convenient launching base for visitors with limited time.

Ban Chiang: This important archaeological site, where the world's first Bronze Age civilization flourished some 6,000 years ago, is primarily of interest to archaeologists.

Surin: Visitors from around the world arrive each November to attend the enormously popular Elephant Round-Up of Surin.

Ubon Ratchathani: Famous for its Candle Festival, which marks the beginning of Buddhist Lent. Festivals are a major attraction in the northeast.

Phu Kradung National Park: A forested plateau situated between 1,200 and 1,500 meters; mysterious, moody, and icy cold at nights.

Southern Thailand

The tropical beaches of southern Thailand are, together with those of the Philippines, the finest in Southeast Asia. All are in various stages of development and appeal to different classes of travelers.

Hua Hin: The first major beach resort south of Bangkok appeals to European families seeking a middle-priced sun-and-fun destination without the tawdriness of Pattaya.

Ko Samui: This Penang-sized island, with its superb beaches and lovely coconut palms, was discovered in the early 1970s by hippie travelers who quietly whispered about the tranquil, virgin hideaway. Twenty years later, commercial developers had constructed international-standard hotels, restaurants, nightclubs, and a small airport to receive daily flights from Bangkok. Despite the changes, Ko Samui remains a destination of great beauty and tranquility.

Phuket: Blessed with magnificent coves and powdery white beaches, Phuket has developed into Southeast Asia's largest and most popular seaside resort—the Waikiki of the East. Although more commercialized than Ko Samui, Phuket offers the upscale visitor an outstanding array of luxurious hotels, superb restaurants, water sports, and nightclubs that go full tilt until sunrise. A wild place for those with enough money to keep the game going. Travelers torn between choosing lively Phuket or idyllic Ko Samui should visit both.

Ko Phi Phi: This exquisite little island located midway between Phuket and Krabi is the first of an archipelago that stretches all the way to Malaysia. Ko Phi Phi is stunning, small, and packed to capacity during the winter tourist season. Travelers are already discovering the more remote, untouched islands to the south.

THAILAND

BANGKOK'S CLIMATE

	JAN.	FEB.	MAR.	APR.	MAY	JUNE	JULY	AUG.	SEPT.	OCT.	NOV.	DEC.
Avg. Maximum C	32°	32°	34°	35°	34°	33°	32°	32°	32°	31°	31°	31°
Avg. Maximum F	90°	90°	94°	95°	94°	92°	90°	90°	90°	88°	88°	88°
Rainy Days	2	1	3	4	18	19	19	19	17	14	4	1

Mongkut learned a dozen languages, studied astronomy and modern history, and, perhaps most importantly, established the Thammayut sect of Buddhism which purified the religion and made it less vulnerable to Western ideology. His search for knowledge convinced him that Thailand's only hope for political independence lay through European-style reforms such as those proposed by his English governess, Anna Leonowens, who eventually penned her fanciful memoirs, *The English Governess at the Siamese Court*. Anna was apparently an unhappy and homesick widow who plagiarized old books on Burma and stitched it all together in her book, which portrayed Mongkut as Rousseau's Noble Savage and Anna as the prim Victorian Christian who single-handedly modernizes the backward nation. Anna's gruesome tales of eastern harem life supported her after she left Bangkok (and certainly made a great deal of money for Yul Brynner), but no race of people enjoy having foreigners laugh at one of their great men—both the book and film have been banned in Thailand. Still, several years ago the present queen took an entourage of 45 people to see Yul Brynner star in the New York stage production!

King Chulalongkorn, 1868-1910

Mongkut's son, Chulalongkorn, continued Mongkut's policies of transforming Thailand from a medieval kingdom into a modern and progressive nation. Chulalongkorn outlawed slavery, developed educational opportunities, and balanced the territorial ambitions of the British and French with modest concessions to both countries. During his 42-year reign—second longest in the country's history—Chulalongkorn completely reorganized its administrative system and abandoned several ancient royal customs including ceremonial prostration. He nevertheless clung to some autocratic customs such as polygamy on a grand scale, keeping a grand total of 92 wives who bore him some 77 children. Chulalongkorn also continued to appoint men of royal descent to high administrative posts, a practice which offended the European-educated elite. Despite his reluctance to grant full democratic rights to his people, his long list of achievements has made him the most honored of all past kings.

Modern Times

Chulalongkorn's bold reforms also created a new bourgeois intelligentsia unhappy with its lack of power within the royalist government. The pressure cooker finally blew in 1932 when a bloodless coup d'etat instigated by French-educated Thai intellectuals supported by the military toppled the absolute monarchy. A constitutional government headed by an army general was formed and Siam was renamed Thailand. The Thai government declared war on the Western allies in 1941 after the Japanese invaded, a face-saving formality which allowed them to recover territories lost to the French and British. With the defeat of the Japanese, a group of Free Thai politicians seized power and placed King Rama VII on the throne. This experiment with democracy ended when the young king was mysteriously murdered in his bed and a military dictatorship seized power. Except for a three-year hiatus of democratic rule in the mid-1970s, Thailand has largely been ruled by an alliance of military and civilian politicians.

Chuan Leekpai and the Economic Meltdown

To no one's surprise, Chuan Leekpai returned to the position of prime minister in November 1997 during a period of economic collapse unparalleled in the history of the country.

The crisis began in January 1997 when a medium-size Thai property firm defaulted on US$80 million worth of convertible Eurobonds.

From that relative matchstick roared a consuming conflagration as attention turned to the overbuilt Bangkok property market, overextended property developers and finance houses, and exactly how much private foreign debt was actually due to be paid in 1997.

The crisis emerged slowly at first as speculators began hammering the *baht* in February. The Bank of Thailand beat them back at first, but the attacks kept coming until they peaked in May. The following month Thailand's finance minister—a key cabinet member who had staunchly argued against the devaluation of the *baht*—resigned. In June, the Thai Central Bank suspended operations of 16 cash-strapped finance companies as then Prime Minster Chavalit Yonchaiyudh assured the nation in a televised address that there would be no devaluation of the *baht*. Two days later the Bank of Thailand announced a managed float of the *baht* and called on the International Monetary Fund for "technical assistance." The announcement effectively devalued the *baht* by 20% as it fell to a record low of 28.80B to the U.S. dollar.

What started as merely a bad exchange rate dream turned into a full-blown nightmare in the summer of 1997. Many Southeast Asian economies had pegged their currencies to the U.S. dollar, but the links started to fray once it became clear that high current-account shortfalls, inflation, and asset bubbles left many economies out of sync with America's economic fundamentals. Further, Asian financial institutions had borrowed massively overseas to take advantage of relatively low rates and as local currencies fell, foreign obligations swelled. The borrowers bought dollars, seeking to hedge against further devaluation, but the move only fulfilled the worst fears.

Meanwhile, most of the borrowed money had been misdirected into unsaleable property or uneconomic factories through cronyism, corruption, or plain bad business. The crisis was also fueled by Bangkok politicians, many of whom had links to bad financial institutions.

In August 1997, the IMF approved a US$17 billion bailout package for Thailand. In November, Chavalit resigned as prime minister after intense public pressure and just 11 months in office. The opposition Democrat Party then formed a new coalition government, and Parliament soon asked Chuan Leekpai to return to his post. The

baht fell to a record low of 44B per dollar in early December.

Along with the collapse of the *baht*, Leekpai also had to deal with the IMF bailout package which required a hefty budget surplus in the forthcoming annual economic report. This meant that the government's revenues would have to exceed its expenditures by a significant amount—60 billion *baht* to be precise. This led to huge cuts in government expenditures, an increase in the value-added tax (VAT) from 7 to 10%, and stiff new taxes on luxury items.

Prime Minster Chuan Leekpai, unlike Suharto in Indonesia, bit the bullet and made the adjustments required by the IMF. By the end of January 1998, it was apparent that Thailand had turned the corner on the economic crisis and that its economy would eventually recover from the devastation of the previous year.

Leekpai made a very successful trip to the United States in March 1998 where he was praised for his reforms by American businessmen, the U.S. media, and President Clinton. He was able to renegotiate the purchase of jet warplanes and find American investors for several new electric power projects. The Peace Corps cancelled their plans to leave Thailand and the U.S. government agreed to finance rural health programs in Thailand.

GOVERNMENT

Thailand is a constitutional monarchy with a bicameral legislature consisting of a Senate appointed by the king and a National Assembly elected by the people. The National Assembly is composed primarily of the liberal-leaning Chart Thai, Social Action, and Democrat parties, three political groups who often form coalitions to work with the military. Both chambers elect a prime minister who chooses a cabinet of 20 ministers. Thailand's leading political figure of the early 1980s was smiling Prem Tinsulanonda, a handsome enigma who confounded the critics by holding the job of prime minister for almost eight years—an amazing accomplishment when you consider that Thailand since 1932 has suffered through a dozen coups and 13 constitutions. Nineteen eighty-eight proved to be a watershed in Thai politics after public pressure for an elected

THAILAND

CONTEMPORARY BUDDHISM IN THAILAND

Modern Buddhism is divided into the Theravada school adopted in Sri Lanka, Thailand, and Myanmar, and the Mahayana version favored in China and Japan. Thais further subdivide Theravada into the less-rigorous Mahanikaya order, the majority cult, and the stricter Thammayut order followed by less than 10% of the population. Thailand's Buddhist *sangha* is currently headed by Somdej Pra Yanasangworm, the same monk who supervised the young King Bhumipol during his 15-day residency at Wat Bowornives in Bangkok. As one of the most powerful individuals in the country, Somdej faces several thorny challenges: the declining interest in Buddhism among the young, the corrupting influence of *phi* propitiation (see below), and widespread decadence within the Buddhist *sangha*. Today in Thailand, it's not uncommon for monks to predict lottery outcomes, practice faith healing, distribute phallic symbols, sell magical charms, and charge hefty fees for ceremonial services. The country's monastic image was further damaged after it was revealed that several monasteries were selling bogus royal decorations.

Rebellion against conventional Buddhism is symbolized by Pra Bodhirak, an unorthodox but immensely popular and charismatic rebel who preaches his iconoclastic viewpoints from the Santi Asoke (Peace, No Sorrow) headquarters on the eastern outskirts of Bangkok. Defrocked and under heavy legal pressures from the government, Bodhirak insists that Thai Buddhism has been badly corrupted by the decadent practices and superstitious beliefs mentioned above. His message of nonmaterialism and religious purity has hit home: popularity has soared and even the current governor of Bangkok supports Bodhirak's platforms of religious reform.

Spirit Propitiation

Buddhism might be Thailand's dominant faith but it has never completely replaced older religious traditions such as Hinduism and spiritualism. Hindu ceremonies still play an important role in Thai society, largely because ceremonies for life passages such as births, deaths, and marriages were never prescribed by the Buddha. Brahmanic astrologers also prepare the national calendar and preside over annual rice-planting ceremonies.

But more important are the powers of astrology, the occult, and wandering supernatural spirits called *phi*, homeless and unhappy apparitions who can cause great harm to the living unless appeased with frequent offerings. *Phi* are propitiated (not worshipped) for dozens of reasons: they are asked to influence the future, to grant wishes, to guarantee the success of a financial venture, to help one pass a school exam, to restore health to a sick family member, or to help a worshipper win the weekly lottery. Believed to exist in all shapes and sizes, some *phi* enjoy a permanent existence unbounded by the law of karma while others are reincarnations of dead human beings who have returned to haunt the living. People who died violently or whose funeral rites were improperly performed are especially dangerous, since witches can force them to consume the internal organs of the living. Others can make you remove your clothes in public! Although these practices are not in accordance with the teachings of the Buddha (karma teaches individual responsibility; spirit propitiation places responsibility on outside forces), *phi* homage doesn't necessarily conflict

young monks in Sukothai

with the reverence that Thais feel for Buddhist philosophy. The average Thai is a Buddhist who was married according to Hindu rituals but makes frequent offerings to placate animist spirits.

Spirit Houses

One of the most powerful forms of *phi* are the guardian spirits called *chao phi*, of which the guardian spirit of the house (*chao thi* or *pra phum* in Khmer) is the most important. Thais believe that every plot of land harbors a spirit who must be provided with a small doll-like house. This curious spirit home, located on the exterior lawn where no shadow will ever fall, is furnished with a replica of the residing spirit holding a double-edged sword and a big book which lists deeds of the occupants. Other figurines include slaves, elephants, and sensuous dancing girls . . . to keep the ghost happy! After proper installation by a Brahman priest at the auspicious place and time, human occupants continue to make daily offerings of flowers, joss sticks, and food to placate the touchy spirit.

Thais also honor eight other household spirits including one troublesome fellow who resides in the door threshold. That's why it is proper behavior to step *over* rather than *on* the threshold. In recent years it has become popular to erect extremely elaborate shrines dedicated to the four-faced Hindu god, Lord Brahma. Thailand's most famous Brahmanic image is displayed at the Hyatt Grand Erawan Hotel shrine in Bangkok, although in the strictest sense this is not a spirit house, but in a category all its own.

Monkhood

To gain heavenly merit, improve their karma through correct living, and bring honor to their parents, many young Thai men elect to become monks for periods from a few days to several months. Initiates take vows of poverty and are allowed few possessions: three yellow robes, an alms bowl, and a strainer to filter any living creature from the water. Final daily meals are eaten before noon, while the remainder of the day is spent meditating and studying Buddhist scriptures. Although instructed to remain unemotional and detached about worldly concerns, many are surprisingly friendly to Westerners and quite anxious to practice their English. The Golden Mount in Bangkok is an excellent place to meet the monks.

leader brought the arrival of Chatichai Choonhavan, a business-minded politician who favors democracy over military rule. Chatichai fell from power in 1992 during a military coup in which dozens of citizens were murdered near Democracy Monument in Bangkok.

Chatichai was replaced by Chuan Leekpai, leader of the Democrat Party and the first non-military Thai to ever serve as prime minister. His rule ended in May 1995 after a scandal over a land-reform program revealed several wealthy families on Phuket had benefited from the government program, which was intended to redistribute land to poor families. Although he was not implicated in the scandal, his five-party coalition collapsed and fresh elections were held.

The July 1995 elections witnessed the rise of Banharn Silpa-archa as the new prime minister and leader of the resurgent Chart Thai Party. Banharn, a Chinese billionaire from Suphanburi presided over a hopelessly disorganized government that finally collapsed in 1997 after a series of economic crises threatened to throw Thailand into complete bankruptcy. To the surprise of few, during the period of economic collapse unparalleled in Thailand's history, new national elections saw the return of Chuan Leekpai to the position of prime minister.

The Monarchy

The most stabilizing factor in Thailand is the overwhelming prestige of the royal family. Although the monarchy was shorn of its powers half a century ago, the Thais continue to view their king as a near-divine being who carries the real force of governmental power. The present ruler, Bhumipol Adulyadej, was born in 1927 in Cambridge, Massachusetts, where his father was studying medicine at Harvard University. Adulyadej received his education in Switzerland before claiming the throne as Rama IX in 1950. Not only amiable and intelligent, he is also a gifted painter and a talented jazz saxophonist who has led all-star jam sessions with such luminaries as bandleader Les Brown and singer Patti Page! His jazz compositions include "Hungry Man's Blues" (can you imagine Queen Elizabeth writing a jazz ballad?) and the three-move-

THAILAND

ment "Manora Ballet," previewed in Vienna during a royal visit. Despite an automobile accident which took an eye, his deft handling of a sailboat won him the gold medal at an international yachting competition.

In what is now the longest reign of any Thai king, Bhumipol has earned immense popularity as the working monarch who guides and unifies the nation as head of state and protector of national traditions. Based on Thailand's laws of succession, Crown Prince Maha Vajiralongkorn, the king's only son, will succeed his father to the throne, although his sister, Princess Maha Chakri Sirindorn, enjoys great popularity among the Thai people.

Portraits of the king, queen, and royal family are seen everywhere in Thailand. All foreign visitors are expected to behave respectfully toward the royal family, an acceptable caveat since there is little doubt that the Thai monarchy has *earned* this honor.

THE PEOPLE

The Thais

Thailand is one of the most racially homogeneous countries in Southeast Asia: about 82% of the country's 60 million inhabitants are Thai. This Mongoloid race largely speaks a common language, shares a unified script, and follows the same Buddhist faith. As a racially tolerant people they have assimilated large numbers of Mons, Khmers, Chinese, and other smaller groups to a degree which precludes any typical Thai physiognomy or physique. Thais generally speak one of four dialects which are mutually intelligible with some degree of difficulty. Central Thai, the official dialect of government and business, has come to dominate over the northern dialect spoken in Chiang Mai and the northeastern dialect laced with Khmer loanwords. A southern dialect is spoken near the Malay border.

Thais on the whole are a delightful race of people who believe life is to be enjoyed so long as no one impinges on another's rights. Many decline to be fanatical about productivity or deadlines. Foreign visitors are often perplexed with their stubborn resistance to the Westerner's fast-paced, ulcer-prone life. This attitude is epitomized by the phrase *mai pen rai* (never mind).

Thais have personal first names such as Porn ("Blessings"), Boon ("Good Deeds"), Sri or Siri ("Glory"), Som ("Fulfillment"), and Arun ("Dawn"). Since Thais are normally addressed by their first names rather than their family names, don't be surprised if they call you "Mr. John" or "Miss Judy." The prefix *khun* is the ubiquitous title which substitutes for Mr. or Mrs. Affectionate nicknames such as Frog, Rat, Pig, Fat, or Shrimp are more popular than first names!

Perhaps because of their Buddhist upbringings, Thais detest any form of conflict and will go to great pains to avoid confrontation and preserve harmony. This attitude—*jai yen* (cool heart)—is strongly favored over *jai rohn* (hot heart). One form of violence you *must* avoid is face-to-face criticism. Unlike Westerners, who criticize friends without ruining relationships, Thais see criticism as highly personal attacks which often lead to grave consequences. To make friends and enjoy yourself in Thailand, keep a *jai yen*.

Thais are also a race of people obsessed with social ranking. Correct social conduct only happens after superior-inferior roles have been determined through direct questions such as "How much do you earn?" and "How old are you?" Westerners should consider such inquiries as friendliness or a form of flattery rather than an invasion of privacy. Social ranking is also reflected in the Thai language, including dozens of ways to say "I" depending on the speaker's social status. The top of the structure is fairly obvious: the king, his family, and the Buddhist priesthood. Below that are the variables of age, social connections, lineal descent, earnings, and education.

The Chinese

Thailand's largest and most important minority group are the Chinese. Early immigrants included the Hokkiens, who arrived during the late 18th century (Rattankosin Period) to serve as compradores and tax collectors for the Thai royalty, and the near-destitute Teochews, who became the leading merchants in early Bangkok. Later arrivals included thousands of economic refugees fleeing massive crop failures and widespread starvation in 20th-century China. As elsewhere in Southeast Asia, Chinese immigrants worked hard, educated their children, and today completely dominate the trade and finance sectors of the local economy. It has been estimated that 60% of Thailand's largest companies are controlled by Sino-Thais (Thai nationals of Chinese descent), and almost 100% of Thai banks are controlled by a handful of extremely wealthy Sino-Thai families.

But unlike in other countries in Southeast Asia, the massive concentration of wealth in Chinese hands has not brought widespread racial conflicts or discriminatory legislation. Thailand's racial harmony is perhaps the result of widespread intermarriage. According to legend, King Mongkut (himself of Chinese lineage) encouraged Chinese immigration and intermarriage with Thai women, social intercourse which he hoped would give future generations the traditional Chinese qualities of industry and thrift. As a result, it is now difficult if not impossible to distinguish ethnic Thais from Sino-Thais; perhaps 50% of Bangkok's population is ethnically Chinese. Sino-Thais have taken on Thai surnames and speak Thai rather than Chinese. Consequently, the Thai government has rarely been motivated to pass discriminatory laws but has let the Chinese help build the economic miracle of modern Thailand.

Other Peoples

Nearly one million Malay Muslims live in the southern provinces bordering Malaysia. Many are fishermen or rubber tappers who sometimes view public education as an attack on their cultural autonomy. Muslim separatist movements such as the United Pattani Freedom Movement have largely been suppressed by the Thai government.

Inhabiting the hills near Chiang Mai are some half-million seminomadic tribespeople who migrated down from southern China over the last few centuries. The 20 distinct tribes range from sophisticated groups like the Meos to primitive peoples like the Phi Tong Luang. All were relatively isolated from the outside world until commercialized trekking and government assimilation programs began in the 1970s. More information under "Chiang Mai."

FESTIVALS

Most Thai festivals are connected with either Buddhism, the annual cycle of rice planting, or commemorations honoring past kings. Religious festivals are movable feasts dated by the Thai lunar calendar; state holidays follow the Western calendar. Exact dates should be checked with the Tourist Authority of Thailand (TAT). Current listings are also given in the *Bangkok Post.*

January

Don Chedi Memorial Fair: The decisive battle of King Naresuan v. the Burmese is reenacted each year 24-30 January. Don Chedi is west of Bangkok near Kanchanaburi.

Pra Nakhon Khiri Fair: Phetburi, a small town south of Bangkok, sponsors a light and sound presentation that illuminates its outstanding monuments.

February

Maha Puja: Buddha's revelations to his 1,250 disciples at Bodgaya are marked with merit-making ceremonies such as releasing of caged birds, burning of incense, and a lovely procession of flickering candles around the temple. Held on the full moon of the third lunar month.

Pra That Phanom Chedi Fair: This important festival held in Nakhon Phanom (northeastern Thailand) honors a holy relic of the Buddha.

Chiang Mai Flower Festival: This popular fair features a beauty pageant, a floral float parade, and cultural entertainment. Visitors should be prepared for enormous crowds.

Red Cross Fair: This commercialized, crowded, and somewhat disappointing festival in Bangkok offers nightly dance performances, music, and exciting *takraw* competition.

March

Pra Buddha Baht: Buddhist devotees gather at the shrine of the holy footprint near Saraburi for religious rites and a bazaar.

Thao Suranari Fair: This festival honors the national heroine who rallied local people to repel invaders from Vientiane. An homage-paying ceremony and victory procession are held at her memorial in Korat (Nakhon Ratchasima), northeastern Thailand.

April

Pattaya Festival: Thailand's major beach resort hosts a weeklong festival complete with

THAILAND

beauty queens, floral floats, fireworks, cultural dancing, kite flying, and motorcar races. One of the biggest festivals in Thailand.

Chakri Day: This national holiday, held on 6 April to commemorate the reign of Rama I (founder of the Chakri dynasty), is the only day of the year when Bangkok's Pantheon at Wat Pra Keo is opened to the public.

Songkran Festival: Thailand's New Year is celebrated nationwide as the sun moves into Aries. Buddha images are purified with holy water, young people honor their parents by pouring perfumed water over their hands, and traditional sand pagodas are built in the temples. Fun-loving Thais have cleverly turned this religious ritual into a wild and crazy water-throwing festival during which everyone is smeared with white powder and drenched with buckets of ice-cold water. Unsuspecting tourists are a prime target—leave the camera at your hotel!

Pra Pradang Songkran Festival: The Mon community in Samut Prakan south of Bangkok sponsors a Mon festival with parades, Mon beauty queens, and continual deluges of water-throwing. Organized tours of this unusual festival can be booked through the Siam Society in Bangkok.

May

Coronation Day: King Bhumibol's coronation is celebrated on 5 May with a private ceremony in the royal chapel.

Royal Ploughing Ceremony: This elaborate Hindu ritual marks the beginning of the rice-planting season. A richly decorated plough is pulled by a garlanded Brahman across the Sanam Luang in Bangkok, while Brahman priests solemnly plant sacred rice seeds and predict the success of the coming harvest.

Visaka Puja: This most sacred of all Buddhist holidays commemorates the birth, death, and enlightenment of Buddha. Merit-making ceremonies are identical to the Maha Puja.

Rocket Festival: People of the dry northeast hold this festival to ensure plentiful rains. Bamboo rockets are launched into the sky before the nighttime activities of music, dancing, and drinking. Held the second weekend in May throughout the Issan. The town of Yasothon hosts the most famous of all rocket festivals, complete with beauty queens and an elaborate parade.

July

Asalha Puja: Commemorates Buddha's first sermon to his five disciples and marks the beginning of the annual three-month rains retreat. During this Khao Phansa (Buddhist Lent), many young Thai males temporarily enter the Buddhist priesthood. Held on the full moon of the eighth lunar month.

Candle Festival: Ubon Ratchathani celebrates the beginning of Buddhist Lent with a gigantic procession of floats carrying huge candles designed to burn for its duration.

August

Longan Fair: Lamphun celebrates the popular fruit with a Miss Longan Beauty Contest, agricultural displays, and a small parade.

Queen's Birthday: Municipal buildings are illuminated with colored lights during this national holiday held 12 August.

September

Phuket Vegetarian Festival: Islanders of Chinese ancestry follow a strict vegetarian diet for nine days. The festival begins with a parade of white-clothed devotees who walk across fire and drive spears through their cheeks—the Chinese version of Hindu Thaipusam.

October

Tod Kathin: The end of Buddhist Lent and the rainy season is celebrated with elaborate boat races in Nan, Surat Thani, Nakhon Phanom, and Samut Prakan. Highlighted by a procession of royal barges down the Chao Praya to Wat Arun, where the king presents new robes to the monks.

Wax Candle Festival: The end of the Buddhist rains retreat is celebrated in Sakhon Nakhon with a parade of beautifully embellished beeswax floats in the form of miniature Buddhist temples.

Chonburi Buffalo Races: Local farmers sponsor races and a beauty contest for decorated buffalo.

Chulalongkorn Day: Thailand's beloved king is honored with a national holiday on 23 October. Wreaths are laid at his equestrian statue in Bangkok's Royal Plaza.

Pra Chedi Klang Nam Festival: The riverside *chedi* in Samut Prakan, some 30 km south of

Bangkok, hosts a popular festival with colorful processions and boat races.

November
Loy Kratong: Thailand's most famous and charming festival honors both the Buddha and ancient water spirits. Banana-leaf boats, each carrying a single candle, are floated in the rivers and lakes—a wonderful and delicate sight. Loy Kratong is celebrated in both Sukothai and Chiang Mai, although Sukothai is a better venue because of the smaller crowds. It's sometimes possible to see both festivals since Sukothai's is often held the previous night.

Golden Mount Fair: Bangkok's most spectacular temple fair features folk drama, barkers, freak shows, countless foodstalls, and a lovely candlelight procession around the temple.

Ayuthaya Boat Races: An international event that attracts both local and foreign crews.

Deepavali: The Hindu Festival of Lights is celebrated at a small ornate Indian temple on Silom Road in Bangkok. Religious zealots perform amazing feats of self-mutilation.

Surin Elephant Roundup: Over 100 elephants engage in staged hunts, comical rodeo and elephant polo, and a tug-of-war between a lone elephant and 100 men. Visitors can ride the pachyderms around town. Held in Surin on the third Saturday in November.

Pra Pathom Fair: Folk dramas, beauty pageants, and a parade take place in Nakhon Pathom at Pra Pathom Chedi, the world's tallest Buddhist monument.

River Kwai Bridge Week: A nightly son et lumière relates the grim history of this world-famous bridge. Visitors can ride WW II-vintage steam engines across the bridge.

December
King's Birthday: Bhumibol's birthday on 5 December is celebrated with a grand parade and citywide decorations of flags, portraits of the king, and brilliantly colored lights.

Tourism Festival: The Tourist Authority of Thailand promotes the nation's number-one industry with dance performances, regional cultural shows, and a fireworks display in Bangkok.

ON THE ROAD

GETTING THERE

Air
Thailand is served by over 50 international airlines from major world capitals and cities in Southeast Asia. Most visitors arrive at Bangkok's Don Muang International Airport (see "Bangkok" for arrival information and further transportation arrangements), although flights are also available to Phuket and Hat Yai from Malaysia; the Penang-to-Phuket flight is highly recommended since it's reasonably priced and saves a full day of land travel.

Travelers with limited time should purchase a roundtrip ticket from their home country and buy any additional tickets in Thailand. Travelers with more time should purchase one-way tickets to Bangkok and make all future travel arrangements in Thailand, an option which adds flexibility and saves money since Bangkok travel agents sell some of the world's cheapest airline tickets.

From the U.S.: Thai International, Korean Air, Pan Am, Northwest, and China Air all offer super-APEX flights to Bangkok for US$900-110 from U.S. West Coast cities. Discounted flights for US$750-850 are available from agencies which advertise in major metropolitan newspapers. Because flights are often fully booked and discounted seats sell quickly, it's very important to book at least two months before your intended departure date. Budget agencies are described in the main Introduction.

From England: Thai International, British Airways, Philippine Airlines, and Qantas offer direct flights from London to Bangkok. If you don't mind time-consuming plane changes, cheaper fares are available from Kuwait Airlines, Gulf Air, and Royal Jordanian. Budget tickets are available from Trailfinders, Council Travel, Campus Travel, STA and other agencies listed in *Time Out* and *TNT* magazines.

From Australia: One-way economy tickets from Sydney and Melbourne cost A$1100 and A$950 from Perth and Cairns. Advance-purchase one-way tickets cost only A$600-700 from

SUGGESTED TIMETABLES FOR THAILAND

DESTINATION	1 MONTH	2 MONTHS	3 MONTHS
Bangkok	1 week	1 week	2 weeks
Chiang Mai	7 days	3 weeks	3 weeks
Sukothai/Ayuthaya	1 day	3 days	4 days
Kanchanaburi	4 days	1 week	10 days
East Coast	2 days	4 days	1 week
Northeast	—	4 days	2 weeks
Ko Samui	1 week	1 week	10 days
Phuket	—	3 days	4 days

Sydney when purchased at least 21 days in advance. Cheap-flight specialists include STA, Travel Specialists, and Sydney Flight Centre.

Train

The International Express (IE) departs Singapore every morning and arrives in Kuala Lumpur by nightfall. Visitors may overnight in the Malaysian capital or continue north by night train to Butterworth, the terminus for Penang. The IE departs Butterworth the following day around 1300, crosses the Thai border, and arrives in Hat Yai about three hours later. The IE departs Hat Yai at 1700 and arrives in Bangkok early the following morning.

Schedules change frequently and should be double-checked with the stationmasters in Singapore or Malaysia. The IE is limited to first and second class and somewhat expensive because of supplemental charges for a/c, superior classes, and sleeping berths. While the International Express from Singapore to Bangkok has romantic appeal and is probably the most luxurious train in Southeast Asia, it's a long and exhausting journey best experienced in shorter segments.

Ordinary diesel trains from Butterworth terminate at the border town of Padang Besar. Travelers can walk across to Thailand and wait for public transport. This transfer is very time-consuming and most travelers prefer buses or shared taxis. More details in the Malaysia chapter.

Bus

Crossing the Thai border by public bus can be tricky. Most buses on the west coast of Peninsular Malaysia terminate at Changlun, a small and isolated Malaysian town some 20 km from the border. From Changlun, you must attempt to hitchhike the distance to Sadao in southern Thailand—not an easy task. Private buses are easier. Buses direct from Penang to Hat Yai, Ko Samui, and Phuket can be booked through travel agents in Penang.

Public transport on the east coast is fairly straightforward. Ordinary buses from Kota Bharu terminate at the Thai border, a one-km walk along the train tracks from Sungai Golok in Thailand. Both trains and public buses leave Sungai Golok for Hat Yai and Bangkok. Immigration can be fairly lax at this border; be sure to get your passport stamped.

Taxi

Crossing the border by public bus or ordinary train can be a haphazard and time-consuming ordeal. Most independent travelers prefer private buses direct to their Thai destinations or share taxis, which are fast, comfortable, and well priced. This also avoids getting stranded at the border waiting for a bus or a train. These lumbering old Mercedes or Chevys can be found in Penang at the waterfront taxi stand and in Georgetown downstairs from the bus terminal. Budget hotels in Penang can arrange pick-up directly from your hotel. Share taxis can also be chartered in Kota Bharu.

Sea

Looking for something unusual? Ferries sometimes operate from Langkawi to Satun in northwestern Malaysia to Satun in southern Thailand, a useful service for visitors coming from Langkawi. Be sure to have your passport stamped by immigration officials. Buses continue up to Hat Yai and points north.

GETTING AROUND

Air

Domestic flights are provided by Thai Airways International, which merged with Thai Airways several years ago. The consolidation greatly benefits international travelers, who can now purchase all necessary tickets in one package, thus ensuring a worry-free trip with guaranteed connections and seats. Major destinations are served by Airbuses and Boeing 737s, while smaller towns are reached with Shorts 330 aircraft. Internal flights are fairly expensive when compared to rail travel, but highly recommended on those routes not served by train or luxury buses. For example, the flight from Chiang Mai to Mae Hong Song takes only 30 minutes and costs 360B while the bone-crushing bus ride takes a full 12 hours and costs 150B. Bangkok Airways, Thailand's only sizeable domestic airline, flies six times daily from Bangkok to Ko Samui and several times daily between Samui, Phuket, and Hat Yai.

Train

Trains are the best form of transportation in Thailand. Not only are they comfortable, punctual, and inexpensive, they're much safer than buses and an excellent way to meet people. The drawbacks? Trains are slow, they don't go everywhere (but you'd be amazed the places they do go!), and they're often fully booked during holidays. Trains from Bangkok to Chiang Mai in the north or to Hat Yai in the south should be booked well in advance.

Types and Classes: Thai trains come in four types. Diesel railcars and ordinary trains stop at every single town and are very, very slow—avoid these except on short journeys. Rapid trains are almost twice as fast as ordinary trains and have a modest 20B supplemental charge. Express trains have a 30B supplemental charge and are slightly faster than the rapid trains.

Trains are also divided into three classes. Third class is the cheapest but the seats are hard and sleeping facilities are limited to floor-space although this class may prove adequate on all but the longest journeys. Second class offers padded seats and more legroom, costs double the price of third class (about the same price as an a/c bus), and can be reserved with sleeping berths. First class's comfortable reclining seats are double the price of second class. Put this all together and the fastest/ cheapest train ticket is third class on a rapid train. Best choice for overnight travel is second class with a lower sleeping berth.

Charges: Supplementary charges are placed on all trains except for diesels and ordinary services. Rapid trains are 20B extra; express costs 30B more, 2nd class a/c is an extra 50B. Sleeping berths also carry supplemental charges. Second class, non-a/c is 70B in the upper and 100B in the lower berth. Second class a/c is 170B lower and 200B upper berth. Take the lower berth; it avoids the noisy overhead fan. First class with a/c is 250B double cabin and 350B single cabin. To compute the final cost, you must know the type of train (ordinary, rapid, express), the class (first, second, third), and whether you want a/c or a sleeping berth.

Timetables: Train schedules, available free of charge from the Rail Travel Aids counter in Bangkok's Hualampong Station, are among the most important pieces of travel information in Thailand. Purple brochures list condensed timetables for the southern train line; blue brochures list the north, northeastern, and eastern lines. Other information on exact fares, refunds, breaks in journeys, ticket alterations, and validity of return tickets is also described. Complete timetables for each trunk line are sold at the same counter.

Thailand Rail Pass: Blue 20-day rail passes which cost 1,500B include unlimited second- and third-class travel; supplemental charges not included. Red passes cost 3,000B; all supplemental charges are included.

Bus

Bus transport in Thailand is fast, clean, and reasonably comfortable on shorter journeys. Most buses provide reclining airline-style seats and video movies (porn and kung fu are popular), plus smiling hostesses who crank up the air-conditioning and serve icy drinks. Seats are often reserved—a great relief from the disorganized condition of most Asian buses.

Both a/c and non-a/c buses are available on major routes. Cheapest are the ordinary coaches operated by the government bus company called Bor Kor Sor (also called Baw Kaw Saw). Departures are usually from city terminals located on the outskirts of town. Air-conditioned buses operated by independent companies are usually 30-70% more expensive than government buses, but complimentary meals and transportation from your hotel to their bus terminal is often included. Finding the correct bus is straightforward, since somebody will nearly always materialize to show the way; gum salesmen expect you to purchase a pack in exchange for directions!

Buses are convenient but there are some drawbacks. Coaches constructed for Thai body sizes are ridiculously cramped for long-legged Westerners. There are also safety concerns. Far too many drivers behave like suicidal maniacs hellbent on destruction. Sensible precautions include never sitting in the front row or riding with drivers who plaster Rambo photographs all over the front window. More problems, especially on luxury buses in the deep south, are armed robberies and confidence artists who use knockout drugs. Thai police videotape passengers to discourage robbery but, like your mother once told you: *never accept food or drink from strangers.*

THAI DIPLOMATIC OFFICES

Australia: 111 Empire Circuit, Canberra, ACT 2600, tel. 273-1149
Exchange Bldg., 56 Pitt St., Sydney
464 Saint Kilda Rd., Melbourne

Canada: 85 Range Rd., #704, Ottawa, Ontario, K1N8J6, tel. (613) 237-0476
250 University Ave., 7th floor, Toronto 110
1155 Dorchester Blvd., #1005, Montreal 102
700 W. George St., 26th floor, Vancouver

China: 40 Guang Hua Lu, Beijing, tel. 521903, 522282

Denmark: Norgesmindevej 1B, 2900 Hellerup, Copenhagen, tel. 01-62-50-10

France: 8 Rue Greuze, Paris 75116, tel. 4704-3222

Germany: Ubierstrasse 65, 53173 Bonn 2, tel. (0228) 355065

Hong Kong: 8 Cotton Tree Dr., 8th floor, Central, tel. 521-6481

India: 56 Nyaya Marg, Chankyapuri, Delhi 110021, tel. 605679
18-B Mandeville Gardens, Calcutta 7000019, tel. 460836

Italy: Via Nomentana 132, 00162 Rome, tel. 832-0729

Japan: 14-6 Kami Osaki 3-Chome, Shinagawa-ku, Tokyo, tel. 441-1386

Laos: Thanon Phonkheng, Vientiane Poste 128, tel. 2508, 2543

Malaysia: 206 Jalan Ampang, 504505 Kuala Lumpur, tel. 488222
1Jalan Tunkoabdul Rahman, Penang, tel. 23352
4426 Jalan Pengkalan Chepa, Kota Bharu, tel. 782545

Myanmar: 91 Pyi Rd., Yangon, tel. 82471, 76555

Netherlands: Buitenrustweg 1, 2517 KD, Den Hague, tel. (070) 345-2088

New Zealand: 2 Cook St., Karori, Wellington 5, tel. 735385

Philippines: 107 Rada St., Makati, Manila, tel. 815-4219

Singapore: 370 Orchard Rd., Singapore 0923, tel. 737-2158

Switzerland: Eigerstrasse 60, 3007 Bern, tel. (031) 462281

United Kingdom: 30 Queens Gate, London SW7 5JB, tel. (01) 589-2834

U.S.A.: 2300 Kalorma Rd. NW, Washington, D.C. 20008, tel. (202) 482-7200
801 N. Labrae Ave., Los Angeles, CA 90038, tel. (213) 937-1894
53 Park Place #505, New York, NY 10007, tel. (212) 732-8166

Vietnam: So Nha El, Kho Ngoai Giao Doan, Hanoi, tel. 56043

Car Rental

Thailand is an outstanding country to tour with rented transport. Contrary to popular belief, traffic is moderate and manageable throughout the country, with the exception of Bangkok. Highways are in good condition and most directional signs are labeled in English. Familiar agencies such as Avis and Hertz maintain offices in the larger towns. Less expensive rentals are available from local agencies, but carefully check the car's condition before handing over your money. Many offer reduced monthly rates which include insurance and unlimited mileage. Split by four people, this can be an economical and flexible way to tour Thailand. An International Driver's License may be required and insurance is mandatory.

Motorcycle Rental

Bikes can be rented in Chiang Mai, Chiang Rai, Mae Hong Son, Sukothai, Ayuthaya, Kanchanaburi, Ko Samui, and Phuket. Motorcycles are unavailable in Bangkok, but long-term rentals of larger bikes are possible in Pattaya. Rates start at 150B for motorscooters and climb sharply for larger bikes. In most cases, a 100cc motorscooter is completely adequate for local touring.

Experienced motorcyclists should have few difficulties with the traffic, though Thailand is no place for beginning cyclists; far too many Westerners have ended their vacations in the hospitals of Ko Samui and Phuket. No matter how experienced you are you should drive defensively, never operate a motorcycle while high, and always wear a helmet, long pants, a long shirt, and hard shoes to prevent injury on minor spills.

VISAS

All visitors to Thailand must have valid passports. Those who intend to stay less than 30 days and have proof of onward passage may enter the country without visas. Extensions are *not* allowed but it has been reported that visitors who overstay are fined approximately 100B per day at the airport.

Foreign nationals intending to stay longer than 30 days must obtain visas in advance from a Thai diplomatic mission. The most popular option is the 60-day tourist visa, which costs US$20 and can be extended once for 30 days at the discretion of Thai immigration. Applications for extensions should be made two to three days in advance at the Immigration Division on Soi Suan Plu off Sathorn Road in Bangkok or at any of the regional offices located throughout the country.

TOURIST INFORMATION

The Tourist Authority of Thailand (TAT) is courteous, efficient, and sincerely interested in helping you have the best possible time in the country. TAT offices, located in major towns throughout the country, are well supplied with accurate travel and hotel information. Ask for the schedule of upcoming festivals and events; useful for planning your vacation. Colorful brochures can be requested from overseas TAT offices listed below. Bangkok's main TAT office is located at 372 Bamrung Muang Road.

Maps

Thailand Travel Atlas: Lonely Planet produces the best map on Thailand although the atlas format may not be for everyone.

Periplus Map of Thailand: This outstanding map can be purchased at bookstores throughout the country. Maps published by Shell and Esso are poor.

Latest Tours Guide to Bangkok and Thailand: Lists major bus routes in Bangkok—an absolute necessity for bus riders in Bangkok.

Nancy Chandler Maps: Nancy's *Market Map of Bangkok* and *Map of Chiang* are immensely useful and highly recommended maps created by artist Nancy Chandler, a longtime resident who offers her trustworthy advice on public markets, restaurants, and tourist attractions.

INTERNATIONAL CLOCK FOR THAILAND

San Francisco	-15
New York	-12
London	-7
Paris	-6
Sydney	+3

THAILAND

TOURIST AUTHORITY OF THAILAND OFFICES

OVERSEAS OFFICES

Australia: TAT, Royal Exchange Bldg., 7th floor, 56 Pitt St., Sydney, NSW 2000, tel. (02) 247-7549, fax 251-2465

France: TAT, 90 Ave. de la Champs Elysees, 75008 Paris, tel. (01) 4562-8656, fax 4563-7888

Germany: TAT, Bethmannstrasse 58, 60311 Frankfurt/Main, tel. (069) 295704, fax 281468

Hong Kong: TAT, Fairmount House, Room 401, 8 Cotton Tree Dr., Central, tel. (852) 868-0732, fax 868-4585

Italy: TAT, Via Barberini 50, 00187 Rome, tel. (06) 487-3479, fax 487-3500

Japan: TAT, Hibiya Mitsui Bldg., 1-2 Yurakucho 1-chome, Chiyoda-ku, Tokyo 100, tel. (03) 3580-6776, fax 3580-7808

TAT, Hiranomachi Yachiyo Bldg., 5th floor, 1-8-14 Hiranomachi, Chuo-ku, Osaka 541, tel. (06) 231-4434, fax 231-4337

Korea: TAT, Coryo Daeyungek Center Bldg., Room 2003, Chungmu-Ro, Chung-Ku, Seoul 100-706, tel. (02) 779-5417, fax 779-5419

Malaysia: Royal Thai Embassy, 206 Jalan Ampang, 504505 Kuala Lumpur, tel. (093) 248-0958, fax 241-3002

Singapore: Royal Thai Embassy, 370 Orchard Rd., Singapore 0923, tel. (65) 235-7694, fax 733-5653

Taiwan: Thai Trade & Economic Office, 2B Central Commercial Bldg., 16-18 Nanking East Rd., Taipei 105, tel. (02) 778-2735, fax 741-9914

United Kingdom: TAT, 49 Albemarle St., London WIX 3FE, tel. (0171) 499-7679, fax 629-5519

U.S.A.: TAT, 5 World Trade Center, Suite 3443, New York, NY 10048, tel. (212) 432-0433, fax 912-0920

TAT, 3440 Wilshire Blvd., Suite 1101, Los Angeles, CA 90010, tel. (213) 382-2353, fax 389-7544

TAT, 303 East Wacker Dr., Suite 400, Chicago, IL 60602, tel. (312) 819-3990, fax 565-0359

TRAVEL PRACTICALITIES

Currency

Thailand's basic unit of currency, the *baht* (B), has fluctuated wildly in value vis-à-vis the dollar since 1997 when the Thai currency crisis saw the *baht* plunge from 25 to 45 per dollar by the end of the year. It's impossible to guess the rate for the future, but the good news is that the declining value of the *baht* means that all goods and services in Thailand are now 40-60% cheaper than they were a few years ago.

Each *baht* is divided into 100 *stang*. Coins come in 25-*stang*, 50-*stang*, one-*baht*, two-*baht*, and five-*baht* denominations. Only the one- and five-*baht* pieces are in common circulation. Thai coinage is confusing to Westerners since it's labeled only in Thai script and identical coins have been minted in different sizes. For example, the five-*baht* coin has progressively shrunk from a monstrous nickel-and-copper heavyweight down to the size of an American quarter.

There is no currency black market. Traveler's checks can be cashed at banks throughout Thailand—even the smallest towns have foreign-exchange services. Surprisingly, Thai banks rather than independent money changers offer the best rates. Foreign banks sometimes charge a 12B service charge; take your business to Thai banks only.

International Telephone

Thailand has one of the best phone systems in Southeast Asia. Connections are clean and crisp. International calls can be made from Thailand by dialing the international access code for calls from Thailand (001), followed by the country code, area code, and local number. Calls can also be made from central telephone offices located in most larger towns. Minimum charge is for three minutes. Station-to-station calls cost

DOMESTIC OFFICES

Ayuthaya: Si Samphet Rd., Ayuthaya 13000, tel. (036) 442768, fax 422769

Bangkok: 372 Bamrung Muang Rd., Bangkok 10100, tel. (02) 226-0060, fax 224-6221

Cha Am: 500/51 Petchkasem Hwy., Phetburi 76000, tel. (032) 471005, fax 471502

Chiang Mai: 105 Chiang Mai-Lamphun Rd., Chiang Mai 57000, tel. (053) 248604, fax 248605

Chiang Rai: 448/16 Singhalkla Rd., Chiang Rai 57000, tel. (053) 717433, fax 717434

Hat Yai: 1 Soi 2, Niphat Uthit 3 Rd., Hat Yai 90110, tel. (074) 243747, fax 245986

Kanchanaburi: Saengchuto Rd., Kanchaburi 71000, tel. (034) 511200, fax 511200

Khon Kaen: 15/5 Prachasamosorn Rd., Khon Kaen 40000, tel. (043) 244498, fax 244487

Lopburi: Provincial Hall, Narai Maharat Rd., Lopburi 15000, tel. (036) 422768, fax 422769

Nakhon Phanom: Provincial Hall, Abhibanbancha Rd., Nakhon Phanom 48000, tel. (042) 513490, fax 513492

Nakhon Ratchasima: 2102 Mittraphab Rd., Nakhon Ratchasima 30000, tel. (044) 213666, fax 213667

Nakhon Si Thammarat: Ratchadamnern Klang Rd., Nakhon Si Thammarat 8000, tel. (075) 346515, fax 346517

Pattaya: 382/1 Chai Hat Rd., Pattaya 210000, tel. (038) 428750, fax 429113

Phitsanulok: 209/7 Boromatrailokanat Rd., Phitsanulok 65000, tel. (055) 252743, fax 252742

Phuket: 73 Phuket Rd., Phuket 83000, tel. (076) 212213, fax 213582

Rayong: 300/77 Liang Muang Rd., Rayong 21000, tel. (038) 611228, fax 611228

Surat Thani: 5 Talat Mai Rd., Surat Thani 84000, tel. (077) 282828, fax 282828

Ubon Ratchathani: 264/1 Khuan Thani Rd., Ubon Ratchathani 34000, tel. (045) 243770, fax 243771

Udon Thani: Provincial Hall, Phosi Rd., Udon Thani 41000, tel. (042) 241968, fax 24196

about US$10 per three minutes, the cheapest in Asia except for Singapore and Hong Kong.

To call Thailand from the United States, dial the U.S. international access code (011), the country code for Thailand (66), the area code for the particular city (drop the zero), and finally, the local number. Note that you don't dial the zero in the area code; when you see the Bangkok area code (02), you drop the zero and dial 011-66-2 and then the phone number. The zero is only used for long-distance calls within the country.

ETIQUETTE AND CUSTOMS

Thais are an extremely tolerant and forgiving race of people blessed with a gentle religion and an easygoing approach to life. And yet, visitors would do well to observe proper social customs to avoid embarrassment and misunderstandings.

Royalty: Thais hold their Royal Family in great reverence. All visitors are expected to show respect to all royal images, including national anthems preceding movies and royal portraits on Thai currency. While many Thais will cheerfully criticize their national and local governments, Thai royalty is never openly criticized. Friends come fast when you praise the king and wear an amulet of his lovely wife!

Buddha Images: Thais are a deeply religious people who consider all Buddhist images extremely sacred—no matter their age or condition. Sacrilegious acts are punishable by imprisonment . . . even when committed by foreign visitors. Several years ago a group of tourists posed for photographs on top a Buddha image in Sukothai. The developing lab in Bangkok turned the negatives over to a Bangkok newspaper, which published the offending photographs on the front page. Public outrage was so strong that the foreigners were arrested and put in jail. More recently *Sports Illustrated* was refused permission

THAILAND

TELEPHONE AREA CODES WITHIN THAILAND

BANGKOK

02: Bangkok, Thonburi, Nonthaburi, Prathum Thani, Samut Prakan

BANGKOK VICINITY

034: Kanchanaburi, Nakhon Pathom, Samut Sakhon, Samut Songkhram
035: Ang Thong, Ayuthaya, Suphanburi
036: Lopburi, Saraburi, Singburi

EAST COAST

038: Chachoengsao, Chonburi, Pattaya, Rayong, Si Racha
039: Chantaburi, Trat

CENTRAL THAILAND

055: Kamphang Phet, Phitsanulok, Sukothai, Tak, Mae Sot, Uttaradit
056: Nakhon Sawan, Petchabun, Phichit, Uthai Thani

NORTHERN THAILAND

053: Chiang Mai, Chiang Rai, Lamphun, Mae Hong Son
054: Lampang, Nan, Phayao, Phrae

NORTHEASTERN THAILAND

037: Nakhon Nayok, Prachinburi, Aranyaprathet
042: Loei, Chiang Khan, Mukdahan, Nakhon Phanom, Nong Khai, Sakon Nakhon, Udon Thani
043: Kalasin, Khon Kaen, Mahasarakham, Roi Et
044: Buriram, Chaiyaphum, Nakhon Ratchasima (Korat)
045: Si Saket, Surin, Ubon Racthathani (Ubon), Yasothon

SOUTHERN THAILAND

032: Phetburi, Cha-Am, Prachuap Khiri Khan, Pranburi, Ratchburi
073: Narathiwat, Sungai Kolok, Pattani, Yala
074: Hat Yai, Phattalung, Satun, Songkhla
075: Krabi, Nakhon Si Thammarat, Trang
076: Phang Nga, Phuket
077: Chaiya, Chumphon, Ko Samui, Ranong, Surat Thani

to use religious shrines as backdrops for its 1988 swimsuit issue, and a *Vogue* model was arrested the following year for posing beside a religious monument in Phuket.

Temple Dress Codes: All Buddhist temples in Thailand have very strict dress codes, similar to Christian churches in the West. *Shorts are not acceptable attire in Buddhist temples—men should wear long pants and clean short-sleeved shirts.* Women are best covered in either pants or long skirts, and shoulders should not be exposed. Leather sandals are better than shoes since footwear must be constantly removed. Rubber flip-flops are considered proper only in the bathroom, not in religious shrines. Buddhist temples are extremely sacred places; please dress appropriately.

Monks: Buddhist monks must also be treated with respect. Monks cannot touch or be touched by females, or accept anything from the hand of a woman. Rear seats in buses are reserved for monks; other passengers should vacate these seats when necessary. Never stand over a seated monk since they should always remain at the highest elevations.

Social Customs

Modest Dress: *Shorts are considered improper and low-class attire in Thailand,* only acceptable for schoolchildren, street beggars, and common laborers . . . not wealthy tourists! Shorts and bathing suits are fine at beach resorts, but no matter how hot the weather, long pants and dresses should be worn in urban environments. Public displays of affection and beach nudity are also offensive.

Emotions: Face is very important in Thailand. Candor and emotional honesty—qualities highly prized in Western society—are considered embarrassing and counterproductive in the East. Never lose your temper or raise your voice no matter how frustrating or desperate the situation. Only patience, humor, and *chai yen* (cool heart) bring results in Thailand.

Personal Space: Thai anatomy has its own special considerations. Thais believe that the head—the most sacred part of the body—is inhabited by the *kwan,* the spiritual force of life. Never pat a Thai on the head even in the friendliest of circumstances. Standing over someone—especially someone older, wiser, or more enlightened than yourself—is also considered rude behavior since it implies social superiority. As a sign of courtesy, lower your head as you pass a group of people. When in doubt, watch the Thais.

Conversely, the foot is considered the lowest and dirtiest part of the body. The worst possible insult to a Thai is to point your unholy foot at his sacred head. Keep your feet under control; fold them underneath when sitting down, don't point them toward another person, and never place them on a coffee table.

A Graceful Welcome: Thailand's traditional form of greeting is the *wai*, a lovely prayerlike gesture accompanied with a little head nodding.

MOVIES FILMED IN THAILAND

More than 100 films and documentaries have been shot in Thailand over the last few decades, primarily Vietnam War pictures that substituted Thailand's topography for Vietnam's.

Man With the Golden Gun: Chase scenes in this James Bond flick were filmed in Phangnga Bay near Phuket. One towering limestone pinnacle has been renamed James Bond Rock, a standard attraction on every tour of the bay.

Deer Hunter: Many of the exciting river scenes (falling from the helicopter, held captive in submerged bamboo cages) were filmed along the River Kwai just west of Kanchanaburi. Bar scenes were shot inside the Mississippi Queen on Patpong Road in Bangkok.

Good Morning Vietnam: Robin Williams wakes up the troops in this 1987 film. The Minh Ngoc Bar was actually a little food store converted into a GI bar complete with American flags and jukebox. Bangkok's notorious Patpong Road served as Saigon's Tu Do Street, complete with fiberglass replicas of the old blue-and-yellow Renault taxis.

Killing Fields: Hua Hin's Railway Hotel served as Phnom Penh's leading hotel. Some of the beach scenes were filmed at Bang Tao Bay on Phuket. Spaulding Gray's monologue *Swimming to Cambodia* provides humorous commentary on the filming.

Casualties Of War: Much of the 1990 hit starring Michael Fox and Sean Penn, and directed by Brian De Palma, was filmed in Thailand.

Social status is indicated by the height of your *wai* and the depth of your bow: inferiors initiate the *wai,* while superiors return the *wai* with just a smile. Under no circumstances should you *wai* waitresses, children, or clerks—this only makes you look ridiculous! Save your respect for royalty, monks, and immigration officials.

CAUTIONS

Theft

Theft in Thailand is usually by stealth rather than by force, and armed robbery is rare except in isolated situations. The biggest problem is razor-blade artists on public buses in Bangkok; carry your bag directly in front of you and be extra alert whenever somebody presses against you.

Protecting valuables by keeping them in hotel safes is sensible, but be cautious about dishonest hotel employees who steal cash or surreptitiously use credit cards. American Express reports that Thailand has the highest ratio of fraudulent-to-legitimate card use of all its markets, second highest in monetary value only to that of the United States. Hotel fraud is a major problem in Chiang Mai guesthouses, where dishonest hotel clerks sometimes remove credit cards from stored luggage and run up large bills with the cooperation of unscrupulous merchants. Credit cards should be sealed to discourage unauthorized charges, and a complete receipt of stored goods including the serial numbers of traveler's checks should be obtained.

Knockout drugs are another problem. Large numbers of Western visitors are robbed each year by sleeping drugs administered by professional con artists who often spend hours (even days!) gaining their confidence. Never accept food or drinks from a stranger and be wary of anyone who offers tours of the city or private boat cruises in Bangkok.

AIDS

Love and lust in Thailand have taken an ugly turn since authorities first detected AIDS in 1984. According to a United Nations report released in 1997, move than 800,000 people carry HIV and a further 60,000 have been diagnosed with AIDS. Most of those who are HIV-positive have not yet developed symptoms and continue to engage in gay and heterosexual prostitution, unwittingly infecting their customers. Thailand's roaring sex-for-money trade will probably continue growing into the next century. And so will AIDS. Sexually active Westerners and Thais alike would obviously do well to exercise caution.

Drugs

Thailand also suffers from a soaring drug problem. Local law-enforcement officials make little distinction between grass and heroin. Penalties are harsh: over 700 foreigners are now incarcerated in the Bangkok and Chiang Mai prisons on drug charges—not pleasant places to spend 10 years of your life. Raids conducted at popular travelers' hotels in Bangkok and Chiang Mai often involve drugs planted by overzealous police officers. Arrested, booked, and fingerprinted, the frightened Westerner spends a night in jail before posting a US$2,000 bail and passport as collateral. Even the smallest quantities bring mandatory jail sentences; life imprisonment is common for sizable seizures. The obvious message with drugs in Thailand is *don't*.

BANGKOK AND VICINITY

Thailand's sprawling, dynamic, and frustrating capital offers more variety, sights, and wonders than any other destination in Asia. Far too many visitors, hearing of the horrendous traffic jams and searing pollution, stop only long enough to glimpse a few temples and pick up cheap air tickets before departing for more idyllic environs.

To some degree this is understandable. Packed into the sweltering plains of the lower Chao Praya are some 10 million residents, 80% of the country's automobiles, and most of the nation's commercial headquarters—a city strangled by uncontrolled development. Without any semblance of a city center or urban planning, traffic grinds to a standstill during rush hours and dissolves into a swamp after summer monsoons. Worse yet is the monotonous sprawl of Chinese shophouses and faceless concrete towers that more closely resemble a Western labyrinth than anything remotely Eastern. It's an unnerving place.

To appreciate the charms and fascinations of Bangkok you must focus instead on the positive: dozens of magnificent temples that form one of Asia's great spectacles, countless restaurants with superb yet inexpensive food, legendary nightlife to satisfy all possible tastes, excellent shopping, and some of the friendliest people in the world. Nobody enjoys the heat, humidity, or traffic jams, but with patience and a sense of *mai pen rai*, Bangkok will cast an irresistible spell.

ATTRACTIONS

Admission Fees

The Grand Palace/Wat Pra Keo Complex will probably be your first experience with the notorious two-tier fee system for selected temples, museums, and historical sites in Thailand. In late 1985 the Fine Arts Department began charging foreigners significantly higher admission fees than Thais. For example, entrance to the Grand Palace is 100B for foreigners but free for Thais. Although rarely noticed by tourists (lower entrance fees for locals are posted only in Thai script), this double standard has proven contentious for Western travelers, who resent the gouge-the-rich-tourist mentality. Complaints should be directed upstairs at the Bangkok TAT office.

Touts and con artists are plentiful around the Grand Palace; be extra cautious about free boat rides, invitations to lunch, or suspicious money-making schemes.

Dress Regulations

Please remember that foreign visitors to Buddhist temples must be properly dressed. *Shorts are never appropriate*. Long pants or long dresses should be worn instead. Women should be well covered. Visitors wearing dirty jeans, T-shirts, or halter tops will be refused admittance. Sandals are preferable to rubber slippers. Photographers should ask permission before taking flash photos inside temples.

THAILAND

CENTRAL BANGKOK

10
11

★ WAT INDRARAM

★ PRA ARHIT OLD FORT

BANGLAMPOO

RAJADAMNERN NOK AVE.

★ TOURIST OFFICE

9

ROYAL BARGES ★

★ WAT CHANA SONGKRAM

★ WAT BOWONIVET

KHAO SAN RD.

LARN LUANG RD.

★ NATIONAL GALLERY

BANGKOK NOI TRAIN STATION

8

NATIONAL THEATER ★

★ NATIONAL MUSEUM

RAJADAMNERN AVE.

DEMOCRACY MONUMENT

★ WAT RAJANADA

★ OLD FORT

★ GOLDEN MOUNT (WAT SAKET)

THAMMASARAT UNIVERSITY

★ WAT MAHATHAT

SANAM LUANG

★ EARTH GODDESS STATUE

LOHAPRASAT

AMULETS

7
6

SILAPKORN UNIVERSITY

LAK MUANG

★ GIANT SWING

BAMRUNG MUANG RD.

★ MONK'S BOWL VILLAGE

5

★ WAT PRA KEO

★ WAT RAJAPRADIT

★ WAT SUTHAT

★ GRAND PALACE

★ WAT RAJABOPIT

LUANG RD.

CHAO PRAYA RIVER

★ WAT PO

4

SAMPENG LANE

TRIPET RD.

★ NAKHON KASEM MARKET

CHAROEN KRUNG RD.

★ WAT ARUN

THONBURI

3

PAK KLONG TALAAT MARKET

■ INDIAN RESTAURANTS

★ PAHURAT MARKET

YAOWARAJ RD.

CHINATOWN

2

★ WAT KALA YANAMIT

MEMORIAL BRIDGE

SONGWAT

★ CHURCH OF SANTA CRUZ

BOAT STOPS

1. Ratchawong (Chinatown)
2. Saphan Phut (Memorial Bridge)
3. Rachini (produce marktet)
4. Tien (Wat Po, Wat Arun)
5. Chang (Grand Palace)
6. Maharaj (museum)
7. Prannok
8. Rot Fai (train station)
9. Arthit (Banglampoo)
10. Daowadung
11. Samphya

0   0.5 km

N

THAILAND

© MOON PUBLICATIONS, INC.

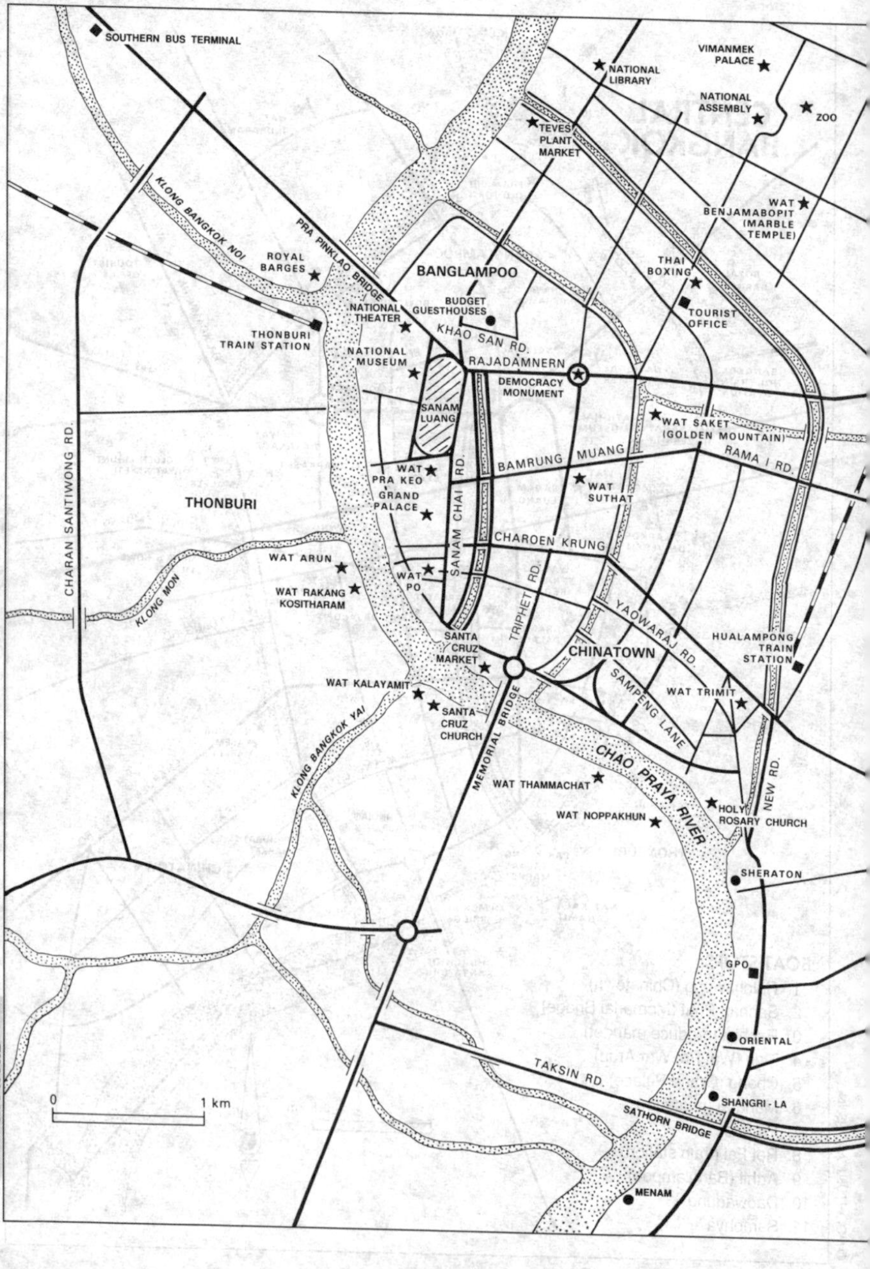
SOUTHERN BUS TERMINAL
NATIONAL LIBRARY
VIMANMEK PALACE
NATIONAL ASSEMBLY
ZOO
TEVES PLANT MARKET
KLONG BANGKOK NOI
PRA PINKLAO BRIDGE
WAT BENJAMABOPIT (MARBLE TEMPLE)
ROYAL BARGES
BANGLAMPOO
THAI BOXING
TOURIST OFFICE
NATIONAL THEATER
BUDGET GUESTHOUSES
THONBURI TRAIN STATION
KHAO SAN RD.
NATIONAL MUSEUM
RAJADAMNERN
DEMOCRACY MONUMENT
SANAM LUANG
WAT SAKET (GOLDEN MOUNTAIN)
CHARAN SANTIWONG RD.
BAMRUNG MUANG
RAMA I RD.
WAT PRA KEO
GRAND PALACE
WAT SUTHAT
SANAM CHAI RD.
THONBURI
CHAROEN KRUNG
WAT ARUN
WAT PO
WAT RAKANG KOSITHARAM
KLONG MON
TRIPHET RD.
YAOWARAJ RD.
HUALAMPONG TRAIN STATION
SANTA CRUZ MARKET
CHINATOWN
SAMPENG LANE
WAT KALAYAMIT
WAT TRIMIT
SANTA CRUZ CHURCH
MEMORIAL BRIDGE
KLONG BANGKOK YAI
CHAO PRAYA RIVER
WAT THAMMACHAT
HOLY ROSARY CHURCH
NEW RD.
WAT NOPPAKHUN
SHERATON
GPO
ORIENTAL
TAKSIN RD.
0
1 km
SHANGRI - LA
SATHORN BRIDGE
MENAM

THAILAND

© MOON PUBLICATIONS, INC.

BANGKOK

CHATUCHAK WEEKEND MARKET
NORTHERN BUS TERMINAL

CHITRALADA
PALACE

RAJAVITHI RD.

TO AIRPORT

TUM NAK THAI REST.

VICTORY
MONUMENT

THAILAND
CULTURAL CENTER

AYUTHAYA RD.

EXPRESSWAY

SUAN
PAKKARD
PALACE

PETCHBURI RD.

PRATUNAM
MARKET

PRATUNAM
MARKET

NEW PETCHBURI RD.

THAI
CRAFTS

JIM
THOMPSON'S
HOUSE

SIAM
SQUARE

RAMA VI RD.

STADIUM

SIAM
SQUARE

PLOENCHIT RD.

SUKUMVIT

PAYATHAI RD.

CHULALONGKORN
UNIVERSITY

GRAND
HYATT ERAWAN

SIAM SOCIETY

SOI. 21

LANDMARK

SUKUMVIT RD.

H. DUNANT RD.

RAJADAMRI RD.

WIRELESS RD.

KAMTHIEMG
HOUSE

SOI
COWBOY

A.U.A.

TO EASTERN
BUS TERMINAL

SIPHYA RD.

RAMA IV RD.

LUMPINI PARK

SNAKE
FARM

SURAWONG RD.

PATPONG

DUSIT
THANI

EXPRESSWAY

SILOM RD.

SILOM

THAI
BOXING

SATHORN NUA RD.

MALAYSIA

BUDGET
GUESTHOUSES

RAMA IV RD.

SATHORN TAI RD.

MOON

IMMIGRATION

THAILAND

Wat Pra Keo and the Grand Palace

Unquestionably one of the most magnificent sights in all of Asia if not the world is Wat Pra Keo and the adjoining Grand Palace—a scene of almost unbelievable brilliance: golden spires and wonderfully ornate pavilions guarded by strange mythological creatures.

The interior cloister murals depict tales from the Ramakien, the Thai version of the Ramayana. Originally painted in 1850 and restored for the Rattankosin bicentennial in 1982, the story begins by the north gate with the discovery of Sita and advances through various adventures of her consort Rama and his assistant, the white monkey god Hanuman. The murals surround the Golden Chedi, erected by King Mongkut and modeled after Ayuthaya's Pra Sri Ratana, and a *mondop,* a richly carved library with a solid-silver floor and interior set with a mother-of-pearl chest filled with sacred texts.

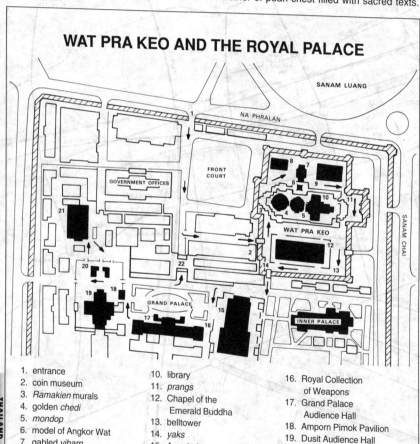

WAT PRA KEO AND THE ROYAL PALACE

1. entrance
2. coin museum
3. *Ramakien* murals
4. golden *chedi*
5. *mondop*
6. model of Angkor Wat
7. gabled *viharn*
8. Royal Mausoleum
9. Royal Pantheon
10. library
11. *prangs*
12. Chapel of the Emerald Buddha
13. belltower
14. *yaks*
15. Amarinda Audience Hall
16. Royal Collection of Weapons
17. Grand Palace Audience Hall
18. Amporn Pimok Pavilion
19. Dusit Audience Hall
20. courtyard doorways
21. Wat Pra Keo Museum
22. double gates

© MOON PUBLICATIONS, INC.

THAILAND

TEMPLE ARCHITECTURE

Thailand has over 30,000 Buddhist temples, which share, to a large degree, common types of structures. The following descriptions will help sort through the dazzling yet bewildering buildings found throughout the country.

The Wat

The entire religious complex is known as a *wat*. This term does not properly translate to "temple," since temple implies a singular place dedicated to the worship of a god, while *wats* are multiple buildings dedicated to the veneration—not worship—of the Buddha. *Wats* serve as religious institutions, schools, community meeting halls, hospitals, entertainment venues, and homes for the aged and abandoned. Some even serve as drug-rehabilitation centers.

Wat titles often explain much about their history and function. Some are named after the kings who constructed them, such as Ayuthaya's Wat Pra Ram, named for King Ramatibodhi. Others use the word Rat, Raja, or Racha to indicate that Thai roy-

alty either constructed or restored the building. Others are named for their Buddha images, such as Wat Pra Keo in Bangkok, which holds the Keo or Emerald Buddha. Pra (also spelled Phra)—the term that often precedes important Buddha images—means "honorable." Thailand's most important *wats* are called Wat Mahathat, a term that indicates they hold a great *(maha)* relic *(that)* of the Buddha. Wat Mahathats are found in Bangkok, Chiang Rai, Sukothai, Ayuthaya, Phitsanulok, Phetburi, Nakhon Si Thammarat, Yasothon, and Chai Nat.

Bot

Bots, the most important and sacred structure in the religious compound, are assembly halls where monks meet to perform ceremonies and ordinations, meditate, give sermons to lay people, and recite the *patimokkha* (disciplinary rules) every fortnight.

The Exterior: Ground plans vary from quadrilateral *cellas* with single doors to elaborate cruciform designs with multiple entrances. All are identified by *bai sema,* eight boundary stones which define the consecrated ground and help ward off evil spirits. *Bai semas* are often protected by small tabernacles richly decorated with spires and runic symbols. *Bot* window shutters and doors are often carved and decorated with gold leaf and mirrored tiles or engraved with mother-of-pearl designs. But the most arresting sights are the multitiered roofs covered with brilliant glazed tiles. Roof extremities end with *chofas,* graceful curls that represent *nagas* or mythological *garudas.* Wriggling down the edges of the bargeboards are more *nagas,* which act as heavenly staircases between earthly existence and Buddhist nirvana. Some of the best artwork is found in the triangular pediments: images of Vishnu riding his Garuda or Indra riding elephant-headed Erawan.

The Interior: Stunning interior murals often follow identical arrangements. Paintings behind the primary Buddha image depict scenes from the Traiphum, the Buddhist cosmological order of heaven, earth, and hell. Have a close look at the punishments of the damned—they might remind you of Hieronymus Bosch's painting of Dante's *Inferno* (devils dancing around, people being speared or boiled alive, etc.). Less interesting side walls are decorated with incidents from the life or earlier in-

(continues on next page)

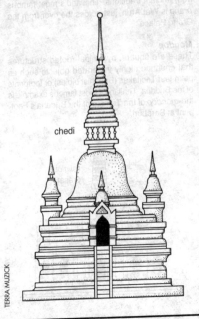

chedi

TERRA MUZICK

THAILAND

TEMPLE ARCHITECTURE

(continued)

carnations of the Buddha. The most spectacular murals, always located on the front wall above the main entrance, depict the Buddha's enlightenment or his temptation by Mara. Shoes must be removed before entering all *bots* in Thailand.

Viharn

Secondary assembly halls where laymen pay homage to the principal Buddha image. *Vihams* are architecturally identical to *bots* except for the lack of consecrated boundary stones. Larger *viharns* are surrounded by magnificently decorated cloisters filled with rows of gilded Buddha images.

Chedi

Chedi is the Thai term for the Indian stupa. In ancient times, these dome-shaped monuments held relics of the Buddha such as pieces of bone or hairs. Later prototypes were erected over the remains of kings or saints, and today anybody with sufficient *baht* can have one constructed for his or her ashes. *Chedis* consist of a three-tiered base representing heaven, hell, and earth, and a bulbous stupa placed on top. The small pavilion (*harmika*) near the summit symbolizes the Buddha's seat of meditation. Above this is a multitiered and highly stylized umbrella ringed with moldings representing the 33 Buddhist heavens. Pinnacles are often capped with crystals and precious jewels. The world's largest *chedi* is located in Nakhon Pathom, one hour west of Bangkok.

Prang

These towering spires, some of the most distinctive and exciting monumental structures in Thailand, trace their architectural heritage back to the corner towers of Cambodian temples. Although these phallic-shaped structures are set on a square base like the *chedi*, many have achieved a more elegant and slender outline than Kampuchean prototypes. Lower tiers are often ringed by a frieze of demons who appear to be—depending on your perspective—either dancing or supporting the tower. Summits are typically crowned by the Hindu thunderbolt, symbol of Shiva and religious holdover from ancient traditions. Thailand's most famous *prang* is Wat Arun, just across the river from the Grand Palace.

Mondop

These are square, pyramidal-roofed structures that enshrine highly venerated objects such as palm-leaf Tripitakas (Buddhist bibles) or footprints of the Buddha. Thailand's most famous example is the *mondop* of the Temple of the Buddha's Footprint at Saraburi.

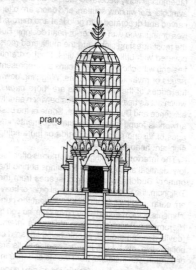

prang

religious prasat

TERRA MUZICK

THAILAND

Prasat

These elegant little buildings have ground plans in the form of Greek Crosses. *Prasats* may serve either religious or royal functions. Those designed for secular or royal purposes are capped with familiar multiple rooflines; religious *prasats* are crowned with *prangs*. Thailand's most famous *prasat* is located at Bang Pa In, one hour north of Bangkok.

Other Structures

Sala: Open-walled structures used by pilgrims to escape the heat and by monks as casual dining rooms. *Salas* also serve as overnight shelters for pilgrims during temple festivals.

Ho Rakang: Bell or drum towers that summon monks to services and meals.

Ho Trai: Elevated, graceful libraries that house Buddhist canonical texts. *Ho trai* are built on stilts to prevent rats and white ants from devouring the precious manuscripts.

Kuti: Monk's quarters. Often the simplest yet most attractive buildings in the *wat* complex. Older *kutis* are frequently on the verge of collapse; those in Phetburi are most evocative.

Kanbarien Hall: Used for religious instruction.

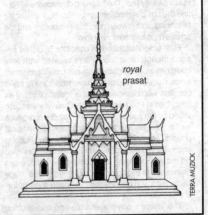

royal prasat

TERRA MUZICK

Gracing the four corners are exquisite Buddha statues carved in a 14th-century Javanese style and miniature sacred white elephants, symbols of royal power. Normally closed to the public.

The nearby model of Angkor Wat was constructed by Rama IV when Kampuchea was a vassal state of the Thai empire. Looming over the southern side are a series of giant Khmer *prangs* covered with glazed ceramic tiles and erected by Rama I as symbols of the eight planets.

You then enter Wat Pra Keo, the Chapel of the Emerald Buddha and Thailand's most important and sacred *wat*. Constructed at the end of the 18th century by King Rama I, this splendid example of Thai aesthetics and religious architecture houses the Emerald Buddha, the most venerated image in the country.

You then exit the grounds of Wat Pra Keo and enter the adjacent grounds of the Grand Palace, an intriguing blend of Italian Renaissance architecture and classical Thai roofing constructed 1783 by King Rama I and improved upon by subsequent rulers. If Wat Pra Keo evokes the Orient, then the Grand Palace will remind you of Europe.

Highlights include the Amarinda Audience Hall, the Grand Palace Audience Hall (eccentric, half-Western and half-Oriental), Amporn Pimok Pavilion, and the Dusit Audience Hall, considered Thailand's finest example of royal architecture.

Attractions in Central Bangkok

Lak Muang: Across the road from the Grand Palace stands a marble pavilion housing a *lingam*-shaped monument covered with gold leaf and adorned with flowers. This foundation stone, from which all distances in Thailand are measured, was placed here by King Rama I to provide a home for the unseen landlord-spirits of the city. Thais believe these magical spirits possess the power to grant wishes, win lotteries, guarantee healthy children, and protect the fate of the city. Thai classical-dance performances take place in the rear pavilion.

National Museum: This museum, the largest and most comprehensive in Southeast Asia, serves as an excellent introduction to the arts of Thailand—it should not be missed. Collections are open daily except Mondays and Fridays 0900-1200 and 1300-1600. Detailed information is provided in the *Guide to The National Museum Bangkok* sold at the front desk.

Wat Mahathat: The "Temple of the Great Relic" serves as one of Thailand's great cen-

THAILAND

ICONOGRAPHY OF THE BUDDHA IMAGE

Visitors to the National Museum and temples of Thailand are often confused by the variety of Buddhas they find. The following descriptions will define the basic symbolism and describe the delicate balancing act between religious symbolism and the artist's urge to create new forms.

First-time visitors often consider Buddhist images monotonous look-alikes created with little imagination or originality, a not unfair judgment since Buddhist sculptors have traditionally been copyists who depicted Buddha images exactly as described in Pali religious texts. Creativity was also stifled by the sculptor's desire to exactly reproduce earlier images which had demonstrated magical powers. According to legend, an authorized Buddha image carved during Sakyamuni's lifetime absorbed his magical potency; sculptors believed that exact likenesses of the original would share these magical powers and provide the pious with supernatural protection.

The image's comprehensible and undisturbing symbolism is conveyed in dozens of ways: feet must be engraved with 108 auspicious signs; toes and fingers should be of equal length; hands should resemble the opening of lotus buds; arms should extend all the way to the knees; the magical spot between the eyes and protuberance from the forehead must represent enlightenment.

Despite these religious straitjackets, Thai artists successfully created a half dozen unique styles which stand today as some of Asia's most refined art.

Mudras of the Buddha: Buddhist images throughout Thailand share common body positions (seated, standing, walking, and reclining) and hand gestures (mudras) which symbolically represent important events in the life of Buddha. Standing images depict Sakyamuni taming evil forces and bestowing blessings. Walking figures illustrate the Buddha returning to earth after preaching to his mother and deities in heaven. Reclining images embody the

Calling the Earth to Witness

Buddha at the exact moment of nirvana—not sleeping, as visitors often assume. Sitting Buddhas represent various stories: meditating, witnessing divinity, or setting in motion the "Wheel of the Law." Understanding the following mudras will prove invaluable when examining Buddha images throughout the country.

Calling the Earth to Witness Mudra

Seated in either a full- or half-lotus position, the Buddha is shown reaching forward to touch the ground with his right hand. This immensely popular mudra symbolizes the Buddha's victory over the demons of Mara and testifies to his enlightenment.

Dispelling Fear Mudra

Either the left, right, or both hands are held at shoulder level with the palms turned outward. Rendered in both walking and standing Buddhas, this mudra evolved from a legend in which the Buddha raised his hand to subdue a rampaging elephant intent on

Reclining

TERRA MUZICK

THAILAND

Meditation

his destruction. Also called the "Triumph over Evil" or "Giving of Protection" mudra.

Meditation Mudra

With one hand resting on the other and both legs crossed in a lotus position, this classic attitude represents the final meditation and enlightenment under the bodhi tree. Eyes are closed and breath is held to concentrate on the truth.

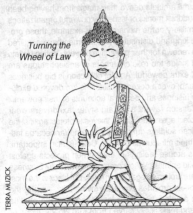

Turning the Wheel of Law

TERRA MUZICK

Adoration Mudra

Generally performed by bodhisattvas or lesser angels giving homage to the Buddha, this hand gesture is formed by joining both hands together vertically at the level of the breast—exactly like the Buddhist *wai*.

Dispensing Favors Mudra

Almost identical to the position of "Dispelling Fear" except the palm is completely exposed, open, and empty, this mudra symbolizes the Buddha's vows of assistance and gifts of truth.

Turning the Wheel of the Law Mudra

Both hands are held before the chest with the thumb and forefinger of the right hand forming a circle. Representing the position that set in motion the wheel of the Buddhist law, this indestructible wheel also symbolizes karma, samsara, and the reality of nirvana.

Dispelling Fear

ters of Buddhist learning and national head-quarters for the Mahanikaya sect practiced by over 90% of the Buddhist population. Vipassana ("Insight") meditation techniques are a specialty of the amazingly friendly head abbot; visitors can obtain further information from the office in Section five. A small *soi* (alley) through the back entrance crosses Maharat Road and opens into the temple's most famous sight: a plaza filled with shops selling Buddhist amulets, freshly cast Buddha images, and monk accessories such as begging bowls and orange robes.

Wat Po: Bangkok's oldest and largest temple complex was founded in the 16th century and radically remodeled two centuries later by Rama II into an open-air university for his Thai subjects. Crammed into the courtyards are a bewildering number of chapels, rock gardens, bizarre statuary (Chinese guards wearing European top hats), educational tablets, belltowers, and dozens of small *chedis;* student guides can be hired. The most famous sight is the gigantic 46-meter Reclining Buddha housed under a claustrophobic shed in the western courtyard. Just as intriguing is the College of Traditional Medicine, a mini-university of massage, herbal medicine, and Chinese acupuncture that offers inexpensive, traditional Thai rubs.

Wat Arun: This monumental 86-meter Khmer-style *prang,* one of the largest religious monuments in the country, towers above the Chao Praya to form Bangkok's most impressive and famous landmark. Better known as the Temple of the Dawn, Wat Arun symbolically represents the Buddhist universe, with its trident-capped central tower indicating Mount Meṛu, and the four smaller towers depicting the four worldly oceans. Take a ferry from the Tha Tien Pier behind Wat Po.

Wat Rajapradit: Constructed in 1864 by King Mongkut to complete the holy triumvirate of Ayuthayan temples, this picturesque *wat* is noted for its inte-

rior murals with clear views of Bangkok during the 1860s.

Wat Rajabopit: Constructed in 1863 by King Chulalongkorn just as Western influence arrived in Thailand, this architectural curiosity features unusual relief carvings of impassive European soldiers, a tall *chedi* encasing a Buddha seated on a Khmer-style *naga,* and a royal cemetery filled with tombs styled after Indian *chedis* and miniature Gothic cathedrals.

Wat Suthat: Constructed in the second quarter of the 19th century, this rarely visited complex is chiefly known for its huge bronze 15th-century Sukothai Buddha located in the *viharn* and exquisite frescoes which adorn the walls of the *bot.* These fabulous murals—considered among the finest in Thailand—were painted during the reign of Rama II with flat tints and primitive perspectives which predate Western influences.

Giant Swing: Opposite Wat Suthat tower a pair of red teak pillars once used for the Brah-

THAILAND

MAGICAL MEDALLIONS

Thais believe protection against malevolent spirits, reckless *phis,* and black magic can be guaranteed with amulets, small talismanic icons worn around the neck or waist. Extraordinarily powerful amulets derive their magic from having been blessed by Buddhist monks or issued by powerful organizations such as the military or the monarchy. For example, those produced by the king and distributed to policemen have acquired considerable renown for their protective powers. Votive tablets found buried inside the relic chambers of ancient stupas are also deemed extra powerful. Amulet collection is big business here in Thailand; over a dozen publications are devoted exclusively to their histories and personal accounts of their powers.

Each profession favors a certain style: taxi drivers wear amulets to protect against accidents, thieves to protect against the police; American soldiers during the Vietnam War became fascinated with their miraculous powers. Color is also important: white amulets arouse feelings of love, green protects against ghosts and wild animals, yellow promotes successful business deals, red offers protection against criminals. But black is the most powerful color—it provides *complete* invincibility. Among the more bizarre amulets are those fashioned after the phallus *(palad khik)* and realistically carved from rare woods, ivory, or horn. Related to Hindu lingam worship, *palad khik* are attached to cords and worn around the waist. A great way for Westerners to make friends and influence people is to proudly wear an amulet of the king or queen.

manic "Ceremony of the Swing." Before being banned in 1932, teams of young Hindu priests would swing a full arch of 180 degrees and try to snatch a bag of gold coins between their teeth. Some bit the gold, others bit the dust.

Wat Rajanada and the Amulet Market: Wat Rajanada is chiefly noted for its popular amulet market at the far left end of the courtyard. Buddhist amulets make great gifts and, unlike Buddha images, may be legally taken out of the country without official permits.

Lohaprasat: To the rear of Wat Rajanada stands a curious pink building which resembles, more than anything else, an ornate wedding cake festooned with 37 candle-spires. Lohaprasat was designed to resemble ancient temples in Sri Lanka and India which, according to legend, served as mansions for the Buddha and his disciples.

Golden Mountain: One of the few places from which to peer (smog permitting) over sprawling Bangkok is high atop the 78-meter artificial mountain just outside the ancient capital walls. Visitors climbing the 318 steps are often approached by young monks anxious to practice their English and older, cynical monks more interested in rock music than nirvana. Wat Saket, at the foot of the mount, sponsors Bangkok's liveliest temple festival each November.

Wat Bowonivet: Somewhat off the familiar tourist route, Wat Bowonivet is the immensely prestigious retreat where Prince Mongkut (of *The King and I* fame) founded the Thammayut sect of Thai Buddhism and served as chief abbot during a portion of his 27-year monkhood. Wat Bowonivet is perhaps the most popular temple in Bangkok for meditation instruction; ask at the international section.

Chinatown

Raucous and seething Chinatown is your best bet if you're looking for the old East in Bangkok.

Wat Trimit: The "Temple of the Golden Buddha" and its three-meter golden image have a story as fabulous as their reputation. Covered with stucco to disguise its value from Burmese invaders, this Sukothai-style Buddha lay neglected until its transfer in 1953 to a neighboring temple. The statue fell from the crane, the plaster cracked, and workmen discovered the wondrous image inside—five tons of solid gold. Open daily; no admission charge.

Yaowaraj Road: Walk slowly to appreciate the spectacle: dazzling gold stores with mirrored interiors and richly carved wooden chairs, traditional calligraphers working on the sidewalk, herbal stores with displays of antler horn and strange roots, restaurants, and neon signs flashing Chinese characters—sensory overload to rival anything in Asia.

Sampeng Lane: Much too narrow for cars, this canvas-roofed lane is crammed with shopkeepers, gold stores, clothing merchants, prewar architecture, and porters hauling heavy loads. Once known as the Green Light area from the lanterns which illuminated the brothels and opium dens, this *highly recommended* alley epitomizes what is most alluring about Chinatown. Be sure to visit the century-old gold shop at the corner of Mangkon Street.

Pahurat Indian Market: Sampeng Lane terminates at the old cloth market where Sikh and Chinese merchants peddle Indian saris, Malaysian batiks, and Thai silks from enormous open-air tables.

Nakhon Kasem Market: Once Bangkok's antique center, most of the dealers have since moved to shopping centers near the tourist centers. A few dusty stores hold on, surrounded by hardware shops and copper merchants.

Attractions in Northern Bangkok

Wat Benjamabopit: Designed by the half-brother of King Chulalongkorn and erected at the turn of the century, the "Marble Temple" is considered one of the great sights of Bangkok. Chiefly known for its superb harmony and pleasing symmetry, it also offers an outstanding collection of 52 Buddha statues, both originals and quality reproductions, carefully labeled as to the country of origin and period; better than art school!

Vimanmek Palace: Designed by a German architect named Sandreczki and once the residence of Rama V, this well-restored palace now serves as a private museum displaying a rich collection of royal regalia. Inside the world's largest golden teak structure is the eclectic assemblage of King Chulalongkorn, including period furniture, the country's first shower, and a photograph of Thomas Edison signed "to the King and Queen of Siam." Open daily except Sundays 0930-1630; included in the admission fee to the Grand Palace and Wat Pra Keo.

THAILAND

Attractions near Sukumvit Road

Jim Thompson's House: Jim Thompson was the legendary American architect-entrepreneur who settled in Thailand after WW II and almost singlehandedly revived the moribund silk industry. No trace was found of Thompson after he disappeared in 1967 while hiking near Cameron Highlands. Jim's maze of seven Thai-style teak houses has since been converted into a small private museum filled with his priceless collection of Asian antiques, pottery, and curiosities. Open daily except Sundays 0900-1600; admission is 130B.

Phallic Shrine: Dedicated to Chao Tuptim (Pomegranate), a Thai female spirit, this tangled mini-jungle shrine has become somewhat notorious in the foreign press for its hundreds of stylized and realistic phalluses contributed by childbearing devotees. Considered a combination fertility-prosperity shrine since the lingam symbolizes both regeneration and good fortune, Bangkok's strangest shrine is located on the grounds of the Hilton at the end of Soi Som Si next to Klong Saen.

Siam Society: Thailand's premier research group publishes the scholarly *Journal of the Siam Society,* restores deteriorating murals, and maintains a 10,000-volume library of rare and valuable editions. Of special interest to foreign visitors is the Society Travel Club, which sponsors professionally led excursions to important temples, archaeological digs, and noteworthy festivals—some of the best available in Thailand. On the grounds is the Kamthieng House, a restored century-old residence noted for its ethnological artifacts and teak lintels which hold ancestral spirits and guarantee the virility of the inhabitants. Located on Soi 21 just off Sukumvit Road. Open daily except Sundays and Mondays 0900-1200 and 1300-1700; admission 30B.

Suan Pakkard Palace: The royal residence of Princess Chumbhot, one of Thailand's leading art collectors, offers an eclectic range of Thai artifacts from Ban Chiang pottery to Khmer sculpture. Disassembled and brought down from Chiang Mai, the complex of traditional Thai homes also includes the 450-year-old Lacquer Palace transferred from Ayuthaya. Open daily except Sunday 0900-1600; admission 100B.

Snake Farm: King cobras, green pit vipers, and banded kraits are milked daily at 1100 and 1400 (weekends at 1100 only) inside Thailand's Pasteur Institute. The extracted venom forms the basis for snakebite serum. Cholera, smallpox, typhoid inoculations, and rabies treatments are also available. Open daily 0830-1600; admission 50B.

Erawan Shrine: Thailand's devotion to animist spirits and Hindu deities is best appreciated in the famous shrine on the grounds of the Grand Hyatt Erawan. The memorial was erected after hotel construction halted from a series of seemingly random disasters: the marble for the lobby disappeared at sea, workmen died under mysterious circumstances, and cost overruns threatened to crush the hotel project. After spirit doctors summoned for advice informed the hotel owners that they must erect a shrine to Brahma, the mishaps ended and word of the miracle spread throughout Thailand. Today, it's a continual circus of devotees, incense, flowers, images of the elephant god Erawan (the three-headed mount of Brahma), plus free performances of Thai dance—a crazy and magical place.

More Attractions

Bangkok Floating Market: Thonburi's floating market epitomizes what is most crass and callous in the tourist trade. Once an authentic and colorful scene, the market completely died out in the '60s as modernization forced boat vendors to leave town and move into modern shopping centers. Threatened with the loss of revenue, tour operators came up with a rather awful solution: hire a few Thai ladies to paddle around and *pretend* to be shopping. Disneyland feels genuine when compared to this outrage, perhaps the most contrived rip-off in the East.

Canal Tours: Bangkok's waterways offer exceptional sightseeing opportunities and reveal what is most attractive about the city. Canal enthusiasts should purchase *50 Trips Through Siam's Canals* by George Veran or the recently published *Bangkok's Waterways* by William Warren. The *Thonburi Canal* map by the Association of Architects is also useful.

Chartered longtail boats from the landing stages at Tha Saphan Phut (*tha* translates to pier) and Tha Tien are somewhat expensive at 150-200B per hour. Less pricey and much more authentic are the ordinary longtail river taxis

THAILAND

which race up and down all the smaller canals, picking up and dropping off passengers until they finally turn around and return to their starting points. Prices average about 5B in each direction or 10B roundtrip. These boats leave regularly from Tha Saphan Phut, Tha Tien, and Tha Maharaj. Boatmen rarely speak English, but it's almost impossible to get lost. Just sit down, smile, and enjoy the ride.

Warning: Beware of slick professionals who offer free guided tours and then blackmail you for a 1,000B gasoline fare in the middle of the river. Never get into a longtail boat alone.

Chao Praya Express Boat: One of the cheapest, easiest, and most relaxing water journeys in Bangkok is on the public boat which shuttles up and down the Chao Praya River daily from 0600 to 1800. The boat continues 18 km north to Nonthaburi and makes 35 stops on both sides of the river; visitors can alight and return at any point. Government-controlled rates vary depending on the distance.

Budget All-day River Trip: Each Saturday and Sunday at 0800 a sleek boat leaves from the Maharaj Pier behind Thammasarat University, stops briefly at the Thai Folk Arts and Crafts Center, and reaches the Royal Summer Palace at Bang Pa In shortly before noon. The return journey visits the fascinating Wat Pailom Stork Sanctuary before arriving back in Bangkok around sunset.

Attractions outside Bangkok

Damnern Saduak Floating Market: Much less touristy than Bangkok's tawdry affair is the Damnern Saduak *klong* market, 109 km southwest of Bangkok. Between 0600 and 0900 dozens of vendors conduct business from their sampans filled with fruits, vegetables, and noodles. The TAT encourages visitors to visit this market rather than the Bangkok fraud; they provide maps and transportation information. Arrive early to beat the tour groups! Public buses leave from the Southern Bus Terminal every 20 minutes from 0600 and take two hours. From the Damnern Saduak Bus Station, either walk along the canal or take a taxi boat to the market. To see the markets at daybreak, spend the night in Damnern Saduak or hire a motorcycle from Kanchanaburi.

Ancient City: Muang Boran, 33 km south of Bangkok, is a 200-acre outdoor park and archi-tectural museum filled with full-sized and reduced-scale replicas of Thailand's 65 most important monuments and temples. The entire park is enormous, somewhat neglected, rarely visited, and murderously hot in the summer. Take a bus from the eastern bus terminal to Samut Prakan, where minibuses continue to Ancient City

Crocodile Farm: Also near Ancient City, the Crocodile Farm has over 30,000 crocodiles lounging around murky swimming pools inside the world's largest reptile farm. Wrestling matches are staged hourly; daily feedings at 1700. Touristy and weird. Located six km before Ancient City. Open daily 0800-1800; admission 100B.

Rose Garden: This upscale resort, 32 km west of Bangkok on the road to Nakhon Pathom, features landscaped gardens, a modern hotel, a lake, restaurants, a swimming pool, an 18-hole golf course, and replica of a Thai village. Open daily 0800-1800; the 150B admission fee includes a cultural show at 1500. Buses leave from the southern bus terminal in Thonburi.

Safari World: Asia's largest wildlife park opened several years ago in a Bangkok suburb at Kilometer 9 on Ramintra Road. Attractions include a wildlife section toured by free coaches, a Bird Park with walk-in aviary, restaurants, and an amusement park. Open daily 1000-1800; admission 100B.

ACCOMMODATIONS

Bangkok in many ways resembles Los Angeles—an urban nightmare spread across vast flatlands without a recognizable city center. For quick orientation, think of the city as individual neighborhoods with distinct personalities, hotel price ranges, and styles of restaurants and nightclubs. The old royal city along the banks of the Chao Praya holds most of the temples and sightseeing attractions. Banglampoo, near the old city, and the area surrounding the Malaysia hotel cater to budget travelers. Silom Road and Siam Square are the upscale tourist districts lined with luxurious accommodations and fine restaurants. Sukumvit is a middle-priced neighborhood of good-value hotels, restaurants, shopping, and lively nightlife.

THAILAND

Banglampoo—Budget

Bangkok's headquarters for backpackers and budget travelers is centered around this friendly little neighborhood just a few blocks from the temples and museums in the royal city. Most guesthouses, restaurants, and travel agencies are located on Khao San Road, a term synonymous with Banglampoo. Some guidebooks have complained that Banglampoo isn't very Thai, but it's much more authentic than other tourist areas in Bangkok! From the airport, take ordinary bus 59, a/c bus 3AC, taxi for 150-200B, or minibus for 100B.

At last count, Banglampoo had over 80 guesthouses, which charge about 60-100B for dorms, 120-250B for singles, and 200-450B for doubles. The most obvious drawbacks are the extraordinarily small rooms, problems of theft, and the terrible noise from the motorcycles which race around late at night. For a good night's sleep, it's important to find a clean and comfortable room tucked away on a side street rather than directly on Khao San Road. Most guesthouses fill by early afternoon; do your room search in the early morning when travelers depart for the airport and bus stations. Most Banglampoo guesthouses are identical in cleanliness and size, but a handful of superior choices are shown on the "Banglampoo" map and listed here.

Buddy Guesthouse: Midway down Khao San Rd., Buddy Guesthouse is a good place to begin your room search. Though the rooms are perpetually filled, you can drop your bags and enjoy a quick meal in the comfortable cafe in the rear. A less-packed restaurant is upstairs. Buddy Guesthouse, like most other guesthouses in Banglampoo, has a variety of rooms from basic cubicles to small a/c rooms with private bath. 137 Khao San Rd., tel. (02) 282-4351, 60-250B.

Hello Guesthouse: A 30-room guesthouse with a popular streetside cafe. 63 Khao San Rd., tel. (02) 281-8579, 60-150B fan, 180-250B a/c.

Ploy Guesthouse: A big place with very large rooms with private bath. Entrance is around the corner from Khao San Road. The second-floor lobby includes a small cafe and the coldest soft drinks in Bangkok. Recommended. 2 Khao San Rd., tel. (02) 282-1025, 60-200B.

Chart Guesthouse: An easy-to-find 20-room guesthouse with a great cafe. All rooms have fans; no a/c. 61 Khao San Rd., tel. (02) 281-0803, 60-140B.

C.H. Guesthouse: Big and popular place with 27 rooms and a packed video cafe on the ground floor. Recommended. 216 Khao San Rd., tel. (02) 282-2023, 60-150B fan, 200-220B a/c.

Lek Guesthouse: One of the original guesthouses in Banglampoo. Always filled, but worth checking with Mr. Lek Saranukul. 125 Khao San Rd., tel. (02) 281-2775, 80-140B.

Central Guesthouse: Both Central and Privacy guesthouses to the east of Tanao Rd. are quiet and somewhat run-down but exude a

THAILAND'S FUTURISTIC ARCHITECTURE

From Hong Kong to Singapore, economic success has dramatically transformed Asian skylines from low-rise colonial to high-tech Houston. But Bangkok's boom has unleashed a wave of innovative architecture unrivaled anywhere else in the region. Refusing to clone Western prototypes, the architects of Bangkok have invented some amazing fantasies: corporate headquarters that resemble Roman palaces, condo complexes that fuse art-deco facades with Thai rooflines, fast-food emporiums buried inside rocket ships, Mediterranean stucco homes, Bavarian half-timbered cottages—Hollywood holograms in the City of Angels.

This new and exciting movement is led by an iconoclastic architect named Sumet Jumsai and an innovative design firm called Plan Architect. Sumet's Bank of Asia Robot building near Silom Road—a humorous mixture of an external skeleton fitted with giant nuts and bolts—illustrates the marriage of high-tech themes with cartoon consciousness. The postmodern McDonald's on Ploenchit Road combines gleaming glass walls with Roman columns. Suburban developments include English castles complete with moats and the new headquarters for the *Nation* newspaper, an 11-story sculpture inspired by the whimsical designs of cubist painter Georges Braque. Bangkok is now more than just Thai temples and nocturnal delights, it's home to some of the most creative modern architecture in the world.

THAILAND

BANGLAMPOO

CHAO PRAYA RIVER

YOK YOR REST.
VISUT KASAT PIER
CHARASRI GH
WAT INDRAVIHARN
VISUT KASAT RD.

SOI 5
SOI 8
TATUM GH
AP GH
PARLIAMENT HOTEL
THAI HOTEL

WAT
SOI 3
SOI 6
RIVER GH
HOME & GARDEN GH
MITPAISARN HOTEL
PRADHATHI RD.

SOI 4
CHAN GH
VIMOL GH
SOI 2
DACHANEE REST.

SOI SAMSEN 1
WET GH
TRULY YOURS GH
NEW WORLD HOUSE

PRA ARTHIT FORT

A-A GH
A.V. GH
APPLE 2 GH
NEW WORLD SHOPPING CENTER
KRAI SI REST.
WAT BOWONIVET

PRA ARTHIT RD.

POST OFFICE

PRASUN GH
MAJESTIC HOTEL

CHUSRI GH
GARDEN GH
TANI RD.
VIENGTAI HOTEL
CENTRAL GH
PRIVACY GH
POST OFFICE
BONGO CLUB
VIJIT REST.

PRA ARTHIT PIER
MERRY V GH
RAMBUTRI RD.
DEMOCRACY MONUMENT
MUANG BORAN

MANGO GH
WAT CHANA SONGKRAM
BUDDY GH
KHAO SAN PALACE
SORN DAENG REST.

PEACHY GH
ROOF GARDEN GH
POLICE
KHAO SAN RD. CHADA
PLOY GH TOP GH
THAI CAFES.
MARIA REST.

DINSO RD.

CHAI'S GH
NAT'L GALLERY
RAJADAMNERN KLANG AVE.

PINKLAO HWY.
P. GH
CITY HALL

WANG NAR REST.
ROYAL HOTEL
WAT MAHAPARAM
PARK

NAT'L THEATER
TORANI STATUE
CHINESE TEMPLE
HINDU SHRINE
GIANT SWING

NAT'L MUSEUM
TANAO RD.
BAMRUNG MUANG RD.
WAT SUTHAT

AMULETS
SANAM LUANG
KANIT'S REST.

THAMMASART UNIV.
0   0.25mi
0   0.25km

MAHATHAT PIER
RACHINI RD.
ATSADANG RD.
BAN MO RD.

WAT MAHATHAT
LAK MUANG

MAHARAJ PIER
SILAPAKORN UNIV.
SANAM CHAI RD.
GOLDEN BOAR STATUE
WAT RAJABOPIT

LONGTAILS
WAT PRA KEO
WAT RAJAPRADIT
WAT RAJABOPIT
CHAROEN KRUNG RD.

CHANG PIER
NA PRALAN RD.
MAHARAJ RD.
SARAN ROM RD.
ROYAL PALACE

THAILAND

© MOON PUBLICATIONS, INC.

homey Thai feeling. Alleys branching off Khao San have several more peaceful guesthouses. 69 Tanao Rd., tel. (02) 282-7028, 60-120B.

Apple 2 Guesthouse: For a slightly Felliniesque experience, walk past the grazing cows and horses of Wat Chana Songkram (an animal refuge in the middle of Bangkok!) to the alleys and guesthouses which surround the temple. Apple 2 is a long-running favorite located in a quiet back alley. The big rambling teak house with songbirds and upstairs rooms is also called "Mama's." 11 Trok Kai Chae, tel. (02) 281-1219, 70-120B.

Peachy Guesthouse: Slightly more expensive than Khao San cubicles, but the rooms are clean, spacious, and furnished with writing tables and standing closets. Air-conditioned rooms are available. Perpetually filled, but sign the waiting list. Avoid rooms facing Pra Arthit Rd. or adjacent to the TV room. 10 Pra Arthit, tel. (02) 281-6471, 100-160B.

Merry V Guesthouse: One of the best guesthouses behind Wat Chana Songkram has clean rooms and a very comfortable restaurant. 35 Soi Chana Songkram, tel. (02) 282-9267, 60-160B.

Truly Yours Guesthouse: Some of Banglampoo's quietest guesthouses are located across the bridge north of Khao San Road. All provide an opportunity to experience Thai homestays in a traditional neighborhood. Samsen 1 Rd. has Truly Yours and Villa guesthouses, while Samsen 3 Rd. has the River, Clean and Calm, and Home and Garden guesthouses. Worth the walk. All charge 60-120B.

Tavee Guesthouse: To really escape the travelers' scene in Banglampoo, walk north up Chakrabongse Rd. and turn left on Sri Ayuthaya Rd. at the National Library. Near the river are three idyllic guesthouses including the Shanti, Sawatdee, and Tavee. The latter is at 83 Sri Ayuthaya Rd., tel. (02) 282-5349, 60-120B.

Banglampoo—Moderate
Khao San Palace Hotel: The dark and small rooms, probably the cheapest a/c rooms in Bangkok, come equipped with private baths, warm water, and horizontal mirrors geared to short-time business. 139 Khao San Rd., tel. (02) 282-0578, 280-340B fan, 360-420B a/c.

Nith Charoen Hotel: Another good mid-priced hotel located in the heart of Banglampoo. Com-

---

RAJADAMNERN AVENUE BUSES

3AC, 59	Airport
12AC	New Phetburi
39AC	Northern Bus Terminal
45	Rama IV
15, 121	Silom
7AC	Southern Bus Terminal
2, 11AC	Sukumvit, Eastern Bus Terminal

---

fortable lounge with a useful bulletin board. 183 Khao San Rd., tel. (02) 281-9872, 300-460 a/c.

A-A Guesthouse: One of Banglampoo's best-value guesthouses has five floors of rooms ranging from common-bath cheapies on the fourth and fifth floors to private-bath a/c rooms on the lower floors. Quietly tucked away in a small alley. 84 Pra Sumeru Rd., tel. (02) 282-9631, 120-480B.

New World House: A large, modern apartment complex with luxury features at a bargain price. All rooms are air-conditioned, with private bath, telephone, laundry service, and views over Banglampoo. Recommended for anyone who intends to stay a week or longer. Located just across the river. 2 Samsen Rd., tel. (02) 281-5596, 300-800B.

Royal Hotel: This well-priced hotel is within walking distance of Bangkok's attractions—an excellent place in a great location. Reservations can be made from the hotel counter at the airport. Budget travelers and overheated travel writers often spend their mornings in the a/c coffee shop reading the *Bangkok Post.* 2 Rajadamnern, tel. (02) 222-9111, fax (02) 224-2083, 1,400-1,800B.

Malaysia Hotel Area
Surrounding the Malaysia Hotel are about 20 budget guesthouses which comprise Bangkok's once-great traveler's center. Most backpackers have deserted the area for Banglampoo, though the neighborhood remains popular with first-time visitors. Soi Ngam Duphli is a short taxi ride from the nightlife areas of Patpong and Sukumvit but distant from the temples in old Bangkok. From the airport take a/c bus 4AC, taxi from the highway for 150-200B, or the direct minibus for 100B.

Freddy's #2 Guesthouse: A clean and friendly guesthouse recommended by many travelers.

Freddy runs two other guesthouses in the neighborhood, though #2 is the best of the lot. Soi Si Bamphen, 60-80B s, 100-120B d.

Madam Guesthouse: The area's quietest guesthouses are located in a back alley and cul-de-sac off Soi Si Bamphen. All can be recommended for their solitude rather than for their cleanliness. Madam is a cozy if rustic homestay known for its friendly proprietor. Ramshackle rooms in the old house go from 60-100B.

Lee #3 Guesthouse: Adjacent to Madam Guesthouse and far removed from the horrendous traffic that blasts along Soi Si Samphen is another old house converted into a backpackers' crash pad. A popular place to nod out in the sunshine. Rooms cost 60-100B.

Honey Guesthouse: The latest addition to the guesthouse scene is this modern, clean, and comfortable 35-room building just down from the Malaysia Hotel. Rooms are available with common or private bath, with fan or a/c. Hefty discounts are given for monthly residents. The adjacent Greco-Roman style Diana Inn is also recommended. 35 Soi Ngam Duphli, tel. (02) 286-3460, 120-240B.

Malaysia Hotel: A decade ago, the legendary Malaysia was the favored gathering place for budget travelers, who enjoyed the low rates, a/c rooms, swimming pool, and 24-hour room service. A large and very famous noticeboard offered tips on visas, crash pads, and how to see the world on a shoestring. Today, the noticeboard is gone, the coffee shop doubles as a video arcade, and the "Day Off Pub—Paradise for Everyone" features freelance prostitutes and nightly girlie shows. 54 Soi Ngam Duphli, tel. (02) 286-3582, 520-800B.

Privacy Hotel: If the scene at the Malaysia

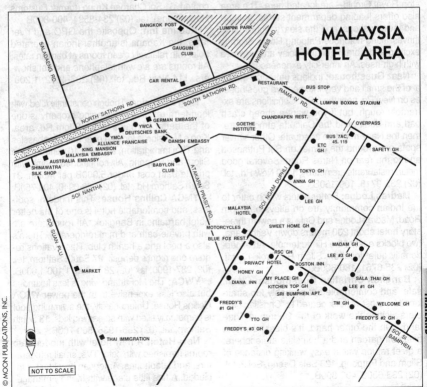

MALAYSIA HOTEL AREA

NOT TO SCALE

© MOON PUBLICATIONS, INC.

THAILAND

turns you off, try this less expensive but very run-down alternative. 31 Soi Ngam Duphli, tel. (02) 286-2339, 220-360B.

Boston Inn: Once the best-value hotel in the neighborhood, the Boston Inn now seems about to collapse into a heap of concrete. Perhaps a Thai experiment: how long can a hotel survive without even the most rudimentary maintenance? The noticeboard has sadly declined into nothingness, the once-popular travel agency has fled, and the a/c rooms have been closed down. Whew! Soi Si Bamphen, tel. (02) 286-1680, 120-180B.

Silom Road—Moderate

Once a luxurious residential neighborhood for wealthy merchants, the Silom-Surawong area has since grown into Bangkok's premier financial and commercial district. Some of the city's finest luxury hotels—the Oriental, the Shangri-La, and the Sheraton Royal Orchid—are located here. The area also offers leading department stores, antique and jewelry shops, and the sleazy nightlife that thrives along notorious Patpong Road. Silom is exciting and vibrant but also noisy and crowded with high-rises. An inner-city experience.

Naaz Guesthouse: Indians patronize several of the small and very inexpensive guesthouses on New Rd. near the GPO. Conditions are extremely rough, but if you want a cheap crash pad and don't mind the Calcutta atmosphere, then the Naaz might be adequate. Other similar spots are around the corner on Soi Puttaosod and to the rear on Nares Road. Several good Indian restaurants are nearby. 1159 New Rd., tel. (02) 235-9718, 100-150B.

Madras Lodge: Better hotels which cater to the Indian community are on alleys off Silom Road. Madras Lodge and Cafe is a newish three-story hotel about 200 meters down Vaithi Lane, two blocks east of the Hindu temple. An exceptionally quiet location. Silom Rd. Trok 13, tel. (02) 235-6761, 180-600B.

Bangkok Christian Guesthouse: Clean, safe, and comfortable but probably too strait-laced for most visitors: geared to "Christian travelers visiting the work of the Church in Thailand." On the other hand, it's blessed with a pleasant garden and a homelike atmosphere; a quiet refuge within easy walking distance of Silom and Patpong. 123 Sala Daeng, Soi 2, tel. (02) 233-6303, 400-800B.

RAMA IV ROAD BUSES

5	Siam Square, Banglampoo
115	Silom, General Post Office
7AC	Train Station, Royal Palace

Swan Hotel: This inexpensive little hotel is ideally located within walking distance of the GPO, inexpensive Indian restaurants, and river taxis behind the Oriental. All rooms include private bath and telephone, plus there's a small pool and an adequate coffee shop. The Swan needs some obvious improvement, but it remains excellent value for budget travelers. Reservations are accepted for a/c rooms only, and flight number and arrival time are required. Credit cards and traveler's checks are not accepted. 31 Soi Charoen Krung (former Customs House Lane), tel. (02) 234-8594, 400-800B.

Kabana Inn: Opposite the GPO and river taxis, the Kabana is another Indian-operated hotel with relatively clean rooms at bargain rates. All rooms are a/c with telephone and hot showers. 114 New Rd., tel. (02) 233-4652, 1,200-1,500B.

King's Mansion: Though constantly filled with long-term residents, this aging property is one of the better bargains in the Silom Rd. area. King's Mansion is located near many embassies and Thai Immigration, and only 10 minutes from Silom and Patpong. Air-conditioned rooms with private bath cost under 5,000B per month. 31 South Sathorn Rd., tel. (02) 286-0940, 400-750B.

YMCA Collins House: This modern, spotless, and comfortable hotel is one of the better hotel bargains in Bangkok. All rooms are a/c with private bath and mini refrigerator. There's also a pool and a health club. Reservations require one night's deposit. 27 South Sathorn, tel. (02) 287-1900, fax (02) 287-1996, 1,100-1,600B.

YWCA: The McFarland wing is less luxurious but also less expensive than the newer YMCA Collins House. Unfortunately, the swimming pool is perpetually filled with screaming kids. 13 South Sathorn, tel. (02) 286-1936, 500-700B.

New Hotel: A new hotel with modern a/c rooms furnished with color TVs, small refrigerators, and telephones. American breakfast is included. A fine little place with friendly manage-

THAILAND

SILOM - SURAWONG

CHAO PRAYA RIVER

SHANGRI-LA HOTEL
EAST ASIATIC BLDG.
TINA TOWER INN
ORIENTAL PIER
AMAR GH
ORIENTAL HOTEL
OLD CUSTOMS HOUSE
WAT MUANG KAI PIER
WAT CATHEDRAL
FRENCH EMBASSY
MOSQUE
ROYAL ORCHID SHERATON HOTEL
SI PHAYA PIER
RIVER CITY SHOPPING CENTER

NEW RD. (CHAROEN KRUNG RD.)

SWAN HOTEL
NEW ROTEL
GPO
SALLIM REST.
WOODLANDS HOTEL

HIMALI CHA CHA
TROCADERO HOTEL
RAMADA HOTEL
NAAZ GH
KABANA INN

SIMLA CAFE
FUJI HOTEL
MAMEE 2 GH

VICTORY HOTEL
SILOM PLAZA HOTEL

SURASAK RD.
BAN CHIANG REST.
HOLIDAY INN
CENTRAL DEPT. STORE
MANOHRA HOTEL
DESIGN THAI

PRAMUAN RD.
PENINSULA HOTEL

THAN YING REST.
SILOM VILLAGE

ST. LOUIS CHURCH
SAVOURY REST.
MYANMAR AIR
HINDU TEMPLE

MYANMAR (BURMA) EMBASSY
PAN RD.
NELSON HAYS LIBRARY

MADRAS LODGE
NARAI HOTEL

SURAWONG RD.
NARET RD.

ROBOT BLDG.
NIAGARA HOTEL
TOWER INN

MAHANAKON RD.

SILOM RD.

SATHORN SOUTH RD.
SATHORN NORTH RD.

CHINESE CEMETERY

ALL GAENGS REST.
SIPHAYA RD.

WESTERN CEMETERY
ONCE UPON A TIME REST.
SHANGRILA REST.
PLAZA HOTEL

SILOM PLAZA
THAI INTERNATIONAL
SUB RD.
RAMA IV RD.

TRINITY COMPLEX

GORDO'S REST.
MANDARIN HOTEL
PHYATHAI RD.

TAWANA RAMADA HOTEL

ROSE HOTEL

SILVER PALACE REST.
D.K. BOOKS

BUSSARACUM REST.
MALAYSIA TOURIST OFFICE
PATPONG 1
MONTIEN HOTEL

U.S.I.S.
PATPONG 2
SAWASDEE REST.
McDONALD'S

SORRENTO REST.
SARAH JANE'S REST.
CHARUVAN DUCK SHOP
WALL ST. HOTEL

ELEPHANT HOUSE
ROME DISCO

SHINAWATRA SILKS
SWISSOTEL
THANIYA RD.
JIM THOMPSON SILK
SNAKE FARM

→ TO IMMIGRATION
BANGKOK CHRISTIAN GH
CHULALONGKORN UNIVERSITY

RUENG PUENG REST.
HENRI DUMANT RD.

KING'S MANSION
ALLIANCE FRANCAISE

YMCA
SALADAENG RD.
SILOM COMPLEX
ROBINSONS DEPT. STORE

YWCA
DUSIT THANI HOTEL
RAJADAMRI RD.

SUKOTHAI HOTEL
LUMPINI PARK

© MOON PUBLICATIONS, INC.

0   100m

THAILAND

SIAM SQUARE

SRI AYUTHAYA RD.

FLORIDA HOTEL

SIAM CITY HOTEL

★ SUAN PAKKARD PALACE

PHYATHAI RD.

EXPRESSWAY

PETCHBURI RD.

MAKKASAN RD.

MAKKASAN TRAIN STATION

BAIYOKE TOWER

INDRA HOTEL

FIRST HOTEL

SAVOY INN

INDONESIAN EMBASSY

ASIA HOTEL

PRATUNAM MARKET

RAJAPRAROB RD.

BANGKOK PALACE HOTEL

PANTIP PLAZA

PETCHBURI RD.

★ JIM THOMPSON'S HOUSE
BED & BREAKFAST GH

A-ONE INN
RENO HOTEL
PRANEE BLDG.
MUANGPHOL LODGING
KRIT THAI MANSION

WORLD TRADE CENTER

ANOMA PAVILION HOTEL

CHITLOM RD.

HILTON HOTEL

SIAM CENTRE

SIAM INTERCONTINENTAL HOTEL

ZEN CENTRAL

NARAYANA PHAND

MOON SHADOW

MERIDIEN HOTEL

CENTRAL DEPT. STORE

SWISS EMBASSY

TOKYU DEPT. STORE

NOVOTEL HOTEL

SIAM SQUARE

RAMA 1 RD.

BRITISH EMBASSY

BRITISH COUNCIL

SEE FAH REST.

COCA GARDEN NOODLES

ERAWAN SHRINE ★

AMARIN PLAZA

PLOENCHIT RD.

DUTY FREE

HENRI DUNANT RD.

GRAND HYATT ERAWAN

PENINSULA PLAZA

IMPERIAL HOTEL

VIETNAM EMBASSY

VINOTHEK

REGENT HOTEL

RAJADAMRI RD.

ROYAL BANGKOK SPORTS CLUB

ISRAEL EMBASSY

SPANISH EMBASSY

NEW ZEALAND EMBASSY

AMERICAN EMBASSY

CHULALONGKORN UNIVERSITY

LANG SUAN RD.

WHOLE EARTH REST.

DIETHELM TRAVEL

WIRELESS RD.

RUAM RUDI RD.

A.U.A.

SOI TONSIN

BROWN SUGAR NIGHTCLUB

OLD WEST SALOON

NEIL'S TAVERN

SOI SARASIN

LUMPINI PARK

THAILAND

MOON

0   0.25mi

0   0.25km

© MOON PUBLICATIONS, INC.

ment. 1216 New Rd., tel. (02) 233-1406, fax (02) 237-1102, 800-1,200B.

Swissotel: Formerly the Swiss Guesthouse under the direction of Andy Ponnaz, this recently renovated and reconstructed Swiss-managed hotel has 57 air-conditioned rooms with all the amenities. Good location, with swimming pool and restaurant. 3 Convent Rd., tel. (02) 233-5345, fax (02) 236-9425, 3,200-3,800B.

Siam Square—Moderate

This centrally located neighborhood, named after the Siam Square Shopping Center on Rama I, is the city's premier shopping district and home to several of Bangkok's most exclusive hotels. The 62-story World Trade Center and several new hotels have brought fresh energy to this otherwise neglected neighborhood. All of the inexpensive hostels and hotels are situated opposite the National Stadium on Rama I Road.

The Bed and Breakfast Guesthouse: A small and absolutely spotless guesthouse. All rooms are a/c with hot showers and telephone. Continental breakfast is included. Recommended. 36/42 Soi Kasemsan 1, Rama I Rd., tel. (02) 215-3004, fax (02) 215-2493, 400-550B.

A-One Inn: Another new and very clean guesthouse with friendly management and quiet location down Soi Kasemsan 1. All rooms are a/c with private bath and telephone. Very safe since "my husband is the police man and stay at A-One along the time." Excellent value. 25/13 Soi Kasemsan 1, Rama I Rd., tel. (02) 215-3029, fax (02) 216-4771, 450-600B.

Muangphol Lodging Department: Somewhat ragged but recommended if the Bed and Breakfast or A-One Inn is filled. All rooms are air-conditioned. 931 Rama I, tel. (02) 215-3056, 450-550B.

Pranee Building: An older hotel operated by a motorcycle collector; check his fine collection of Triumphs. Inexpensive monthly rentals. 931/12 Soi Kasemsan 1, tel. (02) 280-3181, 350-500B.

Krit Thai Mansion: This clean and modern hotel is entered through the lobby restaurant and coffee shop. Easy to find since it faces Rama I Road. 931 Rama I, tel. (02) 215-3042, 900-1,200B.

Sukumvit—Moderate

Thailand's longest road (it stretches all the way to Cambodia!) is quickly becoming the tourist cen-

ter of Bangkok. The neighborhood is very distant from Bangkok's temples, but it's less hectic than Silom Road and the middle-priced hotels which line the road from Soi 1 to Soi 63 are exceptionally good value. Sukumvit also offers great sidewalk shopping between Soi 3 and Soi 11, dozens of outstanding and modestly priced restaurants, English pubs, great bookstores, countless shoe merchants and tailor shops, discount travel agencies, and a nightlife scene second only to Patpong's.

Miami Hotel: An old hotel with dozens of decent rooms overlooking the courtyard swimming pool. Fan rooms are very basic, but all a/c rooms include TV, private bath, and maid service. One of the most popular cheapies on Sukumvit Road. Reservations can be made from the hotel counter at the Bangkok airport. Soi 13, tel. (02) 253-0369, fax (02) 253-1266, 200-650B.

Crown Hotel: Another old hotel constructed for the American GI trade in the 1960s. Very funky, but the small pool provides a refreshing dip in the hot afternoon. All rooms are a/c; a longtime favorite with many visitors. Soi 29, tel. (02) 258-4438, 450-650B.

Uncle Rey's Guesthouse: A clean but cramped high-rise with small, fully furnished a/c rooms with private bath and hot showers. Tucked away in an alley opposite the Nana Hotel. No pool, no yard. Soi 4, tel. (02) 252-5565, 400-550B.

Happy Inn: A small and very simple hotel with clean rooms and a good location near the nightlife and shopping centers. Soi 4, tel. (02) 252-6508, 500-600B.

Atlanta Hotel: An old travelers' favorite that hangs on with a minimum of maintenance. The dreary lobby is compensated for with fairly clean rooms, a cheery little cafe, and a surprisingly good pool in the backyard. Proprietor Dr. Charles Henn, son of the German immigrant who founded

---

SUKUMVIT ROAD BUSES

1AC	Chinatown, Wat Po
2	Banglampoo
8AC	Siam Square, Grand Palace
11AC	Banglampoo, National Museum
13AC	Northern Bus Terminal, Airport

SUKUMVIT

DUTY FREE

IMPERIAL HOTEL

WIRELESS RD.

NEW PETCHABURI RD.

BURMRUNGRAD HOSPITAL

SOI 1

RUAM RUDI RD.

WORLD FELLOWSHIP OF BUDDHISTS ★

NANA INN

SOI 2

SOI 3

AKBAR REST.

GRACE HOTEL

GOLDEN GATE HOTEL

SAHARA HOTEL

NANA HOTEL

RAJAH HOTEL

NANA PLAZA ★

DYNASTY INN

POST OFFICE

SOI 5

BOULEVARD HOTEL

GREEN ROUTE

EXPRESSWAY

ATLANTA HOTEL

HAPPY INN

SOI 4

UNCLE REY'S GH

SOI 7

PARK HOTEL

WHITE INN

LANDMARK HOTEL

MAXIM'S INN

FEDERAL HOTEL

MANDALAY REST.

SOI 9

SOOKSWASDI GH

MOGHUL ROOM

WORLD INN

SOI 11

SWISS PARK INN

MERMAID'S REST.

AMBASSADOR HOTEL & FOOD CENTER

PRESIDENT INN

LE BANYAN REST.

SOI 13

MIAMI HOTEL

THERMAE COFFEE SHOP

SOI 8

D.K. BOOKS

SOI 15

YONG LEE CAFE

MANHATTAN HOTEL

GREEN ROUTE

CONSORT INN

SOI 12

ASIA BOOKS

TO NEW PETCHBURI RD.

CABBAGES & CONDOMS REST.

TIMES SQUARE SHOPPING CENTER

SOI 17

SOI 19

SINGHA BIER HAUS

SOI ASOKE

SOI 10

ROBINSON'S DEPT. STORE

NONG KEE REST.

QUALITY INN

LEE DALAT REST.

SIAM SOCIETY ★

0   100m

SOI 14

SOI 21

KAMTHIENG HOUSE

CUE REST.

SOI COWBOY

RUEN PAK REST.

THONG U RAI RESTAURANT

SEAFOOD MARKET REST.

POST OFFICE

WANAKARM RESTAURANT

TO RAMA IV RD.

RAJADPISEK RD.

SOI 16

SOI 18

SOI 23

PUENG KAEW REST.

BISTANGO REST.

SEPTEMBER REST.

SOI 25

SOI 27

GREEN TAMARIND REST.

TOLLGATE REST.

WINDSOR HOTEL

SOI 20

CROWN HOTEL

DJIT POCHANA REST.

BEI OTTO REST.

SOI 29

REGENCY PARK HOTEL

SOI 22

WASHINGTON SQUARE ★

SOI 31

GREEN ROUTE

THAILAND

© MOON PUBLICATIONS, INC.

the Atlanta in 1952, is now renovating the property with attention to the increasingly rare '50s decor. The cheapest hotel in the Sukumvit neighborhood. Soi 2, tel. (02) 252-1650, 150-600B.

White Inn: A beautiful and unique lodge decorated in an olde English-Tudor style with a/c rooms, swimming pool, and sun terrace. Highly recommended. Soi 4, tel. (02) 252-7090, 650-900B.

Dynasty Inn: Fine little place with comfy cocktail lounge, CNN on the cable TV, and very clean a/c rooms. Excellent location just opposite the Nana Hotel; often filled by noontime. Soi 4, tel. (02) 250-1397, fax (02) 252-9930, 800-900B.

Nana Hotel: A big hotel with all the standard facilities such as nightclubs and restaurants. Recently refurbished a/c rooms include private bath, TV, and refrigerator. The Nana is conveniently located within easy walking distance of the nightlife and shopping districts; one of the better middle-priced spreads on Sukumvit. Recommended for visitors who want a big hotel at a decent price. Soi 4, tel. (02) 252-0121, 850-1,000B.

Golden Gate Hotel: A basic but clean hotel with a/c rooms, TV, massage parlor, and 24-hour coffee shop. Soi 2, tel. (02) 251-5354, 800-900B.

Maxim's Inn: Sukumvit in recent years has added a dozen small hotels in the *sois* near the Ambassador Hotel, especially between Sois 9 and 13. All are clean and comfortable, but Maxim's is more luxurious and has a better location at the end of a short alley. If filled, check the adjacent World Inn; same price range. Soi 9, tel. (02) 252-9911, fax (02) 253-5329, 900-1,200B.

President Inn: Several new, small inns are in the short alleys near Soi 11. Most were constructed in the early 1990s, so the rooms and lobbies remain in good condition. Choices include the President Inn, the Business Inn, the Bangkok Inn (German management), the Comfort Inn, and the Swiss Park Inn. All charge 800-1,200B for clean a/c rooms furnished with color TV, telephone, and mini refrigerator. Soi 11, tel. (02) 255-4230, fax (02) 255-4235, 800B-1,200B.

RESTAURANTS

Banglampoo

Al-fresco dining along Khao San Road is a pleasant way to meet other travelers and exchange information, though none of the cafes will win any awards for great cuisine or elaborate atmosphere. Banglampoo's other problem, besides the mediocre food, is the presence of noisy video cafes that ruin good conversation and turn otherwise colorful people into boob-tube junkies. A pleasant escape, but hardly a reason to visit Asia! The solution to this disturbing problem is to patronize those restaurants that are video-free.

Buddy Cafe: One of the more elegant cafes on Khao San Rd. is tucked away behind the Buddy Guesthouse. The Thai food is bland but safe, a good introduction for first-time visitors fearful of chilies. The upstairs restaurant provides a pleasant escape from the mayhem of Khao San Road. Inexpensive.

Thai Cafes: Several unpretentious cafes around the corner from Khao San on Chakrabongse Rd. offer a good selection of unusual dishes. Best in the morning when the food is freshest. Very inexpensive.

Night Foodstalls: Authentic Thai food is found nightly in the foodstalls at the west end of Khao San Rd. and a few blocks north toward the New World Shopping Center. Inexpensive.

New World Shopping Center: Nearly every shopping center in Thailand has a food complex on its top floor. Prices are rock bottom, the quality is generally good, and the service is instantaneous since most are self-service foodstalls. Inexpensive.

Krai Si: Small, clean, and very chilly restaurant with Japanese sushi, sashimi, tempura, and Western specialties. Look for the sidewalk sushi man. Moderate.

Royal Hotel Coffee Shop: Travelers in Banglampoo will find this the closest restaurant in which to escape the searing heat. An excellent place to relax in the morning, enjoy a good cup of coffee, and read the *Bangkok Post*. Moderate.

Wang Nar: Located underneath the Thonburi Bridge, this riverside restaurant is an outstanding spot for authentic, reasonably priced Thai food. Patrons can sit outdoors on the deck or inside the a/c restaurant to the rear. Super atmosphere. 17 Chao Fa Road. Moderate.

Yok Yor: Also on the banks of the Chao Praya, Yok Yor serves Thai, Chinese, and Japanese dishes in a rather wild atmosphere: waitresses are dressed in sailor outfits and passengers disembarking from the river taxi saunter right through the restaurant! Try *hoh mok,* duck

THAILAND

FOOD AND DRINK

Whether enjoyed in a first-class restaurant or from a simple streetside stall, the cuisine of Thailand is unquestionably one of the great culinary treats of the East. Thai food—a hot and spicy spectrum of exotic flavors—takes its roots from the best of neighboring countries: smooth coconut creams from Malaysia, rich peanut sauces from Indonesia, fiery curries from India, sweet-and-sour sauces from China. Thai cuisine derives its essential character from local ingredients such as coconut milk, lemon grass, tamarind, ginger, coriander, basil, and peanuts blended together with the ubiquitous and intimidating chili. Adorning nearly all dishes to some degree, Thai chilies vary in pungency in inverse proportion to their size. The tiny ones called *prik kee noo* (ratshit peppers) are treated with respect even by the Thais. On the other hand, the large green and yellow *Capsicum annum* are noticeably less aggressive. To survive the heat, remember that even the hottest of chilies lose much of their fierce flavor when safely cocooned in a mouthful of rice. When in doubt, do as the Thais do—eat more rice.

Ordering a meal outside a tourist venue can, at times, be difficult, since few restaurants offer English-scripted menus or have English-speaking waiters. The best solution is to indicate a dish being served to other Thai patrons, or wander in the kitchen, peer in the pots, and point to whatever looks promising. Westerners who find chopsticks the major challenge of Eastern dining will happily note that Thais—being an immensely practical people—eat with forks and spoons, the spoon being the main implement rather than the fork. Tables are generally set with a variety of condiments: fermented fish sauce made from anchovies or shrimp paste called *nam pla*, a hot, pungent sauce known as *nam prik*, and a vinegar-green chili extract called *nam som*. Tamarind sauces and cucumbers fried in coconut oil are other popular accompaniments.

The perfect complement to a Thai dinner is an ice-cold bottle of either Singha or Kloster, light, smooth, and tasty beers brewed according to German recipes. Two spirits to approach with extreme caution are Mekong and Kwang Tong, 70-proof molasses-based spirits that pack an abnormal, almost psychotropic wallop—the tequila of Thailand. Moonshine whiskey is popular since distillers can easily undercut by five times the price of heavily taxed legal whiskey. It's said that only two households in each village don't make moonshine: the government's excise office and the Buddhist *wat*.

A THAI MENU

Meat, Chicken, and Fish
gai: chicken
mu: pork
nua: beef
pet: duck
kung: prawns
pla: fish

Cooking Methods, Condiments, and Sauces
pat: fried
yang: barbecued or roasted
nam pla: fish sauce
nam prik: red spicy sauce
nam som: vinegar with chili sauce
nam buay wan: sweet plum sauce
nam yam hai: oyster sauce
nam king: ginger sauce
nam preo wan: sweet-and-sour sauce

Soups
tom kha kai: a rich chicken-and-coconut-milk soup flavored with lemon grass, lime leaves, galangal, and shallots. Thailand's greatest soup is served throughout the country.
tom yam: a hot-and-sour broth prepared with lemon grass, lime leaves, and chili. Called *tom yam kung* with shrimp and *tom yam kai* with chicken. Almost as good as *tom kha kai*.
kow tom: thick rice soup
kow tom pla: thick rice soup served with fish
kow tom mu: thick rice soup served with pork
kow tom kung: thick rice soup served with prawns
kang chut: a mild flavored soup with vegetables and pork
kang liang: a spicy soup with shrimp, vegetables, basil, and pepper

Rice Dishes
kow pat: fried rice
kow pat kai: fried rice with chicken
kow pat mu: fried rice with pork
kow pat kung: fried rice with shrimp
kow na: steamed rice

THAILAND

kow na kai: steamed rice with sliced chicken
kow na pet: steamed rice with roast duck

Noodle Dishes
kuay teow: wide rice noodles
kuay teow ratna: rice noodles in a meat gravy
kuay teow hang: rice noodles with meat and vegetable served without the meat gravy
kuay teow pat thai: rice noodles fried Thai style
bah mee: wide yellow wheat and egg noodles
bah mee ratna: wheat noodles in meat gravy
bah mee hang: wheat noodles with meat and vegetable served without the meat gravy

Curry Dishes
kang pet: spicy curry made from sweet coconut milk flavored with lemon grass, chilies, and shrimp paste. Served with either pork, chicken, beef, fish, or prawns. Perhaps the most popular dish in Thailand.
kang matsaman: a milder version of Muslim curry laced with beef, potato, onion, coconut milk, and peanut
kang wan: Green curry thickened with coconut milk, eggplant, sweet basil, and lime leaves. Be careful with this one.
kang kari: Yellow curry with tumeric; a mild version of an Indian curry
kang baa: Thailand's hottest curry—for veteran fire-eaters only

Salads
yam: salad
yam nua: beef salad with mint, basil, spring onion, garlic, and chili
yam het: mushroom salad
yam mamuang: green mango salad
yam tang kwa: cucumber salad

yam hoi: cockle salad

Drinks
nam plao: plain water
nam tom: boiled water
nam cha: tea
nam manao: iced lime juice
nam som khan: fresh orange juice
nom: milk
coffee ron: hot coffee with milk
coffee yen: iced coffee with milk
o liang: iced black coffee with sugar
Mekong: Thai whiskey distilled from grains and molasses
sang som: rum liquor made from sugarcane
lao kao: rice liquor, locally produced

Sidewalk Snacks and Desserts
satay: barbecued skewers of meat served with peanut sauce and cucumbers in vinegar and sugar
sang kaya: custard made from coconut milk, sugar, and eggs
chow kway: black-grass pudding shredded and mixed with a sugar syrup over ice
boh bok: green-grass drink made from crushed vines and sugar water. Bitter.
roti sai mai: small flat pancakes with strands of green or pink spun sugar wrapped inside
kanom buang: miniature tacos. Made from batter poured on a hot griddle and then folded over and filled with shredded coconut, egg yolk, and green onions.
tong krob: golden yellow balls made from egg yolks and rice flour, then dusted with sugar
kao glab pat maw: thin crepe filled with fried shrimp, pork, peanuts, sugar, coconut, and even fish sauce. Delicious.

curry, and *noi na* ice cream for dessert. Yok Yor is on Wisut Kaset Rd., down from the National Bank, a very pleasant 30-minute walk through back alleys which skirt the river. Moderate.

Maria Restaurant: Rajadamnern Avenue serves as an administrative center during the day, as restaurant row in the evening. Scattered along the broad avenue are a half-dozen moderately priced restaurants popular with Thai civil servants and businesspeople. Maria's is a large a/c place with both Chinese and Thai specialties. Rajadamnern Avenue. Moderate.

Kanit's: Both French specialties and Italian pizzas are served in elegant surroundings. Considered the best European restaurant in this section of town. Owned by a friendly Thai lady and her German husband. 68 Ti Thong Rd., near the Giant Swing and Wat Suthat. Moderate to expensive.

Malaysia Hotel Area
Blue Fox: A crazy scene of slightly bent Thais and travelers escaping the searing heat. Good Western food but the Thai dishes are bland and monotonous. Inexpensive.

THAILAND

streetside delights

Foodstalls: A large collection of tasty, authentic, and inexpensive Thai foodstalls is located just across Rama IV near the Lumpini Boxing Stadium. Point to a neighbor's dish or look inside the pots. Great atmosphere. Inexpensive.

Silom Road

Serious gourmets should purchase the *Bangkok Restaurant Guide* published by Asia Books. Although somewhat dated (the first and final edition was published in 1988), the maps and descriptions of dishes are immensely helpful.

Patpong Restaurants: Almost a dozen excellent restaurants are on Patpong Road. Expatriates gather on Sunday evenings in the English pub at Bobby's Arms for a round of draft and Dixieland music. Trattoria d'Roberto is known for its Italian specialties such as veal dishes and chocolate desserts. The Australian Club is a comfortable a/c lounge with imported beers from Down Under, plus helpful literature on local nightlife spots. Dating from the days of the

Vietnam War, the venerable Thai Room remains an expat/Peace Corps hangout that serves Thai-Mex and Italian specialties. Most Patpong restaurants are open until midnight. Moderate.

Charuvan Duck Shop: Around the corner from Patpong is an old travelers' favorite with, what else, duck specialties over rice and inexpensive curries. An a/c room is behind the open-air cafe. 70 Silom Road. Inexpensive.

Himali Cha Cha: The long-running Himali Cha Cha, located up a small alley off New Rd. near the GPO, is known for its tasty curries, *kormas*, fruit-flavored *lassis*, tandoori-baked breads, and North Indian specialties served in an informal setting. Cha Cha, owner and head chef at Himali's, was once Nehru's private chef. 1229 New Rd., tel. (02) 235-1569. Moderate.

Simla Cafe: The less expensive Simla Cafe, off Silom Rd. in a small alley behind the Victory Hotel, is another popular choice for Indian and Pakistani dishes. 382 Soi Tat Mai, tel. (02) 234-6225. Inexpensive.

Budget Indian Cafes: Cheap open-air Muslim cafes on New Rd. serve delicious *murtabaks* and *parathas,* but noxious fumes blowing in from the road could kill you. A filling lunch or dinner costs under 50B per person. Indian street vendors sometimes gather opposite the Narai Hotel near the small Hindu temple. The Chandni, on the second floor at 422 Surawong Rd. next to the Manohra Hotel, has great food served under a video screen blasting out wild Hindu films. Madras Cafe in the Madras Lodge is also recommended for its authentic atmosphere and South Indian specialties. Perhaps the best choice for excellent Indian and Malay food at rock-bottom prices is the Sallim Restaurant, adjacent to the Woodlands Hotel near the GPO. Inexpensive.

Robinson's Department Store: For a quick bite at bargain prices, try the Dairy Queen on the main floor. A well-stocked grocery store is located downstairs. Silom Center, Silom at Rama IV roads. Inexpensive.

Once Upon A Time: A wonderful romantic restaurant with outdoor dining under little twinkling lights. Nicely located in a quiet back alley, but within walking distance of most hotels. Decho Rd., Soi 1. Moderate to expensive.

All Gaengs: Unlike most Thai restaurants, All Gaengs has been stylishly decorated with art-deco touches and a shiny baby grand piano.

Along with the jazz, enjoy shrimp curry, *yam* dishes, and *nuea daed dio*, a beef dish served with a spicy dipping sauce. Surawong Road. Moderate.

Siam Square

Many of the best restaurants in this neighborhood are located in luxury hotels or the a/c shopping centers of Siam Square, Siam Center, and Peninsula Plaza.

Tokyu Food Centre: Shopping centers are your best bets for quick, inexpensive Thai and Western dishes. Tokyu Department Store, at the intersection of Rama I and Phyathai roads, features a roomy, a/c, sixth-floor dining emporium with dozens of great foodstalls.

Coca Garden Noodles: A colossal, noisy restaurant packed with Chinese families and groups of hungry teenagers. Serves a wide variety of inexpensive noodle dishes, along with chicken, fish, and seafood specialties. 461 Henri Dunant Rd. at the southeast corner of Siam Square Shopping Center, tel. (02) 251-6337. Moderate.

Blue Moon and Moon Shadow: In the short alley adjacent to the Meridien Hotel are two small cafe-clubs modeled after American Western saloons. The Blue Moon bar features some of the best jazz and R&B combos in Thailand, while the downstairs Western cafe specializes in seafood entrees. Try the *pla krai* in green chili curry. 145 Gaysorn Rd., tel. (02) 253-7552. Moderate.

Old West Saloon: A mini nightlife and restaurant scene has sprung up in recent years along Soi Sarasin, south of Siam Shopping Center near Lumpini Park. Old West, one of the oldest Western clubs in Bangkok, features Thai-cowboy grub and live country music behind the swinging saloon doors. 231 Soi Sarasin, tel. (02) 252-9510. Inexpensive.

Whole Earth Restaurant: Outstanding if slightly expensive vegetarian and Thai specialties accompanied by classical guitar or folk music. 933 Soi Languan, Ploenchit Road. Moderate.

Sukumvit

Ambassador Food Center: Over 50 fast-food-stalls serve up Thai, Japanese, and Western dishes at reasonable prices. This is a great place to look at and learn about Thai dishes and begin your food crawl in the Sukumvit neigh-

borhood. Most dishes cost under 30B, and you pay by coupon. The streetside Bangkapi Terrace is a good place to escape the midday heat and enjoy a very cheap luncheon buffet. Soi 11. Inexpensive.

Cabbages and Condoms: Owned and operated by Mechai Viravaudya, "Condom King" and former director of the national birth-control center (next door), this curiously named place offers excellent food in a/c comfort plus some truly strange items at the front desk . . . condom keychains and T-shirts you won't find back home! Highly recommended. Soi 12, tel. (02) 252-7349. Moderate.

Yong Lee Restaurant: A very funky cafe popular with budget travelers and local *farangs* who rave about the Thai and Chinese specialties. Soi 15. Inexpensive.

Thong Lee Restaurant: A very popular and simple shophouse with good food at low prices. Try the *muu phad kapi* (spicy pork in shrimp paste) and the *yam hed sot* (fiery mushroom salad). Soi 20. Inexpensive.

Night Foodstalls: Some of the best food in Bangkok is found in the foodstalls along Sukumvit Road. Many of the dishes are precooked and displayed in covered pots. Also try *som tam*, a spicy salad made from shredded raw papaya and palm sugar, fried chicken with sticky rice, and *pad thai*, saut—ed bean sprouts with chicken and peanuts. Delicious! Foodstalls are near the Grace Hotel, the infamously seedy Thermae Coffee Shop, both ends of Soi Cowboy, Washington Square nightlife center, and on Sukumvit at Soi 38. Wonderful food and a great way to mix with the locals.

Lemongrass Restaurant: Embellished with antiques in both the interior dining room and exterior courtyard, Lemongrass offers atmosphere and regional dishes from all parts of Thailand. Try the hot fish curry, barbecued chicken, *larb pla duk yang* (smoked catfish in northeastern style), and *nam takrai*, a cool and sweetish drink brewed from lemongrass. Soi 24 near the Calypso Cabaret, tel. (02) 258-8637. Moderate.

Seafood Market Restaurant: This *very* upscale seafood restaurant is worth taking a look at, even if the prices can cause heart failure. Don't miss the enormous Phuket lobsters and giant prawns. Soi 16 at Soi Asoke, tel. (02) 258-0218. Expensive.

THAILAND

Soi 23 Restaurants: Almost a dozen popular restaurants are down Soi 23, a few blocks off Sukumvit Road. Ruen Pak is an excellent-value cafe located in a renovated wooden house. Best bets include Thong U Rai with live music, Cue for French cuisine, Le Dalat Vietnamese restaurant, Wanakarm Restaurant with traditional dishes in a/c dining rooms, Pueng Kaew's experimental Thai-Western dishes, September for art-deco 1930s atmosphere, Bistango steak house, and Black Scene with live jazz. An excellent place to wander and snack in the late evening.

Djit Pochana: One of the most successful restaurant chains in Thailand has three outlets in Bangkok that serve authentic Thai dishes without compromise to Western palates. Try their excellent-value luncheon buffet. Soi 20, tel. (02) 258-1605. Moderate.

Robinson's Department Store: Cheap eats are available in this pricey emporium from McDonald's on the main floor and a downstairs Food Court with several self-service cafes that serve Thai and Japanese dishes. Sukumvit Soi 19.

Green Route Restaurants: Many of Bangkok's finest restaurants are on the so-called Green Route, a street which runs between Sois 39 and 63, midway between Sukumvit and New Phetburi roads. Try Gourmet Gallery at Soi 49, the Library at Soi 49, Laicram at Soi 49, or Piman on Soi 49. All provide expensive but elegant dining experiences.

Soi 55 Restaurants: Another concentration of fine restaurants is on Soi 55 (Soi Thonglor) between Sukumvit and the Green Route. Favorites include the Art House in a lovely country house, funky Barley House with nightly jazz, L'Hexagone French restaurant, simple Sanuk Nuek, and an English pub called the Witch's Tavern.

Tum Nak Thai: According to the *Guinness Book of World Records,* Tum Nak Thai is the world's largest restaurant: 10 acres of land, a capacity of 3,000 seats, over 100 professional chefs, and 1,000 servers decked out in national costumes. Some waiters use roller skates to speed up service! A classical dance show is given nightly at 2000. Take a taxi from your hotel. 131 Ratchadapisek Rd., tel. (02) 277-8833. Moderate.

CULTURAL ENTERTAINMENT

Thai Dance

Lak Muang Shrine: Amateurish but authentic *likay* is sponsored around the clock by various donors; have a quick look after touring the Grand Palace.

Erawan Hotel Shrine: The famous pillar in the courtyard of the Grand Hyatt Erawan is among the more intriguing scenes in Bangkok. No matter the hour, a steady stream of devotees arrives to offer flowers, wooden elephants, and hire the somewhat unenthusiastic dancers. Most active in the early evening and just before the weekly lottery.

Center of Traditional Performing Arts: Outstanding performances of Thai dance, drama, and traditional music are given each Friday at 1700 on the fourth floor of the Bangkok Bank, Parn Fah Branch, just off Rajadamnern in the Banglampoo district. The room is dull but the performances are quite good—so good, in fact, that shows are always packed; arrive an hour early or expect to stand in the back. Upcoming performances are listed on the noticeboard in the TAT office.

National Theater: Thai classical dance performances are given at the National Theater's outdoor stage at irregular intervals between November and May. Sunday afternoons are the most likely times to find performances. Check the *Bangkok Post* or the noticeboard at the TAT office, or just walk by and see if a crowd is gathering. Shows are free but it helps to bring a blanket and claim a spot in the early afternoon. Full-length *khon* performances are given several times yearly by the Fine Arts Department inside the theater, an expensive but unforgettable spectacle.

Dinner/Dance Shows

First-time visitors who wish to sample an overview of Thai dance can attend performances in almost a dozen a/c Thai restaurants. Brief demonstrations of *khon, lakhon,* and *likay* folk dancing, Thai martial arts, puppetry, and sword-fighting follow a northern Thai *khon toke*-style dinner. Prices range from 250B to 500B; transportation is often included. Performance times and prices can be double-checked by calling

PERFORMING ARTS

Khon

The glory of Thai classic theater is the *khon,* a stunning spectacle of warriors, demons, and monkeys who perform acrobatics and highly stylized movements while wrapped in brilliant costumes. *Khon* has its roots in court-sponsored ballets which thrived under royal patronage until the military revolution of 1932 ended Thailand's absolute monarchy. Accompanied by the surrealistic sounds of the Thai *pipat* orchestra, the *khon* typically takes its storyline from either the Javanese Inao legend or the Indian Ramayana, called the Ramakien ("Glory of Rama") in Thailand. Actors and actresses never speak but rather mime narration provided by professional troubadours and choruses. Originally a masked drama, modern *khon* has unmasked heroes and celestial beings, though demons and monkeys continue to wear bizarre head coverings. *Khon* is also an endangered artform, the only remaining venue in Thailand being Bangkok's National Theater. Performances are sponsored several times yearly—an superb theatrical experience not to be missed.

Lakhon

While *khon* is male-oriented and relies on virtuosity in strength and muscular exertion, the courtly *lakhon* impresses its audience with feminine grace and elegant fluidity. *Lakhon* presents episodes from the Ramakien, Manora folktales of southern Thailand, and Lakhon Jatri, itinerant folk dances used to exorcise evil spirits. Lakhon is traditionally accompanied by a chorus and lead singers instead of *khon*-style recitation, though these distinctions are no longer strictly followed. The costumes of elaborately embroidered cloth and glittering ornaments surpass the brilliance of even the *khon.* Unlike the *khon,* actresses are unencumbered by masks, allowing them to combine singing and dialogue with their dance postures. Highly refined body gestures display a complex encyclopedia of movements, while emotion is conveyed by the demure dartings of the eyes and highly stylized, very specific movements of the hands. The dance itself lacks the dramatic leaps and whirling pirouettes of Western ballet—the feet are kept firmly planted on the stage—but a great deal of dramatic tension and sensuality are achieved by the movement of the upper torso. *Khon* and *lakhon* are often combined into grand shows for the benefit of both visitors and Thais.

Likay

If *khon* and *lakhon* are classical art, then *likay* is slapstick comedy performed for the masses. The obvious lack of deep artistic talent is made up for with unabashed exuberance and a strong sense of earthiness. As a form of people's theater performed at most provincial fairs, *likay* relies heavily on predictable plots, outrageous double entendres, and lowball comedy. Performers interact directly with the audience, which responds with raucous laughter at their political sarcasms and sexual innuendo. Costumes worn by the untalented but enthusiastic actors run from gaudy jewelry to heavy makeup. It is ironic that television, the universal destroyer of traditional theater, has actually helped keep *likay* alive with daily performances of soap-opera sophistication.

Thai Puppetry

A third type of court drama is the *nang,* or shadow play, which enjoyed great popularity during the

(continues on next page)

Thai dancers

THAILAND

PERFORMING ARTS

(continued)

reign of King Mongkut. Thai puppetry is occasionally performed in three versions at dinner dance shows.

Nang Yai: This form of puppetry uses larger than life-sized leather puppets painted with vegetable dyes for daytime performances and left translucent for nighttime shows. Oxhide figures are manipulated in front of the screen by puppeteers and illuminated by candles that cast eerie colored shadows. Examples of this vanished art are displayed in the *wayang* room of the National Museum.

Nang Talung: This variation, closely related to the *wayang kulit* of Indonesia, uses smaller and more maneuverable puppets. Still popular in southern Thailand where performances are occasionally given during temple festivals.

Hun Krabok: This version, a vanished art, uses rod puppets similar to Chinese stick puppets. Puppets are still created by the famous Thai painter, Chakrabhand Posayahrit.

Popular Dance

Fawn Lep: Ladies from the north of Thailand perform classical movements while wearing long artificial fingernails.

Ram Wong: A slow and graceful dance that cleverly fuses traditional *lakhon* hand movements with Western dance steps. Performed at most informal gatherings and *very* popular after a few shots of Mekong whiskey! Westerners who try the *ram wong* always appear incredibly clumsy, although their comical efforts are appreciated by the gracious Thais.

Sword Fighting—*Krabi Krabong*

Originally devised by warriors to practice combat techniques, sword fighting is only performed today in conjunction with a dinner-dance show. A complete cycle begins with sharpened swords and then moves through combat with poles, knives, and finally hand-to-hand combat. Real swords give the fighters deadly potential in this skillful and exciting sport.

Traditional Music

Backing up the *khon, lakhon,* and *likay* is the music of the *pipat,* Thailand's strange but captivating orchestra. Most Westerners find the surrealistic flavor of Thai music difficult to appreciate, as it seems to lack harmony or melody. Traditional Thai music is based on a five-tone diatonic scale with neither major nor minor keys—more closely related to medieval Christian music or the abstract compositions of Ravel than conventional Western compositions. Similar to Javanese and Balinese *gamelan,* the Thai percussive orchestra is composed of five to 15 instruments such as drums, xylophones, gongs, metallophones, woodwinds, strings, and flutes. Musical passages indicate specific actions and emotions (marching, weeping, anger) that are immediately recognized by the dancers. Thai music is abstract, highly syncopated, and emotionally charged, but delightfully moving with repeated hearings.

the restaurant or inquiring with the TAT. Some find these highly abbreviated performances artificial and unsatisfying, but the glittering costumes and elegant dance styles are most impressive.

Baan Thai: Like most Thai restaurants with dance performances, Baan Thai recreates a traditional Thai house with polished teakwood floors, elegant furnishings, and tropical gardens. Nightly shows from 1900. 7 Sukumvit Soi 32, tel. 258-5403.

Piman: One of Bangkok's more elegant and expensive shows takes place inside this beautiful reproduction of a Sukothai-era house. Admission 500B. 46 Sukumvit Soi 49, tel. 258-7866.

Chao Praya Restaurant: Travelers staying in the guesthouses of Banglampoo often attend the cultural show across the Pinklau Bridge in Thonburi. Packages sold by travel agents include transportation, dinner, show, and possibly a cocktail in the adjacent Paradise Music Hall.

Hotel Shows: Dance performances are also given in the Sukothai Restaurant of the Dusit Thani Hotel and in the Sala Thai on the rooftop of the Indra Regent.

Oriental Hotel Photo Show: Photographers will enjoy the Kodak Siam Show given at poolside every Sunday and Thursday between 1100 and 1200; admission 100B.

THAILAND

Thai Kick Boxing

Thai boxing is the street fighter's dream of Western boxing mixed with karate and a bit of *tae kwon do.* Barefoot pugilists prior to WW II wrapped their hands in hemp mixed with ground glass and the fight went on for as long as anyone could stand . . . or had any blood left. Today the boxers wear lightly padded gloves and a few rules have been introduced to control the carnage.

Thai kick boxing can be experienced at the Lumpini Stadium on Rama IV Road (near the Malaysia Hotel) every Tuesday, Friday, and Saturday at 1800 and at 1330 on Saturdays. Superior boxers meet at Rajadamnern Stadium (near the TAT office) every Monday, Wednesday, and Thursday at 1800, and on Sundays at 1700 and 2000. Admission is 80-400B. Thai boxing goes center stage on TV every Sunday afternoon.

NIGHTLIFE

Bangkok's nightlife is perhaps the most notorious in the world. Bars, brothels, live sex shows, massage parlors, gay nightclubs, roving transvestites, sex cabarets, all-night coffee shops, child prostitutes, and barber shops that provide more than just haircuts—the range of sexual services is simply amazing. Bangkok alone has an estimated 500,000 prostitutes, and it's said that almost one-third of all visitors to Thailand come for sex. Despite AIDS, local opposition, and the conservative moral attitudes of the Thai people (the vast majority are incredibly puritanical), Thailand's roaring sex industry seems destined to remain a major attraction well into the next millenium.

Patpong

Bangkok's most notorious red-light district is located on Patpong 1 and 2 between Silom and Surawong roads. Once owned by the Patpong family and made popular by American soldiers on leave from Vietnam, this infamous collection of go-go bars, cocktail lounges, live shows, street vendors, pushy touts, and pre-teen hustlers forms a scene straight from Dante's *Inferno.* Less intense bars are located in the Sukumvit district at Washington Square, inside the Nana Entertainment Complex, and along Soi Cowboy, a small lane between Soi 21 and 23.

During the day Patpong is almost deserted except for a pair of excellent bookstores and several cozy pubs which screen the latest videos in a/c comfort. Between 1800 and 2000 the bars spring to life with smaller crowds and happy-hour prices—an excellent time to look around without draining your wallet. From 2000 until around 0100, some 30-50 go-go bars and live-show nightclubs operate at full tilt, packed with both overseas visitors and Thais.

Among the better clubs are King's Castle, Queen's Castle, and the Mississippi Club, where scenes from *The Deer Hunter* were filmed. Patpong also served as Saigon's Tu Do Street for Robin Williams's *Good Morning Vietnam.* On Sundays, the Napoleon Lounge has a music fest of straight-ahead mainstream jazz performed by both Western and Thai artists.

The most irritating sidelights to Patpong are the hordes of overly aggressive barkers who accost Westerners with offers of private shows featuring young girls whose special talents are explicitly listed on calling cards. Very few visitors enjoy these shows, but if you must, be sure to establish the total cover charge and price for drinks *before* going upstairs for the show—misunderstandings are common. Massage parlors and "barber" shops are also found in Patpong, while the gay clubs on Patpong 3 feature transvestites *(gatoeis)* in hilarious follies revues.

Sukumvit

Soi Cowboy: Bangkok's second most active bar area is located off Sukumvit Road between Sois 21 and 23. The area gets its name from a black American nicknamed "Cowboy" who owned one of the first bars on the street. Soi Cowboy is a refreshing change from the hype and hustle of Patpong, more relaxed and low-key with less pressure to spend or buy the girls drinks. Crowds tend to be smaller and made up of locals rather than tourists. Also set with terrific foodstalls and friendly British pubs, Soi Cowboy is the slow and sleazy counterpoint to the flash and glitter of Patpong.

Nana Plaza: Bangkok's newest and liveliest go-go-bar scene features three floors of clubs, cafes, and rock 'n' roll cabarets with outstanding sound systems. Woodstock and Asian Intrigue are the current favorites.

Washington Square: Another low-key

nightlife scene is located on Sukumvit Road between Sois 22 and 24. The mixture of bars, restaurants, foodstalls, and cinemas has a somewhat American atmosphere with names like the Texxan Restaurant and Ex-Pats Retreat. Darts, snooker, videos, and Sunday afternoon barbecues are the main attractions rather than go-go girls and sex shows.

Grace Hotel: A 24-hour coffee shop located on the ground floor of the Grace Hotel and a noisy dive always jammed with freelancers too wild or independent to be employed by any self-respecting bar or nightclub. Four jukeboxes at the four corners play four different tunes simultaneously . . . just too weird.

Massage Parlors: Countless massage parlors, Turkish baths, and steam baths are found throughout Bangkok. Large numbers have cropped up in the last few years on lower Sukumvit and along New Phetburi Road, north of Sukumvit. Filled with numbered ladies patiently waiting in viewing rooms, these giant pleasure palaces are absolutely guaranteed to infuriate Western women.

NIGHTCLUBS AND DISCOS

Discos

Discotheques in Bangkok are absolutely astounding, rivaled in the East only by the clubs of Manila. Cover charges run 60-100B during the week, 120-300B on weekends; a complimentary drink or two (or three) is usually included.

Rome Club: A relatively small but exceedingly hot videotheque frequented by fashionably dressed gays, trendy art-club types, and *gatoeis* who hang out in the upstairs annex until the midnight transvestite revue. Rome Club is located in the gay nightlife district of Patpong 3.

Freakout: Trendy young Thais favor the heterosexual discos and pubs on both sides of Silom Plaza. Dining tables in the plaza provide good people-watching, while adjacent discos such as Virgin and Freakout Supertheque pack in the young crowds. Silom Plaza on Silom Rd., near Thai International Airlines.

NASA Spacedrome: Bangkok's flashiest disco is a multimillion-dollar dance emporium that packs in over 2,000 sweating bodies every weekend. At midnight, a spaceship descends to

THAILAND

LIVE THAI ROCK 'N' ROLL

Unlike those in Manila, most of the clubs in Bangkok feature recorded music rather than live entertainment. The scene, however, has improved with the arrival of *dontree pher cheevit,* a fresh musical force that breaks away from the traditional love themes to raise issues of social injustice. Early efforts at political consciousness by a group named Caravan proved too radical for public airing, but Carabao in the late '80s caused a major sensation with their song "Made in Thailand." The hit both ridiculed Thai obsession with foreign-made goods and inadvertently promoted the government's Buy-Thai program! Other Carabao songs have described the plight of Bangkok's prostitutes and poor rural farmers. Instead of simply plagiarizing Western pop melodies to back up Thai lyrics, Carabao has successfully fused American country rock with traditional Thai music. Remember the 1986 disco hit "One Night in Bangkok"? Banned in Thailand.

the floor amid smoke, flashing lights, and the theme song from *2001: A Space Odyssey.* For sheer spectacle, nothing else compares in Thailand. Ramkamheng Rd., 100 meters north of New Phetburi Rd. in the Bangkapi neighborhood.

The Palace: Perhaps the trendiest of all Bangkok discos, the Palace is frequented by young Thais who hail from the country's wealthiest families. 379 Vipavadee Rangsit Hwy., on the road to the airport.

Paradise Music Hall: Another gigantic dance emporium with the standard amenities of flashing lights, laser videos, and booming disco music. Arun Amarin Rd. in Thonburi, just across the bridge from Banglampoo; a good choice for travelers staying on Khao San Road.

Bars

Bangkok has few bars in the traditional sense, largely because any ordinary restaurant, including the smallest streetside noodle shop, can legally sell beer and other spirits. However, a new breed of nightery has emerged in the early 1990s that caters to foreigners and English-speaking Thais who appreciate tavern ambience.

Soi Sarasin: A very welcome addition to Bangkok's night scene is the collection of intimate nightclubs and cozy restaurants located on Soi Sarasin, just off Rajadamnern Rd. and immediately north of Lumpini Park. Modeled after European bistros with clean decor and sidewalk tables, these clubs appeal to young Westerners and professional Thais rather than the go-go crowd. Best bets include the Brown Sugar, with good jazz, and the Old West Saloon, which re-creates an American Wild West atmosphere.

Soi Lang Suan: Around the corner from Soi Sarasin is another street with a good selection of pubs favored by expats and yuppie Thais. Among the most popular are Round Midnight for jazzophiles and the trendy European-run Vinothek with its extensive wine cellar.

Soi Gaysorn: In the short alley adjacent to the Meridien Hotel (Siam Square area) are two small cafe-clubs modeled after American Western saloons. The Blue Moon bar features some of the best jazz and R&B combos in Thailand, while the downstairs western-style Moon Shadow Cafe specializes in seafood entrees.

Sukumvit Soi 33: Cozy clubs curiously named after European painters are tucked away in a quiet *soi* off Sukumvit Road. All offer happy-hour drink specials and are popular with Western expatriates who live nearby. Try the Vincent Van Gogh or Renoir Club.

SHOPPING

Bangkok enjoys a well-deserved reputation as the Shopping Capital of Asia. Popular products include Thai silks, gemstones, tailor-made suits and dresses, inexpensive shoes, bronzeware, and traditional handicrafts. Imported items such as electronics, watches, cameras, and film are much cheaper in the duty-free ports of Hong Kong or Singapore. Prices are fairly uniform across town, but selection varies between neighborhoods: Chinatown is best for gold chains, Silom Road for silks and antiques, Sukumvit for leather goods and tailors, Siam Square for high fashion and cheap clothing, Banglampoo for handicrafts and tribal artifacts. Anyone seriously interested in shopping should purchase Nancy Chandler's outstanding *Market Map of Bangkok*.

Local Markets

Weekend Market: Among the more fascinating shopping experiences are the simple markets packed with foods, flowers, clothing, and more exotic items. The granddaddy of all Thai flea markets is Chatuchak's monstrous affair out near the airport on Paholyothin Road. Take a bus and watch for the large carnival tent on the left. Open weekends 0900-1800.

Pratunam Market: A sprawling rabbit warren of clothing shops, hygienic foodstalls, vegetable wholesalers, and shoe merchants is located at the intersection of Phetburi and Rajaprarop roads. Open 24 hours; perhaps the single best place in Bangkok to shop for inexpensive clothing. Don't get lost!

Banglampoo Market: Conveniently located near the budget guesthouses on Khao San Road; check the alleys packed with inexpensive clothing and the main floor bargains in the New World Department Store. An inexpensive self-serve cafeteria is on top.

Pak Klong Market: Bangkok's most colorful and smelly vegetable and fruit market hangs over the riverbanks near the Memorial Bridge.

Teves Flower Market: A permanent sidewalk market with plants and (occasionally) flowers flanks a canal one km north of Banglampoo.

Thieves' Market: Touted in many tourist books as an antique shopping district, though the only antiques and thieves are the shopkeepers.

Shopping Tips

Bargaining: Absolutely necessary except in the large department stores. It's challenging and fun— *if* you keep your sense of humor. Haggle with a smile; let the shopkeeper laugh at your ridiculous offer while smiling back at his absurd asking price. Bargaining is a game, not a life-or-death struggle. Expect a discount of 20-30%, not the 50% discount given in some tourist centers such as Bali. As elsewhere in Asia, knowing a few numbers and key phrases will send prices plunging.

Refunds, Receipts, and Guarantees: As a general rule, goods once purchased cannot be exchanged or returned. Deposits are also non-refundable. Carefully examine all merchandise since receipts and guarantees issued by local retailers are of dubious value after you have returned home.

THAILAND

Bangkok silhouette

Touts: Touts are paid commissions for rounding up customers. All expenses, including taxi rides and lunches, are added to your bill. Avoid them.

Fakes: Thailand also enjoys a reputation as the Counterfeit Capital of Asia. Most fakes, such as Lacoste shirts and Cartier watches, are advertised and sold as fakes. More dangerous to your pocketbook are colored glass being peddled as rubies and newly manufactured Buddhas sold as genuine antiques. Experts at Bangkok's National Museum estimate that 90% of the items sold at the city's antique stores are counterfeit! Unless you are an expert or prepared to gamble large sums of money, a sound policy is to shun expensive antiques and simply purchase reproductions.

SERVICES

Tourist Information

The Tourist Authority of Thailand (TAT) at 372 Bamrung Muang Road is well organized and very helpful, but only if you request specific information. Their bulletin board lists upcoming festivals, dance performances, and warnings about safety and rip-offs. Useful publications available from major hotels and the TAT include *Bangkok This Week,* the *Sightseeing and Shopping Map of Bangkok, Thaiways, Pattaya,* and *Where.* The publications department sells large-scale highway maps and souvenir slides.

All TAT offices in the country are open Monday-Saturday 0830-1630. Bus passengers should also pick up *Latest Tour's Guide to Bangkok and Thailand* or *Latest Edition Bangkok Thailand* for current routings. Complaints about unfair business practices can be directed to the Tourist Assistance Center located next door to the TAT office; open daily 0800-midnight.

Bookstores

Bangkok's bookstores are among the finest in Southeast Asia. Best selections are found at Asia Books on Sukumvit Soi 15, D.K. Book House in Siam Square, and Bookseller on Patpong Road. Asia Books in the Galerie Lafayette on Rajadamri Avenue has an exceptional collection of books on Asian art. Used books are sold at Chalermnit Books on Ploenchit near the Grand Hyatt Erawan and in the small bookstore on Soi 24 near the Impala Hotel. The National Library and Chulalongkorn University Library are open to the public, as is the AUA Library on Rajadamri. The Siam Society library on Sukumvit Soi 21 is open to members only.

Visas

Bangkok is a popular place to pick up visas for onward travel. Most embassies accept visa applications from 1000 to 1200 only, and they will often require your passport overnight. Nepalese visas are issued on the spot but must be used within 30 days. Philippine visas should be obtained before arriving to avoid the byzantine procedures at Manila's immigration department. Indonesian entry permits are now granted on arrival, making visas unnecessary for most visitors. The Indian Embassy is a disorganized mess with hordes of impatient people getting their first tastes of Indian bureaucracy. Embassies for Vietnam, Cambodia, and Laos are also located here.

Embassies are spread out all over town and extremely time-consuming to reach. It's *much* easier to let a travel agency obtain your visa.

Communications

Telephone: International telephone calls can be made 24 hours a day, seven days a week from the telecommunications annex next to the General Post Office. Calls to North America and Europe cost about US$10 for the first three minutes. Local phone calls cost 1B at red phones and 3B from private phones in stores and restaurants.

Mail: The General Post Office on New Road is open 0800-2000 Monday-Friday and 0800-1300 on weekends and holidays. The GPO also offers a wrapping service for parcels . . . don't you wish all GPOs in Asia had this? Their poste restante isn't quite as organized as Singapore's, but at least they appear to be keeping track of all those letters.

Newspapers: Thailand's two major English-language papers, the *Bangkok Post* and the *Nation,* are an invaluable source of information on events, festivals, local gossip, international events, and sports back home. The *Bangkok Post* wins my vote for best English-language newspaper in Southeast Asia.

Travel Agents

Bangkok has a wide choice of travel agencies dealing everything from nightclub tours to jungle safaris. Local sightseeing tours can be arranged through most agencies, but major destinations are best purchased from Diethelm Travel (tel. 252-4041) at 544 Ploenchit Road, World Travel (tel. 233-5900) at 1053 Charoen Krung Road, and Sea Tour (tel. 251-4862) in the Siam Center on Rama I Road.

Discount travel agencies located near the guesthouses on Khao San Road and the Malaysia Hotel are excellent sources for cheap flights, visas, discount bus and train travel, and counterfeit student cards. Recommended bucket shops in Banglampoo include Ronny's Tours

and Overland Travel, an honest, courteous, and well-organized outfit. Student Travel Australia adjacent to the Viengtai Hotel is honest and dependable but crowded, slow, and more expensive than other agencies. The STA office (tel. 233-2582) in the Silom district at 33 Surawong Road is faster and less hectic.

Take precautions! Never hand over your money until you have carefully examined your ticket for price, expiration dates, and endorsements. It also helps to check the airline's reservation list before parting with your money.

Other Services

Medical: Excellent medical facilities and English-speaking doctors are available in the Bangkok Christian Hospital at 124 Silom Rd. (near Patpong) and the Bangkok Nursing Home on Convent Road.

Language Instruction: The American University (AUA) at 170 Rajadamri Rd. offers comprehensive group lessons, sells language tapes, has a cheap cafeteria, and operates a public library filled with Western books and magazines. Private language instructors also advertise in the *Bangkok Post.*

Educational Tours: Bangkok's Siam Society sponsors bimonthly group tours to important historical and archaeological sites in Thailand. Led by experts in their fields, these outstanding and reasonably priced tours are highly recommended for all visitors. Also check the Fine Arts Department at Bangkok University and the bulletin board in the National Museum. Unique, free, and personalized tours of Bangkok temples, plus overnight visits to nearby villagers, can be arranged through the Volunteer Guide Group, Box 24-1013, Ramkamheng Rd., Bangkok 10241.

Buddhist Meditation

Increasing numbers of travelers are investigating Buddhism and *vipassana* (insight) meditation during their visits to Thailand. The International Buddhist Meditation Centre (Dhamma Vicaya Hall) in the rear of Wat Mahathat provides information on retreats and weekly lectures on Thai Buddhism and its significance to Thai culture. Upcoming English-language lectures are listed in the *Bangkok Post.* Call (02) 511-0439 or (02) 511-3549 for more information.

THAILAND

Another source is the World Fellowship of Buddhists, where English-language meditation classes for Western visitors are held on the first Sunday of every month 1400-1730. Sukumvit Rd. between Soi 1 and Soi 3.

For excellent up-to-date descriptions of all meditation temples in Thailand, read *A Guide to Buddhist Monasteries and Meditation Centres In Thailand* by Moon author Bill Weir. The authoritative tome is available from the World Fellowship of Buddhists on Sukumvit Rd., Asia Books, Dharma Seed in Massachusetts, and Insight Meditation West (P.O. Box 909, Woodacre, CA 94973). Insight Meditation West (tel. 415-

488-0170) is America's best resourse for retreats, books, and other information on *vipassana* meditation.

TRANSPORTATION

Airport Arrival

Bangkok's Don Muang International Airport, 25 km north of the city, is a busy, modern place with a post office, left-luggage facilities, international phones, and several restaurants including an inexpensive dining area on the top floor. After immigration and custom formalities, ex-

A/C BUS SERVICE FROM BANGKOK

DESTINATION	TERMINAL	KM	HRS	FARE (B)	DEPARTURES
Ayuthaya	Northern	74	1.5	35	every 10 minutes
Ban Phe (Samet)	Eastern	223	3	80	0700, 0800, 0900, 1600
Bang Pa In	Northern	63	1	30	every 20 minutes
Chiang Mai	Northern	713	9	280	0900-1000 (4 x), 2000-2145 (8 x)
Chiang Rai	Northern	844	13	300	1930, 1945, 1950, 2000
Hat Yai	Southern	1031	14	380	every 15 minutes 1730-2015
Hua Hin	Southern	201	3	90	hourly
Kanchanaburi	Southern	129	2	60	hourly
Kamphang Phet	Northern	358	5	150	1200, 2230
Korat	Northern	256	4	100	every 15 minutes
Krabi	Southern	867	14	300	1900, 2000
Lampang	Northern	668	8	220	0930, 1100, 2030, 2130, 2200
Lopburi	Northern	153	3	80	every 20 minutes
Nakhon Pathom	Southern	56	1	30	every 30 minutes
Pattaya	Eastern	132	2	60	every 40 minutes
Phetburi	Southern	135	2	60	hourly
Phitsanulok	Northern	498	5	90	hourly
Phuket	Southern	891	14	300	0800, 1830, 1900, 1930, 2000, 2030
Rayong	Eastern	182	3	80	hourly
Sukothai	Northern	440	5	160	1040, 2220, 2240
Samui Island	Southern	779	16	290	2000
Surat Thani	Southern	668	12	230	2020, 2040
Surin	Northern	451	6	170	1100, 2130, 2200, 2210
Tak	Northern	420	5	150	1300, 2210, 2230
Trat	Eastern	315	7	120	hourly 0600-1000, 2000-midnight

THAILAND

change some money at the currency booth (good rates), then visit the tourist information center for maps and magazines. Hotel reservations at better hotels in Bangkok, Pattaya, Chiang Mai, and Phuket can be made at the Thai Hotel Association booth in the arrival lounge. The adjacent Airport Hotel has rooms from 1,800B plus free transportation into the city.

Bangkok's hotels are 30-90 minutes from city center depending on traffic. Minibus and limousine tickets are sold from a special counter in the arrival section. Minibuses are reasonably priced and take you directly to your hotel. Airport taxis waiting out front are somewhat more expensive than ordinary taxis flagged down on the highway, 50 meters out the front door. Ordinary non-a/c buses—crowded and slow but very cheap—can be flagged down on the highway. Air-conditioned buses listed below are less frequent but much more comfortable; expect a wait of 15 to 30 minutes.

Getting around Bangkok

Bangkok is a hot, bewildering metropolis without any recognizable city center—a place where only the certified insane attempt to walk any great distance. Aside from roaming the neighborhood near your hotel, a taxi, *tuk tuk,* or bus will be necessary. The good news is that public transportation is very cheap; the bad news is that traffic in Bangkok is among the world's worst. Avoid rush hours (0800-1000 and 1500-1800), when the entire city grinds to a complete standstill.

Taxis: Air-conditioned taxis are plentiful and metered although many drivers refuse to use their meters during rush hours. During those precious moments, all fares must be negotiated in advance. Medium-length journeys (e.g. Sukumvit to Silom) should cost 60-100B, while longer trips (outer Sukumvit to the Grand Palace) average 120-150B. Never pay more than 200B to go *anywhere,* and ignore those absurd fares (often double or triple) posted in the luxury hotels. So much for the old saw about asking hotel employees for correct taxi prices!

Tuk Tuks: Affectionately named after their obnoxious sounds, motorized *samlors* are noisy three-wheelers that race around at terrifying speeds, take corners on two wheels, and scream through seemingly impossible gaps. *Tuk tuks,*

the cheapest form of private transportation in Bangkok, cost 30-50% less than taxis but you must bargain hard and settle all fares in advance. Since few drivers speak any English or understand a map, be sure to have your destination written down in Thai or know how to pronounce it properly. If you can't speak Thai, raise a few fingers: two for 20B, three for 30. Smile and grin during price negotiation. If the driver won't come down to a reasonable price then do the taxi ballet . . . walk away shaking your head until he pulls up and waves you inside. Then hold on to your seat.

Ordinary Buses: Non-a/c buses are unbelievably crowded, but they cover a very comprehensive network and cost only two *baht.* The oddly named *Latest Tour's Guide to Bangkok & Thailand* shows most bus routes. Signs at bus stands also help. Service is sporadic (especially in the evening), so write down several different bus numbers unless you care to wait a long, long time. *Beware of thieves using razor blades,* especially on crowded buses.

Air-conditioned Buses: Air-conditioned buses are *much* more comfortable than ordinary buses, plus you have a reasonably good chance of finding a seat. Air-conditioned buses cost 8-205B depending on the distance; destinations are listed in English on the exterior of the bus. Service ends nightly at 2000.

River Boats: The Chao Praya Express Boat is hands-down the *best* way to get around Bangkok. These open-air boats are fast, cheap, exciting, and a refreshing escape from the horrors of land transportation. Boats operate daily from 0600 to 1800 and charge 3-15B depending on the distance—especially useful between Banglampoo and the GPO. Two other types of boats work the river: short and stubby ferries which shuttle across the river and longtailed boats *(hang yao)* that race up and down the smaller canals.

Leaving Bangkok by Bus

Provinces throughout Thailand can easily be reached with public and private buses. Bangkok has three public bus terminals which serve different sections of the country. Each station has different departments for ordinary and air-conditioned buses. All are well organized and have English-language signs over most ticket windows. Departures are frequent for most destinations throughout Thailand; the most difficult task is reaching the terminal!

Northern/Northeastern Bus Terminal: Destinations in the north and northeast are served by two sprawling adjacent terminals on Paholyothin Rd., on the highway toward the airport near Chatuchak Market. Take any bus going toward the airport and look for the modern complex on the right side of the highway. The Northern Terminal is divided into two wings. The first section on the right is for air-conditioned coaches, the second for ordinary buses.

Southern Bus Terminal: All buses to southern Thailand depart from the new terminal on Nakhon Chaisri Rd. in Thonburi. Tickets are sold from the windows near the main road.

Eastern Bus Terminal: The Eastern Bus Terminal on Sukumvit Rd. near Soi 63 serves east-coast resorts such as Pattaya, Rayong, Ko Samet, and Ko Chang. Take any bus going down Sukumvit and watch for the small terminal on the right.

Private Buses: In addition to these three government terminals, a dozen-plus small, independent bus companies operate from private terminals located throughout the city. Private buses are 30-50% more expensive than government buses, but complimentary meals and hotel pick-up are often provided, an important consideration in Bangkok. Private buses can be booked through travel agents, but compare prices carefully as they vary enormously.

By Train: Bangkok has two train stations. Hualampong Station handles trains to the north and northeast and *most* services to the south. The Thonburi or Bangkok Noi station handles some trains to the south. Travelers going south must carefully check on the correct station. Trains from Bangkok should be booked well in advance, especially for popular destinations such as Chiang Mai, Surat Thani (junction for Ko Samui), and Hat Yai. Time and hassles can be avoided by making seat reservations from a travel agent. Tickets are also sold directly at Hualampong Station in the Advance Booking Office to the *right* of the entrance; people in the long lines to the left are purchasing same-day tickets. Be sure to pick up condensed timetables—extraordinarily useful pieces of paper.

By Air: Taxis to the airport cost 200-250B and take 30-90 minutes depending on traffic.

EAST COAST

PATTAYA

Once a "sleepy fishing village" popular with harried Bangkokians and American GIs on R&R, Pattaya has since mushroomed into a major beach resort covered with high-rise hotels, roaring discos, fine restaurants, throbbing go-go bars, and lively transvestite clubs that comprise Thailand's original sex capital.

Today, this low-powered Riviera of Southeast Asia is undergoing an image change as it transforms itself from a bachelor's paradise to a sophisticated retreat catering to middle-aged couples and families. Although it's still fashionable to condemn Pattaya as superficial, overbuilt, unplanned, congested, polluted, tawdry, and having nothing to do with the *real* Thailand (all true), most of the three million annual visitors seem to come away satisfied with its wide range of hedonistic offerings.

Attractions

Named after the southwestern monsoon wind that sweeps the east coast during the summer months, Pattaya is a beach resort dedicated to the pursuit of pleasure and love of *sanuk*. The range of activities is nothing short of amazing—sunbathing, parasailing, skin diving, golf, game fishing, zoos, night markets, and the world-famous nightlife. Pattaya divides itself into North Pattaya (deluxe hotels, fine restaurants, low-key nightlife), South Pattaya (moderate hotels and restaurants, notorious nightlife), and Jomtien Beach (family resort hotels and water sports).

Beaches: Pattaya's biggest disappointments are the narrow and brownish beach—vastly inferior to the crystalline shores of Phuket or Samui—and the polluted waters, which were recently declared a "hazardous zone" by a government-sponsored study on environmental pollution. For better sand and a sense of privacy, try an offshore island or Wong Amat Beach in North Pattaya.

Water Sports: Pattaya has eight scuba-diving shops, including the Seafari Sports Center in the Royal Garden Resort and the Scuba Professionals in the Dusit Resort Hotel. Basic courses start from 2,000B per day. Visitors undeterred by the pollution can rent windsurfers, waterscooters, parasailers, Lasers, and Hobie Cats. Check fuel supplies and condition of equipment, and never sign papers which promise liability; fleecing ignorant tourists is big business here in Pattaya.

Outer Islands: Islands near Pattaya offer better sand and diving than the mainland beaches. Converted fishing trawlers leave from South Pattaya piers, opposite Soi 14, and adjacent to Tangkae Restaurant, daily at 0830. Travel agents arrange glass-bottom boat trips, and prices vary depending on quality of meals, diving equipment, and number of islands visited. Tours usually include Ko Rin or Ko Pai before stopping at Ko Larn (Coral Island), a highly developed resort fixed with several upscale hotels, pricey restaurants, a golf course, and dive shops. Pack food and drinks if you're counting *baht*.

Pattaya Water Park: An enormous beachfront park with waterslides, swimming pools, and restaurants—perfect for families.

Budget Accommodations

Almost 300 guesthouses and hotels are operating in and around Pattaya, grouped together in several areas. Wong Amat Beach in the far north offers luxurious hotels tucked away in a semirural setting on the best beach in the area. North Pattaya has a good selection of moderate to luxury hotels while those in central Pattaya are conveniently located near the markets. South Pattaya hotels are inexpensive and noisy but popular with single males.

Pattaya's cheapest hotels are on Pattaya 2 Road just opposite Soi 11—basic concrete cubicles only adequate for short stays. To the south are luxury hotels such as the Royal Cliff and facilities along Jomtien Beach, a family area lined with moderately priced hotels. Tariffs vary according to day and season. Weekdays are cheaper; rates are cut about 40% during the slow season from May to October. Pattaya's cheapest hotels are on Soi Post Office, Soi Yamato, and Pattaya 2 Rd. opposite Soi 11.

Soi Post Office: Post Office Alley has several good travel agencies, the well-stocked D.K.

PATTAYA

WONG AMAT BEACH

WONG AMAT

MINI SIAM ★

TO BANGKOK

SUNSHINE GARDEN

A C BUS TO BANGKOK

N. PATTAYA RD.

CITY HALL

RESORT HOTEL

ORCHID LODGE

PALM GARDEN
TIFFANY'S SHOW

COTTAGE

REGENT

SOI 1

CABANA

ROYAL CRUISE

SOI 2

COUNTRY

WEEKENDER
ALCAZAR SHOW

NORTH PATTAYA

ROYAL NIGHT BUNGALOW

SOI 3

SOI 4

SOI 5

GRAND SOLE

PATTAYA PALACE

SOI 6

NOVOTEL

SUMMER PLACE

TO SIAM COUNTRY CLUB, RACE CIRCUIT, ELEPHANT VILLAGE

MERLIN PATTAYA

MONTIEN

NIGHT MARKET

CENTRAL PATTAYA RD.

BUS TO RAYONG

BUSES TO NORTH & NORTHEAST

SOI 7

SOI 8

TOURIST OFFICE

OCEAN VIEW

SOI 9

IMMIGRATION

CAESAR'S PALACE

CHEAP HOTELS

SIAM BAYVIEW

SOI 10

HONEY INN

SOI 11

SOI 12

DIANA INN

SOUTH PATTAYA

SOI 13 LEK

POST OFFICE

SOI YAMATO

ROYAL GARDEN

GUESTHOUSES
PALM VILLA

P.K. VILLA

RUEN THAI REST.

BUS TO BANGKOK

GRACE DISCO

ROYAL PALACE

DONGTAN BEACH

ROYAL WING

MARINE BAR

SIMON CABARET

PLAZA

SOI 14

S. PATTAYA RD.

ROYAL CLIFF

SEAFOOD REST.

SOI 15

SOI DIAMOND

BEVERLY PLAZA

BEER BARS

CK

SIAM BAYSHORE

DREAM VILLA

VIEW POINT

MIDTOWN

YACHT CLUB

JOMTIEN BAYVIEW

ASIA

BIG BUDDHA

THEP PRASIT RD.

PATTAYA WATER PARK

CONDOTEL

ROYAL JOMTIEN RESORT

MERMAID'S BEACH RESORT

CASA JOMTIEN

TO KO SAMET, RAYONG, CHANTABURI, TRAT

GUESTHOUSES

SWAN BEACH RESORT

JOMTIEN BEACH

BUS TO BANGKOK

SIGMA RESORT

BEACH RD.

PATTAYA 2 RD.

MOON

NOT TO SCALE

© MOON PUBLICATIONS, INC.

THAILAND

Books, and almost a dozen small hotels with decent fan-cooled rooms for 200-250B and a/c rooms for just 300-350B. Best bets include Sureena, Thips Guesthouse, Post Stuben Guest Haus, French-owned Riviera Beach Hotel, Swedish favorite Hasse Erickson, and Malibu at the end of the road.

Soi Yamato: Named after a Japanese restaurant on the left, this alley has eight hotels in the 200-350B price range, such as Porn Guesthouse, German-operated Eiger Bar, Norwegian Hotel Norge, Texxan Inn, owned by a retired USAF officer, upscale Meridian Hotel, and other cheapies such as PS, Siam, and Nipa guesthouses.

Pattaya 2 Road Guesthouses: Ten inexpensive hotels are located back on Pattaya 2 Rd. just opposite Soi 11. Small rooms with fans cost 150-200B or 200-300B for a room with air-conditioning.

Sea & Sun Inn: Small but clean hotel in a good location and friendly management. 325 South Pattaya Rd., tel. (038) 422945, 300-450B.

Diana Inn: Simple rooms and a good pool make this a popular spot for budget travelers who want basic frills at low cost. Pattaya 2 Rd., Soi 11, tel. (038) 429675, 350-600B.

Palm Villa: Pattaya's best budget hotel has all a/c rooms and an attractive swimming pool and is within easy walking distance of the bars. Pattaya 2 Rd., Soi 13, tel. (038) 429099, 400-600B.

Moderate Accommodations

Most Pattaya hotels priced in the 600-1,000B price range include air-conditioned rooms with private bath, a restaurant, and a small swimming pool. Some charge an additional 20% for tax and service.

Honey Inn: A clean, quiet, and well-located hotel with a spacious swimming pool and discounts for long-term visitors. 529 Soi 10 Pattaya 2 Rd., tel. (038) 421543, fax (038) 421946, 550-800B.

P.K. Villa: Superbly located right on the beach, Pattaya's largest villa has a good pool, a breezy restaurant, and a friendly atmosphere. 595 Beach Rd., South Pattaya, tel. (038) 428462, fax (038) 429777, 500-900B.

Lek House: A new hotel with a large swimming pool, a billiards hall, and a rooftop terrace. All rooms furnished with TV, refrigerator, and

transvestite follies

hot showers. Pattaya 2 Rd. and Soi 13, tel. (038) 425550, 800-1,000B.

Caesar's Palace Hotel: Las Vegas comes to Pattaya in this pseudo-Romanesque 200-room hotel. The compound includes a large pool and tennis courts. Pattaya 2 Rd. Soi 10, tel. (038) 428607, fax (038) 422140, 900-1,200B.

Nightlife

South Pattaya between Soi 13 and Soi 16 is a nonstop barrage of heady go-go bars, seedy nightclubs, high-tech discos, and outrageous live shows that cater to every possible sexual persuasion. No matter how you feel about flesh for sale, it's an amazing experience to wander down Pattaya Beach Road past mud wrestlers, Thai kick boxers, open-air cinemas, touts, transvestite clubs, and whatever new gimmick sweeps the night scene.

A good place to start is on Soi Diamond, a small and totally crazy lane opposite the huge Grace Disco. Lively ladies working the street

THAILAND

drag reluctant customers up to the bar stools and push them into the better bars such as Caligula (live shows), Blackout (better furnishings), Firehouse (not as good as Manila's), and Limmatquai (inexpensive drinks). Despite all the sex and sin, Pattaya nightlife is light-hearted and good-natured, lacking the depressing pathos of Western red-light districts.

Transvestite Shows: South Pattaya's best entertainment options are the hilarious transvestite shows that take place nightly in the Simon Cabaret and the monstrous Marine Bar that caters to "girls, guys, and in-betweens." If you haven't noticed by now, transvestites (gatoeis) are plentiful here in Pattaya. Since most Westerners have a difficult time distinguishing between girls and gatoeis, proceed with caution unless you seek a wild war story. Professional shows are given at Tiffany's and Alcazar Cabaret, which bills itself as having the largest transvestite troupe on Earth!

Services
The TAT office on the beach has maps, hotel lists, and free magazines such as *Explore Pattaya* and *What's On,* two great sources for shopping and nightlife venues. The *Pattaya City Map* produced by the local Rotary Club is also recommended.

Visas may be extended at Thai immigration on Soi 8. International phone calls can be made 24 hours daily from the exchange service at the corner of South Pattaya and Pattaya 2 roads—and from Simon Cabaret! Pattaya Police urge visitors not to carry too much money around, never to accept drinks or food from strangers, to keep off motorcycles unless experienced, and to check prices before buying *anything.*

Transportation
From Bangkok: Air-conditioned buses from Bangkok's Eastern Bus Terminal depart every 30 minutes between 0630 and 2100 and terminate at the poorly located station on North Pattaya Road. Private a/c buses from major Bangkok hotels cost 120-150B. Buses depart from the Bangkok airport at 0900, 1200, and 1900; tickets are sold at the Thai Limousine desk.

Leaving Pattaya: Blue and silver a/c buses depart for Bangkok's Eastern Bus Terminal every 30 minutes from the station on North Pattaya

Road. Air-conditioned buses run on the hour direct to Bangkok's Northern Bus Terminal; there are frequent direct connections to Chiang Mai.

Other services are provided by Diamond Coaches from Nipa Lodge and Erawan buses from the Siam Bayview. Buses to the airport leave hourly between 0700 and 1700 from the Regent Marina Hotel. Orange public buses to Rayong and Ko Samet can be hailed on the main highway.

KO SAMET

This hot and dry island lying 6.5 km offshore is blessed with fine white beaches and clear blue waters sandwiched between craggy headlands. Thais know Samet as the island where Sunthorn Phu, Thailand's greatest poet, based his most famous work, *Pra Apaimanee.*

Ko Samet's great appeal is its easy accessibility to Bangkok and the complete lack of commercialization: the ax-shaped island was declared a national park in 1981 to prevent overdevelopment. As a result the island is blessedly free of high-rises, discos, traffic jams, prostitutes, and other distractions. The downside is that most bungalows are overpriced and some even lack water.

Though the squeaky sand is about the finest in Thailand and the beautifully shaped coves are inviting, Samet sorely needs some attention before it will begin to approach the comfort and attractiveness of Ko Samui or Phuket.

Accommodations
Samet's eastern seaboard is partitioned into a series of beaches and coves filled with bungalows of varying quality. Those on the northern beaches are the most developed; those to the south are generally primitive bamboo huts priced at 80-150B per person. Prices rise sharply during the winter and on weekends, when Thai teenagers, hippies, gays, and folk musicians pack the island. Camping is legal and free anywhere on the island—bring a tent and improve your lifestyle. Better bungalows in the 250-800B range are described below.

Hat Sai Kao: "Diamond Sand," Ko Samet's longest and most impressive beach, is popular with families with children and tourists down from

Pattaya. Located 10 minutes by foot from Na Dan ferry landing, Sai Kao Beach offers over a dozen moderately priced bungalows with restaurants and water-sports facilities that face the broad beach. As with nearly all places on Ko Samet, most bungalow operations have old huts constructed a decade ago and new bungalows erected just last month. All charge 150-300B for simple huts with common bath and 300-600B for individual bungalows with fan and private bath.

Pai Beach: Pai Beach (also called Phai Beach) is a small cove with several bungalows, travel offices such as Citizen Travel, and a small

KO SAMET

TO BAN PHE

KHAM BEACH

SAMET VILLAGE
(125 l)

POND
BIG BUDDHA

PRA BEACH
(112 m)

HAT SAI KAO BEACH

PAI BEACH

TUP TIN BEACH

PUDSA BEACH

TARNTAWAN BEACH

VONG DEUAN BEACH

CANDLELIGHT BEACH

(56 m)

WAI BEACH

KIU NA NAI BEACH
(62 m)

KIU BEACH

(54 m)

KARANG BEACH

KO CHANG

NOT TO SCALE

© MOON PUBLICATIONS, INC.

post office with poste-restante facilities. Popular guesthouses include Naga's Bungalows for freshly baked goods and a sprawling library of yellowing paperbacks, Samed Villa with a good restaurant with bamboo furniture, noisy Sea Breeze Bungalows, Ao Pai Huts with over 70 rooms, and lovely Nop's Restaurant with blinking lights, Buddhas, Balinese music, and lovely views. A great place to dine.

Tup Tin and Pudsa Beaches: Two small bays with several sets of bungalows are located over the craggy headlands. Tup Tin Bungalows is a very popular place on a good beach blessed with hanging palms. Recommended.

From Tup Tin Bungalows, the road veers right to cross the island and dead-end at Ao Pra, where a pair of bungalows stands on Samet's only readily accessible west-coast beach. Excellent sunsets.

Tarntawan Beach: "Sunflower Beach" is dominated by Tarntawan Bungalows, with huts for 100-600B. Tarntawan Beach manages to retain a hippie atmosphere compared to Diamond and Wong Duan beaches.

Vong Deuan Beach: Ko Samet's second-most-popular beach (after Hat Sai Kao) is on a beautifully arched bay bisected by a rickety pier. This is actually a yuppie destination filled with tourists from Pattaya and Europeans on package holidays. Vong Deuan can be reached directly from the Ban Phe pier, but you'll need to inquire about the correct boat.

The beach has five mid-priced-to-expensive bungalows such as Malibu Garden Resort, Sea Horse, the relatively luxurious Vong Deuan Resort, and Vong Deuan Villa with a miniature golf course, and billiards tables.

Candlelight Beach: This long and rocky beach has two sets of primitive bungalows that offer an escape from the commercialism of other beaches.

Wai Beach: A fairly nice beach dominated by the upscale Samet Ville Resort.

Kiu Beach: Ko Samet's most attractive beach is clean, quiet, and graced with a beautiful row of swaying palm trees. Enjoy sunsets from the western beach and from the hillside viewpoint. Kiu Coral Beach Bungalows charges 80-500B in better chalets. Ao Kiu is a very long walk from Hat Sai Kao Beach, but well worth the trouble if you're looking for peace and solitude.

THAILAND

Transportation

Air-conditioned buses leave every two hours for Ban Phe from the Eastern Bus Terminal in Bangkok and hourly to Rayong, from where minibuses continue for Ban Phe. Boats to Ko Samet leave regularly from the Ban Phe pier.

Be careful climbing onto these converted fishing boats—mishaps are common. Some boats go to Samet Village; others go directly to Hat Sai or Vong Deuan Beach. Unless you enjoy long and dusty hikes, take a boat directly to one of the latter beaches. Minibuses return from Ban Phe back to Rayong until sunset. Don't believe taxi driver scare stories, "Last bus already go."

TRAT

Trat, 312 km from Bangkok, remained almost completely off the tourist trail until the discovery of Ko Chang in the early 1990s. Trat now chiefly serves as a transit point for visitors heading to Ko Chang and other islands in the southeast. Trat is an ordinary town with an extraordinary future; you can almost feel the heady air of prosperity.

Accommodations

Max and Tick's Guesthouse: This place wanders around town, but is currently located in a small alley off Tat Mai Road. Good information, assuming Max or Tick are actually around. 1 Soi Luang Aet, tel. (039) 520799, 100-140B.

Foremost Guesthouse: Recommended by many travelers for the friendly Swedish owner who helps with travel tips, provides hot showers, and gives off congenial vibes. 49 Tha Charoen Rd., tel. (039) 511923, 40B dorm, 60-120B private rooms.

Windy Guesthouse: Same owners as Foremost; they also rent motorcycle and canoes. 37 Tha Charoen Rd., tel. (039) 511923, 40B dorm, 60-120B private rooms.

Trad Hotel: The Trad (also called the Meuang Trat) is your best choice for better rooms; the small but decent coffee shop faces the morning market. 4 Sukumvit Rd., tel. (039) 511091, 200-350B fan, 450-750B a/c.

Transportation

Travel agencies on Khao San Road in Bangkok have small minibuses direct to Laem Ngop, the port town for Ko Chang. Services are provided by both Sea Horse and S.T. Travel. Minibuses are convenient, but the air-conditioning rarely works and they travel at frightening speeds. Both services will attempt to put you on private boats that take you to remote beaches where you become a captive audience. Skip this scam and take another boat to the beach of your choice.

Public buses from Bangkok's Eastern Bus Terminal to Trat are both safer and more comfortable for the full-day journey. Minibuses from the main road in Trat continue the 17 km south to Laem Ngop and charge just 10B per passenger.

Ordinary and a/c buses depart throughout the day for Pattaya and Bangkok. The Sea Horse minibus departs daily for Bangkok at 1145.

KO CHANG

Ko Chang ("Elephant Island") is, after Phuket, Thailand's second-largest island, some 30 km in length and eight km broad at its widest point. Covered with dense jungle and bisected by a steep wall of mountains, Chang remained almost completely untouched until the early 1990s.

By 1992 the island had achieved fame as Thailand's next major resort destination. Local authorities jumped on the tourism bandwagon. The Thai government constructed a large pier on the east side of Ko Chang and then blasted a concrete road which now encircles most of the island. Ko Chang today resembles the early stages of Ko Samui: a tropical island firmly mesmerized by the promise of mass tourism.

Despite all the construction and development, Ko Chang remains one of the most beautiful islands in Thailand. Most accommodations still are simple bamboo bungalows rather than concrete hotels filled with package tourists, and a majority of Chang's 5,000 residents still make their living from fishing rather than tourism. Discos, nightly videos, noisy motorcycles, and beer bars are still several years away. Ko Chang is a wonderfully refreshing change from the hustle of Samui and Phuket. The time to visit Ko Chang is *now*.

West Coast Beaches

Ko Chang's best beaches are all on the west coast. Most accommodations are simple bamboo bungalows with mattresses on the floor and illuminated by oil lamps. Restaurants are funky places with good food but rudimentary service; you'll probably be ignored to the point of starvation until you approach the front counter.

Construction of new bungalows is going on at a furious pace as professionals from Bangkok arrive to milk the tourist boom, so expect major changes from the following descriptions. In general, you should take a ferry to the beach of your choice and then wander around to inspect a few places. Most bungalows are filled during the high season from October to March, but tents can be rented while waiting for vacancies. Ko Chang is, technically speaking, a national park where camping is legal anywhere.

White Sand Beach: Hat Sai Khao, the longest and most popular beach on Ko Chang, is the original escape on the island. The concrete road which skirts the back side of the beach goes south to Klong Prao Beach and cuts through the mountains at the northern end to Klong Son Beach. Alternatively, a narrow trail heads north over the ridgetop and brings you to Klong Son in one hour. White Sand Beach is a good place to enjoy the sand and meet other travelers.

Over a dozen bungalows are spread along the beach. All charge 60-100B for bamboo huts with mattresses on the floor and common bathrooms located back toward the road.

Klong Prao Beach: The road from White Sand Beach veers inland and skirts the rocky cape at Chai Chet until it approaches the coastline near Klong Prao River. Klong Prao Beach is a long and relatively undeveloped beach with huge tracts of property covered with little more than coconut groves and wild vegetation. Some great hikes can be made east into the mountains which bisect the island. The path to Klong Prao Waterfall is two km south from Coconut Beach Bungalows. Accommodations are widely scattered along Klong Prao Beach.

Kai Bae Beach: The last major beach on the west coast has a narrow strip of sand crowded with over a dozen bungalows, including Coral Bungalows on the rocky promontory, Nang Nuan 2, Kae Bae and Kae Bae Beach Bungalows, recommended Porn Guesthouse, and finally Nang Nuan 1.

Transportation

Fishing trawlers converted into ferryboats leave from Laem Ngop daily from 0900 to late afternoon. Prices are fixed and it's best to purchase tickets directly from the boat owner rather than the middleman who operates a counter at the pier.

Boats from Ko Chang back to Laem Ngop leave twice in the mornings around 0830 and 1100. Exact departures are posted at most guesthouses. Completion of the concrete road around the island will dramatically change the transportation scene.

WEST OF BANGKOK

NAKHON PATHOM

Your first glimpse of the massive *chedi* at Nakhon Pathom is staggering. Soaring over 125 meters into the hot blue skies, this is the most sacred Buddhist monument in Thailand and the world's largest *chedi*, surpassing even the gilded wonder in Yangon. Although the dome-shaped reliquary lacks the staggering detail of Yangon's Shwedagon, its fairyland of auxiliary *bots, ubosots,* Buddha images, and curious substructures makes for a fascinating afternoon of exploration. For best impact, approach the *chedi* from the north side facing the train station.

Accommodations

Although usually just a stopover en route to Kanchanaburi, good hotels in all price ranges are available.

Mit Thaworn: Two cheap hotels are located near the train station. The **Mit Thaworn** and adjacent **Mit Phaisal** have rooms acceptable for a short stay. Both are located up a short alley off the busy street market. 305 Rot Fai Rd., tel. (034) 243115, 120-250B.

Nakorn Inn: Best upscale choice in town is the Nakorn Inn off the main road. This hotel has a coffee shop, convention room, and 70 a/c rooms. 55 Rajwithi Rd., tel. (034) 251152, fax 254998, 500-800B.

Transportation

Buses leave from Bangkok's Southern Bus Terminal and take an hour. To return to Bangkok, take bus 81 from the north side of the *chedi*, next to the canal. For Kanchanaburi, take bus 81 from the southeast corner of the pagoda. Trains from Thonburi and the south also stop here.

KANCHANABURI

Kanchanaburi is known for the bridge made famous by Pierre Boulle's celebrated novel of WW II, *The Bridge Over the River Kwai*, and the subsequent Academy Award-winning motion picture directed by David Lean in which William Holden and Alec Guinness whistled a very popular musical score. The rather ordinary bridge is nothing special, but Kanchi's relaxed atmosphere and nearby waterfalls, caves, and river trips make this one of *the* most enjoyable destinations in Thailand. Travelers intending to stay just a day or two often extend their visits to a week or more.

Attractions

War Museum: Before going out to the bridge, be sure to visit the JEATH Museum, its name an acronym for the primary nations (Japan, England, America/Australia, Thailand, Holland) that participated in local action. Modeled after POW camps of the period, the simple bamboo structure contains war memorabilia, photographs, personal recollections, and graphic descriptions of tortures committed by the Japanese.

The Bridge over the River Kwai: The world-famous bridge, five km from the center of town, was constructed in just over 12 months by some 60,000 Allied prisoners from Singapore and another 250,000 slave laborers from Japanese-occupied countries. Although an estimated 50,000-100,000 lives were sacrificed, the project was not a success; the bridge was only used *once* before British bombers from Sri Lanka destroyed the fourth, fifth, and sixth spans on 13 February 1945. The Japanese replaced the missing girders with two square beams, ironically stamped, Made in Japan.

Kanchanaburi War Cemetery: With its neatly arranged tombstones and poignant messages, this final resting place for 6,982 Allied war prisoners forms one of the most moving tableaux in Southeast Asia. The adjacent Chinese Cemetery is a study in contrasts; pauper tombs hidden away against the walls, tombstones of the wealthy elevated like Chinese pagodas.

Kao Poon Cave: Limestone caves near Kanchanaburi often serve as Buddhist temples filled with Buddhist and Saivite images illuminated with electric lights.

Chung Kai War Cemetery: Two km closer than Kao Poon and almost identical to its counterpart in town.

Temples on the Hill: Situated on a hilltop about 20 km south of Kanchanaburi is a pair of impressive but half-completed temples. Wat

farang river life

THAILAND

KANCHANBURI

TO THREE PAGODAS PASS

TO ERAWAN FALLS & SRI NAKARIN LAKE

FAMILY CAMP

RAILWAY STATION

BRIDGE OVER THE RIVER KWAI

ART GALLERY

KANCHANABURI WAR CEMETERY

SHERATON

U.T. GH

BAMBOO GH

CHINESE CEMETERY

LUXURY HOTEL

JOLLY FROG GH

P.S. GH

RICK'S GH

V.N. GH

RIVER GH

BAN NUER RD.

PUNEE REST.

PRASOBSUK HOTEL

SUNYA REX REST.

RAMA RIVER KWAI HOTEL

RIVER KWAI 2 HOTEL

VL. GH

CHAO KUNEN RD.

MINIBUS TO BRIDGE

NITAYA GH

TELEPHONE

U-THONG RD.

TO SUPHANBURI & SUKHOTHAI

SAM'S PLACE

PAK PRAEK RD.

SONGWAI RD.

SUPRAKORNCHAI GH

MARKET

TAXIS

AC BUS TO BANGKOK

BUS TERMINAL

SPORTS HALL

POST

HONDA

B.T. GH

FERRY

TOWN GATE

LAK MUANG

T.A.T.

TO BANGKOK

FLOATING RESTAURANTS

SUNYA RAFT HOUSE

NITA RAFT HOUSE

SHELL STATION

NITA GH

THAI SEREE HOTEL

VISUTHARARANGSI RD.

DUCK RAFT HOUSE

JEATH WAR MUSEUM

WAT CHAICHUMPOL

KWAI NOI RIVER

RIVER KWAI YAI

CHAICHUMPOL RD.

GPO. TELEPHONE

FERRY

KASEM ISLAND OFFICE

TO BANGKOK

SANGCHUTO RD.

CHUNG KAI WAR CEMETERY

KAO POON CAVE

KASEM ISLAND RESORT

STONE GARDENS

WAT THAM MONGKAM TONG

BRIDGE

NOT TO SCALE

© MOON PUBLICATIONS, INC.

THAILAND

TRANSPORT AROUND KANCHANABURI

DESTINATION	BUS	HRS.
Bangkok	81	3
Nakhon Pathom	81	1.5
Nam Tok	8203	1
Sai Yok Falls	8203	2
Three Pagodas	8203	6
Ratchaburi	461	2
Suphanburi	411	2.5
Bophloi	325	1.5
Erawan Falls	8170	2

Tam Sua, the Chinese-style pagoda to the left, is fronted by a fat, jolly Buddha surrounded by 18 superbly carved figures. To the right is Wat Tam Kao Noi, which, perhaps in a show of religious competition, is separated from the adjacent temple by a concrete wall. Don't miss the gigantic Buddha complete with automated treadmill to help expedite monetary donations!

River Trips: Three-hour sunset cruises in longtail boats cost 100B to visit the bridge and Chung Kai War Cemetery. Alternatively, you can go to Pak Sang Pier near Namtok some 60 km upriver from Kanchi and hire fast eight-man longtails to visit the upriver caves and waterfalls. Prices from Pak Sang Pier are posted at the train station.

Accommodations

Local accommodations can be divided between floating guesthouses on the Kwai Yai River and a variety of conventional hotels on Sangchuto Road. River-based guesthouses in the center of town are pleasant during the week but incredibly noisy on weekends when Bangkokians flood the region. To escape the all-night parties and blasting disco boats, try the guesthouses north of the park toward the bridge.

Nita Raft House: Several floating crash pads are located along the banks near the city park. Nita's is a popular choice, but store your valuables at her guesthouse for safety reasons. 27 Pakprak Rd., tel. (034) 514521, 50-100B doubles.

Sam's Place: One of the better riverside choices in central Kanchanaburi features a beautiful foyer and a cozy restaurant (with a *farang* menu), wooden reclining chairs facing a pond filled with ducks, and several detached bamboo bungalows with small porches. Songkwai Rd., tel. (034) 513971, 60-300B.

Nitaya Guesthouse: At the north end of the riverside park is an old favorite with over a dozen rickety bamboo bungalows, a disco boat, and river tours at 1300 daily. Songkwai Rd., tel. (034) 513341, 60-180B.

River Guesthouse: Several new guesthouses have recently opened on Soi 2 to the north of central Kanchanaburi. 42 Rongheeboi Rd. Soi 2, tel. (034) 512491, 50-100B.

P.S. Guesthouse: Excellent views and a cozy restaurant make this a good choice. 54 Rongheeboi Rd. Soi 2, tel. (034) 513039, 50-150B.

Jolly Frog Guesthouse: The largest guesthouse in Kanchanaburi has over 50 rooms facing a central courtyard filled with palms and grass. Features include motorcycle rentals, a spacious circular dining hall, German management, and minibuses to Bangkok daily at 1100 and 1430. 28 Maenamwae Rd., tel. (034) 514579, 50-150B.

U.T. Guesthouse: A genuine homestay in a light blue, modern, two-story house about 100 meters back from the river. Peaceful, friendly, and cozy. 275 River Kwai Rd., tel. (034) 513539, 60-100B per person.

Bamboo Guesthouse: The most idyllic guesthouse in Kanchanaburi is at the end of a dirt road about 300 meters before the bridge. Big lawn with a small pond; often filled but otherwise highly recommended. 3-5 Soi Vietnam, tel. (034) 512532, 60-250B.

V.L. Guesthouse: The only other land-based budget guesthouse worth recommending is this modern place opposite the River Kwai Hotel, an excellent deal for anyone who dislikes riverside accommodation. 18/11 Sangchuto Rd., tel. (034) 513546, 120-300B.

Restaurants

Krua Thien Tong and Ruen Ploy: Kanchanaburi's best restaurants are the half-dozen floating cafes tied up at the south end of fitness park. Arrive for the sunset and try deep-fried freshwater catfish or frog legs fried in garlic.

Pae Karn: Another floating restaurant known for its *log tong* and country-style Thai dishes such as *tom yam pla* made with giant river carp.

Unfortunately, the highly prized *pla yi sok* fish (Julien carp, the fish used for those terrific street signs), favored for its fatty and succulent meat, has been hunted nearly to extinction. Other species now substitute.

Cheap Eats: Cheap meals are found at the outdoor foodstalls on Sangchuto Road near the bus terminal. Sunya Rex is a favorite travelers' hangout, as is the lively Cowboy Club located between the bus station and the river.

Transportation

Buses to Kanchanaburi leave every 30 minutes from the Southern Bus Terminal in Bangkok and take three hours. Trains for Kanchi leave three times daily from Thonburi Station.

Biking is the perfect way to get around Kanchi. Ratty old bikes can be rented from most guesthouses and just opposite the War Museum. Motorcycles cost 150B per day at the Honda dealer.

A slow but romantic alternative is the funky third-class train which leaves Kanchanaburi daily at 0600 and 1030 and arrives in Namtok two hours

later. Visit the river or a nearby waterfall before catching the 1520 train back to Kanchanaburi.

Ordinary Bus 81 for Bangkok and Nakhon Pathom departs from the main bus terminal while a/c buses leave from the office on Sangchuto Road. To Ayuthaya, take Bus 419 to Suphanburi (two to three hours), then yellow Bus 703 to Ayuthaya (45 minutes). To Sukothai, take Bus 487 to Nakhon Sawan (four hours), then Bus 99 to Sukothai (three hours). To the floating market at Damnern Saduak, take Bus 461 to Bang Phya intersection, walk down the road, then take Bus 78 or the minibus to the last stop in Damnern. The market is 1.2 km south. Alternatively, take Bus 81 to Nakhon Pathom and then Bus 78 to Damnern Saduak.

KANCHANABURI REGION

The waterfalls, limestone mountains, caves, and other natural wonders around Kanchanaburi comprise one of the loveliest regions in Thailand.

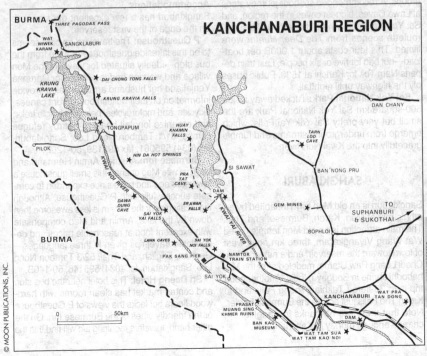

KANCHANABURI REGION

Attractions to the Northwest

Ban Kao Museum: One fortunate outcome of the railway's construction was the discovery by a Dutch prisoner of some important Neolithic artifacts in 1943. A Thai-Danish archaeological team continued the excavations in 1961, and today a small museum near the original excavation site exhibits some of their findings.

Prasat Muang Singh Khmer Temple: What were Cambodians doing so far west? This marvelous Khmer temple complex and military outpost, 45 km from Kanchi, was constructed in the 12th century to guard against Burmese invasion. Now completely restored, the City of Lions marks the westernmost advance of Cambodian power.

Nam Tok River Trip: Several good explorations start from Nam Tok, the railway terminus for visitors coming from Kanchanaburi. The best option is to hire a tricycle from the train station and go downhill to Pak Sang Pier where eight-man longtail boats can be hired for upriver journeys. Boat prices, listed at the train station, are prohibitively expensive except for larger groups. A recommended six-hour journey stops at Lawa Caves, biggest caves in the region, and Sai Yok Yai Falls, where the famous Russian-roulette scenes from *The Deer Hunter* were filmed. This tour costs about 1,000B per boatload—not bad for five or six people. Last train departs Nam Tok for Kanchi at 1530. Public buses ply the highway until nightfall.

Sai Yok National Park: Tucked away inside 500-square-km Sai Yok National Park are the small but very pretty Sai Yok Yai Falls, which emerge from underground streams and tumble gracefully into the Kwai Noi River.

SANGKLABURI

Sangklaburi is an old Mon town inhabited by an ethnic mix of Mon, Karen, Burmese, and Thai. The main attraction is an old Mon temple called Wat Wang Vivangkaram, three km southwest of town toward the reservoir, and a newer stupa, Chedi Luang Paw Utama, modeled after the Mahabodhi shrine in Bodgaya, India. Another good trip is to 36-tiered Takhian Thong Falls and to Kroen Tho Falls just across the Burmese border. Note that there are no banks in Sangklaburi; change enough money in Kanchanaburi.

Three Pagodas Pass

The border crossing into Myanmar at Three Pagodas Pass, 22 km from Sangklaburi, is named after a trio of historic cone-shaped *chedis* known as Pra Chedi Sam Ong. Centuries ago this was the spot from where marauding Burmese armies marched into Thailand on their traditional invasions. Today the small trading post at the pass is a sleepy place.

Locals can point out the few sights around town: the three whitewashed pagodas, the site of the old station that marked the end of the Death Railway, and the track itself, which according to Thai archaeologists follows a route that dates back to the earliest human settlement in the region.

Westerners are occasionally allowed to cross the border and visit the adjacent Burmese village where handicrafts, cheroots, and silver jewelry are sold in the local market. Conditions change with the season and should be double-checked with other travelers and the TAT office in Kanchanaburi.

Accommodations

Sangklaburi has a few excellent guesthouses on the edge of the vast reservoir.

P Guesthouse: The travelers' favorite seems to be this lakeside guesthouse one km from the bus stop—ideally situated for views of the Mon village and wooden bridge. Proprietor Darunee Yenjai and her husband arrange treks; provide information on their bulletin board; rent canoes, bicycles, and motorcycles; help with jungle treks; and organize longtail boats to nearby refugee camps. 81/1 Tambon Noog Loo, Sangklaburi, tel. (034) 595061, fax 595139, 50-120B.

Burmese Inn: Austrian Armin Hermann and his Thai wife Meo opened this small guesthouse a few years ago and have since expanded to compete successfully with P Guesthouse. Although the location near the stream is less awesome than down by the lake, Armin and Meo compensate with excellent food at reasonable prices and dependable travel tips given in three languages—German, English, and Thai. 52/3 Tambon Nong Loo, Sangklaburi, tel. (034) 595146, 50-140B.

Sri Daeng Hotel: This hotel near the bus stop and central market has clean rooms with hardwood floors but lacks the views of P Guesthouse or the friendly vibes of the Burmese Inn. On the other hand, travelers requiring a/c will find this the

THAILAND

only choice in town. 1 Sangklaburi, tel. (034) 595039, 160-380B.

Transportation
Sangklaburi is 220 km from Kanchanaburi. Bus 8203 departs Kanchanaburi daily at 0645, 0900,

1045, 1315, and takes about five hours to reach Sangklaburi. Motorcyclists should allow a full day with stops at Ban Kao Museum, Muang Sing Khmer ruins, Nam Tok, and a brief swim at Sai Yok Yai Falls. Gasoline stations are located in Nam Tok, Tongpapum, and Sangklaburi.

NORTH OF BANGKOK

BANG PA IN

This strange collection of palaces and pavilions in Thai, Italian, Victorian, and Chinese architectural styles once served as summer retreat for Thai kings. Highlights include a delicate water pavilion replicated for international expositions, an elaborate pavilion modeled after a Chinese royal palace, and a six-sided Gothic-style tower. The white marble memorial across the small bridge honors Chulalongkorn's first queen, who tragically drowned in full view of her entourage. At the time of the 1881 incident, royal law demanded death for any commoner who dared touch royalty. The law was changed soon afterwards. A fun cable car whizzes across the river to Thailand's only European-styled Buddhist temple.

Bang Pa In is more odd than amazing, but it's an easy stopover between Bangkok and Ayuthaya, 20 km north. Visitors with limited time should spend their time fully exploring Ayuthaya. Buses leave from Ayuthaya and Bangkok's Northern Bus Terminal.

AYUTHAYA

Ayuthaya, 72 km north of Bangkok, served as Thailand's second capital for over four centuries. The city's scattered ruins, colossal Buddhas, decaying *chedis,* and multitude of soaring *wats* restored by the Fine Arts Department provide eloquent testimony to the splendor of this medieval metropolis. Recently declared a national historic park, Ayuthaya has been successfully developed into one of the country's major tourist attractions—a must-see for all visitors to Thailand. Though Ayuthaya is often a day-trip from Bangkok, it really takes two days of leisurely wandering to properly appreciate the sense of

history evoked by the far-flung ruins. Travelers who enjoy romantic ruins or have an interest in Thai history should allow two full days *each* to Ayuthaya and Sukothai.

Attractions
Chandra Kasem Museum: King Thammaraja constructed this 17th-century palace for his son, who subsequently claimed the throne as King Naresuan. Partially destroyed by the Burmese, the palace was reconstructed by King Mongkut and later converted into one of Ayuthaya's two museums.

Wat Rajaburana: King Boromaraja II constructed this temple in 1424 to commemorate his two brothers who died on elephantback fighting for the throne; Boromaraja wisely skipped the battle. Inside the Khmer-style *prang,* a secret crypt once guarded dozens of 15th-century murals, 200 Lopburi bronzes of Khmer-Bayon style, 300 rare U-Thong Buddhas, 100,000 votive tablets, and a fabulous treasure trove of priceless gold objects. Thailand's equivalent of the Tutankhamen treasure lay untouched until 1957 when scavengers stumbled on the buried crypt.

Wat Mahathat: King Boromaraja constructed his "Temple of the Great Relic" in 1374 to honor his dream about a Buddha relic. Many valuable artifacts, including a tiny gold casket said to contain Boromaraja's holy relics, were discovered during a 1956 restoration project conducted by the Fine Arts Department.

Wat Pra Ram: Ramesuan, second king of Ayuthaya, constructed this beautiful temple in 1369 as the burial spot for his father, King Ramatibodhi. The elegant Khmer-style *prang* casts a beautiful reflection in the placid lily ponds.

Chao Sam Phya National Museum: Thailand's second best museum was constructed in 1959 from sale proceeds of the Wat Rajabu-

THAILAND

AYUTHAYA

TO CHANG MAI

TO BANGKOK

TO BANGKOK

THAILAND

© MOON PUBLICATIONS, INC.

Wat Yai Chai Mongkol

Wat Panam Chong

Japanese Settlement

Portuguese Settlement

Boat Building School

Rim Nam GH

Railway Station

Tevaraj Rest.

Pakunkao Rest.

Old Fortress

Ruenpae Rest.

Ruanrom Ayuthaya Youth Hostel

Pai Tong GH

Wat Suwan Daram

Krung Kao Rest.

Wang Fa Hotel

Raja Rest.

Riverside Rest.

Govt. House

Chao Praya River

St. Joseph's Cathedral

Wat Buddhasawan

GPO

Ayuthaya Historical Study Center

Chao Sam Phya National Museum

Historical Park

U Thong Rd.

Wat Chao Prob

Ferry

Ferry

Ferry

Ferry

Elephant Kraal

Night Market

Market

Market

Boats Around The Island

U Thong Hotel

Cathay Hotel

GPO

Rodeo Saloon

Chandra Kasem Museum

Sri Samai Hotel

Ayuthaya GH

Buses

Van's GH

Pra Preo Rd.

Som Rest.

BJ. GH

Siam Rest.

Horattanachai Rd.

Bangsean Rd.

Pathom Rd.

Rajana Rd.

Chi Kun Rd.

Wat Rajaburana

Bin Bar Rest.

Wat Mahathat

Wat Thammikarat

U Thong Rd.

Naresuan Rd.

Antique Shops

Rama Lake

Viharn Pra Mongkol Bopit

Chao Sam Phya National Museum

Ayuthaya Historical Study Center

GPO

City Hall

Lak Muang and Ayuthaya Model

Khum Khum House

Wat Pra Sri Samphet

Royal Palace Ruins

Watana Praman

Reclining Buddha

Pu Kao Tong (Golden Mount)

500m

0

Chedi Sri Suriyathai

Wat Kasatraram

Wat Chai Wattanaram

Chao Praya River

Buddha head in the clutches of a banyan tree at Wat Mahathat

rana votive tablets. The main floor holds dozens of statues, votives, lacquer cabinets, decorated palm-leaf manuscripts, and priceless objects discovered inside the left shoulder of the Pra Mongkol Bopit Buddha. All major art styles are represented—Dvaravati, Lopburi, U-Thong, Sukothai; Ayuthayan kings were apparently avid collectors of early Thai art.

Lak Muang and Khum Khum House: Ayuthaya's modern city pillar is nothing special but the interior scale model will help with your orientation. The Khum Khum House, constructed in 1894 as the city jail, is an outstanding example of traditional Thai architecture. The Fine Arts Department is located here.

Viharn Pra Mongkol Bopit: Thailand's largest Buddha image is crammed into this modern, claustrophobic temple. After the original structure was destroyed in 1767, the immense statue sat outdoors until the present building was erected in 1951. Perhaps the black statue with its mysterious mother-of-pearl eyes should have been left alone—an image of this size and power needs a great deal of *room.*

Wat Pra Sri Samphet and the Royal Palace: Wat Pra Sri Samphet, a famous trio of 15th-century Sri Lankan-style *chedis,* once the royal temple within the walls of the palace, enshrines the ashes of three Ayuthayan kings. Their perfect symmetry has made them one of the most photographed scenes in Ayuthaya; the very essence of Middle Kingdom architecture. To the north are the ruins of the old Royal Palace destroyed by the Burmese. Nothing remains except for a few scattered foundations.

Watana Praman: This tremendous *bot,* originally constructed in 1503 as a royal monastery and completely rebuilt in 1987, is one of the most impressive temples in Ayuthaya—a must-see for all visitors. The combination of striking architecture and pleasant country surroundings makes Watana Praman a refreshing change from monuments controlled by the Fine Arts Department. Inside the first temple stands a fabulous gold-leaf, six-meter Ayuthaya-style Buddha surrounded by painted pillars, highly polished floors, and roofs carved with concentric lotus buds. A truly magnificent room!

Reclining Buddha: This smiling Buddha image, heavily restored in 1956, is perhaps the most attractive reclining image in Thailand. Cows occasionally graze in front of the yellow-robed image once covered by a wooden *viharn.*

Wat Chai Wattanaram: This magnificent temple complex was constructed in 1630 by King Prasat Tong and restored a few years ago. Fantastic at sunset.

North of Ayuthaya

The following attractions can only be reached with hired *tuk tuk* or *samlor.*

Pu Kao Tong (Golden Mount): To commemorate the 2,500th anniversary of Buddha's birth in 1956, this large temple almost five km outside the city walls was capped with a 2.5-kg solid-gold orb. Somebody immediately stole it, but views from the top of the 80-meter *chedi* are still outstanding.

Elephant Kraal: Wild elephants were once battle trained inside this teak stockade. Old-fashioned elephant roundups were re-created here in 1891 for Czar Nicholas II and in 1962 for Danish royalty.

THAILAND

pre-restoration Wattanaram

South of Ayuthaya

St. Joseph's Cathedral: A classical 17th-century Catholic church constructed by Monsignor de Beryte during the reign of King Narai.

Wat Buddhasawan: Ramatibodhi lived here during construction of his new capital. The general layout is derived from Angkor Wat. A large central *prang* represents Buddhist Mt. Meru; the six smaller *prangs* signify the outer heavens; the mangy dogs represent nothing.

Portuguese and Japanese Settlements: King Narai encouraged foreign traders to set up residential centers south of Ayuthaya. Most were burned by the Burmese and little remains except for memorial plaques.

Wat Panom Chong: Home to the Thailand's largest single-cast bronze Buddha, a 14th-century 20-meter image donated by a Chinese emperor whose daughter had married a local Thai prince.

Wat Yai Chai Mongkol: King Naresuan constructed this temple to commemorate his victory over the Burmese in 1592 and his slaying of the crown prince in a dramatic elephant duel. Encircling the massive *chedi* are some 135 Buddhas and a reclining image with Naresuan's personal spirit house.

Wat Suwan Daram: Among the most fascinating temples in Ayuthaya. The curving, concave foundation of the boat-shaped exterior illustrates mankind's voyage toward nirvana while elaborate doors and interior murals, usually shown by young monks anxious to practice their English, rank among the best in Thailand. A wonderful little gem.

Accommodations

Several new guesthouses have opened in recent years to provide cheap accommodations for backpackers.

Ayuthaya Guesthouse: Formerly known as B.J. Guesthouse, Ayuthaya's original homestay is 50 meters up a small alley running north from Naresuan Road. Great atmosphere plus bicycles for rent. 76/2 Chao Prom Rd., tel. (035) 251468, 50-80B.

B.J. Guesthouse: The most popular guesthouse in Ayuthaya has 20 rooms in a cinderblock building about 10 minutes west of the market. Banjong, the lady owner, is a good cook and can help with travel tips. 19/29 Naresuan Rd., tel. (035) 251512, 60-80B.

Ruandrum Ayuthaya Youth Hostel: Perhaps the most beautiful lodging in Ayuthaya is located in a series of teak houses overlooking the river. The central wing was built by an Ayuthayan aristocrat in the traditional central Thai *panya* style. The owner, Praphan Sukarechit (Kimjeng), has renovated the adjacent homes and refurbished all the rooms with antiques and curiosities. 48 U-Thong Rd., tel. (035) 244509, 200-300B. The dormitory will cost around 100B per person.

Pai Tong Guesthouse: A floating hotel on a reconstructed barge. Rooms are small and the atmosphere is strange, but two good restaurants are located nearby. U-Thong Rd., 60-100B.

Sri Samai Hotel: Ayuthaya's central hotel was once a clean and comfortable place with a fairly decent restaurant. Standards, unfortunately, have dropped, and the hotel can no longer be recommended for any reasons aside from its convenient location near the marketplace. 12 Chao Prom Rd., tel. (035) 245228, 300-400B fan, 400-500B a/c.

Wang Fa Hotel: Although this hotel serves the short-time trade for locals, the clean and modern rooms make this the best budget hotel in Ayuthaya—better than the Sri Samai or the U-Thong. All rooms have large beds with adequate furniture and private bath. 1/8 Rajana Rd., tel. (035) 241353, 150-200B fan, 250-300B a/c. Three-hour room rentals cost 100B.

U-Thong Hotel: A rudimentary hotel for those who want traditional facilities at moderate cost. The U-Thong has rather dirty rooms with fan and common bath and a few a/c rooms with private bath. Avoid rooms facing the street. The nearby Cathay Hotel is similar in quality and price. 86 U-Thong Rd., tel. (035) 251505, 120-300B.

Ayuthaya Grand Hotel: A recent addition to the luxury hotel market in Ayuthaya, this hotel has all the standard facilities such as a pool, snooker hall, and travel services. 55/5 Rajana Rd., tel. (035) 335483, fax 335492, tel. (02) 511-1029 in Bangkok, 800-1,500B.

Restaurants

Most travelers dine in their guesthouse or at the market, though several good restaurants are along the river and near the monuments on Chi Kun Road.

Night Market: The old night market has been relocated from downtown to a new location on the river across from the Chandra Kasem Museum. A small selection of foodstalls complements the hawkers' emporiums. A comfortable place to spend an evening.

Pakunkao Floating Restaurant: The better of Ayuthaya's two floating restaurants is hardly spectacular, but the atmosphere is relaxed and the food is tasty. U-Thong Road. Moderate.

Krung Kao Restaurant: A small, modern, and air-conditioned spot with Thai specialties and an English-language menu. Try the pepper steak or chicken sautéed with garlic. On Rajana Rd. near the bridge. Budget.

Youth Hostel: Kimjeng's wife operates a well-appointed restaurant furnished with antiques and knickknacks. The menu includes both Thai and Western dishes. 48 U-Thong Road. Moderate.

Binlar Restaurant: A large, open-air nightclub with rock music and Thai cabaret singers. Good food at reasonable prices, a popular hangout in the evenings. Naresuan Road. Budget to moderate.

Raja Restaurant: Dine outdoors surrounded by ponds filled with water lilies. Great atmosphere in a very quiet location. Rajana Road. Moderate.

Getting There

Buses leave every half-hour from Bangkok's Northern Bus Terminal and take one hour. Stay on the bus until it arrives in the center of town; get

off at the bridge and you are fed to mercenary taxi drivers. Trains leave Bangkok ten times daily. From the station, stroll to the river and ferry across the river. Minibuses from Ayuthaya to Bang Pa In leave from Naresuan Road. Buses to Sukothai leave at 1020, 1235, and 1500. Trains go north five times daily.

Getting Around

Most visitors attempt to see Ayuthaya on a single day-trip from Bangkok—a serious mistake. Ayuthaya is a sprawling place with dozens of great temples. Forget about walking; rent either a bicycle, a motorcycle, a longtail boat, or a mini-truck. Bicycles are highly recommended. B.J. Guesthouse rents bikes for 30B and motorcycles for 120B daily. Six-man longtail boats chartered from the landing stage near the U-Thong Hotel cost 150-200B for the standard three-hour circular tour. Minitrucks cost 150-200B for an afternoon tour, which should include the Golden Mount, Wat Chai Wattanaram, St. Joseph's Cathedral, and Wat Panom Chong. Central temples can be reached by foot.

LOPBURI

Lopburi is a pleasant and friendly little town with enough historic architecture to merit an overnight stop en route to Sukothai or Khao Yai. All major attractions are centrally located within the old town; hurried visitors can visit them on a three-hour walking tour. Hotels are within easy walking distance of the train station, but Lopburi's main bus terminal is located in the new town, about three km east of the old historic center. Minibuses shuttle west to the old town.

Attractions

Royal Palace: Buildings inside the enormous enclosure were constructed by Narai, King Rama III, or King Mongkut in the 1860s. The Chantom Pisan Pavilion on the right once served as King Narai's royal residence but today it's the Lopburi National Museum, with an indifferent collection of Lopburi and Dvaravati images. Narai's Suttha Vinchai Pavilion on the left now serves as an extension of Bangkok's National Museum but the meager collections are less impressive than the statuary placed on the palace grounds.

THAILAND

The eerie hollow shell to the left originally served as an audience hall for ambassadors and high-ranking foreign visitors. To truly understand the grandeur of the royal court, imagine it laid out with gardens, fountains, and statues surrounded by sumptuously dressed royalty, military leaders, and lovely concubines.

Wat Mahathat: Lopburi's finest architectural treasure is the 12th-century Khmer temple just opposite the train station. Within the temple grounds are Khmer *prangs* embellished with outstanding stucco lintels, a large brick *viharn* dating from King Narai's reign, and *chedi* constructed in the Sukothai style. Admission is 20B at the northern entrance; this one is worth the fee.

Monkey Shrine: Dozens of monkeys scamper around this shrine dedicated to Kala, Hindu god of time and death. Behind the old Khmer shrine is a modern temple with a highly revered four-armed Buddhist image. Hold on to your camera.

Prang Sam Yot: Thailand's 500-*baht* currency note pictures this Khmer shrine.

Phaulkon's Residence: Chao Praya Wichayen, the Greek adventurer's home, was constructed by Narai as residence for important Western visitors. Although recently restored, there's little of interest here. Save 20B and look from the street.

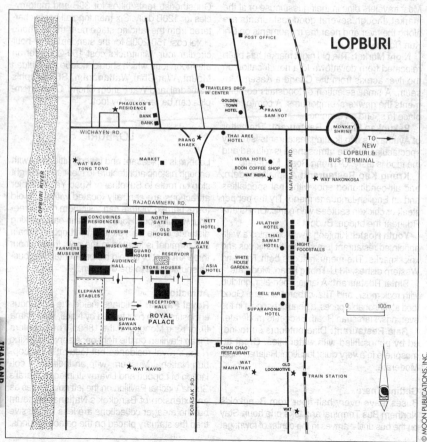

THAILAND

Accommodations

Traveler's Drop In Center: Lopburi's small but popular travelers' center is actually an English-language school with two small communal bedrooms upstairs and two rooms for singles or doubles. Richard, the friendly Thai citizen who runs the school, often invites foreign visitors and Thai students out for dinner and conversation in local nightclubs. 34 Wichayen Rd., Soi 3, no phone, 40B dorm, 60-80B private room.

Asia Lopburi Hotel: Comfortable lodgings assured in this basic hotel opposite the Royal Palace. 1 Sorasak, tel. (036) 411892, 130-350B.

Naprakan Road Hotels: Several inexpen-sive hotels are strung along Naprakan Road just opposite the train station. Rooms at the Su-parapong, Thai Sawat, Julathip, and Indra start from 120B fan and 250B a/c. Ask for the cheap-est room rather than accept the more expen-sive options offered by the manager.

Nett Hotel: Tucked away in a quiet alley, this convenient hotel has large, clean rooms and homey decorations. 17/1 Rajadamnern Rd., tel. (036) 411738, 120-350B.

Rama Plaza Hotel: A new business travel-er's hotel with better rooms than those in the older places in town. 4 Banpong Rd., tel. (036) 411663, 180-400B.

CENTRAL THAILAND

PHITSANULOK

Central Thailand's largest commercial center is also one of the country's oldest and most historic cities. Straddling the Nan River some 400 km north of Bangkok, Phitsanulok served as an important trading post of the Sukothai empire and as a provincial capital of the Ayuthaya empire. While most visitors enjoy the genuine Thai atmosphere and complete lack of tourists, few are impressed with the concrete shophouses put up after the disastrous 1959 fire that leveled the wooden town. The town's saving graces are magnificent Wat Mahathat and the extraordinarily friendly people.

Central Thailand's transportation hub can be reached by air, train, or buses from Bangkok's Northern Terminal. Buses terminate at either the downtown train station or the main bus terminal northwest of town. Minibuses shuttle to city center.

Attractions

Wat Mahathat: Phitsanulok's major spectacle is the Jinaraj Buddha inside Wat Mahathat, one of the few Ayuthayan-period temples to survive the catastrophic fire. Regarded as one of Thailand's most beautiful and sacred images, the highly polished late-Sukothai bronze has been reproduced for Bangkok's Marble Temple and the Thai temple at Bodgaya. Fine interior murals and elaborate mother-of-pearl inlays are also worth noting; a small museum stands to the left.

Wat Rajaburana: The nearby temple and its partially reconstructed Ayuthayan-period *chedi* boasts an interior nothing short of spectacular.

Dr. Tawee's Folklore Museum: An astounding assembly of agricultural and household instruments can be seen in the Folklore Museum inside Dr. Tawee's home on Visut Kasat Road, two km south of the train station. Opposite the folklore museum is a thriving Buddha factory where you can watch the casting of giant bronze Buddhas.

Information on other nearby temples and monasteries is available from the regional TAT office at 209 Boromtrailokanat Road in the Surasi Trade Center, two blocks south of the clock tower.

Accommodations

Two guesthouses have opened in the last few years, and several low-end hotels are located near the train station.

Youth Hostel: Phitsanulok's official youth hostel is somewhat isolated but otherwise an excellent place to stay. The hostel is two km south of the train station, one km from the airport, and four km from the bus terminal. A *samlor* should cost 10B from the train station or airport, 25B from the bus terminal. Bus 3 goes from the bus terminal to the hostel. From the train station, take bus 4 south down Ekathotrot Rd., then left on Ramesaun Rd., then right on Sanambin Road. 38 Sanambin Rd., tel. (055) 242060, 50B dorm, 100-200B.

Green Guesthouse: This lovely teakwood home is on the left side of Ekathotrot Rd., about two km north of the big traffic circle. Bus 4 from the city bus terminal near the train station goes up Ekathotrot Rd. and passes the poorly marked guesthouse. Bus travelers coming from Sukothai should get off after the bridge but before the traffic circle and take a *songtao* going up Ekathotrot Road. 11/12 Ekathotrot Rd., tel. (055) 252803, 60-120B.

Sombat Hotel: Inexpensive hotels in the 80-150B range are near the train station on Sairuthai and Phayalithai roads. All are conveniently located in the center of town, but none are clean or very quiet; Sombat is probably the best of a somewhat dismal lot. 4 Sairuthai Rd., tel. (055) 258179, 100-180B.

Rajapruk Hotel: The best luxury choice in town has 110 a/c rooms, a Thai-Chinese restaurant, a nightclub, car rentals, and a swimming pool. The owner's wife is an American, and English is spoken by some of the staff. The main drawback is the poor location outside town center, across the train tracks. 99 Pra Ong Dum Rd., tel. (055) 258477, 800-1,000B.

Restaurants

Phitsanulok has a wide selection of restaurants, from a/c dining in upscale hotels to alfresco meals down by the river.

Floating Restaurants: Several popular floating restaurants are tied up just south of the bridge. Than Tip has been recommended as the best, followed by Yardfan Floating Restaurant and then the Songkwae Houseboat. The boats wait for a full house, then serve meals as they slowly sail up and down the Nan River. Puttabucha Road. Moderate.

Hern Fa Restaurants: Perhaps more fun than the floating restaurants are the hilarious food vendors who set up their shops each evening on the banks of the Nan River. A brilliant display of cooking and acrobatics is included with every order. First, the cook fires up the wok and sautées a mixture of vegetables and meats. A waiter then climbs to the top of a nearby truck and attempts to catch the mixture flung skyward by the chef. Misses are fairly common, but the best is when a drunken Westerner takes the role of waiter and attempts to catch the flying morning glory. Inexpensive.

Night Market: Over a dozen good foodstalls are on the riverbanks just south of the Hern Fa restaurants. Inexpensive.

Top Land Arcade: A welcome relief from the daytime heat is provided in the a/c restaurant on the top floor of Phitsanulok's largest shopping center. Boromatrailokanat Road. Inexpensive.

Transportation

Phitsanulok serves as the transportation hub for central Thailand. Thai Airways flies from Bangkok and Chiang Mai daily. All trains from Bangkok stop in Phitsanulok. Phitsanulok can also be reached by train from Ayuthaya and Lopburi, a pleasant alternative to the hot and rather boring bus journey. The train station is conveniently located in the center of town.

Ordinary and a/c buses leave hourly from the Northern Bus Terminal in Bangkok and take five hours to reach Phitsanulok. The government bus terminal is on Highway 12 about three km east of downtown.

SUKOTHAI

Thailand's original capital and birthplace of the Thai nation is one of the preeminent archaeological sites in Southeast Asia. Situated 450 km north of Bangkok where the northern mountains intersect

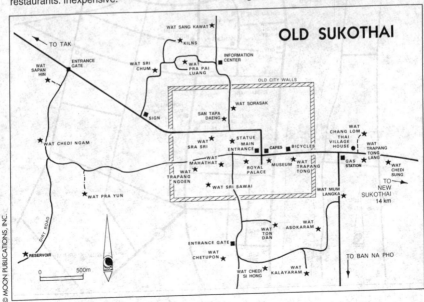

OLD SUKOTHAI

© MOON PUBLICATIONS, INC.

THAILAND

NEW SUKOTHAI

SKY HOUSE

BYPASS RD.

TO SI SATCHANALAI 56KM

0 — 100m

RAJ THANEE HOTEL

TO OLD SUKHOTHAI 14 KM, TAK 78 KM

BUSES TO OLD CITY

WAT KUA SAWAN

YOM RIVER

TANEE RD.

BANK

MARKET

#4 GH

SOMPRASONG GH

O2 GH

RAJUTHIT RD.

YUPA GH

WAT RAJTHANI

MARKET

TO SI SATCHANALAI 56 KM

RIVER VIEW HOTEL

CHINAWAT HOTEL

DREAM CAFE

NIGHT MARKET

WIN TOURS

THEATER

SUKOTHAI HOTEL

CHAROTVITHIWONG RD.

GOVT. BUSES

ISAN RESTAURANT

BUSES TO TAK

TRICHOT RD.

CHOON RESTAURANT

NORTHERN PALACE HOTEL

SAWASDIPONG HOTEL

PRAVET NAKORN RD.

LITHAI RD.

NAKORN KASEM RD.

SINGHAWAT RD.

MAHARAJ RD.

BAN MUANG RD.

DREAM CAFE #2

POST OFFICE

SAN MER YA SHRINE

12

TO PHITSANULOK 56 KM

© MOON PUBLICATIONS, INC.

THAILAND

the central plains, Sukothai is to Thailand what Angkor is to Cambodia, Borobudur is to Indonesia, and Pagan is to Myanmar. Spread out over the 70-square-km National Historic Park are dozens of magnificently restored temples, palaces, Khmer *prangs,* gigantic Buddha images set with enigmatic smiles, and a fine museum which safeguards the grandeur of ancient Sukothai.

The town also offers several good guesthouses, friendly little cafes, and opportunities to become acquainted with the local Thais. Sukothai is also a convenient base for exploring the nearby ruins of Si Satchanalai and Kamphang Phet. Sukothai is the best stop between Bangkok and Chiang Mai—don't miss it.

Orientation

Sukothai is divided into two sections. The unattractive new town has the hotels, restaurants, and transportation facilities. Old Sukothai with the museum and ruins is 14 km west. Minibuses to the old city leave across the bridge about 200 meters on the right side, just beyond the police station.

Old Sukothai ruins have been divided into five zones lettered A through E, with zones A, B, and D each charging a 20B admission fee. Sukothai's ruins are widely scattered; hire a *tuk tuk* at 30-50B per hour, a five-passenger taxi for 500B for a full day, or a bicycle for 20B from the stores just opposite the museum. Visitors on foot are limited to central ruins inside zone A. Determined bicyclists who don't mind working up a sweat can reach all major monuments in a single day, including those to the far west and south.

Please remember that all Buddhist images—no matter their age or condition—are considered sacred objects to the Thais. Visitors should be properly dressed and never touch or climb on any image. This is no joke! Several years ago, a few Westerners—dressed only in shorts—posed for photographs on the shoulders of a Buddha. A national scandal erupted after the Bangkok photo lab turned the negatives over to a local newspaper, which then printed them on the front page. The Westerners were thrown in jail.

Ramkamheng National Museum

Located inside the old city walls and just before the entrance gate to zone A, Sukothai's museum offers an outstanding introduction to the arts and

THE ARTS OF SUKOTHAI

Sukothai blossomed during the reign of Ramkamheng into a grand city of palaces, temples, monasteries, and wooden homes protected behind imposing earthen walls. Unlike Ayuthaya, which was destroyed by the Burmese, much of Sukothai's great architecture and art still stands in good condition.

Architecture: Sukothai's superb range of religious and secular buildings—from Khmer *prangs* covered with terrifying *nagas* to Sinhalese *chedis* capped with distinctive lotus-bud towers—has been restored with varying results by UNESCO and the Fine Arts Department. Some have retained their original flavor and still show ancient craftsmanship; others have been insensitively restored with heavy-handed techniques.

Sculpture: Sukothai's crowning artistic achievement was sculpture, most notably the sensual, otherworldly walking Buddha. Often cast of bronze using the *cire perdu* (lost-wax) method, the typical walking Buddha image is elongated with a flowing, androgynous body and hand raised in the attitude of calming fears and giving reassurance. The other arm hangs rhythmically and follows the sensual curve of the torso, while the head is shaped like a lotus bud capped by the flame of enlightenment. Perhaps the most intriguing feature is the enigmatic smile, which somehow reflects a state of deep inward contentment and spirituality. The total effect is one of marvelous power and sensitivity; rarely has any religious image so successfully conveyed the unspeakable faith of the creator.

Stucco: A combination of lime, sand, and sugarcane juice was used to create Buddha images and the exquisite moldings that decorated many of Sukothai's finest architectural monuments. Since stucco hardens in just a few hours, the artists were forced to work quickly but with great care.

Paintings: All paintings in Sukothai have been destroyed by the elements or stolen by art collectors, except for a handful of ornamental designs and stone engravings. Thai painting came of age during the Rattanakosin or Bangkok period.

Ceramics: Great quantities of high-quality ceramics were produced in nearby Sawankalok. See **Si Satchanalai.**

crafts of historic Sukothai. Inside the spacious building are Khmer statues, Sukothai Buddhas, Sawankalok ceramics, and other archaeological artifacts. Facing the front entrance stands a bronze walking Buddha, considered the finest example of its kind in the country. Open daily except Mondays and Tuesdays 0900-1200 and 1300-1600.

Central Sukothai (Zone A)

Statue of King Ramkamheng: Sukothai's great ruler sits on a replica of the historic Manangasila throne, discovered a century ago and now kept in Bangkok's Grand Palace Museum. The stone slab is charged with enough magic and mystical potency to make it an object of reverence to many Thais. Visitors can summon the ghost of Ramkamheng by ringing the bell on the right!

Wat Mahathat: Sukothai's principal monastery and royal temple once contained 185 *chedis,* a dozen *viharns,* and a central *bot* gilded with stucco surrounded by reflective moats. Most structures have collapsed and wooden buildings have been destroyed by fire or insects, but large Buddhas and fine stucco remain intact.

Royal Palace: Ramkamheng's great palace is marked only by its foundations.

Wat Si Sawai: This well-preserved Khmer sanctuary, surrounded by two concentric enclosures and a deep moat, was originally constructed by the Khmers prior to the founding of Sukothai. Some original *nagas* and *garudas* still cling to the pediments, but much of the stucco exterior has been poorly restored with rough concrete. Many wish the ruins had been left untouched except for necessary support work.

Wat Trapang Ngoen: This well-placed *chedi,* on a small island in the center of Silver Lake, is the focal point for Sukothai's Loy Kratong Festival.

Wat Sra Si: Simplicity of design and elegance of location make this one of Sukothai's most attractive temples. The central tower, with its bell-shaped dome, square base, and tapering spire, is typical of the Sinhalese style adapted by Sukothai's Theravadan architects.

North of the City (Zone B)

Wat Pra Pai Luang: This unrestored 12th-century "Temple of the Great Wind," about one km north of Wat Mahathat, was originally constructed by the Khmers as a Hindu sanctuary in the center of

their military stronghold. Triumphant Thais later converted it to a Buddhist monastery second in religious importance only to Wat Mahathat.

Pottery Kilns: Archaeologists have uncovered several large kilns that once produced the most famous celadons in all of Southeast Asia. An informative display on these enormous walk-in kilns can be seen in the Sukothai Museum.

Wat Si Chum: Sukothai's most impressive Buddha, a monumental 15-meter image seated in the subduing Mara pose, is a must-see for all visitors to the city. It's a lively scene as Thai pilgrims arrive to pray, make offerings, and burn incense in front of the enormous and superbly modeled hand. A narrow and claustrophobic passageway leads partway to the roof past slate slabs engraved with Jataka scenes.

West of the City (Zone C)

Wat Sapan Hin: The 12-meter standing Buddha overlooking the scattered ruins of Sukothai seems to bless the entire region. Good views are guaranteed visitors who survive the hot climb up the jumble of stone slabs. The brick-paved floor of the adjoining *chedi* has been raided by temple robbers—a depressing but familiar sight at many remote and unprotected temples.

Wat Chedi Ngam: The dirt road winds past several more temples before turning left and returning to the city. This round Sinhalese-style *chedi* has also been vandalized by thieves who burrowed a deep hole in the backside. Afterwards, enjoy a swim in the reservoir farther down the road.

South of the City (Zone D)

Wat Chetupon: Entrance to the southern monuments is made through the admissions gate near this temple. Wat Chetupon is chiefly known for its pair of 10-meter stucco Buddhas; the walking image is considered one of the finest in Thailand.

Wat Chedi Si Hong: Decorating the base of this *chedi* currently under restoration are stucco elephants and *garudas* molded with great imagination. The dirt track continues past several small temples before intersecting the road north to the city.

East of the City (Zone E)

Wat Trapang Tong: This *chedi,* surrounded by a symmetrical pool called the Golden Lake, contains a footprint of the Buddha honored each year during Loy Kratong.

Wat Trapang Tong Lang: A panel on the southern side shows the descent of Buddha to earth surrounded by angels and bodhisattvas. Sukothai's most famous stucco relief has tragically deteriorated and lost much of its artistic appeal. A reproduction is displayed in the museum.

Wat Chang Lom: This circular Sinhalese-design *chedi,* supported by a ring of 36 sculpted and ruined elephants, can be reached by walking through the grounds of the Thai Village House.

Wat Chedi Sung: Considered the finest *chedi* of the Sukothai period. Easily visible from Wat Trapang Tong Lang.

Accommodations

Most guesthouses and hotels are in new Sukothai, a nondescript town of concrete shophouses and streets too wide for the traffic. All charge 60-120B for single rooms and 80-150B for doubles.

Lotus Village Guesthouse: Formerly Number 4 Guesthouse, Lotus Village was started by four local schoolteachers. This lovely teakwood home is clean, quiet, and immensely popular with budget travelers. 170 Tanee Rd., tel. (055) 611315, 50-120B private rooms.

Yupa Guesthouse: Sukothai's original guesthouse is in a private home on a small road west of town with an open-air restaurant, laundry facilities, motorcycles and bikes for rent. 44 Pravet Nakorn Rd., tel. (055) 612578, 50-150B.

Sky House: Though somewhat distant from downtown, Wattana's place is actually a modern townhouse converted into backpackers' quarters after the units failed to sell. The Sky office near the bus terminal provides free transportation. 58 Bypass Rd., tel. (055) 612237, 50-250B.

O2 Guesthouse: O2 is a genuine homestay operated by a Thai history teacher and a Thai cooking instructor. The 12-room teakwood home sits in a lovely compound of old residences inhabited by the extended family of aunts, uncles, and grandchildren. 26/4 Rajuthit Rd., tel. (055) 612982, 60-100B.

Somprasong Guesthouse: Another guesthouse across the river near the Yupa Guesthouse with shiny wooden floors, a large porch on the second floor, rooms separated by short walls and chicken wire, free bicycles, and motorcy-

cles for hire. 32 Pravet Nakorn Rd., tel. (055) 611709, 50-100B.

Chinawat Hotel: The best budget-to-moderate hotel in Sukothai is well located in the center of town near the bus terminals and restaurants. Chinawat serves as Sukothai's information center, with a wide range of maps, brochures, and travel tips on buses and nearby attractions. 1 Nakorn Kasem Rd., tel. (055) 611385, 80-120B fan, 160-220B a/c.

River View: A somewhat luxurious hotel on the banks of the Yom River with clean rooms, private baths, a patio restaurant, and lobby with TV. 92 Nakorn Kasem Rd., tel. (055) 611656, fax 613373, 250-350B.

Restaurants

All of the hotels in Sukothai have restaurants, but smaller cafes offer a unique culinary and aesthetic experience.

Night Market: Cheap eats are plentiful at the market which sets up nightly in the alley near Win Tours and the Rainbow Cafe. Popular dishes include *pad thai, gawetio thai nam* (noodle soup with peanuts and greens), *yam nom tok* (spicy beef), and *kanom jinn* (Thai spaghetti). Other choices include mussel omelettes, thick rice soups, ice *kachang,* and *won ton* dishes.

Take-away Foodstalls: Across the street from the night market are several foodcarts that serve food to go wrapped in plastic bags. Simply point to the more appealing dishes and say *ha baht.* A grand total of 25 *baht* will guarantee a delicious and filling meal that you can consume back at your guesthouse. Take-away dishes are often more tasty and varied than stir-fried food from the night market.

Rainbow Cafe: Next to the bus station is a popular open-air restaurant with European fare, Thai noodles, and terrific ice cream.

Dream Cafes: Sukothai's most eclectic restaurants are the brainchildren of Ms. Chaba Suwatmaykin, who has outfitted her cafes with an amazing collection of memorabilia such as old telephone sets, bottles, and ancient gramophones.

Transportation

Buses leave from Chiang Mai's main terminal and Bangkok's Northern Bus Terminal 10 times daily. The nearest train terminus is at Phitsanulok, 60 km from Sukothai. Buses leave Phitsanulok for Sukothai from the Soon Bus Terminal northeast of town.

Win Tours has three a/c buses daily for Bangkok and Chiang Mai. Ordinary buses operated by the government leave eight times daily for Bangkok and six times daily for Chiang Mai. Buses to Si Satchanalai and Sawankalok leave across the street from the Chinnawat Hotel. Buses to Tak leave four blocks up the main street. Buses to old Sukothai leave from the dirt yard 200 meters across the bridge. Don't get suckered into an expensive *tuk tuk* or taxi ride.

SI SATCHANALAI

The evocative ruins of old Si Satchanalai rest 56 km north of Sukothai between Sawankalok and the new town of Si Satchanalai. Once a provincial capital and twin city for the Sukothai empire, Si Satchanalai eventually fell to Burmese attack and was absorbed into the Ayuthayan empire. Although less extensive than the ruins at Sukothai, the superb setting, absence of tourists, and lonely sense of the past makes Sri Sat (the local term) a most memorable place.

Attractions

Three areas interest visitors: the Old Town with the ruins, Wat Mahathat to the south, and pottery kilns to the north. The local office of the Fine Arts Department contains a relief model of the city.

Wat Chang Lom: Supported by 39 crumbling and headless stucco elephants, this Sinhalese-style *chedi* was constructed in 1285 by King Ramkamheng and possibly modeled after Wat Mahathat at Nakhon Si Thammarat.

Wat Chedi Chet Teo: Seven rows of lotus-bud *chedis* around the main structure replicate important shrines from neighboring monasteries. Formerly the burial grounds of Sukothai princes, the monument's large central *chedi* was modeled after Sukothai's Wat Mahathat.

Wat Kao Panom Pleung: Satchanalai's hilltop "Temple of the Mountain of Fire" shows Lanna influence and offers fine views across the hazy valley. Another ruined *chedi* caps the loftier hill to the rear.

Wat Nang Phya: Near the southern wall stands a 15th-century *viharn* famed for excellent stucco floral moldings which imitate Ayuthayan woodcarvings.

Wat Kok Sing Karam: Slit windows of Khmer design and original stucco characterize this ancient sanctuary one km south of old Si Satchanalai. Follow the path along the river. Farther south and set back from the river is another large Khmer tower with finely carved Buddhas.

Wat Sri Ratana Mahathat: No visit to Si Satchanalai would be complete without a stop at this remarkable temple. Situated on a promontory in the bend of the Yom River, this Ayuthayan-style *prang* was erected in the 15th century over an important Khmer sanctuary and embellished with outstanding stucco reliefs and superb walking Buddha images cast in various styles. From here, walk to the main highway and flag down a bus to Sukothai.

Pottery Kilns: Si Satchanalai potters during the 14th and 15th centuries produced the finest glazed ceramics in Southeast Asia. Pottery aficionados can wander around dozens of ruined but systematically excavated kilns which once produced world-famous Sawankalok stoneware, celadon, and decorated vases with distinctive blue-gray glaze.

Transportation

Buses leave opposite the Chinnawat Hotel and take an hour to reach the ruins, 18 km beyond Sawankalok. New Si Satchanalai is 12 km further. Chinnawat Hotel sponsors a six-hour tour for 160B to the Old City, Ko Noi Kiln, and weaving factories at Hat Sieo. Most visitors return to Sukothai before nightfall, but simple hotels are found in both Sawankalok and New Si Satchanalai.

KAMPHANG PHET

Kamphang Phet is an old garrison town on the banks of the Ping River some 85 km from Sukothai. Established in 1347 by King Li Thai, the small town served as a regional capital for the Sukothai empire until 1378, when the final sovereign surrendered to Ayuthaya.

Attractions

Modern Kamphang Phet is a completely ordinary place, but inside the trapezoid walls of the old northern city are several intriguing *wats* in various states of repair and restoration, a worthwhile National Museum organized by the Fine Arts Department, and other *chedi* and sculpture of great historical significance. The museum provides quick historical background and general orientation to the widely scattered monuments.

Wat Pra Sri Iriyabot and Wat Chang Rob—Kamphang Phet's three best monuments—are outside the crenellated ramparts to the northwest. Many of the outlying *wats* and Buddhist monasteries predate even Sukothai but were heavily restored during Ayuthayan occupation. Taken together, Kamphang Phet serves as the third most important historical and archaeological site in central Thailand.

Accommodations

Kamphang Phet has an inexpensive Chinese hotel near the bridge and several mid-priced hotels in the new section of town, about four km from the bus terminal. Minibuses from the bus terminal go across the river and down Ratchadamnoen Rd. to the hotels and the information center.

The Guest House: Budget spot opposite the police station. Thesa Road, Soi 2, tel. (55) 712295, 120-250B.

Ratchadamnoen Hotel: Like most other hotels in Kamphang Phet, the Ratchadamnoen is an older property with both fan and a/c rooms in a variety of price ranges. Hotel owners assume that all Western travelers are rich and want an expensive a/c room rather than a cheaper fan-cooled room. 114 Ratchadamnoen Rd., tel. (055) 711029, 100-280B.

Phet Hotel: The best hotel in town has 235 a/c rooms, a coffee shop, a small swimming pool, and the Princess nightclub. 99 Vichit Rd. Soi 3, tel. (055) 711283, Bangkok reservations (02) 215-2920, 350-600B.

Transportation

Kamphang Phet is 85 km southwest of Sukothai. Most visitors take a bus from Sukothai and spend a single night before continuing northwest to Tak and Mae Sot. The bus terminal is inconveniently located three km from town on the west side of the river. Travelers coming from Sukothai might get off the bus at the ruins and continue into town with a *samlor* or public minibuses.

TAK

Tak is a provincial capital 423 km north of Bangkok on the east bank of the Ping River. The town is at the intersection of Hwy. 1, which connects Bangkok with Chiang Mai, and the Pan-Asian Hwy., which in a more perfect world would link Singapore with Istanbul.

Tak is rarely visited by Western tourists, though the town has some outstanding teakwood architecture and is known throughout Thailand as the birthplace of King Taksin. The town also serves as a useful base for excursions to the hilltribe center and waterfalls of Lansang National Park (19 km west), the traditional riverine settlement of Ban Tak (23 km north), and water sports at Bhumibol Dam (65 km north), the largest artificial lake in Southeast Asia.

Accommodations

Tak Hotel: A popular choice for budget travelers with 29 fan-cooled rooms. 18 Mahathai Bamroong Rd., tel. (055) 511234, 100-150B.

Mae Ping Hotel: Down the road is a slightly larger hotel with somewhat cheaper rooms. 231 Mahathai Bamroong Rd., tel. (055) 511807, 80-120B.

Sanguan Thai Hotel: Near the central market and shopping district. 619 Taksin Rd., tel. (055) 511265, 100-180B.

Viang Tak 1 Hotel: Top-end choices are the two branches of the Viang Tak. The original branch has 100 a/c rooms in an older neighborhood. 25 Mahathai Bamroong Rd., tel. (055) 511910, 500-800B.

Viang Tak 2 Hotel: The best hotel in Tak is on the main drag near the river. Facilities include a comfortable restaurant, a small nightclub, and a dining verandah overlooking the river. Chompol Rd., tel. (055) 512686, fax (02) 235-5138, Bangkok reservations (02) 233-2690, 500-800B.

Transportation

Most visitors reach Tak by bus from Sukothai or Kamphang Phet. The bus terminal is northeast of town across ultrabroad Highway 1. *Songtaos* shuttle into town. Air-conditioned buses to Bangkok can be booked from the private bus office off Mahathai Bamroong Rd. just north of the Viang Tak 1 Hotel.

THAILAND

MAE SOT

Mae Sot is one of the most intriguing towns in the region and a great place to experience Thailand off the beaten track. Initial impressions are that Mae Sot has little of real interest aside from some dusty Burmese architecture, food, and customs which have spilled over the border. A closer look, however, reveals a complex society composed of Burmese, Thais, Chinese, and tribal minorities such as Karen and Hmong. Mae Sot also benefits from its isolated location and almost complete absence of Western tourists.

The opening of the road from Mae Sot north to Mae Sariang now presents a unique way to reach Chiang Mai from central Thailand. The journey is long and rough but covers some beautiful countryside rarely seen by Western travelers. From Mae Sariang, buses continue to Mae Hong Song, Pai, and finally Chiang Mai.

Attractions

Temples: *Wats* and monasteries in Mae Sot reflect Burmese influence brought across the nearby border. Wat Chumphon Khiri, the largest *chedi* in town and visible from the morning market, is covered by brass brickwork and surrounded by 20 smaller plaster *chedis*.

Markets: Two of the chief attractions in Mae Sot are the morning market, which occurs in the narrow alleys near the Porn Thep Hotel, and the central market on the southern road. Both are filled with a gaggle of Thai, Burmese, Chinese, and Muslim traders who compete with the gem vendors operating from nearby shops.

Burmese Border: Five km west of Mae Sot is one of the three direct highway links between Thailand and Myanmar, the other two being Hwy. 106 north of Chiang Mai and north of Chiang Rai at Mae Sai. The trading post is commercialized and overrun with tourist shops, but visitors can gaze across the narrow Moi River to watch local merchants conduct the carefully regulated trade between Myawaddy and Rim Moi.

Accommodations

Mae Sot Guesthouse: Backpackers generally stay in this lovely teakwood house west of town in a quiet residential neighborhood. The owners can help with free maps and information on trekking in nearby provinces. 736 Indrakiri Rd., 40B dorm, 60-90B.

Mae Sot House: Maesot Travel Centre operates a small guesthouse on the highway just outside town. 14/21 Asia Hwy., tel. (055) 531409, 40-60B.

First Hotel: An old favorite opposite the former bus terminal. Rooms are large and clean with private bath. Keys are provided on small piston rods. 444 Indrakiri Rd., tel. (055) 531233, 140-180B fan, 220-300B a/c.

Siam Hotel: The most popular mid-priced hotel in Mae Sot has a shopping center, a cafe, and an outlet for SP Tours. 185 Prasat Vithi Rd., tel. (055) 531376, 120-180B fan, 220-350B a/c.

Transportation

Mae Sot is served by bus from Sukothai, Tak, Bangkok, or Chiang Mai. Thai Airways flies four times weekly from Chiang Mai and Phitsanulok.

Leaving Mae Sot is problematical since buses leave from several different locations. Tickets can be purchased and timetables checked at the Siam and First hotels. Government buses to Bangkok depart three times nightly between 2000 and 2100 from the office on Indrakiri Road. Sukothai Tours opposite the First Hotel has buses to Tak every 30 minutes and service to Phitsanulok at 0930. Tranjit Tours in the First Hotel also goes to Bangkok. Tavorn Frame Tours in the Siam Hotel has buses to most destinations including Tak, Phitsanulok, and Bangkok. The Mae Sot Guesthouse can help with details.

MAE SOT TO MAE SARIANG

One of the most adventurous journeys in Thailand is along the winding road which leads north from Mae Sot to Mae Sariang. This route provides a unique way to reach the far north since it avoids backtracking to Tak or Phitsanulok. The road skirts the banks of the Moi River, a geographical oddity which flows north through the Dawna Range until it intersects the Salween, which in turn continues south though the Burmese Shan states.

Accommodations

Several guesthouses and resorts have recently opened on the highway between Mae Sot and

Mae Sariang. Tan Song Yang, a rather prosperous village some 83 km north of Mae Sot, has three guesthouses. Chao Doi House, one of the most remote but memorable lodges in central Thailand, is on a mountaintop some 15 km east of Mae Salit. Ask the bus or *songtao* driver to drop you at the police box near Mae Salit, then hitch a ride up the mountain. Chao Doi House has been highly recommended by several travelers. Mon Krating Resort, an upscale resort on a hilltop east of Mae Salit and 135 km north of Mae Sot, is for group tours.

Transportation

Highway 1085 is now fully paved, though direct bus service from Mae Sot to Mae Sariang is still under development. As of this writing, the journey can only be completed with a series of buses and *songtaos* which cover limited segments of the highway. *Songtaos* depart in the early morning from Mae Sot and terminate at the small village of Mae Salit, slightly north of Tha Song Yang. Travelers often spend the first night at Chao Doi House (see above).

From Mae Salit to Ban Tha Song Yang (not to be confused with Tha Song Yang) a chartered *songtao* will probably be necessary and cost about 100B per person. Public buses and *songtaos* from Ban Tha Song Yang to Mae Sariang cost an additional 50B. Travelers have reportedly done the entire journey in a single day, but it's a long and very tough haul.

NORTHERN THAILAND

Northern Thailand's cool mountainous landscapes, friendly people, unique arts and architecture, dazzling handicrafts, unsurpassed ethnological variety, and superb shopping make it one of the highlights for any visitor to Thailand. While the region has lost some of its innocence to commercialization and modern developments, much of it remains a pristine destination still rich with distinctive customs and cultures. Best of all, the pace of life has stayed delightfully measured and people continue to exude the warmth and hospitality that first popularized the north.

Routes

Chiang Mai can be reached directly from Bangkok by air, train, or bus, but stopovers in Ayuthaya and Sukothai are highly recommended for visitors interested in history and archaeology. Travelers in Kanchanaburi can avoid backtracking to Bangkok by busing directly to Ayuthaya via Suphan Buri.

Dozens of routes are possible from Chiang Mai. Tribal trekking into the neighboring hills has become somewhat commercialized in recent years, but most travelers who undertake a five- to seven-day adventure still seem satisfied with their experiences. Lampang and Lamphun are two outstanding side trips from Chiang Mai.

Mae Hong Son, a western frontier town with mountainous scenery and Burmese temples, attracts travelers who enjoy venturing slightly off the beaten track and want to trek a more remote, untouched region. An exhausting but rewarding bus journey loops through Mae Sariang and Mae Hong Son before returning to Chiang Mai via Pai. Pai is one of the author's favorite spots to avoid tourists and relax in one of the least disturbed regions in Northern Thailand.

Then it's off to the Golden Triangle. The standard journey begins with a four-hour bus ride to Thaton, where longtail boats load up passengers and depart at 1300 for an exciting but deafening five-hour downriver trip to Chiang Rai. Before returning to Chiang Mai, a few days can be spent visiting the villages, hilltribes, and historic ruins in the region. Then it's back to Bangkok or a detour to the northeast via Phitsanulok. Another option is to do a Mekong River journey or head directly to Laos via Nong Khai in northeastern Thailand.

CHIANG MAI

Chiang Mai, principal city of the north, is the favorite destination for many travelers to Thailand. Situated on the banks of the River Ping and surrounded by green hills and lazing rivers, this thriving city is blessed with a mellow flavor and a cool, dry climate—the perfect remedy to the sweltering cities of the south. It's a world apart. With its

THAILAND

CHIANG MAI

TO CHIANG RAI

TO CHIANG RAI

HIGHWAY 1019

SUPERHIGHWAY

TO BORSANG & SAN KAMPHANG

TO BANGKOK

HIGHWAY 1006

POY LUANG HOTEL

CHIANG MAI BUS ARCADE (BANGKOK, CHIANG RAI, MAE HONG SON, ETC.)

TRAIN STATION

McCORMICK HOSPITAL

G.P.O.

MENGRAI KILNS

AMERICAN BAPTIST MISSION

BUSES TO BORSANG & SAN KAMPANG

GYMKHANA CLUB

BIG TREE

THAI TRIBAL CRAFTS

BOXING STADIUM

TO LAMPHUN

HIGHWAY 106

INDIAN CONSULATE

RIVERSIDE REST.

BUS TO LAMPHUN

TAT

MENGRAI BRIDGE

PING RIVER

NANG NUAL RESTAURANT

CHARON PRATET RD.

SUPERHIGHWAY

WAT PA PAO

WAT CHAI SRI PHUM

DARETS GH

TAPAE GATE

NIGHT MARKET

EMPRESS HOTEL

RIM PING HOTEL

WAT KU TAO

WAT CHIANG MAN

MOON MUANG RD.

BUSES TO DOI INTHANON & HANG DONG

CHIANG MAI GATE

NATIONAL THEATER

LANNA HOSPITAL

CHANG PUAK GATE

CHIANG MAI CULTURAL CENTER

OLD CHIANG MAI

TO FANG & THATON

HIGHWAY 107

CHANG PUAK BUS TERMINAL (FANG, THATON)

BUSES TO DOI SUTHEP

THAI AIRWAYS

JAIL

WAT CHEDI LUANG

WAT MENGRAI

SILVER SHOPS

SUAN PRUNG GATE

HIGHWAY 108

BANYEN ANTIQUES

LIBRARY

FANTASTIC ROOM

WAT PRA PONG

SUAN DOK GATE

WAT PRA SINGH

WAT PUAK HONG

RINCOME HOTEL

YMCA

MARBLE PUB

CHIANG MAI ORCHID HOTEL

THE PUB

HENNESY NIGHTCLUB

WAT SUAN DOK

TO HUAI KEO RD.

CHIANG MAI NATIONAL MUSEUM

WAT CHET YOT

SUTHEP RD.

WAT UMONG

TO DOI SUTHEP PALACE

ZOO

CHIANG MAI UNIVERSITY

TRIBAL RESEARCH CENTER

IMMIGRATION

AIRPORT

TO HOT, DOI INTHANON, HANG DONG & MAE HONG SON

500m

0

© MOON PUBLICATIONS, INC.

THAILAND

unique forms of architecture, dance, music, food, and festivals, Chiang Mai has always been a region both physically and emotionally separated from the remainder of Thailand. The people not only consider themselves superior to their cousins in Bangkok, they also happily agree with the national consensus that their fair-skinned ladies are the most beautiful in the country.

While Chiang Mai provides a refreshing change from the ordeals of Bangkok, travelers expecting a charming little village of wooden houses and rural lanes are in for a rude surprise. Commercial development and the rise of mass tourism have brought not only comfortable hotels and quality restaurants, but also concrete highrises and traffic jams in even the smallest of *sois*.

Nevertheless, Chiang Mai still retains enough traditional charm and warmth to make it one of Southeast Asia's most enjoyable destinations.

Attractions

Chiang Mai's temples range stylistically from early Mon and Sukothai prototypes to Ayuthayan and Burmese-style monuments. Northern architects characteristically favored large multilayered roofs that swoop down lower than those of Bangkok temples and muted exterior colors that typically employ less of the brazen reds, yellows, and blues found on southern temples. Northern architecture is also noted for flamboyant decoration and woodcarving such as filigree umbrellas and long-necked lions which reflect its two centuries of Burmese occupation. Some of the following temples stand in original condition while many others have been heavily restored in unrepresentative styles. Older temples have largely disappeared except for their crumbling *chedis,* which often predate by several centuries the primary *bot* and *viharn.*

The following walking tour describes temples on Tapae Road, followed by those inside and outside the old city walls. Chiang Mai has 80 registered temples and over 1,000 in the province, but the best monuments for rushed visitors are Wat Pra Singh, Wat Chedi Luang, Wat Chiang Man, Wat Chet Yot, and Wat Suan Dok.

Tapae Road Temples

Four temples of varying architectural interest are on Tapae Rd. between the shopping district and Tapae Gate.

Wat Saen Fang: Approached up an undulating *naga*-flanked lane that parallels new construction and crumbling old walls, Wat Saen Fang features a Burmese-style *chedi* decorated with corner cannons and whitewashed *singha* lions, a Burmese-style building used as a monks' residence, and a brightly painted *viharn* fronted by modernistic, abstract *nagas.*

Wat Bupparam: Three interior *viharns* illustrate the past, present, and future of Thai religious architecture. To the left is a soaring, garish, and ostentatious monument to bad taste that displays every gimmick used in modern Thai architecture. Other buildings make better impressions, especially the tiny, three-centuries-old wooden *viharn* to the right.

Wat Mataram: The Burmese-style *viharn* is distinguished by an entrance doorway beautifully carved with the Buddha preaching to the animals, and small tinkling bells which dangle from roof *nagas.* Don't get killed crossing Tapae Road to the next temple.

Wat Chettawan: This sanctuary attains great charm from its secluded location and broad lawns that support a family of hens and roosters. Note the moral sayings tagged to the trees: "If everything is gotten dreamily, it will go away dreamily too."

Central Temples

Wat Chedi Luang: Named after the massive but partially ruined *chedi* behind the modern *viharn,* this famous monument was erected in 1401 by animist King Sam Feng Ken, allowed to fall into ruin, then restored by Sam Feng Ken's son King Tiloka, who raised the monument to 90 meters. An earthquake in 1546 partially destroyed the *chedi,* although the well-preserved foundations still give a strong impression of its architectural magnitude.

Wat Mengrai: Some say the 4.5-meter bronze Buddha inside this rather ordinary temple is a life-size model of King Mengrai himself. As noted above, the gigantic but luckless king was killed by lightning just a few blocks away.

Wat Chiang Man: Wat Chiang Man was constructed by King Mengrai in 1296, but all of the present structures, aside from the ancient *chedi* in the rear, are reconstructions which date from the 19th and 20th centuries. Directly through the entrance gates stands an older *viharn* with an

THAILAND

elaborate gable richly carved with images of Erawan, the three-headed elephant which is now the symbol of royal patronage.

The building to the right is chiefly known for its pair of sacred images protected behind glass doors and two iron gates. To the left is the Crystal Buddha, Pra Setang Khamani, an image miraculously endowed with rainmaking powers and the centerpiece for the annual Songkran Festival. The Marble Buddha on the right, Pra Sila, is an Indian bas-relief image carved in the Pala style of the 8th century. To the left of the central *viharn* is a small modern chapel and an old *bot* with a fine collection of Lanna and U-Thong bronzes.

Between the old *bot* and the rear-side *chedi* stands an elevated *ho trai* (library), considered a masterpiece of woodcarving and lacquer decoration despite a recent repainting in gaudy colors. Behind the modern *viharn* towers one of the more interesting buildings in the complex, a 15th-century square *chedi* supported on the backs of 15 life-size stucco elephants.

Wat Pra Singh: Wat Pra Singh ("Monastery of the Lion Lord") was founded in the 14th century to house the ashes of King Kham Fu and serve as the principal religious center of the Lanna kingdom. The complex is composed of several buildings of varying architectural and artistic merit that form the most famous *wat* in Chiang Mai. The library, a registered historical monument, features outstanding stucco devas and scrollwork around the concrete foundation which supports the delicate wooden building. Directly behind the central *viharn* stands a Lanna-style *bot* constructed entirely of wood with an impressive entrance of stucco and gold leaf.

The most famous and beautiful structure at Wat Pra Singh—and among the most elegant structures in all of northern Thailand—is the small chapel in the southwest corner of the *wat* compound. The exterior is a remarkable mélange of fine proportions and delicate woodcarvings in the window frames and ancient doorways. Interior murals, though dimly lit, remain the best preserved in Chiang Mai and provide a glimpse of the religious and civil traditions of 19th-century Siam.

Attractions outside Town

Chiang Mai National Museum: Tribal costumes and a small collection of Buddha images are housed in this well-maintained but rather unimpressive museum. Kilns which once fired the famous Thai celadons have been reconstructed on the front courtyard. Open Wednesday-Sunday 0900-1200 and 1300-1600.

Wat Chet Yot: From both historical and architectural standpoints, this temple, also known as the Seven Spires Monastery, is considered the most important in Chiang Mai. Founded by King Tiloka in 1455 and modeled after the Bodgaya monument where Buddha attained enlightenment, Wat Chet Yot served as a monastery and center of Lanna Thai Buddhism for several centuries. In 1457, Tiloka convened the Eighth Buddhist Council here to commemorate the 2,000th anniversary of the Buddhist era. Mounted on the walls of the small but beautiful seven-spired Mon-Burmese *bot* are 12 stucco figures of seated divinities framed by standing figures. As unified ensembles, they form the finest stucco figures in Thailand.

Wat Umong: Most of this forest *wat,* located five km outside of town, has disappeared, except for ruined *chedis* and meditation grottoes dating back to 1265. A large map at the entrance describes the layout and bizarre highlights like the Spiritual Mural Painting Hall and Herb's Garden. Scattered around the grounds are trees thoughtfully tagged with amusing admonitions, fragments of Buddhist statuary, and old-style meditation huts built without the use of nails.

Wat Suan Dok: This monumental but completely ordinary temple is chiefly known for its beautiful Chiang Saen-style bronze Buddha cast in 1504.

Other Attractions

Tribal Research Center: Chiang Mai University's small museum and research library provides an excellent introduction to the various hilltribes. Located in building 15 at the far end of campus; pick up a map from the rector's office. Open Monday-Friday 0830-1200 and 1300-1700.

Chiang Mai Zoo: Thailand's largest zoo, with an arboretum and an enormous open-air bird sanctuary, was founded by a Westerner who donated hundreds of endangered animals to the local government. Open daily 0800-1700.

Old Chiang Mai Cultural Center: Handicrafts are hawked during the day from replicas of hilltribe dwellings; northern Thai-style *khan tok* banquets and hilltribe dancing are presented each evening. (See "Nightlife," below.) Laddaland, another hilltribe theme park with morning dance demonstrations, is disappointing.

West of Chiang Mai

Wat Phratat: One of northern Thailand's top attractions is the pair of golden 16th-century stupas which overlooks Chiang Mai from the summit of Doi Suthep. According to legend, the shrine was erected in 1383 after a wandering white elephant carrying a sacred Buddha relic stopped here, trumpeted three times, and promptly died—an auspicious sign by Thai standards. In 1935, Lamphun abbot Sri Vinchai announced the construction of the winding road up to the 1,000-meter summit and, with the help of thousands of volunteers, completed the project in just six amazing months.

The stupa is approached up a monumental, heart-pounding, 290-step staircase flanked by tremendous mythical *nagas* which symbolize man's progress from earth into nirvana. The present temples are rather ordinary, but on clear days views over the misty valley are absolutely spectacular.

Doi Suthep is 20 km west of Chiang Mai. Minibuses leave from the Chang Puak gate (north gate) and cost 35B up and 25B down. Bring warm clothing.

Royal Palace: Pu Ping Palace, official winter residence of the royal family, is generally closed to the public, but the beautiful gardens of roses, orchids, and bougainvillea are open weekends and holidays from 0830 to 1630. Five km beyond and a short minibus ride from Wat Doi Suthep.

East of Chiang Mai

Borsang Village: Thailand's famous umbrella village is located nine km east of town, just beyond the handicraft shops, remaining monkeypod trees, cool streams, and small villages constructed of teak. Borsang is a touristy but nevertheless pleasant place to photograph umbrellas drying in the sun and watch the lovely ladies deftly paint the satin, cotton, and paper parasols. Red-and-white minibuses leave from Charon Muang near Bumrung Raj road.

San Kamphang: Northern Thailand's silk and cotton-weaving village is where, in a show of pure concentration, young girls weave cloth on primitive handlooms while ignoring the tourists. Four km beyond Borsang. Same minibuses as above.

South of Chiang Mai

Hang Dong: Craftsmen in this town produce both bamboo baskets and woodcarvings from old tree stumps and paddy mortars. Thirteen km south of town.

Chom Tong: This small junction town is chiefly known for Wat Pra Tat Sri Chom Tong, a beautiful Burmese-style temple on the left side of the main road. Constructed between 1451 and 1516, this well-maintained temple features a central facade and gilded gables carved with remarkable skill. Fifty-eight km from town.

Doi Inthanon National Park: Often hidden behind a swirling mass of fog and rain, Thailand's highest mountain (2,565 meters) offers beautiful scenery, evergreen montane forests, dwarf rhododendron groves, rare birdlife, and impressive waterfalls: 20-meter Mae Klang Falls located 10 km from the park turnoff, Wachiratan Falls 20 km from Chom Tong, and Sri Phum Falls at Kilometer 31. Since regular transportation is sporadic, you must go on motorbike or charter a pickup in Chom Tong for 500-600B. Hitching is possible on weekends from the turnoff, one km before Chom Tong.

Budget Accommodations

Chiang Mai's 100-plus guesthouses comprise one of the finest accommodation scenes in all of Asia. Guesthouses, ideally, are teak houses owned and operated by local families with fewer than a dozen rooms that face a courtyard filled with flowers, books, and lounge chairs. A perfect guesthouse is also a source of trekking services, bike rentals, and advice on sightseeing, restaurants, and shopping. Genuine guesthouses—a marvelous experience for everyone no matter their age or wealth—have become so popular that many of Chiang Mai's conventional hotels are now calling themselves "guesthouses."

Guesthouses and hotels are located in four areas of town. Those on the east bank of the Ping River are comfortable and quiet, but a bicycle (often provided free) is necessary to get around. Between the Ping River and Moon Muang Rd. are mid-priced guesthouses and hotels ideally located within walking distance of

THAILAND

CENTRAL CHIANG MAI

★ WAT KU TAO

NEW LAMDUON FAHAM REST.

HOLLANDA GH

HIGHWAY 106

BUS TERMINAL NORTH TO FANG, THATON

FAMILY HOUSE

HIGHWAY 107

PUN PUN GH

WANG GH

JE T'AIME GH

MINIBUSES TO DOI SUTHEP

WAT CHIANG YUEN

WAT PA PAO

YOUR PLACE BAR

RIVER RESTAURANT

CHIANG PUAK GATE

HIGHWAY 1009

CHIANG MAI PRESIDENT HOTEL

HONEY CHICKEN

CITY OFFICES

CHARONNRAJ RD.

KHUM KAEW PALACE KHANTOKE REST.

U.S. CONSULATE

THAI AIRWAYS

WAT CHIANG MAN

WAT CHAI SRI PHUM

MEE GH

WANG KEO RD.

RAJPRANIKAI RD.

WAT DUAN CHANG

BAIN GARDEN

COLONIAL HERITAGE RESTAURANT

TAI WANG RD.

MOON MUANG RD.

RAJWITHI RD.

CHIANG MOI RD.

THE GALLERY RESTAURANT

CHAIYAPOON RD.

WAT DUANG DI

★ MARKET

WAT SAEN FANG

POST

RIVERSIDE CAFE

RAJADAMNERN RD.

WAT CHETTAWAN

D.K. BOOKS

TELEPHONE

TAPAE RD.

LA VILLA PENSION

WAT PAN TAO

TAPAE GATE

WAT MATARAM

WAT BUPPARAM

MOSQUE

BUS TO LAMPHUN

WAT CHEDI LUANG

CHIANG MAI RESTAURANT

GALARE GH

RAJAMANKA RD.

CHIANG INN

PORN PING HOTEL

RIVER VIEW

CHIANG MAI TEA HOUSE

WAT MENGRAI

ANODARD GH

NAT GH

AARON RAI RESTAURANT

DIAMOND HOTEL

TAT

PRA POKLAO RD.

LOI KROA RD.

NIGHT MARKET

NOVOTEL SURIWONGSE HOTEL

LE CHALET REST.

CHUMPOL GH

CHIANG MAI GH

GARDEN RESTAURANTS

LANNA THAI GH

BLUE MOON NIGHTCLUB

DUSIT INN

BANG KEO RESTAURANT

BUSES SOUTH TO HOT. CHONG THOM

ANSURAN NIGHT MARKET

CHIANG MAI GATE

SRI DON CHAI RD.

CHIANG MAI PLAZA HOTEL

SILVER SHOPS

SURIWONG BOOKS

WHOLE EARTH RESTAURANT

ALLIANCE FRANCAISE

WUA LAI RD.

BAN KAEW GH

WAT CHAI MONKOL

PING RIVER

0   300m

MOON

CHANG KLAN RD.

SEASON SHOPPING CENTER

CHARON PRATET RD.

NATIONAL THEATER

EMPRESS HOTEL

LANNA PALACE HOTEL

© MOON PUBLICATIONS, INC.

THAILAND

the night market and shopping centers. Inside the old city walls is the largest concentration of guesthouses, especially in the northeast corner. West of town, in the direction of Doi Suthep, are the up-scale hotels, which are quiet and luxurious but far removed from the temples and restaurants.

Guesthouse prices are fairly uniform throughout Chiang Mai. Low-end choices charge 60-120B for simple rooms with fan and common bath or 100-220B with fan and private bath. The emerging trend appears to be better guesthouses with a/c rooms and private bathrooms in the 250-400B range, described below under "Moderate Accommodations." Standards of comfort and cleanliness are similar, but those guesthouses which appear to offer superior ambience have been briefly described below.

The question of which guesthouse to recommend is a difficult one: ask a dozen travelers and you'll get a dozen different selections. The best tactic is to take a minibus from the main bus terminal, or hire a tricycle from the train station, to the general neighborhood and make a walking inspection. Guesthouse touts at the bus and train stations are fairly reliable sources of information. Other travelers throughout Thailand are often happy to make personal recommendations, and these will often prove your best choice.

Daret's Guesthouse: The backpackers' center in Chiang Mai has a popular outdoor cafe with good food and dozens of rooms with fan and private baths. 4 Chaiyapoon Rd., tel. (053) 235440, 80-150B fan.

Moon Muang Golden Court: A new three-story hotel with patio restaurant, travel services, and 30 rooms in various price ranges. 95 Moon Muang Rd., tel. (053) 212779, 140-220B fan, 250-300B a/c.

Rendezvous Guesthouse: Another new hotel on a quiet back street with large rooms, common hot showers, and giant TV in the garden courtyard. Rajadamnern Rd. Soi 5, tel. (053) 248737, 100-150B fan.

Ampawan House: Just across from the Rendezvous is another new place that is modern, clean, and very quiet due to its alley location. Rajadamnern Rd. Soi 5, tel. (053) 210584, 100-150B fan.

Pata Guesthouse: An old wooden house with rustic charm and tree-covered courtyard. Moon Muang Rd. Soi 6, tel. (053) 213625, 60-100B fan.

Moonshine House: A modern hotel just opposite Wat Chiang Man with clean rooms and tasty meals prepared by Duan, wife of the English owner. 212 Rajaphanikai Rd., 80-150B fan.

Racha Guesthouse: Racha and the adjacent Supreme Guesthouse are modern, clean places with good-value rooms; popular with long-term visitors. Moon Muang Rd. Soi 9, tel. (053) 210625, 80-120B fan.

Rose Guesthouse: Popular spot with beer garden decorated with hanging parasols, cane chairs, and other attempts at atmosphere. 87 Rajamanka Rd., tel. (053) 276574, 80-150B fan with common bath.

Moderate Accommodations

Most of the newer guesthouses which have recently opened in Chiang Mai are charging 150-250B for a clean room with fan and private bath, and 250-500B for an a/c room. While somewhat more expensive than the budget guesthouses listed above, the improved cleanliness and touch of luxury make these an outstanding value.

Gap's Antique House: One of Chiang Mai's finest guesthouses offers antique decor with modern amenities, plus a memorable cafe filled with artworks and teakwood carvings. Rajadamnern Rd. Soi 4, tel. (053) 213140, 250-500B a/c.

Fang Guesthouse: Beautiful four-story hotel with small garden, open-air dining room, and outstanding rooms with private bath. 46 Kampangdin Rd. Soi 1, tel. (053) 282940, 200B fan, 300-400B a/c.

Top North Guest House: Not really a guesthouse, but a modern, somewhat clean, decent-value hotel with reasonably priced a/c rooms and less expensive fan rooms. Top North even has a swimming pool. 15 Moon Muang Rd. Soi 2, tel. (053) 278900, fax (053) 278485, 150-250B fan, 300-500B a/c.

Baan Kaew Guesthouse: Tucked away in an alley just south of Alliance Française is this beautiful and quiet guesthouse with spacious gardens and a comfortable restaurant. 142 Charoen Prathet Rd., tel. (053) 271606, 300-350B fan, 400-500B a/c.

Pension La Villa: The somewhat isolated location is compensated by the lovely teakwood house and elevated dining room with some of the best Italian food in Chiang Mai. Italian manage-

THAILAND

ment. 145 Rajadamnern Rd., tel. (053) 215403, 200-250B fan, 250-300B a/c.

Living House: Another modern and very clean guesthouse in a convenient location near Tapae Gate. Tapae Rd. Soi 5, tel. (053) 275370, 200-250B fan, 250-300B a/c.

Lai Thai Guesthouse: A very large 90-room guesthouse which faces the old city and ancient moat. 111 Kotchasan Rd., tel. (053) 271725, fax (053) 272724, 300-350B fan, 400-500B a/c.

YMCA: The Chiang Mai Y has a swimming pool, a restaurant, convention facilities, and over 200 clean and comfortable rooms. Unfortunately, it's outside of city center and isolated from the shops and the night market. 11 Mengrai Rasmi Rd., tel. (053) 221819, fax (053) 215523, 80-200B a/c dorm, 300-600B a/c rooms with private bath.

Riverside Guesthouses

All of the guesthouses which hug the west bank of the Ping River offer either fan or a/c rooms with private baths, comfortable restaurants, and delightful views over the river. As with all other guesthouses and hotels in Chiang Mai, vacancies are scarce during the busy season from Nov. to March and advance reservations are strongly recommended. Reservations by fax are much better than phone calls or relying on the Thai mail system.

River View Lodge: The River View Lodge is nicely decorated with Thai furnishings and traditional woodcarvings and has a wonderful little restaurant. The helpful and courteous owner speaks flawless English. 25 Charoen Prathet Rd., tel. (053) 271109, fax (053) 279019, 1,000-1,800B.

Galare Guesthouse: A modern Thai-style guesthouse with both fan and a/c rooms with private baths. None of the rooms offer river views, but Galare remains a good choice in a great location. 7 Charoen Prathet Rd., tel. (053) 293885, 400-450B fan, 500-700B a/c.

Restaurants

Chiang Mai offers a wide range of dining experiences, from northern Thai dishes to European and Asian specialties. Prices are very low, and dining environments run the gamut from simple street stalls to elaborate teakwood homes and riverside cafes and nightclubs.

Daret's Restaurant: Chiang Mai's most popular travelers' hangout serves fairly good food plus outstanding fruit shakes and smoothies in a friendly atmosphere. Chaiyapoon Road. Inexpensive.

JJ Restaurant: A modern, clean, a/c cafe with bakery, espresso, ice cream, and Thai and American dishes. Great spot for breakfast and the *Bangkok Post.* Montri Hotel. Moon Muang Road. Inexpensive.

Croissant Cafe: Walking tours of Chiang Mai might start with breakfast at either JJ Restaurant, Times Square, or this small a/c cafe near the Tapae Rd. temples. 318 Tapae Road. Inexpensive.

Times Square Roof Garden: Great views and thick coffee can be enjoyed from the rooftop cafe near Tapae Gate. Best at breakfast. Tapae Rd. Soi 6. Inexpensive.

AUM Veggie Cafe: Among the excellent dishes are vegetarian spring rolls, tofu specialties, and meatless entrees; great food at rock-bottom prices. Moon Muang Rd. just south of Rajadamnern. Inexpensive.

Thai German Dairy: Excellent Western dishes such as muesli, homemade yogurt and breads, porridge, and pizza. Moon Muang Rd. Soi 2. Inexpensive.

Aaron Rai: Some of the city's best northern Thai dishes are served in this simple cafe near Tapae Gate. An English-language menu is available. Native specialties include *gang hang ley* (pork curry), *nam prik* (spicy salsa), and *kao neow* (sticky rice). Be sure to try the unlisted regional favorite, *laab,* a dish of diced pork mixed with chilies, basil, and sautéed onions. Other selections include *tabong* (fried bamboo shoots) and *sai owa* (sausage stuffed with pork and herbs). Brave souls can feast on *jing kung* (roasted crickets) and other exotic specialties. 45 Kotchasan Road. Inexpensive.

Bierstube: Ask a local where to dine and the answer will often be this cozy restaurant in the center of Chiang Mai. Though the German and American dishes are popular, Bierstube cooks some of the best Thai dishes in town. 33 Moon Muang Road. Moderate.

The Pub: Superb English and French meals served in a homey place considered one of the most genial gathering spots in town. The Pub is decorated in English fashion with darts, old beer signs, a collection of cigarette packs, and a

THAILAND

roaring fireplace in the winter months. Outside town but worth the *tuk tuk* ride. Huay Kaeo Rd. near the Rincome Hotel. Moderate.

Whole Earth Restaurant: Thai, vegetarian, and Pakistani dishes served in a beautiful Thai building surrounded by lovely gardens. Nightly entertainment ranges from Indian sitar to Thai folk guitar. 88 Sri Donchai Road. Moderate.

Bankao Restaurant: Upscale and memorable, the teakwood "Old House" near the Ansuran night market is a romantic spot with loads of atmosphere. Sit upstairs for piano music, photographs of the royal family, and decent entrees, well priced. Ansuran Road. Moderate to expensive.

Chalet: French dishes served in a genuine old northern teak mansion. Chef John Evalet operates one of Asia's most famous French restaurants on the banks of the Ping River. 71 Charoen Prathet Road. Expensive.

The Hill Restaurant: Somewhat reminiscent of a Tom Sawyer house, the Hill is a weird multilevel treehouse situated in a small forest. Food is only average but the atmosphere is unique and prices are low. 122 Suan San Sai Road. Inexpensive.

Markets

Chiang Mai has one major night market and several small spots popular with Thais and budget travelers.

Ansuran Night Market: Chiang Mai's most lively and authentic dining experience is the food market which operates nightly on Ansuran Rd. between Chang Klan and Charoen Prathet roads, just around the corner from the night bazaar. Dozens of stalls prepare a wide range of inexpensive dishes such as rich mussel omelettes, steamed crabs large enough for two people, and grilled fish served with your choice of sauces. Ansuran Road. Inexpensive.

Thor Loong Market: Budget travelers staying in the guesthouses near Tapae Gate often frequent the street stalls and cafes of Thor Loong. Chaiyapoon Road. Inexpensive.

Restaurants East of the Ping River

Some of the best restaurants are across the river in the old neighborhood once favored by foreign missionaries and diplomats.

Riverside Cafe: Probably the most popular *farang* hangout in Chiang Mai offers relaxed dining on its Thai entrees, then stay for the live music which ranges from light folk to heavy rock. 9 Charoenraj Road. Moderate.

Gallery Restaurant: This outstanding place combines an art gallery with a beautiful garden in a renovated Chinese shophouse. Superb atmosphere and pleasant views. 25 Charoenraj Road. Moderate.

Bain Garden: In the compound of the old Bombay-Burma teak consortium is a simple cafe with low-priced meals. Across from an imposing mansion owned by a Chinese jade merchant (not Khun Sa). 2 Wat Gate Rd. Soi 1. Inexpensive.

Colonial Heritage: An old mansion converted into an upscale restaurant with a spacious backyard dining area. 8 Wat Gate Rd. Soi 1. Moderate.

Dinner Dance Shows

Chiang Mai's classic dining experience is *khantoke,* a traditional northern buffet accompanied by a brief demonstration of Thai dance. It's completely touristy but also fun, reasonably priced, and one of the few opportunities in Thailand to see traditional dance. *Khantokes* cost 200-300B and reservations should be made in advance.

Old Chiang Mai Cultural Center: Since 1971, the complex south of downtown has been presenting meals and dance shows in its teakwood compound. After a very mild but unlimited meal, northern Thai dances are presented in the dining room, followed by hilltribe and folk dances in the adjacent amphitheater. 185 Wulai Road. 300-350B.

Khum Kaew Palace: A large teakwood residence near Thai Airways also presents *khantoke* meals and traditional dance. Rajaphanikai Road. 250-300B.

Diamond Hotel: The most convenient location for *khantoke* is the teakwood mansion behind the Diamond Hotel and near the banks of the Ping River. Unlike the Old Chiang Mai Center, this is an intimate spot where everyone is guaranteed a close look at the dancers. Diamond Hotel. 350-450B.

Information

Tourist Office: The very helpful tourist office on the Chiang Mai-Lamphun Road has free maps, magazines, and lists of bus and train departures, hotels, guesthouses, and licensed trekking agencies. Open daily 0900-1630. The Tourist Police are also located here.

Mail: Chiang Mai's main post office, on Charon Muang Road near the train station, is open Monday-Friday 0900-1700 and Saturday until noon.

Telephone: Phone calls can be made from the main GPO, the branch on Praisani Road, the airport, and until midnight from the international telephone service at 44 Sri Dornchai Road.

Visas: Visas can be extended at Thai Immigration near the airport. India, Japan, and the U.S. maintain consular posts in Chiang Mai.

Bookstores: Chiang Mai's best bookstore is Suriwong Books on Sri Don Chai Road. Hudson Enterprises on Tapae Road and the bookstore near the Tapae Gate occasionally have large-scale USGS topographical maps. The a/c reading room inside the United States Information Service (USIS) on Rajadamnern Road stocks current magazines and newspapers. David's Traveler Library in the Saithum Guesthouse off Moon Muang Road is a good source of trekking information, while Nancy Chandler's *Map of Chiang Mai* is absolutely indispensable for information on restaurants, local transportation, and important place-names in Thai script—*highly recommended!*

More Tips: McCormick Hospital is the best. Transcendental meditation classes are given at the Whole Earth Restaurant, Wat Ram Poeng near Wat U Mong, and the Buddha Dhamma Center near Laddaland. Runners can join the Hash House Harriers at the Pub. English-language schools sometimes hire native English speakers but at very low pay.

Warnings: Penalties for the use or possession of drugs are extremely severe in Thailand. Tricycle drivers sell the dope and turn you in for the reward. Guesthouses are periodically raided by the police and those who can't immediately settle their fines go directly to jail. Chiang Mai is a town with heavy drug penalties.

Getting There

Chiang Mai is 700 km north of Bangkok and can be reached by air, train, or bus.

Bus: Air-conditioned public coaches depart from Bangkok's Northern Bus Terminal three times daily 0900-1000 and eight times daily 2000-2145, cost 300-350B, and take 10-12 hours. Non-a/c buses depart hourly and cost 180-220B. Most buses stop at Chiang Mai's Arcade Bus Terminal outside town, from where yellow minibuses 3 and 4 continue to hotels and guesthouses.

Alternatively, several private bus companies in Bangkok offer similar service at comparable prices. Book these through travel agents; hotel pick-up is usually provided. Buses are fast and cheap but also cramped, cold, and hair-raising. Valium from local pharmacies will help.

Train: Except for air services, second-class coach with sleeper is the fastest and most comfortable way to reach Chiang Mai. Express trains depart Bangkok's Hualampong Station nightly at 1800, 1940, and 0640, and take 13 hours to reach Chiang Mai. Rapid trains depart at 1500 and 2200 and take 15 hours. Ordinary trains leave throughout the day. Advance reservations are recommended. Tricycles from the station cost 10B to any guesthouse.

By Air: Thai Airways' five daily flights to Chiang Mai take one hour and cost 1,900-2,400B. Taxis from the airport to most hotels cost 50-70B.

Getting Around

Chiang Mai is a compact town and all sights in the central section are within walking distance. To explore the more far-flung destinations, a rented bicycle or motorcycle is recommended. Bikes cost 20-25B and motorcycles 100-250B daily from guesthouses and shops near Daret's Restaurant on Moon Muang Road. Check the condition carefully and drive safely! Tricycles cost 5-10B for most short trips. Local yellow minibuses numbered 1-4 and described on Nancy Chandler's map ply four routes around town.

Leaving Chiang Mai

Public buses for most destinations in Chiang Mai Province leave from the Chang Puak Bus Terminal north of the city. Minibuses to Doi Suthep leave from Chang Puak Gate. Minibuses to points south leave near the southern Chiang Mai Gate. Buses to more distant destinations such as Chiang Rai, Mae Hong Son, Sukothai, and Bangkok leave from the Chiang Mai Arcade Bus Terminal northeast of town.

HILLTRIBE TREKKING

One of Thailand's most memorable experiences is visiting and living briefly among the seminomadic hilltribe people of northern Thailand. Most of these agriculturalists migrated here from Laos and southern China via Burma over the last century. Today, despite the inroads of Westernization and government programs to encourage their assimilation into mainstream Thai society, these groups have to a surprising degree maintained their distinct languages, animist customs, patterns of dress, and strong sense of ethno-consciousness.

Although these packaged adventures are called "treks," they more closely resemble long walks than some Nepalese marathon. Treks generally last three to seven days and involve several hours of daily hiking over foothills, wading across streams, and tramping under bamboo forests before spending the evening in a local village. After a late-afternoon arrival at the village, visitors are welcome to politely wander around, watch the women weave or pound rice, play with the kids, and take a few discreet photos.

Western comforts are rare: accommodations are limited to wooden floors in the headman's house, bathrooms are in the distant bushes, and bathing takes place in nearby streams. Dinner is often a simple meal of sticky rice, boiled vegetables, and hot tea. After the plates are cleared, dozens of villagers, children, curious teenagers, and shy young girls fill the lodge for an awkward but fascinating conversation conducted through your interpreter-guide. You can ask about their customs and beliefs, but be prepared to explain yours and perhaps sing a song! Opium is offered after the villagers wander back to their houses and all the children have been put to bed.

Where to Go

Golden Triangle: Hilltribe villages are scattered over most of northern Thailand but the first trekking, some 20 years ago, was in the Golden Triangle area north of the Kok River. Although the hill people continue to live and dress in traditional manner, some of the more accessible villages have been overtrekked and have become sadly commercialized. This is, however, one of the only areas to visit Akhas and the easiest place to do some self-guided trekking without the use of a guide. Self-guided treks can start here or halfway down the river. Another good spot to start is Mae Salong, a small Kuomintang village northwest of Chiang Rai. Guesthouses in Chiang Dao, Fang, Thaton, Chiang Rai, Chiang Saen, and Mae Salong can help with details.

North of Chiang Mai: The region around Chiang Dao and Wiang Papao, midway between Chiang Mai and Fang, was the next area opened to explorers. Treks typically begin with a three-hour jeep ride to a drop-off point on the Chiang Mai-Fang highway, then half a day of hiking to reach the first village. Trekking groups occasionally pass each other and the villagers are now quite accustomed to Westerners.

Mae Hong Son: The early '80s saw the focus shift west of Chiang Mai toward the isolated town of Mae Hong Son, the newest and least commercialized trekking area in Thailand. Trekking agencies are located in Chiang Mai, Mae Hong Son, Pai, Soppong, and Mae Sariang.

Trekking Tips

Research: Paul and Elaine Lewis's *Peoples of the Golden Triangle* is the best of recently published books. Other useful books include the Time-Life publication of Frederic Grunfeld's *Wayfarers of the Thai Forest,* which details Akha lifestyles, and *Highlanders of Thailand,* which provides a comprehensive collection of well-edited essays, including a chapter on the effects of tourism. These books are difficult to find in Chiang Mai and should be read in advance. *People of the Hills* by Preecha Chaturabhand is somewhat trashy (sex lives of the Akhas) but available locally and small enough to be carried on the trek. A few hours browsing in the Tribal Research Center at Chiang Mai University will also help.

When to Go: Winter months (late October to early February) are the ideal time to enjoy the cool nights and warm days without the threat of rain; also the best season to find poppies in full bloom. The rainy months (June to September) can be difficult if not impossible.

Group or Self-guided Tour?: Organized treks are best because of language difficulties, security problems, and the possibility of getting lost on the winding trails.

THAILAND

PEOPLES OF THE HILLS

Inhabiting the hills of northern Thailand are thousands of hilltribe peoples who struggle to maintain their traditional lifestyles against poverty, overpopulation, and the pressures of encroaching civilization. Most of these semi-nomadic tribes are of Tibetan-Burmese or Tibetan-Chinese origin, having migrated across the border from southern China via Myanmar less than 100 years ago. Today they wander from camp to camp employing slash-and-burn (swidden) farming techniques to cultivate rice, vegetables, and their most famous crop: opium. Swidden agriculture typically begins in January, when secondary or tertiary forests are cut down and left to dry before being burned in March or April. Rice is planted in the fertilizer ash after the monsoon rains break in June. Rice stalks are cut four months later with small hand sickles, then threshed and winnowed to remove the chaff. Opium and maize are planted in October and harvested during a 10-week period from December to January. Although one of the world's oldest agricultural techniques, slash-and-burn farming is extremely destructive since it depletes the soil of important nutrients and leaves the fields abandoned to useless shrub such as *lalang*. It also perpetuates tribal migrations, making it impossible to divide the region into neatly defined ethnic districts.

Thailand's hilltribes are sometimes described as peaceful people living in idyllic harmony with nature—something of a forgotten Shangri-La—but nothing could be further from the truth. Most are extremely poor and live in dirty wooden shacks without running water, adequate sanitation, medical facilities, or educational opportunities for their children. Illiteracy, disease, opium addiction, and deforestation are other problems. Uncontrolled erosion and soil depletion have reduced crop yields, while land, once plentiful and rich, has become scarce from tribal overpopulation and the arrival of land-hungry lowlanders. Royal aid projects provide help and discourage opium production in favor of alternative cash crops, but tribal political power remains minimal since tribespeople are stateless wanderers, not Thai citizens. The Thai government recognizes six major groups of hilltribes, subdivided into dozens of subtribes with distinct language, religious beliefs, customs, costumes, and historical backgrounds. The following descriptions include those tribes most likely to be encountered by trekkers. The Western tribal designation is given first, followed by the local Thai terminology.

Akha

TERRA MUZICK

Akha (Ekaw)
Population: 27,000
Origin: Yunnan, China
Location: Golden Triangle

Considered among the poorest and least sophisticated of all hilltribes, the Akhas are also among the most dazzling in costume. Women's dress typically includes a long-sleeved jacket and a short skirt woven from homespun cotton dyed dark blue with indigo. The crowning glory is the Akha headdress, an elaborate pile of cloth stretched over a bamboo frame festooned with bird's feathers, iridescent wings of beetles, silk tassels, dog fur, squirrel's tails, and Indian silver rupees. Leggings are worn to protect against brambles and thorns. The shy and retiring Akhas construct their villages at high elevations to escape neighbors and provide privacy for opium cultivation. Primitive wooden figures flanking the village entrance gates are carved with prominent sex organs to ensure fertility and ward off evil spirits. Don't touch these talisman gates or the bamboo spirit houses scattered throughout the village. Most villages have giant swings used during festivals, and courting grounds where young people meet to find mates.

Homes are enormous structures divided into separate sleeping quarters for males and females. Like most tribespeoples, Akhas are animists who believe that the spirits of nature, departed ancestors,

THAILAND

and graveyard-dwelling malevolent ghosts must be appeased with frequent animal sacrifice. Despite efforts to preserve their traditional lifestyle, Akhas face the challenges of poverty, political impoverishment, deforestation, overpopulation, and discrimination from other tribespeople, who consider them the bottom of the social order.

Hmong (Meo)
Population: 65,000
Origin: Laos
Locations: Chiang Mai, Laotian border

The Hmong, called Meo by the Thais, are a fiercely independent people who fled Chinese persecution over the last century for the relative peace of northern Thailand. Today the second largest tribal group in Thailand, the Hmong have become the country's leading opium producers by establishing their villages on mountain tops—higher elevations are considered best for opium cultivation. Thai Hmong are subdivided into White and Blue, color distinctions that refer to costume hues rather than linguistic or cultural differences. Despite their isolation, Hmongs are not shy or rare; you will see them in Chiang Mai's night market selling exquisite needlework and chunky silver jewelry. Traditional female costume includes a short jacket of Chinese design, circular silver neck rings, and a thickly pleated dress handwoven from cannabis fiber. Their striking and voluminous hairstyle is made by collecting old hair and braiding it together into a bun.

Karen

Young people enjoy a degree of sexual freedom. Courting begins during the New Year festivals when teenagers meet and make arrangements to rendezvous again during rice-planting season. All this ends when the prospective husband makes a monetary offering of five silver ingots to the girl's parents.

Karen (Yang, Kariang)
Population: 275,000
Origin: Myanmar
Location: Thai-Myanmar border

Thailand's largest hilltribe is the only group not heavily engaged in opium cultivation. Settlements are so numerous that most trekking groups pass through at least one of several subdivisions. Karens are divided into the Sgaw, who live near Mae Hong Son, and the Pwo to the south of Mae Sariang. Smaller Burmese groups include the Kayahs (Karenni or Red Karens) in Kayah State (just across the border from Mae Hong Son) and the Pao who live in southern Shan state.

Karens are a peaceful, honest, and hardworking people who use sound methods of swidden agriculture to save topsoil and minimize cogon growth. Their women are superb weavers whose multicolored skirts, blouses, and wedding garments have become prized collectors' items. Female dress often denotes marital status: young girls wear white cotton shifts while married women wear colored sarongs and overblouses. Multiple strands of beads
(continues on next page)

Hmong

TERRA MUZICK

THAILAND

PEOPLES OF THE HILLS
(continued)

are popular, but most women shun the heavy silver jewelry favored by other tribal groups. Males are often covered with elaborate tattoos that permanently satisfy ancestral spirits and eliminate expensive spirit ceremonies.

Religious beliefs run the gamut from animism and Buddhism to visionary millennial movements that prophesy a future, messianic king. Karen Christians call him the final Christ, Buddhists call him the fifth and final incarnation.

Lahu (Musser)
Population: 45,000
Origin: Southwestern China

Locations: Chiang Dao, Fang, Golden Triangle
Lahus are one of the most assimilated of all northern tribes. Most belong to the Black (Lahu Na) or Red (Lahu Nyi) linguistic groups while a minority speak two dialects of the Yellow (Lahu Leh and Shi). Older Lahus, who haven't yet adopted modern costume, dress in black robes richly embroidered with red zigzagged stitching and silver ornaments. Children often wear Chinese beanies sprouting red puff balls.

Like most tribals, Lahus are animists who believe their village priests can exorcise evil spirits with black magic and heal the sick with sacred

Lisu

TERRA MUZICK

amulets. And like the Karens, they anticipate a messianic movement lead by Guisha, the supreme Lahu God who created the heavens. Their most famous postwar messiah was Maw Naw, the Gibbon God who failed in his attempts to restore true Lahu religion and lead his people back into Myanmar.

Ceremonial life revolves around the lively New Year festival in which, after dancing, top spinning, and other games, males court females by blowing gourd signals and poking them with sticks through the slats of the bamboo floor. Special pavilions are available for marriage proposals and lovemaking.

Lisu (Lisa)
Population: 20,000
Origin: Myanmar

Locations: Chiang Dao, Fang, Mae Hong Son
Thailand's premier opium cultivators and the most culturally advanced of all hilltribes are an outgoing, friendly, and economically successful group of people. While most hilltribe villages are poor and dirty, Lisu villages are often clean and prosperous, loaded with sewing machines, radios, motorcycles, and perhaps a Datsun truck. Terrific salespeople, they enjoy setting up stalls and selling their handicrafts in Chiang Mai's night market.

Lahu

THAILAND

Their enthusiasm and determination to outshine every other tribal group are reflected in their beautiful and extremely stylish clothing. Females typically wear brilliant blue skirts topped with electric red blouses and rakish turbans festooned with long strands of multicolored yarn. This dazzling costume is complemented by a cascade of silver buttons and long dangling ornaments that hang over the chest.

Lisu religion revolves around the familiar animist spirits, but also weretigers and vampires that might take possession of a person. Lisus are also noted for their complicated marriage rituals and hedonistic New Year festival of endless dancing, drinking, and religious rituals.

Mien (Yao)

Population: 35,000
Origin: Southern China
Location: Chiang Rai Province

Mien

TERRA MUZICK

Mien are a hard-working and materially advanced people whose Chinese characteristics have made them the cultural sophisticates of Thai tribals. Called Yao by the Thai, the Mien originated in southern China as a non-Han group before migrating into Thailand via Laos between 1910 and 1950. Most have dutifully kept their Chinese cultural links such as Chinese script and Taoist religion. Sacred scrolls that function as portable icons (similar to Tibetan *tankas*) are their great artistic creations. When unrolled and hung up, these Taoist tapestries change ordinary rooms into temporary temples. Tragically, most have been sold to Bangkok antique merchants by impoverished Mien.

Yao women wear large black turbans, distinctive red boas around their necks, and loose-fitting pants embroidered with stunning pastiches of triangle, tie-dye, and snowflake designs.

Selecting the Trekking Agency: Chiang Mai's 40 registered trekking agencies meet together monthly to make reports to the police department, set agreements on rates, and discuss problems. Neither the TAT nor the Tribal Research Center makes specific recommendations on trekking agencies, but everyone agrees that the most important factors are the qualifications of the guide. Meet with him to determine his age, maturity, trekking experience, knowledge of tribal customs and local dialects, and sensitivity to the hilltribes.

Trek Details: Make a firm agreement on all services the trekking company will provide. How many days will the trek last? Since it takes at least two days to reach the relatively untouched villages, a trek of five to seven days will prove much more rewarding than shorter treks. How big will the group be? Groups of more than six people are large and unwieldy and should be avoided. What areas will be visited? Everybody promises the "newest untrekked area," but exactly how many other trekking groups will be in the region with yours? Crossing tracks with another group is to be expected, but it should still be held to a minimum. What hilltribes will be visited? Ideally you should visit three or four distinct groups rather than just five Karen groups in five days. What about the price? Rates set by the Chiang Mai Trekking Guide Association average 1,000-1,800B for a five-day trek, but special trips with elephant rides and river rafting are much more expensive. What else is included? Lodging, food, and transportation are normally factored with the package price, but check on exclusions. Rucksacks and sleeping bags for cooler winter months may also be provided.

Behavior: Experts emphasize the importance of remembering that hill people are human be-

THAILAND

ings with customs, values, and emotions just as valid as those of the tourist. Visitors should act politely and observe local customs. Your guide can advise on local taboos such as avoiding villages marked with bamboo crosses or touching the fertility symbols which guard some villages. Modesty should always be observed. Revealing halter tops on the ladies and nude bathing in the local streams are definitely taboo. Before unpacking the camera, establish some kind of rapport with the villagers. Most tribespeople allow photos when taken discreetly, but it's best to ask permission. Rather than handing out sweets, cigarettes, cheap trinkets, or money for photos, offer food, Band-Aids, disinfectants, soap, toothpaste, and other necessities.

Warning: Should the trekking company or guesthouse offer to keep your valuables, both parties should prepare a complete list of valuables and issue an itemized receipt. Some travelers report that stored valuables, such as traveler's checks or camera equipment, have disappeared during their trek. Even worse, trekkers' credit cards have been surreptitiously used to purchase goods in Bangkok with the cooperation of agreeable shopkeepers—a theft undetected until your Visa bill arrives back home. To prevent this type of fraud (more common than robbery during the trek), make a detailed report and leave all valuables in a locked bag for which you have the only key.

LAMPHUN

Thailand's oldest town makes a fine day outing from Chiang Mai. According to Siamese chronicles, the ancient 7th-century city was founded by a wandering hermit named Suthep who invited Lopburi's Mon princess Chama Devi to reign as the city's first queen. During the next six centuries, Lamphun (then known as Haripunchai) served as capital for an independent Mon kingdom until it fell to King Mengrai's Lanna Thai kingdom in 1281 and was occupied by the Burmese in 1556. Most of the present attractions date from the early 16th century except for one amazing temple which dates from the Mon (Dvaravati) period.

Lamphun is 26 km south of Chiang Mai and can be reached by green buses which leave

every 30 minutes from Lamphun Road near Nawarat Bridge. Visitors with extra time might stop en route at the McKean Leper Rehabilitation Institute, four km off the main road and open Monday-Friday 0800-1700, and the basket-weaving village of Saraphi.

Attractions

Lamphun Museum: A small but worthy collection of Lanna Thai art is displayed inside this branch of the National Museum just opposite Wat Haripunchai. Open Wednesday-Sunday 0900-1200 and 1300-1600.

Wat Prathat Haripunchai: Lamphun's royal monastery, on the left side of the main street, was founded in 897 by a Mon king to enshrine a sacred Buddha relic. Of the dozen-plus beautiful buildings, two of the best are the 50-meter Chiang Saen-style *chedi* covered in copper plates and a 19th-century Lanna-style library elevated above the ground to protect against termites. Many of the buildings owe their Burmese flavor to 20th-century reconstructions.

Wat Kukut: Also known as Wat Chama Devi, this intriguing *chedi* is a must-see for all visitors to Lamphun. The taller of the two *chedis* dates from 1218; it's perhaps the finest example of Dvaravati architecture left in Thailand. By constructing this pyramidal *chedi* with five diminishing tiers graced with 15 diminishing Buddhas, Mon architects created both a monument of great artistic merit and a clever optical illusion. Located one km up the small street next to the museum.

Accommodations

Most visitors see Lamphun on a day-trip from Chiang Mai, though a few Thai hotels are scattered around town.

Lamphun Hotel: Simple rooms with common or private baths are available in the yellow building four shops down from the corner. 51 Inthayong Rd., tel. (053) 511176, 80-150B.

Sawat Ari Hotel: Another hotel marked only with a Thai sign, near Wat Kukut. Chamdevi Rd., 80-100B.

LAMPANG

Lampang, 100 km southeast of Chiang Mai on the arterial highway between Bangkok and the

THAILAND

north, was once a sleepy town known for its temples and nostalgic horse-drawn carriages. Today it's a busy commercial center of 50,000 residents with some of the finest Burmese-style temples in Thailand.

Lampang is a very long day-trip from Chiang Mai or an excellent one-day stopover between Chiang Rai and points south. Buses from Chiang Mai take three hours and leave from the Arcade Terminal and the bus stop on Charonraj Road just across the Ping River. Maps to the following hotels and attractions can be obtained at the Lampang tourist office at the eastern end of Thakrownoi Road, a 15-minute tricycle ride east from the bus or train terminals.

Attractions

Wat Chedi Sao: Located across the Wang River and outside the city limits, this rather unimpressive temple is saved by its peaceful location among the rice paddies. The tourist map shows it as temple number one.

Wat Pra Keo Don Tao: Although located in the middle of a disorienting neighborhood and difficult to find, this Burmese shrine with its massive *chedi*, well-carved Burmese-style chapel, small museum, and Thai-style temple is worth seeking out.

Wat Pra Fang: Central Lampang has three magnificent temples that rank among the finest Burmese structures in the country. Wat Pra Fang, just opposite the Thai Airways office, features a delicate *chedi* surrounded by seven small chapels filled with alabaster Buddhas that represent the seven days of the week.

Wat Sri Chum: Excellent woodcarving and inlaid colored glass make Sri Chum one of Lampang's great sights.

Wat Sri Rong Muang: Lampang's most awesome Burmese sanctuary dazzles the visitor with its glittering multicolored exterior of carved wood and corrugated iron, superb interior woodcarving, and vast collection of sacred images donated by wealthy patrons.

Attractions near Lampang

Wat Prathat Lampang Luang: One of northern Thailand's finest monuments is the 11th-century walled temple located 20 km southwest of Lampang. The massive complex includes a pair of modern Chinese temples, sagging *bodhi*

trees supported by pilgrim posts, dozens of Buddha images including an effigy carved from jade, six *viharns* with outstanding facades, and a monumental 45-meter *chedi*.

Minibuses from Lampang reach Koh Ka, a small town four km off the main road. From Koh Ka, take a motorcycle taxi or walk three km to the monastery.

Elephant School: Thailand's official elephant training camp is located between Chiang Mai and Lampang. Here in a beautiful wooded basin, mahouts train young pachyderms each morning 0700-1100, except on Buddhist holidays and during the hot season from March to June. This is the real thing—not a tourist performance! Take an organized tour from Chiang Mai.

Pha Thai Caves: Some 339 steps lead up to this 400-meter cave filled with limestone formations, stalagmites, and Buddha images illuminated by a string of electric lights. Entrance is 800 meters off highway H1 just past kilometer stone 665, 66 km north of Lampang. Buses can be flagged down in Ban Pang La.

Accommodations

Lampang has about 20 hotels in all price ranges. Most are in the downtown district on Boonyawat and Robiwang roads.

Sri Sanga Hotel: Just east of the Lampang Hotel is a small hotel with inexpensive fan-cooled rooms and better a/c rooms. 213 Boonyawat Rd., tel. (054) 217070, 100-220B.

No 4 Guesthouse: Nobody speaks English, but the place, formerly Thai Guesthouse, has several teakwood cabins and a communal longhouse in a wonderful location on the northern side of the Wang River. Pongsanuk Rd., 80-150B.

Asia Lampang Hotel: Centrally located, the remodeled Asia Lampang has conference facilities, a "Sweety" Room, and the Kumluang Restaurant with "Thai, Chinese and Uropean food by the professional cookers." 229 Boonyawat Rd., tel. (054) 217844, 280-330B.

MAE SARIANG

This small town, midway between Chiang Mai and Mae Hong Son, serves as a good base for treks and river adventures down the Yuam and Salween rivers, which separate Thailand from

Myanmar. Progress has arrived slowly to the region, a blessing for the town, which has retained many of its fine old wooden buildings and simple temples constructed in Burmese-Shan style.

A quick stroll around town turns up a few temples of fairly recent vintage, but the main reason to visit Mae Sariang is to enjoy a boat ride down the Salween or Yuam rivers. Excursions can be organized at most of the guesthouses in town.

Accommodations

Mae Sariang has a handful of simple guesthouses and hotels that cater to the steady trickle of Western tourists.

Riverside Guesthouse: Best choice in town is the lovely guesthouse overlooking the Yuam River. The breezy restaurant is a great place to relax after a long bus ride. 85/1 Lang Panit Rd., tel. (053) 681188, 60-350B.

Kamolsorn Hotel: A new and modern three-story hotel with big fan-cooled rooms and private baths. Very clean and comfortable. Wai Seuksa Rd., 200B.

Transportation

Mae Sariang is 200 km southwest of Chiang Mai and 165 km from Mae Hong Son. Buses leave the Arcade Bus Terminal in Chiang Mai every two hours and take four or five hours to reach Mae Sariang. The same service is offered from the bus terminal in Mae Hong Son.

MAE HONG SON

Tucked away close to the Burmese border and hemmed in by the mountains surrounding the Pai River Valley, this small and somnambulant town is rapidly developing into one of Thailand's more popular off-the-beaten-track destinations. Before the tortuous 369-km road from Chiang Mai was completed in 1965, the town served as a convenient dumping ground for disgraced bureaucrats, who nicknamed it the Siberia of Thailand. Today it can be reached by air in 30 minutes and is promoted as Thailand's Shangri-La—complete with lost valleys, tribal trekking, caves, rivers, and waterfalls.

While not the mystical vision described in tourist literature, the attractive scenery and sense of remoteness make it a welcome change from the more touristy destinations in Thailand. Mae Hong Son now has several hotels, two dozen guesthouses, several banks that cash traveler's checks, trekking agencies, a handicraft center, and motorcycle-rental shops.

Attractions

Not everybody enjoys the noisy and unattractive town of Mae Hong Son, but there's enough of interest to make it worth a few days.

Doi Mung Kung: Top draw is the 424-meter peak at the north end of town, which offers great views and a modest *chedi* constructed by Governor Singnatraja in 1874, the same year Mae Hong Son was declared an official Thai settlement.

Wats Chong Kam and Chong Klang: Picturesquely located on the banks of placid Jongkum Lake are two Burmese-style *chedis* which provide outstanding photographs in the misty morning hours. The latter temple contains a famous collection of 35 wooden figures *(tukatas)* inspired by the Buddhist Vessantara Jataka.

Trekking: Villages near Mae Hong Son are now well trekked but less deluged than those near Chiang Mai. Jeep excursions can also be arranged to a small village where several Paduang women now reside under controversial conditions.

Accommodations

Mae Hong Son's soaring popularity has brought dozens of guesthouses, several middle-priced hotels with a/c rooms, and a few luxury hotels and countryside resorts.

Sang Tong Huts: Great views over ricefields and banana plantations make this somewhat remote guesthouse one of the best in Mae Hong Son. Pracha Uthit Rd., 100-200B.

Golden Huts: Adjacent to Sang Tong is a series of individual *nipa* huts clinging to the hillside amid trees, ferns, and winding walkways. Pracha Uthit Rd., 100-150B.

Mae Hong Son Guesthouse: Also about 15 minutes from town is another popular guesthouse with small huts and nine wooden rooms. Pracha Uthit Rd., 50-100B.

Garden Guesthouse: Back in town is a quiet spot with solid, dark rooms covered with teak paneling and a great reception area. Khunlum Prathat Rd., 140-180B.

Sabanga Guesthouse: Centrally located and placed nicely back from the street with a small garden and an elevated patio. Udom Chowne Rd., 100-120B.

Jungle King Guesthouse: Offers five excellent teak rooms with mosquito nets and mattresses on the floor. Pradit Jongkam Rd., 40-60B.

Chong Kham Lake Guesthouses: Several small places surround the wonderful lake and fitness park in the center of town; these include Baitong, Rose, Chong Kham, and Rim Nong Guesthouses. 50-150B.

Pen Porn Guesthouse: Clean and modern spot up the hill and away from the noise. Doi Kong Mu Rd., 150-200B low season, 200-250B high season.

Getting There

Buses leave Chiang Mai's Arcade Terminal six times daily and take 8-10 grueling hours to reach Mae Hong Son via the southern route. An overnight pause in Mae Sariang is a good way to break the ordeal. Public buses along the northern route through Pai are somewhat quicker and pass through more attractive scenery.

The most comfortable options are the daily air flights which take 30 minutes and cost 380B. Tickets in both directions are heavily booked, so it's best to confirm reservations immediately upon arrival in Chiang Mai or Mae Hong Son. A popular compromise is to take the bus to Mae Hong Son and return by air.

PAI

Pai is one of the most beautiful destinations in Thailand. Situated in a broad valley surrounded by mountains and rivers, the idyllic landscape and easygoing pace of life remind you of Chiang Mai several decades ago. This is the kind of place where days lead into weeks and weeks into . . . you get the idea.

Pai offers a few small temples, several waterfalls, hot springs, trekking, and river trips

down the Pai River all the way to Mae Hong Son—just about everything you want to do in Thailand.

Accommodations

The dusty town of Pai has over a dozen modest guesthouses on the main road and down by the river.

Charlie's Guesthouse: Conveniently near the bus stop, Charlie's is a clean and comfortable place with friendly management. Rungsiyanon Road. Rooms cost 40-250B.

Big Guesthouse: Also on the main road is another clean guesthouse with a small cafe over a pond. Rungsiyanon Road. 50-100B.

Nunya's Guesthouse: A two-story hotel with rooms tucked away in the back courtyard. 84 Rungsiyanon Rd., 50-150B.

Pai River Lodge: River Lodge has a dozen bamboo huts arranged in a semicircle around the central dining area. Run-down but a good location facing the Pai River. Huts cost 50-80B.

Shan Guesthouse: A series of individual wooden huts at the south end of town near some beautiful ricefields, run by a Shan whose business card reads: "You can check out any time you like . . . but you can never leave." A good slogan for a town like Pai. Rungsiyanon Rd., 60-120B.

Transportation

Buses from the Arcade Bus Terminal in Chiang Mai take four hours to cover the 134 km to Pai. Minitrucks from Mae Hong Son to Pai also take four hours and leave several times daily between 0700 and 1300. The road from Mae Hong Son is incredibly rugged and winding but has spectacular views over some of the most isolated regions of Thailand.

Buses from Pai to Chiang Mai depart hourly from 0630 to 1430. An a/c bus departs once daily around 1130. Passengers should arrive early and grab the first available seats. Minitrucks to Soppong and Mae Hong Son depart every two hours between 0700 and 1430.

THAILAND

CHIANG RAI AND THE GOLDEN TRIANGLE

Thailand's infamous Golden Triangle—properly located on the Mekong where Myanmar, Laos, and Thailand intersect—is the mysterious and untamed land where powerful opium warlords, remnants of Chiang Kai-Shek's Kuomintang army, and communist insurgency groups once fought for control of Southeast Asia's immensely lucrative opium traffic. The Triangle's Wild West image attracts large numbers of curious travelers who come searching for caravans of mules hauling tons of high-grade opium.

The reality is somewhat different. Smuggling continues to some degree, but visitors should also prepare themselves for modern towns, lines of tour buses, and a countryside completely in touch with the 20th century. Don't be discouraged by the commercialization—the varied scenery and sense of remoteness still make the region along the Mekong River an enjoyable destination.

Most travelers take an early morning bus (0600-0730) from Chiang Mai directly to Thaton to catch the 1300 longtail boat ride down to Chiang Rai—the most popular river journey in northern Thailand.

THATON AND KOK RIVER

Thaton, a picturesque town on the banks of the Kok River, chiefly serves as a launching point for downriver trips to Chiang Rai. An imposing white Buddha, who seems to be contemplating the steady stream of Western travelers, dominates the town. Hike up for excellent views over the valley. Self-guided treks to nearby villages are easy but less than pristine since this region has been trekked for over 20 years. Robberies are commonplace; be careful.

Accommodations
Cheap guesthouses include the highly recommended Thips Travelers House upriver from the bridge, the quiet Chan Kasem 2 across the river, and the Siam Kok adjacent to the boat launch. More affluent travelers might splurge for the upscale Mae Kok River Lodge across the river

where attractive Thai-style chalets cost 800-1,400B.

River Trip to Chiang Rai
Longtail boats leave Thaton at 1300, cost 160B, and take four hours down the Kok River to Chiang Rai. Brief stops are made at Mae Salak for police registration and photos of the hanging bridge and at the Highland Forestry Development Project for cold drinks. Early stages of the journey are relatively uncommercialized, but lower sections toward Chiang Rai are plagued with refreshment stalls, souvenir shops, TV antennas, and tacky signs announcing Lahu Village.

Longtail boat rides are exciting and provide a glimpse of the countryside, but not everyone is thrilled with the speed, noise, and cramped quarters. Bamboo houseboats, constructed per order in Thaton, are excellent alternatives. Six-man bamboo rafts with cabin and primitive lavatories cost 2,500B per boat and take three relaxing days to Chiang Mai . . . if they aren't capsized on the rocks.

CHIANG RAI

Chiang Rai is a peaceful and easygoing town without the hustle—or the great sights—of Chiang Mai. Despite the lack of any major attractions, tourism is on a sharp rise, as indicated by the new tourist office and the amazing hotel developments being laid on the bewildered little town.

The city was founded in 1262 by King Mengrai as the nation's first independent kingdom, but the fickle king later moved his forces south to Lamphun and finally Chiang Mai. Each year in February the city sponsors a week of traditional northern culture during the colorful Wai Samae Fah Luang Festival.

Attractions
Chiang Rai's modest monuments include Wat Pra Keo, where Bangkok's Emerald Buddha was discovered in 1436, and a reproduction of the sa-

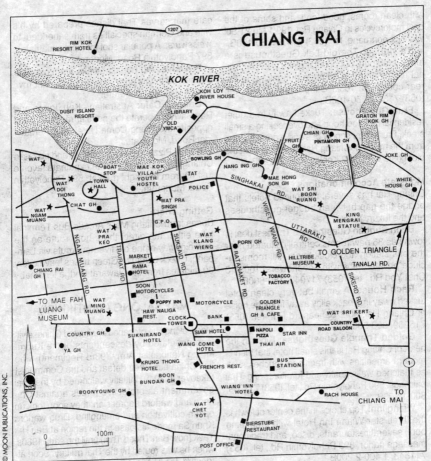

CHIANG RAI

cred Chiang Mai Buddha inside Wat Pra Singh. Wat Chet Yot was copied from the seven-spired monument of the same name in Chiang Mai.

Also worth checking out are the panoramic views from City Hall and the fat, jolly Buddha who sits in the Wat Klang Wieng courtyard. Believe it or not, this is the fifth and final Buddha!

Budget Guesthouses

Chiang Rai has exploded with dozens of new guesthouses in recent years. Operators are always on hand to greet boat arrivals from Thaton and bus customers from Chiang Mai.

Chat Guesthouse: Several years ago the old Chat moved to a much nicer location in a small alley near the boat landing. Chat has a cozy cafe, laundry services, and information on trekking. Trairat Rd. Soi 1, tel. (053) 711481, 50-150B.

Koh Loy River House: A new place on the river behind the old YMCA, with spacious grounds and a pleasant restaurant overlooking a tributary of the Kok River. 485 Tanam Rd., tel. (053) 715084, 120-240B.

Pintamorn Guesthouse: Operated by some Germans and a Hawaiian named Bob Watson, Pintamorn compensates for its isolated location

© MOON PUBLICATIONS, INC.

THAILAND

with clean rooms, good food, and some of the best motorcycles in Chiang Rai. 199/1 Mu 21 Soi Wat Sriboonruang, tel. (053) 714161, 60-180B.

Ya House: The old Lek Guesthouse is a funky, cramped, but popular place with communal rooms and five bamboo bungalows in the rear courtyard. 163/1 Banphaprakan Rd., tel. (053) 713368, 50-100B.

Fruit Guesthouse: Tucked away in a quiet residential neighborhood and overlooking a small creek, Fruit offers good vibes and a great escape from the hustle of Chiang Rai. A tricycle from the pier costs 10B. 91/2 Kohloy Rd., 60-120B.

Moderate Accommodations

Chiang Rai has several mid-priced hotels that bridge the gap between budget guesthouses and the luxury hotels.

Boon Bundan Guesthouse: The best deal in town has 36 new rooms centrally situated near the bus station and clock tower. All rooms include private baths with hot showers. 1005/13 Chet Yod Rd., tel. (053) 717040, 150-600B.

Rach House: A small but very clean hotel tucked away in a back alley away from the noise of Chiang Rai. 90/2 Sanpanard Rd., tel. (053) 715969, 300-500B.

Golden Triangle Guesthouse: Right in the heart of Chiang Rai is this small hotel that blends modern amenities with traditional touches such as thatched walls, teakwood furniture, and Thai paintings. 590 Paholyothin Rd., tel. (053) 711339, 800-1,200B.

Wiang Inn: Top choice in the center of town is the three-star Wiang Inn Hotel with swimming pool, several restaurants, disco, and traditional massage parlor. 893 Paholyothin Rd., tel. (053) 711543, 1,400-2,200B.

Restaurants

Most of the restaurants in town are in the alleys near the Wang Come Hotel.

Night Market: Though it pales in comparison to the grand affair in Chiang Mai, a small but lively night market with foodstalls operates on Trairat and Tanari roads near the Wang Come Hotel.

Cheap Cafe: The corner cafe just east of the clock tower has great dishes for just 20B, plus a friendly manager who cooks, serves, and collects the money. Clock Tower Circle. Inexpensive.

Bierstube: Karl Leinz from Mainz runs a small cafe that serves Thai dishes prepared by his wife and German specialties from sauerkraut to *weisswurst.* A popular spot for local expatriates. 897 Paholyothin Road. Moderate.

French's: Big buffalo steaks and cold beer are served in this cozy cafe on restaurant row. Chet Yot Road. Moderate.

Baitong Cafe: Australians Ken Jones and Ray Sawyer operate the popular restaurant just opposite the Wang Come Hotel. 869 Pemawipat Road. Moderate.

Napoli Pizza: Best Italian dishes and pizzas in Chiang Rai are served in the expatriate favorite just up from the night market. 595 Paholyothin Road. Moderate.

Getting There

Buses from Chiang Mai's Arcade Bus Terminal take either the direct three-hour route on the new highway or the old five-hour route via Lampang. Check carefully. Green buses leave every 30 minutes from the Nawarat Bridge terminal.

MAE SALONG (SANTIKHIRI)

Mae Salong is a precariously situated Chinese village populated by descendants of the Kuomintang Nationalist Army (93rd Regiment), who fled China after their defeat and the Communist takeover in 1949. Initially welcomed by the Thai government as protective forces against Chinese and warlord aggression, they soon took up opium cultivation and smuggling. Drug warlord Khun Sa made his base in the region at Ban Hin Taek (now Ban Thoed Thai) until the early 1980s, when he was routed by the Thai military. Soon afterward, the Thai government officially renamed the Kuomintang village Santikhiri, a pleasant term which means "Mountain of Peace."

Mae Salong today is a sleepy—and often cold—place where Mandarin is still spoken by the older residents and homes remain guarded by ancient protective talismans.

Attractions

Mausoleum: The most striking landmark in Mae Salong is the mausoleum of General Duan Xi Wen, the former chief of staff of China's 93rd Regiment who led 2,000 Chinese Kuomintang soldiers and their families into Thailand.

Trekking: Mae Salong is an excellent place to begin self-guided treks to nearby hilltribe villages. Rough but adequate maps of the region can be picked up from Rainbow, Mae Salong, and Shin Shane guesthouses.

Accommodations

Mae Salong Guesthouse: Up the hill and on the left is a small guesthouse (tel. 053-712962) with trekking information, a fading but useful map posted on the wall, and horseback tours to nearby villages. Rooms cost 80-120B with hot showers outside the compound.

Shin Shane Guesthouse: Another bare-bones guesthouse just off the main road in an old wooden Chinese home. 50-80B.

Rainbow Guesthouse: A rudimentary spot with views from the cafe and a solitary room with three beds. 40-60B.

Mae Salong Resort: The best hotel in town is wonderfully located up a steep road with views over the entire valley. Popular with visiting Chinese and Thais. Mae Chan, tel. (053) 713400, 400-600B.

Transportation

Mae Salong lies 36 km west of Pha Sang (Basang or Pasang) on top of Doi Mae Salong, 1,418 meters above sea level. From Chiang Rai, hire a motorcycle or take the green bus to Pha Sang, three km beyond Mae Chan, from where minibuses continue up the winding road to Mae Salong. Minitrucks from Pha Sang run from 0800 to 1700 and cost 40B up, 30B down.

MAE SAI

Mae Sai, 891 km from Bangkok, is the northernmost town in Thailand and the final stop before crossing the Mae Sai River into Myanmar. Mae Sai claims a mysterious location, but it's hardly more than a nondescript town of concrete shophouses, video stores, souvenir shops, and Chinese restaurants with little appeal except for the bridge to Myanmar and views from Wat Doi Wao.

Attractions

Myanmar: The border crossing into Myanmar is where Thai citizens arrive searching for Chinese goods, sweet orange wine, and Burmese cheroots, while Burmese from Tha Khi Lek and Kengtung (100 km north) cross the bridge for shaving blades, pens, and Western medicines—a strange collision of cultures. Westerners can now cross the bridge, obtain a Burmese visa in Tha Khi Lek, and continue by truck or jeep to Kengtung—one of the newest travel destinations in Southeast Asia. More details in the Myanmar chapter.

Wat Prathat Doi Wao: A long flight of over 200 steps and a *naga*-flanked balustrade lead up a small hill with views of white pagodas, a Chi-

---

THE OPIUM TRAIL

In Homer's *Odyssey*, Helen of Troy mixes a potion "to quiet all pain and strife, and bring forgetfulness of every ill." Thomas De Quincey, author of *Confessions of an English Opium Eater*, tells how he experienced music like perfume and ecstasies of divine enjoyment, living a hundred years in one night. Southeast Asia is the world's largest source of illicit opium, producing an estimated 1,000-2,000 tons annually from Myanmar, Laos, and northern Thailand.

The opium trail begins in the early spring as farmers scour the countryside looking for highly alkaline soils best suited for cultivation. Some say the sweeter taste of limestone soil can actually be recognized by the discriminating palate! Fields are cleared of standing trees by a spectacular burnoff, and planting begins in September after the tree ash has dissolved into natural fertilizers. The soil is chopped, turned, and strewn with select poppy seeds. By January, bright red and white flowers appear, blossom, and then drop away to reveal an egg-shaped bulb filled with resinous opium.

The bulb is scored (like a Vermont maple or Malay rubber tree) with a three-bladed knife, and the milky sap then rises to the surface before turning into brownish-black droplets. Tribeswomen return the following morning to scrape the bulb and deposit the residue into a cup hanging around their necks. The sticky gum is then packed into banana leaves, tied into bundles, and sold to Chinese middlemen who refine it to morphine or heroin and export it to Western countries. The upward spiral of its value is amazing: one kilo of raw opium worth only US$200 in Myanmar brings US$250,000 as heroin in the West.

THAILAND

nese cemetery, and the tin roofs of Tha Khi Lek inside Myanmar.

Guesthouses

Most visitors spend a few hours at the bridge and perhaps climb the hill for views, then head east to Sop Ruak or the idyllic town of Chiang Saen. If you decide to stay, Mae Sai has several well-placed guesthouses down near the river and a handful of better hotels on the main road.

Mae Sai Guesthouse: The best place to escape the concrete drabness of Mae Sai and relax in a riverside setting is the series of bungalows about one km west of the bridge. A *samlor* costs about 15 *baht.* 688 Wiang Pakam Rd., tel. (053) 732021, 50-200B.

Mae Sai Plaza Guesthouse: A decent place much closer to town but with less atmosphere than the Mae Sai Guesthouse. Some 100 bungalows hang precariously from the cliff which rises sharply from the left side of the road. 386 Sairomjoi Rd., tel. (053) 732230, 80-250B.

Chad Guesthouse: The second-best place in Mae Sai is a favorite of motorcyclists, who can obtain good maps and helpful advice from the Thai-Shan family of owner Khun Chad. Located in a quiet neighborhood about two km southwest of the bridge. Soi Wangpan, 50-120B.

Top North Hotel: A 32-room hotel just 100 meters from the bridge. Convenient to reach and popular with mid-level travelers. 306 Paholyothin Rd., tel. (053) 731955, 200-450B.

Transportation

Buses to Mae Sai leave every 15 minutes from Chiang Rai and take about 90 minutes. Both buses and minitrucks reach Mae Sai from Chiang Saen and Sop Ruak. Siam First Tours on the main road has nightly a/c buses direct to Bangkok.

CHIANG SAEN

The once-powerful city of Chiang Saen is one of Thailand's oldest and most historic towns. Founded in the 10th century by Thai commanders as the first independent principality in northern Thailand, Chiang Saen was later destroyed by Khmer forces but re-established by King Mengrai in 1259. It was then abandoned in favor of

Chiang Mai but revived in the 14th century by Mengrai's grandson, a devout Buddhist who constructed most of the existing *stupas* and *chedis.*

Today, over 100 monuments in varying states of collapse and restoration bear witness to the city's turbulent history. None compare with those in Sukothai or Ayuthaya, but the sleepy atmosphere and outstanding location make Chiang Saen a fine spot to relax for a few days.

Attractions

Chiang Saen offers a great little museum and several restored temples that bear witness to the city's turbulent history.

Chiang Saen National Museum: This museum, on the main road near the old west gate, provides an excellent introduction to the handicrafts, carvings, and splendid Buddhas of the Chiang Saen Period, considered among the most beautiful in Thailand.

Wat Chedi Luang: Behind the museum towers an immense 58-meter octagonal *chedi* (spelled Wat Jadeeloung on the sign) perhaps constructed in 1331 by King Saen Phu but reconstructed in 1551 shortly before the Burmese seized Chiang Saen.

Wat Pasak: Beyond the reconstructed walls of ancient Chiang Saen lies the city's oldest surviving *chedi,* constructed in 1295 and a testament to the importance of the valley before the rise of Chiang Mai and the Lanna kingdom.

Wat Prathat Chom Kitti: Two km northwest of town, on a hill with good views over the Mekong River, Wat Prathat Chom Kitti and the small ruined *chedi* of Wat Chom Chang are old monuments which scholars believe also predate the founding of Chiang Saen.

Tobacco Kilns: The rich soil and climatic conditions of Chiang Saen have long made the region a principal source of Virginia tobacco and temperate vegetables such as cabbages and tomatoes. Some of the most interesting sights near Chiang Saen are the tobacco kilns northwest of town on the road to the Golden Triangle. Visitors are welcome to wander through the yards and inspect the smoking kilns kept fired with prodigious amounts of coal.

Wat Prathat Pha Ngao: One of the most awesome and mysterious Buddha images in Thailand is displayed inside a temple 4.2 km east of Chiang Saen on the road to Chiang

Khong, an amazing image that has rarely been mentioned in travel literature on Thailand.

Accommodations
Chiang Saen offers several basic but relaxing guesthouses on the banks of the Mekong River. Mid-level guesthouses are now appearing as the focus slowly shifts from budget to better-quality digs.

Chiang Saen Guesthouse: Not much atmosphere, though the rooms are fairly clean and manager Chan Chai is friendly. Good central location. 45 Rimkhong Rd., 40-100B.

Siam Guesthouse: An old and run-down dive with three bungalows crammed together. 294 Rimkhong Rd., 60-80B.

Gin Guesthouse: Two km west of town is a wonderful place with A-frame chalets facing grassy lawns and an inner orchard filled with lychee and mango trees. 60-350B.

Transportation
Buses from Chiang Rai to Chiang Saen take about an hour and pass through countryside where villagers still harvest rice without the use of machinery. Chiang Saen can also be reached by minitrucks from Mae Sai. *Songtao* service to the Golden Triangle is sporadic and not as reliable as a rented motorcycle or bicycle. Minitrucks to Chiang Khong leave in the mornings from the market along the river.

SOP RUAK

Thailand's notorious Golden Triangle is centered at Sop Ruak, a haphazard collection of teetering shops, simple restaurants, overpriced hotels, and tacky souvenir stalls on the banks of the Mekong River. The actual intersection of Thailand, Laos, and Myanmar is conveniently framed by a modern signpost—worth a photo for friends back home.

Although the mysterious scenery encourages fantasies about drug smugglers and opium warlords, modern Sop Ruak is more popular with tour groups than armed terrorists.

Accommodations
Few visitors overnight in this one-horse town, but if you must, there's a handful of overpriced

guesthouses and hotels strung along the road that parallels the Mekong River. Golden Hut Guesthouse now charges an unreasonable 150-250B for rudimentary rooms while old concrete cubicles about to fall into the river cost 100-150B at the Golden Triangle Guesthouse. Tour groups obviously avoid these death traps and instead blow their savings at the immense white-elephant Delta Golden Triangle Resort Hotel where rooms go from 2,500-4,000B.

CHIANG KHONG

Most travelers return to Chiang Rai from Chiang Saen, but motorcyclists and those intrigued with the more remote destinations in northern Thailand can continue east to the small town of Chiang Khong, located on the banks of the Mekong River and directly opposite the Laotian town of Ban Houei Sai. The chief interest in Chiang Khong is simply sitting at a cafe or on the lawn of the Mae Khong Resort and watching the river flow.

Accommodations
Ban Tam Mi La Guesthouse: Best choice in town is the small Thai-style guesthouse on the main road near Wat Kao. The owners can help with sightseeing excursions to nearby waterfalls, caves, tribal villages, and the historical sights at Doi Patang. 8/4 Sai Klang Rd., 100-250B.

Mae Khong Resort: Great views and a comfortable cafe make this resort a popular, if somewhat expensive, alternative to the Ban Tam Mi La. Sai Klang Rd., 260-450B.

Transportation
Chiang Khong is about 75 km east of Chiang Saen. Minitrucks leave in the morning from the riverside market in Chiang Saen.

PHAYAO

Phayao is a medium-sized town on Hwy. 1 midway between Lampang and Chiang Rai. Though rarely visited by Westerners, Phayao has several worthwhile temples and a magnificent location on the edge of Phayao Lake.

Attractions

Wat Sikhom Kham: The principal temple in Phayao and among the most significant sanctuaries in northern Thailand, Wat Sikhom Kham is highly regarded by scholars for its 400-year-old Buddha image housed inside the central *viharn*. Outside and on the grounds to the north is another of those bizarre collections of stucco statues so popular in modern Thailand.

Modern Temple: Don't miss the exquisite murals which grace the modern *viharn* back by the lake. The *viharn* itself is a masterpiece of architectural design, blessed with great symmetry and a wonderful location on the edge of the lake. Inside the dazzling *viharn* are some of the finest modern murals in all of Thailand, designed and painted under the supervision of an extremely talented artist named Angkarn Kalyanaponsga.

Accommodations

Chalermsak Hotel: The cheapest place in town is directly across from the minibus station and very close to the bus terminal. 915 Phahonyothin Rd., tel. (054) 431063, 80-160B.

Tharn Thong Hotel: Phayao's largest hotel has 96 rooms with fans or a/c. 55 Donsanam Rd., tel. (054) 431772, 180-460B.

PHRAE

Phrae is a modern provincial capital made prosperous from coal mining and the logging industry. The city once served as a Burmese outpost during their occupation of Thailand and today is known for its temples, which uniquely combine Burmese and Laotian styles.

Attractions

Wat Chom Sawan: The Burmese heritage of Phrae is demonstrated by this Shan-style temple constructed some 80 years ago outside the old city walls.

Wat Sra Bo Kaew: Another Burmese-style temple with a Shan *chedi* and richly decorated altars inside the modern *viharn*.

Wat Prabat Ming: Near the center of town, Wat Prabat Ming Muang Vora Viharn features a modern *viharn* and an 18th-century *bot* constructed in the Laotian style with sloping columns and a slate-covered roof.

Wat Luang: Chief interest here are the Burmese-style *chedi* and decorated wooden beams inside the central *viharn*.

Ban Prathup Teakwood House: Certainly the most curious sight in Phrae is the old teakwood home in Ban Prathup (also called Ban Sao Roi Tan), about one km west of town. Constructed from an almost unbelievable amount of precious wood, the opulent home and private museum is a testament to the breathtaking beauty of teakwood and man's insatiable lust for the precious commodity.

Wat Prathat Choe Hae: Phrae's most famous temple is eight km west of town, about one km beyond the village of Padang, at the top of a teak-clad hill cut by two stairways flanked by Burmese lions and guardian *nagas*.

Muang Phi (Ghost City): Eighteen km from Phrae, off Hwy. 101 on a side road just before Km 143, is an eerie natural wonder created by soil and wind erosion: surrealistic chimneys, magic mushrooms, or asteroid dwellings . . . depending on your perspective.

Accommodations

Number 4 Guesthouse: A teakwood home tucked away in a quiet residential neighborhood; motorcycle rentals and trekking services available. 22 Soi 1 Yantara Kitkosol Rd., 50-120B.

Charoen Road Hotels: The Sri Wattana, Ho Fa, and Thep Wiman hotels all have basic rooms at basic prices. 153 Charoen Muang Rd., tel. (054) 511047, 80-220B.

Nakhorn Phrae Hotel: Western travelers who need a better hotel with standard amenities stay at the Nakhorn Phrae just opposite Thai Airways. The hotel offers tourist information, maps, and guided tours from the *samlor* drivers who hang out at the front door. 69 Rajadamnern Rd., tel. (054) 521901, 240-280B.

Transportation

Ordinary buses from the Arcade Bus Terminal in Chiang Mai depart for Phrae daily at 0800, 1100, 1500, and 1700. Air-conditioned buses depart at 1000 and 2200. Each service takes about four hours. Train commuters should alight at Den Chai, from where minitrucks shuttle up to Phrae.

NAN

Situated in the most remote region of northern Thailand, Nan ranks high among travelers, who regard it as similar to Chiang Mai of three decades ago. The landscape combines the mountain vistas of Chiang Mai with the bucolic charms of the lazy, brown river which slowly winds to the east.

Attractions

Nan National Museum: An excellent starting point for an exploration of Nan is the centrally located museum, recently opened in a palace (Ho Kham) constructed in 1903 by Prince Phalida.

Wat Chang Kham Vora Viharn: Across from the museum stands a temple and *chedi* constructed in 1547 with elephant buttresses around the perimeter.

Wat Phumin: The finest architectural piece in Nan dates from 1603, with extensive restorations in 1867 and 1991. The temple is chiefly noted for its outstanding murals, which provide a historical study of local society some 100 years ago.

Wat Suan Tan: Highlights include a 40-meter *prang* with a spire of Khmer design and a 15th-century *viharn* which enshrines an important Buddha image named Pra Chao Thong Tip.

Mrabi Hill Tribe: Phrae and Nan both serve as launching points for excursions to the Mrabi tribes, called Phi Thong Luang by the Thais and nicknamed the Spirits of the Yellow Leaves from the color of their temporary leaf huts. The Mrabi are elusive nomadic hunters whose very existence remained mythical until their discovery by a jungle expedition several decades ago.

Accommodations

Doi Phukha Guesthouse: Nan's best guesthouse in a quiet neighborhood inside an old teak house with gardens and a wooden pavilion. The owner is a great source of local information plus he puts tours together in conjunction with a local travel agency. 94/5 Sumonthiwarat Rd., tel. (054) 771442, 70-150B.

Kiwi Guesthouse: Nan's first guesthouse is operated by a Kiwi named Peter who provides trekking information, bicycle and motorcycle rentals, and tips on nearby waterfalls and border excursions. Mahawong Rd., tel. (054) 710658, 40-80B.

Sukasem Hotel: A simple Thai hotel conveniently near the bus terminal and across from the night market. 119 Anathat Wararicharad Rd., tel. (054) 710141, 100-160B.

Devaraj Hotel: Nan's best hotel offers large, clean rooms with hot showers, a popular cafe with cabaret singers in the evening, and tourist information. 466 Sumon Devaraj Rd., tel. (054) 710094, 200-450B.

Transportation

Nan is 668 km north of Bangkok and 318 km southeast of Chiang Mai. Thai Airways flies once daily from Chiang Mai (400B) and Phitsanulok (425B) via Phrae. Ordinary buses depart from Chiang Mai at 0800, 1100, 1500, and 1700, and take eight hours along the old route via Lampang and Phrae. Air-conditioned buses leave at 1000 and 2200. Buses from Chiang Rai depart at 0930 and take four hours to cover the 270 kilometers.

The nearest train terminus to Nan is at Den Chai, 20 km south of Phrae. Minitrucks and buses from the Den Chai train station head north to Phrae and Nan.

NORTHEASTERN THAILAND

Known as the Issan, northeastern Thailand is a vast and arid limestone plateau bounded by the Mekong River to the north and small mountains to the south and west. An unfortunate combination of sandy soil and overpopulation has brought droughts, floods, poverty, and political discontent to the region. The government has responded by building new roads and a making a concerted effort to sell the area as a tourist destination.

The relative lack of historical or cultural attractions and the large distances between points of interest makes this a tough job, though the Issan is unquestionably the most authentic and untouched region in the country. Top draws include dozens of colorful festivals and a rich collection of restored Khmer temples which, taken together, form the finest spectrum of Cambodian architecture in the world. Naturalists will enjoy trekking around Phu Kradung National Park or simply gazing across the Mekong River from Nong Khai.

The opening of Laos has increased tourism—at least on the route from Bangkok to Nong Khai—plus the near-complete absence of Western visitors carries strong appeal to those travelers who enjoy getting off the beaten track and want to find the "real" Thailand.

Routes

Several routes are possible depending on your interests and time. Visitors keen on Khmer architecture but with a limited schedule should use Korat as a base for short side trips to the nearby monuments.

Visitors with 10-14 days can complete a western loop through Korat, Khon Kaen, Udon Thani, Nong Khai, Chiang Khon, Loei, and Phu Kradung National Park before exiting west to Phitsanulok. This abbreviated loop covers a few Khmer temples and provides a quick look at the Issan.

Travelers with over three weeks can circumnavigate the entire region through Korat, Khon Kaen, Udon Thani, Sakhon Nakhon, That Phanom, Ubon Ratchathani, and Surin.

KHAO YAI NATIONAL PARK

Thailand's most popular national park, south of Pak Chong and 200 km northeast of Bangkok, is a world of rich and diverse flora, from evergreen and rainforest to *lalang* and rolling hills of tropical grasslands. A small visitor center a few kilometers north of the closed Khao Yai Motorlodge offers some haphazard but informative displays on local wildlife and hiking trails.

Attractions

Waterfalls: Hiking trails starting from the visitor center lead to several waterfalls and limestone caves. Most are difficult to find and best reached with private vehicles or tours organized by the park or a private company such as Jungle Adventures in Pak Chong.

Hiking Trails: A guide distributed at the headquarters describes 12 hiking trails originally made by wild elephants. Trails near the visitor center are in good condition, but distant trails are often buried under wild vegetation and difficult to follow.

Wildlife: Wildlife inside the 2,168-square-km park, such as wild elephants and birds such as hornbills, are extremely shy and rarely seen. Best bets are "Night Shining" truck drives organized by the motor lodge.

Tours

Park Tours: Day tours sponsored by park rangers to various waterfalls and viewpoints leave daily around 0900 and 1300 from the visitor center.

Jungle Adventures: Several private companies in Pak Chong, such as Wildlife Safari at 39 Pak Chong Road and Khao Yai Wildlife Tours in the Khao Yai Garden Lodge, organize tours for Westerners. Tours generally include breakfast, guide services, and guesthouse accommodations in Pak Chong.

Accommodations

Most travelers visit Khao Yai on day-trips from Pak Chong although the Forestry Department operates a dormitory in the park.

THAILAND

Park Headquarters: Simple dorm beds are available at park headquarters for 20B per person. Bring your own bedding; a small cafe serves reasonably priced meals.

Khao Yai Garden Lodge: Popular spot run by a German-Thai couple on the road to Khao Yai. Call from town for a free pickup or take local transport toward the park and look for the sign. Khao Yai Rd., tel. (044) 313567, 100-650B.

Jungle Adventures Guesthouse: The small private tour operator in Pak Chong operates a small guesthouse in an alley due south of the stoplight. 752/11 Kongvaksin Rd. Soi 3, Pak Chong, tel. (044) 313836, 80-250B.

Getting There

Khao Yai is 200 km northeast of Bangkok on the road to Nakhon Ratchasima. Buses from Bangkok's Northern Bus Terminal to Pak Chong take three or four hours on the Friendship Highway, constructed during the Vietnam War by the Americans. Note the changes: the Khao Yai region has gone from untamed wilderness to condo/golf course hell in just 10 years.

The turnoff to Khao Yai is five km before Pak Chong. Since only limited bus service is available from Pak Chong, independent travelers should ask the bus driver to stop at the small Khao Yai signpost on the right side of the road and then wait for a minitruck or hitchhike up to the park.

FESTIVALS OF THE NORTHEAST

Northeast festivals are some of the most colorful, authentic, and lively in the country. A perfect visit would include at least one of the following events. The Bangkok TAT has a complete list with exact dates.

Yasothon Rocket Festival: Issan Thais fire homemade rockets into the clouds during the dry season to bring rain and ensure a bountiful harvest. The Yasothon Festival, Thailand's most spectacular pyrotechnic display, begins on Saturday morning with a parade of enormous rockets elaborately decorated with *nagas*, traditional Thai orchestras, and lovely *serong* dancers. Rockets are launched on Sunday; duds are dumped in mudholes. Second weekend of May.

Ubon Candle Festival: The commencement of Thai rains retreat for young monks (*phansa*) is celebrated in Ubon Ratchathani by over 4,000 participants who haul enormous wax candles carved with *garudas*, elephants, and heroes from Thai mythology. A Miss Candlelight pageant is also held. Late June or early July.

Sakhon Nakhon Wax Temple Festival: Large and elaborate beeswax temples are paraded to honor ancestors and the Buddha. Full moon of the 11th lunar month, often mid-October.

Nakhon Phanom Boat Races: Rainy season ends with dozens of boats, shaped like mythological *nagas*, furiously paddled by teams of 40 men and women. Phimai sponsors races on a smaller scale.

Surin Elephant Round-up: One of the most popular and highly promoted festivals in Thailand. The big day starts with an elephant round-up using lassos and a well-trained female as bait and continues with elephant races, dances, a tug-of-war between one elephant and 70 men (guess who wins), and hilarious elephant soccer matches. Festivities end with a colorful procession of pachyderms and mahouts dressed in 17th-century costume. Tours organized by Bangkok travel agents should be booked well in advance. Third weekend in November.

KORAT (NAKHON RATCHASIMA)

Korat, officially called Nakhon Ratchasima, is the region's largest city and gateway to the northeast. The modern town has little charm, but it's an ideal base from which to explore the nearby Khmer ruins and rest up after a long bus or train ride from Bangkok. Korat was established during the reign of King Narai, but its heyday was during the early '70s when it served as a major base for U.S. forces assigned to the Vietnamese conflict. Massage parlors, racy nightclubs, and Turkish baths are the most telling legacies. Korat made international news in August 1993 when the Royal Plaza Hotel suddenly collapsed, killing almost 90 people.

The TAT office is inconveniently located on Mukmontri Road at the extreme west end of town, three km west of the train station. Take any local bus going in that direction.

Attractions

Khunying Mo Statue: Modern Korat spreads around a statue honoring Thao Suranari, the national heroine who in 1826 convinced Korat ladies

THAILAND

KORAT (NAKHON RATCHASIMA)

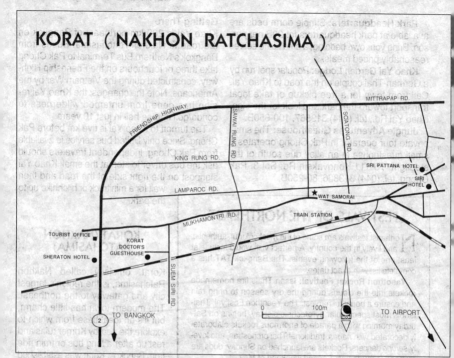

to seduce and then murder invading Laotian soldiers. Complete with a strange but once-fashionable haircut, her highly revered image is a constant source of veneration; stages for itinerant musicians and local dancers are nearby.

Korat Museum: A small branch of the National Museum which displays Khmer artifacts and prehistoric earthenware is located in the compound of Wat Suthachanda.

Nightclubs: Korat's most dubious attractions are the enormous nightclubs and massage parlors left over from the Vietnam War era.

Pakthongchai: Thailand's best-quality silk is produced in the silk-weaving village of Pakthongchai, some 30 km south of Korat.

Accommodations

Korat Doctor's Guesthouse: Dr. Sunan's hostel is Korat's first spot geared for backpackers rather than tourists with information on tours to nearby Khmer monuments, motorcycle rentals, laundry service, and transportation schedules. 78 Sueb Siri Rd. Soi 4, tel. (044) 255846, 80-250B.

Rattana Guesthouse: Somewhat farther down the road is another backpackers' spot with similar services. Sueb Siri Rd., Soi Suksan 39, tel. (044) 927-0354, 80-200B.

Siri Hotel: Korat's most memorable hotel/pub is constantly filled with budget travelers, Vietnam vets, foreign-service employees, and American GIs doing temporary duty at the nearby Thai airbase. The downstairs VFW restaurant has great Western food, sizzling T-bone steaks, and ice-cold beer—the best place to hang out and throw darts in Korat. 167 Poklang, tel. (044) 242831, 120-350B.

Korat (K Star) Hotel: Popular with group tours, this old hotel features a nightclub and a massage parlor that roar on weekends. 191 Atsadang, tel. (044) 242260, 200-550B.

Restaurants

Night Market: Foodstalls are plentiful in the night market on Manat Rd. just north of the

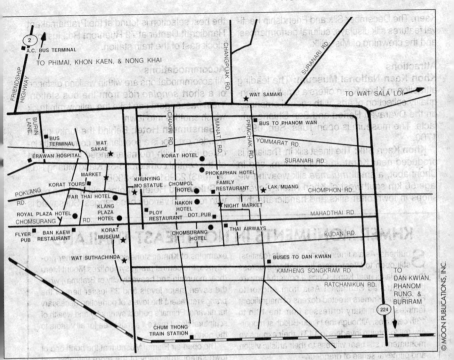

Chomsurang Hotel and in the day market just west of the Thao Suranari Statue. Try the fresh fruit shakes and point-and-order foodstalls.

VFW Cafe: Certainly the most curious restaurant in the northeast is the small, crowded cafe on the ground floor of the Siri Hotel. As the name implies, the cafe serves as headquarters for the Veterans of Foreign Wars (VFW) and is the gathering point for dozens of American veterans who served in the Vietnam conflict and then retired here in Korat. The a/c cafe resembles an American truck stop and serves good burgers, beer, and T-bone steaks in three sizes. Moderate

Transportation
Korat is 256 km northeast of Bangkok. Thai Airway flies four times weekly from Bangkok for 650B. Ordinary and a/c buses from the Northern Bus Terminal in Bangkok leave every 15 minutes and take four hours to reach Korat. Thirteen trains a day depart from Hualampong Train Station in Bangkok. Most convenient are the rapid

trains at 0615 and 0650, express at 0820, and ordinary diesels at 0910, 1105, 1145, and 2225.

Korat has an ordinary bus terminal in Burin Lane near the First Hotel and Erawan Hospital, and an a/c bus terminal on the Friendship Hwy. (Mittrapap Road) about 500 meters north of town. The ordinary terminal has buses to nearby sights such as Ban Don Kwian and Phimai, plus major towns in the northeast such as Udon Thai and Nong Khai. Bus Terminal II on Friendship Hwy. serves all major towns in the northeast.

KHON KAEN

Khon Kaen, 449 km from Bangkok and strategically located at the intersection of Friendship Hwy. and National Rd. 12, is an important crossroads and gateway for visitors arriving from Korat, Phitsanulok, and northern Thailand.

A TAT office opened several years ago in the municipal offices in the north section of Khon

Kaen. The December Silk and Friendship Festival features silk displays, cultural performances, and the crowning of Miss Silk.

Attractions

Khon Kaen National Museum: The leading attraction in Khon Kaen offers a small but high-quality collection of arts, with special emphasis on the Dvaravati Period and Ban Chiang artifacts. The museum is open Tues.-Sun. 0900-1700.

Khon Kaen Silk: The finest silk in Thailand is produced near Korat, in Chaiyaphum, and in Chonnabot, a small *mut mee* silk-weaving village 56 km southwest of Khon Kaen. Several shops in town offer silks and handicrafts, but the best selection is found at the Prathamakant Handicraft Center at 79 Ruenrom Rd., just one block east of the train station.

Accommodations

All accommodations are within walking distance or a short *songtao* ride from the bus station. Train passengers can take the yellow minitruck which shuttles into town.

Sansumran Hotel: Behind the funky green wooden exterior is a popular and conveniently located hotel with rooms arranged left and right off the central corridor. 55-59 Klang Muang Rd., tel. (043) 239611, 160-300B.

Suksawad Hotel: Another old wooden place with rooms in various price ranges. Suksawad is

---

KHMER MONUMENTS IN NORTHEAST THAILAND

Southeast Asia's finest Khmer *prasats* (castles) still open to Westerners lie scattered across the dry plains near Korat. Once a powerful empire that controlled Southeast Asia from Angkor to Burma, the Khmers erected dozens of magnificent temples and military fortresses from the 10th to 13th centuries. Although the Hindu-Buddhist monarchy fell to foreign invaders in 1431, their expansive monuments still bear witness to their artistic vision and primeval sense of grandeur.

Phimai is an easy day-trip from Korat, but the remainder of the following monuments are widely scattered and difficult to reach without an organized tour. Bangkok's Siam Society and National Museum occasionally sponsor group excursions; day tours can be arranged in Korat through travel agents and first-class hotels.

Prasat Hin Phimai

Thailand's most accessible and best-preserved *prasat hin* (stone castle) is located 46 km north of Korat. Dating from the end of the 11th century, the sandstone complex of Phimai is contemporary with and may have been modeled after Angkor Wat. The complex was magnificently restored by Bernard Groslier, the former director of restoration at Angkor who wisely insisted that stucco work be left in original condition. Bravo!

Entrance is through a southern gateway flanked by stone-barred windows—one of the more distinctive features of Khmer architecture. The cruciform central sanctuary with its carved doorways and Ramayana lintels is considered one of Thailand's finest examples of Khmer stonework. As with other prototypes, the central *prang* symbolizes Mount Meru (holy mountain and heavenly city of Brahma), while the seven major levels and 33 lesser tiers of the *prangs* represent the levels of perfection necessary for nirvana. Phimai's perfect symmetry and wealth of sculptural detail make it a must-see for all visitors to the northeast.

The open-air Phimai Museum at the north end of town safeguards many of the more valuable and well-carved lintels. A gigantic banyan tree *(Ficus benjamini)* spreads its branches one km northeast of town. Buses leave Korat hourly. The Phimai Hotel south of the ruins has fan-cooled rooms from 100B.

Prasat Panom Wan

Set in an evocative and tranquil setting 20 km north of Korat, this small but attractive Khmer temple can be visited in conjunction with Phimai. Originally built as a Hindu temple, the 10th-century *panom* (hill) sanctuary follows the standard layout of a courtyard dominated by a central *prang* surrounded by four smaller towers.

Direct buses leave from Wat Samakkhi in Korat, or take a Korat-bound bus from Phimai; ask the bus driver to let you off at Ban Long Thong, and then walk or hitch the remaining six kilometers.

Prasat Panom Rung

Perhaps the most striking and complete Khmer temple in Thailand is this 12th-century hilltop monument located 84 km east of Korat. Like most *prasats,* Panom Rung was originally dedicated to

THAILAND

well located in a quiet alley, and the managers seem friendly if somewhat disorganized. 2 Klang Muang Rd., no phone, 80-200B.

Roma Hotel: The old favorite has been renovated and improved with a new lobby, elevators, and reconditioned rooms. 50 Klang Muang Rd., tel. (043) 236276, 250-400B.

Phu Inn: Tucked away in a small alley near the central market is a cozy, clean, and modern hotel with coffee shop, business services, and 98 a/c rooms. 26-34 Sathid Juthithum Rd., tel. (043) 243174, 500-750B.

Transportation

Khon Kaen is 449 km northeast of Bangkok, 190 km north of Korat, and 115 km south of Udon Thani. Thai Airways flies three times daily from Bangkok for 1,300B and three times weekly from Chiang Mai for 1,400B.

Five trains leave daily from Bangkok and take seven hours by express or eight hours on rapid train. Trains depart Korat at 0600, 0823, 1145, 1226, and 1515. Buses leave hourly from the ordinary bus terminal in Korat and take about three hours to reach Khon Kaen.

UDON THANI

This busy commercial center, 560 km northeast of Bangkok, served as home to thousands of American servicemen until 1975 when the base

---

Shiva but later converted to Buddhist use after Mahayanism was adopted by Jayavarman VII. Staircases leading up the temple are flanked by ruined *nagas* which, like Chiang Mai's *wat* on Doi Suthep, symbolically transport the visitor from the realm of the earth to the world of the gods. The magnificent location atop a volcanic mountain offers splendid views south to the Cambodian border and traces of the Khmer highway that once connected Angkor with Phimai.

The completion of the 38-million *baht* restoration project in 1988 culminated with the return of the valuable Narai Banthomsin lintel. Apparently stolen by art collectors in the early '60s, spirited away to America, and sold to the Chicago Art Institute, the stone crosspiece was subsequently spotted by an archaeologist who contacted the Thai government. A trade was negotiated for an artifact of equal artistic merit; the lintel now surmounts the main eastern entrance. The remainder of Panom Rung boasts a great deal of remarkably clear and delicate stonework. From Korat, take a bus east to Nang Rong, minibus to Ban Taepek, and then walk or hitch the remaining seven kilometers. All tours include this temple.

Prasat Muang Tam

Although older and less well preserved than Panom Rung, this 10th-century fortress also offers outstanding carvings and intriguing architectural symbolism. Clusters of *nagas* ring the inner ponds (the primordial oceans of Hindu-Buddhist cosmology), while window mullions and delicately carved lintels relate themes from Hindu mythology. Restoration,

partially funded by the German government, was completed a few years ago.

Prasat Muang Tam is five km southeast of Panom Rung. From Prakon Chai, take a bus southwest and hitchhike eight km from the signpost. Tours from Korat often include this temple.

Prasat Hin Ban Pluang

As with other major Khmer monuments in the Issan, this small but beautiful 11th-century Khmer temple was constructed on the royal road that once connected Angkor with Phimai. Located 30 km south of Surin and four km south of a small town called Prasat.

Prasat Kao Pra Viharn

One of the most spectacular but inaccessible jewels of Khmer architecture appears ready to welcome visitors after a span of nearly three decades. In 1962 the World Court ruled that the famous *prasat* was in Cambodian territory despite the main entrance being located on Thai soil. The disputed ownership and political problems held tourism to a trickle until 1990, when Khao Pra Viharn was finally cleared of landmines and wire fences and reopened to the public.

Constructed between the 11th and 13th centuries, the temple is laid out in a series of courts and *gopura* on a spur of the Dongrek mountain range. Hindu myths are depicted in the rich craftsmanship of the stairways, lintels, and pediments situated on three levels connected by paved stone avenues. Travel agents in Korat and other cities near the site can help arrange transportation.

was closed and returned to the Thai government. A legacy of sorts continues, with Western military advisers and diplomatic personnel still stationed here and the massage parlors and nightclubs now popular with Thai businessmen. Tourist information can be picked up at the Charoen Hotel, the Bangkok Bank, the Governor's Office, and the small tourist office just opposite the bus terminal. Udon's train station is two km away; take a trishaw.

Attractions

Udon Thani: The city's few sights are limited to a popular Weekend Market which runs in the *very* early morning hours and Wat Muchimawat opposite the Technical College.

Ban Chiang: Udon's top draws are the archaeological excavations, pottery, and Bronze-Age artifacts discovered at Ban Chiang, 58 km east of Udon Thani. Among the world's oldest, these important findings have prompted many scholars to rethink Southeast Asian history and challenge the traditional notion that civilization began in the Middle East or China. A small and meager museum open Wednesday-Sunday only displays the *in situ* diggings. Direct buses leave from Udon's terminal; or take any bus east, change at the Ban Chiang turnoff near Nong Han, and continue the remaining five km by trishaw.

Erawan Caves: The stalactite caves of Tham Erawan, 50 km west of Udon, are filled with Buddha images illuminated by electric lights. Take a bus and look for the Tham Erawan sign.

Accommodations

Sri Sawat Hotel: Budget travelers usually stay in this small hotel just up from the clock tower. 123 Prachak Rd., tel. (042) 221560, 100-300B.

Pracha Pakdee Hotel: Across the street is this clean and modern hotel with good-value rooms. 156 Prachak Rd., tel. (042) 221804, 150-350B.

Queen Hotel: An older joint that absorbs the overflow crowd from the Sri Sawat and Pracha Pakdee. 6 Udon Dusadi Rd., tel. (042) 221451, 100-260B.

Charoen Hotel: Tour groups en route to Ban Chiang usually stay at the Charoen, considered the best in town. 549 Pho Sri Rd., tel. (042) 248115, 750-1,400B.

NONG KHAI

Nong Khai rates as the most popular destination in the northeast. Superbly located at the terminus of the Friendship Hwy. and nestled on the banks of the Mekong River, the comfortably small and rather sleepy town is chiefly known as an important link with Laos and the national capital, Vientiane.

A highly recommended journey west from Nong Khai to Chiang Khan passes through great landscapes, a culturally diverse environment, and charming towns almost completely unaffected by tourism. You can then visit Loei, perhaps trek in one of the nearby national parks, and return to Nong Khai or head off to northern Thailand via the back roads.

Attractions in Town

The River: A new bridge completed in 1994 with the help of the Australian and Lao governments will probably phase out the boat crossing in Nong Khai, but the riverbank trailhead is still a popular spot at which to enjoy a meal from the cantilevered restaurant.

Wat Po Chai: Tucked away in a back alley east of the bus terminal, Wat Po Chai houses a highly venerated solid-gold statue called Luang Pho Phra Sai, cast in Laos and brought here from Vientiane by General Chakri.

Wat Khaek: Certainly the most bizarre and memorable temple in northeastern Thailand is the strange Hindu-Buddhist wonderland of Wat Khaek (also called Wat Phuttama Makasamakhom), located four km east of town at the end of a dusty side road, a few hundred meters beyond St. Paul School. Look for the sign marked "Sala Kaeoku."

Attractions outside Town

Wat Bang Puan: Eighteen km southwest of Nong Khai is a modern Laotian-style *chedi* built by a ruler from Vientiane and reconstructed in 1978 by the Fine Arts Department. Wat Ban is unimpressive aside from several Buddhas displayed under open tin roofs and a small museum filled with wooden figurines. Wat Bang Puan can be reached with a *songtao* to Ban Nong Hong Song and a second minitruck west to the compound.

Wat Prathat Buakok: Far more interesting than Wat Bang Puan is this Laotian stupa and historical park 55 km southwest of Nong Khai.

Ban Phu Historical Park: A dirt road shortly before Wat Buakok leads two km uphill to one of the most curious geological sights in Thailand. An information center at the park entrance shows hiking trails through the bizarre rock formations named after Buddhist legends and ancient folk tales. The historical park, 13 km from the town of Ban Phu, can be reached by *songtao* from either Nong Khai or Si Chiang Mai.

Across to Laos

Visas should be obtained whenever possible in advance from the Laotian Embassy or the Laotian Consulate in Khon Kaen. Guesthouses and travel agencies in Nong Khai such as The Meeting Place on Soi Chuenjit just south of Wat Si Chom Cheun can help with border formalities, but expect to wait several days for your visa. The best strategy is to first check with travel agencies and guesthouses in Bangkok, especially around Khao San Road.

Accommodations

Mut Mee Guesthouse: Probably the most popular guesthouse in town, Mut Mee is favored for its beautiful outdoor restaurant overlooking the Mekong, excellent meals, and reliable information provided by the management. 1111 Kaeworawut Rd., no phone, 80-250B.

Sawasdee Guesthouse: Nong Khai's newest and cleanest guesthouse provides 16 rooms in a convenient location near the center of town. 402 Meechai Rd., tel. (042) 412502, 80-350B.

The Meeting Place: Offerings here include a few rooms, an expat bar, plus help with Laotian visas. 1117 Soi Chuenjit, tel. (042) 421223, 100-150B.

Mekong Guesthouse: Basic but clean rooms overlooking the river. Rimkhong Rd., tel. (042) 412119, 60-180B.

Rimkong Guesthouse: Another riverside guesthouse with small but acceptable rooms. Rimkhong Rd., tel. (042) 421229, 80-200B.

Nong Khai Grand Hotel: Nong Khai tourism came of age in 1993 with the opening of several luxury hotels including this one with swimming pool and other upscale amenities. Highway 212, tel. (042) 420003, 1,600-2,400B.

Transportation

Nong Khai is 615 km northeast of Bangkok, 356 km north of Korat, 51 km north of Udon Thani, and 20 km southeast of Vientiane.

Trains from Bangkok depart daily at 0615, 1900, and 2030, and take 10-12 hours to Nong Khai. Sleepers are available on the 2030 service. Ordinary and a/c buses depart hourly from 0530 to 0800 and 2000 to 2130 from the Northern Bus Terminal in Bangkok.

SI CHIANG MAI

Si Chiang Mai is a thriving commercial center 58 km west of Nong Khai and just across the river from Vientiane. Most of the population are Lao and Vietnamese citizens who fled here after the Communist takeover of Laos and today remain stateless people without passports or land-ownership rights.

Top draws include a roaring business in the production of spring-roll wrappers and Wat Aranyabanpot, about 10 km west of town. Temple fans may also want to visit Wat Hin Mak Peng, west of Si Chiang Mai and 30 km before Sang Khom, a peaceful forest monastery known for its rigorous precepts followed by a large community of monks and *mae chis.*

Accommodations

Tim Guesthouse: Several years ago a Swiss citizen named Jean-Daniel Schranz opened a small guesthouse on the riverfront road between Sois 16 and 17. Rimkhong Rd. Soi 16, tel. (042) 451072, 60-150B.

SANG KHOM

The atmosphere improves considerably in the small town of Sang Khom, 63 km west of Nong Khai. Populated by Thais rather than the Laos and Vietnamese, Sang Khom is a useful base from which to visit the region's waterfalls, temples, and caves.

Accommodations

Several guesthouses are on the riverbanks or back from the main road in Sang Khom. All have simple bungalows priced from 50-100B.

THAILAND

River Huts: Back from the main road but with huts overlooking the river plus services such as boat trips down the Mekong, bicycle rentals, rough maps, and "lice removal—one *baht* each." Sang Khom Rd., 60-100B.

Bouy Guesthouse: Popular spot right on the river with a useful wall map, herbal saunas, and expert Issan dinners prepared by the owner. Seven bungalows, but only two face the river. 190 Rimkhong Rd., tel. (042) 412415, 80-120B.

PAK CHONG

The Lao village of Pak Chong is the prettiest and most laid-back town between Nong Khai and Chiang Khan. Travelers seeking to discover what is most authentic and charming about rural Issan will enjoy a few days gazing at the river and wandering around the surrounding countryside. A wonderful, almost completely untouched destination.

Accommodations
Pak Chom Guesthouse: The best place in town has a dozen bamboo bungalows at the end of a dirt trail at the north end of Pak Chong. The locale and atmosphere of the Maekhong will remind you of the Golden Triangle before the arrival of mass tourism. Walk west of town until you reach the small signpost on the right. 60-100B.

Chumpee Guesthouse: The only alternative to the Maekhong is the rather dismal collection of bamboo huts thoughtlessly crammed together near the river two blocks east of the main intersection. 60-100B.

CHIANG KHAN

Chiang Khan is a fairly large town on the banks of the Mekong River. Almost entirely constructed of teakwood homes now covered with a fine patina of red dust, Chiang Khan guarantees a refreshing change from Thai towns created from concrete and cinderblock.

Attractions
River Trips: Guesthouses in Chiang Khan arrange upriver boat trips through sublime scenery to Menam Heuang and the point where the Mekong turns north into Laos.

Kaeng Khut Ku: A large set of rapids and a scenic overlook are located five km east of Chiang Khan at the end of a very long side road. Kaeng Khut Ku can be reached from Chiang Khan by *songtao, tuk tuk,* rented bicycle, or boats chartered from local guesthouses.

Accommodations
Nong Sam Guesthouse: The friendliest place in Chiang Khan is operated by a Brit named Rob, his Thai wife Noi, and their two children (Nong and Sam) who look Thai but have the frantic energy levels of Western kids. The place is west of town right on the river. 120-180B.

Chiang Khan Guesthouse: A large and comfortable place that runs a close second to Nong Sam. Chai Khong Rd. Soi 19, tel. (042) 821029, 60-100B.

Transportation
Chiang Khan is 50 km north of Loei and about 160 km west of Nong Khai.

Buses from Nong Khai to Chiang Khan and all other towns on the Mekong leave from the street just beyond the Suzuki dealership. Direct service to Chiang Khan takes about five hours but is available only in the early morning.

LOEI

Midway between the north and the northeast on the western edge of the Issan plateau, the provincial capital of Loei is an important transit spot for visitors arriving from northern Thailand and a useful base for visiting Phu Kradung National Park.

Attractions
The region's principal sights are the three national parks outside town.

Phu Kradung National Park: This outstanding park, on a sloping plateau 82 km south of Loei, is a high-elevation retreat set with pine trees, tall grasses, six waterfalls, dozens of hiking trails, and fields of springtime azaleas and rhododendrons. The park closes from July through October when monsoon rains reduce the trails to muddy quagmires. The trail begins at the base of the mountain at Ban Si Than, where the Park

Service operates an information center with maps, a restaurant, and bungalows. The total distance of about nine km takes four or five hours.

Park headquarters at the summit has a small shop with basic provisions, another restaurant with hot meals, bungalows, tent sites, and maps which describe the 50 kilometers of trails. Visitors should bring warm clothes, extra food, flashlights, candles, and insect repellent. Accommodations include 16 10-man bungalows that cost 500-1,500B. Tents cost 50B per night. Bedding and blankets can be hired.

Reservations can be made in Loei inside the provincial offices on the main highway.

Phu Luang National Park: An 848-square-km wildlife reserve controlled by the Forestry Department to help protect the remaining wildlife. Accommodations are similar to Phu Kradung's, with group bungalows from 500B and tents onsite for 50B. Reservations can be made at the provincial offices in Loei. Bring food, drink, warm clothes, a flashlight, and candles.

Phu Luang is 26 km south of Loei down Hwy. 201 and then 15 km west from Wang Saphung. Although somewhat closer than Phu Kradung, Phu Luang is more difficult to visit because of its inaccessibility and lack of organized transportation. The easiest option is a tour arranged by the Forestry Department at the Loei Provincial Office.

Tha Li: Another lovely town somewhat similar to Pak Chong is eight km south of the Heuang River in a remote valley about 50 km west of Chiang Khan and 45 km north of Loei.

Dan Sai: About 86 km west of Loei is the small town of Dan Sai, an important junction point chiefly known among the Thais for its strange ghostly procession called Pi Ta Khon ("Dance of the Ghosts").

Lom Sak: Lom Sak is a small town in a fertile valley between the Phang Hoei Mountains to the east and the southern extension of the Luang Prabang Range to the west. Lom Sak is a major transit point for visitors traveling between Phitsanulok and Loei and Khon Kaen.

Accommodations
Muang Loei Guesthouse: Budget travelers usually stay in the guesthouse two blocks east of the bus terminal. Services include bicycle and motorcycle rentals and organized tours to the

nearby national parks. Ruamchai Rd., Soi Ruamjai, tel. (042) 812302, 60-100B.

Friendship Guesthouse: Another budget option inconveniently located in the southern part of town past the post office. 257/41 Soi Buncharoen, tel. (042) 832408, 80-250B.

Phu Luang Hotel: A middle-quality hotel with big rooms, private baths, and acceptable cafe. 55 Charoenraj Rd., tel. (042) 811570, 400-750B.

Udom Thai Hotel: Loei's most popular hotel is similar to the Phu Luang and King hotels but has better prices and a better location in the center of town. 112 Charoenraj Rd., tel. (042) 811763, 250-450B.

Transportation
Loei is 520 km northeast of Bangkok, 344 km north of Korat, and 269 km east of Phitsanulok. Buses leave eight times daily from the Northern Bus Terminal in Bangkok. Loei can also be reached by bus from Phitsanulok via Lom Sak.

BEUNG KHAN

Highway 212 leaves Nong Khai and continues 135 km east to the small town of Beung Khan, on the Mekong River just opposite the Laotian village of Muang Paksan.

Attractions
Phu Wua Wildlife Park: A small nature park on Phu Wua Mountain, 45 km southeast of town, features several waterfalls, crumbling cliffs, and a small forest *wat.*

Wat Phu Tauk: Formally known as Wat Chedi Kiri Viharn, Wat Phu Tauk (or Phu Tok) is one of the most sacred forest temples in the northeast. It is also among the most spectacular in location, being on a sandstone mountain which soars vertically from the flat dry plains. The complex is 47 km southeast of Beung Khan. Take a bus or minitruck south from Beung Khan 25 km down to Ban Siwilai, from where *songtaos* continue 22 km east on the dirt road to the temple. Visitors can spend the night.

Accommodations
The Santisuk, Somanmit, and Neramit hotels on Prasatchai Road in Beung Khan have fan-cooled rooms for 80-200B.

THAILAND

SAKHON NAKHON

Sakhon Nakhon is a provincial center 647 km from Bangkok, perched on the edge of 32-square-km Nong Han Lake, Thailand's largest natural lake.

Attractions

Wat Chong Chum: Sakhon Nakhon's major religious monument features a modern white-washed Laotian *chedi* that encases a 10th-century Khmer *prang*.

Wat Pa Suthawat: A small temple and modern museum opposite the provincial hall displays the paraphernalia and wax figure of Achaan Man, the fierce meditation master whose intensity is reflected in his lifelike image.

Wat Pa Udom Somphon: Buddhist pilgrims visit this temple to honor and view the religious emblems of Achaan Fan, a *vipassana* master whose life-size wax image is displayed inside the central *viharn*. The temple is three km outside of town.

Phu Phan National Park: Seventeen km southwest of town on Hwy. 213, this 645-square-km nature preserve offers hiking trails, three waterfalls, and forest cover over a vast expanse of remote mountains.

Accommodations

All of the following hotels are within a few blocks of the bus terminal on Raj Pattana Road.

Araya I Hotel: Two blocks northeast of the bus terminal in the center of town. Prem Prida Rd., tel. (042) 711416, 150-300B.

Krong Thong Hotel: Four blocks northeast of the bus terminal. 645/2 Charoen Muang Rd., tel. (042) 711097, 120-280B.

Imperial Hotel: Sakhon Nakhon's best hotel along with the newer Dusit. 1892 Sukkasem Rd., tel. (042) 711119, 300-750B.

Transportation

Sakhon Nakhon is 145 km southeast of Bung Khan, 117 km west of Nakhon Phanom, and 155 km east of Udon Thani. Direct buses are available from Ubon Ratchathani, Nakhon Phanom, That Phanom, Kalasin, Korat, and Bangkok.

NAKHON PHANOM

Nakhon Phanom is set along the banks of the Mekong River, across from the small Laotian town of Muang Ta Kaek (Muang Khammouan). Attractions in town include the modern murals inside Wat Sri Thep—and simply gazing across the river into Laos.

Nakhon Phanom makes a convenient crossing point over to Laos assuming that you have obtained your visa in advance from a Laotian embassy or consulate. A bridge is now under construction across the river.

Accommodations

River Inn Hotel: Budget hotel on the river with a terrace restaurant serving good food and providing views across to Laos. 137 Sunthon Wichit Rd., tel. (042) 511305, 160-350B.

First Hotel: A good alternative to the River Inn is provided by the large hotel across from the clock tower and close to the river and the immigration office. 370 Si Thep Rd., tel. (042) 511253, 150-250B.

THAT PHANOM

That Phanom, a small town on the banks of the Mekong River midway between Nakhon Phanom and Mukdahan, is a major pilgrimage site and home to the most sacred religious monument in the northeast.

Attractions

Wat Prathat That Phanom: Highly venerated by both Thai and Laotian citizens, the Laotian-style *chedi* of That Phanom forms the talismanic symbol of the Issan people and a source of magical power for the residents of Laos. Disaster struck in 1975 when the principal tower collapsed after heavy rains, but local authorities have since reconstructed the monument.

Renu Phanom: Renu Phanom is a small village renowned for the quality of its weaving of cottons, silk fabrics, and a rare version of Thai *ikat*. The turnoff to Renu Phanom is 12 km north of That Phanom and 44 km south of Nakhon Phanom.

Accommodations

Niyana Guesthouse: Lovely and vivacious Niyana operates a popular guesthouse with kitchen facilities, a garden, and information on boat trips for travelers. The author stayed in her Nong Khai guesthouse way back in 1987. 73 Weteshawrachon Rd., no phone, 50-100B.

Hotels: Chai Von Hotel at Phanom Phanarak Rd. has 20 fan-cooled rooms for 80-120B. Saeng Thong Hotel, on the same street but after a right turn through the archway, has similar facilities at identical prices.

Transportation

That Phanom is 52 km south of Nakhon Phanom and 225 km north of Ubon Ratchathani. Buses and *songtaos* from the junction near the Nakhon Phanom Hotel in Nakhon Phanom take about 90 minutes to reach the *chedi* in That Phanom. Buses from the terminal in Ubon Ratchathani to Nakhon Pathom pass through That Phanom.

YASOTHON

Yasothon is rarely visited except during the Rocket Festival held in mid-May to celebrate the end of the dry season and ensure heavy rains throughout the region. Book rooms well in advance or join one of the many tours organized by travel agencies in Bangkok.

Accommodations

Yasothon has six small hotels in the center of town on Chang Sanit and Uthai Ramrit roads. Surawet Wattana Hotel at 128 Chang Sanit Rd. has 30 fan-cooled rooms that cost 150-200B. On the same street you'll find other hotels in the same price range, such as Suk Niran, Serm Siri, and Phan Pricha. Yot Nakhon Hotel at 141 Uthai Ramrit Road is the largest in town and the only place with a/c rooms from 250-350B.

UBON RATCHATHANI

Ubon Ratchathani—often called simply Ubon—is a major destination being positioned as the international gateway to Laos, Cambodia, and Vietnam. Ubon is a major economic center with an international airport, industrial estates, a new

university, and major hotels earmarked for both business and leisure visitors. The TAT office (tel. 045-243770) at 264 Kuan Thani Rd. has maps and sponsors weekend tours to the sights near the Mekong River.

Attractions

National Museum: A good overview of the historical development of the lower Issan and a broad selection of Khmer and Thai artifacts are displayed in the 19th-century building once used as the office of the provincial governor.

Wat Supatnaram: Dedicated to the Thammayut sect of Buddhism, Wat Supatnaram on the Moon (Mun) River reflects the complex interaction of religious traditions in Southeast Asia.

Wat Tung Sri Muang: Constructed during the reign (1824-51) of King Rama III, this *wat* is renowned for its Tripitaka library elevated in the middle of a small pond, ancient *mondop*, and erotic wall murals.

Wat Ba Na Muang: Four km northeast of town on the road past the airport, the latest addition to the *wat* scene is this exotic creation covered with dark red glazed tiles and fronted by an eccentric royal barge filled with dozens of red-tiled boatmen.

Wat Nong Pa Pong: This temple served as the residence of a meditation master named Achaan Cha, a disciple of the famous Achaan Man (1870-1949), who is credited as the inspiration for over 40 forest monasteries located throughout the Issan. Achaan Cha died in 1992 after a long illness. Wat Nong Pa Pong can be reached by *songtao* or bus from Ubon, 15 km northwest.

Wat Pa Nanachat: Westerners interested in Buddhism and *vipassana* meditation are advised to visit the forest monastery across the road from Wat Nong Pa Pong. This is a Western-oriented temple with a Canadian abbot, a Japanese vice-abbot, and several dozen European and American monks who speak English. Laypeople are welcome to stay as guests and conduct brief studies of Buddhism and insight meditation.

Accommodations

Ubon has over 20 hotels that charge 150-250B for fan-cooled rooms and 250-550B for a/c rooms with private baths.

Tokyo Hotel: A clean and popular hotel in the center of town two blocks north of the park.

178 Upparat Rd., tel. (045) 241739, 150-350B.

Racha Hotel: A bit north of city center is a low-priced hotel with both fan and a/c rooms. 149 Chaiyangkun Rd., tel. (045) 254155, 220-450B.

Ratchathani Hotel: A very large hotel nicely situated in the center of town across from the tourist office and the National Museum. Probably the best mid-priced place in Ubon. 229 Kuan Thani Rd., tel. (045) 244388, 280-640B.

Transportation

Ubon is 629 km northeast of Bangkok and 370 km east of Korat. Thai Airways flies once daily from Bangkok. Ubon is connected by rail with Bangkok via Korat, Buriram, and Surin. Seven trains leave Bangkok daily. An express train with sleepers departs at 2100 and arrives in Ubon the next morning at 0705. Rapid trains without sleepers leave at 0650, 1845, and 2245. Rapid trains leave Korat at 1136 and 2356. The train station is five km southwest of town in the suburb of Warin Chamrun. Take a taxi, *tuk tuk,* or bus.

Buses leave every 15 minutes from the Northern Bus Terminal in Bangkok and take 12 hours to reach Ubon. Air-conditioned buses leave Bangkok from 1900 to 2130. The Ubon Bus Terminal is on Chaiyangkun Rd. about four km north of city center. Take public bus 2 or a *songtao* for 20 *baht.* An a/c bus terminal is on Palo Rungrit Rd., two blocks north of the TAT office.

SURIN

Most visitors associate Surin with its famed Elephant Fair, held on the third weekend in November. Though the festival is certainly the highlight, Surin is well located near several Khmer temples and serves as a base for visits to an elephant camp, basketry and silk-weaving villages, and, with special permission, a Cambodian refugee camp.

Attractions

Elephant Fair: Perhaps the most internationally famous festival in Thailand, Surin's annual weeklong Elephant Fair is something like the Super Bowl but without the bowl, beer, or football. Tours with transportation and accommodations can be booked through the TAT and several tour operators in Bangkok.

Tha Klang Elephant Village: City ordinances prohibit Surin citizens from keeping elephants as house pets, so most elephants live in Tha Klang, 58 km north of Surin. Overnight homestays can be arranged by Mr. Pirom at Pirom Guesthouse in Surin.

Silk-weaving Villages: Two villages which specialize in traditional silk production and weaving are within 20 km of Surin. Khawao Sinarin, north of Surin on Hwy. 214, and Ban Chanron, east of town on Hwy. 2077, both produce and sell hand-woven silks.

Prasat Sikhoraphum: Thirty km east of Surin near the town of Sikhoraphum is an 11th-century Khmer *prasat* recently restored by the Fine Arts Department. Note the Shiva lintel over the central *prang.*

Prasat Pluang: Twenty km south of Surin near the silk-weaving town of Ban Pluang is another restored *prasat,* constructed in the late 11th century during the reign of King Suriyavoraman I.

Prasat Ta Muen And Muen Tom: Two clusters of recently opened Khmer ruins are exactly on the Thai-Cambodian border, some 55 km due south of Surin and close to the ruins at Muang Tam and Phanom Rung. Both ruins are inaccessible by public transportation but can be reached with a private car hired in Surin or Buriram.

Prasat Phanom Rung And Muang Tam: Prasat Phanom Rung is widely considered the most impressive Khmer monument in Thailand. Muang Tam is about nine km southeast of Phanom Rung. Both monuments can be visited on day excursions from Surin or Buriram.

Accommodations

Pirom Guesthouse: The backpackers' hotel scene in Surin improved dramatically several years ago with the opening of this guesthouse, two blocks west of the market and 500 meters from the bus terminal and train station. Mr. Pirom has converted his six-room teakwood house into a very cozy place with the best travel information in the province. 272 Krung Sri Rd., tel. (045) 515140, 60-150B.

Country Roads Guesthouse: Small guesthouse owned and operated by a Texan and his Thai wife with good information on nearby sights plus a cafe popular with local expats. 165/1 Sirirat Rd., tel. (045) 515721, 100-150B.

Memorial Hotel: A clean and well-priced hotel well in the center of town near the temples and restaurants. 186 Lak Muang Rd., tel. (045) 511637, 260-540B.

Tarin Hotel: Top hotel south of city center. 60 Sirirat Rd., tel. (045) 514281, 900-1,600B.

Transportation

Surin is 457 km northeast of Bangkok and 198 km east of Korat. Surin is connected by rail with Bangkok via Korat and Buriram. Seven trains leave Bangkok daily. Buses leave every 15 minutes from the Northern Bus Terminal in Bangkok and take 10 hours to reach Surin.

BURIRAM

Although Buriram lacks any great attractions within the city boundaries, the town can serve as a base for exploring the numerous Khmer monuments located south along the Cambodian border. Archaeologists have identified over 50 *prasats* in Buriram Province, of which almost a dozen have been restored by the Fine Arts Department.

Accommodations

Several places can be reached on foot within a few minutes from the train station.

Chai Charoen Hotel: Just opposite the train station is an acceptable spot for an overnight crash. 114 Niwat Rd., tel. (044) 611640, 80-150B.

Thai Hotel: Somewhat better rooms about three blocks from the train station. 38 Romburi Rd., tel. (044) 611112, 150-380B.

Buriram Plaza Hotel: The newest addition to the upscale scene in the center of town. Buriram-Surin Rd., tel. (044) 411123, 850-1,400B.

SOUTHERN THAILAND

The long and narrow peninsula of southern Thailand offers a dazzling array of thick jungles, rugged mountains, limestone pinnacles and emerald-blue bays, fishermen and sea gypsies, graceful temples, coral reefs, colorful marinelife, and some of the most spectacular beaches in Southeast Asia. Landscapes, religions, languages, and even the people change as you travel deeper into the south: rice paddies give way to rubber plantations, Muslim mosques outnumber Buddhist temples, even the beaches seem to change . . . they get better!

Southern Thailand's two most popular destinations are the tropical islands of Phuket and Ko Samui. Both have distinct personalities which appeal to slightly different types of travelers. Phuket, the more developed of the two, offers a stunning combination of superb beaches, upscale hotels, outstanding seafood restaurants, sports activities from parasailing to scuba diving, and raunchy nightlife rivaled only by Bangkok's or Pattaya's. Most of the island is highly commercialized but a few beaches are still pristine . . . at least for the moment.

Ko Samui is a relatively simple and absolutely beautiful island on the east side of the peninsula. Though rapidly approaching saturation point, the atmosphere remains much less frantic than on Phuket. In fact, deserted beaches in southern Thailand have become much harder to find, but with nearly 2,000 km of coastline and hundreds of untouched islands, a few gems still await discovery.

Routes

Most visitors head directly to Phuket or Samui from Bangkok, but travelers intrigued with Thai architecture and painting should visit Phetburi for a recommended four-hour walking tour, described below. Those who prefer a more leisurely approach can also try the family-oriented beach resorts of Hua Hin or Cha Am. One possible route is an early-morning bus to Phetburi for the walking tour, then afternoon bus to Hua Hin.

Visitors with limited time can reach Phuket and Samui directly by air on either Thai Airways International or Bangkok Airways. Bangkok Airways flies twice daily between Samui and Phuket. Four rapid and three express trains leave Bangkok daily for Surat Thani, the launching point for ferries over to Samui. Phuket is off the rail line but can be reached by air or bus.

THAILAND

PHETBURI

© MOON PUBLICATIONS, INC.

Advance reservations from Bangkok's Hualampong Station or a travel agent are strongly recommended on all trains going south.

Regular and a/c buses leave frequently from Bangkok's Southern Bus Terminal, while private buses can be booked through travel agents.

PHETBURI

Phetburi (also spelled Phetchburi, Petchaburi, Petchburi, and Petburi!), 126 km south of Bangkok, is a charming town with a half-dozen outstanding temples. All can be easily visited on the four-hour walking tour described below.

Much of the city's superb art and architecture reflect its long and rich history. Founded as a Mon city which traded with Europe during the Middle Ages, Phetburi fell to the Khmers in the 12th century, to Sukothai a century later, and to

Ayuthaya in 1350. The town is a treasure house of historical artifacts from nearly all possible eras: Mon sculpture unearthed within the ancient city walls; a small but intriguing Khmer temple in a quiet neighborhood; monastery walls gilded with Thailand's finest Ayuthaya-period murals; Wat Mahathat's 19th-century *prang* soaring into the sky; a hilltop palace of neoclassical inspiration.

Day-trippers can store their bags at the train station or in the small office at the bus station.

Attractions

Wat Yai Suwannaram: Phetburi's artistic fame is chiefly due to the murals here and at Wat Ko Keo Sutharam. Thai murals typically date from the fall of Ayuthaya in 1767 until about 1910, when royal patronage ended. Those in Ayuthaya were almost completely destroyed by the Burmese; only Phetburi murals survive to illustrate early Thai painting. Among the best are the 17th-century worshipping divinities in the small *bot* of Wat Yai Suwannaram. Most are chipping and desperately need attention, although the interior door murals are still in good condition. The adjacent wooden *sala*, supported by wooden pillars, is one of Thailand's few surviving examples of this genre.

Wat Borom: This small but attractive temple back toward the railway tracks shows finely plastered roses around the windows and a whitewashed exterior slowly fading into psychedelic patterns.

Wat Trai Lok: A typical monk's quarters complete with TV antennas, sleeping dogs, and a pet monkey in the tree.

Wat Kamphang Lang: Three Khmer towers are the oldest structures in Phetburi. Original stucco can still be seen on the back side of the central *prang*. The adjoining *wat* is a wildlife refuge for wild turkeys, roosters, and other unidentifiable birds.

Wat Pra Song: Two unique and rather strange belltowers face the primary *bot*. Although in danger of falling down, the wonderful old monks' quarters to the right are more appealing than the modern replacements to the rear of the courtyard.

Wat Ko Keo Sutharam: Don't miss Phetburi's most famous temple! Some of Thailand's finest, best-preserved, and oldest murals, dated by inscription to 1734, are guarded inside the small *bot*. Side walls of dramatic triangles show scenes from the life of the Buddha and comical figures of Arab merchants, a Jesuit wearing the robes of a Buddhist monk, and other big-nosed *farangs*. Facing the Buddha is a wall of Buddhist cosmology (this scene is usually *behind* the Buddha image), while the posterior wall shows Buddha's victory over the temptations of Mara. Just below Buddha is Torani, the Earth Goddess so impressed by Buddha's willpower that she washed away Mara's evil armies by wringing water from her hair. The superb execution, careful attention to detail, and high degree of originality make these murals among the great achievements of Thai art. Wat Ko Keo Sutharam is located back down a side alley and somewhat difficult to find. Look for the small blue plastic signs. Ask a monk to unlock the door and watch carefully—it's a strange kind of lock.

Wat Mahathat: The enormous white *prang* of Wat Mahathat (Monastery of the Great Relic) dominates tiny Phetburi like a giant rocketship resting on a launch pad. Climb the late-Ayuthayan style *prang* for views over the town. Outside the temple enclosure near the east entrance is a *bot* with impressive Buddha images and patches of remaining murals.

Khao Wang Palace: A steep and ungraded path leads up the hill past fat monkeys to a neoclassical palace constructed in the 19th century by King Mongkut. Outstanding views from the observation platform. Wat Kao Bandait, another beautiful temple with historical significance, is three km west of town at Bandait hill. Of Phetburi's dozen caves filled with Buddhas, stalactites, and *chedis*, the most famous is Khao Luang, two km north of town.

Accommodations

Chom Klao Hotel: Simple rooms one block east of the bus terminal. Pongsuriya Rd., tel. (032) 425398, 100-150B.

Khao Wang Hotel: Mid-level place two blocks northwest of the bus terminal. Rajawitee Rd., tel. (032) 425167, 200-600B.

HUA HIN

Hua Hin, 170 km south of Bangkok on the sunrise side of the gulf, is a mellow, middle-class Thai beach resort favored by families and travelers seeking peace and quiet. The beach is unspectacular and the modern town undistinguished, but the beautiful bay and the picturesque backdrop of green hills make this a fine place to relax for a few days.

During the day there's little to do but relax, read a book, wander around the beach, and perhaps visit the quaint building next to the train station which once served as the private waiting room for Thai royalty. Nightlife revolves around seafood dinners and drinks at simple open-air cafes. Popular restaurants are found near the guesthouses on Naretdamri alley, at the fishing piers, and at the night market.

One of the area's major attractions is Sam Roi Yot National Park 35 km south, a wonderland of limestone caves, strangely disfigured mountains, and secluded beaches. Tours can be

THAILAND

arranged at the travel agency opposite the tourist office, or you can hire a motorcycle from the nearby shop. More information on trekking, local transportation, and train departures is available from the tourist office.

Accommodations

Hua Hin's dozen-plus guesthouses are tucked away in the alleys one block back from the beach. Rooms during the low season and midweek start from 100B, while weekend, holiday, and high-season rates (Oct.-March) are 300-450B.

Beach Road Guesthouses: Sriosrapusin, Europa, and Sunee guesthouses have simple fan-cooled rooms for 150-250B. Cheaper rooms

are found in the private homes down the alley at the S.M., M.P., and Pattana Thai-Dutch guesthouses. M.P. Guesthouse features a useful noticeboard and a cozy verandah.

One block north is another narrow alley with several inexpensive guesthouses such as Crocodile, Phuen, and Ban Pak; most charge 100-250B.

Thai Tae Guesthouse: A newer place in a quiet location slightly back from the street. 6 Damnern Kasem Rd., tel. (032) 511906, 150-450B.

All Nations Guesthouse: Aussie-run guesthouse with clean rooms and ice-cold beer. 10 Decharnchit Rd., 150-250B.

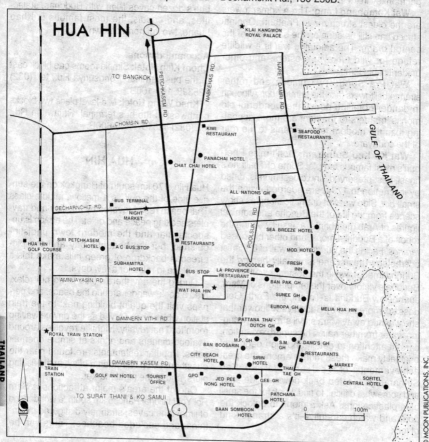

Subhamitra Hotel: An older six-story hotel with a small pool and clean, large rooms. Away from the action, but a good-value choice. Amnuayasin Rd., tel. (032) 511208, 200-500B.

Jed Pee Nong Hotel: Popular spot with swimming pool and great outdoor cafe. 13/7 Damnern Kasem Rd., tel. (032) 512381, 450-550B.

Sirin Hotel: An attractive and spotlessly clean cantilevered hotel centrally located near the beach and restaurants. Very luxurious. Damnern Kasem Rd., tel. (032) 511150, 950-1,200B.

Sofitel Central Hotel: Hua Hin's most famous hotel is the grand old dame constructed in 1921 by Prince Purachtra. Formerly known as the Railway Hotel, the European-style hotel has been completely renovated and redecorated by a French hotel firm. Damnern Kasem Rd., tel. (032) 512021, 3,400-6,500B.

PRACHUAP KHIRI KHAN

One of the more delightful and untouristy towns in the northern third of southern Thailand is the unassuming village of Prachuap Khiri Khan, situated on a magnificently arched bay flanked by towering limestone peaks. Prachuap Khiri Khan ("Town Among Mountains") lacks historical monuments, and the beach inside the city limits is disappointing, but the genuine Thai feel and nearby geological attractions make it an excellent stop for visitors with extra time.

Attractions
Khao Chong Krachok: Looming over the northern end of the bay is a limestone buttress called Mirror Tunnel Mountain after an illuminated arch which appears to reflect the sky. Visitors can climb the stairway to enjoy the panoramic views over the bay.

Ao Noi Beach: Fairly clean and white beaches are located both north and south of town. Ao Noi, six km north and reached by minitrucks heading up Chai Thale Rd., has several small spots such as Ao Noi Beach Bungalows, where a Thai-German couple rents rooms from 450B.

Accommodations
Yutichai Hotel: The first hotel near the train station has decent rooms in a convenient location. 35 Kong Kiat Rd., tel. (032) 611055, 100-200B.

Inthira Hotel: Directly across from the night market is a popular spot with inexpensive rooms. No English sign, but look for the car in the lobby. Phitak Chat Rd., no phone, 100-200B.

Thetsaban Mirror Mountain Bungalows: Facing the bay in the north end of town is a collection of seaside bungalows owned and operated by the city. Suseuk Rd., tel. (032) 611150, 300-600B.

Had Thong Hotel: The newest hotel in Prachuap features a small swimming pool, a comfortable cafe, and well-furnished a/c rooms. 7 Suseuk Rd., tel. (032) 601150, 600-850B.

Transportation
Prachuap Khiri Khan is 252 km south of Bangkok and 82 km south of Hua Hin. Trains from Bangkok's Hualampong Station leave nine times daily from 0900 to 2155. Buses leave regularly from Bangkok's Southern Bus Terminal and from the bus station on Sasong Road in Hua Hin.

CHUMPHON

Almost 500 km south of Bangkok and situated on the Kra Isthmus, Chumphon is an extremely drab provincial capital. Chumphon offers little of interest to most visitors, aside from the several fine beaches on the eastern perimeter and scuba diving considered among the finest in Thailand.

Boat to Ko Tao
Chumphon serves as a departure point for boats to Ko Tao, an option which saves heading down to Surat Thani. The ordinary boat leaves daily at midnight from the Ko Tao pier, 10 km southeast of town, while a speedboat departs daily at 0930 from the Tha Yang pier. All of the guesthouses in Chumphon can help with transportation to the proper pier.

Accommodations
Infinity Travel Service: One of the many guesthouses to open in recent years, chiefly to serve the travelers passing through on their way to Ko Tao. One block north of the bus terminal. 68/2 Tha Taphao Rd., tel. (077) 501937, 70-140B.

Sooksamer Guesthouse: Another budget option in the northeast corner of town. 118/4 Suksamoe Rd., tel. (077) 502430, 120-150B.

Si Taifa Hotel: An old Chinese hotel with decent restaurant, balcony views, and 20 fan-cooled rooms, one block east of the bus terminal. 74 Saladaeng Rd., tel. (077) 511063, 150-200B.

Jansom Chumphon Hotel: The best hotel in town opened in 1991 just down from the large Ocean Shopping Center. Facilities include a restaurant on the lobby floor, a massage parlor, and the Town Disco. 188/65 Saladaeng Rd., tel. (077) 502502, 950-1,400B.

SURAT THANI

Located on the southeastern coast of southern Thailand 644 km from Bangkok, the prosperous port of Surat Thani chiefly serves as a launching point for ferries to Ko Samui, Thailand's third-largest island and one of Southeast Asia's leading tourist destinations.

The Surat Thani TAT office is inconveniently located at 5 Talad Mai Rd. in the east end of town. An excellent resource for exploring Surat Thani Province and the nearby islands is the *Map of Koh Samui, Koh Tao & Koh Phangan* published by Prannock Witthaya Publications.

Wat Suan Mok

Wat Suan Mokkhablarama—the Garden of Liberation—is a monastery near Chaiya dedicated to the study of *dhamma* and *vipassana* meditation. Today, Wat Suan Mok is the most popular temple in Thailand for Westerners to study Buddhism and traditional forms of Thai meditation.

Both novice and experienced practitioners of *vipassana* are invited to join other Westerners during the 10-day meditation retreats held on the first day of each month. Instruction is provided in English and a daily donation of 50B is requested to cover food costs.

Wat Suan Mok is on Highway 41, about 50 km north of Surat Thani and four km south of the junction to Chaiya. Buses from the main bus terminal in Surat Thani take about 50 minutes to reach the temple entrance. Taxis can be hired from the train station at Phun Phin. Buses and *songtaos* also connect central Chaiya with Suan Mok.

Budget Accommodations

Most visitors head directly to Ko Samui, but late arrivals may need to overnight near the train station in Phun Phin or in downtown Surat Thani.

Lipa & Kasem 2 Guesthouses: Adjacent to the bus terminal are several small guesthouses acceptable for an overnight crash. Both have cafes and travel agencies with tickets to Ko Samui, Phuket, and Krabi. 120-240B.

Thai Thani Hotel: Also next to the bus terminal is this sprawling old hotel with amazing wooden furniture on the ground floor and reception facilities on the third floor. 442 Talad Mai Rd., tel. (077) 272977, 260-380B.

Bandon Hotel: A very clean hotel entered through a Chinese coffee shop. 168 Na Muang Rd., tel. (077) 272167, 160-280B.

Wang Tai Hotel: The best hotel in Surat is inconveniently located south of town near the tourist office but offers a swimming pool, a cabaret nightclub, and a restaurant overlooking the Tapi River. 1 Talad Mai Rd., tel. (077) 283020, 750-950B.

Accommodations in Phun Phin

The train station for Surat Thani is 14 km west in the town of Phun Phin. Except for the very late trains, all arrivals are met by buses which connect directly with the boats to Ko Samui. Late-night arrivals can take a taxi into Surat Thani or stay at one of the guesthouses opposite the train station. Among the choices with rooms from 150B are Tai Fah, Sri Thani, and Kaew Fah guesthouses.

Transportation

Surat Thani is 644 km south of Bangkok and two hours by boat from Ko Samui.

Train: Trains depart nine times daily 0900-2155 from Hualampong Station in Bangkok. The 1630 and 1920 overnight trains with sleepers are recommended, since they arrive in the early morning and allow plenty of time to catch a boat to Ko Samui. Reservations are strongly recommended. The State Railways also sells combination tickets to Ko Samui which include all necessary train, bus, and boat connections.

Trains for Surat Thani terminate 14 km west in Phun Phin. Buses wait for passengers and then connect directly with Ko Samui. Advance reservations for trains departing from Phun Phin can be made at travel agencies on Ko Samui and in Surat Thani at Panipat Tours near the bus terminal.

Bus: Air-conditioned and ordinary buses depart from the Southern Bus Terminal in Thonburi daily 0700-0830 and 1900-2100, arriving in Surat Thani 11 hours later. Private bus companies in Bangkok offer VIP coaches with fewer seats and extra leg room. Most sell all-inclusive packages which include boat transportation to Ko Samui.

Boats to Ko Samui: Boat tickets to Ko Samui can be purchased at **Samui Tours** on Talad Mai Rd. and slightly pricier **Songserm** agents near the waterfront on Na Muang Road. Boats depart daily 0730-1600 from either Don Sak Pier, 50 km east of Surat, or Khanom, 60 km east. A slow overnight boat departs at midnight from the pier in Surat Thani.

Tickets to Ko Phangan are sold at the office near the pier. The head office of Songserm Travel at 295 Talad Mai Rd. also sells tickets to Ko Samui and Ko Phangan.

KO SAMUI

Thailand's third largest island, 247 square km, lies in the warm seas of the gulf some 560 km south of Bangkok. With its long beaches of dazzling white sand, aquamarine waters, and sleepy lagoons fringed with palm trees, this tropical retreat has justifiably become one of Southeast Asia's premier beach resorts.

The island opened up several decades ago and is now a major tourist destination with some 500,000 visitors a year and over 240 hotels and bungalows currently lining the beaches.

For better or for worse, Samui is now caught somewhere in the middle between being a backpacker's paradise and an upscale resort with all the glitz, glamour, and problems that plague Pattaya and Phuket. The island's remote location once held overbuilding and commercialization to a tolerable level, but this happy state of affairs ended with the opening of an airport in 1989.

Samui is best between January and September, when the monsoons begin. Torrential rains often lash the island from October until late December; try Phuket. Accommodations are fully booked during July, August, and Christmas holidays.

Attractions

Samui's claims to fame are sandy beaches, clear waters, and a thriving coconut industry, which provides the main occupation of most of Samui's 35,000 residents. At times it seems the entire island is yanking down coconuts with long swaying sticks or burning huge piles of coconut shells! Watch for trained *ling gang* monkeys which deftly climb the palm trees, spin the coconut until it falls to the ground, and then return for their reward. Nearly every part of the coconut is used: flesh for eating, milk for cooking, and fiber for thatching and bed stuffing.

Around The Island: Samui is about 70 km in circumference and can be easily toured in a single day. The following sights are described in counterclockwise order starting from Chaweng Beach. Samui's splendid scenery is best seen by rented car or motorcycle—but first, a word of caution: Motorcycle touring is deceptively dangerous. Far too many Westerners are killing or badly crippling themselves on the two-lane highway that circles the island. Please drive slowly, stay sober, and wear long pants, shoes, and a shirt to prevent sunburn and protect against minor scrapes.

North Coast: Begin your tour with a motorcycle ride along the coastal road to Chong Mon

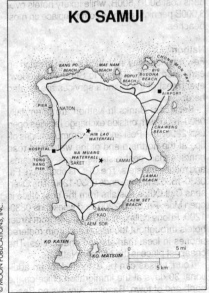

KO SAMUI

BANG PO BEACH
MAE NAM BEACH
BOPUT BEACH
BIG BUDDHA BEACH
CHONG MON BAY
AIRPORT
PIER
NATON
CHAWENG BEACH
HIN LAO WATERFALL
HOSPITAL
NA MUANG WATERFALL
SAKET
TONG YANG PIER
LAMAI
LAMAI BEACH
LAEM SET BEACH
BANG KAO
LAEM SOR
KO KATEN
KO MATSUM
0   5 mi
0   5 km

© MOON PUBLICATIONS, INC.

THAILAND

Bay—a highly recommended route through fabulous scenery. Samui's famous 12-meter Big Buddha statue, surrounded by meditation huts elevated on stilts, is a few kilometers west. The Boput Beach intersection is marked with a bewildering collection of identical Buddhas neatly arranged before a small temple.

Naton: Ko Samui's main commercial center and primary arrival/departure point is an unappealing hodgepodge of overpriced hotels, restaurants, travel agencies, souvenir shops, banks, and other necessary services such as immigration and police.

West Coast: Hin Lad Waterfalls and bathing pools, two km south of Naton, can be reached with a half-hour hike up a narrow pathway through thick jungle. Other west coast bays such as Ta Ling Ngam and Leaen Hin Khom have little of interest aside from their peace and solitude.

South Coast: Na Muang Waterfall and bathing pools (nothing special) lie at the end of a narrow road through durian plantations. Laem Sor Pagoda forms a picturesque setting against the blue waters.

East Coast: Chaweng and Lamai—Ko Samui's two largest and most popular beaches—are located on the east coast. A large and humorously mislabeled sign—"Wonderfull Rock"—shows the way to phallic-shaped formations. Lamai town preserves a small cultural hall filled with old lanterns, gramophones, and agricultural implements used in the coconut industry. Locals sponsor lively buffalo fights during major festivals several times yearly.

Ang Thong Marine National Park: This archipelago of 40 islands west of Ko Samui can only be visited by organized tour. Bring equipment for the outstanding diving, and allow time to climb Uttihayan Hill and swim in the blue lagoon. Accommodations at park headquarters include tents and bungalows.

Accommodations

Ko Samui has a half-dozen beaches in various stages of development and with distinct personalities. Chaweng Beach and Lamai Beach on the east coast are the most popular for good reasons: best sand, longest uninterrupted terrain, and ideal climate. North-coast beaches such as Bophut and Menam are quieter and less expensive, but the sand isn't as white or as plentiful. Robinson Crusoe types might check the isolated bungalows on the west and south coasts.

Each beach appeals to different types of travelers, depending on their finances and desired ambience. One possible plan of action is to spend your first few days on Chaweng or Lamai, then move to a more isolated beach if you crave solitude and want to escape the beer gardens, discos, and pick-up bars.

Ko Samui beaches offer all ranges of accommodations, from cheap shacks under 100B to luxurious hotels with landscaped gardens and swimming pools. Basic wooden huts with electricity, mosquito nets, and common bath charge 100-150B. Most of these original hippie huts have been torn down and replaced with better bungalows with tiled rooms, verandahs, private baths, and comfortable mattresses. These cost 400-800B during the slow season, and generally double in the high summer months and Christmas holidays. Many of these middle-priced bungalows represent extraordinary value when you consider the comfort level and fabulous beach just a few steps away. Air-conditioned bungalows with fancy restaurants and manicured gardens cost 800-1,500B, while luxury hotels over 3,000B per night are now commonplace on most beaches.

Nathon

Few travelers stay in Nathon except to catch an early morning boat back to Surat Thani. However, most of the island's services are located here.

Services: Banks in Nathon are open daily 0800-1600, with outside exchange facilities open until 2200. The Post and Telecommunications office at the northern end of the waterfront road handles mail, post restante, faxes, telegrams, and money transfers. The GPO is open Mon.-Fri. 0830-1630 and weekends 0830-1200. The Overseas Call Office upstairs from the post office is open Mon.-Fri. 0700-2200, and weekends 0830-1200. Phone calls can also be made from larger hotels throughout the island and from metered phones in local markets and pharmacies. The cheapest place is the office in Nathon.

Tourist visas can be extended for an additional 30 days at the immigration office on the north end of town. Bangkok Airways on Beach

Rd. distributes a timetable for flights to Bangkok (six times daily) and Phuket (once daily at 1230).

Travel Agents: Songserm Travel Center on the beachfront road is the largest outlet in town for boats to Surat Thani and Ko Phangan. World Travel Service is another major tour operator that can book transportation, confirm airline tickets, and book rooms at Samui hotels if you arrive without reservations. Phantip Travel sells car-ferry tickets to Surat Thani.

Seaview Guesthouse: An inexpensive guesthouses on the main road. Thawi Ratchaphakdi Rd., tel. (077) 420052, 150-250B.

Chao Koh Bungalows: North of town past the post office is a quiet operation with 20 comfortable if somewhat expensive bungalows. North Nathon, tel. (077) 421214, 300-800B.

Seaside Palace Hotel: The best place in town is overpriced but conveniently located near the pier and restaurants. 152 Beach Rd., tel. (077) 421079, 300-600B.

Chaweng Beach

The six-km curving beach at Chaweng is divided into three sections: Chaweng Noi (Little Cha-

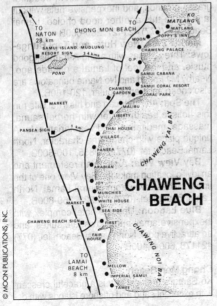

weng, to the south), Chaweng Yai (Big Chaweng, in the center), and North Chaweng Yai (Big Chaweng, to the north). The minitruck from Nathon takes the southern turnoff to the beach near First Bungalows and continues north up the beachside road until it terminates at Samui Cabana. Tell the driver which hotel to stop at or expect to be dropped at the northern end. Charlies is a centrally located guesthouse with over 100 low-priced rooms; a good place to start your bungalow search.

First Bungalows: Popular with budget travelers for over two decades but now fairly expensive. 600-800B.

Fair House: A very popular midlevel spot on squeaky-clean sand. Like most other bungalows at Chaweng, Fair House has older huts in the bargain category and more expensive chalets added in the last few years. 4/3 Chaweng Beach, tel. (077) 421373, 450-1,200B.

White House and the Village: The White House and two nearby properties—the Village and Princess Village (see below)—are the best mid-priced places on Chaweng Beach. The White House and the Village are identically priced; the Village is a newer and better choice. Chaweng Beach, tel. (077) 421382, 1,200-1,800B.

Munchies Resort: A longtime favorite whose name harks back to the days of mushroom omelettes and magic brownies, which are no longer available in their cozy restaurant. 17 Chaweng Beach, tel. (077) 421374, 300-1,500B.

Samui Pansea Resort: A stunning set of bungalows connected with wooden walkways and surrounded by tropical foliage. Tons of charm; a much better choice than the expensive hotels to the north. 38/2 Moo 3 Chaweng Beach, tel. (077) 421384, 2,200-3,800B.

Princess Village: A rare chance to sleep in traditional teak houses from Ayuthaya, restored and elevated over lily ponds. This unique creation of Thai architect Patcharee Smith has great character. Chaweng Beach, tel. (077) 422216, 2,400-3,600B.

Charlies Bungalows: The largest travelers' center on Ko Samui now has three extremely popular branches with over 100 low-priced bungalows. Still owned and operated by the famous Teera, also known as Mama. Chaweng Beach, no phone, 100-350B.

© MOON PUBLICATIONS, INC.

coconut collectors

JR Bungalows: Beautiful shady courtyard, palms, and ferns make this an excellent low-priced choice. 90/1 Chaweng Beach, tel. (077) 421401, fax (077) 421402, 250-550B.

Lucky Mother: Very popular and well-priced bungalows facing a beautiful sandy courtyard and swaying palms. 300-600B.

The Island: Quality rooms at reasonable prices. Chaweng Beach, tel. (077) 421288, 400-900B.

JR Palace: Wild architecture and creative interior decorations distinguish this well-priced set of bungalows. 450-800B.

K John Bungalows: Unusual octagonal bungalows, pet monkey, and friendly management. 200-450B.

Marine Bungalows: Another inexpensive place with decent bungalows. As at most other Chaweng spots, videos are shown nightly in their breezy restaurant. 250-500B.

Lamai Beach

Ko Samui's second-most-popular beach has been developed in a rather haphazard manner with little thought to traffic patterns or hotel aesthetics. The beach is long and beautiful, and a visit can be made to the fishing village at the north end, but bungalows in the central region are packed closely together and the nightlife is turning toward noisy discos and bar girls—a bad sign.

Dozens of bungalows crowd the center, but those isolated on the hills to the east are quieter and more relaxing. Unlike Chaweng Beach, Lamai still has a good supply of inexpensive bungalows in the 100-200B range. Budget travelers should check the western end of the beach (Noi, White Sand, Samui Pearl) and just east of the central beach (Marine Park, My Friend, New Huts, Tapi).

Rocky Chalet: Just beyond Lamai is a popular and very clean place run by two Germans, Linn and Erwin Werrena, on a private beach with scuba-diving facilities. 438 Lamai Beach, 500-900B.

Noi Bungalows: Many of the cheaper places are at the south end of Lamai on narrow but very private beaches. Noi is owned by a Thai-Swiss couple who cater to singles and families. 120-400B.

White Sand Bungalows: Backpackers' favorite with cheap huts. 60-150B.

Casanova Resort: Huge rooms elevated on a hillside, a lovely restaurant, and a stunning swimming pool make this a good choice in the middle price range. Lamai Beach, tel. (077) 421425, 900-1,600B.

Lamai Inn 99: Central location, beautiful grassy grounds, and inexpensive huts without fans make this another good choice. Lamai Beach, tel. (077) 421427, 250-600B.

Marine Park, New Huts, and Tapi Bungalows: Three places with aging A-frames, good music, and the feel of Lamai a decade ago. Nearby My Friend and No Name bungalows are also cheap and very popular. 120-180B.

The Spa: An American and his Thai wife run this holistic health center with herbal sauna, massage, meditation, and vegetarian cafe. A unique place with charm and character. North Lamai Beach, tel. (077) 230855, 100-600B.

Bay View Villa: A stunning restaurant and an idyllic location make the Bay View one of the finest places away from central Lamai. North Lamai Beach, tel. (077) 272222, 250-600B.

Blue Lagoon: Upscale hotel complex with inexpensive small bungalows, a/c suites, and an attractive pool. North Lamai Beach, tel. (077) 421178, 600-2,400B.

Chong Mon Beach

Ko Samui's prettiest bay is a graceful crescent with excellent sand and offshore islands with deserted beaches. Chong Mon was considered well off the beaten track until the 1990 opening of the immense Imperial Chong Mon Resort, which creatively utilized the old fishing boats which once lined the bay. Chong Mon now has regular minitruck service from Nathon and Chaweng Beach.

Sun Sand Resort: A superb arrangement of 33 individual bungalows, a breezy restaurant, and stunning views over Chong Mon Bay have made this resort a popular choice with European group tours. Chong Mon Beach, tel. (077) 421024, 950-1,600B.

P.S. Villa: The spotless bungalows, spacious lawns, and bamboo restaurant make this the best bargain on the beach. Chong Mon Beach, tel. (077) 286956, 250-600B.

Choeng Mon Bungalows: Three classes of bungalows which increase in price the closer to the beach. Chong Mon Beach, no phone, 200-700B.

Imperial Tongsai Bay: A super-exclusive Mediterranean-style hotel with 24 hotel rooms and 48 individual a/c cottages overlooking a private beach just north of Chong Mon Bay. One of the most spectacular resorts in the world. Ban Plailaem, Bophut, tel. (077) 421451, 4,800-8,000B.

Big Buddha Beach

Ao Bang Rak—more commonly called Big Buddha after the nearby image—offers almost a dozen inexpensive to moderate bungalows on an arching beach which is narrow and brownish but generally deserted. Bungalows are clean and comfortable, though beach conditions and noise from highway traffic here make Bophut and Mae Nam beaches more idyllic locations.

Boats to Ko Phangan depart near the Buddha daily at 1530 and return from Had Rin on Ko Phangan at 0930.

Farn Bay Resort: An expensive hotel with Thai dance shows on weekends. But, as their brochure claims, "No more hustle-bustles, no more pollution, no more rat-race." Big Buddha Beach, tel. (077) 273920, 1,000-1,600B.

Nara Lodge: An American-operated hotel with renovated rooms, pool, and ambience popular with families. P.O. Box 9, tel. (077) 421364, 950-1,500B.

Big Buddha Bungalows: Large new wooden bungalows and friendly management make

this one of the best bargains on the beach. Big Buddha Beach, no phone, 300-600B.

Bophut Beach

Travelers who want to escape the congestion of Chaweng or Lamai will find Bophut an acceptable alternative. The narrow and coarse beach isn't as impressive as Chaweng or Lamai, but many visitors consider the friendly people and sense of isolation adequate compensation. Bophut also has wonderful sunsets.

Cafes here once served the most potent magic-mushroom soups on the island, but the banning of psychedelics in 1989 forced the trade over to Ko Phangan and Ko Tao.

Bophut is a convenient departure point for Ko Phangan. The *Hadrin Queen* departs daily at 0900 and 1300 for Had Rin Beach on the southeast corner of the island.

Smile House: At the edge of town is a very clean place with small fan-cooled bungalows and pricier a/c chalets, plus a wonderful pool surrounded by palms. Bophut Beach, tel. (077) 421361, 350-1,250B.

Ziggy Stardust: Beautiful Lanna-style bungalows, a lovely garden, and a popular restaurant make Ziggy's a great choice for midlevel travelers. Bophut Beach, no phone, 450-1,250B.

Peace Bungalows: A longtime favorite located away from town on a quieter stretch of sand. Low-end bungalows are dismal, but those in the 250-400B range are clean and comfortable. Bophut Beach, tel. (077) 421357, 200-800B.

World Bungalows: One of the most popular and reasonably priced places at Bophut features a small swimming pool, lush gardens, and a luxurious restaurant facing the deserted beach. Bophut Beach, tel. (077) 421355, 200-1,000B.

Mae Nam Beach

Mae Nam is an isolated and relatively undeveloped beach midway between Nathon and Chaweng Beach. Over a dozen inexpensive to midlevel bungalows on this beach are signposted on the main highway. Beaches are narrow, but the solitude and remote location are quite appealing.

Laem Sai and Mae Nam Villa: Both of these inexpensive and very popular guesthouses are at the end of the cape which forms the extreme southern end of Ao Mae Nam (Mae Nam Bay). Mae Nam Beach, no phones, 120-350B.

Rainbow: Good-value bungalows constructed with brick and wood. Bophut Beach, 100-300B.

Moon Huts: Attractive bamboo bungalows, an elevated restaurant with views, and a brilliant stretch of sand make well-named Moon a good choice. 67/2 Mae Nam Beach, no phone, 200-450B.

Lolita Bungalows: Lolita boasts an excellent beach with stunning palms, easy access to the town of Ban Mae Nam, and decent bungalows in all possible price ranges. Mae Nam Beach, no phone, 150-700B.

Mae Nam Resort: Beautiful bungalows, comfortable restaurant, and grassy landscapes make this the best mid-priced resort at Mae Nam Beach. Mae Nam Beach, tel. (077) 272222, 250-800B.

Shangrila: Inexpensive bungalows, new restaurant, and safe swimming make Shangrila popular with families. Mae Nam Beach, no phone, 120-300B.

Coco Palms Village: Escape the crowds at the west end of the beach. Coco Palms is a friendly place with great meals prepared by a Western chef. Good value, plus dazzling aquamarine waters. Mae Nam Beach, no phone, 400-900B.

Getting There

Ko Samui is 644 km south of Bangkok and 84 km northeast of Surat Thani.

Travel agents in Bangkok sell package tickets which include all necessary transfers and boat connections. Although tours are the easiest way to reach Ko Samui, independent travelers will have few problems reaching the island on their own. Ko Samui is a major tourist destination, and transportation touts are always there to greet you, take your hand, guide you to the appropriate connection, show you to your seat, collect your money, and deliver you to Samui. No need to worry about confusing place-names or variable schedules—someone is *always* there to point the way. Don't you just love Thailand?

Air: Bangkok Airways flies from Bangkok to Ko Samui six times daily and once daily from Phuket.

Train: The State Railway has rapid trains with sleepers from Bangkok to Surat Thani (Phun Phin Station) at 1730, 1830, and 1920. All arrive early enough to catch the 0730 boat to Ko Samui. Overnight trains with sleepers are com-

fortable and very popular; advance reservations are *absolutely* necessary. The State Railways also sells package tickets direct to Samui.

Bus: Four ordinary and a/c buses depart from the Southern Bus Terminal in Thonburi nightly between 1900 and 2030. Buses arrive the next morning in Surat Thani, from where minibuses continue to the ferries to Ko Samui.

Ferry: Several different types of boats go from Surat Thani to Ko Samui. Express boats leave from Tha Thong pier, six km east of Surat Thani, and arrive at Nathon three hours later. Minitrucks continue to the beaches. Car and passenger ferries depart from Don Sak pier, one hour east of Surat, and terminate three hours later at Thong Yang jetty, about four km south of Nathon. Finally, a slow boat leaves from the harbor in Surat Thani nightly at midnight.

Samui Tours and Songserm Travel in Surat Thani are the principal operators, with different departures during the day. Buses depart from the Samui Tours office on Talad Mai Road in Surat Thani daily at 0650, 0830, 1030, 1230, and 1530. Buses depart daily at 0730, 1130, and 1400 from the Songserm head office and from a stop near the harbor.

Leaving Ko Samui

Express ferries leave Nathon daily at 0730, 1200, 1330, and 1530. Exact departure times are listed at travel agencies near the pier. Night ferries leave around 2300 and arrive in Surat the following morning. Travel agents on Ko Samui sell direct tickets to Bangkok, Phuket, Krabi, Hat Yai, Penang, and even Singapore. Air-conditioned buses from Nathon are about twice as expensive as public non-a/c buses from the Surat terminal. Night departures are also offered.

Ordinary buses from the Surat Thani bus terminal to Bangkok take about 10 hours and depart five times daily from 0700 to 1230, and every half hour from 1700 to 2100. Buses for Phuket take seven hours and depart eight times daily from 0530 to 1300. Buses to Hat Yai take five hours and leave at 0830 and 1130.

Train service from Surat Thani can be tricky since advance booking is necessary to reserve a seat. Tickets can be purchased from small travel agents at the beaches and from larger agencies such as Songserm Travel in Nathon.

KO PHANGAN

Phangan Island, 20 km north of Ko Samui, is a wild and primitive place with isolated beaches, tropical jungles, and arching coves accessible only by long hikes or chartered boats. For those searching for the Samui of a decade ago, Ko Phangan seems a return to the mid-1970s, with its colonies of gypsyish travelers bedecked with amulets and beads, more concerned with blazing sunsets and local herb than raucous nightclubs and air-conditioned resorts.

During the day there's little to do but relax on the beach and perhaps rent a motorcycle to visit some of the local waterfalls. Nightlife remains limited to a few video shows. Ten-day meditation retreats are directed by Buddhist monks at Wat Khao Tam.

The best sand is found on the southern and eastern sides of Ko Phangan. Beaches to the north and west are narrow and spotted with mangrove swamps, but they offer coral beds and the best sunsets on the island.

Thong Sala

Thong Sala is the main port and commercial center of Ko Phangan. No one stays in Thong Sala, but all necessary services are near the pier and the main street along the beach, including a bank which changes money at fair rates and several travel agencies which sell tickets to Surat Thani, Ko Samui, and Ko Tao. A post office and an overseas phone office are just south of the pier on the first paved street. Several shops rent motorcycles at 150-250B per day.

Transportation

Thong Sala and other beaches on Ko Phangan can be reached by boat from Surat Thani, Nathon, Bophut, and Big Buddha Beach.

From Surat Thani: Phangan Ferry Company boats depart from Surat Thani daily at 0720 and arrive at Thong Sala at 1100. Tickets are sold at their office at 10 Chon Kasem Rd. just across from the pier. Songserm Travel also serves Ko Phangan via Ko Samui. A night ferry departs at 2300 and arrives at dawn at Thong Sala. Boats return twice daily to Ko Samui from Thong Sala and Had Rin Beach.

From Nathon: Songserm Travel boats depart daily at 1000 and 1530 from Nathon and arrive in Thong Sala about one hour later. Tickets can be purchased at the Songserm Travel office near the pier.

From Bophut Beach: The *Hadrin Queen* departs daily at 0930 and 1530 from the small pier in the town of Bophut and takes about 45 minutes to Had Rin Beach. This is the most convenient option for travelers staying at Chaweng and beaches on the north coast of Samui.

From Big Buddha Beach: A fishing boat to Had Rin Beach departs from the east end of Big Buddha Beach daily at 1530.

South Coast Beaches

Thong Sala Beach: Also called Ao Bang Charu, Thong Sala Beach has mediocre sand but is a convenient place for early boats to Ko Tao or back to Ko Samui. Like all of Ko Phangan's beaches, Thong Sala has a continuous string of wooden bungalows in the 80-250B price range. Charm Beach Resort is a typical example, with primitive shacks from 80B and deluxe chalets with toilet, shower, and fan from 300B. Chokana Resort is similar.

Ban Tai Beach: The beach starts to improve about two km east of Thong Sala, near the small villages of Ban Tai and Ban Khai. Just east of town are several inexpensive bungalows such as Birdsville, SP Resort, Pink's, Triangle Lodge, Liberty, and Mac Bay Resort with rooms for 100-250B.

Ban Khai Beach: Ban Khai is the last town before the road ends at the rocky headlands. Beaches here are narrow but very quiet, clean, and dotted with impressive granite boulders. Sabai, Baan Kai Bay Huts, Phangan Lodge, Lee Garden, Free Love, Copa, Pan Beach, Rainbow, Golden Beach, and Boom's all have bungalows for 80-250B. Better chalets for 250-450B are available at Lee Garden, Green Peace, Golden Beach, Sun Sea Resort, and Thong Yang.

Had Rin Beach West: Had Rin West and East were the first beaches to open up on Ko Phangan some 10 years ago. Both have excellent sand and aquamarine waters but suffer from overdevelopment and piles of trash which wash up on the shore. Bungalows at the end of the rocky coastline are now being torn down for more expensive places.

THAILAND

Star, Bird, Sun Beach, Sandy, Seaside, Rainbow, Coral, Palm Beach, Neptune's, Black and White, and Friendly House have huts for 80-250B.

East Coast Beaches

Had Rin Beach East: The eastern side of the craggy peninsula features white powder sand, arched in a curving cove flanked by rocky cliffs. Scuba diving is fairly good, and the surf gets high during the stormy months from October to February. Boats from Mae Nam and Big Buddha beaches on Ko Samui head directly to Had Rin East. The beach can also be reached with longtails from Thong Sala, Ban Tai, and Ban Khai.

Over a dozen bungalows occupy virtually every square centimeter of the original and most popular beach on Ko Phangan. Bungalows from south to north include Tai Chi Chuan, Paradise, Sea Garden, Haad Rin, Tommy's, Palita, Seaview, Mountain Sea, and Serenity Hill.

Yang Beach: Six km north of Had Rin and about midway up the east coast is a lovely little cove with coconut palms and sparkling sand. Sea Hill Hat Yang Bay Resort has several bungalows for 80-150B.

Sadet Beach: Had Sadet and nearby Had Thong Reng are now receiving some visitors who arrive by longtail from Had Rin or public minitruck from Thong Sala. The road from Thong Sala ends a few kilometers beyond Ban Thong Nang, making the beach a long hike or a treacherous motorcycle ride. Bungalows include Pra Thip, Ka Wao, and several places aptly called No Name Bungalows.

Ta Pan Beach: Thong Ta Pan Bay is formed by two small bays, Ta Pan Noi to the north and Ta Pan Yai on the south. Ban Thong Ta Pan can be reached by truck from Thong Sala. Bungalows near the village on Ta Pan Yai Beach include Pen's, Pingjun Resort, and Chanchit Dreamland. Ta Pan Noi Beach has Thong Ta Pan Resort at the northern end and Panviman Resort in the south.

North Coast Beaches

Bottle Beach (Khuat Beach): The far northeastern corner of Ko Phangan offers an immaculate and isolated beach with squeaky white sands and excellent swimming in the protected cove. Bottle Beach—the perfect place to *really*

escape civilization—can be reached by longtail boats from Chalok Lam or Had Rin beaches. Sea Love, Bottle Beach, and O.D. bungalows at the northern end have wooden shacks for 80-150B.

Chaloklum Bay: The north-shore fishing village of Chaloklum (Chalok Lam) faces a curving bay ringed with emerald-green mountains. Beaches near the town are brownish but improve sharply to the east, especially at Khom Beach. Trucks take about 90 minutes from Thong Sala. Thai Life, Fanta, and Chalok Lam Resort near the town have acceptable bungalows for 80-150B. Wattana Resort at the west end of the bay has over a dozen huts in various price ranges.

West Coast Beaches

Mae Hat Beach: Similar to the situation on Ko Samui, beaches on the west coast tend to be brown and coarse but compensate with coral beds and blazing sunsets. Mae Hat Bungalows and Mae Hat Villa are on the beach path to the north. Both have huts for 50-100B. Better operations on the southern side include Mae Hat Bay Resort and Island View Cabanas. Both have older huts for 80-150B and newer chalets with private bath and fan for 250-450B.

Yao Beach: Bungalows on the small cove include Sandy Bay, Ibiza, Had Yao, Blue Coral Beach, Phong Sak, and Dream Hill Bungalows.

Chao Phao Beach: The beach at Chao Phao is somewhat brownish and dotted with mangrove trees, but coral beds and spectacular sunsets make this a popular alternative to Had Rin Beach. Bungalows for 80-150B include Bovy Resort in the south, Seetanu, and Sea Flower.

Si Thanu Beach: The circular cove of Si Thanu is near the small fishing town of Si Thanu. Beachside bungalows include Loy Fah at the southern end of the cape, Ladda Guesthouse near the town, and Sea View and Laemson on the northern stretches.

Wok Tum Bay: Bungalows at the southern end include the O.K., Kiat, Darin, and Tuk.

Pla Laem Beach: The four-km road north of Thong Sala passes some decent beaches almost continuously lined with inexpensive bungalows and better spots with private bath and fans. A track behind the main road leads up to Mountain View Resort and Bungtham Bungalows. Beachside bungalows include Beach, Cookies, Sea Scene, and Darin.

THAILAND

Nai Wong Beach: The rocky beach just north of Thong Sala is a convenient location for travelers taking early morning boats to Ko Samui and Ko Tao. Phangan Bungalows has basic huts and more luxurious chalets with private baths. Charn and Siriphun are low-end favorites, while Tranquil Resort at the north end has a popular restaurant and bungalows in all price ranges. All bungalows are within walking distance of the Thong Sala pier.

KO TAO

Tiny Ko Tao is 38 km north of Ko Phangan and 58 km from Ko Samui. Named after its peculiar shape, which resembles a kidney bean or an abstract turtle shell, Ko Tao measures just seven km long and three km wide, for a total area of 21 square km. The population of 750 is occupied with coconuts, fishing, and bungalow operations, which attract a steady trickle of world travelers. The island is chiefly known for its outstanding coral beds off nearby Ko Hang Tao and Ko Nang Yuan and a half-dozen beaches with fairly good sand and crystal-clear waters.

All of the beaches now offer bungalows that charge 40-80B for rooms with common baths and more expensive operations with private bath and fans.

Ban Mae Hat

Ban Mae Hat is the principal town and arrival point for all boats from Surat Thani, Ko Samui, Ko Phangan, and Chumphon. The town has several cafes, dive shops that organize trips to Nang Yuan Island, and travel agents who sell boat tickets to Chumphon and points south. Exchanging money on Ko Tao can be costly, so bring plenty of small bills.

Accommodations on the northern beach include Nuan Nang, Dam, and Khao Bungalows. All have small huts for 80-120B and larger rooms for 120-200B.

West Coast Beaches

Sai Ree Beach: North of Ban Mae Hat is Laem Choporo Cape, followed by a long stretch of sand called Sai Ree Beach and the fishing village of Ban Hat Sai Ree. Accommodations include Sai Ree and O Chai Cottages near Ban Hat Sai

Ree. The trail continues north to Sun Lodge, Mahana Bay, and C.F. Bungalows just opposite Ko Nang Yuan.

Sai Nuan and Sai Nual Beaches: Hikers can follow the seaside trail south to a pair of small coves with several inexpensive bungalows: Neptune, Somat, and Cha bungalows on Sai Nuan, quickly followed by Sai Thong, Sabai, and Char Huts over the cape.

South Coast Beaches

Chalok Ban Kao Bay: Bungalows west of town include Laem Klong, Tarporn, Laem Tap, and Sunset on Chun Chua Beach. South of town are K. See, Koh Tao Cottages with superior bungalows at higher prices, Tato Lagoon, and Freedom Bungalows.

Thianok and Sai Daeng Beaches: Thianok (Thien Ok) has Niyom Huts and Rocky Resort, while Sai Daeng has Kiat and Bai Sai Daeng bungalows. All cost 60-150B.

East Coast Beaches

All of the following beaches can only be reached on foot or on longtails leaving from Ban Mae Hat and Chalok Ban Kao. Every possible cove now has simple bungalows which charge 50-80B, plus big discounts for travelers staying several weeks.

Luk Beach: Ao Luk Resort sits on a small beach reached by trail from Chalok Ban Kao.

Tanot Beach: Tanot Bay and Diamond bungalows have huts for 60-100B on the 100-meter beach.

Mao Beach: Three km east of Ban Mae Hat are several small coves for the determined escapist. Laem Thian, about 900 meters south of Mao, has one set of bungalows.

Hin Wong Beach: Four km northeast of Ban Hat Sai is a curving bay with a very narrow beach. Sahat Huts cost from 60B.

Ma Muang Beach: The northern tip of Ko Tao has Mango Bay Resort with wooden bungalows from 60B.

Ko Nang Yuan

Some of the finest diving in the region is found on three interconnected islands off the northwest corner of Ko Tao. Dive companies on Ko Samui arrange three-day dive packages for about 5,000B, including all equipment, transportation, and lodging. Rooms at Nang Yuan Bungalows cost 80-100B.

Transportation

Ko Tao is midway between Ko Samui and the mainland town of Chumphon. As of this writing there are no direct boat services from Surat Thani.

From Ko Samui: Subject to seasonal weather patterns, Songserm has an express boat to Ko Tao daily at 0900 from Nathon pier. Slower boats are available from Ko Tao Tours.

From Ko Phangan: Songserm Travel and Ko Tao Tours have boats to Ko Tao from Thong Sala. Services are subject to cancellation during the rainy season from October to January.

From Chumphon: Back-door services are available from Chumphon, an option which saves traveling down to Surat Thani or Ko Samui. Schedules change frequently and should be checked with Chumphon Travel Service at 66 Thatapao Rd. just north of the bus station and Thatapao Hotel. Fishing boats currently depart from Chumphon harbor at midnight on Monday, Tuesday, Thursday, and Friday.

PHUKET

The island of Phuket—Southeast Asia's most popular beach resort—is located in the sparkling green Andaman Sea, 885 km south of Bangkok. Like all other successful beaches in Asia, Phuket was discovered by backpackers searching for an escapist holiday of simple huts, local food, and cheap grass. Facilities were limited or nonexistent; early arrivals slept on the sand or lived with locals. The scene was so idyllic that William Duncan wrote in his 1976 guide that "for a few years more, Phuket may be allowed to sleep undisturbed, for this island province is not yet ready to cater to the needs of foreign tourists. There are no first-class hotels or restaurants . . ." But word of the tropical paradise spread among world travelers, and soon a steady trickle of curious visitors tiptoed down to Phuket, hoping to beat the rush and inevitable commercialization.

In the remarkably short span of just one decade, the island has transformed itself from hippie paradise to yuppie nirvana. Present-day Phuket will disappoint travelers who dislike commercial development and find perverse pleasure in running down resorts once they become popular. Yet Phuket remains an outstanding holiday destination. First, few islands in the world can boast of so many excellent beaches in so small an area. Comparisons between Phuket and Ko Samui are almost inevitable, but I'd say that Phuket's half-dozen beaches are just as beautiful as, and certainly more plentiful than, the handful on Ko Samui. Secondly, Phuket's enormous size has allowed the beaches to absorb a great deal of development without being completely overwhelmed. Areas such as Patong have suffered badly from cheap hotels and noisy bars, but other regions have generally been spared the tourist-ghetto fate of Pattaya and Puerto Galera. Besides all this, Phuket offers outstanding scuba diving, a national park, several waterfalls, tin mines, pearl farms, Buddhist temples, villages of sea gypsies, deserted beaches where turtles come to lay their eggs, and bizarre limestone formations used in the filming of *The Man with the Golden Gun.*

Attractions

Visitors to Phuket generally spend the first few days relaxing on the beach and working on their tans, but to discover the beauty of the island you should rent a motorcycle or car and visit the remoter regions. The following attractions are described in clockwise fashion starting from Patong Beach.

Ban Thalang: About 50 meters south of the central intersection stands 200-year-old Wat Pra Na Sang and its modern counterpart on the left. Exterior doors of the modern *bot* feature well-carved guardians on the right, while the older structure features *bai sema* that resemble giant pawns from a monstrous chess set.

Wat Pra Thong: One of the most bizarre Buddha images in Thailand lies half-buried in the middle of an otherwise ordinary temple about one km north of Thalang.

Khao Prapa Tao National Park: Four km east of Thalang is one of the most spectacular scenes on Phuket: an awesome park which provides a rare opportunity to experience the splendor of an endangered rainforest. This might be your *only* chance to see a rainforest; don't miss it.

Pearl Farm: Ao Po is the departure point for visits to Naga Island Pearl Farm on Naka Noi Island. Phuket travel agents can arrange tours to

PHUKET ISLAND

MAI KHAO BEACH

TO BANGKOK

AIRPORT

402

4027

BAN PO

PO BAY

NAI YANG BEACH

KO NAKA YAI

NAITON BEACH

4031

TON SAI WATERFALL

WAT PRA THONG

KHAO PRAPA TAO NATIONAL PARK

NAGA NOI PEARL FARM

KO NAKA NOI

BAN THALANG

BAN DON

BANG TAO BAY

4030

4025

THALANG NATIONAL MUSEUM

MONUMENT

SURIN BEACH

KAMALA BEACH

ISLAMIC SCHOOL

SAPUM BAY

MAPRAO ISLAND

KATHU WATERFALL

PATONG BEACH

4029

PHUKET TOWN

KO SIRAY

FISHING VILLAGE

4022

4021

KARON BEACH

WAT CHALONG

MAKHAM BAY

4023

PHUKET PORT

KATA YAI BEACH

4028

TO KO PHI PHI

KATA NOI BEACH

CHALONG BAY

PEARL FARMS

AQUARIUM

LONE ISLAND

NAI HARN BEACH

RAWAI BEACH

PROMTEP CAPE

0   2 km

© MOON PUBLICATIONS, INC.

THAILAND

PHUKET TOWN

ISLAND

KHAO RANG

TUNG KA CAFE

KAO RANG RESTAURANT

THAI VILLAGE & ORCHID GARDEN

KOMARA PAT RD.

TO SURIN BEACH, AIRPORT & BANGKOK

WAT LANG SAN

PROVINCIAL COURT

TOWN HALL

CHINESE CEMETERY

POLICE

CHOOMPORN RD.

DAMRONG RD.

WAT KHUN CHEE

BANGKOK AIRWAYS

PHUKET MERLIN HOTEL

THARA HOTEL

MAELUAN RD.

THOONG KHA RD.

SUTHAT RD.

NARISORN RD.

A

A

A

DEEBUK RD.

WAT MONGKOL NIMIT

SAMJAO SAM SAN SHRINE

A ★ A

A ★ ★ A

KRABI RD.

THALANG RD.

BUS TERMINAL

4020 VICHITSONGKHRAM RD.

ON ON HOTEL

SINTAVEE GH

SIAM HOTEL

G.P.O.

TO KO SIRAY

TO PATONG BEACH

RANONG RD.

THAI AIRWAYS

PHANGNGA RD.

TELEPHONE

PU JAO AND JUI TUI TEMPLES

WASANA GH

RASDA RD.

IMPERIAL HOTEL

CENTRAL TOURS

BUSES TO PATONG, KARON & KATA BEACHES

MARKET

THAVORN HOTEL

PEARL HOTEL

MONTRI RD.

THAI INTERNATIONAL

JANARAI RD.

BUSES TO NAI HAM & RAWAI BEACHES

TOURIST OFFICE

METROPOLE HOTEL

BANGKOK RD.

TAKUA PA RD.

OCEAN DEPT. STORE

PHUKET RD.

CROCODILE FARM

PHATIPHAT RD.

POONPHOL RD.

THAVORN GRAND HOTEL

NIGHT MARKET

PHUKET TRAVEL SERVICE

KING RAMA IX PARK

CHINESE TEMPLE

BANGYAI RD.

4021

TO KARON, KATA NAI HARN & RAWAI BEACHES

4023

TO MAKHAM BAY, AQUARIUM, CAPE PANWA, & PHUKET PORT

IMMIGRATION

BOXING STADIUM

★ A = NOTEWORTHY ARCHITECTURE

NOT TO SCALE

© MOON PUBLICATIONS, INC.

THAILAND

the farm that provide insight into the considerable skills of pearl cultivation.

Thalang National Museum: This museum, 100 meters east of the Heroines Monument, is a new attraction with displays on local history, industry, the environment, and a highly prized 9th-century Vishnu image discovered near Takua Pa. Open Tues.-Sat. 0900-1630.

Ko Siray: Ko Siray is an extremely disappointing fishing village consisting of dusty roads, rough tin huts, and kids yelling "ten *baht*, ten *baht*"—an experience best avoided.

Panwa Cape: Phuket's Marine Biology Research Center and Aquarium on the south coast contains displays of tropical sealife and fishing devices. On the grounds of the Cape Panwa Sheraton Resort stands a classic Sino-Portuguese mansion filled with a quality collection of antique furniture and art objects.

Wat Chalong: The largest and most sacred temple of the 29 monasteries on Phuket.

Seashell Museum: An impressive collection of shells is exhibited in the modern, blue-tiled building on Hwy. 4021 just north of Rawai Beach.

Rawai Beach and Tristan Jones: West of the fishing village is the small boat which crossed the Kra Isthmus in 1987 with a crew of disabled sailors, including a blind German and a one-legged Englishman named Tristan Jones.

Promtep Cape: Promtep Cape and the viewpoint at the south end of Kata Noi Beach are the best spots on Phuket for spectacular sunsets.

Phuket Town

The capital of Thailand's only island province has great shopping, dependable communication facilities, and delightful examples of Indo-Portuguese mansions constructed by Chinese barons who found their fortunes in tin and rubber rather than tourism. Though not as impressive as Penang's Malaccan-style terrace houses, they add charm and atmosphere to an otherwise ordinary city. The Provincial Town Hall might look familiar—it served as the French Embassy in the film *The Killing Fields*.

The Phuket Tourist Office has maps and information on upcoming festivals, discounts at newly opened hotels, and schedules for weekend Thai boxing. Open daily 0800-1600.

Thai immigration on Phuket Road south of town can extend visas. Phuket town also has a post office on Montri Road and 24-hour telephone services around the corner.

Accommodations

Few visitors stay in Phuket town unless they arrive late or need to catch an early bus.

On On Hotel: Established in 1929, the historic On On is the best choice for budget travelers and a popular spot at which to hang out and wait for evening buses. 19 Phangnga Rd., tel. (076) 211154, 100-350B.

Wasana Guesthouse: The only other budget spot worth mentioning is just past the market. A clean place with friendly managers. 159 Ranong Rd., tel. (076) 211754, 200-300B.

Thavorn Hotel: A convenient midlevel hotel in the center of town near shops and restaurants. Facilities include a coffee shop, a lounge, and a swimming pool. All rooms are a/c. 74 Rasada Rd., tel. (076) 211333, 350-750B.

Phuket Merlin: The finest hotel in Phuket town is just north of downtown. 158/1 Yaowaraj Rd., tel. (076) 212866, 1,800-2,800B.

The Beaches

Phuket's major beach resorts are all located on the western coast of the island. Each differs from the other in natural setting and degree of development, but all offer superb sand, warm waters, and endless sports activities. Most hotels charge 400-800B for clean, modern rooms, and up to 2,000B in super-luxurious resorts with all possible amenities. Contrary to popular belief, simple bungalows under 150B are still available at many beaches. An easy way to locate a hotel is to tell your minitruck driver which beach you want and what price range you can afford.

Phuket's hotels use a double-pricing system. Rates are highest during the high season (November-May), when Europeans flood the island, but discounted 30-50% during the rainy season (May-October), when tropical storms lash the west coast. Rainy-season refugees should flee east to the drier island of Ko Samui.

Phuket's most popular beaches are, in order, Patong, Karon, and Kata.

Patong Beach

This crowded yet beautiful four-km-long beach is the island's liveliest and most popular, the Pattaya of Phuket. Although it's fashionable to con-

PATONG BEACH

TO KAMALA BAY, SURIN BEACH, & BANG TAO BEACH

TO PHUKET TOWN

PRA BARAMI RD.

TEMPLE ★

THAVEWONG RD.

RACHAUTIT RD.

SAINAMYEN RD.

HOSPITAL

HIDE AWAY BAR

200 YEAR RD.

FOODSTALLS

POST OFFICE

GOLDEN LAND SHOPPING

SONG ROI PI RD.

GERMAN BAKERY

HOSPITAL

SIMON CABARET ★

TO KARON & KATA BEACHES

0   200m

© MOON PUBLICATIONS, INC.

THAILAND

PATONG BEACH

1. Thavorn Bay
2. Nerntong Resort
3. Patong Lodge
4. Diamond Cliff
5. Panorama Beach
6. Best Gh
7. Similan
8. A.A. Villa
9. Sunset Mansion
10. Eden
11. P.S. 2
12. Patong Penthouse
13. Swiss Mansion
14. Shamrock
15. Berliner GH
16. Beau Rivage
17. Patong Seaview
18. Patong Grand Condotel
19. Odin's GH
20. Star
21. Ladda Apts.
22. Patong Bayshore
23. Club Andaman
24. Casuarina
25. Jeep 2
26. William Swiss
27. Phuket Cabana
28. Thara Patong
29. Nipha
30. Vises
31. New Tum
32. Royal Crown
33. Asia Guesthouse
34. Royal Paradise Hotel
35. K.S.R.
36. Patong Bay
37. Patong Beach Bungalow
38. Patong Bay Garden
39. Patong Villa
40. Islet Mansion
41. Safari Beach
42. Sandy House
43. Swiss Garden
44. Jeep 1
45. Valentine & Nordic
46. Neptuna
47. K
48. C & N
49. P.S.
50. Expat
51. Suksan Mansion
52. Super Mansion
53. Jagerstube
54. Summer Breeze
55. Duck Tonight
56. Ban Sukothai
57. Tropica
58. Patong Inn
59. Patong Beach
60. Palace
61. Patong Resort
62. Patong Ko
63. Banthai Beach
64. Club Oasis
65. Happy Home
66. Paradise Hotel
67. Holiday Inn
68. Patong Merlin
69. Holiday Resort
70. Thamdee
71. Seagull Cottages
72. Swiss, Bay View, Patong, & K.V.
73. Coconut Village
74. Holiday
75. Duang Chit
76. Coconut Cottages
77. Coconut Village
78. Coral Beach
79. Patong Hill
80. Le Meridian

demn Patong as overdeveloped, raunchy, polluted, expensive, and the worst example of unplanned madness (all true), the beach is outstanding and daytime activities run the gamut from sailboarding and snorkeling to parasailing and sunbathing. Your impression will largely depend on what you expect from Phuket: Patong is a place for parties and good times, not solitude and contemplation!

Soi San Sabai: Although budget travelers avoid Patong and generally head to Karon-Kata, over a dozen bungalows still survive with rooms for 250-400B. The best hunting ground is on Soi San Sabai, the eastern extension of Bangla Rd. in the central beach area. Soi San Sabai is a good location since it's within walking distance of the beach and Soi Bangla nightclubs but somewhat removed from the general mayhem.

Best bets include Summer Breeze Pension with a/c rooms from 500B, Suksan Mansion with fan rooms from 300B and a/c rooms from 400B, and Duck Tonight and Charlies Tonight at 250-350B for fan-cooled rooms.

Bangla Road: Soi Bangla is the heart of the beast—a nonstop string of honky-tonk bars, wild nightclubs, pick-up joints, raging discos, and lowlife restaurants. Hence, bungalows are noisy, but easy to find after consuming a case of Singha. Swiss Garden, Jeep 1, Valentine, and Nordic Bungalows cost 250-350B fan and double for a/c.

Rachautit Road: Several inexpensive hotels are north of Bangla Road. Expat Hotel is quiet but has somewhat overpriced a/c rooms from 800B facing a small pool. P.S. and C & N bungalows cost 300-600B. Farther north are Jeep 2, Star, Scandinavian-run Odin's Guesthouse, and the spotless Ladda Apartments with rooms from 350-800B.

Lower Thavewong Road: A half-dozen small, inexpensive hotels are tucked away at the south

KARON AND KATA BEACHES

TO PATONG BEACH

KARON BEACH

HOSPITAL

CLUB 44

BAR BEER

KARON - KATA

EASY RIDER BAR

POST OFFICE

TO PHUKET TOWN →

KATA YAI BEACH

KATA NOI BEACH

SWISS

TO NAI HARN BEACH & PROMTHEP CAFE

4028

0   500m

THAILAND

© MOON PUBLICATIONS, INC.

KARON AND KATA BEACHES

1. Karon On Sea
2. Kampong Karon
3. Karon Viewpoint
4. Lume & Yai
5. Phuket Ocean Resort
6. Coco Cabana
7. Dream Huts
8. Phuket Golden Sand
9. Karon Hotel
10. Karon Guesthouses
11. Crystal Beach Hotel
12. Karon Bungalow
13. Much My Friend Guesthouse
14. South Seah Resort
15. Karon Villa
16. Royal Wing
17. Sand Resort
18. Karon Sea View
19. Phuket Arcadia
20. Thavorn Palm
    Beach Hotel
21. Karon Inn
22. Karon Village
23. Green Valley Bungalows

24. Holliday Village
25. Sandy Inn
26. Brazil
27. Jor Guesthouse
28. Phuket Island View
29. Krayoon Bungalow
30. Ruam Thep Inn
31. Karon Beach Hotel
32. Marina Cottages
33. Kata Villa
34. Kata Tropicana
35. Garden Resort
36. Happy Huts
37. Fantasy Hill
38. Kampong Kata
39. Hallo Guesthouse
40. Kata On Sea
41. Peach Hill Hotel
42. Lam Sai Village
43. Rose Inn
44. Dome
45. Inter House
46. Kock Chang
47. Bougainvillea

48. Club Med
49. Sawasdee Guesthouse
50. Kata Sanuk Village
51. Kata Beach Resort
52. Kata Plaza
53. Sea Bees
54. Bell Guesthouse
55. P&T Katat House
56. Hayashi
57. Friendship Guesthouse
58. Sea Wind
59. Chao Kheun
60. Boat House
61. Cool Breeze Bungalow
62. Kata Delight
63. Pop Cottages
64. Chins, Sweet Home,
    Mr. At Guesthouse
65. Kata Thani
66. Island Bungalow
67. Kata Noi Riviera
68. Mansion
69. Kata Noi Club
70. Chew Bungalows

end of the beach road, variously spelled Thave-wong, Thawiwong, Taweewong, and Tavee-wong! Swiss Hotel costs 1,500-1,800B, Bay View House 1,000-1,200B, Patong Bed & Break-fast 800-1,000B, and K.V. House 800-1,000B.

On the Beach: Several mid-priced hotels are right on the beach. Sandy House lacks beach views but has cheap a/c rooms for 700-900B. Islet Mansion has rooms without views from 700B, and seaside vistas for 1,000-1,200B.

Patong Beach Hotel: A gorgeous pool, out-standing views from the top floors, and spacious rooms make this deluxe hotel one of the better bargains at Patong. Bananas Disco is also rec-ommended. 94 Patong Beach, tel. (076) 321301, 1,500-2,400B.

K Hotel: Beautiful gardens, a small pool, and efficient German management make this another good choice; popular with European group tours. Rachautit Rd., tel. (076) 321124, 800-1,400B.

Neptuna Hotel: A lovely French-owned hotel with sculpted gardens, an intimate French cafe, and a small but acceptable pool. Recommended.

82/49 Rachautit Rd., tel. (076) 321188, 1,400-1,800B.

Ban Sukothai: Ban Sukothai is something different: an attempt at traditional Thai architec-ture with pavilions and cottages in a landscaped tropical garden. A welcome change from the concrete cubicle. 95 Rachautit Rd., tel. (076) 321195, 1,800-3,000B.

Karon Beach

Phuket's second most popular beach remains beautiful, despite the rising tide of hotel con-struction and the creeping presence of night-clubs and so-called Bar Beers. Karon is probably 80% upmarket hotels, but a handful of inexpen-sive bungalows under 300B are located at the south end, on a hill usually called Karon-Kata (or Kata-Karon) Beach. None are great value, but they're cheap enough to allow you to check out Phuket without wrecking your budget.

Kata-Karon Hill: The largest bungalow op-eration on Phuket is a sprawling complex of over 100 huts called Kata Tropicana, located up a dirt road opposite Ruamthep Inn. Rooms cost 150-600B.

Kata Villa on the main road costs 180-200B, but the huts are quickly falling down. Kampong Kata has six beautiful elevated bungalows with porches and flowers for 350-450B, plus a stunning restaurant decorated with Burmese antiques. Su's Pool Hall has, logically enough, a pool hall on the main floor and 10 rooms upstairs which cost 250-300B with fan and 450-550B a/c. Fantasy Hill only costs 200-250B, but most of the rooms are in an ugly concrete longhouse.

On the Beach: A handful of other inexpensive bungalows still exist on Karon Beach. Krayoon Bungalows, just north of Kata-Karon Hill, is a clean place with small huts from 150B and larger chalets with private bath from 300B. Dream Huts in the north is friendly, cheap, and well removed from the crowds of central Karon. Original hippie huts here cost 180-280B.

Several inexpensive places are in central Karon near the raging Club 44 Disco, including Robin House, Sandy Inn, Brazil, and Jor Guesthouse. All cost 250-600B.

Karon Hotel: A modern, clean hotel in the new shopping development at the north end of Karon Beach. Manager Eric Conger runs one of the better-value places. 33/76 Patak Rd., 300-400B.

Karon Guesthouse: Spotless rooms and friendly management make this another good-value place in north Karon. Rooms with fan and private bath cost 250-350B depending on length of stay.

Crystal Beach Hotel: A large, modern hotel with restaurant, travel facilities, and well-priced rooms. 36-10 Patak Rd., tel. (076) 381580, 350-700B.

Thavorn Palm Beach Hotel: Four swimming pools, five restaurants, luxurious rooms, and enormous grounds (just try to find the reception desk!) make this the best upscale choice on Karon Beach. 128/10 Moo 3 Karon Beach, tel. (076) 381034, 3,400-6,000B.

Kata Beach

Kata's two beaches—Kata Yai in the north and Kata Noi to the south—once served as Phuket's main hippie area until Club Med opened its facilities in 1978. Now, both have been largely blanketed with upscale hotels and expensive restaurants. Kata Yai is almost completely dominated by Club Med, though public access is provided by a beachside road. Kata Noi is a cozy cove with good sand and plenty of inexpensive bungalows.

Contrary to popular folklore, over a dozen bungalows and small hotels on Kata Beach have rooms for 300-500B. Most are on Kata Noi Beach near the expensive hotels, or at the south end of Kata Yai near Kata Plaza.

North Kata Yai Beach: Several small spots near the clubs and Easy Rider Bar have acceptable if sometimes noisy rooms. Hallo Guesthouse is a modern high-rise with clean fan and a/c rooms for 350-700B. Good value. Nearby Rose Inn, Dome Bungalows, Kata On Sea, and Inter House are nothing special but have cheap rooms from 300B. Sawasdee Guesthouse is another choice with clean and modern well-priced a/c rooms for 350-600B.

South Kata Yai Beach: Several inexpensive places are near Kata Plaza. Best choice is Kata Sanuk Village, with a small pool, a comfortable restaurant decorated with European porcelains, and decent bungalows for 600-700B. Friendship, Sea Bees, and Bell Guesthouse have rooms for 300-600B. Longtime favorite Bell offers older *nipa* huts for just 150-200B.

Kata Noi Beach: Hippiedom survives in several bungalows wedged back from the big hotels that dominate the beach. Cool Breeze on the hill behind Kata Inn has four bungalows for 100B, three at 200B, and eight for 500B. Chin's above the Western Inn Restaurant and nearby Sweet Home Bungalows costs 200-300B. Chew Bungalows are run-down but situated on a great stretch of beach far removed from the hordes of tourists. Rooms cost just 200-300B.

Peach Hill Hotel: A clean and modern hotel with a Chinese restaurant, a snooker hall, and 40 a/c rooms. Centrally located on Kata-Karon Beach. 113/16 Patak Rd., tel. (076) 381603, 600-800B including breakfast.

Kata Noi Riviera: Several good-value hotels are at the south end of Kata Noi, including the Riviera just opposite the deserted beach. 3/21 Moo 2 Karon Beach, tel. (076) 381726, 300-700B.

Getting There

Air: Phuket is a direct air flight from Bangkok, Hat Yai, Surat Thani, Penang, and Ko Samui. Travelers coming from Penang should take advantage of the inexpensive flight, which avoids a full day of overland travel. Limousines from the airport to the town of Phuket cost 50B; taxis are 150B per carload.

Bus: Direct a/c buses from Bangkok, Ko Samui, Hat Yai, and Penang can be arranged through travel agents. Ordinary buses leave every 15 minutes 1800-2200 from Bangkok's Southern Bus Terminal in Thonburi. Night buses are fast and cheap but tiring because of wild driving and freezing a/c. Knockout drugs are commonplace; *never accept food or drinks from strangers in Thailand.* Buses terminate at the main bus stop in Phuket town, a few blocks east of the tourist office.

Getting Around

Privately operated minibuses from Phuket town to Patong, Kata, and Karon beaches cost 10-30B depending on your bargaining abilities. Drivers generally collect commissions from hotels and guesthouses. Less-expensive public minibuses to the same beaches leave from the local bus station on Ranong Road beyond the public market. Go here if private charters ask outrageous prices. Minibuses to Rawai and Nai Harn beaches leave from Bangkok and Ranong roads. *Tuk tuks* and minibuses within Phuket town cost 5B. Taxis are unmetered and expensive, but cars and motorcycles can be rented in town and at most beaches—a great way to get around and avoid the hassles of public transportation.

PHANGNGA

The surrealistic and unforgettable limestone mountains in Phangnga Bay costarred with James Bond (if you consider Roger Moore the *real* James Bond) in *The Man with the Golden Gun.*

Boat Excursions

A typical excursion glides through mangrove swamps, countless limestone outcroppings, and caves with prehistoric rock paintings, and stops briefly at Ko Panyi, a commercialized Muslim sea-gypsy village constructed entirely on stilts. Nearby Khao Ping Gan (Leaning Mountain) is James's famous cliff. Boat tours last four to six hours, cost 350-400B per person

from Phuket agents, and leave in the mornings 0800-1000 from the port of Tha Don, 10 km from Phangnga town.

Independent travelers can cut costs dramatically by joining an organized party directly at the launching point. First, take an early-morning bus from Phuket town to Phangnga (93 km), then minibus to the boat dock at Tha Don. Early-morning bus arrivals between 0600 and 0800 are often met by Sayan Tamtopol, who has been leading excellent tours for almost 10 years. The 200B price includes the boat tour, a seafood dinner, and a memorable night in a Muslim fishing village. An early start from Phuket is essential, but a better strategy is to spend a night in Phangnga and hook up with Sayan the following morning. Otherwise, 10-man longtail boats chartered directly from the boatmen cost 300-400B with bargaining.

Accommodations

Phangnga town is supplied with several small and inexpensive hotels on the main street, such as Ruk Phangnga and Ratanapong near the bus stop. Phangnga Bay Resort in Tha Don has a swimming pool, a restaurant, and a/c rooms from 660B.

KO PHI PHI

Phi Phi's almost indescribable combination of powdery white sands, brilliant blue waters, soaring limestone cliffs, and colorful corals makes it one of the most beautiful islands in all of Asia. Ko Phi Phi (spelled Pee Pee and Pi Pi in other guidebooks) is now deluged with over a quarter-million annual visitors who completely pack every square centimeter of land and sand. Despite the almost unbelievable ecological devastation, many visitors still regard the island as a wonderful place to laze in the sun, snorkel around the coral beds, and perhaps enjoy spectacular views from the limestone peak behind the small village.

Attractions

The primary island of Phi Phi Don is an hourglass-shaped islet with narrow crescent bays wedged between soaring limestone mountains. To appreciate the beauty of the island, take the

THAILAND

path from the back side of Tonsai village to the mountain **viewpoint** where a thatched hut restaurant sells expensive soft drinks.

Boat Tour: For most visitors, the highlight of Ko Phi Phi is an all-day boat tour from Tonsai Beach to coral beds including a one-hour stop at stunning Bamboo Island and a jaunt around Phi Phi Ley, an uninhabited island whose pristine beauty surpasses even that of Phi Phi Don. All tours feature stops at amazing Maya Bay for skin diving, fiordlike Lo Samah Bay, and an hour-long visit to famous Viking Cave, an immense cathedral named after cave pictographs which vaguely resemble ancient Viking ships.

Budget Accommodations

Bungalows and resorts are located on Lo Dalam Bay (200 meters north of the boat dock), throughout the interior (follow the path to the right of the dock), Tonsai Beach (both directions from the dock), and along Long Beach (20-minute walk east from the pier). Cheap rooms on Phi Phi are almost extinct.

Lo Dalam Bay: Gift Bungalows has rudimentary huts for 100-150B, though the place is usually full and the owners are impossible to find. Nearby Chong Khao has similar digs for 150-250B. Charlie's Resort is a low-priced, acceptable-quality complex with rooms for 400-800B. The overflow is handled by adjacent Krabi Pee Pee Resort with 60 rooms for 300-600B.

Interior Bungalows: Probably the best midlevel place on the island is a cantilevered hillside complex called P.P. Viewpoint Resort where individual bungalows connected by rickety wooden walkways cost 650-900B. Great place. Another excellent choice is Rimna Villa, with well-spaced clean bungalows for 500-800B overlooking a small valley. Nearby Gipsy Village has 30 bungalows in perfectly straight lines from 250-400B.

Tonsai Beach: Phi Phi Don Resort has small bamboo bungalows back from the water for 150-200B and large concrete cubicles facing the water for 350-500B. Pee Pee Andaman Resort is a large operation with over 100 huts in all price ranges. Their primeval shacks cost 100-150B, good-value huts with private bath are 200-250B, and better beachside chalets with private bath cost 400-500B. Pee Pee Andaman has some good-value bungalows for 400-600B.

Long Beach: Farther east on Had Yao (Long Beach) are Funnyland, Viking Village, and Long Beach Bungalows with bamboo huts and wooden A-frames for 200-450B, plus newer rooms at twice the price.

P.P. Paradise Pearl is an old favorite with over 100 bungalows priced 350-800B.

Transportation

Ko Phi Phi is 40 km southeast of Phuket and 42 km southwest of Krabi. The island is served by an amazing variety of boats from both Phuket and Krabi. Daily boat service runs during the dry season from October to June, with limited crossings during the monsoons from July to October.

From Phuket: Songserm has 10 boats that cost 200-350B each way, take two hours, and depart several times daily from Phuket harbor at Ao Makham. Travel agents on Phuket sell tickets which include transportation to Phuket pier.

From Krabi: Transportation from Krabi includes over a dozen daily departures on anything from fishing boats to sleek cruisers. Krabi guesthouses sell tickets, or you can wander down to the pier and take the next available boat.

KRABI

Krabi Province is one of the most geologically interesting and scenically stunning landscapes in Thailand. Krabi town is a pleasant place but has little to offer except for a good selection of guesthouses and transportation connections to nearby destinations such as Ko Phi Phi, Pranang Cape, and Ko Lanta.

Attractions

Wat Tham Sua: Tiger Cave Monastery, seven km east of Krabi, is a decade-old meditation retreat set in a natural amphitheater of caves and gigantic trees. Thailand's most important forest *wat* welcomes Western visitors. From Krabi, take a minitruck to the junction at Talat Kao, then any bus heading south to the turnoff to the monastery. The monastery is two kilometers up the road.

Reclining Buddha: Most of the attractions are well off the main highway and best reached with rental motorcycle. A colorful concrete Buddha lies serenely under a pair of limestone peaks on Hwy. 4034.

Shell Cemetery: Su San Noi is a famous shoreline collection of fossilized seashells at Laem Pho, 19 km west of Krabi. Although a rare geological phenomenon, Su San Noi actually resembles a slab of parking lot that fell into the ocean; unimpressive and hardly worth the effort.

Accommodations

The best guesthouses are on the new street of Ruen Rudee, or outside town in quieter locales.

K.R. Mansion: Slightly outside town is a very comfortable guesthouse with fully furnished rooms, spotless bathrooms, and a popular cafe. A recommended escape from downtown Krabi. 52/1 Chao Fah Rd., tel. (075) 612761, 120-500B.

Krabi Thai Hotel: Krabi's best has less expensive rooms in the old building and more luxurious choices in the newer wing. 7 Isara Rd., tel. (075) 611122, 250-800B.

Transportation

Krabi is 815 km south of Bangkok, 176 km east of Phuket, 211 km southwest of Surat Thani, and 282 km north of Hat Yai.

Boat: By far the most interesting approach to Krabi is by sea from Phuket via Ko Phi Phi. Boats depart 0700-1100 from Phuket and take about three hours to Ko Phi Phi. Boats continue from Ko Phi Phi to Krabi at 0900 and 1300. A better option is direct boat from Ko Phi Phi to Ao Pranang (Pranang Cape), the premier beach destination near Krabi.

Bus: Most buses from Bangkok, Phuket, Surat Thani, Ko Samui, Trang, and Hat Yai drop passengers in Talat Kao (Krabi junction), a small town five km north of Krabi. Minitrucks continue south to town for five *baht*.

AO NANG (BEACH)

Geographical terminology is somewhat confusing around Krabi. Ao Nang Beach, 17 km northwest of Krabi, is a disappointing stretch of sand that caters mostly to group tourists shuttled here by uninformed travel agents. Hat Nopharat Thara is a somewhat better beach to the north. Pranang Cape—also called Ao Phra Nang (Pranang Beach) or Laem Phra Nang (Pranang Cape)—is one of the most stunning destinations in Thailand and the focal point for informed visitors.

Longtail boats to Pranang Beach leave on demand from the waiting shed in the middle of the beach. Ao Nang is best considered an overnight stop en route to Pranang Beach.

Accommodations

Bungalows are springing up weekly to serve the ever-increasing crowds. Minitrucks from Krabi pause at the Bank of Siam and the boat launch to Pranang Beach, then continue west past the bungalows facing the beach. The best spots appear to be P.S. Cottages (directly on the beach), Coconut Garden with simple huts arranged around a landscaped courtyard, and semiluxurious Krabi Resort for upscale visitors.

Transportation

Ao Nang can be reached from Krabi in 40 minutes with minitrucks leaving from Uttaradit Rd. near Chan Phen Tours.

PRANANG

Pranang is comparable only to the wonders of Ko Phi Phi: an amazing landscape of soaring limestone mountains, aquamarine waters, and squeaky white sand in an outlying corner of paradise. The special grandeur of Pranang comes from the limestone cliffs encrusted with vegetation that resembles an instant designer garden, and pinnacles leeched by rains into phantasmagoric shapes not unlike embryonic dollops of dripped wax. Pranang Beach is composed of silken sand so white it almost hurts your eyes. Few places in Thailand offer such a stunning combination of water, sand, and land.

Compared to Phuket or Ko Samui, Pranang is still somewhat off the beaten track, but the pace of change has accelerated in recent years, and it seems inevitable that serious damage will be done unless government officials stem the uncontrolled development. Bungalows are now packed together and occupy almost every square centimeter of available land, while discos blast away until dawn. Pranang—like Ko Phi Phi—is a very small place that has quickly become overwhelmed without any signs of government intervention.

THAILAND

KRABI

TO MAIN HIGHWAY,
KRABI JUNCTION,
PHUKET, & TRANG

SANONG RD.

UTTARADIT RD.

SNOOKER
HALL

GAS
STATION

LANTA VILLA
OFFICE

HEMATANON RD.

BOXING
STADIUM

SUKHON RD.

TO
AO NANG BEACH

BANK

KRABI
RIVER

MARKET

CHAN PHEN
TOURS

SRISAWAT RD.

REAN PARE
RESTAURANT

BANK

PATANA RD.

SUZUKI
BIKES

KRABI
RESORT

MINIBUS TO
MAIN HIGHWAY

CINEMA

PRACHA CHUEN RD.

CHAO FA
PIER

RUEN RUDEE RD.

BOOKS

TO
KO
LANTA

WAT KORAVARAM

ISARA RD.

NIGHT MARKET

TO
KO PHI PHI

POST OFFICE

SOI RUAM CHIT

ISARA RD.

WANAPUK RD.

SAMUSAN RD.

CITY HALL

SOI RUAM CHAI

IMMIGRATION

CHAO FA RD.

VICHIT RD.

KRABI RD.

PROVINCIAL
HALL

TELEPHONE

CHAMAI RD.

POLICE

0   100m

THAILAND

© MOON PUBLICATIONS, INC.

KRABI

1. Rong's Guesthouse
2. Ban Sib Guesthouse
3. Vieng Thong Hotel
4. Jungle Guesthouse
5. B&B Guesthouse
6. New Hotel
7. K.P.B. Guesthouse
8. Coconut Guesthouse
9. Walker Guesthouse
10. K.L. Guesthouse
11. Mark and May Guesthouse
12. Pine Guesthouse
13. Seaside Guesthouse
14. Krabi Thai Hotel
15. L.R.K. Guesthouse
16. Thammachat Guesthouse
17. Songserm
18. Sea Tours Guesthouse
19. Kanaab Maw Guesthouse
20. Cha Guesthouse
21. Ruamjid Guesthouse
22. Lek Guesthouse
23. New Best Guesthouse
24. Sunshine Guesthouse
25. Friendly Guesthouse
26. Chao Fa Valley Resort
27. R.R. Mansion

Accommodations

Pranang Cape is divided into three beaches with distinct price classes. Pranang Beach at the south end has the most expensive digs, Railey West is mid-priced, while Railey East is the last refuge of cheap bungalows under 200B. Bungalows are filled to capacity during the high season from November to March, when visitors must sometimes camp out under the coconut trees while waiting for a vacancy.

Railey Beach East: Also called Nam Mao Beach, Railey East has several bungalows that cost 100-600B.

Pranang Beach: The south end of the cape offers the finest sand, the best swimming, yachts bobbing in the blue lagoon, and the very, very up-scale Dusit Rayavadee, where rooms start at 8,000B.

Railey Beach West (Lailei Beach): The longest and most popular beach, with several bungalows and private homes at the northern edge. Railey Bay Bungalows and Railey Village offer bungalows for 200-450B.

Transportation

Pranang Cape is 15 km northwest of Krabi and can only be reached by longtail boat from Krabi or Ao Nang Beach. Don't confuse Ao Nang with Pranang; if you are on a beach with a road, you haven't reached the latter.

Boats from Krabi take about 45 minutes. Ask to be dropped on Railey Beach West, not the first stop at Pranang Beach. Boats from Ao Nang take about 15 minutes.

KO LANTA

The search for an undiscovered paradise is quickly pushing travelers south from Krabi toward the Malaysian border and dozens of islands near Trang and Satun. Ko Lanta today has over a dozen bungalows stretched along the west coast, from the northern village of Ban Sala Dan down to Ban Sangka U at the southern tip.

Ko Lanta has a few drawbacks, such as its isolated location that demands long travel, inconsistent sand, murderously hot weather or summer monsoons, a lack of organized transportation, and a lack of imaginatively constructed bungalows. And although the island also lacks the stunning topography and pristine beaches of Ko Phi Phi and Pranang Cape, visitors searching to escape the crowds and willing to endure some transportation hassles will probably enjoy their discovery.

Accommodations

Ban Sala Dan: The largest village on Ko Lanta is where most boats from Krabi and Ko Phi Phi terminate. Ban Sala Dan is a typical Thai fishing village, with several cafes, travel agencies, and motorcycle rentals.

Kor Kwang Beach: Deer Neck Cabanas and Kar Kwang Beach Bungalows are west of town on the rocky promontory called Laem Kor Kwang.

Klong Dao Beach: Almost a dozen bungalows are in northwestern Ko Lanta, including Lanta Villa, Lanta Charlie Bungalows, Sea House, and attractive Lanta Garden Bungalows. All cost 200-450B.

Palm Beach: South of Klong Dao is a beautiful four-km beach with excellent pure-white sand and small surf in the winter months. Mr. Bat at Lanta Palm Beach Bungalows rents simple but decent bamboo huts for 150-250B. Let's hope future hotel owners are blessed with some sense of aesthetics.

Klong Khong Beach: Nine km south of Ban Sala Dan is a small beach with limited sand but plenty of offshore corals for diving exploration and an excellent grove of swaying palms. Marina Huts, just south of the small village of Ban Klong Khong, is a beautifully situated guesthouse with about 30 A-frame bamboo huts for 100-300B, plus a tent campsite on grassy lawns. Recommended.

Klong Nin Beach: Klong Nin is a five-km-long, perfectly straight, and absolutely deserted beach with a handful of fishing boats pulled up over tons of white sand. Great potential here. Lanta Andaman Bungalows is an ugly dive without views of the beach. Lanta Paradise Island offers about 40 bungalows priced 180-350B. Huts, unfortunately, are unimaginatively packed together in rows four deep, and the restaurant is nothing short of tacky.

Kan Tiang Beach: Eighteen km south of Ban Sala Dan is the final series of coves and deserted beaches. Sun Sea Bungalows on Had Kan Tiang offers bamboo huts for 100-180B.

Transportation

Ko Lanta Yai is 100 km southeast of Krabi, 77 km northwest of Trang, and 12 km from the mainland pier at Ban Bo Muang. The most convenient way to reach Lanta is by direct boat from Krabi or Ko Phi Phi. Travel agents sell tickets and can advise on the latest schedules.

TRANG

Trang is the gateway to one of the newest tourist regions in Thailand. The town itself is reasonably clean and within a day's journey of 20 waterfalls within national parks, limestone caves filled with Buddhist images, wildlife sanctuaries, broad and deserted beaches on the western coastline, and a half-dozen small islands with pure-white beaches and outstanding diving. Great potential here.

Accommodations

Koh Teng Hotel: Trang's backpackers' center offers a very useful bulletin board with maps and bus schedules, photos of nearby beach resorts, and a notebook with firsthand tips on current travel conditions throughout Trang Province. The hotel has been closed for a while but is expected to reopen in the near future. 77-9 Rama VI Rd., tel. (075) 218622, 180-250B.

Queen Hotel: A good-value hotel near several decent restaurants and nightclubs. Visetkun Rd., tel. (075) 218522, 260-380B.

Thumrin Hotel: Trang's only luxurious hotel features a comfortable cafe, convention facilities, and a limited amount of tourist information from the front desk. Thumrin Square, tel. (075) 211011, 600-1,200B.

Transportation

Trang is 870 km south of Bangkok, 136 km south of Krabi, and 163 km northwest of Hat Yai.

Rapid train no. 41 departs from Bangkok's Hualampong Station at 1830 and takes 16 hours to Trang. The train back departs at 1400. Air-conditioned buses from Bangkok's Southern Bus Terminal take about 14 hours to Trang. Direct bus service is also available from Krabi, Satun, and Hat Yai.

Motorcycles are a handy way to quickly tour the region. Bikes can be rented from the Koh Teng Hotel, from freelance operators who hang out in the market, and from a fellow named Prechai at the Pak Meng bus stop.

KO TARUTAO NATIONAL PARK

The 61-island archipelago of Tarutao comprises one of the final frontiers in Thailand untouched by mass tourism. The remote location at the extreme southwestern corner of Thailand—only five km from the Malaysian island of Langkawi—has served to maintain the pristine nature of Tarutao, which remains a wild and relatively untouched destination blessed with stunning beaches, tranquil bays, and a seemingly endless number of deserted islands. Go now and avoid the rush.

The Islands

Ko Bulon Lae: This small island is reached from Pakbara. Pansand Resort on the beach facing the mainland offers campsites and private bungalows for 150-600B.

Tarutao Island: Ko Tarutao is the largest and closest island to the mainland port of Pakbara. Boats from Pakbara land at Pante Malacca Bay on the north coast, where park rangers rent bungalows and tents, maintain a visitor center with displays on local ecology, and raise endangered hawksbill turtles. Visitors can hire longtails or walk south at low tide to Ao San, eight km south of Pante, where campsites are located near a small fishing settlement. Visitors can also camp on Tala Wao Bay or stay in primitive longhouses for about 80B. Tala Wao is a four-hour hike from Pante Bay.

Ko Adang: Adang Island, 43 km west of Tarutao and about 80 km from Pakbara, is the archipelago's third-largest island. Laem Son at the south end of Ko Adang has a national-park office with bungalows for 600B and campsites from 60B.

Ko Lipe: South of Ko Adang lies a four-square-km islet, the archipelago's only populated island aside from Tarutao. Visitors can camp at the park office or rent a bungalow from the local sea gypsies. The island can be reached by longtail from Ko Adang.

Ko Rawi: The second-largest island in the Tarutao archipelago is uninhabited, aside from visiting fishermen.

Accommodations

The National Park Service operates bungalows and campsites on several islands. Four-man concrete bungalows cost 600B, deluxe 10-man bungalows cost 800B, and campsites cost 60B. Bungalows and campsites are at Pante Malacca Bay on the north side of Tarutao Island, at Laem Son at the south end of Ko Adang, and on the east side of Ko Lipe. Backpackers can camp at almost any beach. Reservations can be made at national park headquarters in Bangkok or at the Pakbara office near the pier.

Transportation

Tarutao Island is 28 km from Pakbara, a mainland port 65 km north of Satun and 100 km south of Trang.

Buses south from Trang take two hours to Langu (La Ngu), from where minitrucks and motorcycle taxis continue west to Pakbara. Langu

has a bank, so change enough money and bring along extra food and drink.

Direct connections from Krabi are provided by Leebi Travel on Isara Road. Pakbara can also be reached via Langu with public transportation from Satun and Hat Yai. Travel agents in Hat Yai arrange escorted tours on weekends which include transportation and accommodations. Alternatively, take a bus from Hat Yai toward Satun but get off in the dusty village of Chalung, from where *songtaos* continue north to Langu.

Boats to Tarutao depart daily from Pakbara at 1030 and 1400, but only during the tourist season from November to May. Tarutao National Park is *closed* during the May-Nov. monsoon season.

SATUN

Satun is a small town which chiefly serves as a departure point for sea travel south to Langkawi and Kuala Perlis in Malaysia. Travelers heading from Hat Yai to Tarutao National Park need not stop in Satun but can change buses in Chalung, an intersection town about 20 km north of Satun.

The Thai Immigration Office on Buriwanit Rd. near the canal might be the most important place in town. All travelers leaving Thailand by sea *must* obtain an exit stamp from this office. Immigration can also help with quickie Malaysia visas.

Accommodations

Satun Thani Hotel: While not the cheapest spot in town, this small hotel has a cozy a/c cafe, friendly management, and very clean rooms with private baths. 90 Satun Thani Rd., tel. (074) 711010, 150-360B.

Oasis Guesthouse: Rudimentary digs with mattresses on the floor. Run by an ex-accountant who speaks decent English. Riverside Rd., no phone, 100-150B.

Wang Mai Hotel: Satun's only luxurious hotel has a coffee shop, a disco, and 108 a/c rooms. 43 Satun Thani Rd., tel. (074) 711607, 600-900B.

Transportation

Bus: Buses from Hat Yai leave from the bus terminal on the outskirts of town. Easier but somewhat more expensive options are share taxis which depart opposite the post office near the railway station.

THAILAND

BUSES TO SONGKHLA

TO BANGKOK

TO SONGKHLA

PETCHKASEM RD.

NIGHT FOODSTALLS

TO SONGKHLA

TO IMMIGRATION, WAT NAI YAI, AIRPORT, & PHUKET

SUPHANSAN RANGSAN RD.

FUENG FAH RESTAURANT

PETCHKASEM RD.

SOPHIA FABRICS

1

2

DUANG CHAN RD.

TAXIS

HAT YAI

POST OFFICE

3

OCEAN DEPT. STORE

BIRD'S NEST RESTAURANT

5

4

SAENG CHAN RD.

PRACHA THIPAT RD.

6

10

D.K. BOOKS

ZODIAC DISCO

11

NASATANI RD.

NIPHAT UTHIT 2 RD.

NIPHAT UTHIT 1 RD.

7

12

HOLLYWOOD DISCO

15

RATAKAN RD.

8

9

16

13

17

14

MAE TIP RESTAURANT

DIM SUM CAFE

THAMNOEN VITHI RD.

CAFE

21

25

24

FOODSTALLS

TRAIN STATION

19

20

O CHA RESTAURANT

22

26

27

FOODSTALLS

D.K. BOOKS

23

18

HAAD YAI DEPT. STORE

OSMAN'S RESTAURANT MOTORCYCLES

SANEHANUSORN RD.

KIMPRADET RD.

MANASRUDE RD.

BANK

28

HILLMAN RESTAURANT

29

CHINESE TEMPLE

30

KLONG TOEY

PREDAROM RD.

TECK NGEE RESTAURANT

THAI AIR

31

SEAFOOD GARDEN

NAKORN NAI CAFE

NIYOMRAT RD.

32

MAE TIP RESTAURANT

RELAX PUB

MUSLIM CAFES

33

ANIRATANAKORN RD.

NIPHAT UTHIT 3 RD.

PADUNG PAKDEE RD.

WANG MAI HOTEL

35

SOI 2

34

BIRD SHOP

BEST CAFE

TOURIST OFFICE

THAI NIGHTCLUBS

GAS

CAKE HOUSE

36

SRIPOONAVART RD.

TO BUS TERMINAL & MALAYSIA

37

38

0   100m

THAILAND

© MOON PUBLICATIONS, INC.

HAT YAI

1. Singapore Hotel
2. Inter Hotel
3. Asian Hotel
4. Regency Hotel
5. L.K. Hotel
6. Mandarin Hotel
7. Yong Dee Hotels
8. Park Hotel
9. Savoy Hotel
10. Central Sukhotha Hotel
11. Grand Plaza Hotel
12. Tong Nam Hotel
13. Metro Hotel
14. Laem Thong Hotel
15. Indra Hotel
16. Prince Hotel
17. Nora Hotel
18. Rajthanes Hotel
19. Lada Guesthouse
20. Louise Hotel
21. Cathay Hotel
22. Montien Hotel
23. King's Hotel
24. Sakoi Hotel
25. Kim Hua Hotel
26. Oriental Hotel
27. Rado Hotel
28. Pacific Hotel
29. New World Hotel
30. B.P. Grand Tower Hotel
31. Central Hotel
32. Sakura Hotel
33. Emperor Hotel
34. Scala Hotel
35. Kosit Hotel
36. Lee Gardens Hotel
37. Amarin Hotel
38. Florida Hotel

Boat: Boats to Kuala Perlis in Malaysia take about 90 minutes and leave from two locations. Longtails depart several times daily from the city pier on Klong Bambang near the Rain Thong Hotel. Larger boats leave from Tammalang Pier in the estuary 15 km south of Satun.

More useful than boat travel to Kuala Perlis is direct service to Langkawi Island, a well-developed Malaysian resort destination just 90 minutes south of Satun. Boats to Langkawi depart daily at 1600 from Tammalang pier and return from Langkawi daily at 1300. Tickets can be purchased on the ship or from Charan Tours near the Thai Airways office.

HAT YAI

Hat Yai—the dynamic commercial center and transportation hub of southern Thailand—receives wildly divergent reviews from visitors. Many feel the city is monotonous and oversized and lacks any compelling reason for one to stay more than a few hours. Others enjoy the outstanding shopping, lively street markets, and heady nightlife, and don't mind that Hat Yai is a clean and well-ordered city rather than some romantic fishing village.

Travelers from Malaysia who have little interest in Hat Yai can proceed directly to Songkhla, Krabi, Phuket, or Ko Samui by changing buses, taking the next train, or waiting for a share taxi near the train station. Schedules can be quickly checked at the score of travel agents near the Cathay Hotel, three blocks east of the train station.

Thai Immigration is on Nasatani Rd. near the Utapao Bridge. The Malaysian Consulate is in Songkhla.

Accommodations

Most of Hat Yai's 60-plus hotels are in the center of town along the three Niphat Uthit roads, also called Sai Nueng (Rd. 1), Sai Song (Rd. 2), and Sai Sam (Rd. 3). Train arrivals are within easy walking distance of most hotels. Buses from the Malaysia border usually stop at the main bus terminal outside town, from where minitrucks continue to city center. Bus arrivals from Songkhla can walk or take any songtao heading south.

Cathay Guesthouse: Hat Yai's traveler center is a friendly and clean place with a popular cafe. The bulletin board and travelers' logs are gold mines of information on upcoming beaches, new guesthouses, and travel tips on visas and shopping. Overall, the best-value spot in Hat Yai. Arrive early to find a room. 93/1 Niphat Uthit 2 Rd., tel. (074) 243815, 120-380B.

King's Hotel: An older hotel centrally located near the train station and popular Washington Nightclub. 126 Niphat Uthit 1 Rd., tel. (074) 243966, 250-400B.

Tong Nam Hotel: Small and clean, the Tong Nam has a good fast-food cafe on the first floor, "Ancient Massage" in the lobby, and some of the cheapest a/c rooms in Hat Yai. 118-120 Niphat Uthit 3 Rd., tel. (074) 244023, 150-280B.

Montien Hotel: Adjacent to the King's is a high-rise hotel with sparsely furnished but large and comfortable a/c rooms. 120 Niphat Uthit 1 Rd., tel. (074) 234386, 440-800B.

Central Sukhontha Hotel: A small swimming pool, the Zodiac disco, and brightly decorated rooms make the Sukhontha a popular choice. Sanehanusorn Rd., tel. (074) 243999, 600-950B.

Regency Hotel: Teakwood lobbies, a restaurant-cum-cabaret, and very large rooms make the Regency the best in town. 23 Pracha Thipat Rd., tel. (074) 234400, fax (074) 234515, 1,200-1,600B.

Restaurants

Foodstalls: A small but lively market sets up nightly in the northeast corner of central Hat Yai, on Suphansan Rangsan Road. Other foodstalls are located on Sheuthit Rd., opposite the Oriental Hotel. Inexpensive.

Fueng Fah Restaurant: A small, clean a/c cafe with buffalo steaks and other Western specialties. Suphansan Rangsan Road. Moderate.

Osman's Restaurant: A small Malay cafe with regional specialties such as *soup daging, udang goreng, nasi etek,* and *telor bungkus.* A pleasant change from Thai fare. Niphat Uthit 2 Road. Inexpensive.

Muslim Cafes: Tasty Muslim and Indian dishes are prepared at three simple cafes at the south side of central Hat Yai. Aberdeen, Sharefa (Ruby's), and Mustafa 2 have English menus listing vegetable *korma,* mutton curry, and fish *marsala* served with fresh *chapatis.* An even *better* change from Thai fare. Niyomrat Road. Inexpensive.

Getting There

Air from within Thailand: Thai Airways International flies twice daily from Bangkok via Phuket, and weekly from Pattani and Narathiwat.

Air from Malaysia: Thai Airways and Malaysian Air fly once daily from Phuket and Kuala Lumpur. The Hat Yai airport, 12 km west of town, is served by inexpensive minitrucks and private limousines.

Train from Bangkok: Trains from Hualampong Station to Hat Yai depart at 1235 (rapid), 1400 (special express), 1515 (special express), and 1600 (rapid). The 1515 and 1600 departures are recommended, since they arrive at 0704 and 0850. Sleepers are available on all trains. Advance reservations from the Bangkok station or a travel agent are *strongly* recommended on all trains going south, especially on weekends and holidays.

Train from Malaysia: The International Express leaves Butterworth (the train terminus for Penang) daily at 1340, crosses the Thai border, and arrives in Hat Yai three hours later. The IE is limited to first and second class and somewhat expensive because of supplemental charges for a/c and superior classes. Reservations can be made from Penang travel agents.

Ordinary trains no longer connect Butterworth with Hat Yai but rather terminate at the Malaysian border town of Padang Besar. Walk across the border, have your passport stamped, and catch a bus to Hat Yai.

Taxi from Malaysia: Share taxis are an important travel component in southern Thailand since they are fast, comfortable, and relatively inexpensive—about the same price as an a/c bus. Share taxis leave 0600-1000 from the Butterworth station just across the channel from Penang. Share taxis from Kota Bharu terminate at the border, from where you have your passport stamped and continue to Sungai Golok by rickshaw or *tuk tuk.*

Bus from Malaysia: Bus 29 from Kota Bharu terminates in the Malaysian border town of Rantau Panjang, where you have your passport stamped and continue to the Sungai Golok train or bus station by *tuk tuk* or trishaw.

Leaving Hat Yai

Train: Trains going north to Phattalung, Surat Thani, and Bangkok depart at 1534, 1617, 1814, and 1849. Sleepers are available on all trains. Trains going south to Sungai Golok on the Malaysian border near Kota Bharu depart at 0452, 0605, 0810, 1035, and 1322. Trains to Padang Besar and Penang depart once daily at 0704.

Taxi: Hat Yai has several share-taxi stands that specialize in specific destinations. Taxis to Phattalung, Nakhon Si Thammarat, Trang,

Narathiwat, and Sungai Golok leave near the night market.

Bus: The public bus terminal (tel. 074-232789) is in a remote spot in the southeast corner of Hat Yai. An easier if somewhat more expensive option is private service arranged through travel agents near the Cathay Hotel.

SONGKHLA

Songkhla is a deceptively sleepy beach resort picturesquely situated between the Gulf of Thailand and a saltwater sea called Thale Sap ("Inland Sea") or Songkhla Lake. Somewhat off the beaten track and overshadowed by the economic powerhouse of Hat Yai, Songkhla has largely escaped commercialism and blessedly remained a pleasant and charming town of Sino-Portuguese buildings, bobbing fishing boats, and beaches filled with Thai families rather than Western tourists.

Songkhla facilities include a post office, several banks, a Malaysian Consulate at 4 Sukum Rd., and a tax-clearance office near the golf course. The American Consulate closed in 1992.

Attractions
Songkhla National Museum: The regional history of Songkhla and the deep south can be traced in this 19th-century Sino-Portuguese mansion, constructed as a private residence for a wealthy Chinese merchant who later served as governor of Songkhla Province. Open Wed.-Sun. 0900-1600.

Old Town: For an interesting hour long walk through the old town start at the museum and proceed south along the waterfront.

Wat Machimawat: Wat Klang—the oldest and most important temple in Songkhla—features beautiful murals of 19th-century life in Songkhla and episodes from the Jatakas.

Samila Beach: The focal point of Songkhla is the eight-km stretch of sand dotted with seafood restaurants, a municipally owned hotel, and hardly any tourists, since Thais leave sunbathing to mad dogs and unenlightened backpackers.

Ko Yoh: Yoh Island is known for its seafood restaurants, traditional weavings, and the Institute of Southern Thai Studies with its newly opened Folklore Museum.

Khu Khut Bird Sanctuary: A large 520-square-km wildlife refuge, similar to Thale Noi near Phattalung, is 50 km north of Songkhla near the town of Sathing Phra. Accommodations and boat tours of the inland lake are available at park headquarters. Buses from Songkhla stop at Sathing Phra, from where motorcycles continue three km to park headquarters.

Accommodations
Amsterdam House: Clean place owned and operated by a Dutch woman and her Thai partner. 15/3 Rong Muang Rd., tel. (074) 322999, 150-250B.

Holland House: Cozy spot near the clock tower in the center of town. 28 Ramvithi Rd., tel. (074) 322738, 200-400B.

Narai Hotel: The backpackers' favorite is somewhat isolated but compensates with travel tips, bicycle rentals, and decent rooms in the yellow building with a red-tiled roof. 14 Chai Khao Rd., tel. (074) 311078, 120-250B.

Suksomboon 1 Hotel: Acceptable rooms in a small place near the clock tower. 40 Phetchkiri Rd., tel. (074) 311049, 180-320B.

Transportation
Songkhla can be reached from Hat Yai in 30 minutes by green buses which depart on Petchkasem Rd. near the Hat Yai Plaza Theater. Share taxis leave from the President Hotel. Buses stop at the clock tower and then continue to a halt on Saiburi Rd. near Wat Chang. Thai Transportation Company in the Chok Dee Hotel sells a/c bus tickets to Bangkok.

NARATHIWAT

This small and sleepy fishing village is the most pleasant stop between Hat Yai and Sungai Golok. The town itself lacks any great monuments or historical sites, but the undisturbed wooden architecture, deserted beaches, and laid-back atmosphere make it a wonderful spot to escape the more congested and touristy towns of southern Thailand.

Attractions
Walking Tour: A very agreeable three-hour walking tour can be made starting from the clock

THAILAND

tower and heading north along the riverfront road toward the Muslim fishing village and cafes at Narathiwat Beach. You'll pass bird shops on the left, brightly painted *kolae* fishing boats at the north end, Narathiwat Mosque, and then, across the bridge, a typical Muslim fishing village where kids yell "Hello good morning," and several cafes with English-language menus.

Wat Khao Kong: Six km south of Narathiwat is a small hill called Khao Kong on which local Buddhists have constructed the largest seated Buddha in Thailand. Take any bus or minitruck heading south down Hwy. 42 toward Sungai Golok.

Accommodations

Narathiwat Hotel: The cheapest spot in town is the yellow wooden hotel marked with a small English sign. Rooms fronting the street are noisy and need renovation, but rooms facing the Bang Nara River are good value and worth requesting. 341 Phupa Pakdee Rd., tel. (073) 511063, 120-150B.

Bang Nara Hotel: Another budget spot similar to the Narathiwat but without the river-view rooms. Hok Huay Lai and Cathay hotels are in the same price range. 174 Phupa Pakdee Rd., tel. (073) 511036, 120-150B.

Yaowaraj Hotel: Narathiwat's second-largest hotel offers clean rooms with private bath at reasonable prices. 131 Pichit Bamrung Rd., tel. (073) 511148, 150-380B.

Tan Yong Hotel: Narathiwat's finest hotel features a snooker hall, Ladybird ancient massage, and a popular restaurant with live cabaret with young girls dressed as cheerleaders. 16/1 Sopa Prisai Rd., tel. (073) 511477, 650-900B.

Transportation

Share taxis from Sungai Golok leave from the train station and take about one hour to Narathiwat. Taxis from Hat Yai depart on Niphat Uthit 2 Rd. near the Cathay Hotel. Buses leave every two hours from the halt in the south end of Sungai Golok. Buses from Hat Yai leave from the main bus terminal in the southeastern outskirts of town.

SUNGAI GOLOK

Sungai Golok (or Sungai Kolok) is the final town for visitors heading south from Thailand to the east coast of peninsular Malaysia. Aside from its immigration functions, the town serves as a short-time brothel for Malaysian males who pack the hotels, nightclubs, and massage parlors on weekends. Sungai Golok offers nothing for Western travelers except for a small but useful tourist office at the border.

Warning: The Thai border closes nightly sometime between 1700 and 2100, depending on the whim of immigration officials and border guards. Unless you care to spend a night in Sungai Golok—not a pleasant thought—arrive early enough to conduct border formalities and catch a share taxi down to Kota Bharu.

Accommodations

The local tourist office claims that Sungai Golok has 44 hotels in all price categories. Most cost 120-180B fan, 250-450B a/c, or 550-800B in better hotels.

Budget Hotels: Travelers arriving late at night can quickly locate an inexpensive hotel on Charoenkhet Rd. or the parallel avenues to the west. Hotels on Charoenkhet Rd. with rooms for 150B include the Chiang Mai, the Pimarn, the Shanghai, the Asia with a tiled lobby and aquariums, and the Savoy with potted plants on the balcony. The very inexpensive Thaliang (Thai Lieng) has rudimentary rooms from 120B and a small coffee shop with caged songbirds.

Merlin Hotel: A very large and central hotel whose brochure shows photos of lovely girls taking soapy baths, cutting hair, and sitting in bedrooms dressed in blue party dresses. You get the idea. 40 Charoenkhet Rd., tel. (073) 611003, 320-500B.

Transportation

Buses from Hat Yai can be arranged through travel agents near the Cathay Hotel, though most services head southwest toward Penang and Kuala Lumpur. Ordinary buses leave from the Hat Yai bus terminal on the outskirts of town.

Bus: Buses generally arrive and depart from the train station in Sungai Golok, adjacent to the Valentine Hotel, or from the bus terminal on the south end of town near the cinema and An An Hotel. Ordinary buses to Bangkok leave throughout the day until 1630 from both locations.

Taxi: Share taxis are the fastest way to travel in the deep south. Share taxis from Hat Yai,

Satun, Pattani, and Narathiwat stop at the train station in Sungai Golok, from where *tuk tuks* and pedicabs continue east to the Malaysian border.

Share taxis to all towns in the deep south leave from 0700 to 1600 from the Sungai Golok train station. Travelers arriving from Malaysia should proceed directly to the train station and find the next available taxi.

Train: Train arrivals in Sungai Golok are greeted by trishaw drivers who continue to the border. There is no direct train service between Sungai Golok and Kota Bharu.

Getting to Malaysia

The border is about two km from the train station in Sungai Golok. Thai Immigration will check your visa expiration date and charge 100B per day for overstays beyond the allotted period.

Malaysian authorities across the Sungai Golok River grant free entry permits to most Western visitors on arrival. You then walk into the small Malaysian border town of Rantau Panjang. To the right is a small cafe where you can dine and wait for the next available share taxi to Kota Bharu. The cafe manager and taxi drivers accept Thai *baht* at fair exchange rates.

The Westerner is drawn to the tradition of the Easterner, and almost covets his knowledge of suffering, but what attracts the Easterner to the West is exactly the opposite— his future, and his freedom from all hardship. After a while, each starts to become more like the other, and somewhat less like the person the other seeks. The New Yorker disappoints the locals by turning into a barefoot ascetic dressed in bangles and beads, while the Nepali peasant frustrates his foreign suppliants by turning out to be a traveling salesman in Levi's and Madonna T-shirt. Soon, neither is quite the person he was, or the one the other wanted. The upshot is confusion.

—Pico Iyer,
Video Night in Kathmandu

One of the chief delights and benefits of travel is that one is perpetually meeting men of great abilities, of original mind, and rare acquirements, who will converse without reserve.

—Disraeli,
Coningsby

Etymologically a traveler is one who suffers travail, a word deriving in its turn from Latin tripalium, a torture instrument consisting of three stakes designed to rack the body.

—Paul Fussell,
Abroad

VIETNAM

VIETNAM

Travel is not really trade; it's communication between people. Just as travel promotes understanding, understanding promotes peace.

—LARS-ERIC LINDBLAD

Let the tourist be cushioned against misadventure. Your true traveler will not feel that he has had his money's worth unless he brings back a few scars.

—LAWRENCE DURRELL,
SPIRIT OF PLACE

One who has hotel reservations and speaks no French is a tourist.

—PAUL FUSSELL,
ABROAD

INTRODUCTION

Vietnam. The name alone evokes unforgettable images: a young girl running down a country road, an execution on the streets of Saigon, helicopter evacuations on the roof of the American Embassy, Tank no. 843 crashing through the gates of the Presidential Palace, boatloads of refugees fleeing for the political freedoms and economic promises of the West.

Despite two decades of peace, it seems that many Westerners still think of Vietnam as a war rather than a country, a misconception fueled by international agendas and Vietnam's reticence to reveal itself to the outside world. As a result, Vietnam remains one of the world's final enigmas, a land we claim to understand but, in reality, know almost nothing about.

Memories of the war and fears of the unknown have long held tourism to a bare minimum. Fortunately—and for good reasons—this seems to be changing.

Vietnam is a destination considered by many veteran travelers among the most beautiful in all of Southeast Asia. The country offers over 2,000 km of magnificent coastline almost completely untouched by mass tourism. There are misty rainforests in the west and north where

you find minority tribes and remote hill stations constructed out of old French villas peeling behind coconut palms and rubber plantations. There are exquisite temples and remains of an ancient Cham civilization, narrow streets illuminated by oil-lit lamps that remind you of the Indochina of your dreams, and, most importantly, some of the most hospitable and cultured people you will ever meet.

Twenty years after the end of the war, Vietnam has healed its wounds and learned to forgive and forget. Westerners ready to return the favor should include Vietnam in their travel plans.

THE LAND

Arched like a two-headed Chinese dragon, Vietnam stretches over 1,600 km from the border of China to the Gulf of Thailand in the far south. Vietnam is roughly the size of Japan or California. Endowed with great physical beauty and surprising geographic diversity, the country vaguely resembles a pair of roundish rice baskets balanced at the ends of a long and narrow bamboo pole.

VIETNAM

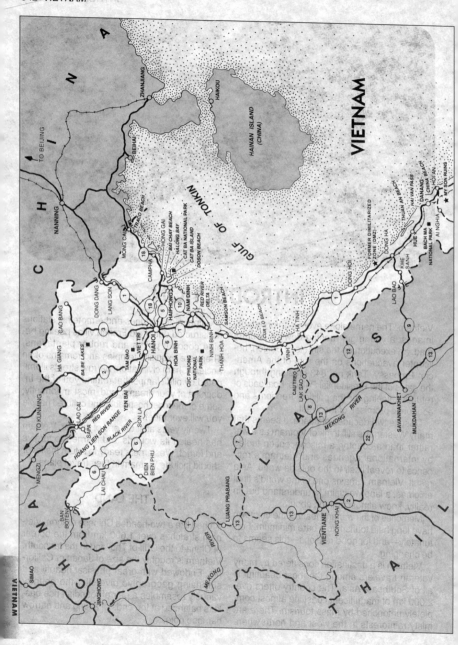

© MOON PUBLICATIONS, INC.

CHU LAI
QUANG NGAI
SA HUYNH BEACH
BINH DINH
QUI NHON
DAI LANH BEACH
VAN PHONG BAY
TUY HOA
NINH HOA
NHA TRANG
CAM RANH BAY
PHAN RANG
CA NA BEACH
PHAN THIET
VUNG TAU
CON DAO ISLANDS

SOUTH CHINA SEA

DAK TO
KONTUM
PLEIKU
CENTRAL HIGHLANDS
BUON MA THUOT
DALAT
BAO LOC
BIEN HOA
VUNG TAU

BAN DON

CAMBODIA

MEKONG RIVER
PHNOM PENH
LAKE TONLE SAP
BATTAMBANG

TAY NINH
MOC BAI
CU CHI
SAIGON
BAVET
MYTHO
VINH LONG
TRA VINH
MEKONG DELTA
SOC TRANG
CHAU DOC
LONG XUYEN
CANTHO
MEKONG RIVER
HA TIEN
RACH GIA
U-MINH MANGROVE FOREST
CAMAU
PHU QUOC ISLAND

GULF OF THAILAND

TO BANGKOK
TO BANGKOK

0   100 km

VIETNAM

SIGHTSEEING HIGHLIGHTS

Despite Vietnam's great number of attractions, the disadvantages are just as plentiful. Whether you arrive as an independent traveler or on an escorted tour, Vietnam can be an expensive and frustrating destination. Group tourists are often charged unreasonable rates for rudimentary hotels, uninspired food, inadequate air and land transport, and an absence of reliable financial and communication systems. Just as disturbing is the apparent greed of tourist authorities and Vietnamese citizens who seem determined to mine, without conscience, the pocketbooks of the foreign tourist. Even sightseers with minimal expectations of comfort and convenience will find Vietnam a challenging destination.

And yet tourism continues to boom, as thousands of Europeans, American veterans, and Vietnamese expatriates arrive to discover the mystique of Asia's final frontier. The bottom line is that jaded travelers, who despair of ever finding any place fresh or unspoiled, will find Vietnam a sparkling revelation, limited in amenities but full of the qualities that their absence encourages.

Ho Chi Minh City (Saigon)

Most visitors arrive in the vibrant former capital of South Vietnam, renamed Ho Chi Minh City (HCMC) after the war, though everyone still calls it Saigon. The city itself is a startling study in contrasts between the poverty of socialism and the heady spirit of capitalism which seems to infect every nook and cranny of the city.

Vietnam's largest city and principal seaport still shows some of the old French-colonial charm in its faded architecture, long tree-lined avenues, and sidewalk cafes that serve up cafe lattes and croissants. More contemporary attractions include an informal "war tour" of the museums and other public buildings which figured so prominently in the American conflict. Saigon also offers religious shrines, excellent shopping, and all sorts of nightlife from seedy nightclubs to splashy cabarets.

Vung Tao

Two hours southeast of Saigon is a popular seaside resort with a fairly good stretch of sand plus inexpensive restaurants, cafes, and colonial villas converted into hotels and guesthouses. A convenient side trip from Saigon, Vung Tao also has a temple consecrated to the whale cult and other oddities such as a 30-meter statue of Christ erected by the Americans in 1971.

Mekong Delta

The vast alluvial delta of the Mekong River offers a great deal to the traveler: beautiful scenery, friendly people, and an almost complete lack of Western tourists. Visitors can spend a few days in the villages nearest Saigon, such as Mytho, Vinh Long, and Cantho, or make a longer excursion to the more remote and almost completely untouched villages of Long Xuyen, Chau Doc, and Rach Gia, all located toward the Cambodian border.

Dalat

A highlight of any visit to Vietnam, Dalat is an old French hill station nestled amid rolling hills, pine-covered valleys, and lakes in the central highlands some 300 km northwest of Saigon. Dalat's bracing temperatures and quiet beauty guarantee a welcome relief from the heat and noise of Saigon.

Sights around town include some old French-colonial cathedrals, seminaries, and romantic old villas, many of which have been converted into cozy hotels. Outside town are natural attractions such as the Valley of Love and the Lake of Sorrows.

Nha Trang

Nha Trang is an important seaport known for its six-km white-sand beach and warm waters popular with scuba divers and fishermen. The town has a vaguely Mediterranean feel and one of the better beaches located within an urban area in Vietnam, plus Buddhist pagodas, a Christian cathedral, a limited amount of war nostalgia, and ancient Cham towers.

Hoi An

Visitors who enjoy old towns should visit this crumbling village, 32 km south of Danang. Once a major trading port, Hoi An now features fine Chinese temples and one of the largest arrays of prewar architecture in Vietnam. Modernization has changed Hoi An's character in recent years, yet it remains a recommended stop.

Danang

Danang, Vietnam's fourth-largest city, is perhaps best known abroad as the seaport where American Marines first landed in March 1965 to secure an air base and initiate the American conflict. Danang is also the former homeland of the Chams, who once controlled Vietnam from Hue to Vung Tao. The Cham Museum provides a good introduction.

Other attractions include the Marble Mountains and the famous Vietnam-era resort of China Beach.

Lang Co Beach

Several dazzling beaches are located about 35 km north of Danang and just beyond Hai Van Pass, the rugged limestone karst which once formed the physical barrier between ancient Vietnam to the north and the Champa Kingdom in the south.

Lang Co Peninsula is highly recommended to all lovers of tropical beauty. The sparkling 10-km beach is wonderfully set between the emerald-blue waters of the South China Sea and an idyllic lagoon which washes up toward the mountains—perhaps the most spectacular beach in Vietnam.

Hue

Hue is Vietnam's artistic, cultural, and historical center, having served as the imperial capital of the Nguyen kings for almost 150 years. The town's main attractions are the baroque tombs of the Nguyen emperors, the remains of the old Imperial City, and its superbly romantic location on the banks of the Perfume River.

Demilitarized Zone (DMZ)

The DMZ, which once served as the boundary between North and South Vietnam, is defined by the Ben Hai River, which follows the 17th parallel.

Among the most famous sites are the battlefield at Khe Sanh; Vinh Moc Tunnels, where hundreds of Vietnamese lived during the war; Doc Mieu Base, former headquarters for American electronic surveillance; Con Thien Firebase, the primary base for an elaborate military barrier designed to detect enemy incursions across the DMZ; Truong Son National Cemetery; Camp Carroll; and Hamburger Hill, scene of a terrible 1968 battle in which 241 Americans died in less than one week.

Most of the war memorabilia has been dismantled and hauled away by Vietnamese scrap collectors, though American veterans and anyone else intrigued by the war will enjoy a visit to the DMZ.

Hanoi

Hanoi, the capital of the Socialist Republic of Vietnam, is a decrepit but atmospheric city of tree-lined boulevards, narrow alleys mercifully free of traffic, and weathered colonial buildings still unchanged from the days of the French. The major attractions—Ho Chi Minh's Mausoleum and an assortment of religious shrines—are secondary to the timeless ambience found in the streets of the Old City.

Halong Bay

Halong Bay and Cat Ba National Park are undoubtedly Vietnam's most magnificent natural marvels. Centerpiece of the movie *Indochine*, Halong Bay is a stunning combination of over 1,000 limestone islets rising dramatically from an iridescent sea—a visual wonderland comparable only to Guilin in China.

The beaches are disappointing and facilities are simple by Western standards, but visitors with sufficient time will find Halong a welcome change from the urbanized destinations in Vietnam.

The principal physiographic features are the 1,200-km Annamite (Troung Son) Cordillera, which dominates the interior, and the two alluvial deltas formed by the Red River (Son Hong) in the north and Mekong River (Song Cuu Long) in the south.

The Mekong, one of the world's longest rivers, snakes over 4,100 km from the mountains of Tibet into the South China Sea, finally forming a vast delta which comprises one of the great rice bowls of Asia. Less well known but just as important is the delta of the Red River, which supports over nine-tenths of northern Vietnam's population.

Climate

Vietnam probably has a greater diversity of climates than most other Southeast Asian destinations due to its immense length and variations in elevation.

Northern Vietnam is influenced by the winds from China, which bring bitter cold from November to January and heavy rains coupled with higher temperatures from June to October. Central Vietnam is a transitional zone with light but steady rains throughout the year. Southern Vietnam is a typical subequatorial region with a dry season from November to May and monsoon climate from June to October.

VIETNAM

The drier months from November to May are the best times to visit Vietnam, though warm clothing will be necessary in the north.

HISTORY

Vietnam's earliest history and the origins of the Vietnamese people remain somewhat hypothetical despite a large number of ethnographic and archaeological studies. Most scholars believe the earliest inhabitants were Negritos who disappeared from Vietnam with the later arrival of Indonesians, who settled in the Red River delta, and refugees from southern China.

Racial and linguistic characteristics indicate that later peoples were a mixture of Mon-Khmers who contributed the basic language, Thais who introduced tonality, and the Chinese who left behind not only their script but also their vocabulary of government, literature, and philosophy.

The end result was a distinct ethnic group which practiced Bronze Age culture several centuries before Christ in the Red River delta of northern Vietnam and left behind a culture distinct from that of China, mainland Southeast Asia, or the Indian subcontinent.

Chinese Rule (200 B.C.-A.D. 939)

The beginning of recorded Vietnamese history begins with the arrival of the Chinese, who ruled most of Vietnam for over a millennium. Sometime during the early Chinese rule, a local emperor named his kingdom the land of "Nam Viet," a term which refers to the people living south of China proper. A subsequent ruler called his empire Annam ("Pacified South") to indicate complete Chinese domination.

China's main interest in Vietnam was to establish a stopover for ships engaged in trade with the Spice Islands, India, and even the Middle East. They also imposed their models of government and technical innovations, which made the Vietnamese among the most advanced civilizations in Southeast Asia. Despite their contributions, the long period of Chinese occupation was marked by numerous insurrections by Vietnamese who disliked foreign domination and refused to wholeheartedly accept assimilation into Chinese culture—a legacy which still shapes contemporary Vietnamese identity.

The fall of the Tang Dynasty (618-907) culminated in a series of political uprisings and the disastrous defeat of the Chinese in 939, the year which marks the beginning of an independent Vietnam.

Independent Vietnam (939-1860)

Vietnam, from the defeat of the Chinese to the arrival of the French, was ruled by a series of dynasties based in Hanoi and Hue.

Ly Dynasty (1009-1225): The state of general anarchy which characterized the early years of independence lasted until the rise of the Ly Dynasty, rulers of most of Vietnam from their capital at Hanoi for over two centuries. During their reign, the Lys gradually replaced the local warlords with a hierarchy of state officials trained in Confucian philosophy while at the same time vigorously promoting Buddhism and a fierce resistance to Chinese influence.

Tran Dynasty (1225-1400): Vietnam's second great epoch was that of the Tran Dynasty, which not only overthrew the Lys but also successfully defended their country against Kublai Khan and his half-million Mongol warriors, who attacked in the late 13th century. Tran Hung Dao, the Tran general who defeated the Mongolian invaders, is still venerated as one of Vietnam's greatest military heroes.

Le Dynasty (1428-1776): The decline of the Tran Dynasty was followed by yet another Chinese invasion and a Ming-directed administration which ruthlessly exploited the hapless country. Hatred of Chinese occupation forces led to the rise of Emperor Le Loi, who established the Le Dynasty and drove the Chinese from Vietnam. For his remarkable military accomplishments, Le Loi is also honored as one of Vietnam's great heroes in the ongoing struggle against Chinese hegemony.

The Le Dynasty also pursued a policy of territorial expansion which drove the Chams from southern Vietnam and integrated Saigon into a unified nation shortly before 1700.

Nguyen Dynasty (1802-1883): Vietnam after the Le Dynasty was carved up into two divisions which lasted until 1802, when Emperor Gia Long established the Nguyen Dynasty—the final Vietnamese dynasty—from his royal capital at Hue. Gia Long captured Hanoi and, once again, reunified the country under a single ruling family.

VIETNAM

Today, the Nguyen era is regarded as the artistic culmination of modern Vietnamese history.

French Rule (1860-1954)

France's role in Vietnamese history was an outgrowth of the rising hostility of Vietnamese Mandarins against Catholic missionaries who were having great success in the Buddhist country. After the execution of 25 European priests and 30,000 Vietnamese Catholics between 1848 and 1860, French forces attacked Saigon and forced Emperor Tu Duc to cede three southern provinces and create the French colony of Cochin China. In 1883, Vietnam was formally divided into the French protectorates of Tonkin (North Vietnam), Annam (Central Vietnam), and Cochin China (South Vietnam), though the entire region was simply known as French Indochina.

French rule improved the physical infrastructure and brought a degree of stability to the country, though ill-conceived policies devastated the peasantry, who fell farther into debt and servitude. As elsewhere in Southeast Asia, heavy-handed policies of the colonial masters led to the rise of revolutionary movements such as the Indochina Communist Party, established in 1930 by Ho Chi Minh.

The defeat of French colonial forces at Dien Bien Phu in 1954 marked the end of the First Indochina War, while a joint French-Vietnamese conference in Geneva the same year divided Vietnam along the 17th parallel into two countries. An all-Vietnamese election scheduled for 1956 to unify the country was never approved by either the U.S. or South Vietnam, as it was believed the vote would have gone to the communists in the north.

The American Conflict (1954-75)

The withdrawal of the French was countered by the arrival of the Americans, who assumed responsibility for the survival of South Vietnam by providing financial aid and military advice for the anticommunist government. In 1954, a Roman Catholic Confucian named Ngo Diem returned from his self-imposed exile in the U.S. to become president of South Vietnam. Although the situation was stable for several years, the insurgency waged by the underground Viet Minh (called the Viet Cong by the Americans) and an unhappy military elite led to the overthrow of Diem in 1963. Nine changes of government followed before the military regime of Nguyen Ky and Thieu seized control in 1965.

South Vietnam continued to deteriorate. Buddhist priests opposed to Thieu's government were soon burning themselves in public spectacles that shocked the viewers of American television and galvanized the world on the troubles of a distant Asian land. The U.S. government responded on 7 March 1965 by sending 3,500 Marines to the beaches of Danang in an effort to protect an endangered airfield. By July the number had reached 75,000 and by early 1968, over 500,000 American soldiers were stationed in Vietnam.

The Vietnam War reached a climax with the Tet Offensive of February 1968, when the Viet Minh attacked more than 100 cities and military bases in the south. Although the offensive was a devastating military defeat for the communists, it was an important psychological victory which convinced many Americans that total victory in Vietnam would require unacceptable sacrifices. Chicago rioted, Watts burned, Lyndon quit, and the Americans withdrew from Vietnam shortly before Tank no. 843 crashed through the gates of the Presidential Palace. The Vietnam War was soon over.

Reunified Vietnam

Victory by the Viet Minh did not signal better days but rather a period of political revenge, in which tens of thousands were exterminated or sent off to reeducation camps, and a period of economic collapse which has made Vietnam among the world's poorest countries. No matter your feelings about the war, the reunified government of Vietnam has mismanaged the country, repressed human rights, alienated the most important segments of its population, created over a half-million political and economic refugees, and, finally, inflicted on the nation one of the world's most disastrous economic models.

Twenty years of failure seems finally to be having an effect on the rulers of Vietnam, who announced a policy of economic *doi moi* (new life) in 1991.

Recent changes on a social level are even more startling: today, you can purchase war-era Zippos in Hanoi, listen to the Doors wail in Saigon's Apocalypse Cafe, or sign up for the annual surfing contest at China Beach.

VIETNAM

President Clinton granted full recognition to Vietnam a few years ago—a formality which allows American investors to enter what is expected to be one of the new economic tigers of Southeast Asia. And in 1997, Clinton appointed onetime fighter pilot Pete Peterson as the first postwar U.S. ambassador to Vietnam, a country where Peterson was imprisoned and tortured for over six years.

THE PEOPLE

Vietnam is the world's 12th-most-populous country, with about 70 million people who primarily reside along the coast and in the lowland provinces of the Red and Mekong river deltas. Overall population density of 200 people per square km and urban density of over 1,000 people per square km make Vietnam among the world's most densely populated agricultural countries. The problem is exacerbated by high birth rates and the fact that over 50% of the population is under 20 years of age.

Vietnamese

An estimated 85% of the population are ethnic Vietnamese (Viet Kinh), who were Sinicized during the 1,000 years of Chinese rule but who have successfully maintained their cultural and ethnic identity. Ethnolinguistic studies indicate that the Vietnamese are a mixture of migrants from southern China, Mon-Khmers, and Thais from the west, and Malayo-Indonesians who arrived over two millennia ago. Originally residing in the Red River delta of northern Vietnam, the Vietnamese progressively moved south to populate central Vietnam around A.D. 1000 and the Mekong River delta in the 17th century.

Chinese Vietnamese

Vietnam's largest ethnic minority are the Chinese (Viet Kieu), who number about four million and primarily live in southern urban areas such as the Cholon District in Saigon. Most have adopted Vietnamese nationality but retain their ethnic identity through language, school systems, and social organizations arranged around their dialect and provincial origins.

Successful at commerce, banking, and finance, Chinese Vietnamese have long been Vietnam's most energetic but persecuted minority. Government persecution after the Viet Minh victory forced almost two million Chinese to flee Vietnam between 1975 and 1990—a full one-third of the Chinese population. Some say the exodus was seen by the government as an easy way to confiscate the wealth of the emigrants and purge the country of its ethnic minority.

Fortunately, the Vietnamese government now recognizes their importance in the national economy and encourages the return of overseas Chinese who are largely responsible for the economic miracle of the south.

Montagnards (Highland Peoples)

Vietnam's 54 ethnic minority groups—called Montagnards by the French—total roughly eight million people or about 13% of the national population. Most of these minorities dwell in the northern mountains near the Chinese border and in the Central Highlands, which comprise about 75% of Vietnam's land area.

Centuries of isolation ended abruptly in the 1940s, when Vietnamese revolutionaries established their resistance bases in highland areas and recruited minority soldiers for their war of national liberation. Other highland groups such as the Montagnard FULRO guerrillas were enlisted by the U.S. military and the South Vietnamese government in the war against the Viet Minh. Today, most have returned to their simple lives as mountain farmers who use slash-and-burn techniques to raise rice, vegetables, and a bit of opium.

The highland groups are often grouped according to their ethnolinguistic roots and geographic locations. Major groups in the northern mountains include the Thai (Black, Red, and White Thai), who number almost one million, the Nung, who have been considerably influenced by Viet culture, and smaller groups such as the Hmong, who share cultural roots with the hilltribe peoples of northern Thailand.

Central Highland groups such as the animist Jarai and Raday are often seen in the marketplaces of Dalat and Bon Me Thout, the capital of Dac Lac Province.

Minorities in the far south include the Chams, who were driven from the coastal homelands by the Vietnamese in the 16th century, and the Mon-Khmers, who are descendants of the Khmer civilization that once stretched from the South China Sea to Angkor.

ON THE ROAD

A State of Flux

Special note must be made about travel restrictions and conditions in Vietnam. All writers discussing travel details about a rapidly changing country such as Vietnam are at the mercy of government agencies, which often make sudden changes in the rules and regulations. For example, the first edition of this book stated that all visitors to Vietnam must sign up with an organized tour arranged through Vietnam Tourism. Six months later this restriction was dropped and independent tourism became a viable option. The following year, the Vietnamese government dropped the permit system for outlying provinces; visitors can now travel freely except in military zones and other restricted areas.

Another problem is that the rules are interpreted throughout Vietnam by different officials in various ways. Government officials and policemen often view the fining of Western tourists as a convenient way to supplement their meager incomes. While it's best to follow the rules, everyone should also be prepared to bargain down bribes while understanding the motivation behind the shakedown.

For these reasons, the following advice on visas, permits, transportation, money, and other travel details is subject to change and should be confirmed with travel agencies that specialize in Vietnam, especially the budget outfits on Khao San Road in Bangkok.

As always, your best sources of current information will be other travelers who have just returned from Vietnam. Final details can be ironed out after arrival in Saigon.

GETTING THERE

By Air

Bangkok is the most convenient embarkation port for flights to Saigon. Thai International, Air France, and Bangkok Airways fly daily to Saigon for US$180 one-way and US$360 roundtrip. Other services include Philippine Airlines from Manila, MAS from Kuala Lumpur, Cathay Pacific from Hong Kong, Garuda from Jakarta, Singapore Airlines from Singapore, and JAL from Tokyo.

Travel to Saigon on Vietnam Airlines (Hang Khong, known among connoisseurs as "Hang On Vietnam") is a frightening experience best left to those unable to fly on airlines with better safety records.

Air services are also available from Bangkok to Hanoi, but most travelers fly to Saigon and then overland to Hanoi before flying on to Laos or back to Bangkok. Travel agents on Khao San Road charge about US$350 for a visa and airfare for Bangkok-Saigon and Hanoi-Vientiane.

Airport departure tax is US$7, payable in U.S. dollars or Vietnamese *dong.*

From Cambodia

Buses depart daily from Phnom Penh in the early morning and take about 12 hours to reach Saigon. The a/c bus costs US$12 and the ordinary bus is US$5.

Travelers must have the proper endorsements on their visas or run the risk of being turned back at the border. Exit and entry stamps can be changed in Phnom Penh. See the Cambodia chapter for details.

Buses from Saigon to Phnom Penh leave from 155 Nguyen Hue Blvd., adjacent to the Rex Hotel, daily at 0600 except on Sunday. Travelers whose visas state their point of exit as Saigon or Hanoi airports can change this at several Saigon travel agencies, such as Ann Tourist on Ton That Tung St. and Vacation Planners on Tran Nhat Dvat Street.

From Laos

Highway 9: The most popular route is on Highway 9 from Savannakhet in southern Laos through Khe Sanh in central Vietnam and then to the coast at Dong Ha, just north of Hue. This option makes it possible to tour northeast Thailand, southern Laos, and Vietnam before continuing overland across Cambodia and back to Bangkok.

Buses can be picked up in Savannakhet. In Vietnam, you can find buses leaving from Dong Ha, Danang, and Lao Bao, the Vietnamese border town.

VIETNAM

Highway 7: Another possible land route is from the Plain of Jars in northeastern Laos to Vinh in Vietnam via Highway 7. This route has been open for several years though only group tours have been allowed to make this crossing.

Highway 6: Certainly the most fascinating and ultimately useful route is between Luang Prabang and Hanoi via the famous battleground of Dien Bien Phu in northwestern Vietnam. This intriguing land crossing would allow you to transit the entire length of Vietnam without having to backtrack or skip a large portion of the country—a complete circuit of Indochina from Nong Khai to Laos and northern Vietnam, including the vast length of coastal Vietnam. As of this writing, this border crossing remains closed but may open in the near future.

From China

Highway 1 from Hanoi to southern China opened to Western travelers several years ago and it's now possible to travel between the two countries with the proper visas and endorsements. Most travelers take the four-hour train ride from Nanning, capital of Guangxi Province, to the border crossing at Dong Dang, also known as "Friendship Gate." After border formalities, the train continues to Lang Son in Vietnam and then southwest to Hanoi. To enter Vietnam via this route, you'll need a Vietnamese visa marked Huu Nghi Quan (Friendship Gate).

Another train service connects Kunming (Yunnan Province) with Hanoi via border crossings at Hekou in China and Lao Cai in Vietnam.

GETTING AROUND

Getting around Vietnam can be frustrating and time-consuming due to the sad state of the roads

SAMPLE TRAVEL TIMES BY BUS

Saigon-Nha Trang.	12 hours
Nha Trang-Danang	12 hours
Danang-Hue.	3 hours
Hue-Vinh	14 hours
Vinh-Hanoi.	14 hours

and the disorganized condition of buses and trains. Another problem is the government bureaucracy, which remains suspicious about Westerners freely wandering around the country. Bring along plenty of patience.

Fortunately, Vietnam has an extensive bus network which reaches every accessible corner of the country, and a dependable—if slow—train service from Saigon to Hanoi. Vietnam Airlines is the quickest way to get around, though routes are limited to major towns and flights are often booked weeks in advance.

By Air

Vietnam Airlines and Pacific Airlines operate daily flights between Saigon and Hanoi with stops in Danang. Most of the smaller destinations are only served once or twice weekly—a big problem for visitors with limited time. For example, Vietnam Airlines flies once weekly from Saigon to Dalat, Hue, Nha Trang, and Qhi Nhon. From Hanoi, Vietnam Airlines flies once weekly to Dien Bien Phu, Dalat, Hue, Nha Trang, Pleiku, and Vinh.

Reservations should be made as soon as you arrive in Vietnam and reconfirmed within 48 hours of departure. Tickets are payable in U.S. dollars, but traveler's checks are sometimes accepted. Overbooked flights are common, though cancellations and no-shows allow most travelers to sign the waiting list and make their flight. Flights generally leave mornings before 0700.

Pacific Airlines, a new service inaugurated in 1993, flies many of the same routes as Vietnam Airlines at the same price, but with better planes and better service.

By Bus

Buses and minibuses serve most major destinations in Vietnam. Service is slow since less than 20% of the nation's roads are surfaced and many of the bridges destroyed during the war are still down. Be prepared for breakdowns and impromptu stops for engine repairs. On the other hand, overland travel is the best way to see the country and experience Vietnam off the beaten track.

The best roads are in the south, while those in the north are dismal to nonexistent. For this reason, many travelers take a bus from Saigon to Danang or Hue and continue by train up to Hanoi.

Bus stations are usually located on the outskirts of town and departures are in the early-morning hours from 0400 to 0600. Minibuses with reserved seating and a/c now serve many of the more important destinations. Advance booking of express buses and minibuses is recommended whenever possible. Prices are low despite the fact that foreign tourists are sometimes charged an extra fee over local rates.

See the "Sample Travel Times by Bus" chart for an idea of what to expect.

By Train

The Reunification Express, connecting Saigon to Hanoi, is a slow, crowded service that passes through some of the best scenery in the region.

Choices include ordinary trains, which have hard wooden benches and take 68 hours, express trains (TN2 and TN4), which have padded couchettes and take 58 hours, and a so-called special express (TBN8), which covers the 1,730 kilometers in about 48 hours, provided the train isn't derailed or struck by a typhoon.

Train travel is an outstanding way to go, but fares are not cheap, since Western visitors are charged about four times the official rate. This makes train travel almost as expensive as air transport. For example, Saigon to Hanoi on the express a/c train with soft sleeper costs US$150 while the airfare is US$175.

Some travelers have reportedly been able to buy train tickets at Vietnamese rates with the aid of local contacts. A student ID purchased in Bangkok may also help obtain lower rates.

Car Rental

Cars with drivers are a sensible option for groups who wish to travel from Saigon to Hanoi in relative comfort. Cars rented from Vietnam Tourism are very expensive, but from smaller outfits in Saigon the cost can be quite reasonable. For example, a seven-day tour of South Vietnam and the Central Highlands costs US$350-450, while a 16-day journey from Saigon to Hanoi is US$500-650. Split among four travelers this is a great way to explore the country. Guesthouses in Saigon can locate the cheaper car-rental agencies.

Local Transportation

Local transportation in major cities is provided by old Russian Volga taxis, tricycles known as cy-clos which cost about US$.50 per hour, and bi-cycles rented from guesthouses and rental shops.

Travel Tips

Independent travel is now permitted in Vietnam despite the usual hassles with internal transportation and obtaining services at local, not tourist, rates. The rule that all visitors must enter on a group tour was dropped several years ago. Today, most travelers pick up their visa and air tickets from a budget travel agency on Khao San Road in Bangkok and are on their way within a few days.

The most popular package sold by travel agents includes a Vietnamese visa, an air ticket to Saigon, overland transport to Hanoi, and a flight to Vientiane, all for about US$350. Those who wish to include Cambodia can fly to Siem Reap or Phnom Penh and then continue overland to Saigon.

The Vietnamese actually love independent travelers, viewing them as easy sources of extra cash through penalties, permits, and all sorts of fines. The vagueness of Vietnamese laws regarding tourism and the poverty of most government officials has created a cottage industry of ongoing fines and bribes.

Visitors should not uniformly accept these shakedowns. Keep calm and smile, insist on your innocence, and ask for a reduction in the fine. Most fines in the US$45-200 range can be talked down to US$10-20, a sizable sum in a country where the average monthly income is just US$15.

TRAVEL PRACTICALITIES

Visas

All visitors to Vietnam must have a visa—arranged by travel agents or tour operators, or obtained directly from a Vietnamese embassy. Visas are good for 30 days and cost US$50-100, depending on the travel agency or whether you obtain your visa directly from a Vietnamese diplomatic office.

Note that your visa will show both the anticipated date of entry and anticipated date of exit from Vietnam. If your plans change and you arrive late in Vietnam, you will forfeit any missed days—so plan carefully.

VIETNAM

The Vietnamese Embassy in Bangkok at 83/1 Wireless Rd., tel. 251-7201, grants visas during office hours, 0830-1100 and 1300-1600. Other Vietnamese diplomatic offices are located in Phnom Penh, London, Paris, Berlin, Jakarta, Rome, Tokyo, Vientiane, Kuala Lumpur, and Manila.

Visas should be obtained on photocopies of your passport rather than stamped directly into your passport. This allows you to deposit a photocopy rather than your original passport with hotel managers and other entities requiring proof of legal entry. When you apply for your visa in Bangkok or Hong Kong, give the travel agency several photocopies of your passport, not the original document.

Allow 2-3 weeks to obtain a visa in the U.S. or Australia and 3-5 days in Bangkok and Hong Kong. Travel agencies and tour operators in all these countries can quickly obtain visas for a reasonable service charge.

Recent reports indicate that visas are *sometimes* granted on arrival at the Saigon airport. This formality should be confirmed with a Vietnamese diplomatic office prior to departure for Vietnam.

Visa Extensions

Visas can sometimes be extended at immigration police offices in Saigon, Hanoi, and other larger towns. Technically, visa extensions are only granted with the purchase of a tour, though travel agents in Saigon and Hanoi are able to work around this rule. Many of the budget guesthouses in Vietnam are now affiliated with travel agencies that obtain visa extensions at reasonable cost—a sensible option which avoids much of the bureaucratic red tape which strangles the Vietnamese tourist industry.

Two-week extensions cost US$20-30 and the process can usually be repeated several times for a total travel time of up to two months.

It is advisable to bring along six passport-size photos and make several photocopies of your visa, passport, and entry/exit card to show—and leave—with immigration officials and police. Whenever possible, hand over these photocopies rather than the original documents; Vietnamese officials often hold passports in an attempt to extort extra payments from tourists.

The government policy on visa extensions seems to change at random; extensions are gleefully granted one year and forbidden the next.

Entry and Exit Stamps

Vietnamese visas include your points of entry and exit, usually the airports in Saigon or Hanoi. Travelers intending to enter or exit the country overland from Cambodia, Laos, or China should be sure to obtain the correct entry and exit stamps at the Foreign Ministry offices in Saigon and Hanoi if they decide to change travel itineraries after arrival in Vietnam.

Airport Arrival and Customs

All visitors must fill in a detailed customs report which must be shown to customs officials when they leave the country. Customs forms and currency declarations are rarely checked on departure, but it's a good idea to keep currency-exchange receipts and other records in order. Also see "Changing Money."

Photographers should note that the X-ray machines in Vietnam are antiquated and all film should be hand-carried through customs. The same rule applies on departure.

Internal Travel Permits

Foreigners in Vietnam are no longer required to obtain internal travel permits. This restriction was dropped in early 1993, after complaints by potential investors trying to check out Vietnam's emerging economy, and due to the fact that almost nobody was checking these permits.

Visitors, however, are barred from some border districts, military zones, and other areas deemed sensitive by the government. Local police sometimes require travel permits to visit certain minority villages around Dalat, Pleiku, and the Demilitarized Zone (DMZ).

Tourist Information

State-run tourist offices are located in nearly every major destination but they essentially serve to sell organized tours to wealthy tourists rather than offer any assistance to independent travelers. Provincial tourism offices located outside the main towns can sometimes help with travel arrangements but are more anxious to sell you an overpriced tour.

MONEY

The unit of currency is the *dong*, though the U.S. dollar is widely accepted throughout the country.

American dollars, most European currencies, and traveler's checks can be exchanged at banks, hotels, shops, and money vendors who work on the streets of Saigon and Hanoi. There is no currency black market in Vietnam. Black-market rates quoted by independent vendors may appear tempting, but not worth the risk due to rip-offs and possible legal consequences.

Changing Money

Exchange rates have risen dramatically from 900 *dong* per dollar in 1989 to over 12,000 *dong* in recent years. Vietnam's steep inflation rate hardly affects Western visitors since most hotels, guides, and taxi drivers in major tourist destinations quote their rates in dollars and not *dong*. On the other hand, *dong* are the accepted form of currency outside Saigon and Hanoi, where it can be difficult or impossible to exchange traveler's checks. This chapter quotes rates in dollars to sidestep problems with the declining *dong*.

Receipts should be retained for reexchange on departure from Vietnam and to satisfy customs officials who sometimes check currency-declaration forms.

Reexchange may be impossible at the airport; spend *all* your *dong* prior to departure. One strategy is to bring along a handful of American dollars and cover any shortages with traveler's checks.

Credit Cards

Visa and MasterCard are accepted by larger hotels and restaurants in Vietnam. Cash advances on Visa cards can be obtained from Vietcombanks in Saigon and Hanoi at a four percent service charge.

Costs

On a local level, Vietnam is one of the best travel bargains in Asia. Budget travelers who can obtain local rates can easily travel for under US$15 per day, including hotels, food, and transportation.

Unfortunately, tourist prices in Vietnam are linked to what the traffic will bear. For example, a hotel room in Saigon that costs US$20 for the Western visitor costs a Vietnamese just US$3, a US$90 plane ticket sold to a Westerner costs just US$30 for a Vietnamese citizen, and train tickets for Westerners are subject to a 400% tourist tax. Essentially, you will be overcharged for almost everything you buy.

The Vietnamese government has a no-apologies policy of grabbing as much Western money as possible. This rip-off mentality also applies to private citizens who feel justified charging up to 10 times the local rate to wealthy Western visitors. And since few prices are written down outside the main tourist centers, a journey through Vietnam quickly becomes an adventure in trying to guess and obtain the local rate.

No matter the length of your journey, it's important to negotiate and set prices before ordering meals or venturing forth on a cyclo or in a taxi. Written agreements regarding prices and services often prevent misunderstandings.

Accepting the unfair prices charged throughout Vietnam will only perpetuate the situation and make it more difficult for the next traveler to obtain local prices. Both tourists and travelers should attempt to pay local prices while realizing that modest surcharges are inevitable throughout Vietnam.

OTHER PRACTICALITIES

Health

Vaccinations are not required for entry to Vietnam, but immunizations against cholera, hepatitis, typhoid, tetanus, and polio are recommended. The most serious health risk is malaria, which remains widespread outside the major cities. Malaria tablets such as Mefloquine or Halfan are recommended for anyone venturing off the beaten track.

Food is relatively safe, but drink only bottled water or soft drinks.

AIDS is a major problem among the estimated 10,000 prostitutes in Saigon and the government-supervised brothels in Hanoi.

Time

Vietnam is seven hours ahead of Greenwich Mean Time. Noon in Vietnam is 0100 in New York, 2200 in San Francisco, 0500 in London, and 1500 in Sydney.

Government Hours
Government offices are open Mon.-Fri. 0800-1200 and 1300-1630. Banks are open the same hours, plus Saturdays 0800-1200. Museums are open Tues.-Sun. 0900-1200 and 1300-1630.

Telecommunications
International calls and faxes are best made from the better hotels in Saigon and Hanoi. Calls can also be made from general post offices, but delays are common and connections can be poor. All calls must be made as collect calls, which cost US$3-4 per minute and a hefty deposit must be left with the cashier prior to attempting any international call. Vietnamese operators routinely charge Westerners for wrong numbers and disconnects—an infuriating practice.

Vietnam's international access code is 84.

Crime
Vietnam is a very poor country with more than its fair share of beggars, pickpockets, and con artists. Drive-by thieves on motorcycles and bag snatchers in trains are also common. Although Vietnam is actually much safer than your hometown and armed robbery is virtually unheard of, anyone who leaves bags unattended at the train or bus station should kiss them good-bye. Whenever possible, valuables should be stored in hotel safe-deposit boxes.

Don't trust strangers with stories about inexpensive gems, rare antiques, old Zippos, and other collectibles that will fetch great prices back home. *All* are fakes.

SOUTH VIETNAM
HO CHI MINH CITY (SAIGON)

Ho Chi Minh City (HCMC)—Saigon until 1975—is the heart and soul of the new Vietnam, the economic engine that drives the rest of the country. Visitors expecting to discover a sleepy colonial relic or Vietnam War leftover will find Saigon a complete surprise. This is a city on the *move*—one of the most energetic and madcap destinations in Southeast Asia.

Saigon offers plenty of formal attractions, from French-colonial architecture to ancient pagodas, but the chief interests in this city of four million are the sharp contrasts between East and West, and the all-encompassing love of *song voi*, or living quickly. Flashy discos, cafes serving angel-hair pasta, and armies of cruising motorcycles are the essential experiences of Saigon, not the socialist ideology of the north.

Saigon is also a place where you must clear your mind of all preconceptions. First, Americans need fear nothing aside from the incessant curiosity and overwhelming goodwill offered by almost every resident of the city. There is nothing to fear from government officials and local denizens who, at times, seem to love the foreign visitor more than their rulers in the north. Saigon has a mind-frame far removed from hardship and war: this vibrant city is among the most peaceful yet exciting in the East.

There are problems, of course: decaying hotels, dismal restaurants, and an ungodly number of beggars working the streets. And yet, despite these hassles and headaches, Saigon remains a completely sassy town, where girls flounce around in lovely *ao dais*—the traditional tight-fitting dress unequaled throughout the East—where young kids shout "Hello Mister You American?" and where the black market continues to flourish as strongly as it did back in 1968. Here in Saigon, everyone is on the make and on the take.

Hold on to your wallet. Saigon is a very *wild* place.

ATTRACTIONS IN CENTRAL SAIGON

Saigon is divided into 12 districts, including the central *quan* of Saigon which gives the metropolis its name. The following list of sights is grouped into three sections: "Central Saigon," "Cholon" (the Chinese district), and "Around Saigon."

A walking tour of central Saigon can be completed in a single day starting from the Saigon Floating Hotel. Cyclos are unnecessary but a rented bicycle is a great way to reach the attractions listed below under "Attractions Around Saigon."

Saigon River
Across from the floating hotel (towed from Australia) is a statue honoring Tran Hung Dao, a Vietnamese general who opposed the Mongol invasion of Kublai Khan in the 13th century.

Ferries across to several popular floating restaurants leave from piers just south of the hotel.

Dong Khoi Street
Dong Khoi (Simultaneous Uprising) St.—the Fifth Avenue of Saigon—was called Rue Catinat during the French era and Tu Do (Freedom) St. during the Vietnam conflict, when it served as a nightclub and brothel area for American soldiers. Shaded by large trees, the boulevard has many grand old sites such as the renovated Majestic Hotel (renamed the Cuu Long), Maxim's Restaurant, Caravelle Hotel (Doc Lap), which once operated as the U.S. press-corps headquarters, and Continental Hotel, constructed in 1885 during the belle époque days and a star of the French film *Indochine*.

The street also has an inordinate number of beggars, con artists, wheelers and dealers, pickpockets, Amerasian hustlers, transvestites, and other varieties of shamsters. Be careful.

(continues on page 960)

VIETNAM

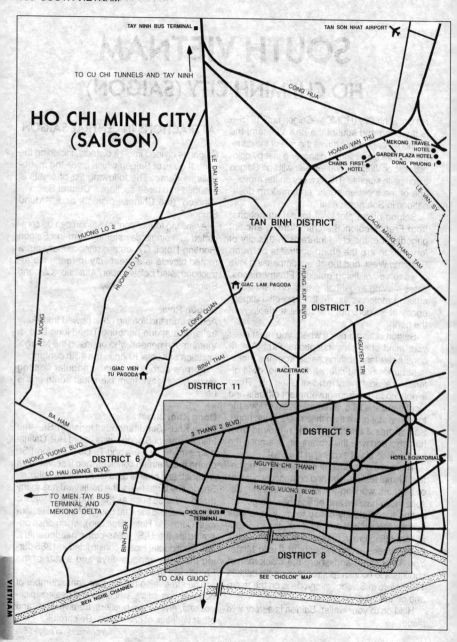

HO CHI MINH CITY (SAIGON)

TAY NINH BUS TERMINAL

TAN SON NHAT AIRPORT

TO CU CHI TUNNELS AND TAY NINH

CONG HUA

HOANG VAN THU

MEKONG TRAVEL HOTEL
GARDEN PLAZA HOTEL
CHAINS FIRST HOTEL
DONG PHUONG

LE VAN SY

LE DAI HANH

CACH MANG THANG TAM

HUONG LO 2

TAN BINH DISTRICT

THUNG KIAT BLVD.

HUONG LO 14

GIAC LAM PAGODA

DISTRICT 10

AN VUONG

LAC LONG QUAN

GIAC VIEN TU PAGODA

BINH THAI

NGUYEN TRI

DISTRICT 11

RACETRACK

BA HAM

3 THANG 2 BLVD.

DISTRICT 5

HUONG VUONG BLVD.

DISTRICT 6

HOTEL EQUATORIAL

LO HAU GIANG BLVD.

NGUYEN CHI THANH

TO MIEN TAY BUS TERMINAL AND MEKONG DELTA

HUONG VUONG BLVD.

BINH TIEN

CHOLON BUS TERMINAL

DISTRICT 8

SEE "CHOLON" MAP

TO CAN GIUOC

BEN NGHE CHANNEL

VIETNAM

© MOON PUBLICATIONS, INC.

NO TRANG LONG

NGUYEN THAI SON

NGUYEN KIEM

MIEN DONG
BUS TERMINAL

QUOC LO 13

TAN SON NHAT
HOTEL

DAI GIAC
PAGODA

SAIGON OMNI HOTEL

LONDON
HOTEL

LAMBRO
STATION

PHAN DANG LUU

BINH THANH DISTRICT

XO VIET NGHE TINH

DIEN BIEN PHU

NGUYEN VAN TROI

LE VAN DUYET
TEMPLE

THI NGHE CHANNEL

VINH NGHIEM PAGODA

TRAN HUNG
DAO TEMPLE

JADE EMPEROR
PAGODA

TO VUNG TAU AND
THE NORTH

SAIGON LODGE

DISTRICT 3

TRAIN STATION

CAMBODIAN
CONSULATE

HISTORY
MUSEUM

ZOO

VO THI SAU

DIEN BIEN PHU

VIETNAM AIRLINES
DOMESTIC BOOKING

XA LOI
PAGODA

WAR CRIMES
MUSEUM

DISTRICT 1

THICH QUANG
DUC SHRINE

EMPEROR

SAIGON
STAR

VAN HOA PARK

NGUYEN DINH CHIEU

NGUYEN THI MINH KHAI

IMMIGRATION POLICE

HOANG GIA

NGUYEN TRAI

PHAM NGU LAO

SEE "PHAM NGU LAO AREA" MAP

TRAN HUNG DAO

SEE "CENTRAL SAIGON" MAP

0   1 km

BEN NGHE CHANNEL

DISTRICT 4

SAIGON RIVER

TO DUYEN HAI

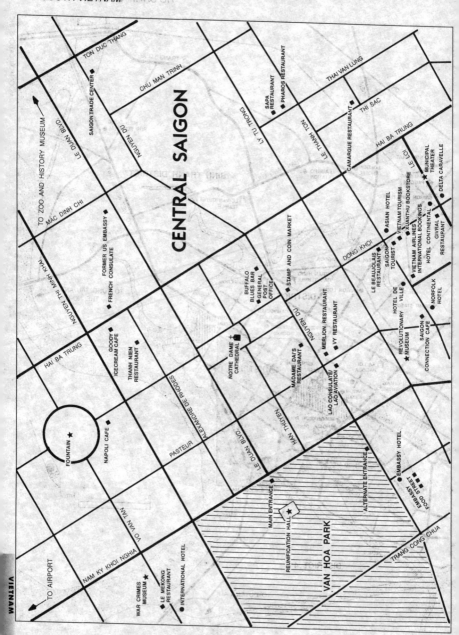

CENTRAL SAIGON

TON DUC THANG

CHU MAN TRINH

SAIGON TRADE CENTER

LE DUAN BLVD.

TO ZOO AND HISTORY MUSEUM

MAC DINH CHI

NGUYEN DU

NGUYEN THI MINH KHAI

FORMER US EMBASSY
FRENCH CONSULATE

HAI BA TRUNG

GOODY ICECREAM CAFE
THANH NIEN RESTAURANT

ALEXANDRE DE RHODES

PASTEUR

VO VAN TAN

NAPOLI CAFE

FOUNTAIN

TO AIRPORT

NAM KY KHOI NGHIA

WAR CRIMES MUSEUM
LE MEKONG RESTAURANT
INTERNATIONAL HOTEL

VIETNAM

THAI VAN LUNG

PHAROS RESTAURANT
SAPA RESTAURANT

THI SAC

LY TU TRONG

LE THANH TON

CAMARGUE RESTAURANT

HAI BA TRUNG

MUNICIPAL THEATER

DELTA CARAVELLE

LE LOI

ASIAN HOTEL
VIETNAM TOURISM
XUANTHU BOOKSTORE
SAIGON TOURIST
VIETNAM AIRLINES/INTERNATIONAL BOOKINGS
HOTEL CONTINENTAL
GIVRAL RESTAURANT

DONG KHOI

STAMP AND COIN MARKET

GENERAL POST OFFICE
BUFFALO BLUES BAR

LE BEAUJOLAIS RESTAURANT
HOTEL DE VILLE

NORFOLK HOTEL

REVOLUTIONARY MUSEUM
SAIGON CONNECTION CAFE

NGUYEN DU

MERLION RESTAURANT
VY RESTAURANT

NOTRE DAME CATHEDRAL

MADAME DAI'S RESTAURANT

HAN THUYEN

LAO CONSULATE/LAO AVIATION

LE DUAN BLVD.

ALTERNATE ENTRANCE

MAIN ENTRANCE

EMBASSY HOTEL

EMBASSY FOOD STREET

REUNIFICATION HALL

VAN HOA PARK

TRANG CONG CHUA

© MOON PUBLICATIONS, INC.

This is a map of Ho Chi Minh City (Saigon) with the following labeled locations:

River/Water features:
- SAIGON RIVER
- BEN NGHE CHANNEL

Ferry/Boats:
- CROSS RIVER FERRY
- HYDROFOIL TO VUNGTAU
- MEKONG DELTA BOATS
- RENTAL BOATS AND BOATS TO CHOLON
- FLOATING RESTAURANTS

Hotels:
- SAIGON HOTEL
- APOCALYPSE NOW
- BACH DANG HOTEL
- RAMADA SAIGON HOTEL
- RIVERSIDE HOTEL
- HUONG SEN
- DONG KHOI HOTEL
- HOTEL MAJESTIC
- SAIGON PRINCE HOTEL
- CENTURY SAIGON HOTEL
- PALACE HOTEL
- REX HOTEL
- SOUTH HAI VAN HOTEL
- CHAMPAGNE HOTEL
- VAN CANH HOTEL
- ART MUSEUM HOTEL
- NEW WORLD HOTEL

Restaurants/Cafes:
- HARD ROCK CAFE
- KIM LONG
- VIETNAM HOUSE
- JARDINE HOUSE
- CITY BAR AND GRILL
- MAXIM'S THEATER/RESTAURANT
- RESTAURANT 13
- RESTAURANT 19
- BRODARD RESTAURANT
- BONG SEN
- MONDIAL RESTAURANT
- LEMONGRASS
- SANTA LUCIA RESTAURANT
- TIN NGHIA VEGETARIAN RESTAURANT
- PHUC LAM MON RESTAURANT

Banks:
- KRUNG THAI BANK
- THAI MILITARY BANK
- VIETCOMBANK

Other:
- STATUE
- CUSTOMS HOUSE
- POST OFFICE
- PANI HINDU TEMPLE
- KIM DO INTERNATIONAL
- SAIGON MINIMART
- KEM BACH DANG
- HO CHI MINH MUSEUM
- BEN THANH MARKET
- BEN THANH BUS TERMINAL
- MARIAMMAN HINDU TEMPLE
- TO GUESTHOUSES
- ARMY SURPLUS MARKET
- PHUNG SON TU PAGODA

Streets:
- TON DUC THANG
- DONG KHOI
- DONG DU
- NGUYEN THIEP
- NGUYEN HUE
- MAC THI BUOI
- TON KHANH
- THI SACH
- HUYNH THUC KHANG
- PASTEUR
- NAM KY KHOI NGHIA
- NGUYEN CONG TRU
- PHO DUC CHINH
- BEN CHUONG DUONG
- NGUYEN TRUNG TRUC
- LE LOI
- CALMETTE
- NGUYEN THAI BINH
- KY CON
- YERSIN
- TRAN HUNG DAO
- PHAM NGU LAO
- LE LAI
- LE THANH TON
- LY TU TRONG
- TRUONG DINH
- THAM
- THO

VIETNAM

The nearby Rex Hotel (Ben Thanh), another old favorite of war correspondents and U.S. officers, offers good city views and cold beer from the terrace on the fifth floor.

City Center

Municipal Theater: This French-era building was once home to the South Vietnamese National Assembly but now functions as a concert hall. Nightly shows (2000-midnight) run the gamut from Vietnamese theater and local acrobats to contemporary dance and cabaret.

City Hall: Constructed from 1901 to 1908 as the Hotel de Ville, this gingerbread yellow-and-white building now serves as the headquarters of the Ho Chi Minh City People's Committee.

Notre Dame Cathedral: Erected between 1877 and 1880 in a grassy central square, Notre Dame has survived a great deal of history to become one of Saigon's most famous landmarks. Masses are held weekday mornings and Sundays at 1600 and 1800.

The adjacent **General Post Office** was completed in 1888.

Revolutionary Museum

Once known as the Gia Long Palace, this neoclassical building currently houses a permanent collection of memorabilia devoted to the national struggle for unification. The building is connected to the Reunification Hall by a network of underground concrete bunkers.

Reunification Hall

Originally the residence of the French governor-general and later the presidential palace of Diem, this reconstructed administrative center is where Viet Cong tanks crashed through the iron gates on 30 April 1975 to end the American experience in Vietnam.

Guided tours visit the banquet room, state chambers, cabinet hall, underground command post, and reception rooms on the upper floors. The hall is open daily except Sunday afternoons, 0800-1000 and 1300-1600.

War Crimes Museum

Constructed on the site of the old U.S. Information Service Office of Saigon University, Saigon's most famous Vietnam War-era sight includes replicas of the infamous "tiger cages" from Poulo Condo Island, American tanks and helicopters, displays on the massacre at My Lai, grisly photos of the effects of napalm and Agent Orange, a guillotine used by the French to execute South Vietnamese dissidents, and some crudely rationalized propaganda. Now called the War Remnants Museum, this is a place for strong stomachs and a sense of historical judgment.

The museum is open Tues.-Sun. 0730-1145 and 1330-1645.

U.S. Embassy

Several former embassies are situated a few blocks north of the cathedral.

Top draw is the former U.S. Embassy, chiefly remembered as the site of frantic rooftop helicopter evacuations and the dramatic finale to the Vietnam War on 30 April 1975. Today, the building contains the offices of Vietnam's State Petroleum Authority and the grounds are frequently cleaned for American and European film crews working on *Rambo*-like epics.

Visitors are admitted through a side door, though there's little to see except for a plaque which commemorates the Tet Offensive of 1968 and the decisive events of 1975.

Military Museum and History Museum

Le Duan Boulevard leads to the Military Museum, with tanks and planes in the front compound, and the History Museum (former National Museum), filled with an outstanding range of artifacts which illustrate the evolution of Vietnamese culture. The Military Museum is disappointing but the History Museum is highly recommended for its extensive collection of Dong Son, Funan, Cham, Khmer, and Vietnamese relics.

Both museums are open Tues.-Sun. 0800-1100 and 1300-1600.

Xa Loi Pagoda

Saigon's best pagodas (temples) are in Cholon, though this modern pagoda on Ba Huyen Thah Quan St. played an important role in the history of the Vietnam War. It was here, on 11 June 1963, that a Buddhist monk named Thich Quang Du from Hue assumed the lotus position, poured gasoline over himself, and committed suicide through self-immolation. The unforgettable image made front-page headlines around the world, electrified the American public, and signaled the beginning of the end for the Diem regime.

The Austin car which transported the monk to Saigon is now displayed in a pagoda in Hue.

Ben Thanh Market
Saigon's Cho Ben Thanh—once the main railway terminal—is the largest and most popular of some 35 markets throughout the city. The market was constructed in 1914 by the French as Halles Centrales and renovated several years ago by city officials, though the clock remains permanently fixed at half past one. Inside you'll find a surprising range of imported goods from Japanese televisions to French perfumes, plus excellent foodstalls and souvenir shops.

Phung Song Tu Temple
A small but attractive temple constructed shortly after WW II by Fukien Chinese to honor Ong Bon, guardian spirit of happiness and virtue. Highlights include the wonderfully illustrated doors and multiarmed image of Kwan Yin, Buddhist goddess of mercy.

Dan Sinh Market
Just around the corner from Phung Song Tu Temple on Nguyen Con Tru St. is an informal market which specializes in American, Chinese, and Russian war surplus, such as dog tags and military hardware. Most of the goods are fake, though authentic memorabilia occasionally passes through the market. Buy with caution.

ATTRACTIONS IN CHOLON

Cholon, Saigon's Chinatown, is home to some half-million Vietnamese of Chinese descent who live and work in the liveliest section of town. Cholon ("Big Market") offers a large number of unique pagodas, superb restaurants, plenty of hotels, and excellent shopping in a half-dozen markets.

The following walking tour takes a half day. The second attraction described below—a temple in the northwest section of Cholon—is worthwhile for temple aficionados but can otherwise be skipped to save time.

Markets: An excellent place to start any tour of Chinatown is in colorful and vibrant **Binh Tay Market** near the Cholon bus terminal. Binh Tay

essentially serves as a wholesale marketplace filled with fruits and vegetables imported from the Mekong River delta. Bring your camera and plenty of film.

Another market worth visiting (exact location unknown) is the very modern **An Duong Market.** Constructed by Chinese investors to signal the return of Chinese power, the shopping emporium is a wonderful place to watch Vietnamese schoolgirls, hand in hand in their pure white *ao dais*, take their first thrilling ride up Vietnam's only functioning escalator.

Khanh Van Nam Vien Pagoda: Constructed by the Cantonese from 1939 to 1942, this is one of the few temples in Vietnam dedicated to Taoism and Lao Tse, its founder. Aside from the usual collection of Chinese deities, the temple features several yin-yang emblems and graphic instructions on breathing exercises and proper diet. Services are held mornings from 0800 to 0900.

Cha Tam Church: Constructed around the turn of the century, Cha Tam (Van Lang) is chiefly noted as the final refuge of President Diem and his brother Nhu, who fled the Presidential Palace during a coup attempt in 1963. The pair negotiated their surrender at the church but were quickly murdered by soldiers on the ride back to the palace. News of the assassination was welcomed by the military, religious leaders, and most citizens of Saigon, who considered Diem a dangerous and deranged despot, better dead than red.

Quan Am Pagoda: Constructed by Fukien Chinese in the early 19th century and dedicated to the goddess of purity and motherhood, Quan Am is among the oldest and most artful temples in the city. Noteworthy features include the traditional ceramic figurines mounted on the roof, front doors decorated with golden lacquered panels, and a broad array of images drawn from Taoist and Buddhist mythologies.

Phuoc An Hoi Quan Pagoda: Another temple erected by the Fukiens and considered one of the most beautifully decorated in Saigon. Dedicated to Quan Cong, a deified Chinese general closely associated with his sacred red horse, the temple is noted for its ceramic rooftop decorations and profuse use of carved wood and gilded figurines.

Thien Hau Pagoda: Constructed by the Cantonese from 1825 to 1830 and among the most

VIETNAM

CHOLON

NOT TO SCALE

© MOON PUBLICATIONS, INC.

VIETNAM

TO CENTRAL
SAIGON

CHOLON HOTEL
CHOLON
TOURIST
MINIHOTEL

SU VAN HANH

TRAN PHU BLVD

AN DONG MARKET

HUNG VUONG BLVD

TO CENTRAL
SAIGON

TRAN HUNG DAO BLVD.

TOKYO HOTEL

NGUYEN TRI PHUONG

AN DUONG VUONG BLVD

NGO GIA TU BLVD

NGUYEN TRAI

BEN HAM TU

KINH TAU HU CANAL

BA HAT

NHAT LO

VINH VIEN

HOA HAO

HANH
LONG HOTEL

NGO QUYEN

DAO DUY TU

NGUYEN KIM

HUONG VUONG BLVD

HONG BANG

NGHIA AN HOI QUAN

CROISSANTS
DE PARIS

ARC EN
CIEL

LY THUONG KIET

TAM SON
HOI QUAN

SAIGON
RACETRACK

GOLDSTAR

PHUOC AN

QUAN
AM

THIEN HAU

LE DAI HANH

CHAU VAN LIEM

PHOENIX
HOTEL

POST OFFICE

DAI LANH
THIEN CLUB

NGUYEN TRAI

KHANH VAN NAM VIEN

NGUYEN CHI THANH

3 THANG 2 BLVD.

NGUYEN THI NHO

CHA TAM
CHURCH

TRAN HUNG DAO BLVD

PHAN VAN KHOE

PHUNG
SON

TRANG TRI

HUONG VUONG

HAU GIANG BLVD

HAI THUONG LAN ON BLVD

CHOLON BUS
TERMINAL

TAY MIEN
TAY BUS
TERMINAL

BINH TAY MARKET

BEN NGHE CANAL

elaborate temples in Saigon, this enormous complex is dedicated to Thien Hau, goddess of the sea and protector of fishermen. Of special note are the rooftop friezes, considered the most complex and richly ornamented in all of Vietnam.

Tam Son Hoi Quan Pagoda: A simple and peaceful temple constructed in the 19th century by Fukien immigrants and dedicated to Chua Thai Sanh, the goddess of fertility. For this reason, the temple is chiefly visited by young women and couples who pray for children.

Nghia An Hoi Quan Pagoda: Among the excellent carvings is a magnificent golden wooden boat which hangs over the entrance and the enormous red horse of General Quan Cong on the left. Chinese believe safe journeys can be insured by praying to the horse and ringing the bell that hangs around its neck.

ATTRACTIONS NEAR SAIGON

The following sights are scattered around the perimeters of Saigon and are best reached by rented bicycle, cyclo, or taxi.

Emperor Of Jade Pagoda: Saigon's most spectacular temple was constructed around the turn of the century by Cantonese Buddhists who dedicated the colorful site to the Emperor of Jade, the supreme god of the Taoists. Inside the wildly decorated sanctuary are dozens of effigies constructed of wood and reinforced paper, which encompass almost the entire religious pantheon of Buddhism, Taoism, and Confucianism.

Among the deities is the King of Hell, the Buddha of the Future, the Goddess of Mercy, a Chinese general who defeated the Green Dragon, the God of Lightning, and of course the Emperor of Jade, flanked by his four guardians. A thick haze of incense smoke completes the surrealistic scene.

Vinh Nghiem Pagoda: The newest and largest temple in Saigon was completed in 1971 with the aid of the Japanese Friendship Association, which accounts for the vaguely Japanese flavor of the architecture. Although this pagoda lacks the historical or artistic significance of others in Saigon, it compensates with some outstanding statuary in the central chapel and on each level of the eight-story tower.

Le Van Duyet Temple: Le Van Duyet was a court eunuch and military leader credited with crushing the Tay Son rebellion in the early 19th century. This temple, dedicated to his memory, contains his tomb and his rather strange collection of memorabilia: a stuffed and moth-eaten tiger, spears, ethnic artifacts, and some of his personal effects.

Giac Vien Tu Pagoda: A Buddhist temple constructed in 1771, this pagoda is considered by many to be among the best-preserved religious sites in the country. Dedicated to the veneration of Emperor Gia Long, this lavishly decorated temple is filled to the brim with over 100 images of divinities and spirits both inspired and demonic. The cast of characters—combined with the darkness and heavy waves of smoke—make this everything you want in the mysterious East.

Giac Lam Pagoda: Giac Lam, the oldest temple in Saigon, is architecturally similar to Giac Vien Tu and perhaps temple overkill for some visitors, but it's worth the trip. Giac Lam is one of the country's purest examples of traditional Vietnamese religious construction and boasts a number of unique features: superb blue-and-white porcelain plates which decorate the roof; hardwood columns engraved with *nom* characters—the Vietnamese script used prior to the introduction of the Roman alphabet in the 17th century; and friendly monks often happy to practice their English with foreign visitors.

ACCOMMODATIONS

Hotels in Saigon include budget guesthouses, old French-colonial hotels in varying states of decay or renovation, hotels constructed during the American era, and another 15 projects scheduled to open within the next few years. Most visitors stay in central Saigon rather than in hotels near the airport or Cholon.

Many of the larger hotels are owned by Saigon Tourism or other government agencies, while smaller hotels are privately operated or joint ventures between Saigon Tourism and outside investors.

Most hotels have been renamed since the events of 1975 but are still called by their old Vietnam War-era titles. Hotel name changes include the Caravelle (new name is Doc Lap Hotel), Continental (Hai Au), Rex (Ben Thanh), Majestic (Cuu Long), Miramar (Bong Sen), Lotus

VIETNAM

(Huong Sen), Palace (Dong Khoi), Liberty (Que Huong), Champagne (Vinh Loi), and Arc En Ciel (Thien Hong) in Cholon.

Pham Ngu Lao Street

The backpackers' headquarters is along Pham Ngu Lao, Saigon's version of Bangkok's Khao San Road—a mad jumble of guesthouses, hotels, travel agencies, transportation companies, motorcycle rentals, money changers, and souvenir shops. You'll also find a rabbit warren of guesthouses on the streets to the south including Do Quang Dau, De Tham, and Bui Vien.

Many of the guesthouses are actually converted homes that post a sign that simply says Room for Rent and call themselves Guesthouse XX, with XX being the street address. Some offer dormitory beds for US$4-6 and the average budget room now costs US$8-12 with fan and US$12-20 with a/c and private bath.

Walking down Pham Ngu Lao Street from Ben Thanh Market, you'll pass Sacombank at the intersection of Nguyen Thai Hoc Street and then come to the guesthouses, mid-level hotels, cafes, and budget travel agencies scattered along the road all the way down to the Thai Binh Market. Be sure to search the alleys and streets to the south where guesthouses and hotels tend to be much quieter than along the heavy construction zone of Pham Ngu Lao.

Generally, guesthouse and hotel quality is fairly uniform within price ranges. The following are described in order as you walk down the street.

Giant Dragon Hotel: Newer hotel with better quality rooms at reasonable prices. 173 Pham Ngu Lao St., tel. 835-3268, US$30-80.

Prince (Hoang Tu) Hotel: Big old hotel and a longtime favorite of travelers. Rooms on the upper floors not served by the elevator are cheaper. 193 Pham Ngu Lao St., tel. 832-2657, US$12-40.

Thanh Thanh 2 Hotel: Simple yet popular spot and one of the few on this street still offering dorm beds. 205 Pham Ngu Lao St., tel. 832-4027, US$4-15.

Hotel 211: Budget option in business for almost a decade with both fan-cooled and a/c rooms. 211 Pham Ngu Lao St., tel. 835-2353, US$8-20.

Hoang Vu Hotel: The former backpacker's favorite is one block past the Prince Hotel and of-

fers a decent cafe, bicycle rentals, and rooms in deteriorating condition. Ask for a discount or try the better-value guesthouses down the side-streets. 265 Pham Ngu Lao St., tel. 839-6522, US$15-40.

Vien Dong Hotel: Another large hotel with over 140 rooms in various price ranges plus Chinese restaurant and karaoke lounge on the first floor. 275 Pham Ngu Lao St., tel. 839-3001, US$20-65.

Thai Binh Hotel: Somewhat run down but with 28 bargain-priced rooms and a few dorm beds. 325 Pham Ngu Lao St., tel. 839-9544, US$4-12.

My Man Mini-Hotel: Tucked away in the alley just before the Thai Binh Market. 375/20 Pham Ngu Lao St., tel. 839-6544, US$10-20.

Bui Vien Street Guesthouses

As Pham Ngu Lao Street continues to go upmarket, guesthouses continue to open to the south, chiefly along Bui Vien Street (one block south) and near Ho Co Giang Street (four blocks south, across Tran Hung Dao Street). Bui Vien Street has almost a dozen inexpensive guesthouses in the US$8-20 price range; a few also offer dorm beds for US$4-6. Guesthouse 64, Guesthouse 70, and Guesthouse 72 are three popular choices in the middle of the block.

Downtown

Most downtown hotels are in the moderate price range with a few luxury hotels near the river.

Dong Khoi Hotel: Good location in central Saigon with rooms inside the French-era hotel that are large, somewhat seedy, perhaps a/c, and with a degree of colonial atmosphere. 8 Dong Khoi St., tel. 829-4046, US$12-25.

Saigon Hotel: Facilities include two restaurants, car rentals, visa services, and a travel agency in a convenient location just opposite the mosque. 41 Dong Du St., tel. 829-9734, US$45-80.

Majestic (Cuu Long) Hotel: A waterfront hotel with swimming pool, breezy Sky Bar on the fifth floor, and 120 a/c rooms with TV and private bath. The more expensive rooms face the river while budget rooms front an inner courtyard. 1 Dong Khoi St., tel. 829-5515, US$135-360.

Bong Sen (Miramar) Hotel: A narrow six-story 85-room hotel right in the heart of central

Saigon with cheaper rooms. 117-123 Dong Khoi St., tel. 829-9744, US$30-160.

Rex (Ben Thanh) Hotel: One of Saigon's most famous hotels features a very small swimming pool on the sixth floor, restaurant and outdoor "buvette" on the fifth (check out the sculptures), and an ornately decorated reception hall with heavy furniture and pseudo-Roman columns on the ground floor. 141 Nguyen Hue, tel. 829-6043, US$80-420.

Continental (Hai Au): Venerable hotel once the favorite watering hole of foreign correspondents and diplomats stationed here during the Vietnam War. The atmosphere from Graham Greene's novel *The Quiet American* remains despite renovation years ago; featured in the film *Indochine.* 132 Dong Khoi St., tel. 829-9201, US$110-240

Saigon Floating Hotel: Formerly moored on Australia's Great Barrier Reef, this US$70-million mobile hotel has served as Saigon's chief accommodation oddity since its arrival alongside Hero Square in 1990. 1 Me Linh St., tel. 829-0783, US$220-440.

RESTAURANTS

Vietnamese cuisine offers a wide variety of fine dishes which combine the flavors of China and ingredients more typical of Thailand. Among the popular dishes are *pho,* a delicious soup of noodles and beef, *ho tieu,* another soup made with fish and aromatic herbs, and the national dish of *cha gio,* spring rolls made from crab and pork mixed with prawns and mushrooms. Other specialties include *nem chua,* fermented pork; *bo bay mon,* a seven-course Chinese beef dish; *chan chua,* tamarind soup; and *cu lao,* beef soup.

Soups and noodle dishes purchased at street stalls or in small cafes should cost well under US$2 while a full meal in a simple cafe should cost US$3-5. It is wise not to drink the water or consume ice. Bottled water and boiled tea are safer options, though few travelers seem to suffer from stomach disorders in Vietnam. Also, all prices should be checked before ordering and the final bill should be scrutinized for mysterious last-minute additions and surcharges.

Restaurant choices include hotel restaurants and a number of privately owned operations.

Rex Hotel: A great escape from the crowds with fine views over Saigon is in the fifth-floor restaurant and open-air cafe in the Rex Hotel. 141 Nguyen Hue Boulevard. Moderate.

Palace Hotel: Some of Saigon's finest panoramic views can be enjoyed from the restaurant on the 15th floor. 56 Nguyen Hue Boulevard. Moderate.

Madame Dai's: Owned and operated by one of Saigon's more famous personalities, Suzi Dai's "La Bibliothèque" serves French cuisine in her private law library, now heavy with old-world ambience. The memorable atmosphere—not to mention the personal service of the Paris-trained lawyer—compensate for the tasty but underspiced food. Ask her about cats, her now-useless law books, her antique ceramics. Conversation is best attempted in French. 84 Nguyen Du Street. Expensive.

Maxim's: Saigon's premier restaurant features a massive menu and live music in a '60s time-warp setting. The place is pricey—figure on US$15-20 per person—but most visitors consider Maxim's a worthwhile splurge. 13 Dong Khoi Street. Expensive.

Cafes

Hotel restaurants are expensive and often a bit bland, but street stalls and simple cafes are plentiful, cheap, and safe to experience despite their spartan setups. Cafes *(nha hang)* are often unnamed but simply identified by their street address, such as Nha Hang 69, or "Restaurant 69."

Pham Ngu Lao Street: Central Saigon's largest collection of foodstalls is located a few blocks west of Ben Thanh Market near the guesthouses. Inexpensive.

Apocalypse Now: Wins best prize for creativity, plus decent food and inexpensive beer. Situated just off Dong Khoi, it's the place to listen to the Doors wail about "The End" and try an Apocalypse Whiskey—bourbon and Chinese herbs mixed with a large cobra. 42 Dong Du Street. Inexpensive.

Givral Patisserie: A government-owned cafe with excellent cakes, pastries, and reasonably priced entrees just across the street from the Continental Hotel. 2 Le Loi Street. Inexpensive.

Lam Son Restaurant: A French-style cafe with both Vietnamese and European dishes at low prices. Good atmosphere. Located near the

VIETNAM

Caravelle Hotel and just across the street from the Municipal Theater. Le Loi Street. Inexpensive.

Nha Hang 95 Dong Khoi: The former Imperial Bar on former Tu Do St. is a pleasant place to relax and watch the parade while enjoying a sizzling steak and an ice-cold beer. 95 Dong Khoi Street. Moderate.

Bordard Cafe: Another time-warp cafe with '60s decor and reasonably good food in a convenient downtown location. 131 Dong Khoi Street. Moderate.

PRACTICALITIES

Tourist Information
Government-operated tourist information centers include Vietnam Tourism at 69 Nguyen Hue Boulevard and Saigon Tourist at 49 Le Thanh Ton Street. Both agencies essentially exist to book expensive tours and provide little assistance or useful information to independent travelers.

Consulates
Most European and Asian countries maintain embassies in Hanoi and consulates in Saigon. The most useful reps for independent travelers are the Cambodian Consulate at 41 Phung Khac Khoan St. and the Laotian Consulate at 181 Hai Ba Trung Street. Both offices are open Mon.-Sat. 0800-1100 and 1400-1700.

Visas for both Cambodia and Laos take about a full week to process. This formality is best completed by guesthouse owners and local travel agencies who understand the paperwork requirements and byzantine mindframes of local bureaucrats.

Money
U.S. dollars, European currencies, and traveler's checks can be cashed at the highest legal rates at the Foreign Trade Bank at 29 Ben Chuong Duong St. and at any branch of Vietcombank. Exchange facilities are also provided at most hotels, a slew of licensed foreign banks, and at legal exchange windows on Dong Khoi Street. Facilities are also found at the Saigon airport.

The official exchange rate is almost equal to black-market rates. American dollars converted on the black market bring somewhat higher

returns, but be cautious when offered outlandish rates by young men working the streets. All are con artists who pass fake *dong* or simply grab your money and run.

Post and Telecommunications
Postal and telecommunication services are available at the General Post Office across from the Notre Dame Cathedral and from the post office branch on Le Loi Boulevard. Most hotels provide the same services for modest charges.

Mail service is fairly reliable, but international phone calls are unrealistically pegged at US$12-20 for the first three minutes.

TRANSPORTATION

Travel Agencies
The problematical transportation system in Vietnam means that many travelers tour the country with the aid of a travel agency, especially one of those located in the backpacker's district along Pham Ngu Lao Street. For a quick look at the various packages, visit Linh Café at 235 Pham Ngu Lao; their all-inclusive tours from Saigon to Hanoi have been recommended by many readers.

Other travel agencies with reasonably priced tours—both local and long-distance—include Ann's Tourist at 58 Ton That Tung Street, Dalat Tourist at 21 Nguyen An Ninh Street, Kim's Café at 270 De Tham Street, and Youth Tourist Company at 292 Dien Bien Phu Street.

Airport Arrival
Saigon is 300 km from Dalat, 445 km from Nha Trang, 965 km from Danang, 1,071 km from Hue, and 1,710 km from Hanoi.

Saigon's Tan Son Nhat Airport, eight km northwest of city center, has a Vietcombank branch with exchange facilities, a post office, airline reservation offices, and Vietnam Tourism and Saigon Tourist information counters. Arriving passengers should be prepared for an inordinate amount of paperwork and remember to keep their sense of humor.

Taxis into town cost US$6-8 and can be shared among several passengers. Cyclos waiting outside the airport are a cheaper option at about US$2 but are suitable only for travelers with little baggage.

Airline Offices

The Vietnam Airlines international booking office at 116 Nguyen Hue Blvd. acts as the general sales agent for Vietnam Airlines, Lao Aviation (Hang Khong Lao), and Cambodia Civil Airlines (Hang Khong Cam Bot). The office is open Mon.-Sat. 0730-1100 and 1300-1600.

Reservations can also be made directly at the offices of Malaysian Airlines at 116 Nguyen Hue, Air France in the Caravelle Hotel, Cathay Pacific at 58 Dong Khoi, Philippine Airlines at 132 Dong Khoi, Singapore Airlines at 6 Le Loi, and Thai Airways International at 65 Nguyen Du Street.

Domestic flights can also be booked at Pacific Airlines at 177 Vo Thi Sau Street.

Getting around Saigon

Most of Saigon can be explored on foot but outlying sights can be quickly reached by cyclo or by a bicycle rented from any number of hotels or guesthouses. Cyclos charge about US$.50 per hour and bikes cost under US$2 per day. Taxi charters for up to four passengers cost US$30-45 per day.

Another option is to purchase a bicycle in Saigon, use it during your travels in Vietnam, and sell it for 70-80% of the original cost in Hanoi.

Public buses to Cholon leave from the Ben Thanh Bus Terminal near the Ben Thanh Market and from Le Loi St. just opposite the Hoang Tu Hotel. Cholon-bound buses also leave from the southern end of Nguyen Hue Blvd. near the river.

Train

The ticket office at the Saigon Railway Station is open daily 0700-1100 and 1300-1500. Tickets for the Reunification Express, which links Saigon with Hanoi, should be purchased several days in advance. Western visitors are charged five times the official rate, which makes train travel almost as expensive as, but certainly safer and more scenic than, domestic air travel.

Buses from Saigon

Saigon has several bus terminals on the outskirts of town.

Mien Tay Bus Terminal: Most buses to points south of Saigon leave from this terminal, situated 10 km west of central Saigon in a suburb called An Lac. The terminal can be reached by city bus leaving from the Ben Thanh Bus Terminal in central Saigon.

Ordinary buses to most destinations leave throughout the day until about 1600. Express buses leave twice daily at 0430 and 1500. Tickets for express buses can be purchased several hours in advance directly at the bus terminal or a day in advance by having a Vietnamese speaker call the station.

Mien Dong Bus Terminal: Most buses to points north of Saigon leave from this terminal situated six km north of downtown on National Highway 13. The terminal can be reached by cyclo or city bus from Ben Thanh Bus Terminal. Express tickets can be reserved a day in advance.

Principal destinations (and travel times): Vung Tau (three hours), Dalat (seven hours), Nha Trang (11 hours), Qui Nhon (18 hours), Pleiku (22 hours), Danang (26 hours), Hue (30 hours), and Hanoi (52 hours).

Express Minibuses: Saigon also has an increasing number of privately owned minibuses which serve all the principal tourist destinations. The office at 39 Nguyen Hue Blvd. is centrally located and very popular with independent travelers. Hotel and guesthouse owners can help find other outlets.

To Cambodia: Buses to Phnom Penh leave from 115 Nguyen Hue Blvd., adjacent to the Rex Hotel, daily at 0600 except on Sunday. Be sure you have your Cambodian visa and that your Vietnamese visa states the correct point of exit from Vietnam. Travelers whose visas state their point of exit as Saigon or Hanoi airports can change this at most Saigon travel agencies.

VIETNAM

VICINITY OF HO CHI MINH CITY

CU CHI TUNNELS

The tunnels of Cu Chi are the famous subterranean creation of the Viet Cong, used during their wars of resistance against French and American forces. The 200-km system of tunnels contained living areas, kitchens, hospitals, printing presses, munitions compounds, and underground street signs designed to help NLF forces find their way. At their greatest expansion, the tunnels stretched from downtown Saigon almost to the borders of Cambodia. When discovered by the Americans, the tunnels were gassed and bombed from above, then brazenly explored by tunnel commandos—a terrifying assignment graphically depicted in the film *Platoon*.

Today, tourists are given a short video presentation and description by local volunteers and then invited to crawl around the claustrophobic maze. Most of the tunnels are now closed and far too narrow for Western tourists, though several segments have been widened to allow passage for hefty foreigners.

Aboveground attractions include a rusting American M41 tank being eaten by weeds and a firing range where for a few dollars you can fire M-16s or AK-47s while pretending to be Rambo, the dimwitted movie idol surprisingly popular in Vietnam. Even the guides find this behavior strange.

Transportation

Cu Chi, 40 km northwest of Saigon city center, can be reached by organized tour, rental car, or public transportation, and is usually combined with a visit to the Cao Dai Cathedral in Tay Ninh. The tunnels are several kilometers outside the town of Cu Chi but are served by motorcycle taxis.

The easiest solution is to organize a party of four passengers and hire a car for the day. Car rentals cost US$30-40 per day—a sensible and cost-effective alternative to overpriced tours or creaky buses. Organized tours are an even better bargain at US$4-5 per person.

Buses to Cu Chi leave Saigon from the Mien Tay Bus Terminal in Cholon and the Tay Ninh Terminal in Tan Binh District.

An intriguing alternative is to hire a bicycle and take it on the bus to Cu Chi, riding from town to tunnels. This option gives you freedom of movement plus the opportunity to explore a bit of Vietnamese countryside.

CAO DAI CATHEDRAL

Tay Ninh, a provincial capital 95 km northwest of Saigon, is home to an indigenous and eclectic religion called Cao Dai which holds services in one of the most remarkable cathedrals anywhere in Asia.

Constructed from 1933 to 1955 in Long Hoa, a small village four km east of Tay Ninh, this rococo fantasy neatly combines Western and Eastern influences into a stunning and completely surrealistic piece of architecture. Cao Dai is Disneyland on the Mekong—a truly unique creation as intriguing as the religion itself.

The Cao Dai sect was founded in 1928 as a mystical synthesis of Confucianism, Buddhism, Taoism, Hinduism, Christianity, and Islam. Among its more esoteric beliefs is the theory that Shakespeare, Lenin, Joan of Arc, Victor Hugo, and other luminaries were Cao Dai messengers capable of communicating with the spiritual world. The equally varied architecture reflects these psychic leaps of logic.

Services are held daily at 0600, 1200, 1800, and midnight. Visitors are welcome to observe from the cathedral balcony and take photographs with permission.

Transportation

Cao Dai is usually combined as part of a visit to the Cu Chi Tunnels (above). Transportation details are listed in that section. Certainly the most convenient option is to join an organized tour arranged by one of the travelers' cafes in Saigon.

VUNG TAO

Vung Tao—the "Bay of Boats"—is a convenient beach resort 110 km southeast of Saigon. Known

VIETNAM

BOAT DOCKS

TO LONGHAI BEACH AND SAIGON

LARGE MOUNTAIN

MARKET

MADONNA AND CHILD STATUE

QUAN AM PAGODA

HUNG TANG TU PAGODA

GUESTHOUSES

BAI DAU BEACH

AIRPORT

VETERANS CLINIC

TRAN PHU

RADAR STATION

VUNG TAU

LE LOI

CAO DAI TEMPLE

LE HONG PHONG

SCHOOL HOTEL

TRUONG CONG DINH

HAISON HOTEL

SEABEE INN RESTAURANT

LIEN HOA HOTEL

KHOI NGHIA

TO PARADISE BEACH

BA CU

BUS TERMINAL

FAR EAST PEARL HOTEL

SOUTHEAST ASIA HOTEL

GPO

TRAN PHU HOTEL

BACH DINH VILLA

CAFES

NAM KY

THUY VAN HOTEL

HOAN MY HOTEL

MARKETS

HAI HA HOTEL

THUY DUONG HOTEL

QUANG TRUNG

REX HOTEL

XO VIET

KIM SON

SAMMY HOTEL

PACIFIC HOTEL

FRONT BEACH

LE LOI

PHUONG DONG HOTEL

VO THI SAU

GRAND HOTEL

PALACE HOTEL

LANG CA ONG PAGODA

HOANG HOA

THANG MUOI HOTEL

THANG MUOI RESTAURANT

NGOC BICH PAGODA

SMALL POST OFFICE

THAM

BEACH MOTEL 29

ROSE HOTEL

LING SON CON TU PAGODA

BACK BEACH

GUESTHOUSE #49/47

CUU LONG CAFE

SOUTH CHINA SEA

HYDROFOIL DOCK

HAI AU HOTEL

LIGHTHOUSE

TRI KY HOTEL

NGA NGHI 72

MY LE HOTEL

FRAVICAM RESTAURANT

QUAN AM PAGODA

SMALL MOUNTAIN

BIEN HUNG HOTEL

SAIGON HOTEL

BEAUTIFUL HOTEL

THUY VAN

HALONG

BAI DUA BEACH

NIET BAN TINH XA TEMPLE

KIM MINH HOTEL

JESUS STATUE

HON BA PAGODA

BAI TAM BEACH

0   1 km

© MOON PUBLICATIONS, INC.

VIETNAM

as Cape Saint Jacques during the French era, Vung Tao has a number of mediocre beaches, but the salty atmosphere and easy access from Saigon might make this a worthwhile escape.

The Bay of Boats is also something of a hedonist escape, with an increasing number of steam baths, massage parlors, and darkened nightclubs filled with Western tourists and city escapees.

Traveler's checks can exchanged at the Vietcombank at 27 Tran Hung Dao Boulevard. The immigration police are at the police station on Truong Cong Dinh St., two blocks back from the beach.

Beaches and Mountains

Vung Tao has four beaches of varying quality, two hills with panoramic views, and an inordinate number of pagodas and temples, few of which are particularly noteworthy.

Front Beach: Just opposite downtown Vung Tao is Bai Truoc, a narrow and silty beach hardly suitable for bathing but worth visiting in the morning to watch the local fishermen unload their catch.

Back Beach: The best stretch of sand is at the northern end of Bai Sau (Thuy Van Beach), while inexpensive bungalows and cafes flank the southern end of the eight-km beach.

Bai Dau (Mulberry Beach): A pleasant and relaxing palm-fringed spot three km north of city center with decent sand plus some of the least expensive guesthouses in Vung Tao.

Nui Nha (Small Mountain): South of downtown lies a rocky hill great for sunsets from either the 1910 lighthouse or from the enormous 30-meter figure of Jesus erected by the Americans in 1971. No, you're not in Rio de Janeiro.

Nui Lon (Large Mountain): The northern hill is circumnavigated by the 10-km Route de la Grande Corniche and capped by a radar station.

Temples and Pagodas

Vung Tao has an estimated 100 pagodas and temples, though only a handful are aesthetic or hold any historical significance.

Lang Ca Ong Pagoda: Perhaps the most intriguing is this pagoda on Hoang Hoa Tham St. across from the Linh Son Temple. Constructed in 1911, the temple is consecrated to the whale cult and contains several whale skeletons displayed in large cabinets. The whale as "Savior of Fishermen" is an ancient belief adopted from the cultures of Champa and Chela.

Niet Ban Tinh Xa Temple: Niet Ban—one of the largest Buddhist temples in Vietnam and the most celebrated shrine in Vung Tao—features a 12-meter reclining Buddha and an enormous bronze bell estimated to weigh over 5,000 kilos.

Thich Ca Phat Dai Park: A hillside park filled with Buddhist statuary and other concrete images fashioned after historical personages. Popular with Vietnamese tourists.

Accommodations

Vung Tao has plenty of hotels and beach bungalows, which are packed with Vietnamese tourists on weekends but largely deserted during the week. Most cost US$8-25 during the week but are somewhat higher on weekends.

Downtown and Front Beach: Several midrange hotels are located in the old Russian Compound, the exclusive neighborhood once the private domain of Soviet oil workers. Most charge US$25-50 depending on facilities. Budget travelers seeking less expensive rooms can check the Thang Long Hotel at 45 Thong Nhat Street where rooms cost US$10-20.

Back Beach: Back Beach has the best sand and the largest selection of beachfront bungalows in Vung Tao. Most, unfortunately, are characterless cubicles adequate only for short stays, but a few clean if somewhat expensive places are located along the northern end of the beach. Choices here include the Bimexco Beach Bungalows, Thuy Duong Hotel, and Saigon Hotel—all with rooms from US$20-40.

Less expensive options include the Beach Motel in the center of the beach with rooms from US$6-20 and the Thang Muoi Hotel with rooms from US$12-25. An enormous Taiwanese-funded resort called Fairyland—a hotel complex of 1,500 rooms, a 27-hole golf course, and a yacht marina—will radically alter the undisturbed stretches of northern Back Beach if completed sometime after the turn of the century.

Bai Dau (Mulberry) Beach: Somewhat isolated but very quiet and set with a half-dozen villas in varying states of collapse and renovation. Mulberry Beach is the cheapest, and in many ways, the most relaxing place in Vung Tao.

Rooms for US$10-25 can be found at Nha Nghi My Tho, Nha Nghi 128, Nha Nghi 29, Nha Nghi DK 142, and Nha Nghi Doan 28.

Transportation

Vung Tao is three hours southeast of Saigon. Buses leave from the Mien Dong and Van Thanh bus terminals in Saigon daily until about 1500. More convenient are the express minibuses which depart hourly from the halt on Dong Du Street near the mosque. Marriage taxis—enormous old American cars—are an alternative from Saigon.

The fastest way to reach Vung Tao is by hydrofoil; it costs US$10 and takes 80 minutes. Tickets can be purchased from the Vina Express Office on Nguyen Tat Thanh Street.

Minibuses back to Saigon leave from the square on Tran Hung Dao Blvd., from Ly Tu Trong St., and from 21 Tran Hung Dao Boulevard. The main bus station is on Nam Ky Khoi Nghia St., about 1.5 km back from the beach.

THE MEKONG DELTA

The vast alluvial delta of the Mekong River offers a great deal to the traveler: beautiful scenery, friendly people, and almost a complete lack of Western tourists. Traditionally the rice basket of not only Vietnam but many other regions in Southeast Asia, the Mekong Delta is a surprisingly prosperous area where the markets are piled high with fresh produce and the people seem satisfied with their relatively high standard of living.

Visitors can spend a few days and visit the villages nearest Saigon, such as Mytho, Vinh Long, and Cantho, or make a longer excursion to the more remote and almost completely untouched villages of Long Xuyen, Chau Doc, and Rach Gia, all located toward the Cambodian border.

Travel is best completed during the dry season from November to April. Heavy monsoons from June to October make transportation difficult though not impossible.

As banks with exchange facilities are in rare supply, visitors should bring along sufficient *dong* or American currency.

Transportation

Transportation is somewhat slow around the region due to the large number of rivers which must be crossed by ferry, but roads are in good condition and buses operate frequently between almost every possible village and hamlet. Plus the scenery is wonderful.

Buses to towns in the Mekong River Delta depart from the Mien Tay Bus Terminal in western Saigon.

Principal destinations (and travel times): Mytho (two hours), Vinh Long (three hours), Cantho (four hours), Long Xuyen (five hours), Bac Lieu (six hours), Chau Doc (six hours), Rach Gia (seven hours), and Camau (eight hours).

A relaxing alternative to the bus is the passenger ferry, which departs Saigon daily in the afternoon from the pier on Ton Duc Thang St. at the end of Ham Nghi Blvd. in Saigon. The boat reaches Mytho in 6-8 hours, Cantho in 15-18 hours, and Chau Doc on the Cambodian border in 30-36 hours.

MYTHO

Mytho (My Tho), the provincial capital of Tien Giang Province, is a small but prosperous agricultural town 71 km southwest of Saigon. A popular stop en route to the deeper delta, Mytho can also be visited on a day-trip from Saigon.

The Tien Giang Provincial Tourist Office is on Hung Vuong St. at the north end of town. Mytho has a few overpriced and poorly maintained hotels; make this a day-trip from Saigon.

Attractions

Like most towns in the Mekong Delta, Mytho has few important pagodas or historical sights, but it is situated among some of the most beautiful countryside in Vietnam. Spend your time exploring the country or taking a boat ride rather than searching for history or religion.

The Central Market and yellow-and-white Mytho Church are worth visiting, but avoid the horrid tourist traps known as Vinh Trang and Quan Thanh pagodas. Both are sad spectacles

VIETNAM

completely devoid of character or authenticity—deplorable and wretched amusement parks whose only purpose is to squeeze dollars from unfortunate victims of escorted tours.

Thirty minutes by boat from Mytho is the island of Con Phung, former home of a charismatic monk who founded a religion which fused Christianity and Buddhism. The place is now largely abandoned to the weeds and perhaps not worth the trip.

Transportation

Buses from the Mien Tay Bus Terminal in Saigon terminate at the Mytho bus halt several kilometers west of town. Minibuses and cyclos continue into town.

VINH LONG

Vinh Long is the next riverside town reached by most visitors heading through the Mekong Delta. Once a Khmer stronghold, Vinh Long later figured in the spread of Christianity throughout the delta and was the site of heavy fighting during the Vietnam conflict.

The Cuu Long Provincial Tourist Office on Thang 5 St. can help with transportation to nearby ruins and boat journeys down the Co Chien River.

The influences of Catholicism and newer sects are seen at the cathedral, the Catholic seminary, and Cao Dai church near the bridge. Most of the Mekong Delta was populated by Khmers until Vietnamese colonizers arrived to construct a network of canals in the 17th and 18th centuries. Khmer ruins are visible four km from town

adjacent to a small lake called Ba Om and south of town near the village of Tra Vinh.

CANTHO

Cantho (Can Tho), the capital of Hau Giang Province, is the largest and most commercially successful city in the Mekong Delta. The town has an airport, a busy shipping industry, and a university that conducts agricultural research.

Hau Giang Provincial Tourist Office is on Chau Van Liem St. near the southern end of the riverside market.

Sights around town include the Central Market on the banks of the Hau Giang (Bassac) River, the Vang Pagoda on Hoa Binh Ave. in the center of town, and a contemporary Khmer-Buddhist sanctuary known as Munikangsyaram Pagoda. Other activities include a visit to the Orchid Gardens northwest of town and a boat ride along the Hau Giang River.

Accommodations

As you might expect, the commercial and transportation center for the Mekong Delta has a large number of hotels in all price ranges. Huy Hoang Hotel on Ngo Duc Ke Street has decent rooms from US$8-12, while Ninh Kieu Hotel on Hai Ba Trung Street has a riverside restaurant and better rooms for US$25-40.

Transportation

Cantho is 165 km from Saigon and 32 km from Vinh Long. The bus terminal is two km northwest of town near the ferry halt. Cantho can also be reached by passenger boat from Saigon.

DALAT TO NHA TRANG

The southern third of Vietnam includes the deltas, coastline, and highlands that lie between the southernmost extension and Qui Nhon in south-central Vietnam.

The South is quite different from the North—differences which range from social and psychological to political and economic. Much of these contrasts can be attributed to the superior economic conditions in the South, its long history of foreign involvement, and its preferable climate. The North is regularly ravaged by

typhoons and has a wet, bitterly cold winter, while the South is blessed with a pleasant tropical climate more conducive to pleasure than work. In addition, the North is much more densely populated, causing serious land shortages and forcing northerners to work harder and then conserve their savings with tightfisted determination.

Furthermore, travelers and even the Vietnamese themselves report significant personality differences between the peoples. South-

VIETNAM

DALAT

TO LAT VILLAGE

TUNG LAM

TO ANCROET FALLS

VALLEY OF LOVE

DA THIEN LAKE

CHIEN THANG LAKE

TO LAKE OF SIGHS

DALAT CEMETERY

PHU DONG THIEN VUONG

NGUYEN TU LUC

MILITARY ACADAMY

NUCLEAR RESEARCH CENTER

DALAT UNIVERSITY

TO LAKE OF SIGHS 2 km

LINH SON PAGODA

GOLF CLUB

LAVY HOTEL
PENSEE 2

PENSEE 10

HUNG VUONG

FLOWER GARDENS

GOLF HOTEL

GOLF COURSE

XUAN HUONG LAKE

TO PHAN RANG (ALTERNATE ROUTE)

MAI HOC DE

HAI BAI TRUNG

GRAND LYCEE YERSIN

KS LAM VIEN

CAM LY FALLS

HOANG VAN THU

GOLF 2 HOTEL

DUY TAN HOTEL

PHAN PHUNG

POST OFFICE

SEE "DOWNTOWN DALAT" MAP

OLD RAILWAY STATION

HOANG HOA TAM

VILLA 27 RESTAURANT

TRAN HUNG DAO

GOVERNOR GENERAL'S RESIDENCE (DINH II)

LAM TY NI PAGODA

PASTEUR INSTITUTE

HANG NGA NHA NGHI SILKWEB MANSION

MINH TAM VILLA

DU SINH CHURCH

XUAN TAM HOTEL

PENSEE 3

PENSEE 6

SAVIMEX

SU NU PAGODA

BAO DAI SUMMER VILLA (DINH III)

TRUNG TAM BUS STATION

DUONG 3/4

KHE SANH

THIEN VUONG PAGODA

CABLE CAR

TO DATANLA FALLS,
PRENN FALLS,
PHAN RANG (101 km),
AND SAIGON (308 km)

20

MINH NGUYET CU SY LAM PAGODA

TRUC LAM MONASTERY

0   500 m

© MOON PUBLICATIONS, INC.

VIETNAM

erners are considered to be friendly, funny, easy-going, open-minded, and adventurous, while northerners sometimes come across as uptight, traditional, and conservative.

Although these differences sharpen as you slowly travel from Saigon north toward Hanoi, the beauty of Vietnam and the essential goodness of the people also make the journey one of the better travel experiences in Southeast Asia.

DALAT

First stop for many travelers from Saigon is the delightfully cool mountain resort of Dalat, 300 km north of the city.

Dalat was founded in the early 1920s by the French, who were enchanted with the region's temperate climate, its pine forests and waterfalls, its alpine vistas and tropical lakes. Inspired by nature and anxious to escape the searing heat of Saigon, they fashioned a romantic piece of Europe 1,500 meters above sea level, a summer retreat rife with exquisite colonial villas, blooming gardens, and broad residential streets overlooking verdant valleys.

Today, Dalat is the honeymoon capital of the South, flush with romantically named hideaways such as the Valley of Love and Lake of Sighs, filled with ducks and tiny sailboats. The region has plenty of attractions but perhaps the greatest draw is simply watching Vietnamese tourists and honeymooners carry on their lives and courtships in such an incongruous place—a taste of France in the mountains of Vietnam.

Dalat has got it all—superb scenery, pleasant climate, colonial atmosphere, cozy cafes, and a broad range of hotels and guesthouses.

Attractions in Town

Xuan Huong Lake: Dalat centerpiece created in 1919 by flooding the west end of the valley; it's now surrounded by a 64-hectare golf course, the Dalat Flower Gardens, and Palace Hotel overlooking the south end of the lake.

French Quarter: French-colonial atmosphere survives in the streets and lanes between the town square and Phan Dinh Phung St., and near the bridge spanning the Cam Ly River. French villas are also located southeast of the lake along Tran Hung Dao Street.

French Governor-general's Residence: Many French-colonial villas are owned by the Provincial Tourism Authority, which rents them to visitors, including this impressive house open for public tours daily 0730-1100 and 1330-1630.

Bao Dai Summer Palace: The 25-room summer residence of Vietnam's last Nguyen emperor, Bao Dai (reigned 1926-45), stands in a large park about two km from city center. Constructed in 1933 and designed by a French architect in the then-popular art-deco style, Dai's retreat is well preserved and worth visiting to view the period interior furnishings and watch the antics of Vietnamese tourists. Open daily 0730-1100 and 1330-1630.

Attractions Outside Town

The following sights are worth visiting if only to see how Vietnam markets its tourist attractions and the impact of clearcut logging on the once-dense forests. All can be reached by bicycle, rented motorcycle, or motorcycle taxi.

Cam Ly Falls: Three km west of downtown are some badly commercialized falls surrounded by souvenir shops and foodstalls. Waterfalls located farther afield are usually less crowded and less commercially exploited.

Valley of Love: An artificial lake formed in 1972, with horse rides and boat rentals.

Lake of Sighs: A well-named natural lake with horses, boats, and small cafes.

Tribal Villages: Dalat is centered amid a number of small villages inhabited by various animist minorities who sometimes visit the weekend market in Dalat. Local officials discourage visits to these villages, which, in most cases, are fairly Westernized and lack the allure of other more remote villages.

Budget Accommodations

Dalat has dozens of guesthouses, villas, and hotels spread across town and in the hills. Many are open to Western visitors, but may be filled on weekends when they also double their rates for tourists. Several inexpensive hotels are near the Central Market and in the old French Quarter just above the market.

Popular backpackers' guesthouses include the Mimosa Hotel II at 170 Phan Dinh Phung St., the nearby Cam Do Hotel at 81 Phan Dinh Phung Street. Both charge US$8-20 for clean

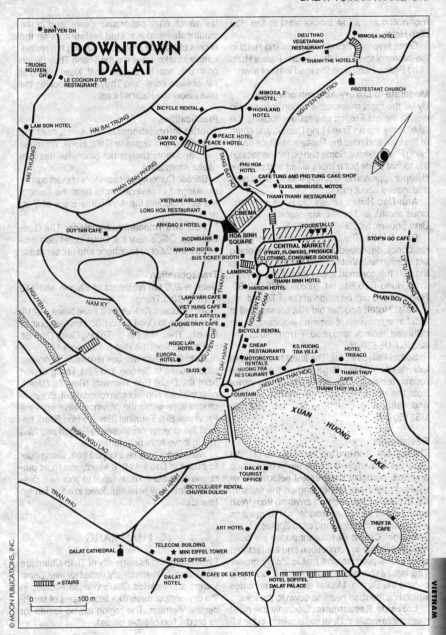

DOWNTOWN DALAT

BINH YEN GH

TRUONG NGUYEN GH

LE COCHON D'OR RESTAURANT

LAM SON HOTEL

HAI BAI TRUNG

HAI THUONG

PHAN DINH PHUNG

TANG BAT HO

CAM DO HOTEL

BICYCLE RENTAL

PEACE HOTEL

PEACE II HOTEL

DIEU THAO VEGETARIAN RESTAURANT

MIMOSA HOTEL

THANH THE HOTELS

PROTESTANT CHURCH

MIMOSA 2 HOTEL

HIGHLAND HOTEL

NGUYEN VAN TROI

PHU HOA HOTEL

CAFE TUNG AND PHO TUNG CAKE SHOP

TAXIS, MINIBUSES, MOTOS

THANH THANH RESTAURANT

VIETNAM AIRLINES

LONG HOA RESTAURANT

ANH DAO II HOTEL

DUY TAN CAFE

INCOMBANK

ANH DAO HOTEL

BUS TICKET BOOTH

CINEMA

HOA BINH SQUARE

LAMBROS

HAISON HOTEL

NAM KY

KHOI NGHIA

LANG VAN CAFE

VIET HUNG CAFE

CAFE ARTISTA

HUONG THUY CAFE

NGOC LAN HOTEL

EUROPA HOTEL

TAXIS

NGUYEN THI MINH KHAI

BICYCLE RENTAL

CHEAP RESTAURANTS

MOTORCYCLE RENTALS

HUONG TRA RESTAURANT

FOUNTAIN

LE DAI HANH

NGUYEN THAI HOC

FOODSTALLS

STOP'N GO CAFE

CENTRAL MARKET (FRUIT, FLOWERS, PRODUCE CLOTHING, CONSUMER GOODS)

THANH BINH HOTEL

LY TU TRUONG

PHAN BOI CHAU

KS HUONG TRA VILLA

HOTEL TRIXACO

THANH THUY CAFE

THANH THUY VILLA

XUAN HUONG LAKE

NGUYEN VAN CU

PHAM NGU LAO

TRAN PHU

LE DAI HANH

DALAT TOURIST OFFICE

BICYCLE/JEEP RENTAL CHUYEN DULICH

TRAN QUOC TOAN

THUY TA CAFE

ART HOTEL

TELECOM. BUILDING

MINI EIFFEL TOWER

POST OFFICE

DALAT CATHEDRAL

CAFE DE LA POSTE

HOTEL SOFITEL DALAT PALACE

DALAT HOTEL

IIIIIIIII = STAIRS

0   100 m

© MOON PUBLICATIONS, INC.

VIETNAM

rooms and are a few blocks west of the Hoa Binh Hotel.

Other favorites include the Highland Hotel in the center of town and the popular Peace Hotel I and Peace Hotel II on the road west of town.

Moderate to Luxury Accommodations

By far the most memorable option is to stay in one of the old French chalets overlooking the lake. Many are on Tran Hung Dao St. just south of the lake and near the Pasteur Institute on Le Hong Phong Street. Some can be rented through the tourist office but a more direct and possibly cheaper approach is to simply knock on the door and inquire about rooms.

Anh Dao Hotel: Lovely old hotel with spacious rooms and terrific atmosphere. 50 Hoa Binh Square, tel. 22384, US$30-55.

Dinh II Villa: The former governor-general's residence described above is quite imposing but overrun with Vietnamese tourists who romp through the common areas during the day. 12 Tran Hung Dao St., tel. 822093, US$40-80. Reservations can be made at Dalat Tourist.

Dalat Hotel: Another old villa constructed in 1907 in a convenient location adjacent to the cathedral; recently renovated. 7 Tran Phu St., tel. 822363, US$30-75.

Sofitel Palace Hotel: The finest hotel in Dalat includes two dozen large and well-appointed rooms, tennis courts, and outstanding views from the restaurant which overlooks the lake and valleys. 2 Tran Phu St., tel. 822203, US$150-395.

Restaurants

The high elevation and moderate climate of Dalat allow the cultivation of a wide range of produce and fruit, probably the greatest selection anywhere in Vietnam. Depending on the season, the market will be filled with anything from fresh strawberries to ripe avocados, not to mention persimmons, cherries, and crisp apples.

Budget Cafes: Restaurant prices are quite reasonable due to competition and the fact that most of the produce and fruit is locally grown. The least expensive options are the foodstalls behind the Central Market and the small cafes which line the road heading down to the lake.

Lakeside Restaurants: Certainly the most memorable meals in Dalat are available in the vil-

las, which offer panoramic views, and in the small cafes and elevated restaurants on the shores of Xuan Huong Lake. Among the restaurants with lake views are the Thanh Thuy on the north side near the bus terminal, Xuan Huong at the western edge, and Thuy Ta overlooking the lake below the Palace Hotel.

Practicalities

Tourist Information: Dalat Tourist, near the post office and opposite Dalat Hotel, arranges tours and rents chalets but otherwise has little useful information

Banks: Currency and traveler's checks can be exchanged at several banks near the Central Market including the Agriculture Bank of Vietnam.

Post and Telecommunications: The General Post Office near the Dalat Hotel also provides international telephone and fax services.

Transportation

Dalat is 300 km northeast of Saigon and 110 km from Nha Trang.

Air: Vietnam Airlines flies three times weekly from Saigon to Dalat Airport, 30 minutes south of the city. Their office is on Truong Cong Dinh St. just across from the Rap 3/4 Cinema.

Bus: Dalat has two bus terminals. Long-distance buses to Saigon and Nha Trang depart from the Dalat Bus Terminal (Ben Xe Dalat), near the lake and fountain roundabout. Buses to destinations within the province leave from the Provincial Bus Terminal (Ben Xe Hoa Binh), behind the cinema. Minibuses to Saigon and Nha Trang leave from both terminals.

Westerners may be stopped from taking public buses in Dalat. In that event, you must purchase a private minibus ticket to your next destination from any hotel registered to admit foreign tourists.

PHAN RANG

Phan Rang and its sister city of Thap Cham are small seaside towns chiefly visited for their Cham towers and isolated Cham villages situated in the dry, almost desertlike landscapes of south-central Vietnam. The region is also famed for its production of table grapes.

Phan Rang is a minor destination though it provides a convenient layover point between Saigon or Dalat and Nha Trang. A small tourist office is located in the Huu Nghi Hotel.

Attractions

Champa was a Hindu-influenced empire which rose around present-day Danang in the late 2nd century and expanded southward to Nha Trang and Phan Rang by the 8th century. Ruled by a series of kings who adopted Hinduism as their religion and employed Sanskrit as the court language, the Cham Empire fell in the 17th century to Vietnamese forces during their southward march toward Saigon.

Po Klang Garai Towers: Phan Rang's claims to fame are the four Cham towers constructed during the 13th century on a boulder-strewn hill some seven km west of town on the road to Dalat. The heavily renovated towers, two km beyond the village of Thap Cham, can be reached by bicycle, cyclo, or any bus heading toward Dalat. Train arrivals can see the towers from the train station in Thap Cham.

Po Ro Me Towers: Another set of Cham towers is situated 10 km south of Phan Rang and five km west of Highway 1. These brick towers were constructed by King Po Ro, the final ruler of an independent Champa, who died a prisoner of the Vietnamese in 1651.

Accommodations

Phan Rang has several hotels about 500 meters south of the main bus terminal. Huu Nghi Hotel in the center of town is convenient and has inexpensive if somewhat grotty rooms from US$10-25. More expensive but a big step up in quality is the Thong Nhat Hotel in the north end of town; refurbished rooms here go for US$35-45. The Ninh Thuan Hotel a block west of the main road also has a/c rooms with satellite TV for US$35-50.

Transportation

Phan Rang is 344 km north of Saigon, 82 km east of Dalat, and 105 km south of Nha Trang. The long-distance bus terminal, located 500 meters north of town, has regular connections with Saigon, Dalat, and Nha Trang. The local bus terminal is on the main road in the south end of town.

The nearest train station is at Thap Cham, about five km west of town. Trains take about 10 hours from Saigon.

NHA TRANG

Nha Trang, a prosperous fishing town of 250,000 people, is known for its collection of restored

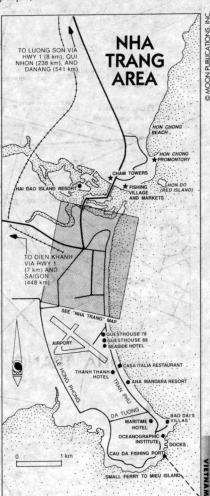

© MOON PUBLICATIONS, INC.

NHA TRANG AREA

TO LUONG SON VIA HWY 1 (8 km), QUI NHON (238 km), AND DANANG (541 km)

HON CHONG BEACH

HON CHONG PROMONTORY

CHAM TOWERS

HAI DAO ISLAND RESORT

FISHING VILLAGE AND MARKETS

HON DO (RED ISLAND)

TO DIEN KHANH VIA HWY 1 (7 km) AND SAIGON (448 km)

SEE "NHA TRANG" MAP

GUESTHOUSE 78
GUESTHOUSE 86
SEASIDE HOTEL

AIRPORT

CASA ITALIA RESTAURANT

THANH THANH HOTEL

ANA MANDARA RESORT

LE HONG PHONG

TRAN PHU

DA TUONG

BAO DAI'S VILLAS

MARITIME HOTEL

OCEANOGRAPHIC INSTITUTE

DOCKS

CAU DA FISHING PORT

0   1 km

SMALL FERRY TO MIEU ISLAND

VIETNAM

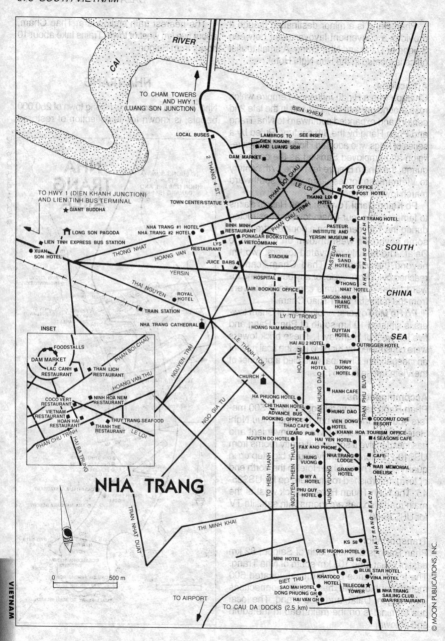

NHA TRANG

RIVER

CAI

TO CHAM TOWERS
AND HWY 1
(LUANG SON JUNCTION)

BIEN KHIEM

LOCAL BUSES

SEE INSET

LAMBROS TO
DIEN KHANH
AND LUANG SON

DAM MARKET

2 THANG 4 ST.

PHAN BOI CHAU

LE LOI

PHAN CHU TRINH

POST OFFICE
POST HOTEL

THANG LOI
HOTEL

TO HWY 1 (DIEN KHANH JUNCTION)
AND LIEN TINH BUS TERMINAL
★ GIANT BUDDHA

TOWN CENTER/STATUE ★

CAT TRANG HOTEL

PASTEUR INSTITUTE AND
YERSIN MUSEUM

NHA TRANG #1 HOTEL
NHA TRANG #2 HOTEL

BINH MINH
RESTAURANT

PONAGAR BOOKSTORE
VIETCOMBANK

LONG SON PAGODA

LIEN TINH EXPRESS BUS STATION

LYS
RESTAURANT

PASTEUR

WHITE
SAND
HOTEL

SOUTH

XUAN
SON HOTEL

THONG NHAT

HOANG VAN

JUICE BARS

STADIUM

YERSIN

HOSPITAL

THONG
NHAT HOTEL

CHINA

THAI NGUYEN

ROYAL
HOTEL

AIR BOOKING OFFICE

SAIGON-NHA
TRANG HOTEL

SEA

TRAIN STATION

NHA TRANG CATHEDRAL

LY TU TRONG

HOANG NAM MINIHOTEL

DUYTAN
HOTEL

NHA TRANG BEACH

HAI AU 2 HOTEL

OUTRIGGER HOTEL

HOA TAM

HAI
AU
HOTEL

THUY
DUONG
HOTEL

LE THANH TON

CHURCH

HANH CAFE

TRAN HUNG DAO

HA PHUONG HOTEL

CHI THANH HOTEL

ADVANCE BUS
BOOKING OFFICE

THAO CAFE

LIZARD PUB

HUNG DAO

VIEN DONG
HOTEL

COCONUT COVE
RESORT

KHANH HOA TOURISM OFFICE
4 SEASONS CAFE

NGUYEN DO HOTEL

FAX AND PHONE

HAI YEN HOTEL

NGUYEN TRAI

NGO GIA TU

NGUYEN THIEN THUAT

HUNG
VUONG

NHA TRANG
LODGE

GRAND
HOTEL

TRAN PHU BLVD.

CAFE

★ WAR MEMORIAL
OBELISK

HUNG
VUONG

MY A
HOTEL

PHU QUY
HOTEL

TO HIEN THANH

THI MINH KHAI

TRAN NHAT DUAT

KS 58

QUE HUONG HOTEL

KS 62

NHA TRANG BEACH

MINI HOTEL

BLUE STAR HOTEL

KHATOCO
HOTEL

VINA HOTEL

BIET THU

SAO MAI HOTEL

DONG PHUONG GH

HAI VAN GH

TELECOM
TOWER ★

NHA TRANG
SAILING CLUB
(BAR/RESTAURANT)

TO AIRPORT

TO CAU DA DOCKS (2.5 km)

NORTH
0   500 m

INSET

FOODSTALLS

DAM MARKET

LAC CANH
RESTAURANT

THAN LICH
RESTAURANT

PHAN BOI CHAU

HOANG VAN THU

COCO VERT
RESTAURANT

NINH HOA NEM
RESTAURANT

VIETNAM
RESTAURANT

HOAN HAI
RESTAURANT

THUY TRANG SEAFOOD

THANH THE
RESTAURANT

LE LOI

PHAN CHU TRINH

HAI BA TRUNG

© MOON PUBLICATIONS, INC.

VIETNAM

Cham towers and the six-km white-sand beach which flanks the eastern edge of the seaport.

Blessed with clean sand and beautiful waters, Nha Trang was popular during the war era with American servicemen stationed at nearby Cam Ranh Bay and later the favorite spot of Soviet sailors who occupied the sprawling naval complex until the early 1990s.

Today an increasing number of visitors are attracted to Nha Trang's long palm-fringed beach and vaguely Mediterranean flavor.

Beaches and Islands

Nha Trang's lovely beach is complemented by a half-dozen nearby islands surrounded by aquamarine, almost transparent waters, which provide some of the best scuba diving in the country. Dive operators here can take you to nearby reefs and islands such as Bamboo (Hon Tre), Ebony (Hon Mun), and Salangane (Hon Yen), a major source of bird's nests for soup and an important sportfishing area.

Po Nagar Cham Temple

Vietnam's more accessible examples of Cham architecture are the four Brahman sanctuaries which rise from a rocky hill two km north of Nha Trang, just beyond the two bridges which cross the Cai River. Flag down a bus or enjoy the walk.

The 23-meter North Tower was constructed in 817 to honor Po Nagar (Thien Yana, or "Mistress of the Kingdom"), the mythical goddess who introduced weaving and new agricultural techniques to the Chams. Today the tower enshrines a black stone image of the goddess—female counterpart to Shiva—and her associated animal. The sculpture was decapitated during the French colonial era and the original head of the statue is now displayed in the Guimet Museum in Paris.

The Central Tower, reconstructed by King Jaya Indravarman in the 12th century, contains a Hindu lingam (phallic symbol) and serves as a fertility temple for childless couples.

More statuary is exhibited in the Cham Museum of Danang.

Long Son Pagoda

A gaily decorated pagoda founded in the 19th century but heavily reconstructed in recent years, the interior sanctuary features murals depicting stories, Chinese dragons which wrap around the columns, and several finely illuminated images of the Buddha.

Behind the pagoda sits an immense white Buddha which contemplates all of Nha Trang from its elevated position. The nine-meter Buddha was constructed in 1965 to commemorate those monks who committed self-immolation and called worldwide attention to the human-rights abuses of the Diem regime.

Pasteur Institute

Nha Trang's Pasteur Institute was founded in 1895 by Dr. Alexandre Yersin, a French military doctor and noted microbiologist who had previously assisted Louis Pasteur in Paris. Credited with the introduction of rubber and quinine-producing trees to Vietnam, Yersin also discovered and then recommended that the French government construct the hill resort at Dalat.

The library on the second floor of the back wing now serves as a museum to Dr. Yersin, who was buried by request on institute land outside Nha Trang.

Vinh Van Phong Beach

The *Master Plan for the Development of Tourism in Vietnam*—a six-volume 1,000-page report financed by the United Nations—called this completely deserted beach "one of the most beautiful sea sites in Asia—of a higher quality than Phuket and comparable to the beautiful beaches in the Seychelles and even of Sierra Leone." A great recommendation despite the complete absence of tourist facilities and access by public transportation.

Vinh Van Phong is 60 km north of town. Ask the tourist office about directions and transportation.

Accommodations

Most hotels are on the beach road or in the center of town just north of the train station. Cyclo drivers at the train station and bus terminal can help find budget places during the high season when most hotels and guesthouses are fully booked.

Huu Nghi Hotel: Long time favorite for backpackers. 3 Tran Hung Dao St., tel. 826703, US$8-30.

Guesthouse 78: Great beachside location with both fan-cooled and a/c rooms. 78 Nha Khach St., tel. 826342, US$8-15.

VIETNAM

Vien Dong Hotel: Popular place with swimming pool, bicycle rentals, and budget rooms on the fourth floor. 1 Tran Hung Dao St., tel. 821506, US$20-65.

Thang Nhat Hotel: Convenient beachfront location with both inexpensive fan-cooled and moderately priced a/c rooms. 18 Tran Phu Blvd., tel. 822966, US$10-25.

Thuy Duong Hotel: Another low-priced hotel on the beach road. 36 Tran Phu St., tel. 822534, US$6-22.

Hai Yen Hotel: An upscale hotel managed by Khanh Hoa Tourism, with 106 a/c rooms, tennis courts, nightclub, and swimming pool. 40 Tran Phu St., tel. 822828, US$20-80.

Nha Trang 2 Hotel: Newly constructed and very clean hotel with spacious rooms. A 10-minute walk from the beach at 21 Le Thanh Phuong St., tel. 822956, US$12-30.

Cau Da Villa: The final word in elegance is this colonial villa constructed in the 1920s as the summer retreat of Bao Dai, final Nguyen emperor, who threw parties here until he fled to France in 1954. Also called Bao Dai Villas, today it is a capitalist retreat with a seedy but memorable French Gothic mood. Tran Phu St., tel. 881049, US$25-80.

Restaurants

Nha Trang is famous for its seafood specialties, such as locally caught lobsters, giant prawns, and horseshoe crabs cooked in garlic and ginger. More adventurous diners might try butter-fried frogs, noodles saut—ed with pig brains, and rabbit simmered in locally produced red wine.

Seaside cafes and open-air restaurants are perfect places to point and order and watch the fishing fleet return to town in the early evening hours.

Many of the better hotels have decent restaurants, including the Hai Yen and the Thang Nhat, known for its fresh crabs and spicy rocket shrimp. Another popular restaurant which provides tableside cooking is the Lac Canh, one block east of Dam Market. This spot offers French, Chinese, and Vietnamese dishes.

Finally, the Cau Da Villa serves elaborate but reasonably priced meals in its restaurant, which overlooks Nha Trang Bay.

Practicalities

Tourist Information: Khanh Hoa Tourism in the Vien Dong Hotel arranges tours, rents cars and boats, and provides services for visa extensions and exit permits. Similar services are also provided by Nha Trang Tourism in the Hung Dao Hotel on Tran Hung Dao Street.

Banks: Traveler's checks and foreign currency can be exchanged at the Vietcombank and at the Foreign Trade Bank on Quan Trung Street.

Post and Telecommunications: The post office is on Tran Phu Street. International phone calls can be made from the GPO and telecommunications office on Le Thanh Ton St., 100 meters from the beach.

Transportation

Nha Trang is 105 km from Phan Rang, 110 km from Dalat, 238 km from Qui Nhon, and 445 km from Saigon.

Air: Vietnam Airlines flies daily from Saigon and Hanoi and twice weekly from Danang. Their office is at 12B Hoang Hoa Tham Street.

Train: Trains heading north leave four times daily and take 10 hours to Qui Nhon and 40 hours to Hanoi. Express trains take 10 hours to Saigon. The ticket office at the train station is open daily 0700-1400.

Bus: Express buses leave from the Lien Tien Bus Terminal in the southwest section of Nha Trang and from another terminal on Le Thanh Ton St. near the Hung Dao Hotel. Long-distance bus services are also available from the centrally located Youth Tourism office just north of Yersin Street. Advance booking is recommended.

Local buses leave from the halt on 2 Thang 4 Street.

CENTRAL VIETNAM
QUI NHON TO HUE

QUI NHON

Qui Nhon, the capital of Binh Dinh Province, is a convenient spot to break the long journey between Nha Trang and Danang. The town was once the center of the Cham kingdom and later

one of four primary deep-water ports used by the American military—the others being Saigon, Danang, and Cam Ranh Bay, 50 km south of Nha Trang.

Vietnamese nationals associate the town with the famous Tay Son Rebellion of 1771-88, during which the Tay Son brothers brilliantly de-

QUI NHON

TO HWY 1 (8km) AND TRAIN STATION (200 m)

SOUTH CHINA SEA

VIET CUONG
BUS TERMINAL
LAMBROS TO DIEU TRI
PHAN DINH PHUNG
MAI XUAN THUONG
TANU BINH
DIEN ANH HOTEL
BINH DINH GUESTHOUSE
VIETINCOMBANK HOTEL
NHA KHACH 264
DONG PHUONG HOTEL
PEACE HOTEL
SAIGON HOTEL
ANH THU MINI HOTEL
POST OFFICE
NGOC LIEN RESTAURANT
HUU NGHI HOTEL
TRAN CAO VAN
STADIUM
AGRIBANK HOTEL
OLYMPIC HOTEL
LONG KHANH PAGODA
VIETCOMBANK
1 THANG 4
CHURCH
TANG BAT HO
LE LOI
TRAN HUNG DAO
CAR RENTAL OFFICE
CENTRAL MARKET
PHAN BOI CHAU
HAI BA TRUNG
TRAN BINH TRONG
POST OFFICE
CAR RENTAL OFFICE
HAI HA MINI HOTEL
BINH DINH TOURISM
QUI NHON TOURIST HOTEL
DIN BO LINH
NGUYEN TRAI
LE HONG PHONG
PHUONG MAI HOTEL
BUS TERMINAL
TRAN PHU
NGUYEN HUE
WAR MEMORIAL
CITY BEACH
ZOO
BINH DINH MUSEUM
0   100 m

© MOON PUBLICATIONS, INC.

VIETNAM

fended their country against Chinese aggression and briefly united Vietnam. The brothers are now revered as among the greatest of all national heroes.

Attractions

Qui Nhon itself offers little of great interest aside from walking along the beach and visiting the market in the early morning hours. Most attractions are located well outside town and are difficult to reach without private transportation.

Lon Khanh Pagoda: Qui Nhon's main religious shrine was founded by a Chinese merchant around 1710 but the present building dates from 1946. Noteworthy features include several large Buddha images and photographs of the monks who committed self-immolation in Saigon to protest the Diem regime.

Cham Towers: Thap Doi are two Cham towers with distinct arching roofs situated three km west of town toward Highway 1. Cham ruins are also located at Cha Ban some 26 km north of Qui Nhon. Thap Duong Long ("Towers of Ivory") are eight km from Cha Ban.

Quang Trung Museum: A small museum dedicated to the most famous of the three Tay Son brothers (Quang Trung) is found 48 km west of Qui Nhon on Highway 19 in the direction of Pleiku.

Accommodations

Several decent hotels are near the bus terminal and within walking distance of the train station. Most accept *dong* and are therefore quite inexpensive.

Bank Hotel: Popular backpackers' spot. 257 Le Hong Phong St., tel. 823591, US$10-30.

Huu Nghi Hotel: Run-down but very cheap rooms. 210 Phan Boi Chau St., tel. 822152, US$6-10.

Peace Hotel: Older hotel with reasonably priced rooms two blocks south of the bus terminal. 266 Tran Hung Dao St., tel. 822710, US$6-15.

Viet Cuong Hotel: About 100 meters south of the train station and north of the bus terminal is a simple place with small but acceptable rooms. 460 Tran Hung Dao St., tel. 822434, US$6-18.

Qui Nhon Tourist Hotel: As the name implies, this hotel is geared toward tourists and therefore demands payment in dollars. The hotel is overpriced but has some of the few a/c rooms in town and faces the best stretch of sand with-

in the municipality. 12 Nguyen Hue St., tel. 822401, US$25-45.

Transportation

Qui Nhon is 238 km north of Nha Trang and 304 km south of Danang.

Train: The Qui Nhon train station is about 1.5 km northwest of city center. Travelers intending to visit Qui Nhon must take one of the slower trains—express services do not stop here. For this reason, most visitors arrive by bus or chartered taxi.

Bus: Long-distance buses leave from the bus terminal on Tran Hung Dao St., about one km northwest of city center, and from the Express Terminal near the Qui Nhon Tourist Hotel. Departures to Nha Trang and Danang are in the early morning around 0500.

QUANG NGAI AND MY LAI

My Lai (Son My)

The massacre at My Lai—a small hamlet near the provincial capital of Quang Ngai—will always be remembered as among the most unfortunate incidents of the Vietnam War. My Lai also signaled a turning point in the war, when many Americans began to question the morality of the Indochinese conflict.

The incident began on the morning of 16 March 1968 soon after paratroopers of the 23rd Infantry Division landed near the village of Son My, under the command of Lt. William Calley. Their assignment was to investigate the earlier deaths of six soldiers who had stumbled across Viet Cong landmines. Instead, Calley and his soldiers proceeded to massacre some 347 unarmed men, women, and children before killing the livestock and torching the village.

Almost every command level of the American Army then became involved in an elaborate plan designed to cover up the crime. The ruse worked until the story was reported by Seymour Hersh in the *New York Times* on 13 November 1968—a full eight months after the massacre. Although Calley was court-martialed and personally convicted of almost 109 murders, Nixon granted a presidential pardon after Calley had served just three years of his sentence. Calley later committed suicide.

Today, the site is commemorated with a large memorial, a small museum, and a few small graves. No less moving are the comments in the visitors' book, many of which are from returning GIs.

Accommodations

Kim Thanh Hotel: Budget hotel one block northeast of the bus terminal. 19 Phan Boi Chau St., tel. 823471, US$8-20.

Hoa Vien Hotel: Somewhat upscale place featuring all a/c rooms on a side street across the road from the Kim Thanh. 12 Phan Chu Trinh St., tel. 823455, US$20-25.

Song Tra Hotel: A high-rise hotel on the northern outskirts of town owned and operated by Quang Ngai Tourism. Quang Trung St., tel. 822665, US$20-30.

Transportation

Quang Ngai is 174 km north of Qui Nhon and 130 km south of Danang.

The bus station is conveniently located in the center of town just off Highway 1. The train station is about three km west.

The turnoff to My Lai, 14 km northeast of Quang Ngai, is indicated by a plaque one km north of town. My Lai can be reached by motorcycle taxi from town.

HOI AN

Hoi An is an ancient city and a living museum nestled on the banks of the Thu Bon River, 28 km south of Danang. The town features some of the best-preserved architecture found anywhere in Vietnam.

Originally a seaport during the Champa era, Hoi An (then called Faifo) served as a thriving port of call for traders from all parts of the world from the 16th to 18th centuries. Portuguese traders and Jesuit missionaries, who arrived after expulsion from Japan, were followed by waves of Chinese entrepreneurs who fled their homeland after the fall of the Ming Dynasty. Japanese merchants also arrived to construct their homes and temples, take Vietnamese wives, and conduct business.

Home to a vibrant, international community of merchants, Hoi An sparkled as one of Vietnam's more important trading centers until the silting of the Thu Bon River forced the community to pull up roots and move north to Danang. The town then went into decline.

Today, Hoi An sleeps on, an undisturbed piece of history largely spared the destruction which has befallen so much of ancient Vietnam. This fact alone makes Hoi An one of the best destinations in central Vietnam.

Hoi An's ancient homes and Chinese assembly halls are concentrated near the riverfront on Tran Phu or Nguyen Thai Hoc streets. A small tourist office is on Tran Hung Dao St. near the Hoi An Hotel.

Attractions

Japanese Covered Bridge: A convenient start for your walking tour is the famous landmark constructed in the 17th century to connect the Chinese quarters with the Japanese settlement on the south bank.

Quang Dong Assembly Hall: Many of the Chinese groups which fled their homeland after the fall of the Ming Dynasty erected elaborate assembly halls to aid their compatriots and honor Quan Cong, a talented general of the Three Kingdoms period, and Thien Hau, goddess of the sea and protector of fishermen. Unlike most other assembly halls in Hoi An, Quang Dong served the economic and religious needs of all Chinese citizens regardless of their region of origin.

Nguyen Thai Hoc Street: Many of the fine old homes erected by wealthy Chinese and Vietnamese merchants have opened their doors to visitors for a small admission charge, including the Tan Ky House at number 101 and the Diep Dong Nguyen House at number 80. All reflect the wealth and refined taste of their owners, who utilized both Chinese and Japanese architectural styles.

Tran Phu Street: Among the highlights on this ancient street are the private homes at numbers 74, 77, and 148, plus several assembly halls erected by Fukien, Hainanese, and Cantonese traders. Many of the elongated homes now function as cotton mills filled with superb old looms which click and clack throughout the day.

Quan Cong And Quan Am Pagodas: A pair of interlinked pagodas—founded in the 17th century but reconstructed in modern times—are

HOI AN

TO CUA DAI BEACH (5 km)

SEA STAR HOTEL

TO CAM NAM ISLAND

CAM NAM BRIDGE

THU BON RIVER

TRAN PHU

PHAN BOI CHAU

HUY HOANG HOTEL

TRIEU CHAU PAGODA

NUY Y (MERMAID) RESTAURANT

FRENCH ARCHITECTURE

PHO HOI HOTEL

COCONUT MILK CAFE

HOANG DIEU

HOSPITAL

NGO GIA TU

QUAN AM PAGODA

MUSEUM AND QUAN CONG PAGODA

BANK

POST OFFICE

NGUYEN HUE

MARKETS

DOCK

BICYCLE RENTAL

CAFE 22
CAFE 24

BICYCLE RENTAL

FUKIEN HALL

CAFE DES AMIS

CROSSRIVER BOAT

LE HONG PHONG

HOI AN HOTEL

HOI AN II HOTEL

DONG PHUONG SEAFOOD

RESTAURANT DU PORT

BOAT RENTALS TO KIM BONG

THANH BINH HOTEL

PEACE BAR

THUY DUONG I HOTEL

TRAN HUNG DAO

RESTAURANTS

NGUYEN THAI HOC

BACH DANG

BOAT RENTALS

NGUYEN TRUONG TO

LE LOI

TRUONG ANCESTRAL HALL

TAN KY HOUSE

HOAI THANH HOTEL

TO CHINA BEACH (19 km) AND DANANG (30 km)

BINH MINH HOTEL

PHAN CHU TRINH

PHU TINH HOTEL

VINH HUNG HOTEL

DIEP DONG HOUSE

BA MA GATE

PHAN DINH PHUNG

QUANG DONG PAGODA

CAFES

NHI TRUNG

HAN HUYEN RESTAURANT

DONG AN CAFE

FOOTBRIDGE

TRADE UNION HOTEL

THIEN TRUNG HOTEL

NGUYEN TMK

TO BUS STATION (500 m) AND HWY 1 (10 km)

SILK AND SOUVENIR SHOPS

JAPANESE COVERED BRIDGE

FLOATING RESTAURANT

AN HOI ISLET

CHURCH

0   100 m

© MOON PUBLICATIONS, INC.

VIETNAM

found at the east end of Tran Phu St. just opposite the Central Market.

French Architecture: Colonnaded and shuttered homes of French inspiration flank the entire length of Phan Bai Chau St. just east of Cam Nam Bridge.

Hoi An Church: Many of the European traders, colonial administrators, and foreign missionaries who once lived in Hoi An are buried in the grounds of this modern church.

Chuc Thanh Pagoda: The oldest pagoda in Hoi An is in the north end of town some 800 meters past the church. Chuc Thanh (also called Phuc Thanh) was founded in 1454 by a Buddhist monk from China.

Phuoc Lam Pagoda: A 17th-century pagoda about 400 meters north of Chuc Thanh.

Accommodations

Hoi An Hotel II: Simple place with inexpensive rooms and shared bathrooms. 92 Tran Phu St., no phone, US$8-12.

Hoi An Hotel: Restored colonial-style building situated amid trees and gardens. 6 Tran Hung Dao St., tel. 861373, US$10-50.

Mai Lan Hotel: Newer property with reasonably clean rooms just opposite the bus terminal. 87 Huynh Thuc Khang St., tel. 861792, US$8-25.

Transportation

Hoi An is 28 km south of Danang, near the mouth of the Thu Bon River.

Buses from both the main and local bus terminals in Danang take about an hour to reach Hoi An, passing through lovely scenery of ricefields and swaying palms.

DANANG

Danang is situated in a region rich with history—both ancient and contemporary. Vietnam's fourth-largest city (population 400,000) rose to prominence in the 2nd century A.D. as the primary port of the Chams, the brilliant Hindu empire which once stretched all the way from Hue in the north to Vung Tao in the south. During the mid-18th century the city was the focus of struggles between Vietnamese and Spanish forces, who ostensibly wished to end mistreatment of

Catholic missionaries by the government of Emperor Tu Duc. By that time, Danang had superseded Hoi Fa as the primary seaport and commercial center between Hanoi and Saigon.

The French began their colonial experience here in August 1858 when French forces fired at Danang's coastal defenses and landed troops to seize the town they subsequently renamed Tourane, a term which roughly described the soup-tureen-shaped bay to the north.

But for Americans, Danang will always be remembered as the site where 3,500 American soldiers landed on 8 March 1965 to signal the official arrival of combat troops—not advisers—into the Vietnam War. During the next decade, Danang grew to become the world's largest Marine base, the "Rocket City" where hundreds of thousands of Americans got their first look at the exotic land of Vietnam.

The fall of Danang to the Communists in 1975 shocked the world with its desperate scenes of panicked refugees trying to board the last planes and ships out of town. Four weeks later, the first rockets fell on Saigon.

Attractions

Despite all the history, Danang offers a limited number of attractions within the city limits. Visitors interested in Cham ruins or beaches must make day-trips from the city.

Cham Museum: A useful introduction to the culture and artistic styles of the Chams is provided in this open-air museum founded in 1916 by the École Française d'Extrême Orient as the world's finest repository of Cham art. The complex includes a number of rooms arranged around different periods and regions of origin, including chambers filled with outstanding sculpture from My Son, Tra Kieu, Dong Duong, and Thap Mam. Indian and Khmer influence is obvious in the later periods. The museum is open Tues.-Sun. 0800-1100 and 1300-1700.

Cao Dai Church: Danang's Cao Dai Church, second largest in the country, is less striking than the sect's headquarters in Tay Ninh but nevertheless worth visiting to see the elaborate interior and the mystical symbols on which the religion is based. Services are held daily at 0600, 1200, 1800, and midnight.

Danang Cathedral: Constructed by the French in 1923, this pink sandstone edifice with its stained-

DANANG

BAY OF DANANG

HAN RIVER

THANH BINH BEACH

THANH BINH GH

CAFE LIEN

SOUP PLACES AND CAFES

DANANG HOTEL (NEW WING)

SAIGON TOURANE HOTEL

DANANG HOTEL (OLD WING)

LAO CONSULATE

TRAN QUY CAP

PEACE HOTEL

COTIMEX HOTEL

THU BON HOTEL

LY THUONG KIET

THUY SAN HOTEL

THUAN AN HOTEL

ELEGANT HOTEL

BACH DANG

HOA CAU BAR

NGUYEN DU

LE LOI

NGUYEN CHI THANH

TRAN PHU

LY TU TRONG

SONG HAN HOTEL

HAI VAN HOTEL

NGOC ANH RESTAURANT

IMMIGRATION OFFICE

QUANG TRUNG

DONG DA

ONG ICH KIEM

AMI HOTEL

ROYAL HOTEL

BINH DUONG HOTEL

BACH DANG HOTEL

FORMER FRENCH CITY HALL

HANA KIMDINH RESTAURANT

THAN LICH RESTAURANT

VIETNAM AIRLINES

VIETCOMBANK

TRAN CHO VAN

TRAIN STATION

HAIPHONG

DIEN LUC HOTEL

CAO DAI TEMPLE

LE DUAN

POST OFFICE

RIVERSIDE HOTEL

SEAMAN'S CLUB

VINAPHA HOTEL

PHAN DINH PHUNG

FERRIES

LE DUAN

NGO GIA TU

NGUYEN THI MINH KHAI

STADIUM

YENBAY

FOOD STREET

NOVOTEL TOURANE HOTEL

THEATER

INCOMBANK

THU DO HOTEL

HUNG VUONG MINI HOTEL

HUNG VUONG

CON MARKET

TO BUS TERMINAL (1 km) AND HWY 1

THANH THANH

LOCAL BUSES

LY THAI TO

ORIENT HOTEL

PACIFIC HOTEL

HUONG VIET RESTAURANT

TRAN QUOC TOAN

DANANG CATHEDRAL

DAI A HOTEL

TAN MINH MINI HOTEL

HAI AU HOTEL

MODERN HOTEL

TU DO AND KIM DO RESTAURANTS

MINH TAM 2 MINI HOTEL

LE HONG PHONG

PHAP LAM PAGODA

HOANG VAN THU

LE DINH DUONG

ONG ICH KIEM

HOANG DIEU

PHAN CHU TRINH

TAM BAO PAGODA

TRUNG NU

FORMER US PRESS CENTER

CHAM MUSEUM. TO MARBLE MOUNTAINS, CHINA BEACH (10 km) AND HOI AN (30 km)

TO AIRPORT

0   500 m

VIETNAM

© MOON PUBLICATIONS, INC.

glass windows and Gothic moodiness is now home to a community of some 4,000 Catholics. Masses are held daily at 0500 and 1700.

American Legacies

Visitors intrigued with signs of colonial occupation and the Vietnam War are often surprised at the near-complete lack of evidence throughout the country. The vestiges are here, though often repainted, renamed, and converted to more utilitarian uses.

American Consulate: Once dubbed the "White Elephant" by U.S. personnel stationed in Danang, this decrepit brick building now houses a small theater and desultory War Crimes Museum which local authorities intend to move soon to another location.

American Navy Club: Now the Seamen's Institute—a curious name for a bar.

Third Marine Amphibious Headquarters: Now a Vietnamese military training center called Nguyen Ai Quoc Academy, named after one of the noms de guerre of Ho Chi Minh.

Danang International Airport: Once among the most active airbases in the world, today the enormous airfield shows little evidence of its turbulent history aside from a few abandoned batteries and rusting carcasses of destroyed jets. According to folklore, most of the scrap was sold to the Japanese, who melted it down and reforged it into automobiles then sold to the Americans—a farfetched tale retold with great relish by many local Vietnamese.

French-era City Hall: The provincial headquarters of the local Communist party.

American Press Center: A shrimp cannery.

Accommodations

Danang has over a dozen hotels, which seem to overcharge less than their counterparts elsewhere in Vietnam. Those which accept *dong* are near the train station and in the north end of town.

Danang Hotel: Inconveniently located in the north end of town, but rooms are clean and low priced—probably because of the location. Take a cyclo or motorcycle taxi from the train station or bus terminal. 3 Dong Da St., tel. 821986, US$8-45.

Huu Nghi Hotel: Simple place adjacent to the Danang Hotel. 7 Dong Da St., tel. 821021, US$6-20.

Hai Van Hotel: Another decent and low-priced hotel with a/c rooms. 2 Nguyen Thi Minh Khai St., tel. 821300, US$12-25.

Song Han Hotel: Modern if somewhat characterless hotel with a restaurant, a nightclub with live music and tiny hostesses, and 40 a/c rooms in three classes. 36 Bach Dang St., tel. 822540, US$25-65.

Hai Au Hotel: Excellent location near the center of town and clean a/c rooms make this one of the most popular hotels in Danang. Unfortunately, the hotel is often booked out and prices have risen sharply in recent years. 177 Tran Phu St., tel. 822722, US$40-65.

Orient Hotel: Vietnam Tourism books tour groups into this centrally located hotel with a/c rooms and rooftop restaurant offering great views over Danang. 93 Phan Chu Trinh St., tel. 821266, US$45-80.

Bach Dang Hotel: Fairly new and very large hotel in a central location with views of the river. 50 Bach Nang St., tel. 823649, US$45-100.

Restaurants

Danang is known for its seafood and locally produced beer, sensibly called Danang Export.

Riverside Restaurants: Certainly the most enjoyable spots to dine are the simple cafes and restaurants facing the Han River along Bach Dang Street. Thanh Lich Restaurant at 48 Bach Dang is somewhat expensive but serves an impressive array of Vietnamese and French specialties. Other riverside choices include the Kim Dinh at 7 Bach Dang and the venerable Seamen's Institute—the former American Navy Club—which hangs right over the water.

City Center: Tu Do (Freedom) Restaurant at 180 Tran Phu St. near the Hai Chu Hotel is generally considered the best in town, with excellent food, friendly staff, and ice-cold beer. Nearby and less pricey places include the Kim Do at 174 Tran Phu and the Thoi Dai at 171.

Services

Tourist Information: Danang Tourist Office at 48 Bach Dang St. arranges tours and car rentals.

Immigration: Visas can (perhaps) be extended at the Immigration Police office at 7 Tran Quy Cap Street.

Banks: Vietcombank at 46 Le Loi St. will exchange most currencies and traveler's checks at standard rates.

Post and Telecommunications: The GPO at the corner of Bach Dang and Le Duan streets also has telex, fax, and international telephone services. Overseas calls can also be made from most hotels.

Transportation

Danang is 108 km south of Hue, 130 km north of Quang Ngai, and almost midway between Saigon and Hanoi.

Air: Vietnam Airlines flies daily from Saigon and Hanoi. The 70-minute flight costs about US$85. Danang International Airport is three km southwest of town. Taxis, motorcycle taxis, and cyclos wait outside the front entrance. Vietnam Airlines booking office is at 35 Tran Phu Street.

Train: Danang train station is on Haiphong St. about 1.5 km from the center of town. Trains take three to four hours to Hue, 14-18 hours to Nha Trang, and 26-30 hours to Saigon or Hanoi.

Train and bus journeys between Danang and Hue are among the most spectacular in Asia, especially when the train skirts the ocean and buses climb over Hai Van Pass, the "Pass of the Ocean Clouds," which cuts through the Truong Son Mountains. Simply amazing.

Bus: The long-distance bus terminal is at 8 Dien Bien Phu St., two km west of city center. Express buses also leave mornings around 0500 from the halt at 52 Phan Chu Trinh St., adjacent to the Thanh Thanh Hotel.

Buses to the Marble Mountains, China Beach, and Hoi An leave from the local bus terminal opposite 80 Hung Vuong Street. The road continues west to become Ly Thai To and finally Dien Bien Phu streets.

ATTRACTIONS NEAR DANANG

Marble Mountains

Eight km southwest of the city rise five limestone peaks nicknamed the Marble Mountains or, in Vietnamese terms, Mountains of the Five Elements—Kim Son (metal), Thuy Son (water), Moc Son (wood), Hoa Son (fire), and Tho Son (earth).

All of the mountains feature eerie caves filled with Buddhist shrines. The most famous is that of Thuy Son, constructed on the site of a much

older Cham shrine and once the spot from which Vietnamese guerrillas mercilessly bombed the Danang airfield. Hence the term, "Rocket City."

Other sanctuaries include Tam Thai Pagoda, constructed in 1852, Linh Ung pagoda on the eastern edge, and Huyen Khong, pierced by chambers which gracefully illuminate the images of Sakyamuni and enlightened Buddhist bodhisattvas. Guides are plentiful but bring a flashlight.

Transportation: Buses to the Marble Mountains leave from the bus terminal on Hung Vuong St. just west of the train tracks.

China Beach

Probably best known to Americans for the short-lived television series of the same name, China Beach (called Non Nuoc by the Vietnamese) is where American troops once relaxed on abbreviated R&R before being helicoptered back to the battle zones.

Things have changed. Several years ago, the Association of Surfing Professionals in Southern California sanctioned a championship surfing contest at China Beach that drew a large number of contestants who found the conditions among the best in the country.

Accommodations: The Non Nuoc Hotel charges US$25-34 for a/c rooms with private bath. Like most other beach resorts operated by Vietnam Tourism, Non Nuoc seems determined to negate its tropical seaside location with the heavy use of colorless concrete and restaurants placed as far away from the sea as possible. Nevertheless, the place is often filled with domestic visitors and foreign tour groups. Call 21470 to check on vacancies.

Transportation: China Beach is one km from the Marble Mountains and can be reached in 20 minutes with buses from the terminal on Hung Vuong Street.

Cham Ruins

Vietnam's largest collection of Cham ruins is located at My Son, 72 km southwest of Danang, and at Dong Duong, 62 km from Danang. Although both sites were heavily damaged during the war, several dozen monuments still stand as testimony to the unique creativity of the Chams.

Both sites are extremely isolated and almost impossible to reach with public transportation.

The only feasible option is to arrange a car and driver through your hotel or the tourist office in Danang.

Lang Co Beach

Some of the most dazzling beaches in central Vietnam are located about 35 km north of Danang and just beyond Hai Van Pass, the rugged limestone karst which once formed the physical barrier between ancient Vietnam to the north and the Champa Kingdom in the south. Lang Co is a dazzling 10-km beach set between the emerald-blue waters of the South China Sea and an idyllic lagoon which washes up toward the mountains. The spectacular peninsula is dotted with palm trees interspersed with tiny villages inhabited by friendly fishermen.

Accommodations: Vietnam Tourism recently opened Lan Co Seaside Resort, but a much better option is to find a homestay in one of the villages which hug the coastline. This may require some ingenuity since many locals are unaccustomed to Westerners and are afraid to offend Vietnamese tourism officials.

Transportation: Situated almost exactly midway between Danang and Hue, Lan Co village can be reached by bus from either town. Alternatively, take a nonexpress train to the Lang Co train station and find a cyclo out to the beach. Cyclo drivers may know about homestays.

HUE

Hue, the famed imperial capital of the Nguyen kings, once was the cultural, religious, and historical center of central Vietnam and is among the highlights of any visit to the country.

The city has dozens of pagodas, temples, and mausoleums superbly situated on the banks of the romantic Perfume River. Hue is also reasonably small and intimate—a relaxing diversion from the larger cities of Vietnam.

History

Hue, in many senses, is a country unto itself. The city was founded in the spring of 1601 by Lord Nguyen Hoang (1524-1613), who erected the Phu Xuan Citadel and Thien Mu Pagoda, which still stands on the left bank of the Perfume River. King Nguyen was the first in a series of 10 kings who fought the Chams and attempted to control the south from Hue to Saigon.

It wasn't until 1802 that the 10th Nguyen ruler crushed the Tay Son uprising, unseated his rival in Hanoi, and proclaimed himself Emperor Gia Long—the formal beginning of the Nguyen Dynasty, which lasted 143 years until the abdication of Emperor Bao Dai in 1945. Brilliant and ruthless, the Nguyen Dynasty for the first time in Vietnamese history united the country from the borders of China to the southern reaches of the South China Sea. Despite its brevity, some scholars consider this era the golden age of Vietnamese creativity, during which 13 emperors constructed more than 300 palaces, temples, mausoleums, libraries, and theaters in and around the Imperial City.

Vietnamese revisionist historians sometimes claim that Nguyen kings were national traitors who in 1884 sold their country to the French and that Hue should be considered secondary in importance to more contemporary and revolutionary landmarks such as Dien Bien Phu and the Ho Chi Minh Trail. Fortunately (especially for architectural conservationists), Hue's status appears to have been upgraded in recent years, as Vietnamese historians reassess the Nguyen Dynasty and delineate the specific roles of each individual king.

Hue was invaded in 1833 by the French and in 1945 by the Japanese, who demanded the resignation of Bao Dai, the final Nguyen king.

Americans remember Hue as the scene of some of the fiercest and most senseless fighting of the entire war. During the Tet Offensive of 1968, Viet Minh forces seized and held the Imperial Citadel for 25 days and massacred perhaps 3,000 Vietnamese civilians, including children, old women, medical personnel, schoolteachers, and missionaries. An estimated 10,000 people died during the battle.

Subsequent American firepower destroyed many monuments in the Citadel, though a great deal survived the tragic episode.

The Imperial City

The Imperial Citadel (Dai Noi) of Hue was constructed in the early 19th century as an almost exact copy of the Forbidden City in Beijing, with an outer wall (Kinh Thanh) enclosing the Yellow City (Hoang Thanh) and the Forbidden Pur-

VIETNAM

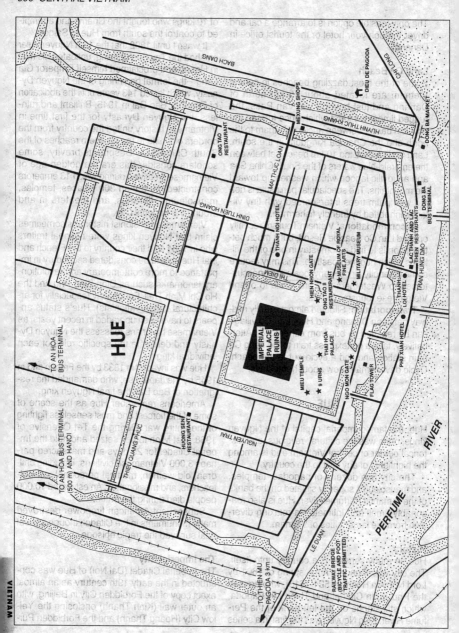

VIETNAM

© MOON PUBLICATIONS, INC.

low City (Hoang Thanh) and the Forbidden Purple City (Tu Cam Thanh). Today it is the major attraction in Hue and among the country's most memorable sights.

Ngo Mon Gate: The richly decorated main entrance is fronted by nine holy cannons, a flag tower which defiantly flew the Viet Minh flag during the 1968 siege, two auxiliary gateways used by common citizens, and the Golden Water Bridge, once reserved exclusively for the emperor.

Thai Hoa Palace: Directly beyond the gate lies the Palace of Supreme Peace, the most significant and best-preserved structure in the Imperial City, constructed in 1805 as the ceremonial quarters and reception room for visiting diplomats.

Forbidden Purple City: Beyond the Red Gate lies the fabled Forbidden Purple City which, unfortunately, has almost completely disappeared over the last century from an onslaught of typhoons, floods, fires, termites, thieves, and firepower provided by French, American, and Viet Minh forces.

The most impressive buildings which have survived the elements and artillery are located west of the royal enclave.

Nine Dynastic Urns: Cast in 1835 and weighing an estimated 2,000 kilos each, these elaborate creations symbolize the divinity of individual Nguyen dynasties and, on a less noble note, were featured in the French film *Indochine*. Some of the recent restorations were financed by the film company.

Mieu Temple: North of the urns is the impressive "Temple of Generations," constructed in 1821 to honor the earliest of the Nguyen emperors.

Museums

As you might expect, Hue has several museums which illustrate the city's history. Although the exhibits here are poorly labeled, the **Hue Imperial Museum** should be visited for its striking architecture and modest collection of ceramics, furniture, and bronzeware.

The nearby **military museum** has the standard array of weapons, tanks, and missiles in the central courtyard. Both museums are open 0830-1700.

Thien Mu Pagoda

This small but well-situated temple on the banks of the Perfume River, four km southeast of Hue,

has an elegant worship chamber and a rather curious sight—the Austin car that carried a 73-year-old Buddhist monk named Thich Quang Duc from Hue to Saigon, where he immolated himself on 11 June 1963 and electrified the world. Malcolm Browne's historic photo of the event is mounted on the front windshield.

The adjacent 21-meter octagonal tower is the unofficial symbol of Hue and among the most famous structures in Vietnam.

Right Bank Attractions

The Imperial City, museums, and royal mausoleums (described below) are probably enough for most visitors, but true culture vultures might explore the sights hidden amid the right bank in modern Hue.

Bao Quoc Pagoda: Founded in 1670 by a Chinese Buddhist monk but renovated in the late 1950s, Bao Quoc features images of Buddhas past, present, and future enshrined on the central altar.

Ho Chi Minh Museum: Small assortment of photographs and personal items less impressive than the counterpart museum in Hanoi. Ho attended nearby Quoc Hoc School along with other notables such as General Giap and President Diem.

Notre Dame Cathedral: A simple single-spired church which combines European architectural styles with Vietnamese elements.

Mausoleums

As the political and spiritual center of the Nguyen Dynasty, Hue features a large number of pagodas and royal mausoleums spread across a wide area south of city center. Most follow a standard arrangement of a paved courtyard flanked by stone figures of elephants and military mandarins, a stele pavilion engraved with the biography of the deceased king, a central temple dedicated to the king, and auxiliary houses constructed by the king for his royal retinue of concubines, servants, and guardian soldiers.

The tombs and pagodas are best reached by rented bicycle, which provides an opportunity to see the countryside. Many are badly damaged or architecturally redundant, making it unnecessary to view the entire selection. Hurried visitors can sign up for a tour or rent a car. The most romantic options are boats rented from docks in

All are open daily 0800-1700 and charge a small admission fee.

Tu Duc Tomb: An architectural masterpiece constructed in the mid-19th century around lakes, pine-covered hills, and pavilions used for relaxation and meditation. Emperor Tu Duc was apparently quite a character: over 100 wives and concubines (but no children), 50 chefs who prepared his daily meals of 50 courses, and hundreds of slaves forced to construct his pleasure palace seven km south of Hue.

Dong Khanh Tomb: Just 500 meters from the tomb of Tu Duc is a small but completely unique mausoleum constructed in 1889 for the nephew and adopted son of Emperor Tu Duc.

Khai Dinh Tomb: Majestically situated on the slopes of Chau Mountain 10 km south of Hue, this royal mausoleum was constructed from 1920 to 1931 as the final monument of the Nguyen Dynasty. Khai Dinh is a contemporary ferroconcrete creation noted for its rather sinister staircase of dragons, ceiling murals, and frescoes made from thousands of ceramic and glass fragments. The overall effect is quite impressive but reflects the gaudy excesses and Eurocentricities of the final Nguyen kings.

Minh Mang Tomb: Minh Mang, 12 km south of Hue, is perhaps the most impressive royal mausoleum in the region. Constructed from 1840 to 1843, the complex is renowned for its harmonious architecture, elaborate decorations, and glaring stone dignitaries set in a majestic site amid peaceful ponds and tributaries of the Perfume River.

Accommodations

Hue has about 20 hotels *(khach san)* and guesthouses *(nha khach)* situated along or near Le Loi St., which skirts the right bank of the Perfume River. Most demand dollars and are overpriced.

Ben Nghe Guesthouse: Popular low-priced hotel. 4 Ben Nghe St., tel. 823687, US$8-18.

Hotel Le Loi Hue: Near the train station, this clean and comfortable hotel offers fan and some a/c rooms. The favorite of many backpackers. 2 Le Loi St., tel. 822153, US$6-40.

Thanh Noi Hotel: Convenient west bank location and sensibly priced rooms. 3 Dang Dung St., tel. 822478, US$10-30.

Guesthouse 5 Le Loi: Former palace with spacious rooms, grand hallways, romantic ambience. 5 Le Loi St., tel. 822155, US$25-75.

Huong Giang (Perfume River) Hotel: Older semiluxurious hotel. 51 Le Loi St., tel. 822122, US$60-220.

Century Riverside Inn: Hue's finest hotel; top-floor rooms overlook the river. 49 Le Loi St., tel. 823390, US$80-200.

Restaurants

Hue offers a number of specialties peculiar to the north: *banh khoi* (deep-fried prawns, pork, and bean sprouts wrapped in a crepe), *banh thit nuong* (meat and vegetables) dipped in *nuoc leo* (spicy peanut and sesame sauce), and *ram* (rice pancake stuffed with pork). Huda 22 is a mild locally produced beer.

Huong Sen Restaurant: Popular spot elevated in a lotus pond in the Imperial Citadel. Serves both Vietnamese and Western dishes. 42 Nguyen Trai Street. Moderate.

Song Huong Floating Restaurant: Central location just downstream from the Trang Thien Bridge. Pleasant ambience. 32 Le Loi Street. Moderate.

Huong Giang (Perfume River) Hotel: Surprisingly good Vietnamese food and outstanding views from its fourth-floor location. 51 Le Loi Street. Moderate.

Tourist Information

Hue Tourist Office at 51 Le Loi St. and Hue City Tourism at 18 Le Loi St. sell package tours and arrange rental cars with drivers and guides. Neither office has much information for independent travelers.

Immigration: Visas can be extended at the immigration police office on Ben Nghe Street.

Banks: The Industrial & Commercial Bank at 2 Le Quy Don St. is open Mon.-Sat. 0800-1130 and 1300-1600. The Huong Giang and Hue hotels also change money.

Post and Telecommunications: The GPO on Hoang Hoa Tham St. offers international phone and fax services.

Transportation

Hue is 108 km north of Danang, 166 km from Dong Hoi, 368 km from Vinh, 664 km from Hanoi, and 1,071 km north of Saigon.

Air: Vietnam Airlines flies twice weekly from Hanoi and Saigon to the Phu Bai Airport, 20 km south of city center. Vietnam Airlines's booking office one block from Dong Ba Market at 16 Phan Dang Luu St. is open Mon.-Sat. 0700-1100 and 1330-1700.

Train: Hue railway station is at the southwestern end of Le Loi Street. Both express and ordinary trains depart several times daily for Hanoi and points south. The booking office is open daily 0700-1700. Advance reservations for sleepers are recommended.

Bus: Hue has three bus terminals. The An Cuu Station at 43 Hung Vuong St. serves destinations to the south. Buses north leave from the An Hoa Station at the northwest corner of the walled citadel. Buses to destinations near Hue leave from the Dong Ba Station on Tran Hung Dao St. near the bridge.

Most departures are in the mornings 0500-0600.

VICINITY OF HUE

QUANG TRI

Highway 1 north from Hue passes through a series of small towns and along a lovely coastline before arriving at the Demilitarized Zone (DMZ), which formed the legal separation between South and North Vietnam from 1954 to 1975. Most visitors head straight across the DMZ and overnight in Vinh, a reconstructed town which provides a useful break on the long journey to Hanoi.

Quang Tri, 59 km north of Hue, served as a citadel city until the spring of 1972, when battles between the Viet Minh and South Vietnamese forces almost completely obliterated the town. The main points of interest are the nearby Vietnam War sites such as Khe Sanh and former American bases now reduced to iron scraps scattered amid a lunar landscape.

DONG HA

The provincial capital of Dong Ha serves as a useful base from which to explore the Demilitarized Zone and war sites to the west. The town has been reconstructed since the war in standard fashion and has little of interest aside from a few surviving blockhouses once used by French and then American military forces.

Dong Ha straddles the intersection of Highway 1 and Highway 9, which leads west to Khe Sanh and the border of Laos. The two-lane asphalt road was originally constructed by the Americans during the war and has been recently upgraded to provide dependable access to landlocked Laos.

Accommodations

Dong Ha Hotel: Convenient location just north of the bus terminal. Highway 1, tel. 852262, US$15-20.

Nha Nghi Du Lich Cong Doan: Another hotel five blocks west of the bus terminal. 4 Le Loi St., tel. 852744, US$10-25.

KHE SANH

Khe Sanh, a remote valley 62 km west of Dong Ha, was the site of one of the most famous battles of the entire Vietnam War. Today a barren plateau surrounded by low hills and tropical vegetation, Khe Sanh marks the spot where the North Vietnamese attempted to inflict the final blow against the Americans—not unlike Dien Bien Phu, which drove the French from Vietnam.

But unlike the French at Dien Bien Phu, American forces were prepared for the assault with an enormous amount of weaponry and firepower. The 77-day attack, now thought to be an elaborate diversion against the upcoming Tet Offensive, made worldwide headlines and was followed by millions of Americans on the nightly news. When the smoke finally cleared and Highway 9 was reopened, 248 Americans and an estimated 10,000 Vietnamese had lost their lives. Khe Sanh was abandoned by the Americans in July 1968 after General Westmoreland reassessed his positions and decided that Khe Sanh held no further strategic importance.

Khe Sanh today shows few signs of battle since most of the military hardware was removed or blown up by the departing Americans. Aside from a handful of American veterans who witnessed combat here, few visitors make the journey to Khe Sanh or other nearby war memorials such as Camp Carroll, the Rockpile, Con Thien Firebase, the Ho Chi Minh Trail, and Hamburger Hill in Ashau Valley.

Accommodations

Two inexpensive guesthouses are located in Khe Sanh town just west of the bus terminal.

Transportation

Buses to Khe Sanh town leave several times each morning from the bus terminals in Hue and Dong Ha. The battle site is located 2.5 km north of town. Since the widely scattered war sites listed above are difficult to reach by public transportation, most visitors hire a car with driver and guide in Hue.

DMZ SITES

The Demilitarized Zone (DMZ), which once served as the boundary between North and South Vietnam, is defined by the Ben Hai River, which follows the 17th parallel. The following sights can be visited on day-trips from Dong Ha, though a better idea is to charter a taxi from Hue and hire a guide who can provide historical backgrounds.

Warning: The entire region was heavily bombed and now resembles some sort of eerie moonscape, complete with a terrible number of live ordnance and mines which continue to kill impoverished peasants in frightening numbers. Anyone touring the region should keep to established paths and never touch any of the mines and bombs which still lie scattered around the battlefields. Anything—ordnance, mines, or shoes—left untouched by scavengers is extremely deadly.

Attractions

Vinh Moc Tunnels: The tunnels of Vinh Moc, just north of the DMZ near the village of Ho Xa, comprise a remarkable testimony to the sacrifice and tenacity of the Vietnamese in their struggle during the war. Although the 2.8-km labyrinth of underground passages has been compared to the tunnels of Cu Chi near Saigon, there is really no comparison. This is the real thing—an

HUE VICINITY

unadulterated and completely untouristed subterranean world once home to some 1,200 villagers who farmed above ground during the day and lived their lives at night in the elaborate complex of passageways and chambers.

Vinh Moc is 13 km east of Highway 1. The turnoff is six km north of the Ben Hai River.

Doc Mieu Base: Once the headquarters for American electronic surveillance, Doc Mieu is now a vast expanse of nothing more than craters filled with rainwater and scattered remnants such as combat boots and live mortars.

VIETNAM

Con Thien Firebase: Con Thien once served as the primary base for the so-called McNamara's Wall, the elaborate military barrier designed to detect enemy incursions across the DMZ. This place is extraordinarily dangerous—even desperate Vietnamese scrap collectors refuse to venture into this no-man's land.

Truong Son Cemetery: Formerly a Vietnamese Army base but now a national cemetery and memorial dedicated to the tens of thousands of Viet Minh soldiers who died at the DMZ and along the Ho Chi Minh Trail. Many of the headstones are labeled *Liet Si*, Unknown Martyr.

Camp Carroll: Once a major American military installation with enormous 175-mm can-

nons, Camp Carroll today is a quiet spot of weeds and craters. Most of the war architecture, including the concrete bunkers and cannons which once shelled Khe Sanh, has been dismantled and hauled away by Vietnamese scrap collectors.

The Rockpile: Former American Marine lookout overlooking old artillery batteries.

Aluoi and Hamburger Hill: Sixty-five km south of Khe Sanh is a lovely valley that was once a major war zone. Among the more infamous battle sites are those at Cunningham, Erskine, Razor, and Hamburger Hill, scene of a terrible 1968 battle in which 241 Americans died in less than one week.

NORTH VIETNAM

Vietnam north of the DMZ but south of Hanoi is a kind of shadowy transition zone between the capitalist South and the socialist North, a land caught in the middle of ideological struggles and tempted to go in either direction.

North-central Vietnam is also one of the country's poorest and most crowded regions. Here, peasants eke out an existence from thin soil and produce only enough food to avoid starvation. The region has some fine beaches and a fair number of monuments which mark the southern expansion of Vietnamese empires, but most visitors bypass this coastal stretch in their hurried journey to Hanoi and the impressive landscapes of the far north.

A few towns are described below in the event that you have enough time or interest to break the journey between Hue and Hanoi.

DONG HOI

Dong Hoi is the provincial capital of Quang Binh Province and an active fishing port heavily damaged during the Vietnam conflict.

Attractions

Dong Hoi is known for its remains of an ancient citadel erected in the early 17th century and for its aromatic wines, distilled from wild strawberries which survive amid the encroaching sand dunes.

Phong Na Caves, 45 km northwest of Dong Hoi, are the premier attraction in the province and widely considered one of the greatest natural wonders of Vietnam. Approached via an underground river, the caves include a series of grottoes once used as Cham religious sanctuaries in the 9th and 10th centuries.

Accommodations

Nhat Le Hotel: Riverside hotel with spacious rooms. 16 Quach Xuan Ky St., tel. 822180, US$10-30.

Phuong Dong Hotel: Another riverside hotel with rooms in various price ranges. 20 Quach Xuan Ky St., tel. 822276, US$10-55.

VINH

Nghe Tinh Province is known throughout Vietnam as the birthplace of several national poets and the father of modern Vietnam, Ho Chi Minh.

The city has variously been destroyed by French aerial bombing in the 1950s, a series of devastating fires in the '60s, and massive naval bombardments from American warships in the '70s. Vinh was almost completely rebuilt with East German assistance after the war in a uniformly depressing style of monolithic socialist architecture. Quang Trung Street, Vinh's main thoroughfare, looks like an Orwellian nightmare on the verge of collapse.

Despite the dreary architecture and utter poverty which grips most of the province, Vinh is a useful stop on the hard journey from Hue to Hanoi.

A tourist office is on Quang Trung St. just north of the Rap 12/9 Cinema.

Attractions

There is nothing of interest in Vinh aside from contemplating the cruel joke which East German architects have sprung on the town.

Ho Chi Minh House: Ho Chi Minh was born in Chua (Kim Lien), 14 km northwest of Vinh, but raised in the nearby village of Sen. Both villages have modest museums and memorials in his reconstructed homes.

Cua Lo Beach: This beach, 20 km east of town, is somewhat narrow but offers clean sand and a complete absence of tourists aside from a few Vietnamese day-trippers. Accommodations at the Cua Lo Hotel. The tourist brochures promises "sun-basking, sea crabs, and Phuc Trach shaddocks." Let me know what you find.

Accommodations

Ben Thuy Hotel: Budget travelers often stay at this friendly hotel about two km from city center. National Highway, tel. 855163, US$10-25.

Bong Sen Hotel: Cheap option in the middle of town. 20 Quang Trung St., tel. 844397, US$8-12.

Thanh Vinh Hotel: Modern hotel with comfortable rooms at decent prices. 9 Le Loi St., tel. 847222, US$25-45.

Kim Lien Hotel: Vinh's luxury spot across from the market and about three blocks south of the bus terminal. Quang Trung St., tel. 844751, US$30-85.

Transportation

Vinh is 368 km north of Hue, 197 km from Dong Hoi, and 291 km south of Hanoi. The train station is in the northwest section of town, three km from city center. Vinh is served by both ordinary and express trains from Hue and Hanoi.

The bus terminal is centrally located a few blocks north of the central market. Express buses to Hanoi and Hue depart around 0500.

THANH HOA

Among the mysterious cultures which fascinate historians and archaeologists concerned with Southeast Asia is that of Dong Son, the civilization of the Ma River which forged the elaborate bronze drums uncovered from north Thailand to the far reaches of eastern Indonesia.

Thanh Hoa served as the capital of Vietnam in the late 14th century and was the site of the Lam Son Uprising (1418-28), during which the Vietnamese expelled Chinese forces from the country. Although much of Thanh Hoa was destroyed in the Vietnam conflict, this remains a region of great historical and cultural significance to the Vietnamese people.

Attractions

Thanh Hoa's only surviving signs of history are the massive city gates, now being excavated with funds provided by UNESCO.

Sam Son Beach: The chief attractions near town are the long and fine beaches at Sam Son, 16 km southeast of town. Beyond the beaches is the Ham Rong Bridge, repeatedly bombed during the war by the Americans and only finally destroyed in 1972 by laser-guided "smart bombs"—a precursor to the technological displays of the 1991 Persian Gulf conflict.

Accommodations at Sam Son include several chalets and hotels in the US$15-45 price range.

Accommodations

Thanh Hoa Hotel: The only place in town. National Highway 1, tel. 852517, US$15-65.

NINH BINH

Ninh Binh is a completely ordinary town situated near some of the most memorable scenery in Vietnam—the eerie limestone mountains and flooded caves at Tam Coc.

Tam Coc

Tam Coc (Three Caves) closely resembles the eerie landscapes of Guilin in the People's Republic of China or perhaps the limestone topography near Krabi in southern Thailand. Visitors to Tam Coc, nine km southwest of Ninh Binh, tour the region by rowboat along the Ngo Dong River. A two-passenger boat costs US$4 for the three-hour excursion, including visits inside the three caves—Hang Ca, Hang Giua, and Hang Cuoi.

Several nearby villages produce embroidered crafts such as napkins, pillowcases, and mittens sold at very reasonable prices.

Tours to Tam Coc can be arranged with travel agencies in Hanoi, though more and more visitors prefer to stay in Ninh Binh and spend a few days exploring the region. Many of the hotels in Ninh Binh also arrange tours of the nearby attractions, or you can rent a motorcycle and enjoy the countryside at a more leisurely pace.

More Attractions

Hoa Lu: Twelve km north of Ninh Binh is another small town surrounded by the same breathtaking scenery found at Tam Coc. Along with limestone karsts, Hoa Lu features several temples dating from the Dinh Dynasty (968-80) and Early Le Dynasty (980-1009).

Kenh Ga: Kenh Ga is one of the few places in Vietnam where almost the entire community continues to live on boats and certainly the only riverine community surrounded by those spectacular limestone mountains that characterize the landscape around Ninh Binh. Kenh Ga is 21 km northwest of Ninh Binh.

Phat Diem: A spectacular Sino-Vietnamese cathedral is located in Phat Diem, 29 km southeast of Ninh Binh.

Accommodations

Star Hotel: Small but comfortable hotel two blocks northwest of the train station and bus terminal with motorcycle rentals and escorted tours. 267 Tran Hung Dao Blvd., tel. 871522, US$6-30.

Ninh Binh Hotel: Good location in the center of town just west of the bus and train stations. 2 Tran Hung Dao Blvd., tel. 871337, US412-20.

Hoa Lu Hotel: Largest hotel in town, with over 100 a/c rooms in the northwest corner of town. Tran Hung Dao Blvd., tel. 873684, US$25-45.

Transportation

Ninh Binh is 90 km south of Hanoi. All trains and buses from Hanoi and from points south stop here.

VIETNAM

HANOI

Hanoi—capital of the Socialist Republic of Vietnam—is a decrepit but romantic city of broad tree-lined boulevards, narrow shophouses, sleepy public squares, misty lakes, and French-era legacies such as colonial villas, universities, museums, hotels, and an opera house. Unlike its brash and commercialized sister city in the south, Hanoi still feels completely authentic, a time-warp destination as yet unchanged by the advent of mass tourism.

Hanoi will strike some as dirty and poor and with far too many rats. The city certainly needs some repairs and a touch of paint, but unlike most other destinations in Southeast Asia, Hanoi retains a timeless charm little altered from the colonial days of the French. There is also the novelty of visiting a place just opening up to the outside world after decades of severe isolation.

History

Founded in 1010 at the beginning of the Ly Dynasty (1010-1225), Hanoi served as the capital of northern Vietnam until 1400, when the Ho Dynasty temporarily transferred the royal city to Than Hoa. The Le Dynasty restored Hanoi's primary diplomatic status in 1428. The city later served as a regional capital after Emperor Gia Long, founder of the Nguyen Dynasty, moved his royal entourage down to Hue. Western traders, diplomats, and missionaries arrived in the early 17th century, though Hanoi remained independent until 1882, when the city fell into the hands of the French.

Pleased with the cooler climate and convenient location on trade routes to China, the French declared Hanoi their Indochinese capital in 1902 and began a construction program which has left the city with much of its rich architectural legacies. Despite widespread destruction during the Vietnam War, older neighborhoods remain museum pieces of weathered shophouses and colonial villas, which taken together form a striking monument to colonial rule.

The French abandoned Hanoi after their defeat at Dien Bien Phu in 1954; the Geneva Conference in the same year partitioned the country into North and South. Hanoi was heavily bombed during the Vietnam War, though signs of destruction are difficult to spot within the city limits.

Today the city appears to be slowly awakening from a long slumber as entrepreneurs cautiously open small businesses and other services aimed at domestic consumers and the burgeoning tourist trade.

CENTRAL HANOI ATTRACTIONS

Not a city of major monuments or great historical ruins, Hanoi displays its charms in the familiar: narrow streets, small shops, old men fixing bicycle tires on the sidewalks, children dressed for school, the smile of a young girl.

Vietnam Tourism conducts tours but the only way to really experience Hanoi is to walk or hire a bicycle. The following walking tour starts in the center of town near the hotels and then winds around toward the sights in northwestern Hanoi.

Hoan Kiem Lake

Named after a legendary incident from the 15th century, a Vietnamese tale of magical swords similar to King Arthur's Excalibur, Hanoi's Lake of the Restored Sword features a somewhat dilapidated Tortoise Tower on a small southern islet and the Jade Hill Pagoda constructed on a northern spit in the early 19th century. The lake is popular with joggers, lovers, and tai chi practioners in the early morning hours.

Old Quarter

Dong Kinh Nghia Thuc, the rabbit warren of narrow alleys situated between Hoan Kiem Lake and Long Bien Bridge, is the most memorable district in Hanoi and among the most evocative urban sights in Vietnam.

The neighborhood originated several centuries ago as an interlinked series of villages set up by guilds to provide handicrafts and consumer goods for the royal court. Even today, many of the streets are defined by their particular crafts and continue to specialize in particular items such as shoes, jewelry, gold, or papier-mâché offerings used in funerals.

Hanoi's so-called 36 Streets District is quite remarkable. Largely erected in the late 19th and early 20th centuries, the neighborhood features hundreds of "tube houses" constructed in an super-elongated style and decorated with red-tiled roofs and bricks held together with sugarcane juice, sand, and lime. The result is a vernacular alchemy of traditional Vietnamese styles mixed with grander French touches such as wrought-iron balconies, windows with louvered wooden shutters, and plaster-relief friezes of flowers and birds.

Tragically, shophouses are now being torn down at a furious pace to be replaced with the same modern concrete cubicles which mar most other cities in Southeast Asia. Architectural conservationists have sounded the alarm but it appears unlikely that they will have any more luck in Hanoi than they had in Singapore's Chinatown.

A hopeful note is provided by the French-era Dong Xuan Market in the northern section of Old Hanoi, whose recent restoration retained the old facade and modernized the interior.

Revolutionary Museum

Vietnam's long history of struggles against Chinese, Japanese, French, and American forces is recounted in a series of rooms arranged chronologically inside the former French Customs House. Displays retell the defeat of Chinese Mongol forces in 938, Japanese atrocities during WW II, the 1954 French defeat at Dien Bien Phu, the American antiwar movement of the 1960s, plus a guillotine, torture devices, and gruesome execution photos best avoided by the squeamish.

History Museum

Formerly the Louis Finot Museum under the supervision of the École Française d'Extrème Orient, Vietnam's leading historical museum features a dazzling if somewhat confusing series of exhibits chronologically arranged around particular dynasties and historical episodes. Highlights include presentations on prehistoric and Neolithic man, bronze Dong Son drums and funerary urns, Cham relics, the Funan culture of the Mekong Delta, Buddhist statuary and bodhisattvas, weapons used in the Tay Son Revolt, displays on the Nguyen Dynasty, and the struggle for national unification.

The museum is open Tues.-Sun. 0800-1200 and 1300-1600.

Municipal Theater

A magnificent Beaux Arts-style building constructed by the French in 1911 as a replica of the Paris Opera House. From this spot, Viet Minh forces announced in 1945 the success of their August Revolution and the liberation of Vietnam from colonial occupation.

Cultural performances are held most evenings 2000-midnight.

Ambassador's Pagoda

Originally constructed as a guesthouse for ambassadors to the court of the Le Dynasty, the Quan Su Pagoda was subsequently destroyed then rebuilt in 1942 as the official center of Buddhism in Hanoi. Interior details include fine stone sculptures and a mural which recounts the enlightenment of Sakyamuni, the historical reincarnation of the Buddha.

NORTHWESTERN HANOI ATTRACTIONS

Army Museum

First stop might be this museum fronted by a Soviet-built MiG-21 which triumphs above a jumbled graveyard of wrecked B-52s and F-111s—thereby setting the tone for subsequent rooms and displays. Perhaps the most poignant revelation is that the American experience formed but a small blip in the 2,000-year history of struggle against outside forces.

The museum is open Tues.-Sun. 0800-1200 and 1300-1600.

Ho Chi Minh Mausoleum

Set on a great boulevard of waving flags and guarded by no-nonsense soldiers is the imposing granite edifice and final resting place of Ho Chi Minh. Modeled after Lenin's tomb in Moscow, this lotus-shaped polygonal structure seems alien to the delicate sensibilities of the Vietnamese people and perhaps even Uncle Ho himself, who almost certainly would have preferred a simpler monument to honor his modest lifestyle.

Visitors must first register at the nearby office and deposit their bags before marching in

VIETNAM

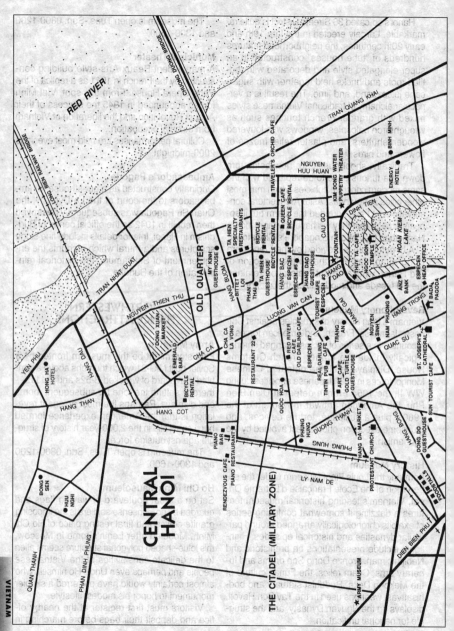

© MOON PUBLICATIONS, INC.

TRAN KHANH DU
TONG DAN
REVOLUTIONARY MUSEUM
HISTORY MUSEUM
LE THANH TONG
CAFE DE PARIS

ITALIAN EMBASSY
CLUB OPERA
BICYCLE RENTAL
Opera House
HANOI OPE..A HILTON HOTEL
GMD/ARMY HOTEL
HOA MA

VIETCOMBANK
LE THACH
POST OFFICE
GOVERNMENT GUESTHOUSE
FORMER TONKIN GOVERNORS OFFICES
IDD/TELECOM
SOFITEL METROPOLE HOTEL
BODEGA CAFE
LOTUS RESTAURANT
TRANG TIEN HOTEL DAN CHU
SMILING PUB
MINIBUSES TO NORTHEAST
VERANDAH BAR AND CAFE
NAM PHUONG RESTAURANT
HANOI TOURISM
PHAN CHU TRINH
LO DUC

HANG KHAY
BODEGA I
BAC NAM
HAI BA TRUNG
NGO QUYEN
LE BISTROT
LE VAN HUU

AIR FRANCE BICYCLE RENTAL
SOPHIA GUESTHOUSE
CENTRAL BUILDING
VIETNAM TOURISM
HOA BINH
HANG BAI
MOTORCYCLE SHOPS

LE THAI TO
NHA CHUNG
HOAN KIEM DISTRICT
BA TRIEU
IMMIGRATION POLICE
ORIENT CAFE
FRENCH EMBASSY
MEETING CAFE
RESTAURANT 202

ESPECEN #1
PHU GIA
GREEN BAMBOO CAFE-BAR
VIETNAM AIRLINES
LOTUS GUESTHOUSE
QUANG TRUNG
NGUYEN DU

19 DECEMBER MARKET
LY THUONG KIET
LAO VISA SECTION

NGUYEN THAI HOC
EDEN HOTEL
QUAN SU PAGODA
HOA SUA BAKERY RESTAURANT
TRAN HUNG DAO
CAMBODIAN EMBASSY
TRAN BINH TRONG
BOSS HOTEL
THIEN QUANG LAKE
CANADIAN EMBASSY

HOAN KIEM GUESTHOUSE
ALPO
BLUE II
INDOCHINE
DONG LOI ROSE HOTEL
SAIGON HOTEL
QUAN SU
MANGO HOTEL
PHAN BOI CHAU
EDEN HOTEL
250 m
VIP CLUB
LENIN PARK

CAFE 252 (BAKERY)
HANOI RAILWAY STATION
30-4 HOTEL
CAPITAL HOTEL
ANN TOURS
LE DUAN
BLUE
LAOTIAN EMBASSY
CIRCUS ARENA

TRAN QUOC PAGODA

HO TAY (WEST LAKE)

TRUC BACH LAKE

NORTHWEST HANOI

QUAN THANH TEMPLE

QUAN THANH

THUY KHUE

HOANG HOA THAM

PHAN DINH PHUNG

BOTANICAL GARDENS

MINISTRY OF DEFENSE

PRESIDENTIAL PALACE

HOANG VAN THU

HO CHI MINH HOUSE ON STILTS & GIFTSHOP

ALTERNATE ENTRANCE FOR HO HOUSE

NGOC HA

HO CHI MINH MAUSOLEUM

NATIONAL ASSEMBLY BUILDING

BAC SON

BA DINH SQUARE

WAR MEMORIAL SHRINE

THE CITADEL (MILITARY ZONE)

ONE PILLAR PAGODA

PARKING CHUA MOT COT

FINISH ENTRANCE

MAUSOLEUM ASSEMBLY POINT (START OF WALK)

PARKING

HO CHI MINH MUSEUM

8 HUNG VUONG BAGGAGE DEPOSIT

5 NGOC HA BAGGAGE DEPOSIT

ARMY CLUB

HOANG DIEU

LE NAM DO

CANADIAN EMBASSY

DOI CAN

DIEN BIEN PHU

LE HONG PHONG

ARMY MUSEUM

FLAG TOWER

HUNG VUONG

LENIN STATUE

KIM MA BUS STATION

RUSSIAN EMBASSY

CHINESE EMBASSY

CHINESE EMBASSY VISA SECTION

MILITARY BANK

THONG TIN MUSEUM

FINE ARTS MUSEUM

MONGOLIAN EMBASSY

GERMAN EMBASSY

THAI EMBASSY

TRAN PHU

MAI ANH HOTEL

CAO BA QUAT

0   100 m

TON DUC THAN

MAIN TEMPLE

NGUYEN KHUYEN

NGUYEN THAI HOC

VAN MIEU

TEMPLE OF LITERATURE

ENTRANCE

QUOC TU GIAM

QUOC TU GIAM HOTEL

□ = ROADBLOCKS

• • • • = WALKING TOUR

⊪⊪⊪⊪ = SEALED OFF AREA

SAO MAI HOTEL

THONG PHONG

QUOC TU GIAM RESTAURANT

© MOON PUBLICATIONS, INC.

VIETNAM

double file to the mausoleum. Inside, Chairman Ho lies embalmed and painted by Soviet technicians to resemble a waxy Vietnamese mummy—despite his specific wishes to be cremated and treated like an ordinary citizen. Above the glass sarcophagus towers a gigantic hammer and sickle, one of the last places in the world to view the symbol of a fallen ideology.

The mausoleum is open Tue.-Sun. 0800-1200.

Ho Chi Minh House

Ho's simple house stands just north of his mausoleum. Ho was born near Vinh on 19 May 1890 into a poor but scholarly family of aristocratic lineage that despised colonial control of Vietnam. He later attended Quoc Hoc College in Hue before leaving for further studies in France and subsequent travels in England, North Africa, and America. During his stay in Paris, Ho studied the works of Marx and joined the French Socialist Party, embracing the radical communist ideology which proved quite popular during the Depression era of the 1930s. Less idealistically, Ho also worked at the Carlton Hotel in London as an assistant pastry chef.

In 1923, Ho moved to Moscow, where he was trained as a communist activist and socialist spy later assigned to an outpost in Canton. His travels from China were varied: Buddhist monk in Thailand, subversive activist in Hong Kong, exiled Vietnamese patriot sentenced in 1930 to death in absentia by the French.

It was not until the early 1940s that the modest village activist assumed the pseudonym by which he is now known—Ho Chi Minh. Ho returned to Vietnam in the 1940s to lead the national struggle for unification until his death in 1969 in the simple house within the former governor's residence.

Presidential Palace

Constructed by the French in 1906 as national headquarters for the governor-general of Indochina, this building is now used for official receptions and other state functions. Rather than living here after his arrival in Hanoi, Ho chose to reside in the servant quarters described above.

West Lake

Just north of the Presidential Palace lies an enormous freshwater lake once encircled by magnificent palaces and pavilions constructed by the early kings of Hanoi. All were destroyed in various feudal wars, but visitors can enjoy the views and tour the Quan Thanh and Tran Quoc pagodas. Tran Quoc, the oldest religious sanctuary in Hanoi, was established in 1639 and completely rebuilt in 1842.

One Pillar Pagoda

Chua Mot Cot, perhaps the most curious structure in Hanoi and among the most ancient and revered monuments in Vietnam, was established in the early 11th century but reconstructed in 1954 after being burned to the ground by departing French troops. The curious name is derived from the singular pillar which supports the little lotus-shaped temple, which symbolizes the sacred blossom rising from the Sea of Sorrow and provides hope in the Buddhist universe.

Ho Chi Minh Museum

Adjacent to the One Pillar is an impressive museum opened in 1990 to commemorate the centenary of Ho's birth. Although the exhibits are labeled in Vietnamese and finding an English-speaking guide can be difficult, the chronological arrangement and historical photographs help you understand the life of Vietnam's most famous patriot.

The museum is open Tues.-Sun. 0800-1200 and 1330-1600.

Fine Arts Museum

Once the French Ministry of Information but today a Vietnamese propaganda museum filled with contemporary socialist-realism art, plus there's a small collection of handicrafts on the second floor.

Temple of Literature

Van Mieu is considered the most important temple complex in Hanoi and among the finest surviving examples of traditional architecture in Vietnam.

The center was founded in 1070 during the reign of Ly Thanh Tong as the national headquarters for the study of Confucianism and as the spiritual center of the Red River delta.

Van Mieu is divided longitudinally by gateways into five courtyards entered through the Van Mieu Gate at the southern end. The Poetry

Balcony above the gate is followed by two large and now-empty squares which were once filled with wooden hostels for students and teachers. Van Mieu's most important artifacts are the 82 stone stelae arranged inside the third courtyard and inscribed with the names and academic records of the laureates who passed the triennial examinations. Beyond this courtyard lie the Dai Thanh ("Great Success Gate") and a series of temples which honor the Chinese philosopher.

ACCOMMODATIONS

If the Western concept of tourism is foreign to Vietnam, then Hanoi has a long way to go before it can offer the standards of service and comfort found elsewhere in Southeast Asia. Most of the following hotels are in rudimentary condition and overpriced by any conceivable benchmark. On the positive side, hotel staffs are often friendly and facilities are slowly improving as more tourists arrive in the nation's capital.

The best neighborhood for visitors is central Hanoi, where most of the moderately priced hotels are located, not in the outskirts of town where Vietnam Tourism often attempts to shuttle Westerners on packaged tours.

Budget
Trang Tien Hotel: Popular guesthouse in the center of town near the Bodega Cafe. 35 Trang Tien St., tel. 825-6341, US$8-50.

Lotus Guesthouse: Small but well-managed guesthouse also in the center of town. 42 Ly Thuong Kiet St., tel. 826-8642, US$6-15.

Hotels near the Railway Station: Some travelers have reportedly had luck at the Railway Hotel (Khach San Ga), Khach San 30, Khach San Chi Long, and Railway Service Company Hotel (Khach San Cong Nhan Duong). All cost US$8-15.

Moderate to Luxury
Several acceptable hotels in the US$25-50 range are conveniently located in the center of town near Hoan Kiem Lake.

Bodega Hotel: Good-value hotel situated above a popular cafe with clean a/c rooms and friendly managers. 57 Trang Tien St., tel. 826-7784, US$20-35.

Dan Chu Hotel: Faded, old colonial-style hotel up the street from the Municipal Theater constructed in the late-19th century and once called the Hanoi Hotel. Now overpriced but all rooms are a/c and breakfast is included. 29 Trang Tien St., tel. 825-4937, US$70-130.

Thang Loi Hotel: Situated in a wonderful location overlooking West Lake (four km from city center), this Cuban-built hotel features all the standard Cuban amenities: a waterless swimming pool, broken a/c units in each room, large mosquitoes, dry rot, and crumbling concrete walls. Tour groups are often exiled out here. Yen Phu St., tel. 826-8211, US$90-180.

Sofitel Metropole Hotel: The only luxury hotel in Hanoi worth considering is the former Thong Nhat, recently refurbished at a total cost of over US$10 million. Originally constructed in 1911 and comparable with the Peninsula in Hong Kong and the Raffles in Singapore, the 300-room Metropole has a swimming pool, French bistro, and all the other amenities. 15 Ngo Quyen St., tel. 826-6919, US$240-380.

RESTAURANTS

Western restaurants are located in all hotels and, unlike the rooms, meals are reasonably priced. However, the best meals are found in streetside stalls in the Old Quarter and small coffee shops in the tourist district.

Dishes to try include *pho* (spicy chicken soup), *cha* (barbecued pork), *ban cuon* (egg rolls filled with minced meats), *nem* (crab and egg pancakes), and *com* (sticky rice).

Bodega Cafe: Popular spot for snacks, drinks, pastries, and ice cream. 57 Trang Tien Street.

Tin Tin Bar & Cafe: Backpacker hangout with road food and nightly entertainment. 14 Hang Non Street.

Real Darling Cafe: Serves decent Western and Vietnamese dishes plus rents out a few rooms upstairs. 33 Hang Quat Street.

Meeting Cafe: Another backpacker haunt with standard fare and a travel agency that can arrange inexpensive tours to most destinations in northern Vietnam. 59 Ba Trieu Street.

Sunset Pub: A Norwegian-run spot with pizzas, hamburgers, and live jazz on weekends. 31 Cao Ba Quat Street.

VIETNAM

Redwoods: An expat favorite for its food and billiards tables. 11 Bao Khanh Street.

Verandah Bar & Cafe: Another watering hole situated in a restored French villa serving Western dishes at reasonable prices. 9 Nguyen Khac Ca Street.

ENTERTAINMENT

Hanoi is a very sleepy town where most cafes and nightclubs are closed by 2100 or 2200. What little nightlife exists is almost exclusively limited to clubs in the major hotels.

Municipal Theater: Entertainment inside this replica of the Paris Opera House ranges from traditional music to revolutionary theater.

Water Puppets: Water puppetry is a folk art unique to northern Vietnam and one of the best entertainments offered in Hanoi. As implied by the name, the performance involves a number of large wooden puppets which are manipulated under the water with long bamboo poles by puppeteers who stand partially submerged behind a bamboo curtain. Performances are held weekly in the Hoan Kiem Lake Theater, established in 1956 by Ho Chi Minh himself.

Circus: Vietnam's amateurish but highly entertaining State Circus performs seasonally near the entrance of Lenin Park. Recommended.

Hotel Nightclubs: For a glimpse into the future, check out the hotel discos and ballrooms packed every weekend with young and trendy Vietnamese. Western residents in Hanoi often join the private clubs at the Australian and Swedish embassies.

OTHER PRACTICALITIES

Tourist Information
Vietnam Tourism at 54 Nguyen Du St. exists solely to sell tours and rent cars and not to aid independent travelers. Hanoi Tourism at 8 To Hien Thanh St. is friendlier and can help with visa extensions, police registration, and changes in departure endorsements.

Many travelers prefer the service and lower prices at privately owned cafes and travel agencies such as Ann Tourist in the Dong Do Hotel, Ecco Vietnam Tours at 50 Ba Trien St., Especen

Tours at 79 Hang Trong St. and Pacific Tours at 58 Tran Nhan Tong Street.

The least expensive options are tours arranged by cafes such as Real Darling Café on Hang Quat St., Lotus Café on Ly Thuong Kiet St., Meeting Café on Ba Trieu St., Queen Café on Hang Bac St., and Red River Café on Hang Bo Street.

Services
Immigration: Visas can be extended with the help of any travel agency in Hanoi. The immigration police on Hang Bai Street do not deal directly with Westerners.

Banks: Cash and traveler's checks can be exchanged at the highest legal rate at the Vietcombank at 47 Ly Thai To St. or at any of the Vietcombank branches located around Hanoi. Bank of America, Barclays, Citibank, and many other Western banks have offices in Hanoi but are forced to collect hefty service fees on all foreign exchange transactions.

Post And Telecommunications: The General Post Office on Dinh Tien Hoang St. also provides international telephone, telex, and fax services at incredibly high rates, though mail service appears reliable. The GPO is open daily 0630-2000.

Embassies: Several countries have embassies in Hanoi, including Cambodia at 71 Tran Hung Dao St., China at 46 Hoang Dieu St., Laos at 22 Tran Binh Trong St., and Thailand at Khu Trung Tu Street.

TRANSPORTATION

Hanoi is 103 km from Haiphong, 165 km from Halong, 420 km from Dien Bien Phu, 658 km from Hue, and 1,710 km from Saigon.

Air
Hanoi's Noi Bai Airport is 35 km north of city center. Taxis cost US$15-20 to city center; purchase your ticket at the taxi booking counter inside the airport. Minibuses operated by Vietnam Airlines cost US$4-5 to city center; once again, purchase tickets at the booking counter inside the airport. From city center, taxis cost US$20 to the airport. Minibuses operated by Vietnam Airlines cost US$4-5; tickets can be purchased in

advance at the Vietnam Airlines International Booking Office on Quang Trung Street.

Hanoi is served by most Asian-based international airlines such as Thai Airways International, Cathay Pacific, Philippine Airlines, Malaysian Airlines, Singapore Airlines, and Garuda.

Vietnam Airlines has two offices, including a domestic office at 60 Quang Trung St. and an international office at the corner of Trang Thi and Quang Trung streets, which handles reservations and ticketing for all international airlines. Thai International, Air France and Aeroflot are adjacent to the Vietnam Airlines international office at 1 Quang Trung Street.

Train

The ticket office at the Hanoi train station is open daily 0730-1130 and 1330-1630. Tickets should be purchased one day in advance. Beware of pickpockets.

Several express trains leave daily for Saigon and points en route. Trains also head east to the port city of Haiphong and northwest to Pho Lu and across the border to Kunming in China.

The main problem with train travel is that Westerners are charged five times the official Vietnamese rate, an outrage which makes trains almost as expensive as air transportation. Despite the surcharge, trains are in almost every respect superior to buses: there's room to stretch your legs, opportunities for conversation, and better scenery since trains typically pass through countryside rather than along crowded roads.

Bus

Hanoi has several bus terminals which serve different destinations. Long-distance buses usually leave mornings 0500-0600 and tickets should be purchased at least one day in advance.

Giap Bat bus terminal, seven km south of the train station, serves points south of Hanoi such as Sam Son Beaches (five hours), Vinh (eight hours), and Saigon (54 hours).

Kim Ma Bus Terminal near the Ho Chi Minh Museum in northwestern Hanoi serves destinations to the west such as Hoa Binh (two hours), Son La (18 hours), and Dien Bien Phu (24 hours).

Gia Lam bus terminal on the east bank of the Red River serves points northeast of Hanoi such as Haiphong (three hours), Halong Bay (five hours), and Lang Son (12 hours) on the border with China.

THE NORTHEAST COAST

HAIPHONG

Haiphong, Vietnam's second-most-important port and third-largest city, is often bypassed by visitors heading directly to the natural wonders of Halong Bay. Admittedly, Haiphong's outer districts are little more than industrialized sprawl, but the colonial architecture which survived the Vietnam War and the general dilapidation of the waterfront area impart a rich atmosphere to the downtown districts.

Haiphong's real charm is found in the French-era warehouses on the Cam River waterfront, the Catholic churches, and other colonial buildings located in the center of town and a few blocks south on Tran Hung Dao Street. Top draw is the former Haiphong Opera House, now the Municipal Theater.

Du Hang Pagoda, Haiphong's most ornate temple, is dedicated to Le Chan, the valiant female warrior who fought with the Trung sisters against their Chinese overlords. The pagoda is one km south of the opera house.

Do Son Beach

Northern Vietnam's most popular beach resort offers fine sand, waving palms, pine-clad hills, and a small selection of hotels once patronized exclusively by French colonialists and high-ranking Vietnamese. Do Son is 21 km southeast of Haiphong. Buses depart from Lach Tay Street.

Accommodations include the 120-room Do Son Hotel run by Haiphong Tourism and a half-dozen beach bungalows favored by expats from Hanoi.

Accommodations

Hoa Binh Hotel: Decent spot just opposite the train station. 104 Luong Khanh Thien St., tel. 846907, US$18-40.

HAIPHONG

CAM RIVER

TO BAI CHAY AND HALONG BAY

BOATS TO HONG GAI AND CAT BA

CAR FERRY

BEN BINH BUS STATION (TO HALONG BAY)

TEXTILE FACTORY

CEMENT WORKS

TO HANOI

TO HANOI

TRAN PHU

VIETCOMBANK

SEE INSET

POST OFFICE

DIEN BIEN PHU

CATHEDRAL

BEN BINH

THANG LONG HOTEL

NGUYEN TRI PHUONG

HOANG VAN THU

BACH DANG

TAM BAC RIVER

HOA BIEN RESTAURANT

NGUYEN DUC CANH

TAM BAC

QUOC HUNG RESTAURANT

SAT MARKET

BINH MINH HOTEL / RESTAURANT

HAITRANG HOTEL / RESTAURANT

HANG KENH CARPET FACTORY

TAM BAC BUS STATION

TON DUC THANG

TO SAIGON

BUS TERMINAL

SAO DEM HOTEL

DU HANG PAGODA

TO HIEU

CAT CUT

HAI BA TRUNG

BONGSEN HOTEL / RESTAURANT

PHU VINH HOTEL

HO SEN

KS CONG DOAN

NGUYEN CONG TRU

HENG KENH PAVILION

TO DOSON (21 km) AND CAT BI AIRPORT

LACH TRAY

LACH TRAY BUS STATION

STADIUM

VIETNAM AIRLINES AGENT

HISTORY MUSEUM

NHA KHACH

THAN LICH HOTEL

BONG SEN HOTEL

KHUBA HOTEL

HANG KENH

LY THUONG KIET

KHANH

LE LOI

PHUONG DONG HOTEL

TRAIN STATION

THIEN

CAT BI HOTEL

VIETNAM AIRLINES

HOA BINH HOTEL

NGUYEN DU PARK

MUNICIPAL QUANG TRUNG THEATER

MINH KHAI

HOANG VAN THU

1 km

© MOON PUBLICATIONS, INC.

VIETNAM

INSET

NGUYEN TRI PHUONG

VIETCOMBANK

HAIPHONG TOURISM

HAI QUAN

BACH DANG

HUU NGHI HOTEL

HOTEL DU COMMERCE

ARTEX SHOP

VID BANK

THANG NAM

QUANG MINH HOTEL

MINH KHAI HOTEL

POST OFFICE

DUYEN HAI HOTEL

HONG BANG HOTEL

DIEM BIEN HOTEL

VIETNAM TOURISM

0   1 km

Thanh Lich Hotel: The least expensive hotel in town is about one km southeast of city center near a public park and several large lakes. 47 Lach Tray St., tel. 847361, US$10-18.

Hotel de Commerce: Formerly the Huu Nghi, this old French-era hotel is one block east of Vietnam Tourism. 62 Dien Bien Phu St., tel. 847206, US$25-45.

Transportation
Haiphong is 103 km southeast of Hanoi.

Bus: Buses from the fountain at the northern end of Hoan Kiem Lake in Hanoi take about three hours to Haiphong. Buses back to Hanoi depart from the halt near the Municipal Theater. Buses south to Thai Binh leave from Tran Nguyen Han Street.

Boat: One of the best reasons to visit Haiphong is to take the four-hour ferry ride to the town of Hon Gai on Halong Bay through a surrealistic landscape of spellbinding limestone mountains and emerald green waters. Ferries depart three times daily from the municipal dock on Ben Binh Street. There's also a hydrofoil which leaves Haiphong four times weekly and takes less than two hours to reach Hon Gai.

HALONG BAY

Halong Bay, considered by many to be the most spectacular landscape in Vietnam, is a watery wonderland of ethereal limestone formations which rise abruptly from perfectly placid waters, isolated coves, breathtaking grottoes, and thousands of misty islets fantastically carved in the shapes of tigers, unicorns, and sea dragons. Ancient junks and simple sampans gliding through placid waters help complete the aquatic terrain, which resembles some sort of Chinese ink painting. Halong is actually the remnant of an ancient seabed which has eroded into the bizarrely sculpted topography found from Vietnam to Guilin, China.

The center of the district is Halong City, a provincial capital split into two parts by a narrow bay. The western half of the city, Bai Chay, has most of the hotels, restaurants, and travel agencies, while the eastern half, Hon Gai, serves as the industrial port for the district. Small boats shuttle back and forth between the two towns.

Boat Tours
Beaches around Halong Bay are disappointing, being both rocky and badly polluted from nearby coal mines. Hire a boat and spend the day touring the region.

Among the more spectacular grottoes are Hang Hanh, which extends almost two km inside a limestone karst; Hang Dau Go, nicknamed "Cave of Wonders" by 19th-century French tourists; and Hang Trinh Nu or "Cave of Virgins," monikered after an old Vietnamese folk story.

Boats can be rented from most hotels and less expensively from independent operators at the boat quays in Bay Chay and Hon Gai, the two towns in Halong Bay. Independent travelers can inquire at larger hotels about joining a tour group.

Another way to have a quick look is with the ordinary ferry which departs mornings from Hon Gai and arrives four hours later in Haiphong.

Bai Chay Accommodations
Halong's main port is in Hon Gai but most hotels are in Bai Chay, a surprisingly large town three km west and a short ferry crossing from Hon Gai. Buses from Hanoi pass through Bai Chay en route to Hon Gai. Bai Chay has almost 100 guesthouses and hotels; competition has kept prices low, at least by Vietnamese standards.

Adjacent to the ferry dock are several basic hotels and newer hotels either owned and operated by the local government or constructed with the aid of Thai or Hong Kong money. Most of the budget places are located in town, two km west of the pier in the direction of Hanoi.

Dozens of small guesthouses, hotels, and mini-hotels are scattered along the main road and side streets of Bai Chay and most charge US$10-20 for an acceptable room with private bath and hot water; the more expensive units often include air-conditioning. There's no need to make an exhaustive listing since hotel touts will approach you immediately as you arrive at Bai Chay by bus or boat.

If the downtown hotels seem somewhat grim, consider one of the hotels just outside town and situated on one of the hills surrounding Bai Chay. To the east of town are a pair of fairly nice mini-hotels with views over the bay—Huong Tram Hotel costs US$10-15 while the adjacent Hai Long Hotel offers superior rooms for US$25-40.

Hon Gai Accommodations

Few travelers stay in this industrial port town, though late arrivals on the boat from Haiphong may need to overnight here before moving across the bay to Bai Chay. Hotels in the center of town include the Hang Hai, Hai Van, Thuong Mai, Huong Lien, Viet Anh, and Queen West Hotels. All have rooms from US$10-25.

Servicable hotels down by the boat pier for Bai Chay include Phuong Nam, Hong Ngoc, and Phuong Lien; same prices as the hotels near city center.

Transportation

Hon Gai is 165 km from Hanoi and 62 km from Haiphong.

Tours: By far the most convenient way to see Halong Bay is with a tour organized in Hanoi. Most of the traveler's cafes put together three-day, two-night tours for US$25-30 which includes transportation, accommodations, and a full-day boat tour of Halong Bay. It's just about impossible to do this excursion any cheaper, and it avoids any potential problems with local police who sometimes shake down tourists for unnecessary fees and travel permits.

Bus: Buses from Hanoi's Gia Lam bus terminal take about five hours to reach Bai Chay. Buses from the bus terminal just across the Cam River in Haiphong take two hours to reach Halong, although most travelers prefer to take the ordinary ferry or hydrofoil.

Travelers heading northeast from Halong can take a bus from the Hon Gai bus terminal to Mong Cai on the Chinese border.

Taxi: Taxis from Hanoi take three hours and cost US$40-80 roundtrip depending on the company and type of car.

Boat: Several ferries depart Haiphong daily

and take five scenic hours to reach Hon Gai. Hydrofoils depart Haiphong several times weekly.

CAT BA NATIONAL PARK

Cat Ba, the largest island within Halong Bay, is famed for its superb beaches and isolated coves, primeval forests and freshwater swamps, and rich diversity of wildlife including hornbills, wild cats, and migratory waterfowl down from China. A small portion of the island was declared a national park in 1986 to protect the fragile ecosystems and endangered wildlife.

Visitors generally stay in Cat Ba town and make day-trips to the beach, or join escorted tours out to Cat Ba National Park, 17 km from town.

Accommodations

Most island residents live along the southern coastline in or around the town of Cat Ba. Several small hotels and an upscale resort are located in town and one km from the Cat Ba dock. Chua Dong, Hoang Huong, Lan Ha, Van Anh, Thuy Linh, and Quang Duc Hotels in Cat Ba charge US$10-30.

There are also some simple cabins right on Cat Ba Beach which cost US$10-15, probably a better option than staying back in town

Transportation

Cat Ba village is 42 km east of Haiphong and 24 km south of Hon Gai. Hydrofoils depart Haiphong in the morning 0600-1200 and take three hours to reach Cat Ba village. Ferries can also be chartered from Halong Bay.

As with Halong Bay, Cat Ba is probably best visited on a package tour from Hanoi which would include transportation, accommodations, and guide services in the national park.

NORTHWEST VIETNAM

Northwest Vietnam is the most isolated and wildly beautiful region in Vietnam. Since the start of World War II, the area had been almost completely isolated from the outside world until early 1993, when French president François Mitterrand made his dramatic visit to the battle site at Dien Bien Phu. After his departure, tourism officials abandoned their discredited system of travel permits and declared the northwest open to Western travelers for the first time since the late 1930s.

Today, the far north provides superb scenery and relatively untouched villages whose tribal inhabitants remain far less commercialized than their cousins in northern Thailand.

The most popular route in this area is west from Hanoi to Hoa Binh and Son La before reaching Dien Bien Phu, site of the decisive 1954 battle between the North Vietnamese and the French. The road from Dien Bien Phu into Laos remains closed to Western visitors, but it will prove immensely convenient for independent travelers as restrictions are slowly lifted. Guesthouse owners and travelers in Hanoi can help with current details.

Westerners are now permitted to depart Vietnam via the town of Lang Son near the Chinese border. Be sure your visa shows Lang Son as your approved departure point, and double check current requirements on travel permits to the Lang Son district.

The Circuit
Surviving some of the terrible roads in the more remote districts of northwestern Vietnam requires a great deal of time and nerves of steel. The road from Hanoi to Tuan Giao is largely sealed and relatively comfortable but sharply deteriorates between Tuan Giao and Dien Bien Phu. Many travelers get discouraged by the road conditions and return to Hanoi after visiting the closer towns of Moc Chau or Son La.

From Dien Bien Phu, you can fly back to Hanoi or attempt to complete the clockwise loop through Lai Chau, Sapa, Lao Cai at the Chinese border, and then back to Hanoi by train. The road from Dien Bien Phu to Sapa and Lao Cai is among the worst in Vietnam and is best attempted with the aid of a hired jeep or motorcycle. When the weather is co-operating, the entire circuit can be completed in about a week.

Russian and Japanese jeeps and 4WD vehicles can be rented in Hanoi and cost US$350-400 for the one-week circular trip.

HOA BINH

Hoa Binh lies in a valley once inhabited by the Lac Viet peoples, who created Dong Son culture and the famous bronze drums now found in museums throughout the world. Hoa Binh is currently home to Hmong and Tai hilltribe peoples, though their proximity to Hanoi has quickly turned these local groups into commercialized parodies of their former selves. Hoa Binh can be a day-trip from Hanoi or a convenient stopping point en route to Dien Bien Phu.

Attractions
All of the following sights are located outside Hoa Binh and are best reached by tour or chartered taxi.

Chua Thay Pagoda: Also known as Thien Phuc Tu ("Heavenly Bliss") Pagoda, this impressive temple complex features three sections filled with images of Buddhas, Vietnamese heroes, and a 12th-century herbalist to whom the temple is dedicated. Chua Thay is 40 km southwest of Hanoi in the village of Sai Son.

Tay Phuong Pagoda: A hillside temple chiefly famed for its collection of 74 wooden effigies of enlightened monks, considered the finest examples of 17th-century woodcarving in Vietnam. The temple is six km southwest of Chua Thay Pagoda in the village of Thac Xa.

Huong Son ("Perfume Mountain"): A superb wonderland of pagodas, shrines, and religious sanctuaries nestled in a spectacular region of limestone mountains and tropical jungle. An important Buddhist pilgrimage center,

Huong Son is widely considered among the most beautiful destinations in the north. The mountain is 60 km southwest of Hanoi and can be toured by boats up the Yen Vi River.

Accommodations
The Hoa Binh Hotel is about two km west of city center on the road to Dien Bien Phu, near a reconstructed Hmong minority village. Hotel guides can arrange visits to nearby minority villages. Rooms in this surprisingly well-maintained hotel cost US$30-45.

Transportation
Hoa Binh is on the banks of the Hac Giang River some 75 km southwest of Hanoi. Buses from Hanoi's Kim Ma terminal take two hours. Tours can also be arranged at most of the cafes and travel agencies in Hanoi.

MAI CHAU

Visitors on a tight schedule who would like to see some of the countryside and perhaps do some trekking will find the Montagnard village of Mai Chau an easy option from Hanoi. The collection of villages which comprise Mai Chau are nothing special but the scenery is magnificent and almost a dozen treks can be made to some surprisingly untouched Montagnard outposts.

Local guides can be hired for US$5 per day. Day hikes to nearby villages are pleasant but you might find longer multi-day treks to remote villages far more rewarding. All treks start from the Mai Chau Guesthouse, which is located in the small hamlet of Ban Lac, five km south of Highway 6 on the Hanoi-Dien Bien Phu route. Longer treks can be arranged in Ban Lac or with the help of the Hoa Binh Provincial Tourist office at the Hoa Binh Hotel.

Accommodations
The Mai Chau Guesthouse just opposite the market costs US$15-20 and is the only officially approved guesthouse in the district. However, most tours and independent travelers continue a few km southwest to Ban Lac village where accommodations are offered in stilt houses for US$4-8 per night. This is also a convenient starting point for treks west to a Xa Linh village inhabited by Hmong.

Transportation
Mai Chau is 135 km southwest of Hanoi and five km south of the Tong Dau Junction on Highway 6. Organized tours can be arranged in Hanoi or you can take a bus to Hoa Binh and continue to Mai Chau by local bus or motorcycle taxi.

SON LA

Son La, two-thirds of the distance from Hanoi to Dien Bien Phu, is the capital of the province of the same name and home to many of Vietnam's ethnic minorities. Son La is an essential overnight stop for any traveler attempting to reach Dien Bien Phu.

Attractions
French Prison: Son La was administered by the Black Thai ethnic minority until the beginning of the 20th century, when the French established control and brutally put down a series of anticolonial revolts. Many of the revolutionaries were executed in the small prison constructed in 1908 on a small hill in the center of town.

Minority Villages: Son La lies near mountainous villages inhabited by ethnic minority groups such as Tai, Hmong, Tay, Zao, and Muong. Many of these peoples have integrated into Vietnamese society and abandoned their traditional lifestyles. Excursions to minority villages in the Mai Chau Valley can be arranged at the Son La Guesthouse.

Accommodations
Several guesthouses and hotels are located along the main highway and on the road heading north toward the To Da River. None are great value but will serve for a single night.

Just opposite the bus stop is Son La Tourism Guesthouse, which is actually a hotel with rooms from US$16-40. At the northwestern end of town you'll find the Hoa Ban Hotel with rooms from US$20-35 and the Phong Lan Hotel with better yet cheaper rooms from US$14-30.

Back in town along Highway 6 is Labor Federation Guesthouse, Song Da Guesthouse, and the People's Committee Guesthouse with rough rooms from US$10-30.

Transportation

Son La is 310 km northwest of Hanoi on the southern banks of the Nam La River. Buses from Hanoi's Kim Ma Bus Terminal take 12-15 hours over increasingly rough roads, sometimes impassable during the rainy season from June to October. The bus from Son La to Dien Bien Phu takes 8-10 hours depending on the weather and road conditions.

DIEN BIEN PHU

Dien Bien Phu was the site of the catastrophic defeat of the French which signaled the end of their colonial empire in Southeast Asia and laid the seeds for subsequent American involvement.

The Indochinese Waterloo began in 1952 when General Giap occupied the remote village of Dien Bien Phu in an elaborate ruse to lure the French into a vulnerable strategic position, with colonial supply lines drawn extremely thin. In 1953 Giap drove into Laos, skirted the French forces on the Plain of Jars, and reached the outskirts of Luang Prabang before pulling back to avoid the summer monsoons. In French eyes, Giap had proven that the Viet Minh could move into Laos with relative impunity and that Dien Bien Phu was a vital barrier from which to block Communist moves into Laos, then a close ally of the French.

In late 1953, French General Henri Navarre proposed that Dien Bien Phu be occupied as a mooring point from which to defend Laos and penetrate the rear guard of the Viet Minh, possibly on a straight march into Hanoi. Despite warnings from other French commanders that Dien Bien Phu would become a "meat grinder" of French battalions rather than a mooring point, Navarre ordered French troops dropped into the valley starting in November 1953. By early 1954 the stage was set: the French had 10,000 combat-trained troops hemmed in a closed valley almost impossible to resupply aside from a massive airlift operation; the Vietnamese had over 50,000 experienced troops and a frightening amount of heavy artillery emplaced in carefully camouflaged positions. It was no contest.

The Viet Minh attacked in March 1954 and by late April it was apparent that the French would soon suffer one of the worst defeats in modern military warfare. On the afternoon of 7 May 1954, the Viet Minh's red flag went up over the French command bunker. A world away on the following morning, nine delegations assembled around a horseshoe-shaped table at the old League of Nations building to settle the question of French authority in Vietnam. On 20 July 1954, members at the Geneva Conference agreed that Vietnam should be divided along the 17th parallel pending elections to determine the future of the country. Nine years of warfare had wiped out almost 95,000 French-colonial troops and an estimated 250,000 Viet Minh.

Dien Bien Phu made international headlines in February 1993 when French President François Mitterrand made a pilgrimage to the battleground and later had an official dinner with Giap in Hanoi. Later that year, Pierre Schoendorffer, a former prisoner of the conflict and now a French film director, released his award-winning *Dien Bien Phu*.

Attractions

Dien Bien Phu today is a quiet valley with little signs of the conflict aside from a small museum and several plaques which show the progress of the battle. The 2,242 French colonial troops who perished and were buried under the rice paddies are commemorated with a simple memorial.

Dien Bien Phu is also home to several minority tribes such as Tai, Hmong, Phu La, and Coong, who often visit the market on weekends and can sometimes be visited on organized treks.

Accommodations

Several guesthouses flank the road coming in from Hanoi. The People's Committee Guesthouse costs US$10-45 and hosts most of the visitors to the region since it has almost 50 rooms in fairly good condition. The nearby Dien Bien Phu Mini-Hotel is smaller, poorly maintained, and has over 20 rooms from US$12-25. More guesthouses will certainly be constructed as tourism in the region continues to increase.

Transportation

Dien Bien Phu is 110 km from Son La and 420 km from Hanoi. Most travelers overnight in Son La and complete the bus journey to Dien Bien Phu the following day.

SAPA

Sapa is a former French colonial hill station nestled in the Tonkinese Alps. Sapa has been the recent recipient of a tourist mini-boom as an increasing number of Western travelers arrive to sample the natural surroundings before mass tourism makes its inevitable mark on the district. Sapa is remote, difficult to reach, and bone-chillingly cold in the winter months but the sheer beauty of the mountains and ethnic flavor provided by the local Montagnards make this one of the upcoming stars of northern Vietnam.

Accommodations

In less than a decade, Sapa has gone from a deserted outpost with a single guesthouse to a major boomtown with an estimated 65 guesthouses and several large concrete hotels now under construction. Most of the guesthouses are very small homestay affairs that charge US$5-10 during the week but often crank up prices to US$10-30 on weekends when Sapa is almost completely inundated with Western and Vietnamese tourists.

The two largest concentrations of guesthouses are at the top of the hill near the post office on the road to Lao Cai and lower in elevation along the main road where you'll find the bus halt for Hanoi.

Transportation

Sapa is 34 km southwest of Lao Cai, the border town and transit point for travelers heading off to China. Minibuses shuttle back and forth between Sapa and Lao Cai and take about two hours to complete the rough but scenic journey straight up the mountain.

Sapa is also 295 km from Hanoi. Most travelers take the train from Hanoi to Lao Cai and head immediately down to Sapa rather than overnighting in the rather dismal border town. Minibuses wait for each train from Hanoi so it's possible to reach Sapa in a single day.

You could also sign up for one of the inexpensive packages sold at many of the backpacker cafes and travel agencies in Hanoi.

LAO CAI

Lao Cai sits right on the Chinese border and serves as the transit point for Westerners traveling between Hanoi and Kunming, China via the Chinese border town of Hekou. Lao Cai is also the entry point for the Red River, which enters Vietnam after flowing 800 km from its source on the Yunnan plateau.

Much of Lao Cai was destroyed in 1979 by the Chinese and the town's reconstruction plan created two zones on either side of the Red River connected by a bridge and a second bridge which crosses a smaller tributary to Hekou.

Money

The bank in Lao Cai will exchange cash but does not accept traveler's checks or credit cards. In fact, the only place in northwestern Vietnam to exchange traveler's checks is in Sapa and only then at a few hotels, which charge commissions of up to 10%. Be sure to bring along plenty of cash or suffer the consequences.

If entering China from Vietnam, you'll find a bank in Hekou near immigration which will exchange traveler's checks and US cash but not Vietnamese currency. If you want to exchange Vietnamese *dong* to Chinese renminbi (RMB), you'll need to deal with the money changers on the streets in the same area.

Border Crossing

The border crossing is open daily 0800-1700. Travelers leaving Vietnam must first visit customs in Lao Cai and then proceed to immigration to show their exit stamp endorsed for Lao Cai—not Ho Chi Minh City or Hanoi. With an improper exit stamp you will almost certainly be denied permission to cross over into China.

After completing formalities on the Vietnamese side, you then walk across the railway bridge to Hekou where you check in at Chinese immigration. The entire process takes about an hour, if all of your paperwork is perfect and the immigration officials on both sides are in a good mood.

Note that there's a one-hour time difference between Lao Cai and Hekou since Hekou runs on Beijing time. If the time is 0900 in Vietnam, it's 1000 in Hekou.

Accommodations

Few travelers stay in Lao Cai, although some guesthouses and hotels are located on the north side near the crossing to China. Among the choices are Song Hong Guesthouse, Hong Ha Hotel, Hanoi Hotel, Vat Tu Hotel, and Post Office Guesthouse. All charge US$10-20 but it's probably best to cross the border and make the run for Kunming.

Transportation

Lao Cai is 355 km from Hanoi. There's an overnight train from Hanoi and a day train, which allows you to see the scenery. Both trains take 10 hours and are met by minibuses that depart immediately for Sapa.

BAC HA

An intriguing alternative to Sapa is this highland town some 65 km west of Lao Cai.

Attractions

Among the activities are trekking to nearby villages inhabited by any one of the 14 regional Montagnard groups. Several of these villages hold markets on various days of the week. Cau Cau, 18 km north of Bac Ha, holds its market on Saturday, while the Bac Ha market operates on Sunday and Thursday. Lung Phin, a small village 10 km north of Bac Ha, holds markets on Saturday and Sunday.

Accommodations

As Sapa goes, so goes Bac Ha, which now has over a dozen guesthouses in the center of town near the market and bus station just opposite the post office. Some of the more attractive guesthouses are east of town near the river and the road that leads north to Cau Cau.

Transportation

Several buses depart Lao Cai daily for Bac Ha or as an alternative you could hire a motorcycle taxi to make the 65 km trip. There are several backpacker cafes and travel agencies in Hanoi that offer four-day package tours to Bac Ha. These include transportation and lodging plus an overnight in Sapa.

The guest is always right—even if we have to throw him out.

—CHARLES RITZ,
NEW YORK TIMES

You can define a good flight by negatives: you didn't get hijacked, you didn't crash, you didn't throw up, you weren't late, you weren't nauseated by the food. And so you are grateful.

—PAUL THEROUX,
THE OLD PATAGONIAN EXPRESS

I have found out that there ain't no surer way to find out whether you like people or hate them, than to travel with them.

—MARK TWAIN,
TOM SAWYER ABROAD

SUGGESTED READINGS

SOUTHEAST ASIA

Buruma, Ian. *God's Dust: A Modern Asian Journey.* New York: Farrar, Straus and Giroux, 1989. Buruma examines a familiar dilemma—can the nations of Southeast Asia modernize without losing their cultural identities?—with great wit, insight, and a sharp sense of humor. His observations on the decline of Myanmar, the confused Filipino sense of history, and the monstrous contradictions of contemporary Singapore make this an excellent resource for all visitors contemplating travel to Southeast Asia.

Eames, Andrew. *Crossing the Shadow Line.* Vermont: Hodder and Stoughton, 1986. Young and talented Andrew Eames spent two years of his life probing the remote corners of Southeast Asia, from northern Thailand's Golden Triangle to an adventurous sail on Makassar schooners between Bali and Irian Jaya. A great tale spiced with prodigious amounts of humor and pathos. Highly recommended.

Fenton, James. *All the Wrong Places.* New York: Atlantic Monthly Press, 1988. James Fenton, journalist, poet, and critic, is one of the new breed of travel writers: jaundiced, self-indulgent, hard-hitting, and more concerned with personal impressions than scholarly dissertation. The result is a mesmerizing book full of great perception, especially his observations of the Philippines.

Iyer, Pico. *Video Night in Kathmandu.* New York: Vintage, 1988. Iyer's incongruous collection of essays uncovers the Coca-colonisation of the Far East in a refreshingly humorous and perceptive style. His heartbreaking accounts of decay in the Philippines, brothels in Bangkok, and cultural collisions in Bali form some of the finest travel writing in recent times. Highly recommended.

Kirch, John. *Music in Every Room: Around the World in a Bad Mood.* New York: McGraw Hill, 1984. An offbeat look at both the pains and the pleasures of contemporary Asian travel. Lively, opinionated, and immensely readable.

Nelson, Theodora, and Andrea Gross. *Good Books For The Curious Traveler—Asia and the South Pacific.* Boulder: Johnson Publishing, 1989. Outstanding in-depth reviews of over 350 books including almost 50 titles to Southeast Asia. Written with sensitivity and great insight. The authors also run a service that matches books with a traveler's itinerary. Write to Travel Source, 20103 La Roda Court, Cupertino, CA 95014, tel. (408) 446-0600.

Reimer, Jo, and Ronald and Caryl Krannich. *Shopping in Exotic Places.* Virginia: Impact Publications, 1987. Step-by-step guide to the secrets of shopping in Southeast Asia. Detailed descriptions of shopping centers, arcades, factory outlets, and exclusive boutiques in Hong Kong, Singapore, Thailand, and Indonesia.

Richter, Linda. *The Politics of Tourism in Asia.* Hawaii: University of Hawaii Press, 1989. A scholarly study of the complex political problems that confront the tourist industries in Thailand, the Philippines, and other Asian destinations. Filled with surprising conclusions about the impact of multinational firms and the importance of targeting grass-roots travelers rather than upscale tourists.

Schwartz, Brian. *A World of Villages.* New York: Crown Publishers, 1986. A superbly written journal of a six-year journey to the most remote villages in the world. Filled with tales of unforgettable people and lands of infinite variety and beauty.

Shales, Melissa, editor. *The Traveler's Handbook.* Connecticut: Globe Pequot Press, 1988. Fifth edition of the award-winning guide, which puts together the contributions of over 80 experienced travelers, all authorities in their particular fields. Practical suggestions on climate, maps, airfares, internal transportation, backpacking, visas, money, health, and theft.

Simon, Ted. *Jupiter's Travels.* New York: Doubleday, 1980. Fascinating account of a 63,000-km motorcycle journey (500cc Triumph Tiger) from Europe, down the continent of Africa, across South America, Australia, and India. And what does Ted do now? Raises organic produce in Northern California!

Theroux, Paul. *The Great Railway Bazaar.* New York: Houghton Mifflin, 1975. One of the world's best travel writers journeys from London to Tokyo and back on a hilarious railway odyssey. Rather than a dry discourse on sights, this masterpiece of observation keeps you riveted with personal encounters of the first order. Highly recommended for everyone!

Various authors. *Culture Shock.* Singapore: Times Books. A series of practical guides to the rules of Asian etiquette, customs, and recommended behavior for every visitor to Asia. Lightweight and well distributed; excellent books to purchase and read while on the road. Highly recommended.

Various authors. Insight Guides. Singapore: APA Publications. Superb photography and a lush text make this the best set of background guides to Southeast Asia. Read before traveling.

Bloodworth, Dennis. *An Eye for the Dragon.* New York: Farrar, Straus and Giroux, 1970. The former Far East correspondent of the *Observer* incisively examines the comedies and tragedies of Asia, from the fanatic wranglings of Sukarno to racial tensions in Malaysia. Bloodworth makes history and politics—often dry and dull subjects—fascinating and memorable.

CAMBODIA

Chandler, David. *The Tragedy of Cambodian History.* New Haven: Yale University Press, 1992. Chandler writes about Sihanouk: "Anyone trying to form a judgment about his years in power must also confront his disdain for educated people, his impatience with advice, his craving for approval, his fondness for revenge, his cynicism, and his flamboyance." The best book about Cambodian politics from 1945 to 1979.

Coedes, George. *Angkor.* Singapore: Oxford in Asia, 1986. Originally published in French in Hanoi in 1943, few guides to Angkor have since equaled the scholarship and insight of this modern-day classic. Visitors are advised to purchase this book in Bangkok prior to departure.

Madsen, Axel. *Silk Roads: The Asian Adventures of Andre and Clara Malraux.* New York: Pharos Books, 1989. Prior to the publication of his classic novel of revolution, *Man's Fate,* the 24-year-old Malraux and his young wife traveled to Cambodia to steal temple ruins and make a quick profit selling the treasures to Western museums. Malraux failed but later organized an anticolonial newspaper in Saigon and eventually served as the French Minister of Culture under Charles de Gaulle.

Mazzeo and Antonini. *Monuments of Civilization: Ancient Cambodia.* New York: Grosset & Dunlap, 1978. The best coffee-table book yet produced on Angkor Wat. Includes a fine introduction by Han Suyin and detailed floor plans of each monument.

Ngor, Haing, with Roger Warner. *A Cambodian Odyssey.* New York: MacMillan, 1987. Haing Ngor is the Cambodian refugee who later served as the principal actor in *The Killing Fields.* An unforgettable look at the Khmer Rouge and their reign of terror from 1975 to 1979.

Parmentier, Henri. *Guide to Angkor*. Phnom Penh: EKLIP, 1959. A small booklet not comparable to Coedes's but often available as a reprint in Phnom Penh.

Sihanouk, Norodom. *My War with the CIA*. New York: Pantheon, 1973. The most important figure in modern Cambodian politics relates the assassination attempts and CIA-backed coup which finally toppled his government in March 1970. A seriously unbalanced but highly entertaining book, much like the author himself.

HONG KONG

Another Hong Kong. Hong Kong: Emphasis, 1989. A guidebook that offers step-by-step walks through the New Territories and Outlying Islands.

Baker, Hugh. *Ancestral Images*. Hong Kong: South China Morning Post, 1979. Reprints of newspaper articles originally published during the late 1970s in a local newspaper. Quirky and highly personalized descriptions of almost everything from Chinese gods to zombies. Hardback sequels include *More Ancestral Images* and *Ancestral Images Again*.

Bloomfield, Frena. *The Book of Chinese Beliefs*. London: Arrow Books, 1983. A brief survey of ancestor worship, *feng shui,* exorcisms, fortune-telling, and other matters of the occult. This easy-to-read and inexpensive little book is an excellent introduction to the mysteries of Chinese religions.

Cameron, Nigel. *Hong Kong: The Cultured Pearl*. Hong Kong: Oxford University Press, 1978. The first half is history but it is the critical second half that holds your interest. Like many other resident writers, Cameron has an obvious love-hate relationship with the place.

Clavell, James. *Tai Pan*. New York: Atheneum and Dell, 1966. Historical fiction based on the founding of Hong Kong. Clavell's *Noble House* describes the wheelings and dealings of Hong Kong *hongs* during the 1960s. Clavell's other Asian-based novels include *Shogun,* set in feudal Japan, and *King Rat,* staged in Singapore during WW II.

Collis, Maurice. *Foreign Mud (Anglo-Chinese Opium War)*. London: Faber and Faber, 1946. The classic retelling of the messy circumstances that led to the founding of Hong Kong. Reprinted by Graham Brash.

Elegant, Robert. *Dynasty*. New York: McGraw-Hill, 1977. Chinese power in Hong Kong during the 20th century. Elegant is a scholar on things Chinese and has written a number of nonfiction books including *China's Red Master, Mao's Great Revolution* and the Time-Life publication *Hong Kong,* an honest look at the author's final days in Hong Kong, where he resided for over 25 years.

Hong Kong. Singapore: APA Productions, 1981. Outstanding photographs and a well-written text. This profusely illustrated book is highly recommended for predeparture reading.

Hughes, Richard. *Hong Kong: Borrowed Place— Borrowed Time*. London: Andre Deutsch, 1968. Although written over 20 years ago, this modern classic remains witty and full of genuine insight.

Mason, Richard. *The World of Suzi Wong*. Glasgow: Collins, 1957. Caucasian businessman falls in love with Wanchai bar girl, one of the great love stories of Southeast Asia. The novel was penned in the Luk Kwok Hotel during the 1950s and later made into the classic movie, which forever sealed the image of Hong Kong.

Morris, Jan. *Hong Kong*. London: Viking, 1988. The famous chronicler of British imperialism has written a marvelously evocative and informative travel companion. Highly recommended.

INDONESIA

More than any other destination in Southeast Asia, Indonesia is the country where advance reading will reap the greatest rewards. The country is far too rich, complex, and expansive to be covered adequately by any singular guidebook to Southeast Asia. This handbook covers the highlights in fairly good detail, but anyone venturing off to explore the outer islands should arm themselves with Bill Dalton's *Indonesia Handbook,* also published by that small but dedicated outfit in Chico, California.

Blair, Lawrence. *Ring of Fire.* New York: Bantam Books, 1988. An extraordinary journey to the most remote corners of the archipelago. This book and the accompanying PBS film series stand as one of the great achievements of contemporary adventure travel. Highly recommended.

Draine, Cathie. *Culture Shock.* Singapore: Times Books, 1986. Another in the outstanding series of handy guides to customs, social etiquette, and world views of the Indonesians. A useful travel companion.

Kallen, Christian and Richard Bangs. *Islands of Fire, Islands of Spice.* San Francisco: Sierra Club Books, 1988. Travel adventure tightly interwoven with historical and cultural observations. Outstanding text marred by dreadful photography.

Koch, Christopher. *The Year of Living Dangerously.* New York: Penguin, 1978. Peter Weir's evocative movie of love and loyalties in Jakarta, 1965, was based on this tightly penned novel.

Lubis, Mochtar. *Twilight in Jakarta.* New York: Vanguard, 1964. Political corruption and the underbelly of Javanese society as viewed by Indonesia's most important modern writer. Mochtar's other works include *The Indonesian Dilemma,* which focuses on the shortcomings of the Indonesian personality, and *A Road With No End,* which established his literary reputation.

McDonald, Hamish. *Suharto's Indonesia.* Australia: Fontana Books, 1980. The best introduction available to the complex world of Indonesian politics, with fascinating accounts of Suharto, corruption, the collapse of Perta-

mina, Timor, and the fate of Indonesia's political prisoners. Highly recommended.

Holt, Claire. *Art in Indonesia.* Ithaca, New York: Cornell University Press, 1967. A modern classic written for the generalist rather than the academic.

Wallace, Alfred Russell. *Malay Archipelago.* Singapore: Graham Brash, 1983. A reprint of the 1869 classic, which, among countless observations, uncovered the orangutan's love for durian. A brilliant, exhaustive, and valid study of natural phenomena as well as an exciting travelogue.

Kahin, Audrey and George. *Subversion as Foreign Policy; The Secret Eisenhower and Dulles Debacle in Indonesia.* New York: New Press, 1995. A startling revelation of the covert intervention by the United States in Indonesia in the late 1950s, an American move that fomented a bloody civil wear, strengthened the Indonesian army, and led to the destruction of parliamentary government.

MALAYSIA

See the Third World While It Lasts. Penang: Consumer's Association of Penang, 1985. A hard-hitting look at the social and environmental impact of tourism. Raises some important and disturbing questions about the effects of mass tourism on third-world countries. Photographs and reproductions of advertisements by Airlanka ("We've put a price on Paradise") and the Shangri-La Hotel ("Don't change your way of life just because you change countries") are alone worth the price.

Hong, Evelyne. *Natives of Sarawak: Survival in Borneo's Vanishing Forest.* Penang: Institut Masyarakat, 1987. A well-argued and liberally illustrated insight into the cultural elimination of Borneo's Penan tribespeoples. Very important reading.

Lat (Mohamad Nor Khalid). *Kampong Boy.* Kuala Lumpur: Straits Times Publishing, 1979. Lat's cartoons of *kampong* life, pop heroes, fat mothers worrying about their rebellious sons, disorganized weddings, comical circumcision rituals, and gentle ribbing of political leaders are hilarious and miraculously reveal the essence of being Malay. Highly recommended.

Mahathir, Dr. Mohammed. *The Malay Dilemma*. Kuala Lumpur: 1970. Malaysia's controversial prime minister talks about race, religion, and politics in his book, which was internally banned for several years.

Mahathir, Dr. Mohammed. *The Voice of Asia*. Kuala Lumpur: 1995. The prime minister argues that Asian values will triumph over the decadence of Western civilizations, a viewpoint shared by several other political leaders in Southeast Asia.

Maugham, Somerset. *Collected Short Stories*. London, 1951. One of the world's great writers describes life in colonial Malaya during the '20s and '30s.

Moore, Donald. *Where Monsoons Meet*. London: George Harrap, 1960. An anthology by various writers on riots, history, and tall tales such as "How to Speak to a Tiger." Used bookstores in Penang and Kuala Lumpur sometimes carry this amusing little paperback.

Naipaul, V.S. *Among the Believers: An Islamic Journey*. London, 1981. A critical but revealing look at Islamic fundamentalism from the Middle East to Indonesia.

Skeat, Walter William. *Malay Magic*. London: Macmillan, 1900. This anthropological classic describes Malaysian folklore, religion, magicians, fire charms, divination, and the black arts with great insight. Comprehensive but less captivating than the similar efforts on Burma by Shway Yoe. Dover republished this book a few years ago.

Winstedt, Richard. *A History of Malaya*. Kuala Lumpur: Marican & Sons, 1982. A classic, but with a rather stuffy introduction. Widely available in the country.

MYANMAR (BURMA)

Visitors with limited time should read *Golden Earth* by Norman Lewis, *Stillwell and the American Experience in China* by Barbara Tuchman, and *The Burman, His Life and Notions* by Shway Yoe. The best source of books on the country is Kiscadale Publications, Murray House, Gartmore, Stirling FK8 3 RJ, United Kingdom.

Aung San Suu Kyi. *Freedom From Fear*. New York: Viking, 1992. The 1991 Nobel Peace Prize winner offers 25 direct and inspirational essays that eloquently convey her belief that democracy and human rights are the birthright of her mother country.

Bixler, Norma. *Burma: A Profile*. New York: Praeger, 1971. One of the best general surveys published, light and easy reading plus a lively style.

Bouchaud, Andre, and Lewis Bouchaud. *Burma's Golden Triangle: The Opium Warlords*. Hong Kong: Asia 2000, 1988. Two French journalists tell of drug dealing in the Golden Triangle and the separatist struggles of the Karens, Karennis, and Kachins.

Bunge, Frederica. *Burma: A Country Study*. Washington, D.C.: United States Government, 1983. A well-organized general study strong on political and military analysis.

Cady, John. *The United States and Burma*. Cambridge: Harvard University Press, 1976. A detailed history that, despite the title, has little to do with the United States, by a former diplomat and professor who authored several books on Burma including *A History of Modern Burma*. Serious and authoritative.

Collis, Maurice. *The Land of the Great Image*. New York: Alfred Knopf, 1943. Collis was a civil-service worker who, during the 1920s and '30s, wrote eight historical-biographical novels set in Burma, including *Siamese White*, *The Lords of the Sunset* about the Shans, and the title piece about a Portuguese Jesuit priest in 17th-century Rakhine.

Khaing, Mi Mi. *The World of Burmese Women.* London: Zed Books, 1984. The author, a well-known Burmese social scientist, concludes that Burmese women are less oppressed than women elsewhere, also author of *Burmese Family* and *Cook and Entertain the Burmese Way*.

Lewis, Norman. *Golden Earth.* London: Eland Books, 1952. Lewis traveled through Burma in the 1950s and observed people, life, and customs with remarkable insight—one of the great travel books on Southeast Asia. Highly recommended.

Lintner, Bertil. *Burma in Revolt: Opium and Insurgency since 1948.* Boulder: Westview Press, 1995. The most comprehensive analysis of the nexus of drugs, insurgency, and politics in Myanmar with insight into the failure of democracy and the triumph of opium politics.

Lintner, Bertil. *Outrage, Burma's Struggle for Democracy.* New York: Review Publishing, 1990. The correspondent for the Far Eastern Economic Review explores the more remote regions of the country and reports on the antics of Ne Win and the return of Aung San Suu Kyi to Yangon and her first speech to an assembly of some half-million citizens.

Orwell, George. *Burmese Days.* London: Penguin, 1982. A sad and biting recollection of Orwell's term as a police official in Mandalay during the 1920s.

Shway Yoe (Sir James George Scott). *The Burman, His Life and Notions.* New York: Norton, 1963. Although written over a century ago, a landmark achievement filled with rare understanding of traditional Burmese culture which remains largely accurate to the current day.

Trager, Frank. *Burma from Kingdom to Republic.* New York: Praeger, 1966. Scholarly and comprehensive look at the early history of Burma.

Smith, Martin. *Burma—Insurgency and the Politics of Ethnicity.* London: Zed Press, 1992.

British journalist Smith has spent more than a decade researching the insurgency groups rarely investigated by mainstream reporters and provides an important document of the final days prior to their accords with the Slorc regime.

Tuchman, Barbara. *Stilwell and the American Experience in China.* New York: MacMillan, 1971. American historian ties together the legends of General Stilwell, Chiang Kai-Shek, Mountbatten, and others in an exciting and well written look at the regional conflicts during World War II. Highly recommended.

U Maung Maung. *General Ne Win.* New York. A revisionist attempt to portray Ne Win as a national hero authored by Burma's former chief justice responsible for Ne Win's constitution. U Maung Maung served as Burma's first civilian president in August 1988 but lasted only nine days before being ousted by the military.

PHILIPPINES

Broad, Robin. *Plundering Paradise: The Struggle for the Environment in the Philippines.* Berkeley: University of California Press, 1993. A call to activists and environmentalists in the West to extend their concern to the Philippines in a collection of vivid tales about courageous Filipinos confronting problems of deforestation and pollution.

Karnow, Stanley. *In Our Image: America's Empire in the Philippines.* New York: Random House, 1989. Having covered Asia for 30 years for *Time, Life,* and the *Washington Post,* the gifted author was in a special position to write this copiously detailed yet highly readable political history of the American experience in the Philippines. Karnow also authored *Vietnam: A History,* whose television companion won six Emmys, and a three-part documentary on the Philippines aired on PBS in 1989.

Manchester, William. *American Caesar.* New York: Little, Brown and Company, 1978. An absorbing biography of General Douglas MacArthur, one of America's last epic heroes.

Roces, Alfredo and Grace Roces. *Culture Shock.* Singapore: Times Books International, 1985. This lively and highly amusing guide to Filipino customs will prove indispensable to understanding the country and the people.

Simons, Lewis M. *Worth Dying For.* New York: William Morrow, 1987. Simon dissects Aquino's rise and People's Power by analyzing the dynamics of Philippine society including the church, the military, business, and the political left. His sensitive vignettes of the common people give great life to what could have otherwise been another clich— about the forces of good and evil.

Steinberg, David Joel. *The Philippines: A Singular and Plural Place.* Colorado: Westview Press, 1982. One of America's leading authorities on the Philippines packs a great deal of insight into this outstanding 150-page book. His chapters on Filipino society, the religious impulse, and the search for a useable past are a superb introduction to the country.

SINGAPORE

Theroux, Paul. *Saint Jack.* New York, Penguin, 1979. Fictional account of an aging American expatriate in Singapore who gets involved with the local prostitution business in the 1970s. Theroux lived in Singapore for almost two years while he taught English at the national university and so the book rings true about many of the more salient aspects of earlier days. The book and subsequent movie directed by Peter Bogdanovich are both banned in Singapore and Theroux is considered *persona non grata.*

Bloodworth, Dennis. *The Tiger and the Trojan.* Singapore: Times Books, 1986. Details the rise of Lee Kuan Yew and his People's Action Party against a powerful communist movement and the British colonial administration.

Clavell, James. *King Rat.* New York: Bantam, 1963. Fictional but evocative account of Clavell's internment at Changi Prison during World War II. After the war, Clavell went into the film business and followed up with his other Asian sagas—*Taipan, Shogun,* and *Noble House.*

Juan, Dr. Chee Son. *Dare To Change: An Alternative Vision for Singapore.* Singapore: Singapore Democratic Party, 1994. Dr. Chee, a neuropsychologist and former lecturer at the National University of Singapore, challenges the ruling party and argues that authoritarian forms of government will ultimately fail as the demands for democracy, free speech, and individual rights spread across modern Asia. Tame by Western standards but one of the few alternative viewpoints available in print.

Leeson, Nick. *Rogue Trader.* London: Little Brown, 1996. Leeson was the British futures trader who single-handedly destroyed one of England's oldest banks by recklessly trading in Japanese stock index futures and Japanese government bonds. According to Leeson, everyone but the author himself was responsible for the disaster, including bosses blinded by profits, the Bank of England, and the Singaporean stock exchange which turned a blind eye to Leeson's flouting of exchange rules on position limits.

Seow, Francis. *To Catch a Tartar: A Dissident in Lee Kuan Yew's Prison.* New Haven: Yale University Press, 1995. One of Singapore's more famous dissidents served as solicitor general and later as the president of the Law Society until 1986 when he was arrested on charges that he interfered in Singapore's internal affairs. After a two-month detention, Seow was released but charged with tax evasion and convicted in absentia. Seow now lives in Massachusetts where he wrote this critical work which is officially banned in Singapore. Widely available in Malaysia.

Sesser, Stan. *The Lands of Charm and Cruelty.* New York: Vintage Press, 1993. Sesser is a former university professor and correspondent for the *New Yorker* who authored this outstanding collection of pieces on the political landscape of modern Southeast Asia. His opening chapter, *Singapore: The Prisoner in the Theme Park,* is stunning—the most elegant analysis of contemporary Singapore in print. Sesser describes both the strengths and weaknesses of Singapore and the People's Action Party. Highly recommended.

Craig, JoAnn Meriwether. *Culture Shock Singapore.* Singapore: Times Editions, 1993. A casual guide to the Singaporean personality which aims to improve cross-cultural awareness between locals and Western expatriates. Strong sections include those on the challenges facing newly arrived expatriates and discussions on social values found in the Business Etiquette and East Meets West chapters. Recommended for Westerners considering a move to Singapore.

Kee, Tan Chong. *The SEF Book; Soc.Culture.Singapore—The Unauthorised Version.* Singapore: Times Books, 1996. Insights, discussions, and flame wars from the internet newsgroup soc.culture.singapore: ministerial salaries, human rights, censorship, and litterbug punishment. Available in Singapore at MPH Books.

Liu, Gretchen. *Pastel Portraits.* Singapore: Singapore Coordinating Committee, 1984. Ian Lloyd's superb photography and Gretchen Liu's thoughtful prose makes this beautiful book a landmark in the field of historical preservation.

Powell, Robert. *Living Legacy.* Singapore: Landmark Books, 1994. The single finest work on the architectural conservation of Singapore features a superb text by a professor of architecture at the National University of Singapore and equally compelling photography by Luca Tettoni and Albert Lim. Published in cooperation with the Singapore Heritage Society and distributed by Select Books in the Tanglin Shopping Centre.

Tyers, Ray. *Singapore, Then and Now.* Singapore: Landmark Books, 1993. A classic photographic study of Singapore which compares the old and new views of many of the island's monuments, churches, buildings, streets, rivers, and neighborhoods. Amazing photos. If you purchase only one book to remember Singapore, make this the one.

Boi, Lee Geok. *The Food of Singapore.* Singapore: Periplus Editions, 1994. The finest book on the Chinese, Malay, and Indian cuisines of Singapore with special sections on the Singapore kitchen, regional spices, and almost 100 recipes accompanied by the stunning photography of Luca Invernizzi Tettoni.

Brazil, David. *Street Smart.* Singapore: Times Editions, 1995. A collection of short and quirky descriptions about the oddities and rarely uncovered folklore of modern Singapore. A great read filled with witty asides and a surprising amount of serious research.

Brazil, David. *No Money, No Honey.* Singapore: Angsana Books, 1993. Singapore's first guidebook to the red-light districts of Singapore was an overnight success despite the refusal of local media to provide all form of review or coverage. Brazil, a British journalist who moved to Singapore in 1988, describes with keen humor the netherworld of prostitution and so proves that Singaporeans are not unlike citizens of the West.

Aitchison, Jim. *Revenge of the Sarong Party Girl.* Singapore: Angsana Books, 1996. Sarong Party Girls are Asian women in Singapore seeking husbands from among European, Australian, or American expatriates who regard the scantily clad lady as the perfect LBFM (little brown fucking machine). Funny text plus racy illustrations by Theseus Chan have made this series a big hit in Singapore.

THAILAND

Some advance reading will go a long way toward understanding Thailand and Thai people. Most of the following are best read before you leave, though *Mai Pen Rai, Culture Shock, Thai Ways,* and *Guide to Thailand* (four highly recommended books) are available in Bangkok.

Blofel, John. *Bangkok, The Great Cities.* New York: Time-Life, 1973. Good local insight into both the upside and the downside of this vibrant metropolis.

Clarac, Achille. *Guide to Thailand.* Malaysia: Oxford University Press, 1981. The most comprehensive traveler's guide to the arts and architecture of Thailand. Rudimentary practicalities, but highly recommended for historical background and cultural coverage.

Cooper, Robert, and Nanthapa Cooper. *Culture Shock.* Singapore: Times Books International, 1982. A humorous paperback which succinctly explains the Thai people, their customs, and hidden rules for correct social etiquette. A delightful book filled with great insight and charm, especially the discussion on Thai smiles.

Geo, Veran. *50 Trips through Siam's Canals.* Bangkok: Duang Kamol, 1979. A fascinating but outdated guide to the confusing labyrinth of rivers and canals that stretch across southern Thailand. Included are over 30 maps, Thai prices, and brief descriptions of the temples.

Hollinger, Carol. *Mai Pen Rai.* Boston: Houghton Mifflin, 1965. The story of an American housewife and her humorous introduction to life in Bangkok. One of the warmest books you will ever read. Highly recommended.

Hoskin, John. *Guide to Chiang Mai and Northern Thailand.* Hong Kong: Hong Kong Publishing, 1984. Detailed and up-to-date information on the attractions of northern Thailand. Oriented toward visitors with rental cars.

Lewis, Paul, and Elaine Lewis. *Peoples of the Golden Triangle.* London: Thames and Hudson, 1984. Paul and Elaine have worked as missionaries among the tribals of northern Thailand since 1947. This lavishly illustrated book is the best available guide to these intriguing peoples.

Segaller, Denis. *Thai Ways.* Bangkok,: Allied Newspapers, 1984. A collection of short essays on Thai ceremonies, festivals, customs, and beliefs. This and his sequel *More Thai Ways* are great books to read while traveling in the country.

Van Beek, Steve, and Luca Invernizzi Tettoni. *Arts of Thailand.* Hong Kong: Travel Publishing Asia Limited, 1985. The best introductory guidebook to Thai arts in print. Great photos!

Warren, William, and R. Ian Lloyd. *Bangkok's Waterways.* Bangkok: Asia Books, 1989. Dependable and well-researched advice on self-guided boat tours on the Chao Praya River and its *klongs*.

Warren, William, and Luca Tettoni. *Legendary Thailand.* Hong Kong: Travel Publishing Asia Limited, 1986. Outstanding photographs and a clean text; a good introduction to the land and people.

INDEX

A

Aberdeen: 134
Abeyadana Temple: 590
Abu Bakar: 450
accommodations: *see specific place*
Aceh State Museum: 289
Adityawarman Museum: 304
Adonara: 344-345
Affandi Art Museum: 192
Agoho: 669
AIDS: 28, 793-794, 953
Air Keroh: 457
air travel: 36-42; Indonesia 157-159, 175-176;
    Laos 383, 384, 393; Macau 412-414;
    Malaysia 446, 447, 469, 492, 517-519, 533,
    536; Myanmar 556, 557, 568, 578; Nusa
    Tenggara 314; Philippines 615, 635-636;
    Philippines 669; Singapore 711; Thailand
    785-786, 787, 830-831; Vietnam 949, 950,
    966-967, 1007-1008
Akha Hill Tribe: 872-873
Alor: 344-345
Alor Setar: 493
Aluoi: 996
A-Ma Temple: 416
Amarapura: 578-579
Ambarawa: 214-215
Ambarita: 297
Ambasing Hanging Coffins: 647
Amed: 273
American Express: 31
Amlapura: 271-272
Ampel Mosque: 217
Ampenan: 317-322

amulets: 804
amusement parks: Indonesia 173, 174, 190-
    192; Malaysia 457, 459, 470-471;
    Singapore 730
Anakalang: 349
Ananda Temple: 586
Anawrahta: 582-583
ancestral poles: 339
Ancient City: 807
Angeles City: 641-642
Angkor: 82-89
Angkor monuments: 85-89
Angkor Thom (Royal City): 86, 88
Angkor Wat: 86-88
animals: Indonesia 150;
antiques: 321, 768-769
Antonio Blanco House: 256
Anturan: 280-281
Ao Nang Beach: 927
Ao Noi Beach: 905
Aquino, Benigno and Corazon: 609
Ardent Hot Springs: 668
area codes: Bali 239; Brunei 49; Hong Kong
    108; Indonesia 239; Macau 415; Malaysia
    449; Myanmar 560; Philippines 622;
    Singapore 715; Thailand 792; Vietnam 954
Armenian Church: 721
art galleries: 769; Bali 263; Penang 481-483
arts: 14
Atambua: 354
ATMs: 32-33
Attapeu: 403
Atumashi Monastery: 575
Aung San Suu Kyi: 552
Ava: 579
Ayala Museum: 653
Ayuthaya: 845-849

ARCHITECTURE

7, 8-9, 11-12
Bagan: 584-585
Kuala Lumpur: 460, 462, 477-478
of temples: 799-801
Singapore: 717-721
Sukothai: 855
Thailand: 808

B

Baa: 353
Baba Nonya Heritage Museum: 456
Babi Besar Island: 501
Bac Ha: 1016
Baclayon Church: 661
Bacolod: 686
Bada Valley: 370

Badian Island: 674
Badoc: 653
Badung: 252-254
Bagan: 550, 582-593
Bagan Lacquerware School and Museum: 592
Bagan Min: 572-574
Bago: 569-570
Baguio: 649-652
Bai Chay: 1010-1011
Baitur Rahman Mosque: 289
Bajawa: 338-339
Bako National Park: 524-525
Bali: 231-283
Bali Janggo: 304
Bali Museum: 252
Balik Pulau: 486
Balina Beach: 270-271
Balingoan: 678
Baluran National Park: 229
bamboo organ: 637
Banaue: 643-644
Ban Chiang: 894
Banda Aceh: 289
Bandar Seri Begawan: 49-52
Bandung: 181-185
Bangar: 53
Bangkok: 794-832
Bangli: 265-266
Bang Pa In: 845
Ban Houei Houne: 403
Ban Kao Museum: 844
bank transfers: 30-31
Ban Mae Hat: 915
Ban Phu Historical Park: 895
Ban Prathup Teakwood House: 886

Bantayan Island: 673
Banten: 177
Bantimurung Falls: 359
Banyuwangi: 230
Banyuwangi Reserve: 229
Bao Dai Summer Palace: 974
Baphuon: 88
Baram River: 530-531
bargaining: 164-165, 827
Basilica of Santo Niño: 670
Batac: 653-654
Batad: 643
Batam Island: 310-312
bathing pools: Langkawi Island 495;
batik: 195, 199, 211, 444-445
Batuan: 255
Batubulan: 255
Batu Caves: 465-466
Batu Ferringhi: 486-487
Batugosok Beach: 337
Batu Kumbung: 322
Batur: 276
Batu Sangkar: 304
Bauang: 652-653
Bau Nyale festival: 326
Bawomataluo: 301
Bayon: 88
Beaufort: 537
Bedugul: 277
Bedulu: 264
Belaga: 528
Bela Vista Hotel: 416
bells: 580-581
Bena: 339
Bengkulu: 308-309
Ben Thanh Market: 961
Berastagi: 290-291
Besakih: 267
Beung Khan: 897
Beverly Hills Taoist Temple: 670
Bhumipol Adulyadej: 781-782
Bidadari Island: 336
Bidwell, Alfred John: 717-721
Big Buddha Beach: 911
Biliran Island: 676
Bima-Raba: 332-333
Binoni: 668
Bintan Island: 312-313
Bintulu: 528-529
Bira: 359-360
Bird Lane: 113

BEACHES

14-16
Brunei: 52
Java: 177, 192
Malaysia: 457, 486-487, 494-496, 503-505, 514
Nusa Tenggara: 336-337, 343-344, 348
Philippines: 655, 658, 663-665, 673-674, 683-685
Thailand: 836-837, 838-839, 905, 907-930
Vietnam: 970, 979, 988-989, 997, 999, 1008

bird parks and sanctuaries: 729-730, 935
Blahbatuh: 255
Blangkejeren: 290
boat trips: Indonesia 159-162, 176; Luzon
    652; Philippines 690-691; *see also specific
    place or* transportation
Boawae: 339
Bocus: 643
Bogor: 178-180
Bohol: 661-665
Bohol Beach: 664
Bokong Falls: 647
Bolovens Plateau: 402
Bonbon: 668-669
Bondomaroto: 349
Bonnet, Rudolph: 256
Bontobangun: 360
Bontoc: 644-646
Bophut Beach: 911
Boracay: 665-667
Borobudur: 202-204
Borsang Village: 865
botanical gardens: Chiang Mai 865; Hong
    Kong 122; Java 178; Macau 419, 420;
    Penang 485; Pyin U Lwin 582; Singapore
    717, 730; Sulawesi 360
Boun Oum Palace: 400-401
Brahma Asrama Vihara: 283
Brastagi: 290-291
Bridge of Whims: 640
Bridge over the River Kwai: 840
Brunei: 43-54
Buddha image: 791-792, 802-803, 855, 847
Buddhism: 593, 780-781, 791-792, 829-830
Buddhist Cave: 502
Bug-ong: 669
Bukit Dharma: 256
Bukit Lawang: 288-289
Bukittinggi: 301-303
bull races/running: 223
Bulukumba: 359-360
Bunaken Sea Gardens: 371
Bundt, Clara: 357
Buntao: 366
Buriram: 801
Burma: *see* Myanmar
Burma city name changes: 548
Burma Road: 581-582
bus travel: *see* transportation *or specific place*
Butuan: 678

C
Cagayan de Oro: 678-679
Cagsawa Ruins: 656-658
Cakranegara: 317-322
Calley, Lt. William: 982
calling cards: *see* telephone communications
Cam Ly Falls: 974
Cambodia: 55-90
Cameron Highlands: 472-474
Caminguin Island: 667-669
Camoes Gardens: 419
Camp Carroll: 996
Camp John Hayes: 649
canal tours: 806-807
Candidasa: 269-271
Candi Sukuh: 208
candis: see temples
Cantarman: 668
Cantho: 972
Cao Dai: 968, 985
Carabao: 826
Carita Beach: 177
Casa Gorodo Museum: 670
Catbalogan: 697-698
Cat Ba National Park: 1011
Causeway Bay: 131-132
Cave Temples: 474
caving: Malaysia 465-466, 474, 502, 529-532,
    540; Laos 396, 399; Philippines 647, 656,
    692; Myanmar 595; Sulawesi 368, 371;
    Thailand 840, 844, 877, 894, 903; Vietnam
    997, 999, 1011
Cebu City: 670-673
Cebu Island: 669-674
Celuk: 255
cemeteries: Imogiri 192; Kuala Lumpur 478,
    483; Macau 420; Malacca 457; Manila 631;
    Thailand 840; Vietnam 996
Centers for Disease Control (CDC): 23-24
ceramics: 856, 858

CUISINE

Laos: 391
Macau: 426
Malaysia: 490
Singapore: 742-743
Thailand: 818-819
see also specific place

Champasak: 401-402
Cham ruins: 988-989
Cham towers: 977, 982
Chan See Shu Yuen Temple: 464
Chandra Kasem Museum: 845
Chang Chi-fu: 553
Chao Sam Phya National Museum: 845-847
Cha Tam Church: 961
Chaweng Beach: 909-910
Chee Swee Cheng Mansion: 456
Cheng Hoon Teng Temple: 456
Cheong Fat Tze Mansion: 483
Cherating: 503-505
Cheung Chau: 139-142
Chiang Khan: 896
Chiang Khong: 885
Chiang Mai: 861-870
Chiang Rai: 880-882
Chiang Saen: 884-885
China Beach: 988
China Hill: 457
Chinese New Year celebrations: 102
Chinese opera: 118
Ching Chung Kong Temple: 137
Chocolate Hills: 664
Choeung Ek: 79
Cholon: 961-963
Chom Tong: 865
Chong Mon Bay/Beach: 907-908, 910-911
Chuan Leekpai: 778-779, 781
Chulalongkorn: 778
Chumphon: 905-906
churches: Macau 416-418, 419, 420, 422;
    Malacca 455; Penang 481; Philippines 626,
    630, 647, 661-663; Singapore 720-722; *see
    also* temples
Cipanas: 180-181
Circle-Pacific airfares: 36, 37
Cirebon: 211-213
Cisarua: 180
cliff burial sites: 365-366
climate: 21, 22; Cambodia 60; Hong Kong 96;
    Indonesia 149-150; Laos 377-379; Macau
    410; Malaysia 434-435; Myanmar 550;
    Philippines 606; Sarawak 517; Singapore
    704; Thailand 778; Vietnam 945-946
coconuts: 907
coffins: 647
Coleman, George: 717-721
Coloane Island: 422
Con Thien Firebase: 996

cons: 624-625, 954, 955
consolidators: 38, 39
Corregidor Island: 637
courier companies: 39, 40
crafts: 14
credit cards: 31-32
Crisologo Museum: 653
crocodile farms: 807
Cu Chi Tunnels: 968
Cua Lo Beach: 997
Cultural Center of the Philippines: 631
Cunningham: 996
currency: 30-33; *see also introduction to
    specific place*

D

Daet: 655
Dalat: 973-976
Danang: 985-988
Dance of the Ghosts: 897
dance performances: *see specific place*
Dan Sai: 897
Dapitan: 679
Davao City: 679-680
Dayabumi Building: 462
demilitarized zones (DMZs): 995
Denpasar: 252-254
Deri: 366
Dhammayangyi Temple: 589
diarrhea: 24
Dien Bien Phu: 1014-1015
Dieng Plateau: 204-206
Dili: 354
diplomatic offices: *see specific place*
Dipolog: 679
Diponegoro: 155
Doc Mieu Base: 995
Doi Inthanon National Park: 865
Doi Mung Kung: 878
Don Khong Island: 404
Dong Ha: 994
Dong Hoi: 997
Dong Khoi Street: 955
Dong Son drum: 360
Donggala: 370
Do Son Beach: 1008
Dr. Tawee's Folklore Museum: 852
dress codes: 792, 794
driving: 30
drugs: 27, 449, 553, 624-625, 794, 870
Dumaguete City: 688-689

Dumai: 525
Durian Monument: 679
Durian Perangin Waterfall: 495
Duyong Besar Island: 508

E

earthquakes: 335
economy: Brunei 47-48; Hong Kong 100-101; Laos 381-382; Macau 410; Myanmar 554; Philippines 610-611
Eindawya Pagoda: 576
El Nido: 693-694
Elephant Festival: 889, 900
Elephant Training Camp: 877
embassies: 31; see also specific place
Emerald Hill: 717
Emperor of Jade Pagoda: 963
endangered species: 35
Ende: 340-341
Enter the Dragon: 130
entertainment: see specific place
Erawan Caves: 894
Erawan Shrine: 806
Ermita: 626-627, 633
Erskine: 996

F

factories: 637
faith healers: 649
feng shui: 113
ferries: Hong Kong 105-106
floating markets: 806-807
Flor de la Mar: 454
Flores: 335-345
food: see specific place

Forbidden Purple City: 989-992
Fort Canning Park: 720
Fort Cornwallis: 481
Fort Margharita: 523
Fort Marlborough: 309
Fort Pilar: 681
Fort Rotterdam: 357
Fort San Pedro: 670
Fort Santiago: 630
Fort Sylvia: 527
Fraser's Hill: 452, 472
funerals: 142, 238
Fung Ying Sing Koon Temple: 138

G

gambling: 428; see also horse racing and greyhound racing
gamelan: 195-196
gardens: see botanical gardens
gatoeis: 836
Gawadapawlin Temple: 588
Gedung Songo: 215-216
Geliting: 342
gems: 566-567
General Luna: 677-678
Genting Highlands: 466
geomancy: 113
Ghost City: 886
Giac Vien Tu Pagoda: 963
Gia Long Palace: 960
Giant Swing: 804
Gianyar: 256
Gili Islands: 323-325
Gilimanuk: 283
Glodok: 173
Goa Gajah: 264-265
Golden Mount: 847
Golden Triangle: 871, 880-887
golf: Boracay 665-667; Cameron Highlands 472
Gomantong Caves: 540
Gorontalo: 373-374
government: Brunei 47; Hong Kong 98-100; Laos 381; Macau 410; Myanmar 552-553; Philippines 609; Thailand 779-782
Gowa Empire: 359
Grajagan: 229-230
Grand Palace: 798-801
greyhound racing: Macau 429
Guguk: 303
Guia Fortress: 421

FESTIVALS

12-13
Brunei: 49
Bali: 237-238
Hong Kong: 102-103
Macau: 413
Malaysia: 442-444
Myanmar: 555
Nusa Tenggara: 326, 346, 348
Philippines: 616-618
Singapore: 707-708, 710
Thailand: 783-785, 889

Guimaras: 695
Guinsiliban: 668
Gulabakul: 349
Gunongan: 289
Gunung Agung: 267
Gunung Kawi: 265
Gunung Mulu National Park: 531-532
Gunung Pengsong: 321
gunungs: see also mountains
Gunung Sitoli: 300

H
Haiphong: 1008-1010
Halong By: 1010-1011
Hamburger Hill: 996
Hang Dong: 865
Hanoi: 1000-1008
Hat Yai: 932-935
Hawaiian Mills: 688
hawker foodstalls: 490; see also specific place
Haw Par Villa: 730
health: 23-28; see also specific place
hepatitis: 24-25
Heritage Museum: 675
Hibok Hibok Volcano: 668
Hidden Valley Springs: 639
highland people: 948, 1013-1014, 1016
Hilisimaetano: 301
hilltribe peoples: 871-876
history: Bali 231-234; Brunei 45-47; Cambodia
    60-63; Flores 335; Hong Kong 96-98;
    Indonesia 151-156, 188; Laos 379-381;
    Macau 409-410; Malaysia 435-438, 454,

HORSE RACING

Hong Kong: 133, 138
Macau: 428
Nusa Tenggara: 321

460, 479-481; Myanmar 550-552, 572-574,
    582-584; Philippines 606-609; Singapore
    704-709; Thailand 773-779; Vietnam 946-
    948, 989, 1000, 1014
Hmong Hill Tribe: 873
Ho Chi Minh: 997, 1001-1005
Ho Chi Minh City: 955-967
Hoa Bin: 1012-1013
Hoa Lu: 999
Hoan Kiem Lake: 1000
Hoang Thanh: 989-992
Hoi An: 983-985
Honda Bay: 691
Hon Gai: 1011
Hong Kong: 91-146
Hong Kong Arts Festival: 102
Hong Kong Island: 134-135
Hong Kong Park: 122
hot springs: Camiguin Island 668; Luzon
    639, 645; Poring 539
hotels: see specific place
Hsinbyume Pagoda: 581
Htilominlo Temple: 588
Hua Hin: 903-905
Hue: 989-994
Hundred Islands: 652
Huong Son (Perfume Mountain): 1012-1013
Huu: 331-332

HIKING

Bangli: 266
Brastagi: 290-291
Luzon: 643, 647
Makale: 363
Hong Kong: 138, 139, 142-143
Nias Island: 301
Ruteng: 338
Samosir Island: 295
Sarawak: 528
Taman Negara :470-471
Thailand: 888
Tioman Island: 499-500
Tirtagangga: 272-273

I
iguanas: 340
Ijen Plateau: 229
ikat weaving: 339, 341-342, 346-348, 403
illness: see health
Iloilo: 694-697
Imogiri Cemetery: 192
Imperial Citadel: 989-992
India Mosque: 465
Indonesia: 147-374; Bali 231-284; Java 166-
    230; Nusa Tenggara 314-354 ; Sulawesi
    355-374; Sumatra 285-313
Inle Lake: 594-597
insurance: 24

International Buddhist Pagoda: 465
international clock: 107
international driving permit: 30
international health certificate: 29
international student identity card (ISIC): 29-30
International Youth Hostel (IYH) card: 30
internet: 34-35
Intramuros: 630, 634
Ipoh: 452, 474-475
Iskandariah Palace: 478
Islamic Museum: 512
Istana: 523
Istana Bukit Serene: 450
Istana Kenangan: 478
Istiqlal Mosque: 171
Iwahig Penal Colony: 691

J
Jagaraja: 278
Jakarta: 168-176
Jalan Tun Tan Cheng Lock: 456
Jamai Masjid Mosque: 109
Jame Asr Hassanil Bolkiah Mosque: 51
Jame Mosque: 460-462
Jao Island: 664-665
Jaro: 695
Java: 164-230
JEATH Museum: 840
Jepara: 216
Jerantut: 471
Jerudong: 52
jewels: 566-567
Johor Bharu: 450-452
Joko Dolog Statue: 217-219
Jones, Tristan: 919
Jopu: 341
Judson, Adoniram: 579
Jurong Bird Park: 729-730
Jurong Crocodile Paradise: 730

K
Kabayan: 649
Kabunduk: 349
Kaeng Khut Ku: 896
Kailala Beach: 348
Kalabahi: 345
Kalaw: 595
Kalibo: 697
Kalibukbuk: 281
Kalinga Province: 645

Kaliuda: 348
Kaliurang: 204
Kamphang Phet: 858-859
Kampong Ayer: 51
Kampong Kling Mosque: 456
Kampot: 81
Kam Tin: 137
Kanchanaburi: 840-843
Kao Poon Cave: 840
Kapal: 254
Kapas Island: 507
Kapit: 527-528
Kapitan Kling Mosque: 484
Karangasem: 271-272
Karen Hill Tribe: 873-874
Karon Beach: 922-924
Karo villages: 291
Kasunanan Kraton: 206-208
Kata Beach: 922, 924
Katibawasan Falls: 668
Kaungmudaw Pagoda: 580
Kawangkoan Caves: 371
Kawasan Falls: 674
Kebun Raya Botanical Gardens: 178
Kek Lok Si Temple: 486
Kelantan Cultural Center: 512-514
Keli Mutu: 341
Kelly's Castle: 474
Kenh Ga: 999
Kep: 81
Kerkhof memorial: 289
Kerta Gosa: 266-267
Keta Kesu: 366
Khao Chong Krachok: 905
Khao Prapa Tao National Park: 916
Khao Wang Palace: 903
Khao Yai National Park: 888-889
Khe Sanh: 994-995
Khmer castles: 892-893, 900
Khmer Rouge: 62-63
Khone Island: 404
Khong Island: 404
Khon Kaen: 891-893
Khon Phapheng Falls: 404
Khoo Kongsi: 484
Khu Khut Bird Sanctuary: 935
Khun Sa: 553
Khun Yam Temple: 464
Khunying Mo Statue: 889-890
kickboxing: 825
The Killing Fields: 76

Kinabalu National Park: 538-539
Kintamani: 276-277
The King and I: 775-778
Klungkung: 266-267
Ko Chang: 838-839
Kok River: 880
Ko Lanta: 929-930
Komodo: 333-335
Komodo dragons: 333-334
Komtar Centre: 484
Ko Nang Yuan: 915
Ko Phangan: 913-915
Ko Phi Phi: 925-926
Korat: 889-891
Ko Samet: 836-838
Ko Samui: 907-912
Kota Belud: 538
Kota Bharu: 512-516
Kota Gede: 192
Kota Kinabalu: 533, 534-537
Ko Tao: 915
Ko Tarutao National Park: 930-931
Kowloon: 108-118
Ko Yoh: 935
Krabi: 926-929
Krakatau Volcano: 177-178
kraton: 195
Kraton Kanoman: 211
Kraton Kasepuhan: 211
Kraton Ratu Boko: 202
Kuah: 495
Kuala Belait: 52-53
Kuala Besut: 510
Kuala Kangsar: 452, 477-478
Kuala Lumpur: 460-469
Kuala Trengganu: 507-509
Kuan Iam Tong Temple: 421
Kuantan: 502-503
Kuan Yin Temple: 483-484
Kubutambahan: 278-279
Kubyaukgyi Temple: 590
Kuching: 520-524
Kudus: 216
Kupang: 351-353
Kuta Beach: 242-248, 326
Kutacane: 290
kutu culture: 468
Kwangdung: 373
Kyaiktiyo: 570-571
Kyauktan: 569
Kyauktawgyi Pagoda: 575, 579

Kythodaw Pagoda: 575

L
Labi Falls: 52
Labuan Island: 537
Labuhanbajo: 336-337
Labuhan Lombok: 329
La Carlotta Mills: 688
lacquerware: 592
Ladelero: 342
La Galigo Museum: 357
Lagundri Beach: 300-301
Lahad Datu: 541
Lahu Hill Tribe: 874
Lai Chi Wan village: 422
Lai Tarung: 349
Lake Batur: 275, 276
Lake Bratan: 277
Lake Chini: 502
Lake Gardens: 459, 465, 478
Lake Limboto: 373
Lake Mananjau: 303
Lake Meribum: 52
Lake of Sighs: 974
Lake Poso: 368
Lake Sebu: 680-681
Lake Taal: 639
Lake Toba: 291-297
Lake Tonando: 371
Lak Muang: 801
La Laguna Beaches: 684
Lamai Beach: 910
Lamalera: 345
Lamma Island: 142-143
Lampang: 876-877
Lamphun: 876
Lam Son Uprising: 998
Lan Xang Kingdom: 380
land: Cambodia 60; Hong Kong 96; Indonesia
    149; Laos 377; Macau 409; Malaysia 433-
    434; Myanmar 549-550; Philippines 601-
    606; Sarawak 517; Singapore 704; Vietnam
    941-945
land mines: 995
Langa: 339
Lang Co Beach: 989
Langkawi Island: 494-496
language: Burmese 559; Indonesia 157;
    Pilipino/Tagalog 613, 623
Lantau Island: 143-145
Lao Cai: 1015-1016

Laos: 375-405
Larantuka: 344
Las Pinas Organ: 637
Laufaushan: 137
La Union: 652-653
Lawa Caves: 844
Leal Senado: 418
leatherback turtles: 505-506
Lee Kuan Yew: 705-709
Legaspi: 656-658
Legian: 242-248
Lembata: 345
Lemo: 366
Le Van Duyet Temple: 963
Lewoleba: 345
Leyte: 675-676
libraries: 587
Limbang: 53
Liminangcong: 693
Ling Nam Temple: 479
Lingsar Temple: 321
Lisu Hill Tribe: 874-875
Loei: 896-897
logging: 521
Loke Chow Kit Emporium and House: 462
Lombok: 315-329
Lom Sak: 897
Londa: 365
Lon Htein: 551-552
Lopburi: 849-851
Lore Lindu: 370
Lou Lim Ioc Gardens: 420
Love is a Many Splendored Thing: 130
Lovina Beach: 279-282
Luang Prabang: 393-397
Lucap: 652
Lukluk: 254
Luzon: 626-659

M
MacArthur, Douglas: 608, 675
Macau: 407-429
Mactan Island: 670
Madura Island: 222-223
Mae Hong Son: 871, 878-879
Mae Nam Beach: 911-912
Mae Sai: 883-884
Mae Salong: 882-883
Mae Sariang: 860-861, 877-878
Mae Sot: 860
magazines: 35

Magellan, Ferdinand: 607, 670
Maha Aungmye Bonzan Monastery: 579
Maha Kalyani Sima: 570
Mahameru: 228-229
Mahamuni Pagoda: 577
Mahinog: 668
Mai Chau: 1013
mail: 33
Majayjay: 640
Majene: 361
Makale: 362-363
Makassar: 357-359
Makati: 631
Malacañang Palace: 630-631
Malacca: 437, 452-459
Malang: 223-225
malaria: 25-27
Malate: 626-627
Malaysia: 431-542
Malincong Rice Terraces: 645
Malino: 359
Mambajao: 667-668
Mambucal: 688
Manado: 371-373
Mandalay: 572-578
Mandalay Hill: 574-575
Mangili: 348
Mangkutana: 367-368
Mangunegaran Kraton: 206
Manila: 626-636
Man Mo Temple: 123
Manuha Temple: 590
maps: see introduction to specific place
Marang: 506-507
Marante: 366
Marapu religion: 348-349
Marble Mountains: 988
Marcos, Ferdinand: 608-609

MOUNTAIN CLIMBING

18
Bali: 267, 274-276
Java: 227-229
Malaysia: 531-533, 538-539
Nusa Tenggara: 327-329, 331, 338, 340, 345
Philippines: 649, 680, 688
Sulawesi: 371
Sumatra: 290-291

Marcos Museum: 653-654
Mardi Gras 616-617
marionettes: 591
Maritime Museum: 416
Marudi: 530-531
Mas: 255
Masingal: 653
Masjid Zahir: 493
Matangkib Cave and Underground River: 647
Matanglag: 643
Mataram: 317-322
Matnog: 658-659
Matutinao: 674
Maumere: 342-343
mausoleums: Thailand 882; Vietnam 992-993, 1001
Mawlamyin: 571-572
Maxwell Hill: 452, 479
Maymyo: 581-582
Mayon Volcano: 656
Mayura Water Palace: 321
Medan: 286-288
meditation retreats: 829-830, 870, 906
Mekong Delta: 971-972
Mekong Islands: 403-404
Melolo: 348
Mengwi: 254-255
Mentawai Islands: 306-307
Merak: 177
Merang Island: 509
Merdeka Building: 181
Merdeka Square: 168-171
Mersing: 498-499
Meru Betiri Reserve: 229
Miagao: 695
Mien Hill Tribe: 875
Minangkabau villages: 303-304
Mindanao: 677-682
Mindon Min: 574
Mindoro: 683-685
Mingalazedi Pagoda: 590
Mingun: 580-581
Minnanthu Village: 589-590
Miri: 530
Moalboal: 674
Mojokerto: 221
Molo: 695
monasteries: Bagan 591; Bali 283; Hong Kong 144; Mandalay 575-576, 579; Thailand 926
money: 30-33; see also specific place

Mong Ha Fortress: 421
Mongkut: 775-778
Moni: 341-342
monkeys: 663, 850
Montagnards: 948, 1016
Monte Fortress (Forleza do Monte): 419
Moriones Festival: 617
motorcycles: 162
Moulmein: 571-572
movies about/filmed in: Cambodia 76; Hong Kong 130; Malaysia 445; Philippines 625; Thailand 793
Mrabi Hill Tribe: 887
Mt. Agung: 267
Mt. Apo National Park: 680
Mt. Batur: 274-276
Mt. Bromo: 227-228
Mt. Ile Ape: 345
Mt. Ipi: 340
Mt. Kanloan: 688
Mt. Kinabalu: 533, 538-539
Mt. Klabat: 371
Mt. Lokon: 371
Mt. Merapi: 204, 304
Mt. Mulu: 531-532
Mt. Phousi: 394
Mt. Popa: 593
Mt. Pulog: 649
Mt. Ranaka: 338
Mt. Rinjani: 327-329
Mt. Semeru: 228-229
Mt. Sibayak: 290-291
Mt. Singabung: 291
Mt. Tambora: 331
Muang Kham: 399
Muang Phi: 886
Muara Siberut: 306-307
Mui Fat Monastery: 137
Murara: 52
museums: Aceh 289; Adityawarman 304; Affandi Art Museum: 192; Ancient City 807; Ayala 653; Baba Nonya Heritage Museum 456; Bagan Lacquerware School and Museum 592; Bali 252; Ban Kao 844; Bengkulu Museum Negeri 309; Bontoc 644-645; Brunei 51; Bukittinggi 301; Cambodia 69; Casa Gorodo 670; Cham Museum 985; Chandra Kasem 845; Chao Sam Phya National Museum 845-847; Chiang Mai 864; Chiang Saen 884; Crisologo 653; Dr. Tawee's Folklore Museum 852; Hanoi

1001, 1005; Heritage Museum, Leyte 675; Ho Chi Minh 1005; Ho Chi Minh City 960; Hong Kong 109; Hue 992; Iloilo 695; Independence Museum, Malaysia 455; Islamic Museum 512; Istana Kenangan 478; JEATH Museum 840; Khon Kaen 892; Korat 890; Kota Bharu Royal Museums 512; Kuala Lumpur 465; Kupang 351; La Galigo 357; Lamphun 876; Laos 386, 393-394; Lopburi 849-850; Malacca Sultanate Palace Museum 456; Marcos Museum 654; Maritime 416; Muzium Negeri 459; Nan 887; *nat* museum, Bagan 593; Neka 256-257; Nusa Tenggara 321; Penang 481-483; Pusat 168; Radyapustaka 208; Ramkamheng National Museum 855-856; Royal Abu Bakar 450; Sabah 534; Sam Tung Uk Folk Museum 136; Sarawak 520-523; Savannakhet 399; Silliman Anthropological Museum 688; Singapore 720-721; Songkhla 935; Sono Budoyo 190; Sulawesi 369; Taiping 478-479; Thalang 919; Tuol Sleng Holocaust Museum 69; Ubon Ratchathani 899; Ubud 256; University of San Carlos 670; Villa Escudero 639; Vredburg Museum 190; Wayang Museum (Jakarta) 186; Yangon 564

Myanmar: 543-597
Mychellin: 668
Myinkaba Village: 590
My Lai: 982-983
Mytho: 971-972

N

Naga: 655-656
Naga Island Pearl Farm: 916-919
Nagayon Temple: 590-591
Nagcartan: 640
Nagore Durga Mosque: 723
Nagoya: 310
Nakhon Pathom: 839-840
Nakhon Phanom: 898
Nakhon Ratchasima: 889-891
Namberala: 353
Nam Tok: 844
Nan: 887
Nanggala: 366
Nanpaya Temple: 590
Narathiwat: 935-936

NATIONAL PARKS

Bako: 524-525
Baluran: 229
Cat Ba: 1011
Doi Inthanon: 865
Gunung Mulu: 531-532
Khao Prapa Tao: 916
Kinabalu: 538-539
Ko Tarutao: 930-931
Mt. Apo: 680
Phu Kradang: 896-897
Phu Luang: 897
Phu Phan: 898
Sai Yok: 844
St. Paul's: 692
Taman Negara: 470-471
Tunku Abdul Rahman: 534
Turtle Island: 540

Narmada Water Palace: 321-322
Nathon: 908-909
nats: 593
Ne Win: 551-553
Negara Brunei Darusalam: *see* Brunei
Negros: 685-689
New Territories: 136-139
Ngarai Canyon: 301-302;
Nggela: 341-342
Ngo Diem: 947, 961
Ngo Mon Gate: 992
Nha Trang: 977-980
Niah Caves: 529-530
Nias Island: 299-301
Ninh Binh: 999
nipa weaving: 664
Nobel Peace Prize: 552
Nong Het: 399
Nong Khai: 894-895
Nongsa: 310-312
Nuabosi: 340
Nusa Dua: 250-251
Nusa Lembongan: 267-268
Nusa Penida: 267-268
Nusa Tenggara: 314-354
Nyaungshwe: 596
Nyaung U: 588-589, 592

O

Ocean Park: 134
oil: 47-48
Old Batavia: 171-173
Old Chiang Mai Cultural Center: 864-865
Olongapo: 642
Omar Ali Saifuddin Mosque: 49-51
opera: 118
opium: 553, 883
orangutans: 533, 540
orchid gardens: 360
Ormoc: 676
Otanaha Fortress: 373
Outlying Islands of Hong Kong: 139-145

P

Pa Umur: 531
packing: 22-23
Padang: 304-306
Padangbai: 268-269
pagodas: see temples
Pagsanjan: 640-641
Pagudpud: 654
Pai: 879
Paigoli: 349
Pak Chong: 896
Pak Ou Caves: 396
Pakse: 400-401
Paksong: 403
Palace in the Sky: 638
Palatoke: 366
Palawa: 366
Palawan: 689-694
Palopo: 360
Palu: 369-370
Panagsama Beach: 674
Panataran: 226-227
Panay: 694-697
Pandaan: 222
Pangandaran: 185-188
Pangkor Island: 475-477
Panglao Island: 663
Pangli: 366
Pangururan: 295
Pantai Trikora: 313
Panwa Cape: 919
Paoay: 654
Papar: 537
Papela: 353
Parangtritis Beach: 192
Pare Pare: 360-361

pasola: 346
passports: 28, 29
Pasteur Institutes: 806, 979
Pathet Lao: 381
Patodawgyi Pagoda: 579
Patong Beach: 919-923
Pattaya: 833-836
Pau: 348
Payakumbuh: 303
pearl farms: 916-919
Pekalongan: 213
Pekanbaru: 307-308
Penampang: 537
Penang: 479-493
Pendolo: 368
Penelokan: 274
Penestanan: 263
Peng Chau Island: 144
Pengosekan: 263
Penha Hill: 416
Penujak: 325-326
people: see population
People's Action Party (PAP): 705-709
performing arts: 12; Thailand 823-824; see
   also specific place
Perhentian Island: 510-511
Pero: 350
Petchburi: 902-903
Petleik Pagodas: 591
Petronas Towers: 465
phallic shrines: 806
Phan Rang: 976-977
Phangnga: 925
Phat Diem: 999
Pha Thai Caves: 877
Phayao: 885-886
Phetburi: 902-903
Philippines: 599-698
Phimenakas: 88
Phitsanulok: 852-853
Phnom Chisor: 80
Phnom Penh: 68-79
Phong Na Caves: 997
Phonsavan: 398
Phrae: 886
Phuket: 916-925
Phu Kradang National Park: 896-897
Phu Luang National Park: 897
Phun Phin: 906
Phu Phan National Park: 898
Phu Wua Wildlife Park: 897

Pi Ta Khon (Dance of the Ghosts): 897
Pindaya Caves: 595
Ping Shan Heritage Trail: 137
Pitakat Taik Library: 587
Plain of Jars: 397-399
Poitan: 643
Po Klang Garai Towers: 977
Po Lin Monastery: 144
Pol Pot: 63
Po Nagar Cham Temple: 979
population: Bali 234-235; Cambodia 63-65;
    Hong Kong 101, 103-104; Indonesia 156-
    157; Laos 382-383; Macau 411; Malaysia
    439-444; Myanmar 554-555; Philippines
    611-614; Singapore 709-710; Thailand 782-
    783, 872-875; Vietnam 948
Poring Hot Springs: 539
Po Ro Me Towers: 977
Port Barton: 692
Poso: 369
pottery kilns: 856, 858
Pousada De Sao Tiago: 416
Prachuap Khiri Khan: 905
Praia Grande: 415
Praijing: 349
Praliu: 348
Prambanan: 201-202
Pranang: 927-929
Prapat: 291-295
prasats: 892-893, 900
Pra That Luang: 386-390
Pratuxai Monument: 386
Praya: 325-326
Probolinggo: 228
Promtep Cape: 919
Pronobaroro: 350
Puerto Galera: 683—685
Puerto Princesa: 691-692
Pu Kao Tong: 847
Pulau Menjangan: 283
Pulau Penyenget: 313
Pulau Weh: 289
Puncak Pass: 180-181
Punta Cruz Watchtower: 663
Pu Ping Palace: 865
puppetry: 823-824
Pura Kehen: 265-266
Pura Meru: 321
Pura Penataran Sasih: 264
Puri Kangiana: 271
Pyin U Lwin: 581-582

Q
Quang Ngai: 982-983
Quang Tri: 994
Quiapo: 630
Qui Nhon: 981-982
quotations: 2, 42, 44, 54, 56, 90, 92, 145, 148,
    374, 376, 405, 408, 429, 432, 542, 544,
    597, 600, 698, 700, 770, 772, 937, 940,
    1016

R
Radyapustaka Museum: 208
Raffles Hotel: 721-722
Raffles, Stamford: 437-438, 455
Raffles, Thomas: 704-705
rainforests: 521
Rambitan: 326
ram fights: West Java 185
Ramkamheng National Museum: 855-856
Ramos, Fidel: 609
Rangoon: see Yangon
Rantau Abang: 505-506
Rantepao: 363-365
Ratenegaro: 350
Rawai Beach: 919
Rawa Island: 501
Razor: 996
reading list: 1017-1025
Redang Island: 509-510
Red Beach: 675
Rejang River: 526-527
religion: Bali 235; Malaysia 441-444; see also
    Buddhism
Rende: 348
Renu Phanom: 898
Repulse Bay: 134
responsible tourism guidelines: 26
restaurants: see specific place
Reunification Hall: 960
Revolutionary Museum, Laos: 386
Rhu Muda: 507
Riau Islands: 310-313
Rio Hondo: 681
Riung: 339-340
river journeys: 19; Kelantan River 514; Sabah
    533, Sekong River 403; see also specific
    place
Rizal Beach: 658
Rizal Park: 626-630
Roti: 353
Round-the-World airfares: 36, 37

Roxas: 692
Roxas City: 685
Royal Abu Bakar Museum: 450
Rua Beach: 349-350
Ruteng: 338

S
Sabah: 532-542
Sabang: 692
Sabang Beach: 684
Sabang Island: 289
Sadan: 366
Sade: 326
Safari World: 807
Sagada: 645-648
Sagaing: 580
Saigon: 955-967
Sai Yok National Park: 844
Sakhon Nakhon: 898
Samal Island: 679-680
Samar: 697-698
Samosir Island: 291-297
Sampaloc Lake: 639-640
Sam Poo Kong Temple: 214
Sam Son Beach: 999
Sam Tung Uk Folk Museum: 136
Sandakan: 539-540
Sandamuni Pagoda: 575
San Fernando: 652-653
Sangeh: 255
Sangiran: 208
Sang Khom: 895-896
Sangklaburi: 844-845
Sangsit: 278

San Isidro Beach: 685
San Kamphang: 865
San Miguel Bay: 655
San Pablo: 639-640
Santandar: 673-674
Santiago Gate: 455
Santikhiri: 882
Santubong: 525
Sanur Beach: 248-250
Sapa: 1015
Sapada Pagoda: 589
Sape: 333
Saraba Gateway: 585-586
Sarao Jeepney Factory: 637
Saravan: 402-403
Sarawak: 517-532
Sarrat: 654
Satun: 931-933
Savang Vatthana: 394
Savannakhet: 399-400
Sawan: 278
Sawangen Monuments: 371
scams: 624-625, 954, 955
sculpture: 855
Sein Lwin: 551-552
Sekong River: 403
Sekupang: 310
Selangor State Secretariat: 462
Selayar Island: 360
Semarang: 214
Semau Island: 351
Seminyak: 242-248
Semonggok Wildlife Rehabilitation Sanctuary: 525
Sempidi: 254
Senggigi Beach: 322-323
Sentosa Island: 730
Sepilok Orangutan Sanctuary: 533, 540
Seremban: 459
Setkyathiha Pagoda: 576
Shatin: 138
Shell Cemetery: 927
Sheung Shui: 138
shopping: 14, *see also specific place*
Shwedagon Pagoda: 562-564
Shwekyimyint Pagoda: 576
Shwemawdaw Pagoda: 569
Shwenandaw Monastery: 575
Shwensandaw Pagoda: 587
Shwezigon Pagoda: 588-589
Siam Society: 806

SCUBA DIVING

16-19
Bali: 240, 283
Bohol: 661, 663-664
Cebu: 669, 673, 674
Gili Island: 324, 325
Mindoro: 683
Nusa Tenggara: 336, 343-344
Palawan: 690
Sabah: 533, 541
Sulawesi: 370, 371
Thailand: 915-916
Tioman Island: 500

Siargao Island: 677-678
Sibolga: 298
Sibu: 526
Sibu Island: 501
Si Chiang Mai: 895
Sidan Pura Dalem: 256
Siem Reap: 82-84
sightseeing highlights: Cambodia 60; Hong
    Kong 98-99; Indonesia 152-153; Laos 379;
    Malaysia 436; Myanmar 549; Philippines
    604-605, 662-663; Southeast Asia 17-19;
    Thailand 776-777; Vietnam 944-945
Sigli: 290
Siguntu: 366
Sihanoukville: 81
Sikka: 342
silk weaving: 579, 892, 900; see also weaving
    villages
Silliman Anthropological Museum: 688
Silvermine Bay: 144
Silver Pagoda: 69
Simanindo: 297
Singapore: 699-770
Singaraja: 278
Singkang: 360
Singki Hill: 366
Singsing Air Terjun: 282-283
Sipadan Islnd: 541
Siquijor Island: 689
Si Satchanalai: 858
Skrang River: 525
snake farms: 806
Snake Temple: 486
snorkeling: Bali 283; see also scuba diving
Soa: 339
Soe: 353-354
Sohoton Park: 675
Solo: 206-211
Solor: 344-345
songket: 445
Songkhla: 935
Son La: 1013
Son My: 982-983
Sono Budoyo Museum: 190
Sop Ruak: 885
Sorsogon: 658
Southeast Asia highlights: 6-11, 17-19
Spies, Walter: 256
Sri Aman: 525-526
Sri Mariamman Temple: 464, 484
Sri Poyatha Vinayagar Moorthi Temple: 456-
    457

Stadthuys: 455
steam trains: 686
Stilwell, "Vinegar" Joe: 551
St. Paul's National Park: 692
stucco: 855
Suan Pakkard Palace: 806
Subic: 642
Suharto: 155-156
Sukarno: 155, 309, 340
Sukawati: 255
Sukothai: 853-858
Sukseskan: 266-267
Sulamani Temple: 589
Sulawesi: 355-374
Sule Pagoda: 564
Sullukang: 366
Sultan Abdul Samad building: 462
Sultan Mosque: 729
Sultan's Palace (Brunei): 51
Sulu Archipelago: 681-682
Sumaging Big Cave: 647
sumarah: 210
Sumatra: 284-313
Sumba: 346-350
Sumbawa: 330-333
Sumbawa Besar: 330-331
Sung Dynasty Village: 113
Sungai Golok: 936-937
Sun Yat-Sen Residence: 420
Surabaya: 217-221
Surakarta: 206-211
Suranadi: 322
Surat Thani: 906-907
Surin: 900
Swimming to Cambodia: 76
sword fighting: 824
Syriam: 569

SURFING

Bali: 240
Java: 229-230
Lagundri Beach: 300-301
Lombok: 325, 332
Mindanao: 677-678
Sumba: 348, 349-350
Timor: 353
Surigao: 677-678
see also beaches

T

Tabaco: 658
Tabon Caves: 692
Tacloban: 675-676
Tad Lo: 403
Tad Phan Waterfall: 403
Tagaytay: 638
Tagbilaran: 661-663
Tai O Village: 145
Taipa Island: 421-422
Taiping: 452
Tai Po: 138
Tak: 859
Talisay: 639
Tam An: 643
Taman Mini Indonesia: 173, 174
Taman Mini Malaysia: 457
Taman Negara: 470-471
Taman Sari: 289
Taman Sari Water Palace: 190-192
Taman Seni Budaya Negeri: 459
Tam Coc (Three Caves): 999
Tampaksiring: 265
Tam Phiu Cave: 399
Tana Beru: 359
Tana Toraja: 361-366
Tanah Lot: 254
Tang Dynasty Village: 730
Tangkuban Crater: 183
Tanjung Aru Beach: 534
Tanjung Bua: 353
Tanjung Kling: 457, 458
Tanjung Pinang: 312-313
Tan Song Yang: 861
Tan Yeok Nee Mansion: 717
Ta Phrom: 79
Ta Prohm: 89
tarsiers: 663
Tarung: 348-349
Tarutao: 930-931
Taunggyi: 595-596
Tawau: 541
Tay Son Rebellion: 981-982
Taytay: 692-693
Telaga Tujuh: 495
telephone communications: 33-34; see also
    introduction to specific place and area
    codes
Teluk Bahang: 486
Teluk Chempedak: 503
Teluk Dalam: 300

Templar Park: 466
temple architecture: 799-801
Temple of 10,000 Buddhas: 138-139
Temple of Literature: 1005-1006
Temple of the Azure Cloud: 486
temples: Bagan 584-591; Java 208,
    394, 396, 399, 401; Malang 226;
    Myanmar 562-564, 569-570, 575-577,
    579-581, 584-591; Prambanan 202;
    Singapore 720, 723; Singaraja 278;
    Thailand 801-805, 845-847, 848, 850,
    852, 856-860, 863-865, 876, 877, 878,
    883-887, 894-895, 897-899, 902-903,
    916-919, 935-936; Vietnam 960-963,
    970, 979, 982, 983-985, 988, 992, 1001,
    1005, 1012-1013; see also specific temple,
    pagoda or wat
Temple Street Night Market: 113, 115-116
Tengah Mosque: 474
Tenganan: 271
Tenom: 537-538
Tentena: 368-369
Tetebatu: 329
Thabyedan Fort: 580
Thai Hoa Palace: 992
Thalang National Museum: 919
Tha Li: 897
Thanh Hoa: 998-999
Thanlyin: 569
Thao Suranari: 889-890
Thap Cham: 976-977
Thatbyinnyu Temple: 586-587
Tha Teng: 403
That Ing Hang: 399-400
Thaton: 880
That Phanom: 898-899
theater: 823-824; Myanmar 571; Singapore
    764; Vietnam 1001
theft: 27, 793, 876, 954
Thein Mu Pagoda: 992
theme travel: 11-19
Theravadism: 593
Thibaw: 574
Thich Quang Du: 960-961, 992
Thompson, Jim: 806
Thong Chai Medical Institution: 723
Thong Sala: 913
Three Pagodas Pass: 844
Tilanga: 365
Timor: 350-354
Timor liberation monument: 354
Tinggi Island: 501

Tin Hau Temple: 109-113
Tioman Island: 499-501
Tirtagangga: 272-273
Tiwi: 658
tobacco kilns: 884
Tolosa: 675
tombs: Thailand 882; Vietnam 992-993, 1001
Tomohon: 371
Tomok: 295
Tonle Bati: 79
Tontonon Falls: 663
Tourist Authority of Thailand (TAT): 789-791, 828
tourist information: *see specific place*
Toya Bungkah: 276
train travel: *see specific place*
Trang: 930
transportation: Laos 383-385, 393; Macau 412-414; Malaysia 446-448, 517-520, 533-534; Myanmar 556-558, 567-568, 578; Philippines 615-619, 635-636, 660, 661, 669-670; Singapore 711-714; Sulawesi 355; Thailand 785-789, 830-832; Vietnam 949-951, 966-967, 1007-1008; *see also specific city or place*
Trat: 838
travel agencies: 41-42
traveler's checks: 30
travel permits: 558
trekking: 18-19; Thailand 871-876, 878, 883; Vietnam 1014, 1016
Tribal Research Center: 864
Trowulan: 222
Trunyan: 276
Truong Son Cemetery: 996
Tsimshatsui: 108-109
Tsuen Wan: 136
Tuaran: 538
Tuban: 243-248
Tu Cam Thanh: 989-992
Tu Do Street: 955
Tuen Mun: 137
Tuk Tuk: 295
Tulamben: 274
Tundung: 366
Tunku Abdul Rahman National Park: 534
tunnels: 968, 995
Tuol Sleng Holocaust Museum: 69
Turtle Islands National Park: 540
turtles: 505-506, 540

U
U Bien Bridge: 579
Ubon Ratchathani: 899-900
Ubud: 256-263
Ubudiah Mosque: 478
Udong: 80
Udon Thani: 893-894
Ujung Kulon Reserve: 178
Ujung Pandang: 357-359
Umabara: 348
umbrella village: 865
Umbu Sawola: 349
Underground River: 692
University of San Carlos: 670
U Nu: 551
Upali Thein Ordination Hall: 588
urns: 992

V
vaccinations: 24, 953
Valley of Love: 974
Van Mieu: 1005-1006
Victoria Mills: 686-688
Victoria Peak: 122-123
Vientiane: 386-393
Vietnam: 939-1016
Vietnam War: 380-381, 947, 982-983, 989, 994-995
Vigan: 653
Viharn Pra Mongkol Bopit: 847
Villa Escudero: 639
Vimanmek Palace: 805
Vinh: 997-998
Vinh Long: 972
Vinh Moc Tunnels: 995
Vinh Van Phong Beach: 979
visas: 28-29; Indonesia 162-163; Laos 384-385, 895; Macau 414; Malaysia 448; Malaysia 520, 533; Myanmar 558; Philippines 619-620, 634; Singapore 714-715; Thailand 789, 828-829; Vietnam 949, 951-952
volcanoes: Gunung Ipi 340; Gunung Ranaka 338; Gunung Tambora 331; Hibok Hibok 668; Keli Mutu 341; Mayon 656; Mt. Klabat 371
Vredburg Museum: 190
Vung Tao: 968-971

WEAVING VILLAGES

Laos: 403
Nusa Tenggara: 338, 341-342, 346-348
Philippines: 643, 647, 649
Thailand: 865, 898, 900
see also ikat and silk weaving

W

Waecicu Beach: 336
Waiara Beach: 343-344
Wailabubak: 348-349
Waingapu: 347
Waiwerang: 345
walking tours: Cheung Chau 141; Hong Kong 123-125, 137; Leyte 675; Narathiwat 935-936; Penang 484-485; Singapore 717-722, 722-725, 726-729; Ubud 257
Wanchai: 127-133
War Crimes Museum: 960
Watampone: 360
Watana Praman: 847
Wat Chayamangkalaram: 485
Wat Chedi Luang: 863
Wat Chet Yot: 864
Wat Chiang Man: 863-864
water palaces: Mayura 321; Narmada 321-322
waterfalls: Bali 282-283; Bantimurung 359; Brunei 52; Cebu 674; Durian Perangin 495; Laos 403-404; Luzon 640, 647; Myanmar 582; Philippines 663; Sai Yok National Park 844; Sarawak 527; Vietnam 974
Wat Ko Keo Sutharam: 903
Wat Ounalom: 69
Wat Phnom: 68
Wat Photiviharn: 514
Wat Phu: 401-402
Wat Pra Keo: 69, 386, 798-801, 880
Wat Pra Singh: 864
Wat Suan Mok: 906
Wat Tham Sua: 926
wats: see temples
Wattansoppeng: 360
Watu Kajiwa: 349
wayang: 186, 196-197; see also specific place
weather: see climate
Western Union: 31
West Java: 177-188
West Lake: 1005
White Beach: 685
wildlife parks: 729-730, 807, 897
Wogo: 339
Wolonjita: 341
Wolowaru: 341
Wong Tai Sin Temple: 114
The World of Suzi Wong: 127, 130
World War II: 438, 608, 705
Wula Padu festival: 348

XYZ

Xa Loi Pagoda: 960
Xang Hai: 396
Xieng Khwang Province: 397-399
Xuan Huong Lake: 974
Yangon: 560-568
Yasothon: 899
Yaumatei: 109
Yeah Peau: 79
Year Zero/Year Ten: 76
Yeh Pulu: 264
Yogyakarta: 188-200
youth hostels: see specific place
Yuen Long: 137
Yumbing: 669
Ywataung: 580
Zamboanga: 681-682
zoos: Chiang Mai 864; Malacca 457; Singapore 729; Surabaya 219

ABOUT THE AUTHOR

Carl Parkes, author of *Southeast Asia Handbook*, *Thailand Handbook*, and *Singapore Handbook*, was born into an American Air Force family and spent his childhood in California, Nebraska, Alabama, and Japan, where his love of Asia first began. After graduating from the University of California at Santa Barbara, Carl traveled throughout Europe and later returned to work in Hawaii, Lake Tahoe, Aspen, Salt Lake City, and finally, San Francisco.

But childhood memories of Asia continued to pull him to the East. After a 12-month journey across Asia, Carl returned to San Francisco to work as a stockbroker and plan his escape from the nine-to-five world. A chance encounter in Singapore with publisher Bill Dalton offered a more intriguing option: to research and write a travel guidebook to Southeast Asia—one that addressed more travel practicalities by exploring the region's rich culture and history.

Carl fervently believes that travel is an immensely rewarding undertaking that affirms the basic truths of life. "Travel is much more than just monuments and ruins. It's an opportunity to reach out and discover what's best about the world. Travel enriches our lives, spreads prosperity, dissolves political barriers, promotes international peace, and brings excitement and change to our lives."

Carl also believes in the importance of political, economic, and environmental issues. "Historical sites and beaches make for wonderful memories, but national agendas such as human rights and rainforest preservation are just as fascinating in their own right. Understanding the contemporary scene enriches travel experiences and opens avenues rarely explored by the visitor."

In addition to his guidebooks from Moon, Carl also writes for Fodor's *Worldview Systems*, *PATA Travel News America*, *Weissmann Travel Reports*, and *Pacific Rim News Service*. Carl has also updated portions of *Indonesia Handbook*, appeared on CNN and the Travel Channel with Arthur From-

mer, and lectured onboard *Pearl*, *Princess*, *Renaissance*, and *Radisson Seven Seas* cruise lines. In 1995, Carl won the Lowell Thomas Award from the Society of American Travel Writers in the travel guidebook category for his *Southeast Asia Handbook*. In 1997, his *Thailand Handbook* won the Lowell Thomas Gold Award in the same category.

Besides travel writing, Carl enjoys straight-ahead jazz, photography, Anchor Steam beer, opera, art openings, poetry readings, and samba nightclubs in his favorite city of San Francisco. Future plans include more books on his favorite destinations in Southeast Asia.

READER SURVEY

Knowing a bit about you and your travel experiences will help me improve this book for the next edition. Please take a few minutes to complete this form and share your tips with the next traveler. Remember to send along corrected copies of photocopied maps from this book and business cards collected from your favorite hotels and restaurants. All contributors will be acknowledged in the next edition.

The author also appreciates correspondence from expatriates and other local residents with special insight into travel conditions. Research correspondents are also needed to help update several Moon Handbooks to destinations in Southeast Asia. You may write to Moon Publications at the address below or contact the author directly via e-mail: cparkes@moon.com.

Send the following survey to:

Carl Parkes/Reader Survey
Southeast Asia Handbook
Moon Publications
P.O. Box 3040
Chico, CA 95927-3040
USA

Date of Letter: _____

1. **Gender:** ☐ male ☐ female
2. **Age:** ☐ under 25 ☐ 25-30 ☐ 31-35 ☐ 36-40
   ☐ 41-50 ☐ 51+
3. **Status:** ☐ single ☐ married
4. **Income:** ☐ $20K ☐ $20-30K ☐ $30-40K ☐ $40-50K
   ☐ $50K+
5. **Occupation:** _____
6. **Education:** ☐ high school ☐ some college ☐ college grad ☐ post grad
7. **Travel style:** ☐ budget ☐ moderate ☐ luxury
8. **Vacations:** ☐ once yearly ☐ twice yearly ☐ 3+ yearly
9. **Why do you travel?** _____

_____

10. **What's best about travel?** _____

_____

11. **What's worst about travel?** _____

_____

12. This Journey:

Length of time: _____

  Enough time? _____

Countries visited: _____

Countries planned for next visit: _____

Season: _____

How was the weather? _____

Travel companions? _____

Do you prefer solo travel or with companions? _____

Purpose of Trip?

  a. ☐ Pleasure b. ☐ Study c. ☐ Work d. ☐ Volunteer e. ☐ Hanging out

Main Activities?

  a. ☐ Sights   b. ☐ Culture c. ☐ Beaches and outdoor activities

  d. ☐ Meeting people   e. ☐ Nightlife and entertainment

  f. ☐ Food and shopping

Main regions? Please give specific locations:

  a. ☐ Cities _____

  b. ☐ Smaller towns _____

  c. ☐ Beaches and islands _____

  d. ☐ Mountains _____

Primary modes of transportation? _____

Expenses:

  a. Total: _____

  b. Average daily expenses: _____

c. Average hotel price: _____

d. Average meal price: _____

e. Total airfare: _____

f. Shopping expenses: _____

Unexpected encounters: _____

13. Favorites:

a. Countries: _____

b. Hotels and guesthouses (include address, price, description): _____

c. Restaurants (address, price range, favorite dishes): _____

d. Airline: _____

e. Cuisine: _____

f. Nightspots: _____

g. Cultural events: _____

h. Outdoor adventures: _____

i. Temples or historical sites: _____

j. Beaches: _____

k. People: _____

_____

14. This Book:

Where did you buy this book? _____

Why did you select Moon Publications? _____

What other Moon Handbooks have you used? _____

What other guidebooks have you used? _____

What is your favorite series of guides? _____

How does this book compare with other guides? _____

Your opinion about the following:

a. Hotel listings (how accurate?) _____

_____

b. Restaurants _____

_____

c. Background information _____

_____

d. Maps _____

_____

e. Charts _____

_____

f. Photography _____

_____

g. Writer's attitude _____

_____

h. Price of this book _____

_____

i. Distribution _____

_____

j. Design and layout _____

_____

How accurate did you find the following information?

a. Hotel prices _____

b. Restaurant recommendations _____

c. Maps _____

d. Charts _____

e. Writer's opinions _____

Favorite introduction section (history, government, etc., none) _____

Did you use the hotel charts? _____

Weakest points of this book: _____

Suggestions for improvements: _____

How does this book compare with the competition? _____

15. Name and Address

_____
_____
_____
_____

Thanks for your help!

www.moon.com

Enjoy our travel information center on the World Wide Web (WWW), loaded with interactive exhibits designed especially for the Internet.

ATTRACTIONS ON MOON'S WEB SITE INCLUDE:

ATLAS
Our award-winning, comprehensive travel guides cover destinations throughout North America and Hawaii, Latin America and the Caribbean, and Asia and the Pacific.

PRACTICAL NOMAD
Extensive excerpts, a unique set of travel links coordinated with the book, and a regular Q & A column by author and Internet travel consultant Edward Hasbrouck.

TRAVEL MATTERS
Our on-line travel zine, featuring articles; author correspondence; a travel library including health information, reading lists, and cultural cues; and our new contest, **Destination X,** offering a chance to win a trip to the mystery destination of your choice.

ROAD TRIP USA
Our best-selling book, ever; don't miss this award-winning Web guide to off-the-interstate itineraries.

Come visit us at: **www.moon.com**

MOON TRAVEL HANDBOOKS

LOSE YOURSELF IN THE EXPERIENCE, NOT THE CROWD

For 25 years, Moon Travel Handbooks have been the guidebooks of choice for adventurous travelers. Our award-winning Handbook series provides focused, comprehensive coverage of distinct destinations all over the world. Each Handbook is like an entire bookcase of cultural insight and introductory information in one portable volume. Our goal at Moon is to give travelers all the background and practical information they'll need for an extraordinary travel experience.

The following pages include a complete list of Handbooks, covering North America and Hawaii, Mexico, Latin America and the Caribbean, and Asia and the Pacific. To purchase Moon Travel Handbooks, check your local bookstore or order by phone: (800) 345-5473 M-F 8 am.-5 p.m. PST or outside the U.S. phone: (530) 345-5473.

"An in-depth dunk into the land, the people and their history, arts, and politics."

—*Student Travels*

"I consider these books to be superior to Lonely Planet. When Moon produces a book it is more humorous, incisive, and off-beat."

—*Toronto Sun*

"Outdoor enthusiasts gravitate to the well-written Moon Travel Handbooks. In addition to politically correct historic and cultural features, the series focuses on flora, fauna and outdoor recreation. Maps and meticulous directions also are a trademark of Moon guides."

—*Houston Chronicle*

"Moon [Travel Handbooks] . . . bring a healthy respect to the places they investigate. Best of all, they provide a host of odd nuggets that give a place texture and prod the wary traveler from the beaten path. The finest are written with such care and insight they deserve listing as literature."

—*American Geographical Society*

"Moon Travel Handbooks offer in-depth historical essays and useful maps, enhanced by a sense of humor and a neat, compact format."

—*Swing*

"Perfect for the more adventurous, these are long on history, sightseeing and nitty-gritty information and very price-specific."

—*Columbus Dispatch*

"Moon guides manage to be comprehensive and countercultural at the same time . . . Handbooks are packed with maps, photographs, drawings, and sidebars that constitute a college-level introduction to each country's history, culture, people, and crafts."

—*National Geographic Traveler*

"Few travel guides do a better job helping travelers create their own itineraries than the Moon Travel Handbook series. The authors have a knack for homing in on the essentials."

—*Colorado Springs Gazette Telegraph*

MEXICO

"These books will delight the armchair traveler, aid the undecided person in selecting a destination, and guide the seasoned road warrior looking for lesser-known hideaways."

—*Mexican Meanderings* Newsletter

"From tourist traps to off-the-beaten track hideaways, these guides offer consistent, accurate details without pretension."

—*Foreign Service Journal*

Archaeological Mexico	$19.95
Andrew Coe	410 pages, 27 maps
Baja Handbook	$16.95
Joe Cummings	544 pages, 46 maps
Cabo Handbook	$14.95
Joe Cummings	272 pages, 17 maps
Cancún Handbook	$14.95
Chicki Mallan	270 pages, 25 maps
Colonial Mexico	$18.95
Chicki Mallan	360 pages, 38 maps
Mexico Handbook	$21.95
Joe Cummings and Chicki Mallan	1,200 pages, 201 maps
Northern Mexico Handbook	$17.95
Joe Cummings	590 pages, 69 maps
Pacific Mexico Handbook	$17.95
Bruce Whipperman	580 pages, 68 maps
Puerto Vallarta Handbook	$14.95
Bruce Whipperman	330 pages, 36 maps
Yucatán Handbook	$16.95
Chicki Mallan	470 pages, 52 maps

LATIN AMERICA AND THE CARIBBEAN

"Solidly packed with practical information and full of significant cultural asides that will enlighten you on the whys and wherefores of things you might easily see but not easily grasp."

—*Boston Globe*

Belize Handbook	**$15.95**
Chicki Mallan and Patti Lange	390 pages, 45 maps
Caribbean Handbook	**$16.95**
Karl Luntta	400 pages, 56 maps
Costa Rica Handbook	**$19.95**
Christopher P. Baker	780 pages, 73 maps
Cuba Handbook	**$19.95**
Christopher P. Baker	740 pages, 70 maps
Dominican Republic Handbook	**$15.95**
Gaylord Dold	420 pages, 24 maps
Ecuador Handbook	**$16.95**
Julian Smith	450 pages, 43 maps
Honduras Handbook	**$15.95**
Chris Humphrey	330 pages, 40 maps
Jamaica Handbook	**$15.95**
Karl Luntta	330 pages, 17 maps
Virgin Islands Handbook	**$13.95**
Karl Luntta	220 pages, 19 maps

NORTH AMERICA AND HAWAII

"These domestic guides convey the same sense of exoticism that their foreign counterparts do, making home-country travel seem like far-flung adventure."

—*Sierra Magazine*

Alaska-Yukon Handbook	**$17.95**
Deke Castleman and Don Pitcher	530 pages, 92 maps
Alberta and the Northwest Territories Handbook	**$17.95**
Andrew Hempstead and Nadina Purdon	530 pages, 72 maps,
Arizona Traveler's Handbook	**$17.95**
Bill Weir and Robert Blake	512 pages, 54 maps
Atlantic Canada Handbook	**$17.95**
Nan Drosdick and Mark Morris	460 pages, 61 maps
Big Island of Hawaii Handbook	**$15.95**
J.D. Bisignani	390 pages, 23 maps
British Columbia Handbook	**$16.95**
Jane King and Andrew Hempstead	430 pages, 69 maps

Colorado Handbook	**$18.95**
Stephen Metzger	480 pages, 59 maps
Georgia Handbook	**$17.95**
Kap Stann	370 pages, 50 maps
Hawaii Handbook	**$19.95**
J.D. Bisignani	1,030 pages, 90 maps
Honolulu-Waikiki Handbook	**$14.95**
J.D. Bisignani	380 pages, 20 maps
Idaho Handbook	**$18.95**
Don Root	610 pages, 42 maps
Kauai Handbook	**$15.95**
J.D. Bisignani	320 pages, 23 maps
Maine Handbook	**$18.95**
Kathleen M. Brandes	660 pages, 27 maps
Massachusetts Handbook	**$18.95**
Jeff Perk	600 pages, 23 maps
Maui Handbook	**$14.95**
J.D. Bisignani	410 pages, 35 maps
Montana Handbook	**$17.95**
Judy Jewell and W.C. McRae	480 pages, 52 maps
Nevada Handbook	**$18.95**
Deke Castleman	530 pages, 40 maps
New Hampshire Handbook	**$18.95**
Steve Lantos	500 pages, 18 maps
New Mexico Handbook	**$15.95**
Stephen Metzger	360 pages, 47 maps
New York City Handbook	**$13.95**
Christiane Bird	300 pages, 20 maps
New York Handbook	**$19.95**
Christiane Bird	780 pages, 95 maps
Northern California Handbook	**$19.95**
Kim Weir	800 pages, 50 maps
Oregon Handbook	**$17.95**
Stuart Warren and Ted Long Ishikawa	588 pages, 34 maps
Pennsylvania Handbook	**$18.95**
Joanne Miller	448 pages, 40 maps
Road Trip USA	**$22.50**
Jamie Jensen	800 pages, 165 maps
Southern California Handbook	**$19.95**
Kim Weir	720 pages, 26 maps
Tennessee Handbook	**$17.95**
Jeff Bradley	530 pages, 44 maps
Texas Handbook	**$18.95**
Joe Cummings	690 pages, 70 maps
Utah Handbook	**$17.95**
Bill Weir and W.C. McRae	490 pages, 40 maps

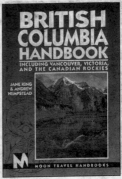

Washington Handbook	**$19.95**
Don Pitcher	870 pages, 113 maps
Wisconsin Handbook	**$18.95**
Thomas Huhti	590 pages, 69 maps
Wyoming Handbook	**$17.95**
Don Pitcher	610 pages, 80 maps

ASIA AND THE PACIFIC

"Scores of maps, detailed practical info down to business hours of small-town libraries. You can't beat the Asian titles for sheer heft. (The) series is sort of an American Lonely Planet, with better writing but fewer titles. (The) individual voice of researchers comes through."

—Travel & Leisure

Australia Handbook	**$21.95**
Marael Johnson, Andrew Hempstead, and Nadina Purdon	940 pages, 141 maps
Bali Handbook	**$19.95**
Bill Dalton	750 pages, 54 maps
Bangkok Handbook	**$13.95**
Michael Buckley	244 pages, 30 maps
Fiji Islands Handbook	**$13.95**
David Stanley	280 pages, 38 maps
Hong Kong Handbook	**$16.95**
Kerry Moran	378 pages, 49 maps
Indonesia Handbook	**$25.00**
Bill Dalton	1,380 pages, 249 maps
Japan Handbook	**$22.50**
J.D. Bisignani	970 pages, 213 maps
Micronesia Handbook	**$14.95**
Neil M. Levy	340 pages, 70 maps
Nepal Handbook	**$18.95**
Kerry Moran	490 pages, 51 maps
New Zealand Handbook	**$19.95**
Jane King	620 pages, 81 maps
Outback Australia Handbook	**$18.95**
Marael Johnson	450 pages, 57 maps
Philippines Handbook	**$17.95**
Peter Harper and Laurie Fullerton	670 pages, 116 maps
Singapore Handbook	**$15.95**
Carl Parkes	350 pages, 29 maps
Southeast Asia Handbook	**$21.95**
Carl Parkes	1,000 pages, 203 maps

South Korea Handbook Robert Nilsen	**$19.95** 820 pages, 141 maps
South Pacific Handbook David Stanley	**$22.95** 920 pages, 147 maps
Tahiti-Polynesia Handbook David Stanley	**$13.95** 270 pages, 35 maps
Thailand Handbook Carl Parkes	**$19.95** 860 pages, 142 maps
Vietnam, Cambodia & Laos Handbook Michael Buckley	**$18.95** 730 pages, 116 maps

OTHER GREAT TITLES FROM MOON

"For hardy wanderers, few guides come more highly recommended than the Handbooks. They include good maps, steer clear of fluff and flackery, and offer plenty of money-saving tips. They also give you the kind of information that visitors to strange lands—on any budget—need to survive."

—*US News & World Report*

Moon Handbook Carl Koppeschaar	**$10.00** 141 pages, 8 maps
Moscow-St. Petersburg Handbook Masha Nordbye	**$13.95** 259 pages, 16 maps
The Practical Nomad: How to Travel Around the World Edward Hasbrouck	**$17.95** 575 pages
Staying Healthy in Asia, Africa, and Latin America Dirk Schroeder	**$11.95** 197 pages, 4 maps

MOONBELT

A new concept in moneybelts. Made of heavy-duty Cordura nylon, the Moonbelt offers maximum protection for your money and important papers. This pouch, designed for all-weather comfort, slips under your shirt or waistband, rendering it virtually undetectable and inaccessible to pickpockets. It features a one-inch high-test quick-release buckle so there's no more fumbling around for the strap or repeated adjustments. This handy plastic buckle opens and closes with a touch but won't come undone until you want it to. Moonbelts accommodate traveler's checks, passports, cash, photos, etc. Size 5 x 9 inches. Available in black only. **$8.95**

ROAD TRIP USA

Cross-Country Adventures on America's Two-Lane Highways

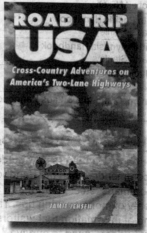

$22.50   800 pages

"For those who feel an adrenaline rush everytime they hear the words 'road trip,' and who understand that getting there is at least half the fun, this is quite simply the best book of its type ever published."

—*Conde Nast Traveler* web site

"Just might be the perfect book about hitting the summoning highway . . . It's impossible not to find something enticing in *Road Trip USA* to add to your next cycling expedition. An encyclopedia of roadside wonders." **—Harley Davidson *Enthusiast***

"For budding myth collectors, I can't think of a better textbook."

—*Los Angeles Times*

"A terrific guide for those who'd rather swat mosquitoes than take the interstate."

—Colorado Springs *Gazette Telegraph*

"Jensen is well-versed in travel, has an enjoyable yet informative style and will guide you along each mile. Don't leave home without it!" **—*Mobilia***

"Zany inspiration for a road Gypsie in search of off-the-beaten-path adventure."

—*The Toronto Globe and Mail*

"A historic journey into the heart and soul of America."
—*Route 66 Magazine*

"Jamie Jensen and the 12 intrepid contributors to *Road Trip USA* have been everywhere and seen everything compiling this exhaustive, delightful, destination-anywhere guide to American road-tripping."

—*Citybooks,* Washington D.C.

"Not only a fantastic guide . . . a great companion!"
—*The Herald,* Columbia S.C.

THE PRACTICAL NOMAD

✈ TAKE THE PLUNGE

"The greatest barriers to long-term travel by
Americans are the disempowered feelings
that leave them afraid to ask for the time off.
Just do it."

✈ TAKE NOTHING FOR GRANTED

"Even 'What time is it?' is a highly politicized
question in some areas, and the answer may
depend on your informant's ethnicity and
political allegiance as well as the proximity of
the secret police."

✈ TAKE THIS BOOK

"Full of hard-won road wisdom."
—*San Francisco Examiner*

$17.95   576 pages

With experience helping thousands of his globetrotting clients plan their trips
around the world, travel industry insider Edward Hasbrouck provides the
secrets that can save readers money and valuable travel time.
An indispensable complement to destination-specific travel guides,
The Practical Nomad includes:

  airfare strategies
  ticket discounts
  long-term travel considerations
  travel documents
  border crossings
  entry requirements
  government offices
  travel publications
  Internet information resources

WHERE TO BUY MOON TRAVEL HANDBOOKS

BOOKSTORES AND LIBRARIES: Moon Travel Handbooks are distributed worldwide. Please contact our sales manager for a list of wholesalers and distributors in your area.

TRAVELERS: We would like to have Moon Travel Handbooks available throughout the world. Please ask your bookstore to write or call us for ordering information. If your bookstore will not order our guides for you, please contact us for a free catalog.

Moon Travel Handbooks
P.O. Box 3040
Chico, CA 95927-3040 U.S.A.
tel.: (800) 345-5473, outside the U.S. (530) 345-5473
fax: (530) 345-6751
e-mail: travel@moon.com

IMPORTANT ORDERING INFORMATION

PRICES: All prices are subject to change. We always ship the most current edition. We will let you know if there is a price increase on the book you order.

SHIPPING AND HANDLING OPTIONS: Domestic UPS or USPS first class (allow 10 working days for delivery): $4.50 for the first item, $1.00 for each additional item.

Moonbelt shipping is $1.50 for one, 50 cents for each additional belt.

UPS 2nd Day Air or Printed Airmail requires a special quote.

International Surface Bookrate 8-12 weeks delivery: $4.00 for the first item, $1.00 for each additional item. Note: We cannot guarantee international surface bookrate shipping. We recommends sending international orders via air mail, which requires a special quote.

FOREIGN ORDERS: Orders that originate outside the U.S.A. must be paid for with an international money order, a check in U.S. currency drawn on a major U.S. bank based in the U.S.A., or Visa, MasterCard, or Discover.

TELEPHONE ORDERS: We accept Visa, MasterCard, or Discover payments. Call in your order: (800) 345-5473, 8 a.m.-5 p.m. Pacific standard time. Outside the U.S. the number is (530) 345-5473.

INTERNET ORDERS: Visit our site at: www.moon.com

ORDER FORM

Prices are subject to change without notice. Be sure to call (800) 345-5473,
or (530) 345-5473 from outside the U.S. 8 a.m.–5 p.m. PST for current prices and editions.
(See important ordering information on preceding page.)

Name: _____ Date: _____

Street: _____

City: _____ Daytime Phone: _____

State or Country: _____ Zip Code: _____

QUANTITY	TITLE	PRICE

Taxable Total_____

Sales Tax (7.25%) for California Residents_____

Shipping & Handling_____

TOTAL_____

Ship: ☐ UPS (no P.O. Boxes) ☐ 1st class ☐ International surface mail

Ship to: ☐ address above ☐ other _____

_____

Make checks payable to: **MOON TRAVEL HANDBOOKS**, P.O. Box 3040, Chico, CA 95927-3040
U.S.A. We accept Visa, MasterCard, or Discover. **To Order**: Call in your Visa, MasterCard, or Discover number,
or send a written order with your Visa, MasterCard, or Discover number and expiration date clearly written.

Card Number: ☐ **Visa** ☐ **MasterCard** ☐ **Discover**

☐ ☐ ☐ ☐   ☐ ☐ ☐ ☐   ☐ ☐ ☐ ☐   ☐ ☐ ☐ ☐

Exact Name on Card: _____

Expiration date:_____

Signature: _____

NOTES

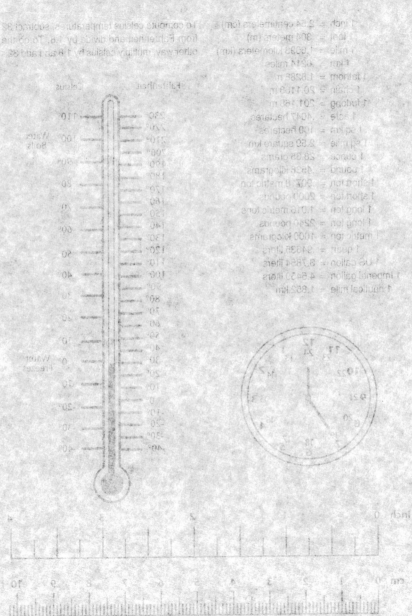

U.S.~METRIC CONVERSION

1 inch	= 2.54 centimeters (cm)
1 foot	= .304 meters (m)
1 mile	= 1.6093 kilometers (km)
1 km	= .6214 miles
1 fathom	= 1.8288 m
1 chain	= 20.1168 m
1 furlong	= 201.168 m
1 acre	= .4047 hectares
1 sq km	= 100 hectares
1 sq mile	= 2.59 square km
1 ounce	= 28.35 grams
1 pound	= .4536 kilograms
1 short ton	= .90718 metric ton
1 short ton	= 2000 pounds
1 long ton	= 1.016 metric tons
1 long ton	= 2240 pounds
1 metric ton	= 1000 kilograms
1 quart	= .94635 liters
1 US gallon	= 3.7854 liters
1 Imperial gallon	= 4.5459 liters
1 nautical mile	= 1.852 km

To compute celsius temperatures, subtract 32 from Fahrenheit and divide by 1.8. To go the other way, multiply celsius by 1.8 and add 32.

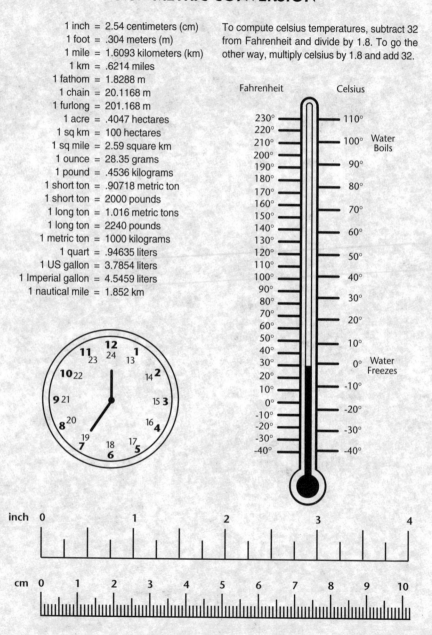